FROMMER'S

COMPREHENSIVE TRAVEL GUIDE

JAPAN '92-'93

by Beth Reiber

PRENTICE HALL TRAVEL

NEW YORK • LONDON • TORONTO • SYDN...

To Joan and Fritz, my parents in Kansas,
who always encouraged me
to look farther than my own backyard

FROMMER BOOKS
Published by Prentice Hall General Reference
A division of Simon & Schuster Inc.
15 Columbus Circle
New York, NY 10023

ISBN 0-13-333485-6
ISSN 1045-6899

Design by Robert Bull Design
Maps by Geografix Inc.

Manufactured in the United States of America

FROMMER'S JAPAN '92-'93
Editor-in-Chief: Marilyn Wood
Senior Editors: Judith de Rubini, Alice Fellows
Editors: Paige Hughes, Sara Hinsey Raveret, Lisa Renaud, Theodore Stavrou
Assistant Editors: Peter Katucki, Lisa Legarde
Contributing Editor: Irene Park
Managing Editor: Leanne Coupe

CONTENTS

LIST OF MAPS

ACKNOWLEDGMENTS

I would like to thank several fine and very special people who graciously offered their help in the preparation of this book: Toshinobu Ikubo, Grace Herget, and Seiko Tanigushi of the Japan National Tourist Organization; and Larry Estes, Debbie Howard, and Evelyn Lenzen for their moral support and editorial advice. I would also like to thank Marilyn Wood and all the other people at Frommer's Guides who helped make this book a reality.

INVITATION TO THE READER

In this guide to Japan, I have selected what I consider to be the best of the many wonderful establishments that I came across while conducting my research. You, too, in the course of your visit to Japan, may come across a hotel, restaurant, shop, or attraction that you feel should be included here; or you may find that a place I have selected has since changed for the worse. In either case, let me know of your discovery. Address your comments to:

Beth Reiber
Frommer's Japan '92–'93
c/o Prentice Hall Travel
15 Columbus Circle
New York, NY 10023

DISCLAIMERS

(1) I have made every effort to ensure the accuracy of the prices as well as of the other information contained in this guide. Yet I advise you to keep in mind that prices fluctuate over time and that some of the other information herein may also change as a result of the various volatile factors affecting the travel industry.

A major problem with regard to prices is the frequent fluctuation in the **exchange rate** between the Japanese yen and the U.S. dollar. The wise traveler will add 15% to 20% to the prices quoted throughout, particularly during the second year (1993) of the lifetime of this edition.

(2) The author and the publisher cannot be held responsible for the experiences of the reader while traveling.

SAFETY ADVISORY

Whenever you are traveling in an unfamiliar city or country, stay alert. Be aware of your immediate surroundings. Wear a money belt and keep a close eye on your possessions. Be especially careful with cameras, purses, and wallets—all favorite targets of thieves and pickpockets. Although Japan is comparatively safe, nonetheless every society has its criminals. It is therefore your responsibility to exercise caution at all times.

JAPANESE SYMBOLS & NAMES

Many hotels, restaurants, and other establishments in Japan do not have signs giving their names in English letters. As an aid to the reader, Appendix C lists the Japanese **symbols** for all such places described in this guide. Each set of symbols has a number, which corresponds to the number that appears inside an oval next to the establishment's boldfaced name in the text. Thus, to find the Japanese symbols for, say, Osaka's **Hotel Hokke Club** ⓘ③⑧, refer to number 138 in the appendix.

In this guide, Japanese personal **names** are given in the Japanese style—family name first, followed by the given name.

CHAPTER 1

GETTING TO KNOW JAPAN

Hardly a day goes by that one doesn't hear something about Japan, whether the subject is trade and fair competition or Japan's increasingly prominent role in world affairs. Yet, although Japan is constantly in the news, it remains something of an enigma to people in the Western world. What, really, is Japan? Is it the giant producer of cars and computers and a whole array of sleek electronic goods that compete favorably with the best in the West? Or is it still, behind its phenomenal economic growth, the land of the geisha and bonsai, the punctilious tea ceremony and delicate art of flower arrangement? Has it become, in its outlook and popular culture, a country more Western than Japanese; or has it retained its unique ancient traditions as it assumes a central place in the modern industrialized world?

Japan, in fact, is an intricate blend of East *and* West, and therefore not an easy nation for Westerners to comprehend. Discovering Japan is like peeling an onion—you uncover one layer only to discover more layers underneath. Thus, no matter how long you stay in Japan, you never stop learning something new about it, and to me that constant discovery is one of the most fascinating aspects of being there. An American journalist, who has lived in Japan more than 20 years and written several books on the land and its people, has told me that she still doesn't understand all the nuances of Japanese culture and customs, and is amazed to find new aspects of the country almost daily.

IMPRESSIONS

This nation is the delight of my soul.
—St. Francis Xavier

? DID YOU KNOW . . . ?

- Although Japan is only about ½₅ the size of the United States, its population of 123 million is about *half* that of the United States.
- Until the end of World War II, Japan had never been conquered or occupied by another nation.
- The Japanese imperial family, which traces its line back to 660 B.C., is the longest-reigning monarchy in the world, with a succession of 125 emperors.
- The written Japanese language consists of some 10,000 pictographs and two phonetic alphabets; yet the literacy rate in Japan is 99%.
- Most streets in Japan are not named.
- The average life span in Japan is 80 years for women and 75 years for men.
- The Japanese business community is dominated by six major corporate groups—Mitsubishi, Mitsui, Sumitomo, Fuyo, Sanwa, and Ichikan—which account for about 16% of the sales of all Japanese companies.
- According to figures released by Japan's Labor Department in 1991, Japanese men earned an average of ¥290,500 ($2,075) monthly, while Japanese women earned ¥175,000 ($1,250).
- Surveys show that some 90% of the Japanese consider themselves members of the middle class.
- Approximately 95% of Japanese households subscribe to a newspaper. The daily *Yomiuri Shimbun* has a circulation of more than 8.5 million, the largest in the world.
- A favorite pastime for many Japanese is playing *pachinko* (an upright, Japanese version of the pinball machine). There are an estimated 3 million pachinko machines in some 16,000 parlors throughout the country; more than 10 million Japanese are said to play pachinko regularly.

Japan '92–'93 is designed to guide you through your own discoveries of this wonderful and enchanting country, however brief—or extended—your visit may be. According to the Japan National Tourist Organization (JNTO), the average length of stay for tourists visiting Japan is 10½ days. To see all the places I describe, however, you would need approximately 3 *months*. So, in planning your itinerary, you should be selective. Decide beforehand what your priorities are—whether you want to concentrate on temples, hot-spring spas, landscape gardens, or breathtaking mountain scenes. Although the Japanese archipelago consists of more than 3,000 islands, I've limited the scope of this book to the main islands of Hokkaido, Honshu, Shikoku, and Kyushu. On these four islands you'll find all of Japan's major cities and historical sights.

As a special aid, this book, unlike most English-language guides to Japan, lists the written Japanese equivalents for the names of hotels and restaurants that do not have signs in English (see Appendix C). After all, nothing is more frustrating than walking down a street where everything is written only in Japanese and not being able to distinguish, at least by name, one locale from the other. Japanese consists mostly of pictographs, called *kanji*, and with a little practice you can probably match up identical kanji. Appendixes A and B, on Japanese vocabulary, should help you further in your travels through Japan.

Even if you have difficulty with the language, however, you'll find Japan navigable. It is one of the safest countries in the world, much safer than the United States or even some European countries. You don't have to worry about muggers, pickpockets, or crooks. The Japanese are honest and extremely helpful toward foreign visitors. Indeed, it's the people themselves who make traveling in Japan such a delight.

Being informed about the country—its history, people, and culture—will greatly enhance your trip. This chapter should serve only as an introduction to the wealth of information available. At the end of the chapter is a recommended reading list for books on Japan.

A WORD ABOUT COSTS

No doubt you've heard horror stories about Japan's high prices, and how hardly anyone visits the country without suffering an initial shock. With the dramatic fall of the dollar against the yen a few years back, Tokyo emerged as one of the world's most expensive cities—if not *the* most expensive city. Food and lodging, for example, are as costly in Tokyo as they are in New York, especially if you insist on living and eating exactly as you do back home.

The secret is to live and eat as the Japanese do. This book will help you do exactly that, with descriptions of out-of-the-way eateries and Japanese-style inns that cater to the native population. By following the book's advice and exercising a little caution on your own, you should be able to cut down on needless expenses and learn even more about Japan in the process. While you may never find Japan cheap, you will find it richly rewarding for all those other reasons that persuaded you to plan a trip there in the first place.

How much should you expect to spend every day for food and accommodations? If you want to travel rock-bottom and are willing to stay in youth hostels and eat inexpensive Japanese food, you can travel in Japan on ¥6,000 ($43) a day, excluding transportation costs. It's best, however, to allow yourself at least ¥10,000 ($71) to ¥14,000 ($100) a day, plus extra for occasional splurges, shopping, and emergencies. That's the budget I follow when I travel in Japan. By sticking to the recommendations in this book, you should be able to do it, too.

While stressing excellent budget choices, I haven't neglected the finest and most expensive places—after all, even though you may flinch at spending $200 for a meal, many such restaurants do exist and you may be interested simply in reading about them. As the recommendations are usually listed in a descending order from the most expensive to the cheapest, you may want to skip to the end of the list for a rundown of budget choices.

Keep in mind, however, that although every effort has been made to be as accurate as possible, prices do change—which means that they go up. Always inquire about prices before checking into a hotel, so that you may avoid embarrassment when it comes time to pay the bill. Furthermore, keep in mind that places do close and change ownership or management.

1. GEOGRAPHY, HISTORY & POLITICS

GEOGRAPHY

Separated from mainland China and Korea by the Sea of Japan, the nation of Japan stretches in an arc about 1,860 miles long from northeast to southwest. Only 250 miles wide at its broadest point, Japan consists primarily of four main islands—

IMPRESSIONS

Japan is essentially a country of paradoxes and anomalies, where all—even familiar things—put on new faces, and are curiously reversed. [The Japanese] write from top to bottom, from right to left . . . and their books begin where ours end, thus furnishing examples of the curious perfection this rule of contraries has attained.
—Sir Rutherford Alcock, *The Capital of the Tycoon*, 1863

Hokkaido, Honshu, Shikoku, and Kyushu—which account for 97% of its 145,000 square miles. Surrounding these large islands are more than 3,000 other, smaller islands and islets, most of them uninhabited; farther to the south are the Okinawan islands, perhaps best known for the fierce fighting that took place there during World War II. If you were to superimpose Japan's four main islands onto a map of the United States, they would stretch all the way from Maine down to northern Florida, which should give you at least some idea of the diversity of Japan's climate, flora, and scenery.

Of the four main islands, Honshu is the largest and the most important historically and culturally—the place where most visitors spend the bulk of their time. Honshu is the home of the ancient capitals of Nara, Kyoto, and Kamakura, in addition to such bustling metropolises as Osaka, Nagoya, Hiroshima, and Tokyo, the modern capital of Japan. Hokkaido, the next largest island, lies to the north of Honshu and is regarded as the country's last frontier, with its wide-open pastures, wildlife, and national parks of mountains, woods, and lakes. The southernmost of the four main islands is Kyushu, with a mild subtropical climate, active volcanoes, and hot-spring spas. Because it's the closest to Korea and China, Kyushu served as a gateway to the continental mainland throughout much of Japan's history, later becoming the springboard for both traders and Christian missionaries from the West. Shikoku, the smallest of the four islands, remains fairly undeveloped and is famous for its 88 Buddhist temples, founded by one of Japan's most interesting historical figures, the Buddhist priest Kukai, known posthumously as Kobo Daishi.

As much as 75% of Japan consists of mountains, most of them volcanic in origin. Altogether, there are some 265 volcanoes, more than 30 of them still considered active. Mt. Fuji (on Honsho), now dormant, is Japan's most famous volcano, while Mt. Aso (on Kyushu) is the largest volcano in the world. In 1991 the eruption of Mt. Unzen (in southern Kyushu) killed more than 30 people. Because of its volcanic origins, the country has been plagued by earthquakes throughout the centuries (the last huge earthquake struck in 1923). Today, Japan's buildings are constructed to withstand the shakes, quakes, and tremors that used to leave towns and villages in ruins.

✪ Japan consists of more than 3,000 islands, most of which are uninhabited.

Even though Japan is only slightly smaller than California in area, it has about *half* the population of the United States. And because three-fourths of the nation is mountainous and therefore uninhabitable, its people are concentrated primarily in only 10% of the country's landmass, with the rest of the area devoted to agriculture. In this island nation—isolated physically from the rest of the world; struck repeatedly through the centuries by earthquakes, fires, and typhoons; and possessing only

---

IMPRESSIONS

Japan offers as much novelty perhaps as an excursion to another planet.
—ISABELLA BIRD, *UNBEATEN TRACKS IN JAPAN*, 1880

[It is] like mental oxygen to . . . breathe in a unique civilization like that of Japan. To feel that for ages millions of one's own race have lived and loved, enjoyed and suffered and died . . . without the religion, laws, customs, food, dress, and culture which seem to us to be the vitals of our social existence is like walking through a living Pompeii.
—W. E. GRIFFIS, *THE MIKADO'S EMPIRE*, 1876

limited space for harmonious living—geography and topography have played a major role both in determining its development and in shaping its culture, customs, and arts.

HISTORY

ANCIENT HISTORY [CA. 30,000 B.C. TO A.D. 710]

According to mythology, Japan's history began when the sun goddess, Amaterasu, sent one of her descendants down to the island of Kyushu to unify the people of Japan. Unification, however, was not realized until a few generations later, when Jimmu, the great-grandson of the goddess's emissary, succeeded in bringing all of the country under his rule. Because of his divine descent, Jimmu became emperor, in 660 B.C. (the date is mythical), thus establishing the line from which all of Japan's emperors are said to derive. However mysterious the origin of this imperial dynasty, it is acknowledged as the longest-reigning such family in the world.

Legend begins to give way to fact only in the 4th century A.D., when a family by the name of Yamato succeeded in expanding its kingdom throughout the country. At the core of the unification achieved by the Yamato family was the Shinto religion. Indigenous to Japan, Shintoism is marked by the worship of nature and the spirits of ancestors and by the belief in the divinity of the emperor.

Although the exact origin of the Japanese people is lost to history, we know that Japan was once connected to the Asian mainland by a land bridge, and that the territory of Japan was occupied as early as 30,000 B.C. From about 10,000 to 300 B.C., hunters and gatherers called the Jomon people thrived in small communities, primarily in central Honshu. They are best known for their hand-formed pottery, decorated with cord patterns. The Jomon Period was followed by the Yayoi Period, which was marked by metalworking, the pottery wheel, and the mastering of irrigated rice cultivation. The Yayoi Period lasted until about A.D. 300. It was after this that the Yamato family succeeded in unifying the state for the first time. Yamato became the ancient name of Japan, which began turning its cultural feelers toward its great neighbor to the west, China.

In the 6th century, Buddhism, which originated in India, was brought to Japan via China and Korea. This was the beginning of large-scale Chinese cultural and scholarly influence, including art, architecture, and the use of Chinese characters for writing. In 604 the prince regent, Shotoku, greatly influenced by the teachings of Buddhism and Confucianism, drafted a document calling for political reforms and a constitutional government. By 607 he was sending multitudes of Japanese scholars to China to study Buddhism. Under Shotoku's guidance a number of Bud-

DATELINE

- **660 B.C.** According to tradition, Japan's first emperor, Jimmu, accedes to the throne.
- **A.D. 538–52** Buddhism is introduced into Japan via China and Korea.
- **607** Prince Regent Shotoku sends the first Japanese envoy to China. Horyuji Temple is completed.
- **710** Nara becomes the country's capital.
- **752** The Great Buddha at Todaiji Temple in Nara is completed.
- **794** Kyoto is declared the national capital.
- **806** Kukai (Kobo Daishi) establishes the Shingon sect of Buddhism.
- **1001** Sei Shonagon completes the *Pillow Book*, her collection of court-life impressions.
- **1011** Murasaki Shikibu completes the world's first major novel, *The Tale of Genji*.
- **1192** Minamoto Yoritomo becomes shogun and establishes his government in Kamakura.

(continues)

DATELINE

- **1274** Mongolian forces, under Kublai Khan, attack Japan but are repelled.
- **1281** The Mongols attack again and are driven back, this time with the help of a typhoon.
- **1333** The Kamakura shogunate falls and the imperial system is restored.
- **1336** The turbulent but culturally fecund Muromachi Period begins.
- **1397** The Kinkakuji, or Golden Pavilion, is built in Kyoto.
- **1489** The Ginkakuji, or Silver Pavilion, is built in Kyoto.
- **1543** Portuguese ships land in Japan, introducing firearms.
- **1549** St. Francis Xavier arrives in Kyushu to spread the teaching of Christianity.
- **1573** Nobunaga Oda overthrows the Muromachi shogunate and tries to unify the country.
- **1582** Nobunaga is assassinated.
- **1585** General Hideyoshi Toyotomi defeats his enemies and begins a campaign to unify the country. Later, he will build a magnificent castle in Osaka.
- **1597** A group of 26 Japanese and

(continues)

dhist temples were built, the most famous of which was Horyuji Temple, near Nara, said to be the oldest existing wooden structure in the world.

THE NARA PERIOD [710 TO 794]

Before the 700s, the site of Japan's capital changed every time a new emperor came to the throne. In 710, however, a permanent capital was established at Nara. Although it remained the capital for only 74 years, seven successive emperors ruled from Nara; the period was graced with the expansion of Buddhism and a flourishing of temple construction throughout the country. Buddhism also inspired the arts, including sculpture, metal casting, painting, and lacquerware. It was during this time that the huge bronze statue of Buddha was cast and erected in Nara. Known as the Daibutsu, it remains Nara's biggest attraction.

THE HEIAN PERIOD [794 TO 1192]

In 784 the capital was moved from Nara to Nagaoka. Ten years later it was moved once again, this time to Heiankyo (present-day Kyoto), where it remained until Tokyo was made the new capital in 1868. Following the example of cities in China, Kyoto was laid out in a grid pattern, with broad roads and canals.

The Heian Period, which lasted from 794 until 1192, was a peaceful time in Japanese history; in fact, Heiankyo means "capital of peace and tranquillity." It was a glorious time, a time of luxury and prosperity, during which court life reached new heights in artistic pursuits. The Chinese alphabet was blended with a new Japanese writing system, allowing for the first time the flowering of Japanese literature and poems. The life of the times was captured in the works of two women: Sei Shonagon, who wrote a collection of impressions of her life at court known as the *Pillow Book,* and Murasaki Shikibu, who wrote the world's first major novel, *The Tale of Genji.*

Because the nobles were completely engrossed in their own luxurious life-styles, however, they failed to notice the growth of military clans in the provinces. The two most powerful warrior clans were the Taira and the Minamoto, whose fierce civil wars tore the nation apart until finally a young warrior named Minamoto Yoritomo established supremacy. (*Note:* In Japan, a person's family name—here Minamoto—comes first, followed by the given name.)

THE KAMAKURA PERIOD [1192 TO 1333]

Wishing to set up rule far away from Kyoto, Minamoto Yoritomo established his capital in a remote and easily defendable fishing village called Kamakura, not far from today's Tokyo. He created a military government, ushering in an era in Japan's history in which the power of the country passed from the aristocratic court into the hands of the warrior class. In becoming the nation's first shogun, or military dictator, Yoritomo laid the groundwork for the military governments that would last for some 700 years, until the imperial court was restored in 1868.

The Kamakura Period is perhaps best known for the unrivaled ascendancy of the warrior caste, known as the samurai. Ruled by a rigid code of honor, the samurai were bound in loyalty to their feudal lord, and as the centuries wore on they became the only caste allowed to carry weapons. They were supposed to give up their lives for their lord without hesitation, and if they failed in their duty they could gain back their honor by committing ritualistic suicide, or *seppuku*. Spurning the soft life led by the noble court in Kyoto, the samurai embraced a harsher and simpler life-style. When Zen Buddhism, with its tenets of mental and physical discipline, was introduced into Japan from China in the 1190s, it appealed greatly to the samurai class.

In 1274, Mongolian forces, under Kublai Khan, made an unsuccessful attempt to invade Japan, then returned in 1281 with a larger fleet. But a typhoon destroyed the whole fleet. Regarding the cyclone as a gift from the gods, the Japanese called it *kamikaze,* meaning "divine wind," a term that took on a different significance at the end of World War II, when Japanese pilots flew suicide missions in an attempt to turn the tide of war. More important, however, is the fact that until U.S. and other Allied forces entered Japan at the end of World War II, the country had never been invaded or occupied by a foreign nation.

THE MUROMACHI & AZUCHI-MOMOYAMA PERIODS [1336 TO 1603]

After the fall of the Kamakura shogunate, a new feudal government was set up at Muromachi, in Kyoto. The next 200 years, however, were marred by bloody civil wars and confusion as *daimyo* (feudal lords) staked out their fiefdoms throughout the land. Similar to the barons of Europe, the daimyo owned tracts of land with complete rule over the people who lived on them. Each lord had his retainers, the samurai, who helped in waging war against his enemies.

These centuries of strife also saw a blossoming of art and culture. Kyoto witnessed the construction of the extravagant Golden and Silver pavilions, as well as the artistic arrangements of the famous rock garden at Ryoanji Temple. Noh drama, the tea ceremony, flower arranging, and landscape gardening became the passions of the upper class. At the end of the 16th century, a number of castles were built across the land, both to demonstrate the daimyo's strength and to defend against the firearms that had been introduced into Japan around 1543 by the Portuguese.

In the second half of the 16th century, a brilliant military strategist by the name of Nobunaga Oda almost succeeded in ending the civil wars by unifying Japan, but in 1582 he was assassinated by one of his own retainers. His campaign was taken up by one of his best generals, Hideyoshi Toyotomi, who had been born a peasant but who had risen up in the ranks of Nobunaga's army. Hideyoshi built a magnificent castle in Osaka, crushed all

DATELINE

European Christians are crucified in Nagasaki.

- **1598** Hideyoshi dies.
- **1600** Tokugawa Ieyasu defeats Hideyoshi's followers and seizes power.
- **1603** Tokugawa becomes shogun and establishes his shogunate in Edo (present-day Tokyo), marking the beginning of a 264-year-long rule by the Tokugawa clan.
- **1615** Tokugawa captures Osaka Castle and wipes out the remaining members of the Hideyoshi clan.
- **1626** Christianity is banned in Japan.
- **1639** Japan closes its doors to the rest of the world, barring all foreigners from landing and all Japanese from leaving. The policy of isolation will last more than 200 years.
- **1853** Commodore Matthew C. Perry of the U.S. Navy arrives in Japan.
- **1854** Perry persuades the Japanese to sign a trade agreement with the United States.
- **1867** The Tokugawa regime is overthrown, bringing Japan's feudal era to a close.
- **1868** Emperor Meiji assumes

(continues)

DATELINE

power, moves his capital to Edo (renamed Tokyo), and begins the industrialization of Japan.

• **1870** Japan's class system is abolished.

• **1877** Saigo Takamori, a disgruntled samurai, leads a rebellion in Satsuma province, but he is defeated and commits ritual suicide with his followers.

• **1894–95** Japan wins a war against China.

• **1904–1905** Japan wins a war against Russia.

• **1910** Japan annexes Korea.

• **1914** World War I breaks out in Europe. Japan sides with the Allies (Great Britain and France) against the Central Powers (Germany and Austria).

• **1923** Tokyo and Yokohama are devastated by a major earthquake.

• **1926** Crown Prince Hirohito succeeds his father, Taisho, as emperor.

• **1931** Japan seizes Manchuria.

• **1933** Japan withdraws from the League of Nations.

• **1937** Japan goes to war against China, occupying Peking (Beijing), Shanghai, and Nanking (Nanjing).

• **1940** As World War II flares in Europe

(continues)

rebellion, and was finally able to unify Japan before he died in 1598.

THE EDO PERIOD [1603 TO 1867]

Upon Hideyoshi's death, power was seized by Tokugawa Ieyasu, a statesman so shrewd and skillful in eliminating enemies that his heirs would continue to rule Japan for the next 250 years. In 1603, Tokugawa set up his shogunate government in Edo (present-day Tokyo), leaving the emperor intact but virtually powerless in Kyoto.

Meanwhile, European influence in Japan was spreading. First contact with the Western world had occurred in 1543, when the Portuguese arrived; they were followed by Christian missionaries. St. Francis Xavier landed in Kyushu in 1549, remaining for 2 years and converting thousands of Japanese to Christianity. By 1580 there were perhaps as many as 150,000 Christians in Japan. Although its rulers at first welcomed the foreigners and trade, they gradually became alarmed at the influence of the Christian missionaries. Hearing about the power of the Catholic Church in Rome and fearing the expansionist policies of the European nations, the shogunate banned Christianity in the early 1600s. In 1597 a group of 26 Japanese and European Christians were crucified in Nagasaki.

The Tokugawa shogunate intensified the campaign against the Christians in 1639, when it closed all its ports to foreign trade. Adopting a policy of total isolation, the shogunate subsequently forbade foreigners from landing in Japan and the Japanese from leaving. Even those Japanese who had been living abroad in overseas trading posts were not allowed to return to their native homes and were forced to live the rest of their days in exile. Those who defied the strict decrees were killed. The only exception to this policy of isolation was in Nagasaki, where there was a colony of tightly controlled Chinese merchants and a handful of Dutch, who were confined to a small trading post on a tiny island.

Thus began an amazing 200-year period in Japanese history, during which Japan's doors were virtually closed to the rest of the world. It was a time of political stability but also a time when personal freedom was strictly controlled by the Tokugawa government. Japanese society was divided into four distinct classes: the court nobles, the samurai, the farmers, and the merchants. Although the nobles occupied the most exalted social position, the real power lay with the samurai, and it was probably during the Tokugawa Period that the samurai class reached the zenith of its glory. At the bottom of the social ladder were the merchants, but as peace reigned on and they began accumulating wealth, new forms of entertainment developed to occupy their time. Kabuki drama and woodblock prints became the new rage, while stoneware and porcelain, silk brocade for elaborate and gorgeous kimonos, and lacquerware improved in quality.

To ensure that no daimyo in the distant provinces would overrun the shogun's power, the Tokugawa government ordered that each daimyo leave his family in Edo to serve as a kind of hostage, and required that he spend every other year in Edo. In expending so much time and money traveling back and forth and maintaining residences both in the provinces and in Edo, the daimyo had no resources left over with which to wage a rebellion. Inns and townships sprang up along Japan's major highways to accommodate these elaborate processions of palanquins, samurai, and footmen traveling back and forth between Edo and the provinces through the rough terrain of Japan's mountains.

Yet, even though the Tokugawa government took measures to ensure its supremacy, by the mid-19th century it was clear that the feudal system was outdated and that economic power was in the hands of the merchants, with money rather than rice becoming the primary means of exchange. Many samurai families were impoverished, and discontent with the shogunate became widespread.

In 1853, Commodore Matthew C. Perry sailed to Japan, seeking to gain trading rights for the United States. The Japanese, however, were reluctant to grant such rights, and Perry departed, his mission unaccomplished. Returning a year later, he succeeded in forcing the shogun to sign an agreement despite the disapproval of the emperor, thus ending Japan's two centuries of isolation. In 1867 some powerful families succeeded in toppling the Tokugawa regime and restoring the emperor as ruler, thus bringing the feudal era to a close.

MODERN JAPAN [1868 TO THE PRESENT]

In 1868, Emperor Meiji moved his imperial government to Edo, renamed it Tokyo (which means "Eastern Capital"), and designated it as the official capital of the nation. During the next few decades, known as the Meiji Restoration, Japan rapidly progressed from a feudal agricultural society of samurai and peasants to an industrial nation. The samurai were stripped of their power and no longer allowed to carry swords. A prime minister and a cabinet were appointed, a constitution was drafted, and a parliament, called the Diet, was elected. With the enthusiastic support of Emperor Meiji for Japan's modernization and Westernization, the latest in technological know-how was imported, including railway and postal systems, along with specialists and advisers. Between 1881 and 1898 as many as 6,177 British, 2,764 Americans, 913 Germans, and 619 French were retained by the Japanese government to help modernize the country.

Meanwhile, Japan made incursions into neighboring lands. In 1894–95 it fought and won a war against China; in 1904–1905 it attacked and defeated Russia; and in 1910 it annexed Korea. After militarists gained control of the government in the 1930s, these expansionist policies continued when it went to war with China in 1937.

On December 7, 1941, Japan attacked Pearl Harbor, entering World War II against the United States. Although Japan went on to conquer Hong Kong, Singapore, Burma, Malaysia, the Philippines, the Dutch East Indies, and Guam, the tide eventually turned and American bombers reduced to rubble every major Japanese city, with the exception of historic Kyoto. On August 6, 1945, the United States dropped the world's first atomic bomb over Hiroshi-

DATELINE

rope, Japan forms a military (Axis) alliance with Germany and Italy and attacks French Indochina.

• **1941** Japan bombs Pearl Harbor, provoking a declaration of war by the United States. Germany and Italy respond by declaring war on the United States.

• **1945** Hiroshima and Nagasaki suffer atomic bomb attacks by American war planes. Japan surrenders unconditionally to Allied forces, which then occupy the country under the command of U.S. Gen. Douglas MacArthur.

• **1946** Hirohito renounces the imperial claim to divinity. Japan adopts a new, democratic constitution; women gain the right to vote.

• **1952** The Allied occupation of Japan ends; Japan regains its independence.

• **1956** Japan becomes a member of the United Nations.

• **1964** The XVIII Summer Olympic Games are held in Tokyo.

• **1972** The XI Winter Olympic Games are held in Sapporo. The Okinawan islands are returned by the
(continues)

DATELINE

United States to Japan.
• **1989** Emperor Hirohito dies, after a reign of 63 years.
• **1990** Hirohito's son and heir, Crown Prince Akihito, formally ascends the Japanese throne, proclaiming the new "Era of Peace" (*Heisei*).

ma, followed on August 9 by a second atomic bomb over Nagasaki. Japan submitted to unconditional surrender on August 14 and soon thereafter American and other Allied occupation forces arrived in the country, where they remained until 1952. For the first time in its history, Japan had suffered defeat and occupation by a foreign power.

The experience had a profound effect on the Japanese people. Emerging from their defeat, they began the long effort to rebuild their cities and economy. In 1946, under the guidance of the Allied military authority, headed by U.S. Gen. Douglas MacArthur, they adopted a new, democratic constitution that renounced war and divested the emperor of his claim to divinity. A parliamentary system of government was set up, and in 1947 the first general elections were held. The following year, the militarists and generals who had carried out the Pacific War were tried and many of them were convicted. To the younger generation of Japanese, the occupation was less a painful burden that had to be suffered than an opportunity to remake their country, with American encouragement, into a modern, peace-loving, and democratic state.

A special relationship developed between the Japanese and their American occupiers. In the early 1950s, as the cold war between the United States and the Communist world erupted in hostilities in Korea, that relationship grew into a firm alliance, strengthened by a security treaty between Tokyo and Washington. In 1952 the occupation ended, and Japan subsequently joined the United Nations as an independent country.

Avoiding involvement in foreign conflicts, the Japanese concentrated on economic recovery. Through a series of policies that favored domestic industries and shielded Japan from foreign competition, they achieved rapid economic growth. By the mid-1960s, they had transformed their nation into a major industrialized power. In 1964, in recognition of Japan's increasing importance, the Summer Olympic Games were held in Tokyo.

○ Japan has the world's longest-reigning dynasty, dating back to 660 B.C., according to legend.

As their economy continued to expand, the Japanese sought new markets abroad; by the early 1970s, they had attained a trade surplus, which they have consistently enjoyed ever since, as Japanese products—cars, electronic goods, computers—attract more and more foreign buyers. Tokyo's trade policies, however, have inevitably caused friction between Japan and the United States, its chief trading partner. In the 1980s especially, as Japanese automobile sales in the United States soared, while foreign sales in Japan continued to be restricted, disagreements between Tokyo and Washington over the issue of fair trade at times strained the alliance.

In the 1990s the demand by the United States—as well as the European Community, another major trading partner—that Japan liberalize its trade policies has been coupled by an appeal that Tokyo take a more active role in world affairs, consonant with its economic power. A principal reason for Tokyo's reluctance to go beyond what Washington calls "checkbook diplomacy" (in 1991, Japan contributed about $13 billion to the Allied effort in the Persian Gulf war but refused to send a

---

IMPRESSIONS

Japan enchants me. Japan has the instant effect upon me of making it imperative to write of it.
—JAMES CAMERON, *POINT OF DEPARTURE*, 1967

token military force) is the constitution's restriction on the use of Japanese military force for any purpose other then national defense.

Yet, as the U.S. defense role in the Pacific, dominant since 1945, begins to recede, Japan may very well be forced by circumstances to assume a greater political, diplomatic, and even, perhaps, military presence in the region.

POLITICS

Japan, under its parliamentary system, has both an emperor, who acts as head of state, and a prime minister, who is head of the government. The constitution, which was adopted in 1946, stipulates that the supreme power of the country resides with the people, who vote for members of the National Diet, the legislative body. The constitution also renounces war—at least one reason why the Japanese have been reluctant to build up their own military since World War II. There are five major political parties, the largest of which is the right-of-center Liberal Democratic Party (LDP). It has never once lost its majority in the Diet since being formed more than three decades ago. Prime ministers generally serve as head of the LDP before assuming the nation's top political position.

2. JAPAN'S FAMOUS PEOPLE

Basho (1644–94) Japan's most famous haiku poet. Basho spent much of his life traveling the country. He left a rich legacy of haiku written about its various regions.

Chikamatsu Monzaemon (1653–1724) Japan's greatest dramatist of the Edo Period. Chikamatsu wrote plays for Kabuki and Joruri (puppet theater). His works reflect the everyday social life of Edo townspeople, including the popular theme of *shinju*, double suicide committed by lovers.

Hideyoshi Toyotomi (1536–98) Son of a poor farmer, Hideyoshi was a popular hero who rose in the military ranks to become one of the nation's greatest leaders. Succeeding Nobunaga Oda, Hideyoshi went on to unify Japan and built himself a magnificent castle in Osaka.

Hokusai Katsushika (1760–1849) A notable and prolific *ukiyo-e* (woodblock print) artist of the late Edo Period, thought to have influenced the French Impressionists. He is especially famous for his 36 landscape paintings of Mt. Fuji.

Ichikawa Danjuro (1660–1704) Kabuki actor of the early Edo Period and originator of red-and-black facial paint and exaggerated movements. In his memory, Kabuki actors through the centuries have adopted his name and acting style, so that today's star actor is the 12th Ichikawa Danjuro.

Izumo-no-Okuni (16th–17th century) An actress, credited with founding Kabuki. According to folklore, she and a troupe of female dancers began performing rather decadent and lewd dances in Kyoto, thereby quickly gaining a wide, appreciative audience. However, the shogun eventually forbade women from the stage. It therefore became necessary for men to assume female roles, and today all Kabuki roles are performed by men.

Kawabata Yasunari (1899–1972) Winner of the Nobel Prize for Literature in 1968 and considered the foremost novelist of modern Japan. Among his most famous works are *Yukiguni* (*Snow Country*) and *Izu-no-Odoriko* (*The Izu Dancer*). He committed suicide at the age of 73.

Kitagawa Utamaro (1753–1806) One of the foremost ukiyo-e painters of his time. He is famous for his pictures of beautiful women, use of limited colors, and backgrounds.

Kukai (774–835) Known posthumously as Kobo Daishi and regarded as the most important Buddhist religious figure in Japan. After studying Buddishm in China,

Kukai returned to his homeland and eventually founded the Shingon Esoteric sect of Buddhism, establishing a seminary on Mt. Koya. He traveled to various parts of the country, teaching, and left behind him many temples, some of which remain today, especially on Mts. Koya and Shikoku.

Emperor Meiji (1852–1912) Japan's 122nd emperor, credited with leading his nation from a feudalistic society into the industrial age. He ascended the throne at 15 and was only 17 at the time of the Meiji Revolution, which restored the imperial family back to power. He went on to create a modern constitution and lead Japan in the Sino-Japanese War (1894–95) and the Russo-Japanese War (1904–1905).

Minamoto Yoritomo (1147–99) Established Japan's first military government and became the nation's first shogun, setting up a shogunate in Kamakura. After both his sons, who succeeded him as shogun, were assassinated, rule passed to the family of his wife, who is remembered in history as having a sharp temper and a calculating, conniving personality.

Mishima Yukio (1925–70) One of Japan's most prominent modern writers, both at home and abroad. Among his most famous works is *Kinkakuji (The Temple of the Golden Pavilion)*, about a young priest who sets fire to Kinkakuji Temple to visualize what he thinks must surely be the most beautiful scene in the world. Mishima shocked the literary world by forming a private radical right-wing movement; after a feeble attempt at a coup, he committed seppuku (disembowelment, followed by decapitation by one of his followers).

Miyamoto Musashi (?–1645) Foremost swordsman of the Edo Period and author of *Gorin-no-sho,* which advises that in order to master the sword, one must first master one's spirit. Miyamoto originated a new technique in fencing, in which a long sword is held in the right hand, a short sword in the left.

Murasaki Shikibu (980–1014) Court lady to the emperor's wife. Her life at the imperial court provided her with much insight for her classic work, *The Tale of Genji*. Regarded as the world's first major novel, it describes the life and love affairs of Hikaru Genji and provides a fascinating look at Japanese nobility in the 11th century.

Natsume Soseki (1867–1918) One of Japan's most prominent literary figures of the Meiji Period, whose portrait appears on the ¥1,000 note. Among his many works, *I Am a Cat* is best known; it is a humorous commentary on human society, written from the viewpoint of a cat.

Nobunaga Oda (1534–82) Considered one of Japan's greatest revolutionists and military strategists, who almost succeeded in putting an end to centuries of bloody civil wars by eliminating his enemies and unifying the country. Nobunaga is also credited with promoting trade with the Portuguese and the Dutch, thereby increasing the flow of tools, arms, foreign knowledge, and Christianity into Japan. He was betrayed and assassinated by one of his own retainers.

Saigo Takamori (1828–77) A popular hero of the Meiji Restoration, which returned power to the emperor. A samurai, Saigo subsequently became disgruntled and led a group of fellow warriors in the Seinan Civil War, in Kyushu, in 1877. Defeated, he and his followers committed suicide. He remains, however, a popular historical figure; all Japanese are familiar with his statue in Ueno Park in Tokyo.

Sen-no-Rikyu (1522–91) Master of the tea ceremony, Rikyu elevated it into an art, utilizing such Zen principles as *wabi* (quiet elegance) and *sabi* (quaintness). Teaching that simplistic beauty is preferable to guady pompousness, Rikyu placed great importance on both the environment and one's mental state during the tea ceremony; the tearoom, the garden, even the tea utensils, he asserted, are significant. Rikyu taught the tea ceremony to both Nobunaga Oda and Hideyoshi Toyotomi and therefore wielded tremendous influence, but he overstepped his boundaries when he had a likeness of himself placed atop the main gate of Daitokuji Temple. Hideyoshi ordered him to commit suicide. After his death, Rikyu's sons founded three different schools of the tea ceremony, all in existence today.

Shotoku Taishi (574–622) Serving as prince regent to the emperor, Shotoku is remembered for his intelligence and virtue and for his promulgation of the Constitution of Seventeen Articles, a code of administrative ethics for court officials that served to strengthen imperial power. Making Buddhism a cornerstone of his government policies, he assured the religion's growth throughout Japan and ordered construction of Horyuji Temple near Nara.

Tokugawa Ieyasu (1542–1616) One of Japan's most famous shoguns, endowed with political genius and strategic ingenuity. Tokugawa ruthlessly eliminated all his enemies, paving the way for his descendants to rule for more than 250 years. James Clavell's *Shogun* is based on the life of Tokugawa. He is entombed in a remarkable mausoleum in Nikko, which remains one of Japan's most visited attractions.

3. ART, ARCHITECTURE & LITERATURE

ART

The Japanese hold aesthetic beauty in such high esteem that the most skilled artists and craftspeople are recognized as "living national treasures." These living national treasures include carpenters, sculptors, swordsmiths, potters, weavers, and creators of Japanese paper and lacquerware.

Japan's first artwork appeared in the form of clay and stone figures during the Stone Age. After the spread of Buddhism in Japan in the 6th century A.D., religious art found expression through architecture, sculptures, and paintings. Other art forms, including lacquerware, ceramics, and bronzes, were first brought to Japan from China. It wasn't until the 1600s that the Japanese began to develop their own styles and techniques for the arts, although they did cultivate their own expressions of beauty through flower arranging, the tea ceremony, Japanese gardens, bonsai, and such sport disciplines as judo and karate. During the Edo Period (lasting until the mid-19th century), traditional arts, such as pottery and lacquerware, received the patronage of feudal lords, which encouraged the spread of various techniques throughout the land. It was also during the Edo Period that ukiyo-e, or woodblock prints, gained popularity among the masses both at home and abroad for their portraits of actors, beautiful women, and landscapes.

Today, the arts thrive in Japan. There are dozens of pottery towns throughout the country, each with its own distinctive style and function. For example, satsuma pottery, in Kagoshima Prefecture in Kyushu, is valued for its whiteness, while Bizen pottery, in Okayama Prefecture, is distinguished for its rough texture, achieved through ash firings. Similarly, lacquerware, coated with lacquer from the Japanese lacquer tree, varies from region to region. Japan is also well known for its regional folk toys and objects, including fans, combs, dolls, and items made of paper.

ARCHITECTURE

Before the modern age, Japanese buildings were made exclusively of wood, regardless of whether they were temples, palaces, or farmers' homes. One reason, of course, was that stone structures would never have withstood the countless earthquakes that shook the land. In addition, wooden buildings could be constructed with sliding

IMPRESSIONS

The light in Japan is always slightly peculiar, different from the light in any other country I know. It has the strange, oblique intensity that often lends subjects a tranced look and gives landscapes momentarily the appearance of being immobilized under glass.
—JAMES KIRKUP, *JAPAN BEHIND THE FAN*, 1970

doors and walls, allowing their occupants to open their homes to the woods and the rest of the natural world around them. Since homes were often expected to last through several generations, rooms could be modified as the need arose, simply by adding or subtracting a paper or wooden wall. There was almost no furniture in a Japanese home. Instead, people sat on *tatami,* or rice mats, usually around a central fireplace. By spreading out *futon,* or mattresses, living rooms could be transformed into bedrooms.

Japan's oldest surviving structures are religious ones. Horyuji Temple near Nara is the oldest wooden structure in the world, built some 1,200 years ago. However, it is Shinto shrines that best reflect pure Japanese architecture, especially the shrines of Ise. Constructed of plain cypress wood with thick thatched roofs, the Ise Jingu Shrines are rebuilt every 20 years according to traditional methods.

During the civil wars of the 15th and 16th centuries, castles were constructed across the land. Although they were originally built on mountains and other places thought difficult to approach, the introduction of firearms to Japan in the mid-1500s necessitated walls thick enough to withstand the volley of gunfire. Eventually, castles were built on the open plains, surrounded by a series of moats. Foundations and walls were made of boulders, but just to be on the safe side, castles often contained such features as entrances that suddenly terminated in tricky dead ends, holes built in the shape of squares or triangles to allow guns or arrows to shoot through, and special chutes through which rocks or scalding water could be dropped on enemies trying to scale the walls. Osaka Castle was the largest castle in all Japan; Himeji Castle is considered one of the most beautiful.

Although traditional Japanese architecture can still be found in the country's many temples, shrines, castles, and private residences, the modern age has taken its toll. After the development of earthquake-resistant buildings in the 1960s, skyscrapers mushroomed in Tokyo and elsewhere, often at the expense of small wooden structures that occupied valuable land.

One of Japan's most famous postwar architects was Tange Kenzo, who designed the Hiroshima Peace Center, the National Indoor Athletic Hall and adjoining gymnasium built for the 1964 Summer Olympics, and the Akasaka Prince Hotel.

LITERATURE

The oldest-known Japanese work of literature is the *Kojiki,* a narrative chronicle on the history of Japan, written in 712. That was followed in 770 by *Manyoshu,* an anthology of more than 4,500 poems composed by emperors, by members of the nobility, and even by common people. Best known today, however, is probably *The Tale of Genji,* written by a lady of the court named Murasaki Shikibu in the 11th century and widely regarded as the world's first major novel.

During the Kamakura and Muromachi periods, from the 12th to the 16th century, glorious war epics were the rage. Stories of the samurai, with themes of revenge, death, and honor, were popular. It wasn't until peace was restored, during the Tokugawa shogunate, that eccentric verse and love stories involving common people came to the fore. Soon the merchant class replaced warriors as a subject for fiction, and commoners' lives were examined instead of the lives of aristocrats. Comedy and amusement were the raison d'être of many

۞ The world's first major novel, *The Tale of Genji,* was written by a Japanese lady of the court in the 11th century.

works, which were set in such popular pleasure districts as Asakusa. Among the many writers of the Edo Period who remain popular today are Shunsui Tamenaga, who depicted the amorous relationships between men and women, and Ikku Jippensha, who wrote about the adventures of two men traveling the famous Tokaido road that connected Kyoto and Edo. Poetry also gained popularity during the Edo Period, especially haiku by the great master Basho. Finally, Kabuki also came into its own.

With the dawning of the Meiji Period and the industrial age, Japan produced its first major novelists since the 17th century. Soseki Natsume, Ogai Mori, and Toson

Shimazaki gained a wide following by writing in everyday speech rather than the ornate prose of earlier writers. The next generation of writers turned their energies to problems faced by a nation trying to bridge two different cultures as a result of the country's Westernization. Kawabata Yasunari, writing about erotic obsession in *Snow Country*, won a Nobel Prize in 1968, while Dazai Osamu wrote about postwar malaise and romantic nihilism in such works as *The Setting Sun*.

Another celebrated Japanese writer of the 20th century was Mishima Yukio, who attained fame with *Confessions of a Mask* and *The Temple of the Golden Pavilion* before taking his own life in a ritualistic suicide. Other prominent writers are Abe Kobo (*Woman in the Dunes*) and Oe Kenzaburo (*Hiroshima Notes* and *A Personal Matter*). In recent years, women writers have added to Japan's literary field, including Uno Chiyo with *The Sound of Rain* and Kono Taeko with *Revolving Door*.

4. RELIGION, MYTH & FOLKLORE

RELIGION

The main religions in Japan are Shintoism and Buddhism, and many Japanese consider themselves believers in both. Whereas Westerners might find it difficult to belong to two completely different religious organizations, the Japanese find nothing unusual about it and incorporate both into their life-style. Most Japanese, for example, are married in a Shinto ceremony, but when they die they'll probably have a Buddhist funeral.

Unlike Westerners, whose churches have religious services weekly, the Japanese generally visit a temple or shrine only for a specific purpose. On New Year's, for example, many of them throng to shrines to pray for good fortune in the coming year, while in mid-July or mid-August they go to pay their respects to their ancestors. As such, neither religion has a great influence in the everyday life of the Japanese. Rather, religion is more a way of thinking, a way of relating to one's world, environment, and family. The Japanese appreciation of natural beauty and strong sense of duty and obligation, for example, have religious roots.

SHINTOISM

A native religion of Japan, Shintoism is the worship of ancestors and national heroes, as well as of all natural things, both animate and inanimate. These natural things are thought to embody gods, called *kami,* and can be anyone or anything—mountains, trees, the moon, stars, rivers, seas, fires, animals, rocks, even vegetables. In this respect, the beliefs of Shintoism resemble those of Native American tribes. Shintoism also embraces much of Confucianism, which entered Japan in the 5th century and stressed the importance of family and loyalty. There are no scriptures in Shintoism, as there is no ordained code of morals or ethics.

The most important goddess in Shintoism is Amaterasu, the sun goddess, who is considered the progenitor of the Japanese imperial family. Central to the principles of Shintoism through the centuries, therefore, was the belief that the emperor was a

IMPRESSIONS

If the most celebrated cathedrals of Europe were situated in the Black Forest, and were all simple wooden structures resembling very large but plain log cabins, Christianity would approximate to Shinto in its aesthetic appeal.
—ALEXANDER CAMPBELL, *THE HEART OF JAPAN*, 1962,
ON THE ISE JINGU SHRINES

living god. Emperors held this revered position for more than 1,500 years, until the end of World War II, when Emperor Hirohito was forced to renounce the claim to divinity and admit that he was an ordinary mortal. At this time, Shintoism also lost its official status as the national religion, a position it had held since the Meiji Restoration (1868). However, Shintoism has not lost its popularity and claims more than 80 million followers in Japan. As for the imperial family, it still occupies a special place in the hearts of the Japanese.

The place of worship in Shintoism is called a *jinja,* or shrine. Every city, town, village, and hamlet has at least one shrine, and to most inhabitants it embodies the soul of their district. The most famous shrines are Meiji Shrine in Tokyo, the Ise Shrines in the Ise-Shima National Park (dedicated to the sun goddess), and Itsukushima Shrine on Miyajima Island.

The most obvious telltale sign of a shrine is its *torii,* an entrance gate, usually of wood, consisting of two tall poles topped with either one or two crossbeams. Sometimes there will be several of these torii spread out over the pathway leading to the shrine, reminding visitors that they are approaching a shrine and giving them time to achieve the proper frame of mind. Before reaching the shrine itself, you'll pass a water trough with communal cups where the Japanese will rinse out their mouths and wash their hands. Purification and cleanliness are important in Shintoism because they show respect to the gods, aspects that have carried over even today in the Japanese custom of bathing and removing shoes indoors.

At the shrine itself, worshippers will throw a few coins into a money box, clap their hands three times to get the attention of the gods, and then bow their heads and pray. Sometimes there will be a rope attached to a gong that's even louder in calling the gods. Worshippers pray for good health, protection, the safe delivery of a child, and that sons get into good universities and daughters get good husbands. Some shrines are considered lucky for love, while others are good against certain ailments. You can ask any favor of the gods. Shrines are also the sites of many festivals and are visited on important occasions throughout one's life, including marriage and on certain birthdays. New Year's is also a popular time to visit famous shrines around the country.

> ✪ **The Japanese people's reverence of nature is part of their native religion, Shintoism, which embraces the worship of all natural things, both animate and inanimate.**

BUDDHISM

Whereas they're called shrines in Shintoism, in Buddhism they're called *otera,* or temples. Instead of a torii, temples will often have an entrance gate with a raised doorsill and heavy doors. Temples may also have a cemetery on their grounds, which Shinto shrines never have, and a pagoda.

Founded in India in the 5th century, Buddhism came to Japan in the 6th century via China and Korea, bringing with it the concept of eternal life. By the end of the 6th century, Buddhism had gained such popularity that Prince Regent Shotoku, one of Japan's most remarkable historical figures, declared Buddhism the state religion and based many of his governmental policies on its tenets. Another important Buddhist leader to emerge was a priest called Kukai, known posthumously as Kobo Daishi. After studying Buddhism in China in the early 800s, he returned to Japan, where he founded the Shingon sect of Buddhism and established his mission atop Mt. Koya. The temples he built throughout Japan, including the famous 88 temples on Shikoku Island and those on Mt. Koya, continue to attract millions of pilgrims even today.

Probably the Buddhist sect best known to the West, however, is Zen Buddhism. Considered the most Japanese form of Buddhism, Zen is the practice of meditation and a strictly disciplined life-style, in the belief that it helps rid one of desire so that one can achieve enlightenment. There are no rites in Zen Buddhism, no dogmas, no theological conceptions of divinity. You do not analyze rationally but are supposed to know things intuitively. The strict and simple life-style of Zen appealed greatly to Japan's samurai warrior class, and many of Japan's arts, including the tea ceremony, arose from the practice of Zen.

As in Shintoism, there are several popular festivals relating to Buddhism. Probably the most widely practiced is O'bon, celebrated in July or August, depending on the region and the time when the spirits of departed ancestors are thought to return home. Many Japanese return to their home towns for O'bon, to visit their ancestors' graves and partake in O'bon dances held at shrines or temples or other public places.

Visitors to Japan who are interested in Buddhism and temples should try to spend at least one night in a temple. The best place is Mt. Koya, known as Koyasan to the Japanese, where approximately 50 temples have opened their doors to overnight guests, offering them simple tatami rooms, vegetarian meals, and the opportunity to join in the 6am service. (For more information, see Chapter 13).

MYTH & FOLKLORE

To the Japanese, as to many people of other cultures, some objects and actions are considered to bring good luck, while others are thought to bring misfortune. Good-luck talismans are often found at shops or stalls on or near the grounds of Shinto shrines, offered to those who hope for a prosperous future, good health, the conception of a child, a bountiful harvest, a successful business, and other wishes.

Some shops and businesses, for example, often display a *manekineko*, a beckoning cat with an uplifted paw, thought to bring in good business. At the start of election campaigns, hopeful candidates always purchase a squat wooden *daruma* doll to paint in one of the eyes that are left blank. If the wish comes true—in this case, of course, to win the election—the candidates paint in the other eye as a sign of gratitude. During New Year's, the Japanese often purchase an arrow, or *hamaya*, that is thought to have the power to exorcise evil spirits. The *inu-hariko*, or papier-mâché god, is a charm considered helpful to women in childbirth and in the raising of their children.

In Japanese fables and folklore, animals and mythical creatures play a significant role. A *kappa* is a mischievous, web-footed creature that lives in rivers and carries on its head a plate filled with water, which is thought to give the kappa its strength. Foxes are considered supernatural in Japan; in ancient times, they were even an object of worship among rural folk. A *tengu* is a mountain goblin that resembles humans but has an extralong nose and wings, giving it the power to fly. Kaminari is the god of thunder, and Japanese parents often warn their children that Kaminari will steal their belly buttons if they stick them out too far. But it's the *oni* that most children fear, a fierce goblin with horns on its head, fangs, and an appetite for human beings. The oni is featured in many Japanese folktales.

5. CULTURAL & SOCIAL LIFE

CULTURAL LIFE

Japan is known around the world for its aestheticism, which is apparent in everything, from its food to its gardens and art. Rich in cultural history, the nation has produced

IMPRESSIONS

This is a child's country. Men, women, and children are taken out of the fairy books. The whole show is of the nursery. Nothing is serious, nothing is taken seriously. . . . Life is a dream, and in Japan one dreams of the nursery.
—HENRY ADAMS, 1886

widely divergent forms of expression—the tea ceremony, sumo, Kabuki, and flower arranging, to name a few—all of which command a large audience even today. In fact, the Japanese think so highly of their artists and performers that masters in many fields have been designated "living national treasures."

Although it's possible to see the performing arts as well as sumo and the tea ceremony in many parts of Japan, Tokyo is your best bet, for it offers the most at any one time. Several of its larger first-class hotels, for example, offer a few hours' instruction in English in the tea ceremony, and sumo matches and Kabuki performances are held several times during the year. For specific information on cultural entertainment in the capital city, see Chapter 9.

TEA CEREMONY

Tea was brought to Japan from China more than 1,000 years ago. It first became popular among Japanese Buddhist priests as a means of staying awake during long hours of meditation. Gradually, its use filtered down among the upper classes, and in the 16th century the tea ceremony was perfected by a merchant named Sen-no-Rikyu. Using the principles of Zen and the spiritual discipline of the samurai, the tea ceremony became a highly stylized ritual, with exact detail given on how tea should be prepared, served, and drunk. The simplicity of movement and tranquillity of setting were meant to free the mind from the banality of everyday life and allow the spirit to enjoy peace. In a sense, it was a form of spiritual therapy.

The tea ceremony, *cha-no-yu,* is still practiced in Japan today and is regarded as a form of disciplinary training for mental composure, as well as a good way to learn etiquette and manners. There are many schools with different methods for performing the tea ceremony throughout the country (see Chapter 17). Several of Japan's more famous landscape gardens have teahouses on their grounds where you can sit on tatami, drink the frothy green tea (called *maccha*) and eat some sweets (meant to counteract the bitter taste of the tea), and contemplate the view.

✪ To the Japanese, the group is more important than the individual—an attitude reflected in their centuries-old system of social etiquette.

IKEBANA

Whereas a Westerner is likely to put a bunch of flowers into a vase and be done with it, the Japanese consider the arrangement of flowers tantamount to an art. Most young girls have at least some training in flower arranging, known as *ikebana*, and there are various schools and differing methods on the subject (see Chapter 17 for a list of schools). First becoming popular among the aristocrats during the Heian Period (A.D. 794–1192) and spreading to the common people in the 14th to the 16th century, traditional ikebana, in its simplest form, is supposed to represent heaven, man, and earth. Department store galleries sometimes have ikebana exhibitions; otherwise, check with the local tourist office.

GARDENS

Nothing is left to chance in a Japanese landscape garden. The shape of hills and trees, the placement of rocks and waterfalls—everything is skillfully arranged by the gardener in a faithful reproduction of nature. To the Westerner, perhaps, it may seem a bit strange to arrange nature to look like nature. But to the Japanese, even nature can be improved upon to make it more beautiful and more pleasing, with the best possible use of limited space. The Japanese are masters at this, as a visit to any of their famous gardens will testify.

In fact, they have been sculpting gardens for more than 1,000 years. At first the gardens were designed for walking and boating, with ponds, artificial islands, and pavilions. As with almost everything else in Japanese life, however, Zen Buddhism exerted an influence on the style of gardens, making them simpler and attempting to create the illusion of boundless space within a small area. To the Buddhist, a garden was not for merriment but, rather, for contemplation—an uncluttered and simple landscape on which to rest the eyes. Japanese gardens often use the principle of "borrowed landscape"—that is, using the surrounding mountains and landscape by incorporating them into the overall design and impact of the garden.

Basically, there are three styles of Japanese gardens. One style, called *tsukiyama,* uses ponds, hills, and streams to depict nature in miniature. Another style, known as the *karesansui,* uses stones and raked sand in the place of water and is often seen at Zen Buddhist temples. It was developed during the Muromachi Period as a representation of Zen spiritualism, with the most famous rock garden being at Ryoanji Temple in Kyoto. The third style, called *chaniwa,* emerged with the tea ceremony and is built around a teahouse, with an eye toward simplicity and tranquillity. Such a garden will often feature stone lanterns, a stone basin filled with water, and water flowing through a bamboo pipe.

Famous gardens in Japan include Kenrokuen and Suizenji parks in Kanazawa, Korakuen Park in Okayama, and Ritsurin Park in Takamatsu. Kyoto alone has about 50 gardens, including the famous Zen rock gardens at Daitokuji and Ryoanji temples, the gardens at both the Golden and Silver pavilions, and those at Heian Shrine, Nijo Castle, and the Katsura Imperial Villa.

ZAZEN

Zazen, or meditation, is practiced by Zen Buddhists as a form of mental or spiritual training. Laymen meditate to relieve stress and clear the mind.

Zazen is achieved if one sits down in a cross-legged lotus position, with the neck and back straight and the eyes slightly open. Usually done by a group—in a semidark room with cushions, facing the wall—meditation is helped along by a monk, who stalks noiselessly behind the meditators. If someone squirms or moves, he is whacked on the shoulders with a stick, which is supposed to help him get back to meditating.

There are several Zen temples where foreigners can join in zazen (see Chapter 7). Through a notice in the *Japan Times,* I spent a weekend at a Zen temple outside Tokyo and tried zazen, ate vegetarian meals, and helped in household chores. If you'd like to try zazen yourself, contact the Tourist Information Center in Tokyo or Kyoto. Check the *Japan Times* also to see whether a session of zazen is being organized with instruction in English for foreigners.

SOCIAL LIFE

As an island nation with few natural resources, Japan has, as its greatest asset, its 123 million people. Hard-working, honest, and proud about performing a task well no matter how insignificant it may seem, the Japanese are well known for their politeness and helpfulness to strangers. Indeed, hardly anyone returns from a trip to Japan without stories of the extraordinary goodness and kindness extended to them by the Japanese.

With approximately 99% of the population consisting of ethnic Japanese, Japan is one of the most homogeneous nations in the world. Originally of Mongoloid stock, with strains of a few other Asian peoples thrown in, the Japanese have had remarkably

IMPRESSIONS

All landscapes acquire the character of their inhabitants, and the Japanese [landscape] is no exception to this rule.
—PETER QUENNELL, *A SUPERFICIAL JOURNEY THROUGH TOKYO AND PEKING,* 1932

little influx of other gene pools into the country since the 8th century. That, coupled with Japan's actual physical isolation as an island nation, has more than anything else led to a feeling among the Japanese that they belong to a single huge tribe that is different from any other people on earth. You'll often hear a Japanese preface a statement or opinion with the words "We Japanese," implying that all Japanese think alike and that all people can basically be divided into two categories, Japanese and non-Japanese.

A characteristic of the Japanese that has received much publicity in recent years, and is seen as at least one reason why their nation has become so powerful economically, is their group mentality. In Japan, consideration of the group always wins out over the desire of the individual. In fact, I have had Japanese tell me that they consider individuality to be synonymous with selfishness and a complete disregard for the feelings of others.

Whereas in the West the attainment of "happiness" seems to be the elusive goal for a full and rewarding life, in Japan it's the satisfactory performance of duty and obligation. From the time they are born, the Japanese are instilled with a sense of duty that extends toward their parents, their husbands or wives, their children, their bosses and co-workers, their neighbors, and the rest of society as a whole.

FAMILY LIFE

In a nation as crowded as Japan, consideration of others is essential. The average Japanese family lives in what Westerners would regard as intolerably tiny living quarters, especially in the larger cities, such as Tokyo and Osaka, where space is at a premium. And in many cases it's still customary for retired parents to live with their eldest son.

The son, however, has very little time to spend at home. If he lives in Tokyo, he spends an average of 3 hours a day commuting on the city's trains and subways to and from work. Commonly called a "salary man" (a description that includes all white-collar company employees), he works long hours, sometimes until 7 or 8pm, often followed by an evening out with his fellow workers, which he considers necessary for promoting understanding, closeness, and a more harmonious working condition. Most likely he'll work for the same company during his entire career, taking only national holidays off and one week of vacation a year. In return, he is assured of lifetime employment (unless his company goes bankrupt), a pay raise according to his age, and promotion according to the number of years he has worked for the company. Although he may secretly complain of the long hours he has to work, he basically accepts the situation because everyone else is doing the same thing.

As for Japanese women, being a housewife and full-time mother is considered the most honored position they can have. Although more women are working outside the home than ever before, they are generally confined to low-paying menial and part-time jobs. Take a look at the employment opportunities in the classified section of the *Japan Times*. There, you'll see that employers can discriminate on the basis of sex, age, and race. Jobs for women are typically as secretaries, waitresses, and teachers, with few jobs open to those over 30. It's still pretty much a man's society when it comes to business in Japan, and a woman's primary obligation is in the home. With few exciting career opportunities easily open to them, it's perhaps understandable why the main goal of most Japanese women is to get married and have children. Those who fail to find a mate during college or the early working years can always find one through arranged marriages, which still make up about 30% of the matches in Japan. The Japanese go all out when it comes to marriage ceremonies—believe it or

---

IMPRESSIONS

In Japan the law of life is not as with us—that each one strives to expand his own individuality at the expense of his neighbor's.
—LAFCADIO HEARN, 1891

not, the cost of an average wedding in Japan, including the honeymoon, is a whopping $30,000.

Of course, the situation is changing in Japan, as elsewhere, and it's no longer safe to talk in stereotypes. In 1986 a new law, the Equal Employment Opportunity Act, went into effect, overturning an earlier law that limited the number of overtime hours women could work (and if you don't work overtime in Japan, there's hardly any chance for promotion). Day-care centers for children are on the increase; young people are moving away and living far from their hometowns; and some young couples are determined to lead different, and separate, lives from their parents. Though rare, you can now find female politicians, doctors, and lawyers who juggle both family and career. In a recent trend, some young Japanese women are putting off marriage until later years; some even say that they never wish to marry, a choice that would have been unthinkable just a decade ago.

But change evolves slowly in Japan. Those who advocate it are in danger of ridicule or, even worse, rejection from the group. Such resistance to change is especially difficult for Japanese who have lived abroad and then return home; unless they slip quietly back into their old mold, they are regarded with suspicion and resentment, as though they have somehow become tainted and are no longer quite Japanese.

FOREIGNERS IN JAPAN

As for foreigners, even though they are treated with extreme kindness during a visit, they soon realize that they will never be totally accepted in Japanese society. They will always be considered outsiders, even if they speak the language fluently. In fact, Japanese-speaking foreigners will tell you that they are sometimes met with suspicion and coldness simply because, to the Japanese mind, foreigners aren't supposed to be able to speak their language. Among the groups most discriminated against are probably the Koreans, many of them second and third generation and the descendants of Koreans who were brought to Japan as forced labor before World War II.

On the other hand, more foreigners live in Japan now than ever before in the country's history. In the past 5 years, the number has quadrupled, and many newcomers are fluent in Japanese. Foreigners are now commonplace in Tokyo. In addition, the Japanese themselves are traveling abroad in ever greater numbers, with the result that they're gaining a greater understanding of other cultures. Old-timers in Japan will tell you that the country has changed dramatically in the past few years.

On a personal level, the Japanese are among the most likable people in the world. They are kind, thoughtful, and adept in perceiving another person's needs. That the country is so safe from violent crime speaks highly of the people. And as for aestheticism, the Japanese have an unerring eye for pure beauty, whether it be in food, architecture, or landscaped gardens. I don't think it would be possible to visit Japan and not have some of the Japanese appreciation of beauty rub off. Having produced the bonsai and the Toyota, the sumo wrestler and the geisha, the Japanese are such a fascinating people that it's impossible not to get hooked. Quite a few foreigners originally come to Japan with the intention of staying only a short while—and they end up living there for years. I was one of them.

MEETING THE JAPANESE

In short, Japan, like every nation in the world, has both its good and bad sides, and the informed visitor should be aware of both. On the whole, however, the visitor will be overwhelmed by the wonderful aspects of the country and by the kindness of the

---

IMPRESSIONS

According to a popular Japanese saying, the four most fearsome things in human life are: earthquake, thunder, fire, and father.
—JAMES KIRKUP, *HEAVEN, HELL AND HARA-KIRI,* 1974

people, which makes traveling in Japan such a delight. By the time you return home, you'll have your own extraordinary stories to tell.

If you're invited to Japan by some organization or business, you will receive the royal treatment, most likely being wined and dined so wonderfully and thoroughly that you'll never want to leave. If you go to Japan on your own as an ordinary tourist, however, chances are your experiences will be much different. Except for those who have lived or traveled abroad, few Japanese have had much contact with foreigners. In fact, even in Tokyo there are Japanese who have never spoken to a foreigner and would be quite embarrassed and uncomfortable if suddenly they were confronted with the possibility. And even though most of them have studied English, few Japanese have had the opportunity to use the language and most feel totally unable to communicate in it. That's one reason why you may find that the empty seat beside you in the subway is the last one to be occupied—most Japanese are deathly afraid you'll ask them a question they won't be able to understand.

In many respects, therefore, it's much harder to meet the inhabitants in Japan than in many other countries, where the people tend to be more gregarious, openly curious, and forward. The Japanese are simply much more shy. Although they will sometimes approach you to ask whether they might practice some English with you, for the most part you are left pretty much on your own, unless you make the first move.

I've found that one of the best ways to meet Japanese is to visit a so-called English-conversation lounge. Such lounges, which are informally set up and often attached to English schools, are intended to give the Japanese an opportunity to converse freely in English with anyone who is there. Most are open in the evenings and offer the chance to play games or read magazines and have drinks of coffee or beer. Usually, foreigners are admitted free of charge; at some lounges you must pay an entrance fee of ¥500 ($4) or so, but it's always less than what the Japanese pay. At any rate, the Japanese who come to these lounges often speak excellent English and will be delighted to talk to you. When I first went to Japan, I visited one of these lounges several times, learning much about Japanese society in the process—everything from the role of women to homosexuality and interracial marriage. I was told that the Japanese feel much more comfortable talking about such subjects in English and would be unable to express themselves as openly in their own language. The *Tokyo Journal,* published monthly to describe what's going on in the capital city, lists conversation lounges in its classified section.

Another way to meet Japanese is to go where they play—namely, the country's countless bars and eateries. There, you'll often encounter Japanese who will want to speak to you if they understand English, and even some slightly inebriated Japanese who will speak to you if they don't. If you're open to it, such chance encounters may prove to be the highlight of your trip, or at the very least an evening of just plain fun.

IMPRESSIONS

The people of this Iland of Iapon are good of nature, curteous above measure, and valiant in warre.
—WILL ADAMS, *TO MY UNKNOWNE FRIENDS AND COUNTRI-MEN,* 1611

The Japanese are in general intelligent and provident, free and unconstrained, obedient and courteous, curious and inquisitive, industrious and ingenious, frugal and sober, cleanly, good-natured and friendly, upright and just, trusty and honest, mistrustful, superstitious, proud, and haughty, unforgiving, brave, and invincible.
—CHARLES PETER THUNBERG, *TRAVELS IN EUROPE AFRICA AND ASIA,* 1795

A race primitive as the Etruscan before Rome was, or more so, adopting the practices of a larger civilization under compulsion.
—LAFCADIO HEARN, 1894, ON THE JAPANESE

ETIQUETTE

Much of Japan's system of etiquette and manners stems from its feudal days, when the social hierarchy dictated how a person spoke, sat, bowed, ate, walked, and lived. Failure to comply with the rules could bring severe punishment, even death.

Of course, nowadays it's quite different, although the Japanese still attach much importance to proper behavior. As a foreigner, however, you can get away with a lot. After all, you're just a "barbarian" and, as such, can be forgiven for not knowing the rules. There are two cardinal sins, however, that you should never commit. One is that you should never wear your shoes inside a Japanese home, traditional inn, or temple; the other is that you should never wash with soap inside a Japanese bathtub. Except for these two horrors, you will probably be forgiven any other social blunder.

As a sensitive traveler, however, you should try to familiarize yourself with the social etiquette in Japan, the basics of which are given below. The Japanese are very appreciative of foreigners who take the time to learn about their country and are quite patient in helping you learn. Remember, if you do commit a faux pas, apologize profusely and smile. They don't chop off heads anymore.

Bowing   The main form of greeting in Japan is the bow rather than the handshake. Although, at first glance, it may seem simple enough, the bow—together with its implications—is actually quite complicated. The depth of the bow and the number of seconds devoted to performing it, as well as the total number of bows, depend on who you are and to whom you're bowing. In addition to bowing in greeting, the Japanese also bow upon departing and to express deep gratitude. The proper form for a bow is to bend from the waist with a straight back and to keep your arms at your sides, but if you are a foreigner, a simple nod of the head is enough. Knowing that foreigners shake hands, a Japanese may extend his hand, although he probably won't be able to stop himself from giving a little bow as well. I've even seen Japanese bow when talking on the telephone. Although I've occasionally witnessed Japanese businessmen shake hands among themselves, the practice is still quite rare.

Visiting Cards   You're a nonentity in Japan if you don't have a visiting card, called a *meishi*. Everyone—from housewives to plumbers to secretaries to bank presidents—carries meishi with him or her to give out during introductions. If you're trying to conduct business in Japan, you'll be regarded suspiciously—even as a phony—if you don't have business cards. As a tourist you don't have to have them, but it certainly doesn't hurt, and the Japanese will be greatly impressed by your preparedness. The card should have your address and occupation on it. You might even consider having your meishi made in Japan, with the Japanese syllabic script (*katakana*) written on the reverse side.

Dining   As soon as you're seated in a Japanese restaurant, you'll be given a wet towel, which will be steaming hot in winter or pleasantly cool in summer. Called an *oshibori*, it's for wiping your hands. In all but the fancy restaurants, men can get away with wiping their faces as well, but women are not supposed to (I ignore this one if I'm hot and sweaty). The oshibori is a great custom, one you'll wish would be adopted back home.

The next thing you'll probably be confronted with are chopsticks. The proper way to use them is to place the first chopstick between the base of the thumb and the top of the ring finger (this chopstick remains stationary) and the second one between the top of the thumb and the middle and index fingers. This second chopstick is the one

IMPRESSIONS

Etiquette is the Kaiser of Japan.
—DOUGLAS SLADEN, *QUEER THINGS ABOUT JAPAN*, 1903

you move to pick up food. The best way to learn to use chopsticks is to have a Japanese show you how. It's not difficult, but if you find it impossible, some restaurants might have a fork as well. How proficiently foreigners handle chopsticks is a matter of great curiosity for the Japanese, and they're surprised if you know how to use them; even if you were to live in Japan for 20 years, you would never stop receiving compliments on how talented you are with chopsticks.

As for etiquette involving chopsticks, if you're taking something from a communal bowl or tray, you're supposed to turn your chopsticks upside down and use the part that hasn't been in your mouth. After transferring the food to your plate, you turn the chopsticks back to their proper position. Never stick your chopsticks down vertically into your bowl of rice and leave them there—that is done only when a person has died.

If you're eating soup, you won't use a spoon. Rather, you will pick up the bowl and drink from it. It's considered in good taste to slurp with gusto, especially if you're eating noodles. Noodle shops in Japan are always well orchestrated with slurps and smacks.

(By the way, it's considered bad manners to walk down the street in Japan eating or drinking. You'll notice that if a Japanese buys a drink from a vending machine, he'll stand there, gulp it down, and throw away the container before going on.)

If you're drinking in Japan, the main thing to remember is that you never pour your own glass. Bottles of beer are so large that people often share one. The rule is that, in turn, one person pours for everyone else in the group, so be sure to hold up your glass when someone is pouring for you. Only as the night progresses do the Japanese get sloppy about this rule. It took me a while to figure this out, but if no one notices that your glass is empty, the best thing to do is to pour everyone else a drink so that someone will pour yours. If someone wants to pour you a drink and your glass is full, the proper thing to do is to take a few gulps so that he or she can fill your glass. Because each person is continually filling everyone else's glass, you never know exactly how much you've had to drink, which (depending on how you look at it) is very good or very bad.

Shoes   Nothing is so distasteful to the Japanese as the bottoms of shoes. Therefore, you should take off your shoes before entering a home, a Japanese-style inn, a temple, and even some museums and restaurants. Usually, there will be some plastic slippers at the entranceway for you to slip on, but whenever you encounter tatami, you should take off even these slippers—only bare feet or socks are allowed to tread upon tatami.

Restrooms are another story. If you're in a home or Japanese inn, you'll notice another pair of slippers—again plastic or rubber—sitting right inside the restroom door. Step out of the hallway plastic shoes and into the bathroom slippers, and wear these the whole time you're in the restroom. When you're finished, change back into the hallway slippers. If you forget this last changeover, you'll regret it—nothing is as embarrassing as walking down the hall in the bathroom slippers and not realizing what you've done until you see the mixed looks of horror and mirth on the faces of the Japanese. Although it might seem like a lot of bother to go through all this ritual with shoes, it actually does make sense once you get used to it.

The Japanese Bath   On my very first trip to Japan, I was certain that I would never get into a Japanese bath. I was under the misconception that men and women bathed together, and I couldn't imagine getting into a tub with a group of smiling and bowing Japanese men. I needn't have worried. The good news (or, I suppose,

---

IMPRESSIONS

It is the man who drinks the first cup of sake, then the second cup of sake drinks the first; then it is the sake that drinks the man.
—Japanese Proverb

bad news for some of you) is that in almost all circumstances bathing is segregated for men and women. There are some exceptions, primarily outdoor hot-spring spas in the countryside, but the women who go to these are usually grandmothers who couldn't care less. Young Japanese women wouldn't dream of jumping into a tub with a group of male strangers.

Japanese baths are delightful—and I, for one, am addicted to them. You find them at Japanese-style inns, at hot-spring spas, and at neighborhood baths (not everyone has his or her own bath in Japan). Sometimes they're elaborate affairs with many tubs, plants, and statues, and sometimes they're nothing more than a tiny tub. The procedure at all of them is the same. After completely disrobing in the changing room and putting your clothes in either a locker or a basket, hold your washcloth in front of you so that it covers the vital parts and walk into the bath area. There, you'll find a plastic basin (they used to be wood), a plastic stool, and faucets along the wall. Sit on the stool in front of a faucet and repeatedly fill your basin with water, splashing it all over you. If there's no hot water from the faucet, it's acceptable to dip your plastic basin into the hot bath. Soap yourself down; then rinse away completely—and I mean *completely*—all traces of soap. After you're squeaky clean, you're ready to get into the bath. When you've finished your bath, do *not* pull the plug.

Your first attempt at a Japanese bath may be painful—simply too scalding for comfort. It helps if you ease in gently and then sit perfectly still. You'll notice all tension and stiffness ebbing away, a decidedly relaxing way to end the day. The Japanese are so fond of baths that many of them take baths every night, especially in the winter, when a hot bath keeps one toasty warm for hours afterward. With time, you'll probably become addicted, too.

Tips on Behavior   Most forms of behavior and etiquette in Japan developed to allow relationships to be as frictionless as possible—a pretty good idea in a country as crowded as Japan. The Japanese don't like confrontations, and although I'm told that fights occur, I've never seen one in Japan.

The Japanese are an emotional people, but they're very good at covering almost all unpleasantness with a smile. Foreigners find the smile hard to read, but a smiling Japanese face can mean happiness, sadness, embarrassment, or even anger. My first lesson in such physiognomic inscrutability happened on a subway in Tokyo, where I saw a middle-aged Japanese woman, who was about to board the subway, being brutally knocked out of the way by a Japanese man rushing off the train. She almost lost her balance, but she gave a little laugh, smiled, and got on the train. A few minutes later, as the train was speeding through the tunnel, I stole a look at her and was able to read her true feelings on her face. Lost in her own thoughts, she knitted her brow in consternation and looked most upset and unhappy. The smile had been a put-on.

Another aspect of Japanese behavior that sometimes causes difficulty for foreigners, especially in business negotiations, is the reluctance of the Japanese to say no when they mean no. They consider such directness poor manners. As a result, they're much more apt to say that your request is very difficult to fulfill, or they'll simply beat around the bush without giving a definite answer. At this point, you're expected to let the subject drop. Showing impatience, anger, or aggressiveness rarely gets you anywhere. Apologizing sometimes does. And if someone does give in to your request, you can't say thank you often enough.

Miscellaneous Etiquette   If you are invited to a Japanese home, you should know that it is both a rarity and an honor. Most Japanese consider their homes too small and humble for entertaining guests, which is why there are so many restaurants, coffee shops, and bars. If you are invited to a home, don't show up empty-handed. Bring a small gift, such as candy, fruit, or flowers. Alcohol is also appreciated. You don't have to fly to Japan more than once to realize that fact—it seems as if every Japanese on board is laden down with his or her three-bottle quota of alcohol. Take your cue from them and stock up on a few bottles on the flight over, especially if you know you'll be visiting someone. Whisky and brandy seem to be the favorites.

When the Japanese give back change, they hand it back to you in a lump sum rather than counting it out. Trust them. It's considered insulting for you to sit there and count it in front of them, because it insinuates that you think they might be trying to cheat you. The Japanese are honest. It's one of the great pleasures of being in their country.

Don't blow your nose in public if you can help it, and never at the dinner table. It's considered most disgusting. On the other hand, even though the Japanese are very hygienic, they are not at all averse to spitting on the sidewalk. And, even more peculiar, the men urinate when and where they want, usually against a tree or a wall and most often after a night of carousing in the bars.

This being a man's society, men will walk in and out of doors and elevators before women, and in subways they will often sit down while their wives stand. Some Japanese men who have had contact with the Western world will make a gallant show of allowing a Western woman to step out of the elevator first. For the sake of Western women living in Japan, such men should be warmly thanked and their behavior greatly encouraged.

6. LANGUAGE

GETTING AROUND

Without a doubt, the hardest part of traveling in Japan is the language barrier. Suddenly you find yourself transported to a crowded land of 120 million people, where you can neither speak nor read the language. To make matters worse, few Japanese speak English. And outside the major cities, the menus, signs at train stations, and shop names are often in Japanese only.

However, millions of foreign visitors before you who didn't speak a word of Japanese have traveled throughout Japan on their own with great success. In fact, I've talked to foreign tourists who told me they thought it was actually quite easy getting around. Much of the anxiety that travelers experience elsewhere is eliminated in Japan, because the country is so safe and the people are so kind and helpful to foreigners. In addition, the Japan National Tourist Organization (JNTO) does a super job of publishing various helpful brochures, leaflets, and maps. Finally, Japan itself has done a mammoth job during the past few years in updating its street signs, subway directions, and addresses in English, at least in the major cities.

If you need to ask directions of strangers in Japan, your best bet is to ask younger people. They have all studied English in school and are most likely to be able to help you. Japanese businessmen also often know some English. And as strange as it sounds, if you're having problems communicating with someone, write it down so that he or she can read it. The emphasis in schools tends to be written rather than oral, with the result that Japanese who can't understand a word you say may know all the subtleties of syntax and English grammar. If you still have problems communicating, you can always call the "Travel-Phone," a toll-free nationwide helpline set up by the JNTO to help foreigners in distress or simply in need of information. (Information on the Travel-Phone is given in the "Fast Facts: Japan" section at the end of Chapter 3.) It also doesn't hurt to arm yourself with a small pocket dictionary.

If you're heading out for a particular restaurant, shop, or sight, it helps to have your destination written out in Japanese. Have someone at your hotel do that for you. If

---

IMPRESSIONS

It has always seemed a grave reflection on the Japanese character that their language, with the exception of the word "fool"—and "countrified fool" is extremely strong—should contain no opportunities for invective.
—PETER QUENNELL, *A SUPERFICIAL JOURNEY THROUGH TOKYO AND PEKING*, 1932

you get lost along the way, look for one of the police boxes, called *koban,* that are found in virtually every neighborhood. They have maps of particular districts and can pinpoint exactly where you want to go if you have the address with you. Remember, too, that train stations in major cities and tourist resort areas have tourist information offices (*kanko annaijo*), which can help you with everything from directions to hotel reservations. The staff may not speak any English, but I don't think you'll have trouble communicating your needs.

Realizing the difficulties that foreigners have with the language barrier in Japan, the JNTO has put out a nifty booklet called *The Tourist's Handbook.* It contains basic sentences in English, with their Japanese equivalents, for almost every activity, from asking directions and shopping to ordering in a restaurant and staying in a Japanese inn. Foreigners traveling around Japan on their own should pick up a copy of this valuable booklet at the Tourist Information Center in either Tokyo or Kyoto. Appendixes A and B in the back of this guide also list some common phrases and words in Japanese to help you get around on your own. *Note:* Japanese nouns do not have plural forms; thus, for example, *ryokan,* a Japanese-style inn, can be both singular and plural. Plural sense is indicated by context.

HISTORY

No one knows the exact origins of the Japanese language, but we do know that it existed only in spoken form until the 6th century. It was then that the Japanese borrowed the Chinese characters, called *kanji,* and used them to develop their own form of written language. Later, two additional character systems, *hiragana* and *katakana,* were added to kanji to form the existing Japanese writing system. Thus, Chinese and Japanese use some of the same pictographs, but otherwise there is no similarity between the languages. While they may be able to recognize some of each other's written language, the Chinese and Japanese cannot communicate verbally.

There are about 10,000 Japanese characters, but the average adult knows only 2,500 or so, which is enough to read newspapers, most books and novels, and other, everyday material. Hiragana and katakana, phonetic alphabets consisting of 46 symbols each, came into use because kanji was considered inadequate to express everything in Japanese thought. Hiragana is used for writing words not expressed in kanji and for verb endings. Katakana is the alphabet used for all foreign words and for telegrams. As a foreigner, for example, if you have visiting cards made up in Japanese, your name will be written in the katakana syllabary.

❂ **Written Japanese uses three different character systems—***kanji, hiragana,* **and** *katakana.*

The Japanese written language—a combination of kanji, hiragana, and katakana—is probably one of the most difficult systems of written communication in the modern world. As for the spoken language, there are many levels of speech and forms of expression relating to a person's social status and sex. It's little wonder that St. Francis Xavier, a Jesuit missionary who came to Japan in the 16th century, wrote that Japanese was an invention of the devil designed to thwart the spread of Christianity. And yet, astoundingly, adult literacy in Japan is estimated to be 99%.

There are at least two ways of pronouncing most kanji in Japanese—one is a Chinese pronunciation from the 6th century, and the other is a Japanese pronunciation. This means that, except by context, one often can't tell by looking at the characters which pronunciation is the proper one. Similarly, if one doesn't know the characters of, say, a restaurant, it may be impossible to find out the telephone number.

JAPANESE PROBLEMS WITH ENGLISH

Despite the fact that Japanese are able to learn their own complicated language, they have much difficulty when it comes to English. Although most students are required to take English for 6 years in school, these studies lean primarily toward entrance exams at universities, which require extensive reading comprehension but almost no practical application. Thus, while many Japanese can read English, few are able to understand spoken English. As I've mentioned elsewhere, if you're having problems communicating with a Japanese, it sometimes helps to write everything down.

Finally, if you're having difficulty communicating with a Japanese, it may help to pronounce an English word in a Japanese way. Foreign words, especially English, have penetrated the Japanese language to such an extent that they are now estimated to make up 20% of the everyday vocabulary. The problem is that these words change in Japanese pronunciation, because words always end in either a vowel or an *n*, and because two consonants in a single syllable are usually separated by a vowel. Would you recognize *terebi* as "television," *koohi* as "coffee," or *rajio* as "radio"?

I'd like to mention here that English words are quite fashionable in Japanese advertising, with the result that you'll often see English on shop signs, posters, shopping bags, and T-shirts. However, words are often wonderfully misspelled, or used in such unusual contexts that you can only guess at the original intent. I don't know how many times my day has been brightened by the discovery of some zany or unfathomable English. What, for example, could possibly be the meaning behind "Today birds, tomorrow men," which appeared under a picture of birds on a shopping bag? In Okayama I saw a shop whose name was a stern admonition to its customers to "Grow Up," while in Kyoto there's the "Selfish" coffee shop and the "Pitiful Pub."

Certainly, the most amusing sign I've seen was at the Narita airport, where each check-in counter displayed a notice advising passengers that they would have to pay a service-facility charge at "the time of check-in for your fright." I was unable to control my giggles as I explained to the perplexed man behind one counter what was wrong with the sign. Two weeks later, when I went back through the airport, I noticed that all the signs had been corrected. That's Japanese efficiency!

7. PERFORMING ARTS & EVENING ENTERTAINMENT

KABUKI

Probably Japan's best-known traditional theater art, Kabuki is also one of the country's most popular forms of entertainment. Visit a performance and it's easy to see why. In a word, Kabuki is fun! The plays are dramatic, the costumes are gorgeous, the stage settings are often fantastic, and the themes are universal—love, revenge, and the conflict between duty and personal feelings. Probably one of the reasons Kabuki is so popular even today is that it developed centuries ago as a form of entertainment for the common people in feudal Japan, particularly the merchants. And one of Kabuki's

---

A NOTE ON JAPANESE SYMBOLS

Many hotels, restaurants, and other establishments in Japan do not have signs giving their names in English letters. As an aid to the reader, Appendix C lists the Japanese symbols for all such places described in this guide. Each set of symbols has a number, which corresponds to the number that appears inside an oval next to the establishment's name in the text. Thus, to find the Japanese symbols for, say, Osaka's **Hotel Hokke Club** ⑬⑧, refer to number 138 in the appendix.

interesting aspects is that all roles—even those depicting women—are portrayed by men.

It didn't start out that way. In Kyoto in the early 1600s, a group of women originated Kabuki by giving performances of erotic dances. Needless to say, the dances were enthusiastically received by the audience, and it wasn't long before there were troupes of women of rather questionable repute giving all kinds of lewd performances. Finally, the shogun decided that the dances were too vulgar and he banned all women from performing. Kabuki was then taken over by all-male companies, who transformed it into the drama it is today.

Kabuki has changed little in the past 100 years. Altogether, there are more than 300 Kabuki plays, all written before this century. For a Westerner, one of the more arresting things about a Kabuki performance is the audience itself. Because this has always been entertainment for the masses, the audience can get quite lively, with yells, guffaws, and laughter from spectators. In fact, old woodcuts of cross-eyed men apparently stemmed from Kabuki—when things got a little too rowdy, actors would stamp their feet and strike a cross-eyed pose in an attempt to get the audience's attention.

Of course, you won't be able to understand what's being said. Indeed, because much of Kabuki drama dates from the 18th century, even the Japanese sometimes have difficulty understanding the language. But it doesn't matter. Many theaters have programs and earphones that describe the plots in minute detail, often in English as well. Thus, you can follow the story and enjoy Kabuki just as much as everyone around you.

NOH

Whereas Kabuki developed as a form of entertainment for the masses, Noh was a much more traditional and aristocratic form of theater. In contrast to Kabuki's extroverted liveliness, Noh is very calculated, slow, and restrained. The oldest form of theater in Japan, it has changed very little in the past 600 years. The language is so archaic that the Japanese cannot understand it at all, which explains in part why Noh does not have the popularity that Kabuki does. *Note:* Don't expect programs in English.

As in Kabuki, all the performers are men. The subject matter of Noh's some 240 surviving plays is usually about supernatural beings, beautiful women, mentally confused people, or tragic-heroic events. Performers usually wear masks.

Because the action is slow, watching an entire evening can be quite tedious unless you are particularly interested in Noh dance and music. You may just want to drop in for a short while. In between Noh plays, there are short comic reliefs called *kyogen,* which usually make fun of life in the 1600s.

BUNRAKU

Bunraku is traditional Japanese puppet theater. But contrary to what you might expect, Bunraku is for adults rather than children, with themes centering on love and revenge, sacrifice and suicide. Many dramas now used in Kabuki were first written for the Bunraku stage.

Popular in Japan since the 17th century, and at times even more popular than Kabuki, Bunraku is fascinating to watch because the puppeteers are right onstage with their puppets. Dressed in black, they are wonderfully skilled in making the puppets seem like living beings. Usually, there are three puppeteers for each puppet, which is about three-fourths the size of a human being. One puppeteer is responsible for movement of the puppet's head, as well as for the expression on its face, and for the

○ **The traditional Japanese puppet theater, Bunraku, is for adults rather than children.**

movement of the right arm and hand. Another puppeteer operates the puppet's left arm and hand, while the third moves the legs. Although at first the puppeteers are somewhat distracting, after a while you forget they're there as the puppets assume personalities of their own. All the talking in Bunraku is provided by a narrator, who tells the story and speaks the various parts as well. The narrator is accompanied by a traditional three-stringed Japanese instrument called a *shamisen*. By all means try to see Bunraku if possible. The most famous presentations are at the Osaka Bunraku Theater, but there are performances in Tokyo and other major cities as well.

8. SPORTS & RECREATION

SUMO

The Japanese form of wrestling known as sumo began perhaps as long as 2,000 years ago, becoming immensely popular by the 6th century. Today, it's still popular, and the best wrestlers are revered as national heroes in Japan, much as baseball players are in the United States. Often taller than 6 feet and weighing well over 300 pounds, sumo wrestlers follow a vigorous training period, which usually begins in their teens. Unmarried wrestlers even live together at their training schools, called sumo stables.

A sumo match takes place on a sandy-floored ring less than 15 feet in diameter. Before each bout, the wrestlers scatter salt in the ring, to purify it from the last bout's loss. They also squat and then raise each leg, stamping it into the ground to crush, symbolically, any evil spirits that may still be lurking there. They then squat down and face each other, glaring to psych each other out. Once they rush each other, the object is for a wrestler either to eject his opponent from the ring or to cause him to touch the ground with any part of his body other than his feet. This is accomplished by shoving, slapping, tripping, throwing, and even carrying the opponent. Altogether, there are 48 holds and throws, and sumo fans know all of them. Most bouts are very short, lasting only 30 seconds or so.

There are six 15-day sumo tournaments in Japan every year. Three are held in Tokyo (in January, May, and September); the others are held in Osaka (in March), Nagoya (in July), and Fukuoka (in November). Matches are widely covered on television as well as on the American armed forces' FEN radio station. If no match is being held during your stay, you may want to drop in on a sumo stable to watch the training.

THE MARTIAL ARTS

Japan's three most popular martial arts—judo, karate, and kendo—all have roots stretching back to the age of the samurai. Judo, the best-known martial art, originated in Japan and is based on jujitsu, a deadly martial art practiced by the samurai as a means of defense. Founded in 1882 by Jigoro Kano, who established the Kodokan Dojo, judo became popular throughout the world after World War II. Judo trains both the body and the mind, with bouts won by one's throwing the opponent or getting hold of him, through several techniques.

Karate, on the other hand, was used as a means of defense and attack, at a time when common people were forbidden from carrying weapons. It developed in ancient China and was imported to Japan via Okinawa. In karate, hands and feet are used to strike vulnerable areas of the opponent, with power achieved through speed and concentration. Although it is generally thought to be an aggressive sport, karate master Gichin Funakoshi, who popularized the sport, emphasized that there was no "first strike" in karate.

The oldest of Japan's martial arts is kendo, an embodiment of the samurai's philosophy of life, combined with swordsmanship. Practiced today with bamboo swords and protective clothing, it, too, emphasizes the training of the mind and body as opponents try to strike each other's mask, arm, or body, using the correct combination of force, bodily posture, and sword position.

Another popular martial art is aikido, which stresses the spiritual aspect of the sport and is said to be "zen in motion." Using the correct breathing and meditation, opponents try to throw or disable each other by attacking weak points.

BASEBALL

Baseball, introduced into Japan from the United States in 1873, is as popular among Japanese as it is among Americans. The playing fields are smaller, but the competition between teams is no less fierce. There are two professional leagues, the Central and the Pacific, which play from April to October and meet in final play-offs. In Tokyo the home teams are the Yomiuri Giants and the Yakult Swallows of the Central League and the Nippon Ham Fighters of the Pacific League. Several American players have gone to Japan to play with Japanese teams and have proved very popular with local fans. Perhaps while you're in Japan you can take in a game and compare it with games you've attended back home. Advance tickets go on sale on Friday two weeks prior to a game and can be purchased at the stadium or, for Tokyo teams, at any Playguide ticket office in the city.

O Baseball is as popular in Japan as it is in the United States, from where it was introduced.

For Tokyo teams, the locations are:

Yomiuri Giants, Tokyo Dome, 1–3 Koraku, Bunkyo-ku (tel. 811/2111). Station: Suidobashi.

Yakult Swallows, Jingu Stadium, 13 Kasumigaokamachi, Shinjuku-ku (tel. 402-2115). Station: A 5-minute walk from Gaien-mae, on the Ginza Line.

Nippon Ham Fighters, Tokyo Dome, 1–3 Koraku, Bunkyo-ku (tel. 811-2111). Station: Suidobashi.

Two other major teams, outside Tokyo, are:

Lotte Orions, Kawasaki Stadium, 2–1–9 Fujimi, Kawasaki-ku, *Kawasaki City,* Kanagawa Prefecture (tel. 044/244-1171). Station: Kawasaki Station, then 5 minutes by bus no. 16, 19, 21, 22, or 23.

Seibu Lions, Seibu Lions Stadium, 2135 Kami Yamaguchi, *Tokorozawa City,* Saitama Prefecture (tel. 0429/25-1151). Station: Seibu Kyujo-mae Station, on the Seibu Sayama Line.

HIKING

Day hiking and backpacking are popular summer recreational activities in Japan, particularly in the Japan Alps and in Hokkaido, where there are cabins in which hikers can stay overnight. Another popular trek is up to the summit of Mt. Fuji (covered later in this book). Check with the Tourist Information Center in Tokyo or Kyoto about details for different parts of the country.

SKIING

With about 75% of Japan's land space consisting of mountains, you can bet that skiing is the country's most popular winter sport. The skiing is so good that Hokkaido, Japan's big northern island, was selected as the site of the 1972 Winter Olympics. With the ski season generally lasting from about mid-December to early April, keep in mind that the slopes—especially those close to a large city—can be very crowded during weekends and holidays. Also, although shops where you can rent skis, boots, and poles for about ¥4,000 ($28.50) to ¥5,500 ($39) a day are plentiful, most don't have shoes larger than about a man's size 9. Day passes for ski lifts generally run about ¥3,500 ($25). For more information, the Tourist Information Centers in both Tokyo and Kyoto have a pamphlet called *Skiing in Japan,* which gives information about ski resorts in northern and central Japan.

There are also a number of skiing areas within easy access of Tokyo and Sapporo. A great plus of many Japanese ski resorts is that they're situated around hot springs—what could be better than soaking in a hot tub after a day out on the slopes?

9. FOOD & DRINK

Whenever I leave Japan, it's the food I miss the most. Sure, there are *sushi* bars and other Japanese specialty restaurants throughout the United States, but they don't offer nearly the variety you can get in Japan. For just as America has more to offer than hamburgers and steaks, Japan has more than just sushi and *teppanyaki*. For both the gourmet and the uninitiated, Japan is a treasure trove of culinary surprises.

FOOD

MEALS & DINING CUSTOMS

Altogether, there are more than a dozen different and distinct types of Japanese cuisine, plus countless regional specialties. A good deal of what you eat may be completely new to you, as well as completely unidentifiable. No need to worry. I've found that sometimes the Japanese don't even know what they're eating, so varied and so wide is the range of edibles. The rule is simply to enjoy—and enjoyment begins even before you raise your chopsticks to your mouth. To the Japanese, presentation of food is as important as the food itself, and dishes are designed to appeal not only to the palate but to the eye. In contrast to the American way of piling as much food as possible onto a single plate, the Japanese use lots of small plates, each arranged artfully with bite-size morsels of food. After you've seen what can be done with maple leaves, flowers, bits of bamboo, and even pebbles to enhance the appearance of food, your relationship with what you eat may be changed forever.

Below are explanations of some of the most common types of Japanese cuisine. Generally, only one type of cuisine is served in a given restaurant—for example, only raw seafood is served in a sushi bar. There are some exceptions to this, especially in those restaurants where raw fish may be served as an appetizer. In addition, some of Japan's drinking establishments offer a wide range of foods, from soups and salads to sushi and skewered pieces of chicken.

For a quick rundown of the various types of Japanese foods, refer to the glossary of menu terms in Appendix B.

Rice There are no problems here—everyone is familiar with rice. The difference, however, is that in Japan it is quite sticky, making it easier to pick up with chopsticks. It's also just plain white rice (called *gohan*)—no salt, no butter, no soy sauce. Like other Asians, the Japanese have used rice as a staple in their diet for about 2,000 years, although not everyone in the old days could afford the expensive white kind. The peasants had to be satisfied with a mixture of white and brown rice, millet, and greens. Today, some Japanese still eat rice three times a day, although the younger ones are now just as apt to have bread and coffee for breakfast.

Kaiseki The king of Japanese cuisine, *kaiseki* is the epitome of delicately and exquisitely arranged food, the ultimate in Japanese aesthetic appeal. It's also among the most expensive and can cost ¥25,000 ($178) or more per person; some restaurants, however, do offer mini-kaiseki courses that are much more affordable. Kaiseki is expensive because so much time and skill are involved in preparing each of the many dishes, with the ingredients cooked so as to preserve their natural flavor. Even the plates are chosen with great care: they are meant to enhance the color, texture, and shape of each piece of food.

Kaiseki cuisine is based on the four seasons, with the selection of food and its

---

IMPRESSIONS

There is a saying that the Chinese eat with their stomachs and the Japanese with their eyes.
—BERNARD LEACH, *A POTTER IN JAPAN*, 1960

presentation dependent on the time of the year. In fact, so strongly does a kaiseki preparation convey the mood of a particular season that the kaiseki gourmet can tell what season it is just by looking at his meal. (The roots of kaiseki go back to the development of the tea ceremony, when monks ate small morsels of food to protect the stomach against the effects of strong tea.)

A kaiseki meal is usually a lengthy affair, with various dishes appearing in set order. First come the appetizer, clear broth, and one uncooked dish. These are followed by boiled, broiled, fried, steamed, heated, and vinegar-ed dishes, and finally by another soup, rice, pickled vegetables, and fruit. Since kaiseki is always a set course, there's no problem in ordering. Let your budget be your guide.

Sashimi & Sushi   It is estimated that the average Japanese eats 70 pounds of seafood a year, six times the amount Americans do. Although this seafood may be served in any number of ways, from grilled to boiled, a great deal of it is eaten raw. Granted, the idea of eating raw fish might seem a little strange at first, but if you'll just try it you'll probably like it.

Sashimi is simply raw seafood. If you've never eaten it, a good choice to start out with is *maguro,* or lean tuna. Contrary to what you might think, it doesn't taste fishy at all and is so delicate in texture that it almost melts in your mouth. The way to eat sashimi is first to mix *wasabi* (pungent green horseradish) into a small dish of soy sauce and then dip the raw fish in the sauce.

Sushi, also called *nigiri-zushi,* is raw fish, seafood, or vegetables placed on top of vinegared rice with just a touch of wasabi. It's also dipped in soy sauce. Use chopsticks or your fingers to eat sushi; remember that you're supposed to eat each piece in one bite—quite a mouthful, but about the only way to keep it from falling apart. Another trick is to turn it upside down when you dip it in the sauce; that way, only the fish and not the rice touches the sauce.

Typical sushi includes flounder (*hirame*), sea bream (*tai*), squid (*ika*), octopus (*tako*), shrimp (*ebi*), and omelet (*tamago*). Ordering is easy because you usually sit at the sushi bar, where you can see all the food in a refrigerated glass case in front of you. You also get to see the sushi chefs at work.

❂ To the Japanese, how a prepared dish looks is at least as important as how it tastes.

The typical meal begins with sashimi and is followed by sushi, but if you don't want to order separately, there are always various set courses.

Tempura   Today a well-known Japanese food, *tempura* was actually introduced by the Portuguese, who came to Japan in the 16th century. Tempura is food that has been coated in a batter of egg, water, and wheat flour, and then deep-fried; it is served piping hot. To eat it, dip it in soy sauce that has been mixed with a fish stock base and flavored with radish (*daikon*) and grated ginger. Various tempura specialties may include eggplant, mushroom, sweet potato, green pepper, sliced lotus root, shrimp, squid, and many kinds of fish. Again, the easiest thing to do is to order the set course, the *teishoku*. If you're still hungry, you can always order something extra à la carte.

Sukiyaki   Until about a hundred years ago, the Japanese could think of nothing so disgusting as eating the flesh of animals (fish was okay). Considered unclean by the Buddhists, meat consumption was banned by the emperor way back in the 7th century. Imagine the horror of the Japanese to discover that Western "barbarians" ate bloody meat! It wasn't until Emperor Meiji himself made a public announcement a century ago that he was going to eat meat that the Japanese accepted the idea. Today, the Japanese have become skilled in preparing a number of beef dishes, and according to a survey conducted a couple of years ago by the Japan Fisheries Association, grilled meat, curried rice, and hamburger were the three favorite dishes among senior high school boys living in Tokyo. The girls, by the way, still preferred sushi.

Sukiyaki is among Japan's best-known beef dishes, and is one many Westerners seem to prefer. Actually, its origins are more Western than Japanese (it was introduced in the last century as a new Western cuisine). To the Western palate, however, it seems distinctly Japanese and today enjoys immense popularity in Japan. Whenever I'm invited to a Japanese home, this is the meal most often served. Like fondue, it's cooked at the table, which makes for an intimate and cozy setting.

Sukiyaki is thinly sliced beef cooked in a broth of soy sauce, stock, and sake, along with scallions, spinach, mushrooms, tofu, bamboo shoots, and other vegetables. All diners serve themselves by taking what they want out of the simmering pot and then dipping it into their own bowl of raw egg. You can skip the raw egg if you want, but it adds to the taste and also cools the food down enough so it doesn't burn your tongue.

Shabu-Shabu   Similar to sukiyaki, *shabu-shabu* is also prepared at your table and consists of thinly sliced beef cooked in a broth with vegetables. (It is named for the swishing sound the beef supposedly makes when cooking.) The main difference between the two dishes is the broth. Whereas in sukiyaki it consists of stock flavored with soy sauce and sake and is slightly sweet, in shabu-shabu it is relatively clear and has little taste of its own. The pots used are also different.

Using their chopsticks, diners hold pieces of meat in the watery broth until they are cooked. This usually takes only a few seconds. Vegetables are left in longer, to swim around until fished out. For dipping, there is either sesame sauce with diced green onions or a more bitter sauce made from fish stock. Restaurants serving sukiyaki usually serve shabu-shabu as well.

Teppanyaki   A *teppanyaki* restaurant is a Japanese steakhouse. As in the famous Benihana restaurants in many U.S. cities, the chef slices, dices, and cooks your meal of tenderloin or sirloin steak and vegetables on a smooth hot grill right in front of you. Because beef is relatively new in Japanese cooking, some people categorize teppanyaki restaurants as "Western." However, I consider this style of cooking and presentation special enough that throughout this book I generally refer to such restaurants as Japanese.

Robatayaki   *Robatayaki* refers to restaurants in which seafood and vegetables are cooked over a *robata* grill. In the olden days an open fireplace (robata) in the middle of an old Japanese house was the center of activity for cooking, eating, socializing, and simply keeping warm. Therefore, today's robatayaki restaurants are like nostalgia trips back into Japan's past, and are often decorated in rustic farmhouse style, with the staff dressed in traditional clothing. Robatayaki restaurants, many open only in the evening, are popular among office workers for both eating and drinking.

There's no special menu in a robatayaki restaurant—rather, it includes just about everything eaten in Japan. The difference is that most of the food will be grilled. Favorites of mine include gingko nuts, asparagus, green peppers, mushrooms, potatoes, and just about any kind of fish. You can usually get skewers of beef or chicken, as well as a stew of meat and potatoes (*nikujaga*), delicious in cold winter months. Since ordering is à la carte, you'll just have to look and point.

Yakitori   *Yakitori* is chunks of chicken or chicken parts basted in a sweet soy sauce and grilled over a charcoal fire on thin skewers. A place that serves yakitori (sometimes called a *yakitori-ya* and often identifiable by a red paper lantern outside its front door) is technically not a restaurant but, rather, a drinking establishment; it usually doesn't open until 5pm. Most yakitori-ya are extremely popular with the working crowd as inexpensive places to drink, eat, and be merry.

Although you can order a set dish of various yakitori, I usually refrain, since this will often include various parts of the chicken like the skin, heart, and liver. You may like such exotica, but they're definitely not for me. If you're ordering by the stick, you might want to try chicken meatballs (*tsukune*), green peppers (*piman*), chicken and leeks (*negima*), mushrooms (*shitake*), gingko nuts (*ginnan*), or chicken breast (*sasami*).

Kushiage   *Kushiage* foods (also called *kushikatsu* or *kushiyaki*) are deep-fried on skewers and include chicken, beef, seafood, and lots of seasonal vegetables (snow peas, gingko nuts, lotus root, and the like). The result is delicious and I highly recommend trying it. I don't understand why this style of cooking isn't better known—maybe someday it will be. Ordering the set menu is easiest, and what you get is often determined by both the chef and the season.

Tonkatsu   The Japanese word for "pork cutlet," *tonkatsu* is made by dredging pork in wheat flour, moistening it with egg and water, dipping it in bread crumbs, and deep-frying it in vegetable oil. Since restaurants serving tonkatsu are generally inexpensive, they are popular with office workers and families. The easiest order is the teishoku, which usually features either the pork filet (*hirekatsu*) or the pork loin (*rosukatsu*). In any case, your tonkatsu is served on a bed of lettuce or shredded cabbage, and two different sauces will be at your table.

Fugu   Known as blowfish, pufferfish, or globefish in English, *fugu* is one of the most exotic and adventurous foods in Japan—if it's not prepared properly, it means almost certain death for the consumer! In the past decade or so, as many as 200 people in Japan have died from fugu poisoning, usually because they tried preparing it at home. The fugu's ovaries and intestines are deadly and must be entirely removed, without puncturing them. So why eat fugu if it can kill you? Well, for one thing, it's delicious, and for another, fugu chefs are strictly licensed by the government and greatly skilled in preparing fugu dishes. You can eat fugu either raw (*sashimi*) or in a stew (*fugu-chiri*) cooked with vegetables at your table. The season for fresh fugu is from October or November through March, but some restaurants serve it throughout the year.

Unagi   I'll bet that if you ate *unagi* without knowing what it was, you'd find it very tasty. In fact, you'd probably be very surprised to find out that you had just eaten eel. Popular as a health food because of its high vitamin A content, eel is supposed to help fight fatigue during the hot summer months, but it is eaten year round. Broiled eel (*kabayaki*) is prepared by grilling filet strips over a charcoal fire; the eel is repeatedly dipped in a sweetened barbecue soy sauce while cooking. A favorite way to eat broiled eel is on top of rice, in which case it's called *unaju*. Do yourself a favor and try it.

Noodles   The Japanese love eating noodles, but I suspect that at least part of the fascination stems from the way they eat them—they slurp, sucking in the noodles with a speed that defies gravity. At any rate, you're supposed to slurp noodles—it's considered proper etiquette. Fearing that it would stick with me forever, however, slurping is a technique I've never quite mastered.

There are many different kinds of noodles—some are eaten plain, some in combination with other foods; some are hot and some are cold. *Soba,* made from buckwheat flour, is eaten hot or cold. *Udon* is a thick, white noodle originally from Osaka; it's usually served hot. *Somen* is a fine, white noodle that is eaten cold in the summer and dunked in a cold sauce.

Okonomiyaki   *Okonomiyaki,* which originated in Osaka and literally means "as you like it," could be considered a Japanese pizza. Basically, it's a kind of pancake to which meat or fish, shredded cabbage, and vegetables are added. Since it's a popular offering of street vendors, restaurants specializing in this type of cuisine are very reasonably priced. At some places the cook makes it for you, but at other places it's do-it-yourself, which can be quite fun if you're with a group.

OTHER TYPES OF CUISINE

During your travels you might also run into these types of Japanese cuisine. *Kamameshi* is a rice casserole with different kinds of toppings that might include seafood, meat, or vegetables. *Nabe,* a stew cooked in an earthenware pot at your table, has ingredients that might consist of chicken, sliced beef, pork, or seafood, and vegetables. *Oden* is fish cakes, *tofu,* and vegetables steeped in broth, served with hot mustard.

Although technically Chinese fast-food restaurants, *ramen* shops are so much a part of dining in Japan that I feel compelled to include them here. Serving what I consider to be generic Chinese noodles, soups, and other dishes, ramen shops can be found everywhere, easily recognizable by their red signs, flashing lights, and quite often pictures of various dishes displayed right by the front door. In addition to ramen (noodle and vegetable soup), you can also get such things as *yakisoba* (fried noodles) or—my favorite—*gyoza* (fried pork dumplings). What these places lack in atmosphere is made up for in price: most dishes average about ¥500 ($3.57).

DRINKS

All Japanese restaurants serve complimentary green tea with meals. If that's a little too weak, you may want to try *sake,* an alcoholic beverage made from rice and served either hot or cold. It goes well with most forms of Japanese cuisine. Produced since about the 3rd century, sake is an integral part of Shinto wedding ceremonies, celebrations, and festivals. Sake varies according to the region in which it is produced and the production method that is involved, differing in alcoholic content, color, aroma, and taste. Altogether, there are about 2,000 brands of sake produced in Japan. Miyabi is a prized classic sake; other popular brands are Gekkeikan, Koshinokanbai, Hakutsuru (meaning White Crane), and Ozeki.

Japanese beer is also very popular. The biggest sellers are Suntory, Kirin, and Sapporo, with a wide variety of choices in each category. In attempt to capture the newest drinking market—Japanese women—beer companies continually come out with new products. Ironically enough, Budweiser is also a big hit among young Japanese. Businessmen are fond of whisky, which they usually drink with ice and water. Although cocktails are available in discos, hotel lounges, and fancier bars, most Japanese stick with beer, sake, or whisky.

Popular in recent years is *shochu,* an alcoholic beverage usually made from rice but sometimes from wheat or sweet potatoes. It used to be considered a drink of the lower classes, but its sales have increased so much that it's threatening the sake and whisky businesses. A clear liquid, it's often combined with soda water in a drink called *chu-hi,* but watch out—the stuff can be deadly.

10. RECOMMENDED BOOKS & FILMS

BOOKS

Japanese society, history, and culture are so rich and extensive that I have been able to give only a short overview in this book. Fortunately, there are vast numbers of books in English covering every aspect of Japan, so you shouldn't have any problem reading up on various subjects in more detail. In particular, Kodansha International, a Japanese publisher, has probably brought out more books on Japan in English than any other company. Available at major bookstores in Japan, its books are distributed in the United States through HarperCollins, 10 E. 53rd St., New York, NY 10022.

For an introduction to Japan's history, a standard work is George B. Sansom's *Japan: A Short Cultural History* (Prentice Hall, 1962), which ranges from antiquity to modern times. A former U.S. ambassador to Japan, Edwin O. Reischauer, gives a detailed look at its history in *Japan: The Story of a Nation* (Knopf, 1974). If you're interested in Japan since World War II, *A History of Postwar Japan* (Kodansha, 1982), by Masataka Kosaka, takes in the enormous changes that have occurred in the country in the past few decades.

A general overview of Japanese history, politics, and society is provided in Reischauer's study *The Japanese* (Harvard University Press, 1977). Delving deeper into Japanese society and psychology are Kurt Singer's *Mirror, Sword and Jewel: The Geometry of Japanese Life* (Kodansha, 1981) and Chie Nakane's *Japanese Society* (University of California Press, 1970). A classic description of the Japanese and their culture is found in Ruth Benedict's brilliantly written book *The Chrysanthemum and the Sword: Patterns of Japanese Culture* (New American Library, 1967), first published in the 1940s but reprinted many times since. For a more contemporary approach, look into *The Japanese Mind: The Goliath Explained* (Linden Press/ Simon & Schuster, 1983), by Robert C. Christopher. I consider this book compulsory reading for anyone traveling to Japan because it describes so accurately the Japanese, the role history has played in developing their psyche, and the problems facing the nation today.

In a more lighthearted vein, a delightful account of the Japanese and their customs is given by the irrepressible George Mikes in *The Land of the Rising Yen*. Because it was published in the early 1970s and is now out of print, I doubt you'll be able to find the book in the United States; it's in major bookstores in Japan, however, and would make enjoyable reading during your trip.

Likewise, the Japan Travel Bureau puts out some nifty pocket-size booklets on things Japanese, including *Eating in Japan, Living Japanese Style,* and *Festivals of Japan.* My favorite, however, is *Salaryman in Japan* (JTB, 1986), which describes the private and working lives of those guys in the look-alike business suits—Japan's army of white-collar workers who receive set salaries. With chapters devoted to life in the salaryman's company, the etiquette of business cards, company trips, the wife of a salaryman, and even the "salaryman blues," this book is both entertaining and enlightening.

If you're interested in women's issues in Japan, read Alice Cook and Hiroko Hayashi's *Working Women in Japan: Discrimination, Resistance and Reform* (ILR Press, 1980). A book seemingly from another era is *Geisha* (Kodansha, 1983), by Liza C. Dalby; it describes her year living as a geisha in Kyoto as part of a research project.

For information on Japanese religions, two beautifully illustrated books are *Shinto: Japan's Spiritual Roots* (Kodansha, 1980) and *Buddhism: Japan's Cultural Identity* (Kodansha, 1982), both by Stuart D. B. Picken, with introductions by Edwin O. Reischauer.

If you find yourself becoming addicted to Japanese food, you might want to invest in a copy of *Japanese Cooking: A Simple Art* (Kodansha, 1980), by Shizuo Tsuji. Written by the proprietor of one of the largest cooking schools in Japan, this book contains more than 220 recipes, as well as information on food history and table etiquette. The history and philosophy of the tea ceremony, beginning with its origins in the 12th century, are given in *The Tea Ceremony* (Kodansha, 1983), by Sen'o Tanaka.

An introduction to Japanese art is provided in Langdon Warner's *Enduring Art of Japan* (Grove Press, 1958). *Japan, A History of Art* (Doubleday, 1971), by Bradley Smith, offers a beautifully illustrated overview and makes an elegant coffee-table book, too. *A Net of Fireflies: Japanese Haiku and Haiku Paintings* (Charles E. Tuttle, 1960) is a charming collection of these typical Japanese art forms. Kabuki and other stage arts are covered in Faubion Bowers's *Japanese Theater* (Greenwood Press, 1976).

Two other informative books are *The World of the Shining Prince: Court Life in Ancient Japan* (Knopf, 1964), by Ivan Morris, and—if you are planning to stay at a ryokan—*The Japanese Inn: A Reconstruction of the Past* (UH Press, 1982), in which Oliver Statler takes you through 400 years of Japanese social history with the family that owned one.

Whenever I travel in Japan, I especially enjoy reading fictional accounts of the country; they put me more in tune with my surroundings and increase my awareness and perception. The world's first major novel was written by a Japanese woman, Murasaki Shikibu, whose classic, *The Tale of Genji* (Knopf, 1978), dating from the 11th century, describes the aristocratic life of Prince Genji. Lafcadio Hearn, a prolific writer about things Japanese in the late 19th century, describes life in Japan around the turn of the century in *Writings from Japan* (Penguin, 1985), while Isabella Bird, an Englishwoman who traveled alone to Hokkaido in the 1870s, writes a vivid account of what life was like for rural Japanese in *Unbeaten Tracks in Japan* (Virago Press Limited, 1984). An overview of Japanese classical literature is provided in *Anthology of Japanese Literature* (Grove Press, 1955), edited by Donald Keene. In Tokyo bookstores, you'll find whole sections dedicated to English translations of Japan's best-known authors, including Mishima Yukio, Soseki Natsume, Kobo Abe, Junichiro Tanizaki, and Nobel Prize–winner Kawabata Yasunari.

Finally, because it was also made into a television miniseries, most Westerners are familiar with James Clavell's *Shogun* (Dell, 1975), a fictional account based on the lives of Englishman William Adams and military leader Tokugawa Ieyasu around

1600. In addition, a vivid history of Japanese woodblock prints from the 17th to the 19th century comes alive in a first-person account written by James Michener in *The Floating World* (University of Hawaii Press, 1983).

For more recent, personal accounts of what it's like for Westerners living in Japan, two entertaining novels are *Ransom* (Vintage, 1985), by Jay McInerney, and *Pictures from the Water Trade* (Harper & Row, 1986), by John D. Morley. Robert J. Collins describes life in Tokyo in *Max Danger: The Adventures of an Expat in Tokyo* (Charles E. Tuttle, 1987).

FILMS

Samurai flicks, which resemble the American western, have never lost their appeal to the Japanese audience. The classic samurai film is probably Kurosawa Akira's *The Seven Samurai*. Other Kurosawa films that deal with feudal Japan include *Kagemusha*, which was cowinner of the Grand Prize at the 1980 Cannes Film Festival, and *Ran*, an epic drama set in 16th-century Japan, based on Shakespeare's *King Lear*.

For a look at Japan's mountain people in the 1880s, nothing can beat Shohei Imamura's *The Ballad of Narayama*, with its unsentimentalized portrait of an elderly woman who goes off into the snowy countryside to die, as was the custom of her people. Another film providing insight into the Japanese psyche is Nagisa Oshima's *Merry Christmas, Mr. Lawrence,* about a P.O.W. camp in Java in 1942; the cast includes rock stars David Bowie and Ryuichi Sakamoto.

Mishima, produced by Francis Ford Coppola and George Lucas and directed by Paul Schrader, relates the bizarre life and death of Mishima Yukio, one of Japan's most famous writers.

Juzo Itami, a well-known Japanese director, created a stir in the film world with *In the Realm of the Senses,* a story of obsessive love between a prostitute and the master of the house. Considered too erotic, it was banned from its premiere at the New York Film Festival in 1976. Juzo Itami's more recent works have been humorous films. *Tampopo* is about a Japanese woman who achieves success with a noodle shop, while *The Funeral* is a comic look at death in Japan, including the surviving family's helplessness when it comes to arranging the complex rituals of the Buddhist ceremony.

CHAPTER 2

PLANNING YOUR TRIP — BEFORE YOU GO

It's quite natural, when you're preparing for a trip abroad, to feel a certain anxiety, especially if your trip is to the other side of the planet, to a country whose language you do not speak and whose customs and traditions may be strange to you. Such fear of the unknown can give even the most seasoned traveler butterflies.

This chapter and the next, therefore, are intended to allay your anxiety by advising you, step by step, on how to plan your trip properly, both before you leave home and after you arrive in Japan. They are designed to answer any questions you may have concerning the what, when, where, and how of foreign travel—from what documents and clothes you should take with you to how to get around Japan easily and economically, despite the language barrier.

In the conviction, however, that familiarity breeds confidence, I recommend that you also read the other chapters in this guide before embarking on your trip. They will advise you on what to expect in the way of accommodations and dining choices, on the best places at which to do your shopping, and on the many attractions that this fascinating country has to offer. The breakdown by price categories will enable you to plan your budget ahead of time.

1. INFORMATION, ENTRY REQUIREMENTS & MONEY

INFORMATION

The **Japan National Tourist Organization (JNTO)** publishes a wealth of free, colorful brochures and maps covering Japan as a whole, Tokyo, and various regions of the country. For general information about Japan, ask for *Economical Travel in Japan,* with money-saving advice on traveling, lodging, and dining; and *The Tourist's Handbook,* a phrase booklet to help foreign visitors communicate with the Japanese.

If you'd like more information on Japan before leaving home, write to or call one of the JNTO offices:

UNITED STATES New York: 630 Fifth Ave., New York, NY 10011 (tel. 212/757-5640). **Chicago:** 401 N. Michigan Ave., Suite 770, Chicago, IL 60611 (tel. 312/222-0874). **Dallas:** 2121 San Jacinto St., Suite 980, Dallas, TX 75201 (tel. 214/754-1820). **San Francisco:** 360 Post St., Suite 401, San Francisco, CA 94108 (tel. 415/989-7140). **Los Angeles:** 624 S. Grand Ave., Los Angeles, CA 90017 (tel. 213/623-1952).

CANADA Toronto: 165 University Ave., Toronto, ON M5H 3B8, Canada (tel. 416/366-7140).

UNITED KINGDOM London: 167 Regent St., London, W1, England (tel. 071/734-9638).

AUSTRALIA Sydney: 115 Pitt St., Sydney, NSW 2000, Australia (tel. 02/232-4522).

In Japan, you'll find tourist offices in nearly all the cities and towns; most of them are located at or near the main train station. Although the staff at a particular tourist office may not speak English and may not be able to provide you with maps in English, it can point you in the direction of your hotel and, in many cases, it can even make bookings for you. Your best bet for information is the **Tourist Information Center (TIC).** Operated by the Japan National Tourist Organization, the TIC has offices in Tokyo, as well as at the Narita airport outside Tokyo, and in Kyoto. It distributes leaflets on destinations throughout Japan, along with information on train, bus, and ferry schedules. Unfortunately, the leaflets are almost never available at the destinations themselves, so you must pick them up at the TIC before leaving Tokyo or Kyoto. Some of the leaflets covering Japan's cities and regions are:

Beppu and Vicinity	*Mt. Fuji and Fuji Five Lakes*
Fukuoka	*Nagasaki and Unzen*
Hakone and Kamakura	*Nagoya and Vicinity*
Hiroshima and Miyajima	*Narita*
The Inland Sea	*Nikko*
Ise-Shima	*Okayama and Kurashiki*
The Izu Peninsula	*Sapporo and Vicinity*
Kagoshima and Vicinity	*Sendai, Matsushima, and Hiraizumi*
Kanazawa	*Shikoku*
Kobe, Himeji, and Takarazuka	*Southern Hokkaido*
Kumamoto and Mt. Aso	*Takayama and Vicinity*
Matsue and Izumo-Taisha	*Walking Tour Courses in Kyoto*
Matsumoto and Kamikochi	*Walking Tour Courses in Nara*
Miyazaki and Vicinity	*Walking Tour Courses in Tokyo*
Morioka and Rikuchu Kaigan	
(Coast) National Park	

The TIC also has leaflets on major attractions and sights—for example, *Japanese Gardens, Japanese Hot Springs,* and *Museums and Art Galleries.* For more information on tourist information centers, see the individual listings for cities.

ENTRY REQUIREMENTS

Americans traveling to Japan as tourists with the intention of staying 3 months or less need only a valid passport to gain entry into the country; visa requirements have been waived by a reciprocal visa-exemption agreement that extends to 1993. Whether visa requirements will then be changed had not been announced by press time, so contact a Japanese embassy or tourist office if you plan on being in Japan beyond 1993.

Note that only American tourists do not need a visa—those in the country for sightseeing, sports activities, family visits, inspection tours, meetings, or short study courses. In other words, you cannot work in Japan or engage in any remunerative activity, including the teaching of English (though many young people ignore the law). No extensions of stay are granted, which means that American tourists must absolutely leave the country after 3 months. If you are going to Japan to work or study and plan on being there for more than 3 months, you will need a visa; contact the Japanese embassy or consulate nearest you.

Australians must possess a passport and a 3-month visa for entry to Japan, and can apply for extensions for longer stays. Canadians and New Zealanders do not need a visa for stays of up to 90 days, while citizens of the United Kingdom and Ireland can stay for up to 180 days without a visa.

If you qualify for an extension of stay in Japan (for example, you are on a working visa or are a Canadian on a tourist visa), you can apply at the nearest immigration bureau in Japan. In Tokyo the place to go is the **Tokyo Regional Immigration Bureau,** 1-3-1 Otemachi, Chiyoda-ku (tel. 03/213-8111), near the Otemachi subway station. Hours are 9am to 5pm (closed from noon to 1pm for lunch) on weekdays and 9am to noon on Saturday. After you've extended your visa, you must also apply for an alien registration card, which all foreigners must carry if they stay in Japan longer than 3 months. Apply at the ward office closest to your home or hotel. (All cities in Japan are divided into wards, called *ku*). The registration card is free, but you'll need two passport-size photos.

Foreigners are required to carry with them at all times either their passports or their alien registration cards. The police generally do not stop foreigners, but if you're caught without the proper identification, you'll be taken to the local police headquarters. It happened to me once, and believe me, I can think of better ways to spend an hour and a half. I had to explain in detail who I was, what I was doing in Japan, where I lived, and what I planned on doing for the rest of my life. I then had to write a statement explaining how it was that I rushed out that day without my passport, apologizing and promising never to do such a thoughtless thing again. The policemen at the station were very nice and polite—they were simply doing their duty.

If you intend to drive in Japan, you'll need either an international or—if you stay longer than a year—a Japanese driver's license.

MONEY
CASH/CURRENCY

The currency in Japan is called the **yen,** symbolized by **¥.** Coins come in denominations of ¥1, ¥5, ¥10, ¥50, ¥100, and ¥500. Bills come in denominations of ¥1,000, ¥5,000, and ¥10,000. Although the conversion rate varies daily, the prices in this book are based on the rate of ¥140 to US$1. In your own rough calculations, therefore, you can generally approximate what things cost by figuring roughly $7 to every ¥1,000. If something costs ¥5,000, for example, you know it's around $35.

Personal checks are virtually useless in Japan. Even if you have an account at a Japanese bank, processing a personal check costs about $20 and takes a couple of weeks. Most Japanese pay with either credit cards or cash—and because the country has such a low crime rate, you can feel safe walking around with lots of money (although, as a rule, you should always exercise caution whenever you're traveling). When I worked as editor of a travel magazine in Tokyo, I was paid in cash; I often left the office for a night on the town with a whole month's salary in my purse. Never once was I afraid of being mugged, and I certainly wasn't the only one. Because the Japanese feel so safe in their own society and carry lots of cash with them, sadly enough they're often easy targets when they travel abroad. The only time you should be alert to possible pickpockets in Japan is when you're riding a crowded subway during rush hour.

If you need to exchange money outside of banking hours, inquire at one of the larger first-class hotels—some of them will cash traveler's checks or exchange money, even if you're not their guest. If you're arriving at the Narita airport outside Tokyo, you can exchange money there from 9am until the arrival of the last flight.

THE YEN AND THE DOLLAR

Note that although the prices quoted in this book were figured at a rate of ¥140 to US$1, the U.S. dollar equivalents given might vary during the lifetime of this edition, due to fluctuations in the exchange rate of the yen. Therefore, the following table should be used only as a rough guide.

¥	US$	¥	US$
10	.07	800	5.70
50	.35	900	6.45
100	.71	1,000	7.15
150	1.07	1,500	10.70
200	1.43	2,000	14.30
300	2.14	5,000	35.70
400	2.85	10,000	71.40
500	3.57	15,000	107.15
600	4.28	20,000	142.85
700	5.00		

TRAVELER'S CHECKS

Traveler's checks can be exchanged for yen at any bank. They generally fetch a better exchange rate than cash.

CREDIT CARDS

As an example of how adaptable the Japanese are, just 5 years ago you'd be hard pressed to find establishments outside hotels, tourist shops, and well-known restaurants that accepted credit cards. Even the most expensive kaiseki meals, which could easily cost upward of ¥20,000 ($143), would usually have to be paid for in cash.

No longer. Credit cards have taken Japan by storm, with the most readily accepted cards being American Express, Visa, and the Japanese credit card JCB (Japan Credit Bureau). Many tourist-oriented facilities also accept MasterCard and Diners Club. Shops and restaurants accepting credit cards will usually post which cards they accept at their front door. However, some establishments may be reluctant to accept cards for small purchases. Inquire beforehand. In addition, note that the majority of Japan's smaller businesses, including noodle shops, fast-food joints, and ma-and-pa establishments, do not accept credit cards.

WHAT THINGS COST IN TOKYO	U.S. $
Taxi from the Narita airport to city center	157.00
Subway ride from Akasaka to Roppongi	1.00
Local telephone call	.07
Double room at the Imperial Hotel (deluxe)	278.00
Double room at the Gajoen Kanko Hotel (moderate)	118.00
Double room at the Ryokan Mikawaya Bekkan (budget)	75.00

	US$
Lunch for one at Gonin Byakusho (moderate)	7.15
Lunch for one at Genrokusushi (budget)	3.50
Dinner for one, without drinks, at Inakaya (deluxe)	71.40
Dinner for one, without drinks, at Seiyo Hiroba (moderate)	39.30
Dinner for one, without drinks, at Irohanihoheto (budget)	10.70
Glass of beer	3.55
Coca-Cola	2.15
Cup of coffee	2.85
Roll of ASA 100 Fujichrome film (36 exposures)	6.40
Admission to the Tokyo National Museum	2.85
Movie ticket	11.40
Theater ticket to Kabuki	14.30

WHAT THINGS COST IN KYOTO — U.S. $

	U.S. $
Airport bus from Osaka International Airport to Kyoto	5.90
Subway ride from Kyoto Station to Karasuma Station	1.15
Local telephone call	.07
Double room at the Miyako Hotel (deluxe)	132.00
Double room at the Holiday Inn Kyoto (moderate)	105.00
Double room at the Matsubaya Ryokan (budget)	57.00
Lunch for one at Okutan (moderate)	23.57
Lunch for one at Musashi (budget)	3.55
Dinner for one, without wine, at Minoko (deluxe)	92.85
Dinner for one, without wine, at Tagoto (moderate)	21.40
Dinner for one, without wine, at Sancho (budget)	12.85
Glass of beer	3.00
Coca-Cola	2.00
Cup of coffee	2.50
Roll of ASA 100 Fujichrome film (36 exposures)	6.40
Admission to Kiyomizu Temple	2.15
Movie ticket	11.40
Theater ticket to Gion Corner	17.85

2. WHEN TO GO — CLIMATE, HOLIDAYS & EVENTS

The Japanese have a passion for travel, and generally they all travel at the same time, resulting in jam-packed trains and hotels. The worst times of year are the New Year's period, from December 28 to January 4; the so-called Golden Week, from April 29 to May 5; and the O'bon Festival time, in mid-July or mid-August—avoid traveling on these dates at all costs.

CLIMATE

Most of Japan's islands lie in a temperate seasonal wind zone similar to the East Coast of the United States, which means that there are four distinct seasons.

Summer, which begins in June, is heralded by the rainy season, which lasts from about mid-June to mid-July. Although it doesn't rain every day, it does rain a lot and umbrellas are imperative. As you walk through all those puddles, remember that this is when Japan's farmers are out planting their rice seedlings. After the rain stops, it turns very hot (in the 80s F) and uncomfortably humid throughout the country, with the exception of the northern island of Hokkaido, such mountaintop resorts as Hakone, and the Japan Alps.

The period from the end of August through September is typhoon season, although most storms stay out at sea and generally vent their fury on land only in thunderstorms. Autumn, which lasts until about November, is one of the best times to travel in Japan. The days are pleasant and slightly cool, with the changing reds and scarlets of leaves giving brilliant contrast to the deep-blue skies. A photographer I know says that autumn is the best season for landscape photography.

Lasting from December to March, winter is marked by snow in much of Japan, especially in the mountain ranges, where the skiing is superb. The climate then is generally dry, and on the Pacific coast the skies are often blue. Tokyo, where the mean temperature is about 40°F, doesn't get much snow.

Spring arrives with a magnificent fanfare of plum and cherry blossoms in March and April, an exquisite time when all Japan is set ablaze in whites and pinks. The cherry-blossom season starts in southern Kyushu toward the end of March and reaches northern Japan in about mid-April. The blossoms themselves last only a few days, symbolizing to the Japanese the fragile nature of beauty and of life itself.

Remember that because Japan's four main islands stretch from north to south at about the same latitudes as Boston and Atlanta, you can travel in the country virtually any time of the year. Winters in southern Kyushu are mild and pleasant, while summers in Hokkaido, in the north, are cool. In addition, there is no rainy season in Hokkaido.

Tokyo's Average Daytime Temperatures & Rainfall

	Jan	Feb	Mar	Apr	May	June	July	Aug	Sept	Oct	Nov	Dec
Temp. °F	37	39	45	54	62	70	77	79	73	62	51	41
Temp. °C	3	4	7	13	17	21	25	26	23	17	11	5
Rainfall (in.)	4.3	6.1	8.9	10	9.6	12.1	10	8.2	10.9	8.9	6.4	3.8

HOLIDAYS

National holidays are January 1 (New Year's Day); January 15 (Adults' Day); February 11 (National Foundation Day); March 20 or 21 (Vernal Equinox Day); April 29 (Greenery Day); May 3 (Constitution Memorial Day); May 5 (Children's Day); September 15 (Respect-for-the-Aged Day); September 23 or 24 (Autumn Equinox Day); October 10 (Health and Sports Day); November 3 (Culture Day); November 23 (Labor Thanksgiving Day); December 23 (Emperor's Birthday). When a national holiday falls on a Sunday, the following Monday becomes a holiday.

Although government offices and some businesses are closed on public holidays, restaurants and most stores remain open. The exception is during the New Year's celebration, from January 1 to 3, when almost all restaurants, public and private offices, and stores close up shop; during that time you'll have to dine in hotels.

As for museums, major museums remain open during public holidays. If a public holiday falls on a Monday (when most museums are closed), most museums will remain open but will close instead the following day, on Tuesday. Note that privately owned museums, such as art museums or special-interest museums, generally close on public holidays.

FESTIVALS

With Shintoism and Buddhism the major religions in Japan, it seems as though there's a festival going on somewhere in the country almost every day. Every major shrine and temple has at least one annual festival, with events that might include traditional dances, archery, or colorful processions in which portable shrines are carried through the streets by groups of chanting Japanese dressed in traditional costumes. Such festivals are always free, though admission may be charged for special exhibitions.

There are also a number of national holidays observed throughout the country, as well as such annual events as cormorant fishing and cherry-blossom viewing. During the summer, festivals are held seemingly everywhere, and you may stumble onto a neighborhood festival just by accident.

As for the larger, better-known festivals, they may be exciting for the visitor but do take some planning, since hotel rooms may be booked 6 months in advance. If you haven't made prior arrangements, you may want to let the following schedule be your guide in avoiding certain cities on certain days. You won't find a hotel room anywhere near Takayama, for example, on the days of its two big festivals. If you plan your trip around a certain festival, be sure to double-check the exact dates with the Japan National Tourist Organization, since these dates can change. And remember, if a national holiday falls on a Sunday, the following Monday becomes a holiday.

JAPAN CALENDAR OF EVENTS

JANUARY

- ☐ **New Year's Day,** the most important national holiday in Japan. Like Christmas in the West, it's a time of family reunions, as well as a time when friends get together to drink sake and eat special New Year's dishes. Streets and homes are decorated with straw ropes and pine or plum branches. Because this is a time that Japanese spend together with their families, and because almost all businesses, restaurants, and shops close down, it's not a particularly rewarding time of the year for foreigners. January 1.
- ☐ **Tamaseseri (Ball-Catching Festival),** Hakozakigu Shrine, Fukuoka. The main attraction here is a struggle between two groups of youths who try to capture a sacred wooden ball. The team that wins is supposed to have good luck the whole year. January 3.
- ☐ **Dezomeshiki (New Year's Parade of Firemen),** Harumi Chuo Dori Avenue, Tokyo. Agile firemen dressed in traditional costumes prove their worth with acrobatic stunts atop tall bamboo ladders—you'd certainly feel safe being rescued by one of them. January 6.
- ☐ **Usokae (Bullfinch Exchange Festival),** Dazaifu Temmangu Shrine, outside Fukuoka. The trick here is to get hold of the bullfinches made of gilt wood that are given away by priests—they're supposed to bring good luck. January 7.
- ☐ **Toka Ebisu Festival,** Imamiya Ebisu Shrine, Osaka. Ebisu is considered the patron saint of business and good fortune, so this is the time when businesspeople pray for a successful year. The highlight of the festival is a parade of women dressed in colorful kimonos and carried through the streets in palanquins. January 9–11.
- ☐ **Adults' Day,** a national holiday. This day honors young people who have reached the age of 20, when they can vote and assume other responsibilities. January 15.

☐ **Grass Fire Ceremony,** Wakakusayama Hill, Nara. As evening approaches, Wakakusayama Hill is set ablaze and fireworks are displayed. The celebration marks a time more than a thousand years ago when a dispute over the boundary of two major temples in Nara was settled peacefully. January 15.

☐ **Toshi-ya,** Sanjusangendo Hall, Kyoto. A traditional Japanese archery contest. January 15.

FEBRUARY

○ *SNOW FESTIVAL, This famous Sapporo festival features huge, elaborate statues and figurines carved in snow and ice, with competitors from around the world.*
Where: Along Odori-Koen Promenade, Sapporo. When: Wednesday to Saturday of 1st week of February. How: Simply walk through this outdoor winter fantasyland.

☐ **Oyster Festival,** Matsushima. Matsushima is famous for its oysters, and this is the time they're considered at their best. Oysters are given out free at booths set up at the seaside park along the bay. 1st Sunday in February.

☐ **Setsubun (Bean-Throwing Festival),** held at leading temples throughout Japan. According to the lunar calendar, this is the last day of winter, and people throng to temples to participate in the traditional ceremony of throwing beans to drive away imaginary devils. February 3 or 4.

☐ **Lantern Festival,** Kasuga Shrine, Nara. A beautiful sight, in which more than 3,000 stone and bronze lanterns are lit. February 3 or 4.

☐ **National Foundation Day (Kigensetsu),** a national holiday. February 11.

MARCH

☐ **Omizutori (Water-Drawing Festival),** Todaiji Temple, Nara. This festival includes a solemn evening rite in which young ascetics brandish large burning torches and draw circles of fire. The biggest ceremony takes place on March 12, and on the next day the ceremony of drawing water is held to the accompaniment of ancient Japanese music. March 1–14.

☐ **Hinamatsuri (Doll Festival),** observed throughout Japan. It's held in honor of young girls to wish them a future of happiness. In homes where there are girls, dolls dressed in ancient costumes representing the emperor, empress, and dignitaries are set up on a tier of shelves, along with miniature household articles. March 3.

☐ **Kasuga Matsuri,** Kasuga Shrine, Nara. With a history stretching back 1,100 years, Kasuga Matsuri features traditional costumes and classical dances. March 13.

☐ **Vernal Equinox Day,** a national holiday. Throughout the week Buddhist temples hold ceremonies to pray for the souls of the departed. March 20 or 21.

☐ **Cherry-blossom season.** This rite of spring begins in late March on the southern islands of Kyushu and Shikoku, travels up Honshu through April, and reaches Hokkaido by the beginning of May. Early to mid-April is when the blossoms burst forth in Tokyo and Kyoto. Popular cherry-viewing spots in Kyoto include Maruyama Park, the garden of Heian Shrine, the Imperial Palace, Nijo Castle, Kiyomizu Temple, and Arashiyama, while in Tokyo people throng to Ueno Park, Yasukuni Shrine, and the moat encircling the Imperial Palace. Late March to May.

APRIL

☐ **Buddha's Birthday,** observed throughout Japan. Ceremonies are held at all Buddhist temples. April 8.

☐ **Kamakura Matsuri,** Tsurugaoka Hachimangu Shrine, Kamakura. This festival honors heroes from the past, including Yoritomo Minamoto, who made Kamakura his shogunate capital back in 1192. Highlights are horseback archery (truly spectacular to watch), a parade of portable shrines, and sacred dances. 2nd to 3rd Sunday.

☐ **Takayama Festival,** Takayama. Supposedly dating back to the 15th century, this festival features a procession of huge, gorgeous floats that parade through the village streets. April 14–15.

☐ **Gumonji-do (Firewalking Ceremonies),** Miyajima. These rites and ancient shrine dances called *bugaku* are held atop Mt. Misen. Walking on fire is meant to show devotion and is also for purification. Mid-April.

☐ **Yayoi Matsuri,** Futarasan Shrine, Nikko. Yayoi Matsuri also features a parade of decorated floats. April 16–17.

☐ **Greenery Day,** a national holiday. The birthday of the former emperor, Hirohito. April 29.

☐ **Golden Week,** a major holiday period throughout Japan. Many Japanese offices and businesses close down, and families go on vacation. It's a crowded time to travel; reservations are a must. April 29 to May 5.

MAY

☐ **Constitution Memorial Day,** a national holiday. May 3.

☐ **Hakata Dontaku,** Fukuoka. Citizens dressed as deities ride through the streets on horseback to the accompaniment of flutes, drums, and traditional instruments. May 3–4.

☐ **Children's Day,** a national holiday. This festival honors young boys, and the most common sight throughout Japan is colorful streamers of carp flying from poles. These fish symbolize attributes desirable for young boys—perseverance and strength. May 5.

☐ **Cormorant fishing,** Nagara River near Gifu. Visitors board small wooden boats at night to watch cormorants dive into the water to catch *ayu*, a kind of trout. Cormorant fishing is also held on the Katsura (also called Oi) River outside Kyoto. Begins May 11, extending to October 15.

☐ **Takigi Noh performances,** Kofukuji Temple, Nara. These Noh plays are presented outdoors after dark, under the blaze of torches. May 11–12.

☼ *Aoi Matsuri (Hollyhock Festival).* This is one of Kyoto's biggest events, a colorful pageant commemorating the days when the imperial procession visited the city's shrines. It supposedly dates from the 7th century, when a ceremony was held to appease the gods following severe storms.
Where: Along the streets near Kyoto's Shimogamo and Kamigamo shrines. *When:* May 15. *How:* Find a spot along the street, but get there early.

☐ **Kanda Festival,** Kanda Myojin Shrine, Tokyo. Held every other year. Portable shrines are carried through the district. Saturday and Sunday closest to May 15.

☐ **Kobe Matsuri,** Kobe. This relatively new festival celebrates Kobe's international past with fireworks at Kobe Port, street markets, and a parade on Flower Road, with participants wearing native costumes. Mid-May.

☐ **Grand Festival of Toshogu Shrine,** Nikko. This festival commemorates the day in 1617 when Tokugawa Ieyasu's remains were brought to his mausoleum in Nikko, accompanied by 1,000 people. This festival re-creates the drama, with more than 1,000 armor-clad people escorting three palanquins through the streets. May 17–18.

☐ ☼ **Sanja Matsuri,** Asakusa Shrine, Tokyo. About 100 portable shrines are carried through the district on the shoulders of men and women in traditional garb. Third Saturday and Sunday in May.

☐ **Mifune Matsuri,** Arashiyama, on the Oi River outside Kyoto. A reproduction of an ancient boat festival. The days of the Heian Period, when the imperial family used to take pleasure rides on the river, are reenacted. Third Sunday in May.

JUNE

☐ **Takigi Noh performances,** Heian Shrine, Kyoto. Evening performances of Noh are presented on an open-air stage in the shrine's compound. June 1–2.

☐ **Sanno Festival,** Hie Shrine, Tokyo. This festival, which first began in the Edo Period (1603–1867), features the usual portable shrines, transported through the busy streets of the Akasaka district. June 10–16.

☐ **Rice-planting Festival,** Sumiyoshi Shrine, Osaka. In hopes of a successful harvest, young girls in traditional farmers' costumes transplant rice seedlings in the shrine's rice paddy to the sound of music and traditional songs. June 14.

☐ **Hyakuman-goku Festival,** Kanazawa. Held only since 1952, the Hyakuman-goku Festival commemorates the arrival of Maeda—a feudal lord who laid the foundations of the Kaga clan—in this castle town. The highlight of the festival is a procession, and in the evening paper lanterns float down the Asano River. Mid-June.

JULY

☐ **Hakata Yamagasa,** Fukuoka. The main event takes place on the 15th, when a giant fleet of floats, topped with elaborate decorations, is paraded through the streets. July 1–15.

☐ **Tanabata (Star Festival),** celebrated throughout Japan. According to myth, the two stars Vega and Altair, representing a weaver and a shepherd, are allowed to meet once a year on this day. If the skies are cloudy, however, the celestial pair cannot meet and must wait another year. July 7.

☐ **O'bon Festival.** This national festival, which takes place in either mid-July or mid-August, commemorates the dead, who, according to Buddhist belief, revisit the world during this period. Many Japanese return to their hometowns for the event, especially if a member of the family has died recently. As one Japanese, whose grandmother had died a few months before, told me, "I have to go back to my hometown—it's my grandmother's first O'bon." Mid-July or mid-August, depending on the area in Japan.

○ *Gion Matsuri   One of the most famous festivals in Japan, it dates back to the 9th century, when the head priest at Kyoto's Yasaka Shrine organized a procession in an attempt to ask the gods' assistance against a plague that was raging in the city. Although the festival is actually celebrated during the whole month of July, the highlight is on the 17th, when spectacular floats wind their way through the city streets. Many foreigners plan their trip to Japan around this event.*
   Where: *Along the main streets of downtown Kyoto.* ***When:*** *July 16–17.*
   How: *Get there early, and find a spot along any of the streets of the procession (inquire at the tourist office for the route).*

☐ **Tenjin Matsuri,** Osaka. One of the city's biggest festivals, it dates back to the 10th century, when the people of Osaka visited Temmangu Shrine to pray for protection against the diseases prevalent during the long, hot summer. They would take pieces of paper cut in the form of human beings and, while the Shinto priest said prayers, would rub the paper over themselves in ritual cleansing. Afterward, the pieces of paper were taken by boat to the mouth of the river and disposed of. Today, the festival reenacts the boat procession with a fleet of more than 100 sacred boats making its way down the river, followed by a fireworks display. July 24–25.

☐ **Kangensai Music Festival,** Itsukushima Shrine, Miyajima. There are classical court music and bugaku dancing, and three barges carry portable shrines, priests, and musicians across the bay, along with a flotilla of other boats. Because this festival takes place according to the lunar calendar, the actual date changes each year. Late July or early August.

☐ **۞ Hanahi Taikai (Fireworks Display),** Tokyo. This is Tokyo's largest summer celebration, and everyone sits on blankets along the banks of the Sumida River near Asakusa. Great fun! Last Saturday of July or early August.

AUGUST

☐ **Oshiro Matsuri,** Himeji. Famous for its Noh dramas, performed on a special stage constructed on the Himeji Castle grounds. On Sunday there's a procession from the castle to the city center, with participants dressed in traditional costumes. 1st Saturday and Sunday of August.

☐ **Waraku Odori,** Nikko. This is a good opportunity to see some of Japan's folk dances. August 5–6.

☐ **Peace Ceremony,** Peace Memorial Park, Hiroshima. Held annually in memory of those who died from the atomic bomb dropped over Hiroshima on August 6, 1945. A similar ceremony is held on August 9 in Nagasaki. August 6.

☐ **Tanabata Festival,** Sendai. Sendai holds its Star Festival one month later than the rest of Japan. It's the country's largest, and the whole town is decorated with colored paper streamers. August 6–8.

☐ **Matsuyama Festival,** Matsuyama. Festivities include dances, fireworks, and a night fair. August 11–13.

☐ **Takamatsu Festival,** Chuo Dori Avenue, Takamatsu. About 6,000 people participate in a dance procession that threads its way along the avenue. Anyone can join in. August 12–14.

☐ **Toronagashi and Fireworks Display,** Matsushima. Held in the evening. First there's a fireworks display, followed by the setting adrift on the bay of about 5,000 small boats with lanterns. Another 3,000 lanterns are lit on islets in the bay. The lanterns, which illuminate the water, are meant to console the souls of the dead. August 15.

☐ **Daimonji Bonfire,** Mt. Nyoigadake, Kyoto. A huge bonfire in the shape of the Chinese character *dai,* which means "large," is lit near the peak of the mountain as part of the O'bon Festival in mid-August.

SEPTEMBER

☐ **Respect-for-the-Aged Day,** a national holiday. September 15.

☐ **Yabusame,** Tsurugaoka Hachimangu Shrine, Kamakura. Archery performed on horseback recalls the days of the samurai. September 16.

☐ **Autumnal Equinox Day,** a national holiday. September 23 or 24.

OCTOBER

☐ **Okunchi Festival,** Suwa Shrine, Nagasaki. This festival illustrates the influence Nagasaki's Chinese population has had on the city through the centuries. A parade of floats and dragon dances are highlights. October 7–9.

☐ **Marimo Matsuri,** Lake Akan, Hokkaido. Marimo is a spherical green weed that grows in Lake Akan. This festival is put on by the native Ainu population. October 8–10.

☐ **Great Festival of Kotohiragu Shrine,** near Takamatsu. The climax of this festival is a parade of *mikoshi* (portable shrines). October 9–11.

☐ **Takayama Matsuri,** Takayama. Similar to the festival held here in April, with huge floats paraded through the streets. October 9–10.

☐ **Health and Sports Day,** a national holiday. October 10.

☐ **Oeshiki Festival,** Hommonji Temple, Tokyo. In commemoration of Buddhist leader Nichiren (1222–82), people march toward the shrine carrying large lanterns decorated with paper flowers. October 11–13.

☐ **Mega Kenka Matsuri** (Roughhouse Festival), Matsubara Shrine, Himeji. Youths shouldering portable shrines jostle each other as they attempt to show their skill in balancing their heavy burdens. October 14–15.

☐ **Autumn Festival,** Toshogu Shrine, Nikko. Armor-clad parishioners escort a sacred portable shrine. October 17.

✪ *Jidai Matsuri (Festival of the Ages)* Another of Kyoto's grand festivals, this is one of its most interesting. Held in commemoration of the founding of the city in 794, it features a procession of more than 2,000 people dressed in ancient costumes representing different epochs of Kyoto's 1,200-year history.
   Where: Heian Shrine. *When:* October 22. *How:* Secure a spot along the main road leading to the shrine.

☐ **Fire Festival,** Yuki Shrine, Kyoto. Long rows of torches are embedded along the approach to the shrine to illuminate a procession of children. October 22.

NOVEMBER

☐ **Ohara Matsuri,** Kagoshima. About 15,000 people parade through the town in cotton *yukata,* dancing to the tune of popular Kagoshima folk songs. A sort of Japanese Mardi Gras, this event attracts several hundred thousand spectators a year. November 2–3.
☐ **Culture Day,** a national holiday. November 3.
☐ **Daimyo Gyoretsu,** Hakone. The old Tokaido Highway that used to link Kyoto and Tokyo comes alive again with a long parade that is a faithful reproduction of a feudal lord's procession in the olden days. November 3.
☐ **Shichi-go-san (Children's Shrine-Visiting Day),** held throughout Japan. Shichi-go-san literally means "seven-five-three" and refers to children of these ages who are taken to shrines by their elders to express thanks and pray for their future. November 15.
☐ **Labor Thanksgiving Day,** a national holiday. November 23.

DECEMBER

☐ **On-Matsuri,** Kasuga Shrine, Nara. This festival features a parade of people dressed as courtiers, retainers, and wrestlers of long ago. December 17.
☐ **Emperor's Birthday,** a national holiday. December 23.
☐ **New Year's Eve.** At midnight many temples ring huge bells 108 times to signal the end of the old year and the beginning of the new. Many families visit temples and shrines on New Year's Eve to pray for the coming year. December 31.

TOKYO
CALENDAR OF EVENTS

JANUARY

☐ **Dezomeshiki (New Year's Parade of Firemen),** Harumi Chuo Dori Avenue. This annual event features agile firemen dressed in traditional costumes who prove their worth with acrobatic stunts atop tall bamboo ladders. January 6.

FEBRUARY

☐ **Hari-kuyo,** Women bring broken pins and needles to Awashimado near Sensoji Temple in Asakusa on this day, a custom since the Edo Period. February 8.

APRIL

☐ **Jibeta Matsuri,** Kanayama Shrine, Kawasaki (just outside Tokyo). This festival extols the joys of sex and fertility, featuring a parade of giant phalluses. Needless to say, not your average festival, and you can get some unusual photographs here. Mid-April.

MAY

☐ **Kanda Festival,** Kanda Myojin Shrine. Held every other year on odd-numbered years. It began during the feudal era as the only time townsmen could enter the shogun's castle and parade before him. It features a parade of dozens of portable shrines, plus a tea ceremony. Saturday and Sunday closest to May 15.

✪ *Sanja Matsuri   One of Tokyo's best-known festivals, it features a parade of 100 portable shrines carried through the streets on the shoulders of men and women dressed in traditional garb.*
    Where: *Asakusa Shrine and Sensoji Temple, Asakusa.* ***When:*** *3rd Saturday and Sunday in May.* ***How:*** *This festival can get quite crowded, but the best viewing spot for the parade is on Nakamise Dori.*

JUNE

☐ **Sanno Festival,** Hie Shrine. This festival, dating from the Edo Period (1603–1867), features the usual portable shrines, transported through the busy streets of the Akasaka district. June 10–16.

JULY

☐ **Ueki Ichi (Potted Plant Fair),** Fuji Sengen Shrine, near Asakusa (on the Ginza subway line). This fair displays different kinds of potted plants and bonsai (miniature dwarfed trees), as well as a miniature Mt. Fuji that symbolizes the opening of the official climbing season. July 1.

☐ **Hozuki Ichi (Ground Cherry Pod Fair),** Sensoji Temple, Asakusa. It features hundreds of stalls selling ground cherry pods and colorful wind bells. July 9–10.

✪ *Hanabi Taikai (Fireworks Display)   This huge fireworks display over the Sumida River in Asakusa is the capital city's largest festival, and it's great fun.*
    Where: *Along the Sumida River, in Sumida Koen Park, near the Kototoibashi and Komagatabashi bridges.* ***When:*** *Last Saturday of July or early August.* ***How:*** *Get there early and spread a blanket along the banks of the Sumida River.*

OCTOBER

☐ **Oeshiki Festival,** Hommonji Temple. This is the largest of Tokyo's commemorative services held for Nichiren, a Buddhist leader. People march to the temple carrying large lanterns decorated with paper flowers. October 11–13.

NOVEMBER

☐ **Tori-no-Ichi (Rake Fair),** Otori Shrine, Asakusa. This fair features stalls selling rakes lavishly decorated with paper and cloth, which are thought to bring good luck and fortune. Based on the lunar calendar, the date changes each year. Mid-November.

DECEMBER

☐ **Hagoita-Ichi (Battledore Fair),** Sensoji Temple, Asakusa. Popular since Japan's feudal days, Hagoita-Ichi features decorated paddles of all types and sizes.

Most have designs of Kabuki actors—images made by pasting together padded silk and brocade—and make great souvenirs and gifts. December 17–19.

☐ **New Year's Eve.** Meiji Shrine is the place to be in Tokyo for this popular family celebration, as thousands throng to the shrine to usher in the new year at midnight. December 31.

3. HEALTH & INSURANCE

HEALTH

You don't need any inoculations for entry into Japan. As for drug prescriptions, they can be filled at Japanese pharmacies. However, it's always better to bring along extra supplies of special medications, especially if you prefer name brands from your own country.

Another consideration for visitors flying to Japan, especially on long flights from North America, is the effects of jet lag. For some reason, flying west has slightly less effect than flying east, which means that the hardest flight to overcome is the journey from Japan back to North America.

To minimize the adverse effects of jet lag—primarily fatigue and slow adjustment to your new time zone—refrain from smoking and alcohol consumption during the flight. In addition, eat light meals high in vegetable and cereal content the day before, during, and the day after your flight. Further, exercise your body during the flight by walking around the cabin every so often and by flexing your arms, hands, legs, and feet. It also helps to set your watch (and your mental clock) to the time zone of your destination as soon as you board the plane.

Once you reach your destination, schedule your day according to your new time zone. Put in a normal day, even if you are tired. Go for a walk in the sunlight, and once in your hotel, turn on the lights as brightly as you can until it's time to go to bed in the evening. If you follow these instructions, your body should be back to normal within 2 days.

INSURANCE

Medical and hospital services are not free in Japan, and they can end up being quite expensive. Before leaving home, therefore, you'd be wise to check with your health-insurance company to see if you are covered for a trip to Japan. If not, you may wish to take out a short-term traveler's medical policy that covers medical costs and emergencies.

You may also want to take extra precautions with your possessions. Is your camera or video equipment insured anywhere in the world through your home insurance? Is your home insured against theft or loss if you're gone longer than a month (some insurance companies will not cover loss for homes unoccupied for a specified length of time)? If you are not adequately covered, you may wish to purchase an extra policy to cover losses.

4. WHAT TO PACK

CLOTHING

A friend and I once spent the better part of an hour trying to list items travelers might need that they wouldn't be able to find in Japan. We finally gave up. With the exception of perhaps some medicines, we decided that virtually everything is available in Japan—the problem lies in choosing the brand. It doesn't make sense, therefore, to pack king-size supplies of toothpaste, shampoo, and other daily necessities. If you run out of something, you'll have no problem finding it in Japan.

One item you should absolutely bring is a pair of good walking shoes. Shoe sizes in Japan are much smaller than in the West, and chances are you won't be able to find Japanese shoes that fit. Keep in mind, too, that because you have to remove your shoes to enter Japanese homes, inns, shrines, and temples, you should bring a pair that's easy to slip on and off. And since you may be walking around in stockinged feet, save yourself embarrassment by packing socks and hose without holes.

Although it might seem superfluous to say this, pack lightly. Struggling through crowded train stations with big bags is no fun, and stations often contain multitudes of stairways and overhead and underground passageways. In addition, trains in Japan do not have large overhead racks.

The Japanese are generally of slighter build than most Westerners, with sizes to match. If you're of large build or simply have big feet, you're going to be tormented by all the wonderful, well-made, and often bargain-priced merchandise you can't fit into. Be sure to pack accordingly.

OTHER ITEMS

As for traveling around Japan, you'll want to have a folding umbrella. It's also a good idea to carry a supply of pocket tissues, since most public restrooms don't have toilet paper. You can pick up pocket tissues at newspaper stands near and in train stations. In the summer, when the weather is hot and extremely humid, you'll see women walking around with wet cotton handkerchiefs that they use to wipe their faces. Try it; it helps keep you cooler.

Although most hotels and Japanese-style inns provide guests with towels, soap, washcloths, toothbrushes and toothpaste, and a cotton kimono called a *yukata,* some of the budget-priced inns do not. If you're traveling on a budget, therefore, carry these items with you. Many hotels and inns also provide a thermos of hot water or a water heater, as well as some tea bags. If you're a coffee addict, you can save money by buying instant coffee and drinking your morning cup in your hotel room.

And at the risk of sounding perverse, I also recommend traveling with your own portable cassette player and headphones. Buy them once you get to Japan—they're inexpensive, are now available at sizes no larger than the cassette itself, and may help preserve your sanity. Many of the buses traveling scenic routes (and tourist boats as well) run continuous commentaries in Japanese at a pitch so high it drives me crazy. I'd much rather look at the scenery to the accompaniment of my own choice of noise. And if you're staying in budget accommodations, chances are there won't be a radio, but only a TV with programs in Japanese. You can buy all kinds of attachments for your portable cassette player, including tiny speakers and even a cord with outlets for two headphones, so that both you and your companion can listen to the music. An alternative to a cassette player is a portable CD player.

While traveling, you'll probably pick up souvenirs, gifts, and other items. I deal with this problem of accumulation by mailing boxes home to myself every 2 weeks or so during the time I'm on the road. All international post offices in Japan sell three sizes of cardboard boxes that come with everything you need for mailing packages abroad. This makes sending packages home a snap. I simply show up with my bag, empty it of all unneeded items, buy a box, and leave the post office feeling pounds lighter.

BAGGAGE TRANSFER SERVICES

If you find yourself encumbered with luggage too heavy to handle, or you simply prefer to travel without bothering with bags, consider sending your luggage on ahead to your next destination through the services of a baggage transfer company. For assistance and information, ask your hotel porter or stop by one of numerous outlets throughout major cities. Among the companies providing this service are Kuroneko and Perikan-bin. The cost of transferring a bag from Tokyo to Kyoto is approximately ¥1,500 ($10.70) for 5 to 10 kilos (11 to 22 pounds) and ¥1,800 ($12.85) for 10 to 20 kilos (22 to 44 pounds).

5. TIPS FOR SPECIAL TRAVELERS

FOR THE DISABLED

For the disabled, traveling can be a nightmare in Japan, especially in Tokyo and other large metropolises. In Tokyo, for example, most subways are accessible only by stairs; many sidewalks can be so jam-packed that getting around on crutches or in a wheelchair is exceedingly difficult. Although Tokyo's subway trains have seating for handicapped passengers—located in the first and last compartments of the train and indicated by a white circle with a blue seat—subways can be so crowded that there's barely room to move. In addition, the seats for the handicapped are almost always occupied by commuters; so unless you look handicapped, no one is likely to offer you his or her seat. Even Japanese homes are not very accessible, since the main floor is always raised about a foot above the entrance-hall floor. Not surprisingly, disabled persons are a rare sight in the larger cities. When I mentioned this once to a Japanese friend, she agreed, saying she was very surprised by the number of disabled people she had seen on a recent trip to the United States. In Japan, handicapped people are likely to be kept at home and cared for by family members.

When it comes to facilities for the blind, however, Japan has a very advanced system. Throughout subway stations and on many major sidewalks in Tokyo and other cities, there are raised dots and lines on the ground to guide blind people at intersections and toward subway platforms. In some cities, street lights chime a certain song when the signal turns green. Even Japanese yen notes are identified, by a slightly raised circle—the ¥1,000 note has one circle in a corner, while the ¥10,000 note has two. And finally, many elevators have floors indicated in braille.

Because Tokyo can be confusing and frustrating even for the able-bodied, disabled travelers may wish to travel to Japan's smaller cities and rural villages. Those using a wheelchair should travel with a compact one.

FOR SENIORS

Senior citizens do not receive discounts in Japan for admission to museums or other places that charge an admission fee. So be prepared to pay full price.

FOR SINGLE TRAVELERS

Traveling alone in Japan poses no difficulty, even for women. The main obstacle, however, is expense, since the price of accommodations is cheaper for couples and groups. Single travelers, therefore, should do what traveling businessmen do: stay at so-called business hotels. With their large number of single rooms, these establishments cater almost exclusively to solo businessmen.

FOR FAMILIES

The Japanese are very fond of children. Visiting children, however, may not be very fond of Japan, especially when it comes to sushi and other Japanese foods. Luckily, Western food is readily available, including McDonald's, but children's menus are rare.

Although children generally pay half fare for transportation and admission fees, prices can still be prohibitively high. You'll need to plan your itinerary with care. To avoid crowds, visit tourist sights on weekdays. Never travel on city transportation during rush hour or on trains during popular public holidays.

FOR STUDENTS

Students sometimes receive discounts at museums, though occasionally discounts are available only to students enrolled in Japanese schools. Further, discounted prices are often not displayed in English. Your best bet is to bring along an **International Student Card** (you can apply for one at your university), along with your university student ID. Show these at the ticket windows of museums to see whether there are student discounts.

6. ALTERNATIVE TRAVEL

EDUCATIONAL/STUDY TRAVEL

Many U.S. universities have campuses in Japan that offer courses in English, or study programs that may range from summer school in Japan to graduate exchange fellowships. Contact your nearest university to inquire about such programs.

In addition, the **National Registration Center for Study Abroad (NRCSA)**, a consortium of more than 80 universities, foreign-language institutes, adult-education colleges and activity centers located in 16 countries around the world, welcomes North Americans to its two member schools in Japan. The **LIC Kokusai Kaiwa Gakuin** in Tokyo provides intensive Japanese-language instruction for 2 to 10 weeks, while the **Eurocentre** in Kanazawa offers a 4-week course consisting of language classes, cultural instruction (ranging from flower arranging to life in Japan), and the opportunity to live with a Japanese family. For more information on these two programs, contact the NRCSA, 823 N. 2nd St., Milwaukee, WI 53202 (tel. 414/278-0631).

If you're interested in learning about Japanese culture but prefer to make arrangements on your own upon arrival in Japan, be sure to pick up the brochure *Explore Japanese Culture* at the Tourist Information Center in Tokyo or Kyoto. It lists a wide range of places that produce Japan's traditional arts, as well as cultural activities that are open to foreigners, including ceramics, origami, flower arranging, the martial arts, zazen meditation, Japanese cooking, sake brewing, and much more. In Kyoto, for example, you can observe the traditional method of *yuzen* dyeing of silk kimonos at several production centers, while in Osaka you can watch Bunraku puppet plays. Contact the Tourist Information Center for more information.

HOMESTAYS

One good way to meet the Japanese is to stay in a *minshuku*, inexpensive lodging in a Japanese home. Usually small, with only a handful of rooms, minshuku often afford the opportunity to meet both the family running the place and the other guests, since meals are usually served in a communal dining room. More information is given about minshuku in the "Where to Stay" section in Chapter 3.

HOME-VISIT SYSTEM

Recognizing the difficulty foreigners may face in meeting the Japanese, the Japan National Tourist Organization has launched a super program called the Home-Visit System, which offers overseas visitors the chance to visit an English-speaking Japanese family in their home. It doesn't cost anything, and the visit usually takes place for a few hours in the evening (dinner is not served). It's a good idea to bring a small gift, such as flowers, fruit, or a souvenir of some kind from your hometown. The system operates in the following 15 cities, for which I've provided the contact telephone numbers: **Tokyo** (tel. 03/3502-1461); **Sapporo** (tel. 011/211-3341); **Narita** (tel. 0476/32-8711 or 24-3198); **Yokohama** (tel. 045/641-5824); **Nagoya** (tel. 052/581-5678); **Otsu** (tel. 0775/23-1234); **Kyoto** (tel. 075/752-0215); **Osaka** (tel. 06/345-2189); **Kobe** (tel. 078/303-1010); **Okayama** (tel. 0862/32-2255); **Kurashiki** (tel. 0864/22-5141); **Hiroshima** (tel. 082/247-6738); **Fukuoka** (tel. 092/291-0777); **Nagasaki** (tel. 0958/24-1111); and **Kagoshima** (tel. 0992/24-1111 or 53-2500). To apply, call the appropriate city at least one day in advance of your intended visit. If you have any other questions, the **Tourist Information Center** in Tokyo (tel. 03/3502-1461) can answer them.

CHAPTER 3

PLANNING YOUR TRIP — ARRIVING IN JAPAN

In Chapter 2 we discussed the preparations you should make before embarking on your trip to Japan. Now we'll consider the various options available for getting to Japan, whether by air or by ship. Once you arrive, you'll find that there are many convenient ways of getting around this island nation, despite the obstacle of language. Japan's extensive transportation system allows for easy access to the places that you may decide to visit; as an aid to English-speaking visitors, the Tourist Information Center in Tokyo offers schedules and other information in English for rail travel, as do major domestic airlines for air travel.

In this chapter you'll find suggestions on the fastest and most economical means of transportation from Tokyo to Japan's principal cities, together with a convenient table of distances and traveling time. To help you plan your itinerary to best advantage, I also offer suggestions, based on my own travels, on what to see and do in Japan, depending on the length of your stay, as well as advice on accommodations and dining choices best suited to your needs. Finally, for quick reference, I provide a list of essential facts about the country that are of special concern to the foreign visitor.

1. GETTING THERE

BY PLANE
THE MAJOR AIRLINES

Most visitors to Japan arrive by air. There are several major carriers that fly from the United States to Japan. Among them are **All Nippon Airways** (tel. 800/235-9262), **American Airlines** (tel. 800/433-7300), **China Airlines** (tel. 800/227-5118), **Continental Airlines** (tel. 800/231-0856), **Japan Airlines** (tel. 800/525-3663), **Delta Air Lines** (tel. 800/241-4141), **Korean Air** (tel. 800/223-1155), **Northwest Airlines,** (tel. 800/225-2525), **Philippine Airlines** (tel. 800/435-9725), **Singapore Airlines** (tel. 800/742-3333), **Thai Airways International** (tel. 800/426-5204), and **United Airlines** (tel. 800/241-6522). Contact your travel agent or specific carriers for current information.

To get a head start on your travel adventure, it seems only appropriate to fly Japan's own Japan Airlines (JAL). An introduction to Japanese culture begins as soon as you enter the plane and are greeted with a bow and a smile by the flight crew. After your craft leaves the ground, you are given a hot, steaming towel, called an oshibori, with which to refresh yourself. In first class and business class, your meal will include both Japanese and Western cuisine selections; in economy class, only Western meals are served.

JAL's gateways in the United States include New York, Washington, D.C., Atlanta, Chicago, Los Angeles, San Francisco, Seattle, Anchorage, and Honolulu. Almost all JAL international flights from North America arrive at the New Tokyo International Airport in Narita, about 40 miles from Tokyo's center. Another international point of entry is Osaka; it's the more convenient gateway if you plan to go straight to either Osaka or Kyoto.

The flying time to Tokyo is about 14 hours from New York, 12 hours 45 minutes from Chicago, 10 hours from Seattle, almost 11 hours from San Francisco, and about 11 hours 20 minutes from Los Angeles.

REGULAR FARES

No matter which airline you fly, there are certain things you should know about airfare structures. While first-, business-, and basic economy-class fares (those with no restrictions) are the same to Japan year round, most airlines charge different APEX (Advance Purchase Excursion) fares according to the season. There are three fare seasons: the **peak season,** which falls usually during the summer months and is the most expensive; the **basic season,** which occurs during the winter and is the least expensive; and the so-called **shoulder season,** which falls in between the other two seasons, both in time and in price. In all three seasons, APEX fares are a little more expensive on weekends.

Listed below are some of the options in fares to Japan from New York, Chicago, and the West Coast as of autumn 1991. Be sure to contact the airlines or your travel agent for an update on prices once you've decided on your exact travel plans.

One way to cut the cost of your flight to Japan is to purchase your ticket in advance and comply with certain restrictions. Reservations, ticketing, and payment for the **APEX** fare usually must be completed no later than 21 days prior to departure, but rules vary depending on the airline. There's a minimum time you can stay in Japan, usually 1 or 2 weeks; the maximum stay may be up to 6 months. Rates vary according to the season, with peak-season rates applied June through August. APEX round-trip fares can run as high as $1,477, for a weekend flight in summer from New York, to as low as $910, for a weekday flight in winter from the West Coast.

The best strategy for securing the lowest airfare is to shop around. On a few airlines you can occasionally purchase a ticket at the very last minute that is lower in price (that is an APEX fare with all the restrictions except the advance-purchase time limit), because if the flight is not fully booked, an airline will discount tickets to try to achieve full-passenger capacity.

In **economy class,** round-trip fares to Tokyo are approximately double. For example, on JAL a round-trip fare is $2,558 from New York, $2,426 from Chicago, and $1,870 from Seattle, San Francisco, or Los Angeles.

Like most carriers, JAL has a **business class,** called "executive class," which has its own airport check-in counter, as well as special executive waiting lounges at the airports in New York and Tokyo. Once on the plane, business travelers are treated to a separate cabin, with seats that recline 40°; complimentary champagne, cocktails, and wine; free use of headphones; a personal 5-inch video screen built into the seat armrest (not available on all flights); and a complimentary travel kit. Meals feature Western and Japanese cuisine, including *jubako* meals (typical Japanese home-cooked food, served in traditional lacquer containers). For health-conscious passengers, there's a special low-calorie menu. JAL's round-trip business-class fares to Tokyo are $3,024 from New York, $2,892 from Chicago, and $2,230 from Seattle, San Francisco, or Los Angeles.

All airlines provide some luxuries to their passengers traveling **first class.** JAL's royal treatment is typically Japanese and begins at the airline's special first-class check-in counter, where your baggage will be loaded into a special container so that it will be taken off first on arrival in Japan. You will also be invited to use the Sakura

Lounge (at major gateways), a special waiting area with free alcoholic drinks, coffee, and soda. On board the plane you'll have a comfortable, electronically operated seat, which inclines to a 60° angle and which, on some flights, contains a personal 5-inch video screen in the seat armrest. You'll be offered a Japanese *happi* coat and slippers for in-flight wear. In addition to complimentary champagne and other alcoholic beverages, travel kits, and the use of headphones, you will be offered a choice of five main courses of Western or Japanese cuisine. JAL's round-trip first-class fares to Tokyo are $5,520 from New York, $5,384 from Chicago, and $4,476 from Seattle, San Francisco, or Los Angeles.

OTHER GOOD-VALUE CHOICES

There are also companies that provide **deeply discounted tickets** (some more than 50% less on economy fares and around 30% less on APEX fares), with no restrictions, depending on availability. You can buy your ticket through them well in advance or, if you're lucky, at the last moment. Among the firms that deal with travel to Japan are **Nippon Travel,** 3408 Wisconsin Ave., Suite 208, Washington, DC 20016 (tel. 202/362-0039); **Japan Associates Travel,** 2000 17th St. NW, Washington, DC 20009 (tel. 202/939-8853); and **Japan Express Travel,** Suite 408, 1150 17th St. NW, Washington DC 20036 (tel. 202/347-7730). Consolidators, such as **C. L. Thomson Express International** in San Francisco and **CNH International** and **Star Tours, Inc.** in Los Angeles, also sell discounted tickets, but only through travel agents.

Many airlines and tour operators also offer occasional **promotional fares,** with tight restrictions, as well as **package tours,** which might be the cheapest way to go, since packages include hotels, transfers, some meals, and more.

Certainly, the best strategy for securing the lowest airfare is to shop around. Consult the travel sections of major newspapers—they often carry advertisements for cheap fares. You may, for example, find bargains offered by so-called **bucket shops,** which sell discounted tickets at reductions of about 20% to 30%. Tickets are usually restrictive, valid only for a particular date or flight, nontransferable, and nonrefundable.

A *warning*: Remember, all fares, rules, and regulations are subject to change. Be sure to contact your travel agent or the airlines for current information.

BY SHIP

There is infrequent **ferry service** connecting ports in Japan with Shanghai, Nakhodka in Russia, Taiwan, and South Korea. The trip from Nakhodka to Yokohama, in operation from May to October, takes 52 hours and costs approximately ¥65,000 ($464) to ¥160,000 ($1,143) one way, depending on the choice of cabin. From Shanghai, ferries travel to Kobe or Osaka in 46 hours and to Yokohama in 60 hours, with fares starting at around ¥25,000 ($178) for Kobe or Osaka and ¥32,000 ($228) for Yokohama. From Pusan, South Korea, ferries take 21 hours to Osaka and cost ¥20,000 ($143) to ¥28,000 ($200) one way.

PACKAGE TOURS

If you're the kind of traveler who doesn't like leaving such arrangements as accommodations, transportation, and itinerary to chance, you may wish to join an organized tour of Japan. Among the many companies offering group tours are **American Express,** American Express Plaza, New York, NY 10004 (tel. 212/323-2291, or toll free 800/241-1700); **Journeys East,** 2443 Fillmore St., San Francisco, CA 94115 (tel. 415/601-1677); **TBI Tours,** 787 Seventh Ave., Suite 1101, New York, NY 10019 (tel. 212/489-1919, or toll free 800/223-0266); and **Visitours, Inc.,**

FROMMER'S SMART TRAVELER: AIRFARES

1. Shop all the airlines that fly to your destination.
2. Keep calling the airlines, since the availability of cheap seats changes daily. As the departure date nears, you might be able to obtain a seat at a discount—an airline would rather sell a seat than have it empty.
3. Read the advertisements in newspaper travel sections; they often offer special deals and packages.
4. You can also save money by buying your ticket as early as possible, since the cheapest fares, such as APEX (Advance Purchase Excursion), usually require 30 days' advance purchase.
5. Ask whether there's a difference in price if you fly on a weekday—weekday flights are sometimes cheaper than weekend flights.
6. Travel off-season if you're trying to save money, since APEX and economy seats often cost less in the off-season.

Olympic Tower, 645 Fifth Ave., 61st floor, New York, NY 10022 (tel. 212/355-6077, or toll free 800/367-4368).

2. GETTING AROUND

BY PLANE

Because it takes the better part of a day and night to get by train from Tokyo down to southern Kyushu or up to northern Hokkaido, you may find it more convenient to fly at least one stretch of your journey in Japan. You may, for example, take a leisurely 2 weeks to travel by train from Tokyo through Honshu and Kyushu and then fly back to Tokyo from Kagoshima. I don't advise flying for shorter distances—say, from Tokyo to Osaka—because of the time spent getting to and from airports. By the way, departures on domestic flights from Tokyo leave from the much more conveniently located Haneda Airport, reached by monorail from Hamamatsucho Station on the Yamanote Line.

Two major domestic airlines are **Japan Airlines** and **All Nippon Airways (ANA),** with networks that stretch all the way from Okinawa to northern Hokkaido. ANA carries more than half of all domestic passengers in Japan and flies to 30 cities throughout the country, including Tokyo, Sapporo, Fukuoka, Hakodate, Takamatsu, Nagasaki, Kagoshima, and Osaka.

Although it's subject to change, the cost of flying from Tokyo to Sapporo in Hokkaido runs about ¥26,000 ($186) one way, while the flight from Tokyo to Kagoshima is about ¥32,000 ($228). It's cheaper, however, if you plan ahead and purchase your domestic flight in conjunction with your international flight to Japan. Contact your travel agent.

BY TRAIN

The most convenient way to travel around Japan is by train. Whether you're being whisked through the countryside aboard the famous Shinkansen bullet train or are winding your way up a wooded mountainside in a two-car electric tram, trains in Japan are punctual, comfortable, dependable, and clean. And because train stations are usually located in the heart of the city, next to the city bus terminal, arriving in a

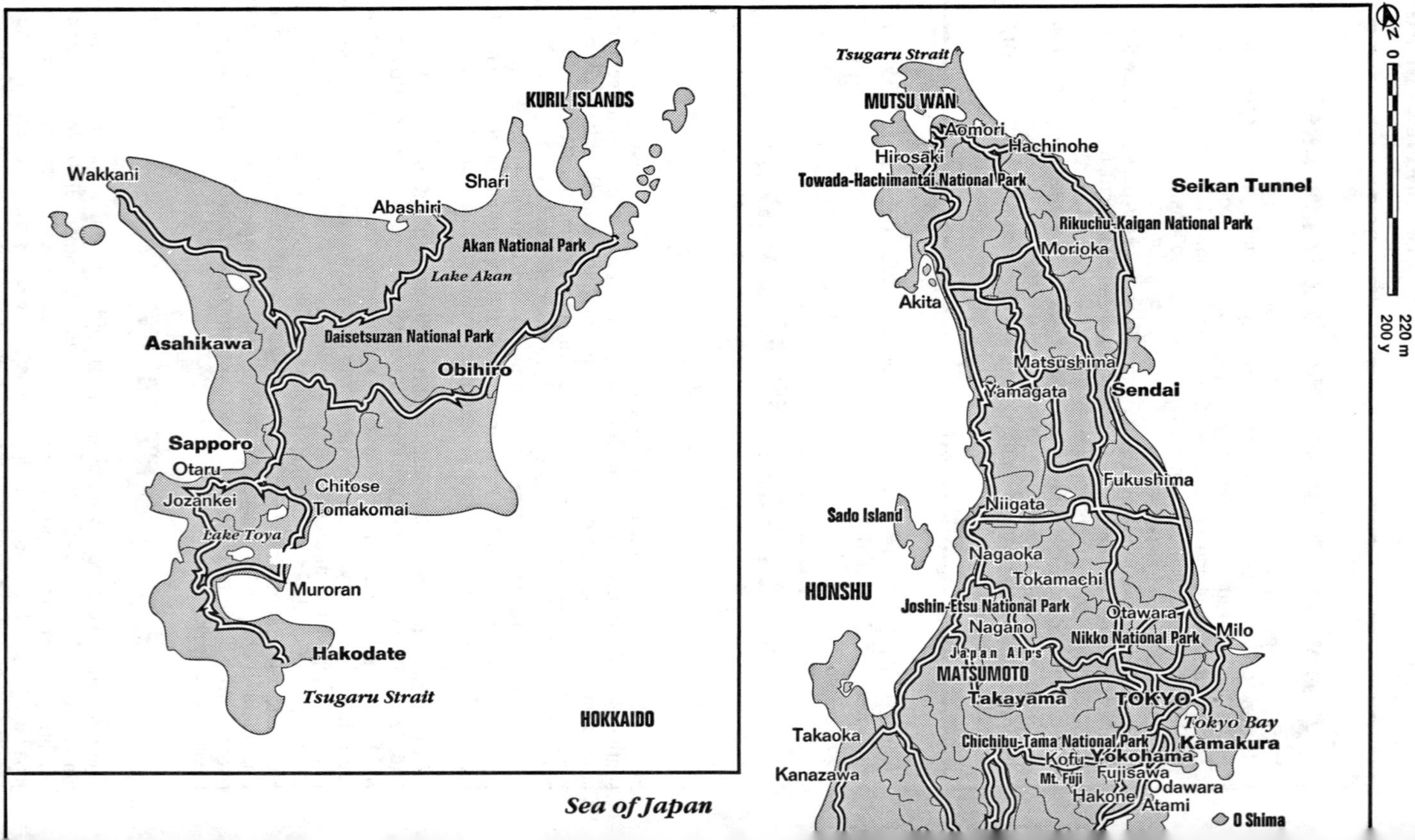

Scale: 0 — 220 m / 200 y

N

Top map (HONSHU):

Seikan Tunnel · Rikuchu-Kaigan National Park · Sendai · Milo · Tokyo Bay · Kamakura · ◇ O Shima

Hachinohe · Morioka · Matsushima · Matsushima · Fukushima · Otawara · Yokohama · TOKYO

Aomori · Hirosaki · Towada-Hachimantai National Park · Akita · Yamagata · Niigata

Nikko National Park · Tokamachii · Nagano · Takayama · MATSUMOTO · Kofu · Hakone · Odawara · Atami · Mt. Fuji · Chichibu-Tama National Park

Joshin-Etsu National Park · Nagaoka · Japan Alps · Sado Island · HONSHU · Takaoka · Kanazawa

Tsugaru Strait · MUTSU WAN

Bottom map (HOKKAIDO):

KURIL ISLANDS · Akan National Park · *Lake Akan* · Shari · Abashiri · Daisetsuzan National Park · Obihiro

Chitose · Tomakomai · Muroran · Hakodate · *Tsugaru Strait*

Asahikawa · Sapporo · Otaru · Jozankei · *Lake Toya* · Wakkani · HOKKAIDO

Sea of Japan

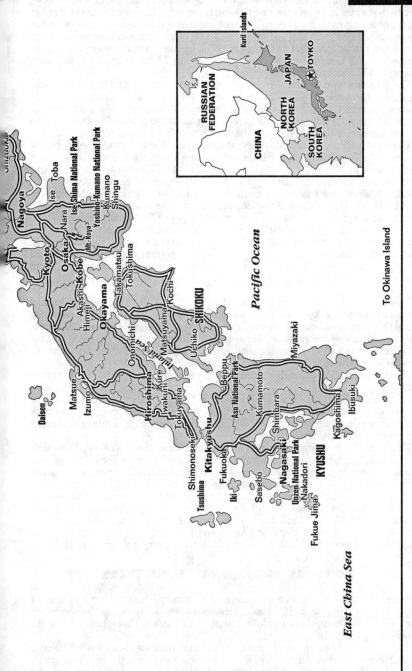

JAPAN

city by train is usually the most convenient way to begin your stay there. What's more, most train stations in Japan's major cities and resort areas have tourist offices that can help with directions to your hotel. The staff may not speak English, but it often has maps or brochures in English. Train stations also often have a counter where hotel reservations can be made free of charge. Most of Japan's trains are run by the **Japan Railways (JR) Group,** which operates as many as 23,400 trains daily, including more than 500 Shinkansen bullet trains.

The **Shinkansen** is probably Japan's best-known train. With a front car that resembles a space rocket, the Shinkansen hurtles 140 m.p.h. through the countryside on its own special tracks. Among the most luxurious Shinkansen trains are the Grand Hikari, a double-decker train that travels between Tokyo and Kyushu, and the Twilight Express, a luxury hotel on wheels that runs from Osaka to Sapporo.

There are three Shinkansen lines operating in Japan. The most widely used line for tourists is the **Tokaido-Sanyo Shinkansen,** which runs from Tokyo Station west to such cities as Nagoya, Kyoto, Osaka, Kobe, Himeji, Okayama, and Hiroshima before reaching its final destination of Hakata/Fukuoka, on the island of Kyushu. The **Tohoku Shinkansen** line runs from Tokyo and Ueno stations to Morioka in northern Japan. The **Joetsu Shinkansen** connects Tokyo and Ueno stations with Niigata, on the Japan Sea coast. There are two types of Shinkansen running along these tracks, one that stops only at the major cities and one that makes more stops and is therefore slightly slower. If your destination is a smaller city on the Shinkansen line, make sure the train you take stops there. As a plus, telephone calls can be made to and from the bullet trains. To reach someone on a bullet train, you can call 107 from anywhere in Japan, provided you know the exact train; announcements are made only in Japanese.

There are also two long-distance trains that operate on regular tracks. The **limited express trains (Tokkyu)** are the fastest after the Shinkansen, while the **express trains (Kyuko)** are slightly slower and make more stops. To serve the everyday needs of Japan's commuting population, **local trains (Futsu)** stop at all stations and are the trains most widely used for side trips outside the major cities. A bit faster are the **rapid trains (Kaisoku),** which stop only at major stations.

There are also some privately owned lines that operate from major cities to tourist destinations.

No matter which train you ride, be sure to hang on to your ticket—you'll be required to give it up at the end of your trip as you exit through the gate. And pack lightly, since porters are rare, overhead luggage space is small, and most rail stations have multitudes of stairs.

The Tourist Information Center in Tokyo has a *Condensed Railway Timetable* giving details, in English, for the Shinkansen and some other major lines. If you plan to do a lot of traveling by train, however, I recommend that you purchase the Japan Travel Bureau's *Mini-Timetable (Speedo Jikokuhyo)* for ¥330 ($2.35); it is published monthly and is available at bookstores or at Japan Travel Bureau offices in big cities. It covers the schedules, in both English and Japanese, for all JR long-distance trains, including the Shinkansen, and for private trains, planes, ferries, and even express buses. It also has maps of Japan, in English and Japanese, with various destinations served by trains. I find this handy little guide invaluable during my trips through Japan.

TRAIN DISTANCES & TRAVELING TIMES

Distances in Japan can be deceiving, since the country is much longer than most people imagine. Its four main islands, measured from the north to the south, are roughly the same distance as from Maine to northern Florida. Thank goodness for the Shinkansen bullet train!

The chart on p. 63 measures the distances and traveling times from Tokyo to principal Japanese cities. Since Tokyo is located approximately in the middle of Japan, you'll most likely change trains there when traveling from north to south and vice versa. Traveling times do not include the time needed for transferring and are calculated for the fastest trains available.

TRAIN TRAVEL FROM TOKYO TO PRINCIPAL CITIES

City	Distance in Miles	Traveling Time
Aomori*	458	4 hr. 43 min.
Atami	65	52 min.
Beppu*	762	7 hr.
Hakata	730	6 hr.
Hakodate*	557	6 hr. 51 min.
Hiroshima	554	4 hr. 37 min.
Kamakura	32	56 min.
Kanazawa*	386	4 hr. 20 min.
Kumamoto*	803	7 hr. 15 min.
Kyoto	318	2 hr. 39 min.
Matsue*	571	6 hr. 25 min.
Matsumoto	146	2 hr. 48 min.
Matsuyama*	587	6 hr. 47 min.
Miyazaki*	897	10 hr. 25 min.
Nagasaki*	825	8 hr. 3 min.
Nagoya	227	1 hr. 49 min.
Narita	42	1 hr. 13 min.
Niigata	207	1 hr. 39 min.
Nikko	93	1 hr. 29 min.
Okayama	454	3 hr. 51 min.
Sapporo*	731	10 hr. 17 min.
Shimoda	75	2 hr. 40 min.
Shin-Kobe	366	3 hr. 12 min.
Shin-Osaka	343	2 hr. 56 min.
Takamatsu*	499	5 hr.
Takayama*	330	4 hr. 52 min.
Toba*	289	3 hr. 59 min.
Yokohama	18	27 min.

*Destination requires a change of trains.

TRAIN RESERVATIONS

You can reserve a seat in advance for the Shinkansen, as well as for limited express and express trains, at any major Japan Railways station for a small fee. The larger stations have special reservation counters or offices that are easily recognizable by their green signs with RESERVATION TICKETS written on them. They're open daily from 10am to 6pm. If you are at a JR station with no special reservation office, you can reserve your seat at one of the regular ticket windows. I recommend that you reserve your seats for your entire trip through Japan as soon as you know your itinerary, especially if you'll be traveling during peak times. However, all trains also have nonreserved cars that work on a first-come, first-served basis.

You can obtain information and buy tickets at any Japan Railways station for JR trains going throughout Japan, including those along the Yamanote Line, which loops around Tokyo. For specific train times, call the Tourist Information Center (tel. 03/3502-1461) or call the JR Group directly in Tokyo for English information (tel. 03/3423-0111), Monday through Friday from 10am to 6pm.

JAPAN RAIL PASS

The Japan Rail Pass is without a doubt the most convenient and most economical way to travel around Japan by train. With the rail pass you don't have to worry about buying individual tickets, and you can reserve your seats on all JR trains for free. The rail pass entitles you to unlimited travel on all JR train lines, including the Shinkansen (except the Twilight Express), as well as on JR buses and ferries.

The Japan Rail Pass is available only to foreigners visiting Japan as tourists and can be purchased only outside Japan from an authorized travel agent or from Japan

Airlines. *You cannot buy a rail pass once you're in Japan,* so you must arrange for one before you leave home. You'll be issued a voucher, which you'll then exchange for the pass itself after you arrive in Japan. You can exchange it either at the JR Information and Ticket Office at the Narita airport or at any of the 12 JR Travel Service Centers in Japan, including Tokyo Station and JR stations in Osaka, Kyoto, Hiroshima, and Sapporo.

There are two types of Japan Rail passes available—one for ordinary coach class and one for the first-class Green Car—and you can purchase passes that are good for 1, 2, or 3 weeks. Rates for the ordinary pass, as of August 1991, are ¥27,800 ($198) for 7 days, ¥44,200 ($316) for 14 days, and ¥56,600 ($404) for 21 days. Rates for the Green Car are ¥37,000 ($264) for 7 days, ¥60,000 ($429) for 14 days, and ¥78,000 ($557) for 21 days. Children pay half fare. Even if you plan to do just a little traveling, you can save quite a bit by purchasing a rail pass. For example, if you were to buy a round-trip ticket on the Shinkansen from Tokyo to Kyoto, it would cost you ¥25,000 ($178.50), which is almost as much as a week's ordinary rail pass. If you plan to see more than just Tokyo and Kyoto, it pays to use a rail pass.

BY BUS

Buses often go where trains don't, and thus may be the only way for you to get to the more remote areas of Japan—as, for example, Shirakawa-go, a picturesque hamlet in the Japan Alps. In Hokkaido and other places, buses are used extensively. When you board a bus, you'll generally find a ticket machine by the entry door. Take a ticket, which is number-coded with a board displayed at the front of the bus. The board shows the various fares, which increase with the distance traveled. You pay your fare upon departure.

In addition to serving the remote areas of the country, long-distance buses (called *chokyori basu*) also operate between major cities in Japan. Although Japan Railways operates almost a dozen bus routes eligible for JR rail pass coverage, the majority are run by private companies. Many long-distance buses travel during the night, saving passengers the price of a night's lodging. There is, for example, a special bus that leaves Tokyo Station every night for Nagoya (¥6,200 or $44.60), Kyoto (¥8,030 or $57.35), and Osaka (¥8,450 or $60.35), arriving the next morning. Similarly, there's also a night bus from Osaka, Kyoto, and Nagoya to Tokyo. If you're on a budget, this is certainly the cheapest way to travel between Tokyo and Kyoto.

BY CAR

Except perhaps in the Izu Peninsula and Hokkaido, driving is not the best way to tour Japan. In cities, streets are often hardly wide enough for a rickshaw, let alone a car, and many roads do not have sidewalks, so you have to dodge people, bicycles, streetlights, and telephone poles. But that's not all—it's not even economical to drive in Japan. Not only is gas expensive, but all of Japan's expressways charge high tolls. The one-way toll from Tokyo to Kyoto, for example, is almost the same as the price of a ticket to Kyoto on the Shinkansen. But whereas the Shinkansen takes only 3 hours to get to Kyoto, driving takes about 8 hours. So, unless there are four of you to split the costs and you are not limited by time, it doesn't make sense to drive.

RENTALS

Car-rental rates vary, but the average cost for 24 hours with unlimited mileage (but not including gasoline) ranges from ¥7,500 ($53.55) for a subcompact to ¥21,500 ($153.55) for a standard-size car. Both **Hertz** and **Avis** can accept reservations for their affiliated car-rental companies in Japan.

Note: If you intend to drive in Japan, you'll need either an international or a Japanese driving license.

GASOLINE

Gas stations are found readily along Japan's major highways. As of this writing, the average cost for regular gasoline is about ¥125 per liter or $3.55 per gallon.

DRIVING RULES

Cars are driven British style, *on the left side of the road,* and signs on all major highways are written in both Japanese and English. You should not have even one drink of alcohol if you plan to drive, and you should wear seat belts at all times.

MAPS

A profusion of maps of Japan are readily available at the major bookstores in Tokyo (refer to the "Fast Facts" section in the next chapter for a list of these stores). The maps include everything from foldouts to *Japan: A Bilingual Atlas,* published by Iris Ltd./Kodansha International. Be sure to purchase a bilingual map, since back roads often have names of towns written only in Japanese.

BREAKDOWNS/ASSISTANCE

The **Japan Automobile Federation (JAF)** maintains emergency telephone boxes along the routes of Japan's major arteries to assist drivers whose cars have broken down or drivers who need help. Calls from these telephones are free and will connect you to the operation center of JAF.

BY FERRY

Because Japan is an island nation, it has an extensive ferry network linking the string of islands. Although it takes longer to travel by ferry, it's also cheaper. For example, you can take the ferry from Tokyo all the way to Hokkaido—a 31-hour trip—for ¥11,840 ($84.55). There are also many ferries plying the waters of the Seto Inland Sea. From Osaka you can take a ferry in late evening and arrive in Beppu, on Kyushu, the next morning for ¥5,870 ($41.90). Contact the Tourist Information Center for more details concerning ferries, prices, and schedules.

HITCHHIKING

Hitchhiking is not common in Japan; in fact, foreigners who have hitchhiked in Japan tell me that some drivers stop simply because they're curious about what the foreigners could possibly want. But even though hitchhiking is uncommon, Japan is probably one of the safest and easiest countries in the world for hitchhiking. Stories abound of how drivers have gone hours out of their way to deposit passengers at their destination.

PLANNING YOUR ITINERARY

Japan, with its rich culture and varied geography, has much to offer the curious visitor, not only in and around the major cities but in many of the outlying regions as well. If you want to see *everything,* however, you should plan on spending at least a year in Japan. More likely, your time there will be more limited—a week or a few weeks. So you'll have to be selective in planning your itinerary. You'll have to decide *beforehand* what your priorities will be—whether, for example, you'll want to spend all your time in Tokyo or divide your time between a stay in Tokyo or another large city and extensive travel around the country. This section offers you some choices that will help you decide on an itinerary.

CITY HIGHLIGHTS

If you visit only one city in Japan, make it Kyoto. In addition to having served as the nation's capital for more than 1,000 years, it has more temples, shrines, and historical sights than any other Japanese city. Other top cities you might include in your travels are Nara, another ancient capital, and Tokyo. Depending on how much time you have, you might also want to visit Mt. Koya, Japan's most revered religious center, where you can sleep in a Buddhist temple; Nikko, site of Shogun Tokugawa Ieyasu's mausoleum; Takayama and Shirakawa-go, two picturesque villages in the Japan Alps; Hiroshima, with its famous Peace Memorial Park and museum of the atomic bomb; and Beppu, a spa renowned for its hot springs. There are, of course, other important destinations.

Note: With the exception of Tokyo and Kyoto, few Japanese cities have tours conducted in English. This book is designed for the individual traveler who prefers sightseeing on his or her own, but if you're pressed for time or don't want to deal with public transportation to sights that may be spread throughout a city, consider joining a Japanese day tour. It's certainly the easiest way to get to the various attractions, and perhaps there will even be a Japanese along who won't mind providing some translations.

SUGGESTED ITINERARIES

IF YOU HAVE 1 WEEK

A week in Japan is surely not enough time even to *begin* to do justice to such an attraction-filled country. Nevertheless, if I had only a week, I suppose I would spend it as follows:

Day 1: Arrive at the Narita airport, from which it's about a 2-hour trip to your hotel in Tokyo. Recuperate from your flight, settle in, and get a feel for the city. Top off the day with a meal in a traditional restaurant.

Day 2: Because of the difference in time zones, you'll probably be wide awake in the wee hours of the morning, so get up and head for Tsukiji Fish Market. After a breakfast of fresh sushi, take the Hibiya Line to Ueno, where you'll find the Tokyo National Museum. From Ueno, hop on the Ginza Line for Asakusa and its famous Nakamise Dori lane, with shops selling traditional products, and its popular Sensoji Temple. If you have time, stroll down Ginza's fashionable shopping district or head toward Harajuku, with its inexpensive clothing boutiques and Oriental Bazaar. Spend the evening in Shinjuku, Roppongi, or another one of Tokyo's famous nightlife areas.

Day 3: Take the 3-hour Shinkansen bullet train to Kyoto early in the morning. Spend the afternoon on a self-guided walk from Kiyomizu Temple to Heian Shrine and the Silver Pavilion, followed by shopping at the Kyoto Handicraft Center. Spend the night in one of Kyoto's many traditional Japanese-style inns.

Day 4: Take in Nijo Castle, Ryoanji Temple, the Golden Pavilion, and a few other sights of your choosing. If you want to see more temples in one of Japan's ancient capitals, head for Nara, where you'll want to spend at least 2 to 3 hours seeing the Great Buddha, Nara Park, and Kasuga Shrine.

Day 5: Leave Kyoto very early in the morning. If you want to spend the night in a Buddhist temple, take the Kintetsu Railways private line (there are only a couple of departures daily, so plan ahead) to Kintetsu Namba Station in Osaka, transferring there to the Nankai Koya Line for the 2-hour trip to Mt. Koya. If you'd rather spend the night in a picturesque town with some museums, board the Shinkansen for Kurashiki—less than 2 hours away; along the way make a 2-hour stopover in Himeji, where you'll find Himeji Castle. If all you want to do is relax at a hot-spring resort, take the Shinkansen back toward Tokyo to Odawara, where you should transfer to a local train bound for Hakone.

Day 6: Spend the day sightseeing, departing by late afternoon for Tokyo. If your plane leaves early the next morning, you may wish to spend the night at Narita.

Day 7: Departure.

IF YOU HAVE 2 WEEKS

If you have 2 weeks, I would expand the above schedule as follows:

Day 1: Arrive at the Narita airport, settle into your hotel, and become acclimated to Tokyo.

Day 2: Spend the day as you would in the 1-week itinerary above.

Day 3: Spend another day in Tokyo—refer to the Tokyo chapter. Or take a day trip to either Kamakura, with its many temples, or Nikko, famous for the mausoleum of Shogun Tokugawa Ieyasu.

Day 4: Early in the morning, take the Shinkansen to Nagoya (about 2 hours), then a 3-hour train ride to Takayama, in the Japan Alps. Explore the picturesque, narrow streets of this old castle town.

Day 5: Before departing Takayama, visit the morning market by the river. Take the 2½-hour bus ride along a winding mountain road to Shirakawa-go, a tiny village of rice paddies and thatched farmhouses. Spend the night in one of these farmhouses.

Day 6: From Shirakawa-go it takes the better part of a day to reach Kyoto, but the scenery is magnificent. From Shirakawa-go you can take a bus back to either Takayama or Nagoya, then transfer to a train for Kyoto.

Days 7 and 8: Spend the 2 days in Kyoto as you would in the 1-week itinerary, above.

Day 9: Early in the morning, set out for Nara, visiting the Great Buddha, Nara Park, and Kasuga Shrine. From Nara you can take the Kintetsu Railways private line (departing from Nara Kintetsu Station) to Kintetsu Namba Station in Osaka, transferring there to the Nankai Koya Line bound for Mt. Koya. If you have a rail pass, you can take Japan Railways trains to Hashimoto, transferring there to the private Nankai Koya Line. Spend the night on Mt. Koya in a Buddhist temple.

Day 10: After visiting Okunoin, the burial grounds of Kobo Daishi, return to Osaka and transfer to the Shinkansen bullet train at Shin-Osaka Station or to a JR train at Osaka Station bound for Kurashiki. Make a 2-hour stopover in Himeji to see the beautiful Himeji Castle. Spend the night in Kurashiki and take an evening stroll along the canal.

Day 11: Take in the sights of Kurashiki, including its many museums. Leave for Hiroshima late in the day (about an hour away by Shinkansen).

Day 12: Spend the morning at Peace Memorial Park, with its museum and statues. Take an afternoon excursion to the tiny island of Miyajima, with its famous Itsukushima Shrine. Take the overnight ferry from Hiroshima to Beppu.

Day 13: Spend a relaxing day in the hot-spring resort of Beppu and either visit the huge baths of Suginoi Palace or take a sand bath at Takegawara Bathhouse. Visit the Hells, boiling ponds created by volcanic activity.

Day 14: Take an early-morning flight from nearby Oita airport to Haneda Airport in Tokyo (the fare is ¥27,000 or $193), transferring to the Narita airport for the flight home.

Needless to say, this is something of a whirlwind trip, but it allows you to take in some of the best that Honshu Island has to offer. If you want to get off the beaten track and if you have more time, refer to the chapters on Shikoku, Kyushu, and northern Japan for more ideas in planning your itinerary.

IF YOU HAVE 3 WEEKS

This itinerary allows you to explore the islands of Hokkaido, Honshu, and Kyushu, at a more leisurely pace. Refer to the 2-week itinerary, above, for more detailed information on day-to-day activities.

Days 1, 2, and 3: Spend the first 3 days in Tokyo as outlined in the 1- and 2-week itineraries, above.

Day 4: Go to Takayama, a picturesque town in the Japan Alps.

Day 5: Spend the day in Takayama.

Day 6: Depart Takayama for Shirakawa-go early in the morning. Spend the night in a thatched farmhouse in a rural setting.

Day 7: Go from Shirakawa-go to Kyoto.

Days 8, 9, and 10: Spend the days in Kyoto and Nara, visiting the many famous gardens, temples, and traditional shops.

Day 11: From Kyoto take an excursion to Mt. Koya, where you can spend the night in a Buddhist temple.

Day 12: From Mt. Koya go to Kurashiki, with a stopover at Himeji Castle.

Day 13: Spend the day in Kurashiki. Leave for Hiroshima late in the day (about an hour away by Shinkansen).

Day 14: After spending the day at Hiroshima's Peace Memorial Park and nearby Miyajima Island, board an overnight ferry for the trip from Hiroshima to Beppu.

Day 15: Spend a relaxing day in the hot-spring resort of Beppu.

Day 16: Take an early-morning flight from Oita to Tokyo, where you can then board a plane bound for Sapporo, on Hokkaido. Take an afternoon stroll through Odori Park and the underground shopping arcades of Aurora Town and Pole Town. Dine on crab, corn on the cob, and other Hokkaido specialties.

Day 17: Start the day with an early-morning tour of the Sapporo Beer Factory, topped off with lunch and a beer at the factory's beer hall or garden. In early afternoon, head for Daisetsuzan National Park.

Day 18: Spend the day at Sounkyo Onsen, skiing, bicycling, or hiking through Daisetsuzan National Park.

Day 19: In the evening, head for Mt. Hakodate, where you can enjoy a great view of the city.

Day 20: Visit the morning market of Hakodate before boarding a train for Matsushima, considered one of the three most scenic spots in Japan.

Day 21: From Matsushima take a return train ride to Tokyo, about a 3-hour trip.

THEMED ITINERARIES

If you're interested in feudal castles, you'll find them in Osaka, Nagoya, Matsue, Matsumoto, Himeji, Kumamoto, Okayama, Hiroshima, and Matsuyama. Japan's most famous gardens are Kenrokuen Garden in Kanazawa, Korakuen Garden in Okayama, and Kairakuen Garden in Mito. Other beautiful gardens are Ritsurin in Takamatsu, on the island of Shikoku; Suizenji Garden in Kumamoto and Iso Garden in Kagoshima, both on the island of Kyushu; and the gardens at the Heian Shrine and Saihoji (Moss Temple), both in Kyoto. Japan's most famous rock garden is probably the one at Ryoanji Temple in Kyoto.

If you're a camera buff, you may want to make a special effort to visit some of the many picturesque towns and villages in Japan. My own personal list includes Kamakura, Takayama, Shirakawa-go, Tsumago, Kurashiki, and the hamlet of Chiran, south of Kagoshima, as well as Mt. Koya. As for towns with historical significance, nothing can beat Kyoto, Nara, and Kamakura, three ancient capitals of Japan. These three towns are also where you'll find a majority of the country's temples and shrines. Other important Shinto shrines in Japan include Meiji Jingu Shrine in Tokyo, the Ise Jingu Shrines located in Ise-Shima National Park, and Itsukushima Shrine on Miyajima Island. Mt. Koya is the place to head if you're interested in spending the night in a genuine Buddhist temple.

If you're considering visiting a spa, you'll find that Japan is blessed with many hot-spring spas. In fact, tourism in Japan began when bathing enthusiasts started traveling to hot springs simply for the joys of the bath. There are open-air spas in forests, sand baths, gigantic public baths, mud baths, sulfur baths, and just plain hot tubs. The hot springs closest to Tokyo are at Hakone and on the Izu Peninsula. Other famous hot springs include Matsuyama's Dogo Spa on Shikoku; the spas at Beppu, Ibusuki, and Unzen, on Kyushu; Toyako Spa and the spas at Noboribetsu, Sounkyo, and Akanko Onsen, on Hokkaido.

3. WHERE TO STAY

JAPANESE INNS

A stay at a Japanese inn, you may be surprised to learn, can prove very expensive. Yet the unique experience of spending at least a single night there makes it worth the splurge. For nothing quite conveys the simplicity and beauty, indeed the very atmosphere, of old Japan than these inns, called **ryokan,** with their gleaming polished wood, tatami floors, rice-paper sliding doors, and meticulously pruned gardens. Personalized service, offered by kimono-clad hostesses, and exquisitely prepared meals are the trademarks of such inns, some of them of ancient vintage. Staying in one of these inns is like taking a trip back in time.

Traditionally, the ryokan are small, only one or two stories high and containing about 10 to 30 rooms, and are made of wood, with a tile roof.

The entrance to a ryokan is often through a gate and small garden. When you enter, you're met by a bowing woman in a kimono. Take off your shoes, slide on the proferred plastic slippers, and follow your hostess down long wooden corridors until you reach the sliding door of your room. After taking off your slippers, step into your tatami room, which is almost void of furniture: a low table in the middle of the room, floor cushions, an antique scroll hanging in an alcove, a simple flower arrangement, and best of all, a view past rice-paper sliding screens of a Japanese landscaped garden with bonsai, stone lanterns, and a meandering pond filled with carp. You notice that there's no bed in the room.

Almost immediately your hostess brings you a welcoming hot tea and a sweet, served at your low table so that you might sit there for a while and appreciate the view, the peace, and the solitude. Next comes your hot bath, either in your own room (if you have one) or in the communal bath. (Be sure to follow the procedure outlined in Chapter 1 in the section on Japanese etiquette, soaping and rinsing yourself *before* getting into the tub.) After bathing and soaking away all tension, aches, and pains, change into your yukata, a cotton kimono provided by the ryokan.

When you return to your room, you'll find the maid ready to serve your dinner, which consists of locally grown vegetables, fish, and various regional specialties, all spread out on many tiny plates. There is no menu in a ryokan but, rather, one or more set courses determined by the chef. Admire how each dish is in itself a delicate piece of artwork, adorned with slices of ginger, a maple leaf, or a flower. It all looks too wonderful to eat, but finally hunger takes over. If you want, you can order sake or beer to accompany your meal.

After you've finished eating, your maid will return to clear away the dishes and to lay out your bed. The bed is really a futon, a kind of mattress with quilts, and is laid out on the tatami floor. The next morning the maid will wake you up, put away the futon, and serve a breakfast of fish, pickled vegetables, soup, dried seaweed, rice, and a raw egg to be mixed with the rice. Feeling rested, well fed, and pampered, you are then ready to pack your bags and pay your bill. Your hostess sees you off at the front gate, smiling and bowing as you set off for the rest of your travels.

Such is life at a good ryokan. Sadly, however, the number of upper-class ryokan diminishes each year. Unable to compete with the more profitable high-rise hotels, many ryokan in Japan's large cities have had to close down, with the result that there are very few left in such cities as Tokyo and Osaka. If you want to stay in a Japanese inn, it's best to do so in Kyoto or at a resort or hot-spring spa.

Altogether, there are approximately 90,000 ryokan still operating in Japan in a variety of different price ranges. Although, ideally, a ryokan is an old wooden structure at least 100 years old and perhaps once the home of a samurai or a wealthy merchant, many—especially those in hot-spring resort areas—are modern concrete affairs with as many as 100 or more rooms. What they lack in intimacy, however, is made up for in such amenities as modern bathrooms and perhaps a bar and outdoor recreational facilities. Most guest rooms are fitted with a color TV, a telephone, and a safe for locking up valuables.

RATES

In a ryokan rates are based on a per-person charge rather than as in Western-style hotels, on a straight room charge, and they include breakfast, dinner, and service charge. Tax is usually extra.

Although rates can vary from ¥8,000 ($57) to ¥60,000 ($429) per person, the average cost is generally ¥10,000 ($71) to ¥20,000 ($143). Even within a single ryokan the rates can vary greatly, depending on the room you choose, the dinner courses you select, and the number of people in your room. If you're paying the highest rate, you can be certain that you're getting the best view of the garden, or perhaps even your own private garden, as well as a better meal than the lower-paying guests. All the rates for ryokan in this book are based on double occupancy; if there are more than two of you in one room, you can generally count on a slightly cheaper per-person rate.

DISADVANTAGES

Although I have heartily recommended that you try spending at least one night in a ryokan, there are a number of disadvantages to this style of accommodation. The most obvious problem may be that you will find it uncomfortable sitting on the floor. And because the futon is put away during the day, there's no place on which to lie down for an afternoon nap or rest except on the hard tatami-covered floor. In addition, some of the older ryokan, though quaint, are bitterly cold in the winter and may have only Japanese-style toilets. As for breakfast, some foreigners might find it difficult to swallow raw egg, rice, and seaweed in the morning. Sometimes you can get a Western-style breakfast if you order it the night before, but more often than not the fried or scrambled eggs will arrive cold, leading you to suspect that they were cooked right after you ordered them.

A ryokan is also quite rigid in its schedule. You're expected to arrive sometime after 4pm, take your bath, and then eat at around 6pm or 7pm. Breakfast is served early, usually by 8am, and checkout is by 10am. That means you can't sleep in, and because the maid is continually coming in and out, you have a lot less privacy than you would in a hotel.

The main drawback of the ryokan, however, is that the majority of them will not take you. They simply do not want to deal with the problems inherent in accepting a foreign guest, including the language barrier and differing customs. I saw a number of beautiful old ryokan that I would have liked to include in this book, but I was turned away at the door. The ryokan in this guide, therefore, are ones willing to take in foreigners, but because management and policies can change, it's best to call beforehand. In fact, you should always make a reservation if you want to stay in a first-class ryokan, and even in most medium-priced ones, because the chef has to shop for and prepare your meals. The ryokan staff members do not look kindly upon unannounced strangers turning up on their doorstep.

You can book a reservation for a ryokan through any travel agency in Japan, such as the Japan Travel Bureau, or by calling a ryokan directly, although it's best if the call is conducted in Japanese. You may be required to pay a deposit.

OTHER TYPES OF ACCOMMODATIONS

There are other kinds of accommodations available in Japan, ranging from inexpensive Japanese-style to large Western-style hotels. Although, theoretically, you can travel throughout Japan without making reservations beforehand, it's essential to do so if you're traveling during peak travel seasons, and recommended at other times. These peak times are the end of April through the first week of May (called Golden Week); the New Year's holiday, from about December 27 to January 4; and mid-July through August, particularly around mid-August.

If you find all my recommendations for a certain city fully booked, there are several ways to find alternative accommodations. Easiest is to book through a travel agency, such as the Japan Travel Bureau. An alternative, especially if you're on a budget, is to book a room through one of three **Welcome Inn Reservation Centers,** located at the Tourist Information Centers in Tokyo and Kyoto and at the Narita airport outside Tokyo. More than 200 modestly priced hotels, business hotels, and Japanese-style inns are members of Welcome Inn and are located throughout Japan. Room rates are ¥8,500 ($61) or less per person per night. There is no fee charged for the reservation service, but applicants must appear in person at one of the three centers. The Tokyo and Kyoto centers are open Monday through Friday from 9am to 5pm; the Narita center is open Monday through Friday from 9am to 8pm. All centers are closed on public holidays. Reservation requests are accepted for up to three locations for one party. Reservations can also be made from abroad before your departure for Japan, but note that you must have a confirmed booking on a flight to Japan. For more information, contact your nearest Japan National Tourist Organization office.

If you arrive at your destination and need help obtaining accommodations, you may inquire about a place to stay in at the hotel and ryokan reservation offices found in most train stations. Although policies may differ from office to office, you generally don't have to pay a fee for their services, but you usually do have to pay a percentage of your overnight charge as a deposit. The disadvantage is that you don't see the locale beforehand, and if there's space left at a ryokan even in peak tourist season, you can guess that there's probably a pretty good reason for it. The two worst places I've stayed in in Japan were booked through one of these reservation offices at a train station (don't worry, I don't recommend them in this book). Although these offices can be a real lifesaver in a pinch, and in most cases may be able to recommend quite reasonable and pleasant places in which to stay, it certainly pays to plan in advance.

JAPANESE STYLE

If you want to experience a Japanese-style inn but can't afford the prices of a ryokan, there are a number of other types of accommodations available. Although they don't offer the personalized service and beautiful setting of a ryokan, they do offer the chance to stay in a simple tatami room, sleep on a futon, and in some cases eat Japanese food. As at a ryokan, prices are per person and include service charge and often two meals as well. English is rarely spoken.

The **Japanese Inn Group** is a special organization of more than 60 Japanese-style inns throughout Japan that offer inexpensive lodging and cater largely to foreigners. Although you may balk at the idea of staying at a place filled mainly with foreigners, you must remember that most of the cheap Japanese-style inns in Japan are not accustomed to guests from abroad and may be quite reluctant to take you in. I have covered many of these Japanese Inn Group members in this guidebook and have found the owners for the most part to be an exceptional group of friendly people eager to offer foreigners the chance to experience life on tatami and futon. In many cases, these are good places in which to exchange information with other world travelers, and they are popular with both young people and families.

Although they call themselves ryokan, they are not ryokan in the true sense of the word, because they do not offer personalized service and many of them do not serve food. However, they do offer simple tatami rooms that generally come with a coin-operated TV and sometimes with a coin-operated air conditioner as well. Some of them have towels and a cotton yukata kimono for your use. Facilities generally include a coin-operated washer and dryer and a public bath. The average cost of a one-night stay is about ¥4,000 ($28.55) to about ¥4,500 ($32.15) per person, without meals.

Upon your arrival in Japan, you can pick up a pamphlet at the Tourist Information Center in Tokyo called *Japanese Inn Group,* which lists the members of this organization. You should make reservations directly with the ryokan in which you wish to stay. In some cases, you will be asked to pay a deposit (equal to one night's stay), which you can do with a personal check, traveler's check, money order, or bank check, but the easiest way is with American Express. If you want more information, the Inn Group's headquarters is at 314, Hayao-cho, Kaminoguchi-agaru,

Ninomiyacho-dori, Shimogyo-ku, Kyoto 600 (tel. 075/351-6748). If you're in Tokyo, there's a liaison office at 03/822-2251, but the Tourist Information Center may be able to answer your questions.

Minshuku   Technically, a minshuku is an inexpensive lodging in a private home. The average per-person cost for one night is about ¥5,500 ($39) to ¥6,500 ($46), including two meals. Because minshuku are family-run affairs, you are expected to lay out your own futon at night, supply your own towel and nightgown, and tidy up your room in the morning. Rooms do not have their own private bathroom, but there is a public bath, and meals are served in a communal dining room. Minshuku can range from thatched farmhouses and rickety old wooden buildings to modern concrete structures. Although, officially, the difference between a ryokan and a minshuku is that the ryokan is supposedly more expensive and provides more services, the difference is sometimes very slight. I've stayed in cheap ryokan that provided almost no service at all and in minshuku too large and modern to be considered private homes.

Since minshuku cater primarily to Japanese travelers, they're often excellent places in which to meet the locals, and I've included in this guide a number of minshuku willing to take in foreigners. For more information, contact the **Japan Minshuku Center,** Kotsu Kaikan Building, Basement 1, 2-10-1 Yurakucho, Chiyoda-ku, Tokyo (tel. 03/3216-6556). It's open every day except Sunday and holidays from 10am to 5pm, and you can make reservations here for member minshuku across the country. Note, however, that reservations are accepted only for two or more persons.

Kokumin Shukusha   A *kokumin shukusha* is public lodging found primarily in resort and vacation areas. Established by the government, there are more than 300 of these facilities throughout Japan. Catering largely to Japanese school groups and families, they offer basic, Japanese-style rooms at an average daily rate of about ¥6,500 ($46) per person, including two meals. Although you don't have to have a reservation to stay in these places, they are usually quite full during the summer and peak seasons. Reservations can be made through a travel agency. The drawback to many of these lodges is that because they are often located in national parks and in scenic spots, the best way to reach them is by car.

Kokumin Kyuka Mura   Similar to a kokumin shukusha, the *kokumin kyuka mura* is a "vacation village" that is government run and located in a national park, but the difference is that it is more expensive—generally around ¥8,500 ($61) per person, with two meals—and offers more recreational facilities. Apply through a travel agency.

Shukubo   These are lodgings in a Buddhist temple. Providing Japanese-style rooms, they are similar to inexpensive ryokan, except that they're attached to temples and serve vegetarian food. There is usually an early-morning service at 6am, which you are welcome to join. Probably the best place to experience life in a temple is at Mt. Koya (described in Chapter 13). Prices at a *shukubo* range from about ¥5,500 ($39) to about ¥11,000 ($79) per person, including two meals.

INTERNATIONAL VILLAS

These small country inns are financed and maintained by the Okayama prefectural government, and are open only to foreigners, although accompanying Japanese guests are welcome. The idea for the inns originated with Okayama's governor, who wanted to repay the kindness of foreigners during his trips abroad as a youth. Each villa is small, with a half dozen or so guest rooms, and equipped with the latest in bathroom and kitchen facilities. You can cook your own meals or visit one of the local restaurants. There are six International Villas, most of them in small villages or rural settings. They are located in Fukiya, Koshihata, Ushimado, Hattoji, Shiraishi Island, and Takebe. The cost for staying at one of the villas is ¥3,000 ($21.40) per person for nonmembers and ¥2,500 ($17.85) for members. To become a member, simply pay ¥500 ($3.55) for a membership card upon check-in at any villa. For more information, refer to the section on Okayama in Chapter 13.

WESTERN STYLE

Lodging in this category ranges from large first-class hotels to inexpensive ones catering primarily to Japanese businessmen. In figuring out your bill, remember that in accommodations costing more than ¥15,000 ($107) per person per night, a 6% local/consumption tax will be added, while in accommodations costing less than ¥15,000, a 3% consumption tax will be added. There will also be a 10% to 15% service charge added to your bill. Although ryokan and some of the less expensive types of lodgings include service and sometimes tax in their prices, most hotels do not. Unless otherwise stated, therefore, you can assume that 16% to 21% will be added to the prices quoted in this book for hotels costing more than ¥15,000 ($107) per person per night. Incidentally, a twin room refers to a room with twin beds, and a double room refers to one with a double bed.

Hotels Both first-class and medium-priced hotels in Japan are known for their excellent service and cleanliness. The first-class hotels in the larger cities can compete with the best hotels in the world, and offer a wide range of services, which may include a health club and massage services (for which there's an extra charge), an executive business center with secretarial services, a guest relations officer to help with any problems you may have, a travel agency, a shopping arcade, cocktail lounges with live music, and fine Japanese- and Western-style restaurants. Rooms have their own private bathroom with a tub and shower combination (since Japanese are used to soaping down and rinsing off before bathing, it would be rare to find tubs without showers; similarly, showers without tubs are practically nonexistent in this nation of bathers). Rooms in this category also have a color television, a clock and usually a radio, a hot-water thermos with tea bags, and a minibar (a refrigerator stocked with beer, soft drinks, bottled water, liquor, and snacks). Because they're accustomed to foreigners, most hotels in this category employ an English-speaking staff. Services provided include room service (usually until midnight, although some Tokyo hotels have 24-hour room service), laundry and dry-cleaning service (note that some hotels do not provide this service on Sundays), and often a complimentary English-language newspaper, such as the *Japan Times*, delivered to guest rooms.

The most expensive hotels in Japan are in Tokyo, where you will pay at least ¥20,000 ($143) for a single room in a first-class hotel. Outside Tokyo, single rooms in this category generally range from about ¥12,000 ($86) to about ¥15,000 ($107), while in medium-priced hotels rooms are usually about ¥2,000 ($14) less. Most first-class hotels offer a variety of rooms in a wide range of prices. The price of a twin-bedded room, for example, may range from about ¥22,000 ($211) to about ¥40,000 ($385) within the same hotel, with the higher price charged for deluxe rooms with more amenities. Standard rooms are usually the lower-priced rooms, but be sure to inquire about the price range when making your reservation.

Business Hotels Catering primarily to traveling Japanese businessmen, a "business hotel" is a no-frills establishment with tiny, sparsely furnished rooms, most of them singles, but usually with some twin or double rooms also available. Primarily just a place to crash for the night, these rooms usually have everything you need but in miniature form—minuscule bathroom, tiny bathtub, small bed (or beds), and barely enough space to unpack your bags. After a while these business hotels all start to look alike. If you're a large person, you may have trouble sleeping in a place like this. There are no bellboys, no room service, and sometimes not even a lobby or coffee shop, although usually there are vending machines that dispense beer and soda. The advantage of staying in business hotels is that they're inexpensive—starting as low as ¥5,500 ($39) for a single—and are often conveniently located next to train and subway stations. Check-in is usually not until 3pm or 4pm and checkout is usually at 10am; you can leave your bags at the front desk. The most sophisticated business hotels can be found in Tokyo, where, because of high prices, they make up the bulk of medium-priced accommodations.

Pensions If you see an accommodation listed as a pension, you know that it is the Western equivalent of a minshuku. Usually containing no more than 10 rooms, these Western-style lodges come with beds and, on the average, charge ¥6,500 ($46) to

¥8,500 ($61) per person, including two meals. Many seem geared to young Japanese girls and are thus done up in rather feminine-looking decor, with lots of pinks and flower prints. They're most often located in ski resorts and in the countryside, sometimes making access a problem.

Youth Hostels There are more than 450 youth hostels in Japan, most of them privately run and operating in locations ranging from temples to concrete blocks. There is no age limit, and although most of them require a youth hostel membership card from the Japan Youth Hostel Association, they often let foreigners stay without one for about ¥500 ($3.55) extra per night. Although there are usually such restrictions as a 9pm or 10pm curfew, meals at fixed times, and rooms with many bunk beds or futon, youth hostels are quite cheap, costing about ¥3,200 ($22.85) per day, including two meals. They're certainly the cheapest places to stay at in Japan, although a Norwegian I met compared life in a youth hostel to that in the military. They're not quite that regimented, but you get the picture.

I've included youth hostels throughout my guide just in case you want to try some of them to keep down costs. If you plan on staying exclusively in youth hostels, however, you should pick up a pamphlet called *Youth Hostel Map of Japan,* available at the Tourist Information Center in Tokyo or Kyoto. You should also get a youth hostel membership card. If you fail to obtain one in your own country, you can get one in Japan for ¥2,800 ($20). The **Japan Youth Hostel Association** is located in the Hoken Kaikan Honkan Building, 1-2 Sadohara-cho, Ichigaya, Shinjuku-ku, Tokyo 162 (tel. 03/3269-5831). Other places in Tokyo where you can buy a youth hostel card are the Youth Hostel information counters on the fourth floor of Keio Department Store in Shinjuku, in the second basement of Sogo Department Store in front of Yurakucho Station, and on the seventh floor of Seibu Department Store in Ikebukuro.

4. WHERE TO DINE

The biggest problem facing the hungry foreigner in Japan is ordering a meal, because few restaurants have English menus. This book alleviates that problem to a large extent by giving some sample dishes and prices for specific restaurants throughout Japan. Another custom that simplifies ordering is the use of plastic food models in glass display cases either outside or just inside the front door of a restaurant. Sushi, tempura, daily specials, spaghetti—they're all there in mouth-watering plastic replicas, along with the corresponding prices. The use of such food models began after Japan opened its doors a century ago and was inundated by all kinds of strange, foreign things. Food was one of them, and the models eased the problems of ordering. Today, those plastic dishes work in reverse, saving the hungry lives of visiting foreigners. Simply decide what you want and point it out to your waitress.

Unfortunately, not all restaurants in Japan have plastic display cases. In such a situation, the best thing to do is to look at what people around you are eating and order what looks best. An alternative is simply to order the teishoku, or daily special (also called "set course" or simply "course"). These are fixed-price meals that consist of a main dish and several side dishes, including soup, rice, and Japanese pickles. Although most restaurants have special set courses for dinner as well, lunch is the usual time for the teishoku, and you can help keep your costs down by eating your big meal in the middle of the day. Even a restaurant that may be prohibitive to your budget at dinnertime may be perfect for a lunchtime splurge, when specials may cost as little as a fourth of what a dinner would be. The usual time for the teishoku is from about 11 or 11:30am to 1:30 or 2pm. Keep in mind that restaurants will add a 6% tax to bills costing ¥7,500 ($53.55) and more, while a 3% tax will be added to bills costing less than ¥7,500. First-class restaurants will also add a 10% to 15% service charge, as do restaurants located in many hotels.

For those of you who may not want to eat Japanese food every day, I've included suggestions throughout this book for non-Japanese restaurants as well. The most popular Western-style restaurants in Japan are Italian and French, although more often than not they cook for the Japanese rather than the Western palate. French nouvelle cuisine matches well the Japanese style of cooking, since both stress presentation, textures, and flavor, and the most expensive foreign restaurants in Japan are nearly all French. Other popular restaurants are Indian, Thai, and Chinese, as well as numerous steakhouses.

The usual opening hours for restaurants in Japan are from about 11am to 10 or 11pm. Of course, some establishments close as early as 9pm, while others stay open past midnight; some close for a few hours in the afternoon. The main thing to remember is that if you're in a big city like Tokyo or Osaka, you'll want to avoid the lunchtime rush, which is from 1 to 2pm. In addition, the closing time posted for most restaurants is exactly that—everyone is expected to pay his or her bill and leave. A general rule of thumb is that the last order is taken about a half hour before closing time. To be on the safe side, therefore, try to arrive at least 30 minutes before closing time. An hour would be even better, giving you time to relax and enjoy your meal.

BUDGET CHOICES

During your first few days in Japan—particularly if you're in Tokyo—money will seem to flow out of your pockets like water. In fact, money has a tendency to disappear so quickly that many people become convinced they must have lost some of it somehow. At this point, almost everyone panics (I've seen it happen again and again), but then slowly realizes that since prices are markedly different here (steeper), all that's required to stay within budget is a bit of readjustment in thinking and habits. Coffee, for example, is something of a luxury, and some Japanese are astonished at the thought of drinking four or five cups a day. By following the advice here, you'll be able to cut down on needless expenses, saving your money for those splurges that are really worth it.

If you're on a budget, avoid eating breakfast at your hotel. Coffee shops offer what is called "morning service" until about 10am; it generally consists of a cup of coffee, a small salad, a boiled egg, and toast for about ¥450 ($3.20). That's a real bargain when you consider that just one cup of coffee usually costs ¥300 ($2.15) to ¥500 ($3.55). If you're addicted to coffee in the morning, you can save money by purchasing instant coffee and drinking it in your hotel room. Many hotels and inns in Japan provide a thermos of hot water or a water heater. Since jars of instant coffee tend to be heavy and bulky, you might want to buy individual packets of coffee, available in cubes, tubes, or so-called coffee sticks, complete with powdered cream and sugar. You'll find instant coffee in the food department of major department stores.

Eat your biggest meal at lunch. Many restaurants offer a daily set lunch, or teishoku, at a fraction of what their set dinners might be. Usually ranging in price from ¥700 ($5) to ¥1,500 ($10.70), they're generally available from 11 or 11:30am to 2pm. A Japanese teishoku will often include the main course (such as tempura, grilled fish, or the specialty of the house), soup, pickled vegetables, rice, and tea, while the set menu in a Western-style restaurant usually consists of a main dish, salad, bread, and coffee. Places in which to look for inexpensive restaurants include department stores (often one whole floor will be devoted to various kinds of restaurants), underground shopping arcades, nightlife districts, and around train and subway stations. Some of the cheapest establishments for a night out on the town are the countless yakitori-ya across Japan—drinking establishments that also sell skewered meats and vegetables.

Noodle shops are generally inexpensive, ranging from stand-up stalls seen around train stations to more traditional restaurants, where guests sit at low tables on tatami. Although noodle and ramen shops are already rock-bottom choices, you can save even more money by avoiding restaurants altogether. There are all kinds of pre-prepared foods you can buy; some of them are complete meals in themselves, perfect for picnics in the park or right in your hotel room.

Perhaps the best known is the *obento,* or box lunch, commonly sold on express trains, on train station platforms, and at counter windows of tiny shops throughout Japan. In fact, the obento served on trains and at train stations are an inexpensive way to sample regional cuisine, since they often include food typical of the region. In Hiroshima, for example, an obento may include oysters. Costing usually between ¥600 ($4.30) and ¥1,200 ($8.55), the basic obento contains a piece of meat (generally fish or chicken), various side dishes, rice, and pickled vegetables. Sushi boxed lunches are also available.

Department stores usually sell pre-prepared foods in their basements, in the food and produce sections; they include such items as tempura, yakitori, sushi, salads, and desserts. These places are very popular with housewives. By the way, most department stores also have inexpensive restaurants, usually on one of the top floors. Since they almost always have plastic food displays, ordering is easy.

Street vendors are also good sources for inexpensive meals. They sell a variety of foods, including oden (fish cakes), okonomiyaki (pancakes with different ingredients), and yakisoba (fried noodles). If you find yourself in real financial woes, you can always subsist on "cup noodle," which you can buy in any food store. Eaten by poor students and workingmen who don't have the time to sit down to a real meal, it's a dried soup that springs to life (well, sort of) when you add hot water—usually readily available if you're staying in a ryokan. The cup noodle comes in a variety of choices, such as curry or chili tomato, and usually costs less than ¥300 ($2.15). Eat too much of it, though, and you'll probably disintegrate.

Japan also has American fast-food chains, such as McDonald's (where Big Macs cost about ¥450 ($3.20), Wendy's, and Kentucky Fried Chicken, as well as Japanese chains—Morninaga, Lotteria, and First Kitchen, among them—that sell hamburgers and french fries.

5. WHAT TO BUY

POSTCARDS

Unless you have a photographic memory and can remember places and names, and how to spell them, chances are that all those snapshots of temples, shrines, and gardens will look distressingly alike once you get your film developed. My mother's solution: Buy postcards of every place you visit. That way you can match snapshots with postcards, many of which may have such useful information as name, location, and correct spelling of the place or object in question. And if your pictures don't turn out, well, you'll always have those postcards.

TRADITIONAL CRAFTS

Traditional crafts are produced throughout Japan, often reflecting the particular style of a region. Those readily available include ceramics and pottery, toys, textiles, products made from Japanese paper (*washi*), Japanese dolls, carp banners, kites, swords, fans, masks (including Noh antique and reproduction masks), lacquerware, items made from bamboo, knives, and artwork. Many prefectural government offices maintain a display room where the local products are offered for sale; otherwise, they can be found in city shops. Refer to the individual city listings for more information. In addition, there are many prefectural display shops grouped together around Tokyo Station, where you can shop for crafts from around Japan. Refer to the Tokyo shopping section for more information. And finally, when it comes to traditional crafts, no city can outdo Kyoto, where many shops have been passed down from generation to generation.

ANTIQUES & CURIOS

Antiques are another good buy in Japan, simply because most are unique to Japan and therefore make memorable souvenirs of your trip. Cast-iron teapots, second-hand kimonos, china, religious statuary, furniture, *hibachi* (charcoal braziers), masks, dolls, mirrors—the list goes on and on. Tokyo is one of the best places in which to pick up antiques, since it has the greatest number of weekend flea markets and antique shops.

FAST FACTS JAPAN

American Express   There are several American Express offices in **Tokyo** (refer to "Fast Facts: Tokyo" in Chapter 4 for offices in the capital). In addition, there are also American Express offices in **Osaka** (tel. 06/264-6300), **Kobe** (tel. 078/392-3431), **Sapporo** (tel. 011/251-0057), **Nagoya** (tel. 052/204-2246), and **Fukuoka** (tel. 092/272-2111). Most are open Monday through Friday from 9am to 5pm and on Saturday from 9am to 1pm.

Business Hours   **Banks** are open Monday through Friday from 9am to 3pm and are closed on Saturday and Sunday. **Government offices** and **private companies** are generally open Monday through Friday from about 9am to 5pm. In reality, however, Japanese businessmen in the private sector tend to work long hours, and it's not unusual to find someone in the office as late as 10pm. To be on the safe side, however, it's best to conduct business before 5pm.

Most **stores** in Japan don't open until 10am, and they close about 8pm. Often they're closed one day a week, and it's not unusual for almost all the shops in a particular neighborhood to be closed on the same day. Some shops, especially those around major train stations and entertainment areas, stay open until 10pm; some convenience stores are open 24 hours. **Department stores** are open from 10am to 6 or 7pm. They close one day a week, but it's different for each store, so you can always find one that's open, even on Sunday.

Restaurants close at exactly the time posted, with the last order taken usually a half hour before closing time (even earlier in kaiseki restaurants). To enjoy your meal fully, therefore, always arrive at a restaurant at least 1 hour before closing.

Similarly, **museums** and **attractions** in Japan close their ticket windows a half hour before closing time.

Calendar Years   The Japanese have their own system for counting years, based on an emperor's reign. The Meiji Period, for example, ran from 1868 to 1912, which translates in the Japanese calendar to Meiji 1–44. Thus, Meiji 10 refers to the 10th year of Emperor Meiji's reign, or 1878. Subsequent periods are Taisaho (1912–26), Showa (1926–89), and Heisei, which began in January 1989, at the beginning of Emperor Akihito's reign. The year 1992, therefore, is Heisei 4.

Cigarettes   A wide variety of both domestic and imported brands are readily available throughout Japan. There are even outdoor vending machines on what seems to be every major city street. (See also "Customs," below.) Unfortunately for nonsmokers, Japan has never had much of an antismoking campaign. Few restaurants, therefore, have nonsmoking sections and only a few enlightened hotels have designated nonsmoking floors. If you want to sit in the nonsmoking car of the Shinkansen bullet train, ask for the *kinensha.*

Climate   See "When to Go" in Chapter 2.

Crime   See "Safety," below.

Currency   See "Information, Entry Requirements & Money" in Chapter 2.

Customs   You can take duty-free into Japan up to 400 non-Japanese cigarettes or 500 grams of tobacco or 100 cigars; three bottles (760cc each) of alcoholic beverages; and 2 ounces of perfume. You can also bring in gifts and souvenirs whose total market value is less than ¥200,000 ($1,429).

A word of caution: Make sure you do not take any pornographic material with you: American magazines, such as *Playboy* and *Penthouse,* that show pubic hair are not allowed into Japan. The Japanese equivalents of these magazines either are much more modest or have the offensive parts blacked out. As for drugs, don't even think about it; penalties for offenders are severe and are strictly imposed (see also "Drug Laws," below).

On your return home, you're allowed by U.S. Customs to bring back duty-free

$400 worth of goods purchased abroad. Beyond that, the next $1,000 worth of goods is assessed at 10% duty. If you're shipping purchases home by mail, you're allowed to send up to $50 per package duty-free. Incidentally, you might want to keep a record of your purchases in Japan, in order to be able to declare the exact value of each item.

Documents Required See "Information, Entry Requirements & Money" in Chapter 2, as well as individual city chapters for local information offices.

Driving Rules See "Getting Around" in Chapter 4.

Drug Laws Drug abuse is not a problem in Japan, simply because there aren't many drugs. Nevertheless, the drug laws are stringent. You'll be fined and deported if you're caught with drugs; if you're caught with harsher drugs, such as cocaine, penalties will be more severe. Don't risk it.

Drugstores Drugstores, called *kusuri-ya*, are found readily in Japan, and they can fill American prescriptions. Nevertheless, it's always best to carry an adequate supply of important medicines with you, particularly since drugstores in Japan do not stay open 24 hours. Convenience stores, which are open day and night, carry such nonprescription items as aspirin.

Electricity The electrical current throughout Japan is 100 volts AC, but there are two different cycles in use. In Tokyo and in regions northeast of the capital, it's 50 cycles, while in Nagoya, Kyoto, Osaka, and all points to the southwest, it's 60 cycles. Leading hotels in Tokyo often have two outlets, one for 110 volts and one for 220 volts; many of them also have hairdryers that you can use for free. Actually, you can use many American appliances, such as radios and hairdryers, in Japan, because the American current is 110 volts and 60 cycles. The only difference is that the appliances may run a little more slowly; the prongs are the same. For sensitive equipment, either have it adjusted or use batteries if it is also battery-operated. The plugs are the same as in the United States.

Embassies and Consulates The embassies of most countries are located in Tokyo and are generally open Monday through Friday from 8:30 or 9am to about 5 or 5:30pm. Most of them close for an hour or so for lunch; their visa or passport sections are open only at certain times during the day. It's best to call in advance. The **U.S. Embassy,** 1-10-5 Akasaka, Minato-ku (tel. 03/3224-5000), close to the Toranomon subway station, is open Monday through Friday from 8:30am to noon and from 2 to 5pm. The **Canadian Embassy,** 7-3-38 Akasaka, Minato-ku (tel. 03/3408-2101), near Aoyama-Itchome Station, is open Monday through Friday from 9am to 12:30pm and from 1:30 to 5:30pm. The **British Embassy,** 1 Ichibancho, Chiyoda-ku (tel. 03/3265-5511), close to Ichigaya, Kojimachi, and Hanzomon stations, is open Monday through Friday from 9am to noon and from 2 to 5:30pm. The **Australian Embassy,** 2-1-14 Mita, Minato-ku (tel. 03/3435-0971), is open from 9am to noon and from 2 to 5pm. The **Embassy of Ireland,** 8-7 Sanbancho, Chiyoda-ku (tel. 03/3263-0695), a 15-minute walk from either Ichigaya or Hanzomon Station, is open Monday through Friday from 9am to 4:30pm. The **New Zealand Embassy,** 20-40 Kamiyama-cho, Shibuya-ku (tel. 03/3467-2271), a 15-minute walk from Shibuya Station, is open Monday through Friday from 9am to noon and from 1:30 to 5pm.

The U.S. Embassy and the British Embassy have consular services in Tokyo as well. They also maintain consulates in some major cities, as do several other embassies; for information regarding location, inquire at the respective embassies.

Emergencies The national emergency numbers are 110 for calling **police** and 119 both for calling an **ambulance** and for reporting a **fire.** Be sure to speak slowly and precisely.

Etiquette See "Cultural & Social Life" in Chapter 1.

Holidays See "When to Go" in Chapter 2.

Information See "Information, Entry Requirements & Money" in Chapter 2, as well as individual city chapters for local information offices.

Language See the "Language" section in Chapter 1.

Laundry All the upper-bracket hotels and even some of the hotels for business travelers have laundry service. Since such service tends to be expensive, you may want to wash your clothes yourself. Not everyone has a washing machine in Japan, so laundromats are abundant. The cost is about ¥200 ($1.40) to ¥300 ($2.15) per load for the washer; the dryer is about ¥100 (70¢) for 10 minutes. Some of the inexpensive Japanese inns that cater to young travelers also have coin-operated laundry machines on their premises.

Liquor Laws The legal drinking age is 20. You'll find vending machines dispensing beer and whisky in almost every neighborhood in Japan, but note that they close down at 11pm. *Note:* If you intend to drive in Japan, however, you are not allowed even one drink.

Mail Citizens of Canada, the United Kingdom, the Republic of Ireland, Australia, and New Zealand can have their mail forwarded to them at their respective embassies in Japan. The U.S. Embassy, however, will not hold mail. Thus, if you don't know where you'll be staying, you can always have your mail sent to the central post office of the major cities you'll be visiting. In Tokyo, have your mail sent c/o Poste Restante, Central Post Office, Tokyo, Japan, which is located just southwest of Tokyo Station.

Although all **post offices** are open Monday through Friday from 9am to 5pm, international post offices are open much later, often until 7 or 8pm. It's only at larger post offices that you can mail packages abroad, and these are often found close to the city's main train station. Conveniently, these branches sell cardboard boxes in three sizes, with the necessary tape and string. Packages mailed abroad cannot weigh more than 20 kilos (about 44 pounds). A package weighing 10 kilos (about 22 pounds) will cost ¥7,150 ($51) if sent to North America via surface mail. As you see, it's very expensive to ship packages abroad.

If you're **mailing a letter,** your hotel may be able to do it for you or direct you to the nearest post office. Airmail letters weighing up to 10 grams cost ¥100 (71¢) to North America and ¥120 (85¢) to Europe. Postcards are ¥70 (50¢) to both. Domestic letters weighing up to 25 grams are ¥62 (44¢); postcards are ¥41 (29¢). It takes approximately 5 to 7 days for letters and postcards to reach North America.

Post offices are easily recognizable by the red symbol of a capital *T* with a horizontal line above it. **Mailboxes** in Japan are painted a bright orange-red.

Maps Maps are readily available at major bookstores that have sections in English. A recent check of Jena bookstore in Tokyo, for example, revealed at least a dozen different maps of the capital city. Some zero in on sightseeing attractions, while others give postal addresses for the various Tokyo wards and are in both Japanese and English. However, unless you're living in Japan or plan on doing extensive sightseeing, I personally believe that the free maps offered by the Tourist Information Center and local city offices are adequate for trips through the country. Free maps at the Tourist Information Center include maps of Japan, Tokyo, and Kyoto.

Measures Before the metric system came into use in Japan, the country had its own standards for measuring length and weight. There's no reason for you to learn these nowadays, but you will hear one way of measuring that is still common—rooms are still measured by the number of tatami straw mats that will fit in them. A six-tatami room, for example, is the size of six tatami mats. A tatami is roughly 3 feet wide and 6 feet long.

Newspapers and Magazines Five English-language newspapers are published daily in Japan. They are the *Japan Times,* the *Mainichi Daily News,* the *Daily Yomiuri,* the *Asahi Evening News,* and the *International Herald Tribune.* Hotels and major bookstores also carry the international edition of such newsmagazines as *Time* and *Newsweek.* For regional publications detailing what's going on in a city, check with the local tourist information office listed in the individual city chapters.

Passports See "Information, Entry Requirements & Money" in Chapter 2.

Pets There is no regulation for bringing a cat into Japan. If you intend to bring a dog with you, however, you must obtain a rabies certificate from the U.S. Department of Agriculture or, if you're a citizen of another country, from the appropriate ministry in your government. For more information, contact the Japanese Embassy or consulate nearest you.

Photographic Needs Japan is the right country to be in if you're looking to buy **cameras** and other photographic equipment. Japanese products are, of course, among the finest in the world, and for that reason they are not cheap. (In fact, you can probably obtain Japanese cameras cheaper in the United States by ordering from one of the many camera catalogues available.) Check the section "Shopping A to Z" in Chapter 8 to find out the location of good camera stores in the capital.

As for **film,** you won't have trouble finding Kodak or the Japanese brand Fuji in Tokyo or other major cities. Outside the big cities, particularly around tourist attractions, it's sometimes difficult to find any film other than Fuji for color prints. If you intend to take a lot of slides, be sure to stock up on film of your choice *before* setting out for remote areas. To have Kodak film processed, you should wait until you return to Tokyo or home before doing so; shops outside Tokyo often send Kodak film to the capital for development, which can take a week.

Police   The national emergency telephone number for police is **110.**

Radio and Television   For English-language radio programs, the **Far East Network,** or **FEN** (at 810 kHz), is the U.S. military station, with broadcasts of music, talk shows, and sports events from the United States, as well as Tokyo sumo matches. **J-Wave** (81.3 FM) is a Tokyo radio station that broadcasts programs in English, with a wide range of music. Upper-bracket hotels in Tokyo also have **KTYO,** a cable radio station broadcasting music, news, and sports around the clock.

If you enjoy watching television, you've come to the wrong country. Almost nothing is broadcast in English; even foreign films are dubbed in Japanese, and the only way to hear them in English is if you have what's called a bilingual television. A few of the best hotels in Tokyo and other major cities do have bilingual televisions, and there are generally one to three English movies on television each week. Major hotels in Tokyo, Osaka, Kobe, and Kyoto also have cable TV with English-language programs, including **CNN** broadcasts from the United States. But even if you don't understand the language, I suggest that you watch television in Japan at least once. Maybe you'll catch a samurai series, which is very popular. Commercials are also worth watching—often they're what I call "mood" advertising, in which the scenery simply sets a mood that has very little to do with the actual product.

By the way, during your travels you may come across rooms in both Western- and Japanese-style establishments that offer video programs with their TVs. These programs are either coin-operated or charged automatically to your bill. Since the descriptions of these programs are usually in Japanese only, I will clear up the mystery—they're generally "adult entertainment" programs. Now you know.

Rest Rooms   If you're in need of a restroom, your best bet is at train and subway stations, big hotels, and department stores. Many toilets in Japan, especially those at train stations, are Japanese style: they're holes in the ground over which you squat facing the end that has a raised hood. Men stand and aim for the hole. Although Japanese lavatories may seem uncomfortable at first, they're actually much more sanitary because no part of your body touches anything. Who knows, you may even come to prefer them over Western-style toilets. To find out if a stall is empty, knock on the door. If it's occupied, someone will knock back. Similarly, if you're inside a stall and someone knocks, answer with a knock back or else the person will just keep on knocking persistently and try to get in.

Don't be surprised if you go into some restrooms and find men's urinals and individual private stalls in the same room. Women are supposed to simply walk right past the urinals without noticing them.

Safety   Japan is one of the safest countries in the world, and the people, for the most part, are honest. These twin attributes of safety and honesty make Japan a particularly attractive place for the tourist. Nevertheless, crime does exist, for every society has its criminals. But it is negligible compared with that in the United States.

As a general policy, therefore, whenever you're traveling in an unfamiliar country, stay alert. Be aware of your immediate surroundings, especially in heavily touristed areas. Wear a moneybelt and don't sling your camera or purse over your shoulder. Men should carry their billfolds in an inner pocket. These elementary precautions will minimize the possibility of your becoming a victim of theft.

Taxes   In 1989 the Japanese government introduced a 3% **consumption tax** on goods and services, including hotel rates and restaurant meals. If you stay overnight in accommodations that cost ¥15,000 ($107) or less per person, a 3% government consumption tax will be added to your bill; if your accommodations cost more than

¥15,000 per person, both a 3% consumption tax and a 3% **local tax** will be added to your bill. Some hotels, particularly business hotels, include the tax in their tariff, while others do not. Be sure to ask, therefore, whether rates include tax. In restaurants, a 3% consumption tax is levied on meals costing ¥7,500 ($53.55) or less per person, while meals costing more than ¥7,500 are subject to a 6% tax (which includes both consumption and local taxes).

In addition to these taxes, a 10% to 15% **service charge** will be added to your bill in lieu of tipping at most of the fancier restaurants and at many hotels. Thus, the 16% to 21% in tax and service charge that will be added to your bill in the more expensive locales can really add up. Most ryokan, or Japanese-style inns, include a service charge but not a consumption tax in their rates. If you're not sure, ask.

As for shopping, a 3% consumption tax is also levied on most goods (some of the smaller vendors are not required to levy tax). Travelers from abroad, however, are eligible for an exemption on goods taken out of the country, although only the larger department stores and specialty shops seem equipped to deal with the procedures. In any case, most department stores grant a **refund** on the consumption tax only when the total amount of purchases exceeds ¥10,000 ($71). You can obtain a refund immediately by having a sales clerk fill out a list of your purchases and then presenting the list to the tax-exemption counter of the department store. You will need to show your passport. Note that no refunds for consumption tax are given for food, drinks, tobacco, cosmetics, film, and batteries.

If you depart Japan from the Narita airport outside Tokyo, you will be charged a ¥2,000 ($14) **service facility fee** (there is no departure tax at any of the other international airports in Japan).

Telephone, Telegram, Telex, and Telefax If you're staying in a medium- or upper-range hotel, most likely you can make local, domestic, and international calls from your room. However, you'd be prudent to ask first whether you can make the call directly, whether you must go through the operator, and whether a surcharge will be added to your bill.

There are several different kinds of **public telephones** in Japan, all color-coded. You can find them virtually everywhere—in telephone booths on the sidewalk, on stands outside little shops, on train platforms, in restaurants and coffee shops. There are even telephones in Japan's bullet trains. The red, pink, and blue telephones take only ¥10 coins, while the yellow and green ones accept both ¥10 and ¥100 coins. A **local call** costs ¥10 (7¢) for the first 3 minutes, after which a warning chime will ring to tell you to insert more coins or you'll be disconnected. I usually insert two or three coins when I make a telephone call so that I won't have to worry about being disconnected; coins that aren't used are always returned at the end of the call.

If you don't want to deal with coins, you can purchase a disposable **telephone card**, which can be inserted into a slot on most of the green telephones. In fact, telephone cards have become so popular in Japan that it's sometimes difficult to find a telephone that will accept coins. Telephone cards are sold at vending machines (located right beside many telephones), at telephone offices, at station kiosks, and even at tourist attractions, where cards are imprinted with photographs of temples, castles, and other sights. The cards come in values of ¥500 ($3.55) to ¥5,000 ($35.70).

For **international calls** made from public telephones, you can make a collect call or place a call through an operator anywhere in Japan by dialing 0051. An operator-assisted **station-to-station call** to the United States costs ¥1,890 ($13.50) for the first 3 minutes. Cheaper, however, are calls made without the assistance of an operator, either through an international green public telephone or through telephones that offer **direct-dial service** (most medium- and upper-range hotels in larger cities offer direct dial, but remember to ask about the surcharge). If a green telephone is equipped to handle international calls, it will have a sign saying INTERNATIONAL AND DOMESTIC CARD/COIN TELEPHONE. This is when those telephone cards really come in handy. You can make a direct-dial call by dialing 001, followed by the code of the country you're calling, the area code, and the telephone number. The direct-dial number for calls to the United States, for example, is 001 + 1 + area code + telephone number. The cheapest time to call is between 11pm and 5am Japan time, when a 3-minute call to the United States costs ¥420 ($3).

If you wish to be connected with an operator in your home country, you can do so from green international telephones by dialing 0039, followed by the country code (for the United States, dial 0039-111). These calls can be used for collect calls or credit-card calls. Some hotels and other public places are equipped with special telephones that will link you to your home operator with the push of a button, and there are instructions in English.

Area codes for all of Japan's cities begin with a zero. Tokyo's area code, for example, is 03, while Osaka's is 06. For other area codes, check the "Orientation" section of each city in this guide. Use the area code only when dialing from outside the area. When calling Japan from abroad, it may be necessary to drop the zero in the area code. When calling from the United States, for example, dial only 3 for Tokyo (not 03) and 6 (not 06) for Osaka. If you have questions, call the international operator in the country from which you are placing your call.

As for **telegrams** and **faxes** (facsimiles) your hotel may be able to handle such services. If not, you can send a telegram or a fax from a **Kokusai Denshin Denwa (KDD)** office. (The name is equivalent to International Telephone & Telegraph.) Ask the hotel clerk where the office nearest your hotel is. KDD offices can also handle phototelegrams, and have booths for international telephone calls and **telex** service. The cost of sending a telegram to the United States is ¥118 (84¢) per word.

Incidentally, Japan leads the way when it comes to faxes. Almost all my friends in Tokyo have a home fax machine, and most businesses cannot survive without one.

Time Japan is 9 hours ahead of Greenwich mean time, 14 hours ahead of New York, 15 hours ahead of Chicago, and 17 hours ahead of Los Angeles. Since Japan does not go on daylight saving time, subtract 1 hour from the above times if you're calling the United States in the summer. Because Japan is on the other side of the international dateline, you lose 1 day when traveling from the United States to Asia. Returning to North America, however, you gain 1 day, which means that you arrive on the same day you left. In fact, it often happens that you arrive in the States at an earlier hour than you departed from Japan.

Tipping One of the delights of being in Japan is that there is no tipping, not even to waitresses, taxi drivers, or bellboys. If you try to tip them, they'll probably be confused or embarrassed. Instead of individual tipping, a 10% to 15% service charge will be added to your bill at the higher-priced hotels and restaurants.

Tourist Offices See "Information, Entry Requirements & Money" in Chapter 2.

Travel-Phone If you're having problems communicating with someone in Japan, are lost, or need information, the Japan National Tourist Organization operates a nationwide telephone system, called Travel-Phone, that provides service every day throughout the year from 9am to 5pm. If you're outside Tokyo or Kyoto, all you have to do is insert a ¥10 coin into a yellow, blue, or green telephone (the coin will be returned to you at the end of the call) and dial one of two numbers. If you want to know something about *eastern Japan* (Tokyo, Yokohama, Matsumoto, the island of Hokkaido), dial 0120-222800; if you have any questions pertaining to *western Japan* (Nagoya, Kanazawa, Kyoto, western Honshu, Shikoku, Kyushu), dial 0120-444800. Toll-free calls can be made only if you're outside Tokyo or Kyoto. If you're in Tokyo, the number to dial is 3502-1461; in Kyoto it's 371-5649. In these two cities you have to pay for the call, which is ¥10 (7¢) for 3 minutes.

Visas See "Information, Entry Requirements & Money" in Chapter 2.

Water The water is safe to drink anywhere in Japan, although some people claim it's too highly chlorinated. Bottled water is also readily available.

Weather The *Japan Times* carries nearly a full page of weather information daily, including forecasts for Tokyo and other major Japanese cities and a weekly outlook. In addition, local weather information can be obtained anywhere in Japan by dialing 177. If you wish to know what the weather is in another part of the country, you must first dial that region's area code. Information is given in Japanese only.

CHAPTER 4

GETTING TO KNOW TOKYO

To the uninitiated, Tokyo may seem like a whirlwind of traffic and people, so confusing that visitors might swear they had somehow landed on another planet. This chapter should make getting settled in Tokyo not only less confusing but more enjoyable as well.

First-time visitors to Tokyo are almost invariably disappointed. They come expecting an exotic Asian city, but instead they find a city that has been Westernized and modernized to the point of ugliness, much of it a drab concrete jungle of unimaginative buildings clustered so close together that there's hardly room in which to breathe.

Simply stated, Tokyo is a crush of humanity. Its subways are often packed, its sidewalks are crowded, its streets are congested, and its air is filled with an irritating amount of noise, pollution, and what can only be called "mystery smells." Almost 12 million people live in its 770 square miles, many of them in so-called bedroom towns, from which they have to commute to work an average of 2 to 3 hours every day. No matter where you go in Tokyo, you are never alone. After you've been here for a while, Paris, London, and even New York will seem like deserted cities.

Tokyo's crowds and ugliness, however, are what you'll see only if you don't bother to scratch beneath the surface. Beautiful in its own way, Tokyo is most definitely a state of mind, and if you open yourself to it you'll find a city humming with energy and vitality, a city unlike any other in the world. People rush around here with such purpose, with such determination, it's hard not to feel that you're in the midst of something important, that you're witnessing history in the making. But before I begin discussing Tokyo's merits, it might help to put the city into historical perspective.

Though today the nation's capital, Tokyo is a relative newcomer to the pages of Japanese history. For centuries it was nothing more than a rather unimportant village called Edo, which means simply "mouth of the estuary." Then, in 1603, Edo was catapulted into the limelight when the new shogun, Tokugawa Ieyasu, made the sleepy village the seat of his shogunate government. From then on, the town developed quickly and by 1787 the population had grown to 1.3 million, making Edo even then one of the largest cities in the world.

The Tokugawas ruled Japan for about 250 years, during which time they adopted a policy of isolation from the rest of the world. When they were overthrown in 1868,

---

IMPRESSIONS

There is no Japan like Tokyo.
—LAFCADIO HEARN, 1895

✔ WHAT'S SPECIAL ABOUT TOKYO

The Nation's Capital
☐ Home of the emperor and the Imperial Palace.
☐ Seat of the Japanese government and the Diet (parliament).
☐ Tokyo National Museum, the largest repository of Japanese art in the world.
☐ Other art museums, from contemporary to those specializing in woodblock prints.
☐ More than a dozen specialized museums, centering on furniture, clocks from the Edo Period, traditional Japanese crafts, Japanese paper, clothing, swords, sumo, and more.

Temples and Shrines
☐ Sensoji Temple, Tokyo's oldest and most important Buddhist temple and one of the city's top attractions.
☐ Meiji Jingu Shrine, Tokyo's most venerable Shinto shrine and one of Japan's best known.

Shopping
☐ Dozens of department stores, so large they're like self-contained cities.
☐ Boutiques of Japan's most famous fashion designers.
☐ Shops specializing in traditional crafts.
☐ Kappabashi, an area selling plastic food and kitchenware.

☐ Akihabara, an area with more than 600 shops selling the latest in electronic and electrical goods.

After Dark
☐ Discos open until dawn.
☐ Jazz clubs.
☐ Summer beer gardens.
☐ A variety of nightlife "neighborhoods," each with its own distinctive atmosphere and clientele.

Food
☐ The largest concentration of Japanese restaurants in the world.
☐ Ethnic diversity, with food ranging from Western (Italian, French, American, and Mexican) to Eastern (Chinese, Thai, and Indian).

Offbeat Attractions
☐ Sumo, with tournaments held three times a year.
☐ Tsukiji Fish Market, Japan's largest.
☐ The Tokyo Stock Exchange, with free tours in English.
☐ Tokyo Disneyland.

Cultural Activities
☐ The best city in Japan for Kabuki and Noh.
☐ Opportunities to partake in the Japanese tea ceremony and ikebana (flower arranging).

the Japanese emperor was restored to power. Although the imperial family had been living in Kyoto all these years, it decided to move the capital to Edo, now renamed Tokyo, "Eastern Capital." Thus, Japan's feudal era came to an end. The country put an abrupt halt to its policy of isolation from the rest of the world and flung its doors wide-open to the West in a scramble to modernize itself.

As the nation's capital, Tokyo was the hardest hit in this new era of modernization, with fashions, architecture, food, department stores, and even people imported from the West. West was best, and things Japanese were forgotten or ignored. It didn't help that Tokyo was almost totally destroyed twice in the first half of this century. In 1923 a huge earthquake struck the city, followed by tidal waves. Almost 150,000 people died and half of Tokyo was in ruins. Disaster struck again in 1945, toward the end of World War II, when Allied incendiary bombs destroyed most of the city.

I guess that's why most visitors are disappointed with Tokyo—there's almost nothing of historical importance to match Kyoto or Kamakura. So put your notions of "quaint Japan" out of your mind and plunge headfirst into the 21st century, because that's what Tokyo is all about. The city is so wired and electric you can feel it in the air.

As the financial nerve center of Japan, Tokyo is where it's happening in Asia. In a nation of overachievers, Tokyo has more than its fair share of intellectuals, academics, politicians, and artists, and it's the country's showcase for technology, fashion, art, music, and advertising.

But even though the city has a fast-paced, somewhat zany side, it also has a quieter and often overlooked aspect that makes the city both lovable and livable. Although formidable at first glance, Tokyo is nothing more than a series of small towns and neighborhoods clustered together, each with its own narrow, winding streets, ma-and-pa shops, fruit stands, and stores. Look for the small things . . . and you'll notice the carefully pruned bonsai adorning the sidewalks, women in kimonos bowing and shuffling down the streets, old wooden houses, neatness and order.

Tokyo is both old and new, both Japanese and Western—but it's definitely more Japanese than Western. The harmonious blending of its two aspects gives it a unique charm and character. I love Tokyo. Although the city is overcrowded, and despite the occasional frustrations one is bound to feel as a foreigner, I find Tokyo exhilarating and fun. It never ceases to be interesting. Best of all, it's one of the safest cities in the world; you can walk without fear anywhere, anytime, night or day. The only thing you may have to watch out for sometimes is the alacrity with which Japanese businessmen who have had a little too much to drink will approach you to practice their English on you. Reserve thrown off after an evening of conviviality, they may prove friendly to a degree that will (pleasantly) surprise you.

1. ORIENTATION

ARRIVING

BY PLANE

NARITA AIRPORT   Most likely you'll arrive at the New Tokyo International Airport in Narita, about 40 miles outside Tokyo. Once you've gone through Customs, you'll exit through automatic doors into the arrival waiting lobby. The arrival lobby is divided into a south and a north wing, both of which have counters for hotel reservations, limousine bus service into Tokyo, and the Keisei Skyliner train to Ueno Station. If you've purchased a Japan Rail Pass, you can turn in your voucher at the Japan Railways (JR), Information and Ticket Office, which is located on the arrival floor, in the corridor connecting the south and the north wings. It's open daily from 7am to 11pm.

The **Tourist Information Center (TIC),** managed by the Japan National Tourist Organization, is located in the south wing of the arrival floor and is open Monday through Friday from 9am to 8pm and on Saturday from 9am to noon. You can pick up a map here and ask for directions to your hotel or inn. If you don't yet have a hotel room and want one at a modest price, you can make reservations here free of charge Monday through Friday between 9am and 7:30pm.

If you need to change money, you can do so at a *bureau de change,* which you'll come across just after you clear Customs and before you enter the arrival lobby. If you forget to change money there, you may do so at counters in the arrival lobby and at a bank in the fourth-floor departure lobby.

Other facilities include a post office in the basement, open Monday through Friday from 9am to 5pm and on Saturday from 9am to 12:30pm, and a post office in the north wing of the departure lobby, open daily from 9am to 8:30pm. Also on the fourth floor is a **Kokusai Denshin Denwa (KDD)** office, where you can make an international call or send a telegram between 9am and 9pm.

Getting from Narita to Tokyo   Everyone grumbles about the Narita airport because it's so far away from Tokyo when compared with the distance of other airports from the capital cities they serve. Obviously, jumping into a taxi and driving straight to your hotel is the easiest way to get to Tokyo, but it's also the most

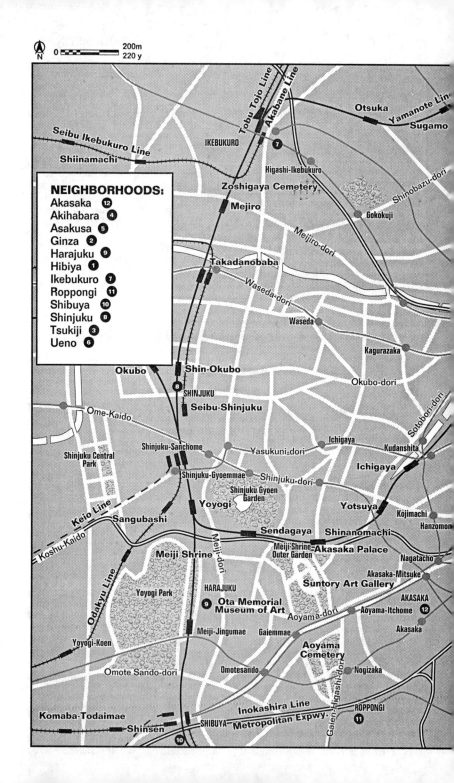

TOKYO ORIENTATION

Komagome
Tabata
Mikawashima
Minami-Senju
Rikugien Garden
Keisei Line
Nishi-Nippori
Joban Line
Meiji-dori
Nippori
Sengoku
Nakasendo
Iriya
Yanaka Cemetery
Uguisudani
Koishikawa Botanical Garden
Kototoi-dori
Hongo-dori
Ueno Park
Hakusan-dori
Kasuga-dori
6 UENO
5
Hakusan
Asakusa-dori
Yushima
Ueno-Hirokoji
Okachimachi
Koishikawa Korakuen Garden
Naka-Okachimachi
Korakuen
Kuramae
Showa-dori
Suidobashi
4 AKIHABARA
Iidabashi
Asakusabashi
Ryogoku
Kitanomaru Park
Jimbocho
Sobu Line
Takebashi
Edo-dori
Bakurocho
National Museum of Modern Art
Awajicho
Nihombashi
Ningyocho
Craft Gallery
Otemachi
Mitsukoshimae
Edobashi
Higashi-Nihombashi
East Garden
Kanda
Shin-Nihombashi
Hamacho Garden
Kyobashi
Imperial Palace
Otemachi
MARUNOUCHI
Nijubashimae
Yurakucho
Tokyo Station
Kayabacho
Kokkai-Gijidomae
1
Hibiya
GINZA
Hibiya Park
2
Toranomon
Higashi-Ginza
Monzen-Nakacho
Eitai-dori
Hibiya-dori
Tsukiji
Sumida River
Tsukiji Fish Market
Kyobashi-dori
Kamiyacho
Shimbashi
3
Onarimon
Hama Detached Palace Garden
Harumi-dori

expensive—and may not even be the quickest if you happen to hit rush hour. Expect to spend ¥22,000 ($157) to ¥24,000 ($171) for a 1- to 2-hour taxi ride from the Narita airport.

The most popular way to get from Narita to Tokyo is via the **Airport Limousine Bus.** Buses, which depart from just outside the arrival lobby, operate most frequently to the Tokyo City Air Terminal, and the trip takes about 70 minutes. Buses also go to Tokyo and Shinjuku stations and more than a dozen of Tokyo's major hotels, but service to these places is less frequent. Check with the staff at the Airport Limousine Bus counter in the arrival lobby to inquire which bus stops nearest your hotel. If you take a bus to the Tokyo City Air Terminal or one of the other destinations, there are plenty of taxis available that can deliver you to your final destination. Fares for the Limousine Bus range from ¥2,700 ($19.30) to ¥3,300 ($23.55), according to the distance. For more information, call 03/3665-7232.

There's another company, called **Airport Shuttle,** that operates buses to more than 20 hotels in Tokyo. Fares for this service begin at ¥2,800 ($20). The company has a counter in the arrival lobby.

Another way to reach Tokyo is by **train,** with several options available. Trains depart directly from the airport's underground terminal, called Narita Airport Station. The JR **Narita Express (NEX)** is the fastest way to reach Tokyo Station, Shinjuku, Ikebukuro, and Yokohoma. The trip to Tokyo Station takes 53 minutes and costs ¥2,890 ($20.65) one way, but if you have a validated JR rail pass, you can ride the NEX free. Note, however, that all seats are reserved, and you must first stop by the NEX counter near the train terminal for a seat assignment. Unfortunately, the NEX is so popular that seats are often sold out in advance. If you want to reserve a seat for your return trip to the Narita airport, you can do so here at the NEX counter or at a travel agency. Otherwise, if NEX is sold out and you're still determined to use your rail pass, you can take the slower JR **rapid train** to Tokyo Station in 83 minutes. If you don't have a rail pass, this rapid train will cost you ¥1,260 ($9).

An alternative is the privately owned **Keisei Skyliner** train, which departs directly from Narita Airport Station and reaches Ueno Station in Tokyo 1 hour later. It's the way I always get to and from the Narita airport. There's a Keisei Skyliner counter in the north and the south wings of the arrival lobby. The fare from the Narita airport to Ueno Station in Tokyo is ¥1,630 ($11.65) one way. Trains depart approximately every 30 or 40 minutes between 7:52am and 10pm. If you're on a budget, you can take one of Keisei's slower **limited express** trains to Ueno Station, with fares starting at ¥910 ($6.50) for the 71-minute trip.

At Ueno Station you can take either the **subway** or the JR **Yamanote Line** to other parts of Tokyo (see "Getting Around" in this chapter). There are also plenty of taxis available.

HANEDA AIRPORT If you're connecting to a domestic flight, more than likely you'll need to transfer to Haneda Airport. The **Airport Limousine Bus** makes runs between Narita and Haneda airports; the fare is ¥2,900 ($20.70), and the trip takes 1 hour or more, depending on the traffic. If perchance you're arriving at Haneda Airport, you can also take the Airport Limousine Bus to Shinjuku and Akasaka.

The locals, however, are more likely to take the **monorail** from Haneda Airport to Hamamatsucho Station on the Yamanote Line, for which the fare is ¥300 ($2.15). The trip takes only 15 minutes, and if you have a validated rail pass, you can use it here.

BY TRAIN

If you're arriving in Tokyo by the **Shinkansen bullet train,** you'll probably arrive at **Tokyo Station** (note that some of the Tohoku and Joetsu Shinkansen lines terminate at Ueno Station). Tokyo Station is easily connected to the rest of the city via JR commuter trains and the subway. If you need assistance or information on Tokyo, stop by the **Information Bureau of Tokyo,** located in Tokyo Station at the Travel Plaza, near the Yaesu Exit. It's open Monday through Saturday from 9am to 6pm; it's closed on Sunday and holidays.

BY BUS

Long-distance bus service from Hiroshima, Nagoya, Osaka, Kyoto, and other major cities delivers passengers to **Tokyo Station,** where they can then use the city's extensive transportation system to reach their destination. Other bus terminals serving the region outside Tokyo include Shinagawa and Shinjuku stations, both of which are served by the JR Yamanote Line, which loops around the city.

BY CAR

The **Chuo Expressway** is the major artery leading into Tokyo from Osaka, Kyoto, Nagoya, and other major cities on the island of Honshu. In any case, all expressways lead toward the heart of the city, Hibiya and Ginza. Parking spaces, however, are scarce, although major hotels have parking garages.

BY FERRY

Long-distance ferries arrive in Tokyo at the **Tokyo Ko Ferry Futo (Tokyo Port Ferry Terminal).** From there passengers can board a bus for Shinkiba JR Station and catch a train to town.

TOURIST INFORMATION

The **Tourist Information Center (TIC),** 1-6-6 Yurakucho, Chiyoda-ku (tel. 3502-1461), can answer all your questions regarding Tokyo and can give you a map of the city, plus various sightseeing materials. It also has more information than any other tourist office on the rest of Japan, including pamphlets and brochures on major cities and attractions. Be sure to stop off here if you plan to visit other destinations, since information in English may not be available at the destination itself. Check the "Information, Entry Requirements & Money," section in Chapter 2 for various pamphlets available on Japan.

The TIC is open Monday through Friday from 9am to 5pm and on Saturday from 9am to noon; it's closed on Sunday and national holidays. The office is near both Hibiya and Yurakucho subway stations (if you're arriving at Hibiya Station, take the A4 or A5 exit). There's also a TIC office at the Narita airport, where you can pick up a map and ask how to get to your hotel. It's open Monday through Friday from 9am to 8pm and on Saturday from 9am to noon.

In addition, the Tokyo Metropolitan Government maintains an **Information Bureau of Tokyo,** located at JR Tokyo Station in a corner of the Travel Plaza, at the Yaesu Exit. It provides all kinds of useful information on the city, including transportation, shopping, accommodations, and sightseeing. It's open Monday through Saturday from 9am to 6pm; it's closed on Sunday and holidays.

If you want to have a quick rundown of what's happening in Tokyo, you can call **3503-2911** for a taped recording in English of what's going on in the city and its environs in the way of special exhibitions, performances, festivals, and events.

Finally, the Nippon Telegraph Corporation and the Kokusai Denshin Denwa Company sponsor a telephone service, the **Japan Hotline** (tel. 3586-0110), which advises callers on Japanese customs and etiquette, gives tips on such aspects of Japanese daily life as education and health services, and answers questions ranging from the availability of instruction on flower arranging to obtaining tickets for Kabuki. Advisers are on duty Monday through Friday, except holidays, from 10am to 4pm.

TOURIST PUBLICATIONS

The best publication for finding out what's going on in Tokyo in terms of contemporary and traditional music and theater, exhibitions in museums and galleries, films, and special events is the *Tokyo Journal*. Published monthly and available for ¥500 ($3.55) at foreign-language bookstores, restaurants, and bars, it also has articles of interest to foreigners in Japan. It even lists department store sales, photography exhibitions, apartments for rent, schools for learning Japanese, and much else. I don't know how foreigners survived in Tokyo before this publication made its debut in the early 1980s.

Another English-language publication of interest to tourists is *Tokyo Time Out,* also published monthly and available for ¥500 ($3.55) at bookstores. The *Tour Companion's Tokyo City Guide* is a weekly tabloid distributed free to hotels, travel agencies, and the TIC; it tells of upcoming events and festivals, as well as other information useful to the visitor. Finally, *Weekender* is another free weekly, one found in supermarkets, hotels, and other places where foreigners hang out. It's best known for its classified ad section, but has articles and features as well.

English-language newspapers such as the *Japan Times* also carry information on the theater, films, and special events.

CITY LAYOUT

Your most frustrating moments in Tokyo will probably occur when you find that you are totally lost. Maybe it will be in a subway or train station when all you see are signs in Japanese. Or perhaps it will be on a street somewhere as you search for a museum, restaurant, or bar. At any rate, accept here and now that you will get lost if you are at all adventurous and strike out on your own. It's inevitable. But take comfort in the fact that Japanese get lost, too. Even taxi drivers get lost and bewildered in Tokyo.

MAIN ARTERIES & STREETS

One factor that makes finding your way around difficult is that hardly any streets are named. Think about what that means—12 million people living in a huge metropolis of nameless streets. Oh, major thoroughfares and some well-known streets in areas like Ginza and Shinjuku might have names that they received after World War II on the insistence of American occupation forces, but for the most part Tokyo's address system is based on a complicated number scheme that must make the postal worker's job here a nightmare. To make matters worse, most streets in Tokyo zigzag—an arrangement apparently left over from olden days (to confuse potential attacking enemies). Today, streets in Tokyo confuse not only foreign tourists but even city residents themselves.

Among Tokyo's most important streets that do have names are **Meiji Dori Avenue,** which runs from Ebisu through Shibuya, Harajuku, Shinjuku, and Ikebukuro; **Yasukuni Dori Avenue** and **Shinjuku Dori Avenue,** which connect Shinjuku with Chiyoda-ku in the heart of the city; and **Sotobori Dori Avenue, Harumi Dori Avenue,** and **Showa Dori Avenue,** which pass through Ginza.

FINDING AN ADDRESS

A typical Tokyo address might read 7-8-4 Roppongi, Minato-ku, which is the address of the Inakaya restaurant. Minato-ku is the name of the ward, which encompasses a large area (altogether there are 23 wards, known as *ku,* in Tokyo). Within that area is the district, in this case Roppongi. Roppongi is further broken down into *chome,* here 7-chome. Number 8 refers to a smaller area within the chome, and 4 is the actual building. Addresses are usually posted on buildings, beside doors, on telephone poles, and by streetlights. In recent years English has been added to street signs in some areas of Tokyo, but usually addresses are written only in Japanese.

As you walk around Tokyo, you will notice maps posted beside sidewalks giving a

---

IMPRESSIONS

The general shape of Tokyo is that of an egg, with the point to the South [and] the butt to the North. The yolk of this egg is the castle, or O Shiro, a work of vast proportions.
—W. E. GRIFFIS, *THE MIKADO'S EMPIRE,* 1876

breakdown of the number system for the area. The first time I tried to use one, I stopped first one Japanese, then another, and asked them to point out on the map where a particular address was. They both studied the map and pointed out the direction. Both turned out to be wrong. Not very encouraging, but if you learn how to read these maps, they're invaluable.

Another invaluable source of information is the numerous police boxes, called koban, spread throughout the city. Police officers have maps of their areas and are very helpful. You should also never hesitate to ask a Japanese the way, but be sure to ask more than one. You'll be amazed at the conflicting directions you'll receive. Apparently, the Japanese would rather hazard a guess than impolitely shrug their shoulders and leave you standing there. The best thing to do is ask directions of several Japanese and then follow the majority opinion. You can also duck into a shop and ask someone where a nearby address is, although it's been my experience that employees may not even know the address of their own store.

NEIGHBORHOODS IN BRIEF

Taken as a whole, Tokyo seems formidable and unconquerable. It's best, therefore, to think of it as nothing more than a variety of neighborhoods scrunched together, much like the pieces of a jigsaw puzzle. Holding the pieces together, so to speak, is the Yamanote Line, a commuter train that makes a loop around the central part of Tokyo, passing through such important neighborhood stations as Yurakucho, Tokyo, Ueno, Shinjuku, Harajuku, and Shibuya along the way.

Hibiya This is one of the financial hearts of Tokyo, together with nearby Marunouchi and Nihombashi. This is where the Tokugawa shogun built his magnificent castle, and was thus the center of old Edo. Today, Hibiya is where you'll find the Imperial Palace and—important for tourists—the Tourist Information Center. Hibiya is located in the Chiyoda-ku ward.

Ginza Ginza is the swankiest and most expensive shopping area in all Japan. When the country opened to foreign trade in the 1860s, following two centuries of self-imposed seclusion, it was here that Western imports and adopted Western architecture were first displayed. Today, Ginza is where you'll find a multitude of department stores, boutiques, exclusive restaurants, art galleries, hostess clubs, and drinking establishments. On the edge of Ginza is Kabukiza, venue for Kabuki productions.

Tsukiji Located only two subway stops from Ginza, Tsukiji is famous for Tsukiji Fish Market, Japan's largest wholesale fish market.

Asakusa Located in the northeastern part of central Tokyo, Asakusa served as the pleasure quarters for old Edo. Today, it is known throughout Japan as the site of the famous Sensoji Temple, one of Tokyo's top attractions. It also has a wealth of tiny shops selling traditional Japanese crafts. When Tokyoites talk about *shitamachi* (old downtown), they are referring to the traditional homes and tiny narrow streets of the Asakusa and Ueno areas.

Ueno Located not far from Asakusa, on the northern edge of Tokyo, Ueno is also considered part of the city's old downtown section. Considered the playground of

---

IMPRESSIONS

That street was typical of the modern Tokyo—not of its main arteries, mushroom offices, and towering [de]partment stores, but of the Tokyo which lies always around the corner, an easy stone's throw from the bright lights and the grinding trams. Vague and slatternly, a sprawling skyline of wooden houses overlooked by a massive procession of telegraph poles that marched—or rather staggered—up its slope, linked together by loose wires in a drooping curve.
—PETER QUENNELL, *A SUPERFICIAL JOURNEY THROUGH TOKYO AND PEKING*, 1932

Tokyo families, Ueno boasts Ueno Park, a huge green space that also contains a zoo, a concert hall, and several acclaimed museums. Among them is the Tokyo National Museum, considered to have the largest collection of Japanese art in the world. North of Ueno is **Nippori,** a residential area of traditional old homes and temples.

Shinjuku An upstart in Tokyo and a district that has been attracting businesses away from the more established Hibiya, Shinjuku is located on the western edge of the Yamanote Line loop. Shinjuku Station, the nation's busiest station, separates Shinjuku into an east and a west side. Western Shinjuku boasts Tokyo's greatest concentration of skyscrapers and a number of hotels, as well as the new City Hall. Eastern Shinjuku is known for its shopping and nightlife, particularly Kabuki-cho, a thriving amusement center.

Harajuku The mecca of Tokyo's younger generation, Harajuku swarms throughout the week with teenagers in search of fashion and fun. Omote Sando Dori is a fashionable tree-lined avenue flanked by trendy shops, sidewalk cafés, and restaurants. Nearby is Takeshita Dori, a narrow pedestrian lane packed with young people looking for the latest in inexpensive clothing. Near Harajuku Station is Meiji Jingu Shrine, built in 1920 to deify Emperor and Empress Meiji.

Ikebukuro Located north of Shinjuku on the Yamanote Line loop, Ikebukuro is the working man's Tokyo, less refined and a bit rougher around the edges. Crowded with commuters who live past Ikebukuro in less expensive areas of the metropolis, Ikebukuro is where you'll find Seibu, one of the country's largest department stores, as well as the Sunshine City Building, Tokyo's tallest skyscraper and home of a huge indoor shopping center.

Akihabara Tokyo's center for electronic and electrical appliances, with more than 600 shops offering a look at the latest in gadgets and gizmos. This is a fascinating place for a stroll, even if you aren't interested in buying anything.

Shibuya Located on the southwestern edge of the Yamanote Line loop, Shibuya serves as an important nightlife and shopping area. There are as many as a dozen department stores here, specializing in everything from designer clothing to housewares.

Roppongi Tokyo's best-known nightlife district for young Japanese and foreigners, Roppongi has more discos and bars than any other district, as well as a multitude of restaurants serving international cuisine. The action here continues until dawn.

Akasaka Another important nightlife district of Tokyo, this one caters more to businessmen. In addition to its expensive hostess bars, Akasaka also has many restaurants and several large hotels.

MAPS

Before setting out on your own, arm yourself with a few maps. Maps are so much a part of life in Tokyo that they're often included in a shop or restaurant advertisement, on a business card, and even in private party invitations. Even though I've spent several years in Tokyo, I rarely venture forth without a map. One I find particularly useful is issued free by the Tourist Information Center; it's called *Tourist Map of Tokyo* and includes smaller, detailed maps of several districts (such as Shinjuku), as well as subway and greater Tokyo train maps. With this map you should be able to locate at least the general vicinity of every place mentioned in the Tokyo chapters of this book.

If you want a map with more detail, head for Kinokuniya, Maruzen, or one of the other bookstores with an English-language section, where you'll be greeted with more than a dozen variations of city maps. Kodanshita's *A Bilingual Map* is a foldout map showing Tokyo's various areas and comes complete with an index to important buildings, museums, and other places of interest. Similarly, *A Great Detailed Map,* published by Nippon Kokuseisha Company, gives the postal addresses for neighborhoods throughout Tokyo and includes bus routes and a subway map. It's useful for finding various addresses in Tokyo.

2. GETTING AROUND

The first rule of getting around Tokyo: It will always take longer than you think. Tokyo is huge and its attractions are far-flung. Learning to gauge the time needed to get from point A to point B can take quite a while. In fact, old Tokyo hands pride themselves on being able to calculate perfectly the amount of time necessary to reach any destination. Arriving late is an unpardonable sin in Tokyo.

For short-time visitors, calculating travel times in Tokyo is tricky business. Taking a taxi can be expensive and involves the probability of getting stuck interminably in traffic. Taking the subway is usually more efficient, even though it's more complicated and harder on your feet: there are often various routes that can be taken, and transfers between lines are sometimes quite a hike in themselves. However, if I'm going from one end of Tokyo to the other by subway, I usually allow anywhere from 30 to 60 minutes, depending on the number of transfers and the amount of walking necessary once I get there. The journey from Roppongi or Shibuya to Ueno, for example, takes approximately a half hour because it's a straight shot on the subway, but the trip from Toranomon to Ueno can take an hour because it requires transfers.

At any rate, the best policy for getting around Tokyo is to take the subway or Japan Railways commuter train to the station nearest your destination. From there you can either walk, asking directions along the way, or take a taxi.

BY PUBLIC TRANSPORTATION

Tokyo's population is served by subway, JR commuter trains (including the Yamanote Line loop), and buses. Of these, the subway is probably the most convenient for visitors. Children younger than 6 can ride free; children 6 to 11 pay half the adult fare.

BY SUBWAY

To get around Tokyo on your own, it's imperative that you learn how to ride its subways. Fortunately, the subway system is efficient, modern, clean, and easy to use, and all station names are written in English. Altogether, there are 10 subway lines crisscrossing underneath the city, and each line is color-coded. The Ginza Line, for example, is orange, which means that all its coaches are orange. If you're transferring to the Ginza Line from another line, just follow the orange signs and circles to the Ginza Line platform.

Vending machines at all subway stations sell tickets, which begin at ¥140 ($1) for the shortest distance and increase according to how far you're traveling. Vending machines give change, and some even accept ¥1,000 notes. To purchase your ticket, insert coins into the vending machine until the fare buttons light up, then push the amount for the ticket you want. Your ticket and change will drop onto a little platform at the bottom of the machine. Fares are posted on a large subway map above the vending machines, but it's in Japanese only. Major stations also post a smaller map listing fares in English, but you may have to search for it. An alternative is to look at your Tourist Information Center subway map—it lists stations in both Japanese and English. Once you know what the Japanese characters look like, you may be able to

IMPRESSIONS

As a city it lacks concentration. Masses of greenery, lined or patched with gray, and an absence of beginning or end, look suburban rather than metropolitan. Far away in the distance are other gray patches; you are told that those are still Tōkiyō, and you ask no more. It is a city of "magnificent distances" without magnificence.
—Isabella Bird, *Unbeaten Tracks in Japan*, 1880

locate your station and the corresponding fare on the huge subway map above the vending machines.

If you still don't know the fare, just buy a basic-fare ticket for ¥140 ($1). When you exit at the other end, the ticket collector will tell you how much you owe. In any case, be sure to hang on to your ticket, since you must give it up at the end of your journey. In recent years, an automated ticketing system has been installed at many subway entrances and exits—simply insert your ticket and the doors to the wicket swing open. Once you reach your destination, if you're confused about which exit to take from the station, ask the ticket collector. Taking the right exit can make a world of difference, especially in Shinjuku, where there are more than 60 exits from the station.

If you think you're going to be using the subways a lot, you can purchase a **one-day ticket** (¥650 or $4.65 for an adult; ¥330 or $2.35 for children), which allows unlimited travel on the Ginza, Marunouchi, Hibiya, Tozai, Chiyoda, Yurakucho, and Hanzomon subway lines. These lines pass through 137 stations in Tokyo, including Hibiya, Ginza, Shinjuku, Tsukiji, Ueno, and major sightseeing destinations. One-day tickets are valuable, however, only if you plan on using the subways for very long distances or more than five times in a day. If so, you can purchase this one-day ticket at more than two dozen subway stations, including Ginza, Shinjuku, Shibuya, and Akasaka-mitsuke. Contact the TIC for more information.

Most subways run from about 5am to midnight, although the times of the first and last trains depend on the line, the station, and whether it's a weekday or weekend. There are schedules posted in the stations, and through most of the day trains run every 3 to 5 minutes. Avoid taking the subway during the morning rush hour, from 8am to 9am. The stories you've heard about commuters packed into trains like sardines are all true. There are even "platform pushers," men who push people into compartments so that the doors can close. If you want to witness Tokyo at its craziest, go to Shinjuku Station at 8:30am—but go by taxi unless you want to experience the crowding firsthand.

BY TRAIN

In addition to subway lines, there are also electric trains operated by Japan Railways (JR) that run above ground. These are also color-coded, with fares beginning at ¥120 (85¢). Buy your ticket the same as you would for the subway. The **Yamanote Line** (green-colored coaches) is the best-known and most convenient JR line. It makes a loop around the city, stopping at 29 stations along the way. In fact, you may want to take the Yamanote Line and stay on it for a roundup view of Tokyo. The entire trip around the city takes about an hour, passing stations like Shinjuku, Tokyo, and Ueno on the way.

Another convenient JR line is the **Chuo Line,** whose coaches are orange-colored. It cuts across Tokyo between Shinjuku and Tokyo stations.

If you think you're going to be traveling extensively on JR trains, you may wish to buy JR's **one-day ticket** (¥720 or $5.15), which allows unlimited travel on all JR trains except express trains. Children pay half price. Called the Tokunai Free Kippu, it's available at JR stations, such as Shinjuku, and at JR travel centers.

If you have a valid Japan Rail Pass, you can travel on JR trains in Tokyo for free.

Transfers   You can transfer between subway lines without buying another ticket, and you can transfer between JR train lines on one ticket. However, your ticket does

IMPRESSIONS

Tokyo is also the city where one encounters at its most intense, its most vital and its most vulgar the kind of society that has resulted from the double impact of industrialization and the West.
—GEORGE WOODCOCK, *ASIA, GODS AND CITIES,* 1966

TOKYO SUBWAY SYSTEM

LEGEND:

- Ginza Line
- Marunouchi Line
- Hibiya Line
- Tozai Line
- Chiyoda Line
- Yurakucho Line
- Hanzomon Line
- Toei Asakusa Line
- Toei Mita Line
- Toei Shinjuku Line
- Junction Connecting to Subways
- Junction Connecting to JNR and/or Private Railways
- National Railways

Tsudanuma
Ahiko
NISHI-FUNABASHI
Barakinakayama
Gyotoku
Urayasu
Kasai
Minami-Sunamachi
OSHIAGE
Honjoazumabashi
Toyocho
Kuramae
ASAKUSA
Higashi-Nihombashi
Hamacho
Morishita
Kikukawa
Sumiyoshi
Nishi-Ojima
Ojima
Higashi-Ojima
Kiba
Monzennakacho
Tawaramachi
Nakaokachimachi
Iwamotocho
Kodemmacho
NINGYOCHO
Bakuroyokoyama
KAYABACHO
Minowa
Inaricho
Bakurocho
NIUOMBASHI
Mitsukoshimae
Hatchobori
Iriya
UENO
KANDA
TOKYO
Kyobashi
Takaracho
Tsukiji
Minami-Senju
Uenohirokoji
Suehirocho
Shin-Ochanomizu
Awajicho
OTEMACHI
HIGASHI-GINZA
KITA-SENJU
AYASE
MACHIYA
Sendagi
Nezu
Yushima
Nijubashimae
GINZA
Ginzaitchome
YURAKUCHO
SHIMBASHI
NISHINIPPORI
HIBIYA
Uchisaiwaicho
KASUMIGASEKI
SHIDOBASHI
Jimbocho
Takebashi
Nagatacho
Sakuradamon
KASUMIGASEKI
MITA
Sengoku
Hakusan
Kasuga
Hongosanchome
IDABASHI
Kudanshita
ICHIGAYA
Kojimachi
AKASAKAMITSUKE
Toranomo
Onarimon
Shibakoen
Daimon
SHIMURA
Shin-Otsuka
Myogadani
Korakuen
Iidagawabashi
YOTSUYA
Yotsuyasanchome
Shinanomachi
AKASAKA
Akasaka
Kamiyacho
SENGAKUJI
SUGAMO
Nishi-Sugamo
Shin-Itabashi
Higashi-Ikebukuro
Waseda
Kagurazaka
Shinjukugyoemmae
Shinjukusanchome
Roppongi
Hiro-O
Takanawadai
GOTANDA
Shimura-Sanchome
Motohasunuma
Itabashikuyaku-shomae
Itabashi-Honcho
Gokokuji
NOGIZAKA
Nagatcho
Shibakoen
Togoshi
IKEBUKURO
TAKADANOBABA
Ochiai
OMOTESANDO
EBISU
NAKAMEGURO
Takanawadai
Magome
Nishi-Magome
Shin-Takashimadaira
Takashimadaira
Shimura-Sakaue
Hasune
Nishidai
SHINJUKU
OGIKUBO
NAKANO
SHIBUYA
YOYOGIUEHARA
Yoyogikoen
Nakanobu
Nishi-Takashimadaira
Minamiasagaya
Shin-Koenji
Higashi-Koenji
Nakano-Fujimicho
Honancho
Nakanoshimbashi
NAKANOSAKAUE
Hiyoshi
Futako-Tamagawaen
Mitaka
Minamiasagaya
Shin-Nakano
Nakanofujimicho
Hon-Atsugi
Nagatsuda
Tamagaween
Higashi-Nihombashi

not allow a transfer between subway lines and JR train lines. You usually don't have to worry about this, though, because if you exit through a wicket and have to give up your ticket, you'll know you have to buy another one. There are instances, however, when you pass through a ticket wicket to transfer between subway lines (for example, when you transfer from the Yurakucho Line to the Hibiya Line at Hibiya Station). In this case, simply show your ticket when you pass through the wicket. The general rule is that if your final destination and fare are posted above the ticket vending machines, you can travel all the way to your destination with only one ticket. But don't worry about this too much—the ticket collector will set you straight if you've made a miscalculation.

BY BUS

Buses are difficult to use in Tokyo because their destinations are often written only in Japanese and most bus drivers do not speak English. If you're feeling adventurous, board the bus at the front and drop the exact fare into a box by the driver. If you don't have the exact fare (usually ¥160 or $1.15), another machine located next to the driver will accept coins only; your change will come out below, minus the fare. When you wish to get off, press one of the buttons on the railing near the door or the seats.

BY TAXI

Taxis are fairly expensive in Tokyo, starting at ¥540 ($3.85) for the first 1¼ miles (2 kilometers) and increasing ¥80 (57¢) for each additional 1,221 feet (370 meters). You can hail a taxi from the street or go to a taxi stand. A red light will show above the dashboard if a taxi is free to pick up a passenger; a green light indicates the taxi is already occupied. Be sure to stand clear of the door—it will swing open automatically. Likewise, it will shut automatically once you're in.

Unless you're going to a well-known landmark or hotel, it's best to have your destination written out in Japanese, since most taxi drivers do not speak English. But even that may not help. Tokyo is so complicated that even taxi drivers are not familiar with much of it, although they do have detailed maps with them. If a driver doesn't understand where you're going, however, he may refuse to take you. (By the way, notice the taxi drivers' white gloves and the way the drivers are always writing things down on a roster—Japanese taxi drivers must write down more information than any other taxi drivers on earth.)

There are so many taxis cruising Tokyo that one is always around and available— except when you need it most. That is, when it's raining and late at night on weekends, after all subways and trains have stopped. Nightlife areas such as Shinjuku, Roppongi, Ginza, and Akasaka are especially bad, and I've waited as long as an hour in each of these places for a taxi after midnight. So if you're out past midnight on Friday or Saturday, you might as well stay out until about 2am or 3am, when it's easier to get a taxi. And from 11pm to 5am, an extra 20% is added to your fare.

The telephone numbers of major taxi companies are **3586-2151** for Nihon Kotsu; **3491-6001** for Kokusai; **3563-5151** for Daiwa; and **3814-1111** for Hinomaru. Note, however, that only Japanese is spoken and that you will be required to pay extra (usually not more than ¥550 or $3.90).

BY CAR

Driving a car in Tokyo can be a harrowing experience. For one thing, the streets are crowded and unbelievably narrow. Then, street signs are often only in Japanese, and

---

IMPRESSIONS

Frequent outbreaks of fire constitute one of the greatest perils to life in Japan. In Tokyo, burning houses are given the poetic name of "the flowers of Edo."
—JAMES KIRKUP, *HEAVEN, HELL AND HARA-KIRI*, 1974

driving is on the left side of the street. Parking spaces can be hard to find, and garages are expensive. Even parking meters along the street run about ¥300 ($2.15) an hour. If you still want to drive, see "Rentals," below.

RENTALS

As I've stressed before, driving a car in Tokyo can make a roller-coaster ride at the local amusement park seem like tame stuff. If you're still not convinced, there are approximately a dozen major car-rental companies in Tokyo, with branch offices spread throughout the city and at the Narita airport. The **Nissan Reservation Center** is in the Landick Iikura Building, 1-5-7 Azabudai, Minato-ku (tel. 03/3587-4123); the **Nippon Rent-A-Car Service** is in the Nippon Rent-A-Car Building, 5-5 Kamiyacho, Shibuya-ku (tel. 03/3468-7126); and **Toyota Rent-A-Lease** is at 1-1-8 Fujimi, Chiyoda-ku (tel. 03/3264-2834). Prices start at around ¥8,000 ($57) for 24 hours. You'll need either an international or a Japanese driver's license.

PARKING

Tokyo residents must have proof of off-street parking before they can buy a car, and yet finding a parking space is still a challenge in Tokyo. You'll pay about ¥300 ($2.15) an hour for the privilege of a metered parking space on the street, and more than ¥500 ($3.55) for a couple hours in a parking garage. Because space is at a premium, parking garages are usually tall and narrow, with cars transported by elevatorlike devices. In many garages, drivers drive onto a platform that can be rotated, since there isn't even enough room to back up and turn around.

DRIVING RULES

Remember, driving in Japan is on the *left* side of the street, and you'll need either an international or a Japanese driver's license. Signs for expressways and major streets are written in English. Because traffic is so horrendous, you should have plenty of time to read them along the way.

FAST FACTS: TOKYO

American Express There are several American Express offices in Tokyo. The head office, and the only one that handles client mail and emergency card-replacement services, is located in Toranomon in the Mitsui Building, 3-8-1 Kasumigaseki, Chiyoda-ku (tel. 03/3508-2400). It's open Monday through Friday from 9am to 5pm and on Saturday from 9am to 1pm; it's closed Sunday and public holidays. The closest subway station is Toranomon. Other conveniently located American Express offices are in Ginza, in the Four Star Building, 4-4-1 Ginza (tel. 3564-4381), open Monday through Saturday from 10am to 6pm; and in Shinjuku, in the Shinjuku Gomeikan Building, 3-3-9 Shinjuku (tel. 3352-1555), open Thursday through Tuesday from 10am to 6pm (closed Wednesday and public holidays). Note that all three offices have outdoor American Express cash machines.

Area Code If you're calling a number in Tokyo from outside the city but within Japan, the area code for Tokyo is 03. If you're calling Tokyo from abroad, it may be necessary to drop the zero and dial only 3, as is the case if you're calling from the United States. If you have any questions, contact your local international operator.

Baby-Sitters Many major hotels in Tokyo provide baby-sitting service. Otherwise, two services that cater to foreigners are **Tokyo Babysitter** (tel. toll free 0120/45-6056) and **Ange Lily Club** (tel. toll free 0120/115-766).

Bookstores There are several very good bookstores in Tokyo with large selections of books written in English about Japan, as well as novels, magazines, and reference materials. On Shinjuku Station's east side, on Shinjuku Dori Avenue, there's the **Kinokuniya Bookstore,** 3-17-7 Shinjuku (tel. 3354-0131). Books in English are located on the sixth floor. This large store is open daily from 10am to 7pm (closed the third Wednesday of the month). Another good bookstore is **Maruzen,** 2-3-10 Nihombashi, Chuo-ku (tel. 3272-7211), with its foreign books located on the second floor; open Monday through Saturday from 10am to 6:30pm (to 6pm on public holidays). The **Yaesu Book Center,** 2-5-1 Yaesu, Chuo-ku (tel. 3281-1811), located close to Tokyo Station, is a five-story bookstore with about a million books, including books in English on the fourth floor; open Monday through Saturday from 10am to 7pm. **Jena,** 5-6-1 Ginza, Chuo-ku (tel. 3571-2980), is conveniently located in the heart of Ginza on Harumi Dori Avenue. Open Monday through Saturday from 10:30am to 7:50pm and on Sunday from noon to 6:30pm (closed on public holidays), it has English paperbacks, magazines, special-interest books, maps, and travel guides. It's located between the Ginza and Hibiya subway stations.

Car Rentals   See "Getting Around" in this chapter.

Climate   See "When to Go" in Chapter 2.

Currency   See "Information, Entry Requirements & Money" in Chapter 2.

Currency Exchange   You can exchange money in major banks throughout Tokyo, often indicated by a sign in English near the front door. The **Bank of America** is located in the Arc Mori Building, 1-12 32 Akasaka, Minato-ku (tel. 3587-3111), and the **Chase Manhattan Bank** is at 1-2-1 Marunouchi, Chiyoda-ku (tel. 3287-4000). Generally speaking, banks give a better exchange rate for traveler's checks than for cash. If you need to exchange money outside banking hours, inquire at one of the larger first-class hotels—some of them will cash traveler's checks or exchange money even if you're not their guest. If you're arriving at the Narita airport, you can exchange money from 9am until the arrival of the last flight.

Dentists and Doctors   Your embassy can refer you to English-speaking doctors, specialists, and dentists. Otherwise, there are a few clinics popular with foreigners living in Tokyo where some of the staff speak English. The **Tokyo Medical & Surgical Clinic,** close to Tokyo Tower in the 32 Mori Building, 3-4-30 Shiba-koen, Minato-ku (tel. 3436-3028), is open Monday through Friday from 9am to 4:45pm (closed 1pm to 2pm for lunch) and on Saturday from 9am to 12:45pm. Appointments are necessary. The **International Clinic,** within walking distance of Roppongi Station, is at 1-5-9 Azabudai, Minato-ku (tel. 3582-2646); open Monday through Friday from 9am to noon and 2:30pm to 5pm and on Saturday from 10am to noon. Only walk-ins accepted here. You can also make appointments to visit doctors in the hospitals listed below under "Hospitals."

Drugstores   There is no 24-hour drugstore in Tokyo, but there are convenience stores throughout the city that carry things like aspirin. (If it's an emergency, I suggest going to one of the hospitals listed below.) If you're looking for specific pharmaceuticals, a good bet is the **American Pharmacy,** Hibiya Park Building, 1-8-1 Yurakucho, Chiyoda-ku (tel. 3271-4034). Open Monday through Saturday from 9am to 7pm and on Sunday from 10am to 7pm, it has most of the drugs you can find at home (many of them imported from the United States) and can fill American prescriptions.

Electricity   See "Fast Facts: Japan" in Chapter 3.

Embassies and Consulates   The addresses, telephone numbers, and open hours for the United States, Canadian, British, Australian, Irish, and New Zealand embassies are given in the "Fast Facts: Japan" section in Chapter 3.

Emergencies   See "Fast Facts: Japan" in Chapter 3.

Eyeglasses   There are optical shops throughout Tokyo, so ask at your hotel which store is nearest you. Otherwise, try the **Tokyo Optical Center,** 6-4-8 Ginza (tel. 3571-7216). An English-speaking staff will assist you in replacing eyeglasses or contact lenses.

Film   See "Photographic Needs" below.

Hairdressers and Barbers   Most first-class hotels have beauty salons and barbershops. In addition, check the advertisements and classified section of the *Tokyo Journal* for more listings of hairdressers used to dealing with foreigners. In any case, you will be pampered to death in a Japanese salon, making it a delightful experience.

Holidays   See "When to Go" in Chapter 2.

Hospitals   In addition to going to a hospital for an emergency, you can also make an appointment at a hospital's clinic to see a doctor. The **International Catholic Hospital (Seibo Byoin)**, 2-5-1 Naka-Ochiai, Shinjuku (tel. 3951-1111), has clinic hours from 8:30am to 11am Monday through Saturday. The closest subway station is Meijiro on the Yamanote Line.

Other hospitals include **St. Luke's International Hospital (Seiroka Byoin)**, 1-10 Akashicho, Chuo-ku (tel. 3541-5151), with clinic hours from 8:30am to 11am Monday through Saturday (closest subway station is Tsukiji on the Hibiya Line); and the **Japan Red Cross Hospital (Nisseki Iryo Center)**, 4-1-22 Hiroo, Shibuya-ku (tel. 3400-1311), with hours from 8:30am to 11am Monday through Friday and from 8:30am to 10:30am on Saturday (closest subway stations are Roppongi, Hiroo, and Shibuya, from which you should take a taxi). No appointments taken here.

Hotlines   At the end of your rope? Have some problems? The **Tokyo English Life Line (TELL)** gives free confidential counseling over the telephone and will listen to your problems and gripes. It's available daily from 9am to 4pm and 7 to 11pm by dialing 3264-4347.

A similar service is provided by **Japan Helpline** (tel. toll free 0120/461997), a 24-hour voluntary service for the foreign community.

For questions in English on anything relating to Japan, call the **Japan Hotline,** (tel. 03/3586-0110), sponsored by KDD, NTT, and IBM. Its staff advises callers on Japanese etiquette and customs; gives tips on daily life, such as health services and transportation; and can answer questions ranging from the availability of instruction in flower arranging to where to obtain tickets to Kabuki. Advisers are on duty Monday through Friday, except national holidays, from 10am to 4pm.

The Tokyo **Tourist Information Center** (TIC) can answer questions relating to tourism and sightseeing in Tokyo and Japan (tel. 3502-1461). Its phone service is available daily from 9am to 5pm.

Information   See "Information, Entry Requirements & Money" in Chapter 2.

Laundry   See "Fast Facts: Japan" in Chapter 3.

Liquor Laws   See "Fast Facts: Japan" in Chapter 3.

Lost Property   If you've forgotten something on a subway, in a taxi, or on a park bench, you don't have to assume it's gone forever. In fact, if you're willing to trace it, you'll probably get it back. If you've lost something on the street, go to the nearest police box (koban). Items found in the neighborhood will stay there for about 3 days. After that, you should contact the **Central Lost and Found Office of the Metropolitan Police Board,** 1-9-11 Koraku, Bunkyo-ku (tel. 3581-4321, ext. 4542 or 4543).

If you've lost something in a taxi or subway, you need to contact the appropriate office: for taxis, it's the **Taxi Kindaika Center,** 7-3-3 Minamisuma, Koto-ku (tel. 3648-0300); for JR trains, it's the **Lost and Found Section** at Tokyo JR Station (tel. 3231-1880) or at Ueno JR Station (tel. 3841-8069); and for Tokyo Metropolitan buses, subways, and streetcars, it's at 1-35-15 Hongo, Bunkyo-ku (tel. 3818-5760). If you've lost something on one of the subways belonging to the Teito Rapid Transit Authority (for example, the Ginza, Marunouchi, Yurakucho, Tozai, or Hanzoman Line), call 3834-5577.

Luggage Storage/Lockers   Coin-operated lockers are located at all major JR stations, such as Tokyo, Shinjuku, and Ueno, as well as at most subway stations. Lockers cost ¥200 ($1.40) to ¥300 ($2.15) per day.

Newspapers and Magazines   Five English-language newspapers are published daily in Japan. They're the *Japan Times,* the *Mainichi Daily News,* the *Daily Yomiuri,* the *Asahi Evening News,* and the *International Herald Tribune.* The international editions of both *Time* and *Newsweek* are also available. For city magazines that describe what's going on in Tokyo, pick up a copy of either the *Tokyo Journal* or *Tokyo Time Out.*

If you're interested in seeing the latest edition of your favorite magazine back home, check one of the bookstores listed above to see whether they carry it. Otherwise, your best bet is to drop in on the **World Magazine Gallery,** 3-13-10 Ginza (tel. 3545-7227). Located behind the Kabuki-za near Higashi-Ginza station, it displays more than 1,200 magazines from 40 countries around the world. Magazines are for reading here only, and are not for sale. It's open Monday through Saturday from 11am to 7pm; closed Sunday and public holidays.

Photographic Needs There are many camera shops on both sides of Shinjuku Station that offer a wide variety of film. As for film development, a reliable store used by professional photographers is the **Image Factory**, 3-2-6 Roppongi, Nishi Azabu, Minato-ku (tel. 3479-3931). Located about a 5-minute walk from Roppongi Station, it's open Monday through Saturday from 9am to 10:30pm; closed the second and fourth Saturdays of the month, every Sunday, and public holidays. See also "Fast Facts: Japan" in Chapter 3.

Police See "Fast Facts: Japan" in Chapter 3.

Post Office If your hotel cannot mail letters for you, ask the concierge where the nearest post office is. The **Central Post Office** is located just southwest of Tokyo Station at 2-7-2 Marunouchi, Chiyoda-ku (tel. 3284-9527). It's open Monday through Friday from 9am to 7pm, on Saturday from 9am to 5pm, and on Sunday and public holidays from 9am to noon. If you need information on postage or mail, contact the **Information Office of the Tokyo International Post Office**, 2-3-3 Otemachi (tel. 3241-4891), located north of Tokyo Station. See also "Mail" under "Fast Facts: Japan" in Chapter 3.

Radio and Television See "Fast Facts: Japan" in Chapter 3.

Rest Rooms If you're in need of a restroom in Tokyo, your best bet is at train and subway stations, big hotels, department stores, and fast-food chains like McDonald's. For an explanation of Japanese toilets, refer to "Fast Facts: Japan" in Chapter 3.

Safety Tokyo is one of the safest cities in the world. Yet there are precautions you should take whenever you're traveling in an unfamiliar city or country. Stay alert and be aware of your immediate surroundings. Wear a money belt and keep a close eye on your possessions. Be especially careful with cameras, purses, and wallets—all favorite targets of thieves and pickpockets—particularly in crowded subways. Be doubly alert when walking along dark streets and in public parks after dark (in fact, if you're alone, it would be wiser to stay out of parks after dark). Every society, even one as relatively safe as Japan's, has its criminals. It's your responsibility to exercise caution at all times, even in the most heavily touristed areas.

Shoe Repairs All department stores have a shoe-repair counter, usually a **Mister Minit**. In addition, stations such as Yurakucho and Shibuya have street-side shoe repairs. Hotels also often offer such services.

Taxes For an explanation of taxes on accommodations, food, and goods, refer to "Fast Facts: Japan" in Chapter 3.

Taxis See "Getting Around" in this chapter.

Telephones, Telegrams, and Telex You can make local and long-distance calls from your room in most tourist hotels in Tokyo. Otherwise, there are public telephones, as well as telephone and telegraph offices throughout the city. The **Kokusai Denshin Denwa (KDD)** office, 1-8-1 Otemachi (tel. 3275-4343), close to Tokyo Station, is open Monday through Friday from 9am to 6pm and on Saturday, Sunday, and holidays from 9am to 5pm. It can handle facsimiles, phototelegrams, ISD calls, and telexes, in addition to telegrams and telephone calls. In Shinjuku there's a telephone and telegraph office at 2-3-2 Nishi Shinjuku (tel. 3347-5000).

There are several English telephone directories that provide addresses and telephone numbers for many businesses, companies, shops, and restaurants in Tokyo. They're *City Source*, the *English Telephone Directory*, the *Japan Times Directory*, and the *Japan Telephone Book Yellow Pages*. If your hotel does not have one of these and you're interested in buying one, they're available at the bookstores listed above. For assistance on directory telephone listings in Tokyo, English-speaking operators can help you if you call 3277-1010. See also "Fast Facts: Japan" in Chapter 3.

TOKYO ACCOMMODATIONS

Tokyo has no old, grand hotels. In fact, it doesn't have many old hotels, period. But what the city's hotels may lack in quaintness or old grandeur is more than made up for in the excellent service for which the Japanese are legendary, and in cleanliness and efficiency. Be prepared, however, for small rooms. Space is at a premium in Tokyo, so with the exception of some of the upper-range hotels, rooms seem to come in only three sizes: minuscule, small, and adequate.

Unfortunately, Tokyo does not have many ryokan, or Japanese-style inns. So I suggest that you wait for your travels around the country to have your ryokan experience. However, realizing that not all visitors have the opportunity to travel outside Tokyo, I've listed medium- and budget-range ryokan that are enthusiastic about foreigners and willing to take them in. In fact, if you're traveling on a budget, a simple Japanese-style inn is often the cheapest way to go. As for upper-range ryokan in Tokyo, none of them accept foreigners. They prefer that guests be introduced through someone they know and simply do not want to deal with the inconveniences and difficulties caused by cultural and language barriers.

Most of the upper-bracket hotels offer at least a few Japanese-style rooms, with tatami mats, a Japanese bathtub (deeper and narrower than the Western version), and futon. Although these rooms tend to be expensive, they are usually large enough for four people.

For each hotel or ryokan listed, I've given the nearest subway station and the walking time required. Remember that in addition to the prices quoted below, upper-class hotels and most medium-range hotels will add a 10% to 15% service charge. Further, rates of more than ¥15,000 ($107) per person per night will require an additional 6% tax; rates of less than ¥15,000 per person will require an additional 3% tax. Unless otherwise stated, the prices given below do not include tax.

Hotels are arranged according to price and are then subdivided according to geographical location, starting with the areas of Ginza and Hibiya in the heart of the city and then fanning out to such other locations as Akasaka and Shinjuku. The **very expensive** hotels are those that charge ¥31,000 ($221) and more for two people per night; the **expensive** hotels are those that charge ¥21,000 to ¥30,000 ($150 to $214) for two people per night; the **moderate** hotels offer rooms for ¥12,000 to ¥20,000 ($86 to $143) for two people per night; and the **budget** accommodations offer rooms for two people per night for ¥11,000 ($78) and less.

Tokyo's very expensive and expensive hotels can rival upper-range hotels anywhere in the world. Although many of the city's best hotels may not show much character from the outside, inside they are oases of subdued simplicity where service and hospitality reign supreme. Rooms in this category are adequate in size—some of them even large by Tokyo standards—and they all come with such amenities as a minibar, bilingual TV with English-language cable and CNN broadcasts from the States, a clock, a radio, cotton kimono, hot water for tea, and countless other personal touches that make staying in Japan a pleasure. Note, however, that while many hotels in this bracket have a health club and a swimming pool, an extra fee is charged for their use, often an exorbitant one.

As for the moderately priced hotels, they vary from Western-style hotels to business hotels to ryokan, with business hotels making up the majority in this category. Popular with Japanese businessmen, these hotels are generally quite small and offer just the basics—a private bathroom, TV, and a telephone—but are usually situated in a convenient location. There's very little to differentiate one business hotel from another—they all look pretty much the same. If you're interested simply in a clean and functional place to sleep in rather than in roomy comfort, a business hotel may be the way to go, although the distinction between a hotel and a business hotel is sometimes a fine one.

If you're looking for rock-bottom prices for rooms, you've come to the wrong city. It's difficult to find inexpensive lodging in Tokyo. The price of land is simply too prohibitive. You can, however, find rooms—tiny though they may be—for two people for less than $60 a night, which is pretty good considering that you're in one of the most expensive cities in the world. Accommodations in this category are basic: a bed and usually a phone, TV, heating, and air conditioning. Facilities are generally spotless, and prices often include tax and service charge. Inexpensive Japanese-style rooms make up the bulk of this category.

Although Tokyo doesn't suffer from a lack of hotel rooms during peak holidays (when most Japanese head for the hills and beaches), there are times when rooms are in short supply because of conventions and other events. And in summer, when there are many foreign tourists in Japan, the cheaper accommodations are often the first to fill up. It's always best, therefore, to make your hotel reservations in advance, especially if you're arriving in Japan after a long transoceanic flight and don't want the hassle of searching for a hotel room. Some of the hotels listed below belong to such well-known chains as Hilton and Holiday Inn, and you can easily make reservations in advance by dialing the hotel's local representative or toll-free number. Reservations for the major hotels can also be made through travel agents. And since most hotels have fax numbers, you can also reserve your room by facsimile. Once you're in Japan, call immediately to reconfirm your reservation.

Finally, a word should be said here about Tokyo's so-called love hotels. Usually found close to large entertainment districts and along major highways, such hotels do not provide sexual services themselves but, rather, offer rooms for rent by the hour to lovers. Altogether, there are an estimated 35,000 such love hotels in Japan, usually gaudy structures shaped like ocean liners or castles and offering such extras as rotating beds and mirrored walls. Love hotels can be found in abundance in Shibuya, Shinjuku, and Asakusa. You'll know that you've wandered into a love-hotel district when you notice discreet entryways and—a dead giveaway—hourly rates posted near the front door.

1. VERY EXPENSIVE

GINZA & HIBIYA

IMPERIAL HOTEL, 1-1-1 Uchisaiwaicho, Chiyoda-ku 100. Tel. 03/3504-1111, or toll free 800/223-5652 in the U.S., 800/223-6800 in the United States and Canada. Fax 03/3581-9146. 1,143 rms. A/C MINIBAR TV TEL **Station:** Hibiya, about a 1-minute walk away.

$ Rates: Main building: ¥29,000–¥55,000 ($207–$393) single; ¥35,000–¥60,000 ($250–$428) double. Tower: ¥34,000–¥51,000 ($243–$364) single; ¥39,000–¥57,000 ($278–$407) double. AE, DC, JCB, MC, V.

A NOTE ON PRICES

The prices quoted in this book were figured at ¥140 = US$1. Because of fluctuations, however, in the exchange rate of the yen (it was 136 to the dollar at press time), the U.S. dollar equivalents given might vary during the lifetime of this edition. Be sure to check current exchange rates when planning your trip. In addition, the rates given below may increase, so be sure to ask the current rate when making your reservation.

A NOTE ON JAPANESE SYMBOLS

Many hotels, restaurants, and other establishments in Japan do not have signs giving their names in English letters. As an aid to the reader, Appendix C lists the Japanese symbols for all such places described in this guide. Each set of symbols has a number, which corresponds to the number that appears inside an oval next to the establishment's boldfaced name in the text. Thus, to find the Japanese symbols for, say, Osaka's **Hotel Hokke Club** ⑬⑧, refer to number 138 in the appendix.

Located across from Hibiya Park within walking distance of Ginza, this is one of Tokyo's best-known hotels, where foreigners (mostly business executives) make up about 50% of its guests. The Imperial's trademark is excellent and impeccable service. Guests are treated like royalty, and the atmosphere throughout is subdued and dignified. The present hotel dates from 1970, with a 31-story tower added in 1983, but the Imperial's history goes back to 1922. That year it opened as a small hotel made of brick and stone, with intricate designs carved into its façade, it was designed by Frank Lloyd Wright. The Imperial won lasting fame when it survived, almost intact, the 1923 earthquake, which destroyed much of the rest of the city. Part of the old structure was moved to Meiji-Mura, a museum village outside Nagoya.

Rooms in the main building are quite large for Tokyo. Tower rooms, while slightly smaller, are higher up, bright, and cheerful; from their floor-to-ceiling bay windows, they offer fantastic views of either the Imperial Palace or Ginza and the harbor. The rooms are equipped with practical writing tables, three telephones, remote-control TV, cotton yukata, terry-cloth robes, a safe, a hairdryer, and all the other amenities you'd expect from a first-class hotel.

Dining/Entertainment: There are 13 restaurants and four bars. The top restaurant, the Fontainebleau, serves exquisitely prepared French cuisine, while the Prunier, founded in 1936, specializes in seafood.

Services: Baby-sitting service, in-house doctor and dentist, limousine and car-rental services, same-day laundry service, free newspaper.

Facilities: Impressive shopping arcade, barbershop and beauty parlor, business center, post office, tea-ceremony room, sauna, and Tokyo's most dramatic swimming pool, located on the 20th floor, with breathtaking views of Tokyo Bay (fee: ¥1,000 or $7.15).

HOTEL SEIYO GINZA, 1-11-2 Ginza, Chuo-ku 104. Tel. 03/3535-1111.
Fax 03/3535-1110. 80 rms and suites. A/C MINIBAR TV TEL **Station:** Ginza-Itchome, a 2-minute walk away.
$ Rates: ¥44,000–¥63,000 ($314–$450) single or double; ¥79,000–¥308,000 ($564–$2,200) suite. AE, CB, DC, JCB, MC, V.
Located about a 5-minute walk from the Ginza 4-chome Crossing, the Seiyo Ginza opened in 1987 as the area's newest luxury hotel. Its room rates are the most expensive in Tokyo, if not in all Japan. Its market is targeted at foreign executives, and with only 80 guest rooms and suites, service is at a premium. The hotel is not open to the public—that is, you must either be a hotel guest or have a reservation at one of its

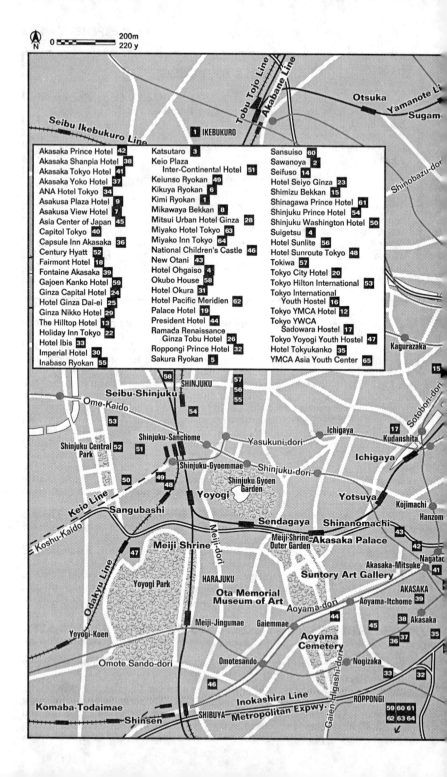

N
0 ─── 200m
    ─── 220 y

IKEBUKURO 1

Akasaka Prince Hotel 42	Katsutaro 3	Sansuiso 60
Akasaka Shanpia Hotel 38	Keio Plaza	Sawanoya 2
Akasaka Tokyo Hotel 41	Inter-Continental Hotel 51	Seifuso 14
Akasaka Yoko Hotel 37	Keiunso Ryokan 49	Hotel Seiyo Ginza 23
ANA Hotel Tokyo 34	Kikuya Ryokan 6	Shimizu Bekkan 15
Asakusa Plaza Hotel 9	Kimi Ryokan 1	Shinagawa Prince Hotel 61
Asakusa View Hotel 7	Mikawaya Bekkan 8	Shinjuku Prince Hotel 54
Asia Center of Japan 45	Mitsui Urban Hotel Ginza 28	Shinjuku Washington Hotel 50
Capitol Tokyo 40	Miyako Hotel Tokyo 63	Suigetsu 4
Capsule Inn Akasaka 36	Miyako Inn Tokyo 64	Hotel Sunlite 56
Century Hyatt 52	National Children's Castle 46	Hotel Sunroute Tokyo 48
Fairmont Hotel 18	New Otani 43	Tokiwa 57
Fontaine Akasaka 39	Hotel Ohgaiso 4	Tokyo City Hotel 20
Gajoen Kanko Hotel 59	Okubo House 58	Tokyo Hilton International 53
Ginza Capital Hotel 24	Hotel Okura 31	Tokyo International
Hotel Ginza Dai-ei 25	Hotel Pacific Meridien 62	Youth Hostel 16
Ginza Nikko Hotel 29	Palace Hotel 19	Tokyo YMCA Hotel 12
The Hilltop Hotel 13	President Hotel 44	Tokyo YMCA
Holiday Inn Tokyo 22	Ramada Renaissance	Sadowara Hostel 17
Hotel Ibis 33	Ginza Tobu Hotel 26	Tokyo Yoyogi Youth Hostel 47
Imperial Hotel 30	Roppongi Prince Hotel 32	Hotel Tokyukanko 35
Inabaso Ryokan 55	Sakura Ryokan 5	YMCA Asia Youth Center 65

TOKYO ACCOMMODATIONS

FROMMER'S SMART TRAVELER: HOTELS

TIPS FOR VALUE-CONSCIOUS TRAVELERS

1. Look for smaller, cheaper rooms in a large hotel, where you can take advantage of the hotel's facilities, which will range from an outdoor swimming pool to one or more restaurants.
2. Does your room have a window facing the street or an inner courtyard? Sometimes the difference in price between a windowless room and one with a window is only a few dollars.
3. Look for hotels outside the city's center. Many are much cheaper and are conveniently accessible by local transportation.
4. Consider taking a room without a private bathroom in the budget accommodations; it will be much cheaper.
5. Japanese-style accommodations are often cheaper than business hotels and sometimes include breakfast and dinner in their price.
6. If you're on a strict budget, you may look for accommodations at youth hostels and the Y, which are open throughout the year.

QUESTIONS TO ASK IF YOU'RE ON A BUDGET

1. Does the price of a room include service charge and tax? If not, what is the *total* charge per night?
2. Is the price different for a double room and a twin-bed room? Some hotels charge more for a twin, others for a double.
3. Is there a room available for a price cheaper than the one quoted? Many hotels have rooms in various price categories but may try to sell the more expensive rooms first, especially if they feel that the cheapest rooms and beds are too small for foreigners.
4. If your hotel has a telephone, how much is the surcharge on local and long-distance calls?
5. If there is parking space at your hotel, what is the charge per day?

exclusive restaurants to go in the main entrance. A hush prevails throughout the hotel, and instead of a front desk there is a comfortable reception room that resembles a living room. As one hotel employee explained, "The hardware is a Western-style hotel, but the software is traditional Japanese service."

Rooms are large and come with humidity-control dials, a safe, and a videocassette player. With the busy executive in mind, telephones have two lines and there are computerized DO NOT DISTURB and MAID SERVICE buttons linked to hotel personnel so that they can respond immediately to the desires of their guests. Bathrooms are huge, with separate shower and tub units and even a mini-TV.

Dining/Entertainment: There are four restaurants serving French, Italian, and Japanese food, including the Pastorale, which specializes in nouvelle cuisine and has one of Japan's largest and best wine cellars, with 300 vintages and 15,000 bottles. Attore serves specialties from northern Italy and is a good place for a business lunch.

Services: 24-hour room service, a personal secretary to organize business needs, travel arrangements, shopping, sightseeing, among other services.

Facilities: Fitness room, two theaters.

TORANOMON

HOTEL OKURA, 2-10-4 Toranomon, Minato-ku 105. Tel. 03/3582-0111, or toll free 800/223-6800 in the U.S., 800/341-8585 in Canada. Fax 03/3582-3707. 898 rms and suites. A/C MINIBAR TV TEL **Station:** Toranomon or Kamiyacho, each about a 10-minute walk away.

$ Rates: ¥30,000–¥66,000 ($214–$471) single; ¥40,000–¥60,000 ($280–$348) double/twin. Japanese-style rooms: ¥36,000–¥70,000 ($257–$500) single; ¥67,000–¥70,000 ($478–$500) double. AE, CB, DC, JCB, MC, V.

★ Located across the street from the U.S. Embassy, this is another venerable Tokyo hotel. Built just before the 1964 Summer Olympics, it has been the favorite hotel of visiting American dignitaries, as well as such celebrities as rock star David Bowie and the late pianist Vladimir Horowitz. Conservative and traditional in décor, the Okura combines Western comfort with Japanese design in the use of shoji screens, flower displays, and a beautifully sculptured garden. This is one of my favorite hotels in Tokyo. In a city where the newest means flashy and borderline pretentious, the Okura comes across as downright old-fashioned.

There are 11 different kinds of rooms, including a dozen Japanese-style rooms with tatami-covered floors, shoji screens, and a Japanese tub. Western-style rooms on the fifth floor feature a good-size balcony overlooking a small but meticulously groomed Japanese garden. TVs receive English-language cable (with CNN) and offer in-house movies.

Dining/Entertainment: There are eight restaurants and four bars, the former including La Belle Epoque, a French restaurant on the 12th floor with views of the city, and the casual Terrace Restaurant, which looks out onto the garden.

Services: Free parking garage for guests, free newspaper.

Facilities: Indoor and outdoor swimming pools (¥1,200 or $8.55 for both), health club and gym (fee charged), shopping arcade of exclusive boutiques (from Hanae Mori to Mikimoto pearls), beauty salon, barbershop, post office.

AKASAKA

AKASAKA PRINCE HOTEL, 1-2 Kioi-cho, Chiyoda-ku 102. Tel. 03/3234-1111, or toll free 800/44-UTELL in the U.S. Fax 03/3262-5163. 761 rms. A/C MINIBAR TV TEL **Station:** Akasaka-mitsuke, a 3-minute walk away.

$ Rates: ¥25,000–¥36,000 ($178–$257) single; ¥34,000–¥41,000 ($243–$293) twin; ¥37,000–¥45,000 ($264–$321) double. AE, DC, JCB, MC, V.

★ This 40-story ultramodern white skyscraper caused quite a stir when it opened in 1983, with some Tokyoites complaining that it was too cold and sterile. In my opinion, however, the Akasaka Prince is just ahead of its time. Japanese style, after all, has always called for simplicity—and this hotel's design is a projection of that simplicity into the world of the 21st century. The lobby is intentionally spacious and empty, lined with almost 12,000 slabs of white marble.

Designed by Kenzo Tange, the hotel's rooms are set on a 45° angle from the center axis of the building's core. This gives each room a corner view, with expansive windows overlooking the city. Rooms are bright, with a lot of sunshine, and color schemes are a soothing powder-blue and white. The single rooms are among the nicest in Tokyo, with three windows forming a pleasant alcove around a sofa. Sinks and vanity desks are located away from toilet and bath areas. Request a room overlooking the Akasaka side and you'll have a view of neon lights down below and Tokyo Tower off in the distance. There's a no-smoking floor.

Dining/Entertainment: There are 12 international restaurants and bars. Le Trianon, the hotel's top Western dining spot, has all the grace, décor, and atmosphere of a fine French restaurant. Other restaurants serve Chinese, Japanese, and continental cuisine, including the Blue Gardenia on the 40th floor, with spectacular views of the city. Also on the 40th floor is Top of Akasaka, one of the city's best cocktail lounges with a view.

Services: 24-hour room service, same-day laundry and dry cleaning service, baby-sitting service, free newspaper, free parking.

Facilities: Business center, travel desk, souvenir shop.

ANA HOTEL TOKYO, 1-12-33 Akasaka, Minato-ku 107. Tel. 03/3505-1111, or toll free 800/ANA HOTELS in the U.S. and Canada. Fax 03/3505-1155. 867 rms, 33 suites. A/C MINIBAR TV TEL **Station:** Roppongi, Akasaka, Kamiyacho, Toranomon, or Kokkai Gijido-mae.

$ Rates: ¥25,000–¥35,000 ($179–$250) single; ¥34,000–¥38,000 ($243–$271) double/twin; from ¥60,000 ($428) suite. AE, CB, DC, JCB, MC, V.

A gleaming white building rising 37 stories above the crossroads of Akasaka, Roppongi, Toranomon, and Kasumigaseki, the ANA Hotel Tokyo has given the Hotel Okura stiff competition since its grand opening in 1986. Its spacious second-floor lobby is of cool, cream-colored marble, with a water fountain serving as a focal point, and the lobby lounge is a favorite among Tokyoites for people-watching. Restaurants, rooms, and even corridors are superbly decorated with artwork and vases.

Rooms are large, with views of Tokyo Bay, Mt. Fuji, or the Imperial Palace. Various types of rooms and suites are available. The 34th floor features special executive quarters, which offer the services of a concierge, free continental breakfast, and an evening cocktail hour.

Dining/Entertainment: There are a dozen restaurants and bars. French, Chinese, and continental food are available, as well as such Japanese favorites as kaiseki, shabu-shabu, sushi, and teppanyaki. The Rose Room is the hotel's signature Western restaurant, while the Unkai serves the best Japanese cuisine. The Astral Bar on the 37th floor provides live music and fantastic views of the city.

Services: Two free newspapers delivered daily, same-day laundry service.

Facilities: Business center with secretarial services, travel desk, shopping arcade, barbershop and beauty salon, sauna (for men only), outdoor swimming pool (fee: ¥2,000 or $14), and baby-sitter's room.

CAPITOL TOKYU, 2-10-3 Nagata-cho, Chiyoda-ku 100. Tel. 03/3581-4511, or toll free 800/888-1199 in the U.S. and Canada. Fax 03/3581-5822. 459 rms and suites. A/C MINIBAR TV TEL **Station:** Kokkai Gijido-mae, a 1-minute walk away.

$ Rates: ¥26,000–¥27,000 ($186–$193) single; ¥36,000–¥42,000 ($257–$300) double/twin. AE, DC, JCB, MC, V.

Another of Tokyo's hotels built just before the 1964 Olympics, this one is located in the Akasaka district, within walking distance of the moat-encircled Imperial Palace. It used to be the Tokyo Hilton until 1984, when the Tokyu hotel chain took over the management. A small hotel by Tokyo's standards, it has the unique ability of making foreign guests feel as if they were in Asia and at home all at the same time. With more than 900 full-time employees, service is at a premium. There are, for example, no cigarette machines in the hotel—instead, guests are requested to ask any employee to fetch them a pack of cigarettes. On its grounds, the Capitol Tokyu boasts a meticulously pruned Japanese garden complete with a pond and golden carp. And if you stay here, be sure to check out Hie Shrine, next door.

Double and twin rooms are comfortably large. There are also 50 single rooms available, although they're fairly small. Rooms come with traditional shoji screens, the best of which overlook a small garden. You can't go wrong staying here.

Dining/Entertainment: The Keyaki Grill, famous for its steaks and continental cuisine, has some of the most attentive waiters in the world, but if it's a view of the garden you want, head for the Origami Restaurant or the Tea Lounge (the latter serves Sunday brunch).

Services: 24-hour room service, free newspaper, same-day laundry service, baby-sitting service.

Facilities: Outdoor swimming pool, steam bath, barbershop, beauty salon, massage, in-house doctor and dentist, shopping arcade, travel agency.

HOTEL NEW OTANI, 4-1 Kioi-cho, Chiyoda-ku 102. Tel. 03/3265-1111, or toll free 800/223-9868 in the U.S., 800/421-8795 in the U.S. and Canada. Fax 03/3221-2619. 1,800 rms. A/C MINIBAR TV TEL **Station:** Akasaka-mitsuke, about a 3-minute walk away; or Yotsuya, a 5-minute walk away.

$ Rates: ¥30,000–¥38,000 ($214–$271) single; ¥34,000–¥44,000 ($242–$314) double/twin. AE, DC, JCB, MC, V.

This is Japan's largest hotel, and its facilities make it seem like a city unto itself. In fact, it's so big that there are two information desks to assist lost souls searching for a particular restaurant or one of the shops in the New Otani's meandering shopping arcade. The most splendid feature of the hotel is its 400-year-old Japanese garden, which sprawls over 10 acres of ponds, waterfalls, bridges, bamboo groves, and manicured bushes.

Accommodations are divided between the main building, built in time for the 1964 Olympics and recently renovated, and a 40-story tower. The rooms are comfortable, most offering the extras of TV with remote control and English-language cable (with CNN), a hairdryer, shoji-like screens on the windows, and bathroom scales. There are no-smoking floors. However, if you don't like crowds and action, stay away from this place.

Dining/Entertainment: With more than 35 restaurants and bars, it's no problem finding a place to eat and drink. Most expensive is La Tour d'Argent, one of Tokyo's most exclusive restaurants, but there's also a Trader Vic's, as well as a teppanyaki restaurant with a lovely setting in the middle of the garden.

Services: 24-hour room service, free newspaper, same-day laundry service.

Facilities: Shopping arcade with 120 stores, medical offices, post office, health club, sauna, tea-ceremony room, indoor and outdoor swimming pools (fee charged) and tennis courts, business center, chapel with daily services, travel agency, art museum, beauty parlor, barbershop, baby-sitting room.

SHINJUKU

CENTURY HYATT TOKYO, 2-7-2 **Nishi-Shinjuku, Shinjuku-ku 160. Tel. 03/3349-0111,** or toll free 800/233-1234 in the U.S. and Canada. Fax 03/3344-5575. 786 rms and suites. A/C MINIBAR TV TEL **Station:** Shinjuku, a 10-minute walk away.

$ Rates: ¥30,000–¥38,000 ($214–$271) single; ¥35,000–¥42,000 ($250–$300) double/twin. Discounts for longer stays. AE, DC, JCB, MC, V.

Located on Shinjuku's west side, this 28-story hotel features an impressive seven-story atrium lobby with three massive chandeliers and an inlaid marble floor. The excellent staff is used to the many foreigners who pass through the hotel's doors. The indoor swimming pool, located on the 28th floor, offers a view of the surrounding area.

Rooms are not only adequately sized but attractively appointed in soft pastels, with TV that offers English-language channels (including CNN) and pay movies. The bathrooms' bright lights are great for applying makeup. Although single rooms are available, their windows are at such an angle in the corner of the rooms that you can hardly see out of them. The twin rooms are better, with big windows that let in a lot of sunshine. Guests in the higher-priced rooms stay on the executive floors, the Regency Club, offering complimentary breakfast and evening cocktails.

Dining/Entertainment: There are a dozen restaurants and bars, including the well-known Hugo's, with its steaks and seafood; a French restaurant, Chenonceaux; and Japanese and Chinese restaurants. On the 27th floor is Rhapsody, featuring live jazz nightly and a view of the city.

Services: 24-hour room service, same-day laundry service, baby-sitting service, in-house doctor, free newspaper, free shuttle bus to Shinjuku Station.

Facilities: Indoor swimming pool (fee: ¥1,500 or $10.70), sauna, business center, shopping arcade, beauty salon, barbershop.

TOKYO HILTON INTERNATIONAL, 6-6-2 **Nishi-Shinjuku, Shinjuku-ku 160. Tel. 03/3344-5111,** or toll free 800/HILTONS in the U.S. and Canada. Fax 03/3342-6094. 808 rms. A/C MINIBAR TV TEL **Station:** Shinjuku, a 10-minute walk away.

$ Rates: ¥28,000–¥37,000 ($200–$264) single; ¥35,000–¥46,000 ($250–$328) double/twin; ¥60,000–¥80,000 ($428–$571) Japanese-style room; from ¥75,000 ($536) suite. AE, DC, JCB, MC, V.

Located down the street from the Century Hyatt, the Hilton relocated here from Akasaka in 1984. As with all Hiltons, the room décor reflects traditional native style: shoji screens instead of curtains, and simple yet elegant furniture. The largest Hilton in the Asia/Pacific area, the S-shaped 38-story structure houses rooms that offer views of either Shinjuku's skyscrapers (a pretty sight at night) or (on clear days) Mt. Fuji. Room rates are based on both size and location, with the more expensive rooms higher up. The most expensive singles and doubles are on the executive floor, with its complimentary breakfast and cocktails. There's also a no-smoking floor.

Dining/Entertainment: Of the hotel's seven restaurants and bars, The Imari is the showcase dining spot, offering grilled foods, seafood, and fine vintage wines. There are also Japanese and Chinese restaurants. St. George's Bar offers draft beer, buffet lunches, and carvery items in the tradition of an English pub, with musical entertainment in the evening.

Services: 24-hour room service, free shuttle bus to Shinjuku Station every 10 minutes, same-day laundry service, baby-sitting service.

Facilities: Excellent fitness center, tennis courts, indoor swimming pool (fee: ¥1,500 or $10.70), sauna, business center.

2. EXPENSIVE

GINZA & HIBIYA

GINZA DAI-ICHI HOTEL, 8-13-1 Ginza, Chuo-ku 104. Tel. 03/3542-5311. Fax 03/3542-3030. 801 rms and suites. A/C MINIBAR TV TEL **Station:** Shimbashi, a 5-minute walk away.
$ Rates: ¥18,000–¥21,000 ($129–$150) single; ¥23,000–¥33,000 ($164–$236) twin; ¥24,000–¥26,000 ($171–$186) double; ¥31,000–¥36,000 ($221–$257) triple; ¥88,000 ($629) suite. AE, DC, JCB, MC, V.

Located on the southern edge of Ginza, with its lobby on the second floor, this hotel offers unexciting but comfortable accommodations, with TVs that carry CNN broadcasts. The bathrooms are tiny, one-piece plastic units. Guest rooms with the best views face Tokyo Bay.

Dining/Entertainment: There are four restaurants and bars. French and Japanese dining establishments on the 15th floor have good views of Tokyo Bay by day and the lights of Ginza by night. The French restaurant, Lumière, specializes in lobsters and steaks, while the Japanese restaurants offer the likes of sukiyaki, shabu-shabu, and tempura. A coffee shop and a sushi bar are also on the premises.

Facilities: Shopping arcade, beauty shop, barbershop, sauna, massage salon, travel agency.

GINZA NIKKO HOTEL, 8-4-21 Ginza, Chuo-ku 104. Tel. 03/3571-4911. Fax 03/3571-8379. 112 rms. A/C MINIBAR TV TEL **Station:** Shimbashi, a 4-minute walk away.
$ Rates: ¥15,500–¥19,000 ($111–$136) single; ¥27,000–¥33,000 ($193–$236) twin. AE, DC, JCB, MC, V.

There's nothing fancy or out of the ordinary about this small business hotel, but it's personable, clean, and conveniently located in southern Ginza. In fact, its location on Sotobori Dori Avenue can't be beat. Built more than a quarter of a century ago, it is one of the oldest hotels in the area.

Dining/Entertainment: There is a coffee shop, plus a bar.
Services: Laundry service, free newspaper.

MITSUI URBAN HOTEL GINZA, 8-6-15 Ginza, Chuo-ku 104. Tel. 03/3572-4131. Fax 03/3572-4254. 252 rms. A/C TV TEL **Station:** Shimbashi, a 1-minute walk away.
$ Rates: ¥11,500–¥15,000 ($82–$107) single; ¥20,000–¥23,000 ($143–$164) double; ¥20,000–¥29,000 ($143–$207) twin. AE, DC, JCB, MC, V.

S Because of its location, convenient to Ginza and to the Kasumigaseki and Marunouchi business centers, this attractive hotel caters to both businessmen and tourists. The lobby, on the second floor, is manned by a friendly staff. The

FROMMER'S COOL FOR KIDS
HOTELS

Tokyo Hilton International *(see p. 109)* This modern hotel in the heart of Shinjuku offers a family plan, with no extra charge for children who occupy the same room as their parents. In addition, baby-sitting is available, and the hotel's in-house movies and indoor swimming pool are sure to keep teenagers happy.

The Keio Plaza Inter-Continental Hotel *(see p. 112)* Parents love this hotel's baby-sitting room, open daily from 10am to 9pm.

National Children's Castle *(see p. 119)* The absolute best place for children, complete with an indoor/outdoor playground and activity rooms for all ages, offering everything from building blocks to computer games.

Sakura Ryokan *(see p. 122)* This modern Japanese-style inn offers a large family room that sleeps up to eight persons in traditional Japanese style, on futon laid out on tatami mats.

guest rooms are small and come with hot water for tea, an alarm clock, a radio, cotton kimono, and color TV offering English-language programs and pay adult entertainment. The bathrooms are larger than in other business hotels. I suggest asking for a room away from the highway overpass that stands beside the hotel.

Dining/Entertainment: There are five restaurants, bars, and lounges. Of these, Munakata is my favorite, a pleasant Japanese restaurant offering reasonably priced mini-kaiseki lunches.

RAMADA RENAISSANCE GINZA TOBU HOTEL, 6-14-10 Ginza, Chuo-ku 104. Tel. 03/3546-0111, or toll free 800/228-2828 in the U.S. Fax 03/3546-8990. 206 rms. A/C MINIBAR TV TEL **Station:** Ginza, a 4-minute walk away; or Higashi-Ginza, a 1-minute walk away.

$ Rates: ¥18,000–¥22,000 ($128–$157) single; ¥30,000–¥33,000 ($214–$236) twin; ¥33,000 ($236) double. AE, DC, JCB, MC, V.

This small, reasonably priced, and personable hotel, located on Showa Dori Avenue behind the Ginza Matsuzakaya department store, employs a full-time staff of 250. About 40% of its guests are foreigners, and half of those are Americans (no group tours are accepted). Each room comes equipped with three telephones, bilingual TV with CNN broadcasts and in-house movies, a radio/music system with a wide variety of music channels, a clothesline and a massage shower head in the bathroom, and a hairdryer. There are also hookups for facsimile machines, which you can use free of charge. A free *Japan Times* is delivered to your room in the morning.

Dining/Entertainment: The five restaurants and bars include an upscale French restaurant, a Japanese restaurant, and a coffee shop that is open 24 hours.

Services: 24-hour room service.

Facilities: Travel and business center, hairdressing salon.

NEAR TOKYO STATION

PALACE HOTEL, 1-1-1 Marunouchi, Chiyoda-ku 100. Tel. 03/3211-5211, or toll free 800/44-UTELL in the U.S., 800/223-0888 in the U.S. and Canada. Fax 03/3211-6987. 404 rms. A/C MINIBAR TV TEL **Station:** Otemachi, a 3-minute walk away.

$ Rates: ¥22,000–¥23,000 ($157–$164) single; ¥28,000–¥55,000 ($200–$393) twin; ¥33,000–¥40,000 ($236–$286) double; from ¥100,000 ($714) suite. AE, DC, JCB, MC, V.

Because of its proximity to Tokyo's business district, this hotel is a favorite among foreign businessmen; in fact, foreigners account for 65% of its guests. The hotel is located across the street from the Imperial Palace and gardens, and its deluxe twin rooms—which are large, face the gardens, and have a balcony—can be highly recommended. Built in 1961, the hotel is small, and repeat guests are rewarded with monogrammed slippers. Rooms are comfortable, with large windows; and there are two no-smoking floors.

Dining/Entertainment: Of its seven restaurants, serving Chinese, Japanese, French, and Italian food, the French-cuisine Crown Restaurant on the 10th floor is the best, offering superb views of the Imperial Palace.

Services: 24-hour room service, free newspaper.

Facilities: Shopping arcade, barbershop, beauty salon.

AKASAKA

AKASAKA TOKYU HOTEL, 2-14-3 Nagata-cho, Chiyoda-ku 100. Tel. 03/3580-2311, or toll free 800/822-0016 or 800/624-5068 in the U.S. Fax 03/3580-6066. 566 rms. A/C MINIBAR TV TEL **Station:** Akasaka-mitsuke, a 1-minute walk away.

$ Rates: ¥21,000–¥26,000 ($150–$186) single; ¥30,000 ($214) double; ¥30,000–¥44,000 ($214–$314) twin. AE, DC, JCB, MC, V.

This hotel boasts an average 89% occupancy, attributed in part to its ideal location. Built in 1969, it is easily recognizable by its candy-striped exterior. The lobby is on the third floor, and rooms were recently renovated to include such features as a hairdryer, a clothesline in the bathroom, shoji screens and window panels that slide shut for complete darkness (even in the middle of the day), a push-button phone, and TV with remote control, pay movies, and CNN cable broadcasts. There are 200 single rooms, but the lower-priced ones are pretty small. Try to get a twin or double room facing Akasaka—the windows can open, a rarity in Tokyo.

Dining/Entertainment: There are more than 14 restaurants in the building, including the French restaurant Gondola on the 14th floor, with a view of glittering Akasaka.

Services: Laundry service Monday through Friday, room service until midnight.

Facilities: Shopping arcade.

SHINJUKU

KEIO PLAZA INTER-CONTINENTAL HOTEL, 2-2-1 Nishi-Shinjuku, Shinjuku-ku 160. Tel. 03/3344-0111, or toll free 800/222-KEIO in the U.S. Fax 03/3345-8269. 1,485 rms. A/C MINIBAR TV TEL **Station:** Shinjuku, a few minutes' walk away.

$ Rates: ¥26,000–¥37,000 ($186–$264) single; ¥28,000–¥40,000 ($200–$285) double/twin. AE, DC, JCB, MC, V.

This hotel has the distinction of being the first skyscraper built in Japan, and at 47 stories it's still Tokyo's tallest hotel—and one of its largest overall. Constructed in 1971, its brilliant white exterior is composed of precast concrete panels, the initial application of this technique in Japan. The room rates are based on size rather than location, so ask for a room higher up, where the view is better. Unfortunately, the recent completion of Tokyo's new City Hall has blocked the hotel's view of Mt. Fuji. Rooms contain TV with remote control, in-house pay movies, and CNN cable broadcasts, as well as a radio, a hairdryer, and a bathroom phone. There's a no-smoking floor.

Dining/Entertainment: There are more than 20 restaurants and bars. Top of the line is Ambrosia, which offers continental food with a view. Other restaurants specialize in steaks, seafood, Chinese and Japanese cuisine. For relaxation, Polestar on the 45th floor offers an unparalleled view of Tokyo.

Services: Medical services, free English newspaper, packing and shipping services.

Facilities: Outdoor swimming pool, sauna, shopping arcade, travel center, beauty parlor, business center, baby-sitting room.

NEAR SHINAGAWA STATION

MIYAKO HOTEL TOKYO, 1-1-50 Shiroganedai, Minato-ku 108. Tel. 03/ 3447-3111, or toll free 800/336-1136 in the U.S. Fax 03/3447-3133. 488 rms and suites. A/C MINIBAR TV TEL **Station:** Takanawadai, about an 8-minute walk away.
$ Rates: ¥22,000–¥24,000 ($157–$171) single; ¥26,500–¥38,000 ($189–$271) double. Japanese-style rooms: ¥27,000 ($193) single; ¥31,000 ($221) double. AE, DC, JCB, MC, V.

⭐ This affiliate of the famous Miyako Hotel in Kyoto was designed by Minoru Yamasaki, the architect of the World Trade Center in New York and the Century Plaza in Los Angeles. The Japanese themselves account for 70% of its guests, and although it's a bit inconveniently located, it offers a free bus shuttle to and from Meguro Station and to Ginza. The lobby overlooks 5½ acres of lush gardens. The guest rooms are large, with huge floor-to-ceiling windows that have views of the hotel's own garden, a garden next door, or Tokyo Tower. There are nine single rooms, all with a semidouble-size bed, but they're usually booked. This hotel is one of my favorites in Tokyo.

Dining/Entertainment: Nine restaurants, bars, and cocktail lounges. La Clé d'Or, serving continental fare, has a view of the hotel's garden, as does the Yamatoya-Sangen, which offers a variety of Japanese cuisine, including shabu-shabu, tempura, kaiseki, sushi, and eel.

Services: Free newspaper, complimentary shuttle bus, same-day laundry service.
Facilities: Health club with both a huge indoor pool that is great for swimming laps and a sauna (fee: ¥2,000 or $14.30), shopping arcade, barbershop, travel agency, medical clinic.

HOTEL PACIFIC MERIDIEN, 3-13-3 Takanawa, Minato-ku 108. Tel. 03/3445-6711, or toll free 800/543-4300 in the U.S. and Canada. Fax 03/3445-5733. 954 rms. A/C MINIBAR TV TEL **Station:** Shinagawa, a 1-minute walk away.
$ Rates: ¥21,500–¥25,800 ($153–$184) single; ¥25,000–¥34,000 ($178–$243) double/twin. AE, DC, JCB, MC, V.
A subsidiary of Air France and located right across the street from Shinagawa Station, this hotel is built on grounds that once belonged to Japan's imperial family. Its coffee lounge looks out onto a peaceful and tranquil garden, and its Blue Pacific lounge on the 30th floor has dynamite views of Tokyo Bay. Approximately 40% of the hotel guests are foreigners. The accommodations are of adequate size, and since rates are based strictly on size, ask for a room on one of the top floors, boasting views of the bay. All rooms come with TV (remote control and English-language cable with CNN broadcasts), a hairdryer, and a clothesline in the bathroom.

Dining/Entertainment: The hotel's 11 restaurants and bars offer Japanese, Chinese, and French cuisine. There is also the Blue Pacific lounge, with its great views.
Services: Free newspaper, same-day laundry service, baby-sitting.
Facilities: Outdoor pool (free for hotel guests), sauna (for men only), shopping arcade.

ROPPONGI

ROPPONGI PRINCE HOTEL, 3-2-7 Roppongi, Minato-ku 106. Tel. 03/ 3587-1111, or toll free 800/542-8686 in the U.S. Fax 03/3587-0770. 216 rms. A/C MINIBAR TV TEL **Station:** Roppongi, a 10-minute walk away.
$ Rates: ¥21,500 ($153) single; ¥24,000–¥27,000 ($171–$193) twin; ¥25,000–¥27,000 ($178–$193) double. AE, DC, JCB, MC, V.
Opened in 1984 (a welcome event in Roppongi, still woefully lacking in hotels), the Roppongi Prince attracts Japanese vacationers aged 20 to 25 and caters to them with a

young and cheerful staff, modern designs, and bold colors. The hotel is built around an inner courtyard, which features an outdoor swimming pool with a heated deck—a solar mirror on the roof directs sun rays toward the sunbathers below. Rooms are small, but are bright and colorful and come with the usual desk, clock, and radio, among other amenities. A good place to be if you want to be close to the action in Roppongi.

Dining/Entertainment: There are Italian, tempura, sushi, and steak restaurants, as well as a coffee shop, bar, and lobby lounge.

Services: Free newspaper.

Facilities: Heated outdoor pool that is open year round (fee: ¥2,000 or $14.30).

ASAKUSA

ASAKUSA VIEW HOTEL, 3-17-1 Nishi-Asakusa, Taito-ku 111. Tel. 03/3847-1111. Fax 03/3842-2117. 350 rms. A/C MINIBAR TV TEL **Station:** Tawaramachi (Ginza Line), an 8-minute walk away.

$ Rates: ¥16,500–¥18,500 ($118–$132) single; ¥23,000–¥31,000 ($164–$221) double; ¥28,000–¥31,000 ($200–$221) twin; ¥35,000 ($250) triple. Japanese-style rooms: from ¥45,000 ($321) for two. AE, DC, JCB, MC, V.

This is the only upper-bracket and modern hotel in the Asakusa area, and looks almost out of place rising among this famous district's older buildings. It's a good place to stay if you want to be in Tokyo's old downtown but don't want to sacrifice any creature comforts. The lobby exudes cool elegance, with a marble floor, an atrium, and hanging chandeliers that hint at art deco. The guest rooms are very pleasant, with sleek contemporary Japanese furnishings and bay windows that let in plenty of sunshine. Rooms facing the front have views of the famous Sensoji Temple. Eight Japanese-style rooms are available, sleeping up to five persons.

Dining/Entertainment: Of the six restaurants and bars, the French restaurant Makie is the best known, featuring Western cuisine served in the delicate style of Japanese kaiseki. Less formal, but with great views of the city, is the Belvedere on the 28th floor; it serves a buffet lunch daily.

Services: Free newspaper, darning and stitching service.

Facilities: Indoor swimming pool with a ceiling opened in summer (fee: ¥3,000 or $21.40), massage, jet bath, shopping arcade, and Japanese-style public bath with wooden tubs (fee: ¥500 or $3.55).

ELSEWHERE IN TOKYO

THE HILLTOP HOTEL, 1-1 Surugadai, Kanda, Chiyoda-ku 101. Tel. 03/3293-2311. Fax 03/3233-4567. 75 rms. A/C MINIBAR TV TEL **Station:** Ochanomizu or Shin-Ochanomizu, each an 8-minute walk; or Jimbocho, a 5-minute walk away.

$ Rates: ¥14,300–¥19,800 ($102–$141) single; ¥23,000–¥25,000 ($164–$178) double; ¥23,000–¥29,000 ($164–$207) twin. AE, DC, JCB, MC, V.

Located, as the name implies, on a hill, this is an old-fashioned, unpretentious hotel with character. Its main building dates back to 1937, with an annex added in the 1970s. Throughout the decades the Hilltop has been a favorite place to stay with writers, including novelist Mishima Yukio. The hotel's brochure maintains that "oxygen and negative ions are circulated into the rooms and its refreshing atmosphere is accepted by many, including prominent individuals, as most adequate for work and rest." I'm not sure exactly what that means but it probably doesn't do any harm. The double rooms are fairly small, and although nothing fancy, they're pleasantly homey and come with cherry-wood furniture (as well as a mahogany desk), fringed lampshades, velvet curtains, a radio, a clock, and old-fashioned heaters with intricate grillwork. There are also small singles.

Dining/Entertainment: The hotel's seven restaurants offer steaks, plus Italian, Chinese, and Japanese cuisine. Its best restaurant, the Yamano-ue, serves excellent tempura.

Services: Same-day laundry service.

3. MODERATE

GINZA & HIBIYA

GINZA CAPITAL HOTEL, 3-1-5 Tsukiji, Chuo-ku 104. Tel. 03/3543-8211. Fax 03/3543-7839. 571 rms (all with bath). A/C TV TEL **Station:** Shintomicho, a 2-minute walk away.

$ **Rates** (including service and tax): Main building: ¥8,200–¥9,000 ($59–$64) single; ¥14,300–¥15,000 ($102–$107) twin. Annex: ¥9,300–¥10,500 ($66–$75) single; ¥15,800 ($113) double/twin, ¥20,500 ($146) triple. AE, DC, JCB, MC, V.

This hotel and its newer annex, called the New Ginza Capital Hotel, offer a total of 571 rooms within a 10-minute walk of Ginza. A modern and efficient establishment with a friendly staff, it has rooms that are clean and bright, even though they are minuscule in size. If being able to look out a window is a big deal to you, stay away from the annex rooms that face north—they have a glazed covering about a foot out from the building, so you can't see anything (heaven knows why); single rooms in the annex face another building and are dark. Otherwise, annex rooms are a bit more modern, but the same size as those in the older, main building. All rooms come with the usual hot water for tea, cotton kimono, alarm clock, radio, and TV with adult movies, but a plus here is the full-length mirrors. The annex has both a Western and a Japanese restaurant; the main building, a Western one.

HOTEL GINZA DAI-EI, 3-12-2 Ginza, Chuo-ku 104. Tel. 03/3541-0111. Fax 03/3541-2882. 82 rms (all with bath). A/C TV TEL **Station:** Higashi-Ginza, a few minutes' walk away.

$ **Rates** (including service and tax): ¥12,800 ($91) single; ¥19,800 ($141) double or twin. Japanese-style rooms: ¥23,900 ($171) for two, ¥28,600 ($204) for three, ¥33,000 ($235) for four. AE, DC, JCB, V.

This typical red-brick business hotel has minuscule rooms that feature a hot-water heater, a cotton kimono, and a desk. A plus, however, is that their windows open. Japanese-style rooms are also available. One restaurant serves Chinese food.

NEAR TOKYO STATION

HOLIDAY INN TOKYO, 1-13-7 Hatchobori, Chuo-ku 104. Tel. 03/3553-6161. Fax 03/3553-6040. 120 rms (all with bath). A/C MINIBAR TV TEL **Station:** Hatchobori, a 3-minute walk away.

$ **Rates:** ¥17,000–¥22,000 ($121–$157) single; ¥19,200–¥24,000 ($137–$171) double. Children under 12 stay free in parents' room. AE, DC, JCB, MC, V.

Located on Shin-Ohashi Dori Avenue in a red-brick building with the familiar Holiday Inn sign, this place is similar to Holiday Inns back home. As many as 30% of its guests are Americans, mainly individual travelers. The rooms in this small hotel are fairly large for Tokyo, and come with the usual desk, clock, radio, TV with remote control and English-language cable, among other amenities. All beds are either double or queen size. There is an outdoor swimming pool, free for hotel guests (open from July to September only); baby-sitters are available on request; and a free *Japan Times* is delivered to your room in the morning. There is one Western restaurant, plus a bar. It's about a 20-minute walk to Ginza.

TOKYO CITY HOTEL, 1-9 Nihombashi Honcho, Chuo-ku 103. Tel. 03/3270-7671. Fax 03/3270-8930. 267 rms (all with bath). A/C TV TEL **Station:** Mitsukoshi-mae, a 2-minute walk away.

$ **Rates** (including service and tax): ¥7,900–¥9,000 ($56–$64) single; ¥12,000–¥13,000 ($86–$93) double; ¥12,500–¥13,800 ($89–$98) twin. AE, MC, JCB, V.

This is a fine, no-nonsense business hotel offering moderately priced rooms in the middle of the city. Its one restaurant serves Western food. Although the single rooms are quite small, the twin rooms are adequate.

AKASAKA

AKASAKA SHANPIA HOTEL, 7-6-13 Akasaka, Minato-ku 107. Tel. 03/ 3586-0811; 03/3583-1001 for reservations. Fax 03/3589-0575. 232 rms (all with bath). A/C TV TEL **Station:** Akasaka, about a 5-minute walk away.

$ Rates: ¥9,500–¥16,000 ($68–$114) single; ¥16,200–¥19,200 ($116–$137) double/twin. AE, DC, JCB, MC, V.

The special feature of this hotel is that 202 of its rooms are singles, a sure sign that it caters primarily to Japanese businessmen. Rooms are minuscule in size, and since the single beds are tiny, you'll probably want to spring for a double bed if you're tall; however, there are only 18 twin-bedded rooms and 12 double-size beds. The higher-priced twins and doubles come with a stocked refrigerator and a hairdryer. Signs in all rooms urge guests to ROCK THE DOOR. There is one restaurant, serving both Japanese and Western food, as well as a bar.

AKASAKA YOKO HOTEL, 6-14-12 Akasaka, Minato-ku 107. Tel. 03/ 3586-4050; 03/3586-8341 for reservations. Fax 03/3586-5944. 245 rms (all with bath). A/C TV TEL **Station:** Akasaka, a 5-minute walk away, on Akasaka Dori St.

$ Rates (including service and tax): ¥9,300–¥10,500 ($66–$75) single; ¥14,300–¥16,500 ($102–$118) twin. AE, MC, V.

In a handy location close to the nightlife of both Roppongi (a 15-minute walk) and Akasaka, this pleasant small business hotel caters primarily to Japanese. For a couple of dollars more in each category you can get a slightly larger room, which may be worth it if you're claustrophobic. In any case, the bathrooms are barely large enough for even one person. If there are two of you who can sleep in one semidouble-size bed, you can stay in the largest single room for ¥13,200 ($94). The hotel has a coffee shop, and there are vending machines that dispense beer and soda.

HOTEL TOKYUKANKO, 2-21-6 Akasaka, Minato-ku 107. Tel. 03/3583- 0451; 03/3583-4741 for reservations. Fax 03/3583-4023. 48 rms (all with bath). A/C TV TEL **Station:** Roppongi or Akasaka, each a 10-minute walk away.

$ Rates: ¥7,700–¥10,200 ($55–$73) single; ¥15,400 ($110) twin. AE, DC, JCB, MC, V.

Close to the ANA Hotel, the Tokyukanko was built at the time of the 1964 Olympics. It shows its age, being a bit worn around the edges, but it remains popular because of its location. In addition, rooms are larger than in some other business hotels, and bathrooms are tiled, not fitted with the usual plastic walls and fixtures. The cheapest singles, however, have a shower instead of a tub and are a bit drab—they face an inner courtyard and have glazed windows. If you like the light of day, it may be worth it to splurge for the single with bathtub. The hotel has one coffee shop and a Japanese restaurant that serves tempura and yakitori.

SHINJUKU

SHINJUKU PRINCE HOTEL, 1-30-1 Kabuki-cho, Shinjuku-ku 160. Tel. 03/3205-1111, or toll free 800/542-8686 in the U.S. Fax 03/3205-1952. 571 rms (all with bath). A/C MINIBAR (in some) TV TEL **Station:** Seibu Shinjuku, beneath hotel; or Shinjuku, a 5-minute walk away.

$ Rates: ¥14,800 ($106) single; ¥17,000–¥27,000 ($121–$193) double/twin. Deluxe rooms: ¥22,000 ($176) twin; ¥24,000 ($192) double. AE, DC, JCB, MC, V.

This business hotel has a great location, just a 5-minute walk north of Shinjuku Station, making it convenient to Shinjuku's nightlife district of Kabuki-cho. A smart-looking streamlined brick building in the heart of Shinjuku, the Prince has shopping arcades and 10 restaurants and bars on its bottom 10 floors, while the rest of its 24 floors hold the guest rooms. The cheapest rooms are small, but all accommodations offer a great view of Shinjuku; those facing Shinjuku Station have double-paned windows to shut out noise. There are no-smoking floors. Services include 24-hour room service, same-day laundry service, and free English newspapers on request. All in all, a good choice in a moderately priced hotel.

SHINJUKU WASHINGTON HOTEL, 3-2-9 Nishi-Shinjuku, Shinjuku-ku 160. Tel. 03/3343-3111. Fax 03/3342-2575. 1,301 rms (all with bath). A/C MINIBAR TV TEL **Station:** Shinjuku, about a 10-minute walk away.

$ Rates: ¥10,500–¥13,500 ($75–$96) single; ¥17,000–¥22,000 ($121–$157) double; ¥17,600–¥40,000 ($126–$286) twin; ¥27,000 ($193) triple. AE, DC, JCB, MC, V.

Opened in West Shinjuku in 1984, with an annex added in 1987, this huge white building reminds me of an ocean liner—even the hotel's tiny windows look like portholes. Inside, everything is bright and white, with a lot of open space. The third-floor lobby features a row of machines for automated check-in and checkout, but there are a few humans there to help you with the process. You'll receive a "card key"—resembling a credit card—which also activates the bedside controls for such things as the TV, radio, and room lights. (The annex has its own check-in desk.) There are no bellboys here, no room service. The small guest rooms remind me of ship cabins, but everything you need is there—a minibar and a radio, among other amenities. There are more than 20 bars and restaurants in the hotel complex, as well as a shopping arcade and a sauna (for men only).

HOTEL SUNLITE, 5-15-8 Shinjuku, Shinjuku-ku 160. Tel. 03/3356-0391. Fax 03/3356-1223. 197 rms (all with bath). A/C TV TEL **Station:** Shinjuku, about a 15-minute walk away; or Shinjuku Sanchome, a 5-minute walk away.

$ Rates (including tax and service): Annex: ¥8,400–¥9,000 ($60–$64) single; ¥13,200 ($94) twin. New building: ¥9,300 ($66) single; ¥14,300 ($102) double; ¥15,400 ($110) twin. AE, JCB, MC, V.

In 1985 this business hotel moved across the street from its old location into a spanking new building, turning the older building into the Hotel Sunlite Annex, with rates slightly lower than those at the newer location. At any rate, all of the rooms are cheerful and clean, although those in the annex are small (its singles are minuscule). Feelings of claustrophobia are somewhat mitigated, however, by the fact that all windows can be opened. The best accommodations are the new building's twin rooms that are situated on the corners and have windows on two sides. Incidentally, if you like to stay out late, beware. Doors here close at 2am and don't reopen until 5:30am. Located on the east side of Shinjuku Station on Meiji Dori Avenue, Hotel Sunlite has one combination bar-lounge and one restaurant serving Western food.

HOTEL SUNROUTE TOKYO, 2-3-1 Yoyogi, Shibuya-ku 151. Tel. 03/3375-3211. Fax 03/3379-3040. 543 rms (all with bath). A/C TV TEL **Station:** Shinjuku, a 2-minute walk south.

$ Rates: ¥11,500–¥15,400 ($82–$110) single; ¥15,400–¥18,700 ($110–$133) double; ¥15,900–¥22,000 ($113–$157) twin. AE, DC, JCB, MC, V.

This hotel attracts a 40% foreign clientele and calls itself a "city hotel," but its rooms resemble business-hotel rather than tourist accommodations. A 15-story white building, it has three restaurants, serving Italian, Chinese, and Japanese cuisine, as well as a pub and a small shopping arcade. The guest rooms may be small, but they are clean, cozy, and attractive.

JAPANESE STYLE

TOKIWA, 7-27-9 Shinjuku, Shinjuku-ku 160. Tel. 03/3202-4321. Fax 03/3202-4325. 50 rms (30 with bath). A/C MINIBAR TV TEL **Station:** Shinjuku Sanchome, a 6-minute walk away; or Shin-Okubo, a 10-minute walk away.

$ Rates (per person, including service): ¥6,000 ($43) room without bath or meals; ¥11,000 ($78) room without bath but with breakfast and dinner; ¥7,200–¥9,600 ($51–$68) room with bath but no meals; ¥13,200–¥16,500 ($94–$118) room with bath and breakfast and dinner. AE, DC, JCB, V.

⑤ Tokiwa, while a bit far from the station, is a good medium-priced ryokan as far
as Tokyo goes. An older building surrounded by a white wall and gate on Meiji
Dori Avenue, this place is actually divided into two parts—a hotel and a
★ ryokan. All 50 rooms, however, are Japanese style. I suggest staying in the
ryokan part—it's more than 40 years old and has a lot more character, with
wooden beams, the earthy smell of tatami, and a quaint old rock-enclosed
public bath. Like most older Japanese buildings, it's cold and drafty in winter, but
each room has a *kotatsu*—a low table with a heating element underneath and a
blanket spread all around it. By sitting at the table with your legs stuck under the quilt,
you can stay pretty toasty. Rates are per person.

NEAR SHINAGAWA STATION

MIYAKO INN TOKYO, 3-7-8 Mita, Minato-ku 108. Tel. 03/3454-3111.
Fax 03/3454-3397. 405 rms (all with bath). A/C MINIBAR TV TEL **Station:**
Tamachi, Mita, or Sengakuji, each within a 6-minute walk.
$ Rates (including tax and service): ¥10,400–¥10,900 ($74–$78) single;
¥16,200–¥33,000 ($115–$236) twin; ¥16,200 ($115) double. AE, DC, JCB,
MC, V.
This combination business and city hotel rises 14 stories high in southern Tokyo.
Rooms on the top floor have the best views, facing either Tokyo Bay or Tokyo Tower
in the distance. All rooms come with the usual minibar, TV (with extra charges for
movies), cotton kimono, alarm clock, and hot-water thermos and tea. Facilities
include Japanese, Chinese, and Western restaurants, a bar, and a travel agency.
Differences in room rates are reflected in the size of the room and the bed.

SHINAGAWA PRINCE HOTEL, 4-10-30 Takanawa, Minato-ku 108.
03/3440-1111, or toll free 800/542-8686 in the U.S. Fax 03/3441-7092. 1,283
rms (all with bath). A/C MINIBAR (in some) TV TEL **Station:** Shinagawa, a
1-minute walk away.
$ Rates: ¥9,200 ($66) single; ¥14,300–¥24,000 ($102–$171) twin; ¥14,300
($102) double.
A gleaming white building just a minute's walk from the station, this hotel complex
consists of a main building, an annex, 13 restaurants and bars, and a sports center
with tennis courts, bowling lanes, and a fitness center (fee charged). The main
building, with 1,016 single rooms, caters to Japanese businessmen on weekdays and
students on weekends and holidays. The annex, added in 1986, has 257 twin and
double rooms. If you're staying in one of the single rooms, ask for a room above the
10th floor, where you have a view of either mountains on the west side or the sea on
the east side. Annex rooms have the extra benefit of a minibar but the views are
unexciting.

ROPPONGI

HOTEL IBIS, 7-4-14 Roppongi, Minato-ku 106. Tel. 03/3403-4411. Fax
03/3479-0609. 182 rms (all with bath). A/C MINIBAR TV TEL **Station:** Roppongi,
a 1-minute walk away.
$ Rates (including service and tax): ¥14,300–¥16,500 ($102–$118) single;
¥19,000–¥28,000 ($136–$200) double; ¥23,000–¥28,000 ($164–$200) twin;
¥29,000 ($207) triple. AE, DC, JCB, MC, V.
If you want to stay close to the night action of Roppongi, the Ibis is about as close as
you can get. It caters to both businessmen and to couples who come to Roppongi's
discos and don't make (or want to make) the last subway home. The lobby is on the
fifth floor, above which are the guest rooms. Small but comfortable they feature
modern furniture, windows that can be opened, and TV with English-language cable
and CNN. On the 13th floor is the Sky Restaurant, an inexpensive French bistro
offering a good view of the surrounding area.

HARAJUKU & AOYAMA

NATIONAL CHILDREN'S CASTLE (Kodomo-no-Shiro Hotel), **5-53-1 Jingumae, Shibuya-ku 150.** Tel. 03/3797-5677. 27 rms (all with bath). A/C TV TEL **Station:** Omote Sando, a 7-minute walk away; or Shibuya, a 10-minute walk away.

$ Rates (including tax and service charge): ¥6,900 ($49) single; ¥14,300–¥15,400 ($102–$110) twin; from ¥19,000 ($136) Japanese-style room. AE, DC, JCB, MC, V.

The National Children's Castle is a great place to stay if you're with children. In addition to containing a small hotel on the seventh and eighth floors, this complex boasts a sophisticated indoor/outdoor playground for children, complete with a clinic and restaurants. Hotel guests range from businesspeople to families and young college students. The rooms, mainly twins, are simple, nice, new, and bright, with large windows to let in the sunshine. The most expensive twins, which face toward Shinjuku, have the best views. Note that the hotel's three singles do not have windows, but you can pay extra to stay in a twin. There are also three Japanese-style rooms, available for three or more persons and great for families wishing to experience the traditional Japanese life-style. Since the number of rooms is limited, it's best to make reservations at least 6 months in advance, especially if you plan on being in Tokyo in the summer. The front desk is on the seventh floor.

PRESIDENT HOTEL, 2-2-3 Minami Aoyama, Minato-ku 107. Tel. 03/3497-0111. Fax 03/3401-4816. 212 rms (all with bath). A/C MINIBAR TV TEL **Station:** Aoyama-Itchome, a 1-minute walk away.

$ Rates: ¥12,000–¥13,700 ($86–$98) single; ¥16,500–¥22,000 ($118–$157) twin; ¥17,500 ($125) double. AE, DC, JCB, MC, V.

Although a small hotel, the President is one of the best deals in town, offering some of the same conveniences as the larger and more expensive hotels (like room service and TV with CNN), plus a great location between Akasaka, Shinjuku, and Roppongi. Its rooms are small but clean, comfortable, and pleasant. They come with hot water for tea, a hairdryer, a radio, and cotton kimono, among other amenities. The lobby, pleasingly elegant but unpretentious, has a somewhat European atmosphere. The President has two very good restaurants, one Japanese and one French. Foreigners constitute 50% of the clientele.

ELSEWHERE IN TOKYO

THE FAIRMONT HOTEL, 2-1-17 Kudan Minami, Chiyoda-ku 102. Tel. 03/3262-1151. Fax 03/3264-2476. 208 rms (all with bath). A/C MINIBAR TV TEL **Station:** Kudanshita, a 10-minute walk away.

$ Rates: ¥10,600–¥21,000 ($76–$150) single; ¥19,800–¥24,000 ($141–$171) twin/double. AE, DC, JCB, MC, V.

This small hotel is beautifully situated on a quiet street opposite the Imperial Palace moat, which is lined with cherry trees—a real treat when the blossoms burst forth in spring. Guests like the Fairmont because it's an older hotel (built in 1952) and because it's conveniently located, yet away from the hustle and bustle of downtown Tokyo. One of the hotel's restaurants, the Brasserie de la Verdure, has a view of the moat, while the French restaurant Cerisiers looks out onto a pleasant small garden with a waterfall. The more expensive rooms are larger and face the palace moat—definitely worth it during cherry-blossom season. All rooms have TV with English-language cable and CNN broadcasts.

GAJOEN KANKO HOTEL, 1-8-1 Shimo-Meguro, Meguro-ku 153. Tel. 03/3491-0111. Fax 03/3495-2450. 100 rms (all with bath). A/C MINIBAR TV TEL **Station:** Meguro, an 8-minute walk away.

$ Rates: ¥10,000 ($71) single; ¥16,500–¥22,000 ($157) twin/double. AE, DC, JCB, MC, V.

★ This older, rather eccentric-looking hotel is one of my favorites in Tokyo. Built in the early 1930s, with a decidedly Asian atmosphere, it boasts wood paneling and Japanese prints on the lobby ceiling and intricately inlaid shell and mother-of-pearl designs in its two old elevators. In its early days it was a hospital; then, after World War II, American army personnel were stationed here for a decade. Over the years the hotel became more and more rundown. In 1986 extensive renovations cleaned up the lobby and guest rooms and added a new wing, and today the hotel caters to a large Chinese clientele. Rooms come in a variety of shapes and sizes, but most have large windows and spacious tiled bathrooms. The best rooms are those on a corner or those facing the backyard, where there are trees. All TVs feature remote control and cable with CNN broadcasts. Facilities include French and Chinese restaurants.

TOKYO YMCA HOTEL, 7 Mitoshiro-cho, Kanda, Chiyoda-ku 101. Tel. 03/3293-1911. Fax 03/3293-1926. 40 rms (all with bath). A/C TV TEL **Station:** Shin-Ochanomizu, a 3-minute walk away; Ogawamachi, a 2-minute walk away; or Awajicho, a 5-minute walk away.
$ Rates: ¥11,000 ($78) single; ¥16,500–¥19,800 ($118–$141) twin. YMCA members receive ¥500 ($3.50) discount. No credit cards.

Where else but in Tokyo would there be a YMCA as expensive as a moderately priced hotel? However, this place is spanking new, modern, and spotless, with an atmosphere better than most business hotels that fall into this price category. Fully carpeted, it has one Western restaurant, a pharmacy, and a beauty salon, and there's laundry service. Both men and women are accepted, and rooms (which are mostly singles) come with hot water and tea, cotton kimono, and bilingual TV with remote control. Vending machines dispense beer and soft drinks.

JAPANESE STYLE

SEIFUSO ①, 1-12-15 Fujimi, Chiyoda-ku 102. Tel. 03/3263-0681. Fax 03/3237-8464. 18 rms (8 with bath). A/C MINIBAR TV TEL **Station:** Iidabashi, about a 7-minute walk away.
$ Rates (per person, including tax and service): ¥8,600 ($61) single without bath, ¥17,400 ($124) single with bath; ¥7,400 ($53) double/triple without bath, ¥13,900 ($99) double/triple with bath. No credit cards.

★ This is an excellent choice for travelers wishing to experience a ryokan for the first time. It's run by Setsuko Fukushima, a warm and friendly woman who doesn't speak a lot of English but who provides a sheet of English-language instructions about such things as the etiquette of the Japanese bath and where and when to wear slippers. More than 30 years old, most of Seifuso's rooms have their own small alcove (with chairs) overlooking a small Japanese garden. If you'd like to have the experience of staying in a ryokan but don't relish the idea of sleeping on the floor, there's one Western-style room with a double bed available. There are also separate public baths for men and women.

Meals range from ¥3,000 ($21.40) for tempura to ¥10,000 ($71) for a Japanese-style dinner, and are served in a dining area that looks out onto the garden. Breakfasts start at ¥1,300 ($9.30). Because Seifuso is a bit hard to find and has a sign in Japanese only, I suggest taking a taxi from Iidabashi.

SHIMIZU BEKKAN ②, 1-30-29 Hongo, Bunkyo-ku 113. Tel. 03/3812-6285. 21 rms (2 with bath). A/C MINIBAR TV TEL **Station:** Hongo Sanchome, an 8-minute walk away.
$ Rates (per person, including tax and service): ¥9,000 ($64) room without bath and meals; ¥10,000 ($71) room with breakfast only; ¥13,500 ($96) room with dinner and breakfast. Room with bath ¥1,000 ($7) per person extra. No credit cards.

Another ryokan that accepts foreigners and has had American guests, it has a variety of rooms available. Several meal options are offered and served in your room, and there are separate public baths for men and women. It's best to take a taxi to get here.

4. BUDGET

SHINJUKU

JAPANESE STYLE

INABASO RYOKAN, 5-6-13 Shinjuku, Shinjuku-ku 160. Tel. 03/3341-9581. Fax 03/3354-3332. 13 rms (all with bath). A/C FRIDGE (in some rooms) TV **Station:** Shinjuku, a 10-minute walk away; Shinjuku Sanchome, a 3-minute walk away; or Shinjuku Gyoen-mae, also a 3-minute walk away.
$ Rates: ¥4,400–¥5,500 ($31–$39) single; ¥8,800–¥10,500 ($63–$75) double; ¥11,500–¥14,800 ($82–$106) triple AE, V.

This ryokan, a member of the Japanese Inn Group, first began receiving foreign guests during the 1964 Olympics, and since then it has had many travelers from North America, Australia, and Europe. The rooms—two of which are Western style, with beds instead of futon—have their own private bath (with Western-style toilet) and bilingual TV. Some rooms have a refrigerator as well, but there's also a communal fridge where you can store food. Facilities include a coin-operated laundry. A Japanese breakfast of rice, bean-paste soup, fish, and ham and eggs is available for ¥600 ($4.30); coffee, toast, and eggs cost ¥300 ($2.15). A Japanese dinner runs ¥1,500 ($10.70).

KEIUNSO RYOKAN, 2-4-2 Yoyogi, Shibuya-ku 151. Tel. 03/3370-0333. 17 rms (3 with toilet only). AE TV TEL **Station:** Shinjuku, south exit, a 3-minute walk away.
$ Rates (per person): ¥6,500 ($46) single; ¥5,500 ($39) double. JCB.

This is one of the least expensive places to stay in Shinjuku, but the English-speaking woman who runs it expressed some reluctance about taking in foreigners who had never stayed in a ryokan before. Another disadvantage to staying here is that guests are requested to leave during the day, from 10am to 5pm. However, Keiunso Ryokan has such a good location that it's worth a try. The rooms are Japanese style, most with their own sink, but the bath is communal. Three of the rooms are Western style, with beds instead of futon.

OKUBO HOUSE, 1-11-32 Hyakunincho, Shinjuku-ku 169. Tel. 03/3361-2348. 76 beds. **Station:** Shin-Okubo, about a 2-minute walk away.
$ Rates: ¥3,300 ($24) single; ¥4,500–¥4,900 ($32–$35) double. Dormitory beds ¥1,900 ($13). No credit cards.

Ⓢ Judging from the number of old Tokyo hands who stayed here when they first arrived in the city, Okubo House has been around forever. It's not a member of the Japanese Inn Group; the owners are sometimes gruff; the place is closed during the day, from 9:30am to 5pm; and the front doors are locked at 11pm—but it's one of the cheapest places to stay in Tokyo. The private rooms are tiny—accommodating just two or three tatami mats—but they all have windows. The majority of beds here are dormitory style, separate for men and women (as are the public baths). Children are not accepted. Cotton kimonos and Japanese tea are provided, but not meals. This place is located one station north of Shinjuku Station on the Yamanote Line. To reach it, turn left out of Shin-Okubo's only exit, then turn left again on the first side street, which runs parallel to the train tracks. Okubo House is on this street, with a sign in English.

ASAKUSA

ASAKUSA PLAZA HOTEL, 1-2-1 Asakusa, Taito-ku 111. Tel. 03/3845-2621. Fax 03/3841-8862. 70 rms (all with bath). A/C TV TEL **Station:** Asakusa, about a 1-minute walk away.
$ Rates: ¥6,000–¥7,300 ($43–$52) single; ¥9,300–¥11,500 ($66–$82) double; ¥11,000–¥13,700 ($78–$98); ¥16,500 ($118) triple. AE, DC, JCB, MC, V.

This hotel is located just a few minutes' walk from the famous Sensoji Temple and

Nakamise Dori shopping street. The simple but adequate rooms come with hot-water pot and tea, as well as cotton kimono, among other amenities. Forty of the rooms are singles, but keep in mind that the cheapest ones don't have windows. The cheapest doubles are with semidouble-size beds. The front desk is on the second floor, and there's a Western-style restaurant specializing in seafood.

JAPANESE STYLE

KIKUYA RYOKAN, 2-18-9 Nishi-Asakusa, Taito-ku 111. Tel. 03/3841-6404. Fax 03/3841-6404. 10 rms (5 with bath). A/C FRIDGE (in rooms with private bath) TV **Station:** Tawaramachi, about an 8-minute walk away.

$ **Rates:** ¥4,600 ($33) single without bath, ¥5,200–¥6,600 ($37–$47) single with bath; ¥8,100 ($58) double without bath, ¥8,500–¥9,300 ($61–$66) double with bath; ¥11,000 ($78) triple without bath, ¥12,000 ($86) triple with bath. AE, MC, V.

This friendly establishment, a member of the Japanese Inn Group, is located in a modern red-brick building about a 10-minute walk from Sensoji Temple, just off Kappabashi Dori Avenue (which is lined with shops selling those plastic-food displays you see in restaurants throughout Japan). There's a communal refrigerator where you can store food and drinks. The front doors close at midnight.

RYOKAN MIKAWAYA BEKKAN, 1-31-11 Asakusa, Taito-ku 111. Tel. 03/3843-2345. Fax 03/3843-2348. 12 rms (none with bath). A/C TV **Station:** Asakusa, a few minutes' walk away.

$ **Rates:** ¥5,700 ($41) single; ¥10,500 ($75) double. Japanese breakfast ¥800 ($5.70). AE, MC, V.

⭐ This ryokan has a great location just off Nakamise Dori, a colorful, shop-lined pedestrian street leading to the famous Sensoji Temple—an area that gives you a feel for the older Japan. The 12 tatami rooms come with coin-operated TV, floor cushions with backrests, and Japanese-style vanity mirrors. A member of the Japanese Inn Group, the ryokan has a small inner courtyard with a goldfish pond, where you can sit outside in warm weather. A Japanese breakfast is available, but a Western-style breakfast of eggs, toast, salad, fruit, and coffee can be arranged for the same price. Doors close at 11:30pm, and to facilitate cleaning, guests are requested to leave their rooms from 10am to noon daily.

SAKURA RYOKAN, 2-6-2 Iriya, Taito-ku 110. Tel. 03/3876-8118. Fax 03/3873-9456. 16 rms (6 with bath). A/C TV TEL **Station:** Iriya, a 5-minute walk away.

$ **Rates:** ¥5,500 ($39) single without bath, ¥6,500 ($46) single with bath; ¥9,900 ($71) double without bath, ¥9,900–¥11,000 ($71–$78) double with bath; ¥13,200–¥14,800 ($94–$105) triple without bath. AE, MC, V.

A relative newcomer to the Japanese Inn Group, this modern concrete establishment is located just off the Kappabashi Dori and Kototoi Dori intersection, about a 10-minute walk from Sensoji Temple. The reception area is on the second floor, and the owner speaks English. A combination business/tourist hotel, Sakura has both Japanese and foreign guests. Rooms are spotless, all of them having a sink and an alarm clock, and guests have use of a coin laundry and an elevator. Half the rooms are Western style, available with or without private bath, while the Japanese-style rooms are all without private bath. Japanese breakfasts cost ¥700 ($5); Western-style breakfasts, ¥600 ($4.28). There's one Japanese-style room large enough for a family of six or seven persons, complete with a terrace.

UENO

HOTEL OHGAISO, 3-3-21 Ikenohata, Taito-ku 110. Tel. 03/3822-4611. Fax 03/3823-4340. 85 rms (all with bath). A/C MINIBAR TV TEL **Station:** Nezu, a 3-minute walk away; or Keisei (Skyliner) Ueno Station, Ikenohata exit, a 7-minute walk away.

$ **Rates:** ¥6,200 ($44) single; ¥11,500 ($82) twin. AE, DC, JCB, MC, V.

This hotel is rather unimaginative, but it's inexpensive, clean, and located across from

Ueno Park. Its rooms come with a desk, a refrigerator, a radio, a coin-operated TV, and a clock, among other amenities. There's a bar for hanging up clothes (no closet), and the windows can be opened. The hotel's single restaurant serves both Japanese- and Western-style breakfasts, as well as tempura, sashimi, and sukiyaki. The front doors close at 2am.

JAPANESE STYLE

KATSUTARO, 4-16-8 Ikenohata, Taito-ku 110. Tel. 03/3821-9808. Fax 03/3821-4789. 7 rms (4 with bath). A/C TV **Station:** Nezu, a 5-minute walk away; or Keisei (Skyliner) Station, Ikenohata exit, a 10-minute walk away.

$ Rates: ¥4,600 ($33) single without bath; ¥8,100 ($58) double without bath, ¥9,200 ($66) double with bath; ¥11,500 ($82) triple without bath, ¥13,800 ($98) triple with bath. Continental breakfast ¥400 ($2.85); Japanese breakfast ¥800 ($5.70). AE, MC, V.

In the neighborhood of Ueno Park is Katsutaro, with Japanese-style rooms that are quite large and have coin-operated TV. Try to avoid rooms that face the main street, as these can be quite noisy. The building itself is about 35 years old, and at least half the guests staying here are Japanese. In addition to the usual Japanese tea available at all Japanese inns, free coffee is on hand throughout the morning and afternoon. The place is a member of the Japanese Inn Group.

RYOKAN SAWANOYA, 2-3-11 Yanaka, Taito-ku 110. Tel. 03/3822-2251. Fax 03/3822-2252. 12 rms (2 with bath). A/C TV TEL **Station:** Nezu, Yanaka exit, about a 7-minute walk away.

$ Rates: ¥4,400–¥4,600 ($31–$33) single without bath; ¥8,000 ($57) double without bath, ¥8,800 ($63) double with bath; ¥10,800 ($77) triple without bath, ¥12,500 ($89) triple with bath. AE.

Although the ryokan itself is relatively modern-looking and unexciting, it's located northwest of Ueno Park in a delightful part of old Tokyo. The staff will give you a map outlining places of interest, as well as pamphlets on inexpensive accommodations throughout Japan; and if you pay for the call, the owner will even make your next reservation for you with another Japanese Inn Group member. Third-floor rooms are the best, in my opinion, because they have their own small balcony; all rooms come with a heater and a sink. Tea and instant coffee are available all day, and facilities include a beer and soda vending machine, a coin-operated washing machine and dryer (with free laundry detergent), a refrigerator, and a public bath. A breakfast of toast and fried eggs is available for ¥300 ($2.15); a Japanese breakfast, for ¥900 ($6.40). Highly recommended.

SUIGETSU, 3-3-21 Ikenohata, Taito-ku 110. Tel. 03/3822-4611. Fax 03/3823-4340. 66 rms (24 with bath). A/C MINIBAR TV TEL **Station:** Nezu, a 5-minute walk away; or Keisei (Skyliner) Ueno Station, Ikenohata exit, a 10-minute walk away.

$ Rates: ¥5,800 ($41) single without bath, ¥18,000 ($128) single with bath; ¥10,300 ($73) double without bath, ¥19,000 ($136) double with bath; ¥12,800 ($91) triple without bath, ¥29,000 ($207). AE, MC, V.

This large, modern ryokan is located behind the Hotel Ohgaiso, a Western-style hotel described above. The two places are under the same management, but each has its own front desk. Suigetsu caters mainly to Japanese families and tour groups. Rooms are Japanese style (some with a balcony) in a hotel-like setting, and come with coin-operated TV (with adult video), a stocked refrigerator, a safe, a mirror, and a table. Most rooms are without bath and are much cheaper than those with. There are three public baths; one for women, one for men, and one for families. A restaurant serves Japanese food and Japanese- and Western-style breakfasts.

HARAJUKU & AOYAMA

ASIA CENTER OF JAPAN, 8-10-32 Akasaka, Minato-ku 107. Tel. 03/3402-6111. Fax 03/3402-0738. 172 rms (100 with bath). A/C TV TEL **Station:** Aoyama-Itchome, about a 3-minute walk away.

$ Rates (including service and tax): ¥5,000 ($36) single without bath, ¥5,900–¥6,800 ($42–$48) single with bath; ¥6,600–¥7,200 ($47–$51) twin without bath, ¥10,000–¥10,500 ($71–$75) twin with bath; ¥7,800 ($56) double without bath, ¥9,300 ($66) double with bath; ¥10,600 ($76) triple without bath, ¥13,200 ($94) triple with bath. No credit cards.

A top choice in this category if you're looking for Western-style accommodations in the center of town. However, it's so popular that it's often fully booked. Everyone—from businessmen to students to travelers to foreigners teaching English—stays here. (I know one teacher who has lived here for years.) Resembling a college dormitory, the Asia Center has rooms with and without private bath, as well as an inexpensive cafeteria and snack bar. Accommodations are basic, no frills, and in the singles you can almost reach out and touch all four walls. Rooms come with the usual bed, desk, heater, and other amenities. The average price of meals served in the cafeteria is ¥600 ($4.30) for breakfast, ¥850 ($6.05) for lunch, and ¥1,500 ($10.70) for dinner. It's about a 15-minute walk to Roppongi, where all the night action is.

OTHER TOKYO ACCOMMODATIONS

JAPANESE STYLE

KIMI RYOKAN, 2-1034 Ikebukuro, Toshima-ku 171. Tel. 03/3971-3766. 41 rms (none with bath). A/C TV (in some rooms) TEL **Station:** Ikebukuro, west exit, about a 5-minute walk away.
$ Rates: ¥3,300–¥4,000 ($23.50–$28.50) single; ¥6,000–¥6,500 ($43–$46) double; ¥6,500–¥7,500 ($46–$53.50) twin. No credit cards.

This place is spotlessly clean, and although it was extensively remodeled in 1986, there are such Japanese touches as sliding screens and traditional Japanese music, playing softly in the hallways. Kimi now caters exclusively to foreigners and is so popular that there's sometimes a waiting list to get in. The tatami-style guest rooms are cheerful and clean. There are coin-operated heaters and air conditioners, as well as coin-operated TVs (in the twin and double rooms). Facilities include a TV lounge, a soda machine, a pay telephone from which you can make international calls, and free tea available throughout the day. The police station to the right of the subway station has maps that will guide you to Kimi. A great place to stay.

SANSUISO, 2-9-5 Higashi Gotanda, Shinagawa-ku 141. Tel. 03/3441-7475. 9 rms (2 with bath). A/C TV **Station:** Gotanda, a 5-minute walk away.
$ Rates: ¥4,700 ($33) single without bath, ¥4,900 ($35) single with bath; ¥8,800 ($63) double without bath, ¥9,200 ($66) double with bath; ¥12,200 ($87) triple without bath. AE, V.
The friendly and accommodating couple who run this place don't speak any English, but they have a poster listing all pertinent questions, such as how many nights will you be staying, etc. The ryokan, which is a member of the Japanese Inn Group, is very clean and rooms come with the usual hot water and tea bags, cotton kimono and towel, coin-operated TV, mirror, heater, and other amenities. Some rooms have a Japanese toilet and bath. There's a midnight curfew.

THE Y'S

YMCA ASIA YOUTH CENTER, 2-5-5 Sarugaku-cho, Chiyoda-ku 101. Tel. 03/3233-0611. Fax 03/3233-0633. 55 rms (all with bath). A/C TV TEL **Station:** Suidobashi, a 5-minute walk away; or Jimbocho, a 10-minute walk away.
$ Rates (including tax): ¥7,400 ($53) single; ¥12,700 ($91) twin; ¥17,500 ($125) triple. YMCA member discount ¥500 ($3.55). No credit cards.
This modern-looking concrete facility opened in 1980. Both men and women of any

age are accepted, and about 30% of the guests are Korean. Rooms are very simple but have all the basics. Japanese or Western breakfasts are ¥1,000 ($7.15), lunches start at ¥1,000 ($7.15), and dinners start at ¥1,500 ($10.70). Facilities include an indoor swimming pool (fee: ¥1,000 or $7.15). There's a midnight curfew.

TOKYO YWCA SADOWARA HOSTEL 4, 3-1-1 Ichigaya Sadowara-cho, Shinjuku-ku 162. Tel. 03/3268-7313. Fax 03/3268-4452. 20 rms (18 with toilet only, 2 with bath). A/C TEL **Station:** Ichigaya, Ichigaya exit, a 7-minute walk away.
$ Rates (including tax): ¥5,800 ($41) single with toilet only; ¥11,300 ($81) twin with toilet only, ¥12,400 ($88) twin with bath. No credit cards.
This YWCA is located in a spotless modern building. In addition to women travelers, it also accepts married couples, but only for one of its two twins that have a private bathroom and a kitchenette. All rooms have a sink. For communal use there's an iron and an ironing board, a kitchen, and a refrigerator. The front doors close at 11pm.

YOUTH HOSTELS

TOKYO INTERNATIONAL YOUTH HOSTEL, 21-1 Kaguragashi, Shinjuku-ku 162. Tel. 03/3235-1107. 138 beds. **Station:** Iidabashi, a 1-minute walk away.
$ Rates (per person): ¥2,600 ($18.50) member; ¥3,300 nonmember. Breakfast ¥400 ($2.85); dinner ¥800 ($5.70). No credit cards.
This hostel is definitely the best place to stay in its price range: it's new, spotlessly clean, and modern, and it offers a great view of Tokyo. No youth hostel card required; no age limit. The lobby is on the 18th floor of the new Central Plaza Building. All 138 beds are dormitory style, with two, four, or five bunk beds to a room. The rooms are very pleasant, with big windows, and each bed has its own curtain for privacy. If there are vacancies, you can stay longer than the 3-day maximum. In summer you must reserve about 3 months in advance. Closed from 10am to 3pm and locked at 10:30pm (lights out). You have free use of a washer and dryer.

TOKYO YOYOGI YOUTH HOSTEL, National Olympic Memorial Youth Center, 3-1 Yoyogi-Kamizono, Shibuya-ku 151. Tel. 03/3467-9163. 150 beds. **Station:** Sangubashi, about a 5-minute walk away.
$ Rates (per person): ¥1,900 ($13.50). No credit cards.
On the west side of Meiji Shrine Outer Garden, in an enclosed complex of buildings surrounded by a fence, this hostel is in Building 14. The whole compound housed American occupation troops after World War II, then accommodated athletes during the 1964 Olympics. It's now devoted to a number of youth activities. There are 150 beds here, for Japan Youth Hostel Association members only. No meals are served, but there are cooking facilities. There's a large Japanese-style bath in a neighboring building. The hostel is closed daily from 10am to 5pm, and the front gate closes at 10pm.

CAPSULE HOTELS

Because Akasaka caters primarily to Japanese businessmen, it doesn't have any budget tourist hotels. Instead, it has what are known as capsule hotels, which became popular in the early 1980s. They are used primarily by Japanese businessmen who have spent an evening out drinking with fellow workers and have missed the last train home—a capsule hotel is cheaper than a taxi home. At any rate, accommodation in one of these establishments is a small unit no larger than a coffin, consisting of a bed, a private color TV, an alarm clock, and a radio. These units are usually stacked two deep in rows down a corridor, and the only thing separating you from your probably inebriated neighbor is a curtain. A cotton kimono and a locker are provided, and baths and toilets are communal. Most capsule hotels do not accept women; the two listed here are no exception.

CAPSULE INN AKASAKA, 6-14-1 Akasaka, Minato-ku 107. Tel. 03/ 3588-1811. 288 beds. A/C TV TEL **Station:** Akasaka, a 3-minute walk away.
$ Rates: ¥4,400 ($31) per person. No credit cards.
Located just off Akasaka Dori Street, this capsule hotel for men offers only a sauna and a public bath. Check-in is after 5pm, and checkout is at 10am.

FONTAINE AKASAKA, 4-3-5 Akasaka, Minato-ku 107. Tel. 03/3583-6554. 367 beds. **Station:** Akasaka, a 2-minute walk away; or Akasaka-mitsuke, 5-minute walk away.
$ Rates: ¥5,300 ($38) per person. AE, DC, JCB, MC, V.
This place is located right in the heart of Akasaka's nightlife—Hitosugi Dori, near the TBS Building. It offers a sauna, a public bath, no-smoking floors, and vending machines selling everything from beer and instant noodles to toothbrushes. Its English brochure says sternly, "Persons whose bodies are tattooed are requested to keep out" (tattoos are associated with Japanese gangsters). Also, "Dead drunks are requested to keep out." Ah, the joys of Japanized English. Check-in is after 5pm, and checkout is at 10am.

5. HOTELS NEAR THE NARITA AIRPORT

If you find yourself on a stopover at the New Tokyo International Airport in Narita for one or two nights, you may not want to take the 1- to 2-hour trip to a hotel in Tokyo. There are a number of nearby Western-style hotels that operate free shuttle buses to and from the airport. Rooms are soundproofed and have the usual conveniences, but otherwise there's nothing that really distinguishes one place from the next. Reservations can be made at the hotel counter in the arrival wing of the airport. The telephone prefix for Narita is 0476, which you needn't dial if you're calling from the airport.

If you find yourself with some spare time, be sure to visit Shinshoji Temple, popularly known as Narita-san, which is located close to the train station in downtown Narita. It's a Buddhist temple dedicated to Fudo, god of fire, and is visited by more than 10 million people each year—usually when they have a favor to ask, whether it be good health, a happy marriage, or success in passing a university entrance exam. Behind the temple is a 40-acre Japanese garden with three ponds and many flowering trees and bushes, including wisteria, plum, and cherry.

ANA HOTEL NARITA, 68 Horinouchi, Narita, Chiba. Tel. 0476/33-1311. Fax 0476/33-0244. 424 rms (all with bath). A/C MINIBAR TV TEL **Transportation:** Free 10-minute shuttle service from airport.
$ Rates: ¥15,900 ($113) single; ¥21,000–¥25,000 ($150–$178) double/twin. AE, DC, JCB, MC, V.
This is one of Narita's newer hotels, a gleaming white establishment located between the airport and the town of Narita. Rooms are comfortable, decorated in soft, warm colors and featuring double-paned windows that open, as well as TV with CNN broadcasts. There are six dining spots, including teppanyaki, Chinese, French, and Japanese restaurants, and a bar on the 17th floor. Facilities include an indoor pool.

HOLIDAY INN—NARITA, 320-1 Tokko, Narita, Chiba. Tel. 0476/32-1234. Fax 0467/32-0617. 280 rms (all with bath). A/C MINIBAR TV TEL **Transportation:** Free 5-minute shuttle service from airport.
$ Rates: ¥14,300–¥18,700 ($102–$133) single; ¥18,700 ($133) double; ¥22,000 ($157) twin. AE, DC, JCB, MC, V.
This hotel, located just a mile from the airport, is similar to Holiday Inns in the United States. Its pleasantly decorated rooms offer TV with cable and CNN broadcasts. Facilities include an outdoor swimming pool, a sauna (for men only), five restaurants (steaks, plus Japanese, Chinese, and Western cuisine), and a bar/restaurant on the ninth floor with views of the airport.

NARITA AIRPORT REST HOUSE, P.O. Box 126, Narita Airport, Chiba.

Tel. 0476/32-1212. Fax 0476/32-1209. 210 rms (all with bath). A/C MINIBAR TV TEL **Transportation:** Free shuttle service from airport.
$ Rates (including service and tax): ¥12,900 ($923) single; ¥16,100 ($115) double; ¥18,100 ($129) twin. AE, DC, JCB, MC, V.

In this square white building located right beside the airport terminal, the rooms are rather sterile but have everything you need, from TV to minibar to alarm clock. Four TV screens in the hotel give the latest information on arrival and departure times for all airlines. There are a Japanese restaurant, a Western restaurant, and a bar in the hotel.

NARITA INTERNATIONAL HOTEL, 650-35 Nanae, Tomisato-mura Inba-gun, Chiba. Tel. 0476/93-1234. Fax 0476/93-4834. 512 rms (all with bath). A/C TV TEL **Transportation:** Free 15-minute shuttle service from airport.
$ Rates: ¥15,400 ($110) single; ¥19,800 ($141) double; ¥24,000 ($171) twin. AE, DC, JCB, MC, V.

This hotel is an affiliate of Northwest Airlines. Its rooms are large for Japan, and the hotel is surrounded by woods and fields. Facilities include an outdoor swimming pool, and Japanese and Western restaurants. There's free shuttle-bus service daily to Narita-san Temple.

NARITA VIEW HOTEL, 700 Kosuge, Narita, Chiba. Tel. 0476/32-1111. Fax 0476/32-1078. 504 rms (all with bath). A/C TV TEL **Transportation:** Free 10-minute shuttle service from airport.
$ Rates: ¥14,300 ($102) single; ¥19,800 ($141) double; ¥24,000 ($171) twin. AE, DC, JCB, MC, V.

Located 10 minutes away from both the airport and the Narita train station. Facilities here include seven restaurants, serving Western, Japanese, Chinese, and French food; one bar and one tea lounge; a sauna, a gym, and indoor and outdoor pools; and a garden.

HOTEL NIKKO NARITA, 500 Tokko, Narita, Chiba. Tel. 0476/32-0032. Fax 0476/32-3993. 528 rms (all with bath). A/C MINIBAR TV TEL **Transportation:** Free 5-minute shuttle service from airport.
$ Rates: ¥14,800 ($106) single; ¥23,000–¥29,000 ($164–$207) double/twin. AE, DC, JCB, MC, V.

This hotel offers an outdoor swimming pool, tennis courts, and two bars and four restaurants, serving Japanese, French, Chinese, and Western cuisine.

TOKYO DINING

From stand-up noodle shops at train stations to exclusive sushi bars, restaurants in Tokyo number at least 45,000, which gives you at least some idea of how fond the Japanese are of food and of eating out. In a city where apartments are so small and cramped that entertaining at home is almost unheard of, restaurants serve as places for socializing, meeting friends, and wooing business associates—as well as excuses for drinking a lot of beer, sake, and whisky. I know people in Tokyo who claim they haven't cooked in years—and that doesn't mean that they're millionaires (although it could mean that they're bad cooks). It just means that they take advantage of one of the best deals in Tokyo—the fixed-price lunch. Called a teishoku in Japanese restaurants, and also variously referred to as a "set lunch," "set course," or simply "course," the fixed-price menu usually includes an appetizer, a main course with several side dishes, coffee or tea, and dessert. Even the most prohibitively expensive Tokyo restaurants often offer set-lunch menus, allowing you to dine in style at very reasonable prices.

To keep your costs down, therefore, try eating your biggest meal at lunch. However, because the Japanese tend to order fixed-price meals rather than à la carte, especially at Western restaurants, set dinners are also usually available (though not as cheap as set lunches).

Although Japanese food is varied, healthful, and delicious, even the most dedicated Japanophile starts craving Western food after a while. In fact, even the Japanese themselves crave it, as shown by the increase in Western restaurants in Tokyo in the past decade. So I have included a goodly number of establishments serving food other than Japanese. The most popular Western restaurants are French and Italian, which can be quite expensive. Other international cuisines tend to be more reasonably priced, including Mexican, Chinese, Thai, Indian, and American. Ethnic restaurants have literally mushroomed in popularity in the past few years; in fact, they have become something of an epidemic. Result? You can dine at French, Indian, and other ethnic restaurants that rival those anywhere else in the world.

Japanese patrons in Tokyo's top restaurants almost never spend their own money, because most of them are on expense accounts, without which many of these establishments wouldn't survive. If you're not on an expense account, however, don't despair. The restaurants I've listed in the **expensive** category will allow you to splurge, to experience some of Japan's most exquisite cuisine without having to mortgage your house upon your return home. And don't forget about those set-lunch courses—great bargains by any standard.

So many of Tokyo's good restaurants fall into the **moderate** category that it's tempting simply to eat your way through the city—and the range of cuisine is so great that you could eat something different at each meal. Be sure to read the list of restaurants in the expensive category—many have great set courses for lunch at very reasonable prices.

Many of Tokyo's most colorful, noisy, and popular restaurants fall into the **inexpensive** category, frequented by the city's huge working population as they catch a quick lunch or socialize with friends after hours. But even if you're on a budget, be sure to read over the restaurants listed in the upper- and medium-range categories—most of them offer great lunches at reasonable prices, which means that you may be able to splurge in style. For the most part, however, keep in mind that you can generally eat more economically at Japanese restaurants than at Western establishments. Remember to check the nightlife section for more suggestions on inexpensive drinking places that serve food.

Also remember that a 3% consumption tax will be added to bills totaling less than ¥7,500 ($53.55). For meals costing ¥7,500 and more, both the 3% consumption tax and a 3% local tax will be added to your bill. In addition, many first-class restaurants, as well as hotel restaurants, will add a 10% to 15% service charge in lieu of tipping. Unless otherwise stated, the prices I've given do not include the extra tax and charges.

See the "Food & Drink" section in Chapter 1 for an explanation of Japanese cuisine.

1. GINZA & HIBIYA

EXPENSIVE

JAPANESE FOOD

KINSEN ③, 4-4-10 Ginza. Tel. 3561-8708.
   Cuisine: KAISEKI. **Reservations:** Recommended for lunch, a must for dinner.
   Station: Ginza, a 1-minute walk away.
$ **Prices** (including tax and service charge): Set dinners ¥10,000–¥13,000 ($71.40–$92.85); set lunches ¥2,600–¥6,500 ($18.50–$46.50) AE, JCB, MC, V.
   Open: Lunch daily 11:30am–2pm; dinner daily 5pm–9pm.
A conveniently located, modern kaiseki restaurant in the heart of Ginza, Kinsen is on Harumi Dori Avenue, on the fifth floor of the Ginza Kintetsu Building, just across the street from Jena Bookstore. There's no English menu, but various courses are available, so simply choose one to fit your budget. Food is served artistically arranged in various bowls and boxes, consisting of elaborate kaiseki meals for dinner and lunch boxes to mini-kaiseki courses for lunch.

KISSO, 4-6-18 Ginza. Tel. 3535-5035.
   Cuisine: KAISEKI. **Reservations:** Recommended for lunch and dinner. **Station:** Ginza, a 1-minute walk away.

A NOTE ON JAPANESE SYMBOLS

Many hotels, restaurants, and other establishments in Japan do not have signs giving their names in English letters. As an aid to the reader, Appendix C lists the Japanese symbols for all such places described in this guide. Each set of symbols has a number, which corresponds to the number that appears inside an oval next to the establishment's boldfaced name in the text. Thus, to find the Japanese symbols for, say, Osaka's **Hotel Hokke Club** ⑬⑧, refer to number 138 in the appendix.

$ Prices: Set-dinner courses ¥6,500–¥9,300 ($46.40–$66.40); set lunches ¥1,500–¥5,500 ($10.70–$39.30). AE, DC, JCB, MC, V.
Open: Lunch Tues–Sat 11:30am–2pm, dinner Tues–Sat 5–9pm.

★ Whereas most kaiseki restaurants imitate traditional Japan in their decor, this kaiseki restaurant flaunts modernity with an artistic flair, reflected in both its interior design and its choice of serving bowls and plates. A small, fifth-floor restaurant located on Chuo Dori Avenue between Mitsukoshi and Matsuya department stores, it has black granite walls, offset by a display of modern sake cups and glasses. It is the sister restaurant of a Kisso establishment in Roppongi, which also sells modern tableware. Only set courses are served, and the restaurant prides itself on presentation. It's a favorite lunchtime haunt of fashionable housewives shopping in Ginza.

SUSHIKO ④, 6-3-8 Ginza. Tel. 3571-1968.
Cuisine: SUSHI. **Reservations:** Required. **Station:** Ginza or Hibiya, less than a 5-minute walk away.
$ Prices: Set courses ¥10,000–¥15,000 ($71.40–$107.15). No credit cards.
Open: Lunch Mon–Sat noon–2pm; dinner Mon–Sat 5–9:30pm. **Closed:** Sun and hols.

If you're in pursuit of exclusive sushi shops in Tokyo, your search will eventually take you here. There's no written menu and its counter seating is for 11 customers only. Owned by a fourth-generation restaurateur, this establishment doesn't display its fish as in most sushi bars but rather keeps the fish freshly refrigerated until the moment it meets the swift blade of the expert chefs. Expect to spend about ¥15,000 ($107) per person on a meal here.

TEN-ICHI, 6-6-5 Ginza, Namiki Dori St. Tel. 3571-1949.
Cuisine: TEMPURA. **Reservations:** Recommended for lunch, a required for dinner. **Station:** Ginza, a few minutes' walk away.
$ Prices: Set dinner courses ¥8,500–¥15,000 ($60.70–$107.14); set lunches ¥6,000–¥13,200 ($42.85–$94.30). AE, DC, JCB, MC, V.
Open: Mon–Sat 11:30am–9:30pm; Sun noon–9pm.

Located on Namiki Dori Street in the heart of the Ginza's nightlife, this is the main shop of a restaurant chain that first served tempura in Tokyo more than 50 years ago and helped this style of cooking gain worldwide recognition by serving important foreign customers. Today Ten-ichi still has one of the best reputations in town for serving the most delicately fried foods, and you can sit at a counter to watch the chef prepare your meal.

There are more than ten Ten-ichi restaurants in Tokyo. Other Ten-ichi restaurants can be found in the Ginza Sony Building on the intersection of Harumi Dori and Sotobori Dori avenues (tel. 3571-8373), the Imperial Hotel's Tower basement (tel. 3503-1001), Akasaka 3-chome, Misujidori (tel. 3583-0107), and both the Shibuya and Ikebukuro Seibu department stores (tel. 3496-5277 and 3984-1930, respectively).

NON-JAPANESE FOOD

MAXIM'S, 5-3-1 Ginza. Tel. 3572-3621.
Cuisine: FRENCH. **Reservations:** Recommended. **Station:** Ginza, 1-minute walk away.
$ Prices: Main dishes average ¥4,900–¥10,700 ($35–$76.40); set-dinner course ¥22,000 ($157); set lunches ¥6,500–¥10,000 ($46.40–$71.40). AE, DC, JCB, MC, V.
Open: Lunch Mon–Sat 11:30am–2:30pm; dinner Mon–Sat 5:30–11pm.

It may seem strange to find a top-class restaurant in the third basement of the Sony Building, but then this is Japan. Opened in 1966 and an exact copy of Paris's famous Maxim's, the Tokyo restaurant is decorated in art-nouveau style. The small dining room is one of the most romantic in town—very French, with gilded mirrors, cut-glass panels, mahogany paneling, and crimson cushions. Service is discreet and professional, as waiters bring you such specialties as goose liver pâté, sole cooked in

French vermouth, sautéed tenderloin with truffle sauce, roast duckling with peaches, or grilled prime rib of Kobe beef. The average à la carte meal is around ¥25,000 ($178.55). The set lunches and set-dinner course change daily. For dinner, men are required to wear a suit and tie.

MODERATE

JAPANESE FOOD

BENIHANA OF NEW YORK, 6-3-7 Ginza. Tel. 3571-9060.
   Cuisine: TEPPANYAKI. **Reservations:** Recommended. **Station:** Hibiya, a 5-minute walk; Ginza, a 10-minute walk away.
$ Prices: Set courses ¥3,800–¥22,000 ($27.15–$157.15); set lunches ¥1,800–¥3,300 ($12.85–$23.55). AE, DC, JCB, MC, V.
   Open: Mon–Sat 11am–10pm, Sun and hols 11am–8pm.

I'm not sure how to categorize this restaurant. With about 50 Benihana restaurants in the United States, most Americans are familiar with this chain and consider it Japanese food. However, the restaurant in Tokyo calls itself Benihana of New York, and what's more, all that theatrical bravado and karate-style knife chops are an American tradition and have very little to do with Japanese food-preparation methods. In any case, teppanyaki steak courses are the specialty here (with Kobe beef featured in the more expensive courses), along with side dishes of seafood that might include lobster, squid, shrimp, scallops, and mussels.

GINZA BENKAY, 7-2-17 Ginza. Tel. 3573-7335.
   Cuisine: JAPANESE. **Reservations:** Recommended for dinner. **Station:** Yurakucho or Hibiya, a few minutes' walk away.
$ Prices: Set-dinner courses ¥4,900–¥10,000 ($35–$71.40); set lunches ¥1,300–¥4,400 ($9.30–$31.40). AE, DC, JCB, MC, V.
   Open: Lunch Mon–Sat 11:30am–2pm; dinner Mon–Sat 5–9:30pm (last order).

This pleasant restaurant is a Japan Airlines affiliate and specializes in teppanyaki, sushi, shabu-shabu, lunch boxes, and kaiseki, each served in its own special dining area and available in a variety of price ranges. Coolly decorated with a stone-and-pebble floor, bamboo, wood, and shoji screens, it offers a variety of set courses. Lunch is the most economical time to come, featuring teppanyaki courses, an assorted plate of sushi, or a small kaiseki lunch box. Dinner courses include teppanyaki, sushi, or kaiseki, and a shabu-shabu course. It's located across from the International Arcade on the Ginza side, just a few minutes' walk from the Tourist Information Center. There's another Ginza Benkay located in the basement of the President Hotel in Aoyama (tel. 3402-0246), with the same hours.

KUSHI COLZA ⑤, 6-4-18 Ginza. Tel. 3571-8228.
   Cuisine: YAKITORI/KUSHIYAKI. **Reservations:** Recommended. **Station:** Hibiya, a 5-minute walk away; Ginza, a 10-minute walk away.
$ Prices: Appetizers ¥500–¥650 ($3.55–$4.65); set-dinner courses ¥3,300–¥4,900 ($23.55–$35). AE, DC, MC, V.
   Open: Mon–Fri 5–10pm; Sat and Sun 5–9pm.

Kikkoman is a well-known brand of soy sauce in Japan, and the Kikkoman company maintains a few restaurants as well, including this one. It serves yakitori and kushiyaki (also grilled meats and vegetables on skewers), delicately seasoned with—what else?—Kikkoman soy sauce. This place is small and pleasant, with an open counter where you can watch the chefs at work preparing your food. An English menu lists three set-dinner courses, which consist of various skewered filets of beef, fish, eel, or pork, along with appetizer, salad, soup, and dessert. A la carte selections for skewered specialties average ¥300 to ¥750 ($2.15 to $5.35) per skewer. Try the vegetable salad with soy sauce dressing.

OHMATSUYA ⑥, 5-4-18 Ginza. Tel. 3571-7053.
   Cuisine: GRILLED DISHES. **Reservations:** A must. **Station:** Ginza, about a 3-minute walk away.

JAPAN
★ TOKYO
GINZA AREA

ACCOMMODATIONS:
Ginza Capital Hotel **27**
Giza Dai-ei **26**
Ginza Dai-ichi Hotel **23**
Ginza Nikko Hotel **10**
Imperial Hotel **1**
Mitsui Urban Hotel
   Ginza **11**
Ramada Renaissance
   Ginza Tobu Hotel **24**
Hotel Seiyo Ginza **20**

DINING:
Attore **20**
Atariya **17**
Benihana of New York **4**
Chiang Mai **2**
Donto **3**
Ginza Benkay **8**
Kinsen **16**
Kisso **21**
Kujaku-cho **25**
Kushi Colza **6**
Maxim's **14**
Munakata **11**
Ohmatsuya **15**
Otako **12**
Rangetsu **19**
Shakey's **18**
Suehiro **22**
Sushi Sei **9**
Sushiko **7**
Ten-ichi **13**
Yakitori under the
   Tracks **5**

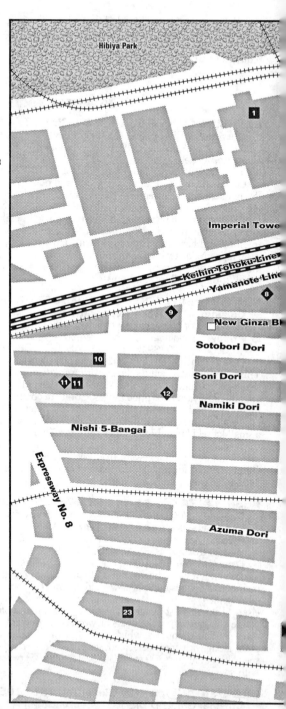

DINING & ACCOMODATIONS IN GINZA & HIBIYA

Hibiya Park

Hibiya Dori

Chiyoda Line

Hibiya Sta.

Yurakucho Sta.

☐ Marunouch Police Station

2

Hibiya Sta.

3

Tourist Information Center

Sogo Dept. Store ☐

Yuraku-cho Sta.

5

4

Sukiyabashi Shopping Center

Hankyu Dept. Store

Nishi Ginza Dept. Store

Hibiya Line

7 **6**

Seibu Dept. Store

☐ Hankyu Dept. Store

14 ☐

Sony Bldg.

13

Miyuki Dori

15

Ginza Sta.

Nishigobangai Dori

16

☐ Hanae Mori Bldg.

17

Chuo Dori

Ginza Sta.

Ginza Line

Matsuzakaya Dept. Store

18 **19**

22

20 **20** →

Harumi Dori

Showa Dori

25

Higashi Ginza Sta.

Toei Asakusa Line

26 **27**

$ Prices: Set-dinner courses ¥5,500–¥7,500 ($39.30–$53.55). AE, DC, V.
Open: Dinner Mon–Sat 5–10pm.

 It doesn't look like much from the outside, but go up the stairs to the second floor and you're instantly greeted by waitresses clad in traditional countryside clothing and by an atmosphere that very much evokes the feeling of an old farmhouse. Little wonder: part of the décor was brought from a 17th-century samurai house in northern Japan. Even the style of cooking is traditional, as customers grill their own food over a hibachi. Sake, served in a length of bamboo, is drunk from bamboo cups. Dinner courses, very reasonably priced, include such delicacies as grilled fish, skewered pieces of meat, and vegetables. This place is a true find—and an easy find at that. It's located on Sony Street, the small side street behind the Sony Building.

RANGETSU, 3-5-8 Ginza. Tel. 3567-1021.
   Cuisine: SUKIYAKI/SHABU-SHABU/KAISEKI/OBENTO. **Reservations.** Recommended. **Station:** Ginza, about a 3-minute walk away.
$ Prices: Set-dinner courses ¥2,400–¥15,000 ($17.15–$107.15); set lunches ¥1,300–¥3,800 ($9.30–$27.14). DC, JCB, MC, V.
   Open: Mon–Sat 11:30am–10pm, Sun and hols 11:30am–9pm.
This well-known Ginza restaurant has been dishing out sukiyaki, shabu-shabu, traditional lunch boxes, and steaks for more than four decades. It uses only Matsuzaka beef (bought whole and then carved up by the chefs), which ranges from the costlier fine-marbled beef to the cheaper cuts with thick marbling. There are also

---

Ⓕ   FROMMER'S SMART TRAVELER: RESTAURANTS

TIPS FOR VALUE-CONSCIOUS TRAVELERS

1. The teishoku, or daily special, is offered by Japanese restaurants for lunch or even the whole day; it's often a complete meal.
2. Lunch menus are offered by most expensive and medium-range restaurants at prices much cheaper than those for dinner menus, making lunchtime a good choice for a splurge.
3. Choose set courses, which are fixed-price meals usually offered for both lunch and dinner.
4. Have at least some of your meals at inexpensive Japanese restaurants selling noodles, sushi, pork cutlets, and other Japanese fare. These establishments are generally cheaper than those serving Western cuisine.
5. For a quick meal, order at takeout counters throughout the city (including most train stations), selling sushi obento lunch boxes.
6. For a snack, go to one of the city's coffee shops, which often offer a "morning service"—consisting of coffee, a small salad, a boiled egg, and toast—for less than ¥500 ($3.55).
7. Drinking establishments, especially yakitori-ya, also offer a variety of inexpensive dishes and snacks.

QUESTIONS TO ASK IF YOU'RE ON A BUDGET

1. Is there a teishoku, daily special, or set course? Since these are complete meals, they're usually cheaper than eating à la carte.
2. If the menu is in Japanese only, what is the price of beer or other alcoholic drinks? Drinks can really add to the bill.
3. Is there a table or snack charge? Some bars and drinking establishments charge extra for such things, so ask before sitting down.

various crab dishes (including a crab sukiyaki), kaiseki, sirloin steaks, and eel dishes. Especially good deals: the obento lunch boxes, available day and night, and the various set courses of tempura or steak offered for lunch. Most set dinner courses average ¥5,000 to ¥8,000 ($35.70 to $57.15). In the basement is a sake bar, with more than 80 different kinds of sake from all over Japan, which you can also order with your meal. Rangetsu is located on Chuo Dori Avenue, across from the Matsuya department store.

SUEHIRO ⑦, **6-11-1 Ginza. Tel. 3571-9271.**
   Cuisine: STEAKS/SUKIYAKI. **Reservations:** A must. **Station:** Ginza, a 5-minute walk away.
$ Prices: Set-dinner courses ¥5,500–¥20,000 ($39.30–$142.85); set lunches ¥2,700–¥8,800 ($19.30–$62.85). AE, DC, JCB, MC, V.
   Open: Daily 11:45am–10pm; Bay of Ginza daily 11:45am–1:30pm and 5:30–10:30pm.

This successful steak-and-sukiyaki chain, established in 1933 and claiming to be the first restaurant in Tokyo to serve sukiyaki, now boasts 17 stores throughout Japan. It recently updated and upgraded its main branch, located behind the Matsuzakaya department store. A shiny new building complete with an information counter on the main floor, it offers several floors of dining. Most formal and expensive is the European-style dining hall on the seventh floor, which serves Matsuzaka beefsteaks and teppanyaki. The sixth floor, featuring traditional Japanese décor, specializes in shabu-shabu and sukiyaki. Least expensive is the Bay of Ginza, in the basement, which offers French cuisine; steaks are the main course here. Of the daily specials, the best are the set steak dinners, which start at ¥5,500 ($39.30) and are available Monday through Wednesday until 7:30pm.

Other conveniently located Suehiro shops are found at 3-16-7 Akasaka (tel. 3585-9855), in the heart of Akasaka on Hitosugi Dori Street; and 4-1-15 Tsukiji (tel. 3542-3951).

SUSHI SEI ⑧, **8-2-13 Ginza. Tel. 3572-4770 and 3571-2772.**
   Cuisine: SUSHI. **Reservations:** Not necessary. **Station:** Hibiya, about a 5-minute walk away.
$ Prices: Sushi à la carte ¥100–¥300 (70¢–$2.15); set-lunch courses ¥1,000–¥2,000 ($7.15–$14.30) (basement only). AE, DC, JCB, MC, V.
   Open: Lunch Mon–Sat noon–2pm; dinner Mon–Sat 5–10:45pm. Closed: Hols.

One of a dependably good chain of medium-priced sushi bars, serving tender cuts of raw fish, this place is a natural for both novice and appreciative sushi fans. The ground-floor bar serves à la carte only; the basement bar is the place to go if you want one of the three lunch teishoku. The chef will prepare your food and place it on a raised platform on the counter in front of you, which serves as your plate. This restaurant is located near the elevated tracks of the Yamanote Line.

NON-JAPANESE FOOD

ATTORE, Hotel Seiyo Ginza, 1-11-2 Ginza. Tel. 3535-1111.
   Cuisine: ITALIAN. **Reservations:** Not necessary. **Station:** Ginza, a 5-minute walk away; or Ginza-Itchome, a 2-minute walk away.
$ Prices: Appetizers ¥900–¥3,500 ($6.40–$25); pasta ¥1,400–¥2,600 ($10–$17.15); main dishes ¥2,400–¥4,400 ($17.15–$31.40); set-lunch courses ¥1,800–¥2,500 ($12.85–$17.85). AE, DC, JCB, MC, V.
   Open: Daily 11am–10pm.

Although the Hotel Seiyo Ginza is one of Tokyo's most expensive and exclusive hotels, this Italian restaurant, located in its basement, serves reasonably priced meals. Modern, cheerful, and pleasant, with an open kitchen separated from the dining hall by a pane of glass, it offers a variety of pasta and main courses—from whole-wheat spaghetti with mushrooms and oven-baked spinach gnocchi with tomato sauce to calamari stuffed with shrimp. If you feel like splurging, there's a second, slightly pricier dining hall, its more elaborate menu including more seafood and meat dishes.

BUDGET

JAPANESE FOOD

ATARIYA ⑨, 3-5-17 Ginza. Tel. 3564-0045.
   Cuisine: YAKITORI. **Station:** Ginza, a 3-minute walk away.
$ **Prices:** Main dishes ¥600–¥1,100 ($4.30–$7.85); yakitori courses ¥1,500–¥2,700 ($10.70–$19.30), individual skewers ¥150–¥400 ($1.05–$2.85). No credit cards.
   Open: Dinner Mon–Sat 5–10pm (last order).

⭐ Because it's open only at night and serves yakitori, this is technically a drinking establishment, but it also makes a good choice for inexpensive dining. You have your choice of table or counter seating on the first floor of this yakitori-ya, while up on the second floor you take off your shoes and sit on split-reed mats. The waiters wear colorful twisted headbands. Since courses will include most parts of the chicken, including the liver, gizzard, and skin, you might wish to order à la carte for your favorites. The shop's name means "to be right on target, to score a bull's-eye," and according to its English pamphlet, eating here is certain to bring you good luck. Atariya is located behind the Wako department store (Suzuran Street).

DONTO, ⑩, **basement of Denki Building, 1-7-1 Yurakucho. Tel. 3201-3021.**
   Cuisine: NOODLES/TEMPURA/OBENTO/SASHIMI. **Station:** Hibiya, a 1-minute walk away.
$ **Prices:** A la carte dishes ¥650–¥2,700 ($4.65–$19.30); set-dinner courses ¥3,500–¥4,400 ($25–$31.40); set lunches ¥750–¥1,600 ($5.35–$11.40). AE, DC, JCB, MC, V.
   Open: Lunch Mon–Sat 11am–2:30pm; dinner Mon–Sat 5–10pm. **Closed:** Hols.

⭐ Located in Hibiya, across the street from the Tourist Information Center, this is a great place for lunch. Popular with the local working crowd and therefore best avoided between 1 and 2pm, it's pleasantly decorated with shoji screens, wooden floors, and an open kitchen. Choose what you want from the plastic display case, which shows various teishoku and set meals. Everything from noodles, sashimi, and tempura to kaiseki is available.

MUNAKATA, basement of Mitsui Urban Hotel, 8-6-15 Ginza. Tel. 3574-9356.
   Cuisine: MINI-KAISEKI/OBENTO/TEMPURA. **Station:** Shimbashi, a 2-minute walk away; or Hibiya, about a 10-minute walk away.
$ **Prices:** Mini-kaiseki lunch ¥3,000 ($21.40); tempura set course ¥2,200 ($15.70). AE, DC, JCB, MC, V.
   Open: Lunch daily 11:30am–4pm; dinner daily 5–10pm.
Kaiseki is one of the most expensive meals you can have in Japan, but there are some lunch specials here that make it quite reasonable. This basement restaurant is cozy, with slats of wood and low lighting that give customers a sense of privacy. In addition to mini-kaiseki meals, there are also tempura and various obento lunch boxes. A great place for lunch.

2. AKASAKA

EXPENSIVE

JAPANESE FOOD

GARDEN BARBECUE, New Otani Hotel, 4-1 Kioi-cho, Chiyoda-ku. Tel. 3265-1111.

Cuisine: TEPPANYAKI. **Reservations:** Recommended for dinner. **Station:** Yotsuya, about a 5-minute walk away; or Akasaka-mitsuke, a 3-minute walk away.

$ Prices: A la carte main dishes ¥1,300–¥9,000 ($9.30–$64.30); set-dinner courses ¥9,300–¥18,500 ($66.40–$132.15); set lunches ¥4,400–¥7,000 ($31.40–$50). AE, DC, JCB, MC, V.

Open: Lunch daily noon–2pm; dinner daily 6–9pm.

Located in the midst of the New Otani Hotel's 400-year-old garden, this teppanyaki restaurant is composed of three glass-enclosed pavilions, all with the same menu of Kobe beef, fish, lobster, and vegetables—cooked on a grill right in front of you. If you order a salad, try the soy sauce dressing; it's delicious. You will eat surrounded by peaceful views, making this place a good lunchtime choice.

HAYASHI ⑪, **4th floor of the Sanno Kaikan Building, 2-14-1 Akasaka. Tel. 3582-4078.**

Cuisine: GRILLED FOODS/RICE CASSEROLES. **Reservations:** A must for dinner. **Station:** Akasaka, a 1-minute walk away.

$ Prices: Set-dinner courses ¥5,500 ($39.30), ¥7,700 ($55), and ¥10,000 ($71.40); lunches ¥1,000 ($7.15). AE, DC, JCB, MC, V.

Open: Lunch Mon–Fri 11:30am–2pm; dinner Mon–Sat 5:30–10pm.

One of the most delightful old-time restaurants I've been to, this cozy, rustic-looking place serves home-style country cooking and specializes in grilled food, which you prepare yourself over your own square hibachi. Altogether, there are 10 grills in this small restaurant, some of them surrounded by tatami mats and some by wooden stools or chairs. As the evening wears on, the one-room main dining area can get quite smoky, but somehow that just adds to the atmosphere (sorry, couldn't resist saying that). Other nice touches are the big gourds and memorabilia hanging about and the waiters in traditional baggy pants. The owner of Hayashi, which opened in 1965, is almost always present and told me that it was his philosophy that the fire in the grills brought people more in touch with their basic feelings. "All mankind loves fire," he said. "For many years man has had a close relationship with fire. It opens our hearts and makes us relax."

Hayashi serves just three set menus, which change with the seasons. The ¥5,500 ($39.30) meal—which will probably end up being closer to ¥8,000 ($57.15) by the time you add drinks, tax, and service charge—may include such items as sashimi and vegetables, chicken, scallops, and gingko nuts, which you grill yourself. The ¥7,700 ($55) and ¥10,000 ($71.40) meals have more items, and may include oysters, abalone, beef, or fresh fish. At lunch, only *oyakodomburi* is served: literally, "parent and child," a simple rice dish with egg and chicken on top.

INAKAYA ⑫, **3-12-7 Akasaka. Tel. 3586-3054.**

Cuisine: GRILLED FOODS. **Reservations:** Accepted only until 7pm. **Station:** Akasaka or Akasaka-mitsuke, each about a 5-minute walk away.

$ Prices: Average meal ¥12,000 ($85.70). AE, DC, JCB, MC, V.

Open: Dinner daily 5–11pm.

Whenever I'm playing hostess to foreign visitors in Tokyo, I always take them to one of the city's three Inakaya restaurants (the other two are in Roppongi), and they've never been disappointed. The drama of the place alone is worth it. Customers sit at a long counter, on the other side of which are mountains of fresh vegetables, beef, and seafood. And in the middle of all that food, seated in front of a grill, are male cooks—ready to cook whatever you point to, in the style of robatayaki. Orders are yelled out by your waiter and are repeated in unison by all the other waiters, with the result that there is always this excited yelling going on. Sounds strange, I know, but actually it's a lot of fun. Food offerings may include yellowtail, red snapper, sole, king crab legs, giant shrimp, steak, meatballs, gingko nuts, potatoes, eggplant, and asparagus, all piled high in wicker baskets and ready for the grill.

UNKAI, ANA Hotel Tokyo, 1-12-33 Akasaka. Tel. 3459-6921.
Cuisine: KAISEKI/VARIOUS TRADITIONAL FOODS. **Reservations:** Recom-

mended for dinner. **Station:** Roppongi, Akasaka, Kamiyacho, Toranomon, or Kokkai Gijido-mae, each within a 15-minute walk away.

$ Prices: A la carte dishes ¥1,000–¥6,500 ($7.15–$46.40); set-dinner courses ¥10,000–¥22,000 ($71.40–$157.15); set lunches ¥3,800–¥12,000 ($27.15–$85.70). AE, DC, JCB, MC, V.

Open: Lunch daily 11:30am–2:30pm; dinner daily 5–10pm.

Another hotel restaurant with a good selection of Japanese food served in a charming setting is the Unkai, overlooking a pond and a waterfall. With a stone pathway leading through the dining area, and a replica of a thatch-roofed house built as a façade into one of the walls, the atmosphere is one of a country village. At midday, there are various set courses available, including a reasonably priced tempura lunch, as well as à la carte selections of tempura, sashimi, seasonal vegetables, and other dishes. The more extensive evening menu includes shabu-shabu and kaiseki.

ZAKURO ⑬, basement of TBS Kaikan Building, 5-3-3 Akasaka. Tel. 3582-6841.
    Cuisine: SHABU-SHABU/SUKIYAKI/TEPPANYAKI. **Reservations:** Recommended. **Station:** Akasaka, TBS exit, a 1-minute walk away.
$ Prices: Set-dinner courses ¥9,300–¥17,500 ($66.40–$125); set lunches ¥1,800–¥5,500 ($12.85–$39.30). AE, DC, JCB, MC, V.
    Open: Daily 11am–10pm (last order).

Serving Kobe beef, this restaurant offers shabu-shabu, sukiyaki, teppanyaki, tempura, and steaks. For lunch it also offers an obento lunch box, as well as inexpensive sukiyaki. Since Zakuro has an English menu, ordering is no problem.

NON-JAPANESE FOOD

ROSE ROOM, ANA Hotel Tokyo, 1-12-33 Akasaka. Tel. 3459-6921.
    Cuisine: FRENCH. **Reservations:** Recommended. **Station:** Roppongi, Akasaka, Kamiyacho, Toranomon, or Kokkai Gijido-mae.
$ Prices: Main dishes ¥5,200–¥10,500 ($37.15–$75); set-dinner courses ¥15,000–¥22,000 ($107.15–$157.15); set lunches ¥5,500–¥11,000 ($39.30–$78.55). AE, DC, JCB, MC, V.
    Open: Lunch daily 11:30am–2:30pm; dinner daily 5–10pm.

It's hard to imagine a more romantic setting than the small and intimate Rose Room. With a huge vase of roses in the center of the dining area, this restaurant is perfect for a tête-à-tête as classical music plays softly in the background. The menu changes twice a year but may include such selections as Beluga caviar, turtle soup lightly seasoned with curry, lobster, rack of lamb, grilled salmon, chicken, and steak. After dinner you may wish to retire to the Astral lounge up on the 37th floor, where you have a good view of the city.

LA TOUR D'ARGENT, New Otani Hotel, 4-1 Kioi-cho. Tel. 3239-3111.
    Cuisine: FRENCH. **Reservations:** Imperative. **Station:** Akasaka-mitsuke, a 3-minute walk away; or Yotsuya, a 5-minute walk away.
$ Prices: Appetizers and soups ¥3,000–¥10,000 ($21.40–$71.40); main dishes ¥7,000–¥15,000 ($50–$107.15). AE, CB, DC, JCB, MC, V.
    Open: Dinner daily 5:30–9:30pm (last order).

This restaurant was rumored to be the most expensive in town when it opened in the New Otani Hotel in 1984, but I doubt it, especially when I consider those exclusive and highly elusive Japanese restaurants with kaiseki cuisine and geisha entertainment patronized by Japan's top corporate management. La Tour d'Argent is sister to the one in Paris, which opened back in 1582 and was visited twice by Japan's former emperor, Hirohito.

Entrance to the Tokyo restaurant is through an impressive hallway with a plush interior and displays of tableware that have been used in the Paris establishment through the centuries. The dining hall looks like a Parisian drawing room, with an elegance a bit too overstated for my taste. The service, however, is superb and the food is excellent. The specialty here is duckling—it meets its untimely end at the age of 3 weeks and is flown to Japan from Brittany—Other dishes on the menu, which changes

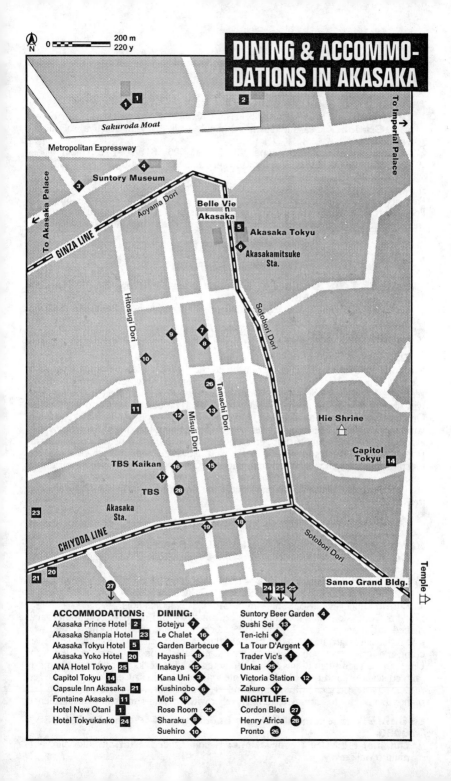

DINING & ACCOMMODATIONS IN AKASAKA

0 ⊨⊨⊨⊨ 200 m
⊨⊨⊨⊨ 220 y

To Imperial Palace →

Sakuroda Moat

Metropolitan Expressway

To Akasaka Palace ←

GINZA LINE

Suntory Museum

Aoyama Dori

Belle Vie Akasaka

Akasaka Tokyu

Akasakamitsuke Sta.

Sotobori Dori

Hitotsugi Dori

Tamachi Dori

Misuji Dori

Hie Shrine

Capitol Tokyu

TBS Kaikan

TBS

Akasaka Sta.

CHIYODA LINE

Sotobori Dori

Sanno Grand Bldg.

Temple

ACCOMMODATIONS:
Akasaka Prince Hotel **2**
Akasaka Shanpia Hotel **23**
Akasaka Tokyu Hotel **5**
Akasaka Yoko Hotel **20**
ANA Hotel Tokyo **25**
Capitol Tokyu **14**
Capsule Inn Akasaka **21**
Fontaine Akasaka **11**
Hotel New Otani **1**
Hotel Tokyukanko **24**

DINING:
Botejyu **7**
Le Chalet **16**
Garden Barbecue **1**
Hayashi **18**
Inakaya **15**
Kana Uni **3**
Kushinobo **6**
Moti **19**
Rose Room **25**
Sharaku **8**
Suehiro **10**

Suntory Beer Garden **4**
Sushi Sei **13**
Ten-ichi **9**
La Tour D'Argent **1**
Trader Vic's **1**
Unkai **25**
Victoria Station **12**
Zakuro **17**
NIGHTLIFE:
Cordon Bleu **27**
Henry Africa **28**
Pronto **26**

with the seasons, may include sea bass, *médaillons* of veal in light curry sauce, young pigeon, beef tenderloin, or fricassee of lobster and morels. For appetizers, I recommend either duck or goose foie gras.

TRADER VIC'S, New Otani Hotel, 4-1 Kioi-cho. Tel. 3265-4708.
   Cuisine: SEAFOOD/STEAKS/INTERNATIONAL. **Reservations:** Not necessary. **Station:** Akasaka-mitsuke, a 3-minute walk away; or Yotsuya, a 5-minute walk away.
$ **Prices:** Appetizers and soups ¥1,500–¥3,500 ($10.70–$25); main dishes ¥4,500–¥9,000 ($32.15–$64.30); set lunches ¥3,900–¥6,500 ($27.85–$46.40). AE, DC, JCB, MC, V.
   Open: Lunch daily 11:30am–2:30pm; dinner daily 5–10pm.
Part of an American chain operating out of California. The décor, as always, is Polynesian, and the extensive menu offers salads, seafood, Chinese dishes, curries, steak, and chicken. The lunch menu includes lighter fare, including sandwiches.

MODERATE

JAPANESE FOOD

KUSHINOBO ⑭, 3rd floor of Akasaka Plaza Building, 2-14-3 Nagato-cho. Tel. 3581-5056.
   Cuisine: KUSHIKATSU. **Reservations:** Not necessary. **Station:** Akasaka-mitsuke, a 1-minute walk away.
$ **Prices:** Skewers à la carte ¥150–¥500 ($1.05–$3.55) (per skewer); set lunches ¥900–¥2,200 ($6.40–$15.70). AE, DC, JCB, MC, V.
   Open: Lunch daily 11:30am–2pm; dinner daily 5–10pm.
Kushinobo is in the building that connects to the Akasaka Tokyu Hotel, on the same floor as the hotel lobby. It's a kushikatsu restaurant, serving skewers of shrimp, vegetables, and meats deep-fried in oil. It's a tiny but popular place, and customers will wait in line to eat at the U-shaped counter. The best thing to do is order the Omakase course, or cook's choice, with the chef supplying skewer after skewer until you simply say stop. I've eaten skewer after skewer of mint leaf, beef, mushrooms, fish, asparagus, chicken, crab, shrimp, green peppers, and pumpkin before crawling away from the table. Sauces in which to dip your skewered goodies include soy sauce, mustard, and vinegar. Expect to spend about ¥5,000 ($35.70) per person for dinner here.
   There's another Kushinobo restaurant in the heart of Akasaka, at 3-10-17 Akasaka (tel. 3586-7390).

NON-JAPANESE FOOD

KANA UNI, 1-1-16 Moto-Akasaka. Tel. 3404-4776.
   Cuisine: FRENCH. **Reservations:** A must. **Station:** Akasaka-mitsuke, about a 3-minute walk away.
$ **Prices:** Soups and appetizers ¥1,000–¥3,800 ($7.15–$27.15); main dishes ¥2,000–¥5,300 ($14.30–$37.85). AE, DC, JCB, MC, V.
   Open: Dinner Mon–Sat 6pm–2am. **Closed:** National hols.
Not far from Akasaka's nightlife district, this cozy and intimate restaurant/bar is owned and managed by a brother and sister who speak excellent English and who love to have foreign guests. In fact, because the place is a little hard to find, they'll even come and fetch you if you call from Akasaka-mitsuke Station. Open since 1966, Kana Uni features such main dishes as sliced raw tenderloin, steaks, beef stew, grilled fish, sautéed scallops, and poached filet of sole with sea-urchin sauce. It's one of the few restaurants in Akasaka still serving food after midnight, and there's even live jazz nightly from 7pm to 2am. After dinner, relax with cocktails and enjoy the ambience.

LE CHALET, basement of Shimizu Building, 3-14-9 Akasaka. Tel. 3584-0080.
   Cuisine: FRENCH. **Reservations:** Recommended. **Station:** Akasaka, a 1-minute walk away.

$ Prices: Appetizers and soups ¥650–¥2,500 ($4.65–$17.85); main dishes ¥2,200–¥3,100 ($15.70–$22.15); set-dinner courses ¥4,900 and ¥7,000 ($35 and $50); set lunches ¥1,600–¥3,600 ($11.40–$25.70). AE, DC, JCB, MC, V.
Open: Lunch daily 11:30am–2pm; dinner daily 5:30–9pm.

A pleasant and modestly priced French restaurant in the heart of Akasaka, with seating for only 30 persons and decorated in an opulent pink and red. The ¥4,900 dinner course includes an hors d'oeuvre, soup, fish, a meat dish, dessert, and coffee. The set lunches are a particularly good bargain.

VICTORIA STATION, 3-15-13 Akasaka. Tel. 3586-0711.
Cuisine: STEAKS/HAMBURGERS. **Reservations:** Not necessary. **Station:** Akasaka or Akasaka-mitsuke, each about a 5-minute walk away.
$ Prices: Main dishes ¥1,600–¥4,100 ($11.40–$29.30); set-dinner courses ¥2,600–¥5,000 ($18.55–$35.70); set lunches ¥850–¥1,300 ($6.05–$9.30). AE, DC, JCB, MC, V.
Open: Daily 11am–11pm.

This is the place to come if you're hungering for American steaks, salads, and soups. Located off Hitosugi Dori on a small side street, opposite the Fontaine Capsule Hotel, it is similar to the approximately 100 Victoria Stations in the United States (and is decorated like a railroad station). Its salad bar is one of the best in town, but it's also known for its steaks (U.S. beef). During lunch, served until 5pm, hamburgers are also available; in fact, the best deal in the house is a hamburger plus a trip to the salad bar for only ¥1,300 ($9.30).

BUDGET

JAPANESE FOOD

Don't forget to consider **Hayashi,** on the fourth floor of the Sanno Kaikan Building, 2-14-1 Akasaka, described above as an expensive restaurant. I mention it again here simply because I don't want those of you on a budget to miss it. This is one of the coziest and most delightful restaurants in town, and although dinner is costly, you can enjoy the same atmosphere for much, much less at lunch, when only one dish, oyakodomburi (rice with chunks of chicken and omelet on top), is served, with pickled vegetables, clear soup, and tea. Open for lunch Monday through Friday from 11:30am to 2pm.

BOTEJYU, 3-10-1 Akasaka. Tel. 3584-6651.
Cuisine: OKONOMIYAKI. **Station:** Akasaka or Akasaka-mitsuke, each about a 5-minute walk away.
$ Prices: ¥750–¥2,600 ($5.35–$18.55); teishoku ¥800–¥950 ($5.70–$6.80). AE, DC, JCB, MC, V.
Open: Daily noon–10:45pm.

This simple second-floor restaurant on Tamachi Dori specializes in okonomiyaki, a Japanese-style pizza/pancake topped with cabbage and a meat such as pork, squid, or shrimp. It also serves fried noodles (yakisoba) and its own creation called tororoyaki, which is a yam okonomiyaki. Its teishoku, served until 3pm, are a great deal and include a main dish such as okonomiyaki, plus rice, soup, and salad.

NON-JAPANESE FOOD

MOTI, 3-8-8 Akasaka (tel. 3582-3620) and 2-14-31 Akasaka (tel. 3584-6640).
Cuisine: INDIAN. **Station:** Akasaka, a few minutes' walk away from both restaurants.
$ Prices: Curries ¥1,100–¥1,500 ($7.85–$10.70); tandoori from ¥1,700 ($12.15); lunch courses ¥990 ($7.05). AE, JCB, MC, V.

Open: Daily 11:30am–10pm.

⭐ This Indian restaurant is so popular that there are two branches in Akasaka alone (a third is in Roppongi). Moti serves vegetable, mutton, and chicken curries, as well as tandoori. An especially good deal is the set lunch, served until 2:30pm, which gives you a curry, along with Indian bread (*nan*) and tea or coffee.

3. SHINJUKU

EXPENSIVE
JAPANESE FOOD

KAKIDEN 7, 3-37-11 Shinjuku. Tel. 3352-5121.
    Cuisine: KAISEKI. **Reservations:** A must for dinner, recommended for lunch.
    Station: Shinjuku, east exit, a 1-minute walk away.
$ Prices: Set-dinner courses ¥6,500–¥16,500 ($46.40–$117.85); set lunch ¥4,400 ($31.40). AE, DC, JCB, MC, V.
    Open: Daily 11am–9pm (last order).

Although located on the eighth floor of a rather uninspiring building on the east side of Shinjuku Station, next to My City shopping complex, Kakiden has a relaxing teahouse atmosphere, with low chairs, shoji screens, bamboo trees, and soothing traditional Japanese music playing softly in the background. Sister restaurant to one in Kyoto, founded more than 260 years ago as a catering service for the elite, this kaiseki restaurant serves set courses that change with the seasons, according to what's fresh and available. The menu is in Japanese only, so simply pick a meal to fit your budget. Some of the more common dishes here will include fish, vegetables, eggs, sashimi, shrimp, and mushrooms, but don't worry if you can't identify everything. I've found that even the Japanese don't always know what they're eating. The set lunch is available until a late 5pm.

SERYNA, 52nd floor of Shinjuku Sumitomo Building, 2-6-1 Nishi-Shinjuku. Tel. 3344-6761.
    Cuisine: SHABU-SHABU/SUKIYAKI/TEPPANYAKI. **Reservations:** Recommended for dinner. **Station:** Shinjuku, west exit, about a 7-minute walk away.
$ Prices: Main dishes ¥6,500–¥12,000 ($46.40–$85.70); set-dinner courses ¥10,000–¥20,000 ($71.40–$142.85); set lunches ¥2,200–¥5,000 ($15.70–$35.70). AE, DC, JCB, MC, V.
    Open: Daily 11:30am–10:30pm.

Perched high above Shinjuku in one of the city's best-known skyscrapers, and offering great views, Seryna serves Kobe steaks, shabu-shabu, sukiyaki, and teppanyaki. There's an English menu, and lunches are especially reasonable, making it a good stopping-off place if you're exploring the west side of Shinjuku.

MODERATE
JAPANESE FOOD

HAYASHI ⑪, Hide Building, 2-22-5 Kabuki-cho. Tel. 3209-5672.
    Cuisine: GRILLED FOODS. **Reservations:** Highly recommended. **Station:** Shinjuku, east exit, about a 10-minute walk away.
$ Prices: Set-dinner courses ¥3,300–¥7,700 ($23.55–$55). AE, JCB.
    Open: Dinner Mon–Sat 5–11:30pm. **Closed:** Public hols.

With a rustic interior imported intact from the mountain region of Takayama, this restaurant specializes in Japanese set courses cooked over your own hibachi grill. It's small and cozy, with women in kimonos who oversee the cooking operations like mother hens, taking over the operation if customers seem the least bit hesitant. Four set courses are offered, and I chose the ¥4,400 ($31.40) course, which came with

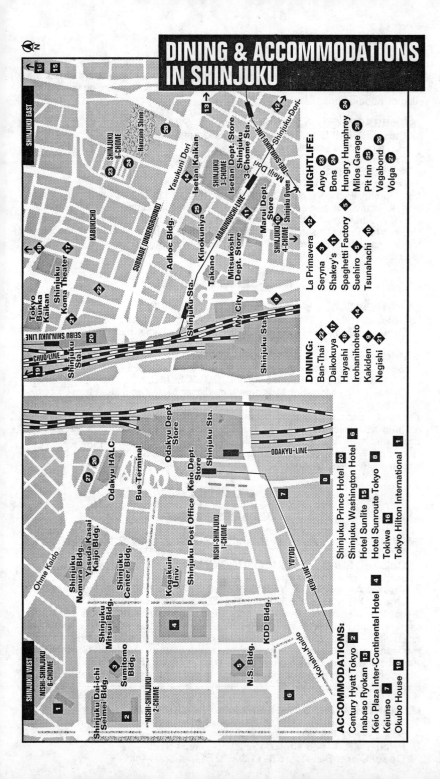

DINING & ACCOMMODATIONS IN SHINJUKU

SHINJUKU EAST

SHINJUKU WEST

NISHI-SHINJUKU 6-CHOME

NISHI-SHINJUKU 2-CHOME

NISHI-SHINJUKU 1-CHOME

SHINJUKU 6-CHOME

SHINJUKU 3-CHOME

SHINJUKU 4-CHOME

KABUKICHO

Ohme Kaido.

Koshu Kaido

Yasukuni Dori

Shinjuku Dai-ichi Seimei Bldg.

Sumitomo Bldg.

Shinjuku Nomura Bldg.

Yasuda Kasai Kaijo Bldg.

Shinjuku Mitsui Bldg.

Shinjuku Center Bldg.

Kogakuin Univ.

Shinjuku Post Office

N.S. Bldg.

KDD Bldg.

Odakyu HALC

Bus Terminal

Odakyu Dept. Store

Keio Dept. Store

Shinjuku Sta.

ODAKYU-LINE

KEIO LINE

YOYOGI

Tokyo Bunka Kaikan

Shinjuku Koma Theater

Adhoc. Bldg.

Kinokuniya

Takano

Isetan Kaikan

Isetan Dept. Store

Shinjuku 3-Chome Sta.

Mitsukoshi Dept. Store

Marui Dept. Store

Shinjuku Gyoen

Hanazono Shrine

My City

Shinjuku Sta.

Shinjuku Sta.

SEIBU SHINJUKU LINE

CHUO LINE

SUBNADE (UNDERGROUND)

MARUNOUCHI-LINE

THE SHINJUKU-LINE

Meiji Dori

Shinjuku-Dori

Yasukuni Dori

ACCOMMODATIONS:

Century Hyatt Tokyo **2**
Inabaso Ryokan **13**
Keio Plaza Inter-Continental Hotel **4**
Keiunso **7**
Okubo House **19**
Shinjuku Prince Hotel **20**
Shinjuku Washington Hotel **15**
Hotel Sunlite **8**
Hotel Sunroute Tokyo **16**
Tokiwa **16**
Tokyo Hilton International **1**

DINING:

Ban-Thai **22**
Daikokuya **17**
Hayashi **18**
Irohanihoheto **14**
Kakiden **9**
Negishi **21**

La Primavera **12**
Seryna **3**
Shakey's **11**
Spaghetti Factory **5**
Suehiro **5**
Tsunahachi **10**

NIGHTLIFE:

Anyo **23**
Bons **24**
Hungry Humphrey **24**
Milos Garage **28**
Pit Inn **25**
Vagabond **26**
Volga **27**

sashimi, yakitori, tofu steak, scallops cooked in their shell, shrimp, and vegetables, all grilled one after the other. Watch your alcohol intake—drinks can really add to your bill. This restaurant is about a 10-minute walk from Shinjuku Station, on the northern edge of Kabuki-cho.

TSUNAHACHI ⑮, 3-31-8 Shinjuku. Tel. 3352-1012.
  Cuisine: TEMPURA. **Reservations:** Recommended. **Station:** Shinjuku, east exit, a 5-minute walk away.
$ **Prices:** Tempura à la carte ¥350–¥1,000 ($2.50–$7.15); teishoku ¥1,200–¥2,000 ($8.55–$14.30). AE, JCB, V.
  Open: Daily 11am–10pm.
A restaurant serving tempura, Tsunahachi first opened in 1923. Now there are more than 40 branch restaurants in Japan, including three in Shinjuku Station alone, and others in Ginza and Akasaka. Hours may vary, but most shops are open daily from 11:30am to 10pm. This main shop, on the east side of Shinjuku, is one of the largest, and its least expensive set meal includes deep-fried shrimp, three kinds of fish, a vegetable, and a shrimp ball.

NON-JAPANESE FOOD

LA PRIMAVERA, 2-5-15 Shinjuku. Tel. 3354-7873.
  Cuisine: ITALIAN. **Reservations:** Strongly recommended, especially for dinner.
  Station: Shinjuku Gyoen-mae or Shinjuku Sanchome, each about a 4-minute walk away.
$ **Prices:** Pastas and pizzas from ¥1,000 ($7.15); main dishes ¥1,200–¥3,000 ($8.55–$21.40); set-dinner courses ¥3,500–¥4,500 ($25–$32.15); set lunches ¥1,100–¥2,200 ($7.85–$15.70). AE, DC, JCB, MC, V.
  Open: Lunch Mon–Sat 11:30am–2pm; dinner Mon–Sat 5:30–11pm.
Since this restaurant opened in 1985, its faithful clientele has been growing steadily. The food is great, the prices are reasonable, and the bread is among the best in town. An intimate locale with only half a dozen tables, each with candles, it offers pastas, pizzas, and main dishes of steak, scallops, and fish. Customers are requested to order more than one dish per person for dinner. Set-lunch courses include steak, stew, homemade sausage, or pasta.

BUDGET

JAPANESE FOOD

DAIKOKUYA, 4th floor of Naka-Dai Building, 1-27-5 Kabuki-cho. Tel. 3202-7272.
  Cuisine: SHABU-SHABU/SUKIYAKI/GENGHIS KHAN. **Station:** Shinjuku, east side, about a 10-minute walk away.
$ **Prices:** All you can eat ¥1,800–¥2,500 ($12.85–$17.85). No credit cards.
  Open: Dinner Mon–Fri 5–11pm, Sat–Sun and hols 3–11pm.
If your forte is eating mountains of food quickly, you won't want to miss this place. It offers only three main dishes—shabu-shabu, sukiyaki, and Genghis Khan (mutton and vegetables)—and as much of it as you can consume within a 2-hour time period. If you want to drink beer, whisky, or shochu with your meal, add ¥900 ($6.40) and you'll be allowed to drink to your heart's content as well. Popular with students and young office workers, Daikokuya is a rather strange but fun place, and needless to say, it can be quite rowdy.

IROHANIHOHETO, 3-15-15 Shinjuku. Tel. 3359-1682.
  Cuisine: YAKITORI/VARIED. **Station:** Shinjuku Sanchome, about a 5-minute walk away; or Shinjuku, less than a 10-minute walk away.
$ **Prices:** ¥350–¥450 ($2.50–$3.20). No credit cards.
  Open: Dinner Sun–Thurs 5–11:30pm, Fri–Sat 5pm–4am.

⭐ Irohanihoheto is a chain of drinking establishments, with a menu so varied, extensive, and cheap that most people eat here as well. Extremely popular with university students, it bills itself as an "Antique Pub," the meaning of which becomes even more elusive once you're inside. The main hall looks imitation barn to me, with rafters, hurricane lamps, and glass lanterns everywhere. A second room is more traditional Japanese, with tatami seating and folkcrafts hanging about. People don't come here for the décor, however, but because of the prices. The menu of Japanese and Western food is in Japanese only, but there are pictures. It includes yakitori, fried noodles, potato salad, sashimi, grilled meatballs, *nikujaga* (potato and meat stew, one of my favorites), and dozens of other dishes. This restaurant with the impossible name is located on Shinjuku's east side, on Yasukuni Dori Avenue, on the sixth floor of a building next to Isetan Kaikan.

NEGISHI ⑯, **2-45-2 Kabuki-cho. Tel. 3232-8020.**
   Cuisine: GRILLED OX TONGUE/OX-TAIL SOUP/BOILED WHEAT WITH YAM.
   Station: Shinjuku or Seibu Shinjuku, each a few minutes' walk away.
$ Prices: Main dishes ¥650–¥1,300 ($4.65–$9.30); lunch teishoku ¥900–¥1,500 ($6.40–$10.70). No credit cards.
   Open: Mon–Sat 11am–10:30pm, Sun and hols 11am–9:30pm.
It would be easy to overlook Negishi, a tiny hole-in-the-wall with just a counter and a few tables, located near America Boulevard, on a tiny side street that runs beside Green Plaza. It would be a shame, however, to miss its healthful, low-calorie foods. It specializes in Japanese stews, ox-tail soup, and *mugi-toro* (boiled wheat with grated yam). You might also want to try *tan-yaki*, grilled ox-tongue, which is low in calories and fat but rich in protein.

NON-JAPANESE FOOD

BAN-THAI, 1-23-14 Kabuki-cho. Tel. 3207-0068.
   Cuisine: THAI. **Station:** Shinjuku, about a 7-minute walk away.
$ Prices: Appetizers and salads ¥1,000–¥1,500 ($7.15–$10.70); main dishes ¥1,100–¥1,900 ($7.85–$13.55). AE, MC, JCB, V.
   Open: Mon–Fri noon–4am, Sat–Sun 11am–4am.
⭐ The Thai staff here prepares and serves excellent and authentic Thai dishes, with 40 mouth-watering items listed on the menu; for the timid, red dots signify the most fiery foods. My favorites are the cold and spicy meat salad, the chicken soup with coconut and lemon grass, and the *pat Thai* (Thai fried rice). There are also lots of pork, shrimp, chicken, and beef dishes. Ban-Thai stands in the seediest part of Kabuki-cho, on a neon-lit pedestrian street that connects the Koma Building with Yasukuni Dori Street. Located on the third floor, it's a bit difficult to find, so look for the numbers of the address on the building.

SHAKEY'S, 3-30-11 Shinjuku. Tel. 3341-0322.
   Cuisine: PIZZA. **Station:** Shinjuku Sanchome, a 1-minute walk away.
$ Prices: All-you-can-eat pizza lunch ¥650 ($4.65). No credit cards.
   Open: Lunch Mon–Sat 11am–2pm (except public hols).
Ⓢ If you want to gorge yourself on pizza, the best deal in town is at one of the 20 or so Shakey's around town, offering a great all-you-can-eat pizza lunch every day except Sunday and holidays from 11am to 2pm. The Shakey's in Shinjuku is across the street from the Isetan department store on Shinjuku Dori Avenue.
   There's another convenient Shakey's in Harajuku at 6-1-10 Meiji-Jingumae (tel. 3409-2405), on Omote Sando Dori Avenue close to the Oriental Bazaar.

SPAGHETTI FACTORY, 29th floor of N.S. Building, 2-4-1 Nishi-Shinjuku. Tel. 3348-1393.
   Cuisine: SPAGHETTI. **Station:** Shinjuku, west exit, an 8-minute walk away.
$ Prices: ¥1,000–¥1,500 ($7.15–$10.70). No credit cards.
   Open: Daily 11:30am–9pm (last order).

Spaghetti with a view is what you get at this casual restaurant. It offers more than 60 pasta dishes with a wide variety of sauces and toppings, from short-necked clams and spicy Chinese cabbage to eggplant with bacon and soy sauce. If all you want is plain meat sauce, you can have that, too. Portions are large. My only complaint is the Japanese pop music the young staff apparently enjoys listening to.

 FROMMER'S COOL FOR KIDS
RESTAURANTS

Hard Rock Café (see page 153) Teenagers will love you for taking them here, where they can eat hamburgers, gaze at famous guitars and other rock-and-roll memorabilia, and, most important, buy that Hard Rock Café T-shirt.

Johnny Rockets (see page 153) The best burgers in town, a 1950s-style diner, and singing waitresses will entertain kids of all ages.

Shakey's (see page 145) When nothing but pizza will satisfy, head for one of these chain pizza parlors for lunch, when great all-you-can-eat bargains are offered.

---

4. ROPPONGI

Because Roppongi is such a popular nighttime hangout for young Tokyoites, as well as for foreigners, it boasts a large number of both Japanese and Western restaurants. To find the location of any of the following addresses, stop by the tiny police station on Roppongi Crossing (Roppongi's main intersection of Roppongi Dori and Gaien-Higashi Dori avenues), where you'll find a map of the area. If you still don't know where to go, ask one of the policemen.

EXPENSIVE
JAPANESE FOOD

FUKUZUSHI ⑰**, 5-7-8 Roppongi. Tel. 3402-4116.**
Cuisine: SUSHI. **Reservations:** Recommended, especially for dinner. **Station:** Roppongi, about a 4-minute walk away.
$ Prices: Set-dinner courses ¥6,500–¥11,000 ($46.40–$78.55); set lunches ¥2,750 ($19.65). AE, DC, JCB, MC, V.
Open: Lunch Mon–Sat 11:30am–2pm; dinner daily 5:30–11pm.
One of the classiest sushi bars in town, tucked underneath Spago restaurant (behind the Roi Building in Roppongi), this place has an entrance through a small courtyard, and an interior of red and black. Some people swear it has the best sushi in Tokyo, although with 7,000 sushi bars in the city, I'd be hard-pressed to say which one is tops. Certainly, you can't go wrong here. The English menu opens up like a fan and offers a variety of choices of sashimi and nigiri-zushi. Most dinners average about ¥10,000 ($71.40), but if you're careful about your drinks and the amount you order, you can eat for less. The set lunch is served every day except Sunday and holidays.

INAKAYA ⑫**, 7-8-4 Roppongi. Tel. 3405-9866.**
Cuisine: GRILLED FOOD. **Reservations:** Not accepted. **Station:** Roppongi, about a 5-minute walk away.
$ Prices: Meals average ¥12,000 ($85.70). AE, DC, JCB, MC, V.
Open: Dinner daily 5pm–5am.

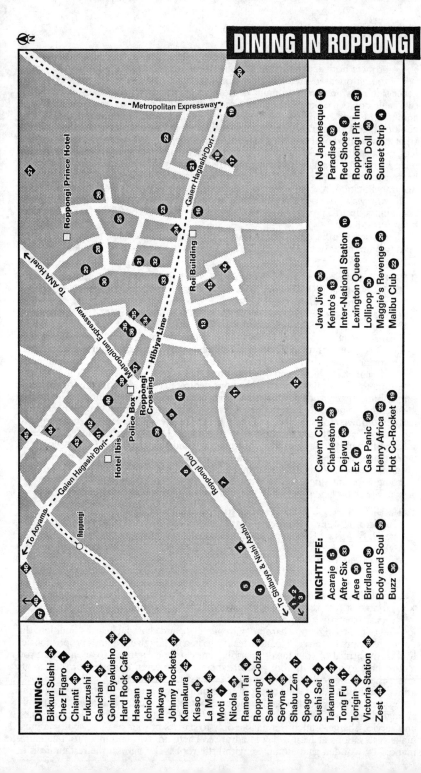

DINING IN ROPPONGI

DINING:
Bikkuri Sushi 24
Chez Figaro 1
Chianti 20
Fukuzushi 44
Ganchan 42
Gonin Byakusho 36
Hard Rock Cafe 15
Hassan 9
Ichioku 45
Inakaya 46
Johnny Rockets 37
Kamakura 42
Kisso 48
La Mex 48
Moti 7
Nicola 34
Ramen Tai 6
Roppongi Colza 8
Samrat 41
Seryna 35
Shabu Zen 47
Spago 12
Sushi Sei 2
Takamura 27
Tong Fu 11
Torigin 43
Victoria Station 38
Zest 44

NIGHTLIFE:
Acaraje 5
After Six 33
Area 30
Birdland 36
Body and Soul 39
Buzz 36

Cavern Club 13
Charleston 28
Dejavu 26
Ex 47
Gas Panic 25
Henry Africa 23
Hot Co-Rocket 19

Java Jive 36
Kento's 13
Inter-National Station 10
Lexington Queen 31
Lollipop 30
Maggie's Revenge 29
Malibu Club 22

Neo Japonesque 16
Paradiso 32
Red Shoes 3
Roppongi Pit Inn 21
Satin Doll 40
Sunset Strip 4

One of Tokyo's best-known Japanese restaurants for grilled foods, Inakaya attracts both Japanese and foreign visitors to the capital. Although definitely tourist-oriented, it's still great fun. Diners sit at a U-shaped counter, on the other side of which are mountains of fresh vegetables, beef, and seafood, as well as two male cooks (cooks in Japan are almost always male), who can sit for inordinate amounts of time on pillows, with their legs tucked neatly underneath them. They cook on a grill in front of them in a style called robatayaki. Customers simply point at what they want. Food offerings may include yellowtail, red snapper, sole, king crab legs, giant shrimp, steak, meatballs, gingko nuts, potatoes, eggplant, and asparagus, all piled high in wicker baskets. Sometimes there are tiny, crunchy crabs you pop whole in your mouth—they tickle all the way down. Inakaya is about a 5-minute walk from Roppongi Station, toward Aoyama-Itchome on Gaien-Higashi Dori Avenue.

If you want to make reservations, you can do so at the two other Inakaya restaurants up to 7pm (whenever a restaurant proves successful in Japan, branches open immediately).

The Roppongi East Branch, 5-3-4 Roppongi (tel. 3408-5040), is also open from 5pm to 5am. Inakaya in Akasaka, 3-12-7 Akasaka (tel. 3586-3054), is open only until 11pm.

KISSO, basement of Axis Building, 5-17-1 Roppongi. Tel. 3582-4191.

Cuisine: KAISEKI. **Reservations:** A must for dinner. **Station:** Roppongi, about a 4-minute walk away.

$ Prices: Set-dinner courses ¥8,800–¥15,000 ($62.85–$107.15); set lunches ¥1,300–¥5,500 ($9.30–$39.30). AE, DC, JCB, MC, V.

Open: Lunch Mon–Sat 11:30am–2pm; dinner Mon–Sat 5:30–9pm (last order).

This thoroughly modern establishment sells Japanese gourmet cookware, including expensive ceramics, utensils, and lacquerware of contemporary design, in its shop up on the third floor. The restaurant, located in the basement of this interesting building filled with shops dedicated to the best in interior design, is simple but elegant, with heavy tables, sprigs of flowers, and soft lighting. The food is kaiseki and comes only in set courses, served (as you might guess) in/on beautifully lacquered bowls/trays, as well as and on ceramic plates. I love eating here because to me Kisso represents all the best that is modern Japan—understated elegance, a successful marriage between the contemporary and the traditional. There should be more places like this in Tokyo. A complete dinner consists of an appetizer, soup, sashimi, a seasonal dish, a baked dish, a boiled dish, tea, rice, and dessert. If you want to come here for lunch, it's very reasonable. From Roppongi Station, walk toward Tokyo Tower on Gaien-Higashi Dori; the Axis Building will be on your right.

TAKAMURA ⑱, 3-4-27 Roppongi. Tel. 3585-6600.

Cuisine: KAISEKI. **Reservations:** Imperative (for lunch, the day before at the latest). **Station:** Roppongi, about a 5-minute walk away.

$ Prices: Set-dinner courses ¥16,500–¥22,000 ($117.85–$157.15); set lunches ¥11,000 and ¥14,000 ($78.55 and $100). AE, DC, JCB, MC, V.

Open: Lunch Mon–Sat noon–3pm; dinner Mon–Sat 5–10:30pm (last order 8pm).

Takamura is a must for everyone who can afford it. Located on the edge of the hot spot that is Roppongi, this wonderful 45-year-old house is like a peaceful oasis that time forgot. Each of its eight rooms is different, with windows looking out onto miniature gardens with bamboo, and charcoal hearths built into the floor. Takamura has a very Japanese feeling to it, a feeling that expands proportionately with the arrival of your meal—seasonal kaiseki food arranged so artfully that you almost hate to destroy it. Your pleasure increases, however, as you savor the various textures and flavors of the food. Specialties here may include quail, sparrow, or duck, grilled on the hearth in your own private tatami room. Seating, by the way, is on the floor, as it is in most traditional Japanese restaurants. The price of dinner here usually averages about ¥25,000 ($178) to ¥30,000 ($214) by the time you add drinks, tax, and service charge. Lunch is available only to parties of four or more, but you must make reservations at least a day in advance. There are two entrances to Takamura, marked by wooden gates complete with little roofs. The sign on the restaurant is in

Japanese only, but look for the credit-card signs. Taxi drivers should have no trouble finding it.

NON-JAPANESE FOOD

SPAGO, 5-7-8 Roppongi. Tel. 3423-4025.
   Cuisine: CALIFORNIAN. **Reservations:** A must. **Station:** Roppongi, about a 4-minute walk away.
$ **Prices:** Appetizers ¥2,000–¥2,600 ($14.30–$18.55); pizza and pasta ¥2,200–¥2,700 ($15.70–$19.30); main dishes ¥3,300–¥4,200 ($23.55–$30); set-dinner course ¥10,000 ($71.40). AE, DC, JCB, MC, V.
   Open: Dinner daily 5:30–11pm (last order 10:30pm).

★ Spago serves Californian cuisine created by its owner, Wolfgang Puck, an Austrian-born chef who has a similar restaurant in Los Angeles. The atmosphere here is bright, airy, and cheerful—very Californian—with huge bouquets of flowers, potted palms, ferns, white walls, and a colorful mural. The menu changes every 3 months to reflect what's in season, but examples of what's been offered in the past include spicy fettuccine with grilled shrimp and fresh basil; sliced breast of duck with Japanese oba leaves and plum-wine sauce; angel-hair noodles with goat cheese, broccoli, and thyme; grilled spicy chicken with garlic and Italian parsley; and roasted baby lamb with a cabernet, mustard, and rosemary sauce. If you order pizza, it will come not with tomato sauce but with olive oil, making it much lighter, so the emphasis is on the toppings. Needless to say, the main dishes are always imaginative, and the service is great. Dining here is a pleasure, and as you might expect, Spago has the largest selection of California wines in town. For dessert, try the restaurant's homemade ice cream. An average dinner check, including wine, tax, and service, is about ¥10,000 ($71.40).

TONG FU, 6-7-11 Roppongi. Tel. 3403-3527.
   Cuisine: CHINESE. **Reservations:** A must. **Station:** Roppongi, about a 2-minute walk away.
$ **Prices:** Main dishes ¥2,000–¥4,500 ($14.30–$32.15); set-dinner courses ¥7,700–¥14,000 ($55–$100); set lunches ¥1,300–¥3,300 ($9.30–$23.55). AE, DC, JCB, MC, V.
   Open: Lunch Mon–Sat 11:30am–2:30pm (last order at 2pm); dinner Mon–Sat 5–10:30pm (last order). Holiday hours: 11:30am–10:30pm.
This is a very trendy Chinese restaurant, with ceiling fans; tablecloths of lime green, orange, purple, or bright yellow; and a fantasy-provoking mural covering one whole wall. In the summertime, there are even a couple of tables outside in a small courtyard under a weeping willow (make a reservation if you want to sit here). Dishes from Shanghai include shark's-fin soup, shrimp in chili sauce, Beijing duck, crabmeat omelet, simmered chili tofu and eggplant, and shredded pork. To reach the restaurant, from Roppongi Crossing take the small diagonal street that leads downhill beside the Almond Coffee Shop; Tong Fu will be on the right side of the street.

MODERATE

JAPANESE FOOD

GONIN BYAKUSHO ⑲, 4th floor of Roppongi Square Building, 3-10-3 Roppongi. Tel. 3470-1675.
   Cuisine: GRILLED FOODS/OBENTO **Reservations:** Recommended for dinner. **Station:** Roppongi, a 3-minute walk away.
$ **Prices:** A la carte dishes ¥650–¥6,000 ($4.65–$42.85); set-dinner courses ¥4,400–¥6,500 ($31.40–$46.40); set lunches ¥850–¥3,800 ($6.05–$27.15). AE, DC, JCB, MC, V.
   Open: Lunch Mon–Sat 11:30am–2pm; dinner Mon–Sat 5–10pm (last order).
   Closed: Hols.

In the midst of all the chic discos in the Roppongi Square Building, you'll find this restaurant, whose name means "five farmers." The atmosphere here is of a farmhouse in the countryside, with the usual heavy beams and thick wooden tables; there's a huge hearth and oven off to one side. You take off your shoes before entering this restaurant and place them in lockers. Most of the food here is charcoal-broiled, and dinner courses may include grilled fish or crab, sashimi, and vegetables. A la carte items on the English menu include yakitori, fresh seafood, charcoal-broiled shrimp, assorted sashimi, and *nabemono* (a pot of boiled chicken and vegetables). Dinner à la carte will probably run about ¥5,000 ($35.70) per person. At lunchtime, there are special obento lunch boxes, as well as tempura and sashimi courses. Highly recommended.

HASSAN ⑳, basement of Denki Building, 6-1-20 Roppongi. Tel. 3403-8333.
   Cuisine: SHABU-SHABU/SUKIYAKI/KAISEKI. **Reservations:** A must for kaiseki. **Station:** Roppongi, a 1-minute walk away.
$ Prices: Shabu-shabu and sukiyaki ¥4,900–¥7,000 ($35–$50); kaiseki ¥7,700–¥13,200 ($55–$94.30); set-lunch courses ¥2,700–¥6,300 ($19.30–$45). AE, DC, JCB, MC, V.
   Open: Lunch daily 11:30am–2pm; dinner daily 4:30–9:30pm (last order).
This modern basement restaurant offers shabu-shabu, sukiyaki, and kaiseki, with various options listed on its English menu. If you plan on eating kaiseki, however, you must make reservations. Lunch specials include choices of shabu-shabu, sukiyaki, obento lunch boxes, and kaiseki. Seating is either in chairs or on tatami mats, waitresses wear kimonos, and *koto* (Japanese zither) music plays in the background. If you take the road toward Shibuya from Roppongi Crossing, Hassan will soon be on your left.

ROPPONGI COLZA, basement of Clover Building, 7-15-10 Roppongi. Tel. 3405-5631.
   Cuisine: TEPPANYAKI/GRILLED SEAFOOD. **Reservations:** Recommended for dinner. **Station:** Roppongi, a 1-minute walk away.
$ Prices: Appetizers ¥1,500–¥3,300 ($10.70–$23.55); main dishes ¥2,200–¥7,500 ($15.70–$53.55); set-dinner courses ¥8,800–¥15,000 ($62.85–$107.15); set lunches ¥1,600–¥4,400 ($11.40–$31.40). AE, DC, JCB, MC, V.
   Open: Lunch Mon–Sat 11:30am–2pm, Sun and hols noon–3pm; dinner Mon–Sat 5–10pm, Sun and hols 5–9pm.
Another Kikkoman restaurant, this locale specializes in teppanyaki steaks and seafood, flavored with Kikkoman condiments. Set courses include various cuts of Matsuzaka beef; seafood, such as scallops, scampi, sole, or turbot; side dishes; and dessert.

SHABU ZEN ㉑, 5-17-16 Roppongi. Tel. 3585-5388.
   Cuisine: SHABU-SHABU/SUKIYAKI. **Reservations:** Recommended. **Station:** Roppongi, a 5-minute walk away.
$ Prices: Shabu-shabu and sukiyaki ¥3,600–¥8,000 ($25.70–$57.15). AE, DC, JCB, MC, V.
   Open: Dinner daily 5pm–midnight.
This restaurant has both an English-speaking staff and a menu in English (along with color illustrations). For ¥4,700 ($37.60) per person you can eat all the shabu-shabu or sukiyaki you want. Shabu Zen also has an all-you-can-eat seafood shabu-shabu for ¥7,000 ($50) per person. The shabu-shabu menu includes an unlimited amount of meat and vegetables, plus two appetizers, sashimi, egg custard, salad, and dessert. Shabu Zen is located behind the Axis Building.

NON-JAPANESE FOOD

CHEZ FIGARO, 4-4-1 Nishi Azabu. Tel. 3400-8718.

Cuisine: FRENCH. **Reservations:** Recommended. **Station:** Roppongi, about a 15-minute walk away; or Hiro, a 7-minute walk away.
$ Prices: Main dishes ¥3,000–¥5,000 ($21.40–$35.70); set-dinner courses ¥6,500 ($46.40); set lunches ¥2,700–¥5,000 ($19.30–$35.70). AE, DC, JCB, MC, V.
Open: Lunch Mon–Sat noon–2pm; dinner Mon–Sat 6–9pm (last order).

Chez Figaro has been serving traditional French cooking since 1969 and is still popular with both foreigners and Japanese. A small and cozy place, it offers such specialties as homemade pâté, escargots, saffron-flavored fish soup, stuffed quail with grapes, steak, and braised sweetbreads with mushrooms. To reach Chez Figaro from Roppongi Crossing, walk toward Shibuya until you come to the second major intersection, at the bottom of a hill. Turn left, and after about 4 minutes you'll see Chez Figaro on your right.

CHIANTI, 3-1-7 Azabudai. Tel. 3583-7546.
Cuisine: ITALIAN. **Reservations:** Recommended for dinner. **Station:** Roppongi, less than a 10-minute walk away.
$ Prices: Appetizers ¥1,000–¥2,000 ($7.14–$14.30); main dishes ¥3,500–¥4,400 ($25–$31.40). AE, DC, JCB, MC, V.
Open: Daily 11:30am–1:45am.

Established in 1960, this is one of the oldest Italian restaurants in Tokyo. Founded by two Japanese who had been living in Europe and who wanted to introduce Western food to the Japanese, it cannot compete with the surge of newer and more authentic Italian restaurants that have opened in the capital in the past decade. Still, it's a good moderately priced restaurant in Roppongi. Dining is either on the second floor or in the more formal basement, which is also more intimate and romantic. The menu, the same for both venues, includes such main dishes as grilled chicken in spicy tomato sauce, veal scaloppine sautéed with vegetables, Milanese veal cutlet, Hungarian beef stew, and braised veal shank in tomato sauce. On the ground floor there's a coffee shop where you can have snacks, salads, and sandwiches. The restaurant is located on the right side of Gaien-Higashi Dori, in the direction of Tokyo Tower and past the big intersection.

VICTORIA STATION, 4-9-2 Roppongi. Tel. 3479-4601.
Cuisine: STEAKS/HAMBURGERS. **Reservations:** Recommended. **Station:** Roppongi, a 1-minute walk away.
$ Prices: Main dishes ¥1,500–¥4,100 ($10.70–$29.30); set-dinner courses ¥2,600–¥5,100 ($18.55–$36.40); set lunches ¥850–¥1,300 ($6.05–$9.30). AE, DC, JCB, MC, V.
Open: Mon–Sat 11am–midnight, Sun and hols 11am–11pm.

If you're hungering for American steaks, salads, and soups, Victoria Station may be the closest you can come. It specializes in roast prime beef and steaks and has one of the best salad bars in town. Hamburgers are available only at lunch; a hamburger plus a trip to the salad bar costs just ¥1,300 ($9.30). If you're interested mainly in beverages or lighter dishes, there's a cocktail bar upstairs with its own menu, offering chicken, teriyaki steaks, and sandwiches, as well as a salad bar. Victoria Station is located close to Roppongi Crossing, almost catercorner from the Almond Coffee Shop.

Another Victoria Station is located in Akasaka, at 3-15-13 Akasaka (tel. 586-0711).

ZEST, 2-13-15 Nishi Azabu. Tel. 3400-3985.
Cuisine: MEXICAN/CALIFORNIAN. **Reservations:** Not necessary. **Station:** Roppongi, about a 10-minute walk away.
$ Prices: Appetizers ¥700–¥1,200 ($5–$8.55); main dishes ¥900–¥3,500 ($6.40–$25). AE, DC, MC, V.
Open: Daily 11:30am–5am (last order 4:15am).

This local group of breezy, trendy Zest restaurants, looking nothing like the usual Mexican variety, specialize in both Mexican and Southern Californian cuisine.

Newest of these is the one located near the intersection of Roppongi Dori and Gaien Nishi Dori streets in Nishi Azabu, about a 10-minute walk from Roppongi Station. Its menu lists burgers, salads, and Mexican dishes, including fajitas, tacos, and burritos. Tacos are rather expensive: three shells and sauce are ¥550 ($3.90), with fillings costing an extra ¥900 ($6.40) and up. But the food is good, the ambience is even better. There's a minimum charge of ¥800 ($5.70) after 6pm, but that's not difficult considering the prices. Cocktails average ¥900 ($6.40). If you want to eat Mexican but don't want to spend a fortune, consider coming for lunch, when specials are offered until 2pm every day except Sunday and holidays, with most dishes costing less than ¥900 ($6.40).

Other Zest restaurants are at 4-11-13 Roppongi (tel. 3478-0222), open from 5pm to 5am; and at 6-7-18 Jingumae in Harajuku (tel. 3409-6268), open from 11:30am to 5am.

BUDGET

JAPANESE FOOD

BIKKURI SUSHI, 3-14-9 Roppongi. Tel. 3403-1489.
   Cuisine: SUSHI. **Station:** Roppongi, about a 3-minute walk away.
$ Prices: Dishes ¥120–¥300 (85¢–$2.15). No credit cards.
   Open: Daily 11am–5am.

In this establishment, plates of sushi move along a conveyor belt past customers seated at the counter. They simply help themselves to whichever plates strike their fancy; this makes dining a cinch, since it's not necessary to know the name of anything. The white plates of sushi are all priced at ¥120 (85¢), while the colored dishes run ¥240 ($1.70) and ¥300 ($2.15). Your bill is tallied according to the number of plates you've taken. One of the cheapest places to eat in this popular nightlife district, it's located on the road leading to Tokyo Tower, on the left-hand side of the road across the street from the Roi Building.

GANCHAN (22), 6-8-23 Roppongi. Tel. 3478-0092.
   Cuisine: YAKITORI. **Station:** Roppongi, about a 5-minute walk away.
$ Prices: Yakitori skewers ¥170–¥300 ($1.20–$2.15); yakitori set course ¥2,700 ($19.30). JCB, V.
   Open: Dinner Mon–Sat 6pm–3am, Sun and hols 6pm–midnight.
One of my favorite yakitori-ya. Small and intimate, it's owned by a friendly and entertaining man who can't speak English worth a darn but keeps trying with the help of a worn-out Japanese–English dictionary he keeps behind the counter. He also keeps an eclectic cassette collection—I never know whether to expect Japanese pop tunes or mellower Simon and Garfunkel. Seating is along just one counter, with room for only a dozen or so people. Though there's an English menu, it's easiest to order the yakitori *seto*, a set course that comes with salad and soup and eight skewers of such items as chicken, beef, meatballs, green peppers, and asparagus with rolled bacon. If you're still hungry, order individual skewers or an item such as tofu steak, pork-and-leek ravioli, or stewed meat with vegetables. To reach this place, take the small street going downhill on the left side of the Almond Coffee Shop; Ganchan is at the bottom of the hill on the right—look for the big white paper lantern.

ICHIOKU 48, 4-4-5 Roppongi. Tel. 3405-9891.
   Cuisine: JAPANESE ORIGINALS. **Station:** Roppongi, about a 4-minute walk away.
$ Prices: ¥700–¥1,400 ($5–$10). No credit cards.
   Open: Dinner daily 6–11:30pm.

One of my favorite restaurants in Tokyo for casual dining, Ichioku opened in the early 1970s. It's a tiny, cozy place with only eight tables, and you fill out your order yourself from the menu in English, complete with pictures, glued onto your table underneath clear glass. The food can best be called Japanese nouvelle cooking, with original creations offered at very reasonable prices. There's tuna and ginger sauté, mushroom sauté, shrimp spring rolls, asparagus salad, fried potatoes, and a dish of crumbled radish and tiny fish. I recommend the tofu steak (fried tofu and flakes of dried fish), as well as the cheese gyoza (a fried pork dumpling with cheese melted on it). The restaurant is tucked away on a side street; look for the neon lights and Japanese flag on its façade.

KAMAKURA, 4-10-11 Roppongi. Tel. 3405-4377.

Cuisine: YAKITORI. **Station:** Roppongi, less than a 2-minute walk away.
$ Prices: Yakitori skewers ¥170–¥300 ($1.20–$2.15); set courses ¥2,500–¥4,700 ($17.85–$33.55). AE, DC, JCB, MC, V.
Open: Dinner Mon–Sat 6–11pm.

Much more refined than most yakitori-ya, this establishment is decorated with paper lanterns and sprigs of fake but cheerful spring blossoms, with traditional koto music playing softly in the background. The English menu lists yakitori set courses, and à la carte sticks include those with shrimp, meatballs, squid, eggplant, and mushrooms. Kamakura is located across from the Ibis hotel, down a side street.

TORIGIN ㉓, 4-12-6 Roppongi. Tel. 3403-5829.

Cuisine: YAKITORI/RICE CASSEROLES. **Station:** Roppongi, a 2-minute walk away.
$ Prices: Yakitori skewers ¥130–¥270 (90¢–$1.90); kamameshi ¥750–¥900 ($5.35–$6.40). No credit cards.
Open: Lunch Mon–Sat 11:30am–2pm; dinner Mon–Sat 5–10:30pm.

Part of a chain of yakitori establishments, this no-frills place is typical of the smaller Japanese restaurants all over the country patronized by the country's salarymen, who stop off for a drink and bite to eat before boarding the commuter trains for home. An English menu includes skewers of grilled chicken, gingko nuts, green peppers, quail eggs, and asparagus with rolled bacon, as well as various kamameshi (rice casseroles cooked and served in their own little pots and topped with chicken, bamboo shoots, mushrooms, crab, salmon, or shrimp).

NON-JAPANESE FOOD

HARD ROCK CAFE, 5-4-20 Roppongi. Tel. 3408-7018.

Cuisine: AMERICAN. **Station:** Roppongi, a 3-minute walk, toward Tokyo Tower, then a right at McDonald's.
$ Prices: Appetizers ¥650–¥1,500 ($4.65–$10.70); main dishes ¥1,500–¥4,200 ($10.70–$30). AE, DC, JCB, MC, V.
Open: Mon–Thurs 11:30am–2am, Fri and Sat 11:30am–4am, Sun and hols 11:30am–11:30pm.

The Tokyo version of this world-famous hamburger joint dedicated to rock and roll. If you have disgruntled teenagers in tow, bring them here to ogle the memorabilia on the walls, chow down on a burger, and look over the T-shirts for sale. In addition to hamburgers, the menu includes salads, sandwiches, steak, barbecued pork ribs, and fajitas. The music, by the way, is loud.

JOHNNY ROCKETS, 3-11-10 Roppongi. Tel. 3423-1955.

Cuisine: HAMBURGERS. **Station:** Roppongi, a 1-minute walk away.
$ Prices: ¥550–¥1,300 ($3.90–$9.30); fixed-price lunch ¥1,000 ($7.15).
Open: Sun–Fri 11am–11pm, Sat 11am–5am.

Quite simply, the best burgers in town. At ¥900 ($6.40) they're also a bit steep. When nothing else will do, however, these are so huge that they'll definitely hit the spot. Perched on the second floor of a building on Roppongi Crossing, Johnny Rockets is decorated like an American '50s diner, and when certain songs come on the jukebox, the waitresses all stop to sing and dance in unison, just like in the movies. Seating is on a first-come, first-served basis at the counters, and smoking is not allowed. Other goodies on the menu include sandwiches, fries (including fries topped with chili), malts, shakes, floats, and pie à la mode. From 11am to 2pm daily, a fixed-price lunch is offered for ¥1,000 ($7.15), consisting of a hamburger, fries, and a drink.

MOTI, 6-2-35 Roppongi. Tel. 3479-1939.
 Cuisine: INDIAN. **Station:** Roppongi, a 3-minute walk away.
 $ Prices: Curries ¥1,100–¥1,800 ($7.85–$12.85); set lunches ¥990 ($7.05). AE, DC, JCB, MC, V.
 Open: Daily 11:30am–10pm.

This is my favorite Indian restaurant in town. Dishes include vegetable curries, chicken and mutton curries (I usually opt for the sag mutton—lamb with spinach), and tandoori chicken. Set lunches, served until 2:30pm, cost ¥990 ($7.05) and offer a choice of vegetable, chicken, or mutton curry, along with Indian bread (nan) and tea or coffee. Moti is on the left side of the street as you walk from Roppongi Crossing toward Shibuya.

There are two other Moti restaurants, both in Akasaka—on the second floor of the Akasaka Floral Plaza, 3-8-8 Akasaka (tel. 3582-3620); and on the third floor of the Kinpa Building, 2-14-31 Akasaka (tel. 3584-6640).

NICOLA, 3rd floor of Roppongi Plaza Building, 3-12-6 Roppongi. Tel. 3401-6936.
 Cuisine: ITALIAN. **Station:** Roppongi, a 1-minute walk away.
 $ Prices: Pizzas ¥1,300–¥3,500 ($9.30–$25); main dishes ¥2,000–¥5,300 ($14.30–$37.85); set-dinner courses ¥3,800–¥5,500 ($27.15–$39.30). AE, DC, JCB, MC, V.
 Open: Dinner daily 5pm–midnight.

One of the oldest pizzerias in town, if not *the* oldest, this place claims to have been the first to bring pizza to Japan, more than three decades ago. At any rate, it offers more than 50 different kinds of pizza in 6-inch, 9-inch, or 12-inch pans, as well as spaghetti, lasagne, cannelloni, chicken parmesan, steak, and other simple fare. From Roppongi Station, walk toward Tokyo Tower; the Roppongi Plaza Building is on the first alley to the left, with Nicola on the third floor. Look for Nicola's sign.

SAMRAT, 4-10-10 Roppongi. Tel. 3478-5877.
 Cuisine: INDIAN. **Station:** Roppongi, a 1-minute walk away.
 $ Prices: Curries ¥1,600–¥2,000 ($11.40–$14.30); set-dinner courses ¥2,100–¥3,800 ($15–$27.15); set lunches ¥900–¥1,400 ($6.40–$10). AE, DC, JCB, MC, V.
 Open: Daily 11am–5am.

Another Indian restaurant, this one located across from the Hotel Ibis and up on the third floor. Small but elaborately decorated, it offers curries and tandoori, as well as fixed-price lunches that are served only Monday through Friday from 11am to 4pm. The restaurant itself is open until dawn for all those Roppongi revelers.

5. TSUKIJI

EXPENSIVE

JAPANESE FOOD

TAMURA ㉔, **2-12-11 Tsukiji. Tel. 3541-2591.**
 Cuisine: KAISEKI. **Reservations:** Required for dinner, recommended for lunch.
 Station: Tsukiji, about a 1-minute walk away.
 $ Prices: Set-dinner courses from ¥30,000 ($214.30); set lunches ¥6,500–¥11,000 ($46.40–$78.55). AE, DC, JCB, MC, V.
 Open: Lunch daily noon–2pm; dinner daily 5:30–10pm (last order 7:30pm).

This modern kaiseki restaurant has a friendly staff of smiling and bowing kimono-clad waitresses and hostesses who make you feel as though they've been waiting all this time just for you. Although the menu is in Japanese only, they'll help you decide what to order, but since there are only set courses, your budget will probably decide for you. Lunch is the most economical time to come, when Tamura is popular with Japanese housewives. You have your choice of either tatami seating or tables and chairs.

MODERATE

JAPANESE FOOD

TENTAKE ㉕, **6-16-6 Tsukiji. Tel. 3541-3881.**
   Cuisine: FUGU. **Reservations:** Not necessary. **Station:** Tsukiji, about a 7-minute walk away.
$ Prices: Main dishes ¥1,000–¥4,900 ($7.15–$35); fugu set courses ¥6,000–¥13,500 ($42.85–$96.40). No credit cards.
   Open: Daily noon–10pm. **Closed:** Sun in Apr–Sept; first and third Wed in Oct–Mar.
People who really know their fugu, or blowfish, will tell you that the only time to eat it is from October through March, when it's fresh. You can eat fugu all year round, however, and a good place to try this Japanese delicacy is Tentake, a place popular with the Tsukiji working crowd. The menu is in Japanese, so if you want suggestions, try the fugu sashimi for ¥2,000 ($14.30) or the fugu-chiri for ¥3,500 ($25). The latter is a do-it-yourself meal in which you cook raw blowfish, cabbage, dandelion leaves, and tofu in a pot of boiling water in front of you. This is what I had, and it was more than I could eat. There are also fugu dishes that come with a variety of side dishes. Or you can order one of the tempura, eel, or crab dishes. The restaurant, a white-and-black mortar building, is located on Harumi Dori Avenue next to a bridge (from Tsukiji Station, walk in the opposite direction of Ginza).

BUDGET

JAPANESE FOOD

Since Tsukiji is where you'll find the nation's largest wholesale fish market, it's not surprising that this area abounds in sushi and seafood restaurants. In addition to the recommendations here, don't neglect the many stalls in and around the market, where you can eat everything from noodles to fresh sashimi.

EDOGIN ㉖, **4-5-1 Tsukiji. Tel. 3543-4401.**
   Cuisine: SUSHI. **Station:** Tsukiji, a 3-minute walk away.
$ Prices: Set-dinner courses ¥1,100–¥2,700 ($7.85–$19.30); lunch teishoku ¥1,500 ($10.70). AE, DC, MC, V.
   Open: Mon–Sat 11am–9:30pm.
There are four Edogin sushi restaurants in Tsukiji, all located within walking distance of one another. Since they're close to the famous fish market, you can be assured that in any of them the fish will be fresh. There's nothing aesthetic about this Edogin—the lights are bright, it's packed with the locals, and it's noisy and busy, with waitresses constantly bustling around. It's particularly packed during lunch- and dinnertime because the food is dependably good and plentiful. The menu is in Japanese only, but there's a glass case outside with some of the dishes displayed. As an alternative, look at what the people around you are eating, or if it's lunchtime, order the teishoku. The restaurant is located near the Harumi and Shinohashi Dori intersection, and anyone in the neighborhood will be able to point you in the right direction; look for the building with a string of Japanese lanterns adorning its façade.

SUSHI DAI ㉗, **Tsukiji Fish Market. Tel. 3542-1111.**
   Cuisine: SUSHI. **Station:** Tsukiji, about a 10-minute walk away.
$ Prices: Sushi à la carte ¥200–¥1,000 ($1.40–$7.15); sushi seto ¥1,200 ($8.55). No credit cards.
   Open: Mon–Sat 5am–1:30pm. **Closed:** Public hols.
Located right in the Tsukiji Fish Market, this restaurant boasts some of the freshest fish in town. The easiest thing to do is order the seto, a set sushi course that usually comes with tuna, eel, shrimp, and other morsels of sushi, along with six rolls of tuna

and rice in seaweed (*onigiri*). Sushi Dai is nestled in a row of barracks housing other restaurants and shops beside the covered market. To find it, cross the bridge that leads to the market grounds, take a right past the various small shops selling knives and fish-related cooking objects, and then your first left. To your right will be the barracks. Sushi Dai is located in Building 6 on the third alley. Look for the blue curtains outside its front door.

6. ASAKUSA

EXPENSIVE

JAPANESE FOOD

MUGITORO ㉘, **2-2-4 Kaminarimon. Tel. 3842-1066.**
 Cuisine: YAMS. **Reservations:** Recommended. **Station:** Asakusa, a 1-minute walk away.
 $ Prices: Set-dinner courses ¥7,500–¥14,000 ($53.55–$100); set lunch ¥5,500 ($39.30). AE, DC, JCB, MC, V.
 Open: Tues–Sun 11:30am–8:30pm (last order).
Founded about 60 years ago but now housed in a new building, this restaurant specializes in *tororo-imo* (yam). Popular as a health food, yams are featured in almost all the dishes; the menu changes monthly. If you're walking here from Sensoji Temple, walk south on Edo Dori Avenue (with your back to Kaminarimon Gate) until you reach the first big intersection. Komagatabashi Bridge will be to your left, and Mugitoro is located right beside the bridge and a tiny playground. Look for the big white lanterns hanging outside.

KUREMUTSU ㉙, **2-2-13 Asakusa. Tel. 3842-0906.**
 Cuisine: KAISEKI/GRILLED DISHES. **Reservations:** A must. **Station:** Asakusa, about a 5-minute walk away.
 $ Prices: Set courses from ¥6,500 ($46.40); kaiseki from ¥8,800 ($62.85). No credit cards.
 Open: Dinner Fri–Wed 4–10pm.
Located just southeast of Sensoji Temple, Kuremutsu is actually a tiny house tucked behind an inviting courtyard with a willow tree, a millstone covered with moss, and an entrance invitingly lit with lanterns. Inside, it's like a farmhouse in the countryside, filled with farm implements, old chests, masks, cast-iron tea kettles, hibachi, and other odds and ends. Traditionally dressed to match the mood, waitresses will bring you fresh grilled fish, the restaurant's specialty, as well as platters of assorted sashimi and kaiseki. The menu is in Japanese only, and since only cash is accepted, make sure you know what you've ordered.

MODERATE

JAPANESE FOOD

KOMAGATA DOJO ㉚, **1-7-12 Komagata, Taito-ku. Tel. 3842-4001.**
 Cuisine: DOJO. **Reservations:** Recommended for dinner. **Station:** Asakusa Station, about a 3-minute walk away.
 $ Prices: Dishes ¥300–¥1,500 ($2.15–$10.70); set-dinner courses from ¥3,800 ($27.15); teishoku ¥2,700–¥7,000 ($19.30–$50). DC, JCB, MC, V.
 Open: Daily 11am–9pm.
Following a tradition spanning more than 185 years, this old-style dining hall specializes in *dojo*, a tiny sardinelike river fish that translates as a "loach." It's served in a variety of styles, from grilled to stewed. Teishoku are available throughout the day. The dining area is simply one large room of tatami mats, with ground-level boards serving as tables and waitresses moving quietly about dressed in traditional dress. To

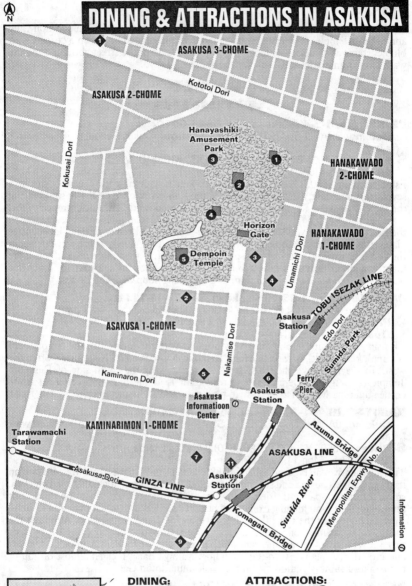

DINING & ATTRACTIONS IN ASAKUSA

ASAKUSA 3-CHOME

Kototoi Dori

ASAKUSA 2-CHOME

Kokusai Dori

Hanayashiki
Amusement
Park

HANAKAWADO
2-CHOME

Horizon
Gate

HANAKAWADO
1-CHOME

Dempoin
Temple

Umamichi Dori

ASAKUSA 1-CHOME

Nakamise Dori

Asakusa
Station

TOBU ISEZAK LINE

Edo Dori

Sumida Park

Kaminaron Dori

Asakusa
Information
Center

Asakusa
Station

Ferry
Pier

Tarawamachi
Station

KAMINARIMON 1-CHOME

Azuma Bridge

Asakusa Dori

GINZA LINE

Asakusa
Station

ASAKUSA LINE

Sumida River

Metropolitan Expwy No. 6

Komagata Bridge

Information

JAPAN
★TOKYO

DINING:
Chinya ➊
Daikokuya ➋
Ichimon ➊
Kamiya Bar ➏
Keyaki ➍
Komagata Mugitoro ➑
Komagata Dojo ➒
Kuremutsu ➌
Namiki ➐

ATTRACTIONS:
Asakusa Shrine ➊
Dempoin Temple ➎
Five-Storied Pagoda ➍
Hanayashiki Amusement Park ➌
Sensoji Temple ➋

reach the restaurant, walk south on Edo Dori Avenue (away from Kaminarimon Gate and Sensoji Temple). The restaurant—a large, old-fashioned house on a corner, with blue curtains at its door—is located on the right side of the street about a 5-minute walk from Kaminarimon Gate, past the Bank of Tokyo.

BUDGET

JAPANESE FOOD

CHINYA ③, 1-3-4 Asakusa. Tel. 3841-0010.
    Cuisine: SHABU-SHABU/SUKIYAKI. **Station:** Asakusa, about a 1-minute walk away.
    $ Prices: ¥1,400–¥2,100 ($10–$15). DC, JCB, MC, V.
    Open: Thurs–Tues 11:30am–9:30pm.

Established in 1880, Chinya is an old sukiyaki restaurant with a new home in a seven-story building, located to the left of the Kaminarimon Gate if you stand facing the famous Asakusa Kannon Temple: look for the sukiyaki sign. The entrance to this place is open-fronted. To the left of this main entrance is another entrance, leading to the basement, where you'll find a small, one-room casual eatery offering inexpensive plates of sukiyaki and shabu-shabu. Seating is around a counter, where you can watch the cooks at work. If you feel like splurging or wish to have a more relaxed meal, the main restaurant upstairs offers a very good shabu-shabu or sukiyaki set lunch for ¥2,500 ($17.85), available until 3pm and including soup and side dishes.

DAIKOKUYA ③, 1-38-10 Asakusa. Tel. 3844-1111.
    Cuisine: TEMPURA. **Station:** Asakusa, about a 5-minute walk away.
    $ Prices: ¥1,300–¥1,800 ($9.30–$12.85). No credit cards.
    Open: Thurs–Tues 11am–8:30pm.

This simple tempura restaurant is very popular with the locals. Try the tempura *ebi* (shrimp), *kisu* (smelt), or *kaki* (oysters). Daikokuya is located off Nakamise Dori to the west. To reach it, take the small street that passes by the south side of Dempoin Temple (also spelled Demboin); the restaurant is at the first intersection, a white corner building with a Japanese-style tiled roof and sliding front door.

KAMIYA BAR, 1-1-1 Asakusa. Tel. 3841-5400.
    Cuisine: JAPANESE/WESTERN. **Station:** Asakusa, less than a 1-minute walk away.
    $ Prices: ¥550–¥1,400 ($3.90–$10). No credit cards.
    Open: Wed–Mon 11:30am–9:30pm (last order).

This inexpensive eatery, established in 1880, serves both Japanese and Western fare on its three floors. The first and second floors offer Western food, including fried chicken, smoked salmon, spaghetti, fried shrimp, and hamburger steak, while the third floor serves Japanese food ranging from udon noodles and yakitori to tempura and sashimi. I personally prefer the third floor, both for its food and atmosphere. Although the menus are in Japanese only, there are extensive plastic-food display cases. In any case, this is a very casual restaurant, very much a place for the locals. It can be quite noisy and crowded. A plain brown-tiled building, Kamiya Bar is located almost on top of the Asakusa subway station, not far from Kaminarimon Gate.

KEYAKI ③, 1-34-5 Asakusa. Tel. 3844-9012.
    Cuisine: EEL. **Station:** Asakusa, a few minutes' walk away.
    $ Prices: A la carte dishes ¥550–¥10,000 ($3.90–$71.40); lunch teishoku ¥1,500–¥1,800 ($10.70–$12.85). No credit cards.
    Open: Lunch Tues–Sun 11:30am–2pm; dinner Tues–Sun 5–10pm.

This eel restaurant is located on the second street that parallels Nakamise Dori Avenue to the east—look for the brown flag with an eel on it and for the fish tank just inside the front door. A small place, with just a counter, a couple of tables, and an adjoining tatami room, Keyaki offers an eel set-lunch course (*unagi seto*) as well as tempura or sashimi courses. Try the house specialty, a sake called *ginjo-shu*.

NAMIKI ③, 2-11-9 Kaminarimon. Tel. 3841-1340.
    Cuisine: NOODLES. **Station:** Asakusa, a 3-minute walk away.

$ Prices: ¥600–¥1,500 ($4.30–$10.70). No credit cards.
Open: Fri–Wed 11:30am–7:30pm.

⭐ Asakusa's best-known noodle shop is this one-room place where prices range from ¥600 ($4.30) for plain noodles in cold or hot stock to ¥1,500 ($10.70) for tempura and noodles. There's an English menu, and seating is either at tables or on tatami mats. Since Namiki is small, don't linger once you've finished your meal if there are people waiting for a table. To reach the restaurant, take the road that leads south and away from Asakusa Kannon Temple and Kaminarimon Gate. Namiki is a brown building on the right side of the street, with some bamboo trees by the front door.

7. UENO

BUDGET

JAPANESE FOOD

IZU'EI ㉟, **2-12-22 Ueno. Tel. 3831-0954.**
Cuisine: EEL. **Reservations:** Recommended. **Station:** JR Ueno Station, a 3-minute walk away.
$ Prices: ¥1,500–¥3,000 ($10.70–$21.40); set courses ¥2,500–¥4,000 ($17.85–$28.55). AE, DC, JCB, MC, V.
Open: Daily 11am–9:30pm.
Put aside all your prejudices about eels and head for this modern, yet traditionally decorated restaurant with a 260-year history dating back to the Edo Period. Since eels are grilled over charcoal, the Japanese place a lot of stock in the quality of the charcoal used, and this place boasts its own furnace in the mountains of Wakayama Prefecture, which produces the best charcoal in Japan. *Unagi donburi* (rice with strips of eel on top), tempura, and sushi are available. Izu'ei is located across the street from Shinobazu Pond and the Shitamachi Museum.

NON-JAPANESE FOOD

MAHARAJA, 3rd floor of Nagafuji Building Annex, 4-6-9 Ueno. Tel. 3835-0818.
Cuisine: INDIAN. **Station:** JR Ueno Station, a 2-minute walk away.
$ Prices: Appetizers and soups ¥450–¥1,800 ($3.20–$12.85); main dishes ¥1,100–¥1,800 ($7.85–$12.85); set lunches ¥850–¥1,600 ($6.05–$11.40). No credit cards.
Open: Daily 11am–9:30pm.
This spotless modern restaurant offers curries and tandoori at prices that are cheaper than those in the majority of Tokyo's other Indian restaurants, with most dishes costing around ¥1,200 ($8.55). Decorated in a cool peach and pink, with etched mirrors and lots of brass, Maharaja is located in a modern building situated between busy Chuo Dori Avenue and the Ameyokocho shopping street.

8. HARAJUKU & AOYAMA

EXPENSIVE

NON-JAPANESE FOOD

L'ORANGERIE DE PARIS, 5th floor of Hanae Mori Building, 3-6-1 Kita-Aoyama, Minato-ku. Tel. 3407-7461.
Cuisine: FRENCH. **Reservations:** A must for dinner, recommended for lunch.
Station: Omote Sando, a 1-minute walk away.

$ Prices: Appetizers and soups ¥2,200–¥4,000 ($15.70–$28.55); main dishes ¥4,600–¥8,000 ($32.85–$57.15); set-dinner course ¥8,800 ($62.85); set lunch ¥4,400 ($31.40). AE, DC, JCB, MC, V.
Open: Lunch Mon–Sat 11:30am–2:30pm; dinner daily 5:30–10pm (last order 9:30pm); Sun brunch 11am–2:30pm.

This well-known Tokyo branch is sister of the Parisian restaurant of the same name. It's located in the chic area of Omote Sando, on the fifth floor of the Hanae Mori Building, which houses fashion designer Hanae Mori's entire collection. The building was designed by Kenzo Tange, who also designed the controversial Akasaka Prince Hotel, as well as a score of other buildings around town. Check out the front shop windows—they're always interesting. The menu changes often, but always offers set-lunch and -dinner courses. The very popular Sunday brunch costs ¥3,700 ($26.40), including tax and service, and seems to attract half the foreign population in Tokyo.

SABATINI, basement of Suncrest Building, 2-13-5 Kita-Aoyama. Tel. 3402-3812.
Cuisine: ITALIAN. **Reservations:** Recommended for dinner. **Station:** Gaienmae, a 2-minute walk away.
$ Prices: Appetizers and soups ¥1,400–¥2,800 ($10–$20); pasta ¥1,800–¥3,400 ($12.85–$24.30); main dishes ¥4,000–¥8,200 ($28.55–$58.55); set lunch ¥4,900 ($35). AE, DC, JCB, MC, V.
Open: Lunch daily 11:30am–2:30pm; dinner daily 5:30–11pm.
The three Italian brothers who own Sabatini have had a restaurant in Rome for more than 30 years. They take turns overseeing the Tokyo store, so one of them is always here, serving food or helping out in the kitchen. This restaurant, with its Italian furniture and tableware and strolling musicians, seems as if it had been moved intact from the Old World. In fact, the only thing to remind you you're in Tokyo are the Japanese waiters. The menu includes soups, spaghetti, seafood, veal, steak, lamb, and a variety of vegetables. You can do it cheaper at lunch with the set menu, which gives you a choice of soup or pasta, fish or meat, and salad and coffee. Sabatini is located on Aoyama Dori Avenue.

MODERATE
NON-JAPANESE FOOD

SABATINI PIZZERIA ROMANA, basement of Suncrest Building, 2-13-5 Kita-Aoyama. Tel. 3402-2027.
Cuisine: ITALIAN. **Station:** Gaienmae, a 1-minute walk away.
$ Prices: Appetizers and soups ¥1,000–¥1,800 ($7.15–$12.85); pasta and pizza ¥1,300–¥1,600 ($9.30–$11.40); main dishes ¥2,700–¥4,400 ($19.30–$31.40); set lunches ¥2,300–¥3,800 ($16.40–$27.15). AE, DC, JCB, MC, V.
Open: Lunch daily 11:30am–2:30pm; dinner daily 5:30–11pm.
This restaurant, opened in 1984 and owned by three brothers from Rome who operate an expensive Italian restaurant (also located in the Suncrest Building), offers the closest thing to real Italian pizza in town. Many ingredients are flown in from Italy, including olive oil, huge slabs of parmesan and other cheeses, as well as the restaurant's large wine selection; they've even shipped in a pasta machine. In addition to pizzas, the place also serves spaghetti, lasagne, fettuccine, and meat dishes. All you need order, however, is pizza. The pizzeria is 1 minute from Gaienmae, at the intersection of Aoyama Dori and Killer Dori avenues.

SELAN, 2-1-19 Kita-Aoyama. Tel. 3478-2200.
Cuisine: FRENCH/NOUVELLE JAPANESE. **Reservations:** Strongly recommended. **Station:** Gaienmae or Aoyama-Itchome, each a 5-minute walk away.
$ Prices: Appetizers and soups ¥750–¥2,000 ($5.35–$14.30); main dishes ¥1,600–¥3,800 ($11.40–$27.15); set-dinner course ¥5,500 ($39.30). AE, JCB, MC, V.
Open: Lunch daily 11:30am–2:30pm; dinner daily 6–10pm.

⭐ It looks like a French restaurant, with its sidewalk seating and pink, chandeliered interior, and the menu offers such fare as steaks, chicken, fish, lobster, and duck. However, the food is cooked using Japanese ingredients and thus may be classified as *"nouvelle japonaise"* cuisine. In any case, it's a successful marriage between French and Japanese cooking, with such innovative dishes as flounder stuffed with chopped shrimp and calamari and topped with sea urchin and vegetables, or seared bonito salad with soy sauce, garlic, and oil dressing. Little wonder that this is fast becoming one of Tokyo's most popular mealtime retreats. Large windows overlook a pleasant tree-lined street. Head upstairs for a meal; if the weather is fine and all you want is a coffee, try to get one of the ground-floor café's outdoor tables.

BUDGET
JAPANESE FOOD

GENROKUSUSHI ㊱, 5-8-5 Jingumae. Tel. 3498-3968.
   Cuisine: SUSHI. **Station:** Meiji-Jingumae, a 1-minute walk away; or Omote Sando, a 5-minute walk away.
   $ Prices: Sushi ¥120 and ¥240 (85¢ and $1.70). No credit cards.
   Open: Daily 11am–9pm.

Ⓢ This is another one of those fast-food sushi bars where plates of food are conducted along the counter on a conveyor belt. Customers help themselves to whatever strikes their fancy. Plates cost either ¥120 or ¥240, and to figure your bill, the cashier simply counts the number of plates you took from the conveyor belt. There are also takeout sushi boxes starting at ¥390 ($2.70), which you might want to eat in nearby Yoyogi Park. Genrokusushi is located on Omote Sando Dori Avenue close to the Oriental Bazaar.

NON-JAPANESE FOOD

BAMBOO SANDWICH HOUSE, 5-8-8 Jingumae. Tel. 3406-1828.
   Cuisine: SANDWICHES. **Station:** Omote Sando, Meiji-Jingumae, or Harajuku.
   $ Prices: ¥450–¥800 ($3.20–$5.70). No credit cards.
   Open: Daily 11am–9pm.

Ⓢ Located off Omote Sando on a side street beside the Paul Stuart shop, this place offers more than 20 sandwich fillings, and you have your choice of white or rye bread. What's more, it's probably the only place in town to offer a bottomless cup of coffee for a mere ¥220 ($1.55), a price that hasn't changed in a dozen years. This is a cheerful place that even boasts outdoor seating.

BEER MARKET DOMA, basement of Ga-Z Building, 6-5-3 Jingumae. Tel. 3498-7251.
   Cuisine: ASIAN. **Station:** Meiji-Jingumae, a 1-minute walk away; or Harajuku, a 3-minute walk away.
   $ Prices: ¥300–¥2,000 ($2.15–$14.30). No credit cards.
   Open: Lunch daily 11:30am–2pm; dinner daily 5–10:30pm.

⭐Ⓢ One of my favorite restaurants in Harajuku, this is a true gem in terms of prices, quality, and atmosphere—it's decorated with an earthen floor (*doma*) and silk cloth draped from the ceiling. The food is a mixture of Chinese, Japanese, Thai, and other Asian cuisine, along with *pao* dishes, originally from the Middle East, featuring such morsels as beef with *kimchi* (spicy Korean cabbage) and fish and curry wrapped in lettuce. In addition to its table-service menu, it has a help-yourself counter with a dozen or so selections ranging from salads, soups, and main dishes to desserts, with most prices under ¥800 ($5.70). This find is located on Meiji Dori toward Shibuya, just off Omote Sando.

EL AMIGO, 4-30-2 Jingumae. Tel. 3405-9996.
   Cuisine: MEXICAN. **Station:** Meiji-Jingumae, a 1-minute walk away.
   $ Prices: Dishes ¥600–¥1,000 ($4.30–$7.15). AE.
   Open: Dinner Mon–Fri 6pm–midnight, Sat–Sun 5pm–midnight.

This is one of the cheapest Mexican restaurants in town. To cut corners, they use cabbage instead of lettuce, but otherwise it's the usual tacos and enchiladas, margaritas and Mexican beer—a lot of people come here just for those margaritas. There's an outdoor patio of sorts, below street level and smothered in plants. The place is cheerful and often crowded. It's located near the Omote Sando Dori Avenue and Meiji Dori Avenue intersection, on a side street beside Wendy's hamburger shop.

EL POLLO LOCO, 1-13-12 Jingumae. Tel. 3408-4024.
  Cuisine: CHICKEN. **Station:** Harajuku or Meiji-Jingumae, each about a 1-minute walk away.
$ Prices: ¥350–¥1,800 ($2.50–$12.85). No credit cards.
  Open: Daily 10am–10pm.
If you're crazy about charbroiled chicken at reasonable prices, head straight for El Pollo Loco, a California fast-food chain specializing in charbroiled chicken served with tortillas and mild salsa. A two-piece combo comes with two pieces of chicken, two tortillas, salsa, rice, and a small side dish. Side dishes include coleslaw, corn on the cob, and potato salad. Also available: a curry chicken burger and an Oriental chicken burger. The place is located on Omote Sando Dori Avenue.

MOMINOKI HOUSE, 2-18-5 Jingumae. Tel. 3405-9144.
  Cuisine: NOUVELLE JAPANESE/FRENCH. **Station:** Harajuku or Meiji-Jingumae, each about a 15-minute walk away.
$ Prices: Dishes ¥1,000–¥2,000 ($7.15–$14.30); set lunches ¥850–¥1,100 ($6.05–$7.85). No credit cards.
  Open: Mon–Sat 11am–11pm (last order 10pm). **Closed:** Hols.
I'm not sure how to categorize Mominoki House. The dishes could be described as French, except that they're the special creations of a chef who uses lots of soy sauce, ginger, and Japanese vegetables. Suffice it to say that Mominoki House is in a category all by itself. Serving macrobiotic foods, this alternative restaurant features hanging plants and split-level dining, allowing for more privacy than one would think possible in such a tiny place. Its recorded jazz collection is extensive, and on weekends there's live music. Dishes may include the likes of tofu steak, duck, sole, escargots, eggplant gratin (baked in a delicious white sauce), salads, and homemade sorbet. An especially good deal is the daily lunch special, featuring brown rice, *miso* soup, salad, fish or another main dish, and a glass of wine. There's an English menu, but daily specials are written on the blackboard, in Japanese only. The chef speaks English, so if in doubt ask him what he recommends. You're best off taking a taxi from either the Harajuku and or the Meiji-Jingumae station.

SHAKEY'S, 6-1-10 Jingumae. Tel. 3409-2404.
  Cuisine: PIZZA. **Station:** Meiji-Jingumae, a few minutes' walk away.
$ Prices: All-you-can-eat pizza lunch ¥650 ($4.65). No credit cards.
  Open: Lunch Mon–Sat 11am–2pm.
Like the other Shakey's around town, this location on Omote Sando Dori Avenue near the Oriental Bazaar offers a buffet of all the pizza you can consume for lunch, a great bargain.

9. SHIBUYA

MODERATE

NON-JAPANESE FOOD

SEIYO HIROBA ㊲**, 5th floor of Prime Building, 2-29-5 Dogenzaka. Tel. 3770-1781.**

Cuisine: MEDITERRANEAN. **Reservations:** Recommended. **Station:** Shibuya, about a 2-minute walk away.
$ Prices: Dinner buffet ¥5,500 ($39.30); lunch buffet ¥2,200 ($15.70). AE, DC, JCB, MC, V.
Open: Lunch daily 11:30am–2pm; dinner daily 6–10pm.

Ⓢ   All-you-can-eat buffets are rare in Tokyo (the idea of piling a plate with food is alien to the Japanese), but this place would stand out even with competition. Its buffet offers a great selection of Mediterranean-influenced French and Spanish cuisine, with an emphasis on fresh fish, salads, and vegetables. Even if you don't eat a lot, this is a great place to come just for the atmosphere. Billing itself as a "resort restaurant," it tries to make customers feel as though they've embarked on a minivacation, with turquoise lighting, potted palms, a spacious dining area, candles on the tables, and free evening entertainment nightly, ranging from music or magic shows to pantomime. This place manages to look romantic even in the middle of the day. Highly recommended, especially if you're in Shibuya on a shopping spree.

BUDGET

JAPANESE FOOD

IROHANIHOHETO 33, 1-19-3 Jinnan, Shibuya-ku. Tel. 3476-1682.
Cuisine: YAKITORI/VARIED. **Station:** Shibuya, about a 10-minute walk away.
$ Prices: ¥350–¥500 ($2.50–$3.55). No credit cards.
Open: Dinner daily 5pm–4am.

Ⓢ   This boisterous drinking establishment offers inexpensive dining and is extremely popular with university students; if you get here after 7pm, you may have to wait for a place to sit. The extensive menu of both Japanese and Western food is in Japanese, but with pictures, and features nikujaga (potato and meat stew), fried tofu, oden (a tofu, fishcake, and vegetable stew), yakitori, fried noodles, potato salad, sashimi, and much more. Less than 10 minutes from the Shibuya subway station, and near the Parco I and II department stores, the restaurant is a little hard to find. Once you get to Parco, you'll probably have to ask someone on the street (it's in the basement of a modern building).

SHUNKASHUUTOU TENMI, 2nd floor of Daiichi Iwashita Building, 1-10-6 Jinnan, Shibuya-ku. Tel. 3496-9703.
Cuisine: MACROBIOTIC VEGETARIAN. **Station:** Shibuya, about a 5-minute walk away.
$ Prices: Most dishes ¥700–¥800 ($5–$5.70); set-dinner courses ¥1,000–¥2,500 ($7.15–$17.85); set lunches ¥1,100–¥1,700 ($7.85–$12.15). AE, DC, JCB, MC, V.
Open: Lunch Mon–Fri 11:30am–2:30pm; dinner Mon–Fri 5–10pm; Sat–Sun and hols 11:30am–7pm. **Closed:** Second and third Wed of every month.

★   If you're a vegetarian or looking for a Japanese health-food restaurant, this place serves traditional Japanese macrobiotic vegetarian food, along with unpolished brown rice. Dishes and set menus include various vegetable, tofu, noodle, and rice combinations. I found the set lunch for ¥1,100 ($7.85), which included brown rice, an assortment of boiled vegetables, seaweed, and miso soup, very satisfying and delicious. There's a health-food shop on the ground floor that sells the ingredients used in the restaurant. It's located near the TEPCO Electric Energy Museum.

NON-JAPANESE FOOD

THE PRIME, 2-29-5 Dogenzaka. Tel. 3770-0111.
Cuisine: INTERNATIONAL. **Station:** Shibuya, a 2-minute walk away.
$ Prices: ¥500–¥1,000 ($3.55–$7.15); set lunches ¥700–¥900 ($5–$6.40). No credit cards.

Open: Daily 11:30am–10pm.

If you find yourself in Shibuya, it's worth checking out The Prime, a great building filled with restaurants and amusements, including movie theaters, a dance and aerobics studio, and a concert and theater-ticket agency. The second floor is a large cafeteria, with various counters offering dishes from around the world, ranging from bagels and sandwiches to Indian curries, Chinese food, sushi, salads, and pastas. In the basement are a number of noodle shops serving Chinese, Singaporean, Kyushu, and Hokkaido styles of noodles. A great place for an inexpensive meal. The Prime is located a few minutes away from Shibuya Station, on Dogenzaka.

10. ELSEWHERE IN TOKYO

NEAR AKIHABARA

MODERATE

Japanese Food

KANDAGAWA ⓷⓼**, 2-5-11 Soto, Kanda. Tel. 3251-5031.**
Cuisine: EEL. **Reservations:** A must. **Station:** Akihabara, about a 5-minute walk away.
$ Prices: Appetizers and soups ¥400–¥600 ($2.85–$4.30); main dishes ¥2,200–¥3,300 ($15.70–$23.55). No credit cards.
Open: Lunch Mon–Sat 11:30am–2pm; dinner Mon–Sat 4:30–8pm. **Closed:** National hols.

This beautiful, old-fashioned, traditional Japanese restaurant has been famous for its eel dishes since the Edo Period. It's actually a Japanese-style wooden house, hidden behind a wooden gate and offering seven private tatami rooms, as well as a larger tatami dining room. The menu, in Japanese only, offers side dishes of soup, rice, and Japanese pickles, and such main dishes as *kabayaki* (broiled and basted eel); *unaju* (broiled eel on rice with a sweet sauce); *shiroyaki* ("white" eel, broiled without soy sauce of oil); and *umaki* (eel wrapped in an omelet). There's also grilled eel's liver, plus sashimi. Expect to spend a minimum of ¥7,000 ($50) per person, including drinks, appetizers, tax, and service. Since no one here speaks English, it's best to have a Japanese make your reservation, at which time you should order the dishes you'd like to be served. This is a great place for a splurge.

BUDGET

Japanese Food

YABU-SOBA ⓷⓽**, 2-10 Awajicho, Kanda. Tel. 3251-0287.**
Cuisine: NOODLES. **Station:** Awajicho, about a 5-minute walk away; or Akihabara, about a 10-minute walk away.
$ Prices: ¥600–¥1,200 ($4.30–$8.55). No credit cards.
Open: Tues–Sun 11:30am–7pm.

Soba (noodle) shops are among the least expensive restaurants in Japan, and this is one of Tokyo's most famous noodle places, established in 1880. Surrounded by a wooden gate and with a small bamboo-and-rock garden, the house features shoji screens, a wooden ceiling, and a dining area with tatami mats and tables. Although the building looks old, it dates only from the 1940s, the previous building having been flattened during World War II. You'll find the restaurant filled with middle-aged businessmen and housewives, and if you come during lunchtime you may have to wait for a seat. There's a menu in English, featuring noodles with shredded yam, topped with crispy shrimp tempura, or served with grilled eel. Listen to the woman sitting at a small counter by the kitchen—she sings out orders to the chef, as well as hellos and goodbyes to customers. Yabu-Soba is located between Awajicho and Akihabara stations, near Sotobori Dori and Yasukuni Dori avenues.

MEGURO

BUDGET

Japanese Food

TONKI ㊵, **1-1-2 Shimo Meguro, Meguro-ku. Tel. 3491-9928.**
Cuisine: TONKATSU. **Station:** Meguro, west exit, a 1-minute walk away.
$ **Prices:** ¥650–¥1,100 ($4.65–$7.85); set course ¥1,500 ($10.70). JCB, V.
Open: Dinner Wed–Mon 4–11pm (last order 10:30pm).

This is probably the best-known tonkatsu (pork cutlet) restaurant in town, and you'll probably have to wait for a seat at the counter. A man will ask if you want the hirekatsu (a filet cut of lean pork) or the rosukatsu (loin cut). If you're uncertain, he'll hold up the two slabs of meat and you just point to one. No matter which you pick, ask for the teishoku, the set meal, featuring soup, rice, cabbage, pickled vegetable, and tea. The man will scribble your order down on a piece of paper and put it with all the other scraps of paper, miraculously keeping track of not only which order belongs to whom but also which customers have been waiting for a seat the longest. The open kitchen behind the counter takes up most of the space in the restaurant, and as you eat you can watch the dozen or so cooks scrambling to turn out orders. Never a dull moment. You can get free refills of tea and cabbage. Tonki is on the side street that runs beside the Mitsui Bank. It has blue curtains over its sliding glass doors.

NEAR TOKYO STATION

BUDGET

Japanese Food

UOGASHI 34, 2-2-3 Nihombashi. Tel. 3271-8833.
Cuisine: SUSHI. **Station:** Nihombashi, a 3-minute walk away; or Tokyo Station, a 5-minute walk away.
$ **Prices:** ¥240 ($1.70) per 4 sushi. No credit cards.
Open: Lunch Mon–Sat 11:30am–2pm; dinner Mon–Sat 4–10pm. **Closed:** Hols.

A sushi bar for the adventurous, this is also one of the cheapest and best sushi places in town. Difficult to find, it's located near the Maruzen bookstore and the Takashimaya department store. First, look for the restaurant with the number 2-3 on it. You'll see display cases with plastic food in front of it, and short blue curtains in front of the sliding door. This is the main restaurant, but you want the stand-up sushi bar to its right, at the end of a short alley. Uogashi is tiny, just two small counters. There are no chopsticks, so you just eat with your fingers, and whatever you order will usually come in a set of four. Keep ordering until you've had your fill. When it's time to pay, your chef will yell your bill to the man beside the door at the cash register, which is just an old wooden box. Truly an experience.

11. SPECIALTY DINING

BEER GARDENS

If you're in Tokyo during the summer months, you should take advantage of the very popular beer gardens. These sprout up all over the city when the weather turns warm, often atop office buildings. In addition to the two establishments described below, another good place for an outdoor beer is Hibiya Park (located across from the Imperial Hotel), where there are various beer gardens and bars; open from about April to October, daily from 11am to 8pm.

HANEZAWA BEER GARDEN, 3-12-15 Hiro, Shibuya-ku. Tel. 3400-6500.
Cuisine: JAPANESE BARBECUE. **Reservations:** A must. **Station:** Ebisu, Omote Sando, or Shibuya; then take a taxi.
$ Prices: Appetizers ¥440–¥750 ($3.15–$5.35); main dishes ¥3,300–¥6,000 ($23.55–$42.85). No credit cards.
Open: Dinner daily 5–9pm (last order). **Closed:** Oct–Mar.

⭐ This is a lovely place to go for a meal and drinks. An outdoor garden spread under trees and paper lanterns, it looks traditionally Japanese and serves sukiyaki, shabu-shabu, Mongolian barbecue (cooked at your table), and a variety of snacks and other dishes. Note that if you want shabu-shabu or sukiyaki, however, you should notify the restaurant the day before. A mug of foaming beer starts at ¥500 ($3.55).

SUNTORY BEER GARDEN, rooftop of Suntory Building, 1-2-3 Moto-Akasaka. Tel. 3401-4367.
Cuisine: JAPANESE BARBECUE. **Reservations:** Highly recommended. **Station:** Akasaka-mitsuke, a 1-minute walk away.
$ Prices: Appetizers ¥500–¥700 ($3.55–$5); main dishes ¥1,300–¥2,400 ($9.30–$17.15). No credit cards.
Open: Dinner Mon–Sat 5–9pm (last order). **Closed:** Public hols and Sept–May.

⭐ With a great view of surrounding Akasaka, this rooftop beer garden is better and more sophisticated than most, with real palms and bushes circling the dining area instead of the plastic vegetation that usually seems to plague such places. Even more astounding, there's no Astroturf! In addition to its draft Suntory beer, which starts at ¥690 ($4.90) for a large mug, it offers a barbecued mix of sirloin, beef, or ram that you grill at your own table, as well as the usual beer snacks listed on an English menu. Purchase what you want from the ticket booth, sit down, and then hand the waiter your ticket.

COFFEE SHOPS

These coffee shops are located in Harajuku, which has the greatest concentration of sidewalk cafés in the capital. They're great for people-watching.

CAFE DE ROPE, 6-1-8 Jingumae. Tel. 3406-684.
Cuisine: COFFEE SHOP. **Station:** Meiji-Jingumae, about a 2-minute walk away; or Harajuku, a 3-minute walk away.
$ Prices: Coffee ¥600 ($4.30); beer from ¥650 ($4.65).
Open: Daily 11am–11pm.
Close to the Meiji–Omote Sando Dori intersection, the oldest outdoor café in Harajuku has long been a place popular with Tokyo's "beautiful people." In the wintertime, heaters and a plastic tarp keep the place in operation. In addition to beer, cocktails, and coffee, there are also cakes and sandwiches.

CAFE HAUS VIE BEN [CAFE B HAUS], ground floor of Vivre 21 Building, 5-10-1 Jingumae. Tel. 3498-2655.
Cuisine: COFFEE SHOP. **Station:** Meiji-Jingumae, a 4-minute walk away; or Harajuku, about a 5-minute walk away.
$ Prices: Coffee ¥500 ($3.55); beer ¥700 ($5).
Open: Daily 10am–10pm.
On Omote Sando Dori, right next to Shakey's pizza parlor, this slick sidewalk café opened in 1985 and features white-tiled floors and sleek black furniture. Probably the best place for people-watching.

DEMEL, Quest Building, 1-13-12 Jingumae. Tel. 3478-1251.
Cuisine: COFFEE SHOP. **Station:** Meiji-Jingumae or Harajuku, each about a 1-minute walk away.
$ Prices: Coffee ¥1,000 ($7.15).
Open: Daily 11am–11pm.

In a relatively new building called Quest, you'll find the exclusive Demel, modeled after Vienna's famous coffee shop. It's not a sidewalk café, but if it's raining or you feel like splurging, come here for sinful desserts.

BREAKFAST/BRUNCH

Sunday brunch is a favorite pastime of Tokyo's expatriate community, but it has caught on only in places where Westerners hang out—Tokyo's hotels and the cosmopolitan area of Aoyama. Below are some of the city's best brunch spots, all of which feature buffets.

AKASAKA

TEA LOUNGE, Capitol Tokyu Hotel, 2-10-3 Nagata-cho. Tel. 3581-4511.
Reservations: Recommended on weekends. **Station:** Kokkai Gijido-mae, a 1-minute walk away.
$ Prices: ¥2,600 ($18.55) per person. AE, DC, JCB, MC, V.
Open: Mon–Fri 7–10:30am, Sat–Sun 7am–noon.
Located just off the lobby, with a view of a traditional Japanese garden, the Tea Lounge is casual and pleasant. Seating is on sofas and overstuffed chairs.

TRADER VIC'S, New Otani Hotel, 4-1 Kioi-cho. Tel. 3265-4707.
Reservations: Recommended. **Station:** Akasaka-mitsuke, a 3-minute walk away.
$ Prices: ¥6,500 ($46.40) per person. AE, DC, JCB, MC, V.
Open: Sun and hols 11:30am–2:30pm.
If you like champagne for breakfast, this is the place, since it includes as much as you want of the bubbly stuff in the price of its buffet. The spread here takes in fresh fish, meats, salads, and desserts, in addition to breakfast foods.

SHINJUKU

MARBLE LOUNGE, in Tokyo Hilton International, 6-6-2 Nishi-Shinjuku. Tel. 3344-5111.
Reservations: Recommended Sun and hols. **Station:** Shinjuku, west exit, a 10-minute walk away.
$ Prices: ¥3,300 ($23.55) breakfast Mon–Sat; ¥4,400 ($31.40) brunch Sun and hols. AE, DC, JCB, MC, V.
Open: Mon–Sat 7–10:30am, Sun and hols 11am–2pm.
Dishes from the United States, Switzerland, Japan, and Indonesia are served in this Sunday buffet, including a German-Swiss porridge, a light stew of tofu with Japanese leeks, cheeses, croissants, omelets, bacon, hash-brown potatoes, and more. On other days, breakfast features waitress service.

HARAJUKU & AOYAMA

BRASSERIE D, Ecsaine Plaza Aoyama, 3-15-14 Kita-Aoyama, Minato-ku. Tel. 3470-0203.
Reservations: A must. **Station:** Omote Sando, a 2-minute walk away.
$ Prices: ¥3,000 ($21.40) per person. AE, DC, JCB, MC, V.
Open: Sun and hols noon–2:30pm.
This restaurant serves a very reasonable Sunday brunch, giving you a choice of beer, wine, kir, or juice, and a choice of omelet, croquette, or eggs Benedict. On the buffet table are a variety of salads, side dishes, and desserts. The nearest subway station is Omote Sando, and as you walk toward Gaienmae, you'll find Brasserie D on the left side of Aoyama Dori Avenue.

L'ORANGERIE DE PARIS, 5th floor of Hanae Mori Building, 3-6-1 Kita-Aoyama. Tel. 3407-7461.
Reservations: An absolute must. **Station:** Omote Sando, a 1-minute walk away.

$ Prices: ¥3,700 ($26.40) per person. AE, DC, JCB, MC, V.
Open: Sun 11am–2:30pm.

⭐ This Sunday brunch seems to attract half the foreign population of Tokyo. A place to see and be seen, it's located on Omote Sando Dori.

SPIRAL GARDEN, Spiral Building, 5-6-23 Minami Aoyama. Tel. 3498-5791.
Reservations: Highly recommended. **Station:** Omote Sando, a 1-minute walk away.
$ Prices: ¥2,700 ($19.30) per person. AE, DC, JCB, MC, V.
Open: Sun 11am–2pm.

Also in Omote Sando but on the other side of Aoyama Dori Avenue, Spiral is in a beautifully designed white building that opened in 1985 and houses galleries, a concert hall and theater, a shop on the second floor that specializes in well-designed kitchenware and household gadgets, and several restaurants. Spiral Garden also offers a brunch that includes a choice of cocktails, one egg dish, and a trip to the buffet. My one complaint is that the eggs almost always arrive cold, but a consolation is the live classical music that accompanies your meal.

LIGHT, CASUAL & FAST FOOD

There are ramen (Chinese noodle) shops all over Tokyo, easily recognizable by their red signs, flashing lights, and pictures of various dishes displayed by the front door. In addition to ramen you can also order gyoza (fried dumplings), fried noodles, and Chinese fast food. Since ramen shops are found on almost every corner in Tokyo, it seems pointless to single any out, but if you want specific addresses, there is one in Roppongi that is easy to find. If you walk from Roppongi Crossing toward Tokyo Tower, within a minute you'll find a ramen shop on your left, at 3-14-10 Roppongi (tel. 3408-9190).

There are also many obento establishments throughout the city, usually tiny hole-in-the-walls selling takeout sushi or box meals. Every neighborhood has such places; train stations are another good place to look. You can also find takeout food at every department store food section, usually located in the basement.

TOKYO ATTRACTIONS

Tokyo hasn't fared very well over the centuries. Fires and earthquakes have taken their toll, old buildings have been torn down in the zeal of modernization, and World War II left most of the city in ruins. The Tokyo of today has very little remaining of historical significance. Save your historical sightseeing for places like Kyoto, Nikko, and Kamakura, and consider Tokyo your introduction to Japan's economic miracle, the showcase of the nation's accomplishments in the arts, technology, fashion, and design. It is the best place in the world for taking in Japan's performing arts, such as Kabuki, and such diverse activities as the tea ceremony and flower arranging. Tokyo also has more museums than any other city in Japan, as well as a wide range of other attractions—from parks to temples. Go shopping, explore mammoth department stores, experiment with restaurants, visit museums, walk around the city's various neighborhoods, and take advantage of its glittering nightlife. There are plenty of things to do in Tokyo. I can't imagine being bored even for a minute.

I am including in this chapter several walking tours through districts in Tokyo that offer the most to tourists in terms of sightseeing and variety. This chapter also covers shopping, Tokyo's nightlife, and such cultural events as sumo and Kabuki.

SUGGESTED ITINERARIES

Two things to remember in planning your sightseeing itinerary are that the city is huge and that it takes time to get form one end to the other. Plan your days so you cover it neighborhood by neighborhood, coordinating sightseeing with dinner and evening plans. To help you get the most out of your stay, the suggested itineraries below will guide you to the most important attractions. Note, however, that some attractions are closed 1 day of the week, so plan your days accordingly.

IMPRESSIONS

Then I saw for the first time the true beauty of Tokyo, and of all Japanese cities. They are only beautiful at night, when they become fairylands of gorgeous neon: towers and sheets and globes and rivers of neon, in stunning profusion, a wild razzle-dazzle of colors and shapes and movements, fierce and delicate, restrained and violent against the final afterglow of sunset.
—JAMES KIRKUP, *THESE HORNED ISLANDS*, 1962

? DID YOU KNOW . . . ?

- Tokyo has been the capital of Japan since 1868 only; before that, Kyoto served as the capital for more than 1,000 years.
- About 10% of Japan's total population lives in Tokyo—12 million residents.
- Tokyo's labor force commutes to work an average of 1½ hours one way; even a 2-hour commute one way is not considered exceptionally long.
- Tokyo has some of the most expensive land in the world. In fashionable Aoyama, near Harajuku, a square meter of real estate costs approximately ¥15,5 million (approximately $110,000).
- Shinjuku Station handles the largest number of train and subway passengers in all Japan, more than a million people a day; more than 60 exits lead out of the station.
- Sunshine City, a 60-story skyscraper in Ikebukuro, is Japan's tallest building (790 feet) and claims to have the fastest elevators in the world, whisking passengers to the top floor in 35 seconds.
- Tokyo Disneyland, which opened in 1983, is 1½ times larger than Disneyland in California; by mid-1991 it had received more than 100 million visitors.

IF YOU HAVE 1 DAY

Day 1: Start by getting up in the wee hours of the morning (if you've just flown in from North America, you'll be suffering from jet lag anyway and will find yourself wide awake by 5am) and head for the Tsukiji Fish Market, Japan's largest wholesale fish market (closed Sunday and holidays). Be brave and try a breakfast of the freshest sushi you'll ever have. By 9am you should be on the Hibiya Line on your way to Ueno, where you should race to the Tokyo National Museum, the country's largest and most important museum (closed Monday). From there you should head to Asakusa for lunch in one of the area's traditional Japanese restaurants, followed by a walk on Nakamise Dori (good for souvenirs) to Sensoji Temple. In the afternoon you might want to go to Ginza for some shopping, followed by dinner in a restaurant of your choice. Drop by a yakitori-ya, a typical Japanese watering hole, for a beer and a snack. You might be exhausted by the end of the day, but you'll have seen some of the city's highlights.

IF YOU HAVE 2 DAYS

Day 1: Because 2 days still isn't much time, get up early and go to Tsukiji Fish Market to eat sushi for breakfast. Next, head for the nearby Hama Rikyu Garden, which opens at 9am (closed Monday). It's about a 20-minute walk from Tsukiji, or a short taxi ride away. After touring the garden, board the ferry that departs from inside the grounds for a trip up the Sumida River to Asakusa, where you can visit Sensoji Temple and shop along Nakamise Dori, followed by lunch in a traditional Japanese restaurant. In early afternoon, head to Hibiya for a glimpse of the Imperial Palace (closed to the public), followed by a stroll through Ginza and some shopping. If there's a performance, drop by the Kabukiza theater for part of a Kabuki play. Have dinner at a Ginza restaurant or at a yaki-tori-ya.

Day 2: On Day 2, head for Ueno, where you should walk through Ueno Park to the Tokyo National Museum. For lunch, board the Yamanote Line and go to Shinjuku Station, where, on the west side, there are a number of skyscrapers with top-floor restaurants that offer panoramic views of the city. After lunch, reboard the Yamanote Line and go two stations south to Harajuku, where you can visit Meiji Jingu Shrine, Tokyo's most famous Shinto shrine; the Ota Memorial Museum of Art, with its collection of woodblock prints; and the Oriental Bazaar, a great shop for souvenirs. Devote the rest of your afternoon to shopping, visiting more museums, or other attractions. Spend the evening in one of Tokyo's famous nightlife districts, such as Shinjuku or Roppongi.

IF YOU HAVE 3 DAYS

Days 1 and 2: Spend the first 2 days as outlined above.

Day 3: Head for Kamakura, one of Japan's most important historical sites. Located an hour south of Tokyo by train, Kamakura served as the capital back in the 1100s and is packed with temples and shrines.

IF YOU HAVE 5 DAYS OR MORE

Days 1–3: Spend the first 3 days as outlined above.

Day 4: Devote this day to pursuing your own interests, such as a visit to the Tokyo Stock Exchange, a trip to one of Tokyo's numerous specialty museums or a sumo stable, an appointment with an acupuncturist, shopping, or following one of the walking tours outlined later in this chapter. This may be the evening to spend in wild partying, staying out until the first subways start running at 5am.

Day 5: You might wish to make an excursion to Nikko, approximately 2 hours north of Tokyo by train. Nikko contains the sumptuous mausoleum of Tokugawa Ieyasu, the powerful shogun who succeeded in unifying Japan in the 1600s under his military rule. As an alternative, you might consider a 2-day trip to Hakone, famous for its open-air sculpture museum. If you have money or want to splurge, Hakone also has some of the best old-fashioned Japanese inns in the vicinity of Tokyo, and if the weather is clear, it offers great views of Mt. Fuji. If you prefer physical activity, you might even wish to climb Mt. Fuji itself. Information on destinations in the vicinity of Tokyo is provided in Chapter 10.

1. THE TOP ATTRACTIONS

THE IMPERIAL PALACE

The Imperial Palace, where Japan's imperial family lives, can be considered the heart of Tokyo. Built on the very spot where Edo Castle used to stand during the days of the Tokugawa Shogunate, it became the imperial home at its completion in 1888. The original structure was destroyed during air raids in 1945, and the palace was rebuilt in 1968. Except on New Year's Day and on the Emperor's Birthday (December 23), when the grounds are open to the public, the palace remains off-limits to visitors. You'll have to console yourself with a camera shot of the palace taken from the southeast side of Nijubashi Bridge, with the moat and the palace turrets showing above the trees. Tourists still like to make a brief stop here, enjoying the view of the wide moat lined with cherry trees, especially beautiful in the spring, or spending an hour walking the 3 miles around the palace and moat.

While in the vicinity of the palace, visit its **East Garden (Higashi Gyoen),** described below. This is where you'll find what's left of the central keep of old Edo Castle—the stone foundation. Built in the first half of the 1600s, Edo Castle was once the largest castle in the world, with an outer perimeter stretching 10 miles and a central keep 168 feet high, offering an expansive view of Edo. As you stand there on top of what's left of the keep's foundation, consider how different things used to look back then—a marsh surrounding the Sumida River, a fishing village where Hibiya now stands. You could see the shore of the bay; what's Ginza today used to be completely under water.

Bijutsukan Kogeikan (Craft Gallery) **13**
Bridgestone Bijutsukan **9**
Hama Rikyu Garden **5**
Hibiya Park **4**
Hie Jinja Shrine **14**
Higashi Goen (East Garden) **3**
Imperial Palace **15**
Japan Sword Museum **17**
Meiji Jingu Shrine **2**
National Science Museum **16**
Nezu Institute of Fine Arts **18**
Ota Kinen Bijutsukan (Ota Memorial Museum of Art) **11**
Riccar Art Museum **12**
Tokyo Kokuritsu Hakubutsukan **1**
Tokyo Kokuritsu Kindai Bijutsukan (National Museum of Modern Art) **10**
Tsukiji Fish Market (Uogashi) **7**
Ueno Park **6**
Yoyogi Park **8**

TOKYO ATTRACTIONS

SENSOJI TEMPLE, 2-3-1 Asakusa, Taito-ku. Tel. 3842-0181.

⭐ Sensoji Temple is Tokyo's oldest temple, dating from A.D. 628. Destroyed during an air raid in 1945, it was rebuilt in 1958. According to popular lore, the temple was erected to enshrine a tiny golden statue of Kannon that was fished out of the nearby Sumida River by two brothers. Kannon is the Buddhist goddess of mercy and happiness, and is empowered with the ability to release humans from suffering. Although the statue is still housed in Sensoji Temple, it is never shown to the public. Worshipers still flock here, however, to seek favors of Kannon and to shop at the traditional shops and souvenir stalls that line colorful Nakamise Dori.

Admission: Free.

Open: 24 hours. **Station:** Asakusa, a few minutes' walk away.

MEIJI JINGU SHRINE, 1-1 Kamizonocho, Yoyogi, Shibuya-ku. Tel. 3379-5511.

⭐ This is Tokyo's most venerable Shinto shrine, opened in 1920 in honor of Emperor and Empress Meiji, who were instrumental in opening Japan to the outside world a hundred years ago. A fine example of dignified and refined Shinto architecture, this shrine is made of Japanese cypress, topped with green-copper roofs. The pathway to the shrine leads through a dense forest of trees and shrubs, donated by people from throughout the country, and past two large torii built of cypress wood more than 1,700 years old (one of them is the largest wooden torii in all Japan). Meiji Jingu Shrine is *the* place to be on New Year's Eve, when more than two million people crowd onto the grounds to usher in the New Year.

Admission: Free.

Open: Daily 9am–5pm (4:30pm in winter). **Station:** Harajuku, a 2-minute walk away.

TOKYO NATIONAL MUSEUM (Tokyo Kokuritsu Hakubutsukan), Ueno Park, Taito-ku. Tel. 3822-1111.

⭐ In addition to being the largest museum in Japan, the Tokyo National Museum has the largest collection of Japanese art in the world. This is where you go to see antiques from Japan's past—old kimonos, samurai armor, priceless swords, lacquerware, pottery, scrolls, screens, ukiyo-e (woodblock prints), and more. Altogether, the museum has about 86,000 items in its collections, including more than 10,000 paintings, 1,000 sculptures, 15,500 pieces of metalwork, 3,000 swords, 3,700 pieces of lacquerware, 27,000 archeological finds, and 7,500 works of foreign Eastern art. Items are moved on a rotating basis, with about 4,000 shown at any one time. Thus, no matter how many times you visit the museum, you'll always see different things.

There are four principal buildings with museum displays. The **Main Gallery (Honkan),** straight ahead as you enter the main gate, is the most important one. Just inside the entrance is a desk where you can buy the *Tokyo National Museum Handbook,* which gives a room-by-room account of various periods in Japanese art history. You'll view Buddhist sculptures dating from about 538 to 1192; armor, helmets, and decorative sword mountings; swords, which throughout Japanese history were considered to embody spirits all their own; textiles; ceramics from prehistoric times; and paintings, calligraphy, and scrolls.

The **Gallery of Eastern Antiquities (Toyokan)** houses art and archeological artifacts from everywhere in Asia outside Japan. There are Buddhas from Pakistan from the 2nd and 3rd centuries; Egyptian relics, including a mummy dating from around 751–656 B.C. and wooden objects from the 20th century B.C.; bronze weapons from Iran; stone reliefs from Cambodia; embroidered wall hangings and cloth from India; Korean bronze and celadon; and Thai and Vietnamese ceramics. The largest part of the collection consists of Chinese art, including jade, glass, stone reliefs, paintings and calligraphy, mirrors, lacquerware, ceramics, and bronzes. China had a tremendous influence on Japan's art, architecture, and religion.

THE TOP ATTRACTIONS • 175

 FROMMER'S FAVORITE
TOKYO EXPERIENCES

A Stroll Through Sensoji Temple More than any other place in Tokyo, Sensoji Temple and the surrounding Asakusa convey a feeling of old Tokyo. Nakamise Dori, the pedestrian lane leading to the temple, is lined with shops selling souvenirs and traditional Japanese goods.

An Evening in a Yakitori-ya There's no better place to observe Tokyo's army of office workers at play than at a yakitori-ya, a drinking establishment that serves skewered foods and bar snacks. Fun, noisy, and boisterous.

A Kabuki Play at the Kabukiza Theater Kabuki has served as the most popular form of entertainment for the masses since the Edo Period. Watch the audience as they yell their approval; watch the stage for its gorgeous costumes, stunning stage settings, and easy-to-understand dramas of love, duty, and revenge.

Sunday in Harajuku Start with a Sunday brunch; then stroll the promenade of Omote Sando Dori Avenue to the Olympic stadiums, where young musicians, dancers, and performers entertain the crowds. Shop the area's boutiques, relax at a sidewalk café.

Tsukiji Fish Market This is Japan's largest fish market, where tuna, salmon, shrimp, squid, octopus, and other creatures from the deep are sold wholesale. The best part of the action is from 4 to 8am; the earlier you get there, the better.

A Day of Sumo Nothing beats watching huge sumo wrestlers, most weighing well over 200 pounds, throw each other around. Matches are held in Tokyo in January, May, and September. Great fun and not to be missed.

Department Store Shopping Tokyo's department stores are huge, spotless, and filled with merchandise you never knew existed. Seibu in Ikebukuro is the city's largest, a virtual city in itself. The greatest concentration is in Shibuya.

A Spin Through Kabuki-cho Shinjuku's Kabuki-cho has the craziest nightlife in all of Tokyo, with countless strip joints, pornography shops, restaurants, bars, and the greatest concentration of neon you're likely to see anywhere. A fascinating place for an evening's stroll.

Discos in Roppongi You can dance the night away in the madness that's Roppongi; most revelers party till dawn.

The **Hyokeikan Gallery** is where you'll find archeological relics of Japan, including pottery and objects from old burial mounds. One room is devoted to items used in daily life by the Ainu, an indigenous ethnic group now confined mainly to Hokkaido (refer to Chapter 16 for more information regarding the Ainu).

The fourth building is the **Gallery of Horyuji Treasures,** which houses a collection from the Horyuji Temple in Nara, including gilt-bronze Buddhist statuettes, other religious objects, and paintings. This building is open only on Thursday, and only then if the weather is dry, since wet weather would damage the fragile contents inside.

Admission: ¥400 ($2.85).

Open: Tues–Sun 9am–4:30pm (enter by 4pm). **Station:** Ueno, about a 7-minute walk away.

2. MORE ATTRACTIONS

FISH MARKET & STOCK MARKET

TSUKIJI FISH MARKET

⭐ This huge wholesale fish market—the largest in Japan—is a must for anyone who has never seen such a market in action, and the action here starts early. At about 3am, boats begin arriving from the seas around Japan, from Africa, and even from America with enough fish to satisfy the demands of a nation where seafood reigns supreme. The king is tuna, huge and frozen, unloaded from the docks, laid out on the ground, and numbered. Wholesalers then walk up and down the rows, jotting down the numbers of the best-looking tuna, and by 6am the auctions for tuna are well under way. The wholesalers then transfer what they've bought to their own stalls in the market, subsequently selling the fish to their regular customers, usually retail stores and restaurants.

This market is held in a cavernous, hangarlike covered building, which means that you can visit it even on a dismal rainy morning. To give you some idea of its enormity, this market handles almost all the seafood consumed in Tokyo.

There's a lot going on—men in black rubber boots rushing wheelbarrows and carts through the aisles, hawkers shouting, knives chopping and slicing. This is a good place to bring your camera if you have a flash: the people working here burst with pride if you single them out for a photograph. Because the floors are wet, leave your fancy shoes at the hotel.

This is also a good place to come if you want sushi for breakfast. Beside the covered market are rows of barracklike buildings divided into sushi restaurants and shops related to the fish trade. Sushi Dai, for example, offers a seto for ¥1,200 ($8.55); it's open every day except Sunday and holidays from 5am to 1:30pm.

As you walk the distance between the Tsukiji subway station and the fish market, you'll find yourself in a delightful district of tiny retail shops and stalls where you can buy the freshest seafood in town, plus dried fish and fish products, seaweed, vegetables, and cooking utensils. In this area and beside the market are stalls selling cheap sushi, noodles, and fish, catering mainly to buyers and sellers at the market who come for a quick breakfast.

There are also a lot of pottery shops and stores that sell plastic and lacquered trays, bowls, and cups. Although they usually sell in great quantities to restaurant owners, shopkeepers will usually sell to the casual tourist as well.

Admission: Free.
Open: Mon–Sat 3–10am (best time 4–8am). **Closed:** Hols, Aug 15, 16.
Station: Tsukiji (Hibiya Line), Honganji Temple exit.

TOKYO STOCK EXCHANGE, 2-1 Nihonbashi-Kabutocho, Chuo-ku. Tel. 3666-0141 (information).

Established in 1878, the Tokyo Stock Exchange vies with that of New York as one of the busiest exchanges in the world. It's located in the Nihombashi/Kyobashi district, a commercial area even during the Edo Period and known today as the Wall Street of Japan. The Tokyo Stock Exchange has some of the shortest trading hours in the world. Visitors, in addition to watching the frenetic trading floor from a glass-enclosed observation deck, can view an excellent display called Exhibition Plaza. On its first floor is a hall that traces the history of the Japanese securities market, while its second floor contains an array of audiovisual displays that enhance the visitor's knowledge of securities and the stock market. What's more, the entire Plaza has explanations in English. A three-dimensional display explains the intricacies of what you see on the trading floor and how it all works, while a robot demonstrates the various hand signals used by the traders. Computers simulate the actual experience

of investing in stock by asking questions and leading the viewer through various procedures.
Admission: Free.
Open: Mon–Fri 9–11am and 12:30–3pm. Free English tours Mon–Fri 9:30am and 1:30pm; about 1 hour. **Closed:** National hols. **Station:** Kayabacho, Exit 11, a 5-minute walk away; or Nihombashi Station, Exit A2, a 5-minute walk away.

PARKS & GARDENS

Although Japan's most famous gardens are not in Tokyo, the first three places listed below use principles of Japanese landscaping and give visitors an idea of the scope and style of these gardens. The fourth listing, Ueno Park, is Tokyo's largest park and contains a number of museums and attractions, making it one of the city's most visited places.

EAST GARDEN (Higashi Gyoen), 1 Chiyoda, Chiyoda-ku. Tel. 3213-1111.

The 53 acres of this formal garden were once part of Edo Castle, of which a stone foundation still remains. A pleasant and peaceful oasis right in the heart of the city, the garden contains sculpted bushes and a pond framed with wisteria. It's east of the Imperial Palace.
Admission: Free.
Open: Tues–Thurs and Sat–Sun 9am–4pm (enter by 3pm). **Station:** Otemachi, Takebashi, or Nijubashi-mae.

HAMA RIKYU GARDEN, 1-1 Hamarikyuteien, Chuo-ku. Tel. 3541-0200.

Considered by some to be the best garden in Tokyo, this was once the site of a villa of a former feudal lord where the Tokugawa shoguns practiced falconry. In 1871 possession of the garden passed to the imperial family, and it was opened to the public after World War II. Come here to see how the upper classes enjoyed themselves during the Edo Period. Surrounded by water on three sides, the garden contains an inner tidal pool, spanned by three bridges draped with wisteria. There are also other ponds, a promenade along the river lined with pine trees, moon-viewing pavilions, and teahouses. From a boarding pier inside the garden's grounds, ferries depart for Asakusa every hour or so between 10:25am (10:15am on weekends and holidays) and 4:05pm; the fare is ¥520 ($3.70) one way.
Admission: ¥200 ($1.40).
Open: Tues–Sun 9am–4:30pm. **Station:** Shimbashi, a 10-minute walk away.

SHINJUKU GYOEN, 11 Naitocho, Shinjuku-ku. Tel. 3350-0151.

Formerly the private estate of a feudal lord and then of the imperial family, this is a wonderful park for strolling because of the variety of its planted gardens—styles ranging from French and English to Japanese traditional. It amazes me every time I go there. The park's 144 acres make it one of the city's largest, and each bend in the pathway brings something completely different: ponds and sculpted bushes give way to a promenade lined with sycamores, which opens up into a rose garden. Cherry blossoms, azaleas, chrysanthemums, and other flowers provide splashes of color from spring through autumn. A greenhouse is filled with tropical plants.
Admission: ¥160 ($1.15).
Open: Tues–Sun 9am–4:30pm (enter by 4pm). **Station:** Shinjuku Gyoen-mae, a 2-minute walk away.

UENO PARK, Taito-ku.

Ueno Park and its many attractions—on the northeast edge of the Yamanote Line—constitute one of the most popular places in Tokyo for Japanese families on a day's outing. Opened in 1873, it was the city's first public park and the first place in Japan to see the establishment of a museum and a zoo. Today, it's one of the largest parks in Tokyo and a cultural mecca with a number of museums, including the prestigious **Tokyo National Museum** and the delightful **Shitamachi Museum,** with its displays of old Tokyo; **Ueno Zoo;** and **Shinobazu Pond,** a bird sanctuary.

A landmark in the park is a **statue of Takamori Saigo,** a samurai born in 1827 near Kagoshima on Kyushu Island. After helping restore the emperor to power after the downfall of the Tokugawa Shogunate, Saigo subsequently became disenchanted with the Meiji regime when rights enjoyed by the military class were suddenly rescinded. He led a revolt that failed, and ended up taking his own life in ritualistic suicide. The statue, erected in 1898, became the center of controversy when Gen. Douglas MacArthur, leader of the occupation forces in Japan after World War II, demanded that the statue be removed because of its ties to nationalism. The Japanese people protested in a large public outcry and MacArthur finally relented. Today, the statue is one of the best known in Tokyo.

Another well-known landmark in Ueno Park is **Toshogu Shrine.** Erected in 1651, it is dedicated to Tokugawa Ieyasu, founder of the Tokugawa Shogunate. Stop here to pay respects to the man who made Edo (present-day Tokyo) the seat of his government and thus elevated the small village to the most important city in the country. The pathway to the shrine is lined with massive stone lanterns that were donated by various feudal lords.

The busiest time of the year at Ueno Park is in April, during the cherry blossom season, and people come here en masse to celebrate the birth of the new season. It's not the spiritual communion with nature that you might think, however. In the daytime on a weekday, Ueno Park may be peaceful and sane enough, but on the weekends and in the evenings during cherry blossom season, havoc prevails as office workers break out of their winter shells. Whole companies of workers converge on Ueno Park to sit under the cherry trees on plastic or cardboard, where they drink sake and beer and get drunk and rowdy. The worst offenders are those who sing loudly into microphones, accompanied by cassettes playing the appropriate instrumental music to each song; this is a popular entertainment called *karaoke,* also found in special clubs devoted to it. At any rate, visiting Ueno Park during cherry blossom season is an experience no one should miss. More than likely you'll be invited to join one of the large groups—by all means do.

Admission: Free to Ueno Park; separate admissions to each of its attractions.

Open: Ueno Park open 24 hours. **Station:** Ueno, a 1-minute walk away.

OBSERVATION PLATFORMS

TOKYO TOWER, 4-2 Shiba Koen, Minato-ku. Tel. 3433-5111.

Japan's most famous observation tower, Tokyo Tower was built in 1958 and modeled after the Eiffel Tower in Paris. Lit up at night, this 1,089-foot tower is a familiar landmark in the city's landscape, but has lost its popularity over the decades with the construction of Tokyo's skyscrapers. The best time of year to go up is supposedly during Golden Week, at the beginning of May. With many Tokyoites gone from the city and most factories and businesses closed down, the air is thought to be the cleanest and clearest at this time, affording views of the far reaches of the city—and exactly how far this city stretches will amaze you.

Admission: Main observatory (492 feet high) ¥720 ($5.15); top observatory (820 feet high) ¥520 ($3.70) more.

Open: Apr–Oct daily 9am–8pm; Nov–Mar daily 9am–6pm. **Station:** Onarimon or Kamiyacho.

OBSERVATORY, Sunshine City Building, 3-1-1 Higashi Ikebukuro.

At the other end of Tokyo is the city's tallest building, the 60-story Sunshine City Building. On the top floor is an observatory. A special elevator—reputedly the world's fastest—whisks you there in 35 seconds. If you want to forgo the price of the observatory and the fast elevator, take one of the regular elevators to the 59th floor, where you can relax over a cup of coffee at Le Trianon Lounge, open daily from 10am to 2am.

Admission: ¥620 ($4.40).

Open: Daily 10am–8pm. **Station:** Ikebukuro, a 5-minute walk away.

SUMITOMO BUILDING, 51st floor, 2-6-1 Nishi-Shinjuku.

This is one of my favorite buildings among the skyscrapers that rise above the west

side of Shinjuku. It's a triangular structure that's hollow inside, and if you stand in the middle of the ground-floor lobby and look up, you can see past the glass roof and more than 50 stories to the sky above. On the 49th to 52nd floors are coffee shops and restaurants. On the 51st floor is a one-room observatory that provides a great view of Tokyo.
Admission: Free.
Open: Daily 10am–10pm. **Station:** Shinjuku, west exit, a 7-minute walk away.

MUSEUMS

Note that most museums are closed on Monday and the first 3 days of the New Year. If Monday happens to be a national holiday, however, most museums will remain open but will close the next day, Tuesday, instead. Call beforehand to avoid disappointment. Remember, too, that you must enter museums at least 30 minutes before closing time. For a listing of current special exhibitions, consult the *Tokyo Journal* or *Tokyo Time Out*, both published monthly.

GOTO ART MUSEUM (Goto Bijutsukan), 3-9-25 Kaminoge, Setagaya-ku. Tel. 3703-0661.
This museum houses fine arts and crafts of ancient Japan, China, and other Asian countries, including calligraphy, paintings, ceramics, and lacquerware. Surrounding the museum is a garden with a teahouse.
Admission: ¥500 ($3.55) and up.
Open: Tues–Sun 9:30am–4:30pm (enter by 4pm). **Closed:** During exhibit changes. **Station:** Kaminoge.

HARA MUSEUM OF CONTEMPORARY ART (Hara Bijutsukan), 4-7-25 Kita-Shinagawa, Shinagawa-ku. Tel. 3445-0651.
Devoted to contemporary international and Japanese art, this pleasant museum is housed in a Bauhaus-style art-deco building that used to be the Hara family home. The building itself is worth the trip. Featuring paintings and sculptures mainly from the 1950s and 1960s by Japanese and foreign artists, it also holds regular exhibitions for rising young artists.
Admission: ¥700 ($5).
Open: Tues–Sun 11am–5pm. **Station:** Shinagawa, then by taxi.

NATIONAL MUSEUM OF MODERN ART (Tokyo Kokuritsu Kindai Bijutsukan), Kitanomaru Koen Park, Chiyoda-ku. Tel. 3214-2561.
This is Japan's best display of modern Japanese art, including paintings, sculptures, prints, watercolors, and drawings, dating from the Meiji Period onward. A few Western artists are also represented.
Admission: ¥400 ($2.85).
Open: Tues–Sun 10am–5pm (enter by 4:30pm). **Station:** Takebashi, less than a 5-minute walk away.

NATIONAL MUSEUM OF WESTERN ART (Kokuritsu Seiyo Bijutsukan), Ueno Park, Taito-ku. Tel. 3828-5131.
With a main building designed by Le Corbusier, this museum features Western art, with a concentration on French impressionism. Artists include Renoir, Monet, Sisley, Manet, Degas, and Cézanne, as well as El Greco, Goya, and Delacroix. The museum is also famous for its 50-odd sculptures by Rodin, the third-largest Rodin collection in the world.
Admission: ¥400 ($2.85).
Open: Tues–Sun 9:30am–5pm (enter by 4:30pm). **Station:** Ueno, 5-minute walk away.

NEZU ART MUSEUM (Nezu Bijutsukan), 6-5-36 Minami Aoyama, Minato-ku. Tel. 3400-2536.
This museum houses a fine collection of Asian art, including Chinese bronzes, Japanese calligraphy, Korean ceramics, and other artwork. The museum is surrounded by a delightful small garden with several teahouses.
Admission: ¥1,000 ($7.15).

Open: Tues–Sun 9:30am–4:30pm. **Closed:** Day following hols, during exhibition changes, and Aug. **Station:** Ōmote Sando, a 10-minute walk away.

OTA MEMORIAL MUSEUM OF ART (Ota Kinen Bijutsukan), 1-10-10 Jingumae, Shibuya-ku. Tel. 3403-0880.

⭐ This great museum features the private ukiyo-e (woodblock print) collection of the late Ota Seizo, who early in life recognized the importance of ukiyo-e as an art form and dedicated his life to its preservation. Exhibitions of the museum's 12,000 prints are changed monthly, with descriptions of the displays in English. The museum itself is small but delightful, with such traditional touches as bamboo screens, stone pathways, and even a small tearoom that sells Japanese sweets.

Admission: ¥500–¥800 ($3.55–$5.70).

Open: Tues–Sun 10:30am–5:30pm (enter by 5pm). **Closed:** From the 24th to the end of every month. **Station:** Harajuku or Meiji Jingumae, each a 2-minute walk away.

RICCAR ART MUSEUM (Riccar Bijutsukan), 7th floor of Riccar Building, 6-2-3 Ginza, Chuo-ku. Tel. 3571-3254.

This is another museum specializing solely in ukiyo-e. It has approximately 6,000 prints in its collection, which it displays on a rotating basis, with displays changed monthly.

Admission: ¥300–¥500 ($2.15–$3.55).

Open: Tues–Sun 11am–6pm. **Closed:** During exhibition changes. **Station:** Ginza or Hibiya, each less than a 5-minute walk away.

SUNTORY MUSEUM OF ART (Suntory Bijutsukan), 11th floor of Suntory Building, 1-2-3 Moto-Akasaka, Minato-ku. Tel. 3470-1073.

Exhibitions change regularly, and may feature ceramics, screens, glass objects, lacquerware, paintings, or prints, on loan from other museums and collections from around the world.

Admission: ¥800–¥1,000 ($5.70–$7.15).

Open: Tues–Sun 10am–5pm (7pm Fri). **Closed:** During exhibit changes. **Station:** Akasaka-mitsuke, a 1-minute walk away.

TOKYO METROPOLITAN ART MUSEUM (Tokyo-to Bijutsukan), Ueno Park, Taito-ku. Tel. 3823-6921.

This museum features modern Japanese works, mainly by 20th-century artists, with temporary exhibitions.

Admission: Separate admission fees for each exhibit, usually ¥500–¥800 ($3.55–$5.70).

Open: Tues–Sun 9am–5pm (enter by 4pm). **Closed:** During exhibit changes. **Station:** Ueno, about a 6-minute walk away.

CRAFTS GALLERY (Bijutsukan Kogeikan), Kitanomaru Koen Park, Chiyoda-ku. Tel. 3211-7781.

Housed in a Gothic-style brick building constructed in 1910 as headquarters of the Imperial Guard, the Crafts Gallery collects contemporary crafts, including lacquerware, ceramics, textiles, bamboo works, and dolls, which it shows in rotating exhibitions.

Admission: ¥400 ($2.85) and up, depending on exhibit.

Open: Tues–Sun 10am–5pm (enter by 4:30pm). **Station:** Takebashi, a 10-minute walk away.

DAIMYO CLOCK MUSEUM (Daimyo Tokei Hakubutsukan), 2-1-27 Yanaka, Taito-ku. Tel. 3821-6913.

This small museum displays about 50 clocks drawn from its extensive collection of clocks made during the Edo Period. Displays change annually.

Admission: ¥300 ($2.15).

Open: Tues–Sun 10am–4pm. **Closed:** Dec 25–Jan 15 and June–Sept. **Station:** Nezu, a 10-minute walk away.

DRUM MUSEUM (Taikokan), **2-1-1 Nishi-Asakusa, Taito-ku. Tel. 3842-5622.**

This new museum houses traditional Japanese drums, including those used in festivals throughout the country, as well as drums from around the world. With the exception of some of the rare, older pieces, many of the drums can be touched and played. There are also videos of drumming from Japan and around the world.
Admission: ¥200 ($1.40).
Open: Wed–Sun 10am–5pm. **Closed:** Hols. **Station:** Tawaramachi, about a 2-minute walk away.

FUKAGAWA EDO MUSEUM (Fukagawa Edo Shiryokan), **1-3-28 Shirakawa, Koto-ku. Tel. 3630-8625.**

This delightful museum reproduces a 19th-century neighborhood in Fukagawa, a prosperous community on the east bank of the Sumida River during the Edo Period. The hangarlike interior contains 11 houses, vegetable and rice shops, a fish store, two inns, and tenement homes. There are lots of small touches and flourishes to make the community seem real and believable—a cat sleeping on a roof, a snail crawling up a fence, a dog relieving itself on a pole, and sounds of birds, a vendor shouting his wares, horse's hooves clattering, and a dog barking. Of Tokyo's museums, this one would probably be the preferred choice of children.
Admission: ¥300 ($2.15).
Open: Daily 10am–5pm. **Station:** Monzen-Nakacho or Morishita, each a 15-minute walk away; from either station, bus no. 33 toward Kiyosumi Garden to Kiyosumi Teien-mae bus stop.

FURNITURE MUSEUM (Kagu no Hakubutsukan), **2nd floor of JIC Building, 3-10 Harumi, Chuo-ku. Tel. 3533-0098.**

Traditional Japanese furniture is preserved and displayed, as well as some antique European furniture.
Admission: ¥400 ($2.85).
Open: Thurs–Tues 10am–4:30pm. **Closed:** Hols. **Station:** Ginza or Tsukiji, then by taxi.

HATAKEYAMA MEMORIAL MUSEUM (Hatakeyama Kinenkan), **2-20-12 Shiroganedai, Minato-ku. Tel. 3447-5787.**

Its emphasis is on tea-ceremony ceramics and other objects, but it also has paintings, calligraphy, sculptures, and lacquerware from ancient Japan and China.
Admission: ¥500 ($3.55).
Open: Tues–Sun 10am–5pm (4:30pm Oct–Mar). **Closed:** Third and fourth weeks in Mar, June, Sept, and Dec, and first week in Jan. **Station:** Takanawadai, a 6-minute walk away.

JAPAN FOLK CRAFTS MUSEUM (Nippon Mingeikan), **4-3-33 Komaba, Meguro-ku. Tel. 3467-4527.**

Folk art gathered from around Japan is displayed in this very special museum, including furniture, pottery, and textiles, many dating from the Edo and Meiji eras. Crafts from other Asian (as well as from European) countries are also on display.
Admission: ¥700 ($5).
Open: Tues–Sun 10am–5pm. **Station:** Komaba-Todaimae (Keio-Inokashira Line), a 5-minute walk away.

KITE MUSEUM (Tako no Hakubutsukan), **5th floor of Taimeiken Building, 1-12-10 Nihombashi, Chuo-ku. Tel. 3271-2465.**

Kites from Japan and countries around the world are displayed.
Admission: ¥200 ($1.40).
Open: Mon–Sat 11am–5pm. **Closed:** Hols. **Station:** Nihombashi, a 3-minute walk away.

NATIONAL SCIENCE MUSEUM (Kokuritsu Kagaku Hakubutsukan), **Ueno Park, Taito-ku. Tel. 3822-0111.**

This sprawling complex covers everything from the evolution of life to electronics in Japan, aircraft, and automobiles. Unfortunately, not all displays are in English, but the museum is worth visiting for its exhibits relating to Japan, including its displays on the origin and development of the Japanese people, examples of Japanese architecture (no nails were used to join heavy wooden beams), the process of making Japanese lacquerware and paper, a "Zero" fighter plane from World War II, and an excellent collection of antique Japanese clocks.
Admission: ¥400 ($2.85).
Open: Tues–Sun 9am–4:30pm (enter by 4pm). **Station:** Ueno, about a 5-minute walk away.

PAPER MUSEUM (Kami no Hakubutsukan), 1-1-8 Horifune, Kita-ku. Tel. 3911-3545.

For enthusiasts of traditional hand-made Japanese paper, this museum displays products and utensils used in its creation.
Admission: ¥2.00 ($1.40).
Open: Tues–Sun 9:30am–4:30pm. **Closed:** Hols. **Station:** Oji, across from south exit.

SHITAMACHI MUSEUM (Shitamachi Fuzoku Shiryokan), Ueno Park, Taito-ku. Tel. 3823-7451.

Shitamachi means "downtown" and refers to the area of Tokyo in which commoners used to live, mainly around Ueno and Asakusa. There's very little left of old downtown Tokyo, and with that in mind, this museum seeks to preserve for future generations a way of life that was virtually wiped out by the great earthquake of 1923 and then by World War II. There are shops set up as they may have looked back then, including a merchant's shop and a candy shop, as well as one of the Shitamachi tenements common at the turn of the century. Long, narrow buildings with one roof over a series of dwelling units separated by thin wooden walls, these were the homes of the poorer people, confined to the narrow back alleys. Everyone knew everyone else's business; few secrets could be kept in such crowded conditions. The alleyways served as communal living rooms. Children played in them and families sat outside to catch whatever breeze there might be. The museum also displays relics relating to the life of these people, including utensils, toys, costumes, and tools, most of which are not behind glass but are simply lying around so that you can pick them up and examine them more closely. The museum's collections were all donated by individuals, many living in Shitamachi.
Admission: ¥200 ($1.40).
Open: Tues–Sun 9:30am–4:30pm. **Station:** Ueno, about a 3-minute walk away.

SUGINO COSTUME MUSEUM (Sugino Gakuen Isho Hakubutsukan), 4-6-19 Osaki, Shinagawa-ku. Tel. 3491-8151.

Clothing of Western Europe from around the 18th century, as well as that worn in Japan and other Asian countries, is displayed. Included are kimonos, samurai outfits, and costumes worn in Noh dramas and the comic kyogen plays that accompany them.
Admission: ¥200 ($1.40).
Open: Mon–Sat 10am–4pm. **Closed:** Hols. **Station:** Meguro, a 7-minute walk away.

SUMO MUSEUM (Sumo Hakubutsukan), 1-3-28 Yokoami, Sumida-ku. Tel. 3622-0366.

Located in the Kokugikan sumo stadium, it shows the history of sumo since the 18th century, with portraits and mementos of past grand champions.
Admission: Free, but during tournaments you must have sumo tickets to enter stadium.
Open: Mon–Fri 9:30am–4:30pm. **Closed:** Hols. **Station:** Ryogoku, a 1-minute walk away.

SWORD MUSEUM (Token Hakubutsukan), 4-25-10 Yoyogi, Sumi-da-ku. Tel. 3379-1386.

This museum pays tribute to Japanese swords, with more than 6,000 in its collection. Considered by the Japanese to embody spirits all their own, Japanese swords rank as an art form in the highest degree, and in feudal Japan swordmakers were respected masters.
Admission: ¥515 ($3.65).
Open: Tues–Sun 9am–4pm. **Station:** Sangubashi (Odakyu Line).

TEPCO ELECTRIC ENERGY MUSEUM, 1-12-10 Jinnan, Shibuya-ku. Tel. 3477-1191.
If you find yourself in Shibuya with nothing to do, or if you're interested in electricity, drop by this new public-service facility of the Tokyo Electric Power Company (TEPCO). Established to teach urban dwellers how electricity is generated, supplied, and consumed, it offers four floors of displays, including a model of a nuclear reactor and a "house of the future," equipped with the latest in appliances and technology. Visitors learn that TEPCO operates 11 nuclear power plants to supply Tokyo and its vicinity with electricity and that by 1994, nuclear power will account for 40% of TEPCO's power supply. An English-language pamphlet describes the displays.
Admission: Free.
Open: Thurs–Tues 10:30am–6:30pm (enter by 6pm). **Station:** Shibuya, a 5-minute walk on Koen Dori.

COOL FOR KIDS

TOKYO DISNEYLAND, 1-1 Maihama, Urayasu-shi, Chiba Prefecture. Tel. 0473/54-0001.
I'm not sure why anyone coming to Japan from the United States would want to spend time visiting Tokyo Disneyland, but in case you do, this one is virtually a carbon copy of the back-home versions. Here you can find the Jungle Cruise, Pirates of the Caribbean, Haunted Mansion, and Space Mountain (okay, I admit that I've been to Tokyo Disneyland three times). The hottest attractions are the park's newest: Big Thunder Mountain, a roller-coaster mining train that winds through a gorge; *Captain EO*, the 3-D space-opera video starring Michael Jackson; Star Tours, a joint venture between George Lucas Productions and Walt Disney Productions that takes visitors on a flight through the *Star Wars* universe; and Splash Mountain, a journey through swamps and down waterfalls.
Opened in April 1983, this Disneyland had already had more than 100 million visitors by May 1991. Tickets for Tokyo Disneyland can be purchased in advance at the Disneyland counter in Tokyo Station (near the Yaesu-guchi exit) and at travel agencies, such as JTB.
Admission: Disneyland Passport, including entrance to, and use of, all attractions: ¥4,400 ($31.40) adults, ¥4,000 ($28.55) junior high and high school students, ¥3,000 ($21.40) children.
Open: Mon–Fri 9 or 10am–7 or 8pm (10pm on weekends in summer), with slightly shorter hours in winter. Schedule is subject to change, so call in advance.
Directions: Shuttle buses run at 10-minute intervals from Tokyo Station directly to Disneyland's front gate in 35 minutes. Bus stop is behind Tekko Building on Yaesu-guchi side of Tokyo Station. One-way fare: ¥600 ($4.30) adults, ¥300 ($2.15) children. You can also take JR Keiyo Line from Tokyo Station to Maihama Station, from which park is a few minutes' walk.

HANAYASHIKI, 2-8-1 Asakusa, Taito-ku. Tel. 3842-8780.
Japan's oldest amusement park is located northwest of the famous Sensoji Temple in Asakusa. Small by today's standards, it offers a small roller coaster and diversions that would appeal to younger children.
Admission: ¥400 ($2.85) adults, ¥200 ($1.40) children.
Open: Wed–Mon 10am–6pm (5:30pm in winter). **Station:** Asakusa, about a 5-minute walk away.

NATIONAL CHILDREN'S CASTLE (Kodomo no Shiro), 5-53-1 Jinguemae, Shibuya-ku. Tel. 3797-5666.
If you have children, you'll want to bring them to the National Children's Castle.

Conceived by the Ministry of Health and Welfare to commemorate the International Year of the Child in 1979, the Children's Castle opened in 1985, its activity rooms designed to appeal to children of all ages. A video library offers videos on everything from fairy tales and Golden Book series to *Sesame Street* and even rock videos. There's a list of videos in English from which to choose, and viewing is in your own private cubicle. A Play Hall features building blocks, a jungle gym, table tennis and football for older kids, a large dollhouse, and computer games. Children can make their own creations in a supervised art room, and on the roof there is a playground.

Admission: ¥410 ($2.90) those over 18, ¥310 ($2.20) children aged 6 to 18, free for children under 6.

Open: Tues–Fri 12:30–5:30pm, Sat–Sun and hols 10am–5:30pm. **Station:** Omote Sando, Exit B2, about a 5-minute walk away.

UENO ZOO, Ueno Park, Taito-ku. Tel. 3828-5171.

Opened back in 1882, Ueno Zoo is small but very popular with Japanese families. The main attractions are two giant pandas that were donated by the Chinese government. These two celebrities are so popular, in fact, that there are always long lines to their cages on weekends, and there are all kinds of souvenirs you can buy with pandas on them. The zoo also has an aquarium, plus a large aviary filled with tropical plants that you can walk through.

Admission: ¥400 ($2.85) adults, ¥100 (70¢) children aged 12 to 14, free for children under 12 and senior citizens.

Open: Tues–Sun 9:30am–4:30pm (enter by 4pm). **Closed:** Some hols. **Station:** Ueno, about a 5-minute walk away.

INTERNATIONAL AQUARIUM, 10th floor of World Import Mart Building, Sunshine City, 3-1-3 Higashi Ikebukuro. Tel. 3989-3466.

Claiming to be the world's highest aquarium, this 20-year-old attraction is located in the Sunshine City complex in Ikebukuro. It's home to more than 20,000 fish and animals, including dolphins, octopuses, eels, piranhas, sea horses, sea otters, seals, giant crabs, and rare species of fish. There are several shows, including performances by the sea lions, but this may be the only place on earth that has a fish performance, featuring an electric eel (which gives off an electric charge) and an archer fish.

Admission: ¥1,500 ($10.70) adults, ¥750 ($5.35) children aged 4 to 12.

Open: Daily 10am–5:30pm. **Station:** Higashi Ikebukuro, a 5-minute walk away; or Ikebukuro, about an 8-minute walk away.

WALKING TOURS

The best way to discover Tokyo, to get a feel of its pulse, is by taking a stroll through the city's major districts. Following are suggested walking tours, as well as some organized tours.

WALKING TOUR 1 — Ginza

Start: Tourist Information Center (TIC).
Finish: Kabukiza.
Time: Allow approximately 2 hours, not including stops along the way.
Best Times: Tuesday through Friday, when most establishments are open.
Worst Times: Monday, when the Riccar Art Museum is closed; Thursday, when the Nihonshu Center (selling sake) is closed; Sunday, when some galleries and shops are closed; the last of each month and the whole month of August, when there are no Kabuki productions.

Ginza is without a doubt the most chic, sophisticated area in all Japan, worth a browse even if you can't afford to buy anything. Ginza is Tokyo's Fifth Avenue, its Champs-Elysées. But rather than just a street, Ginza is a whole area of expensive boutiques, the city's largest concentration of department stores and galleries, excellent restaurants, hostess bars, and coffee shops. Its name means "silver mint," a name that goes back to the days of Tokugawa Ieyasu, when the area was reclaimed from the sea and became the home of a silver mint in 1612. After Japan opened itself up to the rest of the world in 1868, Ginza was the first place to become modernized, with Western-style buildings, and to display goods from abroad. It became a popular place for the upwardly mobile to shop and be seen, amidst brick buildings, gas street lamps, and planted trees. Today, there's no longer a silver mint here, but the coins keep rolling in.

If you're arriving by subway, take Exit A4 of Hibiya Station. It'll take you to the:

1. **Tourist Information Center (TIC),** 1-6-6 Yurakucho, where you should pick up a map of the city and stock up on pamphlets and brochures on Tokyo and Japan if you haven't already done so. From there, take a right out of the TIC, and then another immediate right, following the elevated train tracks. Underneath these tracks is the:

2. **International Arcade,** a long row of shops where you can look for such tax-free items as watches, kimonos, Noritake china, woodblock prints, pearls, cameras, and other souvenirs, as well as clothing, shoes, and accessories. (See Chapter 8 for more details.) Although you can find cheaper prices elsewhere, this may be a good place to wander through if you're in a rush and don't have time to hunt around. Be sure to have your passport with you so that you qualify for duty-free prices.

Located next to the International Arcade and also under the tracks is the:

3. **Nishi-Ginza Electric Center,** where you can shop for radios, cassette players, calculators, CD players, and TVs. (See Chapter 8 for more details.) Just on the other (east) side of the tracks is the:

4. **Riccar Art Museum,** 6-2-3 Ginza, a delightful little museum devoted exclusively to woodblock prints. (See "More Attractions," above, for more details.) It's located on the seventh floor of the Riccar Building (note that the entrance to the museum is not through the main entrance of the Riccar Building but through a much smaller entrance on a side street called Miyuki Dori). The place is so tiny it won't take you long to walk through.

From the Riccar Building, continue walking two blocks east (away from the elevated train tracks), to a large street called Sotobori Dori Avenue, where you should take a right and walk a few blocks, passing art galleries along the way, until you find the:

5. **Takumi Craft Shop** on your left (if you reach Ginza Nikko Hotel, you've gone too far), located at 8-4-2 Ginza. This crafts store stocks Japanese folk art, including ceramics, some kites, umbrellas, lacquerware, textiles, and paper objects. (See Chapter 8 for more details.)

Paralleling Sotobori Dori a couple of blocks east is Namiki Dori Street. On this narrow tree-lined lane, art galleries and exclusive boutiques alternate with pubs and hostess bars; you would find a different atmosphere if you were to return here at night. Some galleries you might want to drop in on include:

6. **Tokyo Gallery,** on the second floor of the Dai Go Shuwa Building, 8-6-18 Ginza (tel. 3571-1808), specializing in avant-garde art;

7. **S. Watanabe,** 8-6-19 Ginza (tel. 3571-4684), dealing mostly in modern and old woodcut prints; and

8. **Yoseido Gallery,** 5-5-15 Ginza (tel. 3571-1312), specializing in modern Japanese woodblock prints, silkscreens, lithographs, copper plates, and etchings.

A REFUELING STOP   If you feel like taking a coffee break, a few shops down from S. Watanabe is one of the cheapest places in the Ginza, **9. Skyaire Pronto,** 8-6-25 Ginza. A coffee shop by day and a bar by night, it offers a cup of coffee for a mere ¥150 ($1.05).

Namiki Dori empties onto Harumi Dori Avenue, a busy street that runs from Hibiya through the heart of Ginza. Turn left here and go two blocks, to the:

10. Sony Building, 5-3-1 Ginza (tel. 3573-2371), which is always crowded because it acts as a meeting place in Ginza, especially in early evening, when couples or friends meet after work for a meal or a drink. As you might expect, Sony displays its products in showrooms (on the first, third, and fourth floors); stop here to see all the latest, from the Walkman to computers to television. Catercorner from the Sony Building, open daily from 11am to 8pm, are two relatively new department stores in Ginza:

11. Hankyu and **Seibu.** Located side by side, they both opened in the mid-1980s with a lot of fanfare. (See Chapter 8 for more details.) Altogether, there are eight large department stores in the Ginza area. They're closed one day a week, but this day is staggered so that you can always find department stores open.

To see more department stores, retrace your steps and walk east on Harumi Dori Avenue. You'll notice a smart-looking two-story:

12. koban, or police box. There are koban all over Japan, but this one, with its copper-plated peaked roof and red-and-brown-striped walls is larger than most and one of the most stylish. Stop here if you need directions. Otherwise, continue on Harumi Dori until you come to Chuo Dori Avenue. This intersection, called:

13. Ginza 4-chome Crossing, is the heart of Ginza, and the subway station here is serviced by three subway lines—the Hibiya, Ginza, and Marunouchi lines. The older building with the clock tower is:

14. Wako, a department store famous for its innovative shop windows (and high prices). Across the street is:

15. Mitsukoshi, another department store. (See Chapter 8 for more details regarding these and other department stores.) There are also many boutiques and shops along Chuo Dori Avenue, including:

16. Mikimoto Shop, 4-5-5 Ginza, Japan's most famous distributor of cultivated pearls, located across the street from Mitsukoshi. (See Chapter 8 for more details.)

A REFUELING STOP One of my favorite places for a break in Ginza is **17. Hill Colonial Tea Garden,** a coffee-and-dessert shop on the second floor of Mitsukoshi department store that serves tea, coffee, and snacks. Open daily from 8:30am to 11:30pm, this place with large windows right above the busy Ginza Crossing affords a vantage point from which to watch the bustling crowds. Prices are a bit expensive, but the view is worth it.

Back at Ginza Crossing, there's an interesting shop, located just a stone's throw east of the crossing on Harumi Dori Avenue, called the:

18. Nihonshu Center, 5-9-1 Ginza, which sells something dear to my heart—the Japanese rice wine, sake (look for the store's sign that says SAKESPO 101). For only ¥300 ($2.15) you can sample five different kinds of sake, and you even get to keep the cup. What a deal! (See Chapter 8 for more details.)

Farther east on Harumi Dori, on the right side of the street, is the:

19. Kabukiza, 4-12-15 Ginza, Tokyo's most famous Kabuki theater. If there's a performance, you can watch part of it for only ¥600 to ¥900 ($4.30 to $6.40), depending on the show. (See Chapter 1 for a description of Kabuki, Chapter 9 for information on Kabukiza.)

FINAL REFUELING STOPS What better way to end the day than at a yakitori-ya, a drinking establishment that sells skewers of chicken and other snacks. **20. Atariya,** 3-5-17 Ginza, is a lively, fun place with an English menu listing all kinds of yakitori. It's located on the side street that runs beside the Wako department store, not far from Ginza Crossing. (See Chapter 6 for more details.) If you prefer something quieter, a great bar in the Ginza is **21. Lupin,** 5-5-11 Ginza, in a small alleyway off Namiki Dori behind the Ketel German

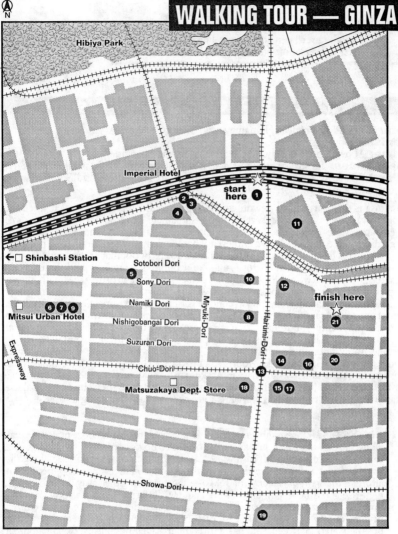

WALKING TOUR — GINZA

N

Hibiya Park

Imperial Hotel

start here ❶

❷ ❸
❹

⓫

← Shinbashi Station

Sotobori Dori

❺ Sony Dori

⓾

⓬

finish here

Namiki Dori

❻ ❼ ❾
Mitsui Urban Hotel

Nishigobangai Dori

❽

㉑

Suzuran Dori

Miyuki-Dori

Harumi-Dori

Expressway

Chuo-Dori

⓭

⓮ ⓰ ⓴

Matsuzakaya Dept. Store

⓲

⓯ ⓱

Showa-Dori

⓳

JAPAN
★TOKYO
GINZA AREA

❶ Tourist Information
  Center (TIC)
❷ International Arcade
❸ Nishi-Ginza
  Electric Center
❹ Riccar Art Museum
❺ Takumi Craft Shop
❻ Tokyo Gallery
❼ S. Watanabe
❽ Yoseido Gallery
❾ Skyaire Pronto
⓾ Sony Building

⓫ Hankyu and Seibu
⓬ Koban
⓭ Ginza 4-chome Crossing
⓮ Wako
⓯ Mitsukoshi
⓰ Mikimoto Shop
⓱ Hill Colonial Tea Garden
⓲ Nihonshu Center
⓳ Kabukiza
⓴ Atariya
㉑ Lupin

restaurant. A tiny basement establishment, it hasn't changed much in decades, and there's never been anything so blasphemous as music within its walls. Great for quiet conversations. (See Chapter 9 for more details.)

WALKING TOUR 2 — Asakusa

Start: Hinode Pier, near Hamamatsucho Station.
Finish: Kappabashi Dori.
Time: Allow approximately 3 hours, including the boat ride.
Best Times: Tuesday through Friday, when the crowds aren't as big.
Worst Times: Monday, when some attractions are closed, and Sunday, when shops on Kappabashi Dori are closed.

Asakusa is the heart of old downtown Tokyo, where the merchants settled when the Tokugawas made Edo the seat of their shogunate government. In those days, merchants were considered quite low on the social ladder and were restricted regarding where they could live and even what they could wear. Gradually, however, the merchants became wealthy, and whole new forms of popular entertainment arose to occupy their time. Theaters for Kabuki and Bunraku were built and flourished in Asakusa. Ukiyo-e (woodblock prints) became the latest artistic rage, with scenes depicting beauties and Kabuki stars, as well as daily life in Edo. To the north of Asakusa was Yoshiwara, the most famous geisha and pleasure district in the city. Unfortunately, Asakusa has not escaped the modernization that swept through Japan over the past century, but more than anywhere else in Tokyo it still retains the charm of old downtown Edo and a festive atmosphere, crowded with stalls and with people visiting its most famous attraction, Sensoji Temple. For Japanese, visiting Asakusa evokes feelings of nostalgia. For tourists, it provides a glimpse of the way things were.

The most dramatic way to arrive in Asakusa is by boat, just as people used to arrive in the olden days (if you want to forgo the boat ride, take the subway to Asakusa Station and start from there). Start this tour, therefore, by boarding a ferry at:

1. **Hinode Pier** (closest subway station: Hamamatsucho). The boat makes its way along the Sumida River, just as in past centuries boats carried wealthy townsmen to the pleasure district of Yoshiwara. Although much of what you see along the river today is only concrete embankments, I recommend the trip because it affords a different perspective of Tokyo—barges making their way down the river, high-rise apartment buildings (with laundry fluttering from balconies), warehouses, and superhighways. The boat passes under approximately a dozen bridges during the 40-minute trip, each bridge completely different. Ferryboats ply the waters between Asakusa and Hamamatsucho about every half hour or hour, but because schedules change it's best to call ahead (tel. 3841-9178 or 3457-7830). Cost of the ferry one way is ¥560 ($4). The first stop on the ferry is at:

2. **Hama Rikyu Garden,** where more passengers are picked up. If you're interested in seeing the garden, considered by many to be Tokyo's finest, you can start your tour here; but you must first pay the ¥200 ($1.40) admission. (See "More Attractions," above, for more details on the garden).

Upon arrival in Asakusa, walk from the boat pier a couple of blocks inland, where you will soon see the colorful Kaminarimon Gate. Across the street from this gate is the:

3. **Asakusa Information Center,** 2-18-9 Kaminarimon (tel. 3842-5566). Open daily from 9:30am to 8pm, it's staffed by English-speaking volunteers until 5pm. Stop here to pick up a map of the area and to ask directions to restaurants and other sights you might be interested in visiting. In addition, note that huge Seiko clock on the center's façade—a mechanical music clock, with performances

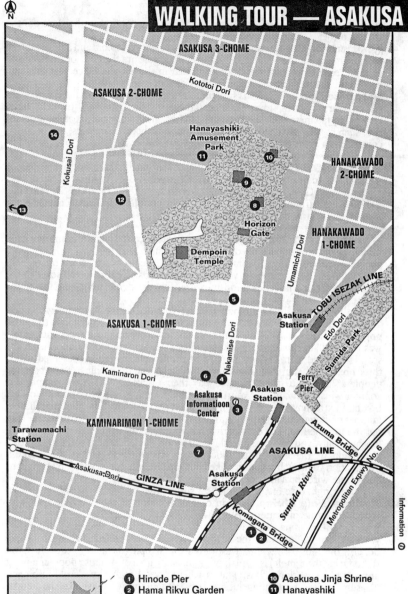

WALKING TOUR — ASAKUSA

N

ASAKUSA 3-CHOME

Kototoi Dori

ASAKUSA 2-CHOME

Kokusai Dori

⑭

Hanayashiki Amusement Park

⑪

⑩

⑨

⑧

HANAKAWADO 2-CHOME

⑫

⑬

Horizon Gate

HANAKAWADO 1-CHOME

Dempoin Temple

Unamichi Dori

ASAKUSA 1-CHOME

Nakamise Dori

⑤

Asakusa Station

TOBU ISEZAK LINE

Edo Dori

Sumida Park

Kaminaron Dori

⑥ ④

Ferry Pier

Asakusa Informatioon Center

③

Asakusa Station

Tarawamachi Station

KAMINARIMON 1-CHOME

⑦

Azuma Bridge

Asakusa-Dori

GINZA LINE

Asakusa Station

ASAKUSA LINE

Komagata Bridge

Sumida River

Metropolitan Expwy No. 6

Information ⊕

① ②

JAPAN ★TOKYO

① Hinode Pier
② Hama Rikyu Garden
③ Asakusa Information Center
④ Kaminarimon Gate
⑤ Nakamise Dori
⑥ Chinya
⑦ Namiki
⑧ Incense burner
⑨ Sensoji Temple
⑩ Asakusa Jinja Shrine
⑪ Hanayashiki
⑫ France-za
⑬ Kappabashi Dori Street
⑭ Belvedere

every hour on the hour from 10am to 7pm. Then it's time to head across the street, to the:

4. **Kaminarimon Gate,** unmistakable with its bright red colors and a huge lantern hanging in the middle. Those statues inside the gate are the gods of thunder and of rain, ready to protect the deity enshrined in the temple. Once past the gate, you'll find yourself immediately on a pedestrian lane called:

5. **Nakamise Dori,** which leads straight to the temple. This lane is lined with stalls selling fabrics, shoes, toys, Japanese crackers (called *sembei*), trinkets, bags, umbrellas, Japanese dolls, clothes, fans, masks, and traditional Japanese accessories, such as brightly decorated straight hairpins, black hairpieces, and wooden combs. It's a great place for souvenir and gift shopping.

REFUELING STOPS If you're hungry for lunch, there are a number of possibilities in the neighborhood. 6. **Chinya,** 1-3-4 Asakusa, located near Kaminarimon Gate, has been serving sukiyaki since 1880. Nearby is 7. **Namiki,** 2-11-9 Kaminarimon, Asakusa's best-known noodle shop. (See Chapter 6 for more details on both these places.)

At the end of Nakamise Dori, as you head toward the temple, is another gate, which opens on a square filled with pigeons and a large:

8. **incense burner,** where worshippers "wash" themselves to ward off or help against illness. If, for example, you have a sore throat, be sure to rub some of the smoke over your throat for good measure. But the dominating building of the square is:

9. **Sensoji Temple,** Tokyo's oldest temple. Founded in the 7th century, Sensoji Temple is dedicated to Kannon, the Buddhist goddess of mercy, and is therefore popularly called the Asakusa Kannon Temple. According to legend, the temple was founded after two fishermen pulled up a golden statue of Kannon from the sea. The sacred statue is still housed in the temple, carefully preserved inside three boxes, and even though it's never on display and the public has never seen it, people still flock to the temple to pay their respects. Within the temple is a counter where you can buy your fortune by putting ¥100 (70¢) into a wooden box and extracting one of the long wooden sticks inside. The stick will have a number on it, which corresponds to one of the numbers on a set of drawers. Take out the fortune from the drawer that has your number. Although it is written in Japanese only, you can take it to the counter on the left, where you can ask for a translation (if the counter is unoccupied, you can also ask at the Asakusa Information Center). If you don't like your fortune, you can negate it by tying it to one of the wires provided or to the twig of a tree.

On the right side of the temple is a shrine, the:

10. **Asakusa Jinja Shrine,** built in commemoration of the two fishermen who found the statue of Kannon. Northwest of Sensoji Temple is:

11. **Hanayashiki,** a small and kind of corny amusement park that opened about 40 years ago and still draws in the little ones. (See "Cool for Kids," above, for more details.) But most of the area west of Sensoji Temple (the area to the left if you stand facing the temple) is a small but interesting area of Asakusa popular among Tokyo's older working class. This is where several of Asakusa's old-fashioned pleasure houses remain, including bars, restaurants, strip shows, traditional Japanese vaudeville, and so-called "love hotels," which rent out rooms by the hour. One of the most famous strip shows is:

12. **France-za,** 1-43-12 Asakusa (tel. 3841-6631). It's located on a small side street that leads west from Sensoji Temple. With four shows daily, beginning at 11am and with the last show at 6:30pm, it charges a ¥3,300 ($23.55) entrance fee—and leaves nothing to the imagination. If you keep walking west, within 10 minutes you'll reach:

13. **Kappabashi Dori Street,** Tokyo's wholesale district for restaurant items. Yes, this is where you can buy models of all that plastic food you've been drooling over in restaurant displays. Ice cream, pizza, fish, sushi, mugs foaming with

beer—they're all here, looking like the real thing. My favorite is one of spaghetti with a fork hovering above it, supported by a few strands of noodles. You'll also find kitchenware, including frying pans, knives, lunch boxes, lacquerware, rice cookers, and *noren,* the curtains hung outside Japanese restaurants. This is where restaurant owners come to purchase items wholesale, but retail sales are made to the public as well.

A FINAL REFUELING STOP   A great place for lunch or for ending the day in Asakusa is 28 floors above ground, at the **14. Belvedere** in the Asakusa View Hotel, on Kokusai Dori Avenue. It serves a lunch buffet of Japanese, Western, and Chinese food daily from noon to 2:30pm for ¥3,300 ($23.55); in the evening, you can listen to music while sipping drinks and watching the sun go down.

WALKING TOUR 3 —— Harajuku

Start: At the Omote Sando Dori and Aoyama Dori intersection (nearest station: Omote Sando).
Finish: Olympic stadiums, Omote Sando Dori.
Time: Allow approximately 3 hours, not including restaurant and shopping stops.
Best Time: Sunday, when you can start with a Sunday brunch and when Omote Sando Dori becomes a pedestrian zone and dancers converge on the scene.
Worst Times: Monday and from the 24th to the end of every month, when the Ota Memorial Museum of Art is closed; Thursday, when the Oriental Bazaar is closed.

Harajuku is one of my favorite neighborhoods in Tokyo. Sure, I'm too old to really fit in. If you're over 25, you're apt to feel ancient here, since this is Tokyo's most popular and trendy place for Japanese high school and college students. The young come here to see and be seen, and there are Japanese punks, girls dressed in black, and young couples in their fashionable best. But I like Harajuku for its vibrancy, its sidewalk cafés, its street hawkers, and its fashionable clothing boutiques. It is also the home of Tokyo's most important Shinto shrine, as well as a woodblock-print museum, an excellent souvenir shop of traditional Japanese items, and a park with wide-open spaces. Formerly the training grounds of the Japanese army and later the residential area of American families during the postwar occupation, Harajuku was also the site of the 1964 Olympic Village.

If at all possible, come to Harajuku on a Sunday. That's when Omote Sando Dori, the tree-lined main thoroughfare bisecting the heart of the area, is closed to vehicular traffic and becomes a pedestrian promenade. Young Japanese dressed to kill walk up and down holding hands (a rather new phenomenon), and in the shadow of the Olympic stadiums is where the crowds are the thickest—for that's where Sunday's most unusual attraction takes place, an open stage for anyone who wants to perform.

Standing on the corner of Omote Sando Dori and Aoyama Dori, you will see boutiques in all directions. This is one of the most fashionable and expensive neighborhoods in Tokyo, with the price for real estate among the highest in the country. If it's Sunday, I suggest you start this tour at the corner of:

1. **Omote Sando Dori and Aoyama Dori.** Within a 2-minute walk from this intersection are three good places for brunch. **2. L'Orangerie de Paris,** located on the fifth floor of the Hanae Mori Building on Omote Sando Dori, is the most expensive and exclusive and seems to attract half the foreign expatriate population for its brunch. **3. Brasserie D** and **4. Spiral Garden,** both on Aoyama Dori Avenue, are slightly cheaper and more casual. Be sure to make reservations beforehand, since these places are popular. (See Chapter 6 for more details.)

After brunch, head west on Omote Sando Dori, where on your left you'll soon see the:

5. Hanae Mori Building, housing the fashions by this famous designer. In the basement is the: **Antique Market,** with individual stallkeepers selling china, jewelry, clothing, watches, swords, and items from the 1930s. (See Chapter 8 for more details.) Almost next door is:

6. Shu Uemura. A very successful chain of makeup products, it features cosmetics, blush, and eyeshadow in incredible rainbow colors. Continuing on Omote Sando Dori, you'll soon come to Harajuku's most famous store, the:

7. Oriental Bazaar, 5-9-13 Jingumae, one of Tokyo's best places to shop for Japanese souvenirs. Three floors offer antique chinaware, old kimonos, Japanese paper products, fans, jewelry, woodblock prints, screens, and more. (See Chapter 8 for more details.) Not far away is:

8. Vivre 21, boasting boutiques showcasing fashions of designers Kenzo, Takeo Kikuchi, and Kensho Abe. (See Chapter 8 for more details.) Also on the left side of Omote Sando Dori is:

9. Kiddy Land, which sells gag gifts and a great deal more than just toys. You could spend hours here, but it's often so packed with giggling teenagers that you end up rushing out.

REFUELING STOPS This is for those of you who didn't eat brunch—ready for lunch? There are several inexpensive restaurants near this stretch of Omote Sando Dori. **10. Genrokusushi,** on Omote Sando Dori near the Oriental Bazaar, is a fast-food sushi bar that uses a conveyor belt to deliver plates of food to customers seated at the counter. Also takeout sushi, in case you want to pack yourself a little something to eat later in Yoyogi Park. **11. Bamboo Sandwich House,** located off Omote Sando Dori on a side street near the Paul Stuart Shop, offers inexpensive sandwiches and coffee, complete with outdoor seating. But my favorite is **12. Beer Market Doma,** located in the basement of the Ga-Z Building, at the intersection of Omote Sando and Meiji Dori, which serves a variety of Asian dishes and is decorated like a Mongolian nomad's tent. (See Chapter 6 for more details on these three places.)

The first big intersection you come to on Omote Sando Dori is Meiji Dori. This crossroad is the heart of Harajuku. If you cross Meiji Dori, you'll arrive almost immediately at a shop with the unlikely name of:

13. Chicago, which nonetheless stocks hundreds of used and new kimonos and yukata in a corner of its basement. (See Chapter 8 for more details.) On the corner of Omote Sando and Meiji Dori intersection is:

14. La Forêt, a building filled with trendy shoe and clothing boutiques. (See Chapter 8 for more details.) Behind La Foret is one of my favorite museums, the:

15. Ota Memorial Museum of Art, 1-10-10 Jingumae. It features the private ukiyo-e (woodblock prints) collection of the late Ota Seizo. Exhibitions of the museum's 12,000 prints are changed monthly. (See "More Attractions," above, for more details.)

Return to Meiji Dori and continue north. If it's the first or fourth Sunday of the month, you might want to go on walking a few minutes until on your left you see:

16. Togo Shrine. A flea market is held on the grounds of the shrine on these days, when everything from old chests, dolls, and inkwells to kitchen utensils and kimonos are for sale, spread out on a sidewalk that meanders under trees to the shrine. Beginning early in the morning, the market usually goes on until about 4pm. Otherwise, turn left off of Meiji Dori onto the first side street past La Foret, a pedestrians-only street called:

17. Takeshita Dori Street. Lined nonstop with stores, it's always jam-packed with young people—usually Japanese teenagers—out hunting for bargains in the shops with doors flung open wide to the crowds. You'll pass record shops, shoe stores, and coffee shops—it's all there if you can only find it through the crowds.

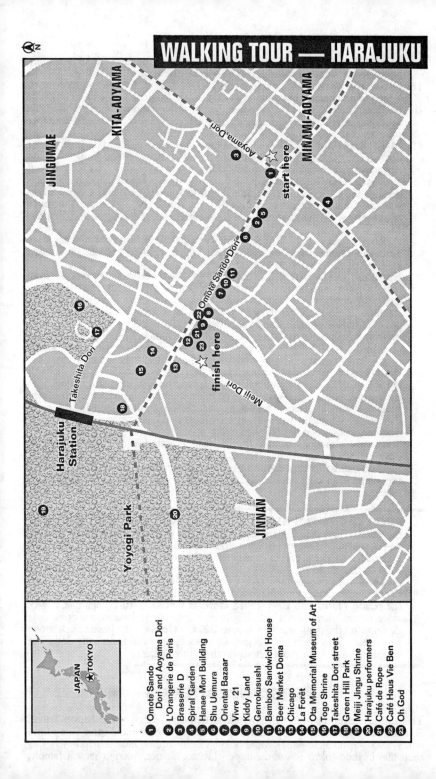

WALKING TOUR — HARAJUKU

JINGUMAE

KITA-AOYAMA

MINAMI-AOYAMA

Aoyama Dori

start here

Omote Sando Dori

Takeshita Dori

Harajuku Station

Yoyogi Park

JINNAN

Meiji Dori

finish here

JAPAN
TOKYO

1. Omote Sando
   Dori and Aoyama Dori
2. L'Orangerie de Paris
3. Brasserie D
4. Spiral Garden
5. Hanae Mori Building
6. Shu Uemura
7. Oriental Bazaar
8. Vivre 21
9. Kiddy Land
10. Genrokusushi
11. Bamboo Sandwich House
12. Beer Market Doma
13. Chicago
14. La Forêt
15. Ota Memorial Museum of Art
16. Togo Shrine
17. Takeshita Dori street
18. Green Hill Park
19. Meiji Jingu Shrine
20. Harajuku performers
21. Café de Rope
22. Café Haus Vie Ben
23. Oh God

At the top end of Takeshita Dori, where you'll see Harajuku Station, turn left. Soon, across from the station, you'll see a small enclosed area called:

18. **Green Hill Park,** where young vendors set up stalls of clothing and accessories. You can find bargains here, although some of the leather-studded items might be too bizarre for the folks back home. Just past the station, turn right and walk over the bridge above the tracks, where you'll then find yourself at the entrance of:

19. **Meiji Jingu Shrine.** The most venerable shrine in Tokyo, Meiji Jingu Shrine opened in 1920, dedicated to Emperor and Empress Meiji. (See "The Top Attractions," above, for more details.) On the way to the shrine you can stop off at the **Iris Garden,** spectacular for its irises in late June. A stream meanders through the garden, and if you follow it to its source, you'll find a spring where you can drink the cold water. North of the shrine complex is the **Treasure Museum,** with the garments and personal effects of Emperor and Empress Meiji.

Retrace your steps back to the entrance to the shrine, turn right, and you'll see a mass of people on the wide boulevard, which is closed to traffic on Sunday. Here, from about noon to 5pm, are the:

20. **Harajuku performers.** In what is Tokyo's best free show, everyone—from rock 'n' rollers and break dancers to roller skaters, rock bands, and pantomime artists—converges on Omote Sando Dori, in the shadow of the Olympic stadiums, to do his or her thing on the street. It all started in the 1970s, when a group of kids got together and began dancing to music they brought with them on their portable cassette players. Gradually, the number of young dancers grew, until by the mid-1980s there were as many as several hundred teenagers dancing in the street, dressed either in styles of the 1950s or in colorful circuslike clothing. Although today the number of dancers has dwindled, a few diehards are still here. Like most undertakings in Japan, this is group participation, with each group having its own cassette player, music, leader, and costumes. Individual dancing is out, and if by chance you simply joined in, the other dancers would regard you with astonishment and consider you slightly weird. The fun consists in simply wandering about, observing group after group. You might also come across a roller-skating club putting on stunts, young boys performing on trick bicycles, a pantomimist, and, in recent years, lots of rock bands. In this carnival-like atmosphere, there are also stalls selling everything from fried noodles to roasted corn on the cob to a kind of Japanese omelet.

FINAL REFUELING STOPS After you've visited Meiji Jingu Shrine, seen the Sunday dancers of Harajuku, and fought your way through the crowds, you're probably ready to imbibe a drink or two. Although Tokyo doesn't have many sidewalk cafés, Harajuku is blessed with several, all on Omote Sando Dori Avenue. Closest to the Meiji–Omote Sando Dori intersection is **21. Café de Rope,** 6-1-8 Jingumae, the oldest outdoor café in Harajuku. Farther east on Omote Sando Dori, right next to Shakey's pizza parlor in the Vivre 21 building, is **22. Café Haus Vie Ben** (called **Café B Haus),** 5-10-1 Jingumae, a slick sidewalk café that opened in 1985. For an indoor bar in the area, walk past Café de Rope (on the small lane beside it) to **23. Oh God,** 6-7-18 Jingumae. It shows free foreign films every night beginning at about 6pm and is decently dark. (See Chapters 6 and 9 for more details on these three places.)

ORGANIZED TOURS

There are several group tours of Tokyo and its environs, offered by the **Japan Travel Bureau (JTB)** (tel. 3276-7777) and such tour companies as the **Japan Gray Line** (tel. 3433-5745 and 3436-6881), with bookings easily made at most tourist hotels. Day tours may include Tokyo Tower, the Imperial Palace district, Asakusa Sensoji Temple,

Meiji Jingu Shrine, and Ginza. There are a number of organized evening tours that take in such activities as Kabuki or a geisha party. If your time is limited, you might be interested in one or more of these day and evening tours, although be warned that they are very tourist-oriented. Prices range from about ¥4,200 ($30) for a half-day tour to about ¥1,400 ($100) for a night tour that includes dinner, a geisha show, and Kabuki.

One tour you might consider joining because you can't do it on your own is the **Industrial Tokyo tour,** offered by JTB twice a week. Plants toured may include the Japan Airlines maintenance plant, an Isuzu Motors factory, or the Tokyo Stock Exchange. The price of this tour is ¥10,900 ($77.85), including lunch.

3. CULTURAL EXPERIENCES

Just walking down the street in Japan can be considered a "cultural experience." However, there are a number of places, aside from museums, where you can get further exposure—as a participant—to this country's fascinating cultural life. While Chapter 1 describes what the tea ceremony, ikebana, and zazen are about, this section will tell you where you can experience these and other distinctly Japanese cultural activities.

IKEBANA

Instruction in ikebana—or flower arranging—is available at a number of schools in Tokyo. Information can be obtained from **Ikebana International,** Ochanomizu Square Building, 1-6 Surugadai, Kanda (tel. 3293-8188). Otherwise, one school particularly good for foreigners is the **Ichiyo School Nakano,** 4-17-5 Nakano (tel. 3388-0141); it provides instruction in English at various sites around Tokyo and will give certifications. Other well-known schools include the **Sogetsuryu Ikebana School,** 7-2-21 Akasaka (tel. 3408-1126; closest station: Aoyama-Itchome), with instructions in English every Tuesday from 10am to noon for ¥4,800 ($34.30); and the **Ohararyu Ikebana School,** 5-7-17 Minami Aoyama (tel. 3499-1200; closest station: Omote Sando), where you can join in lessons Monday through Friday from 10am to noon for ¥3,800 ($27.15) per lesson. Appointments must be made in advance. Flower arranging is also taught for ¥1,650 ($11.80) per lesson at **Sakura Kai,** 3-2-25 Shimoochiai, Shinjuku-ku (tel. 3951-9043), described below in the tea ceremony section.

If you wish to see ikebana, ask at the **Tourist Information Office** whether there are any special exhibitions. Department stores sometimes have special ikebana exhibitions in their galleries. Another place to look is **Yasukuni Shrine,** located on Yasukuni Dori Avenue, northwest of the Imperial Palace (closest station: Ichigaya or Kudanshita). Although dedicated to Japanese war dead, the shrine also has ongoing exhibitions of ikebana on its grounds.

TEA CEREMONY

Several first-class hotels in Tokyo hold tea ceremonies with instruction in English. Since they are often booked by groups, be sure to call in advance to see whether you can participate.

Seisei-an, on the seventh floor of the Hotel New Otani, 4-1 Kioi-cho, Chiyoda-ku (tel. 3265-1111, ext. 2567; closest station: Yotsuya or Akasaka-mitsuke), holds a 30-minute instruction on Thursday, Friday, and Saturday from 11am to noon and again from 1 to 4pm. The cost is ¥1,000 ($7.15).

Chosho-an, on the seventh floor of the Hotel Okura, 2-10-4 Toranomon, Minato-ku (tel. 3582-0111; closest station: Toranomon), gives instruction anytime between 11am and noon and between 1 and 4:30pm. The cost is also ¥1,000 ($7.15).

At **Toko-an,** on the fourth floor of the Imperial Hotel, 1-1-1 Uchisaiwaicho, Chiyoda-ku (tel. 3504-1111; closest station: Hibiya), instruction is from 10am to 4pm, daily except Sunday and holidays. The cost is ¥1,100 ($7.85).

Another place you can enjoy the tea ceremony is at **Sakura Kai (Tea Ceremony Service Center),** 3-2-25 Shimoochiai, Shinjuku ku (tel. 3951-9043, closest station: Mejiro, on Yamanote Line). Instruction is on Thursday and Friday from 11am to noon and from 1 to 4pm. There are various fees, and you can even combine a tea ceremony with a lesson in ikebana (flower arranging) for ¥2,700 ($19.30).

ACUPUNCTURE & JAPANESE MASSAGE

Although most Westerners have heard about acupuncture, they may not be familiar with *shiatsu* (Japanese pressure-point massage). Many first-class hotels in Japan offer shiatsu, as do the two clinics listed below.

There are acupuncture clinics everywhere in Tokyo, and the staff of your hotel may be able to tell you of the one nearest you. If you want a specific recommendation, try **Kojimachi Rebirth,** on the second floor of the Kur House Building, 4-2-12 Kojimachi, Chiyoda-ku (tel. 3262-7561). Hours here are 9:30am to 9pm Monday through Saturday; closed holidays. First-time fee is ¥7,210 ($51.50) for acupuncture and ¥6,690 ($47.80) for a shiatsu massage.

Similarly, in Shinjuku there's the **Seibu Shinjuku Ekimae Clinic,** located above a pharmacy on the fourth floor of the Chiyoda Building, 2-45-6 Kabuki-cho (tel. 3209-9217; closest station: Seibu Shinjuku), across the street from a group of shops called American Blvd. Open Monday through Friday from 9am to 1pm and 2 to 6pm, and on Saturday from 9am to 1pm and 2 to 3pm, it offers treatments in acupuncture, shiatsu, and moxibustion (small cones of wormwood, used on specific points for heat stimulation). A doctor trained in Western medicine is also in residence. A treatment of both acupuncture and shiatsu is ¥5,000 ($35.70).

PUBLIC BATHS

If you won't have another opportunity to visit a communal bath in Japan, I suggest you go at least once to a neighborhood *sento* (public bath). Altogether, Tokyo has an estimated 2,000 sento, which may sound like a lot but is nothing compared to the 20,000 the city used to have. Easily recognizable by a tall chimney and shoe lockers just inside the door, a sento sells about anything you might need at the bathhouse— soap, shampoo, towels, and even underwear.

Since there are so many public baths spread throughout the city, it's best simply to go to the one most convenient to you. If you prefer a suggestion, however, the **Azabu Juban Onsen,** 1-5 Azabu Juban, Minato-ku (tel. 3404-2610; closest station: Roppongi), is the one I used to go to when I lived for a while in an apartment without a tub or shower. Closed on Tuesday but open the rest of the week from 3 to 11pm, it has brownish water that actually comes from a hot spring. Admission here is ¥300 ($2.15).

The **Asakusa Kannon Onsen,** 2-7-26 Asakusa, Taito-ku (tel. 3844-4141), is located just west of Sensoji Temple, described above. This one also boasts water from a hot spring and has the atmosphere of a real neighborhood bath. Closed every first and third Thursday, it opens early, at 6:30am, and closes at 6pm. The fee is slightly higher, at ¥500 ($3.55).

Although it's far from Tokyo, about 1½ hours by train from Shinjuku Station, you may wish to visit **Kappa Tengoku** ④, just for the experience of open-air bathing (tel. 0460-6121). Located in the heart of Hakone, this is the closest open-air bath to Tokyo. Located on a hill directly behind Yumoto Station, it's open daily from 10am to 10pm, and admission is ¥500 ($3.55).

ZAZEN

Sitting meditation is occasionally offered with instruction in English by a few temples in the Tokyo vicinity. **Eiheiji Temple,** 2-21-34 Nishi-Azabu, Minato-ku (tel. 3400-5232), holds a zazen every Monday from 7pm to 9pm, charging ¥100 (71¢).

Instruction here, however, is in Japanese only. For more information, contact the Tourist Information Center.

4. SPORTS

SPECTATOR SPORTS

For current sporting events taking place in Tokyo, check the monthly magazine *Tokyo Journal* for information ranging from kick boxing and pro wrestling to soccer, table tennis, and golf classics.

SUMO

Sumo matches are held in Tokyo in January, May, and September at the **Kokugikan,** 1-3-28 Yokoami, Sumida-ku (tel. 3623-5111; closest station: Ryogoku), a sumo stadium completed in 1985. Matches are held in Tokyo in January, May, and September for 15 consecutive days, beginning at around 10am and lasting until 6pm; the top wrestlers compete after 4pm. The best seats are ringside box seats, but they're bought out by companies and by friends and families of sumo wrestlers. Usually available are balcony seats, which can be purchased at any Playguide (a ticket outlet in Tokyo, with counters throughout the city), or at the Kokugikan ticket office beginning at 9am every morning of the tournament. Prices range from about ¥1,000 to ¥7,000 ($7.15 to $50). Sumo matches are broadcast on Japanese television as well as on the American military FEN radio station.

If no tournament is going on, you might want to visit a sumo stable to watch the wrestlers train. There are more than 30 stables in Tokyo, many of which are located in Ryogoku, close to the sumo stadium. Call first to make an appointment and to make sure the wrestlers are in town. Stables include **Dewanoumi Beya,** 2-3-15 Ryogoku, Sumida-ku (tel. 3631-0090); **Izutsu Beya,** 2-2-7 Ryogoku, Sumida-ku (tel. 3633-8920); **Kasugano Beya,** 1-7-11 Ryogoku, Sumida-ku (tel. 3631-1871); and **Takasago Beya,** 1-22-5 Yanagibashi, Taito-ku (tel. 3861-3210). The Tourist Information Center has a list of other stables as well.

MARTIAL ARTS

If you're interested in the martial arts, including kendo and aikido, stop by the Tourist Information Center for its list of schools that might allow you to watch their practices. If you're interested, you can also join on a monthly basis for instruction.

Otherwise, contact the various federations directly: the **International Aikido Federation** (tel. 03/3203-9236); the **All-Japan Judo Federation** (tel. 03/3818-4199 or 3812-2995; the **World Union of Karate-do Organization** (tel. 03/3503-6637); and the **Japan Kendo Federation** (03/3211-5804). All have member schools in Tokyo. To watch aikido, for example, you can visit the **Nihon Sobukan,** 1-36-2 Uehara, Shibuya-ku (tel. 3468-3944; closest station: Yoyogi-Uehara). It has visitor days several times a week. Telephone to make an appointment.

BASEBALL

The Japanese are so crazy about baseball, you'd think they invented the game. Even the annual high school playoffs keep everyone glued to their TV sets. In Tokyo, the home teams are the **Yomiuri Giants** and the **Nippon Ham Fighters,** both of which play at the Tokyo Dome (tel. 3811-2111); closest station: Suidobashi; and the **Yakult Swallows,** which play at Jingu Stadium (closest station: Gaienmae). Other teams playing in the vicinity of Tokyo are the Lotte Orions, the Seibu Lions, and the Yokohama Taiyo Whales. Advance tickets go on sale on Friday, 2 weeks prior to a game, and can be purchased at the stadium or, for Tokyo teams, at any Playguide office.

CHAPTER 8

TOKYO SAVVY SHOPPING

**1. THE SHOPPING
   SCENE**

2. SHOPPING A TO Z

One of the delights of being in Japan is the shopping, but it's not only the tourists who go crazy. The Japanese themselves are avid shoppers, and it won't take you long to become as convinced as I am that shopping is the number-one pastime in Tokyo. Women, men, couples, and even whole families go on buying expeditions in their free time, making Sunday the most crowded shopping day of the week. With such a discriminating, knowledgeable, and enthusiastic domestic market, it's little wonder that Japanese products have earned respect in international markets around the world. Today, the label MADE IN JAPAN is synonymous with quality, reliability, and superb craftsmanship. Japanese workers take great pride in the goods they produce, whether toys, lacquerware, computers, or cars.

1. THE SHOPPING SCENE

In Tokyo, stores both mammoth and miniature are everywhere, offering everything you can and can't imagine. Traditional Japanese crafts and souvenirs that make good buys include woodblock prints (ukiyo-e), toys and kites, bamboo window blinds, Japanese dolls, carp banners, swords, lacquerware, ikebana accessories, ceramics, fans, masks, knives and scissors, sake, and silk and cotton kimonos. Also popular are products made of Japanese paper (washi), such as umbrellas, lanterns, boxes, wallets, and stationery. And Japan is famous for its workmanship in electronic products, including cameras, stereo and video equipment, computers, and typewriters. However, because of the present exchange rate, you can probably find these products just as cheaply, or even more cheaply, in the United States. If you think you want to shop for electronic products, therefore, it pays to do some comparison shopping before you leave home so that you know what the prices are.

If you have only a few hours to spare for shopping in Tokyo, head for either a department store, one of the larger souvenir/crafts outlets, or a shopping arcade. With a wide selection of goods under one roof, they're the most convenient places to shop if you can't afford to waste a single minute. If your time is limited, a good choice among these is the **International Arcade,** near the Imperial Hotel, with its wide range of everything from cameras to kimonos to watches and chinaware, while the **Oriental Bazaar,** in Harajuku, is excellent for traditional Japanese items. Those of you with more time on your hands might want to explore districts in Tokyo that specialize in certain products—Akihabara, for example, for electronic equipment or Kanda for used books.

Remember that a 3% consumption tax will be added on to the price marked, but all major department stores in Tokyo will refund the tax on purchases amounting to more than ¥10,000 ($80). Ask at the store's information counter (usually located near the main entrance) for the special form to be filled out by the sales clerks and for the location of the refund counter. Be sure to bring your passport.

SALES

Department stores have sales throughout the year where you can pick up bargains on everything from electronic goods and men's suits to golf clubs, toys, kitchenware, food, and lingerie. There are even sales for used wedding kimonos. The most popular—and crowded—sales are for designer clothing, usually held twice a year, in July and December or January. In fact, most people I know living in Tokyo buy their Japanese designer clothing only during these sales. You can pick up fantastic clothing at cut-rate prices—but be prepared for the crowds. To find out about current sales, check the **Tokyo Journal,** the monthly guide to what's going on in Tokyo.

Items on sale in department stores are usually found on one of the top floors, with sometimes an entire floor devoted to the sale. Whenever I go to a department store, I can't resist riding the up escalators until I finally reach the bargain floor. I've come upon sales I never knew existed and ended up buying things I never really needed. The *Tokyo Journal* also lists the various exhibitions being held at department store art galleries.

SHIPPING IT HOME

Many first-class hotels in Tokyo provide a packing and shipping service. In addition, most large department stores, as well as tourist shops such as the Oriental Bazaar and antiques shops, will ship your purchases overseas.

If you wish to ship packages yourself, the easiest method is to go to a post office and purchase an easy-to-assemble cardboard box, available in three sizes (along with the necessary tape and string). Packages mailed abroad cannot weigh more than 20 kilograms (about 44 pounds), and keep in mind that only the larger international post offices accept packages to be mailed overseas. Remember, too, that mailing packages from Japan is expensive. Ask your hotel concierge for the closest international post office.

BEST BUYS

Tokyo is the country's showcase for everything, from the latest in camera or stereo equipment to original woodblock prints. You don't have to spend a fortune shopping, either. You can pick up handmade Japanese paper products or other souvenirs, for example, for a fraction of what they would cost in import shops in the United States. In Harajuku it's possible to buy a fully lined dress of the latest fashionable craze for $40, and I can't even count the number of pairs of shoes I've bought in Tokyo for a mere $16. Used cameras can be picked up for a song, reproductions of famous woodblock prints make great inexpensive gifts, and many items—from pearls to electronic video and audio equipment—can be bought tax free.

Another enjoyable aspect of shopping in Tokyo is that specific areas are often devoted to certain products, sold wholesale but also available to the individual shopper. Kappabashi Dori Avenue, for example, is where you'll find shops specializing in plastic-food replicas and kitchenware, while Kanda is known for its bookstores. Akihabara is packed with stores selling the latest in electronics. Ginza is the chic address for clothing boutiques, as well as art galleries. Shibuya has at least a dozen department stores, while Harajuku is the place to go for youthful, fun, and inexpensive fashions.

2. SHOPPING A TO Z

In addition to the shops listed here, other places to look for antiques include the Oriental Bazaar, described below in the crafts section, and flea markets.

ANTIQUES & CURIOS

ANTIQUE MARKET, basement of Hanae Mori Building, Omote Sando Dori, 3-6-1 Kita-Aoyama, Minato-ku. Tel. 3406-1021.
Individual stall holders here sell china, jewelry, clothing, swords, watches, woodblock prints, and 1930s kitsch; and prices are high. The Hanae Mori Building is located in Harajuku/Aoyama. Open: Daily 11am–8pm. Station: Omote Sando, a 1-minute walk away.

KUROFUNE, 7-7-4 Roppongi. Tel. 3479-1552.
Located in a large house in Roppongi, Kurofune specializes in Japanese antique furniture that has not been refinished but, rather, left in its original condition. The stock also includes fabrics, prints, maps, and folk art. The place is owned by an American who has lived in Japan more than 20 years. Open: Mon–Sat 10am–6pm. Closed: National hols. Station: Roppongi, a 5-minute walk away.

MAYUYAMA, 2-5-9 Kyobashi, Chuo-ku. Tel. 3561-5146.
One of the best-known names in fine antiques, this shop was first established in 1905 and is one of Tokyo's oldest and most exclusive antiques shops. Housed in a distinguished-looking stone building between Kyobashi and Takaracho, within walking distance of Tokyo Station, Mayuyama deals in ceramics and pottery, scrolls and screens from Japan, China, and Korea—at expectedly high prices. Open: Mon–Sat 9:30am–6pm. Closed: National hols. Station: Kyobashi or Takaracho.

TOKYO ANTIQUE HALL [KOMINGU KOTTOKAN], Meiji Dori Street at 3-9-5 Minami Ikebukuro, Toshima-ku. Tel. 3982-3433 or 3980-8228.
One of the best places in town for one-stop antiques hunting, this building has more than 35 antiques dealers' stalls. Although most articles are marked, it's okay to try bargaining. You could spend hours here, looking over furniture, ceramics, woodblock prints, jewelry, lacquerware, swords, china, hair combs, Japanese army memorabilia, kimonos and fabrics, scrolls and screens, samurai gear, clocks, watches, dolls, and other items too numerous to list. Antiques are both Japanese and Western, and dealers here work the flea markets across the country. Open: Fri–Wed 10am–7pm (try to get here before 5pm because some stalls close down early if business is slow). Station: Ikebukuro, a 10-minute walk away. Take a right out of the station's east side, walking south on Meiji Dori; the shop will be on your left.

ARCADES & TAX-FREE SHOPS

Shopping arcades are found in several of Tokyo's first-class hotels. While they don't offer the excitement and challenge of going out and rubbing elbows with the natives, they are convenient, sales clerks speak English, and you can be assured of top-quality merchandise. The **Imperial Hotel Arcade** is one of the best, with shops selling pearls, woodblock prints, toys, antiques, and expensive name-brand clothing like Hanae Mori. The Okura and New Otani hotels also have extensive shopping arcades.

Underground shopping arcades are found around several of Tokyo's train and subway stations, the biggest of which are Tokyo and Shinjuku stations. Serving commuters on their way home, they often have great sales and bargains on clothing, accessories, and electronics. In Ikebukuro, the city's tallest skyscraper, Sunshine City, contains more than 200 shops, including the **World Import Mart,** selling different foods and goods from 50 countries.

Other good places to shop if you're short of time are duty-free stores. To qualify, you must present your passport, whereupon you'll be issued a piece of paper that you surrender at the Customs desk when departing Japan (the Customs desk at the Narita airport is well marked, so you can't miss it). At that time you may also be requested to show the product to Customs officials.

The best-known tax-free arcade is the **International Arcade,** 1-7-23 Uchisaiwaicho, Chiyoda-ku (tel. 3571-1528), located close to the Imperial Hotel (in

Hibiya), under the train tracks. Stores here are open daily from 10am to 6:30pm and include merchandise from pearls and cameras to kimonos, china, woodblock prints, and electronics.

The **Narita airport's duty-free shops** are also good places to shop for alcoholic products, such as sake or whisky.

BOOKS

In addition to the bookstores listed in the "Fast Facts: Tokyo" section in Chapter 4, there's a whole slew of bookstores along Yasukuni Dori Avenue in Jimbocho-Kanda, which no bibliophile should pass up. In this mecca for both new and used books, there are more than 50 shops, several of which deal in books written in English.

KITAZAWA, 2-5 Jimbocho, Kanda. Tel. 3263-0011.

This place has an overwhelming selection of books on Japan, including those most recently published. It also has old and rare books. Open: Mon–Sat 10am–6pm. Station: Jimbocho, a 3-minute walk away.

OHYA SHOBO, 1-1 Jimbocho, Kanda. Tel. 3291-0062.

This shop in Kanda claims to have the largest stock of old Japanese illustrated books, woodblock prints, and maps in the world. Open: Mon–Sat 10:30am–6:30pm. Closed: Hols. Station: Jimbocho, a 3-minute walk away.

TUTTLE BOOK SHOP, 1-3 Jimbocho, Kanda. Tel. 3291-7072.

This shop, the Tokyo branch of a Vermont firm, has a wide selection of books on Japan and the Far East written in English, as well as Japanese-language books. Open: Mon–Fri 10:30am–6:30pm, Sat and national hols 11am–6pm. Station: Jimbocho, a 3-minute walk away.

CAMERAS & FILM

You can purchase cameras at many duty-free shops, including those in Akihabara, but if you're really serious about photographic equipment or want to stock up on film, make a trip to a shop dealing specifically in cameras. If purchasing a new camera is too formidable an expense, consider buying a used camera. New models come out so frequently in Japan that older models can be grabbed up for next to nothing.

YODOBASHI CAMERA, 1-11-1 Nishi Shinjuku. Tel. 3346-1010.

Shinjuku is the photographic equipment center for Tokyo, and this is the biggest store in the area. It ranks as one of the largest discount camera shops in the world, with around 30,000 items in stock, and reputedly sells approximately 500 to 600 cameras daily. In addition to cameras, it also has watches, calculators, typewriters, and cassette players. Its duty-free section is on the second floor, and even though prices are marked, you can bargain here. Come here to stock up on film. Open: Daily 9:30am–8:30pm. Station: Shinjuku, a block west.

CAMERA NO KIMURA, 1-18-8 Nishi Ikebukuro. Tel. 3981-8437.

This store, west of Ikebukuro Station, has a good selection of used cameras. Open: Mon–Sat 8am–8pm, Sun and hols 10am–7pm. Station: Ikebukuro, a 2-minute walk away.

MATSUZAKYA CAMERA, 1-27-34 Takanawa, Minato-ku. Tel. 3443-1311.

This is another shop that deals in used Japanese and foreign cameras. Open: Mon–Sat 10am–7pm, Sun and hols 10am–5pm. Station: Shinagawa, about a 20-minute walk away.

CRAFTS & TRADITIONAL JAPANESE PRODUCTS

If you want to shop for traditional Japanese folk crafts, a number of stores in Tokyo offer such items as fans, paper products, chinaware, lacquerware, kimonos, and

Ando **8**
Hankyu **6**
Imperial Hotel Arcade **1**
International Arcade **3**
Itoya **15**
Matsuya **14**
Matsuzakaya **10**
Mikimoto **13**
Mitsukoshi **11**
Nihonshu Center **9**
Nishi-Ginza Electric
    Center **4**
Printemps **16**
Sakai Kokodo Gallery **2**
Seibu **7**
Takumi **5**
Wako **12**

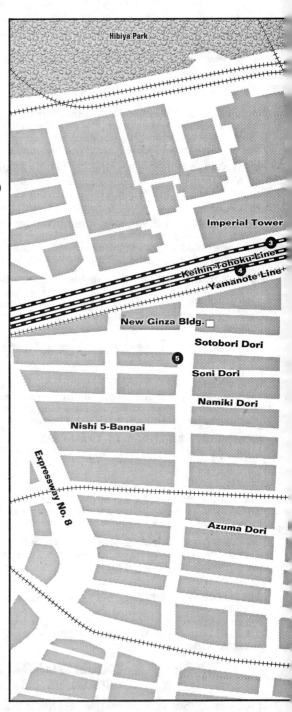

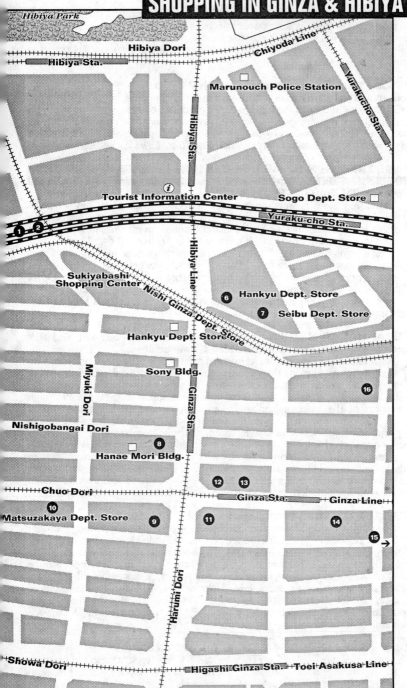

SHOPPING IN GINZA & HIBIYA

Hibiya Park

Hibiya Dori

Chiyoda Line

Hibiya Sta.

Marunouch Police Station

Yurakucho Sta.

Hibiya Sta.

Tourist Information Center

Sogo Dept. Store

Yuraku-cho Sta.

Hibiya Line

Nishi Ginza Dept. Store

Sukiyabashi Shopping Center

Hankyu Dept. Store

Seibu Dept. Store

Hankyu Dept. Store

Miyuki Dori

Sony Bldg.

Ginza Sta.

Nishigobangai Dori

Hanae Mori Bldg.

Chuo Dori

Ginza Sta.

Ginza Line

Matsuzakaya Dept. Store

Harumi Dori

Showa Dori

Higashi Ginza Sta.

Toei Asakusa Line

bamboo products. In addition to the shops listed below, remember that department stores have crafts sections boasting wide selections of everything from kitchenware to lacquerware to kimonos. Also, Nakamise Dori, a pedestrian lane leading to Sensoji Temple in Asakusa, is packed with stalls selling everything from wooden *geta* shoes to hairpins worn by geisha.

BINGOYA, 10-6 Wakamatsucho. Tel. 3202-8778.

Folk art and crafts are sold on six floors of this small building, including traditional toys such as tops and dolls, handmade paper products, baskets, straw boots, items made from cherry bark, chopsticks, pottery, glassware, lacquerware, and fabrics from all over Japan. Open: Tues–Sun 10am–7pm. Station: Akebonobashi, a 15-minute walk away; or Shinjuku, west exit, then bus no. 74 or 76 to Kawada-cho bus stop.

JAPAN TRADITIONAL CRAFT CENTER (ZENKOKU DENTOTEKI KOGEIHIN SENTA), 2nd floor of Plaza 246 Building, 3-1-1 Minami Aoyama. Tel. 3403-2460.

This lovely store is worth a trip even if you can't afford to buy anything. Established to publicize and distribute information on Japanese crafts, it's a great introduction to both traditional and contemporary Japanese design. In addition to its permanent exhibition, it sells various crafts from all over Japan that are changed on a regular basis, which means there are always new items on hand. Crafts for sale usually include lacquerware, ceramics, fabrics, paper products, bamboo items, dolls, writing brushes, metalwork, and more. Prices are high but rightfully so. Open: Fri–Wed 10am–6pm. Station: Gaienmae, a 3-minute walk away. Located on the corner of Gaien-nishi Dori Avenue and Aoyama Dori Avenue, above a Häagen-Dazs ice-cream parlor.

KOKUSAI KANKO KAIKAN, 1-8-3 Marunouchi, Chiyoda-ku; and 9th floor of Daimaru Department Store (same address).

What finds these two places are! Located right beside each other, practically on top of Tokyo Station, they contain tourism promotional offices for every prefecture in Japan—each of which also sells its own special goods and products. Altogether, there are 49 of these little shops, spread along the first through fourth floors of the Kokusai Kanko Kaikan Building and on the ninth floor of Daimaru Department Store. You won't find such a varied collection anywhere else in Japan; and prices are very reasonable, cheaper than at department stores. What's more, no one shops here. You don't have time to go to Okayama to buy its famous Bizen pottery? You forgot to buy your clay *ningyo* doll while in Fukuoka? You can find those here, as well as toys, lacquerware, pottery, glassware, paper products, sake, *kokeshi* dolls, bamboo ware, pearls, china, and everything else Japan makes. Open: Mon–Fri 9am–5pm. Station: Tokyo, Yaesu north exit, less than a minute's walk away.

ORIENTAL BAZAAR, 5-9-13 Jingumae. Tel. 3400-3933.

This is Tokyo's best-known and largest souvenir/crafts shop, selling products at very reasonable prices. It's located on Omote Sando Dori in Harajuku, easily distinguished by its Asian-looking façade of orange and green. I've always been partial to this store and have found great bargains here in used kimonos. It offers three floors of souvenir and gift items, including cotton yukata, polyester and silk kimonos, woodblock prints, paper products, fans, Japanese swords, lamps and vases, Imari chinaware, sake sets, Japanese dolls, and pearls. This store will also ship things home for you. Open: Fri–Wed 9:30am–6:30pm. Station: Harajuku or Meiji-Jingumae, each a few minutes' walk away.

TAKUMI CRAFT SHOP, 8-4-2 Ginza. Tel. 3571-2017.

This two-story shop on Sotobori Dori Avenue in Ginza stocks a variety of Japanese folk art, including rustic ceramics, paper products, fabrics, furniture, and lacquerware. It isn't as large as the shops above, but is definitely worth a stop if you're in the vicinity. Open: Mon–Sat 11am–7pm, hols 11am–5:30pm. Station: Hibiya or Ginza.

DEPARTMENT STORES

Japanese department stores are institutions in themselves. Usually enormous, well designed, and chock-full of merchandise, they have about everything you can imagine, including art galleries, pet stores, rooftop playgrounds or greenhouses, travel agencies, restaurants, grocery markets, and flower shops. You could easily spend a whole day in a department store, eating, attending cultural exhibitions, planning your next vacation, and exploring the various departments. Microcosms of Japanese society, these department stores reflect the affluence of modern Japan, offering everything from wedding kimonos to fashions by the world's top designers. And one of the most wonderful aspects of the Japanese department store is its courteous service.

If you arrive at a store as its doors open, at 10am, you will witness a daily Japanese rite: lined up at the entrance, the entire staff will bow in welcome. Some Japanese shoppers arrive just before opening time so as not to miss this favorite ritual. Sales clerks are everywhere, ready to help you. In many cases you don't even have to go to the cash register once you've made your choice. Just hand over the product, along with your money, to the sales clerk, who will return with your change, your purchase neatly wrapped, and an *"arigatoo gozaimashita"* (thank you very much). A day spent in a Japanese department store could spoil you for the rest of your life.

Department stores are convenient places to shop for traditional Japanese items, including lacquerware, china and kitchenware, trays, gift items, toys, furniture, sporting goods, shoes, cosmetics, jewelry, clothing, sweets, lingerie, belts, hats, and household goods. The basement is usually devoted to foodstuffs: fresh fish, produce, and pre-prepared snacks and dinners. There are often free samples of food. If you're feeling slightly hungry, therefore, walking through the food department could do nicely for a snack. Many department stores include boutiques of such famous Japanese and international fashion designers as Issey Miyake, Rei Kawakubo (whose line is called "Comme des Garçons"), Hanae Mori, Christian Dior, Calvin Klein, and Brooks Brothers, as well as a department devoted to the kimono. To find out what's where, stop by the store's front entrance. Many department stores in the Ginza and Shinjuku areas have floor-by-floor guides in English.

Hours are generally 10am to 7pm, and since department stores close on different days of the week, you can always find several that are open, even on Sunday and holidays (which are major shopping days in Japan).

IN IKEBUKURO

SEIBU, 1-28-1 Minami Ikebukuro. Tel. 3981-0111.

If you want to visit a department store simply for the cultural experience, you might be interested in knowing that Seibu, located practically on top of Ikebukuro Station, claims to be the second-largest department store in the world (the largest is Sogo in Yokohama, which opened a few years back and took the number-one title from Seibu). Just imagine—there are 47 entrances to Seibu, 8,000 sales clerks, 63 restaurants, 12 floors, 31 elevators, and 8 escalators. On an average weekday, 190,000 shoppers pass through the store, a number that swells to 300,000 on a Sunday.

Seibu devotes two basement floors to foodstuffs alone—you can buy everything from taco shells to octopus to seaweed. Dishes are set out so that you can nibble and sample the food as you move along, and hawkers yelling out their wares give the place a marketlike atmosphere. Fast-food counters sell salads, grilled eel, chicken, sushi, and other ready-to-eat dishes. The rest of the floors are devoted to clothing, furniture, art galleries, kitchenware, and a thousand other things, and many of the best Japanese and Western designers have boutiques here. Open: Wed–Mon 10am–7pm. Station: Ikebukuro.

IN GINZA & NIHOMBASHI

The fashionable district of Ginza, along with Nihombashi east of Tokyo Station, has the largest concentration of top-quality department stores in Tokyo.

WAKO, 4-5-11 Ginza. Tel. 3562-2111.

On the corner of Ginza 4-chome Crossing, this is one of the few buildings in the area to have survived World War II. Its distinctive clock tower and innovative window displays are Ginza landmarks. Wako specializes in imported fashions, luxury items, and Seiko timepieces. Certainly one of the classiest stores around, with prices to match. Open: Mon–Thurs 10am–5:30pm, Fri–Sat 10am–6pm. Closed: Hols. Station: Ginza.

MITSUKOSHI, 4-6-16 Ginza. Tel. 3562-1111.

Located right on Ginza 4-chome Crossing, this store is a branch of the famous Mitsukoshi in Nihombashi. Popular with young shoppers. Open: Tues–Sun 10am–7pm. Station: Ginza.

MATSUZAKAYA, 6-10-1 Ginza. Tel. 3572-1111.

Located one block from Ginza 4-chome Crossing on Chuo Dori Avenue in the direction of Shimbashi, this is an older, more established mart, and was the first department store in Japan that did not require customers to take off their shoes at the entrance. Established more than 300 years ago, it appeals to Tokyo's older generation. Open: Thurs–Tues 10am–7pm. Station: Ginza.

MATSUYA, 3-6-1 Ginza. Tel. 3567-1211.

★ In the opposite direction from Ginza 4-chome Crossing, on Chuo Dori Avenue, this is one of my favorite department stores in Tokyo. It has a good selection of Japanese folkcraft items, kitchenware, and beautifully designed contemporary household goods, in addition to the usual clothes and accessories. If I were buying a wedding gift, this is one of the first places I'd look. Open: Wed–Mon 10am–7pm. Station: Ginza.

PRINTEMPS, 3-2-1 Ginza. Tel. 3567-0077.

This store, a branch of Paris's fashionable Au Printemps, is a relative newcomer in the Ginza scene. A fun, young store with announcements in both French and Japanese, it is very popular with Tokyo's young generation. Open: Thurs–Tues 10am–7pm.

SEIBU, 2-5-1 Yurakucho. Tel. 3286-0111.

Located in Yurakucho between the Hibiya and Ginza subway stations, this store consists of two buildings, one selling clothing and accessories, the other specializing in interior design and kitchenware. Open: Fri–Wed 10am–7pm. Station: Yurakucho or Hibiya.

HANKYU, 2-5-1 Yurakucho. Tel. 3575-2233.

Another department store located in Yurakucho between the Hibiya and Ginza subway stations, this relative newcomer to the area has the usual food, clothing, and household goods departments. Open: Fri–Wed 10am–7pm. Station: Yurakucho or Hibiya.

MITSUKOSHI, 1-7-4 Nihombashi Muromachi. Tel. 3241-3311.

In Nihombashi, this is one of Japan's oldest department stores. First opened as a kimono shop back in the 1600s, today it has many name-brand boutiques, including Givenchy, Dunhill, Chanel, Hanae Mori, Oscar de la Renta, Christian Dior, and Tiffany. Its kimonos, by the way, are still hot items. The building itself is old, stately, and attractive, making shopping here a pleasure. Open: Tues–Sun 10am–7pm. Station: Mitsukoshimae (which means "In Front of Mitsukoshi").

TAKASHIMAYA, 2-4-1 Nihombashi. Tel. 3211-4111.

This department store, located near Nihombashi Station, provides stiff competition for the above-listed Mitsukoshi, with a history just as long. It also has boutiques by such famous designers as Chanel, Laroche, Dunhill, Céline, Lanvin, Louis Vuitton, Gucci, Christian Dior, Issey Miyake, and Kenzo. Open: Thurs–Tues 10am–6:30am. Station: Nihombashi.

IN SHINJUKU

ISETAN, 3-14-1 Shinjuku. Tel. 3352-1111.

Isetan is a favorite among foreigners living in Tokyo. It has a good line of conservative clothing appropriate for working situations, as well as contemporary and fashionable styles, including designer clothes. It also has a great kimono section. It's located about a 5-minute walk west of Shinjuku Station on Shinjuku Dori Avenue. Open: Thurs–Tues 10am–7pm. Nearest station: Shinjuku Sanchome.

ODAKYU, 1-1-3 Nishi Shinjuku. Tel. 3342-1111.

Odakyu is hard to miss, since it's located right above Shinjuku Station. Its merchandise is fairly middle-of-the-road. Open: Fri–Wed 10am–7pm. Station: Shinjuku.

KEIO, 1-1-4 Nishi Shinjuku. Tel. 3342-2111.

Another department store right over the station is Keio, which specializes in everyday products for the hordes of commuters passing through. Open: Fri–Wed 10am–7pm. Station: Shinjuku.

IN SHIBUYA

In recent years, Shibuya has emerged as a shopping mecca for the fashionable young, and so many stores have opened in the last few years that there is a bona fide store war going on. Tokyu and Seibu are the two big names, both of which keep opening more and more shops around Shibuya Station. In addition to the big stores here, check the "Fashions" section for Shibuya's fashion department stores.

TOKYU, 2-24-1 Dogenzaka. Tel. 3477-3111.

A conservative, middle-of-the-road department store appealing greatly to middle-aged well-to-do women. Other Tokyu-affiliated stores include a smaller shop right above Shibuya Station, Tokyu Hands (everything imaginable for the hobbyist and the home), and 109 and 109-2 (filled with clothing boutiques). Open: Fri–Wed 10am–7pm. Station: Shibuya.

SEIBU, 21-1 Udagawacho. Tel. 3462-0111.

Similar to the main store in Ikebukuro, it carries everything from accessories and art to stationery and wine. Designer boutiques here include for Comme des Garçons, Giorgio Armani, Issey Miyake, Jun Ashida, Kenzo, and Yohji Yamamoto. Other Seibu stores include Loft (with items for the home and hobbyist, a stiff competitor of Tokyu Hands), Parco, and Seed (the last two are fashion stores, described below). Open: Thurs–Tues 10am–7pm. Station: Shibuya.

DOLLS

Asakusabashi is the place to go for dolls, with several stores lining Edo Dori Avenue. These two stores are among the best known.

KYUGETSU, 1-20-4 Yanagibashi, Taito-ku. Tel. 3861-5511.

Japanese dolls range from elegant creatures with delicately arranged coiffures and silk kimonos to wooden dolls called kokeshi. This is one of the biggest doll shops in Japan, located in front of Asakusabashi Station. Open: Mon–Fri 9am–6pm, Sat–Sun 9am–5pm. Station: Asakusabashi.

YOSHITOKU DOLLS, 1-9-14 Asakusabashi, Taito-ku. Tel. 3863-4419.

Yoshitoku Dolls has had a shop at this location since 1711. One of the largest shops in the area, it sells a variety of Japanese dolls, including Hakata (fired-clay painted dolls representing traditional characters) and kokeshi, as well as kimono-clad babies, Kabuki figures, masks, souvenirs, and some antiques. Open: Mon–Sat 9:30am–5:30pm. Closed: National hols. Station: Asakusabashi, a 1-minute walk away.

ELECTRONICS

The largest concentration of electronics and electrical-appliance shops in Japan is in an area of Tokyo called Akihabara. Although you can find good deals on video and audio equipment elsewhere, Akihabara is special simply for its sheer volume. With more than 600 stores, shops, and stalls, Akihabara accounts for a tenth of the nation's electronics and electrical-appliance sales. An estimated 50,000 shoppers come here on a weekday, 100,000 per day on a weekend. It may surprise you to learn that 80% of Japan's consumer electronics market is domestic.

Even if you don't buy anything, it's great fun walking around (and if you do intend to buy something, make sure you know what it would cost back home—with the present exchange rate, there are few bargains in Japanese electronics products, but you may be able to pick up something unavailable back home). Most of the stores and stalls are open-fronted, many of them are painted neon green and pink, and inside, lights are flashing, fans are blowing, washing machines are shaking and shimmying, stereos are blasting. Salesmen yell out their wares, trying to get customers to look at their rice cookers, computers, video equipment, cassette players, TVs, calculators, and watches. This is the best place to go to see the latest models of everything electronic, an educational experience in itself.

If you purchase anything, make sure it is made for export—that is, that there are instructions in English, that there is an international warranty, and that the product has the correct electrical connectors.

Simply look for signs saying DUTY FREE. Good buys in Akihabara include cassette players, stereo equipment and CD players, watches, calculators, video equipment, and portable electronic typewriters. Be sure to bargain, and don't buy at the first place you go to. One woman I know who was looking for a portable cassette player bought it at the third shop she went to for ¥4,000 ($32) less than what was quoted to her at the first shop. All the larger shops in Akihabara have duty-free floors where the products are designed for export. Some of the largest shops are **Yamagiwa,** 3-13-10 Soto-Kanda (tel. 3253-2111); **Laox,** 1-2-9 Soto-Kanda (tel. 3253-7111); and **Hirose Musen,** 1-10-5 Soto Kanda (tel. 3255-2211). If you're serious about buying anything, comparison-shop at these stores first.

The easiest way to get to Akihabara is via the Yamanote Line or the Keihin Tohoku Line to the JR Akihabara Station. You can also take the Hibiya subway line to Akihabara Station, but it's farther to walk. Most shops are open daily from about 10am to 7pm.

Another place to look for electric and electronic equipment is the **Nishi-Ginza Electric Center,** 2-1-1 Yurakucho (tel. 3503-4481; closest station: Yurakucho or Hibiya). It's located in Ginza, next to the International Arcade and under the train tracks. Shops here sell radios, cassette players, calculators, CD players, and other electrical and electronic gadgets duty free. It's open Monday through Saturday from 10am to 7pm, on Sunday and holidays from 10am to 6pm.

FASHIONS

The department stores listed above are all good places for checking the latest in Japanese fashion. If you want to pick up some fashions that have the Japanese-designer look without the corresponding price tags, the whole area around Harajuku has hundreds of small shops selling inexpensive clothing. Takeshita Dori, a street described in the walking tour of Harajuku, is lined with shops catering to young, fashion-conscious Japanese. Otherwise, Harajuku and Shibuya are the places to go for fashion department stores, which are multistoried buildings filled with concessions of various designers and labels. The stores below are three of the largest.

PARCO, 15-1 Udagawacho, Shibuya. Tel. 3464-5111.

A division of Seibu, Parco is divided into three buildings called Parco 1, 2, and 3. Parco 1 and 2 are filled with designer boutiques for men and women, including such avant-garde Japanese designers and designs as Kansai, Yohji Yamamoto, Nicole, Comme des Garçons, and Issey Miyake, while Parco 3 is devoted to household goods and interiors. Parco has two sales a year that you shouldn't miss if you're here—one in January and one in July. Open: Daily 10am–8:30pm. Station: Shibuya.

SEED, 21-1 Udagawacho. Tel. 3462-0111.

One of Seibu's newer ventures in the store wars of Shibuya, Seed consists of eight floors devoted to the newest of the new in design talent. There will be a lot of names you're probably not familiar with, along with such notables as Paul

Smith, Missoni, Katharine Hamnett, Takeo Kikuchi, Jean Paul Gaultier, and Junko Shimada. Open: Thurs–Tues 10am–7pm. Station: Shibuya.

LA FORET, 1-11-6 Jingumae. Tel. 3475-0411.

This is another good place to shop, near Harajuku's main intersection of Omote Sando Dori and Meiji Dori avenues. In addition to being the largest store in Harajuku, it is also one of the most fashionable. Although some of the boutiques are expensive, there are some great deals to be found here, particularly in the shops in the basement. Open: Daily 11am–8pm. Station: Harajuku or Meiji-Jingumae.

VIVRE 21, 5-10-1 Jingumae. Tel. 3498-2221.

Not far from La Foret is Vivre, a sleek white building filled with fashionable boutiques selling designer clothing and jewelry. Nicole, Kenzo, Montana, Thierry Mugler, Jean Paul Gaultier, and Junko Shimada are just a few of the concessions here. In the basement is a shop selling kitchenware, plus a café. Open: Daily 11am–8pm. Station: Meiji-Jingumae or Omote Sando.

FLEA MARKETS

Flea markets, of course, are good opportunities to shop for antiques as well as for delightful junk. Don't expect to find any good buys in furniture, but you can pick up second-hand kimonos, kitchenware, small chests, dolls, household items, and odds and ends. The markets usually begin as early as 6am and last until 4pm or so, but go early if you want to pick up bargains. Bargaining is expected. There are flea markets every weekend in Tokyo.

In addition to the regularly scheduled ones listed here, there are markets held occasionally at various other places in Tokyo, especially in summer. Check the *Tokyo Journal* for a list of the month's markets.

Togo Shrine (closest station: Meiji-Jingumae or Harajuku), described in the Harajuku section, has a flea market for antiques on the first and fourth Sundays of the month. Since it's held outside, it's canceled in case of rain. It's good for used kimonos, furniture, and curios.

Nogi Shrine (located at Nogizaka Station) has an antiques flea market the second Sunday of the month; this is also canceled in case of rain.

In Roppongi, the steps of the **Roi Building** (closest station: Roppongi) become a market as dealers lay out their wares on the fourth Thursday and Friday of every month. Items here are generally small, since space is limited.

On the second and third Sundays of the month, **Hanazono Shrine,** behind the Isetan department store on Yasukuni Dori in Shinjuku, is the site of a flea market for antiques if it doesn't rain.

Although held irregularly (once or twice a month on a Sunday, from 10am to 4pm), the **Yoyogi Park** flea market (closest station: Harajuku) is the place to go for second-hand goods. Only used items may be sold, and since there aren't many outlets for such goods in Japan, this market resembles a huge American yard sale. Since anyone can buy space here, vendors range from foreigners moving away from Japan who are eager to get rid of what they've accumulated to Japanese families selling unwanted junk. It's held near Yoyogi Park and NHK Hall.

Finally, the closest thing Tokyo has to a permanent flea market is **Ameya Yokocho** (closest station: Ueno), also referred to as Ameyokocho or Ameyacho. Located near Ueno Park, it's a narrow shopping street along the elevated tracks of the Yamanote Line between Ueno and Okachimachi stations. Originally a wholesale market for candy and snacks and later becoming a black market in U.S. Army goods after World War II, Ameya Yokocho today consists of approximately 400 stalls selling discounted items of everything from fish to vegetables to handbags and clothes. Early evening is the most crowded time, as workers rush through on their way home and hawkers shout out their wares. The scene retains something of the shitamachi spirit of old Tokyo. Although housewives have been coming here for years, in more recent times young Japanese have also discovered it as a good bargain for fashions and accessories. Some shops close on Wednesday, but otherwise hours here are from about 10am to 7pm.

FLOWER-ARRANGING & TEA-CEREMONY ACCESSORIES

In addition to this shop, other good places to look for these traditional wares are department stores. In addition, the Japan Traditional Craft Center, described above under "Crafts & Traditional Japanese Products," usually has beautiful bamboo vases and other accessories for flower arranging.

TSUTAYA, 5-10-4 Minami Aoyama, Minato-ku. Tel. 3400-3815.
Tsutaya has everything you might need for ikebana (flower arranging) or the Japanese tea ceremony, including vases of unusual shapes and sizes and tea whisks. Open: 9am–6:30pm. Closed: First and fourth Sun of month. Station: Omote Sando.

INTERIOR DESIGN

The department stores listed above have furniture and interior design sections, and Ikebukuro's **Seibu** (see above) has an especially well-known and popular department. My favorite is the Design Collection on the seventh floor of Ginza's **Matsuya** (see above), which displays items from around the world selected by the Japan Design Committee as examples of fine design. Included may be such goods as the Alessi teapot from Italy, Braun razors and clocks, and Porsche sunglasses.

A very good place for studying the latest in contemporary Japanese interior design is the **Axis Building,** 5-17-1 Roppongi (closest station: Roppongi). Altogether, there are more than two dozen shops here, most devoted to high-tech interior design. The majority of the products are Japanese, but there are also selected goods from the United States and Europe. Shops feature various aspects of contemporary design, from sleek and unusual lighting fixtures to textiles and linens, clocks, kitchenware, office accessories, and lacquered furniture. Don't neglect the shops in the basement. Hours vary for each shop, but most are open from 11am to 7pm; closed on Sunday and holidays. The Axis Building is on your right as you walk on Gaien-Higashi Dori in the direction of Tokyo Tower.

KIMONOS

The Oriental Bazaar, described earlier under "Crafts & Traditional Japanese Products," has a good selection of new and used kimonos, including elaborate wedding kimonos. In addition, department stores sell kimonos, notably Takashimaya and Mitsukoshi in Nihombashi and Isetan in Shinjuku. They have sales on rental wedding kimonos at least once a year (check the *Tokyo Journal*). Flea markets are also good for used kimonos and yukata.

HAYASHI KIMONO, International Arcade, 2-1-1 Yurakucho. Tel. 3501-4012.
Established in 1913, Hayashi Kimono sells silk and polyester kimonos, including wedding kimonos and the short *happi-coat*. It also sells cotton yukata, men's and children's kimonos, and *obi*, the sash worn around a kimono. If you're buying a gift for someone back home, this is the best place to start. Hayashi Kimono has two concessions in the International Arcade. Open: Daily 10am–6pm. Station: Hibiya or Yurakucho.

CHICAGO, 6-31-21 Jingumae. Tel. 3409-5017.
The place to go for used kimonos. Located on Omote Sando Dori in Harajuku, it stocks hundreds of used kimonos and cotton yukata in the very back of the shop, past the 1950s clothing. There are many used kimonos in the ¥2,000 to ¥5,000 ($14 to $35) price range. Open: Daily 11am–9:30am. Station: Harajuku or Meiji-Jingumae.

KITCHENWARE & TABLEWARE

In addition to the department stores listed above, there are two areas in Tokyo with a number of shops filled with items related to cooking and serving. In Tsukiji, along the streets stretching between Tsukiji Station and Tsukiji Fish Market are shops selling pottery, serving trays, bowls, dishes, wonderful fish knives, and lunch boxes.

The second place to look is Kappabashi Dori Avenue near the Tawaramachi subway station, Japan's largest wholesale area for cookware. There are approximately 150 specialty stores selling cookware here, including sukiyaki pots, woks, lunch boxes, pots and pans, aprons, knives, china, lacquerware, rice cookers, and disposable wooden chopsticks. Although stores in Tsukiji and Kappabashi are wholesalers selling mainly to restaurants, you're welcome to browse and purchase as well. Stores in both areas are closed on Sunday.

PAPER PRODUCTS

Folkcraft shops such as Takumi in Ginza and the Oriental Bazaar in Harajuku have items made of Japanese paper.

WASHIKOBO, 1-8-10 Nishi Azabu, Minato-ku. Tel. 3405-1841.

This store deals almost exclusively in handmade Japanese paper and handcrafts from various parts of Japan. It sells paper and cardboard boxes, paper wallets, notebooks, paper lamps, toys, and sheets of beautifully crafted paper. Open: Mon–Sat 10am–6pm. Closed: Second and third Sat of every month, national hols. Station: Roppongi. Washikobo is about 7 minutes on foot from the station, on right side of street as you walk toward Shibuya.

KURODAYA, 1-2-5 Asakusa. Tel. 3844-7511.

If you're visiting Asakusa, you might want to stop in at this shop, located right beside Kaminarimon Gate. First opened back in 1856, it sells traditional Japanese papers, kites, papier-mâché masks, boxes, and other products made of paper. Open: Tues–Sun 11am–7pm. Station: Asakusa, a few minutes' walk away.

PEARLS

A good place to shop for pearls is in the **Imperial Hotel Arcade,** 1-1-1 Uchisaiwaicho (closest station: Hibiya). There are also pearl shops in the Hotel Okura shopping arcade and the International Arcade.

MIKIMOTO SHOP, 4-5-5 Ginza. Tel. 3535-4611.

The first really good cultured pearl was produced back in 1913 by a Japanese man named Mikimoto Koichi. Today, Mikimoto is one of the most famous names in the world of cultured pearls. The main shop is not far from Ginza 4-chome Crossing. Open: Thurs–Tues 10:30am–6pm. Station: Ginza.

Mikimoto has a branch shop at the Imperial Hotel Arcade, Uchisaiwaicho (tel. 3591-5001). Open: Mon–Sat 10am–7pm. Station: Hibiya.

K. UYEDA PEARL SHOP, Imperial Hotel Arcade, 1-1-1 Uchisai-waicho. Tel. 3503-2587.

In business since 1884, this shop has a wide selection of pearls in many different price ranges. Open: Mon–Sat 10am–7pm, Sun and hols 10am–6pm. Station: Hibiya.

ASAHI SHOTEN, Imperial Hotel Arcade, 1-1-1 Uchisaiwaicho. Tel. 3503-2528.

This is another pearl shop in the Imperial Hotel Arcade with a good selection in the modest-to-moderate price range. Open: Daily 9am–8pm. Station: Hibiya.

RECORDS & COMPACT DISCS

WAVE, 6-2-27 Roppongi. Tel. 3408-0111.

This innovative store, a branch of Seibu, is one of the largest shops in town, with a computerized record-reference system and a comprehensive selection of records, cassettes, CDs and videos. On the first floor are headphones to help you select from 200 of the top hits. Come to Wave for jazz, German new wave, reggae, heavy metal, classical, vintage, or the latest in Japanese music. In the basement is Cine Vivant, a minitheater that shows foreign films four or five times daily. Open: Mon–Sat

11am–10pm, Sun 11am–8pm. Closed: First and third Wed of month. Station: Roppongi. Wave is 3 minutes on foot from station, on left side of Roppongi Dori as you walk in direction of Shibuya.

WAVE, 1-19-6 Minami-Ikebukuro. Tel. 3980-0111.
If you're in Ikebukuro, there's a second Wave outlet located across from Seibu department store. Open: Wed–Mon 10am–7pm. Station: Ikebukuro, east exit; turn right and walk south on Meiji Dori Ave.

VIRGIN MEGASTORE, basement of Marui 0101 Fashion Building, 3-30-16 Shinjuku. Tel. 3353-0038.
Located on Shinjuku Dori Avenue, this store stocks more than 150,000 titles. There are several sections where you can listen to selections, and there's even a disc jockey imported from the U.K. who can tell you about the newest hits. Open: Daily 10:30am–7:30pm. Closed: Second and fourth Wed of month. Station: Shinjuku Sanchome.

SAKE

NIHONSHU CENTER, 5-9-1 Ginza. Tel. 3575-0656.
This is a good place to go to learn more about sake, and you can sample five different kinds of the brew for only ¥300 ($2.15)—and you get to keep the sake cup. A great deal. The center sells sake from regions throughout Japan. It's located on Harumi Dori not far from Ginza 4-chome Crossing, in the direction of Higashi Ginza, on the right side of the street (look for a sign that says SAKESPO 101). Open: Fri–Wed 10:30am–6:30pm. Closed: Every fourth Sun, plus hols. Station: Ginza.

SOUVENIRS

The best places to look for souvenir items are the Oriental Bazaar, listed above under the "Crafts & Traditional Japanese Products" section, and the pedestrian shopping lane called Nakamise Dori, described in the walking tour of Asakusa. In addition, the International Arcade, described in the walking tour of the Ginza, is full of shops selling kimonos, china, woodblock prints, pearls, and other Japanese products.

STONE LANTERNS

ISHIKATSU, 3-4-7 Minami Aoyama. Tel. 3401-1677.
Some people are so enamored of the huge stone lanterns they see at shrines and landscaped gardens that they want to take one home. In operation since 1706, this store has a catalog of various stone lanterns to choose from and they'll ship one to you. Open: Mon–Sat 9am–5pm. Closed: Hols. Station: Roppongi or Omote Sando, from which you should take a taxi.

SWORDS

Other places to look for swords include the Oriental Bazaar, the Tokyo Antique Hall, and the Antique Market in the basement of the Hanae Mori Building in Omote Sando.

JAPAN SWORD, 3-8-1 Toranomon. Tel. 3434-4321.
This is the best-known sword shop in Tokyo, also dealing in sword accessories, sword guards, and kitchen cutlery. Coming here to see its displays is like visiting a museum. Open: Mon–Sat 9:30am–6pm. Closed: Hols. Station: Toranomon or Kamiyacho.

WOODBLOCK PRINTS

In addition to the store listed below, other good places for woodblock prints, including original antiques and reproductions, are the Oriental Bazaar and the Antique Market in the basement of the Hanae Mori Building, both on Omote Sando Dori in Harajuku.

SAKAI KOKODO GALLERY, 1-2-14 Yurakuco. Tel. 3591-4678.

This gallery across from the Imperial Hotel claims to be the oldest woodblock print shop in Japan. The first shop was opened back in 1870 in the Kanda area of Tokyo by the present owner's great-grandfather, and altogether four generations of the Sakai family have tended the store. This is a great place for original prints as well as for reproductions of such great masters as Hiroshige. (If you're really a woodblock print fan, you'll want to visit the Sakai family's excellent museum in the small town of Matsumoto in the Japan Alps.) Open: Daily 10am–7pm. Station: Hibiya.

CHAPTER 9

TOKYO EVENING ENTERTAINMENT

By day, Tokyo is arguably one of the least attractive cities in the world. A congested mass of concrete, it has too many unimaginative buildings, too many cars and people, and not enough trees and greenery.

Come dusk, however, Tokyo comes into its own. The drabness fades and the city blossoms into a profusion of giant neon lights and paper lanterns, and its streets fill with millions of overworked Japanese out to have a good time. If you ask me, Tokyo at night is unequivocally one of the craziest cities in the world. It's a city that never gives up and never seems to sleep. The entertainment district of Roppongi, for example, is as crowded at 3am as it is at 3pm. Many establishments stay open until the first subways start running after 5am. Whether it's jazz, reggae, gay bars, sex shows, discos, mania, or madness that you're searching for, Tokyo has it all.

To understand Tokyo's nightlife, you first have to know that there is no one center of nighttime activity. Rather, there are many nightspots spread throughout the city, each with its own atmosphere, price range, and clientele. Most famous are probably Ginza, Akasaka, Shinjuku, and Roppongi. Before visiting any of the locales suggested in this guide, be sure to walk around and absorb the atmosphere. The streets will be crowded, the neon lights will be overwhelming, and you never know what you might discover on your own.

Although there are many bars, discos, and restaurants packed with young Japanese men and women, nightlife in Japan is still pretty much a man's domain, just as it has been for centuries. At the high end of this domain are the geisha bars, where highly trained women entertain by playing traditional Japanese instruments, singing, and holding witty conversations—and nothing more risqué than that. Generally speaking, such places are outrageously expensive and closed to outsiders. As a foreigner, you'll have little opportunity to visit a geisha bar unless you're invited by a business associate, in which case you should consider yourself extremely fortunate.

More common than geisha bars, and generally not quite as expensive, are the so-called hostess bars, many of which are located in Ginza and Akasaka. A woman will sit at your table, talk to you, pour your drinks, listen to your problems, and boost your ego. You buy her drinks as well, which is one reason the tab can be so high. Hostess bars in various forms have been a part of Japanese society for centuries. Most foreigners will probably find the cost of visiting a hostess bar not worth the price, as the hostesses usually speak only Japanese, but such places provide Japanese males with sympathetic ears and the chance to escape the world of both work and family. Men usually have their favorite hostess bar, often a small place with just enough room for regular customers. In the more exclusive hostess bars, only those with an introduction are allowed entrance. And in almost all cases, Japanese companies are picking up the tab.

The most popular nightlife establishments are drinking locales, where the vast majority of Japan's office workers, college students, and expatriates go for an evening out. These places include Western-style bars, as well as Japanese-style watering holes, called *nomi-ya.* Yakitori-ya, restaurant-bars that serve yakitori and other snacks, are included in this group.

At the low end of the spectrum are Tokyo's topless bars, sex shows, massage parlors, and pornography shops, with the largest concentration of such places in Shinjuku.

Keep in mind that taxis—which are seemingly everywhere during the day— suddenly become very scarce after midnight, especially on weekends. In great demand after the subways stop running, they are often impossible to flag down in all entertainment districts of Tokyo, and I've had the unpleasant experience of having to wait 2 hours in the dead of winter before an empty taxi would finally stop to pick me up. If it's a weekend night, you should plan either to catch the last subway home or else resign yourself to staying out someplace until 2am or 3am, when it becomes easier to catch a taxi. And, of course, you can also simply stay out all night, until the first subways start running after 5am. I've listed a number of establishments that stay open until such an ungodly hour.

In addition to the establishments listed here, be sure to check the Tokyo dining chapter. If you're counting your yen, for example, the Japanese restaurants listed under the budget category in Chapter 6 are your best bet for a relatively inexpensive night out on the town. Many places serve as both eateries and watering holes, especially those that dish out skewers of yakitori.

And finally, one more thing you should be aware of is the "table charge" that many bars and cocktail lounges charge their customers. Included in the table charge is usually a small appetizer—maybe nuts, chips, or a vegetable. At any rate, the charge is usually between ¥300 and ¥500 ($2.15 and $3.55) per person. Some establishments levy a table charge only after a certain time in the evening; others may add it only if you don't order food from their menu. If you're not sure and it matters to you, be sure to ask before ordering anything. Some locales call it an *otsumami,* or snack charge. Remember, too, that a 3% consumption tax will be added to your bill. Some establishments, especially nightclubs, hostess bars. and some dance clubs, will also add a 10% to 20% service charge.

1. THE ENTERTAINMENT SCENE

The best publication for finding out what's going on in Tokyo in terms of contemporary and traditional music and theater, exhibitions in museums and galleries, films, and special events is the *Tokyo Journal.* Published monthly and available for ¥500 ($3.55) at foreign-language bookstores, restaurants, and bars, it also has articles of interest to foreigners in Japan. It even lists department store sales, photography exhibitions, apartments for rent, schools for learning Japanese, and many other services. I don't know how foreigners survived in Tokyo before this publication made its debut in the early 1980s.

Another monthly city magazine with articles and information on the performing arts, concerts, theater, and current films is *Tokyo Time Out,* on sale at bookstores for ¥500 ($3.55). You can also pick up a copy of *Tour Companion's Tokyo City Guide,* a weekly distributed free to hotels, travel agencies, and the TIC. It tells of upcoming events and festivals, as well as other information useful to the traveler. *Weekender,* also a free weekly, is found in supermarkets, hotels, and other places where foreigners hang out. It's best known for its classified ad section, but has articles and features as well. English-language newspapers such as the *Japan Times* also carry information on the theater, films, and special events.

To secure tickets, you can always go to the theater or hall itself to buy tickets. However, if you are staying in one of the upper-class hotels, the concierge or guest-relations manager will usually obtain tickets for you. Otherwise, a much easier way to secure tickets is through one of the several ticket services available, although you should have someone who speaks Japanese make the call for you. Ticket services include **Ticket PIA** (tel. 5237-9990); **Ticket Saison** (tel. 3286-5482); and **Playguide** (tel. 3257-9999).

2. THE PERFORMING ARTS

THEATER

KABUKI

Among the several theaters in Tokyo with regular showings of Kabuki, **Kabukiza,** 4-12-15 Ginza (tel. 3541-3131; 5565-6000 for reservations; located above Higashi-Ginza subway station), is the best known. This theater has about eight or nine Kabuki productions a year, each of which runs 25 days (there are no shows in August). Usually, there are two different programs being shown; matinees run from about 11 or 11:30am to 4pm, and evening performances run from about 4:30 or 5pm to about 9pm. It's considered perfectly okay to come for only part of a performance. In addition to English programs explaining the plot, which cost ¥800 ($5.70), there are English earphones you can rent (¥650 or $4.65, plus a deposit) that provide a running commentary on the story, music, actors, stage properties, and other aspects of Kabuki. I strongly suggest that you either buy a program or rent earphones; it will add immensely to your enjoyment of the play.

Tickets generally range from about ¥2,000 to ¥15,000 ($14.30 to $107.15), depending on the program and the seat location. Advance tickets can be purchased at the Advance Ticket Office, to the right side of Kabukiza's main entrance, from 10am to 6pm. Otherwise, tickets for each day's performance are placed on sale 1 hour before the start of each matinee and evening performance.

If you want to come for only part of a performance (say, for an hour or so), you can do so for as little as ¥600 to ¥900 ($4.30 to $6.40) if you're willing to sit up on the

---

MAJOR CONCERT & PERFORMANCE HALLS

Bunkamura (including Orchard Hall and Theater Cocoon), 2-24-1 Dogenzaka Shibuya-ku (closest station: Shibuya). Tel. 3477-3244.

Kabukiza, 4-12-15 Ginza (closest station: Higashi-Ginza). Tel. 3541-3131.

National Theater of Japan (Kokuritsu Gekijo), 4-1 Hayabusacho, Chiyoda-ku (closest station: Hanzomon, Kojimachi, or Nagatacho). Tel. 3265-7411.

NHK Hall, 2-2-1 Jinnan, Shibuya-ku (closest station: Harajuku or Shibuya). Tel. 3465-1751.

Nakano Sun Plaza, 4-1-1 Nakano, Nakano-Ku (closest station: Nakano). Tel. 3388-1151.

Sunshine Gekijo Theater, 4th floor of Sunshine City Bunka Kaikan, 3-1-4 Higashi Ikebukuro (closest station: Higashi Ikebukuro). Tel. 3987-5281.

Suntory Hall, Ark Hills, 1-12-32 Akasaka (closest station: Akasaka or Roppongi). Tel. 3505-1001.

Tokyo Bunka Kaikan, Ueno Park (closest station: Ueno, Koen exit). Tel. 3828-2111.

fourth floor. No earphones are available, but you can still buy a program. These seats are on a first-come, first-served basis.

If you're in Tokyo in August, when there are no Kabuki performances at Kabukiza, you can usually see Kabuki at the **National Theater of Japan (Kokuritsu Gekijo)**, 4-1 Hayabusacho, Chiyoda-ku (tel. 3265-7411; closest station: Hanzomon, Kojimachi, or Nagatacho). Kabuki is scheduled here throughout the year except during May, September, and December, when Bunraku is being staged instead. Ticket prices range from about ¥1,500 to ¥8,000 ($10.70 to $57.15).

NOH

Noh performances are given at a number of locations in Tokyo, with tickets generally ranging from ¥2,000 to ¥5,000 ($14.30 to $35.70). Performances are usually in the early afternoon, at 1pm, or in the late afternoon, at 5 or 6:30pm; but check the *Tokyo Journal* for exact times. Following is a list of several Noh theaters, of which the National Noh Theater is the most famous:

Hosho Nohgakudo, 1-5-9 Hongo, Bunkyo-ku (tel. 3811-5753), about a 5-minute walk from Suidobashi Station.

Kanze Nohgakudo, 1-16-4 Shoto, Shibuya-ku (tel. 3469-5241), a 15-minute walk from Shibuya Station in the area behind the Tokyu Main Department Store.

Kita Nohgakudo, 4-6-9 Kami-Osaki, Shinagawa-ku (tel. 3491-7773), a 10-minute walk from the JR Meguro Station toward Gajoen.

National Noh Theater (Kokuritsu Nohgakudo), 4-18-1 Sendagaya, Shibuya-ku (tel. 3423-1331), near Sendagaya Station.

Tessenkai Butai, 4-21-29 Minami Aoyama, Minato-ku (tel. 3401-2285), about a 5-minute walk from Omote Sando Station (take Exit A4 from the station).

Umewaka Nohgakudo, 2-6-14 Higashi-Nakano, Nakano-ku (tel. 3363-7748), about a 5-minute walk from Nakano Sakaue Station on the Marunouchi subway line, or a 7-minute walk from Higashi-Nakano Station on the JR Sobu Line.

Yarai Nohgakudo, 60 Yaraicho, Shinjuku-ku (tel. 3268-7311), located up the hill from the Yarai exit of Kagurazaka Station on the Tozai subway line.

BUNRAKU

The **National Theater of Japan (Kokuritsu Gekijo),** 4-1 Hayabusacho, Chiyoda-ku (tel. 3265-7411; closest station: Hanzomon, Kojimachi, or Nagatacho), stages about three Bunraku performances a year, in May, September, and December. There are usually two performances daily, with tickets costing ¥4,000 to ¥4,800 ($28.55 to $34.30). Earphones with English explanations are available for ¥650 ($4.65).

CLASSICAL MUSIC

There are several philharmonic orchestras in Tokyo. Among the best known are the **Tokyo Philharmonic Orchestra** (tel. 3256-9696), the **Japan Philharmonic Orchestra** (tel. 3234-5991), the **Tokyo Prefectural Orchestra** (tel. 3822-0727), and the **NHK Philharmonic Orchestra** (tel. 3465-1780). They play in various theaters in Tokyo, with the majority of performances in either Suntory Hall or NHK Hall. Since the schedule varies, it's best to call the orchestra directly or check with the *Tokyo Journal* to see whether there's a current performance.

DANCE

There is a steady stream of dance companies performing in the capital, including Japanese and foreign ballet companies and modern dance groups. One of the best-known forms of modern Japanese dance is Butoh: it features performers, usually painted white, who create their own highly individualistic interpretations. Unfortunately, Butoh is more popular abroad than it is in Japan. To see what is being performed where, check the *Tokyo Journal*.

LOCAL CULTURAL ENTERTAINMENT

Takarazuka Kagekidan is a world-famous all-female troupe that stages elaborate musical revues, with dancing, singing, and gorgeous costumes. The first Takarazuka troupe, formed back in 1912 at a resort near Osaka, gained instant notoriety because all of its performers were women, in contrast to the all-male Kabuki. When I went to see this troupe perform, I was surprised to see that the audience consisted almost exclusively of women.

Performances are held in Tokyo at the **Tokyo Takarazuka Gekijo,** 1-1-3 Yurakucho (tel. 3591-1711; 3201-7777 for reservations) about 6 or 7 months of the year, generally in March, April, July, August, November, December, and sometimes in June. Occasionally a performance is held in the Kabukiza theater in Higashi-Ginza. Inquire at the Tourist Information Center for more information. Tickets generally range from about ¥1,200 to ¥5,000 ($8.55 to $35.70).

3. THE CLUB & MUSIC SCENE

THE ENTERTAINMENT DISTRICTS

Ginza   A chic and expensive shopping area by day, at night Ginza transforms itself into a dazzling entertainment district of restaurants, bars, and first-grade hostess bars. It is the most sophisticated of Tokyo's nightlife districts and also one of the most expensive, so you have to exercise great caution in choosing a place in which to settle down for the evening; otherwise, you might be paying for the experience for a long time to come. Ginza clubs, notorious for being ridiculously expensive, are supported solely by business executives out on expense accounts. Remember that hardly any of the Japanese businessmen you see out carousing in Ginza's expensive hostess bars are paying for it out of their own pockets. The cost is simply too prohibitive, with bills running from $100 to $500 per person. Since I am not wealthy, I personally prefer Shinjuku and Roppongi to Ginza for nighttime entertainment. However, because Ginza does have some fabulous restaurants, I am including some suggestions of things to do in the area if you happen to find yourself here after dinner. Remember, the cheapest way to absorb the atmosphere in Ginza is simply to wander about, particularly around Namiki Dori Street.

Akasaka   Not quite as sophisticated as Ginza, Akasaka nonetheless has its share of exclusive geisha and hostess bars, hidden away behind forbidding walls and exquisite front courtyards. More accessible are the many drinking bars, cabarets, restaurants, and inexpensive holes-in-the-wall. Popular with both executive tycoons and ordinary office workers, as well as foreigners staying in one of Akasaka's many hotels, this district stretches from the Akasaka-mitsuke subway station along three narrow streets, called Hitotsugui, Misuji, and Tamachi, all the way to Akasaka subway station and beyond. For orientation purposes, stop by the koban (police box) at the huge intersection of Aoyama Dori and Sotobori Dori avenues at Akasaka-mitsuke Station.

Shinjuku   Northeast of Shinjuku Station is an area called **Kabuki-cho,** which undoubtedly has the craziest nightlife in all of Tokyo. A world of its own, it's sleazy, chaotic, crowded, vibrant, and fairly safe—block after block of strip joints, massage parlors, pornography shops, peep shows, bars, restaurants, and lots of drunk Japanese men. I wouldn't be surprised to hear that (with the possible exception of Munich's Oktoberfest) there are more drunk people per square meter in Shinjuku than anywhere else in the world. Shinjuku's primary night hot spot has nothing to do with Kabuki. Apparently at one time there was a plan to bring some culture to the area by introducing a Kabuki theater; the plan never materialized, but the name stuck. Although Kabuki-cho has always been the domain of salarymen out on the town, in recent years young Japanese, including college-age men and women, have claimed parts of it for their own, with the result that there are a few inexpensive drinking establishments well worth the visit.

To the east of Kabuki-cho is a smaller district called **Goruden Gai,** which is pronounced "Golden Guy." It's a neighborhood of tiny alleyways leading past even tinier bars, each consisting of just a counter and a few chairs. Closed to outsiders, these bars cater to regular customers. On hot summer evenings the *"mama-san"* of these bars sit outside on stools and fan themselves, soft red lights melting out of the open doorways. Things aren't as they appear, however. These aren't brothels: they are simply bars, and the mama-san—well, they're as likely to be men as women. Unfortunately, Goruden Gai sits on such expensive land that many of the bar owners are being forced to sell their shops. Some of them are already boarded up, awaiting land developers who are itching to build a high-rise. It's a shame, because this tiny neighborhood is one of the most fascinating in all of Tokyo.

Even farther east is **Shinjuku 2-chome,** officially recognized as the gay-bar district of Shinjuku. It's here that I was once taken to a host bar featuring young men in crotchless pants. Strangely enough, the clientele included both gay men and groups of young, giggling office girls. The place has since closed down, but Shinjuku is riddled with places bordering on the absurd.

The best thing to do in Shinjuku is simply to walk about. In the glow of neon light, you'll pass everything from smoke-filled restaurants to hawkers trying to get you to step inside so they can part you from your money. If you're looking for strip joints, topless or bottomless coffee shops, peep shows, or pornography shops, I leave you to your own devices, but you certainly won't have any problems finding them. In Kabuki-cho alone, there are an estimated 200 sex businesses in operation, including bathhouses where women are available for sex, usually at a cost of around ¥30,000 ($214.30). Although prostitution is illegal in Japan, everyone seems to ignore what goes on behind closed doors.

A word of warning for women traveling by themselves—forgo the experience of Shinjuku. Although you're relatively safe here, with so many people milling about, you won't feel comfortable with so many inebriated fellows stumbling around. If there are two of you, however, you'll be okay. I took my mother to Kabuki-cho for a spin around the neon and we escaped relatively unscathed.

Besides walking around and dining in Shinjuku (see Chapter 6), you can also hear music and visit inexpensive drinking establishments. Although most of the night action in Shinjuku is east of the station, the west side also has an area of inexpensive restaurants and bars.

Roppongi   Although perhaps not as well known to the outside world as Ginza and Shinjuku, Roppongi has emerged as the most fashionable and hip place to hang out for Tokyo's younger crowd. It's also a favorite with Tokyo's foreign community, including the many models in the city, businessmen, and English teachers. With more discos than any other place in town, Roppongi also has more than its fair share of jazz houses, restaurants, expatriate bars, and pubs. Some Tokyoites complain that Roppongi is too crowded, too trendy, and too commercialized (and has too many foreigners), but for the casual visitor I think Roppongi offers an excellent opportunity to view what's new and hot in the capital city.

For orientation purposes, the center of Roppongi is Roppongi Crossing (the intersection of Roppongi Dori and Gaien-Higashi Dori avenues), at the corner of which sits the garishly pink Almond Coffee Shop. The coffee shop itself has mediocre coffee and desserts at terribly inflated prices, but the sidewalk in front of the store is the number-one meeting spot in Roppongi. If you're going to meet a friend in Roppongi, this is probably where it will be.

If you need directions, there's a conveniently located koban (police box) catercorner from the Almond Coffee Shop and next to the Mitsubishi Bank. It has a big map of the Roppongi area, showing the address system, and someone is always there.

Harajuku One of the most popular districts for young Japanese by day, Harajuku doesn't have much of a nightlife district because of the city zoning laws. There are a few places scattered through the area, however, that are good alternatives if you don't like the crowds or the commercialism of Tokyo's more famous nightlife districts.

NIGHTCLUBS & HOSTESS BARS

CORDON BLEU, 6-6-4 Akasaka. Tel. 3582-7800 or 3585-6980.

Small and intimate, this well-known 150-seat nightclub in Akasaka features topless Japanese and foreign dancers, and former guests have included boxer Muhammad Ali and the late John Lennon. There are three different admission prices, depending on whether you choose to have dinner or snacks. Open: Daily from 6pm, with shows at 7:30, 9:30, and 11:30pm. Station: Akasaka.

Admission: ¥13,000 ($92.85), including hors d'oeuvres and drinks; ¥16,500–¥19,800 ($117.85–$141.40), including dinner and drinks; ¥10,000 ($71.40), including light dinner and wine (11:30pm show only).

CLUB MAIKO, Suzuran Dori Street, 4th floor of Aster Plaza Building, 7-7-6 Ginza. Tel. 3574-7745.

If you are interested in visiting a hostess bar, one in Ginza that is receptive to foreigners and not prohibitively expensive is this club, located in a modern building in the heart of the area. The hostesses here are geisha and *maiko*, who are young women still training to be geisha. At this small bar, consisting of a few tables and a long counter, the women put on dancing shows and in between performances sit and talk with customers. With its traditional music and atmosphere, this may be the closest you'll get to Japan's geisha bars. Performances are given by the geisha four times nightly. Open: Mon–Sat 6pm–midnight. Closed: Hols. Station: Ginza, a 3-minute walk away.

Admission: ¥8,800 ($62.85) special package deal for foreigners include entrance and show charge, snacks, and three free drinks. **Prices:** Additional drinks ¥1,000 ($7.15) each.

LIVE-MUSIC HOUSES

AFTER SIX, 3-13-8 Roppongi. Tel. 3405-7233.

After Six is a small and intimate jazz club featuring a grand piano, which takes up most of the space. Its musicians are all imported from America. Opened more than 20 years ago, this tiny basement establishment offers live music every night except Sunday. Open: Mon–Sat 8pm–2am (if Sun is a holiday, it remains open on Sun but closes on Mon). Station: Roppongi, less than a 3-minute walk away. Located on left side of Gaien-Hagashi Dori in direction of Tokyo Tower.

Admission: ¥3,300 ($23.55). **Prices:** Beer ¥650 ($4.65); cocktails ¥1,000 ($7.15).

BIRDLAND, Square Building, 3-10-3 Roppongi. Tel. 3478-3456.

Down to earth and featuring good jazz, Birdland is a welcome refuge from Roppongi's madding crowd. It's located in the basement of the Square Building, well known for its eight discos on the upper floors. Small and cozy, with candles and soft lighting, this jazz house features live music performed by Japanese musicians every day of the week. Open: Daily from 5:30pm, with live entertainment Sun–Fri 7–11:30pm, Sat 8:30pm–1am. Station: Roppongi, a 2-minute walk away.

Admission: ¥2,700 ($19.30). **Prices:** Drinks ¥900 ($6.40).

BODY & SOUL, 7-14-12 Roppongi. Tel. 3408-2094.

This no-nonsense and very casual jazz club features mostly Japanese musicians, playing both traditional and modern jazz. There's room for only 50 people, and musicians who have finished gigs elsewhere have been known to jam with the band. Open: Mon–Sat 7pm–2am, with shows usually at 8:30, 10, and 11:30pm. Station: Roppongi, a 1-minute walk on Roppongi Dori in direction of Shibuya.

Admission: ¥2,200 ($15.70). **Prices:** Beer ¥750 ($5.35).

BLUE NOTE, 5-13-3 Minami Aoyama. Tel. 3407-5781.

One of the newest—and most expensive—nightclubs to open in Tokyo in recent years, this sophisticated jazz club is cousin to the famous Blue Note in New York and, with its blue interior, is almost an exact replica. It manages to draw top-notch jazz musicians: Oscar Peterson, Sarah Vaughan, Tony Bennett, Betty Carter, Lou Rawls, Sergio Mendes, and the Milt Jackson Quartet have all performed here. Open: Mon–Sat 6pm–2am, with shows at 7:30 and 10pm. Station: Omote Sando, about a 5-minute walk away.

Admission: ¥7,000–¥13,000 ($50–$92.85), including one drink.

CAVERN CLUB, 5-3-2 Roppongi. Tel. 3405-5207.

If you know your Beatles history, you'll know that the Cavern Club is the name of the Liverpool club where the Beatles got their start. The Tokyo club features house bands that perform Beatles music exclusively, and very convincingly at that. Close your eyes and you might think you've been transported back in time to the real thing. Decorated with photos and memorabilia of the famous four, and extremely popular with both Japanese and foreigners, it's packed on weekends—with long waiting lines. Unfortunately, reservations are not possible. Snacks include mixed pizza, various salads, pasta, and rice dishes. Open: Mon–Sat 6pm–2:30am, Sun and hols 6pm–midnight. Station: Roppongi, about a 4-minute walk away.

Admission: ¥1,400 ($10) music charge, plus a 20% service charge. **Prices:** Beer ¥650 ($4.65); cocktails ¥850 ($6.05).

CROCODILE, 6-18-8 Jingumae. Tel. 3499-5205.

Located on Meiji Dori Avenue between Harajuku and Shibuya, this establishment is popular with the young and describes itself as a casual rock 'n' roll club, with live bands ranging from rock to blues to jazz-fusion, reggae, country, and experimental. It has an interesting interior and a good atmosphere, and the clientele ranges from Japanese with bleached blond hair and earrings to English-language teachers, depending on the concert. Open: Daily 6pm–2am, with live music 8:30–11pm. Station: Meiji-Jingumae, about a 10-minute walk away.

Admission: ¥1,600–¥2,200 ($11.40–$15.70). **Prices:** Beer from ¥600 ($4.30).

KEYSTONE KORNER, 1-19-11 Jingumae. Tel. 3470-6101.

Although open only since 1991, this jazz club has already gained both a following and a reputation for bringing top musicians to Japan, mostly from the United States. Open: Mon–Sat 6pm–midnight, with shows at 7:30 and 10pm. Station: Harajuku, a few minutes' walk away.

Admission: ¥7,500–¥9,000 ($53.55–$64.30), including one drink.

ROPPONGI PIT INN, 3-17-7 Roppongi. Tel. 3585-1063.

Another well-known music house, this is a no-frills basement establishment catering to a younger crowd and boasting some of the finest in native and imported fusion and jazz rock. Open: Daily from 6:30pm, with shows at 7:30 and 9pm. Station: Roppongi, about a 7-minute walk on Gaien-Higashi Dori in direction of Tokyo Tower.

Admission: ¥2,700–¥6,000 ($19.30–$42.85), depending on the band. **Prices:** Beer ¥550 ($3.90).

SATIN DOLL, 3rd floor of Haiyuza Building, 4-9-2 Roppongi. Tel. 3401-3080.

A comfortable and established locale featuring Japanese jazz singers and musicians seven nights a week. The emphasis here is on vocals, with three sets nightly. Open: Daily 5:30pm–midnight. Station: Roppongi, a 1-minute walk away. Located on street behind Victoria Station restaurant.

Admission: ¥1,300–¥2,000 ($9.30–$14.30), depending on the performer. **Prices:** Beer ¥800 ($5.70); cocktails ¥770 ($5.50).

SHINJUKU PIT INN, 3-16-4 Shinjuku. Tel. 3354-2024.

This is one of Tokyo's most famous jazz, fusion, and blues clubs, and features both Japanese and foreign musicians. An institution for more than 20 years, this basement locale with exposed pipes and bare concrete walls places more emphasis on good music than on atmosphere. Since only a few snacks (like potato chips and sandwiches) are available, eat before you come. There are three programs daily—from 11:30am to 2pm, 2:30 to 6pm, and 7:30 to 11pm—making it a great place to stop for a bit of music in the middle of the day. Station: Shinjuku Sanchome, a 1-minute walk away. Located near Isetan department store.

Admission (including one drink): ¥880–¥1,400 ($6.30–$10) for 11:30am show; ¥1,400–¥2,700 ($10–$19.30) for 2:30pm show; ¥2,700–¥4,500 ($19.30–$32.15) for evening show.

DANCE CLUBS & DISCOS

Roppongi is disco heaven, with approximately two dozen establishments clustered in the vicinity. Since the set cover charge often includes drinks and food, they can be the cheapest way to spend an evening. If you prefer to dance to live music, Roppongi has plenty of dance clubs as well. Keep in mind, however, that prices are often higher for men than for women, and are also slightly higher on weekends. Although discos are required by law to close at midnight, many of them ignore the decree and simply stay open until dawn.

AREA, basement of Nittaku Building, 3-8-15 Roppongi. Tel. 3479-3721.
An appropriate name for a disco with the highest ceiling in town, Area has a spaciousness that belies the fact that it's actually in the basement of the Nittaku Building (the same building as Lollipop, described below). This is one of the best discos for dancing and observing—there are elevated blocks for the nerviest of the dancers, who like showing off what they can do. The lighting is good, curtains lower and rise on the dance floor, and the ceiling is mirrored. All in all, this place somehow seems a bit wilder than most, and it's popular mainly with young Japanese women. Open: Sun–Thurs 6pm–2am, Fri–Sat 6pm–4am. Station: Roppongi, a 3-minute walk away.

Admission: Sun–Thurs ¥4,000 ($28.55) for women, ¥4,500 ($32.15) for men, including tickets for about six drinks. Fri, Sat, and eve before hols, add ¥500 ($3.55) extra to above prices.

BUZZ, 5th floor of Square Building, 3-10-3 Roppongi. Tel. 3470-6391.
Buzz is one of several discos located in this building. Using the catchwords "Video & Dance," the gimmick here is the presence of screens that show rock videos, allowing you to dance while watching your favorite performer. For some reason, it's decorated "like a New York rooftop," whatever that is, complete with clouds painted on the walls and—get this—giant flies hanging from the ceiling. Although the "official" closing time is midnight, Buzz actually stays open much later. Open: Sun–Thurs 6pm–3am, Fri–Sat 6pm–5am. Station: Roppongi, about a 3-minute walk away.

Admission: ¥3,000 ($21.40) for women, ¥4,000 ($28.55) for men, including 10 tickets that can be exchanged for drinks. Most drinks require 2 to 5 tickets.

HOT CO-ROCKET, 5-18-2 Roppongi. Tel. 3583-9409.
If you like your music loud, you won't be disappointed at this club, located across from the Porsche dealership as you walk from Roppongi Crossing toward Tokyo Tower. Live reggae bands regale the crowds here, and there's a tiny dance floor. Sunday night features disco music only. Open: Mon–Sat 7pm–3am, Sun 7pm–midnight; music starts at about 8:30pm. Station: Roppongi, a 7-minute walk away.

Admission: ¥3,000 ($21.40) for women, ¥4,000 ($28.55) for men, including two drinks.

JAVA JIVE, basement of Square Building, 3-10-3 Roppongi. Tel. 3478-0088 or 3478-0087.
Of the eight discos in the Square Building, the current favorite remains the immensely popular (and very crowded) Java Jive, actually a two-level establishment, with loose-limbed Jamaican cutouts dancing in silhouette along the wall

(I think you'll have to see this for yourself to understand what I mean). Tropical palms and the flicker of electric candles add to the atmosphere—the dance floor even used to be sand, but it was covered over when it proved too difficult to writhe upon. A live reggae and salsa band is featured every night except disco night, Sunday. (This place is so cavernous and crowded, however, that friends who have been here swear they never even realized there was a live band, though that was probably due to the condition they were in.) Open: Daily 6pm–midnight (officially), 6pm–4am or later (unofficially). Station: Roppongi, a 3-minute walk away.

Admission: ¥3,000 ($21.40) for women, ¥4,000 ($28.55) for men, including 10 tickets for food or drinks. **Prices:** Most drinks take 2 or 3 tickets (beer not included—must buy from vending machines).

KENTO'S, basement of Daini Building, 5-3-1 Roppongi. Tel. 3401-5755.

Kento's was one of the first establishments to open when the wave of 1950s nostalgia hit Japan in the 1980s, and has even been credited with creating the craze. This is the place to come if you feel like dancing and twisting the night away to tunes of the '50s and '60s, played by live bands. It's decorated with posters of such stars as Elvis and Connie Francis, has waiters with slicked-back hair, and even the microphones here are decades old. Although there's hardly room to dance, that doesn't stop the largely over-30 Japanese audience from doing a kind of rock 'n' roll twist in the aisles. If you get hungry, you can order such snacks as chicken, pizza, spaghetti, sausage, salads, and a rather peculiar treat consisting of butter and raisins. There are now other Kento's dance clubs all over Japan, including one in Ginza at 6-7-12 Ginza (tel. 3572-9161). Open: Both places Mon–Sat 6pm–2:30am, Sun and hols 6pm–midnight. Station: Roppongi, about a 4-minute walk away.

Admission: ¥1,400 ($10). **Prices:** Beer ¥650 ($4.60); cocktails ¥850 ($6.05).

LEXINGTON QUEEN, basement of Daisan Goto Building, 3-13-14 Roppongi. Tel. 3401-1661.

Opened in 1980, Lexington Queen is an old-timer in the crazy world of discos, having been the reigning queen for more than a decade. The list of its guests reads like a Who's Who of foreign movie and rock stars who have visited Tokyo—Stevie Wonder, Rod Stewart, Liza Minnelli, Sheena Easton, Joe Cocker, Dustin Hoffman, John Denver, Jacqueline Bisset, Spandau Ballet, and Jennifer Beals, to name a few. One night when I was there the two lead musicians of Wham walked in; another night it was Duran Duran. Popular with foreign models working in Tokyo, Lexington Queen is managed by Bill Hersey, who, appropriately enough, writes a gossip column for the *Weekender*. This is evidently the best place to be on Halloween and New Year's if you can stand the crowds. Note, however, that men unaccompanied by women are not allowed entrance. Open: Daily 6pm–midnight (officially), 6pm–2am or 3am (unofficially). Station: Roppongi, a 3-minute walk away.

Admission: ¥3,000 ($21.40) for women, ¥4,000 ($28.55) for men, including unlimited drinks (except beer, which costs extra) and ¥1,000 ($7.15) worth of sushi.

LOLLIPOP, 2nd floor of Nittaku Building, 3-8-15 Roppongi. Tel. 3478-0028.

Cashing in on the nostalgia craze, Lollipop features a house band that plays hits from the 1960s, Motown, and twist tunes. The dance floor is small and usually crowded, and there are even mirrored disco balls hanging from the ceiling. There's a one-drink minimum. Open: Mon–Sat 6pm–3am, Sun 6pm–3am. Station: Roppongi, a 3-minute walk away.

Admission: ¥1,400 ($10). **Prices:** Beer ¥550 ($3.90).

MALIBU CLUB, 3-3-29 Roppongi. Tel. 3588-8344.

This establishment features live *gaijin* (foreign) and Japanese bands, playing everything from rock 'n' roll to reggae. It has changed names and hands several times in the few years of its existence, due partly to the wild crowd that tends to gather here—and thereafter create havoc in this otherwise rather quiet residential area (a sign outside Malibu's front door pleads with customers to refrain from urinating in the area, giving some indication of the kind of clientele that sometimes gathers here).

The early closing hour is an offering of peace to the neighborhood. Open: Tues–Sat 6pm–2am. Station: Roppongi, about a 10-minute walk away. To reach Malibu, walk toward Tokyo Tower on Gaien-Higashi Dori, turning left when you reach Häagen-Dazs (which will be on your right); then turn right after parking lot.
Admission: ¥1,400 ($10). **Prices:** Drinks ¥850 ($6.05).

NEO JAPONESQUE, basement of Roppongi Forum Building, 5-16-5 Roppongi. Tel. 3586-0050.
I rather like the entrance to this place—through an inner courtyard past slinking black panthers with eyes glowing in the dark. The disco itself changes its decor often to please Tokyo's fickle crowd (which tends to gravitate to the newest hot spot); it even changes its name on occasion. Catering to a slightly older disco crowd than the usual 20-year-olds, and popular with foreigners, this place is also slightly more expensive. Open: Daily 7pm–3am (4am to weekends). Station: Roppongi, about a 5-minute walk. Located on the right side of Gaien-Higashi Dori in the direction of Tokyo Tower.
Admission: ¥3,800 ($27.15) for women, ¥5,500 ($39.30) for men, including 7 tickets good for drinks. **Prices:** Drinks are 1 or 2 tickets; thereafter ¥500–¥1,000 ($3.55–$7.15).

4. THE BAR SCENE

GINZA

HENRY AFRICA, 7-2-17 Ginza. Tel. 3573-4563.
This is one of several Henry Africa pubs in Tokyo. Decorated in the theme of an African hunt, with potted plants, Tiffany-style lampshades, and a wood-plank floor, it is a comfortable place for a drink where visitors will feel right at home. Beer starts at ¥600 ($4.30). Open: Daily 10am–11:30pm. Station: Hibiya or Yurakucho, a few minutes' walk away. Located across from Yamanote elevated tracks (entrance around corner, past tobacco shop).

KIRIN CITY, 8-8-1 Ginza. Tel. 3571-9694.
This relatively new and modern bar features Kirin beer and offers snacks that include assorted sausages, chili beans and crackers, and salads. Beer starts at ¥470 ($3.35). Open: Daily 11:30am–11pm. Station: Ginza, about a 3-minute walk away. Located on Hanatsubaki Dori, just off Chuo Dori near Shiseido boutique.

LUPIN ㊷, 5-5-11 Ginza. Tel. 3571-0750.
If you're looking for a quiet place for a drink, you can't find a more subdued place than Lupin, located in a tiny alley behind Ketel, a German restaurant. This tiny basement bar first opened back in 1928 and has changed little over the decades. Featuring a long wooden bar and wooden booths and cabinets, it's so quiet here you can hear yourself think. As though the world of jukeboxes and stereos has passed Lupin by, no music is ever played here, making it a good place to come if you want to talk. A large bottle of beer starts at ¥880 ($6.30), mixed drinks start at ¥1,000 ($7.15). Open: Mon–Sat 5–11pm. Station: Ginza, a few minutes' walk away.

NANBANTEI, 5-6-6 Ginza. Tel. 3571-5700.
Nanbantei is a chain of yakitori-ya, combining the modern with the traditional in its decor. Its à la carte menu lists skewers of pork with asparagus, Japanese mushroom, large shrimp, quail eggs, gingko nuts, and chicken meatballs, among many other items, with pairs of skewers ranging from ¥500 ($3.55) to ¥1,000 ($7.15). Beer starts at ¥600 ($4.30). Open: Daily 5–11pm. Station: Ginza, a few minutes' walk away.

SAPPORO LION, 7-9-20 Ginza. Tel. 3571-2590.
Sapporo beer is the lure of this small beer hall with its mock Gothic ceiling, located on Chuo Dori Avenue not far from the Matsuzakaya department store. The English-language menu lists snacks ranging from yakitori to salads, spaghetti, and

shrimp with chili sauce. Beer starts at ¥500 ($3.55). Open: Daily 11:30am–11pm. Station: Ginza, about a 3-minute walk away.

SKYAIR PRONTO, 8-6-25 Ginza. Tel. 3571-7864.

Ⓢ Tokyo is filled with so-called "cafébars," which are combination coffee shops and bars popular with young Japanese women and couples. This cafébar in Ginza is easy to find because it's on Namiki Dori Street. It serves as a neighborhood coffee shop until 5pm, with a cup of coffee going for a mere ¥150 ($1.05). From 5:30pm it's a bar, with beer starting at ¥430 ($3.05). Shots are its specialty, costing only ¥380 ($2.70) a glass. Open: Mon–Sat 8am–11pm, Sun 8am–9:30pm. Station: Ginza, a few minutes' walk away.

YAGURA CHAYA 55, basement of Riccar Building, 7-2-22 Ginza. Tel. 3571-3494.

★ If you're looking for a more boisterous drinking atmosphere, I recommend this Japanese-style yakitori-ya in the Riccar Building, not far from the Imperial Hotel. Look for a traditional-looking restaurant, with lockers just inside the door where you're supposed to deposit your shoes. Popular with businessmen, Ⓢ couples, and large groups, it's decorated with antiques and traditional crafts. It offers a large menu (in Japanese only) that includes sashimi, yakitori, fish, oden, and pizza, so technically you could come here for both drinks and dinner. Beer starts at ¥550 ($3.90); sake at ¥580 ($4.15). Open: Daily 5pm–midnight. Station: Hibiya or Ginza, each less than a 5-minute walk away.

AKASAKA

HENRY AFRICA, 2nd floor of Akasaka Ishida Building, 3-13-14
Yet another in this chain of pubs in Tokyo. Besides the usual potted plants and glass lampshades, this one also has elephant tusks. It's popular with young Japanese male and female office workers, and in the evenings there's free popcorn. A good place to meet friends. Beer starts at ¥650 ($4.65), cocktails at ¥800 ($5.70). Open: Mon–Sat 11:30am–11:30pm, Sun 5–11:30pm. Station: Akasaka, a 30-second walk away. Located across from TBS Kaikan television building on Hitotsugi Street.

PRONTO, 3-12-1 Akasaka. Tel. 3582-3717.
Similar to Skyair Pronto in Ginza, this Pronto serves as an inexpensive coffeehouse by day and a bar by night. Although its décor is plain and unexciting, it offers cups of coffee for only ¥150 ($1.05). Open: Mon–Sat 8am–11pm; coffee served 8am–5pm, alcohol thereafter until 11pm, with beer starting at ¥430 ($3.05). Closed: Hols. Station: Akasaka or Akasaka-mitsuke. Located on Tamachi Dori.

SHINJUKU

ANYO ㊸, 1-1-8 Kabuki-cho. Tel. 3209-7253.
★ This tiny bar, with room for only a dozen or so people, is typical of a multitude of miniature establishments that line the alleyways of Goruden Gai, a unique nightlife neighborhood east of Kabuki-cho. However, unlike most of the establishments here, it welcomes foreigners and is run by a very friendly woman who speaks some English. In business for more than 20 years, it attracts a regular clientele that ranges from businessmen to those in the advertising industry. This place is a true find for the opportunity it affords of a different view of Japanese life, but prices can add up. There's a ¥500 ($3.55) table charge, as well as a ¥500 ($3.55) snack charge, per person. Beer ranges from ¥500 ($3.55) to ¥800 ($5.70). Open: Mon–Sat 6:30pm–2am. Closed: Hols and mid-Aug. Station: Shinjuku Sanchome, about a 10-minute walk away.

BON'S, 1-1-10 Kabuki-cho. Tel. 3209-6334.
This is another accessible place if you feel like having a drink in Shinjuku's Goruden Gai, a warren of tiny alleyways and even tinier bars. Bon's is located on its very eastern edge, near Hanazono Shrine. Larger than most of the bars here, the establishment caters to a 30-ish Japanese clientele and boasts a Mickey Mouse collection behind a glass case. Note that there's a table charge here of ¥600 ($4.30);

beer starts at ¥650 ($4.65). Open: Mon–Sat 6pm–5am, Sun and hols 6pm–3am. Station: Shinjuku Sanchome, about a 10-minute walk away.

IROHANIHOHETO, 3-15-15 Shinjuku. Tel. 3359-1682.

If you're young and don't have much money, head for this place, located on Yasukuni Dori Avenue next to Isetan Kaikan, on the sixth floor. One in a chain of inexpensive yakitori-ya that attracts a young college crowd, it offers a multitude of snacks, as well as beer starting at ¥440 ($3.15). Open: Daily 5pm–4am. Station: Shinjuku Sanchome, a 5-minute walk away.

VAGABOND, 1-4-20 Nishi Shinjuku. Tel. 3348-9109.

Although most of the night action in Shinjuku is east of the station, the west side also has an area of inexpensive restaurants and bars. This second-floor establishment is owned by the effervescent Mr. Matsuoka, who can be found either here or over at nearby Volga (described below). Vagabond features a jazz pianist nightly, beginning at 7:30pm. Although there's no music charge per se, there is an obligatory snack charge of ¥500 ($3.55) for the bowl of chips automatically brought to your table. Small and cozy, this place is popular with foreigners who live close to Shinjuku Station and with Japanese who want to rub elbows with foreigners. Its Guinness brings in customers from the United Kingdom. Beer ranges from ¥550 to ¥900 ($3.90 to $6.40). The only drawback is its one bathroom, but as one customer pointed out, the queue is a good place to meet people. Open: Mon–Sat 5:30–11:30pm, Sun 4:30–10:30pm. Station: Shinjuku, west side, a few minutes' walk away. Located on second alley behind Odakyu Halc.

VOLGA ⑭, 1-4 Nishi Shinjuku. Tel. 3342-4996.

Located right down the street from Vagabond, described above, Volga is a yakitori-ya housed in an ivy-covered two-story brick building. It has an open grill facing the street and a smoky and packed drinking hall typical of older establishments across the country. Rooms are tiny and simply decorated with wooden tables and benches, and the clientele is middle-aged. Very Japanese. Skewers of yakitori start at ¥100 (70¢). A huge bottle of beer (enough for two to share) is ¥650 ($4.65). Open: Mon–Sat 5–11pm. Closed: Hols. Station: Shinjuku, west side, a few minutes' walk away. Located on second alley behind Odakyu Halc.

SHINJUKU 2-CHOME

These establishments are located east of Kabuki-cho and Goruden Gai in an area known as 2-chome, which has a mixture of gay and straight bars. The nearest subway station is Shinjuku Sanchome, but if you're walking from Kabuki-cho, walk east on Yasukuni Dori Avenue until you come to a large intersection where you can see a large building called Bygs. These establishments are located on a small street behind Bygs.

KINSMEN, 2-18-5 Shinjuku. Tel. 3354-4949.

This gay bar, located in the building next to 69, up on the second floor, welcomes customers of both persuasions and is a good place to come if you want to hear yourself talk. It's a pleasant oasis in 2-chome, small and civilized, with a huge flower arrangement dominating the center of the room. Beer prices start at a low ¥650 ($4.65), and there's no table charge. Open: Wed–Mon 9pm–5am.

NEW SAZAE, 2nd floor of Ishikawa Building, 2-18-5 Shinjuku. Tel. 3354-1745.

After 69 closes, many who refuse to call it quits migrate around the corner to New Sazae. The place is a dive and the crowd is a bit rowdy, but if you get this far you're probably where you belong. The first drink costs ¥1,000 ($7.15); thereafter, drinks are ¥650 ($4.65). Open: Daily 10pm–6am.

69, basement of Daini Seiko Building at 2-18-5 Shinjuku.

This is one of the undisputed old-timers here, beginning first as a gay bar in this heart of the gay district, but now mainly heterosexual. This is the place people gravitate to after an evening in Shinjuku, moving on from here to the bars that follow. Playing primarily reggae music, this dive is tiny, and often so packed it reminds me of the Yamanote Line during rush hour. It usually has a healthy mix of both foreigners and Japanese, with an atmosphere unlike that of any other place in Tokyo. The first drink costs ¥1,100 ($7.85); thereafter, drinks cost ¥650 ($4.65). Open: Fri–Wed 8pm–2am.

ROPPONGI

CHARLESTON, 3-8-11 Roppongi. Tel. 3402-0372.

Charleston has had its ups and downs in the years it's been open. Starting out as a hip place filled with foreign models, it now has a clientele and corresponding atmosphere that are different every time I come here. Sometimes it's filled with U.S. military men on leave, sometimes with foreign businessmen dressed in suits, and sometimes with characters that must have dragged themselves up from the deep. At any rate, it's almost always filled with men, which may be just what you're looking for, but the recent opening of Déjàvu has given Charleston some pretty tough competition and has stolen away much of its clientele. Who knows, we may be witnessing the demise of one of Roppongi's oldest establishments. Beer is ¥780 ($5.55); cocktails start at ¥880 ($6.30). Open: Daily 6pm–6am; most crowded at 3am. Station: Roppongi, less than a 5-minute walk away. Located beside a graveyard.

DEJAVU, 3-15-24 Roppongi. Tel. 3403-8777.

Although popular nightspots in Tokyo seem to come and go with both the brilliance and the durability of a shooting star, it's worth mentioning that one of the hottest places in Roppongi the past few years has been Déjàvu. Some people find the chaotic and colorful walls gaudy, others find them interesting, but everyone seems to be trying to get into this small place—they'll even line up outside and wait. The clientele is mainly foreign, many of whom seem absorbed in their own importance. Cocktails start at ¥900 ($6.40). Open: Sun–Thurs 8pm–4am, Fri–Sat 8pm–5:30am. Station: Roppongi, about a 4-minute walk away.

EX, 7-7-6 Roppongi. Tel. 3408-5487.

For a bit of old Germany right in the heart of Tokyo, pay a visit to Ex, whose name, appropriately enough, means "bottoms up." Although this is primarily a beer-drinking establishment, owner Horst serves hearty helpings of German food. There's no menu, so you just have to ask Horst what's cooking, but common dishes are schnitzel, various kinds of wurst, boiled ribs of pork, sauerkraut, and fried potatoes. Ex is a tiny place, just a half circle of a bar with enough seating for 15 people, but it's usually packed with German businessmen and expatriates who don't mind standing to drink their favorite brand of German beer. Eating is usually done good-naturedly in shifts. Hanging from the ceiling and on the walls are such German paraphernalia as beer mugs, soccer pennants, and photos of German celebrities who have visited Ex. Beer here starts at ¥600 ($4.30). Open: Mon–Sat 5pm–2am. Station: Roppongi, about a 5-minute walk away. Located on diagonal street across from former Defense Agency as you walk on Gaien-Higashi Dori in direction of Nogizaka.

GAS PANIC, 3-14-8 Roppongi. Tel. 3405-0633.

Opened during the Iraqi invasion of Kuwait, this place didn't waste any money on decoration. It looks like a fallout shelter, with graffiti-filled walls and a clientele that tends to be young and restless. Located near Déjàvu and Henry Africa, it may be destined to last as long as the Middle East conflict itself. Draft beer starts at ¥750 ($5.35). Open: Daily 8pm–5am. Station: Roppongi, about a 4-minute walk away.

THE HARD ROCK CAFE, 5-4-20 Roppongi. Tel. 3408-7018.

If you like your music loud, the Hard Rock Café, easily recognizable by King Kong scaling an outside wall, is the place for you. The inside looks like a modern Yuppie version of the local hamburger hangout joint. The food includes barbecued chicken, burgers, and chili. A beer here starts at ¥850 ($6.05), cocktails at ¥990 ($7.05). Open: Daily 11:30am–2am, Sun until 11:30pm. Station: Roppongi, a 3-minute walk in direction of Tokyo Tower and then a right at McDonald's.

HENRY AFRICA, 3-15-23 Roppongi. Tel. 3405-9868.

Similar to its counterparts in Ginza and Akasaka, Henry Africa is devoted to the spirit of the hunt and even has a real rhinoceros head, purchased in Hong Kong. This was the first of the Henry Africa chain bars (there are now four), and popcorn is served free. Beer ranges from ¥600 to ¥850 ($4.30 to $6.05). Open: Mon–Thurs 6pm–2am, Fri–Sat 6pm–4am, Sun and hols 6–11:30pm. Station: Roppongi, a 3-minute walk away. Located on a cul-de-sac on left-hand side as you walk on Gaien-Higashi Dori in direction of Tokyo Tower.

INTER-NATIONAL STATION, 6-1-5 Roppongi. Tel. 3423-4667.

A very civilized yet casual meeting place. The owner, Hiro, speaks English and serves as the amiable bartender. There are little gadgets and toys to play with if you don't feel like talking, and the music is at a level that allows for conversation if you do. You can come here as a single female and not feel weird. There's a ¥300 ($2.15) per-person cover charge. Beer costs ¥750 ($5.35); cocktails start at ¥900 ($6.40). Open Mon–Thurs 7pm–2am, Fri–Sat 7pm–5am. Station: Roppongi, a 1-minute walk away. Located on diagonal street down from Almond Coffee Shop on right side (across from With disco).

MAGGIE'S REVENGE, 3-8-12 Roppongi. Tel. 3479-1096.

Run by an Australian woman who knows almost all her customers by name, this is another expatriate bar that is also popular with the Japanese. There's live music here every night, usually provided by a guitar or piano soloist. Sometimes the music's good, sometimes not—you take your chances—but since the music charge is only ¥700 ($5), what the heck. In addition to beers starting at ¥660 ($4.70) and cocktails starting at ¥880 ($6.30), this place has a good selection of liqueurs, brandies, and champagnes. Open: Mon–Thurs 6:30pm–3am, Fri–Sat 6:30pm–4am. Station: Roppongi, a 3-minute walk away.

PARADISO, 3-13-12 Roppongi. Tel. 3478-4211.

Popular, chic, and very avant-garde, this basement establishment stretches on and on like an underground cavern. It's a good place for people-watching (the clientele is mainly Japanese), but expensive. This is one of the few bars that levies a hefty table charge, which is ¥1,000 ($7.15), and for some reason it's even more expensive if you sit at one of the counters (¥2,200 or $15.70). Cocktails start at ¥1,300 ($9.30). Open: Mon–Sat 7pm–4am, Sun 7–11:30pm. Station: Roppongi, about a 3-minute walk away.

HARAJUKU & AOYAMA

If the weather is fine, you'll want to sit outdoors at one of Harajuku's many sidewalk cafés, described in the dining section.

OH GOD, 6-7-18 Jingumae. Tel. 3406-3206.

One of the best places to go if you find yourself in Harajuku after nightfall; this mellow, dimly lit bar features a mural of a city at sunset and shows free foreign films every night beginning at 6pm (9pm on weekdays). I've seen everything from James Bond to Fassbinder to grade-B movies here. There are also two pool tables. Beer starts at ¥650 ($4.65), cocktails at ¥750 ($5.35). Open: Daily 6pm–6am. Station: Meiji-Jingumae, a few minutes' walk away. Located at Omote-Sando Dori at the end of an alley behind the Café de Rope.

5. SPECIALTY BARS & CLUBS

COCKTAILS WITH A VIEW

RAINBOW LOUNGE, 17th floor of Imperial Hotel's main wing, 1-11 Uchisaiwaicho. Tel. 3504-1111.

If you're in Hibiya or Yurakucho, you might like to stop at the Rainbow Lounge for a quiet drink and a great view of the city lights stretched below. Cocktails here start at ¥1,200 ($8.55). Open: Daily 11:30am–midnight.

TOP OF AKASAKA, 40th floor of Akasaka Prince Hotel, 1-2

Whenever I go to Akasaka, I like to start out the evening with a quiet drink at this fancy and romantic cocktail lounge. With the city of Tokyo as a dramatic backdrop, I can watch the day fade into darkness as millions of lights and neon signs twinkle in the distance. Cocktails average ¥1,300 ($9.30). Open: Daily 5pm–2am. Station: Akasaka-mitsuke, a 3-minute walk away.

THE GARDEN LOUNGE, Hotel New Otani, 4-1 Kioi-cho. Tel. 3265-1111.

If you'd rather rest your eyes on a Japanese landscape garden than on neon lights, the Garden Lounge looks out over a 400-year-old garden complete with waterfall, pond, bridges, and manicured bushes. Cocktails, which begin at ¥1,400 ($10), are served every evening, and there's live-music entertainment nightly except Sunday, for which there's a ¥300 ($2.15) charge Monday through Friday and ¥600 ($4.30) on Saturday. Open: Daily 6–10pm. Station: Akasaka-mitsuke, a 3-minute walk away.

BEER GARDENS

HANEZAWA BEER GARDEN, 3-12-15 Hiro, Shibuya-ku. Tel. 3400-6500.

If you're in Tokyo in the summer months, a lovely place to go for either a meal or drinks is this outdoor beer garden. For the types of meals served, see Chapter 6. Otherwise, mugs of beer here range from ¥600 ($4.30) to ¥900 ($6.40). Open: Apr–Sept, daily 5–9pm. Station: Ebisu, from which you should take a taxi.

SUNTORY BEER GARDEN, Suntory Building, 1-2-3 Moto-Akasaka. Tel. 3470-1970.

You can enjoy a great view of surrounding Akasaka from the beer garden atop the Suntory Building. This place is classier than most rooftop beer gardens, and you can also come here for a meal or snack, such as barbecued steak, which you cook at your own table (see Chapter 6 for more information). A mug of foaming Suntory beer starts at ¥650 ($4.65). Open: End of May–Aug, Mon–Sat 5–9pm. Station: Akasaka-mitsuke, a 1-minute walk away.

KARAOKE

When I first saw karaoke in Japan in the early 1980s, I was convinced it was too uniquely Japanese for export. Wrong! Sing-along bars are now found throughout Asia, as well as in the Western world. Karaoke allows would-be singers to perform in front of an audience: they select the background music to a song and then sing the words into a microphone. Karaoke translates as "empty orchestra," and there are karaoke bars in virtually every nook and cranny in Japan.

KARAOKE THEATRE, 4-10-3 Roppongi. Tel. 3402-7772.

The Kento's Group does it again. The same company that brought you the 1950s dancing club Kento's and the Cavern Club has now opened a fancy karaoke bar in the heart of Roppongi. It offers the latest in karaoke gadgetry, including video equipment that projects singers onto a screen. There are about 40 English-language songs available, from the ever-popular "Michelle" to "Blue Suede Shoes." If you come here, be prepared to sing—and it doesn't matter how out of tune you are. Beers are ¥650 ($4.65); cocktails ¥750 ($5.35). Open: Mon–Sat 7pm–3am. Station: Roppongi, about a 1-minute walk, on street behind Victoria Station restaurant.

Admission: ¥1,000 ($7.15).

6. MOVIES

Going to the movies is an expensive pastime in Tokyo, with admission averaging about ¥1,700 ($11.40) for adults, ¥1,400 ($10) for university students, ¥1,300 ($9.30) for junior and senior high school pupils, and ¥1,000 ($7.15) for children and senior citizens (past 60). As perhaps an admission that prices are high, some theaters accept credit cards. If you want to see one of Hollywood's latest releases (which usually take a few months to reach Japan), you may also have to contend with long lines and huge crowds. To see what's on where, check the *Tokyo Journal* or *Tokyo Time Out,* both published monthly and sold in bookstores for ¥500 ($3.55). Both publications list more than 100 cinemas in their movie section. Movies are also listed in the *Weekender* and the *Tour Companion's Tokyo City Guide,* tabloids distributed free to hotels, stores, and places where foreigners frequent. Note that theaters in Tokyo close early, with the last showing usually around 7pm. Movies are shown in the original language, with Japanese subtitles.

One of my favorite theaters is **Ciné Vivant,** located in the basement of the Wave Building, 6-2-27 Roppongi (tel. 3403-6061; closest station: Roppongi). It specializes in European films, mostly new works, with about four or five showings daily, starting at 12:40pm and with the same admission prices given above.

Another good place to see movies—albeit mostly of the B-grade variety but sometimes classics—is at **Oh God,** 6-7-18 Jingumae (tel. 3406-3206; closest station: Meiji-Jingumae or Harajuku), in Harajuku. A bar, it charges no admission price, though beer prices start at a high ¥650 ($4.65). Movies, which generally start at 9pm on weekdays and 6pm on weekends, are shown throughout the evening, with the last movie beginning at 3am. I've seen everything from sci-fi horror flicks to James Bond and Fassbinder here. Call to see what's playing.

If you're a fan of Japanese movies, no doubt you'll be disappointed to discover that the big box-office favorites are usually imported from Hollywood. If you're interested in seeing Japanese classics, your best bets are movies shown Saturday and Sunday at the **National Museum of Modern Art,** located in Kitanomaru Koen Park (closest station: Takebashi). Movies include both Japanese and foreign films (some with English subtitles), and programs change often; call the **National Film Center** (a branch of the museum) to see what's playing (tel. 3561-0823) and to check the times. Admission to the movies is ¥400 ($2.85).

7. CASINOS

No doubt you'll notice so-called pachinko parlors as you walk around Tokyo. Usually brightly lit and garish, they're packed with upright pinball-like machines, with row upon row of Japanese businessmen, housewives, and students sitting intently and quietly in front of them. Becoming popular after World War II, pachinko is a game in which ball bearings are flung into the machine, one after the other. Humans control the strength with which the ball is released, but otherwise there's very little to do. Points are amassed according to which holes the ball bearings fall into. Just ¥100 (71¢) gives you 20 ball bearings, which don't last for long. If you're good at it, you win ball bearings back, which you can subsequently trade in for food, cigarettes, watches, calculators, and the like. It's illegal to win money in Japan, but outside many pachinko parlors and along back alleyways, there are tiny windows where you can trade in the watches, calculators, etc., that you won for cash. Police just look the other way. At any rate, there are probably more pachinko parlors in Tokyo than there are streetlights, so you won't have any problem finding one.

CHAPTER 10
EASY EXCURSIONS FROM TOKYO

1. KAMAKURA
2. NIKKO
3. MASHIKO
4. YOKOHAMA
5. KAWASAKI
6. MOUNT FUJI
7. HAKONE
8. THE IZU PENINSULA

If your stay in Tokyo is long enough, you should consider taking excursions to some of the sights in the vicinity. Kamakura and Nikko, for example, rank as two of the most important historical sites in Japan, while the Fuji-Hakone-Izu National Park serves as a huge recreational playground for the residents of Tokyo. Mashiko, a pottery village, can be visited on its own, or it can be seen in combination with Nikko. Kawasaki and Yokohama have a few worthwhile museums and attractions that warrant visits.

Before departing Tokyo, stop by the Tourist Information Center (TIC) for a color brochure called *Side Trips from Tokyo*, which carries information on Kamakura, Nikko, Hakone, and the Mt. Fuji area. The TIC also has a map of Tokyo's vicinity, as well as pamphlets on individual destinations. *Hakone and Kamakura*, for example, includes a map of Kamakura and how to get to some of the village's most important sights by bus.

1. KAMAKURA

30 miles S of Tokyo

GETTING THERE   By Train   To reach Kamakura, take the Yokosuka Line, which departs every 10 to 20 minutes from the Yokohama, Shinagawa, Shimbashi, and Tokyo JR stations. The trip takes 1 hour from Tokyo Station and costs ¥880 ($6.30) one way, 49 minutes from Shinagawa at a cost of ¥680 ($4.85). If you have a full day for sightseeing, I suggest getting off the train at Kita-Kamakura Station, which is just before Kamakura Station. If you have only a few hours, head straight for Kamakura Station and begin your sightseeing there.

ESSENTIAL INFORMATION   The telephone **area code** for Kamakura is 0467.
Before departing from Tokyo, be sure to pick up a pamphlet entitled *Hakone and Kamakura* from the Tourist Information Center. In Kamakura, there's a **tourist information window** (tel. 0467/22-3350) located immediately to the right as you go out from Kamakura Station's east exit in the direction of Tsurugaoka Hachimangu Shrine. Open daily from 9am to 5pm, it sells a color brochure with a map of Kamakura for ¥200 ($1.40), but also has a free map (in both English and Japanese) that it seems reluctant to give out unless you insist. Ask here for directions on how to get to the village's most important sights by bus.

GETTING AROUND   Transportation in Kamakura is by **bus,** as well as a wonderful two-car **train** that will take you from Kamakura Station to Hase Station, where you can see the bronze statue of the Great Buddha and Hase Temple. Kamakura's other major attraction, Tsurugaoka Hachimangu Shrine, is an easy walk from Kamakura Station.

If you take only one day-trip outside Tokyo, it should be to Kamakura, especially if you're unable to include the ancient capitals of Kyoto and Nara in your travels. Kamakura is a delightful hamlet with no fewer than 65 Buddhist temples and 19 Shinto shrines spread throughout the village and the surrounding wooded hills. Most of these were built centuries ago, when a warrior named Yoritomo Minamoto seized political power and established his shogunate government in Kamakura back in 1192. Wanting to set up his seat of government as far away as possible from what he considered to be the corrupt imperial court in Kyoto, Yoritomo selected Kamakura because it was easy to defend. The village is enclosed on three sides by wooded hills and on the fourth by the sea, a setting that lends dramatic background to its many temples and shrines.

Although Kamakura remained the military and political center of the nation for a century and a half, the Minamoto clan was in power for only a short time. After Yoritomo's death, both of his sons were assassinated, one after the other, after taking up military rule. Power then passed to the family of Yoritomo's widow, the Hojo family, who ruled until 1333, when the emperor in Kyoto sent troops to crush the shogunate government. Unable to stop the invaders, 800 soldiers retired to the Hojo family temple at Toshoji, where they all disemboweled themselves in ritualistic suicide known as seppuku.

Today a thriving seaside resort with a population of 175,000, Kamakura, with its old wooden homes, temples, shrines, and wooded hills, makes a pleasant 1-day excursion from Tokyo.

There's a beach in Kamakura called Yuigahama Beach, but I personally find it unappealing. It consists of muddy-looking sand, often strewn with litter, and yet it can be unbelievably crowded in summer. (One friend of mine told me he came to Yuigahama Beach on a hot weekend day and couldn't find enough space on which to spread his towel. Perhaps he was exaggerating, but you get the general idea.) Most amusing are the surfers. The waves are usually nothing more than ripples, but that doesn't stop the surfing fanatics, who promptly fall off if a big wave does roll along unexpectedly.

WHAT TO SEE & DO

Because Kamakura has so many temples and shrines, it's obvious that visitors must limit their sightseeing to those that offer the most in terms of historical and architectural importance. The most worthwhile places of interest in Kamakura are generally considered to be Tsurugaoka Hachimangu Shrine, the Great Buddha, and Hase Temple, while visitors with more time on their hands should take in a few other temples as well. Keep in mind that most temples and shrines open about 8 or 9am and close between 4 and 5pm.

AROUND KITA-KAMAKURA STATION

If you leave the train at Kita-Kamakura Station, within a minute's walk you can reach **Engakuji Temple** (tel. 22-0478). Founded in 1282, this Zen temple was once one of the most important and imposing temples in Kamakura, and although its grandeur has been reduced through the centuries by fires and earthquakes, it's still considered by many to be the best remaining example of architecture from the Kamakura Period. A sacred tooth of Buddha is enshrined on the precinct grounds in a wooden structure called Shari-den. This temple sponsors a 5-day Zen training course at the end of July, as well as intensive zazen meditation courses several times a year.

A 5-minute walk from Kita-Kamakura Station is **Tokeiji Temple** (tel. 22-1663), a Zen temple founded in 1285. Visited now for its flower blossoms of plum

EASY EXCURSIONS FROM TOKYO

Atami 8
Hakone 5
Izu Peninsula 7
Kamakura 4
Kawasaki 2
Mashiko 1A
Mount Fuji 6
Nikko 1A
Shimoda 9
Yokohama 3

(mid-February), magnolia and peach (late March/April), peony (late April/May), and iris (May/June), in feudal times it served as a place of refuge for women fleeing cruel husbands and disagreeable mothers-in-law (it was known as the Divorce Temple). Back in those days, only men could divorce their wives. Women had no legal recourse, but if they could make it to Tokeiji, they were given protection from their husbands and allowed to live among the nuns. Hours are 8:30am to 5pm in summer, shorter in winter.

If you feel like walking, you can hike onward to Tsurugaoka Hachimangu Shrine (see below) in about 30 minutes, stopping in at **Kenchoji Temple** (tel. 22-0981) on the way. Along with Engakuji, Kenchoji is considered among the five best Zen temples in Kamakura. Note the magnificent cedars surrounding it, as well as the ceremonial gate held together with wooden wedges. If you don't feel like walking all the way to Tsurugaoka Hachimangu Shrine, return to Kita-Kamakura Station and go one more stop to Kamakura Station.

AROUND KAMAKURA STATION

✪ About a 10-minute walk from Kamakura Station, **Tsurugaoka Hachimangu Shrine** (tel. 22-0315) is the spiritual heart of Kamakura. It was built by Yoritomo and dedicated to Hachiman, the Shinto god of war who served as the clan deity of the Minamoto family. The pathway to the shrine is along Wakamiya Oji, a cherry-tree-lined pedestrian lane that was also constructed by Yoritomo back in the 1190s, so that his oldest son's first visit to the family shrine could be accomplished in style with an elaborate procession. Along the pathway are souvenir and antique shops selling lacquerware and folk art, and three massive torii gates set at intervals along the route to signal the approach to the shrine.

As you ascend the steps to the vermilion-painted Tsurugaoka Hachimangu Shrine, note the gingko tree to the left. This is supposedly the site where Yoritomo's second son was ambushed and murdered back in 1219. The gingko tree itself is thought to be about 1,000 years old. The shrine grounds are free to the public and are always open (there's a small shrine museum, but with only a handful of displays and only in Japanese, it's not worth visiting).

On the shrine grounds are also the **Kanagawa Prefectural Modern Art Museum (Kanagawa-ken Ritsu-Kindai Bijutsukan)** (tel. 22-5000), which exhibits contemporary art Tuesday through Sunday from 10am to 5pm, and the **Kamakura Municipal Museum (Kamakura Kohokukan)** (tel. 22-0753), which displays a collection of scrolls, urns, carvings, bronzes, swords, calligraphy, lacquerware, and other historical objects from neighboring shrines and temples. This museum is open Tuesday through Sunday from 9am to 4pm; admission is ¥150 ($1.05).

Although it's a little bit far out of the way, it might pay to make a visit to **Zeniarai-Benten Shrine,** about a 20-minute walk west of Kamakura Station and open daily from 8am to 5pm. This shrine is dedicated to the goddess of good fortune, and on Asian zodiac days of the snake, worshippers believe that if you take your money and wash it in spring water in a small cave on the shrine grounds, your money will double or triple itself later on. Of course, this being modern Japan, don't be surprised if you see a bit of ingenuity. My Japanese landlady told me that when she visited the shrine she didn't have much cash on her, so she washed something she thought would be equally as good—her plastic credit card. As a shrine dedicated to the goddess of fortune, it's befitting that admission here is free.

AROUND HASE STATION

To get to the attractions around Hase Station, you can go by bus, which departs from in front of Kamakura Station, or you can go by the Enoden train line, on a two-car train that putt-putts its way seemingly through backyards on its way from Kamakura Station to Hase and beyond (to Enoshima and Fujisawa). Since there's only one track,

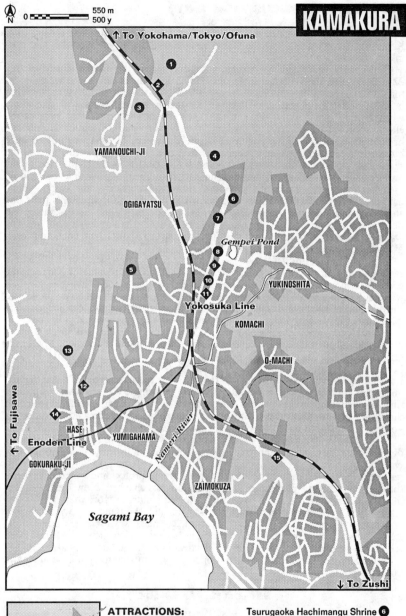

↑ To Yokohama/Tokyo/Ofuna

KAMAKURA

0 ▭▭▭ 550 m
    ▭▭▭ 500 y
N

YAMANOUCHI-JI

OGIGAYATSU

Gempei Pond

YUKINOSHITA

Yokosuka Line

KOMACHI

O-MACHI

↑ To Fujisawa

HASE

Enoden Line

YUMIGAHAMA

GOKURAKU-JI

Nameri River

ZAIMOKUZA

Sagami Bay

↓ To Zushi

JAPAN

★ TOKYO
Kamakura

ATTRACTIONS:
Engakuji ❶
Great Buddha (Daibutsu) ⑬
Hase Kannon Temple ⑭
Kamakura Municipal Museum ❼
Kanagawa Prefectual Modern
   Art Museum ❽
Kenchoji ❹
Tokeiji ❸

Tsurugaoka Hachimangu Shrine ❻
Zeniarai-Benten Shrine ❺

DINING:
Kayagi-ya ❾
Miyokawa ⑫
Monzen ❷
Nakamura-an ⑪
Raitei ⑯

trains have to take turns going in either direction. I would suggest taking the bus from Kamakura Station directly to the Great Buddha, walking to Hase Shrine, and then taking the Enoden train back to Kamakura Station.

✪ Probably Kamakura's most famous attraction is the **Great Buddha** (tel. 22-0703), called the Daibutsu in Japanese. Thirty-seven feet high and weighing 93 tons, it is the second-largest bronze image in Japan. The largest Buddha is in Nara, but in my opinion the Kamakura Daibutsu is much more impressive. For one thing, whereas the Nara Buddha sits enclosed in a wooden structure that reduces the effectiveness of its size, the Kamakura Buddha sits outside against a dramatic backdrop of wooded hills. Cast in 1252, the Kamakura Buddha was indeed once housed in a temple, but a huge tidal wave destroyed the wooden structure and the statue has sat under sun, snow, and stars ever since. I also prefer the face of the Kamakura Buddha. I find it more inspiring and divine, as though with its half-closed eyes and calm, serene face it's somehow above the worries of the world—wars, natural disasters, other calamities, and sorrow. It's as though it represents the plane above human suffering, the point at which birth and death, joy and sadness, merge and become one and the same. If you want, you can go inside the statue—it's hollow. The Daibutsu is open daily from 7am to 5:45pm, closing at 5:15pm in winter. Admission is ¥150 ($1.05), and your entry ticket is also a bookmark, a nice souvenir.

Nearby, **Hase Temple (Hasedera)** (tel. 22-6300), constructed on a hill with a sweeping view of the sea, is the home of an 11-headed gilt statue of Kannon, the goddess of mercy. More than 30 feet high and the tallest wooden image in Japan, it was made from a single piece of camphorwood back in the 8th century. The legend surrounding this Kannon is quite remarkable. Supposedly two wooden images were made from the wood of a huge camphor tree. One of the images was kept in Hase, not far from Nara, while the second image, if you can imagine, was given a short ceremony and then duly tossed into the sea to find a home of its own. The image drifted 300 miles eastward and washed up on shore, but was thrown back in again because all who touched it became ill or incurred bad luck. Finally, the image reached Kamakura, where it gave the people no trouble. This was interpreted as a sign that the image was content with its surroundings, and Hase Temple was erected at its present site. Another statue housed here is one of Amida, a Buddha who promised rebirth in the Pure Land to West to all who chanted his name. It was created by orders of Yoritomo Minamoto upon his 42nd birthday, considered an unlucky year for men.

As you climb up the steps to Hase Temple and its Kannon, you'll encounter statues of a different sort. All around you will be likenesses of Jizo, the guardian deity of children. Although parents originally came to Hase Temple to set up statues to represent their children in hopes that the deity would protect and watch over them, through the years the purpose of the Jizo statues has changed. Now they represent miscarried, stillborn, or, most frequently, aborted children. More than 50,000 Jizo statues have been offered here since the war, but the thousand or so you see now remain only a year before being burned or buried to make way for others. Some of the statues, which can be purchased on the temple grounds for as much as $400, are fitted with hand-knitted caps and sweaters. The effect is quite chilling.

Admission to Hase Temple, which is open daily from 7am to 5pm in summer and until 4:40pm in winter, is ¥200 ($1.40).

WHERE TO DINE
MODERATE

MIYOKAWA ㊺, 1-16-17 Hase. Tel. 25-5556.
   Cuisine: MINI-KAISEKI/OBENTO. **Station:** Hase, about a 5-minute walk away.
$ **Prices:** Mini-kaiseki ¥6,000–¥7,500 ($42.85–$53.55); obento ¥2,500–¥4,000 ($17.85–$28.55); Japanese steak set course ¥3,800 ($27.15). No credit cards.
   Open: Daily 11am–9pm.
This modern restaurant, located on the main road that leads from Hase Station to the Great Buddha and about a 5-minute walk from each, specializes in kaiseki, including beautifully prepared mini-kaiseki set courses that change with the seasons. It also

offers an obento lunch box, the least expensive of which is served in a container shaped like a gourd, as well as a set meal featuring steak prepared Japanese style.

MONZEN ㊻, **Yamanouchi 407. Tel. 25-1121.**
   Cuisine: KAISEKI/OBENTO/VEGETARIAN. **Station:** Kita-Kamakura, a 1-minute walk away.
   $ Prices: Obento teishoku ¥3,300 ($23.55); vegetarian set courses from ¥4,400 ($31.40); kaiseki from ¥5,500 ($39.30). AE, DC, JCB, MC, V.
   Open: Daily 11am–7:30pm.
This modern-looking kaiseki restaurant is located just across the tracks from Engakuji Temple in Kita-Kamakura. The main dining hall is on the second floor, and seating is on tatami mats at low tables. Although there's no English menu, there are pictures of various meals available, including kaiseki, obento teishoku, and *shojin-ryoori*, vegetarian set courses commonly served at Buddhist temples.

INEXPENSIVE

In addition to the suggestions here, there's a pavilion at Hase Temple, described above, that serves oden, noodles, beer and soft drinks, with indoor and outdoor seating. There's a great view from here, making it a good place for a snack on a fine day.

KAYAGI-YA ㊼, **2-11-16 Komachi. Tel. 22-1460.**
   Cuisine: EEL. **Station:** Kamakura, about a 5-minute walk away.
   $ Prices: Dishes ¥1,400–¥2,200 ($10–$15.70); teishoku ¥2,500 ($17.85). No credit cards.
   Open: Sat–Thurs noon–6:30pm.
Closer to Kamakura Station, this modest, older-looking restaurant serves several different kinds of inexpensive eel dishes, my favorite of which is the unagi donburi (eel served on top of rice). The place is located on Wakamiya Oji (on the left side if you're walking from the station to Tsurugaoka Hachimangu Shrine), next to a lumber yard.

NAKAMURA-AN ㊽, **1-7-6 Komachi. Tel. 25-3500.**
   Cuisine: NOODLES. **Station:** Kamakura, about a 3-minute walk away.
   $ Prices: Noodles ¥600–¥1,700 ($4.30–$12.15). No credit cards.
   Open: Fri–Wed noon–6pm.
This noodle restaurant, between Kamakura Station and Hachimangu Shrine, is located on a side street off Wakamiya Oji Avenue. It's easy to spot because of the front window, where you can watch noodles being made. There's also a front-window display of plastic food, so it's easy to make your selection. I can never resist ordering the tempura soba.

RAITEI ㊾, **Takasago. Tel. 32-5656.**
   Cuisine: NOODLES/OBENTO. **Bus:** Takasago stop.
   $ Prices: Noodles ¥750–¥1,500 ($5.35–$10.70); obento lunch boxes ¥3,300–¥4,400 ($23.55–$31.40). AE, DC, MC.
   Open: Daily 11am–sundown (about 6:30pm in summer).
⭐ This is the absolute winner for a meal in Kamakura, and visiting Raitei is as much fun as visiting the city's temples and shrines. It's situated on the edge of Kamakura, surrounded by verdant countryside, and the wonder is that it serves inexpensive soba (Japanese noodles), as well as priestly feasts of kaiseki (which you must reserve in advance, with prices beginning at ¥5,500 or $39.30). To reach Raitei, take a bus from platform 3 in front of Kamakura Station (make sure the bus is going to the Takasago bus stop, since not all buses from this platform go there). Upon entering the front gate, you must pay an entry fee of ¥500 ($3.55), which counts toward the price of your meal at the restaurant. If you're here for soba or one of the obento lunch boxes, go down the stone steps to the back entry of the restaurant, where you'll be given an English menu with such offerings as noodles with chicken, mountain vegetables, tempura, and more. The pottery used comes from the restaurant's own specially made kiln. When you've finished your meal, be sure to walk the path circling

through the garden past a bamboo grove, stone images, and a miniature shrine. The stroll takes about 20 minutes, unless you stop for a beer at the refreshment house, with its outdoor seating and view of the countryside.

2. NIKKO

90 miles N of Tokyo

GETTING THERE   By Train   The easiest, fastest, and most luxurious way to get to Nikko is on the Tobu Line's limited express, which departs from Akasaka Station and costs ¥2,280 ($16.30) one way for the 2-hour trip. Also departing from Akasaka Station are the so-called rapid trains on the Tobu Line, which cost half as much and reach Nikko in about 2 hours and 15 minutes. Trains depart every hour or less, but note that some trains are not direct, requiring a change at Shimo-Imaichi Station. If you have a Japan Rail Pass, you'll probably want to take one of the JR trains departing from Ueno, in which case you'll have to change trains in Utsunomiya. The Tobu and JR stations in Nikko are located almost side by side in the village's downtown area.

ESSENTIAL INFORMATION   The telephone **area code** for Nikko is 0288.
Before leaving Tokyo, pick up a leaflet called *Nikko* from the Tourist Information Center (TIC). It gives the train schedule for both the Tobu Line, which departs from Asakusa Station, and JR trains that depart from Ueno Station. The TIC also has some color brochures with maps of the Nikko area.
When I last checked, no one at the **Nikko Tobu Station tourist information counter** spoke English, but they do have an English map and can point you in the right direction. You can also make hotel and ryokan reservations here and buy bus tickets onward to Lake Chuzenji.
More useful for foreigners is the **Nikko Information Center** (tel. 0288/54-2496), located on the main road leading to Toshogu Shrine. You're more likely to find someone who speaks English here and can pick up more information about Nikko. It's open daily from 9am to 5pm.

GETTING AROUND   You can **walk** from the Nikko train stations to Toshogu Shrine in less than half an hour. From Tobu Station simply walk straight out the main exit, pass the bus stands, and then turn right. There are signs pointing the way in English. Keep walking on this main road (you'll pass the Nikko Information Center about halfway down, on the left side) until you come to a T intersection with a vermilion-colored bridge spanning a river (about a 15-minute walk from the train stations). The stone steps opposite lead up the hill into the woods and to the mausoleum. You can also get to the T intersection by **bus,** getting off at the Shinkyo bus stop.
If you're heading to Chuzenji, buses depart from in front of Tobu Station, with a stop at the Shinkyo bus stop near the mausoleum. You can therefore visit the historical sights in Nikko before boarding the bus and continuing onto Chuzenji.

Since the publication of James Clavell's novel *Shogun,* many people have become familiar with Tokugawa Ieyasu, the real-life powerful shogun of the 1600s on whom Clavell's fictional shogun was based. Quashing all rebellions and unifying Japan under his leadership, Tokugawa built such a military stronghold that his heirs continued to rule Japan for the next 250 years without serious challenge.
If you'd like to join the millions of Japanese who through the centuries have paid homage to this great man, travel 90 miles north of Tokyo to Nikko, where a mausoleum was constructed in his honor in the 17th century and where his remains were laid to rest. *Nikko* means "sunlight," an apt description of the way the sun's rays play upon this sumptuous mausoleum of wood and gold leaf. Surrounding it are thousands of cedar trees in a 200,000-acre national park, home also to a temple, a

NIKKO

Inarigawa River

Daiyagawa River

Shinkyo

Honden

Hongu

Shionryu-ji (former temple)

Shoyo-en Garden

Tomb of Ieyasu

Toshogu Shrine

Butokuden

Sanbutsudo Hall

Rinnoji Temple

Sacred Stable

Five-Story Pagoda

Stone Torii

Abbot's Lodging

Futarasan Shrine

Bronze Torii

Treasury

Hokkedo

Jogyodo

Daiyuin Mausoleum

TOSHOGU SHRINE DETAIL

Tomb of Ieyasu

Offices

Yakushido

Five-Story Pagoda

Treasury

Butokuden

KEY TO SHRINE DIAGRAM:

1 Staircase of the Thousand
2 Stone Torii
3 Sacred Stable
4 Storerooms
5 Fountain
6 Library
7 Bell Tower
8 Drum Tower
9 Yomeimon
10 Haiden
11 Honden
12 Haiden
13 Inukimon

shrine, and another mausoleum. A trip to Nikko can be combined with a visit to Lake Chuzenji, a jewel of a lake about an hour's bus ride from the mausoleum.

WHAT TO SEE & DO

Tokugawa Ieyasu's mausoleum is on the edge of town, which you can reach by foot in about half an hour or by bus from either the Tobu or JR Station in about 10 minutes. The first indication that you're nearing Tokugawa's mausoleum, which is called Toshogu Shrine, is the vermilion-painted **Sacred Bridge (Shinkyo),** arching over the rushing Daiyagawa River. It was built in 1636, and for more than three centuries only shoguns and their emissaries were allowed to cross it. Even today, mortal souls like us are prevented from completely crossing it because of a barrier at one end.

Across the road from the bridge are some steps leading into a forest of cedar, where after a 5-minute walk you'll see a statue of a priest named Shodo, who founded Nikko 1,200 years ago, and the first major temple, **Rinnoji Temple.** You can buy a combination ticket here for ¥750 ($5.35), which allows entry to Rinnoji Temple, Toshogu Shrine, neighboring Futarasan Shrine, and another Tokugawa mausoleum. Once at Toshogu Shrine, you'll have to pay an extra ¥430 ($3.05) to see Ieyasu's tomb. A combination ticket is also sold at the entry to Toshogu Shrine, but at a price of ¥1,030 ($7.35), which also includes admission to the inner recesses of the mausoleum.

At Rinnoji, visit the **Sanbutsudo Hall,** which contains three wooden images of Buddha plated with gold leaves. One of the best things to see at Rinnoji Temple, however, is its **Shoyo-en Garden,** which requires a separate ¥250 ($1.80) admission and is located opposite the Sanbutsudo Hall. Completed in 1815 and typical of Japanese landscaped gardens of the Edo Period, this strolling garden provides a different vista with each turn of the path, making it seem much larger than it actually is. The garden's English pamphlet says that Ulysses S. Grant visited here in 1879, 2 years after leaving the U.S. presidency. ✪ The most important and famous structure in Nikko, of course, is **Toshogu Shrine,** which contains the tomb of Tokugawa Ieyasu. Although Tokugawa died in 1616, construction of the mausoleum did not begin until 1634, when his grandson, Tokugawa Iemitsu, undertook the project as an act of devotion. It seems that no expense was too great in creating the monument. Some 15,000 artists and craftspeople were brought to Nikko from all over Japan, and after 2 years' work they had succeeded in erecting a group of buildings more elaborate and gorgeous than any other Japanese temple or shrine. Rich in colors and carvings, Toshogu Shrine is gilded with 2.4 million sheets of gold leaf (that would cover an area of almost six acres). The mausoleum was completed in 1636, almost 20 years after Ieyasu's death.

Toshogu Shrine is set in a grove of magnificent ancient Japanese cedars planted over a 20-year period during the 1600s by a feudal lord named Matsudaira Masatsuna. Thirteen thousand of the original trees are still standing, adding a sense of dignity to the mausoleum and the shrine and appearing timeless.

You enter Toshogu Shrine via a flight of stairs that pass under a huge stone torii gateway, one of the largest in Japan. On your left is a five-story, 115-foot-high pagoda. Although normally pagodas are found only at temples, this pagoda is just one example of how both Buddhism and Shintoism are combined at Toshogu Shrine. After climbing a second flight of stairs, turn left, where you'll presently see the Sacred Stable, which houses the likeness of a sacred white horse. Look for the three monkeys carved above the stable door, fixed in the pose of "see no evil, hear no evil, speak no evil."

At the next flight of stairs is **Yomeimon Gate,** considered to be the central

---

IMPRESSIONS

The Japanese proverb says Nikko wo minai uchi wa kekko to iu na:
Until you have seen Nikko, do not say kekko, *i.e., grand or splendid.*
—DOUGLAS SLADEN, *QUEER THINGS ABOUT JAPAN,* 1903

showpiece of Nikko and popularly known as the Twilight Gate, implying that it could take you all day (until twilight) to see everything carved onto it. Painted in red, blue, and green, and decorated with gilding and lacquerwork, this gate has about 400 carvings of flowers, dragons, birds, and other animals. It's almost too much to take in at once.

To the left of the gate is the hall where the portable shrines are kept, as well as **Honchido Hall,** famous for its dragon painting on the ceiling. If you clap your hands under the painting, the echo supposedly resembles a dragon's roar. You can visit the shrine's main hall, where guides will explain (in Japanese) its history and main features. To the right of the main hall is a gate with a carving of a sleeping cat above it. Beyond that are 200 stone steps leading past cedars to Tokugawa's tomb, admission to which costs an additional ¥430 ($3.05) if it's not already included in your combination ticket. After the riotous colors of the shrine, the tomb itself seems surprisingly simple.

Toshogu Shrine is open daily from 8am to 5pm (you must enter by 4:30pm), closing earlier in winter (November through March) at 4pm (enter by 3:30pm).

Directly to the west of Toshogu Shrine is **Futarasan Shrine,** the oldest building in the district (from 1617), which has a pleasant garden and is dedicated to the gods of the mountains surrounding Nikko. On the shrine's grounds is the so-called ghost lantern, enclosed in a small wooden structure. According to legend, it used to come alive at night and sweep around Nikko in the form of a ghost. It apparently scared one of the guards so much that he struck it with his sword, the marks of which are still visible on the lamp's rim.

Past Futarasan Shrine is the second mausoleum, **Daiyuin Mausoleum.** It's the final resting place of Iemitsu, grandson of Ieyasu and the third Tokugawa shogun. Completed in 1653, it's not nearly so ornate as Toshogu Shrine nor as crowded, making it a pleasant last stop on your tour of Nikko.

After touring Nikko's shrines, you can catch a bus not far from the vermilion-painted bridge for **Lake Chuzenji** (you can also board it in front of Tobu Station). The ride costs ¥980 ($7) and takes about 50 minutes, winding higher and higher along hairpin roads. The view is breathtaking—I've even seen bands of monkeys along the side of the road. On the shores of Lake Chuzenji are many ryokan, souvenir stores, and coffee shops, making it a popular holiday resort. Things to do include visiting Tachiki Kannon Temple, beside the lake; going on an hourlong boat cruise; and visiting nearby Kegon Falls, a 300-foot waterfall.

WHERE TO STAY

Most ryokan are strung along the shores of Lake Chuzenji at a resort called Chuzenji Onsen. Keep in mind, however, that the majority of them are closed during the winter months and are open only from about mid-April to mid-November. If you want to stay in one of these ryokan, it's best to reserve a room in advance, which you can do at a travel agency. You can also make a reservation upon arrival at Nikko at the accommodation-reservation window inside Nikko Tobu Station; they'll charge a ¥200 to ¥500 ($1.40 to $3.55) fee but will take care of all arrangements for you. Ryokan owners in this area do not speak English and aren't likely to take you in if you simply show up at their door (I've done it this way, but I had to try several places before I finally found a sympathetic manager). If it's peak season, you should definitely reserve a room before leaving Tokyo at a travel agency such as the Japan Travel Bureau. Most ryokan start at ¥10,000 ($71.40) per person, including two meals; rates rise to as much as ¥18,000 ($128.55) per person during peak season. There's little difference in what they offer: basically a tatami room, coin-operated TV, hot tea, breakfast and dinner served in your room, and a cotton kimono. Be sure to specify if you want a lakeside view.

EXPENSIVE

NIKKO KANAYA HOTEL, 1300 Kami-Hatsuishi, Nikko City, Tochigi Prefecture 321-14. Tel. 0288/54-0001. Fax 0288/54-0001. 81 rms (5 with toilet only, 9 with toilet and shower, rest with bathroom). TV TEL **Directions:** About a 15-minute walk or 5-minute bus ride from Nikko stations (get off at the Shinkyo stop).

$ Rates: ¥8,800 ($63) single with toilet only, ¥11,000 ($78.50) single with shower and toilet, ¥14,300–¥25,000 ($102–$178) single with bath; ¥11,000 ($78.50) twin with toilet only, ¥13,200 ($94.30) twin with toilet and shower, ¥14,300–¥30,000 ($102–$214) twin with bathroom. ¥3,000 ($21.40) extra on Sat and evening before national holidays; ¥5,000–¥10,000 ($35.70–$71.40) extra during peak season. AE, DC, JCB, MC, V.

A distinguished-looking old-fashioned place secluded on a hill above the red Sacred Bridge, this is the most famous hotel in Nikko, combining the rustic heartiness of a European country lodge with elements of old Japan. First established in 1873, it has played host to a number of VIPs—Charles Lindbergh, Indira Gandhi, Helen Keller, Eleanor Roosevelt, David Rockefeller, Shirley MacLaine, and Albert Einstein, to name a few.

All rooms are Western-style twins and doubles, the differences in their prices based on room size, view, and facilities. Rooms are rather old-fashioned but cozy, and do not have air-conditioning, since the high altitude of Nikko rarely warrants it.

Dining/Entertainment: The hotel has a small Japanese restaurant (open only in the evening), serving shabu-shabu; a wonderful dining hall, serving Western food; and a coffee shop.

Facilities: Souvenir shops, public bath, small outdoor heated swimming pool, outdoor skating rink, Japanese garden.

NIKKO LAKESIDE HOTEL, 2482 Chugushi, Nikko City, Tochigi Prefecture 321-16. Tel. 0288/55-0321. Fax 0288/55-0771. 100 rms (all with bath). A/C TV TEL **Bus:** A 50-minute ride from Nikko to Lake Chuzenji.

$ Rates: Winter ¥19,800–¥24,000 ($141–$171) double/twin; peak seasons ¥33,000–¥39,000 ($236–$278). AE, DC, JCB, MC, V.

If you want to stay at Lake Chuzenji but prefer a Western-style hotel, this modern hotel is conveniently located on the rim of the lake not far from Kegon Falls. It's open throughout the year. Facilities include tennis courts, a pleasant restaurant with a view of the lake, and a bar.

INEXPENSIVE

PENSION TURTLE, 2-16 Takumi-cho, Nikko City, Tochigi Prefecture 321-14. Tel. 0288/53-3168. Fax 0288/53-3883. 11 rms (3 with bath). TV **Bus:** A 7-minute ride from Nikko stations to Sogo Kaikan-mae bus stop, then a 5-minute walk.

$ Rates: ¥4,200–¥4,800 ($30–$34) single without bath, ¥5,300 ($38) single with bath; ¥7,400–¥8,500 ($53–$61) double without bath, ¥9,600 ($69) double with bath; ¥10,500–¥12,200 ($87) triple without bath. AE, MC, V.

A member of the Japanese Inn Group, this pension is not as picturesque as St. Bois, described below, but it's closer to Toshogu Shrine and is run by the very friendly Fukuda family. Mr. Fukuda speaks English and is very helpful in planning a sightseeing itinerary for the area. In this new two-story house on a quiet side street beside the Daiyagawa River, rooms are bright and cheerful, in both Japanese and Western styles, though the three tatami rooms are without bath. Rooms have coin-operated TV. Japanese dinners for ¥1,500 ($10.70), Western dinners for ¥2,000 ($14.30), and Western breakfasts for ¥500 to ¥800 ($3.55 to $5.70) are available if you order them in advance. This place comes highly recommended from several readers of this book who have stayed here.

ST. BOIS, 1560 Tokorono, Nikko City, Tochigi Prefecture 3212-14. Tel. 0288/53-3399. Fax 0288/53-3399. 11 rms (4 with bath). TV **Directions:** A 15-minute walk from Nikko stations.

$ Rates: ¥4,900 ($35) single without bath, ¥5,500 ($39) single with bath; ¥9,400 ($67) double without bath, ¥10,500 ($75) double with bath; ¥13,500 ($96) triple without bath, ¥15,200 ($109) triple with bath. AE, MC, V.

⭐ Another member of the Japanese Inn Group, this country-style lodge is located atop a hill and nestled in among pine trees on the edge of Nikko. About a 15-minute walk north of Tobu Station and a 30-minute walk from Toshogu Shrine, it's very pleasant and peaceful here, making St. Bois an inexpensive getaway from Tokyo. Of the 11 rooms, 9 are Western style, with beds, and 2 are Japanese style. Five of the rooms that face the front have their own balcony. A Western-style breakfast is available for ¥700 ($5) if you let the manager know the night before, and dinner is available for ¥2,300 ($16.40) if you order it by 3pm.

Youth Hostels

NIKKO YOUTH HOSTEL, 2854 Tokorono, Nikko City, Tochigi Prefecture 321-14. Tel. 0288/54-1013. 50 beds. **Directions:** A 25-minute walk from Nikko stations.
$ Rates: ¥2,300 ($16.40) member and nonmember. Breakfast ¥450 ($3.20), dinner ¥720 ($5.15). No credit cards.

Located north across the river in quiet surroundings, this hostel accepts both Japan Youth Hostel Association (JYHA) members and nonmembers. Sleeping is in bunk beds, with four to eight persons to a room. There's a coin-operated laundry.

DAIYAGAWA YOUTH HOSTEL, 1075 Nakahatsuishi, Nikko City, Tochigi Prefecture 321-14. Tel. 0288/54-1974. 26 beds. **Directions:** A 20-minute walk from Nikko stations.
$ Rates: ¥2,100 ($15) JYHA card-carrying member. Breakfast ¥400 ($2.85), dinner ¥650 ($4.65). No credit cards.

Only JYHA members can stay at this hostel, located right beside the Daiyagawa River. Sleeping is on bunk beds, with four to eight persons to a room. The place is run by a woman who doesn't speak English. The front doors are locked at 9:30pm.

WHERE TO DINE

MODERATE

MAIN DINING HALL, Nikko Kanaya Hotel, 1300 Kami-Hatsuishi. Tel. 54-0001.
Cuisine: WESTERN. **Reservations:** Recommended during peak season.
Directions: A 15-minute walk from Nikko stations, beside Sacred Bridge.
$ Prices: Appetizers and soups ¥850–¥3,800 ($6.05–$27.15); main dishes ¥2,700–¥8,800 ($19.30–$62.85); set lunches ¥3,800 ($27.15). AE, DC, JCB, MC, V.
Open: Lunch daily noon–5pm; dinner daily 6–7:30pm.

⭐ Even if you don't spend the night here, you might want to come for a meal in the hotel's quaint dining hall, one of the best places in town for lunch. Since it's only a 10-minute walk from Toshogu Shrine, you can easily combine it with your sightseeing tour of Nikko. I suggest Nikko's specialty, locally caught rainbow trout, available in three different styles of cooking. I had mine cooked Kanaya style, covered with soy sauce, sugar, and sake, grilled and served whole. Other items on the menu include steak, veal cutlet Cordon Bleu, lobster, chicken, and beef Stroganoff. The best bargain is the set lunch, available to 3pm, which comes with soup, salad, and main dish.

MASUDAYA, 439 Ichiyamachi. Tel. 54-2151.
Cuisine: LOCAL JAPANESE SPECIALTIES. **Reservations:** Recommended for private rooms. **Directions:** A 5-minute walk from Nikko stations, on left side of main street leading to Toshogu Shrine.
$ Prices: Set courses ¥4,200 ($30) and ¥5,500 ($39.30). No credit cards.

Open: Fri–Wed 11am–4pm.

Only two fixed-price meals are served at this Japanese-style, traditional restaurant, both featuring a local specialty, *yuba*. Made from soybeans, yuba could be eaten only by priests and members of the imperial family until about 100 years ago. Now you can enjoy it, too, along with such side dishes of rice, sashimi, soup, fried fish, and vegetables. Dining is either in a common dining hall with chairs or, for the more expensive course, in private tatami rooms, for which you should make a reservation.

BUDGET

GYOZA HOUSE, 257 Matsubara-cho. Tel. 53-0494.
    Cuisine: GYOZA. **Directions:** A 2-minute walk from Tobu train station, on left side of main street leading to Toshogu Shrine.
    $ Prices: ¥350–¥800 ($2.50–$5.70). No credit cards.
    Open: Summer daily 11am–8pm, winter daily 11am–7pm.

Red banners and a red façade signal the existence of this simple restaurant, which offers gyoza (Chinese dumplings) and ramen (noodle and vegetable soup). Gyoza House has an English menu and pictures, listing such unique dishes as curry gyoza, shoyu gyoza (in a soup broth), and spicy ramen. It also offers an obento, for takeout only—which you could eat on the grounds of Toshogu Shrine.

3. MASHIKO

62 miles N of Tokyo

GETTING THERE   By Train   Take the train from either Asakusa or Ueno to Utsunomiya, transferring there to a bus. Or take the Tohoku Line from Ueno to Oyama, changing there for a local train to Mashiko. In either case, the trip from Tokyo to Mashiko takes 3 hours or more.

ESSENTIAL INFORMATION   The telephone **area code** for Mashiko is 02857.

Mashiko is a small village known throughout Japan for its *Mashiko-yaki*, distinctive, heavy, country-style pottery. A visit to Mashiko is usually combined with an overnight trip to Nikko, since both are located not far from the town of Utsunomiya, north of Tokyo. Since the major attraction in Mashiko is its pottery shops and kilns, and there's little in the way of restaurants and accommodations, I suggest coming here just for the day, returning to Tokyo or traveling on to Nikko before nightfall.

Mashiko gained fame back in 1930, when the late Hamada Shoji, designated a "national living treasure," built a kiln in this tiny village and introduced Mashiko ware throughout Japan. Other potters have since taken up his technique, producing ceramics for everyday use, including plates, cups, vases, and tableware. Altogether, there are about 50 pottery shops in Mashiko, along with a number of kilns, where you can simply wander in, watch the craftspeople at work, and even try your own hand at throwing or glazing a pot.

WHAT TO SEE & DO

The whole process of making pottery can be seen at **Tsukamoto Pottery** (tel. 2-3223), and visitors can try their hand at kneading clay, turning the potter's wheel, or hand-molding a pot. At the **Mashiko Reference Collection Museum (Mashiko Sankokan)** (tel. 2-5300), open from 9:30am to 4:30pm every day except Monday, New Year's, and the month of February, you can see works by Hamada, as well as a collection of Eastern and Western glass, ceramics, fabrics, furniture, and paintings. Charging an admission of ¥500 ($3.55), the museum is housed in several thatch-roofed structures, which served as Hamada's workshop. His kilns are still there, built along a sloping hill and once heated with wood.

The main reason people come to Mashiko is to shop. There are more than a dozen shops along the main road of Mashiko, offering a wide variety of pottery produced by the town's potters. Simply wander in and out—you're sure to find something that pleases you.

WHERE TO DINE

There are a number of inexpensive restaurants spread along Mashiko's main street, where the pottery shops are located. They all sell the same types of dishes, including tempura, curry rice, and noodles, with prices ranging from about ¥600 to ¥1,500 ($4.30 to $10.70). Since there's little difference between the restaurants, you should simply try the one closest at hand when hunger strikes.

4. YOKOHAMA

20 miles S of Tokyo

GETTING THERE   By Train   Yokohama is easily reached by train from Tokyo, Shimbashi, Shinagawa, and Yurakucho stations via the JR Keihin-Tohoku Line and Shibuya Station via the Tokyu-Tokyoko Line. It takes about 40 minutes to reach Yokohama Station from Tokyo Station and about 30 minutes from Shinagawa. If you want to go directly to Kannai Station in the old part of Yokohama, where most of its attractions are centered, the Keihin-Tohoku Line from Tokyo Station, with stops in Yurakucho, Shimbashi, Shinagawa, and Yokohama stations, reaches Kannai Station in about 45 minutes. Kannai Station is connected to Yokohama Station by subway, train, bus, and even boat.

In addition to the two train lines above, you can also take the Yokosuka Line that departs from Tokyo, Shinagawa, and Shimbashi stations. Note, however, that it stops only at Yokohama Station.

ESSENTIAL INFORMATION   The telephone **area code** for Yokohama is 045.

The **Yokohama Municipal Tourist Association** is located in the Silk Center, 1 Yamashita-cho, Naka-ku (tel. 045/641-5824), close to the harbor and an easy walk from Kannai Station. This tourist office is one of the best and most efficient I've come across in Japan, and its English map is excellent. The staff speaks English, can give you all kinds of brochures on the city, and can also arrange for you to visit with a Japanese family under Yokohama's **Home Visit System.** Be sure to call to set up the appointment at least a day in advance of your intended visit. The tourist office is open Monday through Friday from 8:45am to 5pm and on Saturday from 8:45am to 12:45pm.

Next door to the city tourist office is the **Kanagawa Prefectural Tourist Office,** where you can also obtain information on Hakone and Kamakura, since they're both in Kanagawa Prefecture. It's open Monday through Friday from 9am to 5pm and on Saturday from 9am to 2pm.

GETTING AROUND   Both the Japan Railways **Keihin-Tohoku Line** and the **Tokyu-Toyoko Line** pass through Yokohama Station and continue on to Sakuragicho and Kannai stations, convenient to most of Yokohama's attractions. Another way to get from Yokohama Station to Kannai is by **shuttle boat.** The boats depart from Sogo department store, across the street from Yokohama Station's east exit. Called the Sea Bass, they deposit passengers at Yamashita Park, described later in this chapter. Boats leave about three times an hour and afford a view of the city from the water. The fare is ¥450 ($3.20), considerably cheaper than the harbor cruises offered.

There are few attractions in Yokohama to warrant a visit by the short-term traveler to Japan. However, if you find yourself in Tokyo for an extended period, Yokohama is a pleasant and easy destination for an afternoon or 1-day excursion.

A rather new city in Japan's history books, Yokohama was nothing more than a tiny fishing village when Commodore Perry arrived in the mid-1800s and demanded that Japan open its doors to trade. Nevertheless, the village was selected by the shogun as one of several ports to be opened for international trade, and in 1859 the first foreign settlers arrived. To accommodate them, Yokohama was divided into two parts—Outside the Barrier (Kangai) and Inside the Barrier (Kannai). A canal was dug between the two and the foreigners were placed in Kannai, ostensibly to protect them from irate samurai, who were disgruntled with these foreign intruders and might try to assassinate them. It's probably not too far-fetched to assume, however, that this separation between foreigner and Japanese was also meant to isolate the strangers. After all, following more than two centuries of isolation from the rest of the world, the Japanese were bound to be at least a little cautious about foreigners and their habits. But as Japan entered the Meiji Period in full swing, relations relaxed and the foreigners moved to a nearby hill known as The Bluff.

Even so, throughout the 19th century the foreigners in Yokohama continued to be a source of great curiosity for the Japanese, who came from as far away as Tokyo to look at them and to see the Western goods that were being imported. Serving as the capital city's port, Yokohama grew by leaps and bounds, becoming so important that the first railroad in Japan linked Tokyo with Yokohama, reducing the 10-hour journey by foot to less than an hour.

Today, Yokohama is still an important international port and still supports a large international community, with many foreigners continuing to reside on The Bluff. Yokohama also has a large Chinese population, descendants of immigrants who moved here shortly after Japan opened itself to trade. With a population of almost three million, Yokohama is Japan's second-largest city.

WHAT TO SEE & DO

Because Yokohama is a relatively new city by Japanese standards, it doesn't have ancient temples or shrines, a castle, or a centuries-old landscape garden. In fact, most Japanese come to Yokohama for the same reason they've always come here—to soak up the cosmopolitan atmosphere created by the city's foreign population.

They visit The Bluff, the nearby Foreign Cemetery, where many of Yokohama's first international residents are buried; Yokohama port; and Chinatown, where there are a number of fine Chinese restaurants. For the foreigner visiting Yokohama, I would say that Kannai (with its Silk Museum), the Yokohama Museum of Art, Chinatown, and the superb Sankei-en Garden are the top attractions in the city.

AROUND YOKOHAMA STATION

The biggest attraction here is **Sogo,** 2-18-1 Takashima (tel. 465-2111), Japan's largest department store. It employs 4,300 sales clerks, who serve as many as 100,000 customers a day—a number that can swell to double that on a weekend. For bargains and promotions, head up to the 8th floor; for its many restaurants, branches of famous restaurants in Japan, go to the 10th floor. Sogo is open Wednesday through Monday from 10am to 7pm; its restaurants stay open until 10pm.

From Sogo you can take the Sea Bass shuttle boat, described above, to Kannai.

AROUND KANNAI STATION

Your first stop in Kannai should be the **Silk Center,** in which you'll find both the tourist office and the **Silk Museum,** 1 Yamashita-cho, Naka-ku (tel. 641-0841). For many years after Japan opened its doors, silk was its major export, and most of it was

---

IMPRESSIONS

Yokohama does not improve on further acquaintance. It has a dead-alive look. It has irregularity without picturesqueness, and the gray sky, gray sea, gray houses, and gray roofs look harmoniously dull.
—ISABELLA BIRD, *UNBEATEN TRACKS IN JAPAN,* 1880

shipped to the rest of the world from Yokohama, the nation's largest raw-silk market. In tribute to the role silk has played in Yokohama's history, this museum has displays showing the metamorphosis of the silkworm and how silk is obtained from cocoons; it also has exhibits of various kinds of silk fabrics, as well as gorgeous kimonos. I was astonished to learn that as many as 10,000 cocoons are needed to make just one kimono. By the way, today Japan produces about 33% of the world's silk, but the Japanese are such avid fans of the expensive fabric that they use 50% of the world's total, which means that they must import silk to satisfy the demand. The Silk Museum is open Tuesday through Sunday from 9am to 4:30pm; admission is ¥300 ($2.40).

Just a few minutes' walk from the Silk Center is **Yamashita Park,** laid out after the huge earthquake in 1923, which destroyed much of Tokyo and Yokohama. Japan's first seaside park, Yamashita Park is a pleasant place for a stroll along the waterfront, where you have a view of the city's mighty harbor. This is also where you'll arrive if you've come to Kannai by the Sea Bass shuttle boat. At one end of the park is the 348-foot-high **Marine Tower,** with an observation platform that provides an excellent view of the city, port, and sometimes even Mt. Fuji. It's open daily from 10am to 9pm (6pm in winter) and charges ¥700 ($5) admission. Moored at a pier off the park is the *Hikawa Maru,* a transoceanic liner built in 1930. Its maiden voyage was to Seattle, after which it crossed the Pacific 238 times until it was retired in 1960. Today, it houses a restaurant and beer garden, but the ¥700 ($5) admission fee may deter you from wishing to dine here.

From Yamashita Park you can also take a sightseeing tour by boat of **Yokohama harbor**—a tour that, according to the boat company's English brochure, "will fill up your complete satisfactions." Tours, conducted in Japanese only, are operated approximately every half hour or hour, from 10:30am to 6:30pm, and start at ¥750 ($5.35) for the 40-minute cruise.

Just a minute's walk from the Silk Center is the **Yokohama Archives of History (Yokohama Kaiko Shiryokan),** 3 Nippon O-dori (tel. 201-2100), with exhibits and pictures relating to the opening of Japan to foreigners and the establishment of Yokohama as an international port. A very small museum, it can be toured quickly just to get an idea of early Yokohama. Open Tuesday through Sunday from 9:30am to 5pm; closed on days following public holidays. The entrance fee is ¥200 ($1.40).

AROUND SAKURAGICHO STATION

If you're really a museum buff, you should wander over to the **Kanagawa Prefectural Museum (Kanagawa Kenritsu Hakubutsukan),** 5-chome Minaminaka-dori (tel. 201-0926). It's a 7-minute walk from Sakuragicho Station, or about a 20-minute walk from the Silk Center. In a Western-style building constructed in 1904 to house the nation's first modern foreign-exchange bank, the museum exhibits items related to natural science, archeology, history, and folklore in Kanagawa Prefecture. Yokohama, incidentally, is Kanagawa Prefecture's chief town. Included in the collection are rooms of a traditional Japanese farmhouse, tools for farming and silk production, and models of both Perry's ships and of Japan's first train, which ran between Tokyo and Yokohama. The museum is open Tuesday through Sunday from 9am to 4pm (closed the last Friday of the month and on days following national holidays), and the entrance fee is ¥200 ($1.40).

IMPRESSIONS

While the quaking was going on [in Yokohama, in October 1884] the fancy came to me that it was a laugh rippling over Mother Earth. Today, being gloomy, it seems more like a sigh heaving her bosom.
—LILIAN LELAND, *TRAVELING ALONE: A WOMAN'S JOURNEY ROUND THE WORLD,*
1890

Also near Sakuragicho Station is the newly opened **Yokohama Museum of Art (Yokohama Bijutsukan)**, 1-4 Midoricho (tel. 221-0300). With an emphasis on works by Western and Japanese artists since the 1850s, the museum's ambitious goal is to collect and display art reflecting the mutual influence between the modern art of Europe and that of Japan since the opening of Yokohama's port in 1859. Designed by Kenzo Tange and Urtec Inc., the museum houses exhibits from its permanent collection—these are changed several times a year—as well as special exhibits on loan from other museums. Thus, no matter how many times you visit the museum, there's always something new to see. Hours here are 10am to 6pm, Friday through Wednesday. Admission is ¥500 ($3.55).

MORE SIGHTS

If you're interested in visiting **The Bluff** and the **Foreign Cemetery,** they're located south of Yamashita Park and across the Nakamura River. From The Bluff you have another view of the harbor from Harbor View Park. Also of interest is **Chinatown,** with about 100 Chinese restaurants and shops selling Chinese food-stuffs and souvenirs. Refer to the dining section, below, for information on the restaurants.

As you gaze out over the harbor from Yamashita Park, you can see one of Yokohama's newest sights, the **Yokohama Bay Bridge.** Designed to ease conges-tion, it also features a 1,000-foot pedestrian walkway on the underbelly of the bridge, which extends to an observation deck, offering views of the harbor. Called the **Sky Walk,** it charges an admission of ¥600 ($4.30) and is open daily from 9am to 9pm in summer, from 10am to 6pm in winter. To reach the Sky Walk, which is on the opposite side of the harbor from Yamashita Park, take bus no. 109 from Sakuragicho Station's platform 6, getting off at the Daikoku bus stop.

✪ In my opinion, **Sankei-en Garden** is the best reason for visiting Yokohama. Although not itself old, this lovely park contains a number of historical old buildings that were brought here from other parts of Japan; they are all situated around streams and ponds. Divided into an Inner Garden and an Outer Garden, the park was laid out back in 1906 by Tomitaro Hara, a local millionaire who made his fortune exporting silk. As you wander along the gently winding pathways, you'll see a villa built in 1649 by the Tokugawa Shogunate clan, tea arbors, a 500-year-old pagoda, and a farmhouse built in 1650 without the use of nails. No matter what the season, the views here are beautiful.

The easiest way to reach Sankei-en Garden is by bus no. 8, which departs from Yokohama Station and winds its way through Kannai and past Chinatown before reaching the Sankei-en-mae bus stop. It's therefore easy to combine Sankei-en and Kannai in a day's sightseeing tour. In fact, you may want to come first to Sankei-en Garden and take the bus back to Kannai, ending up in Chinatown for dinner. Sankei-en is open daily from 9am to 4:30pm (enter by 4pm), and admission is ¥300 ($2.15) for the Outer Garden, another ¥300 ($2.15) for the Inner Garden.

WHERE TO DINE

CHINATOWN [CHUKAGAI], Yamashita-cho, Naka-ku.
    Cuisine: CHINESE. **Station:** Kannai, about a 15-minute walk away; or Ishikawacho, a 10-minute walk away.
$ **Prices:** Most dishes ¥800–¥3,000 ($5.70–$21.40); set lunches ¥600–¥750 ($4.30–$5.35). Larger restaurants accept credit cards; those that do, display them on the front door.
    Open: Most Chinatown restaurants open 11am–8:30pm; some close Wed or Tues, but there are always restaurants open.

★ Chinatown consists of one main street and dozens of offshoots, with restaurant after restaurant serving Chinese food, primarily Cantonese. Most of them have plastic-food displays or pictures of their menu, so let your budget be your guide. Many also have English menus. Altogether, there are about 100 restaurants here, so your best policy is to simply to wander around and choose one that suits your fancy. Among the larger, better-known restaurants are **Manchinro** and **Heichinro,** both of which serve Cantonese food; **Saika,** which specializes in dim sum; and **Kaseiro** and **Peking Hanten,** both of which serve Pekinese food.

SOGO DEPARTMENT STORE, 10th floor, 2-18-1 Takashima, Nishi-ku. Tel. 465-2111.

Cuisine: JAPANESE/WESTERN. **Station:** Yokohama Station, east exit.

$ Prices: Dishes ¥650–¥1,300 ($4.65–$9.30); set courses ¥1,700–¥7,500 ($12.15–$53.55). Some restaurants accept credit cards; those that do, display them on the door.

Open: Wed–Mon 11am–10pm.

There are approximately 40 restaurants and coffee shops here in Japan's largest department store, the best of which are on the 10th floor, called Gourmet Ten. It features branches of many famous restaurants, including **Tenichi,** which serves tempura; **Shisen,** a Chinese restaurant; **Chikuyotei,** a famous eel restaurant; and **Sabatini,** an Italian restaurant from Rome, with a branch also in Tokyo. Other restaurants serve udon noodles, Kyoto specialties, kaiseki, shabu-shabu, sukiyaki, sushi, and Kobe beef. Since all restaurants have plastic-food display cases outside their doors, ordering is easy.

5. KAWASAKI

10 miles S of Tokyo

GETTING THERE   By Train   To reach the open-air museum, take the Odakyu Line from Shinjuku to the Mukogaoka-yuen Station, which is the 18th stop. Minka-en is about a 15-minute walk from the south exit of the station.

ESSENTIAL INFORMATION   The telephone **area code** of Kawasaki is 044.

With a population of almost one million, Kawasaki has pretty much been swallowed up by the Tokyo-Yokohama metropolis, and as you travel by train it's virtually impossible to see where Tokyo ends and Kawasaki begins. A sprawling industrial complex with some of the largest Japanese manufacturing plants located here, Kawasaki is one of those cities better left unseen. ✪ However, tucked away in a corner of woods and hills is a delightful open-air museum called **Nihon Minka-en** (tel. 044/922-2181), where traditional thatched houses and other historical buildings have been preserved. If you don't have the chance to visit Takayama or Shirakawa in the Japan Alps, or a similar museum in Takamatsu, on the island of Kyushu, this may be your only chance to examine closely how rural Japanese lived in centuries past.

Altogether, 22 structures have been brought here from other parts of Japan and artistically situated on various wooded hills. Most of them are heavy-beamed thatched houses, but there are also warehouses, a shrine, and a Kabuki stage from a small fishing village. All the buildings are open to the public, so that you can wander in and inspect the various rooms, filled with items used by rural Japanese during the feudal era. The oldest houses date from about 300 years ago; they were usually homes for extended families, with as many as several dozen family members living under one roof. Imagine how it must have been to live back then, with the family gathered around the central hearth on cold winter nights. An English pamphlet tells about each of the buildings, and there are many explanations throughout in English. Nihon Minka-en is open Tuesday through Sunday from 9:30am to 4:30pm (enter by 4pm) and charges ¥300 ($2.15) admission.

Because there are no special restaurants in this area, I suggest you return to Shinjuku to take advantage of the many wonderful restaurants there. Or, if the weather is fine, you might want to pack a picnic lunch to eat outdoors. There are many fast-food outlets with takeout service in Shinjuku Station, as well as many department stores with food departments selling prepared meats, salads, and other ready-to-eat dishes.

In addition to Nihon Minka-en, there's one other attraction in Kawasaki you might like to know about, although it takes place only once a year, in mid-April. That's the **Jibeta Matsuri festival.** This rather unusual event extols the joys of sex, and points out perhaps better than anything else the differences in attitude that the Japanese and Westerners have had about sex throughout the centuries. Whereas in the West sexuality has had a long history of repression, expressed largely through religious beliefs, the Japanese have always taken a rather open and natural attitude toward sex, without the burden of guilt and without treating it as a moral issue.

At any rate, this festival takes place at Kanayama Shrine, which has on display huge phalluses as well as various other sexual objects, and the highlight of the festival is a parade in which various phallic objects are carried through the streets. As with many festivals in Japan, this one is tied to a legend. According to a well-known Japanese myth, a long time ago there was a beautiful maiden who was afflicted by a terrible demon. Twice she tried to marry, but on both wedding nights her grooms died while they tried to consummate the marriage—the demon had bitten off the symbol of their manhood. As you can imagine, the father of the poor girl was unsuccessful in securing her another husband. Finally, a blacksmith heard about her story and, taking pity, he resolved to help her. He applied for assistance to the metalsmiths' protective deities at his local shrine; there he had a vision that instructed him to create a metal phallus and use that to deflower the girl. The plan worked, the demon broke its teeth on the metal phallus, and everyone lived happily ever after. In gratitude to the deities, the smith presented the metal phallus to the shrine, and from that time on the deities were known as the Deities of the Metal Phallus.

You can get some unusual photographs at this annual event. Inquire at the Tokyo Tourist Information Center for the exact date. To get to Kanayama Shrine, also known as the Shrine of Kanamara-sama, take the Keihin Kyuko Line from Shinagawa Station to Keihin Kawasaki Station, and transfer to the Kawasaki Daishi Line for the 10-minute trip to Kawasaki Daishi Station. From there it's only a few minutes' walk.

6. MOUNT FUJI

62 miles SW of Tokyo

GETTING THERE By Train and Bus   Kawaguchiko Fifth Stage is the starting point for most climbs to the top of Mt. Fuji. The easiest way to reach Kawaguchiko Fifth Stage is by direct bus from either Hamamatsucho or Shinjuku Bus Terminal, in operation several times daily from July 9 to August 31. Less frequent bus service is also available from about the end of April to July and again during September and October. The fare from Hamamatsucho Bus Terminal is ¥2,500 ($16.70) one way, and from Shinjuku Bus Terminal it's ¥2,300 ($16.40) one way. The bus trip takes about 2½ hours from Shinjuku and almost 3 hours from Hamamatsucho. Reservations for the bus, which are required, can be made through a travel agency, such as the Japan Travel Bureau. You can also reach Kawaguchiko Fifth Stage by taking either a bus or a train from Shinjuku Station to Kawaguchiko Station, transferring there for a bus bound for the Fifth Stage. Note that all bus service to Kawaguchiko Fifth Stage is suspended, however, from November to April, when Mt. Fuji is blanketed in snow and is considered too dangerous for the novice climber.

For the return back to Tokyo, buses from Subashiri New Fifth Stage reach Gotember Station in about 65 minutes; the fare is ¥2,400 ($17.15). There is frequent train service from Gotemba to both Shinjuku and Tokyo stations.

More information regarding train and bus schedules can be obtained from the Tokyo Tourist Information Center in leaflets called *Mt. Fuji and Fuji Five Lakes* and *Climbing Mt. Fuji.*

ESSENTIAL INFORMATION   The telephone **area code** for Mt. Fuji is 0555.

Mt. Fuji, affectionately called "Fuji-san" by the Japanese, has been revered as sacred since ancient times. Throughout the centuries Japanese poets have written about it, painters have painted it, pilgrims have flocked to it, and more than a few people have died on it. Without a doubt this mountain has been photographed more than anything else in Japan.

Visible on a clear day from as far as 100 miles away, Mt. Fuji is stunningly impressive. At 12,388 feet it towers far above anything else around it, a symmetrical cone of almost perfect proportions. Mt. Fuji is majestic, grand, and awe-inspiring. To the Japanese it symbolizes the very spirit of their country. Unfortunately, Fuji-san is almost always cloaked in clouds. If you catch a glimpse of this mighty mountain (which you can do from the bullet train between Tokyo and Nagoga), consider yourself extremely lucky.

WHAT TO SEE & DO

Other than admiring it from afar (some of the best views are afforded from Hakone, described below), the most popular thing to do regarding Mt. Fuji is to climb it. Several well-marked trails leading to the top are open throughout the year, but because of snow and inclement weather from fall through late spring, the best time to make an ascent is during the "official" climbing season, from July 1 to August 31. It's also the most crowded time of the year. Consider the fact that there are approximately 120 million Japanese, most of whom wouldn't dream of climbing the mountain outside the "official" 2 months it's open, and you begin to get the picture. More specifically, about 400,000 people climb Fuji-san every year, mostly in July and August and mostly on weekends. In other words, if you plan on climbing Mt. Fuji on a Saturday or a Sunday in summer, go to the end of the line, please. I've seen pictures of a trail leading up to Fuji's summit taken on a hot summer's day—a solid, unbroken line of hikers stretching all the way up the face of the mountain, one right behind the other. It was as though everyone were waiting in a queue to get into a movie being shown at the top, but I have no doubt that these Japanese hikers were enjoying themselves immensely, reveling in the togetherness, happy that they were all partaking in the spirit of the climb up old Fuji-san.

So, unless you climb Mt. Fuji outside the summer months, it will not be a solitary venture. Rather, you should view the experience as something to be shared with a determined group of Japanese who are following in their fathers' footsteps by making the pilgrimage to the top (women, incidentally, weren't allowed to climb Mt. Fuji until 1868). Climbing the mountain is not difficult, but it can be extremely strenuous. You'll be amazed by the number of children and old people doggedly making their way to the top of the highest mountain in Japan.

Mt. Fuji is part of a larger national park called Fuji-Hakone-Izu National Park. Of the handful of trails leading to the top, the most popular ones for Tokyoites are the Kawaguchiko Trail for the ascent and the Subashiri Trail for the descent. All trails are divided into 10 different stages, with the Fifth Stage located about 8,250 feet up. It takes about 5 hours to reach the summit and 3 hours for the descent.

CLIMBING MOUNT FUJI

Don't be disappointed when your bus deposits you at Kawaguchiko Fifth Stage, where you'll be bombarded with an overflow of souvenir shops, restaurants, and busloads of tourists. Most of these tourists aren't climbing to the top, and as soon as you get past them and the blaring loudspeakers, you'll find yourself on a steep rocky path, surrounded only by scrub brush and with hikers on the path below and above you. After a couple of hours you'll probably find yourself above the roily clouds, which stretch in all directions. It will be as if you were on an island, barren and rocky, in the middle of an ocean.

IMPRESSIONS

As time goes on, he becomes an infatuating personality.
—ISABELLA BIRD, *UNBEATEN TRACKS IN JAPAN*, 1880, ON MT. FUJI

You needn't have had climbing experience to ascend Mt. Fuji, but you do need stamina and a good pair of walking shoes. It's possible to do it in tennis shoes, but if the rocks are wet they can get awfully slippery. You should also bring a light plastic raincoat (which you can buy at souvenir shops at the Fifth Stage), a sun hat, and a sweater for the evening. It gets very chilly on Mt. Fuji at night.

As for sleeping, there are about 25 mountain huts along the Kawaguchiko Trail above the Fifth Stage, but they're very primitive, providing only a futon and toilet facilities. The cost without meals is ¥4,000 ($28.55) per person, and with meals it's ¥6,000 ($42.85) per person. When I stayed in one of these huts, dinner consisted of dried fish, rice, bean-paste soup, and pickled vegetables; breakfast was exactly the same.

The usual procedure for climbing Mt. Fuji is to start out in early afternoon, spend the night near the summit, get up early in the morning to watch the sun rise, and then climb the rest of the way to the top, where there's a 1-hour hiking trail that circles the crater. Hikers then begin the descent, reaching the Fifth Stage about noon.

In recent years, however, a new trend has started in which climbers arrive at the Fifth Stage late in the evening and then climb to the top through the night with the aid of flashlights. After watching the sun rise, they then make their descent. That way, they don't have to spend the night in one of the huts.

Climbing Mt. Fuji is definitely a unique experience, but there is a saying in Japan: "Everyone should climb Mt. Fuji once; only a fool would climb it twice."

---

7. HAKONE

60 miles SW of Tokyo

GETTING THERE   By Train   Getting to Hakone is half the fun! Start out by train from Tokyo, then switch to a small two-car train that zigzags up the mountain, change to a cable car and then a smaller ropeway, and end your trip with a boat ride across Lake Ashi, stopping off to see major attractions along the way. From Lake Ashi (from either Togendai or Hakone-machi), you can then board a bus bound for Odawara Station (an hour's ride), where you can then take the train back to Tokyo. From Togendai, there are also buses that go directly to Shinjuku Station.

By Bus   Odakyu buses depart every hour from Shinjuku Station's west exit bound for Togendai on Lake Ashi. The trip takes 2 hours and 10 minutes. Reservations are recommended. Call Odakyu at 03/3481-0061.

ESSENTIAL INFORMATION   The telephone **area code** for Hakone is 0460. Before leaving Tokyo, pick up the *Hakone and Kamakura* leaflet available from the Tourist Information Office. It lists the time schedules for the extensive network of trains, buses, cable cars, and pleasure boats throughout the Hakone area.

GETTING AROUND   The most economical way to see Hakone is via the **Hakone Free Pass,** which despite its name isn't free but does give you a round-trip ticket from Shinjuku Station to Odawara or Hakone Yumoto in Hakone and includes almost all other modes of transportation in Hakone (see "Getting There," above). The pass avoids the hassle of having to buy individual tickets and also provides discounts on several of Hakone's attractions. Valid for 4 days, it costs ¥5,840 ($41.70) if you take the nonstop Odakyu Romance Car and ¥4,600 ($32.85) if you take the slower, ordinary Odakyu express train. The Romance Car travels from Shinjuku all the way to Hakone Yumoto Station in about 1½ hours; the slower train travels from Shinjuku only as far as Odawara in the same amount of time. If you have a Japan Rail Pass, you should take the Shinkansen bullet train from Tokyo Station to Odawara (not all bullet trains stop there, so make sure yours does). From there, you can travel on the private railways, cable cars, buses, and boats for the ¥3,500 ($25) Hakone Free Pass, also valid for 4 days. All passes can be purchased at any station of the Odakyu Railway, including Shinjuku Station.

As part of the Fuji-Hakone-Izu National Park, Hakone is one of the closest and most popular resorts for residents of Tokyo. Blessed with beautiful scenery, Hakone has about everything a vacationer could wish for—hot-spring resorts, mountains, lakes, breathtaking views of Mt. Fuji, and interesting historical sites. You can tour Hakone as a day trip, but adding an overnight stay near Lake Ashi, or in the mountains, where you can soak in the water of hot springs, is much more pleasant. If you plan to return to Tokyo, I suggest leaving your luggage in storage at your Tokyo hotel and traveling to Hakone with only an overnight bag.

WHAT TO SEE & DO

If you plan on spending only a day in Hakone, you should leave Tokyo very early in the morning. If you're spending the night—and I strongly urge that you do—you can arrange your itinerary in a more leisurely fashion and devote more time to Hakone's attractions. You may wish to travel only as far as your hotel the first day, stopping at sights along the way and in the vicinity. The next day you could continue with the rest of the circuit through Hakone. If you want to do most of your sightseeing the first day, you can travel all the way to Lake Ashi and from there take a bus to all accommodations recommended below.

THE TRAIN TRIP

Regardless of whether you travel via Shinkansen, the Odakyu Romance Car, or the ordinary Odakyu express, you will end up at either Odawara Station, considered the gateway to Hakone, or Hakone Yumoto Station. At either station, you can transfer to the **Hakone Tozan Railway,** a small two-car train that winds its way through forests and over streams as it travels upward to Gora, making several switchbacks along the way. The entire trip from Hakone Yumoto Station to Gora takes only 45 minutes, but it's a beautiful ride, on a narrow track through the mountains. The train makes about a dozen stops before reaching Gora, including Tonosawa and Miyanoshita, two hot-spring spa resorts with a number of old ryokan and hotels (refer to my food and lodging recommendations). Some of these ryokan date back several centuries, from the days when they were on the main thoroughfare to Tokyo, the old Tokaido Highway. Miyanoshita is also the best place for lunch.

As for things to do along the way, you can begin your trip with some open-air bathing at the public baths behind Hakone Yumoto Station, called **Kappa Tengoku** (41) (tel. 5-6121). Probably the closest outdoor baths in the vicinity of Tokyo, they're open from 10am to 10pm and charge ¥500 ($3.55) admission. From Hakone Yumoto Station, take a right and go under the train tracks, and then take an immediate right again. Walk uphill and follow the sign (in kanji only) up the steps to what looks like a house. The baths are in the woods behind the house.

✪ The most important stop on the Hakone Tozan Railway is the next-to-the-last stop, Chokoku-no-Mori, where you'll find the famous **Hakone Open-Air Museum** (tel. 2-1161), with more than 100 sculptures by artists from around the world, including Rodin, Henry Moore, Imoto Atusushi, and Yodoi Toshio. Using nature itself as a dramatic backdrop, this museum spreads through glens and gardens and over ponds. There's also an indoor exhibit of paintings and sculptures, including a collection of Picasso's works. You'll want to spend at least a couple of hours here. Open from 9am to 5pm (4pm in winter), the museum charges ¥1,500 ($10.70) admission.

BY CABLE CAR & ROPEWAY

From Gora you can travel by cable car, which leaves every 15 minutes and arrives 9 minutes later at the end station of Sounzan, making several stops along the way. One of the stops is Koen-Kami, which is only a minute away from the **Hakone Art**

Museum (Hakone Bijutsukan) (tel. 2-2623). Open Friday through Wednesday from 9am to 4pm, it displays Japanese pottery and ceramics from the Jomon Period (around 4000 B.C.) to the Edo Period. Included are water jars, terra-cotta vessels taken from burial grounds dating from before the 7th century, Bizen ware from Okayama, and 17th-century Imari ware. A lovely Japanese landscape garden of moss and bamboo is on the museum grounds. Admission is ¥800 ($5.70).

From Sounzan you board a small ropeway for a long haul down the mountain to Togendai, which lies beside Lake Ashi, known as Lake Ashinoko in Japanese. Before reaching Togendai, however, get off at the first intermediary station, Owakudani, the ropeway's highest point. Here you can take a 30-minute hike along a nature path through Owakudani, which means "Great Boiling Valley." Sulfurous steam escapes from fissures in the rock, testimony to volcanic activity still present here. In Owakudani you'll also find the **Natural Science Museum** (tel. 4-9149), with displays on the fauna, flora, geology, and volcanic origins of Hakone. It's open from 9am to 5pm and charges ¥350 ($2.50) admission. Before starting back down on the ropeway, stop off for a drink at the second floor of the ropeway station, where you have fantastic views of Hakone and of Mt. Fuji if it's not covered by clouds.

LAKE ASHI

From Togendai you can take a pleasure boat across Lake Ashi, also referred to as "Lake Hakone" in English brochures. Believe it or not, one of the boats crossing the lake is a replica of a centuries-old man-of-war. It takes about half an hour to cross the lake to Hakone-machi (also called simply Hakone; *machi* means city) and Moto Hakone, two resort towns right next to each other on the southern edge of the lake. This end of the lake affords the best view of Mt. Fuji, a view often depicted in tourist publications.

In Hakone-machi you should visit the **Hakone Checkpoint (Hakone Sekisho)**, a reconstructed guardhouse. Originally built in 1618, it served as a checkpoint on the famous **Tokaido Highway**, which connected Edo (present Tokyo) with Kyoto. In feudal days, local lords, called daimyo, were required to spend alternate years in Edo, and their wives were kept on in Edo as hostages so that the lords wouldn't plan rebellions while in their homelands. This was one of the points along the highway where travelers were checked. Although it was possible to sneak around it, violators who were caught were promptly executed. The checkpoint is open daily from 9am to 4:30pm (4pm in winter) and admission is free.

Not far from the checkpoint is the **Hakone Detached Palace Garden,** which lies on a small promontory on Lake Ashi. Originally part of an imperial villa built in 1887, the garden is open free to the public. It not only offers a fine view of the lake but also displays historical materials relating to the old Tokaido Highway, including weapons, armor, palanquins, and items from life during the Edo Period. For more information on either the Hakone Checkpoint or the Detached Palace Garden, call the Hakone Town Office at 0460/5-7111.

Between Hakone-machi and Moto-Hakone is part of the Tokaido Highway itself. Lined with ancient and mighty cedars, 1¼ miles of the old highway follow the curve of Lake Ashi and make a pleasant stroll (unfortunately, a road of the 20th century has been built right beside the original one). In Moto-Hakone is **Hakone Shrine,** revered by samurai until the Meiji Restoration in 1868. Especially picturesque is its red torii gate, standing in the water.

WHERE TO STAY

Japan's ryokan sprang into existence to accommodate the stately processions of daimyo and shogun as they traversed the roads between Edo and the rest of Japan. Many of these ryokan were built along the Tokaido Highway, and some of the oldest are found in Hakone.

EXPENSIVE

THE FUJIYA HOTEL, 359 Miyanoshita, Hakone-machi, Ashigarashimo-gun 250-04. Tel. 0460/2-2211. Fax 0460/2-2210. 146 rms (all with bath).

A/C MINIBAR TV TEL **Station:** Miyanoshita (on Hakone Tozan Railway), a 5-minute walk away.

$ Rates (single or double occupancy): ¥16,000 ($114) weekdays; ¥24,000 ($171) Sat, day before a national hol, and during Golden Week (Apr 28–May 4); ¥33,000 ($236) during New Year's and July–Aug. AE, DC, JCB, MC, V.

⭐ Established in 1878, it's the grandest, most majestic old hotel in Hakone and one of the oldest Western-style hotels in Japan. It's a lovely establishment, with such Asian touches as a Japanese-style roof, lots of windows, and wooden corridors. It consists of five separate buildings, all different and added on at various times in the hotel's 112-year history. One is shaped like a pagoda, while another has turrets and a roof shaped like that of a Japanese temple. The old-fashioned rooms have high ceilings and wooden furniture. In the back of the hotel are a garden with a waterfall and a pond full of carp. There's an outdoor swimming pool, as well as an indoor thermal pool fed by water from a hot spring. The hotel even has its own greenhouse. The front-desk personnel speak very good English.

Dining/Entertainment: The Fujiya's main dining hall, dating from 1930, is one of the best places for a meal in Hakone. It offers a variety of Western dishes, from spaghetti and sandwiches for lunch to steaks for dinner.

Services: Free newspaper, free shoeshine kit.

Facilities: Shopping arcade, indoor and outdoor swimming pools, hot-spring baths, pleasant garden, golf course.

HAKONE PRINCE HOTEL 67, 144 Moto-Hakone, Hakone-machi, Ashigarashimo-gun 250-05. Tel. 0460/3-7111. Fax 0460/3-7616. 294 rms (all with bath). A/C (except in cabins) MINIBAR TV TEL **Bus:** From Odawara Station or Hakone Yumoto Station to Hakone-en bus stop (last stop).

$ Rates: Ryuguden complex: ¥29,000–¥70,000 ($207–$500) per person, including two meals and service charge; ¥44,000–¥80,000 ($314–$571) during peak seasons (New Year's and summer vacation). Western-style hotel: ¥33,000–¥44,000 ($236–$314) double occupancy; ¥40,000–¥55,000 ($286–$393) mid-July and Aug. Western-style cabins sleeping up to four persons: ¥26,000–¥44,000 ($186–$314); ¥31,000–¥55,000 ($221–$393) mid-July and Aug. AE, DC, JCB, MC, V.

This luxurious hotel is situated on secluded property right on Lake Ashi. The various types of rooms available here are in several differently styled complexes that sprawl over the well-tended grounds.

The Ryuguden complex ⑤⓪, with its Japanese-style tatami rooms, resembles an Asian palace. It's a grand structure, built in 1936, with iron lanterns hanging from its upturned wooden eaves and sculptured bushes gracing its manicured lawns. Prices vary according to the room and the meals ordered.

Not far from the Ryuguden complex is the Hakone Prince's Western-style hotel, designed by Japanese architect Togo Murano in a circular shape so that each room has a different panoramic view, complete with balcony.

And finally, you can also stay in one of the individual pine log cabins (the wood imported from Finland), spread underneath the trees in a kind of village and sleeping up to four persons each.

Dining/Entertainment: Two restaurants serving Japanese, Western, and Chinese food; two bars; and one coffee shop.

Services: Free newspaper (not available in cabins).

Facilities: Gardens, tennis courts (with night lighting), public baths (overlooking lake), outdoor pool, ice-skating rink (winter only), and arboretum.

ICHINOYU ⑤①, 90 Tonosawa, Hakone-machi, Ashigarashimo-gun 250-03. Tel. 0460/5-5331. 22 rms (12 with bath). A/C MINIBAR TV TEL **Station:** Tonosawa (on Hakone Tozan Railway), a 6-minute walk away.

$ Rates (per person, including two meals, tax, and service): ¥18,000–¥22,000 ($128–$157) with bath; ¥16,000–¥20,000 ($114–$143) without bath. AE, DC, JCB, V.

⭐ Ichinoyu, first opened more than 350 years ago, is now in its 14th generation of owners. It claims to be the oldest ryokan in the area and was once honored by the visit of a shogun. Located near Tonosawa Station (on the Hakone Tozan Line), this delightful, rambling wooden building stands on a tree-shaded 💲 winding road that follows the track of the old Tokaido Highway. On the one side of the ryokan is a roaring river.

The oldest rooms here date from the Meiji Period, more than 100 years ago. The two rooms I like the most are called Seseragi and Matsu (rooms are usually named in ryokan). Old-fashioned, they face the river and consist mainly of seasoned and weathered wood. Old artwork, wall hangings, and paintings decorate the ryokan, and some of the rooms have old wooden bathtubs. Both the communal tubs and the tubs in the rooms have hot water supplied from a natural spring.

NARAYA, 162 Miyanoshita, Hakone-machi, Ashigarashimo-gun 250-04. Tel. 0460/2-2411. 20 rms (19 with bath). TV TEL **Station:** Miyanoshita (on Hakone Tozan Railway), a 5-minute walk away.

💲 **Rates** (per person, including two meals and service charge): ¥33,000 ($236). AE, DC, V.

⭐ Across the street from the Fujiya Hotel is Naraya, an elegant traditional Japanese inn with tiled roof, wooden walls, shoji screens, and hot-spring baths. Although the inn's history stretches back several hundred years, the present building is about a century old. The tatami rooms here have inspiring views of a large landscape garden and mountains beyond. This is a great place to relax and revel in nature's beauty, and the meals served are worth the price of staying here.

MODERATE

SUGIYOSHI RYOKAN ㉟, 56 Moto-Hakone, Hakone-machi. Tel. 0460/3-6327. Fax 0460/3-7007. 12 rms (6 with bath). TV TEL **Bus:** From Odawara, 50 minutes to Hakone-machi.

💲 **Rates** (per person, including two meals and service charge): ¥13,000 ($93) without bath; ¥17,000 ($121) with bath. ¥20,000 ($160) peak season. No credit cards.

Located at the southern tip of Lake Hakone, this simple ryokan has rooms in Japanese style. They come with the usual coin-operated TV and fridge, and some of them have lake views. The public baths here are natural hot springs.

INEXPENSIVE

FUJI-HAKONE GUEST HOUSE, 912 Sengokuhara, Kanagawa 250-06. Tel. 0460/4-6577. Fax 0460/4-6578. 12 rms (none with bath). **Bus:** Hakone Tozan Bus (included in Hakone Free Pass) from Togendai (10 minutes) or from Odawara Station (45 minutes) to Senkyoro-mae bus stop. Stop is announced in English, and guesthouse is then only a minute's walk away.

💲 **Rates:** ¥4,900–¥5,500 ($35–$39) single; ¥10,000–¥11,000 ($71–$78) twin; ¥14,000–¥15,000 ($100–$107) triple. AE, MC, V.

⭐ Although it's a bit isolated, this guest house is a member of the Japanese Inn Group and offers inexpensive lodging in tatami rooms. Kept spotlessly clean, this modern house in tranquil surroundings set back from a tree-shaded road is run by a man who speaks very good English. Some of the rooms face the Hakone mountain range. Facilities include a public hot-spring bath, coin-operated laundry and dryer, a large lounge area, and a communal refrigerator. The family running the guesthouse prefer that guests stay at least two nights.

MOTO-HAKONE GUEST HOUSE, 103 Moto-Hakone, Hakone-machi, Kanagawa 250-05. Tel. 0460/3-7880. Fax 0460/4-6578. 5 rms (none with bath). **Bus:** Hakone Tozan Bus (included in Hakone Free Pass) from Odawara Station (1 hour) to Ashinoko-en bus stop; guesthouse is then less than a minute's walk away.

💲 **Rates:** ¥5,500 ($39) single; ¥11,000 ($78) double; ¥15,000 ($107) triple. AE, MC, V.

Conveniently located in Moto-Hakone, less than a 15-minute walk from Lake Ashi, this simple guesthouse offers five Japanese-style tatami rooms, a shared communal bath, and a coin-operated laundry.

WHERE TO DINE

MAIN DINING ROOM, Fujiya Hotel, 359 Miyanoshita. Tel. 2-2211.
　Cuisine: WESTERN. **Station:** Miyanoshita (on Hakone Tozan Railway), a 5-minute walk away.
　$ Prices: Main dinner courses ¥3,000–¥10,000 ($21.40–$71.40), main lunch courses ¥2,000–¥4,000 ($14.30–$28.55). AE, DC, JCB, MC, V.
　Open: Lunch daily noon–2pm; dinner daily 6–8:30pm.

★ 　The Fujiya Hotel, Hakone's grandest hotel and conveniently located near a stop on the two-car Hakone Tozan Railway, is the most memorable place for a meal. The main dining hall, dating from 1930, is very bright and cheerful, with a high, intricately detailed ceiling, large windows with Japanese screens, a wooden floor, and white tablecloths. The views are nice and the service is attentive. For lunch you can have such dishes as pilaf, spaghetti, sandwiches, chicken, rainbow trout, and hamburger steak, while the more expensive dinner menu includes steaks, fish, grilled chicken, and stews.

8. THE IZU PENINSULA

Whenever Tokyoites want to spend a few days at a hot-spring spa on the seashore, they head for the Izu Peninsula. Jutting out into the Pacific Ocean, Izu boasts some fine beaches, verdant and lush countryside, and a dramatic coastline marked in spots by high cliffs and tumbling surf. However, even though the scenery is at times breathtaking, there is little of historical interest to lure the short-term visitor to Japan; make sure you've seen both Kamakura and Nikko before you consider coming here. Keep in mind also that Izu's resorts are terribly crowded during the summer vacation period, from mid-July to the end of August.

The fastest way to reach Izu is by the Shinkansen bullet train from Tokyo Station, an hour's trip to Atami, Izu's main gateway on the east side of the peninsula. From Atami you can travel farther south to Shimoda by limited express train.

The west side of the peninsula is much less developed and in my opinion offers the best scenery in Izu. Since there is no rail service here, transportation is either by bus or by boat. A good choice of a place to stay on the west side is Dogashima, a small fishing village with a good beach, clear waters, and interesting rock formations. A pleasant way to reach Dogashima is either by boat from Numazu or by bus along the coast from Shimoda.

But the best way to enjoy Izu is to drive, making this one of the few times when it may be worthwhile to rent your own car. There's a road that hugs the coast all the way around the peninsula, which you can drive easily in a day. If you're traveling by public transportation, an interesting route is to take the Shinkansen bullet train to Atami, travel by limited express to Shimoda, take the bus from Shimoda to Dogashima, and from there take a boat to Numazu, where you can catch a train back to Tokyo. Before leaving Tokyo, be sure to pick up the leaflet *The Izu Peninsula* at the Tourist Information Center.

If you're traveling during the peak summer season, you should make reservations at least several months in advance. Otherwise, there are hotel, ryokan, and minshuku reservation offices in all of Izu's resort towns which will arrange accommodations for you, but be aware that if a place has a room still open at the last minute in August, there's probably a reason for it—poor location, poor service, or unimaginative décor. I took my chances one August and arrived in Atami without prior arrangements. The "ryokan" arranged by the accommodations office at the Atami train station was the worst I've ever stayed in. It pays to plan ahead. Below are recommended accommodations in Atami, Shimoda, and Dogashima, three towns that provide a good overview of what the peninsula has to offer.

ATAMI
30 miles SW of Tokyo

GETTING THERE   By Train   From Tokyo Station, 1 hour by Shinkansen bullet train (since not all bullet trains stop in Atami, make sure yours does).

ESSENTIAL INFORMATION   The telephone **area code** for Atami is 0557. The **Atami Tourist Information Office** is located at the train station (tel. 0557/81-6002) and is open daily from 10am to 6pm.

---

*A*tami means "hot sea." Legend has it that a long time ago there was a hot geyser spewing forth in the sea, killing a lot of fish and marine life. The concerned fishermen asked a Buddhist monk to intervene on their behalf and to pray for a solution to the problem. The prayers paid off when the geyser moved itself to the beach. Not only was the marine life spared, but Atami was blessed with hot-spring water the townspeople could henceforth bathe in.

Today, Atami—with a population of more than 50,000—is a conglomeration of hotels, ryokan, restaurants, pachinko parlors, souvenir shops, and a sizable red-light district. The city itself is not very interesting, but it's the most easily accessible hot-spring resort from Tokyo and has a wonderful art museum. In fact, the art museum is so famous that Tokyoites will come to Atami on a day trip just to see it.

WHAT TO SEE & DO

Be sure to see the **MOA Art Museum** (tel. 84-2511), located on top of a hill a short bus ride away from Atami Station. Housed in a modern building at the headquarters of the Church of World Messianity, this museum includes woodblock prints, ceramics, lacquerware, and artwork from the collection of Mokichi Okada, leader of this relatively new religion in Japan. The place is open Friday through Wednesday from 9:30am to 4pm (you must enter by 3:30pm), and admission is ¥1,500 ($10.70).

WHERE TO STAY

HOTEL NEW AKAO ⑤③**, Atami-cho 1993-250, Atami City 413. Tel. 0557/82-5151.** 255 rms (all with bath). A/C MINIBAR TV TEL **Directions:** 10 minutes by hotel shuttle bus from Atami Station, with departures once an hour.
$ Rates (per person, including two meals, tax, and service charge): ¥25,000 ($178) weekdays; ¥27,000 ($193) weekends. DC, JCB, V.
This large pleasure hotel is one of the most conspicuous resort hotels on the Izu Peninsula, hemmed in on one side by cliffs and on the other by the blue sea. Rooms in both Japanese and Western style are available, simply but tastefully done, all with large windows facing the water and a private bath. Obviously, what you're paying for here is use of the facilities rather than luxurious rooms. My only complaint about this hotel is that it's so popular and crowded during peak season that the front desk seems too busy to be very accommodating.
   Dining/Entertainment: This hotel has about everything most Japanese want in a vacation, including a fancy dining hall affording an unusual view of surf crashing into cliffs, and two discos.
   Services: Free soft drink.
   Facilities: Swimming pool, roped-off area in the sea for swimming, large hot-spring public bath, outdoor garden complete with arbors and Corinthian pillars, and small miniature golf area.

KIUNKAKU ⑤④**, 4-2 Showacho, Atami City 413. Tel. 0557/81-3623.** 27

rms (21 with bath). A/C MINIBAR TV TEL **Directions:** 8 minutes by taxi from Atami Station.

$ Rates (per person, including two meals and service charge): ¥38,000–¥50,000 ($271–$357).

⭐ One of Atami's oldest ryokan, Kiunkaku has a beautiful garden with a meandering stream, manicured bushes, and stunted pine trees. It has one of the most pleasant coffee shops I've seen in a ryokan, and facilities include hot-spring baths and an outdoor pool. Although rooms encircle the garden, they are artfully concealed from one another and give optimum privacy through the clever use of bushes and mounds. There are various styles of rooms available: the most expensive are those with the best view, the most space, and the best meals. However, there are a few rooms in the lower price range that are comparative bargains. Tamahime, for example, is the name of one of the ryokan's two Western-style rooms and it's changed little over the decades. It sports stained-glass windows, a paneled ceiling, a fireplace (no longer used), a monstrous old dresser, and cozy furniture—plus a good view of the garden. The only reason it's available for ¥35,000 per person is that there is no private bathroom.

NEW FUJIYA HOTEL, 1-16 Ginza-cho, Atami City 413. Tel. 0557/81-0111. Fax 0557/81-8052. 350 rms (all with bath) A/C TV TEL **Directions:** 5 minutes by taxi from Atami Station.

$ Rates: ¥25,000 ($178) per person with two meals; without meals ¥13,000 ($93) single, ¥22,000–¥30,000 ($157–$214) twin. AE, DC, JCB, V.

On a less grand scale but recently renovated, this hotel was built just before the 1964 Summer Olympics. The staff here is friendly and efficient and used to foreigners. Although the New Fujiya is located a few blocks inland, its top-floor rooms have partial views of the water. The cheapest rooms are those that face an inside courtyard. Both Japanese- and Western-style rooms are available.

Dining/Entertainment: In addition to a coffee shop and restaurant, there's a nightclub—usually with performances by rather scantily clad women.

Facilities: Indoor pool, rooftop playground, public bath and sauna, and outdoor hot-spring spa.

SHIMODA

112 miles SW of Tokyo

GETTING THERE   By Train   From Tokyo, take the Shinkansen bullet train to Atami, transferring there to a limited express train bound for Shimoda.

ESSENTIAL INFORMATION   The telephone **area code** for Shimoda is 05582.

The **Shimoda Tourist Office** is located just outside the train station and is open daily from 9am to 5pm (tel. 05582/2-1531). It has some brochures of Shimoda.

Located on the southeast end of the Izu Peninsula, Shimoda is famous as the site where Commodore Perry set anchor in 1854 to force Japan to open its doors to trade. Shimoda is also where the first American diplomatic representative, Townsend Harris, lived before setting up permanent residence in Yokohama.

WHAT TO SEE & DO

Ryosenji Temple, located about a 15-minute walk from Shimoda Station, is where Perry and representatives of the Tokugawa shogunate government signed the treaty to open up Japan. Strangely enough, the temple also houses a small museum of erotica.

Hofukuji Temple, about a 5-minute walk from Shimoda Station, is dedicated to Tojin Okichi, the mistress of Townsend Harris while he lived in Shimoda. Although today no one is exactly certain how it came about that she was chosen, we do know that she ended her life by drowning herself after he left. This temple contains both her tomb and her personal artifacts.

About 20 minutes south of Shimoda by bus is **Yumigahama Beach,** considered by many to be the best public beach in Izu. If you're on a budget, head for **Sotoura,** a small bay on the edge of Shimoda with about 60 minshuku and pensions. It has its own small beach and is popular with young people and families.

WHERE TO STAY & DINE

SHIMODA TOKYU HOTEL, 5-12-1 Shimoda-shi 415. Tel. 05582/2-2411.
Fax 05582/3-2419. 117 rms. A/C MINIBAR TV TEL **Directions:** A 10-minute taxi ride from Shimoda Station.

$ Rates: Western-style rooms: ¥13,000–¥23,000 ($93–$164) single; ¥21,000–¥39,000 ($150–$278) double/twin. Japanese-style rooms: ¥17,000 ($121) for two persons; ¥50,000 ($357) peak season. AE, JCB, V.

This large white hotel occupies the top of a hill not far from the sea. Most of its rooms are Western style, though it does have 10 Japanese-style tatami rooms. Probably the best thing about the hotel is its outdoor bathing possibilities.

Dining/Entertainment: In addition to Western and Japanese dining facilities, from mid-July through August there's an outdoor barbecue.

Services: Free newspaper.

Facilities: Hot-spring spa, outdoor swimming pool, and bathing area in sea.

SHIMODA ONSEN HOTEL HANAMISAKI, 6-12 Takegahama, Shimoda City 415. Tel. 05582/2-3111. 83 rms (all with bath). A/C MINIBAR TV TEL **Bus:** 3 minutes from Shimoda Station.

$ Rates (per person, including two meals and service): ¥20,000 ($143); ¥38,000 ($271) in summer. AE, JCB.

This reasonably priced ryokan opened in 1954. Located an 8-minute walk from Shimoda Station, it has friendly front-desk personnel and features a small outdoor swimming pool and hot-spring baths. Western-style breakfasts are available if ordered the night before.

HAJI ⑤⑤**, 708 Sotoura-Kaigan, Shimoda City. Tel. 05582/2-2597.** 7 rms (4 with toilet only). A/C TV **Bus:** 10 minutes from Shimoda Station.

$ Rates (per person, including two meals): ¥6,500 ($46). No credit cards.

Haji is a small, clean, and simple minshuku with seven rooms, four of which have their own toilet. The owner speaks English and is happy to see foreign guests. His place is located in a part of Shimoda called Sotoura, which boasts its own beach and is popular with vacationing families.

DOGASHIMA

112 miles SW of Tokyo

GETTING THERE By Bus From Shimoda, it takes 1 hour to reach Dogashima by bus.

By Boat There are boats from Numazu to Dogashima.

ESSENTIAL INFORMATION The telephone **area code** for Dogashima is 0558.

The **tourist office** (tel. 0558/52-1268) is located across the street from the bus terminal in a tiny one-room building not far from the boat pier. It's open Monday through Friday from 8:30am to 5pm, and on Saturday from 8:30am to noon; closed national holidays. During July and August, it remains open every day from 8:30am to 5pm.

With its fishing boats, tiny lanes and back alleyways, sandy beach, clear water, and rock formations jutting out of the sea, Dogashima is one of my favorite villages on Izu's west side. There's not much to do here except relax, swim, and walk around—which may be exactly what you're looking for.

WHERE TO STAY

GINSUISO ⑤⑥, **2977-1 Nishina, Nishi-Izu-cho. Tel. 0558/52-2211.** 90 rms (all with bath). A/C MINIBAR TV TEL **Directions:** A 5-minute taxi ride from Dogashima bus stop.

$ Rates (per person, including two meals): Off-season ¥22,000 ($157); summer ¥33,000 ($236). AE, DC, JCB, MC, V.

The excellent service at Dogashima's most exclusive luxury-resort ryokan begins as soon as you arrive, with staff personnel at the door to greet you. This stunningly white hotel sprawls along a cliff over the sea and has its own private beach and outdoor swimming pool. All the rooms come with views of the sea. Because it's popular with large Japanese tour groups, you should book well in advance, particularly in summer.

Dining/Entertainment: In addition to a lounge, there's a cabaret show beginning nightly at 8pm.

Services: Free newspaper.

Facilities: Outdoor swimming pool, private beach.

KAIKOMARU ⑤⑦, **Nishi-Izu-cho, Sawada. Tel. 0558/52-1054.** 8 rms (none with bath). A/C TV **Directions:** A few minutes' walk from Dogashima bus stop.

$ Rates (per person, including two meals): ¥6,500 ($46). No credit cards.

At this tiny family-run minshuku on Dogashima's main road, no one speaks English. But the family, which seems to include everyone from small children to grandparents, is friendly if a bit shy. If you're gregarious and outgoing, you'll like this place. Use of the hot-spring bath costs ¥200 ($1.40) extra.

KYOTO

If you go to only one place in all of Japan, Kyoto should be it. As the only major Japanese city spared bombing attacks during World War II, Kyoto is charming and captivating. As you walk its narrow streets and along its tiny canals, you will be struck with images of yesterday. Old women in kimonos bend over their "garden," which may consist of only a couple of gnarled bonsai beside their front door. An open-fronted shop reveals a man making tatami mats, the musty smell of the rice mats reminiscent of earth itself. Perhaps you'll see a geisha shuffling to her evening appointment in Gion, a small enclave of solemn-brown wooden houses where the sounds of laughter and traditional Japanese music escape through shoji screens. Nijo Castle is still here, built by the Tokugawas and famous for its creaking floorboards, designed to warn of enemy intruders. The famous Ryoanji rock garden is here, a Zen garden of pebbles and stones. There is a pleasant stroll from Kiyomizu Temple to Heian Shrine, with tea gardens, pottery shops, and temples along the way. In the evening in the summertime, couples sit along the banks of the Kamo River, which cuts through the heart of the city.

As your Shinkansen bullet train glides into Kyoto Station, however, your first reaction is likely to be one of great disappointment. There's Kyoto Tower looming in the foreground, looking like some misplaced spaceship. Modern buildings and hotels surround you on all sides, making Kyoto look like just any other Japanese town.

But nestled in between all those buildings are an incredible 1,700 Buddhist temples and 300 Shinto shrines, narrow alleyways and willow-lined canals, gardens of rock and moss, and enough history to fill many volumes. If you stay here long enough, you'll grow to understand why I consider Kyoto Japan's most romantic city.

Kyoto has always led a rather fragile existence, as a look at any of its temples and shrines will tell you. Made of wood, they have been rebuilt countless times, destroyed through the years by man, fire, and earthquake. As a product of the past and the present, Kyoto is a synthesis of all that is Japan in the 20th century. No one who comes to this country should miss the wealth of experience this ancient capital has to offer.

WHAT'S SPECIAL ABOUT KYOTO

Temples & Shrines

☐ 1,700 Buddhist temples, including Kiyomizu Temple, Nanzenji Temple, Ginkakuji (Silver Pavilion), and Kinkakuji (Gold Pavilion).

☐ 300 Shinto shrines, including Heian Shrine.

Palaces, Castles, & Villas

☐ Kyoto Imperial Palace, home of the imperial family for more than 500 years.

☐ Nijo Castle, home of the Tokugawa shogun and considered the quintessence of Momoyama architecture.

☐ Katsura Imperial Villa and Shugakuin Imperial Villa, two of Japan's most famous villas, both with renowned gardens.

Gardens

☐ Heian Shrine Garden, typical of gardens constructed during the Meiji Period.

☐ Nijo Castle Garden, designed by famous gardener Kobori Enshu.

☐ Gardens of Katsura and Shugakuin imperial villas.

☐ Saihoji, famous for its moss garden.

☐ Ryoanji Temple, with the most famous Zen rock garden in Japan.

Japanese-Style Accommodations

☐ Ryokan in all price categories, making this one of the best cities in Japan to experience living as the Japanese do.

☐ The opportunity to spend the night at a temple or shrine.

Cuisine

☐ *Kyo-ryoori,* Kyoto cuisine with regional specialties.

☐ *Kyo-kaiseki,* a variation of kaiseki that includes regional specialties.

☐ Vegetarian tofu dishes, served at Buddhist temples and surrounding restaurants.

Shopping

☐ A mecca for shoppers looking for traditional crafts.

A BRIEF HISTORY

Kyoto served as Japan's capital for more than 1,000 years, from 794 to the Meiji Restoration in 1868. It was laid out in a grid pattern borrowed from the Chinese, with streets running north, south, east, and west. Its first few hundred years, from about 800 to the 12th century, were perhaps its grandest, a time when culture blossomed and the court nobility led luxurious and splendid lives. If you have any fantasies about old Japan, perhaps they fit into the Heian Period. There were poetry-composing parties and moon-gazing events. Buddhism flourished and temples were built. A number of learning institutions were set up for the sons and daughters of aristocratic families, and scholars were versed in both Japanese and Chinese.

Toward the end of the Heian Period, however, military clans began clashing for power, resulting in a series of civil wars that eventually pushed Japan into the feudal era of military government that lasted nearly 680 years—until 1868. The first shogun to rise to power was Yoritomo Minamoto, who set up his shogunate government in Kamakura. With the downfall of the Kamakura government in 1336, however, Kyoto once again became the seat of power for the country. The beginning of this era,

IMPRESSIONS

Temple of all earth's towns; of all the bell
Far-heard clear-calm whatever thunders roll!
—EDMUND BLUNDEN, "VOICE OF KYOTO," A HONG-KONG HOUSE, 1962

known as the Muromachi and Azuchi-Momoyama periods, was marked by extravagant prosperity and luxury, expressed in such splendid villas as Kyoto's Gold Pavilion and Silver Pavilion. Lacquerware, landscape paintings, and the art of metal engraving came into their own. Zen Buddhism was the rage. And despite the civil wars that rocked the nation in the 15th and 16th centuries and destroyed much of Kyoto, culture flourished. During these turbulent times Noh drama, the tea ceremony, flower arranging, and landscape gardening gradually took form.

Emerging as victor in the civil wars, Tokugawa Ieyasu established himself as shogun and set up his military rule in Edo (present Tokyo), far to the east. For the next 250 years Kyoto remained the capital in name only, and in 1868 (which marked the downfall of the Tokugawa shogunate and the restoration of the emperor to power), the capital was officially moved from Kyoto to Tokyo. Thus Tokyo mushroomed into the concrete megalopolis it is today. Kyoto, with a population of about 1½ million people, remains very much a city of the past.

1. ORIENTATION

ARRIVING

BY PLANE

If you're arriving in Japan at Osaka International Airport, there is frequent service to Kyoto via a special **airport bus** that will deliver you to Kyoto Station and major hotels in Kyoto. The trip takes from 60 to 90 minutes, depending on traffic and your destination, and fares average about ¥900 ($6.40).

BY TRAIN

One of the major stops on the Shinkansen bullet train, Kyoto is less than 3 hours away from Tokyo and only 20 minutes from Shin-Osaka Station in Osaka. There are also local commuter lines that connect Kyoto directly with Osaka Station and Sannomiya and Motomachi stations in Kobe. For information on train schedules, drop by the **Travel Service Center** at Kyoto Station or telephone 371-0036 between 10am and 6pm.

BY BUS

There's a **night bus** that departs Tokyo Station every evening for Kyoto, arriving the next morning. The fare is ¥8,030 ($57.35) one way.

TOURIST INFORMATION

The **Tourist Information Center (TIC)** is about a minute's walk from Kyoto Station's north side (take the Karasuma Central Exit out of Kyoto Station). It's located on the ground floor of the Kyoto Tower Building, Higashi-Shiokojicho, Shimogyo-ku (tel. 075/371-5649), with the entrance around the corner on Karasuma Dori Avenue. Open Monday through Friday from 9am to 5pm and on Saturday from 9am to noon, it has a staff that speaks excellent English and can help you with all your questions regarding Kyoto. The TIC distributes a great city map in English, and has brochures and leaflets not only on Kyoto but on other destinations in Japan as well. Be sure to pick up the leaflet *Walking Tour Courses in Kyoto*.

Keep in mind, however, that the TIC is closed on Sunday, Saturday afternoon, and weekdays after 5pm, so plan your arrival accordingly. Otherwise, there's the local

Kyoto City Information Office, also located on the station's north side. No one here speaks English, but you can pick up a map in English and get directions to your hotel. It's open daily from 8:30am to 5pm. You can also call the **Japan Travel-Phone** for any questions you might have regarding Kyoto and the surrounding area at 371-5649, daily between 9am and 5pm.

To find out what's going on in Kyoto in terms of festivals, special events, Kabuki or Noh performances, or exhibitions, call the **Teletourist Service** at 361-2911. This 24-hour service provides 90 seconds of recorded information in English on what's going on during the week.

TOURIST PUBLICATIONS

In addition to the brochures and leaflets distributed by the TIC, there are a couple publications with information on Kyoto. *Discover Kinki,* a monthly distributed free to hotels, travel agencies, and the TIC, tells of upcoming events and festivals in Kyoto and the neighboring cities of Osaka, Kobe, and Nara. Another monthly tabloid distributed free at hotels and restaurants is *The Kyoto Visitor's Guide,* which contains maps, a calendar of events, and information on sightseeing and shopping. In addition, a monthly English magazine called *Kansai Time Out* carries information and articles on Kyoto, Osaka, and Nara. It's available in Kyoto at both the Maruzen and Izumiya bookstores for ¥300 ($2.15).

CITY LAYOUT

Most of Kyoto's attractions and hotels are north of Kyoto Station. The largest concentration of restaurants, shops, bars, and nightlife activity spreads in a radius from the Kawaramachi–Shijo Dori intersection and includes a narrow street called Pontocho and the geisha district of Gion. Temples are sprinkled throughout Kyoto.

FINDING AN ADDRESS

Kyoto's address system is actually quite simple once you understand what the directions mean. Many of its streets are named. Those north of Kyoto Station that run east–west are numbered; for example, the *shi* of Shijo Dori Avenue means "four." *Agaru* means "to the north," *sagaru* means "to the south," *nishi-iru* means "to the west," and *higashi-iru* means "to the east." Thus an address that reads Shijo-agaru means "north of Shijo Dori (or Fourth) Avenue." In addition, many addresses indicate which cross streets a building is near. Therefore, the address for the Hotel Gimmond, which is Takakura Oike Dori, means that the hotel is near the intersection of Takakura Dori and Oike Dori. Complete addresses include the ward, or *ku,* such as Higashiyama-ku.

NEIGHBORHOODS IN BRIEF

Shimogyo-ku   The ward that stretches from Kyoto Station north to Shijo Dori Avenue, catering to tourists with its cluster of hotels and to commuters with its shops and restaurants.

Nakagyo-ku   The central part of Kyoto west of the Kamo River and embracing Kyoto's main shopping and nightlife districts, with most of the action on Kawaramachi and Shijo Dori avenues. In addition to its many shopping arcades, restaurants, and bars, Nakagyo-ku also has a number of exclusive ryokan, tucked away in delightful neighborhoods typical of old Kyoto. Home also of Nijo Castle, Nakagyo-ku is one of the most desirable places to stay in terms of convenience and atmosphere.

Higashiyama-ku   East of the Kamo River, this ward in eastern Kyoto boasts a number of the city's most famous temples and shrines, as well as a number of restaurants specializing in Kyoto cuisine and Buddhist vegetarian dishes. It's a great area for walking and boasts several ryokan as well.

Gion Kyoto's geisha entertainment district, where customers are entertained in traditional wooden geisha houses. These houses are not open to the public, but the area makes for a fascinating stroll.

Pontocho Kyoto's most famous street for nightlife, a narrow lane that parallels the Kamo River's west bank not far from the Kawaramachi–Shijo Dori intersection. It's lined with exclusive hostess clubs, bars, and restaurants that boast outdoor verandas that extend over the Kamo River.

2. GETTING AROUND

BY PUBLIC TRANSPORTATION
BY SUBWAY

There's only one subway line in Kyoto, which is useful only for going to the Imperial Palace. It runs from Kitayama in the north through Kitaoji and Kyoto Station to Takeda in the south. Fares range from ¥160 ($1.15) for the shortest distance to ¥520 ($3.70) from end to end, with service from 5:20am to about 11:20pm.

BY BUS

The easiest way to get around Kyoto is by bus. The city map given out by the TIC shows major bus routes. Some of the buses travel in a loop around the city, while others go back and forth between two destinations. At any rate, get on at the back of the bus. If the bus is traveling a long distance out to the suburbs, there will be a ticket machine right beside the back door—take the ticket and hold on to it. It has a number on it and will tell the bus driver when you got on and how much you owe. You can see for yourself how much you owe by looking for your number on a panel at the front of the bus. Unsurprisingly, your fare rises the longer you stay on the bus. If you're on a loop bus, however, the fare is the same no matter how long you stay on—¥180 ($1.28)—and you pay when you get off. Exact fare is required, which you drop into the machine next to the driver. There's also a change machine for ¥100 and ¥500 coins and ¥1,000 bills. There are no transfer tickets, so you have to pay separately for each ride. For convenience, you may wish to purchase a booklet of seven bus tickets (called *kaisuken*) for ¥1,000 ($7.15), available from bus drivers.

BY TAXI

Taxis in Kyoto come in three different sizes, with correspondingly different fares. Small ones are ¥470 ($3.35) for the first 2 kilometers (1.25 miles), medium-sized ones are ¥480 ($3.40), and large ones are ¥500 ($3.55). Taxis can be waved down, or, in the city center, boarded at marked taxi stands or at hotels.

BY CAR

See "Getting Around" section of Chapter 3.

RENTALS

There are many car-rental agencies in Kyoto. Among them are: **Mazda Rent-A-Car,** Kawaramachi-Nishi-Iru, Gojo-dori, Shimogyo-ku (tel. 361-0201); **Nippon Rent-A-Car,** Higashi-Kujo Muromachi (tel. 671-0919); **Nissan Rent-A-Car,** 26, Nishi-

Kujo-Inmachi, Minami-ku (tel. 661-2161); and **Toyota Rent-A-Lease,** Sanjo-agaru, Karasuma Dori Avenue, Nakagyo-ku (tel. 241-0100).

PARKING

As in the rest of Japan, parking is a problem in Kyoto, especially because many streets are too narrow to accommodate both parking and traffic. There are several parking garages around Kyoto Station, as well as parking lots in Nakagyo-ku. Major hotels also offer parking.

DRIVING RULES

Because Kyoto is laid out in a grid pattern, driving by car is not as difficult as in many Japanese cities. However, with traffic often congested, it ends up being a slow way to get around the city. In addition, there are many one-way streets, particularly in the center of the city. Parking is another headache. You are best off walking and using Kyoto's public transportation.

BY BICYCLE

A popular way to get around Kyoto is by rental bike, made easy because there are few hills and most streets are named. **Rental Pia Service,** located across the street from Kyoto Station's south exit, next to Nippon Rent-A-Car, rents bicycles for about ¥1,200 ($8.55) a day (tel. 672-0662).

 KYOTO

Area Code The area code for Kyoto is **075.**

Baby-sitters Your best bet is to inquire at your hotel. Major hotels can usually arrange a sitter, often a staff member.

Bookstores There are two conveniently located stores selling books in English. **Maruzen,** Kawaramachi Takoyakushi-agaru, Nakagyo-ku (tel. 241-2161), part of a national bookstore chain, stocks novels as well as books on Japan. Located north of the Kawaramachi–Shijo Dori intersection, it's open Thursday through Tuesday from 10am to 7pm (6:30pm on Sunday and holidays). **Izumiya Book Center** is in the Avanti department store just south of Kyoto Station (tel. 671-8998). It's open Friday through Wednesday from 10am to 8pm.

Business Hours Banks are open Monday through Friday from 9am to 3pm. An establishment with longer hours is the High Touch Plaza of the Kyoto Shinyo Kinko Bank, located on Shijo Dori Avenue, Yanagino-banba, Shimogyo-ku (tel. 211-2111). It's open Thursday through Tuesday from 10am to 5pm, including holidays. **Department stores** in Kyoto stay open from 10am to 7pm, while **smaller shops** in the downtown area remain open from about 10am to 8pm.

Car Rentals See "Getting Around" above.

Climate See "When to Go" in Chapter 2.

Currency See "Information, Entry Requirements & Money" in Chapter 2.

Currency Exchange In addition to **banks,** another place to exchange money is at the **large department stores** like Takashimaya, Daimaru, and Kintetsu. If you need to cash a traveler's check outside these hours and your hotel doesn't have the facilities to do so, both the **Grand and New Miyako hotels** will cash traveler's checks even if you are not a hotel guest.

Credit cards are accepted by most major establishments. If you need to use your credit card to obtain a cash advance, Sanwa Bank, Karasuma Shijo, Shimogyo-ku (tel. 211-1111), handles American Express; Tokai Bank, Shijo Karasuma-agaru, Nakagyo-ku (tel. 221-7061), handles MasterCard; and Sumitomo Bank has two locations for VISA—Karasuma Sanjo-agaru, Nakagyo-ku (tel. 221-2111), and Shijo Kawaramachi-nishi, Shimogyo-ku (tel. 223-2821).

Dentist   The **Tourist Information Center (TIC)** (tel. 371-5649) has a list of approximately half a dozen dentists who speak English.

Doctor   The **TIC** (tel. 371-5649) has a list of approximately a dozen doctors who speak English. If the TIC is closed or you'd rather talk to a doctor directly, **Dr. Sakabe**, Gokomachi, Nijo-sagaru, Nakagyo-ku (tel. 231-1624), is an internist who speaks excellent English, and he can refer you to other doctors as well.

Drugstores   Drugstores, called kusuri-ya in Japanese, are open the usual business hours and are found throughout the city. For aspirin and other minor needs, there are convenience stores open late into the night.

Electricity   In both Kyoto and Nara it's 100 volts, 60 cycles, almost the same as in the United States (110 volts and 60 cycles).

Emergencies   The same all over Japan, the national emergency telephone numbers are 110 for police and 119 for calling an ambulance or for reporting a fire.

Film   See "Photographic Needs" below.

Hairdressers and Barbers   Several hotels in Kyoto have both beauty salons and barbershops where you're most likely to find someone who speaks English. Consult the hotel section for hotels with such facilities. Department stores also have beauty salons.

Holidays   See "When to Go" in Chapter 2.

Hospitals   Most hospitals are not equipped to handle emergencies 24 hours a day, but a system has been set up in which hospitals handle emergencies on a rotating basis. If you go by ambulance, it must take you to one of these. The **Kyoto Second Red Cross Hospital (Daini Sekijuji Byoin)**, Marutamachi-sagaru, Kamanza Dori, Kamikyo-ku (tel. 231-5171), is staffed 24 hours a day, but referral by a doctor who knows your problem is expected. English is spoken at **Japan Baptist Hospital** (Nihon Baputesuto Byoin), 47 Yamanomoto-cho, Kitashirakawa, Sa-kyo-ku (tel. 781-5191). Other hospitals in Kyoto include the **Kyoto University Hospital (Kyoto Daigaku Byoin)**, Shogoin Kawahara-cho, Sakyo-ku (tel. 751-3111), and the **Kyoto Municipal Hospital (Kyoto Shiritsu Byoin)**, Gojo Dori Onmae, Nakagyo-ku (tel. 311-5311).

Information   See "Information, Entry Requirements & Money" in Chapter 2.

Laundry and Dry Cleaning   Most hotels provide laundry and dry cleaning services, but usually not on Sunday and holidays. Since laundromats are common in Japan, ask at your hotel for the location of the nearest one.

Lost Property   If you left something on the Shinkansen bullet train, call 691-1000 to see whether it's been found. Items lost at Kyoto Station are turned in to the lost-and-found office (tel. 371-0134). If you lost something along a street or outside, contact the Shichijo Police Station (tel. 371-2111). Forgetting something in a taxi is a bit more complicated—you have to know which taxi company to call. The **MK Taxi Company** number is 721-4141; the privately owned green taxis all report to 314-4481 and 661-2244. Another number to call for items left in taxis is 691-6518. Because it's so difficult to track down items left in taxis, the TIC suggests you visit their office if you have any problems.

Luggage Storage/Lockers   Kyoto Station has lockers for storing luggage beginning at ¥200 ($1.40) for 24 hours.

Newspapers and Magazines   The *Japan Times, International Herald Tribune,* and other newspapers published in Tokyo are available in Kyoto. In addition, *Kansai Time Out,* with information on the arts and entertainment in Kyoto, Osaka, and Kobe, is sold in bookstores.

Photographic Needs   There are many camera and film shops in Nakagyo-ku, especially on Shijo and Kawaramachi Dori avenues and in the covered shopping arcades. Department stores also sell film.

Police   See "Emergencies" above.

Post Office   The **Kyoto Central Post Office** is located just west of Kyoto Station at 843-12 Higashi-shiokoji-cho, Shimogyo-ku (tel. 365-2471). It's open

Monday through Friday from 9am to 7pm, on Saturday from 9am to 5pm, and on Sunday and holidays from 9am to 12:30pm. You can mail packages bound for international destinations here. You can also have your own mail delivered Post Restante here, but you have to pick it up within 1 month if it's international mail and within 10 days if it's domestic.

Prefecture   Kyoto city is the capital of Kyoto Prefecture.

Rest Rooms   Hotel lobbies, fast-food chains, coffee shops, subway stations, and Kyoto Station are the best places to look for restrooms.

Safety   Kyoto, like Tokyo and other cities in Japan, is generally safe. Yet there are precautions you should take whenever you're traveling in an unfamiliar city or country. Stay alert and be aware of your immediate surroundings. Wear a money belt and keep a close eye on your possessions. Be especially careful with cameras, purses, and wallets—all favorite targets of thieves and pickpockets. Be doubly alert when walking along dark streets and in public parks after dark (in fact, if you're alone, it would be wiser to stay out of parks after dark). Every society, even one as relatively safe as Japan's, has its criminals. It's your responsibility to exercise caution at all times, even in the most heavily touristed areas.

Shoe Repairs   Department stores have shoe repair counters.

Taxes   For information on taxes applied to goods, and to hotel and restaurant bills, see "Fast Facts: Japan" in Chapter 3.

Taxis   See "Getting Around" earlier in this chapter.

Television   Major hotels in Kyoto have cable TV, called **ACTV,** available on Channel 5. English-language programs are available throughout the day, including CNN broadcasts and information on local sightseeing.

3. ACCOMMODATIONS

There are many types of accommodations available in Kyoto, from exclusive Japanese inns to business hotels to rock-bottom dormitorylike lodgings. If you've never stayed in a ryokan, Kyoto is probably the best place to do so. With the possible exception of some hot-spring resorts, Kyoto has more choices of ryokan in all price categories than any other city in Japan. Small, usually made of wood, and often situated in delightfully quaint neighborhoods, these ryokan can enrich your stay in Kyoto by putting you in direct touch with the city's traditional past. Remember that in upper- and medium-priced ryokan the room charge is per person, and though the prices may seem prohibitive at first glance, they include two meals and service charge. The meals are feasts, not unlike kaiseki meals you'd receive at a top restaurant. Ryokan in the budget category, on the other hand, usually do not serve meals unless stated otherwise, and they often charge per room rather than per person.

But even if you decide to stay in a hotel, Kyoto has excellent choices in all price ranges (many hotels also have Japanese-style rooms available). Whichever type of accommodation you select, make reservations in advance. Kyoto is a favorite holiday destination for the Japanese, receiving as many as 10 million visitors each year.

Remember that for rooms costing ¥15,000 ($107) and more, a 6% tax will be added to your bill. For rooms costing less than ¥15,000, a 3% tax will be added. In addition, upper-range hotels will add a 10% to 15% service charge.

Because Kyoto is relatively small and is served by such a good bus system, no matter where you stay you won't be too far away from the heart of the city. Most hotels and ryokan, however, are concentrated around Kyoto Station (Shimogyo-ku ward) in central Kyoto, not far from the Kawaramachi–Shijo Dori intersection (Nakagyo-ku ward), and east of the Kamo River (called Higashiyama-ku and Sakyo-ku wards).

FROMMER'S SMART TRAVELER: HOTELS

TIPS FOR THE VALUE-CONSCIOUS TRAVELER

1. Stay at least one night at one of Kyoto's many Japanese-style inns (ryokan), where guests can experience sleeping on a futon in a tatami room.
2. Meals in a ryokan are both elaborate and offer the chance to experience local Kyoto cuisine.
3. Reserve one of the Japanese-style rooms in Western-style hotels; they combine the traditional way of sleeping with the conveniences offered by hotels.
4. Prefer smaller, cheaper rooms in large hotels, where guests can take advantage of facilities ranging from outdoor pools to a variety of restaurants.
5. If you're on a limited budget, order a room without a private bathroom; such rooms are much cheaper.

QUESTIONS TO ASK IF YOU'RE ON A BUDGET

1. Are service charge and tax included in the price? If not, what is the total charge per night?
2. Are meals included in the ryokan price? If so, is it possible to stay without taking your meals there?
3. Are prices different for double and twin-bedded rooms? Some hotels charge more for a twin, others for a double.
4. Is there a cheaper room available than the one at the price quoted? Most hotels and inns have rooms in various price categories, depending on size of room, facilities, and location.
5. How much is the surcharge on local and long-distance telephone calls?
6. Is there parking space at the hotel, and if so, what is the charge per day?

EXPENSIVE

The service and hospitality at Kyoto's first-class hotels and ryokan are legendary. After all, Kyoto has had centuries of practice catering to members of the imperial court, feudal lords, shoguns, and their emissaries. Following in their footsteps, you, too, will be treated like royalty. Western-style hotels in this category have the extra benefit of English-language ACTV cable TV, with CNN newscasts from the United States and information on local sightseeing attractions, plus such services as room service, available usually until midnight; concierge service, with an English-speaking guest-relations officer; and other extras.

WESTERN STYLE
Around Kyoto Station

KYOTO GRAND HOTEL, Horikawa-Shiokoji, Shimogyo-ku, Kyoto 600. Tel. 075/341-2311. Fax 075/341-3073. 506 rms. A/C MINIBAR TV TEL
Transportation: From 8am to 9pm, free hotel shuttle bus every 15 minutes from Kyoto Station's Hachijo Guchi exit; otherwise, a 10-minute walk from Kyoto Station.
$ Rates: ¥13,000–¥18,500 ($93–$132) single; ¥19,800–¥26,000 ($141–$186) double/twin; ¥38,000 ($271) quad. Japanese-style rooms: ¥33,000 ($236) single or double. AE, DC, JCB, MC, V.
Built in 1969 just before the Osaka Expo, this has been one of Kyoto's grand hotels ever since. The building's flat roof and railed ledges resemble traditional Japanese architecture, while the inside is a successful blend of traditional and modern. The

rooms, for example, have shoji screens and fresh-flower arrangements, yet come with remote-control bilingual TV (with CNN) soundproof windows, clock, radio, and other modern conveniences. There's an English-language guest-relations coordinator, and the hotel also issues its own maps and sightseeing information on Kyoto in English.

Dining/Entertainment: Eight superb restaurants are popular with Kyoto's residents, including the city's only revolving restaurant and Gourmand Tachibana, where French food is served kaiseki style.

Services: Free shuttle bus to Kyoto Station, free English-language newspaper, same-day laundry service, baby-sitting service.

Facilities: Indoor swimming pool (fee: ¥1,500 or $10.70), sauna (men only), Jacuzzi (women only), beauty salon, barbershop, souvenir shop, clothing and accessories shop.

Central Kyoto

ANA HOTEL KYOTO, Nijojo-mae, Horikawa Dori, Nakagyo-ku, Kyoto 604. Tel. 075/231-1155, or toll free 800/ANA HOTELS in the U.S. and Canada. Fax 075/231-5333. 303 rms. A/C MINIBAR TV TEL **Bus:** 9 or 52 from Kyoto Station to Nijojo-mae.

$ Rates: ¥11,000–¥17,600 ($78–$126) single; ¥20,000–¥28,000 ($143–$200) twin; ¥23,000–¥25,000 ($164–$178) double. AE, DC, JCB, MC, V.

One of Kyoto's newer hotels, it's located just across the street from Nijo Castle—and some rooms have views of the castle grounds. This property has one of the most stunning lobbies in town, complete with a glass wall overlooking an impressive waterfall and tiny landscape garden. The service is excellent, and there's even a service desk to help you make travel plans for the city and beyond. Rooms are attractive and comfortable, with well-crafted furniture reflecting Asian design and with lots of space in the bathrooms for spreading out cosmetics and toiletries. None of the singles face the castle; twin and double rooms that do so start at ¥25,000 ($178).

Dining/Entertainment: First-rate restaurants serve Japanese, Chinese, and Western cuisine. Particularly outstanding is Nijo, a French restaurant that serves both traditional cuisine and French kaiseki meals.

Services: Free English-language newspaper twice a day, same-day laundry service.

Facilities: Indoor swimming pool and sauna (fee: ¥3,000 or $21.40), baby-sitting room, beauty salon, shopping arcade.

KYOTO BRIGHTON HOTEL, Nakadachiuri, Shinmachi-dori, Kamigyo-ku, Kyoto 602. Tel. 075/441-4411. Fax 075/431-2360. 183 rms. A/C MINIBAR TV TEL **Subway:** Imadegawa Station, an 8-minute walk away.

$ Rates: ¥18,500–¥30,000 ($132–$214) single; ¥24,000–¥36,000 ($171–$257) double; ¥25,000–¥35,000 ($178–$250). AE, DC, JCB, MC, V.

The newest deluxe hotel in Kyoto is near the Imperial Palace. Named after England's seashore resort to evoke a sense of light, airy brightness, the Brighton Hotel flaunts space with a huge, six-story atrium rising above the lobby and glass-enclosed elevators. With space at such a premium in Japan, the air in this atrium is a statement of luxury. The corridors to all rooms ring the atrium and are well lit, so even women traveling alone should feel very safe here. Accommodations are large, the more expensive rooms containing a couch and lounging area separated from the bedroom by a partition. There are no single rooms; rather, people traveling alone can stay in double or twin-bedded rooms at cheaper rates. Needless to say, service is superb, even though this hotel is a bit far from the action. For many guests, that's precisely why they stay here.

Dining/Entertainment: There are seven restaurants serving French, Japanese, and Cantonese food, including Kyoto-style kaiseki.

Services: Free English-language newspaper twice a day, same-day laundry service, baby-sitting service.

Map: Kyoto, Japan

Inset: JAPAN · TOKYO · Kyoto

Hotel Legend:

- Hotel Alpha **37**
- ANA Hotel Kyoto **39**
- Dai-ichi Hotel Kyoto **32**
- Hotel Gimmond **33**
- Higashiyama Youth Hostel **27**
- Hiiragiya Bekkan **36**
- Hiiragiya Ryokan **34**
- Hinomoto **23**
- Hiraiwa Ryokan **13**
- Hotel Hokke Club **5**
- International Hotel Kyoto **40**
- Kinmata **25**
- Kuwacho Ryokan **9**
- Kyoto Brighton Hotel **41**
- Kyoto Central Inn **24**
- Kyoto Central Hotel **7**
- Kyoto Dai-San Tower Hotel **4**
- Kyoto Gion Hotel **22**
- Kyoto Grand Hotel **2**
- Kyoto Holiday Inn **49**
- Kyoto Park Hotel **18**
- Kyoto Royal Hotel **30**

Map labels include: Shugakuin, Ichijoji, Chayama, Takano Bashi, Keifuku Eizan Line, Mototanaka, Chionin Temple, Ginkakuji Temple, Demachiyanagi, Shimogawa Shrine, Aoi Bashi, Kamo Izumoji Ohashi, Kuramaguchi Dori, Kitaoji Bashi, Kamo Ohashi, Marayama Park, Heian Shrine, Okazakimichi, Yoshidahondori, Higashioji Dori, Kamo River, Takano River, Kojin Bashi, Biwako Sosui Canal, Marutamachi Ohashi, Nijo Ohashi, Oike Ohashi, Sanjo Ohashi, Higashiyama Sanjo, Keage, Tozai Line, Kyoto Old Imperial Palace, Karasuma Dori, Imadegawa, Kuramaguchi, Kitaoji Dori, Shimei Dori, Omiya Dori, Kyu Shirakawa Dori, Ichijo Dori, Konoe Dori, Kasugakita Dori, Nijo Dori, Nioman Dori, Teramachi Dori, Gokomachi Dori, Fuyacho Dori, Tominokoji Dori, Yanaginobanba Dori, Sakaimachi Dori, Takakura Dori, Ainomachi Dori, Higashinotoin Dori, Kurumayacho Dori, Muromachi Dori, Koromonodana Dori, Shinmachi Dori, Wakamiya Dori, Ogawa Dori, Aburanokoji Dori, Nishinotoin Dori, Takeyamachi Dori, Ebisugawa Dori, Nijo Dori, Oshikoji Dori, Oike, Aneyakoji Dori, Sanjo Dori, Ryogaemachi Dori, Marutamachi Dori, Shimodachiuri Dori, Imadegawa Dori, Kisse River

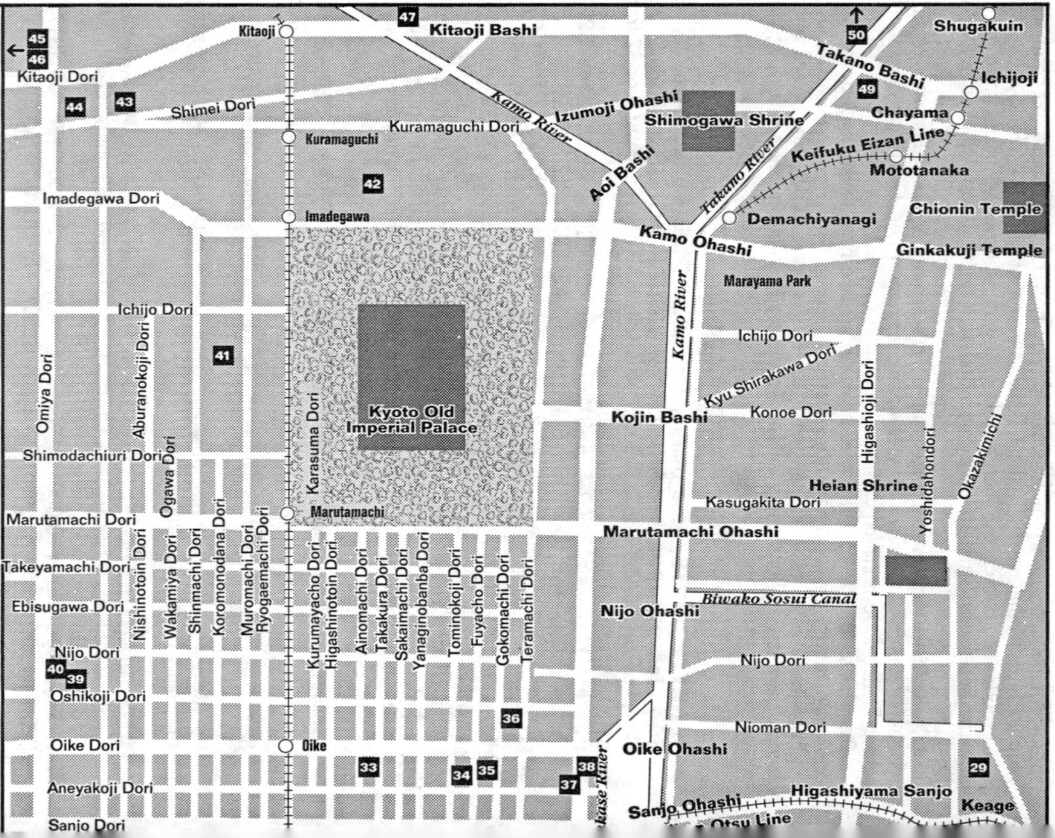

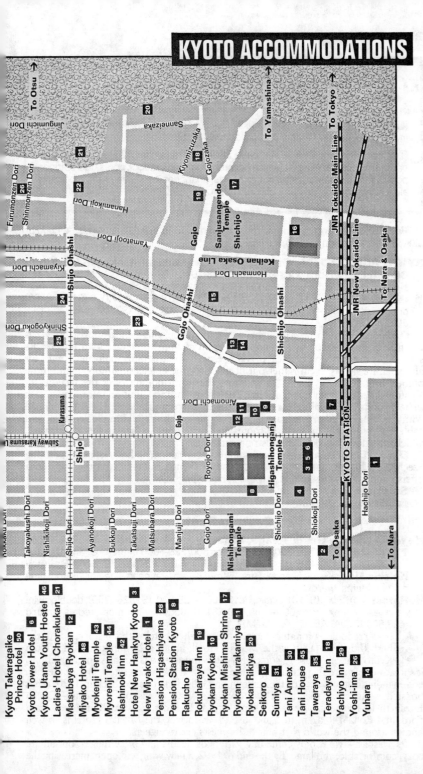

KYOTO ACCOMMODATIONS

Kyoto Takaragaike Prince Hotel 50
Kyoto Tower Hotel 6
Kyoto Utane Youth Hostel 46
Ladies' Hotel Chorakukan 21
Matsubaya Ryokan 12
Miyako Hotel 49
Myokenji Temple 43
Myorenji Temple 44
Nashinoki Inn 42
Hotel New Hankyu Kyoto 3
New Miyako Hotel 1
Pension Higashiyama 28
Pension Station Kyoto 8
Rakucho 47
Rokuharaya Inn 19
Ryokan Kyoka 10
Ryokan Mishima Shrine 17
Ryokan Murakamiya 11
Ryokan Rikiya 20
Seikoro 15
Sumiya 31
Tani Annex 30
Tani House 45
Tawaraya 35
Teradaya Inn 18
Yachiyo Inn 29
Yoshi-ima 26
Yuhara 14

FROMMER'S COOL FOR KIDS
HOTELS

ANA Hotel Kyoto (see page 271) A supervised baby-sitting room and an indoor pool please parents and children alike at this modern hotel.

Kyoto Holiday Inn (see page 280) Children under 12 stay free in their parents' room at this hotel, which boasts indoor and outdoor pools (the outdoor pool is free to hotel guests), tennis courts, an indoor ice-skating rink, a bowling alley, and a mall with many children's favorite, McDonald's.

Facilities: Outdoor swimming pool open only in July and August (fee: ¥4,000 or $28.55), beauty salon, souvenir shop.

KYOTO ROYAL HOTEL, Sanjo-agaru Kawaramachi, Nakagyo-ku, Kyoto 604. Tel. 075/223-1234. Fax 075/223-1072. 331 rms. A/C MINIBAR TV TEL
Bus: 4, 14, or 205 from Kyoto Station to Kawaramachi-Sanjo stop.
$ Rates: ¥10,500–¥17,500 ($75–$125) single; ¥18,500–¥27,000 ($132–$193) double; ¥22,000–¥25,000 ($157–$178) twin; ¥35,000 ($250) quad. AE, DC, JCB, MC, V.
In the heart of Kyoto on Kawaramachi Dori Avenue, this typical tourist hotel has recently undergone complete renovation in an attempt to elevate it to upper-class status. The result is a bit comical in some respects—the bellboy uniforms, a must for all expensive hotels, seem rather out of place for the hotel's small lobby (and those pillbox hats are a bit much). In addition, the Royal doesn't offer the facilities of Kyoto's other top hotels. Still, it has a convenient location, plus an information desk to help guests with local sightseeing. The rooms are comfortable and bright, equipped with the usual hairdryer, extra telephone in the bathroom, alarm clock, radio, and cable TV. Note that most single rooms and some doubles face an inner courtyard, which cuts down on noise but also on sunshine.
Dining/Entertainment: Six restaurants and bars, including restaurants serving Szechuan (Chinese) and Kyo-ryoori cuisine. A French restaurant on the 10th floor offers panoramic views of the city and surrounding hills.
Services: Free newspaper.
Facilities: Gift shop.

Eastern Kyoto

MIYAKO HOTEL, Sanjo Keage, Higashiyama-ku, Kyoto 605. Tel. 075/ 771-7111, or toll free 800/223-6800 or 800/228-3000 in the U.S. and Canada. Fax 075/751-2490. 366 rms. A/C MINIBAR TV TEL **Keihen Electric Railway Keishin Line:** Keage Station. **Bus:** 5 from Kyoto Station to Jingumichi stop, then a few minutes' walk.
$ Rates: ¥16,500 ($118) single; ¥18,500–¥35,000 ($132–$250) double/twin. Japanese annex: ¥26,000–¥49,000 ($186–$350), with most rooms around ¥28,500 ($204) AE, DC, JCB, MC, V.
If you're looking for an older, more established hotel with a history, one of the best known in Japan is the Miyako Hotel, about a 20-minute taxi ride from Kyoto Station. Close to some of Kyoto's most famous temples and attractions, it spreads over more than 16 acres on top of a hill at the northeastern end of the city, commanding a good view of the surrounding hills. First opened back in 1890, it has boasted a guest list that reads like a Who's Who of visitors to Japan—Queen Elizabeth II, Prince Charles and Diana, Anwar El-Sadat, Edward Kennedy, Gerald Ford, and Ronald Reagan, to name just a few. In fact, the Miyako Hotel is so well known around the world that half of its guests are foreigners.

Its Western-style rooms come in a variety of décors and price ranges, but all are cozy, comfortable, and large. By the end of 1992, a new wing will open, increasing the number of rooms to 540. Twenty Japanese-style rooms are available in an annex (connected to the main hotel by a covered passageway) that manages to maintain the atmosphere of a traditional ryokan with views of a Japanese garden.

Dining/Entertainment: Restaurants serve Japanese, Chinese, and Western food. There are also three bars and a lounge.

Services: Free English-language newspaper twice a day, same-day laundry service, baby-sitting service, free parking.

Facilities: Japanese garden, shopping arcade, beauty salon, barbershop, indoor and outdoor swimming pools (by end of 1992).

KYOTO PARK HOTEL, Sanjusangendo Side, Higashiyama-ku, Kyoto 605. Tel. 075/525-3111. Fax 075/551-4350. 300 rms A/C MINIBAR TV TEL **Bus:** 206 or 208 from Kyoto Station to Sanjusangendo-mae stop.

$ Rates: ¥10,000–¥13,200 ($71.40–$94) single; ¥21,000–¥26,000 ($150–$186) twin; ¥22,000 ($157) double. Weekday discount of ¥1,000 ($7.15) available. AE, DC, JCB, MC, V.

Located across the street from the National Museum, this hotel is a good starting point for strolls through eastern Kyoto, including the pleasant walk from nearby Kiyomizu Temple to Heian Shrine. With its stained-glass windows, plants, and statues, it's reminiscent of a European hotel, with grounds that include both a rock garden and one containing a waterfall, cliff, and pond. Flowered wallpaper brightens up the rooms, primarily twins, which come with the usual TV (with ACTV cable), hot-water pot, minibar, and alarm clock. Especially nice are the more expensive twin rooms on the fifth floor, each with a balcony overlooking the garden.

Dining/Entertainment: On the premises are French, Chinese, and Japanese restaurants, a sushi bar, a coffee shop, a lobby lounge, and a bar.

Services: Same-day laundry service, baby-sitting service.

Facilities: Shopping arcade, beauty parlor.

Northern Kyoto

KYOTO TAKARAGAIKE PRINCE HOTEL, Takaragaike, Sakyo-ku, Kyoto 606. Tel. 075/712-1111, or toll free 800/228-3000 in the U.S. and Canada. Fax 075/712-7677. 322 rms. A/C MINIBAR TV TEL **Taxi:** 30 minutes from Kyoto Station.

$ Rates: ¥33,000–¥38,000 ($236–$271) single/double/twin. AE, DC, JCB, MC, V.

Although a bit inconveniently located on the northern fringes of the city, this hotel is useful for those attending conferences in the Kyoto International Conference Hall across the street. Another advantage is nearby Takaragaike Park, complete with jogging paths, pond, botanical garden, and wood-covered hills. If you want the benefits of being in the countryside but don't want to give up the comforts of a first-class hotel, this may be the place for you.

Designed by the famous architect Togo Murano, this imposing circular hotel has the unmistakable touches of a Prince Hotel, including its excellent service, cheerful staff, and its bright color schemes of white, pink, and purple. The rooms are positively palatial, with a sink and vanity area separated from the bathroom. Upon arrival at the hotel, you will be treated to a complimentary tea and sweet, brought to your room by a kimono-clad hostess. With a higher staff-to-guest ratio than any other hotel in Kyoto, it is the only one in Kyoto to offer 24-room service. Should you have any questions regarding the hotel or Kyoto during your stay, there's a guest-relations officer on duty to help arrange everything—from reserving train tickets to arranging picnics in the park.

Dining/Entertainment: Beaux Séjours, under the direction of a French chef, is the hotel's signature restaurant. Other restaurants serve Japanese food, including sushi and tempura, and Chinese cuisine from Peking. There are also a coffee shop and a bar.

Services: Complimentary green tea upon arrival, free English-language newspapers twice a day, 24-hour room service, same-day laundry service, baby-sitting service, free shuttle bus to Kyoto Station.

Facilities: Business center, beauty salon, souvenir shop, traditional tea house (tea ceremony, with tea and sweets, costs ¥1,000 or $7.15).

JAPANESE STYLE
Central Kyoto

HIIRAGIYA RYOKAN, Anekoji-agaru, Fuyacho, Nakagyo-ku, Kyoto 604. Tel. 075/221-1136. Fax 075/221-1139. 33 rms (28 with bath and toilet, 3 with toilet only). A/C MINIBAR TV TEL **Taxi:** 10 minutes from Kyoto Station.

$ Rates (per person, including two meals and service): ¥22,000 ($157) without bathroom; ¥28,000–¥80,000 ($200–$571) with bathroom. AE, DC, JCB, MC, V.

⭐ As fine an example of a traditional inn as you'll find in Japan, this exquisite ryokan opened more than 150 years ago as a seafood merchant's shop, and was converted into an inn in 1861 to cater to visiting merchants. Under the same family ownership for five generations, it offers the ultimate in Japanese-style living, with a very accommodating staff that is helpful in initiating foreigners unfamiliar with Japan to the joys of the traditional inn. Located on the corner of Fuyacho and Oike streets in the heart of old Kyoto, the ryokan hides hidden behind walls of wood and earth-toned yellow mortar, topped by a traditional tiled roof. Entry is through a stone courtyard, with the rest of the ryokan making artful use of wood, bamboo, screens, and stones in creating a haven of simple design.

The best room in the house is number 30, with magnificent views of the garden; at ¥80,000 ($571) per person, however, it is probably a bit out of range for most of us. The next most expensive room is the one I find the most beautiful, a corner room with antiques and plenty of sunshine, going for ¥65,000 ($464) per person. All accommodations are decorated with art and antiques. Even the remote controls for the lights and curtains are artfully concealed in specially made lacquered boxes shaped like gourds (invented by the present owner's great-grandfather). Western-style breakfasts are available upon request. Guests who have stayed here include princes of the Japanese royal family, former Prime Minister Tojo, Charlie Chaplin, and designer Pierre Cardin. The three public baths and the tubs in the guest rooms—all handmade—are of Chinese pine, soft to the touch.

KINMATA ⑱, 407 Gokomachi, Shijo-agaru, Nakagyo-ku, Kyoto 604. Tel. 075/221-1039. Fax 075/231-7632. 6 rms (none with bathroom, 1 with toilet only). A/C TV TEL **Bus:** 4, 5, or 14 from Kyoto Station.

$ Rates (per person, including service charge): ¥13,000 ($93), including breakfast; ¥27,000–¥38,000 ($193–$271), including two meals. No credit cards.

⭐ First opened in the early 1800s, this is a beautiful traditional wooden inn in the heart of Kyoto. Its earliest customers were medicine peddlers, and in the hallway hangs an old sign announcing the house rules of past centuries—no gambling, no prostitution, no mah-jongg, and no noisy parties. The present owner represents the seventh generation of innkeepers here and is renowned as a chef, preparing kaiseki meals for his guests. Even if you don't stay here, you can come just for a meal. With only six rooms, Kinmata is exquisite inside and out, complete with an inner courtyard and peaceful garden. The public bath is of cypress. The place is located just north of Shijo Avenue on Gokomachi Street.

SUMIYA, Fuyacho-dori, Sanjo-sagaru, Nakagyo-ku, Kyoto 604. Tel. 075/221-2188. Fax 075/211-2267. 25 rms (17 with bath) A/C MINIBAR TV TEL **Taxi:** 10 minutes from Kyoto Station.

$ Rates (per person, including two meals and service): ¥33,000 ($236) without bath; ¥44,000–¥75,000 ($314–$536) with bath. AE, DC, JCB, MC, V.

⭐ Another traditional Japanese inn located on Fuyacho-dori Street, this one offers excellent service amid simple yet elegant surroundings. Some rooms have wonderful views of tiny private gardens, with outdoor benches or platforms for sitting. Western breakfasts are available, and meals feature Kyoto kaiseki cuisine. Not far from the other ryokan listed here, Sumiya has a great location in a typical Kyoto neighborhood, and yet is less than a 10-minute walk from downtown Kyoto.

TAWARAYA, Fuyacho, Oike-Sagaru, Nakagyo-ku, Kyoto 604. Tel. 075/ 221-5566. Fax 075/211-2204. 19 rms (all with bath). A/C TV TEL **Taxi:** 10 minutes from Kyoto Station.
$ Rates: ¥24,000–¥35,000 ($171–$250) per person, including two meals; ¥38,000 ($271) double occupancy for room only (no meals). AE, DC, JCB, V.

Across the street from the Hiiragiya is another distinguished, venerable old inn, which has been owned and operated by the same family since it opened in the first decade of the 1700s. The present owner is Mrs. Toshi Okazaki Sato, who represents the 11th generation of innkeepers. Unfortunately, fire consumed the original building, so the oldest part of the ryokan now dates back only 175 years. This inn also has had an impressive list of former guests, including the king of Sweden, former Canadian Prime Minister Pierre Trudeau, Leonard Bernstein, and Barbra Streisand. Saul Bellow wrote in the ryokan's guest book, "I found here what I had hoped to find in Japan—the human scale, tranquillity, and beauty." With refined taste reigning supreme, each room here is different and exquisitely appointed. Some, for example, have glass sliding doors opening onto a mossy garden of bamboo, stone lanterns, and manicured bushes, with cushions on a wooden veranda from which you can soak in the peacefulness.

Eastern Kyoto

SEIKORO, Tonyamachi, Gojo-sagaru, Higashiyama-ku, Kyoto 605. Tel. 075/561-0771. Fax 075/541-5481. 24 rms (all with bath). A/C TV TEL **Bus:** 205 from Kyoto Station to Kawaramachi Gojo stop. **Keihan Electric Railway:** Gojo Station.
$ Rates: ¥22,000–¥60,000 ($157–$428) per person, with two meals and service; ¥27,000–¥44,000 ($193–$314) double occupancy for room only (no meals). AE, DC, JCB, MC, V.

Established in 1831, the present ryokan dates from about a century ago. After passing through a traditional front gate and small courtyard, you'll find yourself in a cozy parlor replete with an eclectic mixture of both Japanese and Western antiques, including an old grandfather clock. The rooms, also decorated in antiques, are very homey and comfortable; some overlook a garden. Rooms in an annex built just before the 1964 Olympics are high enough up so that you can see over the surrounding rooftops, but I always prefer rooms in the oldest buildings. The owner, who speaks good English, doesn't mind if you take your meals elsewhere, especially if you're going to be here for a while. Seikoro is located just a few minutes' walk east of the Kamo River.

YACHIYO INN, 34 Nanzenji-Fukuchicho, Sakyo-ku, Kyoto 606. Tel. 075/771-4148. Fax 075/771-4140. 25 rms (20 with bathroom). A/C TV TEL **Bus:** 5 from Kyoto Station to Hosho Jicho stop.
$ Rates (per person, including two meals and service): ¥22,000 ($157); without meals 30% less. AE, DC, JCB, MC, V.

Located on the approach to Nanzenji Temple, this inn has a large foreign clientele. Formerly a villa (it became a ryokan after World War II), the building is about 100 years old but has been remodeled so that it seems almost new. All accommodations on the ground floor open onto a small garden; less expensive ones are located on the second floor. There are wooden bathtubs in most rooms, along with showers and Western toilets. Rooms also boast transom carvings and ikebana flower arrangements. This ryokan doesn't mind if you prefer to take your meals elsewhere. If you're staying in Kyoto for a few days, you might want to first take breakfast and dinner at the ryokan and then later start going out to Kyoto's many restaurants.

MODERATE

Accommodations in this category are numerous and offer excellent value for the money, with prices lower than those in Tokyo. All the Western-style hotels listed below have private bathrooms connected to all their guest rooms. The Japanese-style ryokan offer rooms with and without a bathroom, as well as communal baths and toilets.

WESTERN STYLE
Around Kyoto Station

KYOTO CENTURY HOTEL, 680 Higashishiokoji-cho, Shiokoji-sagaru, Higashinotoin-dori, Shimogyo-ku, Kyoto 600. Tel. 075/351-0111. Fax 075/343-3721. 243 rms. A/C MINIBAR TV TEL **Directions:** Less than a 2-minute walk east of Kyoto Station.

$ **Rates:** ¥10,000–¥13,500 ($71–$96) single; ¥14,800–¥25,000 ($106–$178) double; ¥20,000–¥23,000 ($124–$164) twin. Japanese-style rooms: ¥38,000–¥60,000 ($271–$428) double or single occupancy. AE, DC, JCB, MC, V.

Located just east of Kyoto Station, this brick hotel features a four-story atrium lobby, five restaurants and bars, a souvenir shop, a hair salon, and an outside swimming pool (fee: ¥2,100 or $15). All rooms include TV (with CNN broadcasts) and minibar, and there are also spacious Japanese-style rooms available that are actually two-room suites with kitchenette. Ask for a room facing east toward Higashiyama-ku. Although the view is nothing special, it's a lot better than the view toward the west, which looks squarely at the rooms of a neighboring hotel. Services here include those at some of the upper-class hotels, including a free English-language newspaper, same-day laundry service, room service, and overnight film development.

KYOTO TOWER HOTEL, Karasuma Shichijo, Shimogyo-ku, Kyoto 600. Tel. 075/361-3211. Fax 075/343-5645. 158 rms A/C TV TEL **Directions:** Across street from Kyoto Station's north side (Karasuma Central exit).

$ **Rates:** ¥7,000–¥10,500 ($50–$75) single; ¥12,500–¥22,000 ($89–$157) twin; ¥14,000–¥18,500 ($100–$132) double; ¥18,000 ($144) triple. Japanese-style rooms: ¥24,000 ($171) double occupancy. AE, DC, JCB, MC, V.

It's hard to miss the Kyoto Tower Hotel, right across the street from Kyoto Station. Topped by Kyoto Tower (with an observation platform), this place was built just before the 1964 Olympics and is now a cross between a tourist hotel and a business hotel. Because of the tower and the connecting souvenir shops, there's a lot of traffic through the lower floors of the hotel, but you'll find the eighth-floor lobby and restaurant a bit more peaceful. Rooms, on the fifth to ninth floors, are soundproof and feature shoji screens, minibar, hot-water pot, and alarm clock, among other amenities. The bathrooms and tubs are tiny.

HOTEL NEW HANKYU KYOTO, Shiokoji-dori, Shimogyo-ku, Kyoto 600. Tel. 075/343-5300. Fax 075/343-5324. 319 rms. A/C MINIBAR TV TEL **Directions:** A minute's walk from Kyoto Station's north side (Karasuma Central exit).

$ **Rates:** ¥10,000–¥12,000 ($71–$86) single; ¥17,500–¥28,000 ($125–$200) twin; ¥20,000–¥22,000 ($143–$157) double. Japanese-style rooms: ¥35,000 ($250) double occupancy. AE, DC, JCB, MC, V.

Across the street from Kyoto Station's north side, this is one of the better hotels in this category. About 20% of its guests are foreigners, and of particular help to visitors is its information desk in the lobby, where the English-speaking staff can answer any questions you might have regarding your stay in Kyoto. The front-desk staff is very efficient and polite. Restaurants include a steakhouse and a Chinese restaurant, as well as a branch of the famous Minokichi Restaurant. Rooms are pleasant, with a décor of subdued colors, and come equipped with the usual minibar, radio, alarm clock, and hot water for tea, as well as a hairdryer and TV (with ACTV cable showing CNN and pay movies). The more expensive twins face the station and have soundproof windows; the doubles all face toward the back of the hotel, which delivers a free English-language newspaper to its guests.

NEW MIYAKO HOTEL, Hachijo-guchi, Kyoto Station, Kyoto 601. Tel. 075/661-7111, or toll free 800/336-1136. Fax 075/661-7135. 714 rms A/C MINIBAR TV TEL **Directions:** A 3-minute walk from Kyoto's south side (Hachijo-guchi exit).

$ **Rates:** ¥7,500–¥10,500 ($53–$75) single; ¥13,200–¥23,000 ($94–$164)

twin; ¥18,500–¥26,000 ($132–$186) double; ¥27,000 ($193) triple. AE, DC, JCB, MC, V.
With the Miyako name behind it, this is one of the most popular hotels in this category. Opened in 1975, it's a sister hotel to the older, first-class Miyako Hotel and is conveniently located just across the street from Kyoto Station's south side. With lower prices than the first-class Miyako Hotel, as well as a modern exterior and simple décor, it appeals widely to younger Japanese, group tours, and individual tourists. A 10-story white building shaped like an H. it has souvenir and gift shops, a beauty salon and barbershop, seven restaurants and bars, as well as a rooftop beer garden that is open every evening (5 to 9pm) from April to September. Rooms are what you'd expect in this price range, coming with the usual cable TV (with CNN English-language broadcasts), radio, minibar, and hot-water pot for tea.

Central Kyoto

HOTEL ALPHA, Kawaramachi, Sango-agaru, Nakagyo-ku, Kyoto 604. Tel. 075/241-2000. Fax 075/211-0533. 119 rms. A/C MINIBAR TV TEL **Bus:** 4, 14, or 205 from Kyoto Station to Kawaramachi-Sanjo bus stop.
$ Rates: ¥7,000–¥8,500 ($50–$61) single; ¥12,000–¥15,500 ($86–$111) double; ¥14,300–¥17,500 ($102–$125) twin. Japanese-style rooms: ¥24,000–¥29,000 ($171–$207) double occupancy. AE, DC, JCB, MC, V.
This small and pleasant brick business hotel, which opened in 1982, has a great location just off Kawaramachi Dori Avenue not far from where it meets Sanjo Dori Avenue. Its entrance is on a side street called Anekoji Dori. Semidouble-size beds are in almost all the rooms, which also have the usual TV with pay video, hot-water pot, and minibar. Hairdryers are available on request. Since the cheapest singles face an inner courtyard and are fairly dark, it may be worthwhile to dish out the extra yen for a brighter room. A few Japanese-style rooms are available. The hotel's one restaurant serves Kyoto cuisine.

DAI-ICHI HOTEL KYOTO, Higashino-toin, Sanjo-sagaru, Nakagyo-ku, Kyoto 604. Tel. 075/252-4411. Fax 075/211-7963. 118 rms. A/C MINIBAR TV TEL **Subway:** Oike Station, a 2-minute walk away.
$ Rates: ¥7,500–¥9,900 ($53–$71) single; ¥17,500–¥24,000 ($125–$171) twin; ¥12,000–¥17,500 ($86–$171) semidouble. AE, DC, JCB, MC, V.
Located near the Museum of Kyoto in the heart of old Kyoto is this pleasant and modern hotel with a bright marbled lobby that features a large ikebana flower arrangement as its focal point. Although it calls itself a tourist hotel, I consider it a business hotel, since 90 of its 118 rooms are singles. Rooms are of adequate size and come with minibar, hot-water pot and tea, radio, TV with pay movies, alarm clock, hairdryer, and cotton yukata, among other amenities. Note that the cheapest doubles are actually semidoubles (that is, rooms with only a semidouble-size bed). Restaurants serve French and Japanese food.

HOTEL GIMMOND, Takakura Oike Dori, Nakagyo-ku, Kyoto 604. Tel. 075/221-4111. Fax 075/221-8250. 145 rms. A/C MINIBAR TV TEL **Subway:** Oike Station, a 3-minute walk away.
$ Rates: ¥8,500–¥9,600 ($61–$68) single; ¥14,300 ($102) double; ¥14,800–¥21,000 ($106–$150) twin. AE, DC, JCB, MC, V.
Situated on Oike Dori Avenue, this smaller hotel calls itself a tourist hotel, although its rooms resemble those of a business hotel, being rather plain and bare but equipped with minibar, alarm clock, and TV with pay video. All rooms are soundproof, but I still think those that face away from Oike Dori Avenue are quieter. There's one restaurant serving Western food, plus one lounge.

INTERNATIONAL HOTEL KYOTO (Kyoto Kokusai Hotel), Horikawa Dori, Aburano Kohji, Nakagyo-ku, Kyoto 604. Tel. 075/222-1111. Fax 075/231-9381. 310 rms. A/C MINIBAR TV TEL **Bus:** 9 or 52 from Kyoto Station to Nijojo-mae.
$ Rates: ¥10,500–¥17,500 ($75–$125) single; ¥15,500–¥29,000 ($111–$207) double; ¥17,500–¥30,000 ($125–$214) twin. AE, DC, JCB, MC, V.

Opening more than 30 years ago in time for the 1964 Olympics and recently renovated, this hotel is located across from Nijo Castle. Despite its name, approximately 90% of its guests are Japanese. Its lobby overlooks a pleasant, lush garden, and facilities include five restaurants, two bars, and a shopping arcade. In summer it has a beer garden open from 5 to 9pm. Rooms are decorated with traditional shoji screens, yet have such modern conveniences as radio, clock, hairdryer, and telephone and clothesline in the bathroom, plus a toilet that sprays water at the push of a button (the Japanese version of the bidet). The higher-priced twins and doubles face the castle, but none of the singles do. Note that with the completion of room renovations, expected by 1993, prices will rise. Until then, the older, unrenovated rooms offer good value for the money.

Eastern Kyoto

KYOTO GION HOTEL, 555 Gion, Higashiyama-ku, Kyoto 605. Tel. 075/ 551-2111. Fax 075/551-2200. 135 rms. A/C MINIBAR TV TEL **Bus:** 206 from Kyoto Station to Gion bus stop.
$ Rates: ¥9,000–¥10,000 ($64–$71) single; ¥15,500–¥16,700 ($111–$119) twin; ¥18,500 ($132) triple. AE, DC, JCB, MC, V.
This is an older, simple hotel with no extra frills but a great location on Shijo Dori in the heart of Gion near Yanaka Shrine. Within easy walking distance of shops, nightlife, and the many sights in Higashiyama-ku, it has a Western and a Japanese restaurant, a bar, and a rooftop beer garden during the summer months. The lobby and front desk are up on the second floor. Rooms are simple, with ceiling-to-floor windows.

Northern Kyoto

KYOTO HOLIDAY INN, 36 Nishihiraki-cho, Takano, Sakyo-ku, Kyoto 606. Tel. 075/721-3131. Fax 075/781-6178. 267 rms. A/C MINIBAR TV TEL **Bus:** 206 from Kyoto Station to Takano bus stop.
$ Rates: ¥10,500 ($75) single; ¥14,800–¥23,000 ($106–$164) double/twin. Children under 12 stay free in parents' room. AE, DC, JCB, MC, V.
Although it's rather inconveniently located in the northeast corner of Kyoto, far from most of the city's sights, this inn provides facilities normally found only at resort hotels, including indoor and outdoor swimming pools (outdoor pool free to hotel guests), tennis courts, an indoor ice-skating rink, a sauna and gym, a golf-driving range, and a 100-lane bowling alley. A shopping and restaurant mall features a dozen different restaurants, ranging from McDonald's to Chinese to steak, and a rooftop beer garden (open from 5 to 9pm in the summer) has barbecued dishes you can cook at your own table. A number of different kinds of rooms are available, and all beds, even those in twin rooms, are of double size. The hotel maintains a shuttle-bus service to Kyoto and Demachiyanagi stations. Parking here is free.

JAPANESE STYLE
Central Kyoto

HIIRAGIYA BEKKAN, Gokomachi Dori St., Nijosagaru, Nakagyo-ku, Kyoto 604. Tel. 075/231-0151. Fax 075/231-0153. 14 rms (10 with toilet only). A/C MINIBAR TV TEL **Taxi:** 10 minutes from Kyoto Station.
$ Rates (per person, including two meals and service): ¥13,000–¥22,000 ($93–$157). AE, DC, JCB, MC, V.
⭐ Under the same management as the exclusive Hiiragiya Ryokan, this is a very good choice among Kyoto's medium-priced Japanese inns. Run by a friendly, accommodating staff, this small ryokan has a warm and homey feel to it. Opened 25 years ago, it's relatively new by ryokan standards but manages to transmit a traditional atmosphere, as most of the rooms open onto a small garden. The management prefers that you take your meals here.

Eastern Kyoto

RYOKAN RIKIYA ⑤⑨, Ryozen Kannon-mae, Higashiyama-ku, Kyoto 605. Tel. 075/561-2814. 10 rms (2 with bath). A/C MINIBAR TV TEL **Bus:** 206

from Kyoto Station to Yasui stop, then a 4-minute walk.

$ Rates (per person): Room only: ¥8,800 ($63) without bath, ¥11,000 ($78) with bath. Room and two meals: ¥20,000 ($143) without bath, ¥22,000 ($157) with bath. AE, DC, JCB, MC, V.

Ryokan Rikiya is located in front of Ryozen Kannon, between Kiyomizu Temple and Maruyama Park. This is a quiet family-run ryokan in a modern building. The best room is named Daiyu, has its own bathroom, and faces toward the front courtyard. This ryokan doesn't mind if you take your meals elsewhere.

YOSHI-IMA, Shinmonzen Street, Gion, Higashiyama-ku, Kyoto 605. Tel. 075/561-2620. Fax 075/541-6493. 20 rms (18 with bath). A/C TV TEL **Taxi:** 10 minutes from Kyoto Station.

$ Rates (per person including two meals and service): ¥20,000–¥33,000 ($143–$236). AE, DC, MC, V.

One of the best things about this ryokan is its location on Shinmonzen shopping street, in a quaint neighborhood of small wooden homes and antiques shops within easy walking distance of Gion and the Kawaramachi district. Much of the ryokan is relatively new and modern, although there are a few older rooms available in a wooden building for the same price. The best room has a view of the garden. Most of the guests here are booked through the Japan Travel Bureau, including foreigners. In fact, sometimes the whole ryokan is filled with foreigners only.

BUDGET

Kyoto abounds in budget accommodations, due in part to the many students and young people who flock to this cultural mecca. Most establishments in this category are Japanese style, but many of the hotels offer both Japanese- and Western-style rooms. Whereas many rooms in the business hotels have a private bathroom, rooms in Japanese-style ryokan often do not.

Remember also that unless otherwise stated, a 3% tax will be added to your bill. Some places also add a service charge.

WESTERN STYLE

These hotels and pensions, though Western-looking in construction and offering Western-style rooms, also offer Japanese-style tatami rooms. For Japanese inns offering a traditional ryokan experience, refer to the listing under "Japanese Style" that follows.

Around Kyoto Station

HOTEL HOKKE CLUB, Higashi-Shiokojicho, Shimogyo-ku, Kyoto 600. Tel. 075/361-1251. Fax 075/361-1255. 134 rms (35 with private bath, 6 with toilet only). A/C TV TEL **Directions:** Across street from Kyoto Station's north side (Karasuma Central exit).

$ Rates (including service): Japanese-style rooms: ¥7,500 ($53) single without bath or toilet, ¥8,300 ($59) single with toilet only, ¥9,000 ($64) single with bathroom; ¥13,500 ($96) double without bath or toilet, ¥14,300 ($102) double with toilet only, ¥15,400 ($110) double with bathroom. Western-style rooms: ¥6,800 ($48) single without bathroom, ¥9,000 ($64) single with bathroom; ¥11,500 ($82) double without bathroom, ¥14,900 ($106) double with bathroom. AE, DC, JCB, MC, V.

Across the street from Kyoto Station, this business hotel also caters to tourists because of its favorable location, and it offers both Japanese- and Western-style rooms. Take off your shoes before entering. The front desk is on the ground floor and the lobby is on the second floor. The ground floor also has a large tatami room used for Buddhist ceremonies twice a day by the hotel's employees, which you're welcome to observe. There are two public baths, large and bright, with windows extending along the length of one wall. You're better off asking for a room on a higher floor. The cheapest Japanese-style tatami rooms, without private bath, tend to be rather small and have tiny windows, but they come with TV (with video), radio, cotton kimono, hot-water pot, and sink. All rooms are very simple, with only the basics, though some have a stocked refrigerator as well.

KYOTO DAI-SAN TOWER HOTEL, Shinmachi-dori, Shichijo-sagaru, Shimogyo-ku, Kyoto 600. Tel. 075/343-3111. Fax 075/343-2054. 122 rms (all with bath). A/C TV TEL **Directions:** A 4-minute walk north of Kyoto Station.

$ Rates: ¥6,500–¥8,800 ($46–$63) single; ¥14,300 ($102) double; ¥11,000–¥15,900 ($78–$113) twin; ¥15,500–¥22,000 ($111–$157) triple. Japanese-style rooms: ¥15,500–¥22,000 ($111–$157) triple occupancy. AE, DC, JCB, MC, V.

Dai-San means "third," referring to the fact that this is the third Tower Hotel in Kyoto (look for the big sign on its façade that reads "3 Tower Hotel"). A simple business hotel, with one restaurant serving Western food, it offers clean Japanese- and Western-style rooms. Some rooms face another building and therefore have glazed windows. If looking outside is important to you, ask for a room with a view of the street. Vending machines dispense beer and soda.

KUWACHO RYOKAN, 231 Shichijo-agaru, Akezu-dori, Shimogyo-ku, Kyoto 600. Tel. 075/371-3191. 14 rms (all with bath). A/C TV TEL **Directions:** A 5-minute walk north of Kyoto Station.

$ Rates: ¥6,000 ($43) single; ¥8,800 ($63) double/twin; ¥13,200 ($94) triple. AE, V.

Despite its name, this place offers both Western- and Japanese-style rooms and is very conveniently located just north of Kyoto Station and east of Higashi Honganji Temple. A modern, concrete three-story building (no elevator), it offers rooms with coin-operated TV, safe for valuables, and cotton kimono, among other amenities. Rooms facing the front even have a small balcony. I prefer the Japanese-style rooms (somehow, bare rooms are more becoming to tatami than Western-style rooms). No meals are served.

PENSION STATION KYOTO, Shichijo-agaru, Shinmachi, Shimogyo-ku, Kyoto 600. Tel. 075/882-6200. Fax 075/862-0820. 16 rms (2 with bath). A/C TV. **Directions:** A 7-minute walk from Kyoto Station.

$ Rates: ¥4,100 ($29) single without bath; ¥8,300 ($59) double without bath, ¥9,900 ($71) double with bath; ¥11,500 ($82) triple without bath, ¥13,200 ($94) triple with bath. AE, MC, V.

A member of the Japanese Inn Group, this pension offers Japanese-style and Western-style rooms, two of the latter sleeping two or three persons and having a private bathroom. Located just west of Higashi Honganji Temple, the place gets a bit carried away in its use of fake flowers as decoration, but is nevertheless cheerful and spotlessly clean. Rooms come with coin-operated TV and heater, among other amenities, and there's a coin-operated laundry. Western breakfasts are available for ¥800 ($5.70), while Japanese dinners cost ¥1,800 ($12.85).

Central Kyoto

KYOTO CENTRAL INN, Shijo Kawaramachi, Nishi-iru, Shimogyo-ku, Kyoto 600. Tel. 075/211-1666. Fax 075/241-2765. 150 rms (all with bath). A/C TV TEL **Bus:** 4, 5, 14, or 205 from Kyoto Station to Shijo-Kawaramachi stop.

$ Rates: ¥6,000–¥7,500 ($43–$53) single; ¥9,300–¥11,000 ($66–$78) double/twin. AE, DC, JCB, MC, V.

As the name implies, this inn is centrally located in the heart of the city, near the intersection of Shijo and Kawaramachi streets. Although it's a business hotel, because it occupies one of the best spots in town, about 50% of its guests are tourists. Rooms are small but adequate, and come with radio, among other amenities. The hotel's coffee shop serves American breakfasts.

Eastern Kyoto

LADIES' HOTEL CHORAKUKAN, Maruyama Park, Higashiyama-ku, Kyoto 605. Tel. 075/561-0001. Fax 075/561-0006. 21 rms (all with toilet only). A/C TV TEL **Bus:** 206 from Kyoto Station to Yasaka stop, then a 7-minute walk.

$ Rates: ¥5,500 ($39) single; ¥9,900 ($71) double. No credit cards.

⭐ This small, eccentric-looking hotel is for women only and has a pleasant location on the edge of Maruyama Park. An imposing Western-style building constructed just after the turn of the century, it has modified its interior so much through the decades, mixing the grand with the gaudy, that the atmosphere is comically bizarre and somewhat quirky. The lobby, for example, has a chandelier and a high gilded ceiling, but the rest of the room sports plastic moldings and decorations. Each guest room is slightly different, and there are two Japanese-style rooms. A hotel with personality, it would make a great set for a comedy. Highly recommended.

PENSION HIGASHIYAMA, Sanjo-sagaru, Shirakawa-suji, Higashiyama-ku, Kyoto 605. Tel. 075/882-1181. Fax 075/862-0820. 13 rms (3 with bath). A/C TV **Bus:** 206 from Kyoto Station to Chion-in-mae stop, then a 2-minute walk.

$ Rates: ¥4,100 ($29) single without bath; ¥8,300 ($59) double without bath, ¥9,900 ($71) double with bath; ¥11,500 ($82) triple without bath, ¥13,200 ($94) triple with bath. AE, MC, V.

Opened in 1985, this clean, cheerful establishment on a small street banked by the Shirakawa River is not far from the Miyako Hotel on Kyoto's east side. Its rooms, some of which overlook the willow-lined stream, are mainly Western style, with flowered wallpaper and quilts on the bed, but three Japanese-style tatami rooms are also available. A few rooms have their own private bathroom. Rooms come with coin-operated TV, and there's a coin-operated laundry on the premises. The front doors are locked at 11:30pm. Pension Higashiyama is under the same management as Pension Station Kyoto and has the same fax number, so be sure to specify which pension you wish to reserve a room in.

JAPANESE STYLE

There isn't much variation in rooms in this category. After all, a tatami room is a tatami room and at this price there usually isn't much else in them. Rooms are fairly bare, with perhaps only a low table, a TV, some cushions, and a futon in the closet that you lay out yourself before retiring. Imparting a feeling of traditional Japan, however, these accommodations are highly recommended.

Around Kyoto Station

HINOMOTO, 375 Kotakecho, Matsubara-agaru, Kawaramachi Dori, Shimogyo-ku, Kyoto 600. Tel. 075/351-4563. Fax 075/351-3932. 6 rms (none with bath). A/C TV TEL **Bus:** 17 or 205 from Kyoto Station to Matsubara stop, then a 3-minute walk.

$ Rates: ¥3,800–¥4,400 ($27–$31) single; ¥7,500 ($53) double; ¥9,900–¥11,500 ($82) triple. Western breakfast ¥300 ($2.15); Japanese breakfast ¥1,000 ($7.15). AE, MC, V.

This ryokan is located a bit far from Kyoto Station (about a 30-minute walk north), but is convenient if you want to stay closer to the action around the Kawaramachi-Shijo Dori intersection. A two-story home, it has a front façade of brick but the rest is of wood. Although the couple running this ryokan do not speak much English, they welcome foreigners. Rooms are pleasant, the location is quiet and convenient, and the public bath is made of wood.

HIRAIWA RYOKAN, 314 Hayao-cho, Kaminoguchi-agaru, Ninomiyacho-dori, Shimogyo-ku, Kyoto 600 Tel. 075/351-6748. Fax 075/351-6969.

21 rms (none with bath). A/C TV **Bus:** 17 or 205 to third stop, Kawaramachi Shomen, then a 3-minute walk.

$ Rates: ¥3,800–¥4,900 ($27–$35) single; ¥8,000–¥8,800 ($57–$63) double; ¥12,000 ($86) triple. Western breakfast ¥300 ($2.15); Japanese breakfast ¥1,000 ($7.15). AE, MC, V.

⭐ This inexpensive ryokan is one of the best-known and oldest members of the Japanese Inn Group, and several feature stories have been published about it and the couple in charge. They speak almost no English and yet have been welcoming foreigners from all over the world for many years. Spread through the main building and a new annex, the guest rooms are spotless and come with towel and cotton kimono. Facilities include coin-operated washer and dryer, and there are even heated toilet seats. Breakfasts are communal affairs around the kitchen table. There are a small public bath and showers, but better still is the neighborhood public bath just around the corner, which charges ¥250 ($1.80). This ryokan is about a 15-minute walk from Kyoto Station, and it locks its front doors at 11pm.

RYOKAN KYOKA, Higashi-iru, Higashinotouin, Shimojuzuyamachi-dori, Shimogyo-ku, Kyoto 600. Tel. 075/371-2709. Fax 075/351-7920. 10 rms (none with bath). A/C TV **Directions:** An 8-minute walk from Kyoto Station.

$ Rates: Japanese-style rooms: ¥3,900 ($28) single; ¥7,900 ($56) double; ¥11,900 ($85) triple. Western breakfasts ¥350–¥700 ($2.50–$5); Japanese breakfasts ¥1,000–¥1,500 ($7.15–$10.70), Japanese dinners ¥3,000–¥5,000 ($21.40–$35.70). AE, MC, V.

This simple ryokan is located east of Higashi Honganji Temple and offers 10 tatami rooms with coin-operated TV. Facilities include a coin laundry, and there are bikes for rent. A member of the Japanese Inn Group, this is one of the few places to offer such an elaborate dinner.

MATSUBAYA RYOKAN, Nishi-iru, Higashinotouin, Kamijuzuyamachi Dori, Shimogyo-ku, Kyoto 600. Tel. 075/351-3727 or 351-4268. Fax 075/351-3505. 11 rms (none with bath). A/C TV TEL **Directions:** An 8-minute walk north of Kyoto Station.

$ Rates: ¥4,000–¥4,400 ($28–$31) single; ¥8,000–¥8,800 ($57–$63) double; ¥11,000 ($78) triple. Western breakfast ¥300 ($2.15); Japanese breakfast ¥1,000 ($7.15), Japanese dinner ¥3,000 ($21.40). AE, MC, V.

⭐ Located just east of Higashi Honganji Temple and a member of the Japanese Inn Group, this 180-year-old traditional ryokan is a great choice in this category. It's owned and managed by the friendly and irrepressibly energetic Mrs. Hayashi, representing the fifth generation of innkeepers. She'll talk on and on to you in Japanese, even if you don't understand, making you wish you did. Her best rooms have wooden balconies facing a miniature inner courtyard. Another good choice: the rooms facing a tiny enclosed garden. Reservations require a deposit equal to one night's lodging, payable by cashier's or traveler's check, international money order, or credit card. Towels and cotton kimonos are provided, and rooms have coin-operated TV. Facilities include two public baths and a coin-operated laundry. Highly recommended.

RYOKAN MURAKAMIYA, 270 Sasaya-cho, Shichijo-agaru, Higashi-notouin-dori, Shimogyo-ku, Kyoto 600. Tel. 075/371-1260. Fax 075/371-7161. 8 rms (none with bath). A/C TV **Directions:** A 7-minute walk northeast of Kyoto Station.

$ Rates: ¥3,900–¥4,400 ($28–$31) single; ¥7,900–¥8,800 ($56–$63) double; ¥10,800–¥11,800 ($77–$84) triple. AE, MC, V.

Not far from Matsubaya, this small and clean ryokan offers nicely decorated rooms—some with old-style ceilings and woodwork—in a 50-year-old traditional wooden building. The owner is friendly and accommodating and does her best to communicate, even though her English is limited. There's a coin-operated laundry, and a Japanese breakfast is available for ¥1,000 ($7.15) if you order it the night before. A member of the Japanese Inn Group, the ryokan locks its front door at 11pm.

YUHARA, Kiyamachi-dori, Shomen-agaru, Shimogyo-ku, Kyoto 600. Tel.

075/371-9583. 9 rms (none with bath). A/C TV **Directions:** A 10-minute walk from Kyoto Station. **Bus:** 17 or 205 from Kyoto Station to Kawaramachi Shomen stop (third stop), then a few minutes' walk.
$ Rates (per person): ¥3,800 ($27). No credit cards.

⭐ This small ryokan has been welcoming guests from all over the world for more than 30 years. Pleasantly located beside a tree-lined narrow canal in a quiet residential area, it's run by an enthusiastic woman who speaks English. There are nice touches everywhere, from the shoji screens and artwork in the rooms to the plants and bamboo decorations in the hallways. One of the rooms is Western style, and three have their own sink. The largest room looks out onto a miniature courtyard.

Central Kyoto

TANI ANNEX, Nishi-minami Kade Gokomachi, Nakagyo-ku, Kyoto 604. Tel. 075/211-5637. 2 rms (both with bath). A/C FRIDGE TV **Bus:** 4, 5, or 14 from Kyoto Station to Shijo-Kawaramachi bus stop.
$ Rates: ¥6,500 ($46) double. AE, DC, MC, V.

Ⓢ If you want to stay close to the action in the center of the city, Mrs. Tani (see also the listing for Tani House, below) rents out two rooms above a shop where her English-speaking daughter works, just off the covered shopping arcade in the center of town. Rooms are often rented out by the week or for longer periods, and there's a coin-operated laundry.

Eastern Kyoto

RYOKAN MISHIMA SHRINE, Umamachi-dori, Higashioji Higashi-iru, Higashiyama-ku, Kyoto 605. Tel. 075/551-0033. Fax 075/531-9768. 8 rms (with toilet only). A/C TV **Bus:** 206 from Kyoto Station to Higashiyama-Umamachi stop, then a 5-minute walk.
$ Rates: ¥4,400 ($31) single; ¥7,500 ($53) double; ¥11,500 ($82) triple. AE, MC, V.

This ryokan, a member of the Japanese Inn Group, is located on the grounds of Mishima Shrine, a small Shinto shrine visited by women who desire children and by women already pregnant who wish to ensure a safe delivery. You can have your picture taken in traditional shrine garb, free if you have your own camera and ¥240 ($1.70) if you have it taken with the shrine's Polaroid. Although the shrine was founded about 150 years ago, the Japanese-style rooms are located in a new building that opened in the mid-1980s. Spotless and simple, the ryokan caters largely to foreigners in the summer and to Japanese in the winter. Cotton kimonos and towels are provided, and rooms have coin-operated TV as well as a private toilet. Facilities include four public baths and a coin-operated washing machine. No meals are served. The family running this place speaks some English.

ROKUHARAYA INN ⑥⓪, 147 Takemuracho Rokuhara, Higashiyama-ku, Kyoto 605. Tel. 075/531-2776. Fax 075/551-2683. 7 rms (none with bath). A/C TV **Bus:** 206 from Kyoto Station to Gojozaka stop, then a 3-minute walk.
$ Rates (per person): ¥4,400–¥4,900 ($31–$35). Breakfast ¥700 ($5); dinner ¥2,000–¥3,000 ($14.30–$21.40). AE, V.

This inexpensive ryokan, located on a small residential street typical of Kyoto, offers just the basics. In my opinion the best rooms are on the second floor of this two-story, wooden building. More foreigners stay here than Japanese. Each room has coin-operated TV but not much more—just your average Japanese tatami room. There's a coin-operated laundry.

TERADAYA INN, 583 Higashi Rokuchome, Gojobashi, Higashiyama-ku, Kyoto 605. Tel. 075/561-3821. Fax 075/551-2683. 5 rms (none with bath). A/C TV **Bus:** 206 from Kyoto Station to Gojozaka stop, then a 5-minute walk.
$ Rates (per person): ¥5,500 ($39) single occupancy, no meals; ¥4,400 ($31.40) double occupancy, no meals. With breakfast ¥5,500 ($39); with dinner ¥8,500 ($61). AE, V.

Under the same ownership as Rokuharaya Inn (above) and therefore with the same fax number, this concrete inn is located just off the sloping approach to Kiyomizu Temple in east Kyoto, about halfway up (look for the large sign in English). Yukata are provided, and TVs and air conditioners are coin operated. Rooms on the second floor are the brightest. Facilities include a public bath and a coin-operated laundry.

Northern Kyoto

MYOKENJI TEMPLE ㉛, Teranouchi Horikawa, Kamigyo-ku, Kyoto 602. Tel. 075/414-0808 or 431-6828. 50 beds. **Bus:** 9 from Kyoto Station to Teranouchi stop, then a few minutes' walk.

$ Rates (per person, including breakfast): ¥4,400 ($31.40). No credit cards.

If you want to stay in a Buddhist temple and don't mind sharing a room, both Myokenji and Myorenji (below) have simple accommodations on their temple grounds. Myokenji, located in a pleasant, quiet residential area in north Kyoto, offers traditional tatami rooms surrounded by moss-covered gardens and bamboo. It is secluded and in a world of its own, almost as if it were out in the country instead of in a bustling city. Since most temples offering accommodations cater largely to groups, you should make a reservation here at least several weeks in advance. Most rooms are large, sleeping as many people as will fit into them; but if no group is booked, you're likely to have the place to yourself. As in all Buddhist temples, the breakfast served here is vegetarian.

MYORENJI TEMPLE ㉜, Teranouchi Horikawa, Kamigyo-ku, Kyoto 602. Tel. 075/451-3527. 40 beds. **Bus:** 9 from Kyoto Station to Teranouchi stop, then a few minutes' walk.

$ Rates (per person, including breakfast and ticket for neighborhood public bath): ¥3,300 ($23). No credit cards.

Not far from the above temple is Myorenji, founded more than 650 years ago and now run by a jolly woman named Chizuko-san, who speaks a little English. Since she manages this place virtually single-handedly, she prefers guests who stay 2 or 3 days and requests them to make reservations at least a week (and preferably a month) in advance. The temple buildings, about 200 years old, offer rooms with a view of gardens, including a rock garden with raked pebbles. Sleeping is on futon spread out in large rooms, and again it's possible that you'll have a room to yourself if no groups happen to be staying here. Since there are no bathing facilities on the temple grounds, guests are given a ticket to use the neighborhood bath. If you're interested in attending services, they're held every morning at 6:30am.

NASHINOKI INN, Agaru Imadegawa Nashinoki Street, Kamikyo-ku, Kyoto 602. Tel. 075/241-1543. 7 rms (none with bath). A/C TV **Subway:** From Kyoto Station to Imadegawa Station, then a 13-minute walk.

$ Rates: ¥5,200 ($37) single; ¥9,200 ($65) double; ¥13,200 ($94) triple. Japanese or Western breakfast ¥1,000 ($7.15). No credit cards.

In a quiet, peaceful neighborhood north of the Kyoto Imperial Palace, this ryokan is run by a warm and friendly older couple who speak some English. Staying here is like living with a Japanese family, since the home looks very lived in and is filled with the personal belongings of a lifetime. Some of the tatami rooms, which feature such touches as vases, Japanese dolls, and pictures, are quite large and adequate for families. Breakfast is served in your room.

RAKUCHO, 67 Higashihangi-cho, Shimogamo, Sakyo-ku, Kyoto 606. Tel. 075/721-2174. Fax 075/791-7202. 8 rms (none with bath). A/C TV **Bus:** 205 from Kyoto Station to Furitsu-Daigakumae bus stop, then a few minutes' walk. **Subway:** Kitaoji Station, then a 10-minute walk.

$ Rates: ¥3,600–¥4,400 ($25–$31) single; ¥7,000–¥8,300 ($50–$59) double; ¥9,900–¥12,200 ($71–$87) triple. AE, MC, V.

Located in north Kyoto, this ryokan is not as conveniently situated as most of the other inns listed above, but all of the rooms here are pleasant and clean, with heating and a view of a small, peaceful garden; some rooms also have a refrigerator. Entrance to the ryokan is through a well-tended tiny courtyard filled with plants. A member of the Japanese Inn Group, the place offers a coin-operated laundry.

TANI HOUSE, 8 Daitokujicho, Murasakino, Kita-ku, Kyoto. Tel. 075/

492-5489. 4 private rms (none with bath); 2 dormitory rms. A/C (in some rooms). **Bus:** 206 from Kyoto Station to Kenkunjinja stop, then a few minutes' walk.
$ Rates: ¥1,500 ($10.70) per person in dormitory room; ¥3,900–¥4,600 ($28–$33) double in private room. AE, DC, MC, V.

If you're looking for lodging at rock-bottom prices, the best place in town is Tani House, near Daitokuji Temple on the northern edge of Kyoto. The entrance of this 50-year-old wooden house is smothered with bamboo. This place, with a reputation that extends far beyond Japan's borders, is popular with young backpackers. Mrs. Tani, who speaks English, keeps the place tidy and clean, and sleeping is either in private rooms or in communal tatami sleeping rooms (separate for men and women). You're supposed to leave during the day, from 11am to 3pm, but rules are otherwise fairly lenient. Although Tani House is a bit far north, the price more than makes up for it.

YOUTH HOSTELS

HIGASHIYAMA YOUTH HOSTEL, 112 **Shirakawabashi-goken-cho, Sanjo-dori, Higashiyama-ku, Kyoto 605. Tel. 075/761-8135.** 130 beds. A/C **Bus:** 5 from Kyoto Station to Higashiyama-Sanjo stop (20-minute ride), then a few minutes' walk.
$ Rates (including breakfast and dinner): ¥3,500 ($25) member; ¥4,000 ($28) nonmember. No credit cards.
Of the several youth hostels in and around the Kyoto area, this is the most convenient and the closest to Kyoto Station. The modern concrete building has bunk beds, and guests are required to take breakfast and dinner here. Be sure to call in advance, since this place is sometimes booked full with school groups.

KYOTO UTANE YOUTH HOSTEL, 29 Nakayama-cho, Uzumasa, Ukyo-ku, **Kyoto 616. Tel. 075/462-2288.** Fax 075/462-2289. 168 beds. A/C **Bus:** 26 from Kyoto Station or 10 from Shijo-Kawaramachi to Youth Hostel–mae stop, then a 1-minute walk.
$ Rates: ¥2,300 ($16.40) member and nonmember. Breakfast ¥400 ($2.85); dinner ¥600 ($4.30). No credit cards.
Located in the northwestern part of the city near Ryoanji Temple, which is famous for its Zen rock garden, this youth hostel is a modern, concrete structure offering bunk-bed accommodation. Facilities include coin-operated laundry, bicycles for rent, tennis courts, and kitchen facilities.

4. DINING

Kyoto's specialties include vegetarian dishes, which arose to serve the needs of Buddhist priests and pilgrims making the rounds of Kyoto's many temples. Called

---

A NOTE ON JAPANESE SYMBOLS

Many hotels, restaurants, and other establishments in Japan do not have signs giving their name in English letters. As an aid to the reader, Appendix C lists the Japanese symbols for all such places described in this guide. Each set of symbols has a number, which corresponds to the number that appears inside an oval next to the establishment's boldfaced name in the text. Thus, to find the Japanese symbols for, say, Osaka's **Hotel Hokke Club** ⟨138⟩, refer to the number 138 in the appendix.

shojin ryoori, these vegetarian set meals include tofu simmered in a pot at your table (*yudofu*) and an array of local vegetables. Kyoto is also known for its kaiseki (Kyo-kaiseki), originally conceived as a meal to be taken during the tea ceremony but eventually becoming an elaborate feast enjoyed by the capital's nobility. Today, Kyoto abounds in restaurants serving both vegetarian tofu dishes and kaiseki courses fit for an emperor. A restaurant advertising that it serves Kyo-ryoori offers a variety of Kyoto cuisine.

Most of Kyoto's traditional Japanese restaurants are located in the heart of the city, in Nakagyo-ku, spreading to the east in areas called Higashiyama-ku and Sakyo-ku. Choices in fast food and reasonably priced set meals abound in restaurants around Kyoto Station, which cater to tourists, commuters, and shoppers. I have divided Kyoto's restaurants according to district, adding some Western-style restaurants as well.

AROUND KYOTO STATION

In addition to the restaurants listed here, a good place for inexpensive dining is **Kintetsu Mall,** located on the west side of Kyoto Station (under the tracks) and offering two dozen restaurants serving a wide variety of inexpensive meals. Check the "Dining Clusters/Complexes" section at the end of this chapter for more information.

EXPENSIVE

MINOKICHI, Hotel New Hankyu Kyoto, basement, Shiokoji Dori. Tel. 343-5300.
    Cuisine: KYO-KAISEKI/KYO-RYOORI. **Reservations:** Recommended. **Directions:** A 1-minute walk from Kyoto Station's north side.
$ Prices: Kyo-kaiseki ¥7,500–¥16,500 ($53.55–$117.85); Kyo-ryoori ¥3,800–¥5,500 ($27.15–$39.30); set lunches ¥2,200–¥3,300 ($15.70–$23.55). AE, DC, JCB, MC, V.
    Open: Daily 11:30am–9pm (last order).
A branch of the famous Minokichi restaurant first established in Kyoto more than 260 years ago, this establishment is designed to resemble a lane in a typical traditional Japanese village, with waitresses in kimonos and Japanese music playing in the background to help set the mood. The menu includes Kyoto-style kaiseki cuisine and

---

FROMMER'S SMART TRAVELER: RESTAURANTS
TIPS FOR THE VALUE-CONSCIOUS TRAVELER

1. Kyoto's many restaurants serve shojin ryoori, a vegetarian meal served in and around Buddhist temples and featuring tofu and local seasonal vegetables.
2. The teishoku, or daily special, is offered by Japanese restaurants at lunch or even the whole day, and usually consisting of a complete meal.
3. Lunch menus offered by most expensive and medium-range restaurants are at prices much cheaper than those charged for dinner menus.
4. Set courses, fixed-price meals, are offered for lunch and dinner.

QUESTIONS TO ASK IF YOU'RE ON A BUDGET

1. Is there a teishoku, daily special, or set course not on the English menu?
2. Is there a service charge? Most expensive restaurants and restaurants located in hotels will add a 10% or 15% service charge to your bill.

typical Kyoto dishes, as well as such Japanese favorites as obento lunch boxes and eel. Set lunches, served Monday through Saturday until 4pm, are especially good bargains, offering everything from eel to mini-kaiseki.

BUDGET

IZUSEN ⑥, **2nd floor of Surugaiya Building, Karasuma Shichijo Dori-sagaru. Tel. 343-4211.**
Cuisine: KYO-RYOORI/VEGETARIAN. **Directions:** A 1-minute walk from Kyoto Station, in building just north of Tourist Information Center, on Karasuma Dori.
$ Prices: Set meals ¥1,900–¥5,800 ($13.55–$41.40). No credit cards.
Open: Fri–Wed 11am–8pm.

Although the décor is simple, the food in this restaurant is great and beautifully presented, featuring local Kyoto and vegetarian dishes. There's an English menu, and seating is either at tables or on tatami mats. There are a variety of fixed-price meals from which to choose, offering soup, appetizer, rice, a main dish, and side dishes. A vegetarian meal for ¥1,900 ($13.55), for example, is a light meal usually served at a tea ceremony. I usually opt for the Matsu course, which costs ¥2,900 ($20.70) and features Kyoto cuisine, including tempura, sashimi, various vegetables, broiled fish, rice, and soup. This is one of my favorite restaurants in Kyoto.

GIO GIONO, 2nd floor of Renaissance Building, 849 Higashi Shiokojicho. Tel. 365-0202.
Cuisine: ITALIAN. **Directions:** A 1-minute walk northeast of Kyoto Station, in Renaissance Building on Shiokoji Dori Avenue.
$ Prices: Pasta and pizza ¥1,000–¥1,400 ($7.15–$10); meat dishes ¥1,400–¥2,200 ($10–$15.70); set-dinner courses ¥2,200–¥8,800 ($15.70–$62.85); set lunches ¥1,000–¥2,700 ($7.15–$19.30). AE, DC, JCB, MC, V.
Open: Daily 11:30am–10pm (last order 9:30pm).

Next to Kyoto Station is a relatively new building called the Renaissance Building, which features several restaurants, including a coffee shop, a Chinese restaurant, and a beer hall. Best for a meal, however, is Gio Giono, an informal Italian restaurant serving pizza, pasta, and such main dishes as fish, chicken grilled with olive-oil sauce, veal cutlet Milanese style, veal saltimbocca, and risotto. There's an English menu. An especially good deal is the ¥1,000 ($7.15) set lunch, available until 2pm and offering a choice of spaghetti, pizza or risotto, as well as salad, dessert, and coffee.

CENTRAL KYOTO

The heart of Kyoto's shopping, dining, and nightlife district is in Nakagyo-ku, especially on Kawaramachi and Shijo Dori avenues and in the many side streets.

EXPENSIVE

MANYOKEN, Fuyacho Shijo. Tel. 221-1022.
Cuisine: FRENCH. **Reservations:** Recommended. **Bus:** 4, 5, 11, 14, 203, or 207 to Shijo-Fuyacho stop.
$ Prices: Appetizers and soups ¥1,400–¥4,000 ($10–$28.55); main dishes ¥4,000–¥12,000 ($28.55–$85.70); set-dinner courses ¥10,000–¥20,000 ($71.40–$142.85); set lunch ¥7,500 ($53.55). AE, DC, JCB, MC, V.
Open: Lunch daily 11:30am–3pm; dinner daily 4:30–8:30pm (last order).

Located on Shijo Dori Avenue, Manyoken is one of Kyoto's best-known restaurants, with more than 70 years of experience serving French cuisine. With its chandeliers, fresh roses, white tablecloths, and drawing-room atmosphere, this elegant restaurant serves a set lunch for ¥7,500 ($53.55) and set dinners, all of which change monthly. A la carte selections include steak, lobster, fish, and chicken. Although the menu changes often, a typical meal here may start out with escargots in bourguignonne sauce, followed by onion soup, sirloin steak cooked with a special house sauce, and then baked Alaska or soufflé in curaçao or chocolate.

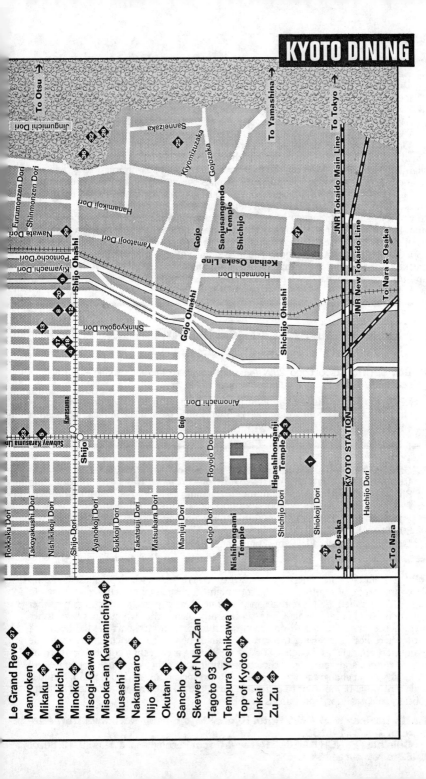

KYOTO DINING

Le Grand Reve **27**
Manyoken **4**
Mikaku **29**
Minokichi **1** **5**
Minoko **25**
Misogi-Gawa **10**
Misoka-an Kawamichiya **18**
Musashi **19**
Nakamuraro **36**
Nijo **28**
Okutan **31**
Sancho **20**
Skewer of Nan-Zan **21**
Tagoto 93 **12**
Tempura Yoshikawa **7**
Top of Kyoto **37**
Unkai **6**
Zu Zu **23**

MINOKICHI, basement under Bank of Tokyo, Kyoto Fukutoku Building, Karasuma Shijo-agaru. Tel. 255-0621.
Cuisine: KYO-KAISEKI/OBENTO/SHABU-SHABU. **Reservations:** Recommended. **Subway:** Shijo Station, a 3-minute walk away.
$ Prices: Kaiseki and dinner shabu-shabu set courses ¥5,500–¥16,500 ($39.30–$117.85); lunch obento and shabu-shabu ¥2,400–¥5,500 ($17.15–$39.30). AE, DC, JCB, MC, V.
Open: Daily 11:30am–9pm (last order).

Open for more than a decade, this is the largest Minokichi branch and has prices slightly lower than those of the main restaurant in Higashiyama-ku. It has low lighting, as well as latticed wood that separates the dining tables from one another, and it serves a variety of typical Japanese cuisine, including shabu-shabu, eel dishes, steak, and a kaiseki menu featuring Kyoto cuisine that changes monthly. If you want to try Kyo-kaiseki but can't afford evening prices, come for lunch and order the mini-kaiseki meal for ¥5,500 ($39.30), available until 3pm. It changes according to what's fresh and in season, but my meal was typical of the variety of dishes you get: appetizer vegetables and sashimi; Japanese potato filled with crabmeat; gelatin with chicken, salmon, and asparagus inside; pumpkin soup; buckwheat noodles with eel and mushroom; a small river fish; tempura; dessert; and Japanese frothy green tea.

FROMMER'S COOL FOR KIDS
RESTAURANTS

Gio Giono (*see page 289*) A casual Italian restaurant serving pizza and spaghetti, conveniently located near Kyoto Station.

El Pollo Loco (*see page 295*) This fast-food chain from California will not stretch your budget as you munch on chicken burgers, chicken legs, tortillas, and salsa.

MISOGI-GAWA ㉔, Sanjo-sagaru, Pontocho. Tel. 221-2270.
Cuisine: FRENCH KAISEKI. **Reservations:** A must. **Bus:** 4, 5, 14, or 205 to Shijo-Kawaramachi intersection, then a 5-minute walk.
$ Prices: Main dishes ¥3,000–¥5,000 ($21.40–$35.70); set-dinner courses ¥16,500–¥33,000 ($117.85–$235.70); set lunches ¥7,500–¥13,000 ($53.55–$92.85). AE, DC, JCB, V.
Open: Lunch daily 11:30am–2pm; dinner daily 4:30–9pm.

Serving nouvelle French cuisine that utilizes the best of Japanese style and ingredients in what could be called French kaiseki, this lovely and exclusive restaurant stands on a narrow street called Pontocho, which parallels the Kamo River and is one of Kyoto's most famous nightlife districts. Located in a century-old renovated wooden building that once belonged to a geisha, who used it as her entertainment house, Misogi-Gawa successfully blends the two cuisines into dishes artfully prepared and served on Japanese tableware. In fact, part of the delight of eating here lies in receiving the various courses of the fixed-price meals, each one exquisitely arranged as though a work of art. Dining is either at a counter or in private tatami rooms, and you have a choice of eating with either chopsticks or knife and fork. The menu changes monthly, and the lunch special for ¥7,500 ($53.55) includes a glass of wine. If you want to order à la carte, the menu (written in French) includes lobster, sole, scallops, and various beef dishes.

NIJO, basement of ANA Hotel Kyoto, Nijojo-mae, Horikawa Dori Avenue. Tel. 231-1155.
Cuisine: FRENCH KAISEKI. **Reservations:** Recommended. **Bus:** 9, 12, 50, or 52 to Nijojo-mae bus stop.

$ Prices: Set-dinner courses ¥11,000–¥16,500 ($78.55–$117.85); set lunches ¥4,400–¥6,600 ($31.40–$47.15). AE, DC, JCB, MC, V.
Open: Lunch daily 11:30am–2:30pm; dinner daily 5–10pm.

Another restaurant serving French food with a twist, Nijo is located on Horikawa Dori, across from Nijo Castle on Horikawa Dori Avenue. It achieves a successful marriage of French cuisine and kaiseki philosophy, serving one dish after the other rather than all of them at once. Portions are small, and each dish is elegantly and artistically arranged. Only set courses, which change with the seasons, are available. If you prefer steaks, there's a separate room with a teppanyaki counter, with a set-lunch course costing ¥4,400 ($31.40) and dinner courses starting at ¥11,000 ($78.55).

TEMPURA YOSHIKAWA, Tominokoji Dori, Oike-sagaru. Tel. 221-5544.
Cuisine: TEMPURA. **Reservations:** A must. **Subway:** Oike Station, a 7-minute walk away.
$ Prices: Tempura dinner courses ¥6,500–¥11,000 ($46.40–$78.55); tempura set lunches ¥2,200–¥4,400 ($15.70–$31.40). AE, DC, JCB, MC, V.
Open: Lunch Mon–Sat 11am–2pm; dinner Mon–Sat 5–8:30pm (last order).

If you're hungering for tempura, this restaurant near Oike Avenue with its sign in English is easy to find. Located in an old-fashioned part of Kyoto that boasts a number of expensive ryokan, it's a tiny, intimate place with a traditional atmosphere, and the counter seats only 12. It serves a tempura lunch for ¥2,200 ($15.70). If you feel like splurging, you can also order a kaiseki meal here—beginning at ¥7,500 ($53.55) for lunch and ¥13,000 ($92.85) for dinner—which will be served in a private tatami room.

UNKAI, ANA Hotel Kyoto, Nijojo-mae, Horikawa Dori Avenue. Tel. 231-1155.
Cuisine: KAISEKI/TEMPURA/VEGETARIAN. **Reservations:** Not necessary.
Bus: 9, 12, 50, or 52 to Nijojo-mae bus stop.
$ Prices: Appetizers ¥550–¥2,200 ($3.90–$15.70); main dishes ¥1,300–¥4,000 ($9.30–$28.55); shabu-shabu ¥8,800 ($62.85); vegetarian set courses ¥6,500 ($46.40); kaiseki ¥11,000–¥13,000 ($78.55–$92.85); set lunches ¥3,300–¥4,400 ($23.55–$31.40). AE, DC, JCB, MC, V.
Open: Lunch daily 11:30am–2:30pm; dinner daily 5–10pm.

In a convenient location across from the main entrance of Nijo Castle, this restaurant has a modern and refined décor, ceiling-to-floor windows, kimono-clad waitresses, and an English menu. The varied menu includes shabu-shabu, kaiseki, a vegetarian set meal typical of Kyoto, tempura, grilled fish, and sashimi.

MODERATE

ASHOKA, 3rd floor of Kikusui Building, Teramachi Dori. Tel. 241-1318.
Cuisine: INDIAN. **Bus:** 4, 5, 11, 12, 14, 203, 205, or 207 to Shijo-Kawaramachi intersection, then a 3-minute walk.
$ Prices: Main dishes ¥1,500–¥2,000 ($10.70–$14.30); set-dinner courses ¥2,700–¥6,000 ($19.30–$42.85); set lunch ¥1,400 ($10). AE, DC, JCB, MC, V.
Open: Lunch Wed–Mon 11:30am–2:30pm; dinner Wed–Mon 5–9pm.

One of Kyoto's most popular Indian restaurants, Ashoka serves vegetarian and meat curries, including mutton, chicken, fish, vegetable, and shrimp selections. I started my meal here with mulligatawny Madrasi, a South Indian soup, and followed with Indian bread stuffed with minced meat along with mutton sagwala (mutton and spinach). Ashoka is located just north of Shijo Dori at the beginning of the Teramachi covered shopping arcade.

IZUMOYA ⑥⑤, Pontocho, Shijo-agaru. Tel. 211-2501.
Cuisine: KAISEKI/SHABU-SHABU/SUKIYAKI/TEMPURA/EEL. **Reservations:** Recommended, especially for kaiseki. **Bus:** 4, 5, 11, 12, 14, 203, 205, or 207 to Shijo-Kawaramachi intersection, then a 1-minute walk.

$ Prices: Set courses ¥2,700–¥4,000 ($19.30–$28.55); shabu–shabu and sukiyaki ¥4,000 ($28.55); kaiseki ¥6,500–¥8,800 ($46.40–$62.85). AE, DC, JCB, V.
Open: Fri–Wed noon–9:30pm.

It's easy to find this restaurant, a many-storied place on Shijo Dori Avenue right beside the bridge spanning the Kamo River. The backside of the restaurant faces the river, and in the summer a wooden veranda is constructed on stilts over the water (open from 5 to 8:30pm). Popular with tourists and groups, Izumoya serves a wide variety of dishes on its various floors. On the third floor, shabu-shabu and sukiyaki are available, while on the second and fourth floors you can dine on set meals of tempura, sashimi, eel, and other Japanese dishes. Only kaiseki meals are served on the outdoor veranda. Although the menu is in Japanese only, there's a large display of plastic food at the front door.

KYOSHIKI, Fuyacho Dori, Sanjo-agaru. Tel. 221-4866.
   Cuisine: KAISEKI/KYO-RYOORI. **Reservations:** Not necessary. **Bus:** 4, 5, 11, 59, or 205 to Kawaramachi-Sanjo stop, then a 5-minute walk.
$ Prices: Set courses ¥3,300–¥8,800 ($23.55–$62.85). AE, DC, JCB.
   Open: Daily 11:40am–8:30pm (last order).

This reasonably priced kaiseki restaurant, just north of Sanjo Dori Avenue on Fuyacho Dori Street, was converted from a private home about 15 years ago by English-speaking Shoichi Hirayama. I recommend the Hisago fixed-price meal offered on the English menu, which is a variety of seasonal food served in individual dishes that stack neatly on top of one another to form a gourd; you take the bowls apart to eat. The atmosphere here is relaxed and comfortable, with regular customers stopping in for a chat with Mr. Hirayama. On Monday and Wednesday free tea and sweets are served with lunch.

TAGOTO 93, Shijo-Kawaramachi, Nishi-iru, Kitagawa. Tel. 221-1811.
   Cuisine: KYO-RYOORI/KAISEKI/OBENTO. **Reservations:** Not necessary.
   Bus: 4, 5, 11, 12, 14, 203, 205, or 207 to Shijo-Kawaramachi intersection, then a 1-minute walk.
$ Prices: Obento and set-price meals ¥3,000–¥3,800 ($21.40–$27.15); Kyo-ryoori ¥6,500–¥8,800 ($46.40–$62.85). AE, DC, JCB, MC, V.
   Open: Lunch daily 11am–3pm; dinner daily 4–8:30pm.

Nestled in an inner courtyard off busy Shijo Dori Avenue and offering a peaceful retreat in the heart of downtown Kyoto, this restaurant has been serving a variety of Japanese food at moderate prices for about 100 years. Its entrance is near the Kyoto Central Inn (look for a tiny door with a white sign; step through and follow the passageway to the back courtyard). The menu includes Kyo-ryoori set meals, tempura, eel dishes, obento lunch boxes, seasonal kaiseki courses, and sashimi. Noodles, costing only ¥750 ($5.35) to ¥1,400 ($10), are served for lunch as well.

BUDGET

BEER MARKET ICHIBA COJI, basement of Withyou Building, Tera-machi. Tel. 252-2008.
   Cuisine: CHINESE/PAO/ASIAN. **Bus:** 4, 5, 11, 12, 14, 203, 205, or 207 to Shijo-Kawaramachi bus stop, then a 4-minute walk.
$ Prices: Appetizers and soups ¥350–¥700 ($2.50–$5); main dishes ¥850–¥1,500 ($6.05–$10.70). AE, DC, JCB, V.
   Open: Daily 11:30am–10:15pm (last order).

It's difficult to classify this place, which calls itself a "Kyoto mini-brewery," serving its own original beer and claiming to have more beer on tap than any other establishment in Kyoto. But it is certainly much more than that. Visually it's the most interesting and exciting new-age restaurant I've seen in Kyoto, reminding me of high-tech establishments in Tokyo. In fact, it looks an awful lot like Doma in Harajuku, which was designed by the same architectural firm. Ichiba Coji features bare cement walls, white pebbles on the floor, black furniture, and an elevated dining platform above a running stream. The waitresses and cooks are all decked out in Asian baggy pants, and the food is eclectic, although I guess it's more Chinese than anything else. The menu includes spring rolls, fresh fish, sweet-and-sour pork, steamed chicken in peanut sauce, and a large variety of salads. The specialty of the house is pao food, morsels wrapped in lettuce leaves; for fillings you can choose from eggplant and pork in miso, boiled duck, white fish in pungent sauce, shrimp in chili sauce, dry curry pilaf, and much more. All the food is seasonal and fresh. Ichiba Coji is located in the Teramachi covered shopping arcade, just north of Nishikikoji Dori.

BIO-TEI ⑥⑥**, southwest corner of Sanjo-Higashinotouin. Tel. 255-0086.**
Cuisine: VEGETARIAN/HEALTH FOOD. **Subway:** Oike Station, less than a 2-minute walk away.
$ Prices: ¥380–¥650 ($2.70–$4.65); lunch teishoku ¥850 ($6.05). No credit cards.
Open: Lunch Mon, Wed–Sat 11:30am–2pm; dinner Mon, Wed–Sat 5–8pm (last order).

If you're yearning for a meal in a health-food restaurant, this second-floor restaurant near the Museum of Kyoto serves a variety of inexpensive dishes from an English menu, including rice balls, soups, tofu salad with Chinese dressing, and fermented soy beans with yam powder. A very informal and casual establishment, it also offers a great daily teishoku lunch that includes several dishes, pickled vegetables, brown rice, and miso soup. Seating is at sturdy wooden tables hewn from Japanese cypress, and meals are served on tableware from local kilns. As befits a health-food restaurant, smoking is not allowed.

EL POLLO LOCO, Kawaramachi-Sanjo. Tel. 225-3122.
Cuisine: CHICKEN. **Bus:** 4, 5, 11, 14, 59, or 205 to Kawaramachi-Sanjo, then a 2-minute walk west.
$ Prices: ¥330–¥1,600 ($2.35–$11.40). No credit cards.
Open: Daily 10am–10pm.
This fast-food chain from California has been a big success in the Japanese market. Its limited menu includes chicken burgers, legs, and wings, along with such side dishes as tortillas, salsa, and rice. The last time I was here, the Japanese staff wore cowboy hats, the reason for which was lost on me. Located just off Kawaramachi in the Sanjo Dori covered shopping arcade.

GANKO SUSHI ⑥⑦**, Kawaramachi-Sanjo, Higashi-iru. Tel. 255-1128.**
Cuisine: SUSHI. **Bus:** 4, 5, 11, 14, 59, or 205 to Kawaramachi-Sanjo, then a 1-minute walk east.
$ Prices: Sushi à la carte ¥280–¥1,400 ($2–$10); set meals ¥1,000–¥2,400 ($7.15–$17.15). JCB, MC, V.
Open: First floor daily 11:30am–10:30pm; second floor and basement daily 4:30–10:30pm. **Closed:** First Mon and third Tues of month.
A popular, lively sushi restaurant located just to the west of the Kamo River on Sanjo Dori Avenue, it offers the usual tuna, eel, bonito, squid, and fish sushi selections, as well as such items as grilled yakitori and kushikatsu, shabu-shabu, tempura, tofu (ranging from fried to grilled), and shrimp or crab dishes. There's an English menu. Behind the sushi counter is a fish tank with some rather large specimens, swimming around happily until their number comes up. On the second floor and in the basement are two robatayaki restaurants which are popular with office workers after work, with an English menu listing grilled vegetables and meats.

GONTARO ⑥⑧**, Fuyacho Dori, Shijo-agaru. Tel. 221-5810.**
Cuisine: NOODLES. **Bus:** 4, 5, 11, or 14 to Shijo Dori, then a few minutes' walk.
$ Prices: ¥330–¥1,600 ($2.35–$11.40). JCB.
Open: Thurs–Tues 11:30am–11pm.
This noodle shop has been serving its own handmade noodles for a mere 70 years. It's located on the west side of Fuyacho Dori Street just north of Shijo Dori Avenue—look for a tiny recessed courtyard, white curtains, and a lone pine tree. A small place, with a modern yet traditional interior, it offers various noodle (soba) dishes, including tempura soba, chicken soba, potato soba, and soba sushi.

MISOKA-AN KAWAMICHIYA, Fuyacho Dori, Sanjo-agaru. Tel. 221-2525.
   Cuisine: NOODLES. **Bus:** 4, 5, 11, 14, 59, or 205 to Kawaramachi-Sanjo, then a 5-minute walk.
$ **Prices:** Noodles ¥500–¥1,300 ($3.55–$9.30); Hokoro ¥3,500 ($25). AE, DC, JCB, V.
   Open: Fri–Wed 11am–8pm.

Charming and delightful, with a central courtyard and cubbyhole rooms, this tiny noodle shop is about 300 years old—and makes a great place for an inexpensive meal in the heart of traditional Kyoto. Located on Fuyacho Dori just north of Sanjo Dori, it offers plain buckwheat noodles for ¥500 ($3), as well as noodles with such adornments as tempura and chicken and onions. Its specialty is a one-pot noodle dish called Hokoro, which includes chicken, tofu, mushrooms, and vegetables.

MUSASHI ⑥⑨, Kawaramachi-Sanjo agaru. Tel. 222-0634.
   Cuisine: SUSHI. **Bus:** 4, 5, 11, 14, 59, or 205 to Kawaramachi-Sanjo intersection, then a 1-minute walk.
$ **Prices:** ¥140 ($1) per plate. No credit cards.
   Open: Thurs–Tues noon–9pm.

For a cheap meal of raw fish, this restaurant can't be beat. With a convenient location on the northwest corner of the Kawaramachi-Sanjo intersection, it offers morsels of sushi via a conveyor belt that moves along the counter. Simply reach out and take whatever strikes your fancy. Plates of tuna, octopus, sweet shrimp, eel, crab salad, and more are offered, all costing the same price. Takeout sushi is also available from the front counter.

SANCHO ⑦⓪, Fuji Ginko Yoko-agaru. Tel. 211-0459.
   Cuisine: SALADS/SANDWICHES. **Bus:** 4, 5, 11, 12, 14, 203, 205, or 207 to Shijo-Kawaramachi intersection, then a 3-minute walk.
$ **Prices:** Salads ¥650–¥900 ($4.65–$6.40); sandwiches ¥850–¥900 ($6.05–$6.40); set meals ¥1,000–¥1,800 ($7.15–$12.85). No credit cards.
   Open: Thurs–Tues 11:30am–9pm.

Although it's a bit difficult to find, Sancho is worth a visit for its hearty portions. Serving inexpensive salads, sandwiches, and fixed-price meals, it's just north of Shijo Dori Avenue on the first side street that parallels Kawaramachi to the west, which is the same street that runs beside Fuji Bank. Look for the sign that says "Salada House," as well as the plastic display case of salads. A small, casual establishment, it has only a long counter and six tables. Salads include such combinations as asparagus and crab, shrimp, and chicken. The English menu also lists hamburgers, teriyaki steak, chicken, and several fixed-price meals.

SKEWER OF NAN-ZAN, Kawaramachi-Sanjo, Futasugi-agaru. Tel. 221-6930.
   Cuisine: YAKITORI. **Bus:** 4, 5, 11, 14, 59, or 205 to Kawaramachi-Sanjo intersection, then a 3-minute walk.
$ **Prices:** ¥330–¥1,600 ($2.35–$11.40). No credit cards.
   Open: Dinner daily 5pm–midnight. **Closed:** Third Sun of month.

This friendly yakitori-ya is owned by a man-and-wife team that speaks English and is delighted to have foreign guests. The English menu lists various kinds of yakitori, including skewers of beef, chicken, squid, bell pepper, mushroom, and eggplant, with prices averaging ¥330 ($2.35) to ¥1,000 ($7.15) for three to five skewers. Also available are beef sushi, salads, soups, and beefsteak cooked Japanese style. I recommend trying the grilled wrapped potato—mashed potato with egg, onion, and bacon. Skewer of Nan-Zan is located close to the Alpha and Kyoto Royal hotels and just a few steps southeast of the Kawaramachi Catholic Church, on Anekoji Dori Street. It's in the basement—don't mistake it for the more expensive Nan-Zan steak house in the same building.

TOHKASAIKAN, Shijo Ohashi, Nishizume. Tel. 221-1147.

Cuisine: CHINESE. **Bus:** 4, 5, 11, 12, 14, 203, 205, or 207 to Shijo-Kawaramachi intersection, then a 1-minute walk.
$ Prices: ¥1,000–¥2,700 ($7.15–$19.30). No credit cards.
Open: Daily 11am–9pm (last order).

This Peking-style Chinese restaurant, on Shijo Dori Avenue just west of the bridge that spans the Kamo River, is in a large yellow stone building (it started out as a Western restaurant). It features an ancient elevator, lots of wood paneling, high ceilings, and old-fashioned décor. From June to mid-September you can sit outside on a wooden veranda (supported by stilts) over the Kamo River. If it's winter or raining, consider sitting in the fifth-floor dining room, which has nice views of the city. The best views, however, are from the rooftop garden, open during the summer, where you can order mugs of beer and dine on dishes from its extensive English menu, including sweet-and-sour pork, cooked shrimp with arrowroot, fried pork meatballs, chicken and green pepper, and pork and vegetable rolled with egg. The service tends to be slow and I've had better Chinese food, but the atmosphere is great and reminiscent of another era. The place is popular with families.

ZU ZU ⑦, **Takoyakushi-agaru, Pontocho. Tel. 231-0736.**
Cuisine: VARIED. **Bus:** 4, 5, 11, 12, 14, 203, 205, or 207 to Shijo-Kawaramachi intersection, then a 5-minute walk.
$ Prices: ¥550–¥1,000 ($3.90–$7.15). AE, MC, V.
Open: Dinner Wed–Mon 6pm–2am.

Staffed by friendly young Japanese, this small and informal restaurant/bar is located on Pontocho, just north of the playground that splits the narrow pedestrian lane in half. It's located on the inland side of the street—keep your eyes peeled for a white stucco façade and a sign that proclaims WELCOME TO THE ORIENTAL RESTAURANT. Its menu mixes Japanese, Chinese, and French food, including rack of roast spare rib, chicken steak, and what the staff calls "garlic food." Since the menu, which is apt to change, is in Japanese only, ask for a translation or look around at what others are eating.

EASTERN KYOTO

Many of the restaurants in this part of town sprang up in connection with the Buddhist temples in the area, serving either vegetarian fare to Buddhist monks and worshippers or traditional Japanese food to sightseers. Kaiseki cuisine and tofu dishes are offered by the majority of restaurants in this area.

In addition to the restaurants discussed below, there are a lot of informal and inexpensive locales in and near Kiyomizu Temple, so you shouldn't have any problems finding a place to eat. If the weather is fine, you might wish to stop for noodles and a beer on the Kiyomizu Temple grounds, where you'll find several tatami-mat pavilions.

EXPENSIVE

HYOTEI ⑫, **Kusakawa-cho 35, Nanzenji. Tel. 771-4116.**
Cuisine: KAISEKI/OBENTO. **Reservations:** A must for kaiseki, recommended for obento. **Bus:** 5 to Nanzenji.
$ Prices: Kaiseki dinner courses ¥22,000 ($157.15); kaiseki lunch courses ¥16,500 ($117.85); obento lunch boxes ¥4,400 ($31.40). AE, DC, MC, MCB, V.
Open: Obento served Mon–Wed and Fri–Sun noon–4pm; Kaiseki served daily 11am–7:30pm, except every second and fourth Tues of month.

✪ East of Shirakawa Dori on the main road leading to Nanzenji Temple (look for a plain façade hidden behind a bamboo fence, with a sign shaped like a gourd), this three-centuries-old restaurant first opened its doors to serve pilgrims and visitors on their way to Nanzenji Temple.

Today, it consists of two parts, one offering expensive kaiseki meals and the other offering seasonal obento lunch boxes. The kaiseki meals are served in separate tiny houses situated around a beautiful garden with a pond, maple trees, and bushes. The oldest house, which resembles a small teahouse, is more than 300 years old. Seating is on cushions on a tatami floor in your own private room, and your food is brought to you by kimono-clad women. The other part of the restaurant serves obento lunch boxes; the menu depends on the season, and seating here is at tables and chairs.

MIKAKU ⑦, **Nawate Dori, Shijo-agaru, Gion. Tel. 525-1129.**
   Cuisine: JAPANESE STEAKHOUSE. **Reservations:** Recommended. **Bus:** 12, 203, or 207 to Shijo Keihan-mae.
$ Prices: Steak and shabu-shabu courses ¥8,800–¥20,000 ($62.85–$142.85); set lunches ¥4,400–¥6,500 ($31.40–$46.40). AE, DC, JCB, MC, V.
   Open: Mon–Sat noon–10pm (last order 9:30pm).

Established about 50 years ago by the present owner's grandfather, this restaurant in the heart of Gion is located in a 100-year-old building that was once a private house but has recently been completely renovated. The house specialty is its *aburayaki* meal, which consists of beef filet cooked with various vegetables and seasoned with soy sauce and wine. Sukiyaki, *mizudaki* (similar to shabu-shabu but stronger in taste), and teppanyaki are also served. If you order sukiyaki or mizudaki, you'll sit in your own private tatami room on the second floor. If you order teppanyaki, you'll sit at a counter where the chef will prepare your food in front of you on a hot griddle. Outside the window is a pleasant view of a canal. There's an English menu.

MINOKICHI OF KYOTO, Sanjo-agaru, Dobutsuen-mae Street. Tel. 771-4185.
   Cuisine: KYO-KAISEKI/SHABU-SHABU/OBENTO. **Reservations:** Recommended for dinner and kaiseki orders. **Bus:** 5 to Jingumichi stop, then a few minutes' walk.
$ Prices: Kyo-kaiseki ¥10,000–¥20,000 ($71.40–$142.85); set-dinner courses from ¥10,000 ($71.40); set lunch ¥5,500 ($39.30). AE, DC, JCB, MC, V.
   Open: Daily 11:30am–8pm (last order).

One of Kyoto's best-known restaurants, Minokichi of Kyoto was first established more than 260 years ago and now has several branches in Japan, including a handful in Kyoto, Osaka, and Tokyo. This flagship restaurant consists of various dining venues in several buildings, the most enjoyable of which is tatami seating in the oldest building, with an open square hearth and views of a graceful bamboo garden. The specialty of the restaurant is Kyoto kaiseki, reflecting the gourmet dining style of the upper classes during the Heian Period more than 800 years ago. Emphasis is on the appearance of the food, with great care given to the selection and preparation of seasonal ingredients.

   Although the dishes themselves change, a kaiseki meal here always consists of eight items: appetizer, raw fish, soup, food cooked in delicate broth, steamed food, broiled food, deep-fried food, and vinegared food. There are also special obento lunch boxes and shabu-shabu. Note that while the restaurant is still open, part of it is undergoing renovation, with an expected completion by the summer of 1992.

MINOKO ⑦, **480 Kiyoi-cho, Shimogawara-dori, Gion. Tel. 561-0328.**
   Cuisine: KAISEKI/OBENTO. **Reservations:** Recommended for lunch, required for dinner. **Bus:** 202, 203, 206, or 207 to Yasaka Shrine/Gion, then a 5-minute walk.
$ Prices: Kaiseki ¥13,000 ($92.85); mini-kaiseki lunch ¥8,800 ($62.85); obento lunch box ¥3,300 ($23.55).
   Open: 11:30am–10pm (last order 8pm). **Closed:** Second and fourth Wed of month.

   Formerly a villa, Minoko is an enclave of traditional Japan, with a simple, austere exterior and an interior of winding wooden corridors, tatami rooms, and a garden. Opened about 70 years ago by the present owner's father, Minoko does its best to retain the spirit of the tea ceremony. For lunch, for example, you can order an informal obento lunch box called *chabako-bento,* named after the lacquered box it's served in, which is traditionally used to carry tea utensils to outdoor tea ceremonies. It's served from 11:30am to 2:30pm. For lunch you can also order the *hiru-kaiseki,* a mini-kaiseki set meal. Lunch is served communally in a large tatami room with a view of a beautiful tea garden. If you come here for dinner, which features kaiseki, you'll eat in your own private tatami room. Elaborate kaiseki dinners include a special kind of kaiseki called *cha-kaiseki,* usually served at tea-ceremony gatherings. Minoko is located just a couple of minutes' walk south of Yasaka Shrine.

MODERATE

LE GRAND REVE, Kyoto Park Hotel, Shichijo Dori. Tel. 525-3111.
   Cuisine: FRENCH KAISEKI. **Reservations:** Not necessary. **Bus:** 206 or 208 to Sanjusangendo-mae bus stop, then a few minutes' walk.
$ Prices: Main dishes ¥2,700–¥7,400 ($19.30–$52.85); set-dinner courses ¥6,500–¥15,000 ($46.40–$107.15); set lunches ¥2,700–¥6,500 ($10.30–$46.40).
   Open: Lunch daily 11am–3pm; dinner daily 5–9pm (last order).
There aren't many restaurants in this vicinity, making this a good place to go for lunch or dinner if you're visiting Sanjusangendo Hall or the Kyoto National Museum. Located on Shichijo Dori Avenue in the Park Hotel, this formal dining hall is small and intimate, overlooking a beautiful garden with a waterfall and pond. It specializes in French kaiseki meals, which is French food prepared with the imagination of kaiseki and eaten with chopsticks. The menu changes with the seasons, but past main dishes have included sautéed chicken and prawn with lobster sauce, fricasseed sweetbreads and scallops, and grilled duck with lemon-and-honey sauce.

HAMASAKU, Mikayo Hotel, Sanjo-Keage. Tel. 771-7111.
   Cuisine: KAISEKI/TEMPURA/SHABU-SHABU/VARIED. **Reservations:** Not necessary. **Bus:** 5 to Jingumichi stop.
$ Prices: Dinner main dishes ¥3,300–¥4,900 ($23.55–$35); tempura ¥4,700–¥6,300 ($33.55–$45); shabu-shabu ¥9,900 ($70.70); kaiseki ¥8,800–¥13,000 ($62.85–$92.85); set lunches ¥3,000–¥4,900 ($21.40–$35). AE, DC, JCB, MC, V.
   Open: Lunch daily noon–2pm; dinner daily 5:30–10pm.
If you're the least bit shy about going into a Japanese restaurant and ordering something without being able to read the menu, the easiest place to enjoy Japanese food in Eastern Kyoto is in the internationally known Mikayo Hotel. In its Japanese restaurant, Hamasaku, you can have a variety of dishes ranging from tempura, sushi, and shabu-shabu to kaiseki cuisine. Lunch is the most economical time to come, when set courses include obento lunch boxes and such main dishes as tempura, sashimi, and eel.

ISOBE ⑦⑤, Maruyama Park, Ikenohata. Tel. 561-2216.
   Cuisine: KAISEKI/OBENTO/TEMPURA/SHABU-SHABU/SUKIYAKI. **Reservations:** Not necessary. **Bus:** 202, 203, 206, or 207 to Gion, then a 10-minute walk.
$ Prices: Set meals ¥2,700–¥16,500 ($19.30–$117.85). AE, DC, JCB.
   Open: Daily 10am–10pm.
A convenient place to stop for lunch if you're walking from Kiyomizu Temple to Heian Shrine, this restaurant is located on the southeastern edge of Maruyama Park (if you're walking from Kiyomizu, take a right at the entrance to the park) and is easily recognized by its outdoor red umbrella (the logo also used for its sign). The same menu is available day and night and includes an obento for ¥2,700 ($19.30), shabu-shabu or sukiyaki for ¥5,500 ($39.30), a tempura set meal for ¥3,600 ($25.70), and kaiseki starting at ¥7,500 ($53.55). This modern, pleasant restaurant offers a nice view of the park from its dining room.

JUNSEI, 60 Kusakawa-cho, Nanzenji. Tel. 761-2311.
   Cuisine: TOFU/KAISEKI/OBENTO/VARIED. **Reservations:** Not necessary. **Bus:** 5 to Hosho Jicho stop.
$ Prices: Set meals ¥2,700–¥12,000 ($19.30–$85.70). AE, DC, JCB, MC, V.
   Open: Daily 11am–8pm (last order).
Located on the road to Nanzenji Temple, this restaurant specializing in tofu dishes opened in 1961, but the grounds and garden were originally part of a private

institution established in the 1830s, during the shogun era. Although Junsei is popular with tour groups and is tourist-oriented, the food is good and an English menu makes ordering easy. There are several buildings spread throughout the grounds and what you eat determines where you go—as soon as you arrive, you'll be given a menu and asked what you want to eat. I chose the yudofu (tofu) set meal for ¥2,700 ($19.30) and was directed to an older building filled with antiques and tatami mats. My meal came with vegetable tempura and various tofu dishes, including fried tofu on a stick and tofu boiled in a pot at my table. Other set meals include kaiseki beginning at ¥10,000 ($71.40), shabu-shabu and sukiyaki priced at ¥8,800 ($62.85), and a tempura set meal for ¥3,800 ($27.15). There are also obento lunch boxes beginning at ¥3,800 ($27.15). After your meal, be sure to take a stroll through the garden.

OKUTAN ⑦⑥, 86-30 Fukuchi-cho, Nanzenji. Tel. 771-8709.
  Cuisine: TOFU/VEGETARIAN. **Reservations:** Recommended. **Bus:** 5 to Eikando-mae stop.
  $ Prices: Yudofu set meal ¥3,300 ($23.55); à la carte prices ¥2,000–¥10,000 ($14.30–$71.50). No credit cards.
  Open: Mon–Wed and Fri–Sun 10:30am–5:30pm (last order).

  ★ This is one of the oldest, most authentic, and most delightful tofu restaurants in Kyoto, located just north of Nanzenji Temple's main gate (called the San Mon Gate). Founded about 350 years ago as a vegetarian restaurant serving Zen dishes to Buddhist monks, this wooden place with a thatched roof serves just one thing, a tofu set meal (yudofu), with the finishing touches provided by a pond, a garden, and peacefulness. Okutan is very simple and rustic, with seating either in tatami rooms or outdoors on cushioned platforms. Women dressed in traditional rural clothing bring your food. The tofu set meal includes boiled tofu, fried tofu, vegetable tempura, yam soup, and pickled vegetables. If you're still hungry, you can order some of the above items à la carte. This restaurant is especially delightful in fine weather. Highly recommended.

BUDGET

LADIES' HOTEL CHORAKUKAN ⑦⑦, Maruyama Park. Tel. 561-0001.
  Cuisine: WESTERN. **Bus:** 202, 203, 206, or 207 to Gion/Yasakai Shrine, then a 5-minute walk.
  $ Prices: Main dishes ¥900–¥1,700 ($6.40–$12.15); set lunch ¥1,500 ($10.70). No credit cards.
  Open: Daily 11am–7:30pm.

There aren't many Western restaurants in eastern Kyoto, but if you're walking from Kiyomizu Temple to Heian Shrine, this informal establishment is tucked away in the southwest corner of Maruyama Park, in a large stone-and-brick Western-style building dating from the Meiji Period, with a huge stone lantern in its driveway. The building features elaborate woodwork and marble, but while the inexpensive Western restaurant downstairs is nothing fancy, it's restful; classical music plays in the background, and there is a view of some maple trees. The dishes include fried or grilled shrimp, grilled chicken with bacon, spaghetti, beef or chicken curry, and sandwiches. There are also lunch specials served from 11am to 3pm, when you have your choice of either a Western-style lunch or a Japanese-style box lunch. After lunch you may wish to retire to the building's coffee shop, a beautiful room reminiscent of European coffee shops.

GOEMONJAYA ⑦⑧, 67 Kukasawa-cho, Nanzenji. Tel. 751-9638.
  Cuisine: TOFU/TEMPURA/NOODLES. **Bus:** 5 to Hosho Jicho stop.
  $ Prices: ¥750–¥2,900 ($5.35–$20.70). No credit cards.
  Open: Daily 11am–7:30pm (last order). **Closed:** First and third Tues of month.
An inexpensive restaurant serving tofu dishes, tempura, and noodles, Goemonjaya is located across the street from Yachiyo Ryokan on the road leading to Nanzenji Temple. Look for its red lantern beside the road and for a display case of plastic food. The restaurant itself is back off the main road, past a red umbrella (summer only), a small garden, and a waterfall and pond (filled with carp). A typical Japanese restaurant

with tatami seating, it offers noodles starting at ¥750 ($5.35), with tempura teishoku going for ¥2,400 ($17.15).

KOAN ⑦⑨**, Shotekiin Temple, Fukuchi-cho, Nanzenji. Tel. 771-2781.**
   Cuisine: TOFU/VEGETARIAN. **Reservations:** Not necessary. **Bus:** 5 to Eikando-mae bus stop.
$ Prices: Yudofu set meals ¥2,200 ($15.70) and ¥2,700 ($19.30); vegetarian dishes ¥3,300–¥4,400 ($23.50–$31.40). No credit cards.
   Open: Mon–Tues and Thurs–Sun 11am–4:30pm.
Located just north of Nanzenji Temple, Koan is a simple restaurant on the grounds of a small temple, beside a large wooden gate that straddles the road. It offers vegetarian and tofu dishes characteristic of Zen temple meals usually served to monks, which you can eat at an open-air pavilion in the shade of a small and peaceful courtyard. There is an English menu.

NAKAMURARO ⑧⓪**, Yasaka-jinja-uchi, Gion. Tel. 561-0016.**
   Cuisine: TOFU/KAISEKI. **Bus:** 202, 203, 206, 207 to Yasaka Shrine/Gion.
$ Prices: *Tofu dengaku obento* ¥3,300 ($23.55); 3 sticks of tofu dengaku ¥400 ($2.85). No credit cards.
   Open: Daily 11:30am–6pm for tofu, to 7pm for kaiseki.
   Closed: Last Thurs of month.
⭐ Opened 400 years ago to serve worshippers on their way to Yasaka Shrine, this tiny one-room teahouse is said to be the oldest restaurant in Japan. (It is now in its 12th generation of restaurateurs.) Located at the south entrance to Yasaka Shrine, right next to the stone torii gate, it has an open façade in summer and specializes in tofu dengaku, skewers of tofu smothered in miso sauce. Best is the tofu dengaku obento, served from 11:30am to 6pm every day except the last Thursday of the month. If you simply want to try the restaurant's specialty but don't want to eat a complete meal, you can order three sticks of tofu dengaku for just ¥400 ($2.85). If you feel like splurging, beside the teahouse is a handsome wooden restaurant, added in the 19th century, where meals are served in lovely rooms overlooking a magnificent garden. You can also order the tofu dengaku obento here until 3pm. In the evenings, kaiseki meals are served, but at ¥20,000 ($143) per person, they're a bit out of our range.

SPECIALTY DINING
DINING WITH A VIEW

On the 14th floor of the Kyoto Grand Hotel, Horikawa Shiokoji (tel. 341-2311), is **Top of Kyoto,** the city's only revolving restaurant. On clear days you have excellent views over the tops of Kyoto's temples to the mountains surrounding the city. Recently remodeled, with marble and décor imported from Italy, this trendy restaurant offers set lunches for ¥3,800 ($27.15) and ¥4,400 ($31.40), and set-dinner courses ranging from ¥5,500 to ¥16,500 ($39.30 to $117.85). A la carte main dishes, ranging from ¥3,300 to ¥11,000 ($23.55 to $78.55), change often but may include lobster with sweetbreads and caviar, smoked Norwegian salmon with papaya, rack of lamb, and steaks. Adjoining the restaurant is a comfortable cocktail lounge, where you can relax with a drink after dinner. Food is served daily from noon to 11:30pm. A Sunday brunch buffet is offered on Sunday between 11am and 2:30pm, and costs ¥3,800 ($27.15). Reservations are recommended for dinner, especially on a Saturday or Sunday evening.

DINING CLUSTERS & COMPLEXES

For inexpensive Japanese restaurants, you might want to check out the seventh and eighth floors of the **Hankyu department store,** on the corner of Shijo and Kawaramachi avenues in central Kyoto. There are lots of restaurants on these two floors serving both Japanese and Western cuisine, and because they have plastic food displays outside their front doors, it's easy to choose both a restaurant and what you want to eat. Choices include sushi, eel, shabu-shabu, sandwiches, Chinese food, steaks, noodles, tonkatsu, and okonomiyaki (a Japanese version of the pancake). Simply wander around and decide what looks best. Most dishes are priced between ¥600 and ¥1,000 ($4.30 and $7.15), with set meals averaging ¥2,500 ($17.85). These restaurants are open daily from 11am to 9:30pm.

If you're waiting for a train or want something inexpensive and fast, head for **Kintetsu Mall,** located on the southern edge of Kyoto Station near the Kintetsu Line, on Hachijo Dori. Stretching under the tracks are about two dozen enterprises, most with plastic display cases, offering everything from tempura and sushi to hamburgers, noodles, spaghetti, sandwiches, tonkatsu, pilaf, and desserts. Most prices fall between ¥600 and ¥1,500 ($4.30 and $10.70), and you can eat well for under ¥1,000 ($7.15). In the morning, coffee shops offer a "morning service" of coffee, toast, and eggs for about ¥450 ($3.20). Hours here are from about 7:30 or 9am to 9 or 10pm. Some establishments are closed on Thursday.

LATE-NIGHT & 24-HOUR ESTABLISHMENTS

If you'd like a snack in the middle of the night, go to the north end of Pontocho—where it joins Sanjo Dori Avenue—to **Karafuneya,** Pontocho, Sanjo-sagaru (tel. 255-1414). This coffee shop with an outdoor veranda overlooking the river is open 24 hours a day every day, and offers various kinds of coffee, tea, sandwiches, ice cream, sundaes, and desserts.

Another place that stays open late is **Irohanihoheto** ⑧①, Sanjo-sagaru, Higashiyama-ku (tel. 541-1683), located on Nawate Dori Street just south of Sanjo-Keihan Station. Popular with students for its inexpensive dishes averaging ¥400 ($2.85) and for its beer starting at ¥420 ($3), it's open daily from 5:30pm to 3:30am (4am on weekends).

Check the nightlife section for more information on these establishments.

5. ATTRACTIONS

Because Kyoto has 1,700 Buddhist temples, 300 Shinto shrines, and numerous gardens, museums, and other worthwhile sights, it's obvious that you must carefully plan your itinerary. Even the most avid sightseer can become jaded after days of visiting yet another temple or shrine—and after a while how much can your memory retain? Be sure to temper your visits to cultural and historical sights with time spent simply walking around. Kyoto is a city best seen on your own two feet, exploring small alleyways and curio shops, pausing to soak in the beauty of its carefully landscaped gardens. If you spend your days in Kyoto racing around in a taxi or a bus from one temple to another, the essence of this ancient capital and its charm may literally pass you by.

SUGGESTED ITINERARIES

IF YOU HAVE 1 DAY

Day 1: If you have only a single day to spend in Kyoto, spend it in eastern Kyoto, including the stroll from Kiyomizu Temple to Heian Shrine, topping it off with a visit to the Silver Pavilion, and, if time permits, a short stop at the Kyoto Handicraft Center for some shopping. In the evening, visit Gion Corner, with its cultural demonstrations, topped with a stroll through Gion—and then start planning for your next trip back to Kyoto.

IF YOU HAVE 2 DAYS

Day 1: Spend Day 1 in eastern Kyoto as outlined above.

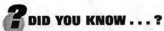

DID YOU KNOW . . . ?

- Kyoto served as Japan's capital for more than 1,000 years, from 794 to 1868.
- There are 1,700 Buddhist temples and 300 Shinto shrines in Kyoto.
- Kyoto is the birthplace of kaiseki, an elaborate meal served in courses and originally offered during the tea ceremony.
- Shojin-ryoori, vegetarian food served in Buddhist temples, originated in Kyoto.

Day 2: Visit Nijo Castle in Central Kyoto, and Ryoanji Temple with its famous rock garden and the Golden Pavilion in northwestern Kyoto. End the day shopping in the Shijo-Kawaramachi shopping district. Eat dinner at a restaurant serving Kyoto cuisine, followed by a stroll down Pontocho. Such a 2-day tour would present you a well-rounded view of Kyoto by giving you the chance to see temples, a shrine, gardens, and a former shogun's palace.

IF YOU HAVE 3 DAYS

Days 1 and 2: Spend Days 1 and 2 in and around Kyoto as outlined above.
Day 3: Head for Nara, Japan's ancient capital, and its many temples and historical attractions. If it's summer, spend the evening in Arashiyama, where you can board a wooden boat and observe cormorant fishing.

IF YOU HAVE 5 DAYS OR MORE

Days 1 and 2: Spend Days 1 and 2 in eastern Kyoto, including both recommended strolls that follow.
Day 3: Add Nijo Castle, Ryoanji Temple, and the Golden Pavilion, as outlined in "If You Have 2 Days," above.
Day 4: Spend Day 4 in Nara.
Day 5: Visit Katsura Imperial Villa, Saihoji Moss Temple, or one of the other recommended destinations in the environs of Kyoto. An alternative is to visit those museums you haven't had time for, shopping, or pursuing your own interests.

THE TOP ATTRACTIONS

Before setting out on your walking tours, be sure to stop by the Kyoto Tourist Information Center (TIC), located across from Kyoto Station in the Kyoto Tower Building, Higashi-Shiokojicho, Shimogyo-ku (tel. 075/371-5649), to pick up a leaflet called *Walking Tour Courses in Kyoto*. It contains four maps for strolling tours of Kyoto, including the walk from Kiyomizu Temple to Heian Shrine and on to the Silver Pavilion, which I've outlined below in more detail. The TIC also has city maps and a colorful brochure listing Kyoto's most important sites.

Keep in mind, too, that you must enter Kyoto's museums, shrines, and temples at least a half hour before closing time.

EASTERN KYOTO

The eastern part of Kyoto, embracing the area of Higashiyama-ku, with its Kiyomizu Temple, and stretching up all the way to the Silver Pavilion (Ginkakuji Temple), is probably the richest in terms of culture and charm. Although the walking-tour leaflet distributed by the TIC claims you can walk from Kiyomizu Temple to Heian Shrine in 50 minutes, I don't see how it would be possible unless you ran the whole way. I've walked this route four times and it's always taken me the better part of a day—perhaps I'm slow, but it's a pace I've found does justice to this wonderful area of Kyoto.

The two strolls I've listed below, one through Higashiyama-ku and the other so-called Philosophers' Stroll, are logical continuations of each other. If you don't finish Higashiyama-ku in one day, therefore, you could start where you left off on the following day and then continue on with the Philosophers' Stroll. In any case, since eastern Kyoto has some of the city's most traditional and beautiful restaurants, be sure to read through the dining section to decide beforehand where you might want to eat lunch or dinner. The majority of the traditional restaurants are in the vicinity of Nanzenji Temple.

FROMMER'S FAVORITE
KYOTO EXPERIENCES

A Night in a Ryokan Kyoto is one of the best places in Japan to experience the traditional inn, where guests sleep on futon in a tatami room and are treated to elaborate Japanese meals.

A Tofu Vegetarian Meal in a Garden Setting Shojin ryoori, vegetarian meals served at Buddhist temples, are one of Kyoto's specialties. They're served at a number of rustic restaurants with outdoor seating in a garden.

A Visit to a Japanese Garden Kyoto has a wide range of traditional gardens, from Zen rock gardens once used by priests for meditation to miniature landscape gardens that once belonged to the ruling classes.

A Stroll Through Eastern Kyoto Temples, shrines, gardens, shops and traditional neighborhoods are highlights of a day spent walking through this historic part of Kyoto.

Nishi-Koji Dori This fish-and-produce market right in the heart of the city puts visitors in direct contact with Kyoto's residents, as both housewives and restaurant owners buy their day's food, just as their ancestors have for more than 300 years.

Shopping for Traditional Crafts Passed down from generation to generation, traditional arts and crafts thrive in Kyoto, with small specialty shops selling everything from fans to wooden combs.

A Visit to Gion Kyoto's traditional pleasure quarter, where geisha entertain businessmen on expense accounts, is fascinating for its austere architecture, hushed atmosphere, and the sight of geishas hurrying to their evening appointments.

Cormorant Fishing There's no more romantic way to spend a summer's evening than drifting down the river in a wooden boat decorated with paper lanterns, watching men at work fishing with the help of cormorants.

An Evening's Stroll Through Pontocho A small, narrow pedestrian lane, Pontocho is lined with hostess bars, restaurants, and drinking establishments. End the evening seated on the banks of the nearby Kamo River, a popular spot for Kyoto's young couples.

WALKING TOUR 1 — Higashiyama-ku

Start: Sanjusangendo Hall, Schichijo Dori Avenue.
Finish: Kyoto Handicraft Center, Kumano Jinja Higashi.
Time: Allow approximately 6 hours, including stops for shopping and museums.
Best Times: Weekdays, when temples and shops aren't as crowded.
Worst Times: Mondays, when museums are closed.

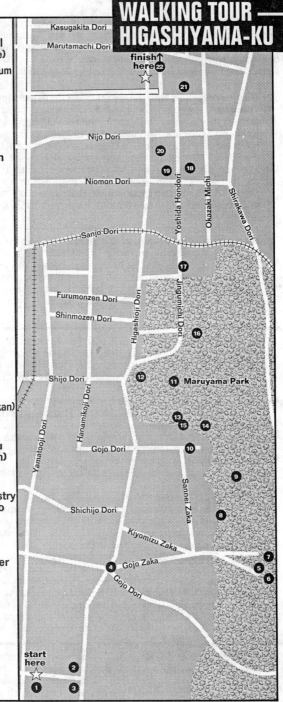

1. Sanjusangendo Hall (Rengeoin Temple)
2. Kyoto National Museum (Kokuritsu Hakubutsukan)
3. Le Grand Rêve
4. Gojo-zaka
5. Kiyomizu Temple
6. An open-air pavilion
7. Jishu Shrine
8. Sannenzaka Slope
9. Ryozen Kannon Temple
10. Kodaiji Rakusho Tea Room
11. Maruyama Park
12. Yasaka Shrine (Gion Shrine)
13. Nakamuraro
14. Isobe
15. Chorakukan
16. Chion-in Temple
17. Shoren-in Temple
18. Kyoto Municipal Museum of Art (Kyoto-shi Bijitsukan)
19. National Museum of Modern Art (Kyoto Kokuritsu Kindai Bijitsukan)
20. Kyoto Municipal Museum of Traditional Industry (Kyoto-shi Dento Sangyo Kaikan)
21. Heian Shrine
22. Kyoto Handicraft Center

A stroll through Higashiyama-ku will take you to Kiyomizu Temple and Heian Shrine, two of Kyoto's most famous attractions, as well as through some of Kyoto's most charming neighborhoods en route. To reach Sanjusangendo Hall, located just south of Shichijo Dori Avenue, a block or so east of the Kamo River, walk 20 minutes from Kyoto Station or take bus no. 206 to Sanjusangendo-mae bus stop.

1. **Sanjusangendo Hall** (tel. 525-0033) is the name popularly given to **Rengeoin Temple.** The hall is only some 50 feet wide, but it stretches almost 400 feet—and it's filled with more than 1,000 images of the thousand-handed Kannon. There are row upon row of these gold figures glowing in the dark hall, and in the middle is a large seated figure of Kannon, flanked by her 28 disciples. The large Kannon was carved in 1254 by Tankei, a famous sculptor from the Kamakura Period, and the hall itself dates from 1266. At the back of the hall is a 130-yard-long archery range, where a competition is held every January 15. Sanjusangendo is open daily from 8am to 5pm (enter by 4:30pm) in summer and daily from 8am to 4pm (enter by 3:30pm) in winter. Admission is ¥400 ($2.85).

Across the street and to the northeast of Sanjusangendo Hall is the:
2. **Kyoto National Museum (Kokuritsu Hakubutsukan),** 527 Chaya machi (tel. 541-1151). Established in the latter half of the last century as a repository for art objects and treasures that belonged to both Kyoto's temples and individuals, it displays historical items, artwork, and handcrafts, including a great collection of ceramics, Japanese paintings, calligraphy, lacquerware, textiles, and sculptures. Admission is ¥400 ($2.85), and the museum is open Tuesday through Sunday from 9am to 4:30pm.

A REFUELING STOP Just past the National Museum is the Royal Park Hotel, where you'll find the delightful 3. **Le Grand Rêve,** a restaurant with views of a beautiful garden and serving French food in the style of kaiseki—that is, served in courses and eaten with chopsticks. (See "Kyoto Dining," above, for more details.)

Just beyond the Royal Park Hotel is Higashioji Dori, where you should take a left and walk 10 minutes or so until you come to the big intersection with the overpass to Gojo Dori. Cross Gojo Dori, walk past the small temple on the right, and then take a right onto the diagonal road leading uphill. Called:
4. **Gojo-zaka,** it is lined with pottery shops, but don't go crazy shopping yet—there are many more shops to come. At the top of Gojo-zaka are stairs leading to:
5. **۞ Kiyomizu Temple** (tel. 551-1234). First founded in 798 and rebuilt in 1633 by the third Tokugawa shogun, Iemitsu, the temple occupies an exalted spot, with a grand view of the city below. The main hall is built over a cliff and features a large wooden veranda supported by 139 pillars, each 49 feet high. The magnificence of the height and view is so well known to the Japanese that the idiom "jumping from the veranda of Kiyomizu Temple" means that they're about to undertake some particularly bold or daring adventure. To appreciate the grandeur of the main hall with its pillars and dark wood, walk to the three-story pagoda, which affords the best view of the main hall, built without the use of a single nail. From the pagoda, descend the steps down to Otowa Fall, where you'll see Japanese lined up to drink from the refreshing spring water. The temple is open daily from 8am to 6pm and charges ¥300 ($2.15) admission.

A REFUELING STOP On the grounds of Kiyomizu Temple, just beside Otowa Fall, is 6. **an open-air pavilion** where you can sit on tatami and enjoy noodles and a beer or shaved ice colored with various flavors. This is a great place to stop (and now you know why this walk takes me all day). If you're lucky to be here in fall, the fiery reds of the maple trees will set the countryside around you on fire. These pavilions are open Friday through Wednesday from 9am to 5pm.

Before departing Kiyomizu Temple, be sure to make a stop at:

7. Jishu Shrine (tel. 541-2097), regarded as a dwelling place of the deity in charge of love and a good match. This vermilion-colored Shinto shrine (free admission) is easy to spot, located as it is behind and to the left of Kiyomizu's main temple hall. There's a pamphlet available in English that gives the history of the shrine, and throughout the grounds are signs and descriptions in English telling about its various parts, so that for once you're not left in the dark as to the purpose of the various statues and memorials and what the Japanese are doing as they make their rounds. Very enriching. You can buy various good-luck charms for everything from a happy marriage to easy delivery of a child to success in passing an examination. On the shrine's grounds are two stones placed about 30 feet apart—if you're able to walk from one stone to the other with your eyes closed, you're supposedly guaranteed success in your love life. It sure doesn't hurt to try.

From Kiyomizu Temple, take the road leading downhill directly in front of the temple's main gate, where you'll find shop after shop selling sweets, pottery, fans, ties, hats, souvenirs, and curios. It's okay to go crazy shopping here, but remember you're going to have to carry whatever you buy. After passing a couple of small shrines nestled in among the shops, you'll come to a split in the road and a shrine on the right shaded by trees in front. Just beside this shrine are steps leading downhill to the right. Called:

8. Sannenzaka Slope, it leads past lovely antiques and curio shops and winds through neighborhoods of wooden buildings reminiscent of old Kyoto. Eventually you'll come to:

9. Ryozen Kannon Temple, with its huge white statue dedicated to Japan's unknown soldiers who died in World War II. Past Ryozen Kannon Temple and just before the street ends at a pagoda with a crane on top, keep your eyes peeled for a teahouse on your right.

REFUELING STOP 10. Kodaiji Rakusho Tea Room ⑧², 517 Washiochiyo (tel. 561-6892), is a lovely place, one of my favorite tearooms in Kyoto. It has a miniature 100-year-old garden, which you can glimpse from the street through a gate and which contains a pond with some of the largest carp I've ever seen, some of which are 20 years old and winners of those many medals displayed in the back room. Stop for somen (finely spun cold noodles), tea, or dessert, and refresh yourself with views of the small but beautiful garden. Open from 9:30am to 6pm.

Continuing on your stroll, take a right at the pagoda and then an immediate left, which marks the beginning of:

11. Maruyama Park. This is one of Kyoto's most popular city parks, filled with ponds, pigeons, and gardens. In spring, this is one of the most popular spots for the viewing of cherry blossoms. Beside Maruyama Park is:

12. Yasaka Shrine, also known as **Gion Shrine** for its close proximity to the Gion district. Its present buildings date from 1654, and its stone torii on the south side are considered among the largest in Japan. Admission here is free.

REFUELING STOPS If you need a meal more substantial than the open-air pavilions at Kiyomizu or the teahouse were able to provide, good choices for Japanese food are **13. Nakamuraro,** a 400-year-old teahouse located next to Yasaka Shrine's stone torii and serving skewers of grilled tofu, and **14. Isobe,** located on the southern edge of Maruyama Park and offering obento lunch boxes, tempura, shabu-shabu, and an assortment of Japanese cuisine. For Western food, there's the **15. Chorakukan,** located in a Meiji-era Building at the southwest corner of Maruyama Park. It offers set lunches priced at ¥1,500

($10.70), as well as such main dishes as spaghetti and sandwiches. (See "Kyoto Dining," above, for more details on all three establishments.)

After taking your time strolling through Maruyama Park, you'll come to:

16. Chion-in Temple (tel. 531-2111), founded in 1234 as a center of the Jodo sect of Buddhism. Famous for its enormous gate, rising almost 80 feet, the temple also has Japan's largest bell, weighing 74 tons. Entrance to the temple precincts is free; if you wish to visit its treasure hall, the admission is ¥300 ($2.15). It's open daily from 9am to 4pm. Just north of Chion-in is:

17. Shoren-in Temple (tel. 561-2345), built as a villa for the abbots of a Buddhist sect. The present buildings date from 1895. The temple has an impressive 15th-century garden, considered one of the best in Kyoto. Open daily from 9am to 5pm (remember, you must enter by 4:30pm), it charges an admission of ¥400 ($2.85).

From Shoren-in Temple, continue walking north on Jingumichi Dori Avenue, passing Sanjo and Niomon Dori (you'll know you're on the right track when you spot the vermilion-colored torii gate straddling a street busy with traffic). You'll soon come to several museums you might want to stop in, among them the:

18. Kyoto Municipal Museum of Art (Kyoto-shi Bijitsukan) (tel. 771-4107), which is the city's repository for local art, while the:

19. National Museum of Modern Art (Kyoto Kokuritsu Kindai Bijutsukan) (tel. 761-4111) offers changing exhibitions of modern art. My favorite, however, is the:

20. ✪ Kyoto Municipal Museum of Traditional Industry (Kyoto-shi Dento Sangyo Kaikan) (tel. 761-3421). Not only is it free, but it sells many of the items displayed. Crafts range from pottery to lacquerware to textiles, bamboo products, damascene jewelry, knives, and dolls. Prices are high, but so is the quality. There are also frequent demonstrations by local artists. It's open Tuesday through Sunday from 9am to 5pm (note that if Monday is a holiday, the museum will remain open but will close the following day). Directly north of the museums is:

21. ✪ Heian Shrine. If orange and green are your favorite colors, you're going to love this shrine, one of Kyoto's most famous. Although it was built as late as 1895, in commemoration of the 1,100th anniversary of the founding of Kyoto, Heian Shrine is a replica of the first imperial palace, built in Kyoto in 794, giving you some idea of the architecture back then. The most important thing to see here, however, is the garden, the entrance to which is on your left as you face the main hall. Admission is ¥500 ($3.55) and daily hours are 8:30am to 5:30pm (5pm in winter). Typical of gardens constructed during the Meiji Era, it's famous for its weeping cherry trees in spring, its irises and water lilies in summer, and its changing maple leaves in fall.

After visiting Heian Shrine, you may want to stop off to do some shopping at the:

22. Kyoto Handicraft Center, (tel. 761-5080), located behind the shrine on its north side, open daily from 9:30am to 6pm (5:30pm December through February). It's the best place in Kyoto for one-stop shopping for souvenirs of Japan, including pearls, kimono and yukata, fans, paper products, and more. (See "Kyoto Savvy Shopping," below, for complete information).

WALKING TOUR 2 — Philosophers' Stroll

Start: Nanzenji Temple.
Finish: Ginkakuji, the Silver Pavilion.
Time: Allow approximately 3 hours, including stops along the way.
Best Times: Weekdays, when it isn't as crowded.
Worst Times: There are no bad times for this stroll.

This stroll takes in two temples and the Silver Pavilion, considered one of the most beautiful structures in Kyoto. Between the temples and the Silver Pavilion is a canal

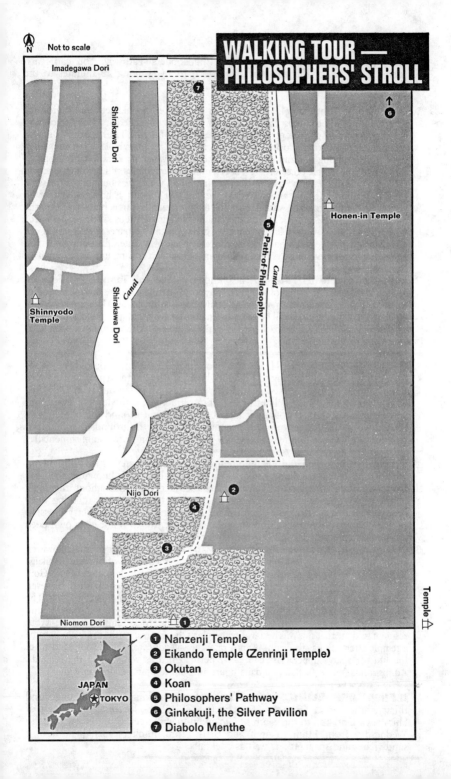

WALKING TOUR —
PHILOSOPHERS' STROLL

Not to scale

Imadegawa Dori

Shirakawa Dori

Canal

Shirakawa Dori

Shinnyodo
Temple

Honen-in Temple

Canal
Path of Philosophy

Nijo Dori

Niomon Dori

Temple

JAPAN
TOKYO

1 Nanzenji Temple
2 Eikando Temple (Zenrinji Temple)
3 Okutan
4 Koan
5 Philosophers' Pathway
6 Ginkakuji, the Silver Pavilion
7 Diabolo Menthe

lined by trees and a path known as the Philosophers' Pathway. You can reach Nanzenji, the start of this tour, by bus no. 5, or by walking 20 minutes to the southeast of Heian Shrine.

1. ✪ **Nanzenji Temple** (tel. 771-0365) is a Rinzai Zen temple set amid a grove of spruce. One of Kyoto's most famous Zen temples, it was founded in 1293. Attached to the main hall is a Zen rock garden, sometimes called "Leaping Tiger Garden" because of the shape of one of the rocks. In the building behind the main hall is a famous sliding door with a painting by Kano Tanyu of a tiger drinking water in a bamboo grove. Spread throughout the temple precincts are a dozen other lesser temples and buildings that you can explore if you have the time, including Nanzen-in, which was built about the same time as Nanzenji Temple and served as the emperor's vacation house whenever he visited the temple grounds. Admission to the temple grounds is free, but entrance to the main hall, with its Zen rock garden and famous sliding door, costs ¥350 ($2.50). For ¥300 ($2.15) more you can have ceremonial green tea and a Japanese sweet served in a tatami room off the main hall with a peaceful view of a waterfall. Daily hours are 8:30am to 5pm (you must enter by 4:30pm). Less than a 5-minute walk north of Nanzenji Temple is:

2. **Eikando Temple** (tel. 761-0007), also known as **Zenrinji Temple** ⑧③. Founded in 856, it features the statue of a Buddha turned so that he looks backward instead of forward, but the main reason everyone comes here is the garden. Upon paying your ¥400 ($2.85) admission, you'll be given an English-language pamphlet and a map of the garden. The Buddha facing backward is in the Amidado Hall. Eikando is open daily from 9am to 4:30pm.

REFUELING STOPS There are two great restaurants located north of Nanjenji on the road leading to Eikando, both of which offer vegetarian and tofu dishes typical of meals served at Buddhist temples. Most famous is 3. **Okutan,** which is one of the most delightful restaurants in Kyoto, with views of a beautiful and peaceful garden. If you can't afford Okutan, right around the corner is 4. **Koan,** which also serves tofu and vegetarian dishes on the grounds of a Buddhist temple. (See "Kyoto Dining," above, for more details on both establishments.)

North of Nanzenji and Eikando temples is a narrow canal, lined with cherry, willow, and maple trees and flanked by a small pathway. It's known as the:

5. **Philosophers' Pathway,** referring to the fact that throughout the ages, philosophers and priests have strolled along the tranquil canal thinking deep thoughts. It is a particularly beautiful sight in spring during the cherry-blossom season. The pathway runs almost a mile, allowing you to think your own deep thoughts before reaching the crown jewel of this walk:

6. ✪ **Ginkakuji, the Silver Pavilion** (tel. 771-5725). Contrary to its name, however, it isn't silver at all. It was built in 1482 as a retirement villa of Shogun Ashikaga Yoshimasa, who intended to coat the structure with silver in imitation of the Gold Pavilion built by his grandfather. He died before this could be accomplished, however, which is just as well because the wood of the Silver Pavilion is beautiful just as it is. The whole complex is designed for the enjoyment of the tea ceremony, moon viewing, and other aesthetic pursuits, with a beautiful garden of sand, rocks, and moss. One Kyoto resident told me that this was his favorite temple in the whole city (the residence became a temple after Ashikaga's death). At any rate, the splendor, formality, and grandeur of the life of Japan's upper class can easily be imagined as you wander the grounds. Admission is ¥400 ($2.85), and daily hours are 9am to 5pm (4:30pm in winter).

A FINAL REFUELING STOP If strolling and thinking made you hungry and thirsty, head for 7. **Diabolo Menthe** (tel. 751-2887), located a block east of Shirakawa Dori and to the south of Ginkakuji-michi Street. Open Friday through Wednesday from 11am to 4pm and 6 to 11pm, it offers such light fare as sandwiches and spaghetti, as well as cocktails.

NORTHWESTERN KYOTO

✪ The inspiration for the Silver Pavilion, described above, was **Kinkakuji, the Gold Pavilion** (tel. 461-0013), which you can reach by taking bus no. 205 from Kyoto Station (platform B3) to the Kinkakuji-michi bus stop. One of Kyoto's best-known attractions, it was constructed in the 1390s as a retirement villa for Shogun Ashikaga Yoshimitsu and features a three-story pavilion covered in gold leaf and topped with a bronze phoenix on its roof. Apparently, the retired shogun lived in shameless luxury while the rest of the nation suffered from famine, earthquakes, and plague. If you come here on a clear day, the Gold Pavilion shimmers against a blue sky, its reflection captured in the waters of a calm pond. However, this pavilion is not the original. In 1950 a disturbed student monk burned Kinkakuji to the ground, a story told by author Mishima Yukio in his *The Temple of the Golden Pavilion*. The temple was rebuilt in 1955. Be sure to explore the surrounding park with its moss-covered grounds and teahouses. Daily hours are 9am to 5:30pm in summer, to 5pm in winter. Admission is ¥300 ($2.15).

✪ About a half-hour walk southwest of the Gold Pavilion is **Ryoanji Temple** (tel. 462-2216), with what is probably the most famous Zen rock garden in all of Japan. Fifteen rocks set in waves of raked, white pebbles are surrounded on three sides by a wall and on the fourth by a wooden veranda. Sit down here and contemplate what the artist was trying to communicate. The interpretation of what the rocks are supposed to represent is up to the individual (to my mind they look like mountains rising up from the sea). My only objection to this peaceful place is that, unfortunately, it's usually not peaceful—a loudspeaker extols the virtue of the garden, destroying any chance for peaceful meditation. If you get here early enough, you may be able to escape both the crowds and the noise. After visiting the rock garden, be sure to take a walk around the 1,000-year-old pond. At one corner is a beautiful little restaurant with tatami rooms and screens where you can eat yudofu (boiled tofu with vegetables) for ¥1,500 ($10.70) or drink a beer and enjoy the view. Note, however, that if you order only a beer, which costs ¥550 ($3.90), an extra ¥300 ($2.15) will be added to the bill. The view, however, is well worth it. Ryoanji is open daily from 8am to 5pm in summer, to 4:30pm in winter. Admission is ¥350 ($2.50).

Ready for some fun? How about going to the **Toei Uzumasa Eiga Mura (Toei Uzumasa Movieland)**, 10 Higashihachigaokacho Uzumasa Ukyo-ku (tel. 881-7716), where many of Japan's samurai flicks are made? Open daily from 9am to 5pm (9:30am to 4pm December through February) and closed December 21 to January 1, it charges an admission of ¥1,800 ($12.85) for adults and ¥800 ($5.70) for children. Resembling an amusement park more than a movie studio, it has both outdoor and indoor sets, and if you're lucky you'll see a movie in the making. Reconstructed houses re-create the mood, setting, and atmosphere of feudal Japan, while indoor museums show miniature castles, houses, and items from the history of Japanese film. Who knows, you may even see a famous star walking around dressed in samurai garb. You can also have a photo taken of yourself decked out in a kimono or samurai gear. Since Movieland is clearly a commercial venture, come here only if you have a lot of time, are sick of temples, or have youngsters in tow. To reach it, take bus no. 71, 72, or 73 to Uzumasa Koryoji bus stop.

CENTRAL KYOTO

Much of central Kyoto has been taken over by the 20th century, but there are a few interesting sites worth investigating. **Kyoto Imperial Palace** (tel. 221-1215), near the Imadegawa subway station, was where the imperial family lived from 1331 until 1868, when they moved to Tokyo. The palace was destroyed several times by fire, and the present buildings date from 1855. You need special permission to see the palace grounds, but that can be obtained the day of your intended visit by dropping by the Imperial Household Agency, located on the grounds. A 30-minute tour is held every morning at 10am—except Sunday and the second and fourth Saturdays of every month—and you must apply to join this tour by 9:40am. Be sure to bring your passport. Another tour in English is held Monday through Friday at 2pm, and for this

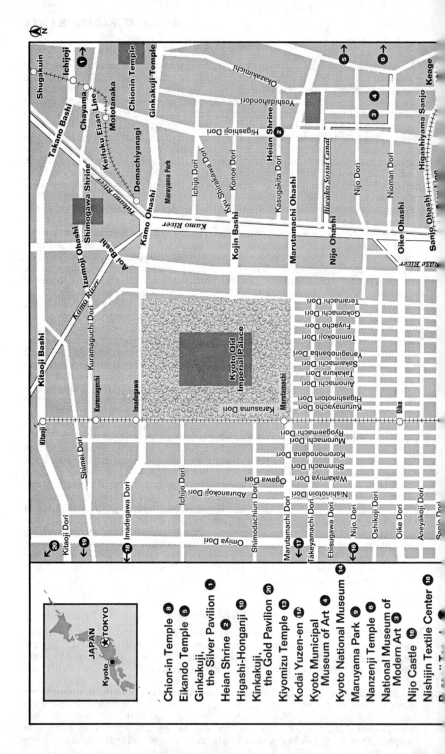

N ↑

Chion-in Temple **8**
Eikando Temple **5**
Ginkakuji,
  the Silver Pavilion **1**
Heian Shrine **2**
Higashi-Honganji **10**
Kinkakuji,
  the Gold Pavilion **20**
Kiyomizu Temple **13**
Kodai Yuzen-en **14**
Kyoto Municipal
  Museum of Art **4**
Kyoto National Museum **14**
Maruyama Park **9**
Nanzenji Temple **6**
National Museum of
  Modern Art **3**
Nijo Castle **16**
Nishijin Textile Center **18**

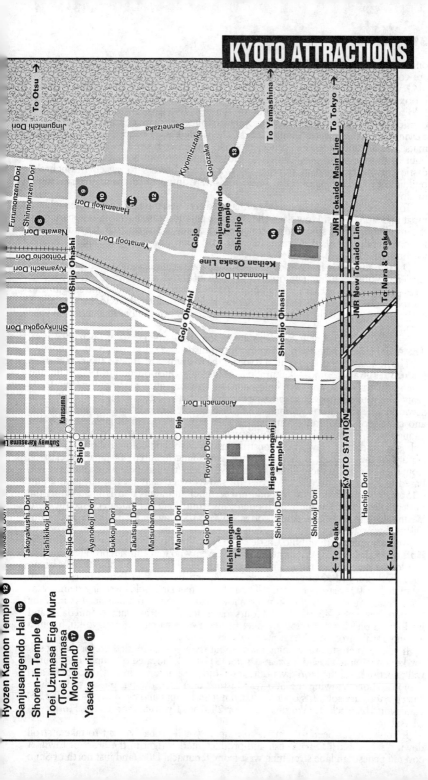

KYOTO ATTRACTIONS

Ryozen Kannon Temple ⑫
Sanjusangendo Hall ⑮
Shoren-in Temple ❼
Toei Uzumasa Eiga Mura
(Toei Uzumasa
Movieland) ⑰
Yasaka Shrine ⑪

one you must apply by 1:40pm. The tours are free, cover just the palace grounds, and are conducted quickly, leaving little time for dawdling or taking photographs.

○ Whereas the Imperial Palace was where the royal family resided, **Nijo Castle,** Horikawa Dori (tel. 341-0096), is where the Tokugawa shogun stayed whenever he left Edo and visited Kyoto. It was built by the first Tokugawa shogun, Ieyasu, and is considered the quintessence of Momoyama architecture, with delicate transom wood carvings and paintings on sliding doors. The castle has 33 rooms, some 800 tatami mats, and an understated elegance, especially when compared to the castles being built in Europe at the same time. All the sliding doors on the outside walls of the castle can be removed in summer, allowing cool breezes to sweep through the building. Typical for Japan at the time, rooms were unfurnished, the mattresses stored in closets.

To protect the shogun from real or imagined enemies, the castle was protected by a moat and stone walls. How deep the shogun's paranoia ran, however, is apparent by the installation of the so-called nightingale floor inside the castle itself. Corridors were fitted with floorboards that squeaked when trod upon, and there were hidden alcoves for bodyguards.

Outside the castle is a garden famous in its own right, designed by the renowned gardener Kobori Enshu. The original grounds of the castle, however, were without trees—supposedly because the falling of leaves in autumn reminded the shogun and his tough samurai of life's transitory nature, making them terribly sad. Incidentally, I prefer Nijo Castle to the Imperial Palace because you can explore its interior on your own.

Nijo Castle is open daily from 8:45am to 4pm; the garden remains open until 5pm. The ¥500 ($3.55) admission covers both the castle and the garden.

The newest attraction in central Kyoto is the **Museum of Kyoto (Kyoto Bunka Hakubutsukan),** Sanjo-Takakura (tel. 222-0888), which opened in 1988. Through video displays, slides, and even holograms, the museum attempts to present the 1,200 years of Kyoto's history. Exhibited are prehistoric relics, glassware, fans, crafts, and artwork. The third-floor exhibition hall displays the works of contemporary artists and craftspeople. My only complaint is that explanations are in Japanese only—if enough people complain, maybe this will be corrected. Be sure to check out the holographic display of workers constructing the vermilion-colored shrine. A special feature of the museum is its film library, containing hundreds of Japanese classics, from silent movies to those filmed up to 20 years ago (the Japanese movie industry was based in Kyoto for decades). Movies are shown twice daily (at last check at 2 and 6:15pm, but you'd be wise to confirm the time) and admission is included in the museum entry fee. The museum is open daily from 10am to 8:30pm; closed the third Wednesday of the month. Admission is ¥500 ($3.55), and it's a 3-minute walk from Oike subway station.

About a mile north of Nijo Castle is the **Nishijin Textile Center (Nishijin-Ori Kaikan)** (tel. 451-9231), dedicated to the weavers who for centuries produced elegant textiles for the imperial family and the nobility. The history of Nishijin textiles began with the history of Kyoto itself back in 794, and by the Edo Period there were an estimated 5,000 weaving factories. The museum regularly holds weaving demonstrations, historical displays, and kimono shows. Admission to the hall itself is free; the kimono show costs ¥360 ($2.55). Hours for the textile hall are 9am to 5pm daily, and it's located on Horikawa-dori Avenue, Imadegawa-minamiiru, Kamigyo-ku, about a 7-minute walk from the Imadegawa subway station.

If you're interested in learning more about the Kyo-Yuzen method for dyeing silk for kimonos, visit **Kodai Yuzen-en** (tel. 811-8101), located a couple of minutes' walk northwest of the Horikawa-dori and Gojo Street intersection. It has displays and demonstrations showing the 300-year history of Yuzen dyeing, plus a shop where Yuzen goods are sold. It's open daily from 9am to 5pm and charges a ¥500 ($3.55) admission. To reach it, take bus no. 9 or 28 from Kyoto Station to the Horikawa-Matsubara stop.

If you've never been to a market in Japan, you'll probably want to take a stroll down **Nishiki-Koji Dori,** a fish-and-produce market right in the heart of town. A covered pedestrian lane stretching west from Teramachi Dori (and just north of Shijo

Dori), Nishiki-Koji has been Kyoto's principal food market for more than three centuries. This is where the city's finest restaurants and inns buy their food, and you'll find open-fronted shops and stalls selling seasonal vegetables, fish, beans, seaweed, pickled vegetables, and more. Shops are open from the early morning hours until about 7 or 8pm; many close on either Wednesday or Sunday.

AROUND KYOTO STATION

Just north of Kyoto Station are two massive temple compounds, **Nishi-Honganji** and **Higashi-Honganji.** They were once joined as one huge religious center called Honganji but split after a disagreement several centuries ago. Higashi-Honganji is Kyoto's largest wooden structure, while Nishi-Honganji is the older temple and represents an outstanding example of Buddhist architecture. Only parts of both temples are open to the public.

North of these two temples, on Horikawa Dori Avenue, is the **Costume Museum,** located on the fifth floor of the Izutsu Building, Shinhanaya-cho kado (tel. 351-6750). Though small, it includes traditional Japanese clothing ranging from hunting outfits worn during the Kamakura Period to ceremonial court dress, including elaborate kimonos. About a 20-minute hike from Kyoto Station, it's open Monday through Saturday from 9am to 5pm; admission is ¥300 ($2.15).

NEARBY ATTRACTIONS

If this is your first visit to Kyoto and you're here only a short while, you should concentrate on the sightseeing sites in Kyoto itself. If, however, this is your second trip to Kyoto or you're here for an extended period of time, there are a number of worthwhile attractions in the region surrounding Kyoto.

Note: Katsura Imperial Villa, Shugakuin Imperial Villa, and Saihoji (popularly called the Moss Temple) all require advance permission to visit. To see Katsura Imperial Villa or Shugakuin Imperial Villa, you can telephone the **Imperial Household Agency** (tel. 211-1211) at least 1 week to 3 months in advance to make an appointment to join a tour. Unfortunately, no one at the office speaks English, so you'll have to find someone to make the call for you in Japanese. If applying by mail, do so 1 to 3 months in advance and include your name, age, sex, occupation, passport number, nationality, home address, and the date and time of the tour you'd like to join. You must be more than 20 years old, and the maximum number of people allowed in your group is four. Tours—in Japanese only—are given at Katsura at 10am and 2pm and at Shugakuin at 9 and 10am and at 1:30 and 3pm. Note that no tours are given on Saturday afternoon, Sunday, national holidays, and the second and fourth Saturdays of every month. When specifying your desired date and time, be sure to include several choices. The address of the Imperial Household Agency is 3, Kyoto-Gyoen, Kamigyo-ku, Kyoto, and once you arrive in Kyoto you should drop by the agency (located at the Kyoto Imperial Palace) at least 1 day prior to the tour to fill out a formal application. Be sure to bring your passport. The tours of the villas are free. For information about applying for a tour of Saihoji, please see the description of the temple further on in this section.

Obviously, it's somewhat of a hassle to visit the imperial villas, and according to the Tourist Information Office, applications by mail are not always acknowledged or successful. Applying by phone is much easier if you can find someone to do so in Japanese. If you're going to be in Japan longer than a week before arriving in Kyoto, you might try calling the Imperial Household Agency as soon as you arrive in Japan. If all time slots are already booked, don't be too disappointed—there are many other sites that are equally enjoyable to visit.

KATSURA IMPERIAL VILLA

Located about a 15-minute walk from Katsura Station on the Hankyu railway line or a 30-minute bus ride from Kyoto Station (take bus no. 33 to Katsura Rikyu Mae bus stop), Katsura Imperial Villa is considered the jewel of traditional Japanese architecture and landscape gardening. It was built between 1620 and 1624 by Prince

Toshihito, brother of the emperor, with construction continued by Toshihito's son. The garden, markedly influenced by Kobori Enshu, Japan's most famous garden designer, is a "stroll garden" in which each turn of the path brings an entirely new view.

The first thing you notice upon entering Katsura is its simplicity—the buildings were all made of natural materials, and careful attention was paid to the slopes of the roofs, and to the grain, texture, and color of the various woods used. A pavilion for viewing the moon, a hall for imperial visits, a teahouse, and other buildings are situated around a pond, and as you walk along the pathway you are treated to views that literally change with each step you take. Islets, stone lanterns, various scenes (representing the seashore, mountains, and hamlets), manicured trees, and bridges of stone, earth, or wood that arch gracefully over the water—everything is perfectly balanced. No matter where you stand, the view is complete and in harmony. Every detail was carefully planned, down to the stones used in the pathways, the way the trees twist, and how scenes are reflected in the water. Little wonder that Katsura Imperial Villa has influenced architecture not only in Japan but around the world.

SHUGAKUIN IMPERIAL VILLA

Located about a 15-minute walk from the Shugakuin Rikyu Michi bus stop (take bus no. 5 from Kyoto Station), the Shugakuin Imperial Villa was built in the mid-1600s for Emperor Go-Mizunoo, who became a monk after his abdication. Its stroll garden, among Kyoto's largest, is divided into three levels. The upper garden, with its lake, islands, and waterfalls, is the most extensive of the three and uses the principle known as "borrowed landscape," in which the surrounding landscape is incorporated into the overall garden design. The gardens are more spacious than most Japanese-style gardens, and the view of the surrounding countryside is grand.

SAIHOJI

Popularly known as Kokedera, the Moss Temple, Saihoji is famous for its velvety-green moss garden spread underneath the trees. Altogether, there are more than 40 different varieties of moss throughout the grounds, giving off an iridescent and mysterious glow that is at its best just after a rain. Because the monks are afraid that huge numbers of visitors would trample the moss to death, prior permission is needed to visit Saihoji, which you can obtain by writing to the temple at least 1 month in advance. The address is Saihoji Temple, Matsuo Kamigaya-cho, Nishikyo-ku, Kyoto (tel. 075/391-3631), and you should give your name, address, nationality, age, sex, and when you'd like to visit. Include a self-addressed return envelop and International Reply Coupons for return postage. The cost of a visit to the temple, which includes Sutra writing demonstrations, is ¥3,000 ($21.40) and can be paid when you pick up your ticket. To reach Saihoji, take bus no. 73 from Kyoto Station to Kokedera stop.

ENRYAKUJI TEMPLE

Along with Mt. Koya, south of Osaka, Enryakuji Temple (tel. 0775/78-0551) is one of the most important centers of Buddhism in Japan. Located atop Mt. Hiei, Enryakuji Temple was founded back in 788 at the order of Emperor Kammu to ward off evil spirits that might come from the northeast. At one time, Enryakuji Temple consisted of as many as 3,000 buildings and maintained an army of warrior monks that made raids on rival temples. Because of the temple's political and military power, an army organized by Nobunaga Oda attacked Enryakuji and destroyed it in 1571. Although some of the temple was subsequently rebuilt, it never again reached its former powerful position. However, there are a number of fine buildings spread out under large cedar trees in a peaceful atmosphere. Open in summer daily from 8:30am to 4:30pm and in winter from 9am to 4pm, it charges a ¥400 ($2.85) admission. To reach it, take bus no. 16 or 17 or the Keihan Electric Railway to Demachiyanagi Station, transferring there to the Eisan Electric Railway Line bound for Yase-yuen, the last stop. There you'll find the Keifuku Cable Car, followed by the Hieizan Ropeway, which will take you to the top. The entire trip takes approximately an hour.

BYODOIN TEMPLE

Located in the town of Uji, about 11 miles southeast of Kyoto, Byodoin Temple (tel. 0774/21-2861) is a good example of temple architecture of the Heian Period. Originally a villa, it was converted into a temple in 1053. Most famous is the main hall, known as Phoenix Hall, the only original building remaining and featured on every ¥10 coin. It has three wings, creating an image of the mythical bird of China, the phoenix, and on the gable ends are two bronze phoenixes. On the temple grounds is one of the most famous bells in Japan, as well as a monument to Yorimasa Minamoto, who took his own life here after being defeated by the rival Taira clan. Byodoin is located about a 10-minute walk from the Uji JR Station (there's a map of the town in front of the station). Admission is ¥400 ($2.85), and though the grounds of the temple are open daily from 8:30am to 5pm, note that Phoenix Hall is open from 9am to 5pm.

FUSHIMI-INARI SHRINE

Just a minute's walk from the JR Inari Station, Fushimi-Inari Shrine has long been popular with merchants, who come here to pray for success and prosperity. One of Japan's most celebrated Shinto shrines, it was founded back in 711 and is dedicated to the goddess of rice. The 2½-mile-long pathway behind the shrine is lined with more than 10,000 red torii gates, presented by worshippers throughout the ages, and there are also stone foxes, which are considered messengers of the gods. It's a glorious walk as you wind through the woods and then gradually climb a hill, from where you have a good view of Kyoto. At several places along the path are small shops where you can sit down for a bowl of noodles or other refreshment. Admission is free, and the expansive grounds never close.

Note: Both Byodoin Temple and Fushimi-Inari Shrine are on the same JR line that continues to Nara. If you plan on spending the night in Nara, you could easily take in these two attractions on the way.

CORMORANT FISHING IN ARASHIYAMA

If you're lucky enough to be in Kyoto during July and August, I highly recommend that you spend one evening on the Oi River, drifting in a wooden boat and watching men fishing with trained cormorants (seabirds). Cormorant fishing is held in Arashiyama every evening (except when there's a full moon or during and after a heavy rain) from July 1 to August 31. You should reach Arashiyama before 7pm, and for a fee of ¥1,400 ($10) you can board a narrow wooden boat gaily decorated with paper lanterns. Along with dozens of others, your boatman will pole you down the river so that you can see the fishing boats lit by blazing torches. The cormorants, with rings around their necks so that they don't swallow the fish they catch, dive under the water for ayu, a small river fish. Water taxis ply the river offering snacks and beer. I find the whole experience of watching the cormorants, and of being a part of the flotilla of wooden boats and paper lanterns, terribly romantic. It's a lovely way to spend a warm summer's evening.

You can reach Arashiyama by bus no. 71, 72, or 73 from Kyoto Station to the Arashiyama bus stop, followed by a 1-minute walk, or by taking the JR Sagano Line from Kyoto Station to Saga Station, from which it's a 15-minute walk.

A MAZE

Just trying to find your way around Japan's big cities can be challenging enough, but if you enjoy frustration at every turn, visit the **Kyoto Daigo Granmaze** (tel. 621-2207), a specially constructed maze for humans. Opened in 1985, the Kyoto Granmaze was the start of the maze craze that has since spread to other parts of Japan. Covering an area about half the size of a football field, this maze features wooden walls about 6½ feet tall, with lookout towers posted every so often to let you survey your position.

Although the record time for finding one's way out is 8 minutes, it takes most people about an hour. If you take longer, don't feel bad—one person wandered around for 4 hours and 34 minutes before reaching the finish line. To get to the Granmaze, take the Keihan Uji Line to Rokujizo Station, from which it's about a 7-minute walk north of the station (make sure you have the right line—otherwise you might well end up in Osaka, with more frustration than you bargained for). The Granmaze opens daily at 9am, and lost souls are flushed out at sunset. Admission is ¥600 ($4.28).

COOL FOR KIDS

There are several attractions listed above that would appeal to children. If they need to run and play, take them to **Maruyama Park,** described in "Walking Tour 1." An alternative is the **Philosophers' Stroll,** a 1-mile walk along a tree-lined canal; see "Walking Tour 2." The **Toei Uzumasa Eiga Mura (Movieland)** in northwestern Kyoto, where samurai flicks are filmed, is Japan's answer to Hollywood's MGM Studios. Your youngsters will be able to wander through a mock feudal village and see people dressed in period costumes. For teenagers, cormorant fishing in Arashiyama may be a fun way to spend an evening. The Rapids Shooting Tour, described below, provides a different kind of river excitement.

ORGANIZED TOURS

Although I believe that being herded around Kyoto's temples in a large group can never compete with the experience of wandering around at your own leisure, you may find yourself so short of time that you feel compelled to join an organized tour of Kyoto. Both morning and afternoon tours are offered by the **Japan Travel Bureau** (tel. 341-1413) and the **Kintetsu Gray Line** (tel. 691-0903). Sites visited may include the Imperial Palace, Nijo Castle, the Golden Pavilion, Heian Shrine, Sanjusangendo Hall, and Kiyomizu Temple. Three-hour tours cost about ¥5,200 ($37.15).

For those who want a more personalized tour, **student guides** from Kyoto, Doshisha, and Kyoto Women's universities are available through the **Tourist Information Center (TIC),** Kyoto Tower Building, Higashi-Shiokojicho, Shimogyo-ku (tel. 075/371-5649). (Students are happy to act as voluntary guides because they can practice their English.) You must apply at the TIC 1 or 2 days in advance, and you're expected to pay for the student's transportation, entrance fees to shrines and temples, and lunch.

Another tour that you may consider joining is the **Rapids Shooting Tour** (tel. 07712/2-5846). March through November, flat-bottomed wooden boats depart from Kameoka seven times daily, with fewer departures in heated boats during the winter months. The trip lasts about 2 hours and covers approximately 10 miles of the Hozu River, ending in Arashiyama. The rapids are not dangerous (in fact, most of them are nothing more than small riffles), and the trip is a very pleasant and relaxing way to see something of the surrounding countryside of wooded hills and a winding gorge. Cost of the trip is ¥3,400 ($24.30) for adults and ¥2,000 ($14.30) for children. To reach Kameoka, take the San'in JR Line from Kyoto Station to Kameoka Station, from which it's an 8-minute walk. For more information on the tour or how to get to Kameoka, contact the TIC.

6. SAVVY SHOPPING

As the nation's capital for more than 1,000 years, Kyoto became home to a number of crafts and exquisite art forms that catered to the elaborate tastes of the imperial court and the upper classes. Today, you can shop for everything from Noh masks to silk to cloisonné and lacquerware in Kyoto.

THE SHOPPING SCENE

There are a number of tiny specialty shops in Kyoto, the majority situated in Gion, along **Shijo Dori Avenue,** and in the area of Kawaramachi Dori Avenue. The square formed by **Kawaramachi Dori, Shijo Dori, Sanjo Dori,** and **Teramachi Dori,** for example, includes a covered shopping arcade and specialized shops selling lacquerware, combs and hairpins, knives and swords, tea and tea-ceremony implements, and more. If you're looking for antiques, woodblock prints, and art galleries, head toward **Shinmonzen Street** in Gion, which parallels Shijo Dori to the north on the east side of the Kamo River. Pottery shops are found in abundance on the roads leading to Kiyomizu Temple in Higashiyama-ku.

For clothing, accessories, and modern goods, Kyoto's many department stores are good bets and are conveniently located near Kyoto Station or in the heart of Nakagyo-ku near the Shijo-Kawaramachi intersection. In addition, there's a huge underground shopping mall called **Porta** that radiates from the Karasuma (north) side of Kyoto Station, with boutiques selling everything from clothing and shoes to stationery.

SHOPPING A TO Z

CRAFTS & SPECIALTY SHOPS

ARITSUGU, Nishiki-Koji Dori, Gokomachi Nishi-iru, Nakagyo-ku. Tel. 221-1091.

The fact that this family-owned business is located near the Nishiki-Koji market is appropriate, since it sells hand-wrought knives and other handmade cooking implements, including sushi knives, bamboo steamers, pots, pans, and cookware used in the preparation of traditional Kyoto cuisine. In business for 400 years, the shop counts the city's top chefs among its customers. Open: Mon–Sat 9am–5:30pm. Directions: At east end of Nishiki-Koji Dori, a block north of Shijo Dori Avenue.

KYOTO HANDICRAFT CENTER, Kumano Jinja Higashi, Sakyo-ku. Tel. 761-5080.

For one-stop shopping under one roof, your best bet is this huge crafts center, located just north of Heian Shrine on Marutamachi Dori Avenue. Seven floors of merchandise contain almost everything Japanese imaginable—pearls, lacquerware, dolls, kimonos, woodblock prints, pottery, cameras, cassette players, items made of Japanese paper, swords, lanterns, silk and textile goods, painted scrolls, and music boxes. And that's just for starters. You can even buy the socks to be worn with geta wooden shoes and the obi sashes to be worn with the kimono. You can easily spend an hour or two here wandering around, and there are also demonstrations showing artisans at work on various crafts, including hand-weaving, woodblock printing, and the production of damascene. Open: daily 9:30am–6pm (5:30pm Dec through Feb). Closed: Dec 31 through Jan 3. Bus: 206 to Kumano-jinja-mae.

KYOTO CRAFT CENTER, 275 Gion, Kitagawa, Higashiyama-ku. Tel. 561-9660.

Whereas the Kyoto Handicraft Center, described above, is good for souvenirs and inexpensive gifts for the folks back home, this crafts center features beautifully designed and crafted items by local and famous artisans. Located on Shijo Dori Avenue east of the Kamo River in the heart of Gion, the Kyoto Craft Center devotes its two floors to a wide range of products, including jewelry, scarves, pottery, glass, fans, damascene, baskets, and much more. This is the place to shop for wedding gifts or something very special for yourself, and since the products are continually changing, there's always something new. Open: Thurs–Tues 10am–6pm. Bus: 12, 203, or 207 to Gion Ishidanshita bus stop.

KYOTO MUNICIPAL MUSEUM OF TRADITIONAL INDUSTRY (Kyoto-shi Dento Sangyo Kaikan), 9-2 Seishoji-cho, Okazaki, Sakyo-ku. Tel. 761-3421.

Described earlier under the walking tour of eastern Kyoto, the Kyoto Municipal Museum of Traditional Industry is a crafts museum that also sells many of the items displayed. Lacquerware, textiles, bamboo products, cloisonné, damascene jewelry, knives, dolls, and more are for sale. Admission to the museum is free. Open: Tues–Sun 9am–4:30pm. Bus: 5 to Kyoto Kaikan Bijutsukan-mae bus stop, or 206 to Higashiyama Nijo.

JUSAN-YA, Otabi-cho, Shijo Dori, Shinkyogoku Higashi-iru, Shimogyo-ku. Tel. 221-2008.

Handcrafted boxwood hair combs and ornamental hairpins, made by a fifth generation of comb makers, are on display at this shop in central Kyoto. Open: Daily 10am–8:30pm. Directions: On Shijo Dori Avenue, west of Kawaramachi Dori Avenue.

INABA CLOISONNE, Sanjo Shirakawabashi. Tel. 761-1161.

This store is one of Japan's most famous shops and has been dealing in cloisonné and artistic enamelware for about a century. Its showroom displays jewelry, vases, trays, and other products. There's a workshop here where you can watch women producing various cloisonné wares. The shop is located west of the Miyako Hotel on Sanjo Dori Avenue, not far from the Shirakawa River. Open: Mon–Sat 9am–5:30pm. Closed: hols. Bus: 206 to Chion-in-mae bus stop.

MIYAWAKI BAISEN-AN 102, Tominokoji-nishi, Rokkaku-dori, Nakagyo-ku. Tel. 221-0181.

This elegant shop has specialized in handmade fans since 1823, especially fans characteristic of Kyoto. English is spoken. Open: Daily 9am–5pm. Directions: On Rokkaku-dori, just west of Tominokoji.

SAWAKICHI STONE STORE, 551 Gojozaka, Higashiyama-ku. Tel. 561-2802.

If you want to decorate your garden back home with a Japanese stone lantern, drop by this store located on a large intersection just west of the approach leading to Kiyomizu Temple. It offers a variety of styles and sizes in stone lanterns. Open: Daily 9am–6pm. Bus: 202, 206, or 207 to Gojozaka stop.

TANAKAYA ⑧⑷, Shijo Dori, Yanaginobanba-higashi. Tel. 221-1959.

If you're interested in Japanese dolls, this is a good place to browse for Kyoto-style dolls, Noh masks, and inexpensive miniature animals. The shopkeepers speak English. Open: Thurs–Tues 10am–7pm. Directions: On Shijo Dori Avenue, just east of Yanaginobanba.

YAMATO MINGEI-TEN, Kawaramachi Dori, Takoyakushi-agaru, Naka-gyo-ku. Tel. 221-2641.

This shop has been selling folkcrafts and folk art from all over Japan for more than four decades, including ceramics, glassware, lacquerware, textiles, paper products, baskets, and other handcrafted items. Open: Wed–Mon 10am–8:30pm. Directions: On Kawaramachi Dori, next to Maruzen bookstore.

ZOHIKO LACQUERWARE, Okazaki Park near Heian Shrine. Tel. 761-0212.

This store carries on the tradition of Kyoto lacquerware, which has been produced in the ancient capital for 1,000 years. The showroom offers various lacquer products for sale. Open: Mon–Sat 9:30am–5:30pm. Closed: National hols. Bus: 5 or 206.

DEPARTMENT STORES

Department stores are good places to shop for Japanese items and souvenirs, including pottery, lacquerware, and kimono. Since department stores are closed different days of the week, you'll always find several open.

TAKASHIMAYA, southwest corner of Shijo and Kawaramachi intersection. Tel. 221-8811.

In the heart of Kyoto, Takashimaya is one of Japan's oldest and most respected department stores. It has a good selection of traditional crafts. Open: Thurs–Tues 10am–7pm.

HANKYU, southeast corner of Shijo and Kawaramachi intersection. Tel. 223-2288.

Just across the street from the department store above, Hankyu offers seven floors of fashion, housewares, and food. The top two floors are devoted to restaurants, offering a variety of food at reasonable prices. Open: Fri–Wed 10am–7pm.

DAIMARU, Shijo Dori Avenue. Tel. 211-8111.

Located farther west than the two stores listed above, this smaller store sells everything from clothing and food to electronic goods. Open: Thurs–Tues 10am–7pm.

KINTETSU, Karasuma, Shichijo-sagaru, Shimogyo-ku. Tel. 361-1111.

Located across the street from Kyoto Station's north exit, this is a convenient store for all those necessities, from film to toiletries and food. Its foreign-exchange service on the first floor is a good place to exchange money after the banks close. Open: Fri–Wed 10am–7pm.

A FLEA MARKET

On the 21st of each month a flea market is held at **Toji Temple,** located about a 15-minute walk southwest of Kyoto Station. Japan's largest monthly market, it's also one of the oldest, with a history stretching back more than 700 years. The market began in the 1200s as pilgrims began flocking to Toji Temple to pay their respects to Kobo Daishi, who founded the Shingon sect of Buddhism. Today, Toji Temple is still a center for the Shingon sect, and its monthly market is a colorful affair with booths selling antiques, old kimonos, and other items. Worshippers come to pray before a statue of Kobo Daishi and to have their wishes written on wooden slats by temple calligraphers. Even if you don't buy anything, the festive atmosphere of the market and booths makes a trip here a memorable experience.

7. EVENING ENTERTAINMENT

Nothing beats spending a fine summer's evening strolling the streets of Kyoto. From the geisha district of Gion to the bars and restaurants lining the narrow street of Pontocho, Kyoto at night is a city utterly charming and romantic. Begin your evening with a walk along the banks of the Kamo River—it's a favorite place for young couples in love. In the summer, restaurants along the river stretching north and south of Shijo Dori Avenue erect outdoor wooden platforms on stilts over the water. Illuminated with paper lanterns, they look like images from Kyoto's past.

Gion is a small district of Kyoto, an area of plain wooden buildings devoid of flashing neon signs. In fact, as the geisha entertainment district of the city, there's something almost austere and solemn about Gion, as though its raison d'être were infinitely more important and sacred than that of mere entertainment. Gion is a shrine to Kyoto's past, an era when geishas numbered thousands in the city. Now there are only a mere couple of hundred. After all, in today's high-tech world, few women are willing to undergo the years of training to learn how to conduct the tea ceremony, to play the samisen (a three-stringed musical instrument), or to perform ancient court dances. And contrary to popular Western misconceptions, geishas are not prostitutes. Rather, they are trained experts in conversation and coquettishness, and their primary role is to make men feel like kings while in the soothing enclave of the geisha house.

As you stroll the narrow streets of Gion, perhaps you will see a geisha or maiko (a young woman training to be a geisha) clattering in her wooden shoes on her way to her

IMPRESSIONS

Kyoto—or, for that matter, any Japanese city—is a barfly's Valhalla.
—TRUMAN CAPOTE, *THE DOGS BARK*, 1974

evening appointment. She will be dressed in a brilliant kimono, her face a chalky white, and her hair adorned with hairpins and ornaments. From geisha houses music and laughter lilt out from behind paper screens, but you cannot enter without being invited. Not even the Japanese will venture inside without proper introductions. If it will satisfy your curiosity, however, I will tell you that on my fourth visit to Kyoto I was finally invited to one of Gion's geisha houses—and found it to be much like any other hostess bar in Japan. The women pour the drinks, the men drink, and everyone is lighthearted and happy.

Gion is located in Higashiyama-ku on the east side of the Kamo River, about a 5-minute walk from the Shijo-Kawaramachi intersection. To reach it, walk west on Shijo, and then take a right on Hanamikoji Dori.

Pontocho is a narrow street that parallels the Kamo River's west bank and stretches north from Shijo Dori to Sanjo Dori. Riddled with geisha houses, hostess bars, restaurants, and bars that fill every nook and cranny, Pontocho makes for a fascinating walk as you watch groups of Japanese enjoying themselves.

Although many of these restaurants lining the river have outdoor verandas in summer, I was able to include only a couple of them in this book, which you'll find listed in the "Kyoto Dining" section of this chapter. Unfortunately, most of the restaurants in Pontocho are unreceptive to foreigners, and I was turned away from establishment after establishment with the excuse that the place was full—even when I could see that it was not. The Kyoto Tourist Information Center (TIC) informed me that they do not recommend Pontocho to foreigners simply because of the cold reception. However, I think it's worth walking through Pontocho because the area is so interesting and so Japanese. Although most of the bars and clubs are virtually impossible to enter without an introduction, you might want to come here for a meal at one of the restaurants recommended in this book. And if you're feeling adventurous and are determined to find seating under the paper lanterns on one of the open verandas, maybe you'll be lucky. Once in a while, restaurants that do not want the publicity of a guidebook will accept the occasional lone foreigner.

Another good place to look is Kiyamachi, a small street that parallels Pontocho to the west and runs beside a small canal.

THE ENTERTAINMENT SCENE

To find out what's going on in Kyoto in terms of festivals, special events, Kabuki or Noh performances, or exhibitions, call the **Teletourist Service** at 361-2911. This 24-hour service provides 90 seconds of recorded information in English on what's going on during the week.

To find out what's being performed where in Kyoto, purchase the monthly magazine called *Kansai Time Out,* available in Kyoto at both the Maruzen and Izumiya bookstores and costing ¥300 ($2.15). Although major concerts are infrequent in Kyoto (they're usually held in nearby Osaka), the magazine is the best source for finding out what's going on in the classical and modern music scene.

Discover Kinki, a monthly distributed free to hotels, travel agencies, and the TIC, tells of upcoming events and festivals in Kyoto and the neighboring cities of Osaka, Kobe, and Nara. Another monthly tabloid distributed free at hotels and restaurants is *The Kyoto Visitor's Guide,* which contains maps, a calendar of events and performances for the month, and information on sightseeing and shopping.

Finally, don't forget the TIC itself, which has information on Noh performances; Kabuki drama, which is staged in Kyoto several times a year; and such special events as court music that may be taking place at one of the city's shrines.

THE PERFORMING ARTS

GION CORNER, Yasaka Hall, Hanamikoji Dori, Shijo-sagaru. Tel. 561-1119.

After strolling around Gion, visit Gion Corner, located on Hanamikoji Dori south of Shijo Dori. Special variety programs are held every night from March 1 to November 29, with demonstrations of the tea ceremony, flower arrangement, *koto* (Japanese harp) music, *gagaku* (ancient court music and dance), *kyogen* (Noh comic play), *kyomai* (Kyoto-style dance, performed by maiko), and Bunraku (puppetry). This is an excellent way to see a variety of ancient Japanese entertainment in a short period of time. There are two shows nightly, at 7:40 and again at 8:40pm. Reservations are not necessary, but get there early since the 250 seats are on a first-come, first-served basis.

Prices: Tickets ¥2,500 ($17.85). Tickets are available at most hotels, travel agencies, and at Gion Corner itself.

THE CLUB & LIVE MUSIC SCENE

IMAGIUM, Shijo Dori, Kobashi-nishi-iru. Tel. 223-2911.

If you like your entertainment in one spot, head for this multientertainment building, just north of Shijo and west of Kiyamachi in the nightlife district. It offers eight floors of evening activity, from eating, drinking, and playing pool to dancing. In the basement is Disco Gaia; on the first floor is a karaoke bar, where you can sing along into a microphone; on the fifth floor is a pub that plays oldies but goldies; on the seventh floor is a pool hall; and on the eighth is another disco. Imagium is the glitziest thing to hit Kyoto in a long time and looks as if it had been imported straight out of Tokyo—and Kyoto purists grumble that Tokyo is exactly where it belongs. Most locales are open only in the evenings, from 6 or 7pm to 3am or later.

Admission: Different admissions for each locale; Disco Gaia charges ¥2,200 ($15.70) on weekdays, ¥3,300 ($23.55) on weekends, including two drinks; Karaoke Pub Rheia charges ¥3,300 ($23.55), which includes all the singing you care to do.

ROCK

TAKU TAKU ⑧⑤**, Tominokoji-Bukkoji. Tel. 351-1321.**

If you want to hear live music, head for this old sake warehouse with a plain décor. Featuring heavy metal, rock, soul, blues, reggae, jazz, and punk rock, it caters mainly to Kyoto's college students. To find Taku Taku, walk south from Shijo Dori Avenue on Tominokoji Dori Street for about 3 minutes. It's just past the red-and-white spiral of a barbershop, on the right-hand side of the street behind a small parking lot. Listen for the music. Open: Daily 6pm–11pm, with live music usually from 7–9pm.

Admission: ¥1,600 ($11.40), including one drink; ¥6,000 ($42.85) for occasional bands from England or the U.S. **Prices:** Beer ¥550 ($3.90).

JAZZ

JAZZ CLUB SUNNYSIDE, 5th floor of Kyoto Art Center Building, Furumonzen Dori Street, Yamato-oji, Higashiyama-ku. Tel. 525-0910.

Located just east of the Kamo River a minute's walk south of Sanjo Keihan Station, this informal and cozy place seats less than 20 people and is owned by Watanabe Fumihiro, who also provides the entertainment by singing and playing the piano. His repertoire centers on American jazz and popular hits of the 1940s, and there's a tiny dance floor. The place is popular with a middle-aged crowd. Open: Tues–Sun 7pm–1am.

Admission: ¥2,000 ($14.30) music charge, including one drink, snack, and tip. **Prices:** Beer ¥600 ($4.30).

KYOTO CAVERN CLUB AND KENTO'S, Hitotsume-nishi-iru, Hanamikoji Dori, Shijo-sagaru. Tel. 551-1369 (Cavern Club), 551-2777 (Kento's).

Located in the heart of Gion, this is the Kyoto branch of two popular Tokyo entertainment clubs, under the same ownership. The Cavern Club, as its name implies, features a house band that plays exclusively Beatles songs. Kento's is where enthusiasts of yesterday come to hear oldies but goldies of the '50s and '60s. The clubs are located just off Hanamikoji, in a plain building in keeping with Gion's atmosphere. Open: Both establishments daily 6:30pm–2am.

Admission: Separate admission of ¥3,800 ($27.15) for either club, plus a one-drink minimum, ¥550–¥1,000 ($3.90–$7.15), and a one-dish minimum, ¥650–¥1,200 ($4.65–$8.55), per person.

DANCE CLUBS/DISCOS

CHINA EXPRESS, basement of Sanjo Terrace Building, Sanjo Kiya-machi-sagaru. Tel. 241-3870.

Catering to a young crowd in their 20s is China Express, located on the first street south of and paralleling Sanjo Dori Avenue, between Kawaramachi and Kiyamachi streets. Its entryway is a bit futuristic, with a clear floor suspended above huge ball bearings. Inside is a small dance floor with mirrors so you can watch yourself dance and an interesting Chinese-like decor. In an effort to attract an international crowd, foreigners pay a lower admission than do Japanese. Open: daily 6pm–midnight.

Admission: ¥3,000 ($21.40) for Japanese, including 20 tickets for drinks; ¥2,000 ($14.30) for foreigners, which includes tickets worth ¥1,500 ($10.70) for drinks. **Prices:** Beer 6 tickets, cocktails 6 or 7 tickets.

THE BAR SCENE

YAKITORI-YA

SUISHIN HONTEN ⑧⑥, Pontocho, Sanjo Dori-sagaru. Tel. 221-8596.

This inexpensive yakitori-ya, part of a chain of Suishin yakitori restaurants, is very popular with young Japanese. It's located on the west side of Pontocho, just south of Sanjo Dori Avenue. Look for a big white sign, red curtains hanging outside the front door, and a large display case of plastic food. Three skewers of chicken yakitori or grilled fish (*yakizakana*) cost ¥380 ($2.70), while a plate of assorted sushi costs ¥800 ($5.70). This is a good place to stop off for a beer. Be sure to remove your shoes at the entryway and place them in one of the lockers provided. Small mugs of beer cost ¥400 ($2.85). Open: Daily 4:30–11:30pm.

SKEWER OF NAN-ZAN, Kawaramachi-Sanjo, Futasugi-agaru. Tel. 221-6930.

⭐ This friendly yakitori-ya is located just off Kawaramachi Dori, on a tiny street called Anekoji Dori, south of the Kawaramachi Catholic Church. It's a tiny basement establishment (don't confuse it with the Nan-Zan steakhouse on the ground floor of the same building), consisting of just one long counter and a couple of tables. The owner has studied English, is a big baseball fan, and is delighted to have foreign guests. The English menu lists various kinds of yakitori, including skewers of beef, chicken, squid, bell pepper, mushroom, and eggplant, as well as sushi, salads, soups, and beefsteak cooked Japanese style. Draft beer here costs ¥450 ($3.20). Open: daily 5pm–1am. Closed: Third Sun of month.

IROHANIHOHETO ⑧①, 5th floor of Akua Building, Sanjo-sagaru, Yamato-oji Dori, Higashiyama-ku. Tel. 541-1683.

Ⓢ Another popular place among Kyoto's college crowd, Irohanihoheto is located on Nawate Dori Street on the fifth floor of a white-tiled building just south of Sanjo-Keihan Station (look for a sign on the building's ground floor that says Colorado Coffee Shop). One of a chain of drinking establishments with headquarters in Hokkaido, Irohanihoheto is known for its rustic décor, which always includes heavy wooden beams held together with ropes to give it a country atmosphere, shoji screens, and crafts hanging down from the ceiling. It's also known for its low prices. The extensive Japanese menu with pictures includes yakitori, gyoza, soba noodles, sashimi, salads, and vegetables, with most items costing less than ¥400 ($2.85). Beer starts at ¥400 ($2.85). Open: Daily 5:30pm–3:30am (5am on weekends).

BARS

AFRICA, Shijo-Kawaramachi. Tel. 255-4518.

This comfortable and pleasant bar caters to a 20- to 30-year-old Japanese and foreign crowd and is a good place to meet friends or while away the evening over a few beers. It's filled with all kinds of knickknacks, stuffed animals, masks, junk, and stained-glass lamps. A video screen shows old and recent American movies, TV shows, and rock videos, and there are also a Foosball table and backgammon sets you can use. Snacks include pizza, gratin, spaghetti, seafood, roast beef, fried chicken, and pilaf. Africa is located on a side street just northeast of the Shijo-Kawaramachi intersection. Beer and cocktails start at ¥550 ($3.90). Open: Daily 6pm–2am.

RUB A DUB, Sanjo-sagaru, Kiyamachi. Tel. 256-3122.

If you like to listen to reggae, one more bar worth mentioning is this tiny basement establishment, unpretentious and primitive. In fact, this could be the only bar in the world that *tries* to imitate the poverty of Jamaica, with a corrugated tin wall and a thatched roof over the bar. The music isn't live, but prices are cheap. It's located on Kiyamachi Street, a couple of shops south of Sanjo Dori Avenue, below a drugstore. Beer and cocktails are ¥650 ($4.65). Open: Daily 6pm–2am.

CAFES

FRANCOIS SALON DE THE, Shijo Kobashi nishizume-minami. Tel. 351-4042.

If evening entertainment to you means a cup of coffee or tea or a drink in quiet surroundings, this is the place for you. Located on a small street running along the west side of a tiny canal just a minute's walk southwest of the Shijo Avenue Bridge, which spans the Kamo River, François Salon de Thé is more than 50 years old. Its façade resembles a miniature castle, while the small interior has an atmosphere similar to that of an old Viennese coffeehouse. A domed ceiling, dark-wood paneling, stained-glass windows, heavy red-cushioned chairs, and classical music make drinking a cup of coffee here a pleasant and relaxing experience—and a good place to escape the crowds. Tea and coffee start at ¥450 ($3.20); beer is ¥650 ($4.65). Open: Daily 9:30am–11pm (11:30pm on Sat).

KARAFUNEYA, Pontocho, Sanjo-sagaru. Tel. 255-1414.

If you yearn to sit under the stars on one of the verandas overlooking the Kamo River, this coffee shop is Pontocho's most accessible establishment. Unfortunately, patrons wishing to sit outside are also obligated to order something from its special veranda menu, which includes an iced coffee and ice cream for ¥800 ($5.70) and a combination beer and french fries for ¥1,000 ($7.15). Still, it's a small price to pay for the chance to relax outdoors, and what I like most about this place is its location right beside a small fall in the river, which produces a roar loud enough to obliterate all traffic noises. Open: 24 hours a day.

BEER GARDENS

TENDAN, Keihan Shijo, Minamizayoko-kudaru. Tel. 551-1196.

This rooftop beer garden, on the east bank of the Kamo River, south of Shijo Dori on Kawabata Dori, offers the usual beer and snacks and a panoramic view of downtown Kyoto. Beer here starts at ¥600 ($4.30). Open: June–Aug, daily 5–10pm.

ANA HOTEL KYOTO, Nijo-Castle-Mae, Horikawa Dori, Nakagyo-ku. Tel. 231-1155.

A good place to top off a late-afternoon visit to Nijo Castle is this rooftop beer garden on the ANA Hotel, located on Horikawa Dori and offering a view of the castle. Beer starts at ¥600 ($4.30). Open: End of May–Aug, daily 5:30–9pm.

NEW MIYAKO HOTEL, Hachijo-guchi, Kyoto Station. Tel. 661-7111.

A good place for a beer if you're in the vicinity of Kyoto Station is this rooftop beer garden at the New Miyako Hotel. Beer starts at ¥550 ($3.90). Open: May–Aug, daily 5:30–9:30pm.

8. AN EXCURSION TO NARA

Nara is celebrated as the cradle of Japanese culture. The Japanese flock here because it gives them the feeling that they are communing with their ancestors. Foreigners come here because Nara offers them a glimpse of a Japan that was.

NARA

26 miles S of Kyoto

GETTING THERE   By Train   Nara is easily reached in about 33 minutes from Kyoto Station on the Kintetsu Limited Express of Kinki Nippon Railways, which whisks you directly to Nara Kintetsu Station. If you have a Japan Rail Pass you can take the slower JR train from Kyoto Station to Nara JR Station in about an hour. You can also reach Nara from Osaka in about 30 to 50 minutes, depending on the train and the station from which you leave.

ESSENTIAL INFORMATION   The **area code** for Nara is 0742.

Pick up brochures and information on Nara before leaving Kyoto at the Tourist Information Center. The Kyoto map distributed there also has a map of Nara on the reverse side. Be sure also to pick up the leaflet *Walking Tour Courses in Nara.*

In Nara itself, there are **tourist information offices** at both JR Station (tel. 0742/22-9821), open daily from 8am to 6pm, and Kintetsu Station (tel. 0742/24-4858), open daily from 9am to 5pm. Both have good brochures and maps, with useful information on how to get around Nara by bus. For more detailed information on Nara, visit the **Nara City Tourist Center,** 23-4 Kamisanjo (tel. 0742/22-3900), located in the heart of the city on Sanjo Dori, about a 5-minute walk from both train stations. It's open daily from 9am to 9pm. Finally, there's a **fourth tourist office,** located at Sarusawa-ike Pond, not far from Nara's many tourist attractions. It's open daily from 9am to 5pm.

If you'd like your own personal guide of Nara, volunteer **Goodwill Guides** will be glad to show you the sights in exchange for the chance to practice their English. One guide each is posted at both the JR and Kintetsu station tourist offices and is available to the first tourists who show up any day except Sunday. If you'd like to reserve a guide in advance, call 0742/45-0221 the day before to arrange a time. The service is available Monday through Saturday from 9:30am to 3pm.

To find out about festivals and exhibitions in Nara, call 0742/27-1313 for a 2-minute taped recording in English.

GETTING AROUND   Nara's Kintetsu and JR stations are about a 10-minute walk of each other. Most of Nara's sites are located to the east of the two stations, within easy **walking** distance. To visit the areas of Horyuji and Nishinokyo, take a **bus,** no. 52, from either JR Station or Kintetsu Station. It has announcements of its stops recorded in English. Other buses bound for the Horyuji and Nishinokyo temple areas are indicated on the brochure of Nara available at the Nara tourist offices.

In the beginnings of Japanese history, the nation's capital was moved to a new site each time a new emperor came to the throne. In 710, however, the first permanent Japanese capital was set up at Nara. Not that it turned out to be so permanent—after only 74 years the capital was moved first to Nagaoka and shortly thereafter to Kyoto, where it remained for more than 1,000 years. What's important about those 74 years is that they witnessed the birth of Japan's arts, crafts, and literature, as Nara imported everything from religion to art to architecture from China. Even the city itself, laid out in a rectangular grid pattern, was modeled after Chinese concepts. It was during the Nara Period that Japan's first historical account, first mythological chronicle, and first poetry anthology (with 4,173 poems) were written. Buddhism flourished and Nara grew as the political and cultural center of the land.

Remarkably enough, many of Nara's buildings and temples remain intact, and long ago someone had enough foresight to enclose many of these historical structures in the quiet and peaceful confines of a large and spacious park. Although most visitors come to Nara on only a day trip from Kyoto, there is more than enough here to occupy 2 full days. For that reason, I've included some recommendations in accommodations. If you stay here overnight, be sure to take advantage of an evening or early-morning stroll through Nara Park.

WHAT TO SEE & DO

The best way to enjoy Nara is to arrive early in the morning before the first tour buses start pulling in. If you don't have much time, the most important sites to see are Todaiji Temple, Kasuga Shrine, and Kofukuji Temple, which you can see in about 2 or 3 hours. If you have more time, add Horyuji Temple.

Around Nara Park

With its ponds, grassy lawns, trees, and temples, Nara Park covers about 1,300 acres and is home to more than 1,000 deer, which roam freely through the park. As you walk east from either the JR or the Kintetsu train station, the first temple you reach is **Kofukuji Temple** (tel. 22-7755), founded in 710 as the family temple of the Fujiwaras, the second most powerful clan after the imperial family. At one time as many as 175 buildings were erected on the Kofukuji Temple grounds, but through centuries of civil wars and fires most of the structures were destroyed. Only a handful of buildings still remain, but even these were rebuilt after the 13th century. The five-story pagoda, first erected in 730, was burned down five times. The present pagoda dates from 1426 and is an exact replica of the original; at 164 feet tall, it's the second-tallest pagoda in Japan (the tallest is at Toji Temple in Kyoto). The temple's **Treasure House,** charging an admission of ¥400 ($2.85) and open daily from 9am to 5pm, displays many statues and works of art originally contained in the temple's buildings, the most famous of which is a statue of Ashura carved in the 8th century.

To the east of Kofukuji is the **Nara National Museum (Nara Kokuritsu Hakubutsukan)** (tel. 22-7771), which houses invaluable Buddhist art and archeological relics. Many statues and other items originally contained in Nara's many temples are now housed here, including sculptures, paintings, calligraphy, and archeological objects. Open Tuesday through Sunday from 9am to 4:30pm, it charges ¥360 ($2.55) admission.

✪ **Todaiji Temple** (tel. 22-5511), along with its **Daibutsu (Great Buddha),** is Nara's premier attraction. When Emperor Shomu ordered construction of both the temple and the Daibutsu back in the mid-700s, he intended to make Todaiji the headquarters of all Buddhist temples in the land. As part of his plans to create a Buddhist utopia, he commissioned work on an overwhelmingly huge bronze statue of Buddha. It took eight castings to finally complete this remarkable work of art, which remains the largest bronze statue of Buddha in Japan. At a height of more than 50 feet, the Daibutsu is made of 437 tons of bronze, 286 pounds of pure gold, 165 pounds of mercury, and 7 tons of vegetable wax. However, because of Japan's frequent natural calamities, the Buddha of today isn't quite what it used to be. In 855, in what must have been a whopper of an earthquake, the statue lost its head. It was repaired in 861, but alas, the huge wooden building housing the Buddha was burned twice during wars, melting the Buddha's head. The present head dates from 1692.

The wooden structure housing the Great Buddha, called Daibutsuden, was destroyed several times through the centuries; the present structure dates from 1709. Measuring 161 feet tall, 187 feet long, and 164 feet wide, it's the largest wooden structure in the world—but only two-thirds its original size. Be sure to walk in a circle around the Great Buddha to see it from all different angles. Behind the statue is a huge wooden column with a small hole in it near the ground. According to popular belief, if you can manage to crawl through this opening you will be sure to reach enlightenment. The Daibutsuden and Great Buddha are open daily from 7:30am to 4:30pm. Admission is ¥400 ($2.85).

✪ A stroll through Nara Park will bring you to **Kasuga Shrine** (tel. 22-7788), one of my favorite Shinto shrines in all Japan. Originally the tutelary shrine of the Fujiwara family, it was founded in 768 and, according to Shinto concepts of purity, was torn down and rebuilt every 20 years in its original form until 1863. Nestled in the midst of verdant woods, it's a shrine of vermilion-colored pillars and an astounding 3,000 stone and bronze lanterns. The most spectacular time to visit the shrine is in mid-August or the beginning of February, when all 3,000 lanterns are lit. One of the fun things to do at Kasuga Shrine is to pay ¥100 (70¢) for a slip of paper on which your fortune is written in English. If the fortune is unfavorable, you can conveniently negate it by tying the piece of paper to the twig of a tree. The grounds of Kasuga Shrine are free. If you want to visit its museum, open daily from 9am to 4pm and charging an admission of ¥350 ($2.50), you'll see the shrine's treasures, including armor, swords, and Noh masks.

A 10-minute walk to the southwest of Kasuga Shrine brings you to **Shin-Yakushiji Temple** (tel. 22-3736), built in the middle of the 8th century by the Empress Komyo to obtain the gods' help in the recovery of Emperor Shomu from an eye disease (Yakushi is the name given to the Healing Buddha). Only the main hall remains, the other buildings having been destroyed and rebuilt after the 13th century. The main hall contains a statue of Yakushi-nyorai surrounded by 12 pottery figures, 11 of which are originals and are considered national treasures. Admission is ¥400 ($2.85), and the temple is open from 8:30am to 5:30pm.

Horyuji Temple Area

Founded in 607 by Prince Shotoku as a center for Buddhism in Japan, **Horyuji Temple** (tel. 07457/5-2555) is one of Japan's most significant gems in terms of both architecture and art. It was from here that Buddhism blossomed and spread throughout the land. Today, about 45 buildings remain, some of them dating from the end of the 7th century and comprising what are probably the oldest wooden structures in the world. At the western end of the grounds is the two-story, 58-foot-high **Golden Hall (Kondo)**, which is considered the oldest building at Horyuji Temple. Next to the main hall is a five-story pagoda, which dates from the foundation of the temple. It contains four scenes from the life of Buddha, including Buddha's cremation and entry into Nirvana. The **Great Treasure House (Daihozoden)**, a concrete building constructed in 1941, contains temple treasure, including statues and other works of art from the 7th and 8th centuries. On the eastern precincts of Horyuji Temple is an octagonal building built in 739 called **Yumedono Hall,** or **Hall of Dreams.** Supposedly Prince Shotoku used this building for quiet meditation.

Admission to Horyuji Temple, the Treasure House, and Hall of Dreams is ¥700 ($5). The grounds are open daily from 8am to 4:30pm.

East of Yumedono is **Chuguji Temple,** a nunnery built for members of the imperial family. It contains two outstanding works of art. The wooden statue of Miroku-bosatsu, dating from the 7th century, is noted for the serene and compassionate expression on its face. The Tenjukoku Mandala, the oldest piece of embroidery in Japan, was originally 16 feet long and created by Shotoku's widow and her female companions, with scenes depicting life of the times. Only a replica of the fragile embroidery is now on display. Admission here is ¥300 ($2.15).

Nishinokyo Area

If you still have time to spend in Nara, it's worth making a trip to the vicinity of Nishinokyo Station to visit two more temples. **Toshodaiji Temple** (tel. 33-7900) was founded in 759 by Ganjin, a high priest from China who was invited to Japan by the emperor to help spread Buddhism. Ganjin's initial attempts to reach Japan were thwarted by pirate attacks, storms, and five shipwrecks. During one of these voyages,

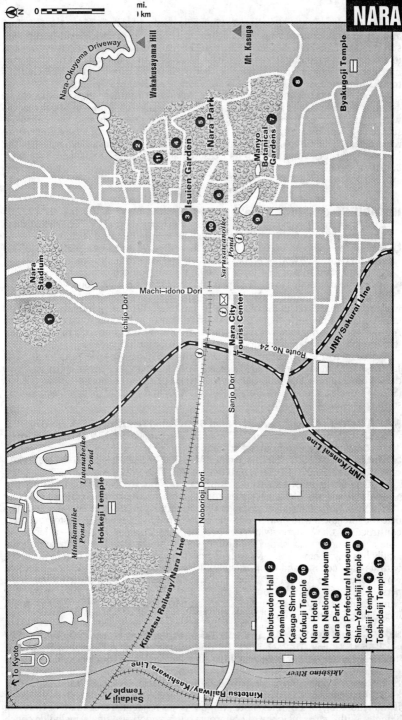

NARA

Post Office ☒ Information ⊘

- Daibutsuden Hall ❷
- Dreamland ❶
- Kasuga Shrine ❼
- Kofukuji Temple ❿
- Nara Hotel ❾
- Nara National Museum ❻
- Nara Park ❺
- Nara Prefectural Museum ❸
- Shin–Yakushiji Temple ❽
- Todaiji Temple ❹
- Toshodaiji Temple ⓫

Ganjin lost his sight through disease. He finally reached Japan in 754 at the age of 66 and set to work constructing this magnificent temple. Its main hall and lecture hall still stand and are both national treasures. The main hall contains various statues and its front pillars are thought to resemble Greek architecture, the concept of which may have been brought to Japan via the Silk Road. Also on the temple's grounds is Ganjin's tomb. Admission is ¥300 ($2.15). Daily hours are 8:30am to 4:30pm.

About 800 yards south of Toshodaiji is **Yakushiji Temple** (tel. 33-6001), which contains more Buddhist statues. It was erected by Emperor Tenmu in hopes that his wife would recover from illness—and must have worked because she ended up succeeding him to the throne. Its three-story pagoda, the only original structure remaining, is believed to date from 698 and looks as if it has six stories because of the intermediate roofs. Admission to its treasure hall is ¥400 ($2.85). Open daily from 8:30am to 5pm.

WHERE TO STAY

KIKUSUIRO ⑧⑦**, 1130 Takahata Bodaimachi, Nara 630. Tel. 0742/23-2001.** 14 rms (8 with bath). A/C MINIBAR (in some rooms) TV TEL **Directions:** A 15-minute walk from JR Station, 10 minutes from Kintetsu Station.
$ Rates (per person, including two meals and service charge): ¥33,000 ($235) without bath; ¥38,000–¥65,000 ($271–$464) with bath. No credit cards.

If you want to stay in a Japanese-style ryokan, you can't find a more beautiful example than this lovely 120-year-old inn, located not far from Nara Park. An imposing structure with an ornate Japanese-style roof and surrounded by a white wall, it makes artful use of various woods to create pleasing forms of decoration in its tatami rooms, including delicately carved transoms. Rooms, some of which face Ara-ike Pond, are outfitted with scrolls and antiques and are connected to one another with rambling wooden corridors. There is also a beautiful garden.

Adjacent to the ryokan are both Western- and Japanese-style restaurants. The Japanese restaurant is new and decorated with bamboo and paper lanterns. Open daily from 11am to 8:30pm, it features sukiyaki or shabu-shabu starting at ¥7,500 ($53.55), obento mini-kaiseki for ¥5,500 ($39.30) and ¥6,500 ($46.40), and kaiseki starting at ¥22,000 ($157).

NARA HOTEL, Nara-Koennai, Nara 630. Tel. 0742/26-3300. Fax 0742/23-5252. 132 rms (all with bath). A/C MINIBAR (new wing only) TV TEL **Directions:** A 10-minute taxi ride from either station.
$ Rates: ¥12,000 ($86) single; ¥20,000–¥38,000 ($143–$271) twin; ¥22,000–¥23,000 ($157–$164) double. AE, DC, JCB, MC, V.

One of the most famous places to stay in Nara, the Nara Hotel was built in 1909 and sits like a palace on top of a hill overlooking several ponds. Near Nara Park, and similar to Japan's other hotels built decades ago to accommodate the foreigners who poured into the country following the Meiji Restoration, it is constructed as a Western-style hotel but has many Japanese features—a Japanese-style roof, wooden eaves, the use of fine woods throughout. The Japanese imperial family has stayed here. You have your choice of staying in the old section of the hotel, with its high ceilings and comfortable old-fashioned décor, or in the new addition, which opened in 1984 and offers pleasant and modern rooms with verandas. I personally prefer the older rooms—they're also less expensive than those in the new wing. Facilities include a souvenir shop and two restaurants serving Western food, including a beautiful main dining hall.

HOTEL SUNROUTE NARA, 1110 Takabatake-cho, Nara 630. Tel. 0742/22-5151. Fax 0742/27-3759. 95 rms (all with bath). A/C MINIBAR TV TEL **Directions:** A 10-minute walk from Kintetsu Station, a 15-minute walk from JR Station.
$ Rates: ¥7,500 ($53) single; ¥14,800 ($105) double; ¥14,300–¥16,000 ($102–$114) triple. AE, DC, JCB, MC, V.
If you're looking for a business hotel, this one is in a residential area south of Kofukuji Temple. With a cheerful lobby, the Sunroute offers a good-size single, including couch

and chairs. All rooms have a minibar and a one-cup water heater with tea bags, among other amenities. This hotel features a pleasant restaurant serving Western breakfast, lunch, and dinner, and a coffee shop.

SEIKANSO, 29 Higashi-Kitsuji-cho, Nara 630. Tel. 0742/22-2670. Fax 0742/22-2670. 13 rms (none with bath). A/C TV **Directions:** A 15-minute walk from Kintetsu Station, a 25-minute walk from JR Station.

$ Rates (per person): ¥3,800 ($27). Western breakfast ¥350 ($2.50); Japanese breakfast ¥700 ($5). AE, MC, V.

This is a beautiful place to stay if you're on a budget and like Japanese-style accommodations. In fact, it's one of the most beautiful ryokan in the Japanese Inn Group that I've seen. Located in a quiet neighborhood, it dates from 1916 and is owned by a friendly young couple who speak English. The ryokan, a traditional Japanese building, wraps itself around an inner garden complete with azalea bushes and manicured trees. Some rooms face the garden—request one of these when making your reservation.

FURUICHI ⑧, **Higashitera Hayashimachi, Nara 630. Tel. 0742/22-2440.** Fax 0742/23-7808. 15 rms (5 with bath). A/C TV TEL **Directions:** A 10-minute walk from Kintetsu Station, a 15-minute walk from JR Station.

$ Rates (per person): ¥3,800 ($27) without bath; ¥5,500 ($39) with bath. Including two meals, ¥8,800 ($63) per person. MC, V.

This budget accommodation looks modern and unexciting from the outside, but its Japanese-style rooms are very pleasant, with traditional shoji screens and seating space beside the windows. Some rooms have a bathroom, and all have a sink, as well as a heater and a safe, among other amenities. Furuichi is located close to Sarusaw-ike Pond (not far from the Hotel Sunroute, above) and Nara's many attractions. The only drawback is that no one here speaks English.

WHERE TO DINE

HARISHIN ⑧⑨, **15 Nakashinya-cho. Tel. 22-2669.**
Cuisine: OBENTO. **Directions:** A 5-minute walk south of Sarusawa-ike Pond, on road that leads south from east edge of pond (stop at tourist office here for directions).

$ Prices: Obento ¥2,700 ($19.30). No credit cards.
Open: Lunch Tues–Sun 11:30am–3pm (last order). If Mon is a national holiday, it remains open and closes on Tues instead.

This restaurant is located in a lovely part of old Nara that many tourists never see, near Gangoji Temple. The restaurant itself is a 200-year-old house of ocher-colored walls and a wood-slat façade, and dining is on tatami with a view of a garden. Only one thing is served—an obento that changes with the seasons. On my last visit, my meal included an appetizer of pumpkin gelatin, strawberry wine, soup, vegetables, and various exquisitely prepared dishes.

MIKASA, Nara Hotel, Nara-Koennai. Tel. 26-3300.
Cuisine: FRENCH/WESTERN. **Directions:** Less than a 5-minute walk south of Nara Park.

$ Prices: Main dishes ¥2,900–¥3,800 ($20.70–$27.15); set-dinner courses ¥5,500–¥8,800 ($39.30–$62.85); set lunch ¥4,400 ($31.40). AE, DC, JCB, MC, V.
Open: Lunch daily 11:30am–2pm; dinner daily 5:30–8pm.

The main dining room of the Nara Hotel is a good place to come for lunch or dinner. Decorated in old drawing-room fashion—heavy curtains, wood paneling, a super-tall ceiling, and a view of a peaceful pond—it has the feel of a country lodge. The menu changes often and includes steaks and seafood.

THE JAPAN ALPS

Lying in the central part of Honshu, the Japan Alps consist of several volcanic mountain ranges. With the exception of Japan's tallest mountain, Mt. Fuji, all of Japan's loftiest mountains are in these ranges, making the Japan Alps a popular destination for hikers and nature-lovers. Some of the villages nestled in the mountains remain relatively unchanged, giving visitors the unique opportunity to see how mountain people have lived through the centuries.

SEEING THE REGION

Because towns and villages in this region are spread out—with lots of mountains in between—the traveling isn't as fast in this part of the country as on Honshu's broad plains. If you're coming from Tokyo, your best strategy is to start with a direct train from Shinjuku Station to Matsumoto. From there, take the Chuo Honsen Line early in the morning to Nakatsugawa, where you can then board a bus for Magome and spend the day hiking to Tsumago. By late afternoon, you should be back on the Chuo Honsen Line bound for Nagoya, where you then change trains for Takayama, reaching it in time for dinner. Takayama is the best starting out point for bus rides to Ogimachi (in Shirakawa-go). From Ogimachi, buses depart for Nagoya and Kanazawa.

1. TAKAYAMA

330 miles NW of Tokyo; 103 miles NE of Nagoya

GETTING THERE   By Train   The easiest way to get here is by direct train from Nagoya, with about eight departures daily for the two-and-a-half-hour trip. There is also a direct train from Osaka via Kyoto, which takes five hours.

ESSENTIAL INFORMATION   The **area code** for Takayama, lying in the northern part of Gifu Prefecture, is 0577.

The local **tourist office** (tel. 0577/32-5328) is located in a wooden booth on the east side of Takayama Station. You can pick up an English brochure and a map of the town. The office is open daily from 8:30am to 6:30pm (5pm in winter).

GETTING AROUND   Most of Takayama's attractions lie to the east of the train station and are easily reached **on foot.** An alternative is to rent a **bicycle** from one of the many rental shops ringing the station, the cost of which averages ¥300 ($2.15) per hour or ¥1,400 ($10) for the whole day.

Located in the Hida Mountains of the Japan Alps, Takayama is surrounded by 10,000-foot peaks, making the train ride here breathtaking. The village, located on a wide plateau, was founded back in the 16th century by Lord Kanamori, who

WHAT'S SPECIAL ABOUT THE JAPAN ALPS

Natural Spectacles

☐ Some of the highest mountains in Japan.

☐ Good hiking trails through beautiful countryside, including the hike between Magome and Tsumago; for more serious hikers, trails leading out of Kamikochi.

☐ Breathtaking train rides.

Great Towns/Villages

☐ Takayama, with its preserved merchants' homes, its museums, and its unique food and architecture.

☐ Shirakawa-go, nestled in a valley hemmed in by mountains, with more than 150 thatched farmhouses, barns, and sheds set in the midst of paddies.

☐ Matsumoto, a castle town.

☐ Magome and Tsumago, two old post towns linked by a 5-mile pathway.

Architectural Highlights

☐ Merchants' homes in Takayama, built in the 18th century and typical of classical design of the region.

☐ Thatched farmhouses, most more than 200 years old and some of them converted to minshuku accommodations.

☐ Matsumoto Castle, built in 1504 and possessing the oldest existing keep in Japan.

Regional Food and Cuisine

☐ *Hoba miso*, a specialty of Takayama served at breakfast, consisting of soy-bean paste mixed with scallions and other ingredients; cooked on a magnolia leaf at your table.

☐ Rice sake of Shirakawa-go, famous for its milky color, potency, and thickness (provided by rice kernels).

☐ *Sansai*, fresh mountain vegetables.

---

selected the site because of the impregnable position afforded by the surrounding Hida Mountains. Modeled after Kyoto but also with strong ties to Edo (the former name of Tokyo), Takayama borrowed from both cultural centers in developing its own architecture, food, and crafts, much of them still preserved today because of its centuries of remote isolation in the Japan Alps.

The heart of Takayama is delightful, with homes of classical design typical of 18th-century Hida. The streets of the old town are narrow and clean, flanked on both sides by tiny canals of running water. Rising up from the canals are one- and two-story homes and shops of gleaming dark wood with overhanging roofs. Latticed windows and slats of wood play games of light and shadow in the white of the sunshine. Strips of blue cloth flutter in the breeze of open shop doors. As you walk down the streets, you'll notice huge cedar balls hanging from the eaves in front of several shops, indicating a sake factory. Altogether, there are eight sake factories in Takayama, most of them small affairs. Go inside, sample the sake, and watch men stirring rice in large vats. Takayama is a town that invites exploration.

WHAT TO SEE & DO

Takayama's main attraction is its old merchants' houses, which are clustered together in the old town on narrow streets called Sannomachi and Ninomachi. Be sure to allow time for just wandering around. Shops in the area sell Takayama's specialties, including sake, yew wood carvings, and a unique lacquerware called *shunkei-nuri*. Almost all the attractions listed below are closed during the New Year's holidays.

HIDA MINZOKU MURA FOLK VILLAGE. Tel. 33-4714.

Popularly called Hida no Sato, Hida Minzoku Mura Folk Village is an open-air museum of more than 30 old thatched farmhouses, showing how farmers and artisans used to live in the Hida Mountain region. The whole village is picturesque, with swans swimming in the central pond, green moss growing on the thatched roofs, and flowers blooming in season. Some of the houses have *gassho-zukuri* style roofs, built steeply to withstand the heavy snowfalls. The tops of the roofs are said to resemble hands joined in prayer. There are shingle-roofed homes, houses with earthen floors, a woodcutter's hut, a grain storehouse, and a house where the second floor was used as a silkworm nursery. All the structures, which range in age from 100 to 500 years, are open to the public and are filled with utensils, tools, and furniture used in daily life. On display, for example, are old spindles and looms, utensils for cooking and dining, instruments used in the silk industry, farm tools, sleds, and straw boots and capes worn to fend off wet snow.

Workshops have been set up in one corner of the village grounds to demonstrate textile dyeing and weaving, lacquerwork, and wood sculpture. Within walking distance of the folk village is the **Hida Folklore Museum (Hida Minzoku-kan),** with more displays on life in the Hida region. Next to the folklore museum is the **Museum of Mountain Life,** with displays on the history of mountaineering in the Japan Alps and regional flora and fauna.

Admission: ¥500 ($3.55), which includes entrance to all museums and to folk village.

Open: Daily 8:30am–5pm. **Directions:** To reach Hida Minzoku Mura Folk Village, take bus departing from platform 2 in front of Takayama Station to last stop. Otherwise, it's about a 20-minute walk from train station.

MORNING MARKETS

One of the things you should be sure to do in the morning is to head for the east bank of the Miyagawa River, where women sell flowers, vegetables, and local produce at a colorful local market. Another market takes place every morning also in front of Takayama Jinya.

Admission: Free.

Open: Both markets, summer daily 6:30am–noon; winter daily 8:30am–noon.

MERCHANTS' HOUSES, on north end of Shimo-Ninomachi Street.

⭐ Located side by side, **Yoshijima-ke (Yeshijima House)** (tel. 32-0038) and **Kusakabe Mingeikan** are two merchants' mansions that once belonged to two of the richest families in Takayama. Of the two, the Yoshijima House is my favorite. With its exposed attic, heavy cross-beams, sunken fireplace, and sliding doors, it's a masterpiece of geometric design. It was built in 1907 as both the home and factory of the Yoshijima family, well-to-do brewers of sake in Takayama. Notice how the beams and wood of the home gleam, a state attained through decades of polishing as each generation of women did their share in bringing the wood to a luster. Yoshijima-ke is also famous for its lattices, typical of Takayama yet showing an elegance influenced by Kyoto.

Not quite as rustic, the Kusakabe Mingeikan merchant house is more refined and imposing, built in 1879 for a merchant dealing in silk, lamp oil, and finance. Its architectural style is considered unique to Hida, and on display are items handed down through the generations, arranged just as they would have been in the 18th and 19th centuries.

Admission: Yoshijima-ke, ¥250 ($1.80); Kusakabe Mingeikan, ¥309 ($2.20).

Open: Summer: both houses, daily 9am–5pm. Winter: (Dec–Feb): Yoshijima-ke, Wed–Mon 9am–4:30pm; Kusakabe Mingeikan, daily 9am–4:30pm.

MORE MUSEUMS

FESTIVAL FLOATS EXHIBITION HALL (TAKAYAMA YATAI KAIKAN), 178 Sakura-machi. Tel. 32-5100.

Not far from the merchants' houses is this exhibition hall, where you can see some of the huge, elaborate floats used for Takayama's famous parade in its autumn festival. Most of them date from the 17th century and were built by famous craftspeople of the village. Special features include marionettes, which are made to dance through the streets during festival time. The hall also contains Japan's largest portable shrine.

Admission: ¥460 ($3.30).

Open: Mar–Nov daily 8:30am–5pm; Dec–Feb daily 9am–4:30pm. **Directions:**

Located on precincts of Sakurayama Hachimangu Shrine, about a 5-minute walk from old town or a 15-minute walk from train station.

LION DANCE CEREMONY EXHIBITION HALL [SHISHI KAIKAN], 53-1 Sakura-machi. Tel. 32-0881.

More than 800 lion masks, used in Japanese festivals around the country, are on display here, including those of the Hida region. There are video presentations of local folk dances, as well as demonstrations of marionettes used in Takayama's two festival parades.
Admission: ¥430 ($3.05).
Open: Daily 8:30am–5pm. **Directions:** Just a minute's walk from Takayama Yatai Kaikan, above.

HIDA FOLK ARCHEOLOGICAL MUSEUM [HIDA MINZOKU KOKOKAN], 82 Kamisanno-machi. Tel. 32-1980.

In the heart of Takayama on Sannomachi Street, this interesting old house once belonged to a doctor and contains a number of trick devices, including secret passageways and a hanging ceiling. Imagine inviting an enemy to your home, offering him the best room in the house, and then secretly sneaking upstairs to chop the rope that has been holding up the suspended ceiling. The ceiling plunges down with a loud thud, neatly crushing your enemy to death. Rather dramatic, don't you think? And of course, very effective. Back in the old days of Japan's constant civil wars, trickery was sometimes the only way to survive the constant power struggles. This museum also has a collection of earthenware and folk tools.
Admission: ¥300 ($2.15).
Open: Summer daily 8am–6pm; winter daily 9am–5pm. **Directions:** In heart of old town, about a 10-minute walk from train station.

FUJI FOLK CRAFT MUSEUM [FUJI BIJUTSU MINGEI-KAN], 60 Kamisanno-machi. Tel. 32-0108.

Just down the street from the Hida Folk Archeological Museum on Sannomachi Street is this gallery, which contains a varied collection of furniture, clothing, combs, dolls, pottery, and lacquerware, most dating from the Edo Period. Included are some beautiful *tansu* (chests), smoking utensils, belt pouches with netsuke, swords, paper-covered lamps, farming tools, and spinning wheels. Many items are identified in English, and the entrance gate was once the outer gate of Takayama Castle, which is no longer in existence. A very worthwhile museum.
Admission: ¥300 ($2.15).
Open: Daily 9am–5pm. **Directions:** A 10-minute walk from train station.

TAKAYAMA MUSEUM OF LOCAL HISTORY [TAKAYAMA KYODOKAN], Kami-Ichi-no-Machi Street. Tel. 32-1205.

Another good museum, housed in a 100-year-old building, this one displays antiques, traditional arts and crafts, and folklore items handed down from generation to generation, as well as work by Hida craftspeople.
Admission: ¥200 ($1.40).
Open: Mar–Nov Tues–Sun 8:30am–5pm; Dec–Feb 8:30am–4:30pm. **Directions:** A 10-minute walk from train station.

TOY MUSEUM [KYODO GANGU-KAN], Kami-Ichi-no-Machi Street. Tel. 32-1183.

Across the street from the history museum (above), this museum houses a collection of dolls and folk toys from around the country, dating from the 17th century to today.
Admission: ¥200 ($1.40).
Open: Daily 9am–5pm. **Directions:** A 10-minute walk from train station.

HISTORICAL GOVERNMENT HOUSE [TAKAYAMA JINYA], 1-5 Hachiken-machi. Tel. 32-0643.

Once a manor house for administrators in Takayama, this is the only building of its kind in Japan. Constructed like a miniature castle with an outer wall and imposing entrance gate, it contains a rice granary (rice was collected as a tax), chambers and courts, and historical records. An English-language pamphlet describing the history of the building and its purpose is available.

Admission: ¥300 ($2.15).

Open: Apr–Oct 8:45am–5pm; Nov–Mar 8:45am–4:30pm. **Directions:** A 10-minute walk from train station.

WHERE TO STAY

There are by far more minshuku and ryokan in Takayama than hotels, making it the perfect place to stay in a traditional Japanese inn. In fact, staying in a tatami room and sleeping on a futon are the best way to immerse yourself in the life of this small community.

And the best news is that there are places to fit all budgets. All rates below for ryokan and minshuku follow the Japanese system in that they are on a per-person basis and include breakfast, dinner, and service charges. Tax is extra. You should be aware that in peak season (August and during festival times in April and October), prices will be higher, generally between 10% and 20% more.

A NOTE ON JAPANESE SYMBOLS

Many hotels, restaurants, and other establishments in Japan do not have signs giving their name in English letters. As an aid to the reader, Appendix C lists the Japanese symbols for all places described in this guide. Each set of symbols has a number, which corresponds to the number that appears inside an oval next to the establishment's boldfaced name in the text. Thus, to find the Japanese symbols for, say, Osaka's **Hotel Hokke Club** ⑬⑧, refer to the number 138 in the appendix.

RYOKAN

KINKIKAN ⑨⓪**, 48 Asahimachi, Takayama 506. Tel. 0577/32-31311.** 15 rms (11 with bath). A/C MINIBAR TV TEL **Directions:** A 6-minute walk from train station.

$ Rates (per person, including breakfast, dinner, and service): ¥16,500–¥25,000 ($118–$178). AE, JCB, V.

Kinkikan is right in the center of old Takayama, set back from a small side street and surrounded by a wall. Dating from the Edo Period and once owned by Lord Kanamori, it later served as a restaurant and today is still famous for its meals. The small lobby, full of furniture made of shunkei-nuri lacquerware crafted in Takayama, opens up to a delightful 300-year-old garden, just the kind of place that invites relaxation. Most of the guest rooms were built about a decade ago, each one utilizing Japanese craftsmanship in its own distinctive interior design. One room, for example, has shoji screens and wall trimmings in shunkei-nuri lacquer, while another room is decorated with the wood of local trees. Three rooms on the ground floor have peaceful views of the garden. All rooms have private toilet and most have private bath as well. As with all ryokan, however, there's a public bath for communal bathing, this one brand new.

ASUNARO ⑨①**, 2-96-2 Hatsuda-cho, Takayama 506. Tel. 0577/33-5551.** 20 rms (14 with bath). A/C MINIBAR TV TEL **Directions:** A 5-minute walk northeast of Takayama Station.

$ Rates (per person, including breakfast, dinner, and service): ¥16,500–¥30,000 ($118–$214). ¥2,000 ($14.30) extra during peak season. DC, JCB, MC, V.

This modern ryokan, recently renovated, offers fairly standard tatami rooms, all with their own toilet and most with bath as well. The higher rates during peak season are due in part, the management says, to more elaborate meals.

RYOKAN HISHUYA ⑨₂, 1-464 Kami-Okamoto-cho, Takayama 506. Tel. 0577/33-4001. Fax 0577/34-5065. 14 rms (all with bath). A/C MINIBAR TV TEL **Bus:** From platform 2 at Takayama Station to last stop, then a 1-minute walk.
$ Rates (per person, including breakfast, dinner, and service): ¥14,000–¥19,000 ($100–$136). ¥3,000 ($21.40) extra during peak season. AE, DC, JCB, MC, V.
Built a little more than a decade ago and possessing all the grace and charm you'd expect from a first-class ryokan, this place is just a minute's walk from the Hida Minzoku Mura Folk Village on the quiet outskirts of town. Its rooms have views of either the garden surrounding the ryokan or the distant mountain peaks. Five rooms have their own wooden bathtub and are more expensive; the other rooms all have the smaller unit bathroom typically found in a business hotel. Dinner is served individually in the guest rooms, while breakfast is served in a communal dining hall. If you request it in advance, you can get a Western breakfast of scrambled eggs, toast, ham, coffee, and juice. If requested in advance, shabu-shabu is served to guests who stay a second night.

SEIRYU ⑨₃, 6 Hanakawa-cho, Takayama 506. Tel. 0577/32-0448. Fax 0577/35-2345. 24 rms (all with bath). A/C MINIBAR TV TEL **Directions:** A 6-minute walk from Takayama Station.
$ Rates (per person, including breakfast, dinner, and service): ¥11,000 ($78); ¥16,500 ($118) in peak season. JCB, MC, V.
Down the street from Kinkikan (described above), in the center of Takayama, is this modern ryokan. Two of the rooms combine beds with a separate tatami section, making them good choices if you want the feel of living on tatami but prefer the comforts of a bed. Although dinner is served in your own room, breakfast is served in a tatami dining hall, with each person receiving his own little tray. Western breakfasts are available on request.

HIDA GASSHOEN ⑨₄, 3-829 Nishinoishiki-cho, Takayama 506. Tel. 0577/33-4531. 24 rms (5 with bath). MINIBAR TV TEL **Directions:** A 10-minute walk from Takayama Station.
$ Rates (per person, including breakfast, dinner, and service): ¥7,500 ($53) without bath; ¥8,800–¥13,700 ($63–$98) with bath. Rates 10% higher during festivals and Aug. No credit cards.
Another ryokan close to the Folk Village, Hida Gasshoen is secluded on a hillside, and its approach has one of the most impressive stone walls I've ever seen—massive boulders, some of which measure 10 feet high, all neatly piled on top of one another. The main building, housing most of the guest rooms, was built in 1980 and was designed to resemble an old gassho-zukuri farmhouse. Meals are served in a genuine 200-year-old thatched farmhouse. Rooms in a separate ancient house have their own private bath and toilet, and one of the five rooms with bath is a combination room, with both a bed and tatami.

MINSHUKU

HACHIBEI ⑨₅, 1-389 Kami-Okamoto-cho. Tel. 0577/33-0573. 32 rms (none with bath). A/C TV TEL **Transportation:** Hachibei has its own shuttle bus and will pick you up if you call from the station.
$ Rates (per person, including breakfast, dinner, and service): ¥7,500 ($53). V.
A few minutes' walk from the Hida no Sato Folk Village, this minshuku is a big old house with a new addition and a rather nice (and overgrown) garden. It also has a pleasant open hearth where guests can sit and socialize in the evening. Most of those staying here are young Japanese. The public baths are large and lined with rock walls.

MATSUYAMA, 5-11 Hanasato-cho. Tel. 0577/32-1608. Fax 0577/35-0737. 24 rms (none with bath). A/C TV TEL **Directions:** A 2-minute walk from Takayama Station.
$ Rates (per person, including breakfast, dinner, and service): ¥6,500 ($46); ¥4,900 ($35) without meals. ¥500 ($3.55) extra during peak season. No credit cards.

Matsuyama is conveniently located near the train station in a nondescript building, with tatami rooms that are rather bare and plain and come with just the basics of coin-operated TV, heater, fan, and air conditioning.

MINSHUKU SOSUKE, 1-64 Okamoto, Takayama 506. Tel. 0577/32-0818. 13 rms (none with bath). A/C TV TEL **Directions:** An 8-minute walk southwest of Takayama Station; across from Green Hotel.

$ Rates (per person, including breakfast, dinner, and service): ¥6,500–¥8,800 ($46–$63). No credit cards.

The entryway of this delightful minshuku resembles those of farmhouses on display at the Folk Village, filled with country knickknacks and exuding a warm and friendly atmosphere. There's an old open-hearth fireplace, called an **irori,** in the communal room to the left as you enter—if it's chilly you'll be invited to sit down and warm yourself. The couple running this minshuku are outgoing and friendly. Mealtimes are especially fun. Everyone is seated around one long table, where each person introduces himself or herself. Since most of the guests are Japanese, this is a good opportunity to learn about other parts of the country. Although the building housing the minshuku is 150 years old, the inside has been remodeled and all the rooms are spotlessly clean.

YAMAKYU, 58 Tenshoji, Takayama 506. Tel. 0577/32-3756. Fax 0577/35-2350. 28 rms (none with bath). A/C TV TEL **Directions:** A 5-minute taxi ride from Takayama Station.

$ Rates (per person, including breakfast, dinner, and service): ¥6,500 ($46). No credit cards.

Yamakyu has a deserved reputation for serving the best meals in town in its price range. Although it's located a bit far from the station—about a 20-minute walk or a 5-minute taxi ride—it's only a 10-minute walk to the old part of town. As with most minshuku, the Japanese-style rooms are without private bathroom, but the public baths are large and pleasant. Display cases line the corridors, showing off a collection of glass bowls, vases, clocks, and lamps.

HOTELS

HIDA HOTEL PLAZA, Hanaoka-cho 2, Takayama 506. Tel. 0577/33-4600. Fax 0577/33-4602. 152 rms (all with bath). A/C MINIBAR TV TEL **Directions:** A 4-minute walk from Takayama Station.

$ Rates: Western-style rooms: ¥8,800 ($63) single; ¥17,500–¥33,000 ($125–$236) double/twin. Peak season rates about 20% higher. Japanese-style rooms (including two meals): ¥16,500 ($118) per person. AE, DC, MC, V.

About four blocks northeast of Takayama Station is the Hida Hotel Plaza, consisting of an older annex and a newer, contemporary high-tech addition—you'll find the front desk in the new wing. All rooms come with radio, minibar, and hot-water pot and tea bags, among other amenities. The newer addition has Western-style rooms. The hotel's 55 Japanese-style tatami rooms are clean and simple, the way Japanese-style rooms should be; note, however, that meals are served in a communal dining hall.

Facilities include an attractive wood-beamed shopping arcade, rental bicycles, a black-marble–and–stainless-steel public bath, an indoor swimming pool, a sauna and steambaths (extra fees charged), five restaurants, and a bar. During the summer months there's a rooftop beer garden open nightly from 5 to 9pm, offering panoramic views of Takayama and surrounding hills.

TAKAYAMA GREEN HOTEL, 2-180 Nishinoishiki-cho, Takayama 506. Tel. 0577/33-5500. Fax 0577/32-4434. 171 rms (146 with bath). A/C MINIBAR TV TEL **Directions:** An 8-minute walk west of Takayama Station.

$ Rates (per person, including two meals): ¥20,000 ($143) single; ¥17,500 ($125) twin; ¥15,500 ($111) triple. 20% extra during peak season. AE, DC, JCB, MC, V.

The largest hotel in town, this is the place to stay if you like all the conveniences in one building—restaurants, bar, beer garden (open summers only), shopping, beauty and barber salons, bike rentals, tennis courts, public bath, tea lounge, and sushi bar.

YOUTH HOSTEL

**YOUTH HOSTEL TENSHOJI TEMPLE, 83 Tenshoji-machi, Takayama 506.
Tel. 0577/32-6345.** 150 beds. **Directions:** A 20-minute walk east of
Takayama Station.
$ Rates (per person, including breakfast and dinner): ¥3,200 ($23) member,
¥3,700 ($26) nonmember. No credit cards.
This youth hostel is located in a temple a good hike from the station. Unfortunately,
there is no bus to the hostel. Sleeping is on futon in tatami rooms.

WHERE TO DINE

Takayama has some local specialties that you should try while you're here. The best
known is hoba miso, which is soy-bean paste mixed with dried scallions, ginger, and
mushrooms and cooked on a dry magnolia leaf at your table above a small clay
burner. Sansai are mountain vegetables, including edible ferns and other wild plants,
and ayu is river fish, grilled with soy sauce or salt.

EXPENSIVE

KAKUSHO ⑨⑥**, 2-98 Babacho. Tel. 32-0174.**
    Cuisine: VEGETARIAN. **Reservations:** A must. **Directions:** On eastern edge
    of city, a few minutes' walk from old town.
    $ Prices: Set course ¥10,000 ($72); tax and service charge extra. No credit cards.
    Open: Lunch 11:30am and 1:30pm. **Closed:** Sometimes Wed, sometimes Thurs.
For the big splurge, you should dine at Kakusho, which offers local vegetarian fare
called shojin-ryoori, typically served at Buddhist temples. Situated on the slope of a
hill on the eastern part of town, this 250-year-old building with heavy wooden beams
and ocher-colored walls is surrounded by a mossy garden and a clay wall. You must
make a reservation to dine here, and there's only one meal available, served twice a
day, at either 11:30am or 1:30pm. It's served in private tiny tatami rooms, in a separate
old building in the back with its own view of the mossy garden. This place is worth the
price of the various mountain vegetables, mushrooms, nuts, and tofu you'll be served.

MODERATE

BANDAI KADO MISE ⑨⑦**, Hanakawa-cho. Tel. 33-5166.**
    Cuisine: LOCAL SPECIALTIES. **Directions:** A 5-minute walk from station, near
    Kokubunji Street.
    $ Prices: Set meals ¥1,500–¥3,000 ($10.70–$21.40); mountain vegetable
    teishoku ¥2,200 ($17.60). No credit cards.
    Open: Lunch Thurs–Tues 11am–3pm; dinner Thurs–Tues 5–8pm.
If Suzuya, described below, is closed or crowded, a restaurant close by is Bandai Kado
Mise, located across the street and a few shops down. It doesn't have an English
menu, so the easiest thing to do is to order one of the obento box meals for ¥1,500
($10.70) or the mountain vegetable teishoku for ¥2,400 ($17.15). Tempura or Hida
beef teishoku are also available.

SUZUYA ⑨⑧**, 24 Hanakawa-cho. Tel. 32-2484.**
    Cuisine: LOCAL SPECIALTIES. **Directions:** A 5-minute walk from Takayama
    Station.
    $ Prices: Set meals ¥1,000–¥4,000 ($7.15–$28.55). V.
    Open: Wed–Mon 11am–8pm.
This place, which specializes in Takayama cuisine, is easy to recognize by the
curtains hanging above the front door and the cedar ball hanging from the
eaves. Inside, it's darkly lit, with shoji screens covering the windows, wooden
beams above, and traditional Takayama country décor. This place is so popular
that if you come for lunch between noon and 1pm, you'll probably have to wait
for a table. There's an English menu, with such local specialties as mountain

vegetables, hoba miso, ayu river fish, and Takayama-style buckwheat noodles, Hida beef, and *tobanyaki,* which is a stew of leek, Japanese green pepper, mushrooms, and various chicken parts (including liver, gizzard, skin, and meat), which you cook at your table in your own personal cooker. Also cooked at your table is the *sansai-misonabe,* a stew with Chinese cabbage, chicken, and various mountain vegetables flavored with miso. This place is highly recommended.

BUDGET

ICHOO, Sowacho. Tel. 33-8913.
   Cuisine: PIZZA. **Directions:** A 3-minute walk from Takayama Station.
$ **Prices:** Pizza ¥700–¥900 ($5–$6.45). No credit cards.
   Open: Tues–Sun 8am–9pm.
If you're staying in a ryokan or a minshuku and hunger for something different from what you had for breakfast and dinner, maybe homemade pizza will hit the spot. This small coffee shop is located on Kokubunji Dori Street, about halfway between the station and the river. Pizzas are large, with a generous amount of cheese.

JIZAKE-YA ⑨, Suehiro Nibangai. Tel. 34-5001.
   Cuisine: VARIED JAPANESE. **Directions:** A 5-minute walk east of Takayama Station.
$ **Prices:** ¥600–¥1,400 ($4.30–$10). No credit cards.
   Open: Daily 5pm–2am. **Closed:** Third Sun of month.
Technically a drinking place because of the dozen different varieties of sake it sells, Jizake-ya also serves a wide variety of Japanese food, including tofu steak, tempura, noodles, and river fish. A large room with tatami and low tables, this place has a convivial drinking-hall atmosphere.

KOFUNE ⑩, Hanasato-cho 6-6. Tel. 32-2106.
   Cuisine: NOODLES. **Directions:** Exit from station and keep walking 2 minutes toward river; noodle shop will be on your left.
$ **Prices:** Noodle dishes ¥550–¥1,200 ($3.90–$8.55). No credit cards.
   Open: Daily 10:30am–6pm.
If you're looking for an inexpensive meal, this homey, pleasant noodle shop is just a few minutes' walk from the station. It has an English menu offering such dishes as noodles served plain or with river fish, tempura, or mountain vegetables.

2. SHIRAKAWA-GO

With its thatch-roofed farmhouses, rice paddies trimmed with flowerbeds, roaring river, and pine-covered mountains rising on all sides, Shirakawa-go is one of the most picturesque regions in Japan. Sure, it has its share of tour buses, especially in May, August, and October, but because of its rather remote location and because it's accessible only by bus, Shirakawa-go still remains off the beaten path for most tourists in Japan. A visit to this rural region could well be the highlight of your trip.

Stretching almost 5 miles beside the Shokawa River and squeezed to a width of only 1.8 miles between towering mountains, Shirakawa-go is a tiny region with a population of 2,000 living in several small communities. Because Shirakawa-go is hemmed in by mountains, land for growing rice and other crops has always been scarce and valuable. As a result, farmhouses were built large enough to hold extended families, sometimes with as many as several dozen family members living under one roof. Because there was not enough land available for young couples to marry and build houses of their own, only the oldest son was allowed to marry. The other children were required to spend their lives living with their parents and helping with the farming. But even though younger children were not allowed to marry, a man was allowed to choose a young woman, visit her in her parents' home, and father her children. The children then remained with the mother's family, becoming valuable members of the labor force.

Before the roads came to Shirakawa-go, winter always meant complete isolation, as snow 6 feet deep blanketed the entire region. Open-hearth fireplaces (irori) were commonplace in the middle of the communal room. They were used both for cooking and for warmth, and because there were no chimneys, smoke simply rose into the levels above. So the family lived on the ground floor, with the upper floors used for silk cultivation and storage of utensils. Because of the heavy snowfall, roofs were constructed at steep angles, known as gassho-zukuri in reference to the fact that the tops of the roofs look like hands joined in prayer.

Today, there are about 150 thatched farmhouses, barns, and sheds in Shirakawa-go, most of them built about 200 to 300 years ago. The thatched roofs are about 2 feet thick and last about 50 years. The old roofs are replaced in Shirakawa-go every April, when one to four roofs are replaced on successive weekends. The whole process involves about 200 people, who can replace one roof in a couple of days.

OGIMACHI

347 miles NW of Tokyo

GETTING THERE   By Bus   The most common way of reaching Ogimachi is by bus from Takayama, with a change of buses in Makido. The entire trip takes about 3 hours along winding mountain roads and costs ¥3,000 ($21.40) one way. If you have a JR Rail Pass, however, you can use it between Makido and Ogimachi, in which case you'll need to buy a ticket only for the stretch between Takayama and Makido, which costs ¥1,740 ($12.40). Buses run throughout the year, with about three to five departures from Takayama daily, depending on the season. You can also reach Ogimachi by JR Tokai bus from Nagoya, available from July to November and costing ¥4,320 ($30.85) one way. From Kanazawa, Meitetsu buses depart for Ogimachi July to November and cost ¥1,880 ($13.40) one way.

ESSENTIAL INFORMATION   The **area code** for Ogimachi, lying in Gifu Prefecture, is 05769.

There's a **tourist office** (tel. 05769/6-1751 or 6-1013) located in a small square in the center of the town. You can reserve a room in a minshuku here if you have not already done so, as well as pick up a pamphlet in English. If you want to make the tourist office your very first stop upon arrival in Shirakawa-go, get off at the bus stop called Gassho-Shuraku. The tourist office is about a minute's walk away and is open daily from 8:30am to 5pm.

The address for all establishments listed below is Shirakawa Mura, Ogimachi, Ono-gun, Gifu.

GETTING AROUND   Your own two feet can do it best. You can **walk** from one end of the village to the other in about 10 minutes.

SPECIAL EVENTS   The **Doburoku Matsuri Festival** is held at Shirakawa-go every year from October 14 to 19.

The most important village for visitors is Ogimachi, with its 800 residents. It has minshuku and a couple of museums, including an open-air museum of old thatched

IMPRESSIONS

But how sweet the Japanese woman is! All the possibilities of the race for goodness seem to be concentrated in her.
—LAFCADIO HEARN, 1891

farmhouses depicting how life used to be in the region before roads opened it up to the rest of the world.

WHAT TO SEE & DO

✪ To see how rural people lived in past centuries in the Japan Alps, visit the **Shirakawa-go Gassho no Sato Village,** an open-air museum with 25 gassho-zukuri houses and sheds filled with implements and tools. In some of the buildings, artisans are engaged in woodworking, pottery, basket-weaving, and toy-making. All the buildings are open to the public, and you are allowed to wander at will. The village is located about a 5-minute walk from Ogimachi along a footpath that takes you over a suspension bridge and through a narrow tunnel. Hours are 8:30am to 5pm most of the year; in the winter, from December through March, they are 9am to 4pm, while in August they are 8am to 6pm. The entrance fee is ¥500 ($3.55).

In addition to the open-air museum, there are several other old farmhouses in Ogimachi open to the public. **Seikatsu Shiryokan** ⑩ (tel. 6-1818), open daily from 8:30am to 5pm April through November, displays farm implements and folkcrafts, including cooking utensils, lacquerware, household items, and clothing. The upstairs is crammed with all kinds of farming tools and items used in everyday life, including mountain backpacks, hatchets, handmade skis, saddles, and implements for silk cultivation. Charging an admission of ¥200 ($1.40), Seikatsu Shiryokan is located on the southern edge of town, past the Juemon minshuku (described under the "Where to Stay," below). **Myozenji** ⑩ (tel. 6-1009) is a 170-year-old house with farm equipment, straw raincoats, palanquins, and other relics on display. You can walk around upstairs and inspect how the roof looks from the inside. If a fire is burning in the downstairs irori, you can also see how smoky the upstairs can get. Attached to the house is the main hall of Myozenji Temple, which is more than two centuries old. Hours here are generally 7:30am to 5pm, with shorter hours in winter, and admission is ¥200 ($1.40). Myozenji is located in the heart of Ogimachi.

Not far from Myozenji is a relatively new museum, **Doburoku Matsuri no Yakata** ⑩ (tel. 6-1655), erected in honor of the Doburoku Matsuri Festival, held in Shirakawa-go every year from October 14 to 19. Centering on a locally produced and potent sake, the festival is held just outside the museum's grounds at Hachimanjinja Shrine. The ¥310 ($2.20) entrance fee allows you to see some of the costumes worn during the festival and to try some of the festive sake. The highlight of the museum, however, is the hourlong video that shows the festival activities, including dances, parades, and plenty of drinking. Although the video is rather corny in parts, it's probably the next best thing to being at the festival itself. The museum is open daily from 8:30am to 4:30pm (9am to 4pm in winter).

And finally, for an overview of the entire village, walk along the gently sloping road that leads from the north of Ogimachi to the **Ogimachi Viewing Point.** There's a restaurant up here, but in my opinion the best thing to do is bring your own snack and walk to the hill's westernmost point (that is, toward the river, where there are some secluded benches). From here you have a marvelous view of the whole valley.

WHERE TO STAY

Because huge extended families living under one roof are a thing of the past, many residents of Ogimachi have turned their gassho-zukuri homes into minshuku. There are more than two dozen minshuku in Ogimachi, giving visitors the unique chance to stay in a thatched farmhouse with a family that might consist of grandparents, parents, and children. English is limited to the basics of "bath," "breakfast," and "dinner," but smiles go a long way. Most likely the family will drag out their family album with its pictures of winter snowfall and the momentous occasion when their thatched roof was repaired.

All minshuku charge approximately ¥6,000 to ¥6,500 ($43 to $46) per person, including two meals. Tax is extra. Most of them are fairly small affairs, with about five to nine rooms open to guests. Rooms are basic, without bath or toilet, and you're expected to roll out your own futon. Although there's little difference between the minshuku, some of them do not have thatched roofs. Below is a list of those that do.

KANDAYA ⑩④. **Tel. 05769/6-1072.** 9 rms (none with bath). **Directions:** In middle of village, a few minutes' walk from Ogimachi bus stop, away from river.
$ Rates (per person, including breakfast and dinner): ¥6,000 ($43). No credit cards.
This 200-year-old house with an irori is the largest minshuku in Ogimachi. Some of its rooms are in a separate building. It's located in the middle of the village and has a nicely remodeled bathroom and toilet area with wooden floors and walls.

MAGOEMON ⑩⑤. **Tel. 05769/6-1167.** 6 rms (none with bath). **Directions:** A few minutes' walk from bus stop, toward river.
$ Rates (per person, including breakfast and dinner): ¥6,000 ($43). No credit cards.
Magoemon stands by the suspension bridge on the way to the open-air museum. One of its rooms overlooks the Shokawa River. About 300 years old, it features a cozy living room with open-hearth irori, wooden communal bathtub, and Western-style flush toilets.

OTAYA ⑩⑥. **Tel. 05769/6-1425.** 5 rms (none with bath). **Directions:** On north end of village, less than a 5-minute walk from bus stop.
$ Rates (per person, including breakfast and dinner): ¥6,000 ($43). No credit cards.
Otaya is located on the northern edge of the village, giving it a little more privacy. A couple of the rooms face a small river that cuts deep into a ravine. A pond outside the front door contains the fish you'll have for dinner.

YOSOBE ⑩⑦. **Tel. 05769/6-1172.** 4 rms (none with bath). **Directions:** A few minutes' walk from bus stop, near tourist office.
$ Rates (per person, including breakfast and dinner): ¥6,000 ($43). No credit cards.
Yosobe, a small minshuku, has a communal dining area that is small and friendly, with an irori in the middle of the room. The rooms facing the front of the house open onto wooden verandas, polished smooth by years of wear. In case it matters, the toilets here are nonflush in the Japanese style.

JUEMON ⑩⑧. **Tel. 05769/6-1053.** 10 rms (none with bath). **Directions:** Located on south edge of Ogimachi, near Doburoku Matsuri-no-kan bus stop.
$ Rates (per person, including breakfast and dinner): ¥6,500 ($46). No credit cards.
Located on the other end of the community, this minshuku features an irori in the dining room and recently remodeled bathroom facilities. Juemon is a favorite place for young foreigners traveling in Japan, and the outgoing woman who runs this place is quite a character.

WHERE TO DINE

Since all minshuku and ryokan serve breakfast and dinner, the only meal you have to worry about is lunch.

IRORI ⑩⑨. **Tel. 6-1737.**
   Cuisine: LOCAL SPECIALTIES. **Directions:** On Ogimachi's main road, a few minutes' walk from tourist office.
$ Prices: ¥450–¥1,600 ($3.20–$11.40). No credit cards.
   Open: Daily 8:30am–11pm in summer, daily 10am–11pm in winter.
This place is easy to spot because of a huge block of gnarled wood beside its front door. The inside of this gassho-zukuri house is appropriately rustic and even has an irori where you can fry your own fish on a skewer. The menu, in Japanese only, includes fresh river fish (ayu), wild mountain vegetables called sansai, hoba miso (soybean paste cooked on a magnolia leaf over a small clay pot), unagi donburi (eel on rice), yakisoba (fried noodles), and *sansai-soba* (mountain vegetables and noodles). I opted for the tofu teishoku set meal, which consists of fried tofu covered with fish flakes, vegetables, rice, and soup. You might also want to come here for a nightcap. Beer starts at ¥550 ($3.95) and sake at ¥440 ($3.15).

KITANOSHO ⑩⑩. **Tel. 6-1506.**
   Cuisine: LOCAL SPECIALTIES. **Directions:** On southern edge of Ogimachi, about a 10-minute walk from tourist office, on right side; across from Juemon minshuku.

$ Prices: Noodles ¥600 ($4.30); teishoku ¥1,000–¥1,600 ($7.15–$11.40). No credit cards.
Open: Daily 10am–5pm. **Closed:** Dec–Mar.

Another large thatched farmhouse that has been turned into a restaurant, this one is on the other side of town. It also has an irori, found in the middle of a large tatami room. From the dining hall you can look out over the Shokawa River. When you finish your meal, climb the steep stairs to have a look at the second floor, where the heavy wooden beams are held together with just rope. Dishes include river fish, bear stew (called *kumanabe teishoku* and available in spring and autumn only), *sansai udon* (noodles and mountain vegetables), curry rice, hoba miso, and *oyakodon* (chicken and egg on rice). The menu is in Japanese only, so look around at what others are eating. Otherwise, complete meals are available by ordering the *sansai teishoku* for ¥1,000 ($7.15) or the *iwana teishoku* (river fish) for ¥1,600 ($11.40).

GASSHO (tel. 6-1419) and KODAIJI (Tel. 6-1154), Shirakawa-go Gassho no Sato Village.
Cuisine: NOODLES/OBENTO/LOCAL SPECIALTIES. **Directions:** Located at front gate to open-air museum.
$ Prices: ¥600–¥1,500 ($4.30–$10.70). No credit cards.
Open: Daily 8:30am–5pm for both.

Finally, if you're visiting the open-air museum and want a quick lunch or snack, next to the museum's entrance you'll find two thatch-roofed establishments that combine modern restaurants with souvenir shops. Simple places, they offer noodles, obento lunch boxes, and sansai or hoba miso teishoku. Gassho offers a *gassho teishoku* for ¥1,500 ($10.70), with mountain vegetables, while Kodaiji offers a *hoba miso teishoku* for ¥1,200 ($8.55). There's not much difference between the two.

3. MATSUMOTO

146 miles NW of Tokyo

GETTING THERE   By Train   There's a direct JR line to Matsumoto from Tokyo's Shinjuku Station. The Limited Express Azusa reaches Matsumoto in about 3 hours, while the Express Alps takes a bit longer, at about 5 hours. There's also a direct train from Nagoya, which takes about 2¼ hours.

By Bus   From Tokyo, the bus takes about 3¼ hours at a cost of ¥3,400 ($24); from Nagoya, 3½ hours at a cost of ¥3,400 ($24); from Osaka, 5½ hours at a cost of ¥5,500 ($39).

ESSENTIAL INFORMATION   The **area code** for Matsumoto, lying in Nagano Prefecture, is 0263.

Before departing from Tokyo, be sure to pick up a sheet called *Matsumoto and Kamikochi* at the Tourist Information Center. It gives the latest train schedules, as well as information on sights in and around Matsumoto. It also recommends hiking trips (lasting 2 to 4 hours) from Kamikochi, a small village that you can reach in a little over 2 hours via train and bus from Matsumoto.

In Matsumoto itself, the **tourist information window** is on the east side of Matsumoto Station (tel. 0263/32-2814). Open daily from 9:30am to 8pm in summer (9am to 6pm in winter), it has a good pamphlet with a map of the city (destinations are written in English). Its English-speaking staff will also help with accommodations.

GETTING AROUND   You can **walk** to Matsumoto Castle, just a mile northeast of the station. If you want to visit the other sights, however, you'll have to go by **bus** or **taxi.**

Located in the middle of a wide basin about 660 feet above sea level and surrounded on all sides by mountain ranges, Matsumoto boasts a fine feudal castle with the oldest existing donjon (keep) in Japan, as well as an outstanding woodblock-print museum. Although the city itself (population 200,000) is modern, with little remaining from its castle days, I find the town pleasant, the air fresh, and its people among the nicest I've encountered in Japan. Most travelers pass through Matsumoto on their way to more remote regions of the Japan Alps. Encircled with towering peaks, sparkling mountain lakes, and colorful wild flowers, Matsumoto serves as the gateway to hiking trails in the Japan Alps and in nearby Chubu Sangoku National Park.

WHAT TO SEE & DO

✪ Originally built in 1504, when Japan was in the throes of bloody civil wars, **Matsumoto Castle** (tel. 32-2902) is a fine specimen of a feudal castle, with the oldest existing donjon in the country. Surrounded by a willow-lined moat with ducks and white swans, the outside walls of the donjon are black, earning the place the nickname of Karasu-jo, or Crow Castle. It's a rather small castle, dark and empty inside. Take your shoes off at the entrance and walk in stocking feet over worn wooden floors and up steep and narrow steps until you finally reach the sixth floor, from which you have a nice view of the city. The castle grounds are open daily from 8:30am to 5pm. An entrance fee of ¥500 ($3.55) includes admission to the **Japan Folklore Museum,** located next to the castle. A rather eclectic museum, it has displays relating to archeology, history, and the surrounding region, including armor, an ornate palanquin, clothing, farming equipment, butterflies from around the world, insects, animals of the Japan Alps, and a wonderful collection of old clocks from Japan and other nations.

✪ The **Japan Ukiyo-e Museum,** 2206-1 Koshiba, Shimadachi (tel. 47-4440), is one of the best museums of woodblock prints in Japan. It houses the ukiyo-e collection of Tokichi Sakai, which contains more than 100,000 prints, including representative masterpieces of all known ukiyo-e artists. It is believed to be the largest collection of its kind in the world. The exhibition changes every 2 months, so there's always something new to see. On one of my visits, for example, the masterpieces of Hokusai were being shown, including his series on famous Japanese bridges and waterfalls. A 10-minute slide show with explanations in English introduces the current exhibition, and a pamphlet in English describes the history of the collection and how woodblock prints are made. The museum is open Tuesday through Sunday from 10am to 4:30pm and charges ¥600 ($4.30) admission. Unfortunately, there's no convenient way to get to the museum by public transportation, but the ¥1,000 ($7.15) taxi ride is worth it.

One more museum worth visiting if you have time is the **Matsumoto Folkcraft Museum (Matsumoto Mingei-kan),** ⑪ (tel. 33-1569), located about 15 minutes by bus or taxi from Matsumoto Station (if you're going by bus, get out at the Shimoganai Mingeikan Guchi bus stop). Open Tuesday through Sunday from 9am to 5pm, it contains products of wood, glass, bamboo, and porcelain from Japan and foreign countries. Particularly beautiful are its wooden chests. Admission is ¥200 ($1.40).

If perchance you studied violin when you were young, maybe you were one of the countless children around the world who learned by the well-known Suzuki Method. In Matsumoto is the famous **Suzuki Shin-ichi Talent Education Institute,** where young and old alike from around the world come to study violin, piano, cello, and flute. Dr. Suzuki, founder of the method, is now in his 90s but is still actively involved in the daily lessons. Group and private lessons for both pupils and teachers of the Suzuki Method are held throughout the week, and guests are welcome to watch. There are also periodic concerts given by graduating musicians of the institute. For more information, call the institute any time between 9am and 5pm Monday through Saturday at 32-7171. Dr. Suzuki's group lesson is generally held from 9 to 10:30am, but it would be wise to check the time beforehand.

If you find yourself with extra time on your hands, you might want to take a trip to **Alps Park,** located on one of Matsumoto's surrounding wooded hills, where you'll find the Alps Dream Coaster. I don't know who thinks up these names, but this one is a toboggan run and doesn't allow much time for dreaming. The race down the hill and around curves takes only a few minutes, during which time you swear you're going to fly off course. Closed in the winter, it's open the rest of the year from 9am to 5pm, and one trip down costs ¥300 ($2.15). To reach Alps Park, take the bus from Matsumoto Station bound for Alps Koen; the trip takes about 25 minutes. Since there are only five buses daily, ask for the timetable at the tourist office. A restaurant and hiking trails are located in the park.

WHERE TO STAY

Because Matsumoto is popular primarily with hikers used to roughing it along nature trails, there are no luxury hotels in the city, and facilities are geared mainly toward convenience.

MODERATE

HOTEL NEW STATION, 1-1-11 Chuo, Matsumoto 390. Tel. 0263/35-3850. 103 rms. A/C TV TEL **Directions:** A 1-minute walk from Matsumoto Station.

$ Rates (including tax and service): ¥6,500–¥7,200 ($46–$51) single; ¥12,500–¥14,300 ($89–$102) double/twin. AE, DC, JCB, MC, V.

This business hotel, which opened in 1985, offers a very pleasant and good-size single with print comforter, large desk, and hot-water heater for tea. All rooms come with bathroom and coin-operated TV. The front-desk personnel are very helpful and accommodating, but not much English was spoken here during my last visit.

MATSUMOTO TOKYU INN, 1-3-21 Fukashi, Matsumoto 390. Tel. 0263/36-0109. Fax 0263/36-0883. 160 rms (all with bath). A/C MINIBAR TV TEL **Directions:** A 2-minute walk from Matsumoto Station.

$ Rates: ¥8,500 ($61) single; ¥14,900 ($106) double/twin; ¥25,000 ($178) deluxe twin. AE, DC, JCB, MC, V.

Matsumoto Tokyu Inn is a practical, clean, and pleasant business hotel conveniently located close to Matsumoto Station. The front desk is on the second floor. Four kinds of rooms are offered: a nicely decorated single with semidouble-size bed; a double-bedded room; a twin; and a deluxe twin with sofa, chairs, and a separate vanity area with its own sink. Similar to other business hotels in the nationwide Tokyu Inn chain, this place offers rooms decorated in beige and brown and equipped with desk or table, clock, fridge, tea server, and TV with pay video, including movies from the United States. Facilities include the Shangri-La restaurant, serving Western and Japanese meals, a bar/lounge, and vending machines on the fifth and eighth floors. As a service to the forgetful, rugs in the elevator tell what day of the week it is and are changed daily.

BUDGET

ENJYOH BEKKAN, 110 Utsukushigahara-onsen, Satoyamabe-ku, Matsumoto 390. Tel. 0263/33-7233. Fax 0263/36-2084. 19 rms (8 with bath). TV **Bus:** A 20-minute ride from Matsumoto Station to Utsukushigahara-onsen Bus Terminal.

$ Rates: ¥5,200 ($37) single without bath, ¥6,200 ($44) single with bath; ¥9,900 ($71) twin without bath, ¥11,300 ($81) twin with bath; ¥13,500 ($96) triple without bath, ¥16,000 ($114) triple with bath. Breakfast ¥800 ($5.70); Japanese-style dinner ¥2,500 ($17.85). AE, MC, V.

Although it's a bit far from the center of Matsumoto, this simple ryokan is a member of the Japanese Inn Group and offers simple and clean tatami rooms. What's more, it's located near a hot spring and offers hot-spring bathing 24 hours a day.

HOTEL IKYU ⑫, 1-11-13 Honjo, Matsumoto 390. Tel. 0263/35-8528. 19 rms (all with bath). A/C MINIBAR TV TEL **Directions:** An 8-minute walk from Matsumoto Station.

$ Rates (per person): ¥4,400 ($31) without meals; ¥6,500 ($46) including breakfast and dinner. No credit cards.

A bit on the old side but very reasonably priced and run by friendly people, the Hotel Ikyu is housed in a concrete building fairly close to the train station. It's popular with young Japanese. Fourteen tatami rooms and 5 Western-style rooms are available, all with heater, stocked fridge, hot-water pot for tea, and coin-operated TV, among other amenities. There are lots of windows in this place and added touches like plants in the stairwell. Meals are served in a small dining hall adjoining the hotel.

MATSUMOTO TOURIST HOTEL, 2-4-24 Fukashi, Matsumoto 390. Tel. 0263/33-9000. 96 rms (37 with bath). A/C TV TEL **Directions:** A 6-minute walk from Matsumoto Station.

$ Rates (including service): ¥5,200 ($37) single without bath, ¥6,000–¥6,400 ($43–$46) single with bath; ¥12,000 ($86) double/twin with bath. Japanese-style tatami rooms: without private bath ¥5,500 ($39), one person; ¥9,300 ($66), two; ¥12,000 ($86), three. AE, DC, JCB, MC, V.

This business hotel has one restaurant serving both Western and Japanese food, a public bath, and a vending area. Its staff is very friendly, but again, no one speaks much English. All rooms are simple but tastefully decorated, and include TV and a hot-water heater for tea. Some rooms have a refrigerator. The majority of rooms are Western-style singles, with and without bathroom, as well as twins or doubles, all with bathroom. There are also eight Japanese-style tatami rooms, none with private bath but each offering a private sink.

NISHIYA RYOKAN ⑬, **2-4-12 Ote, Matsumoto 390. Tel. 0263/33-4332.** 15 rms (none with bath). **Directions:** About an 8-minute walk from Matsumoto Station toward Matsumoto Castle.

$ Rates (per person): ¥3,500 ($25) without meals; ¥4,000 ($28) with breakfast. No credit cards.

Nishiya Ryokan offers just the basics of Japanese-style tatami rooms outfitted both with fans for cooling and with kotatsu (heaters underneath low tables draped with a blanket, to keep your legs warm) to ward off cold winters. Only breakfast is served.

Youth Hostel

ASAMA ONSEN YOUTH HOSTEL, 302-1 Asama-Onsen, Matsumoto 390-03. Tel. 0263/46-1335. 150 beds. **Directions:** A 20-minute bus ride from Matsumoto Station, then a 5-minute walk.

$ Rates (per person, including sheets): ¥2,500 ($17.85) member; ¥3,100 ($22.15) nonmember. Japanese breakfasts ¥450 ($3.20). No credit cards.

The closest youth hostel, Asama Onsen Youth Hostel offers rooms filled with bunk beds, with eight people to a room. No dinner is served.

WHERE TO DINE

TAIMAN, 4-2-4 Ote. Tel. 32-0882.
Cuisine: FRENCH. **Reservations:** Recommended. **Directions:** A 10-minute walk from Matsumoto Station.

$ Prices: Appetizers ¥1,500–¥2,000 ($10.70–$14.30); main dishes ¥3,000–¥6,000 ($21.40–$42.85); set courses ¥5,500–¥16,500 ($39.30–$117.85). AE, DC, JCB, MC, V.

Open: Lunch daily 11:30am–2pm; dinner daily 5–9pm (last order 8pm). **Closed:** First and third Wed of month.

If you feel like treating yourself to a wonderful French meal in rustic yet elegant surroundings (not far from Matsumoto Castle), this is an excellent choice. The inside of this ivy-covered building has heavy wooden beams, high ceilings, fresh flowers on the tables, and elaborate cutlery. Set dinners with changing menus are available, as well as less expensive fixed-price meals of either sole or stewed beef, which are always on the menu and come with soup and dessert. For à la carte dishes such as roast lamb, steak, chicken, or sole, expect to spend at least ¥8,500 ($60.70).

One way to eat inexpensively is to come here for the special lunch, which costs ¥5,000 ($35.70). For example: My luncheon, which included bread or rice, started with an hors-d'oeuvre plate of marinated squid, lox, cream cheese, capers, and grated onion. The next course was crab gratin, cooked in a cheese-and-tomato base, resembling lasagne. The main dish was sautéed pork wrapped in bacon and topped with cheese. Also included in the price were salad, dessert, and coffee.

KAJIKA 135, 1-2-21 Fukashi. Tel. 35-7632.
Cuisine: KAISEKI/VARIED JAPANESE. **Reservations:** Required for dinner.
Directions: A 4-minute walk from Matsumoto Station.
$ Prices: Kaiseki ¥7,000–¥15,000 ($50–$107.15); lunch teishoku ¥2,000–¥3,000 ($14.30–$21.40). No credit cards.
Open: Lunch Mon–Sat 11:30am–2pm; dinner Mon–Sat 5–10pm (last order 9pm). **Closed:** National hols.

If you'd rather have Japanese fare, Kajika is on the fourth floor of the Cosmo Building behind the bus terminal. It's a modern restaurant decorated in stained dark wood and cool white walls. The lunch menu is quite reasonable, with various kinds of teishoku available, ranging from the ubiquitous obento lunch box to sashimi, tempura, and soba set meals. At dinnertime, only kaiseki is served.

SHIKIMI 136, 1-5-5 Chuo. Tel. 35-3279.
Cuisine: EEL/SUSHI. **Directions:** A 4-minute walk from Matsumoto Station.
$ Prices: Unagi donburi (eel on rice) ¥1,600 ($11.45); platters of assorted sushi **(moriawase)** ¥1,600–¥3,300 ($11.45–$23.55). No credit cards.
Open: Fri–Wed noon–10pm.

For inexpensive Japanese fare close to Matsumoto Station, try Shikimi, which specializes in eel and sushi. Although relatively new, it manages to evoke an atmosphere of old Japan with its traditional tiled roof and its cast-iron lanterns hanging from outside eaves. The inside is a successful blend of the old and new, tastefully decorated with wooden sliding doors, small tatami rooms, a wooden counter, and paper lanterns. I recommend the unagi donburi (strips of eel on rice), which comes with soup and pickled vegetables. If sushi is more to your liking, try one of Shikimi's platters of assorted sushi, called moriawase, available in three different sizes.

NAJA, 4-3-20 Ote. Tel. 36-9096.
Cuisine: VEGETARIAN. **Directions:** About a 10-minute walk from Matsumoto Station toward castle.
$ Prices: Main dishes ¥450–¥800 ($3.20–$5.70); set meals ¥650–¥750 ($4.65–$5.35). No credit cards.
Open: Lunch Mon–Sat 11:30am–3pm; dinner Mon–Sat 5–9pm.

If you're a vegetarian or fan of natural foods, head for Naja. A tiny place with only three tables, it looks and sounds as if it had been transported from a commune in the woods of California—dried flowers hanging from the walls, a plain wooden décor, and music from the '60s playing in the background. Its English menu lists a daily brown-rice set meal, as well as such offerings as soy-bean curry with yogurt, noodles, tofu steak, and brown-rice porridge. Since it's on a tiny alley, ask the tourist office to pinpoint its exact location on your map.

---

4. MAGOME & TSUMAGO

Approximately 61 miles E of Nagoya; 55 miles SW of Matsumoto

GETTING THERE   By Train and Bus   Since neither Magome nor Tsumago is directly on a train line, you'll have to make the final journey by bus. To reach Magome, take the Chuo Honsen Line (which connects Nagoya and Matsumoto) to Nakatsugawa Station, from which it's a 35-minute bus ride to Magome. Nakatsugawa Station is 1 hour from Nagoya and about 1¼ hours from Matsumoto. Tsumago is only a 7-minute bus ride from Nagiso Station, which is also on the Chuo Honsen

Line. Note that not all trains stop in Nagiso or Nakatsugawa, so make certain that your train stops where you want to go. Note also that buses are not very frequent, so you might want to inquire about bus schedules beforehand (because it's in the same prefecture, the Matsumoto Station tourist office has information on bus schedules). If you don't feel like walking the distance between Magome and Tsumago, there's also a bus that travels between the two villages.

ESSENTIAL INFORMATION   The **area code** for both Magome and Tsumago, lying in Nagano Prefecture, is 0264.

Your best bet for information on Magome and Tsumago is at the Tourist Information Center in Tokyo or Kyoto, where you can pick up a pamphlet called *Kiso Valley*. It provides a rough sketch of the 5-mile hiking path between the two villages.

The **information office** for Magome itself is at Yamaguchi-mura, Kiso-gun (tel. 0264/59-2336); and for Tsumage, at Nagiso-machi, Kiso-gun (tel. 0264/57-3123).

If you have luggage, you might be interested in knowing that a **luggage-transfer service** between Magome and Tsumago is available daily from July 20 through August, and on Saturday, Sunday, and national holidays from March 21 to July 19 and from September through November. Luggage is accepted at either town's tourist office no later than 9am for morning delivery and no later than 1pm for afternoon delivery. It would be prudent, however, to verify this beforehand by calling the Magome or Tsumago tourist office, but note that only Japanese is spoken on the telephone.

If you're traveling between Nagoya and Matsumoto, you'll most likely pass through the Kiso Valley in the mountainous Nagano Prefecture. Surrounded by the towering Japan Alps, the deep valley formed by the Kiso River has always served as a natural passageway through the hills. In fact, it was one of the two official roads that linked Kyoto with Edo (present-day Tokyo) back in the days of The Tokugawa shogunate (the other route was the Tokaido Highway, which passes through Hakone). Known as the Nakasendo Highway, it was the route of traveling daimyo (feudal lords) and their entourages of samurai retainers as they journeyed between Japan's two most important towns. To serve their needs, 11 post towns sprang up along the Nakasendo Highway. Back then, it took 3 days to travel through the valley.

Of the old post towns, Magome and Tsumago are two that still survive, with many of the old buildings left intact. A 5-mile pathway skirting the Kiso River links the two villages, providing hikers with the experience of what it must have been like to travel the Nakasendo Highway back in the Edo Period. Visits to the picturesque villages, as well as the hike, can easily be accomplished in a 1-day excursion from Nagoya or Matsumoto.

WHAT TO SEE & DO
IN MAGOME

Magome, the southernmost post town, has old inns and souvenir shops that line both sides of a gently sloping road. It takes about 20 minutes to stroll through the town. Halfway up the slope you'll see a museum dedicated to Shimazaki Toson (1872–1943), a noted novelist and poet born in Magome.

IN TSUMAGO

Tsumago, the second post town from the south, is in my opinion the more beautiful and authentic. Threatened with gradual decline and desertion after the Chuo Line was constructed in 1911, thus bypassing Tsumago, the town experienced decades of neglect—probably what ultimately saved it. Having suffered almost no modernization in the zeal of the 20th century, Tsumago was a perfect target for renovation and restoration in the early 1970s. In a rare show of insight (I say rare because this has hardly ever happened in Japan), electrical wires, TV antennae, and telephone poles were hidden from sight along the main road. Tsumago looks much as it did back in the days of Edo.

On the main street of Tsumago, be sure to stop off at **Waki-honjin Okuya,** an officially appointed inn, once serving as a way station for daimyo and court nobles. It was also home of a sake brewery. The present house dates from 1877, rebuilt with *hinoki* cypress trees, which has a special significance for this region. For centuries, all the way through the Edo Period (1603–1867), the people of the Kiso Valley were prohibited from cutting down trees, even if they were on private property. When the Meiji Period dawned and the ban was finally lifted, wealthy landowners were quick to rebuild their homes in a more stately manner. This house, rebuilt in the style of a grand old castle, was visited by Emperor Meiji himself in 1880. Today, it serves as a local museum, with displays of rice bowls, hair combs, books with ukiyo-e prints, and other items relating to the Edo Period. Be sure to check out the daimyo's bathtub and toilet.

THE HIKE

Allow about 3 hours for the hike between Magome and Tsumago, although you can probably do it in 2 hours. It doesn't matter which town you start from, since either way it's a beautiful walk, tracing the contours of the Kiso Valley and crisscrossing the stream over a series of bridges. The trail is mainly a footpath, although at times it follows a paved road. In any case, the signs are in Japanese, so familiarize yourself with the kanji for Magome ⑭ and Tsumago ⑮. As the trail does go up some steep inclines, be sure to wear your walking shoes. And have fun—this is a great walk.

CHAPTER 13

THE REST OF HONSHU

In addition to Tokyo, Kyoto, and the Japan Alps, Honshu has numerous other towns and attractions that are well worth a visit. As the largest of Japan's islands, centrally situated, Honshu is where many of the country's most important historical events took place and is thus the home of many castles, gardens, temples, shrines, and other famous sights linked with the past. Honshu offers enough variety to satisfy the whims of every traveler: from the bustling modern cities of Osaka and Nagoya to the sacred shrines of Ise-Shima National Park and Miyajima; from Kurashiki, with its quaint historic districts, to the religious sanctuaries atop Mt. Koya; from the great ports of Kobe and Hiroshima, with their heavy industries, to the outlying forests and agricultural districts, where the bulk of the country's tea and silk are produced, along with rice and cotton. Little wonder that many travelers to Japan never make it farther than the shores of Honshu.

Honshu is where more than 80% of the Japanese people live. Its climate ranges from snowy winters in the north to subtropical weather in the south. The middle of the island is traversed by Japan's longest river, the Shinano.

1. NAGOYA

227 miles W of Tokyo; 92 miles E of Kyoto; 116 miles E of Osaka

GETTING THERE   By Train   The Shinkansen bullet train takes 2 hours from Tokyo, 43 minutes from Kyoto, and 1 hour from Shin-Osaka Station.

By Bus   The Tomei Highway Bus takes 5 hours and 40 minutes from Tokyo. The Meishin Highway Bus takes 2 hours and 25 minutes from Kyoto and 3 hours and 15 minutes from Osaka.

ESSENTIAL INFORMATION   The **area code** for Nagoya, lying in Aichi Prefecture, is 052.

Before leaving Tokyo or Kyoto, drop by the Tourist Information Center to pick up a free leaflet called *Nagoya and Vicinity,* which has a map of the city and a list of attractions in Nagoya and the surrounding area.

Nagoya itself has one of the best tourist information facilities in Japan. The **Nagoya International Center** is on the third floor of the Nagoya International Center Building, 1-47-1 Nagono (tel. 052/581-0100), a 10-minute walk from the train station. Open daily from 9am to 8:30pm, this modern facility has an English-speaking staff, a lounge area with a TV featuring CNN newscasts from the United States, and information on the city, including a free monthly publication called *Nagoya Calendar.* The center also advises foreign residents on how to get a visa, where to find an apartment, and which doctors speak English. Be sure to pick up a city map, as well as a map of the underground shopping arcade radiating out from Nagoya Station.

There's also a **tourist information center** at the central concourse of Nagoya

Station (tel. 541-4301), open from 9am to 5pm. It has pamphlets and maps of Nagoya, and its staff speaks English.

ORIENTATION & GETTING AROUND Clustered around JR Nagoya Station are the Shinkansen Station, the Meitetsu Bus Terminal, Meitetsu Shin-Nagoya Station, the city bus terminal, and Kintetsu Station, as well as many hotels and a huge underground shopping arcade. The city's downtown area is called Sakae and has many shops, restaurants, and department stores.

The easiest way to get around is via the city's **subway** system, which is simple to use because stations have names written in both English and Japanese. Probably the most important line for tourists is the **Meijo Line,** which runs through Sakae. It takes you to both Atsuta Jingu Shrine (stop: Jingu-Nishi) and to Nagoya Castle (stop: Shiyakusho); and if you take this line all the way to the end you'll end up in Ozone—no kidding!

Although it's Japan's fourth-largest city, with a population of 2.1 million, Nagoya is a place most foreigners never stop to see. True, it doesn't have the attractions of many of the nation's cities, but it does have a castle originally built by the first Tokugawa shogun, as well as one of Japan's most important Shinto shrines.

You can visit the world-famous Noritake chinaware factory, observe summer cormorant fishing, and visit an open-air architectural museum with structures dating from the Meiji Period. Nagoya, capital of Aichi Prefecture, also serves as the gateway to Toba and Ise-Shima National Park. Incidentally, Nagoya is the birthplace of pachinko, the upright Japanese pinball machine now found in the farthest corners of the islands. Its industries include automobile manufacture, chinaware, shipbuilding, and aircraft construction. Almost completely destroyed during World War II, Nagoya was rebuilt with wide, straight streets, many of which are named.

WHAT TO SEE & DO

THE TOP ATTRACTIONS

⭐ Built for his ninth son by Tokugawa Ieyasu, the first Tokugawa shogun of Japan, **Nagoya Castle,** 1-1 Honmaru, Naka-ku (tel. 231-1700), was completed in 1612 and served as both a stronghold and a residence for members of the Tokugawa family for almost 250 years, until the Meiji Restoration ended Tokugawa rule in 1868. Tokugawa, a shrewd and calculating shogun, forced feudal lords throughout Japan to contribute to the castle's construction, thereby depleting their resources and making it harder for them to stage rebellions.

Although Nagoya Castle was destroyed in World War II, it was rebuilt in 1959 and is almost a carbon copy of the original. Like most reconstructed castles in Japan, this one is made of ferroconcrete, and even has an elevator up to the fifth floor, where you have fine views of Nagoya and beyond.

The 154-foot donjon houses treasures that escaped the bombing during World War II, including beautiful paintings on sliding doors and screens. On top of the donjon roof are two golden dolphins, thought to protect the castle from dreaded fires. The dolphins each weigh about 2,650 pounds and are made of cast bronze covered with 18-karat gold scales. The castle is open daily from 9:30am to 4:30pm, and the entrance fee is ¥400 ($2.85).

East of the castle is **Ninomaru Garden,** one of the few remaining castle gardens in Japan. Besides providing a beautiful setting, it served as an emergency shelter for the lord in case of enemy attack. Stop by the Ninomaru Tea House—it's said that if you drink tea here, 5 years will be added to your life.

The **Tokugawa Art Museum,** 1017 Tokugawa-cho, Higashi-ku (tel. 935-6262), houses thousands of documents, armor, swords, helmets, pottery, lacquerware, and paintings that once belonged to the Tokugawa family. The museum's most famous exhibits are picture scrolls of *The Tale of Genji* (*Genji Emaki*)—but they're displayed only 1 week a year, in November. Closed during exhibition changes, the museum is open Tuesday through Sunday from 10am to 5pm; the entrance fee is ¥1,000 ($7.15).

Because it contains one of the emperor's Three Sacred Treasures, **Atsuta Jingu Shrine,** 1-1-1 Jingu, Atsuta-ku (tel. 671-4151), is revered as one of the three most important shrines in Japan. It enshrines the Kusanagi-no-Tsurugi (Grass-Mowing Sword), and even though the sword isn't on public display, Japanese make pilgrimages here to pay their respects. (The other two sacred treasures are the Sacred Mirror, which is in the Ise Jingu Shrines, and the Jewels, which are kept in the Imperial Palace in Tokyo.)

Atsuta Shrine was founded in the 2nd century and was rebuilt in 1965. According to legend, the Grass-Mowing Sword was presented to an ancient prince named Yamato-Takeru, who used it during a campaign against rebels in eastern Japan. The rebels set a field of grass on fire and the prince used the sword to mow down the grass, thereby quelling the fire. *Atsuta* means "hot field" in Japanese.

If you like high places, you may be interested in knowing that the **Nagoya TV Tower,** 3-6-15 Saki, Nishiki, Naka-ku (tel. 971-8546) was the first such tower in Japan. Since it opened in 1954, more than 25 million visitors have ridden its glass-enclosed elevators to its observation platform, approximately 300 feet above the ground, for a bird's-eye view of the sprawling city. Used jointly by Nagoya's five television stations, the tower is located about a 2-minute walk from Sakae subway station in the heart of Nagoya. It's open daily from 10am to 10pm in summer and from 10am to 5:50pm in winter (7pm on Sunday and holidays). Admission is ¥600 ($4.30) for a visit to the observation platform.

FACTORY VISITS

For centuries Nagoya has been a pottery and porcelain production center, and today the city and its vicinity manufacture 50% of Japan's total export chinaware. The largest chinaware company in Japan is Noritake, known the world over for its fine tableware. Founded in 1904, Noritake now exports to 110 nations around the world.

✪ The **Nagoya Noritake Factory,** located about a 10-minute walk north of Nagoya Station, offers two free tours daily Monday through Friday at 10am and 1pm. Conducted in English, the tours last about an hour, but you must reserve in advance (tel. 562-5072). The tour begins with an excellent film that depicts the history of Noritake and describes the manufacturing and decorating processes involved in making porcelain. After the film ends, you're led on a trip through the various production stages of the Diamond Collection, Noritake's best porcelain line. Unlike most modern-day factories, where work is largely automated, almost all the work here is still done by hand. If you're interested in buying some porcelain, there are two shops located next to the plant that sell Noritake ware at reduced prices. Ask your guide to point you in the right direction.

In addition to its chinaware, Nagoya and its vicinity also rank first in the nation in the production of cloisonné, and the Nagoya International Center has a 14-minute videotape demonstrating its production. You can also visit the **Shippo-Cho Industrial Hall (Shippo Sangyou Kaikan),** Tojima Shippo-cho (tel. 441-3411). Open Wednesday through Monday (closed national holidays) from 9am to 5pm, it's free of charge to the public and contains exhibits of cloisonné ware. If you want to see demonstrations of how cloisonné is made, the Industrial Hall can arrange an appointment with one of the area's many cloisonné factories. To reach the Industrial Hall, take the Meitetsu bus from the Meitetsu Bus Terminal (in the Melsa Building, next to Nagoya Station) to the Yasumatsu bus stop. From there it's a 15-minute walk.

NEARBY ATTRACTIONS

Meija Mura

If architecture is your passion, you'll find a lot to delight in at this open-air museum. Called Meiji Mura (tel. 0568/67-0314), it features more than 50 buildings and structures dating from the Meiji Period (1868–1912). Before Japan opened its doors in the mid-1800s, unpainted wooden structures dominated Japanese architecture. After Western influences began infiltrating Japan, however, stone, brick, painted wood, towers, turrets, and Victorian features came into play. Contained on the grounds of this 250-acre museum are Western homes that once belonged to foreigners living in Nagasaki and Kobe; official government buildings and schools; two Christian churches; a post office; a Kabuki theater; a brewery; and even a prison. Don't miss the front façade and lobby of the original Imperial Hotel in Tokyo, designed by American architect Frank Lloyd Wright.

To get to Meiji Mura, take a direct bus from the Meitetsu Bus Terminal's third floor in the Melsa Building. Buses leave every 30 minutes (even more frequently on weekends) and the trip to Meiji Mura takes just over an hour. The round-trip bus ticket costs ¥2,240 ($16); admission to Meiji Mura is ¥1,240 ($8.85). Meiji Mura is open daily from 10am to 5pm (4pm from November through February).

Cormorant Fishing

There are two places near Nagoya where you can watch **cormorant fishing** every night (except during a full moon) in summer. In this ancient Japanese fishing method, trained cormorants (seabirds) dive into the water in search of ayu, a small Japanese trout. To ensure that the cormorants don't swallow the fish, the birds are fitted with rings around their necks.

The city of **Gifu** features cormorant fishing on the Nagaragawa River from May 11 to October 15, and you can view the whole spectacle aboard a small wooden boat. To reach Gifu, take the Meitetsu Main Line train from Meitetsu Shin-Nagoya Station to Shin-Gifu Station. From there, switch to a local train or bus heading for Nagara Kitamachi and get off at Nagarabashi Station. You'll see the ticket office (Gifu-shi Ukai Kanransen Jimusyo) after exiting the station. Ticket sales begin at 5:30am, but you can call in advance to reserve your ticket (tel. 0582/62-0104). The price of a ticket is ¥2,700 ($19.30) in May, June, and October, and ¥2,900 ($20.70) in July, August, and September.

The other site for cormorant fishing is in the town of **Inuyama,** from June 1 to September 30. Take the Inuyama Line of the Meitetsu Railways from Meitetsu Shin-Nagoya Station to Inuyama Yuen Station. From there it's a 5-minute walk. Tickets are sold throughout the day beginning at 9am, and the action starts after 6pm. Call ahead to make reservations at 0568/61-0057. Tickets cost ¥2,500 ($17.85) in June and September, and ¥2,800 ($20) in July and August.

Inuyama City

There are several attractions in Inuyama that might interest you—come here for the day and top it off with the cormorant fishing described above. Just a 10-minute walk from Inuyama Yuen Station, for example, is **Inuyama Castle,** which was constructed in 1537 and is Japan's oldest castle. Admission is ¥300 ($2.15), and it's open daily from 9am to 5pm. Another popular activity is to **shoot the rapids** of the Kiso River. Boats depart approximately every 30 or 60 minutes for the 1-hour trip, priced at ¥2,900 ($20.70). For more information, call the Nihon-Rhine Kanko Company at 0574/26-2231.

WHERE TO STAY

Most hotels are near Nagoya Station, with the rest located east of the station near Sakae and Nagoya Castle. As with most cities in Japan, Nagoya does not have many ryokan—the cost of personal service and the price of land are simply too prohibitive.

EXPENSIVE

HOTEL NAGOYA CASTLE, 3-19 Hinokuchi-cho, Nishi-ku, Nagoya 451.
Tel. 052/521-2121. Fax 052/531-3313. 241 rms. A/C MINIBAR TV TEL
Subway: Sengencho Station (Tsurumai Line), a 10-minute walk away.
$ Rates: ¥11,000 ($78) single; ¥19,800–¥34,000 ($141–$243) twin; ¥22,000–¥27,000 ($157–$193) double. AE, DC, JCB, MC, V.
This hotel is just west of Nagoya Castle, offering wonderful views of the castle from

its higher-priced twins and doubles. Rooms come equipped with the usual TV (with CNN broadcasts; bilingual TV also available) and minibar, and facilities include a range of restaurants and athletic diversions.

Dining/Entertainment: There are two restaurants serving Western food, a Chinese restaurant, a Japanese restaurant, and one bar.

Services: Free newspaper, free shuttle bus from hotel to Nagoya Station.

Facilities: Indoor swimming pool, sauna and gym (fee: ¥3,000 or $21.40), shops, business center.

NAGOYA HILTON, 1-3-3 Sakae, Naka-ku, Nagoya 460. Tel. 052-212-1111, or toll free 800/HILTONS. Fax 052/212-1225. 453 rms. A/C MINIBAR TV TEL **Subway:** Fushimi Station, a 2-minute walk away.

$ Rates: ¥16,500–¥23,000 ($118–$164) single; ¥24,000–¥30,000 ($171–$214) double/twin. Executive floor: ¥27,000 ($193) single, ¥35,000 ($25) double/twin. AE, DC, JCB, MC, V.

One of Nagoya's newest hotels, the Nagoya Hilton is a gleaming white-tiled building that soars 28 stories above the heart of the city. A 5-minute taxi ride from Nagoya Station, it is one of the city's tallest buildings and bases its room rates according to height. The most expensive accommodations are the Executive rooms on the 25th and 26th floors, offering a private lounge and concierge, complimentary continental breakfast, and evening cocktails. All rooms are luxuriously appointed, with tradition-al shoji screens, bilingual TV (with CNN broadcasts from the United States and in-house movies), hairdryer, and a phone in the bathroom, among other amenities.

Dining/Entertainment: Of its four restaurants, The Seasons is the most elegant and serves continental cuisine, while the Genji offers a diversity of Japanese food. After dinner, retire to the Windows of the World on the 28th floor, offering great views of the city and nightly entertainment.

Services: 24-hour room service, free newspaper, baby-sitting, in-house physician.

Facilities: Indoor swimming pool and health club (extra fees for pool and gym), shopping arcade with 23 boutiques, beauty salon, business center.

NAGOYA KANKO HOTEL, 1-19-30 Nishiki, Naka-ku, Nagoya 451. Tel. 052/231-7711. Fax 052/231-7719. 505 rms. A/C MINIBAR TV TEL **Subway:** Fushimi Station, a few minutes' walk away.

$ Rates: ¥12,000–¥14,800 ($85–$106) single; ¥22,000–¥31,000 ($157–$221) double/twin. AE, JCB, MC, V.

Located between Nagoya Station and Sakae, this first-class hotel offers many conveniences in one place, including a variety of restaurants and a shopping arcade. First opened in 1934 and completely renovated in 1985, it has a huge lobby featuring white brick, natural woods, brass, and contemporary glass chandeliers. All rooms are nicely appointed and come with TV (with CNN broadcasts; bilingual TV available upon request) and minibar.

Dining/Entertainment: Five restaurants serve French, Japanese, and Chinese cuisine, including the 18th-floor Aurora with its views of the city. There's one bar.

Services: Free newspaper.

Facilities: Shopping arcade, barbershop.

MODERATE

HOTEL CASTLE PLAZA, 4-3-25 Meieki, Nakamura-ku, Nagoya 450. Tel. 052/582-2121. Fax 052/582-8666. 262 rms. A/C MINIBAR TV TEL **Directions:** A 6-minute walk from Nagoya Station.

$ Rates: ¥8,200–¥10,500 ($58–$75) single; ¥14,300–¥16,500 ($102–$118) double; ¥14,300–¥20,000 ($102–$143) twin. AE, DC, JCB, MC, V.

Under the same management as the first-class Hotel Nagoya Castle, this 10-year-old hotel has more facilities than you'd expect from a moderately priced establishment, including a dozen restaurants and a shopping plaza. The swimming pool, sauna, gym, and jogging track can be used for ¥2,700 ($19.30). The hotel is decorated in classy contemporary designs of glass and mauve coloring, and the rooms are bright and cheerful. The most expensive twins have good views of the city, plus a separate entrance foyer and semidouble-size beds.

MEITETSU GRAND HOTEL, 1-2-4 Meieki, Nakamura-ku, Nagoya 450. Tel. 052/582-2211. Fax 052/582-2230. 242 rms. A/C MINIBAR TV TEL
Directions: A 1-minute walk from Nagoya Station.
$ Rates: ¥9,900 ($71) single; ¥17,500–¥25,000 ($125–$178) twin; ¥20,000 ($143) double. AE, DC, JCB, MC, V.

Built in 1967, this hotel is conveniently located right above Meitetsu Station. In addition to its three restaurants, one lounge, and a beer garden open in the summer, it has shops on the first several floors. The check-in desk is on the 11th floor. Singles are comfortably decorated with semidouble-size bed, desk, chair, and table, and all rooms have TV and minibar. The most expensive twin is a large room featuring an entry foyer, a separate vanity area, semidouble-size beds, and a sitting area with couch, chairs, and table separated from the sleeping area by a glass partition.

MONT BLANC HOTEL, 3-14-1 Meieki, Nakamura-ku, Nagoya 450. Tel. 052/541-1121. Fax 052/541-1140. 281 rms. A/C MINIBAR TV TEL **Directions:** A 2-minute walk from Nagoya Station.
$ Rates (including tax): ¥7,400–¥8,500 ($53–$61) single; ¥12,500 ($89) double; ¥12,500–¥14,800 ($89–$106) twin; ¥17,600 ($126) triple. AE, DC, MC, V.

Built in 1980 and renovated in 1985, this small business hotel is clean, bright, conveniently close to Nagoya Station, and has both Western and Japanese restaurants. It has mostly singles, but there are also 47 twins, 12 doubles, and a few Japanese-style rooms, all of which come with radio, clock, TV with pay video, and minibar. Bathtubs in the cheapest singles are extremely narrow; if you're a big Westerner, you may have an uncomfortable bath. Some of the twins features both beds and a separate tatami sitting area.

NAGOYA MIYAKO HOTEL, 4-9-10 Meieki, Nakamura-ku, Nagoya 450. Tel. 052/571-3211. Fax 052/571-3242. 400 rms. A/C MINIBAR TV TEL
Directions: A 5-minute walk from Nagoya Station.
$ Rates: ¥8,500–¥13,000 ($61–$93) single; ¥16,500–¥22,000 ($118–$157) twin; ¥20,000–¥22,000 ($143–$157) double. Japanese-style rooms: ¥20,000–¥27,000 ($143–$193) single or double occupancy. AE, DC, JCB, MC, V.

This is one of the best hotels in this price category. As in all Miyako hotels, service is excellent, and all rooms have recently been refurbished. The hotel has an attractive white-marble lobby; a rooftop beer garden open in summer; Chinese, Japanese, and Western restaurants; and an underground shopping arcade with passageways to the Meitetsu Bus Terminal, Kintetsu Station, and Nagoya Station. Rooms are comfortable, with wooden furniture, minibar, hot-water thermos, TV with video and CNN, clock, and radio. Rates are based on room size. Most of the singles face an inner courtyard—no view, but the rooms are quiet. Some of the Japanese-style rooms have bathtubs made of cypress. Guests receive a free newspaper.

HOTEL SUNROUTE NAGOYA, 2-35-24 Meieki, Nakamura-ku, Nagoya 450. 052/571-2221. Fax 052/571-2235. 276 rms. A/C MINIBAR TV TEL
Directions: A 3-minute walk from Nagoya Station.
$ Rates: ¥7,400–¥8,800 ($53–$63) single; ¥12,500–¥14,800 ($89–$106) twin; ¥15,400–¥15,900 ($110–$113) double. AE, DC, JCB, MC, V.

Opened in 1985, this hotel is one of Nagoya's best and most conveniently located business hotels. A handsome brick building, it features a spacious lobby with an atrium and marbled fountain and restaurants serving Japanese and Western food. As with many business hotels, the majority of its rooms are singles. White walls make the simply decorated accommodations bright and pleasant, while TV with pay video, minibar, radio, alarm, and hot-water pot and tea add to the comfort.

BUDGET

NAGOYA DAINI WASHINGTON HOTEL, 3-22-12 Nishiki, Naka-ku, Nagoya 460. Tel. 052/962-7111. 320 rms (all with bath). A/C TV TEL **Subway:** Sakae, a few minutes' walk away.

$ Rates: ¥5,800–¥7,800 ($41–$56) single; ¥12,000–¥14,300 ($86–$102) double/twin. AE, DC, JCB, V.

This hotel is near Sakae and its restaurants and bars. Unlike most business hotels, which have few facilities, it features four restaurants serving Japanese, Chinese, and Western food; there is also a sauna. Even the cheapest singles manage to maintain a cheerful atmosphere, even though they're small and windowless. Twins and doubles are small but functional, with single and narrow beds, a small writing area, and two chairs. Machines selling soda and beer are located on the fifth and eighth floors.

NAGOYA PLAZA HOTEL, 3-8-21 Nishiki, Naka-ku, Nagoya 460. Tel. 052/951-6311. Fax 052/951-6319. 173 rms (all with bath). A/C MINIBAR TV TEL **Subway:** Sakae Station, a 3-minute walk away.

$ Rates (including tax and service): ¥5,500–¥6,500 ($39–$46) single; ¥9,900–¥11,000 ($71–$78) double; ¥10,500 ($75) twin. AE, DC, JCB, MC, V.

Also located in Sakae, this business hotel offers just the basics and is cheap. The décor could use some updating, but the staff is friendly and the location convenient. Rooms come with coin-operated TV, minibar, and desk. The cheapest single is rather bare, with just a bed and wall hooks for clothes. The hotel's one restaurant serves breakfast only, with the price running ¥800 ($5.70).

RYOKAN MEIRYU, 2-4-21 Kamimaezu, Naka-ku, Nagoya 463. Tel. 052/331-8686. Fax 052/321-6119. 23 rms (none with bath). A/C TV TEL **Subway:** Kamimaezu station, a 3-minute walk away.

$ Rates: ¥4,900 ($35) single; ¥8,800 ($63) twin; ¥11,500 ($82) triple. Japanese breakfast ¥500 ($3.55), Japanese dinner ¥2,200 ($15.70). AE, V.

Another Japanese Inn Group member, this one has been a family-owned operation for more than 40 years, but the present building is concrete—a no-nonsense business accommodation. Most customers are Japanese businessmen, some of whom have lived here for years during the week, commuting home to their families on weekends. Rooms come with safe for valuables, bilingual TV, cotton kimono, and combination air conditioner/heater, among other amenities. The men's public bath also has a sauna (they don't have many female guests at this ryokan, but there is a separate public bath in case the lone female makes an appearance).

RYOKAN OYONE, 2-2-112 Aoi, Higashi-ku, Nagoya 461. Tel. 052/936-8788. Fax 052/936-8883. 18 rms (none with bath). A/C TV **Subway:** Higashiyama Line from Nagoya Station to Chikusa Station, then a 5-minute walk. Or take the JR Chuo Line (bound for Kozoji) to Chikusa Station.

$ Rates: ¥4,100–¥4,900 ($29–$35) single; ¥8,200–¥9,300 ($58–$66) twin; ¥11,500–¥12,000 ($82–$85) triple. Western breakfast ¥300–¥500 ($2.15–$2.55); Japanese breakfast ¥700 ($5), Japanese dinner ¥1,500 ($10.70). AE, MC, V.

A member of the Japanese Inn Group, this ryokan offers inexpensive tatami rooms. The building itself is rather characterless, but rooms are clean and come with heater and coin-operated bilingual TV.

Youth Hostels

THE NAGOYA YOUTH HOSTEL, 1-50 Kameiri, Tashirocho, Chikusa-ku, Nagoya 464. Tel. 052/781-9845. 102 beds. A/C **Subway:** 16 minutes from Nagoya Station to Higashiyama Koen, then a 10-minute walk.

$ Rates: ¥1,800 ($12.85) member and nonmember. Breakfast ¥400 ($2.85) extra. No credit cards.

As in most youth hostels, life here is fairly regimented: the front doors close at 9pm, lights are out at 10pm, and rising time is 6:30am. Dinner runs ¥600 ($4.30).

YOUTH HOSTEL AICHI-KEN SEINEN-KAIKAN, 1-18-8 Sakae, Naka-ku, Nagoya 460. Tel. 052/221-6001. 60 beds. A/C **Bus:** 50 to Nayabashi stop, then a 3-minute walk.

$ Rates: ¥2,570 ($18.35) member; ¥3,900 ($27.85) nonmember. Breakfast ¥450 ($3.20) extra. No credit cards.

It's worth a try to see whether there's room at this hostel, but it's so centrally located that it's usually full. Dinner choices range from ¥850 ($6.05) to ¥1,600 ($11.40).

WHERE TO DINE

One of Nagoya's specialties is *kishimen* (white) noodles. It's also famous for *miso nikomi udon*—udon noodles served in a bean-paste soup and flavored with such ingredients as chicken and green onions. There are also fine restaurants serving kaiseki, tempura, and other Japanese cuisine.

AROUND NAGOYA STATION

NAGOYA MIYAKO HOTEL BEER GARDEN, 4-9-10 Meieki, Nakamura-ku. Tel. 052/571-3211.

Cuisine: TEPPANYAKI/WESTERN. **Directions:** A 5-minute walk from Nagoya Station.

$ Prices: Main dishes ¥500–¥2,000 ($3.55–$14.30); teppanyaki course ¥3,900 ($27.85). No credit cards.

Open: Summer daily 5–9pm.

For outdoor summer dining, head for the Miyako Hotel's beer garden. Pop music plays from a loudspeaker, and there's a plastic-food display case to help you make your selection—anything from frankfurters to sushi. The teppanyaki course (strips of beef that you grill at your table) includes all the beer or fruit juice you can consume. If you go the à la carte route, beer starts at ¥850 ($6.05).

YAMAMOTO-YA HONTEN ⑪⑥, Sakura Dori St., basement of Horiuchi Building. Tel. 565-0278.

Cuisine: UDON NOODLES. **Directions:** A 3-minute walk from Nagoya Station, near Hotel Castle Plaza.

$ Prices: Udon soup ¥680 ($4.85); udon with chicken ¥1,000 ($7.15). No credit cards.

Open: Daily 10:45am–7:30pm.

This chain noodle shop specializes in miso nikomi udon. Its noodles, all handmade, are thick, hard, and chewy and are served in a type of bean paste special to Nagoya. If you like your noodles spicy, you can add a mixture of spices to your food from the large bamboo container on your table. If you want to try these noodles in Sakae, there's another shop just a couple of minutes from the Sakae subway station, in the basement of the Chu-Nichi Building (tel. 263-7519), open 11am to 8:30pm.

IN SAKAE

YAEGAKI TEMPURA HOUSE ⑪⑦, 3-17-28 Nishiki, Naka-ku. Tel. 951-3250.

Cuisine: TEMPURA. **Reservations:** Recommended for dinner. **Subway:** A 6-minute walk from Sakae Station.

$ Prices: Set-dinner courses ¥7,500 ($53.55); set lunch ¥5,500 ($39.30). AE, JCB, V.

Open: Lunch Mon–Sat 11:30am–2pm; dinner Mon–Sat 5–9pm.

Closed: National hols.

This well-established tempura restaurant in Sakae's nightlife and restaurant district has been serving fresh seafood and vegetables for more than half a century and features open kitchens so that guests can watch the action. The staff here is very friendly, and there's an English menu for the seasonal offerings, which may include shrimp, oyster, smelt, Japanese trout, gingko nuts, or lotus root. It's easiest to order the set dinner, which consists of hors d'oeuvres, four shrimp, six pieces of varied seasonal fish, vegetables, rice, soup, pickled vegetables, and fruit.

KISOJI ⑪⑧, **3-20-15 Nishiki, Naka-ku. Tel. 951-3755.**
   Cuisine: SHABU-SHABU. **Reservations:** Not necessary. **Subway:** A 5-minute walk from Sakae Station.
$ Prices: Set-dinner courses ¥5,500–¥10,400 ($39.30–$74); set lunch ¥1,400 ($10). AE, JCB, V.
   Open: Lunch Mon–Sat 11:30am–3pm; dinner Mon–Sat 5–10pm; Sun noon–9:30pm.

This restaurant specializes in shabu-shabu. In business for more than 20 years, it evokes a countryside atmosphere with traditional, comfortable décor; dining is either at tables or on tatami. There's an English menu, but the kimono-clad waitresses are unable to elaborate on what the various courses entail, so choose according to your budget. For dinner, the Shabu-Shabu Special includes hors d'oeuvres, shabu-shabu, rice, pickles, and ice cream, while the Shabu-Shabu Keyaki features hors d'oeuvres, shabu-shabu, sashimi, tempura vegetables, rice, pickles, and dessert.

KISHIMENTEI ⑪⑨, **3-20-4 Nishiki, Naka-ku. Tel. 951-3481.**
   Cuisine: KISHIMEN NOODLES. **Subway:** A 5-minute walk from Sakae Station.
$ Prices: Noodles ¥600–¥1,800 ($4.30–$12.85). No credit cards.
   Open: Mon–Sat 11am–8pm.

Kishimentei is a small hole-in-the-wall that has been offering Nagoya's specialty for more than 70 years—kishimen noodles. It even sells packages of noodles in case you want to take some home with you. There's no English menu, but plastic food is displayed in the window. Meals include kishimen noodles with pork, tempura shrimp, or vegetables.

SPECIALTY DINING

For a wide choice of inexpensive dining, a good bet is the ninth floor of the **Meitetsu department store,** the shiny white building next to Nagoya Station. Approximately 10 small restaurants are scattered along the ninth floor, offering everything from noodles and sushi to Chinese cuisine, tempura, eel, and spaghetti. You can dine here Friday through Wednesday from 10:30am to 7pm for ¥600 ($4.30) to ¥1,600 ($11.40).

SHOPPING

If you're a real Noritake fan, you might want to make a trip to the company's largest store in Japan, located at 2-1 Shinsakae-Machi, Naka-ku (tel. 951-0561). The closest subway station is Sakae, and the store is open daily from 10am to 5:30pm; closed on national holidays.

---

2. ISE-SHIMA NATIONAL PARK

289 miles W of Tokyo; 62 miles S of Nagoya

GETTING THERE   By Train   The easiest way to get to Ise-Shima is from Nagoya on the private Kintetsu Ise-Shima Line (Kinki Nippon Railway), which departs about every 30 minutes or so from the Kintetsu Station next to the Japan Railways' Nagoya Station. It takes about 1 hour and 30 minutes to reach Ise (Ujiyamada Station), about 1 hour and 40 minutes to reach Toba, and 2 hours to reach Kashikojima. A ticket from Nagoya to the end of the line in Kashikojima costs ¥3,000 ($21.40) one way. There are also Kintetsu lines to Shima Peninsula from both Kyoto (2 hours and 15 minutes to Toba) and from Osaka's Kintetsu Station in Namba (2 hours to Toba).

   If you're on a Japan Rail Pass, you can also reach Ise-Shima by Japan Railway, although trains are not as frequent or convenient. There is only one train from Kyoto, and if you're coming from Nagoya you'll have to change in Taki. Note that JR trains pass through Ise (Iseshi Station) and terminate in Toba. If you want to go on to Kashikojima, therefore, you'll have to switch in Toba to the Kintetsu private line.

ESSENTIAL INFORMATION   Ise-Shima National Park lies in Mie Prefecture. Be sure to drop by the Tourist Information Center in Tokyo or Kyoto to pick up the free leaflet *Ise-Shima*. It lists train schedules from Osaka, Kyoto, and Nagoya, and gives information on the park's main attractions.

Blessed with subtropical vegetation, small islands dotting its shoreline, and the most revered Shinto shrine in Japan, Ise-Shima National Park merits a one- or two-night stopover if you're anywhere near Nagoya. Located on Shima Peninsula and covering 200 square miles, this national park has bays and inlets that are the home of the Mikimoto pearl, Japan's famous women divers, and thousands of oyster rafts. Although you could conceivably cover the major attractions on a day's outing from Nagoya, I've included recommended accommodations in case you'd like to take in the sights at a more leisurely pace.

Ise-Shima's major attractions are concentrated in the small towns of Ise, Toba, and Kashikojima, all in Mie Prefecture. Ise, for example, is where you'll find the Ise Jingu Shrines; Toba contains the Mikimoto Pearl Island, with a pearl museum and demonstrations by women divers; and in Kashikojima you can visit the Shima Marineland or take boat trips around Ago Bay, perhaps the most scenic spot in the park.

Transportation inside Ise-Shima National Park is either by local train or by bus. You might also consider joining a sightseeing tour. Although they're conducted in Japanese only, tours provide a convenient way of seeing the park's far-flung attractions.

WHAT TO SEE & DO

The easiest way to see the sights of Ise-Shima National Park is to start in Ise and work your way down the peninsula to Kashikojima.

ISE

✪ Ise, the northern gateway to Ise-Shima National Park, is famous for the **Ise Jingu Shrines,** also called the Grand Shrines of Ise. The grounds consist of the Outer Shrine, the Inner Shrine, and more than 100 minor shrines.

The **Outer Shrine (Geku)** is just a 10-minute walk from either Ujiyamada or Iseshi Station. Founded in 478, it's dedicated to the Shinto goddess of harvest and agriculture. The **Inner Shrine (Naiku)** was founded a few centuries earlier and is dedicated to Amaterasu, the sun goddess. Since the shrines are about 4 miles apart, walk first to the Outer Shrine and then take a bus to the Inner Shrine. Buses run between the two shrines about every 15 minutes; the fare is ¥350 ($2.50).

The Ise Jingu Shrines are some of the few Shinto shrines in Japan without any Chinese Buddhist influences. Constructed of plain cypress wood, with thick thatched roofs, they are starkly simple and do not have any ornamentation except for gold and copper facing on their beams and doors. In fact, if you've come all the way to Shima Peninsula just to see the shrines, you may be disappointed—there is nothing much to see. The shrines are so sacred that no one is allowed close to them—no one except members of the imperial family and high Shinto priests. Both shrines are surrounded by four wooden fences and we lesser mortals are allowed only as far as the third gate. Because of the fences you can't see much, but that doesn't stop the estimated six million Japanese who come here annually. They come because of what the shrines represent, which is an embodiment of the Japanese Shinto religion itself. The Inner Shrine is by far the more important because it's dedicated to the sun goddess, considered the legendary ancestress of the imperial family. It contains the Sacred Mirror (Yata-no-Kagami), one of the Three Sacred Treasures of the emperor.

According to legend, the sun goddess sent her grandson to Japan so that he and his descendants could rule over the country. Before he left she gave him three insignia—a mirror, a sword, and a set of jewels. As she handed him the mirror, she is said to have remarked, "When you look upon this mirror, let it be as if you look upon me." The mirror, therefore, is considered to embody the sun goddess herself and is regarded as the most sacred object in the Shinto religion. The mirror is kept in the deep recesses of the Inner Shrine in a special casket and is never shown to the public. The sword is in the Atsuta Shrine in Nagoya and the jewels are in the Imperial Palace in Tokyo.

Even though you can't see much of the shrines themselves, they're still the most important stops in Ise-Shima. The Inner Shrine is surrounded by old cypress trees. Watch how the Japanese stop after crossing the second small bridge on the approach to the shrine to wash and purify their hands and mouth with water from the Isuzu River. Its source lies on the Inner Shrine grounds itself and it's considered sacred. You'll also see a couple of white royal horses, kept near the shrine for the use of the sun goddess. Perhaps the most amazing thing about the Outer and Inner Shrines is that even though they were founded centuries ago, the buildings themselves have never been more than 20 years old. Every 20 years they are completely torn down and rebuilt exactly as they were on neighboring sites. The present buildings were built in 1973 for the 60th time. No photographs of the shrines themselves are allowed.

ISE-SHIMA SKYLINE HIGHWAY

Near the front entrance of the Inner Shrine are buses that depart for Toba, traveling on the Ise-Shima Skyline highway. About 10 miles long, it rises up over Mt. Asama, on top of which is **Kongoshoji Temple.** You can get off the bus here, visit the temple, and then catch the next bus on to Toba. Kongoshoji Temple is renowned for the vermilion-painted Moon Bridge, which forms a circle as it reflects in a pond, and for a huge footprint said to be Buddha's. Behind the temple is a pathway lined with poles erected in memory of departed loved ones. The entire ride from the Inner Shrine to Toba takes about 45 minutes and costs ¥1,030 ($7.35).

TOBA

Toba's best-known attraction is the **Mikimoto Pearl Island** (tel. 0599/25-2028), just a few minutes' walk from Toba Station and connected to the mainland via a short bridge. Open daily from 8:30am to 5pm (from 9am to 4:30pm November 20 to February 28) and charging ¥850 ($6.05), it's geared entirely toward tourists but is still quite enjoyable, especially if you have a weakness for pearls or have ever wondered how they're cultivated. In addition to a pearl museum and a shop, there's a demonstration hall where the processes of culturing pearls and sorting and stringing them are explained in live demonstrations. Most fascinating in my opinion is the **Mikimoto Memorial Hall,** chronicling in flawless English the attempts, failures, and final success of Kokichi Mikimoto to cultivate pearls. The son of a noodle-shop owner, Mikimoto went to Yokohama as a young man and was surprised to see stalls selling pearls with great success. Mikimoto reasoned that if oysters produced pearls as the result of an irritant inside the shell, why couldn't man introduce the irritant himself and thereby induce oysters to make pearls?

It turned out to be harder than it sounded. Oysters used in Mikimoto's experiments kept rejecting the foreign material and dying. It wasn't until 1893, 5 years after he started his research, that Mikimoto finally succeeded in cultivating his first pearl. In 1905, Mikimoto was able to cultivate his first perfectly round pearl, after which he built what is probably the most successful pearl empire in the world. Mikimoto, who died at the age of 93, was a remarkable man and a real character. His favorite expressions included "Have you anything worth talking about?" and "Make the most of it." Nothing disgusted him more than wastefulness. He once said to Emperor Meiji: "I want to adorn the neck of every woman in the world with a pearl necklace."

As for the **Pearl Museum,** it examines the relationship between humanity and pearls since ancient times. On the second floor you'll find various models made with pearls. The Pearl Pagoda, for example, has 12,760 Mikimoto pearls and took 750 artisans 6 months to complete, after which it was exhibited at the Philadelphia World Exhibition in 1926. The Liberty Bell, a third the size of the original, has 12,250 pearls and was displayed at the New York World's Fair in 1939.

Also at Mikimoto Pearl Island, women divers, wearing traditional white outfits, demonstrate how women of Shima Peninsula have dived through the ages in search of abalone, seaweed, and other edibles. At one time there used to be thousands of women divers, known for their skill in going to great depths for extended periods of time. Today's tourist brochures say that there are still 2,500 of these women divers left—but I've seen them only at demonstrations given for tourists. If you happen to see women divers working in earnest, consider yourself lucky.

If you have more time in Toba, visit **Toba Aquarium,** with its otters, seals, and sea cows, and **Brazil Maru,** a moored ship that took Japanese immigrants to Brazil from 1954 to 1974.

FUTAMIGAURA

If you're at all sentimental, make a trip to Futamigaura, which you can reach by either bus or train from Ise or Toba. There you'll find a pair of large rocks that jut out of the sea not far from shore. Known as the **Wedded Rocks,** they represent man and wife and are joined by a thick braided rope, the same kind you see extended from torii gates at Shinto shrines. The best time to visit the rocks is at dawn: in this Land of the Rising Sun, the spectacle of the sun rising between these two rocks is a favorite among Japanese.

KASHIKOJIMA

At the southern end of Shima Peninsula, the last stop on the Kintetsu Line is Kashikojima. Here you can visit **Shima Marineland,** open daily from 8:30am to 6pm in summer and 9am to 5pm the rest of the year. It describes the fish and plant life of the region and beyond, and also has demonstrations given by women divers. Although explanations are in Japanese only, it's a fun place for children. Entrance is ¥1,000 ($7.15) for adults, ¥600 ($4.30) for children.

The main attraction of Kashikojima, however, is its **boat cruises of Ago Bay.** Vessels leave from the boat dock, about a 2-minute walk from the train station. The cost of the cruise is ¥1,500 ($10.70) and you'll pass oyster rafts, fishing boats, and many small islands along the way. The trip lasts approximately an hour, with boats departing every hour or so between 9am and 3:30pm in the summer. For more information or inquiries about the winter schedule, call the Kintetsu Shima Kanko Kisen Co. at 05994/3-1023.

If you're desperate for a dip in salt water, the most popular beach in the area is **Goza.** The boat from Kashikojima to Goza takes about 25 minutes and costs ¥600 ($4.30) one way, passing oyster rafts, their cultivators, and the sweeping mountainous terrain of the region. The boat ride is enjoyable but the beach itself is a bit disappointing after coming all that distance. There are certainly prettier beaches in the world, but this one is okay for a quick fix.

WHERE TO STAY

There are resort and hotel establishments throughout Shima Peninsula that offer wonderful seafood dining. Kashikojima is the best place to go if you want to escape the crowds and relax in a rural setting, while Toba has the most attractions. Not considered as much a resort area as Toba and Kashikojima, Ise has more reasonably priced accommodations.

IN ISE

YAMADAKAN (120), **13-1 Honmachi, Iseshi 516. Tel. 0596/28-2532.** 23 rms (6 with bath). A/C TV TEL **Directions:** A 3-minute walk from Iseshi Station, on road leading to Outer Shrine.
$ Rates (per person, including two meals): ¥9,900–¥18,500 ($71–$132). No credit cards.

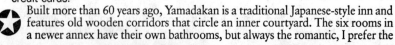
Built more than 60 years ago, Yamadakan is a traditional Japanese-style inn and features old wooden corridors that circle an inner courtyard. The six rooms in a newer annex have their own bathrooms, but always the romantic, I prefer the

older rooms without bathrooms. It's a convenient place to stay for visiting Ise's shrines.

ISE CITY HOTEL ⑫, **1-11-31 Fukiage, Iseshi 516. Tel. 0596/28-2111.** Fax 0596/28-1058. 94 rms (all with bath). A/C TV TEL **Directions:** A 3-minute walk from Ujiyamada or Iseshi Station.
$ Rates (including tax and service): ¥7,000–¥7,200 ($50–$51.40) single; ¥14,300–¥15,400 ($102–$110) twin. AE, JCB, MC, V.

Of the business hotels in the area, your best bet is Ise City Hotel, which opened in 1985 and is right beside the railroad tracks between Iseshi and Ujiyamada stations. The adequately sized rooms are clean and cheerful, with flowered wallpaper and tiled bathrooms. Amenities include TV with pay video, a radio, a clock, and hot-water pot with tea. All of the single rooms feature a semidouble-size bed. Facilities include a Western-looking Japanese restaurant serving shabu-shabu, plus a bar.

HOSHIDEKAN ⑫, **2-15-2 Kawasaki, Iseshi 516. Tel. 0596/28-2377.** 13 rms (none with bath). A/C TV **Directions:** Less than a 10-minute walk from Iseshi or Ujiyamada Station.
$ Rates (per person): ¥3,800 ($27.15). AE, MC, V.

Catering to a young traveling crowd, this inexpensive 70-year-old ryokan has several rooms with windows framed with gnarled roots and bamboo (they simply don't make windows like that anymore). This ryokan is run by a group of women who are strong advocates of macrobiotic vegetarian cooking, which they serve in a simple tatami room connected to the ryokan. Open Monday through Saturday from 11am to 2pm and 5 to 8pm, it offers a vegetarian course (Genmae teishoku) for ¥750 ($6), vegetarian pilaf for ¥550 ($3.90), and noodles, tempura, tofu dishes, raw wheat beer, and natural raw sake.

IN TOBA

TOBA HOTEL INTERNATIONAL, 1-23-1 Toba, Toba 517. Tel. 0599/25-3121. Fax 0599/25-3129. 130 rms (all with bath). A/C MINIBAR TV TEL **Directions:** A 20-minute walk or 5-minute taxi ride from Toba Station.
$ Rates: Twin and Japanese-style rooms: ¥26,000 ($186). Combination rooms: ¥70,000 ($500). AE, DC, JCB, MC, V.

Perched on a hill above the city, this hotel offers both twin and Japanese-style rooms for the same price, as well as deluxe combination rooms with both Western-style beds and a separate tatami area. Some rooms have a balcony, and there are great views of the water, oyster rafts, fishing boats, and islands.

Facilities here include an outdoor swimming pool and French and Japanese restaurants. Most unique, perhaps, is the floating seafood restaurant, Shioji, which features a large fish tank in the middle of its dining room. Your fish couldn't be fresher. The dinner menu, served from 5:30 to 8pm, has courses that start at ¥9,000 ($64.30). The Shioji dinner, for example, includes an appetizer, sashimi, tempura, both broiled and boiled shellfish, soup, and fruit. If you're on a budget, consider coming for lunch, served from 11:30am to 2pm, when a set menu costs ¥3,800 ($27.15).

KIMPOKAN ⑫, **1-10-38 Toba, Toba 517. Tel. 0599/25-2001.** 44 rms (all with bath). A/C MINIBAR TV TEL **Directions:** A 2-minute walk from Toba Station.
$ Rates (per person, including two meals and service): ¥14,000–¥27,000 ($100–$193). AE, DC, MC, V.

Although this ryokan is 100 years old and boasts of being the oldest Japanese inn in Toba, its present white-concrete building is much more recent, now catering largely to Japanese groups. All rooms face the water, but because it's a little inland the views aren't that grand. Rooms come with Western-style toilet, minibar, safe for valuables, TV with pay video, and shoji screens. Western breakfasts are served on request.

IN KASHIKOJIMA

SHIMA KANKO HOTEL, Ago-cho, Kashikojima, Shima-gun, Mie 517-05. Tel. 05994/3-1211. Fax 05994/3-3538. 202 rms (all with bath). A/C MINIBAR TV TEL **Directions:** A 5-minute walk from Kashikojima Station.

$ Rates: ¥15,500 ($111) semidouble; ¥20,000 ($143) double; ¥20,000–¥27,000 ($143–$193) twin. Japanese-style rooms: ¥20,000–¥25,000 ($143–$178) up to four persons. ¥3,000 ($21) extra July–Aug, New Year's. AE, DC, JCB, MC, V.

⭐ Sitting on a hill above Ago Bay with its many oyster rafts, this is a resort hotel in the old tradition, boasting impeccable service. Although it's just a few minutes' walk from the train station, for example, hotel buses meet each Kintetsu train. Rooms are spacious, and despite recent remodeling they retain a healthy old-fashioned atmosphere with their shoji screens and wooden furniture. Some of the twins have a balcony, and rooms facing the bay have a splendid view. There are no single rooms, but since the semidouble rooms have very small beds, they're probably best used by single travelers. There's a pathway leading from the hotel through its garden to its own private dock, where you can sit and watch the pearl cultivators at work on their rafts.

Dining/Entertainment: There are several fine Western and Japanese restaurants, described in the "Where to Dine" section, below.

Services: Free shuttle bus to station.

Facilities: Large outdoor swimming pool, garden, beauty salon.

ISHIYAMA-SO ⑫₄, **Yokoyama-jima, Ago-cho, Kashikojima, Shima-gun, Mie 517-05. Tel. 05995/2-1527.** Fax 05995/2-1240. 11 rms (3 with bath). A/C TV **Directions:** A 2-minute boat trip from Kashikojima pier.

$ Rates (per person, including Western-style breakfast): ¥4,400 ($31) room without bath; ¥5,500 ($39) room with bath. AE, MC, V.

If you're looking for an inexpensive place to stay, a good choice is the family-run Ishiyama-So, located on a small island just a stone's throw from the Kashikojima pier, which can be reached only via the hotel's own private boat—you pull up right at the ryokan's front door. If you call ahead, they'll even come fetch you at the train station and lead you to their boat. Although the building itself is concrete, the rooms are tatami and feature a heater and a safe for valuables, among other amenities. Japanese dinners are available for ¥1,500 ($10.70). You can swim right off the dock here, and footpaths cross the small island. One of the family members here speaks good English.

IN FUTAMIGAURA

FUTAMIKAN, 569-1 Ko, Futami-cho, Watarai-gun, Mie 519-06. Tel. 05964/3-2003. Fax 05964/2-1224. 43 rms (21 with bath). A/C MINIBAR TV TEL **Directions:** A 20-minute walk from Futamigaura JR Station, or a 20-minute bus ride from Ujiyamada Station.

$ Rates (per person, including two meals and service): ¥15,400–¥33,000 ($110–$236). MC, V.

⭐ Futamikan, a grand, traditional Japanese-style inn, has even hosted the imperial family. The oldest part of the ryokan is more than 100 years old and features beautifully carved transoms and sitting alcoves overlooking the garden. Since they didn't make private bathrooms back then, you might prefer rooms in the newer annex; these also have a small balcony—ask for a room on the fifth floor, where you have a sweeping view of the sea. But no matter where you stay, explore. On the second floor of the old building is one of the most beautiful banquet rooms I have ever seen—it has wooden railings outside its sliding glass windows, chandeliers, and 120 tatami mats. As for the town itself, it's small and peaceful. The famous Wedded Rocks are only a 5-minute walk away.

Youth Hostel

YOUTH HOSTEL TAIKOJI ⑫, 1659, Ei, Futami-cho, Mie 519-06. Tel.
05964/3-2283. 28 beds. **Bus:** From Futamigaura Station (a 4-minute ride),
then walk 5 minutes.
$ Rates: ¥1,800 ($12.85) card-carrying member, ¥2,400 ($17.15) nonmember.
Breakfast ¥400 ($2.85); dinner ¥650 ($4.65). No credit cards.

Located in a temple not far from the famous Wedded Rocks, this small youth hostel
offers accommodation for only 28 people, with sleeping on futon in tatami rooms.

WHERE TO DINE

LA MER, Shima Kanko Hotel, Kashikojima. Tel. 05994/3-1211.
   Cuisine: FRENCH. **Reservations:** Required for set-dinner course. **Directions:** A few minutes' walk from Kashikojima Station.
$ Prices: Main dishes ¥5,500–¥8,000 ($39.30–$57.15); set-dinner courses
   ¥22,000–¥29,000 ($157.15–$207.15); set lunches ¥6,500–¥13,000 ($46.40–
   $92.85). AE, MC, V.
   Open: Lunch daily 11:30am–2pm; dinner daily 5–9pm.

Since Kashikojima is surrounded by water, you can safely assume that the seafood
here is fresh and excellent. One of Ise-Shima's most famous restaurants, La Mer has a
well-deserved reputation for serving its own delightful recipes created by its
well-known chef. The specialty is lobster, served in a Western dining hall with
chandeliers, wooden floor, white tablecloths, and tables overlooking the bay and
oyster rafts. A fixed-price lobster menu includes abalone, while other meals include
steak as well. The small à la carte menu offers main dishes of lobster, shrimp, or beef.
Set lunches have beef or seafood as the main dish. If you've never had abalone, this is a
great, albeit expensive, place to try it.

HAMAYU, Shima Kanko Hotel, Kashikojima. Tel. 05994/3-1211.
   Cuisine: KAISEKI/SEAFOOD. **Reservations:** Recommended. **Directions:** A
   few minutes' walk from Kashikojima Station.
$ Prices: Seafood dishes ¥2,500–¥7,000 ($17.85–$50); kaiseki dinners
   ¥15,000–¥18,000 ($107.15–$128.55). AE, MC, V.
   Open: Dinner daily 6–8:30pm.

Designed like a country lodge, with a high slanted roof of thick beams supported by
large pillars and a wooden floor, this pleasant Japanese restaurant is open for dinner
only. It serves kaiseki, as well as seafood dishes that include abalone, lobster, shrimp,
sashimi, and fried fish.

---

3. KANAZAWA

386 miles NW of Tokyo; 140 miles NE of Kyoto

GETTING THERE **Train** There are direct trains from Osaka via Kyoto and
Nagoya that depart hourly; the ride takes almost 4 hours. From Tokyo, take the
Shinkansen to either Maibara or Nagaoka, switching there for a local line to
Kanazawa. Either way, the trip takes about 4½ hours.

By Bus Buses depart daily from Tokyo's Ikebukuro Station (trip time: 7 hr. 30
min.), Nagoya Station (trip time: 3 hr. 42 min.), and Kyoto Station (trip time: 4 hr. 8
min.).

ESSENTIAL INFORMATION The area code for Kanazawa, the capital of
Ishikawa Prefecture, is 0762.
   Before leaving Tokyo or Kyoto, be sure to pick up the flyer *Kanazawa* at the
Tourist Information Center.

In Kanazawa itself, the **tourist information** window is just outside Kanazawa Station as you exit from the east side (tel. 0762/31-6311). Open from 8am to 8pm (8:30am to 7:30pm in winter), it distributes a map in English and will also book hotel rooms.

GETTING AROUND   Kanazawa's attractions spread south and southeast from the station (take the station's east exit). Kenrokuen Garden, for example, is 1½ miles southeast of Kanazawa Station, easily reached by **bus** (no. 10, 11, or 12 from the station). You can also take a bus from the station to the Kosen Pottery Kiln. Other attractions can be covered **on foot** in 1 day.

On the northwest coast of Honshu on the Sea of Japan, Kanazawa is a gateway to the rugged, sea-swept Noto Peninsula. It was the second-largest city (after Kyoto) to escape bombing during World War II, and some of the old city has been left intact, including a few samurai houses, old geisha quarters, and tiny narrow streets that run crooked without rhyme or reason (apparently to confuse any enemies foolish enough to attack). Kanazawa is most famous for its Kenrokuen Garden, one of the most celebrated gardens in all of Japan. If your time in Japan is limited, however, and you're mainly interested in traditional Japanese buildings and neighborhoods, my own opinion is that Kyoto or Takayama in the Japan Alps has more to offer. On the other hand, if you are a big fan of Japanese gardens, Kenrokuen is one of the best. It's the main reason people come here.

Kanazawa first gained notoriety about 500 years ago, when a militant Buddhist sect joined with peasant fanatics to overthrow the feudal lord and establish its own autonomous government, an event unprecedented in Japanese history. The independent republic survived almost 100 years before it was attacked by an army of Nobunaga Oda, who was trying to unite Japan at a time when civil wars wracked the nation. Kanazawa was subsequently granted to one of Nobunaga's retainers, Toshiie Maeda. The Maeda clan continued to rule over Kanazawa for the next 300 years, amassing wealth in the form of rice paddies and encouraging development of the arts. All through the Tokugawa shogunate era the Maedas remained the second most powerful family in Japan after the Tokugawas themselves and controlled the largest domain in the country. About 1 million *koku* of rice (equaling 5 million bushels of rice) were produced here annually. The arts of Kutani ware, Yuzen silk dyeing, and Noh theater flourished—and enjoy success and popularity even today.

WHAT TO SEE & DO

Much of Kanazawa's charm lies in the atmosphere of its old neighborhoods. Be sure to wear your good walking shoes, since the best way to explore the city is via your own two feet.

KENROKUEN GARDEN & VICINITY

At one time Kanazawa possessed an impressive castle belonging to the powerful Maeda clan, but it was destroyed by fire in 1881. One of the few structures left standing is the **Ishikawamon Gate,** which used to be the south entrance to the castle. Looking at how big and grand the gate is, you can appreciate the size of the original Maeda castle.

✪ Just south of Ishikawamon Gate is **Kenrokuen Garden,** Kanazawa's main attraction. The largest of the three best landscape gardens in Japan—the other two are Kairakuen Garden in Mito and Korakuen Garden in Okayama—it's considered by many to be the grandest. Its name can be translated as "a refined garden incorporating six attributes"—spaciousness, careful arrangement, seclusion, antiquity, elaborate use of water, and scenic charm. Ponds, trees, streams, rocks, mounds, and footpaths have all been combined so aesthetically that the effect is spellbinding. Altogether, it took about 150 years to complete the garden. The fifth Maeda lord started construction in the 1670s, and successive lords added to the garden according to his own individual tastes. The garden as we now see it was finished by the 12th

Maeda lord in 1822. Only after the Meiji Restoration was the garden opened to the public. Admission is ¥300 ($2.15), and hours are 6:30am to 6pm daily (8am to 4:30pm in winter).

You may want to arrive at dawn or near the end of the day, since the garden is a favorite destination of Japanese tour groups, led by guides who explain everything in detail—through loudspeakers. I don't know how they affect you, but loudspeakers drive me to absolute distraction.

In the southeast corner of Kenrokuen Park, charging a separate admission of ¥500 ($3.55), is **Seisonkaku Villa** (tel. 21-0580), built in 1863 by the 13th Maeda lord as a retirement home for his widowed mother. Elegant and graceful, this villa has a distinctly feminine atmosphere, with delicately carved wood transoms and shoji screens painted with various designs. The villa's bedroom is decorated with tortoises painted on the shoji wainscoting (tortoises were associated with long life, and it must have worked—the mother lived to be 84). Open Thursday through Tuesday from 8:30am to 4pm.

✪ Next to Seisonkaku Villa is the **Ishikawa Prefectural Museum for Traditional Products and Crafts** (tel. 62-2020), open Friday through Wednesday from 9am to 4:30pm. Admission is ¥250 ($1.80). Opened in 1984, it houses locally produced lacquerware, wood carvings, folk toys, pottery, silk, washi (Japanese paper), and hats and baskets made from cypress. Here you can also see the famous Kutani pottery, first produced under the patronage of the Maeda clan in the 1600s. There are also displays of Yuzen dyeing, with its bold and clear picturesque designs. A pamphlet and explanations in English of the various displays make a visit here worthwhile.

South of Kenrokuen Park and not far from Seisonkaku Villa are a few more museums. The **Ishikawa Prefectural Art Museum (Ishikawa-ken Bijutsu-kan)** (tel. 31-7580), open daily from 9:30am to 4:30pm and charging a ¥300 ($2.40) admission, houses a small collection of antique Kutani pottery, samurai costumes, and decorative art, most dating from the Edo Period. Several rooms are also devoted to modern and contemporary paintings, sculptures, and other works by local artists, with exhibitions changed monthly. Close by is the **Honda Museum,** which displays samurai outfits, weapons, artwork, and the personal effects of the Honda clan, one of Lord Maeda's chief retainers. Open daily from 9am to 5pm (closed on Thursday from November through February), it charges ¥500 ($3.55) admission. A third museum, the **Ishikawa Prefecture History Museum (Reikishi Hakubutsukan)** (tel. 62-3236), exhibits artifacts dealing with the history of the prefecture from prehistoric to modern times. Housed in a handsome red-brick building that was built to stock guns and gunpowder before the turn of the century, it contains archeological finds from the region, items from the Edo Period, and folkloric objects. There are even samurai outfits you can try on for size—they weigh up to 44 pounds. Open daily from 9am to 5pm, the museum charges ¥250 ($1.80) admission.

Since it would be tiring (and expensive) to visit all the museums described above, you might want to limit your selection to one or two. My own personal favorite is the Ishikawa Prefectural Museum for Traditional Products and Crafts.

NAGAMACHI SAMURAI DISTRICT

About a 20-minute walk west of Kenrokuen Garden is the Nagamachi Samurai District, which should be visited just to soak up the atmosphere, since most of the homes are still privately owned and are not open to the public. Furthermore, despite the name, many of these homes were built during the Meiji Period and never belonged to samurai at all.

The Nagamachi Samurai District is basically just one street, lined with beautiful wooden homes hidden behind gold-colored mud walls. An unhurried stroll in the neighborhood is the main source of entertainment here. One home open to the public is the **Nomura Samurai House,** open daily from 8:30am to 5pm (4:30pm in winter) and charging ¥400 ($2.85) admission. Its drawing room is of Japanese cypress, with elaborate designs in rosewood, and its shoji screens are painted with landscapes. There's also a small, charming garden containing a miniature waterfall, a winding stream, and stone lanterns.

Another old home in the Nagamachi Samurai District has been converted into a silk center, where you can watch artists at work painting intricate designs on silk. Open Friday through Wednesday from 9am to noon and 1 to 4:30pm, the **Yuzen Silk Center (Saihitsu-an)** (tel. 64-2811) charges ¥500 ($3.55) admission, which includes a welcoming tea and a sweet. A video shows the process of Yuzen dyeing, and a pamphlet in English describes the steps in detail. It can take up to 6 months to make one kimono of Yuzen hand-painted silk.

From the Nagamachi District it's just a few minutes' walk to **Oyama Jinja Shrine,** built in 1599 in honor of the first Maeda lord, Toshiie Maeda. Its three-story gate was designed by a Dutchman in 1875, with stained-glass windows on the third floor.

OTHER SIGHTS

If your interest lies in pottery, it's worth a visit to the **Kosen Pottery Kiln (Kutani Kosengama),** 20 minutes by bus from Kanazawa Station to the Nomachi bus stop (tel. 41-0902). It's the only kiln within Kanazawa and shows the entire process of producing Kutani ware. Admission is free, and it's open daily from 9am to 5pm.

Myoryuji Temple, 15 minutes by bus from Kanazawa Station to the Nomachi-Hirokoji bus stop and then a 5-minute walk, is popularly known as Ninja-dera (or Temple of the Secret Agents) because of its secret chambers, hidden stairways, tunnels, and trick doors. The temple was constructed as an escape route for the Maeda lord in case his castle was attacked. A well at the temple was supposedly connected to the castle via a secret tunnel. You must make a reservation to see it (tel. 41-2877), and you'll probably be able to go the same day you call. Admission is ¥500 ($3.55). To make sure you don't get lost (which would be quite easy because of all the trick doors), you will be grouped with other visitors and led by a guide who, unfortunately, describes everything in Japanese only. Tours, given daily from 9am to 4pm, last 30 minutes.

If you're in Kanazawa for more than one day, consider taking an outing to Yuwaka Spa, where you'll find the **Edo-Mura Village.** About a 40-minute bus ride from Kanazawa Station, this is an open-air architectural museum with a collection of some 20 buildings from the Edo Period, including a samurai mansion, farmhouses, and shops. This museum provides unique insight into how the various social classes lived back in the feudal days. Open daily from 8am to 6pm (5pm in winter), it charges ¥1,100 ($7.85) admission.

WHERE TO STAY

Most of Kanazawa's hotels are clustered conveniently around Kanazawa Station. There are also a few ryokan in the city, located in the older sections of town.

EXPENSIVE

All the rates given below for expensive accommodations are those charged during peak season, which is New Year's, Golden Week, July 25 to the end of August, and the month of October. During the off-season, you can expect rates to be ¥1,000 ($7.15) to ¥2,000 ($14.30) lower than those given here.

ANA HOTEL KANAZAWA, 16-3 Showa-machi, Kanazawa 920. Tel. 0762/24-6111, or toll free 800/44-UTELL in the U.S. Fax 0762/24-6100. 255 rms. A/C MINIBAR TV TEL **Directions:** A 1-minute walk from Kanazawa Station's east exit.
$ Rates: ¥12,000–¥14,300 ($86–$102) single; ¥21,000–¥25,000 ($150–$178) double; ¥21,500–¥44,000 ($153–$314) twin. AE, JCB, DC, MC, V.
This is Kanazawa's newest deluxe hotel, opened in 1990. A sleek, white building that soars above Kanazawa Station, it features a huge atrium lobby with a marble floor, chandeliers, plants, and a fountain. Rooms are simple, comfortable, and uncluttered, with everything you'd expect from one of Kanazawa's best hotels.
Dining/Entertainment: Seven restaurants and bars, including the popular

Unkai, serving Japanese specialties; Karin, a Cantonese restaurant; and the elegant C'est la Vie, a French restaurant. The Astral Bar on the 19th floor offers the best panoramic views of the city.
Services: Free newspaper.

HOLIDAY INN KANAZAWA, 1-10 Horikawa-cho, Kanazawa 920. Tel. 0762/23-1111. Fax 0762/23-1110. 174 rms. A/C MINIBAR TV TEL **Directions:** A 1-minute walk from Kanazawa Station's east exit.
$ Rates: ¥10,000 ($71) single; ¥13,000–¥18,500 ($93–$132) double; ¥15,000–¥20,000 ($107–$143) twin. AE, DC, JCB, MC, V.
Located right in front of Kanazawa Station, this hotel was built in the late 1970s and is similar to most Holiday Inns in Asia; foreigners should feel readily at home. All rooms have a minibar, cable TV, and a water heater and tea bags, among other amenities. The cheapest double room contains only a double-size bed; the higher-priced doubles contain a queen-size bed. Children 12 and under stay free in their parents' room.
  Dining/Entertainment: The hotel has six restaurants and bars, including a Western-style restaurant on the 14th floor with good views of the city and evening piano music. Kitano Shoya, the hotel's Japanese restaurant, is decorated in the style of a rustic farmhouse and features fresh seafood.

KANAZAWA MIYAKO HOTEL, 6-10 Konohanacho, Kanazawa 920. Tel. 0762/31-2202. Fax 0762/23-2856. 200 rms. A/C MINIBAR TV TEL **Directions:** A 1-minute walk from Kanzawa Station's east exit.
$ Rates: ¥11,000 ($78) single; ¥15,000 ($107) double; ¥20,000–¥27,000 ($143–$193) twin. AE, DC, JCB, MC, V.
This conveniently located hotel, constructed in the 1960s and remodeled in the 1980s, is part of the famous Miyako hotel chain and features comfortable rooms, all well designed with attractive wood furniture and large windows. Each room comes with hot-water pot, alarm clock, double glass windows to shut out offending traffic noise, bilingual TV, and minibar.
  Dining/Entertainment: Belle Vue, on the seventh floor, is the hotel's signature restaurant, serving French cuisine. Kakitsubata, a Japanese restaurant, also on the seventh floor, specializes in seafood and local Kanazawa dishes. In summer there's a beer garden on the roof, open every evening in fine weather and offering a great view.
  Services: Free newspaper.
  Facilities: Shopping arcade, delicatessen, beauty salon.

KANAZAWA TOKYU HOTEL, 2-1-1 Kohrinbo, Kanazawa 920. Tel. 0762/31-2411. Fax 0762/63-0154. 250 rms. A/C MINIBAR TV TEL **Bus:** A 15-minute ride from Kanazawa Station to Kohrinbo.
$ Rates: ¥12,000–¥15,500 ($86–$111) single; ¥23,000–¥24,000 ($164–$171) double; ¥21,000–¥24,000 ($150–$171) twin. AE, DC, JCB, MC, V.
Opened in 1985, the Kanazawa Tokyu Hotel is one of the newest places to stay in town and is a good choice if you prefer being in the heart of the city rather than near the train station. A 16-story brick building, it's convenient to Kanazawa's nightlife and department stores and is within walking distance of the Nagamachi Samurai District and Kenrokuen Garden. The lobby and front desk are on the second floor. Rooms are small and simple but pleasant, with good views of the city. Rates are based on room size as well as height. Regardless of which price category you select, ask for the highest floor available, where the views are much better.
  Dining/Entertainment: Of the seven food-and-beverage outlets, there are two coffee shops, a Japanese restaurant, and a bar.
  Services: Free newspaper.
  Facilities: Convenience store, beauty salon.

MIYABO ⑫⑥, **3 Shimo Kakinokibatake, Kanazawa 920. Tel. 0762/31-4228.** 28 rms (25 with bath). A/C MINIBAR TV TEL **Bus:** A 10-minute ride south of Kanazawa Station.
$ Rates (per person, including two meals and service): ¥18,000–¥30,000 ($128–$214). AE, DC, JCB, MC, V.

⭐ In the heart of the city, Miyabo is a beautiful Japanese-style inn near Katamachi Shopping Street and within walking distance of Kenrokuen Garden. It boasts one of the oldest private gardens in Kanazawa, and part of the ryokan used to be the private teahouse of Kanazawa's first mayor after the feudal age came to an end. Most of the ryokan dates from before World War II, although there is also a newer section. The lowest price is for a room in the newer section. The lowest price is for a room in the newer section, while the top price is for a room with private view of the garden and more elaborately prepared meals. My favorite room is one that used to be the mayor's tea-ceremony room. Named Bunte, with maroon walls, it's secluded from the rest of the ryokan, right in the middle of the garden.

MODERATE

GARDEN HOTEL, 2-16-16 Honcho, Kanazawa 920. Tel. 0762/63-3333. 147 rms. A/C MINIBAR TV TEL **Directions:** A 1-minute walk from Kanazawa Station's east exit.
$ Rates: ¥7,200 ($51) single; ¥12,000 ($85) double; ¥14,500 ($103) twin. AE, DC, JCB, MC, V.
Located across from the train station next to the Miyako Hotel, the Garden Hotel caters primarily to Japanese businessmen. It opened in the mid-1980s and has a small contemporary lobby with a restaurant that serves breakfast, lunch, and dinner. Singles are tiny but nicely decorated, and have semidouble-size beds. Rooms are equipped with minibar, hot-water pot and tea, TV with adult video, music, alarm clock, windows that can be opened, and panels that can be closed for complete darkness.

KANAZAWA CASTLE INN ⑫, 10-17 Konohanamachi, Kanazawa 920. Tel. 0762/23-6300. 136 rms. A/C MINIBAR TV TEL **Directions:** A 3-minute walk from Kanazawa Station.
$ Rates (including tax and service): ¥6,600 ($47) single; ¥11,200 ($80) double/twin. AE, JCB, MC, V.
A practical and attractive business hotel that offers simple but cheerful rooms. The bathtubs are miniature, but amenities include minibar, hot-water pot and tea, and TV with adult video. Singles have a semidouble-size bed.

BUDGET

OKA HOTEL, 5-2 Horikawa, Kanazawa 920. Tel. 0762/63-5351. 51 rms (45 with bath). A/C MINIBAR TV TEL **Directions:** A 5-minute walk from Kanazawa Station.
$ Rates (including service): ¥4,400 ($31) single without bath, ¥5,800–¥6,400 ($41–$46) single with bath; ¥10,500 ($75) double with bath; ¥9,000 ($64) twin without bath, ¥12,900 ($92) twin with bath. JCB, MC, V.
Less than a block away from the Castle Inn, and offering the same basic amenities, is the Oka Hotel. Although the front-desk staff doesn't speak much English, they are accommodating and friendly. This simply decorated business hotel, which opened in the early 1980s, has one restaurant that serves both Japanese and Western selections, and there's a public bath. Doubles have a semidouble-size bed, which may be too small if you like room.

RYOKAN MURATAYA, 1-5-2 Katamachi, Kanazawa 920. Tel. 0762/63-0455. 11 rms (none with bath). A/C TV TEL **Bus:** 20, 21, 22, 30, 31, 32, 40, 41, 44, or 45 from Kanazawa Station to Katamachi-Kingeki-mae, then a 3-minute walk.
$ Rates: ¥4,600 ($33) single; ¥8,800 ($63) twin; ¥11,500 ($82) triple. Western breakfast ¥400 ($2.85); Japanese breakfast ¥800 ($5.70). AE, MC, V.
This ryokan is in the heart of Kanazawa, not far from Katamachi Shopping Street and within walking distance of Kenrokuen Garden. A member of the Japanese Inn Group, it's modern and rather uninteresting from the outside, but comfortable and pleasant inside. All rooms come with heating, among other amenities. One of its rooms is Western style, with one single bed. There's a coin-operated laundry.

YOGETSU ⑫⑧**, 1-13-22 Higashiyama, Kanazawa 920. Tel. 0762/52-0497.** 5 rms (none with bath). A/C (in some rooms) TV **Bus:** 10-minute ride from Kanazawa Station. **Directions:** A 20-minute walk east of Kanazawa Station.
$ Rates (per person): ¥4,000 ($28) without meals, ¥6,000 ($43) with two meals. No credit cards.

⭐ This delightful little minshuku is in the middle of the old Higashiyama district, set aside in the 1820s by the local government as a place where geishas could entertain. Run by a jovial woman, Yogetsu is a 100-year-old house that used to belong to a geisha. The rooms are rather plain, but the quiet, quaint surrounding atmosphere makes up for the lack of décor.

Youth Hostels

KANAZAWA YOUTH HOSTEL ⑫⑨**, 37 Suehirocho, Kanazawa 920. Tel. 0762/52-3414.** 120 beds. A/C **Bus:** A 25-minute ride from Kanazawa Station.
$ Rates (per person, including breakfast and dinner): ¥3,600 ($26) member, ¥4,350 ($31) nonmember. No credit cards.
Although this youth hostel is a bit far from all the attractions, it still has a nice location. Rooms here are both tatami and Western style; only the Western-style rooms have TV. Nonmembers are not accepted during the busy summer season. There's a coin laundry.

MATSUI YOUTH HOSTEL ⑬⓪**, 1-9-3 Katamachi, Kanazawa 920. Tel. 0762/21-0275.** 30 beds. A/C **Bus:** 20 from Kanazawa Station to Katamachi bus stop, then a few minutes' walk.
$ Rates (per person): ¥2,500 ($17.85) member, ¥700 ($5) extra nonmember. Breakfast ¥450 ($3.20); dinner ¥850 ($6.05). No credit cards.
More centrally located, this youth hostel offers accommodations in tatami rooms, with about six people to a room. There are laundry facilities.

WHERE TO DINE

Kanazawa's local specialties are known collectively as *Kaga no aji* and consist of seafood such as tiny shrimp and winter crabs, as well as freshwater fish and mountain vegetables.

AROUND KENROKUEN GARDEN

MIYOSHIAN ⑬①**, 1-11 Kenrokumachi. Tel. 21-0127.**
Cuisine: KAGA CUISINE. **Reservations:** Necessary for dinner, not accepted for lunch. **Directions:** Located inside Kenrokuen Garden, about a 10-minute bus ride or a 20-minute walk from Kanazawa Station.
$ Prices: Lunch teishoku ¥1,600–¥3,300 ($11.40–$23.55); Kaga cuisine ¥5,500–¥11,000 ($39.30–$78.55). No credit cards.
Open: Lunch daily 10am–5pm; dinner kaiseki daily 4–8:30pm.

⭐ A great place to try the local Kaga cuisine is right in Kenrokuen Garden itself at this 100-year-old restaurant. It consists of three separate wooden buildings, the best of which is a traditional room that extends over a pond. This is where you'll probably dine, seated on tatami with a view of an ancient pond (giant carp swim in the murky waters). In addition to the local Kaga cuisine, you can also order such à la carte dishes as *jibuni* stew (a chicken and vegetable stew eaten primarily in winter) for ¥770 ($5.50) and shrimp sashimi for ¥550 ($3.90). Set obento lunches range from ¥1,600 to ¥3,300 ($11.40 to $23.55). A jibuni teishoku, which includes chicken stew, sashimi, pickled vegetables, rice, and soup, is available for ¥1,600 ($11.40). In the evening, only kaiseki is served, with meals easily costing ¥20,000 ($143).

TOZAN ⑬②**, 8-30 Koshomachi. Tel. 63-8666.**
Cuisine: KAGA CUISINE. **Reservations:** Recommended. **Directions:** Bus from Kanazawa Station to Kenrokuen, or a 20-minute walk from Kanazawa Station.
$ Prices: Set meals ¥2,200–¥5,500 ($15.70–$39.30). AE, JCB, V.
Open: Daily 11am–5pm.

Another restaurant serving Kaga specialties is Tozan, located just outside the north entrance of Kenrokuen Garden. Catering largely to Japanese groups, it has a dining hall on the second floor with tatami mats, shoji screens, and a wooden ceiling. Outside the front door you'll see the dishes named in English, so ordering is easy here.

KANKO BUSSANKAN, 2-20 Kenrokumachi. Tel. 22-7788.
> **Cuisine:** VARIED JAPANESE/KAGA CUISINE. **Bus:** From Kanazawa Station to Kenrokuen Garden.
> **$ Prices:** Set meals ¥1,300–¥2,500 ($9.30–$17.85). MC, V.
> **Open:** Daily 10am–6pm. **Closed:** Thurs Nov–Mar.

Located on the second floor of the Ishikawa Prefectural Products Center, near Kenrokuen Garden's main entrance, this traditionally decorated restaurant offers reasonably priced Japanese food. There are fixed-price meals, with main dishes consisting of sashimi, tempura, noodles, and other common Japanese dishes, including Kaga cuisine. The most popular set lunch is the Kaga Sanmi with local cuisine, priced at ¥2,000 ($14.30). Although the menu is in Japanese only, there are pictures of set meals and a plastic-food display case.

TAKEDA ⑬, 2-12 Kenrokumachi. Tel. 21-3662.
> **Cuisine:** NOODLES. **Bus:** From Kanazawa Station to Kenrokuen Garden.
> **$ Prices:** ¥600–¥1,500 ($4.30–$10.70). No credit cards.
> **Open:** Mon–Thurs and Sat–Sun 10:30am–5pm.

This simple restaurant, with only a few tables and tatami seating, serves inexpensive udon noodles. It's located between Kenrokuen Garden's north entrance and the Ishikawa Prefectural Products Center. Look for the black curtains hanging at its front door and a plastic-food display case of noodles.

KATAMACHI AREA

Just east of the Saigawa Ohashi Bridge is an area full of restaurants and drinking establishments, radiating out from Katamachi Shopping and Chuo Dori streets.

ZENIYA ⑭, 2-29-7 Katamachi. Tel. 33-3331.
> **Cuisine:** KAISEKI. **Reservations:** Required. **Bus:** from Kanazawa to Katamachi.
> **$ Prices:** Kaiseki meals ¥11,000–¥16,500 ($78.55–$117.85). AE, DC, JCB, MC, V.
> **Open:** Lunch daily 11am–2pm; dinner daily 5–9pm. **Closed:** Last Sun of month.

One of Kanazawa's best-known and most exclusive restaurants, it serves seasonal kaiseki meals of local specialties in cool, elegant surroundings. Lunch is less expensive, with obento meals starting at ¥5,500 ($39.30) and mini-kaiseki offerings for ¥8,800 ($62.85). The presentation of each dish, naturally, is spectacular. Zeniya is tucked away on a small side street, in a traditional Japanese house with a small court entryway.

HAMACHO ⑮, 2-31-32 Katamachi. Tel. 33-3390.
> **Cuisine:** JAPANESE SEAFOOD. **Reservations:** Recommended. **Bus:** From Kanazawa Station to Katamachi.
> **$ Prices:** Set meals ¥4,000–¥8,000 ($28.55–$57.15). DC, V.
> **Open:** Dinner Mon–Sat 5–11pm. **Closed:** Hols.

Down the street from Zeniya, on the opposite side of the street, Hamacho offers seafood and vegetables in season. The menu, written on a blackboard but in Japanese only, changes according to what's fresh and available and may include *imo* (Japanese potatoes), freshly picked mushrooms, vegetables, various seafood selections, and sashimi. Most courses average ¥6,000 ($42.85). Just tell Mr. Ishigami, the owner and chief chef, how much you want to spend and he'll do the rest. If there's anything you don't like, be sure to tell him. Sit at the counter, where you can watch the preparation of your set course, which may include grilled fish or shrimp, noodles, tofu, sashimi, soup, and vegetables.

KITAMA ⑯, 2-3-3 Katamachi. Tel. 61-7176.
> **Cuisine:** VARIED JAPANESE/KAGA CUISINE. **Bus:** From Kanazawa Station to Katamachi.

$ Prices: Set meals ¥1,300–¥3,000 ($9.30–$21.40). DC, V.
Open: Thurs–Tues 11:30am–9:30pm.
Sitting on tatami mats, you'll have a pleasant view of a small moss-covered 100-year-old garden of tiny pines, stone lanterns, and rocks. I ordered the jibuni teishoku, which came with chicken stew, clear soup, pickled vegetables, rice, and hors d'oeuvres. My friend opted for the Kojitsu Obento, served in an upright lunch box; it featured such delicacies as sashimi, small pieces of pork and fish, fried shrimp, a soybean patty, and various seasonal vegetables. Most meals here cost less than ¥3,000 ($21.40).

KAGA TOBI ⑬⑦, **Kohrinbo 109 department store, 2-1 Kohrinbo. Tel. 62-0535.**
Cuisine: VARIED JAPANESE/KAGA CUISINE. **Directions:** Bus from Kanazawa Station to Kohrinbo, or a 20-minute walk from Kanazawa Station.
$ Prices: Set meals ¥2,000–¥3,000 ($14.30–$21.40); teishoku ¥850–¥1,500 ($6.05–$10.70). MC, V.
Open: Lunch Thurs–Tues 11am–2pm; dinner Thurs–Tues 5–10pm.
This restaurant is easy to find, located right beside the Tokyu Hotel in the Kohrinbo 109 department store. To reach the restaurant, however, don't enter the department store; rather, walk around the building to the tiny back street flanking a narrow canal. You'll find very reasonable set lunches. For ¥850 ($6.05) you can choose a main course of sashimi, tempura, or eel, which will come with side dishes. If you'd like to try Kaga cuisine, order the Shokado Teishoku. There's also mini-kaiseki for only ¥2,700 ($19.30).

AROUND KANAZAWA STATION

KAKITSUBATA, Kanazawa Miyako Hotel, 6-10 Konohanacho. Tel. 31-2202.
Cuisine: KAISEKI/VARIED JAPANESE. **Directions:** A 1-minute walk from Kanazawa Station's east exit.
$ Prices: Kaiseki ¥6,500–¥11,000 ($46.40–$78.55); set lunches ¥1,600–¥3,300 ($11.40–$23.55). AE, DC, JCB, MC, V.
Open: Lunch daily 11:30am–2pm; dinner daily 5–10pm.
Located on the seventh floor of the Miyako Hotel, this Japanese restaurant is simply decorated, with the emphasis on the panoramic views of the city. Kakitsubata serves kaiseki, as well as sashimi and fresh seafood, from shrimp and crab to yellowtail. You can also come here for lunch, when eel, sashimi, or tempura set meals and obento lunch boxes are offered on an English menu.

BELLE VUE, Kanazawa Miyako Hotel, 6-10 Konohanacho. Tel. 31-2202.
Cuisine: FRENCH/CONTINENTAL. **Directions:** A 1-minute walk from Kanazawa Station's east exit.
$ Prices: Main dishes ¥2,500–¥4,000 ($17.85–$28.55); set-dinner courses ¥4,500–¥9,000 ($32.15–$64.30); set lunches ¥2,000–¥4,500 ($14.30–$32.15). AE, DC, JCB, MC, V.
Open: Lunch daily 11:30am–2pm; dinner daily 5–10pm.
Also on the seventh floor of the Miyako Hotel, with panoramic views of the city, this restaurant is decorated in soft plum colors. Comfortable cushioned chairs and chandeliers provide a romantic setting, and piano music serenades on Saturday and Sunday nights. Although the menu changes often, main dishes are likely to include sole, steak, veal, lamb chops, and other seasonal choices. The fixed-price dinners and lunches are reasonably priced and include appetizers, salad, and dessert.

SPECIALTY DINING

You can save even more money by going underground. There's an underground passageway leading from Kanazawa Station to the nearby bus depot and to the

Miyako Hotel; the entrance is a bit difficult to find in the station itself, so look for the stairway outside the station or in front of the Miyako Hotel. You'll also find a slew of tiny holes-in-the-wall and diners here serving tempura, noodles, sushi, spaghetti, and the usual train-station fare designed to meet the needs of hurried commuters. You can easily dine for less than ¥1,200 ($8.55), but don't expect much in the way of atmosphere except that provided by the locals.

SHOPPING

The most famous products of Kanazawa are its Kutani pottery, with bright five-color overglaze patterns, and its hand-painted Yuzen silk. Kanazawa also produces toys, lacquerware, and wooden products.

    ✪ For one-stop shopping, visit the **Ishikawa Prefectural Products Center (Kanko Bussankan)** (tel. 22-7788), near Kenrokuen Garden (if you're arriving at Kenrokuen Garden via bus no. 10, 11, or 12 from Kanazawa Station, you'll get off the bus just a few steps away from the Bussankan). The ground and basement floors sell local products, the second floor is a restaurant, and the third floor houses the Ishikawa Prefectural Museum of Handicrafts, which charges a ¥200 ($1.40) admission fee to see artisans produce crafts of the area, including Kutani pottery, Japanese cakes, and lacquerware. Hours are 9am to 6pm; closed Thursday during the winter.

4. OSAKA

341 miles W of Tokyo; 26 miles SW of Kyoto; 212 miles E of Hiroshima

GETTING THERE By Plane If you arrive at Osaka International Airport, you can take one of the airport limousine buses that make frequent runs to Shin-Osaka, Osaka, and Namba stations. The trip to Osaka (Umeda) Station takes about half an hour and costs ¥410 ($2.90).

By Train Osaka is 3 hours from Tokyo by Shinkansen bullet train. All Shinkansen bullet trains arrive at Shin-Osaka Station, at the city's northern edge. To get from Shin-Osaka Station to Osaka Station and other points south, the most convenient public transportation is the Midosuji subway line. The subway stop at Osaka Station is called Umeda Station. Japan Railways trains also make runs between Shin-Osaka and Osaka stations. Note that if you need to turn in your voucher for your Japan Rail Pass, you can do so only at Osaka Station, at the JR Travel Service Center, from 10am to 6pm.

    If you're arriving in Osaka from Kobe or Kyoto, you're much better off taking one of the local commuter lines, since these will deliver you directly to Osaka Station in the heart of the city. The San-yo Line, for example, is convenient from both Kyoto Station (about 35 minutes) or Sannomiya Station in Kobe (about 30 minutes).

By Bus Night buses depart from both Tokyo and Shinjuku stations every evening, arriving in Osaka the next morning.

Although its history stretches back about 1,500 years, Osaka first gained prominence when Hideyoshi Toyotomi built Japan's most magnificent castle here in the 16th century. To develop resources for his castle town, he persuaded merchants from other parts of the nation to resettle in Osaka. During the Edo Period the city became an important distribution center as feudal lords from the surrounding region sent their rice to merchants in Osaka, who in turn sent the rice onward to Tokyo and other cities. As the merchants prospered, the town grew and such arts as Kabuki and Bunraku flourished. With money and leisure to spare, the merchants also developed a refined taste for food.

    Nowadays Osaka, in Osaka Prefecture on the southern coast of western Honshu, is an industrial city with a population of almost 2.8 million, making it the third-largest city in Japan (after Tokyo and Yokohama). With inklings of their merchant beginnings

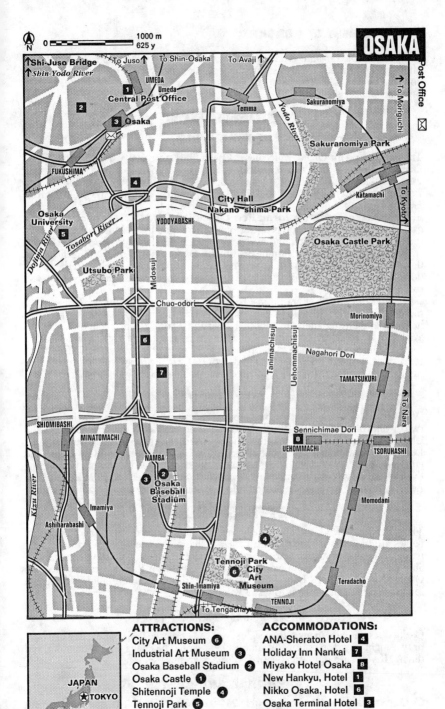

OSAKA

Post Office ⊠

ATTRACTIONS:
City Art Museum ❻
Industrial Art Museum ❸
Osaka Baseball Stadium ❷
Osaka Castle ❶
Shitennoji Temple ❹
Tennoji Park ❺

ACCOMMODATIONS:
ANA-Sheraton Hotel 4
Holiday Inn Nankai 7
Miyako Hotel Osaka 8
New Hankyu, Hotel 1
Nikko Osaka, Hotel 6
Osaka Terminal Hotel 3
Plaza 2
Royal Hotel 5

JAPAN
★TOKYO
Osaka

still present, Osakans are usually characterized as being rather money-minded, and often greet one another with a saying that translates as "Are you making any money?" Today, Osaka has a reputation throughout Japan for its food, its castle, and its Bunraku puppet theater.

ORIENTATION

INFORMATION

The **area code** for Osaka, which lies in Osaka Prefecture, is **06**. The **Central Post Office (Osaka Chuo Yubinkyoku)** (tel. 06/347-8006) is located a minute's walk west of Osaka Station. The post office is open Monday through Friday from 9am to 7pm, on Saturday from 9am to 5pm, and on Sunday and holidays from 9am to 12:30pm.

The **Osaka Tourist Information Office** (tel. 06/345-2189) is located at the east exit of Osaka Station and is open from 8am to 7pm. Its staff speaks English, gives out good maps of the city, and assists in securing hotel rooms. **Another tourist office** is located near the central exits of Shin-Osaka Station, on the third floor (tel. 06/305-3311). Note that if you're arriving by Shinkansen, you'll be up on the fourth floor, so simply go down one flight to the tourist office, which is open daily from 8am to 8pm.

To find out what's going on in Osaka, pick up a copy of *Kansai Time Out*, a monthly magazine with information on sightseeing, festivals, restaurants, and other items of interest pertaining to Osaka, Kobe, and Kyoto. Costing ¥300 ($2.15), it's available at bookstores, restaurants, and places frequented by English-speaking tourists. Other good sources of information are *Discover Kinki!*, available free at the tourist offices and at many hotels, and *Meet Osaka*, a quarterly with information on sightseeing, Bunraku, festivals, concerts, and special exhibits and events.

CITY LAYOUT

With regard to hotels, shopping, restaurants, and nightlife, Osaka can be divided into two distinct parts: **Kita,** the North Ward, which embraces the area around Osaka and Umeda stations; and **Chuo-ku,** the Middle Ward, which is in the center of the JR Loop Line and includes the Shinsaibashi shopping district and a lively eating and entertainment district clustered around a narrow street called Dotonbori. Connecting the two areas is a wide boulevard lined with gingko trees called Midosuji Dori Avenue, running from Osaka Station one way south all the way to Namba Station.

GETTING AROUND

The **subway** network is easy to use because all lines are color-coded and the station names are in English. The **Midosuji Line** is the most important one for visitors; it passes through Shin-Osaka Station and then goes to Umeda (close to Osaka Station), Shinsaibashi, Namba, and Tennoji. There's also a Japan Railways train called the Osaka Kanjo Line, or JR Loop Line, which passes through Osaka Station and makes a loop around the city; take it to visit Osaka Castle.

WHAT TO SEE & DO

Osaka does not have many tourist sights; you can cover the basics of the city in a one- or two-night stay. Top priority on your list here should be Osaka Castle, Bunraku, and dining. If you have more time, visit Osaka Aquarium.

AROUND OSAKA CASTLE

✪ **Osaka Castle (Osaka-jo)** (tel. 944-0546 or 941-3044) is one of the most famous castles in Japanese history. It was first built in the 1580s on the order of Hideyoshi Toyotomi, who requisitioned materials from his feudal generals. The most conspicuous of these materials were huge stones; the largest, 19 feet high and 48 feet long, is known as the "Higo-ishi." Upon its completion, Osaka Castle was the largest castle in Japan, a magnificent structure used by Hideyoshi as a military stronghold against rebellious feudal lords. By the time he died in 1598, Hideyoshi had succeeded in crushing his enemies and unifying Japan under his command.

After Hideyoshi's death, Tokugawa Ieyasu seized power and established his shogunate government in Edo. Hideyoshi's heirs, however, had ideas of their own and, considering Osaka Castle impregnable, they plotted to overthrow the Tokugawa government. In 1615, Tokugawa sent troops to Osaka, where they not only defeated the Hideyoshi insurrectionists but destroyed Osaka Castle. Although the Tokugawas rebuilt the castle, they burned it down in 1868 during the Meiji Restoration, as they made their last retreat.

The present Osaka Castle dates from 1931. Built of ferroconcrete, it's not as massive as the original but is still impressive. Its eight-story donjon, or keep, rises 130 feet and houses a museum with displays relating to the Hideyoshi clan and old Osaka, including armor, fans, and personal belongings. Hours are 9am to 5pm (enter by 4:30pm) and admission is ¥400 ($2.85). To reach Osaka Castle, take either the JR Loop Line to Morinomiya or Osakajokoen Station, or the subway to Temmabashi, Tanimachi 4-chome, or Morinomiya Station.

Just a few minutes' walk from the castle is the **O-Kawa River,** one of the many waterways that once served as important transportation avenues back in Osaka's merchant days. Although O-Kawa doesn't look anything like it used to, glass-enclosed boats ply the river throughout the year, departing from a dock close to the castle. Rides last an hour and cost ¥1,600 ($11.40). Boats depart once an hour (at last check, on the hour; but double-check) from 10am to 4pm (longer hours in summer). The trip is beautiful (and therefore crowded) during the cherry-blossom season. For information or reservations, call **Osaka Aqua Bus** at 942-5511.

Also just a few minutes' walk from Osaka Castle are the Twin 21 buildings, 2-1-61 Shiromi, easy to spot because they are two identical-looking structures among the several skyscrapers that make up Osaka's recently developed business park. On the second floor of the National Tower Building is **Panasonic Square,** a hall filled with electronics of various fields, including communications (such as the TV telephone) and games. Although it's designed for the Japanese (with most things explained in Japanese), there's enough to interest everyone, especially children. A robot, for example, can draw your portrait, while a periscope mounted on the building's roof lets you scan Osaka's panorama. Panasonic Square is open daily from 10am to 6pm, and admission is ¥300 ($2.15) for adults and ¥200 ($1.40) for children. For more information, call 949-2122.

AROUND SHITENNOJI TEMPLE

Shitennoji Temple (tel. 771-0066) was first built in 593 at the order of Prince Shotoku and is believed to be one of the oldest Buddhist temples in Japan (it was founded more than a decade before Horyuji Temple, outside Nara, was constructed). Popularly known as Tennoji Temple and considered to represent the birthplace of Buddhism in Japan, it has been destroyed by fire many times through the centuries; none of the original structures remain. However, it does have a Treasure House, which contains a large collection of religious artwork. Shitennoji is open daily from 8am to 4:30pm (4pm in winter); the Treasure House is closed on Monday. The nearest station is JR Tennoji Station or Shitennoji-mae Subway Station on the Tanimachi Line.

Southwest of the temple is **Tennoji Park,** where you can visit a zoo, botanical

IMPRESSIONS

In trade it is a Chicago. In situation it is a Venice.
—JOHN FOSTER FRASER, *ROUND THE WORLD ON A WHEEL*, 1899, ON OSAKA

gardens, and the Municipal Art Museum, with both ancient and modern Asian art. **Tennoji Zoo,** opened in 1915, is home to 1,000 animals, including kiwis, Tasmanian devils, and rare Mongolian gazelles. It's open Tuesday through Sunday from 9:30am to 5pm and charges a ¥400 ($2.85) admission. If you wish to visit only Tennoji Park, admission here is ¥150 ($1.70), waived if you're visiting the zoo. The park is open Tuesday through Sunday from 9:30am to 9pm in July and August, and from 9:30am to 5pm the rest of the year. To reach Tennoji Park, take the subway or JR Loop Line to Tennoji Station; if you're main destination is the zoo, head for Dobutsuen-mae Station.

OSAKA AQUARIUM

The Osaka Aquarium (tel. 576-5500 or 576-5501) the city's newest attraction, is one of the world's largest aquariums, encompassing 286,000 square feet and containing 2.9 million gallons of water. It is constructed around the theme "Ring of Fire," which refers to the volcanic perimeter encircling the Pacific Ocean. Visitors begin their tour with a walk through a room that contains a video of erupting volcanoes, followed by an escalator ride to the eighth floor. From there, visitors pass through 14 different habitats as they follow a spiraling corridor back to the ground floor, starting with the daylight world above the ocean's surface and proceeding to the depths of the ocean floor. Arctic, Antarctic, tropical, and temperate zones are all represented, in exhibits ranging from the Gulf of Panama and Monterey Bay to the Great Barrier Reef. The walls of the aquarium tank are constructed of huge acrylic glass sheets, imparting a sense of being immersed in the middle of the ocean. Visitors look at 18,000 specimens, including penguins, sea otters, sharks, stingrays, dolphins, giant spider crabs, sea turtles, and myriad fish. Allow about 1 to 2 hours to tour the aquarium, avoiding weekends. It's open daily from 10am to 8pm (9pm in July and August); closed every third Wednesday between December and February and on New Year's Eve. Admission is ¥1,950 ($13.90) for adults, ¥900 ($6.40) for children aged 7 to 15, and ¥400 ($2.85) for children aged 4 to 6. To reach it, take the Chuo Subway Line to Osakako Station, from which it's about a 5-minute walk.

BUNRAKU

The **National Bunraku Theater,** 1-12-10 Nipponbashi, Chuo-ku (tel. 212-2531), was completed in 1984 and presents traditional puppet theater six times a year, with most productions running for 2 to 3 weeks at a time. Tickets usually range from ¥3,600 to ¥4,400 ($25.70 to $31.40), with performances usually held daily at 11am and 4pm. To find out whether a performance is being held, contact the Osaka Tourist Information Office. The National Bunraku Theater is located about a 10-minute walk from the Namba subway station on the Midosuji Line, or a 5-minute walk from Nipponbashi Station on the Kintetsu Line.

TAKARAZUKA

Takarazuka is a town northwest of Osaka, but its name is synonomous with the all-female **Takarazuka Troupe.** Founded in 1914 to attract vacationers to Takarazuka, the troupe proved instantly popular with the general public, which had slowly been turning away from traditional forms of Japanese drama to lively Western musicals and entertainment. Combining Japanese and Western elements in its performances, the Takarazuka Troupe today consists of about 400 women, who perform musicals, classical Japanese drama, folk dances, and modern revues in Takarazuka and Tokyo and on tours around the world.

Performances are held at the Takarazuka Revue Hall most days throughout the year, with the exception of Wednesdays, with tickets ranging from about ¥800 to ¥4,100 ($5.70 to $29.30). Note, however, that the hall is located on the grounds of an amusement park called **Takarazuka Family Land,** admission to which is an additional ¥1,200 ($8.55) and includes access to a zoo and botanical garden. The amusement park is open Thursday through Tuesday from 9:30am to 5:30pm; performances by the Takarazuka Troupe are usually at 1pm on weekdays, and at 11am and 3pm on weekends and holidays. It takes approximately 45 minutes to reach Takarazuka Station from Umeda Station via the private Hankyu Line, followed by an 8-minute walk. For more information, call 0797/84-0321.

WHERE TO STAY

Like Tokyo, Osaka has a wide range of hotels, from first-class accommodations to business hotels. Most are concentrated around Osaka Station, while the rest stretch to the south and around Shin-Osaka Station.

EXPENSIVE

In Kita-ku [Near Osaka Station]

ANA-SHERATON HOTEL, 1-3-1 Dojimahama, Kita-ku, Osaka 530. Tel. 06/347-1112. Fax 06/348-9208. 500 rms. A/C MINIBAR TV TEL **Directions:** A 15-minute walk south from Osaka Station, or a 5-minute taxi ride.

$ Rates: ¥16,500–¥21,000 ($118–$150) single; ¥27,000–¥31,000 ($193–$221) double; ¥27,000–¥34,000 ($193–$243) twin. AE, DC, JCB, MC, V.

Opened in 1984, this sleek white first-class hotel emphasizes running water, greenery, and ample sunlight in its architectural philosophy, evident as soon as you enter the impressive lobby. An inner courtyard stretches up to a skylight on the sixth floor, from which water trickles along extended chains to a pond below; nearby, water trickles over a rock sculpture. Built on the banks of the Dojima River, the ANA-Sheraton offers everything you'd expect from a first-class hotel, including a guest-relations desk to help with everything from restaurant reservations to sightseeing. The guest rooms are large and comfortably designed, and feature bilingual cable TV with CNN broadcasts and sightseeing information in English, minibar, and plug-in hot-water thermos, among other amenities. I prefer rooms that face the Dojima River.

Dining/Entertainment: There are five restaurants, two bars, and a lobby lounge, as well as an outdoor beer garden open in summer. The Rose Room is one of Osaka's best French restaurants.

Services: 24-hour rooms service, English-language newspapers delivered twice a day, same-day laundry service.

Facilities: Indoor swimming pool and sauna (fee: ¥3,000 or $21.40), business center, travel agency.

HOTEL OSAKA GRAND, 2-3-18 Nakanoshima, Kita-ku, Osaka 530. Tel. 06/202-1212. Fax 06/227-5054. 348 rms. A/C MINIBAR TV TEL **Station:** Higobashi, about a 5-minute walk away.

$ Rates: ¥11,000–¥16,500 ($78–$118) single; ¥19,800–¥26,000 ($141–$186) double/twin. AE, DC, JCB, MC, V.

This is a fine small hotel on the island of Nakanoshima in the heart of Osaka, with a location close to Osaka's Festival Hall that makes it a favorite of concert-goers and musicians. Dating from 1960, it's also one of Osaka's older hotels and has aged gracefully. The small, cozy lobby, with its high ceiling and old décor, evokes a European atmosphere of days gone by. With prices lower than other hotels in this category (and with no facilities outside its restaurants), it offers rooms with radio, clock, TV with bedside control buttons, pot for hot water, and bathroom covered with tile instead of the usual plastic. I prefer the rooms that face the river—although there's little traffic on the river and nothing really to see, it at least affords a bit of spaciousness.

Dining/Entertainment: The seven bars and restaurants include a popular Western-style dining spot on the 14th floor that offers buffet lunches and dinners.

Services: Same-day laundry service.

OSAKA HILTON, 1-8-8 Umeda, Kita-ku, Osaka 530. Tel. 06/347-7111, or toll free 800/HILTONS in the U.S. and Canada. Fax 06/347-7001. 526 rms. A/C MINIBAR TV TEL **Directions:** A 3-minute walk from central exit of Osaka Station. **Station:** Yotsubashisen Subway Station, beneath the hotel.
$ Rates: ¥22,000–¥38,000 ($157–$271) single; ¥29,000–¥44,000 ($207–$314) double/twin. AE, DC, JCB, MC, V.

Not to be outdone is the Osaka Hilton International, the closest luxury hotel to Osaka Station. A sleek silver-gray tower that is connected to the Hilton Plaza with its shopping arcade and restaurants, it conveys an international atmosphere. Rooms, with rates based on height and therefore view, are decorated in subtle blends of Japanese and Western styles, featuring soothing color combinations of pale peach and celadon green, shoji screens, and large, full-length mirrors. Bilingual TV (CNN newscasts, remote control, in-house movies) and a radio are among other amenities. The most expensive rooms are those on the four executive floors, with separate check-in facilities, private lounge, and complimentary breakfast and cocktails. The hotel's only no-smoking floor is on an executive floor. There is no extra charge for children sharing a room with parents, but the maximum occupancy is three persons to a room.

Dining/Entertainment: There are a multitude of restaurants in the Hilton and the Hilton Plaza. The Seasons is the hotel's showcase restaurant, while the Genji features Japanese food in a traditional setting. Windows on the World on the top floor features a restaurant and music lounge with views of the city.

Services: 24-hour room service, free newspaper delivered twice a day, same-day laundry service.

Facilities: Fitness center (fee: ¥4,000 or $28.55) with indoor pool, tennis court, sauna, and gym; shopping arcade; business center; barbershop; beauty salon.

OSAKA TERMINAL HOTEL, 3-1-1 Umeda, Kita-ku, Osaka 530. Tel. 06/344-1234. Fax 06/334-1130. 644 rms. A/C MINIBAR TV TEL **Directions:** Located above Osaka Station.
$ Rates: ¥13,000–¥17,500 ($93–$125) single; ¥19,800–¥33,000 ($141–$236) twin; ¥22,000–¥29,000 ($157–$207) double. AE, DC, JCB, MC, V.

Since it towers above Osaka Station, this hotel is very convenient for a single night's stay in the city. But because its lobby is on the ground floor, with doors that open right into the train station, it's also very hectic and busy. Thankfully, its guest rooms, with soundproof windows, are on the 21st to 26th floors. Opened in 1983, this tourist hotel caters to a 10% foreign clientele, with rooms that are cheerful and have a pot for heating water, a radio, an alarm clock, a minibar, and TV with CNN and pay video. The cheapest singles and twins face an inner courtyard—they're quieter, but you're missing a great view of the city. Also in the same building is Daimaru department store, a good place to shop for all those traveling necessities.

Dining/entertainment: There are eight restaurants and bars, many of them located on the 19th floor, with good views of the city.

Services: Free newspaper, no-smoking rooms.

Facilities: Beauty parlor, drugstore.

PLAZA, 2-2-49 Oyodo-Minami, Kita-ku, Osaka 531. Tel. 06/453-1111, or toll free 800/223-6800 in the U.S. and Canada. Fax 06/454-0169. 535 rms. A/C MINIBAR TV TEL **Station:** Fukushima on the JR Loop Line. **Bus:** Free shuttle bus from Osaka Station to the hotel every 15 minutes.
$ Rates: ¥16,500–¥23,000 ($118–$164) single; ¥25,000–¥29,000 ($178–$207) double/twin. AE, DC, JCB, MC, V.

Opened in 1970, this was one of Osaka's first deluxe hotels and remains in high standing as a member of the Leading Hotels of the World. Although relatively close to Osaka Station and only a 15-minute taxi ride from Osaka's airport, it's far enough away that it's out of the mainstream of human traffic. Further, it has none of the decorating pretentiousness that sometimes afflicts modern hotels. Foreigners constitute about 30% of the Plaza's guests. Rooms are large and comfortable, and amenities include hot-water pot, bilingual TV with CNN, radio, hairdryer, and magnifying makeup/shaving mirror in the bathroom. No-smoking rooms are available.

Dining/Entertainment: There are six restaurants, one lounge, and two bars. The Rendezvous French restaurant on the 23rd floor is one of Osaka's best.

Services: 24-hour room service, free newspaper, same-day laundry service, baby-sitting, in-house doctor, free shuttle bus to Osaka Station every 15 minutes.

Facilities: Outdoor swimming pool (free of charge), business center.

ROYAL HOTEL, 5-3-68 Nakanoshima, Kita-ku, Osaka 530. Tel. 448-1121, or toll free 800/937-5454 in the U.S. Fax 06/448-4414. 1,116 rms. A/C MINIBAR TV TEL **Subway:** Yodoyabashi Station on Midosuji Line, then free shuttle bus from Yodoyabashi Station to hotel, with departures every 20 minutes. **Taxi:** Less than a 10-minute ride from Osaka Station.

$ Rates: ¥14,300–¥19,000 ($102–$136) single; ¥26,000–¥45,000 ($186–$321) double; ¥27,000–¥45,000 ($193–$321) twin. AE, DC, JCB, MC, V.

One of Osaka's most established hostelries, the Royal was first opened more than 55 years ago and remains among the city's largest hotels. Located on Nakanoshima, an island in the middle of the Dojima River in the heart of Osaka, it has been completely remodeled and updated, with a striking lobby that has a "stream" running through it and views of a waterfall surrounded by trees. Its rooms sport large windows and bilingual TV with CNN.

Dining/Entertainment: There are almost two dozen restaurants, the most renowned of which is the Chambord, a French restaurant on the 29th floor with views of the city.

Services: 24-hour room service, free newspapers delivered twice daily, same-day laundry service, baby-sitting, no-smoking floor.

Facilities: There is a beautifully designed swimming pool (one of the largest hotel pools in Osaka) and sauna (fee: ¥2,000 or $14.30), a shopping arcade with more than 40 boutiques, business center, beauty salon, barbershop.

In Chuo-ku [the Middle Ward]

NANKAI SOUTH TOWER HOTEL OSAKA, 5-1-60 Namba, Chuo-ku, Osaka 542. Tel. 06/646-1111. Fax 06/648-0331. 548 rms. A/C MINIBAR TV TEL **Station:** Namba, a 1-minute walk away.

$ Rates: ¥16,500–¥22,000 ($118–$157) single; ¥27,000–¥39,000 ($193–$278) double/twin. AE, DC, JCB, MC, V.

This very modern hotel, open since 1990, towers above Namba Station in an area expected to grow in strategic importance with the completion of a new airport in 1995. Its marbled lobby is up on the sixth floor, with an atrium and a spaciousness that come as a surprise in an area so high off the ground. Guest rooms are on floors 14 through 34, with prices based on size and height; they offer everything from cable TV with remote control to outlets for fax machines and a phone in the bathroom.

Dining/Entertainment: There are 11 restaurants and bars serving French, Chinese, and a wide range of Japanese food, including sukiyaki, sushi, tempura, teppanyaki, and kaiseki. The Sky Lounge on the 36th floor offers breathtaking views of Osaka.

Services: 24-hour room service, free newspapers delivered twice a day, same-day laundry service, baby-sitting room.

Facilities: Fitness center indoor pool, gym and sauna (fee ¥3,500 or $25), shopping arcade, business center, travel counter.

HOTEL NEW OTANI OSAKA, 1-4 Shiromi, Chuo-ku, Osaka 540. Tel. 06/941-1111. Fax 06/941-9769. 559 rms. A/C MINIBAR TV TEL **Station:** Osakajokoen (JR Loop Line), a 3-minute walk away.

$ Rates: ¥26,000–¥33,000 ($186–$236) single; ¥30,000–¥38,000 ($214–$271) double; ¥30,000–¥44,000 ($214–$314) triple. AE, DC, JCB, MC, V.

Another relatively new hotel—and Osaka seems to have a lot of them—is the Hotel

New Otani Osaka, near Osaka Castle. Its location near Osaka's new business park—with corporate headquarters for KDD, NEC, Sumitomo, and other big companies—assures it a steady business clientele, while its proximity to Osaka Castle brings in the tourists as well. Everything about this hotel is visually pleasing, right down to the elevators. The marbled lobby boasts a four-story atrium, with a clever use of mirrors and skylights to give it an added airiness.

Rooms are pleasant and comfortable, equipped with semidouble-size beds, bilingual TV with CNN newscasts from the United States, radio, and hairdryer, among other amenities, plus windows that open. Rates are based on room size and view, with the more expensive rooms providing a view of Osaka Castle.

Dining/Entertainment: Among the hotel's 18 restaurants and bars is the ever-popular Trader Vic's, as well as restaurants serving Chinese, continental, Italian, and Japanese cuisine. The Four Seasons is a piano bar with views of Osaka Castle.

Services: 24-hour room service, free newspaper delivered twice a day, same-day laundry service.

Facilities: Fitness club with indoor and outdoor swimming pools and tennis courts (fee charged), shopping arcade with designer names, business center, travel agency, beauty salon, medical clinic.

HOTEL NIKKO OSAKA, 1-3-3 Nishi-Shinsaibashi, Chuo-ku, Osaka 542. Tel. 06/244-1111. Fax 06/245-2432. 665 rms. A/C MINIBAR TV TEL **Station:** Shinsaibashi Subway Station, beneath the hotel.
$ **Rates:** ¥16,500–¥22,000 ($118–$157) single; ¥27,000–¥31,000 ($192–$221) double; ¥27,000–¥33,000 ($192–$236) twin. AE, DC, JCB, MC, V.

Just a few years older than the newer hotels and owned by Japan Airlines, the elegant Hotel Nikko Osaka is located on fashionable Midosuji Boulevard and is easily recognized by its striking architectural design, with slanted walls. It's only a 7-minute walk from the hotel to Dotonbori Street, the heart of Osaka's nightlife and restaurant district. About 30% to 40% of the hotel's guests are foreigners, mainly Americans, who are drawn by its excellent service, great location, and fine facilities. A guest-relations desk will answer any questions regarding Osaka or the hotel. Rooms are equipped with bilingual TV featuring CNN and in-house movies. The 27th floor has rooms designed by Hanae Mori, one of Japan's best-known fashion designers, while the top three floors have executive rooms.

Dining/Entertainment: Included among the eight restaurants and bars is the popular Benkay Japanese restaurant with its kaiseki and tempura selections. The Jet Stream, a sky lounge on the 32nd floor, boasts live entertainment.

Services: 24-hour room service, free newspaper delivered twice daily, same-day laundry service, no-smoking floor.

Facilities: JAL office, barbershop, beauty salon, shopping arcade.

Elsewhere in Osaka

MIYAKO HOTEL OSAKA, 6-1-55 Uehommachi, Tennoji-ku, Osaka 543. Tel. 06/773-1111, or toll free 800/336-1136 in the U.S. Fax 06/773-3322. 608 rms. A/C MINIBAR TV TEL **Station:** Uehommachi Station on the Kintetsu Line, or Tanimachi 9-chome Subway Station.
$ **Rates:** ¥16,500–¥21,000 ($118–$150) single; ¥24,000–¥29,000 ($171–$207) double/twin. AE, DC, JCB, MC, V.

This hotel was designed by the well-known Japanese architect Togo Murano, renowned for his ability to combine Japanese simplicity and tradition with modern efficiency. He was the interior designer as well, reflected in his preferences for light, muted colors and wooden furniture. Chandeliers are in every guest room. He died recently at the age of 91, so this Miyako Hotel was his last complete architectural achievement.

Guest rooms come with all the comforts you'd expect from a first-class hotel, including bilingual TV with CNN cable broadcasts from the United States and a closed-circuit media system that provides timely reports on weather, traffic conditions, tourist information, and other services. In addition, there are also packets of soup and coffee, along with tea; a well-stocked minibar; and both a hairdryer and a clothesline in a roomy bathroom. Beds are decked with quilts instead of the usual heavy blankets. Room rates are based on the size of the room, with the highest rates charged for the executive floors on the 17th and 18th floors, offering free breakfast and cocktails.

Dining/Entertainment: The 13 restaurants and bars offer everything from Japanese and Chinese to French cuisine. La Mer is an exclusive, expensive seafood restaurant, while the Ciel Bleu on the 21st floor offers French dishes and a grand view. In the basement are inexpensive restaurants, including those specializing in buckwheat noodles, tofu, and okonomiyaki, a local dish described later in the "Where to Dine" section. Service is excellent.

Services: English-language newspapers delivered twice a day, 24-hour room service, same-day laundry service, baby-sitting.

Facilities: Health club (charge begins at ¥4,000 or $28.55) with exercise gym, swimming pool, racquetball courts, and sauna.

MODERATE

There are a few hotels located near Shin-Osaka Station, but because the area is unexciting and industrial I suggest staying at one of the other hotels listed here. All rooms in this category come with private bath.

In Kita-ku [Near Osaka Station]

HOTEL KITAHACHI, 7-16 Doyama-cho, Kita-ku, Osaka 530. Tel. 06/361-2078. Fax 06/361-7468. 38 rms. A/C MINIBAR TV TEL **Directions:** A 10-minute walk from Osaka Station's east exit, on Shinjido-suji Street.

$ Rates (including service): ¥6,500–¥7,300 ($46–$52) single; ¥11,000–¥13,200 ($78–$94) double; ¥13,200–¥15,900 ($94–$113) twin; ¥19,200 ($137) triple. AE, DC, JCB, MC, V.

Located within easy walking distance of Osaka Station, Kitahachi opened as a ryokan in 1946 and then converted to a Western-style hotel in the early 1980s. Half of the rooms at this small, personable hotel are singles with semidouble-size beds, but they are often fully occupied because of their low prices. Twins are usually available. Rooms are larger than those of most business hotels; they are more tastefully furnished as well. All rooms have double doors to block out corridor noise and are equipped with coin-operated TV, radio, clock, minibar, and hot-water pot. At last check, no one here spoke any English—try to have a Japanese make your reservation. There's one restaurant serving Western food, and a bar that stays open until 2am.

HOTEL NEW HANKYU (Shin Hankyu Hotel), 1-1-35 Shibata, Kita-ku, Osaka 530. Tel. 06/372-5101. Fax 06/374-6885. 947 rms. A/C MINIBAR TV TEL **Directions:** A few minutes' walk from Osaka Station.

$ Rates: ¥11,000–¥14,300 ($78–$102) single; ¥18,000–¥33,000 ($128–$236) twin; ¥23,000–¥28,000 ($164–$200) double; ¥29,000 ($207) triple. AE, DC, JCB, MC, V.

Opened in 1964 but so well maintained it doesn't seem nearly that old, this hotel is part of the conglomerate that owns Hankyu Railways, Hankyu department stores, restaurants, and even Takarazuka Family Land. Rooms have cable TV with CNN and pay video, clock, music, and double-pane windows. Vending machines dispense soda and beer. The simple décor resembles that found in business hotels. Altogether, there are 23 bars and restaurants in the hotel and in the neighboring Hankyu complex, and in the Hotel New Hankyu Annex, a few minutes' walk away, guests can use a fitness club with pool and gym for ¥4,000 ($28.55).

OSAKA TOKYU INN, 2-1 Doyama-cho, Kita-ku, Osaka 530. Tel. 06/315-0109. Fax 06/315-6019. 402 rms. A/C MINIBAR TV TEL **Directions:** A 10-minute walk west of Osaka Station.

$ Rates (including service charge): ¥9,300–¥11,000 ($66–$78) single; ¥16,500 ($118) double; ¥16,500–¥17,500 ($118–$125) twin. AE, DC, JCB, MC, V.

Part of a nationwide chain, this is your typical standard business hotel. Its one restaurant serves Western food, and its rooms are quiet and clean, featuring clock, desk, TV with remote control and pay video, minibar, hot-water pot and tea, and small unit bathroom made of plastic. The cheapest singles and twins face an inner courtyard with absolutely no view. My favorite rooms are those that face the front, where you can look down on a small and tidy temple and cemetery that look slightly out of place among Osaka's office buildings—typical Japan. Vending machines are on the seventh floor. The hotel is a bit confusing to find because the most direct way to get there is via an underground passageway lined with shops. Follow the signs that say OGIMACHI until they bring you above ground at the W31 exit—you should be able to spot the Tokyu from there. Your best bet is to stop by the tourist office in the train station, where they can give you a map showing the way to the hotel.

In Chuo-ku [Middle Ward]

HOTEL CALIFORNIA, 1-9-30 Nishishinsaibashi, Chuo-ku, Osaka 542. Tel. 06/243-0333. Fax 06/243-0148. 54 rms. A/C MINIBAR TV TEL **Station:** Shinsaibashi, a few minutes' walk away.

$ Rates: ¥8,200 ($58) single; ¥12,000–¥15,500 ($86–$111) double; ¥14,300–¥18,500 ($102–$132) twin. ¥1,000 more on Sat and evening before a hol. AE, DC, JCB, MC, V.

This place tries to evoke images of sunny California through its use of whites and greens, plants, and brass railings. Rooms are cheerfully decorated with soft pastels and rattan furniture, and they come with TV with pay video, radio, clock, hot-water pot, and minibar. Hotel California is conveniently located in Chuo-ku, not far from the Nikko Hotel, and has one Western-style restaurant, called California Garden, and one American-style bar.

HOLIDAY INN NANKAI, 2-5-15 Shinsaibashisuji Chuo-ku, Osaka 542. Tel. 06/213-8281, or toll free 800/HOLIDAY in the U.S. and Canada. Fax 06/213-8640. 229 rms. A/C MINIBAR TV TEL **Station:** Namba, a 3-minute walk away.

$ Rates: ¥14,300–¥20,000 ($102–$143) single; ¥17,500–¥26,000 ($125–$186) double/twin. Children up to 12 stay free with parents. AE, DC, JCB, MC, V.

This hotel has a very convenient location close to Dotonbori and Osaka's nightlife district right on Midosuji Dori Avenue. The lobby is on the fifth floor, and the rooftop pool, open free to hotel guests during July and August, is a plus. There's also an outdoor beer garden on the third floor, open daily from 5 to 9pm from the end of May to the end of August. Four restaurants serve French, Chinese, American, and Japanese cuisine. As with all Holiday Inns, all beds are double size, even those in single rooms, and the rooms are large. Guests receive a free newspaper, and room service is available until 11pm.

Near Shin-Osaka Station

NEW OSAKA HOTEL, 5-14-10 Nishi-Nakajima, Yodogawa-ku, Osaka 532. Tel. 06/305-2345. Fax 06/305-2388. 304 rms. A/C MINIBAR TV TEL. **Directions:** A 2-minute walk from Shin-Osaka Station's central exit.

$ Rates: ¥7,000–¥8,800 ($50–$63) single; ¥14,800 ($106) twin; ¥14,800–¥16,500 ($106–$118) double. AE, DC, JCB, MC, V.

If you find it more convenient to stay close to where the Shinkansen bullet trains pull in at Shin-Osaka Station, you might try this hotel, which caters almost exclusively to Japanese businessmen (most of its rooms are singles). Rooms are simply decorated and come with minibar and TV with pay video. Because the building is sandwiched in between two other buildings, all but 76 of the rooms face a wall. If you want to have more of a view, be sure to ask. A restaurant on the 13th floor serves Chinese and Western food; there's also a Japanese restaurant.

SHIN-OSAKA STATION HOTEL, 1-16-6 Higashi-Nakajima, Higashi-yodogawa-ku, Osaka 533. Tel. 06/325-0011. Fax 06/325-3366. 90 rms A/C MINIBAR TV TEL **Directions:** A 2-minute walk from Shin-Osaka Station's central exit, to the left over the pedestrian bridge over the railroad tracks.

$ Rates (including tax and service charge): ¥6,500–¥7,500 ($46–$53) single; ¥12,000 ($86) double; ¥14,300 ($102) twin; ¥17,500 ($125) triple. No credit cards.

This is one of the newest inexpensive business hotels to open near Shin-Osaka Station. Don't confuse this hotel with the much older, smaller one just in front of it with the exact same name (the older hotel is identified only in Japanese, while the newer one has an English sign). Rooms are small but adequate, coming with TV with pay video, minibar, clock, and hot-water pot with tea. There's one restaurant serving Western food.

Near Osaka International Airport

CREVETTE, 1-9-6 Kuko, Ikeda-shi, Osaka 563. Tel. 06/843-7201. Fax 06/843-0043. 188 rms. A/C MINIBAR TV TEL **Directions:** A 5-minute walk from Osaka International Airport.

$ Rates: ¥7,000–¥9,600 ($50–$68) single; ¥13,200–¥17,000 ($94–$121) twin; ¥17,000 ($121) double. Japanese-style rooms: ¥17,000 ($121) double occupancy. AE, DC, JCB, MC, V.

Crevette (pronounced Kurebe in Japanese) caters to businesspeople with early-morning flights out of Osaka's airport. Rooms are simple, with just the basics, and facilities include one Western restaurant and one bar.

OSAKA AIRPORT HOTEL, Osaka International Airport Building, Osaka 560. Tel. 06/855-4621. Fax 06/855-4620. 105 rms. A/C MINIBAR TV TEL **Directions:** Located in center of third floor of Osaka International Airport Building.

$ Rates: ¥10,500 ($75) single; ¥17,000–¥24,000 ($121–$171) twin; ¥19,000 ($136) double. AE, DC, JCB, MC, V.

If you find yourself with a stopover at Osaka International Airport, this hotel should fit the bill for both convenience and comfort. Rooms come with the usual minibar and hot-water pot with tea, and facilities include eight restaurants and bars.

Elsewhere in Osaka

HOTEL INTERNATIONAL HOUSE, 8-2-6 Uehommachi, Tennoji-ku, Osaka 543. Tel. 06/773-8181. Fax 06/773-0777. 50 rms A/C TV TEL **Directions:** A 5-minute walk from Uehommachi Station of the Kintetsu Line; a 7-minute walk from Tanimachi 9-chome and Shitennoji-mae subway stations.

$ Rates (including tax and service): ¥6,700 ($48) single; ¥13,500 ($96) twin. The hotel is closed Dec 29–Jan 3. AE, DC, JCB, MC, V.

The International House is a new facility used for international seminars, conventions, and meetings. It includes the Hotel International House, used mainly by those attending seminars but also open to the public—try to book well in advance. Rooms, which have that spartan look you'd expect from such a facility offering inexpensive accommodations, come with hot-water pot and tea, desk, alarm clock, and small unit bath with a clothesline. Forty of the 50 rooms here are singles, making it a great place to stay for the single traveler. One restaurant serves Western-style foods at very reasonable prices, and there are two bars. It's managed by the Miyako Hotel Osaka, so service is above what you'd find at most hotels at these prices.

BUDGET

In Kita-ku [Near Osaka Station]

HOTEL HOKKE CLUB ⑬, 12-19 Togano-cho, Kita-ku, Osaka 530. Tel. 06/313-3171. Fax 06/313-4637. 247 rms (none with bath). A/C MINIBAR TV TEL **Directions:** A 10-minute walk east of Osaka Station.

$ Rates (including service charge): ¥5,700 ($41) Japanese- or Western-style single; ¥9,300 ($66) Japanese-style double occupancy; ¥10,200 ($73) Western-style twin. Breakfast ¥680 ($4.86). AE, DC, JCB, MC, V.

First opened about 37 years ago, this hotel is one of Osaka's oldest business hotels. Its small but clean and adequate rooms, available in both Western and Japanese style, are without private bathrooms, but there are large, separate public baths for men and women. If you're taking a single, request a corner room, since the other singles face an inner courtyard and are dark. There's one Japanese-style restaurant, and vending machines dispense beer and soft drinks. To reach the hotel, take the underground passageway lined with shops from Osaka Station, heading toward signs that read OGIMACHI until you come aboveground at the W32 exit. It's a 2-minute walk from there. Ask the tourist office at the station for a map of the area.

Near Shin-Osaka Station

SHIN-OSAKA SEN-I CITY ⑬⑨, **2-2-17 Nishi-Miyahara, Yodogawa-ku, Osaka 532. Tel. 06/394-3331.** Fax 06/394-3335. 70 rms (12 with bath). A/C MINIBAR TV TEL **Directions:** A 10-minute walk northwest of Shin-Osaka Station, or take the free shuttle bus from Shin-Osaka Station's central exit.
$ Rates: ¥4,500 ($32) single without bath; ¥7,400 ($53) twin without bath, ¥8,500–¥8,800 ($61–$63) twin with bath. AE, DC, JCB, MC, V.

This very simple business hotel is easy to spot with its green-and-blue sign and clock on the top of the building. The lobby is on the sixth floor and guest rooms are on the sixth and seventh floors. The rooms are a few decades away from being modern, but they're clean, good for the price, and fairly large as far as business hotels go. They come with stocked refrigerator, hot-water pot with tea, and coin-operated TV with pay video. All the singles and most twins are bathless, but there are public baths. Those twins that do have private bathrooms have Western-style toilets and deep, Japanese-style bathtubs. Shuttle buses bound for Sen-i City depart every 10 minutes or so from the lowest level of the Central Exit—turn right out of the station and walk to the end of the row of buses.

1 SUNNY STONE HOTEL, 10-3 Hiroshiba-cho, Suita City, Osaka 564. Tel. 06/386-0001 or 385-1281. 414 rms (148 with toilet only, 366 with bath). A/C TV TEL **Directions:** A 2-minute walk from Esaka, two stops north of Shin-Osaka Station on the Midosuji Line.
$ Rates: ¥4,400 ($31) single without bath, ¥5,500 ($39) single with bath; ¥7,400 ($53) twin without bath, ¥8,800 ($63) twin with bath; ¥12,000 ($86) triple with bath. JCB, V.

This business hotel, with both Japanese-style tatami rooms and Western-style bedrooms, is located in north Osaka. About 20 years old, it shows its age and offers very simple rooms. The cheapest are those with toilet but no bath, but note that all of these face another building, so that if you're claustrophobic, you may want to spring for one of the Western- or Japanese-style rooms with bath and toilet. The hotel's one restaurant serves both Japanese and Western food.

2 SUNNY STONE HOTEL, 1-22-4 Esaka-cho, Suita City, Osaka 564. Tel. 06/386-3200. 132 rms (all with bath). A/C TV TEL **Directions:** A 2-minute walk from Esaka, two stops north of Shin-Osaka Station on the Midosuji Line.
$ Rates (including tax and service charge): ¥6,300 ($45) single; ¥9,900 ($71) twin. AE, DC, JCB, MC, V.

Catercorner from 1 Sunny Stone Hotel is this business hotel, which opened in the mid-1980s. Rooms here are slightly larger. Six of the twins feature bunk beds that have curtains for more privacy, reminding me of train sleeping compartments. At any rate, be warned that neighboring buildings have been built only a few feet from the hotel itself, obstructing all views.

Elsewhere in Osaka

EBISU-SO RYOKAN, 1-7-33 Nipponbashi-Nishi, Naniwa-ku, Osaka 556. Tel. 06/643-4861. 15 rms (none with bath). A/C TV **Directions:** A 5-minute walk from Ebisucho Station, or a 10-minute walk from Nipponbashi on the Kintetsu Line.
$ Rates: ¥4,600 ($30) single; ¥8,000 ($57) twin; ¥12,000 ($86) triple. AE, MC, V.

This Japanese-style inn is a member of the Japanese Inn Group, and is more cluttered and run-down than most (it's been an inn for 35 years and no one speaks English). It reminds me of a small apartment house where young single Japanese often live—a narrow corridor flanked on both sides with 4½- and 6-tatami rooms. I have friends who say they like living in a 4½-tatami room because they can reach everything without having to move. Rooms come with coin-operated TV, fan, and heater, and there's a public bath. The ryokan is located near Den Den Town, Osaka's electronics shopping region.

Youth Hostels

HATTORI RYOKUCHI YOUTH HOSTEL ⑭⓪**, 1-3 Hattori-ryokuchi, Toyonaka-shi, Osaka 540. Tel. 06/862-0600.** Fax 06/863-0561. 108 beds. A/C **Subway:** Midosuji Line from Umeda Station to Ryokuchi-koen Station (45-minute ride), then a 10-minute walk.
$ Rates (per person): ¥1,600 ($11.40) member and nonmember. Breakfast ¥410 ($2.90); dinner ¥720 ($5.15). Sheets ¥100 (70¢). No credit cards.
This youth hostel, although a bit far from the center of Osaka, is located in Hattori-Ryokuchi Park, which has a swimming pool and an open-air museum of old Japanese farmhouses. The front doors close at 9:30pm and lights-out is at 10pm.

OSAKA-SHIRITSU NAGAI YOUTH HOSTEL ⑭⓵**, 1-1 Nagai-Koen, Higashi-sumiyoshi-ku, Osaka 546. Tel. 06/699-5631.** 100 beds. A/C **Subway:** Midosuji subway line to Nagai Station (20-minute ride from Umeda Station, 30 minutes from Shin-Osaka); then a 15-minute walk.
$ Rates (per person): ¥1,900 ($13.55) member and nonmember. Sheets ¥100 (70¢) extra. Breakfast ¥350 ($2.50); dinner ¥600 ($4.30). No credit cards.
This youth hostel, more centrally located, is on municipal sports grounds. You don't need a membership card to stay here, but the maximum stay is 3 nights. The front door closes here at 9pm, with lights-out at 10pm.

WHERE TO DINE

There's a saying among Japanese that whereas a Kyotoite will spend his last yen on a fine kimono, an Osakan will spend it on food. You don't have to spend a lot of money to enjoy good food in Osaka, however.

Most of Osaka's restaurants are found either in Kita-ku near Osaka Station or in Chuo-ku on or near Dotonbori Street. The best Western-style restaurants are in Osaka's first-class hotels. Be sure to check the many restaurant/bars described in the "Evening Entertainment" section, below.

Specialties of Osaka include sushi, udon (noodles) with white soy sauce, and *takoyaki* (cooked dumplings made of octopus). It is probably best known, however, for okonomiyaki, which literally means "as you like it." Its origins date from about 1700, when a type of thin flour cake cooked on a hot plate was served during Buddhist ceremonies. The cake was filled with a bean paste called miso. It wasn't until this century that it became popular, primarily during food shortages. At first it was a simple dish consisting only of flour, water, and a sauce, but gradually other ingredients, such as pork, egg, and vegetables, were added. Today, Osaka is literally riddled with okonomiyaki restaurants offering very inexpensive dining.

IN KITA-KU

LE RENDEZVOUS, 23rd floor of Plaza Hotel, 2-2-49 Oyodo-Minami, Kita-ku. Tel. 453-1111.
Cuisine: FRENCH. **Reservations:** A must. **Transportation:** Free shuttle bus or 5-minute taxi ride from Osaka Station.
$ Prices: Appetizers ¥2,400–¥3,800 ($17.15–$27.15); main dishes ¥4,400–¥6,500 ($31.40–$46.40); set-dinner courses ¥16,500–¥22,000 ($118–$157). AE, DC, JCB, MC, V.
Open: Dinner daily 5:30–10:30pm.
★ Le Rendezvous is one of the most famous—if not the most famous—of Osaka's French restaurants. It receives advice on its creations from internationally known chef Paul Bocuse and was the first of only two Asian restaurants that are members of Traditions et Qualité, a prestigious gastronomical association of

French restaurants (the second restaurant is Tour d'Argent in Tokyo). With windows overlooking Osaka, this small and intimate restaurant serves seasonal dishes that in the past have included such selections as Kobe sirloin and tenderloin steaks, duck, sole stuffed with artichoke and basil, young rabbit leg, and turbot cooked in champagne. Men must wear dinner jackets.

ROSE ROOM, ANA-Sheraton Hotel, 1-3-1 Dojimahama. Tel. 347-1112.
   Cuisine: FRENCH. **Reservations:** Strongly recommended, especially on weekends. **Directions:** A 5-minute taxi ride or 15-minute walk south of Osaka Station.
$ **Prices:**   Appetizers   ¥3,300–¥5,000   ($23.55–$35.70);   main   dishes ¥4,600–¥10,000   ($32.85–$71.40);   set-dinner   courses   ¥14,300–¥22,000 ($102–$157); set lunches ¥6,500–¥8,800 ($46.40–$62.85). AE, DC, JCB, MC, V.
   Open: Lunch daily 11:30am–2:30pm; dinner daily 5:30–10pm.
This elegant French restaurant serving nouvelle cuisine is popular with local Osakans. Its chef, Tomoyoshi Yokota, studied in France for 6 years and worked at Le Rendezvous in the Osaka Plaza Hotel before joining the Sheraton as grand chef in 1984. Small, with seating for only 59 diners, the restaurant features a huge bouquet of roses as its focal point; soft lighting and candles assure intimate dining. You might want to start your meal with one of the hotel's specially made cocktails—Rose d'Or is a mixture of three different kinds of wine, while Symphonie en Rose combines Campari and white wine. For dinner you can start with Norwegian smoked salmon with capers, followed by chilled lobster soup with sour cream. The seafood selection includes turbot with sea urchin, fresh seasonal fish, and lobster au gratin with spinach. Main dishes include hashed duck and sweetbreads with mashed potatoes, roasted rack of lamb, pigeon, and steak.

UNKAI, 6th floor of ANA Sheraton Hotel, 1-3-1 Dojimahama. Tel. 347-1112.
   Cuisine: KAISEKI/SUSHI/TEMPURA/VARIED JAPANESE. **Reservations:** Recommended for dinner on weekends. **Transportation:** A 5-minute taxi ride or a 15-minute walk south of Osaka Station.
$ **Prices:** Appetizers ¥650–¥1,600 ($4.60–$11.40); shabu-shabu ¥7,500 ($53.55); set-dinner courses ¥11,000–¥22,000 ($78–$157); set lunches ¥3,300–¥6,500 ($23.55–$46.40). AE, DC, JCB, MC, V.
   Open: Lunch daily 11:30am–2:30pm; dinner daily 5:30–10pm.
Serving everything from sushi to tempura to shabu-shabu, Unkai is a good place to go if you can't decide on just one type of cuisine. This simple, pleasant restaurant has both a sushi and a tempura counter, where the food is prepared in front of patrons, as well as individual tables and chairs. A sushi teishoku set meal is served at lunch only, for ¥3,300 ($23.55); obento lunch boxes are ¥4,900 ($35). Evenings are more expensive, with shabu-shabu starting at ¥7,500 ($53.55) and tempura set courses and kaiseki starting at ¥11,000 ($78). You can also order sushi or tempura à la carte, or order a platter of assorted sashimi for ¥3,000 ($21.40).

KAEN ⑭²⁾, 3rd floor of Steak Ron Building, 1-10-2 Sonnezaki-shinchi. Tel. 344-2929.
   Cuisine: FRENCH KAISEKI. **Reservations:** Essential. **Directions:** A 2-minute walk from Yotsubashi Subway Station, or a 10-minute walk south of Osaka Station and Dai Ni Building.
$ **Prices:** Set-dinner courses ¥10,000–¥16,500 ($71.40–$117.85). AE, DC, JCB, MC, V.
   Open: Lunch Mon–Sat 11:30am–2pm; dinner Mon–Sat 5–9pm (last order).
   One of the most popular new forms of cuisine to hit the Japanese culinary scene in recent years is French food presented in the Japanese kaiseki manner. The food is French, but each course is served separately using Japanese plates and dishes, and guests use chopsticks instead of forks. Each plate is chosen to enhance the food that's on it, according to color, texture, and the seasons. This refined, modern restaurant serves only set meals, which are changed twice a month. Highly recommended.

GRAND SKY RESTAURANT, 14th floor of Osaka Grand Hotel, 2-3-18 Nakanoshima. Tel. 202-1212.
  Cuisine: CONTINENTAL BUFFETS. **Station:** Higobashi, a 5-minute walk away.
  $ Prices: Lunch buffet ¥2,500 ($17.85); dinner buffet ¥5,500 ($39.30). AE, DC, JCB, MC, V.
  Open: Lunch Mon–Sat 11:30am–2pm, dinner daily 5–9:30pm. **Closed:** Lunch on national hols.

Buffets are a rarity in Japan, especially for lunch and dinner, so if you have a big appetite or want to take advantage of a variety of dishes, head to this restaurant with a view of Osaka. Tablecloths and flowers adorn each table, and the hearty buffet spreads include everything from cold cuts and salads to at least a half dozen selections in main courses and desserts.

VICTORIA STATION, second basement of Hilton Plaza, next to Hilton Hotel, 1-8-8 Umeda. Tel. 347-7470.
  Cuisine: AMERICAN. **Directions:** A 1-minute walk from Osaka Station.
  $ Prices: Set-dinner courses ¥2,600–¥5,000 ($18.55–$35.70); set lunches ¥1,400–¥2,000 ($10–$14.30). AE, DC, JCB, MC, V.
  Open: Daily 11am–11pm.

If you're looking for casual, inexpensive dining, Victoria Station serves a mean hamburger plus a trip to the salad bar for ¥1,300 ($9.30) daily until 5pm. If you're ecstatic about finding a salad bar (they're still fairly rare in Japan) and want that as your sole meal, you can have that for only ¥1,100 ($7.85) for lunch. Other lunch selections include teriyaki beefsteak, sirloin steak, broiled chicken, crab quiche, and swordfish, available with or without the salad bar. The dinner menu includes steaks, roast prime rib, teriyaki chicken, and lobster. Set-dinner courses include a trip to the salad bar, soup, and more.

AB PUB RESTAURANT, 19th floor of Osaka Terminal Hotel, 3-1-1 Umeda, Tel. 344-1234.
  Cuisine: INTERNATIONAL. **Directions:** Above Osaka Station.
  $ Prices: Lunch smörgåsbord ¥1,600 ($11.40). AE, DC, JCB, MC, V.
  Open: Lunch daily 11am–2pm.

This informal locale is actually a bar, but it also offers a very reasonably priced lunch buffet daily. Dishes are mainly casseroles and easy-to-prepare food, including noodle and rice dishes, and a salad bar, soups, and desserts. The food is fairly mediocre, but what it lacks in imagination is made up for by the price, the unlimited quantity afforded by a smörgåsbord, its convenient location, and its great view of Osaka. It's especially popular with housewives and female office workers, so get here by 11:30am if you don't want to wait for a table.

OKONOMIYAKI MADONNA, second basement of Hilton Plaza next to Hilton Hotel, 1-8-8 Umeda. Tel. 347-7371.
  Cuisine: OKONOMIYAKI. **Directions:** A 2-minute walk from Osaka Station.
  $ Prices: ¥1,000–¥1,600 ($7.15–$11.40). AE, DC, JCB, MC, V.
  Open: Daily 11am–11pm.

At this modern and with-it okonomiyaki restaurant served by a young and friendly staff, ingredients change with the seasons but may include pork, beef, squid, octopus, shrimp, potato, mushroom, or oyster. Fried noodles are also available. Madonna is located across from Victoria Station, described earlier in this chapter, in the basement of Hilton Plaza beside the Hilton Hotel. It has an English menu, and diners sit around a counter watching their food being prepared. Very casual.

BOTEJYU, second basement of Hankyu Sanbangai Building. Tel. 374-2254.
  Cuisine: OKONOMIYAKI. **Directions:** A 2-minute walk from east exit of Osaka Station.
  $ Prices: ¥700–¥1,300 ($5–$9.30). No credit cards.
  Open: Daily 10am–10pm. **Closed:** Third Wed of month.

One of the best-known okonomiyaki chain restaurants, this informal eatery is located in the second basement of the Sanbangai Building, in a restaurant mall called Gourmet Museum (if you can find a map here, Botejyu is number 16). Its window display shows okonomiyaki filled with pork and egg, squid, shrimp, noodles, and pork, and many other ingredients in various combinations. I tried the *omu soba*, a type of omelet filled with cabbage, wheat noodles, and pork and smothered in ketchup and mayonnaise. Cooking is done on a hot griddle right in front of you, and dishes are served on sheets of aluminum foil.

IN CHUO-KU

Dotonbori Street, a narrow pedestrian lane flanking the south bank of the Dotonbori River, is lined with restaurants and drinking establishments.

MOTI, 3rd floor of Dohton Biru Building, 1-6-15 Dotonbori. Tel. 221-6878.
  Cuisine: INDIAN. **Station:** Namba, a 3-minute walk away.
$ Prices: Main dishes: ¥1,300–¥2,000 ($9.30–$14.30); set meals ¥2,500–¥5,500 ($17.85–$39.30). AE, DC, JCB, V.
  Open: Daily noon–10pm.
This small, comfortable, and casual restaurant with an Indian décor offers various meat and vegetable curries, as well as tandoori. Its Indian chefs bake nan and prepare food behind a plate-glass window.

EBI DORAKU ⑭³, 1-6-2 Dotonbori. Tel. 211-1633.
  Cuisine: SHRIMP. **Directions:** A 4-minute walk from Namba Station.
$ Prices: ¥1,100–¥6,800 ($7.85–$48.55). AE, DC, JCB, MC, V.
  Open: Daily 11am–11pm.
Ebi is the Japanese word for shrimp, and this restaurant has a big wriggling shrimp on its façade to advertise that the crustacean is its specialty, prepared in a number of different ways. There's no English menu here, so make your selections from the plastic-food display case. Dishes include *ebi-shi* (a shrimp sukiyaki), ebi tempura, fried shrimp, ebi gratin, and ebi sushi. If you feel like overdosing, the kaiseki ebi teishoku for ¥3,800 ($27.15) features nine different kinds of shrimp dishes. If you're lucky, you'll get a table overlooking the canal and its fountains.

KANI DORAKU ⑭⁴, 1-6-18 Dotonbori. Tel. 211-8975.
  Cuisine: CRAB. **Station:** Namba, a 3-minute walk away.
$ Prices: Crab dishes ¥1,100–¥2,500 ($7.85–$17.85); crab set meals ¥5,000–¥6,500 ($35.70–$46.40). AE, DC, JCB, MC, V.
  Open: Daily 11am–11pm.
Under the same management as Ebi Doraku but specializing in *kani* (crab), this restaurant would be difficult to miss because of the huge model crab on its façade (it moves its legs and claws). The restaurant is part of a chain originating in Osaka a couple of decades ago, with more than 55 stores now spread throughout Japan. Its dishes range from crab-suki and crab-chiri (a kind of crab sukiyaki) for ¥4,900 ($35) and fried crab dishes for ¥2,700 ($19.30), to crab croquette, roasted crab with salt, crab salad, crab sushi, and boiled king crab. Located on Dotonbori right beside the bridge over the canal, the restaurant occupies several floors, with some tables offering a view of the water.

KUIDAORE ⑭⁵, 1-8-25 Dotonbori. Tel. 211-5300.
  Cuisine: VARIED JAPANESE. **Station:** Namba, a 3-minute walk away.
$ Prices: Dishes ¥700–¥1,300 ($5–$9.30); set courses ¥2,400–¥3,500 ($17.15–$25). AE, JCB, MC, V.
  Open: Daily 11am–10:30pm; 2nd-floor pub daily 4–11pm.
One of the best-known restaurants on Dotonbori, this place is famous for its clown model outside the front door, which has been beating a drum and wiggling its eyebrows ever since the place first opened in 1949. There's an extensive plastic-food display case by the front door, which is one good indication of the wide variety of food this restaurant serves, including tempura, sashimi, charcoal-broiled beef, shabu-shabu, udon, eel, sukiyaki, yakitori, noodles, and even Western food. Altogeth-

er, there are four floors of dining, with prices increasing the higher up you go. On the ground floor is a modern family-style dining area, where you can order such things as spaghetti, sushi, tempura, and noodles, with prices under ¥1,400 ($10). On the second floor is a nomi-ya, or pub, where you can order a beer, yakitori, and snacks. The fourth floor is for nabe (one-pot stews), including shabu-shabu starting at ¥4,200 ($30), and the fifth floor is for set courses.

BOTEJYU, 2nd floor of Dohton Biru Building, 1-6-15 Dontonbori. Tel. 211-3641.
  Cuisine: OKONOMIYAKI. **Station:** Namba, a 3-minute walk away.
$ Prices: ¥700–¥1,300 ($5–$9.30). No credit cards.
  Open: Daily noon–10:30pm.
Another okonomiyaki restaurant, this one is located on Dotonbori near the bridge that crosses the canal. Its display case shows fried noodles, okonomiyaki with noodles, and okonomiyaki with ham and noodles.

NEAR THE CASTLE

TRADER VIC'S, New Otani Hotel, 1-4 Shiromi. Tel. 941-1111.
  Cuisine: INTERNATIONAL. **Station:** Osakajo-koen, a 3-minute walk away.
$ Prices: Appetizers ¥1,500–¥2,900 ($10.70–$20.70); main dishes ¥3,500–¥6,500 ($25–$46.40); set lunch ¥2,000 ($14.30). AE, DC, JCB, MC, V.
  Open: Mon–Sat noon–midnight; Sun and hols 11:30am–midnight.
This is a great choice for lunch if you're sightseeing at Osaka Castle. Decorated in Polynesian style typical of Trader Vic's restaurants around the world, it offers dining with a view of the castle, the park, and the river. There's a luncheon special served Monday through Saturday until 2:45pm, as well as a lunch menu that includes hamburgers, club sandwiches, pasta, chicken, lamb curry, and other international selections. Dinners offer a wider selection, including salads, a good selection of vegetable side dishes, curries, steaks, seafood, and Chinese dishes. If you feel like a splurge, come for the Sunday champagne brunch, served from 11:30am to 2:45pm and costing ¥4,400 ($31.40).

SPECIALTY DINING

Another choice for dining close to Osaka Castle is the **Twin 21 Buildings,** located near the New Otani Hotel in Osaka's newly developed business park. Identical structures standing side by side, the Twin 21 Buildings are joined by what is called Gallery Twin 21, offering three floors of dining in all categories. You'll find a Dunkin' Donuts, McDonald's, and restaurants serving sandwiches, curry rice, Italian food, steaks, ramen noodles, okonomiyaki, sushi, tempura, and Chinese food. Daily hours are 11am to 10pm; closed the first and third Thursdays of the month.

If you want inexpensive dining with a view, there are many restaurants on the top four floors of the **Hankyu Grand Building** (also called 32 Bangai), located just a minute's walk east of Osaka Station. On the 28th floor, for example, there are Japanese restaurants serving everything from shabu-shabu and eel to tonkatsu (pork cutlet), kaiseki, tempura, and sashimi. On the 29th floor you'll find a mixture of Japanese and Western restaurants, while the 30th and 31st floors serve Western food only. Altogether, there are more than 30 choices in eating places, all of which have plastic-food displays, so ordering is no problem. Prices are generally low, with most meals costing about ¥1,000 ($7.15) to ¥2,000 ($14.30). Daily hours for most of the restaurants on the 28th floor are 11am to 8:45pm, but some restaurants on other floors remain open until 11pm.

Den Den Town is Osaka's electronics shopping region, similar to Tokyo's Akihabara (*Den* is short for "electric"). There are more than 150 shops here dealing in electrical and electronic equipment, from rice cookers to cassette players and personal computers. Most stores here are open daily from 10am to 7pm. The nearest subway station is either Nipponbashi or Ebisucho.

If you're in the market for dolls or toys, you'll want to visit **Matsuyamachi Street,** located near Tanimachi 6-chome and Nagahoribashi stations. This street is lined with wholesale and retail outlets selling everything from elaborate Japanese dolls to yo-yos. Shops here are open from 9:30am to 5:30pm; some shops are closed different days of the week, so you're sure to find some always open.

SHOPPING

Osaka must rank as one of the world's leading cities in underground shopping arcades. The **Umeda Chika Center** is a huge subterranean shopping mall that connects Osaka and Umeda stations to a number of buildings, including the Hanshin and Hankyu department stores, Hankyu Sanbangai, and the Hankyu Grand Building. It caters primarily to local workers and is so massive and complicated that you'll probably get lost in the maze. Other shopping areas include the underground mall at **Namba** and an aboveground covered shopping street near Shinsaibashi subway station. Paralleling Midosuji Dori Avenue to the east, it runs south all the way past Dotonbori and on to Namba.

EVENING ENTERTAINMENT

Osaka's liveliest—and most economical—nightlife district radiates from a narrow pedestrian lane called **Dotonbori,** which flanks the south bank of the Dotonbori River. About a 3-minute walk from Namba Station or less than a 10-minute walk from Shinsaibashi Station, it's lined with restaurants and drinking establishments.

THE CLUB & MUSIC SCENE

THE JET STREAM, 32nd floor of Nikko Hotel, 1-3-3 Nishishinsaibashi. Tel. 244-1111.
This sophisticated nightclub, located in the Nikko Hotel on Midosuji Dori Avenue, is the best place to begin an evening of carousing. More than 360 feet high, the Nikko Hotel is the tallest building in the area, which means that the Jet Stream provides a dynamite view of the city, perfect for watching the sun go down and the lights of the city come on. Romantic, with soft candlelight, it offers Twilight Dinners every day from 5 to 7pm for just ¥2,700 ($19.30) and ¥3,800 ($27.15), including a choice of main dish, salad, bread, and coffee. From 7:30 to 11pm, Jet Stream features live jazz and popular music, for which it levies an admission charge. Food is also available at this time, with most main dishes averaging between ¥2,200 and ¥6,500 ($15.70 and $46.40) for such items as fried chicken, steak teriyaki, fish and scallops au gratin with mushroom sauce. Open: Daily 5pm–midnight.
    Admission: Sun–Wed ¥1,000 ($7.15); Fri–Sat ¥4,000–¥5,500 ($28.55–$39.30), depending on visiting band and event. **Prices:** Beer ¥850 ($6.05), cocktails ¥1,500 ($10.70).

MAHARAJA, 5th floor of Diamond Building, 1-5-12 Shinsaibashisuji. Tel. 213-7090.
    At the more frenzied end of the scale is Maharaja, serving the needs of disco maniacs. The music is loud, and there are lots of mirrors so you can watch yourself dance. Maharaja is located on the first street paralleling Dotonbori River to the north, identified by a big sign that says SOEMON-CHO. Open: Daily 7pm–midnight.
    Admission: ¥5,000 ($39.30) males; ¥4,500 ($32.15) females. Sat and eve before a hol, ¥500 ($3.55) extra for males. Entrance fee includes 10 tickets for drinks. **Prices:** Drinks, 2 tickets each.

THE BAR SCENE

SOLAR BEER GARDEN, Holiday Inn Nankai, 2-5-15 Shinsaibashisuji, Chuo-ku. Tel. 06/213-8281.
    For outdoor drinking in the summer, head for the Holiday Inn on Midosuji Dori

(not far from Dotonbori), where you'll find a beer garden on its third-floor patio. A snack menu includes green salad, french fries, cheese and crackers, smoked salmon, mixed nuts, and sausages. Draft beer costs ¥750 ($5.35). Open: June–Aug, daily 5–9pm.

IROHANIHOHETO, basement of Awajiya Building, 2-4-5 Shinsaibashi-suji. Tel. 213-1683.

This inexpensive yakitori-ya, billing itself as an "Antique Pub" and decorated with traditional memorabilia, serves beer and a wide assortment of snacks, including yakitori, sashimi, salads, and vegetables, with most items costing less than ¥600 ($4.30). Beer costs ¥450 ($3.20). Part of a chain of drinking establishments, it's popular with younger Japanese and is located on the first street paralleling the Dontonbori River to the north. Open: Weekday 5:30pm–3:30am (5am Fri–Sat).

KIRIN CITY, Kirin Plaza Osaka, 2-46-1 Shinsaibashisuji. Tel. 212-6572.

Owned by the Kirin beer company, Kirin Plaza Osaka is a futuristic black, chrome, and glass building rising up from the banks of the Dotonbori River in the heart of the nightlife district. On the second floor is Kirin City, one of a chain of modern beer halls seemingly found in every hamlet of the country. On the ground floor is a café, with a few tables on a terrace with a view of the Dotonbori River. Kirin beer costs ¥450 ($3.20); coffee, ¥270 ($1.90). Open: Daily noon–11pm.

NEWZ BAR, 2-6 Shinsaibashisuji. Tel. 212-6063.

A casual, trendy café/bar, Newz Bar is located right on Midosuji Dori Avenue, just north of the Holiday Inn (on the same side of the street), in a building called intriguingly enough Gourmet Tower Across—but across from what remains a mystery. Fashionable, with bare white walls, a marbled floor from Italy, and outdoor sidewalk tables, it's a good place from which to observe the world go stumbling by. Its food, mostly in the ¥1,000 to ¥1,500 ($7.15 to $10.70) price range, includes spaghetti, steaks, salmon steak, and snacks. There is a daily table charge of ¥200 ($1.40) from 6 to 10pm; beer and wine cost ¥550 ($3.90). Open: Mon–Thurs 11am to 5am (6am Fri–Sat, 11pm Sun).

PIG AND WHISTLE, 2nd floor of Is Building, 2-1-32 Shinsaibashisuji. Tel. 213-6911.

If all you want to do is drink, this is probably the best-known expatriate bar in Osaka. It's located a few blocks north of Dotonbori (nearest station: Shinsaibashi). However, because there aren't that many foreigners living in the city, the majority of customers here are Japanese. Munchies include pizza and fish and chips, and there's a dart board for entertainment. A large draft beer is ¥700 ($5). Open: daily 4pm–midnight (1am on weekends).

STUDEBAKER'S, 2-4-12 Nakazakinishi. Tel. 372-1950.

If you happen to be much farther north, in the vicinity of Osaka Station, this is an enthusiastic re-creation of an American 1950s diner, complete with lots of chrome; red, white, and blue; and booths and counters. A member of a chain with similar diners in Houston and Dallas, it features a disc jockey who plays golden oldies. The minimum age for admittance is 20. The place offers a lunch buffet daily from 11:30am to 2pm, and this costs ¥950 ($6.80) Monday through Friday and ¥1,400 ($10) on Saturday, Sunday, and holidays. In the evenings, an all-you-can-eat buffet is available until 8pm, included in the price of admittance. Studebaker's is located about an 8-minute walk east of Osaka Station, past Hankyu department store and Shinmidosuji Dori Avenue. Open: Daily 11:30am–midnight.

Admission: After 5:30pm Sun–Thurs ¥3,300 ($23.55). Fri–Sat ¥3,800 ($27.15). Charge includes an all-you-can-eat buffet until 8pm and ¥1,500 ($10.70) worth of tickets good for drinks.

WINE BAR, 3rd floor of Awajiya Building, 2-4-5 Shinsaibashisuji. Tel. 211-7736.

Part of a chain that has more than 15 locations in Japan, the Wine Bar serves wine by the glass and is popular with young Japanese. If you get a window seat, you'll have a view of the river and bridge. It's located on the first street paralleling the Dotonbori

River to the north, in the same building as Irohanihoheto (described above). Along with wines from France, Germany, and California, it also offers such dishes as chicken, spareribs, salads, gratin, and snacks. There is a table charge of ¥500 ($3.55); wine costs ¥400–¥650 ($2.85–$4.65). Open: Daily 5pm–1am.

5. KOBE

365 miles W of Tokyo; 47 miles W of Kyoto; 19 miles W of Osaka

GETTING THERE By Train Shinkansen bullet train takes 3½ hours from Tokyo, 33 minutes from Kyoto, and 15 minutes from Osaka. All Shinkansen trains arrive at Shin-Kobe Station, about a mile northwest of Sannomiya Station, which is considered the heart of the city. Shin-Kobe Station is linked to Sannomiya Station via a 3-minute subway ride (or a 20-minute walk). If you're arriving from nearby Osaka, Himeji, or Okayama, however, it's easiest to take a local commuter train that stops directly at Sannomiya Station. Incidentally, there are several terminals in Sannomiya, including stations for Japan Railways (JR), Hankyu, and Hanshin. There are also buses from Sannomiya bound for Osaka International Airport, leaving approximately every 20 minutes. The trip takes 40 minutes and costs ¥700 ($5).

By Bus Buses depart from Tokyo Station's Yaesu south exit for Kobe every night (trip time: 8 hours, 20 minutes).

ESSENTIAL INFORMATION The **area code** for Kobe, lying in Hyogo Prefecture, is 078.

There are **tourist information offices** in both Shin-Kobe Station (open 10am to 6pm) and Sannomiya Station (open 9am to 6pm), where you can pick up a map and ask for directions to your hotel. (The tourist office at Sannomiya Station is on the second floor of the Kobe Kotsu Center and is rather difficult to find; if you get lost, the telephone number is 078/392-0020.) Current information on Kobe's sights, festivals, and attractions appears in a monthly magazine called *Kansai Time Out,* which you can pick up at bookstores, restaurants, and tourist-oriented locations for ¥300 ($2.15).

ORIENTATION & GETTING AROUND Squeezed in between hills rising in the north and the shores of the Seto Inland Sea in the south, Kobe stretches some 18 miles along the coastline, but in many places it is less than 2 miles wide. It is made up of many wards (ku), such as Nada-ku, Chuo-ku, and Hyogo-ku. The heart of the city lies around the Sannomiya and Motomachi stations in the Chuo-ku ward. It's here that you'll find the city's nightlife, its port, its restaurants and shopping district, and most of its hotels. Many of the major streets here have names with signs posted in English.

Because the city is not very wide, you can **walk** to most points north and south of Sannomiya Station. South of Sannomiya Station are the Sannomiya Center Gai covered-arcade shopping street and a flower-lined road leading straight south, toward the port—called, appropriately enough, Flower Road. North of Sannomiya Station are bars and restaurants clustered around narrow streets like Higashimon Street and Kitano-Zaka. About a 10-minute walk west of Sannomiya Station is Motomachi Station, south of which lies Chinatown.

Blessed with the calm waters of the Seto Inland Sea, Kobe has served Japan as an important port town for centuries. Even today its port is the heart of the city, its raison d'être, and the people of Kobe are proud of their city, content with where they are. One of the first ports to begin accepting foreign traders in 1868, following Japan's two centuries of isolation, this vibrant city of 1.5 million inhabitants is quite cosmopolitan, with 45,000 foreigners living here. There are a number of fine restaurants serving Western, Japanese, Chinese, Korean, and Indian food, not to mention the many steakhouses offering the famous Kobe beef. Equally famous is Kobe's wonderful nightlife, crammed into a small, navigable, and rather intimate quarter of neon lights, cozy bars, brawling pubs, and sophisticated nightclubs. As one resident of Kobe told me, "We don't have a lot of tourist sights in Kobe, so we make up for it in nightlife."

WHAT TO SEE & DO

SEEING THE PORT

I find Kobe's port fascinating. Unlike many harbor cities where the port is located far from the center of town, Kobe's is right there, demanding attention and getting it. For a bird's-eye view of the whole operation, go to the **Port Tower** at Naka Tottei Pier. Opened in 1963, the tower is designed to resemble a Japanese drum, a cylindrical shape with the middle squeezed together. Almost 600 feet tall, its glass-enclosed five-story observatory can be reached by two elevators. It's open daily from 10am to 9pm.

Right beside the Port Tower is the newly developed **Meriken Park,** along with the **Kobe Maritime Museum,** which has a roof shaped like a ship. Open Tuesday through Sunday from 10am to 5pm, the museum's exhibits recount the history of Kobe's port, as well as ports and harbors around the world. At the push of a button, models of port activities spring to life, along with a spoken commentary in English. A combination ticket for both the Port Tower and the Maritime Museum is ¥700 ($5). If you buy the tickets separately, they're ¥500 ($3.55) each. The closest station is Motomachi.

Next to Port Tower are boats offering **cruises of the harbor.** Costing ¥1,030 ($7.35), the trip lasts 50 minutes and takes you to Kawasaki and Mitsubishi shipyards, the container yard, Port Terminal, and Port Island. Although the commentary is in Japanese only, it's well worth it. Departures are every hour on the hour from 10am to 4pm on weekdays and Saturday, and every 30 minutes on Sunday and holidays. For more information, call 391-8633.

Another interesting way to see the harbor is by taking the computer-controlled **Portliner monorail** from Sannomiya Station out to **Port Island,** an artificial island complete with amusement park, luxury hotel, high-rise condominiums, exhibition grounds, and convention halls. This is a great ride even if you don't get off the monorail. It takes about a half hour to make the whole loop around the island, passing bridges, ships, tankers, tugboats, barges, and stacked containers along the way. If you're up to an outing, get off at Shimin Hiroba Station and go to the Portopia Hotel for a meal or a cup of coffee. It's quite an interesting hotel, with a dramatic lobby. From there you can walk to the amusement park. The monorail costs ¥210 ($1.50) no matter how far you go, and announcements are in English.

OTHER SIGHTS IN TOWN

If you want to learn more about the history of Kobe, visit the **Kobe City Museum (Kobe Shiritsu Hakubutsukan)** (tel. 391-0035), next to the Oriental Hotel, about a 10-minute walk south of Sannomiya Station. Open Tuesday through Sunday from 10am to 5pm, it displays the history and folklore of Kobe, including 16th- and 17th-century Japanese paintings and art objects showing decidedly European influences. Admission here is ¥200 ($1.40). Chinese bronzes, ceramics, and lacquerware are displayed at the **Hakutsuru Art Museum** (tel. 851-6001), a 15-minute walk from Mikage Station on the Hankyu Line, while the **Hyogo Prefecture Ceramic Museum,** with a collection of Japanese ceramics, is just a 3-minute walk from Motomachi Station.

Another point of interest are some **wooden houses in Kitano-cho,** north of Sannomiya Station, where foreigners used to live after Kobe became an international port. Although it may not hold much interest for foreigners who have come to see Japan, Kitano-cho is very popular with the Japanese, particularly young girls, who flock here in droves. There are a number of houses (most unauthentic) that have opened in the past couple of years and are based on a particular national theme—there are, for example, the Holland House, the Persian House, the American House, and the Meiji-kan (German), where costumes are rented out for picture-taking sessions. Seeing a young Japanese girl decked out in a turn-of-the-century long dress, apron, and blonde wig may be reason enough for making the trip here. Entrance fees, however, are quite high, so it's best just to walk around the steep and narrow roads and take a quick spin through the Kazamidori-no-ie (Weathervane House), built in 1909 by a German trader and open to the public for free.

NEARBY ATTRACTIONS

You might also want to travel to **Sakagura,** where you can visit the **Sawanotsuru Collection Hall** (tel. 822-6333), once a sake cellar and now a museum displaying tools used in sake brewing during the Edo Period. This hall, open free to the public, is close to Oishi Station on the Hanshin Line. It's open Thursday through Tuesday from 10am to 4pm.

Farther away, **Mt. Rokkosan** is a resort high among the peaks, with hiking, golfing, eating, and relaxation as the major forms of entertainment. Serving mainly as an escape for residents of Osaka and Kobe, it is worth a day's outing if you're here for an extended length of time. More convenient for a quick getaway are the hills directly behind Shin-Kobe Station, with hiking trails through woods and streams. You can reach Nunobiki Falls (called Nunobiki-no-taki in Japanese) in less than an hour.

WHERE TO STAY

Most of Kobe's tourist and business hotels radiate north and south of Sannomiya Station within easy reach of Kobe's many restaurants and bars.

EXPENSIVE

KOBE PORTOPIA HOTEL, 6-10-2 Minatojima, Nakamachi, Chuo-ku, Kobe 650. Tel. 078/302-1111. Fax 078/302-6877. 778 rms A/C MINIBAR TV TEL **Directions:** 15-minute taxi ride from Shin-Kobe Station, or a 10-minute ride from Sannomiya Station via Portliner monorail.

$ Rates: ¥10,500–¥15,500 ($75–$111) single; ¥22,000–¥29,000 ($157–$207) twin; ¥24,000–¥30,000 ($171–$215) double. Japanese-style rooms: ¥40,000 ($285) double. AE, DC, JCB, MC, V.

Kobe's most famous and ritziest hotel, the Kobe Portopia Hotel opened in 1981 and is located on Port Island. The most dramatic way to arrive is via monorail—sleek, tall, and white, this first-class hotel looks like some futuristic ship slicing through the landscape. Inside, it flaunts space and brightness, with waterfalls, fountains, lots of brass, marble, and plants. Its rooms, whose large windows face either the sea or Kobe city (some even have a balcony), are elegantly designed with all the amenities and plushness you'd expect from a first-rate hotel, including bilingual cable TV with CNN satellite newscasts.

Dining/Entertainment: There are 15 restaurants, lounges, and coffee shops, including the Alain Chapel on the 31st floor, which serves the creations of French chef Alain Chapel, and Plein d'Etoiles, a sophisticated lounge with views of the harbor.

Services: Free newspaper, same-day laundry service.

Facilities: 27 name-brand shops like Nina Ricci and Givenchy, indoor and outdoor swimming pools, gym, tennis courts, business center.

HOTEL OKURA KOBE, 2-1 Hatoba-cho, Chuo-ku, Kobe 650. Tel. 078/ 333-0111. Fax 078/333-6673. 472 rms. A/C MINIBAR TV TEL **Station:** Motomachi, about a 10-minute walk south.

$ Rates: ¥17,500–¥22,000 ($125–$157) single; ¥24,000–¥34,000 ($171– $243) double/twin. AE, DC, JCB, MC, V.

This magestic 35-story hotel has a grand location right beside Meriken Park and the Port Tower, within easy walking distance of the shopping arcades near Motomachi and Sannomiya stations. Each elegantly appointed room has all the comforts of a first-class hotel, including bilingual cable TV with CNN broadcasts, with the best views afforded by those accommodations that face the harbor.

Dining/Entertainment: There are eight restaurants and bars, with food ranging from French haute cuisine to Japanese and Chinese.

Services: Free newspaper, same-day laundry service.

Facilities: Health club (fee charge) with gym, indoor and outdoor swimming pools, sauna and tennis courts; business center; beauty salon; travel agent.

ORIENTAL HOTEL, 25 Kyomachi St., Chuo-ku, Kobe 650. Tel. 078/331-8111. Fax 078/391-8708. 190 rms. A/C MINIBAR TV TEL **Directions:** A 5-minute taxi ride or a 15-minute walk south of Sannomiya Station.
$ Rates: ¥11,000–¥15,500 ($78–$111) single; ¥22,000–¥27,000 ($157–$193) double/twin. AE, DC, JCB, MC, V.

A handsome brick building, this is one of Kobe's older hotels which has aged well. Its guest rooms are small but comfortable and pleasant, and come with minibar, clock, and radio, among other amenities.

Dining/Entertainment: There are seven restaurants, serving everything from Italian to Chinese to French to kaiseki cuisine.

Services: Free newspaper, same-day laundry service.

SHINKOBE ORIENTAL HOTEL, 1-chome Kitano-cho, Chuo-ku, Kobe 650. Tel. 078/291-1121. Fax 078/291-1154. 600 rms. A/C MINIBAR TV TEL **Directions:** A 1-minute walk from Shin-Kobe Station.
$ Rates: ¥13,000–¥22,000 ($80–$148) single; ¥24,000–¥34,000 ($117–$243) double; ¥24,000–¥39,000 ($171–$278) twin. AE, DC, JCB, MC, V.

⭐ "Grand," "stunning," and "numbing" might describe one of Kobe's newest deluxe hotels. Soaring like a steeple on a hill above the city right next to Shin-Kobe Station, this hotel is huge, with a 10-story atrium and facilities so staggering in scope it would be easy never to leave the premises. You can swim, sweat it out in the gym, go out for dinner, shop until 10pm, and then drink until 4am. This hotel is so popular that it has been almost solidly booked every Saturday night since it opened in 1988. And since it's located next to the Shinkansen station, you can be in Osaka in 15 minutes or Kyoto in 34.

As for the hotel itself, it is decorated with finesse in art deco style, with restaurants designed to complement the food served. The hotel proper starts on the fourth floor, with well-appointed rooms offering great views of the city. They're equipped with bilingual cable TV complete with CNN newscasts and remote control, radio, minibar, and hot-water pot. Incidentally, the hotel complex is linked to Shin-Kobe Station via a covered walkway; Kobe's one subway line begins right in the basement with Shin-Kobe Station.

Dining/Entertainment: There are 10 restaurants and bars—and a whole "city" underneath, with almost 200 additional shops and restaurants.

Services: Free newspaper, same-day laundry service.

Facilities: Indoor pool, gym, and sauna (fee: ¥5,000 or $35.70), shopping arcade, beauty salon, barbershop.

MODERATE

All these hotels offer rooms with private bathroom.

GREEN HILL HOTEL 1, 2-5-16 Kano-cho, Chuo-ku, Kobe 650. Tel. 078/222-1221. 102 rms. A/C TV TEL **Directions:** Between Sannomiya and Shin-Kobe stations, about a 10-minute walk from each.
$ Rates: ¥7,000 ($50) single; ¥13,000 ($93) double/twin. AE, JCB, MC, V.

There's not a lot you can say about the Green Hill Hotels 1 and 2 except that they are both located between Sannomiya and Shin-Kobe stations, and are your typical clean and sparsely furnished business hotels. Green Hill Hotel 1 is slightly older and cheaper and has two restaurants serving Western and Japanese food.

GREEN HILL HOTEL 2, 2-8-3 Kano-cho, Chuo-ku 650. Tel. 078/222-0909. Fax 078/222-1139. 158 rms. A/C MINIBAR TV TEL **Directions:** Between Sannomiya and Shin-Kobe stations, about a 10-minute walk from each.
$ Rates: ¥8,000 ($57) single; ¥15,500 ($111) twin. AE, JCB, MC, V.

This hotel, slightly more upscale than its sister hotel (above), sports modern rooms, which feature shoji screens, minibar, and TV with pay video. It even has a chapel and Japanese wedding room in case you want to tie the knot while staying here (weddings constitute sometimes as much as 25% of a Japanese hotel's profit). It has one Western restaurant and a lounge, and room service is available until 10pm.

HANA HOTEL, 4-2-7 Nunobiki-cho, Chuo-ku, Kobe 651. Tel. 078/221-1087. Fax 078/221-1785. 47 rms. A/C MINIBAR TV TEL **Directions:** A 2-minute walk north of JR Sannomiya Station.

$ Rates (including tax and service): ¥7,700 ($55) single; ¥13,000 ($93) double; ¥14,800 ($106) twin. AE, JCB, V.

Opened in 1986, the Hana Hotel is a cheerful, airy business hotel, with an accommodating and courteous staff. Hana means flower in Japanese, and that's the motif here, on the wallpaper, the furniture, and everywhere the hotel logo is displayed. A small, personable business hotel with only 6 rooms on each floor, it has accommodations that are nicely furnished with minibar, radio, TV with pay video, alarm clock, hairdryer, and windows that open. The front desk is on the second floor, and there's a teppanyaki restaurant serving Kobe beef, a coffee shop, and a bar.

KITAGAMI HOTEL (149), 3-2-3 Kano-cho, Chuo-ku, Kobe 650. Tel. 078/391-8781. 42 rms. A/C MINIBAR TV TEL **Directions:** Less than a 5-minute walk north of Sannomiya Station.

$ Rates (including tax and service): ¥7,300–¥8,000 ($52–$57) single; ¥13,000–¥16,500 ($93–$118) twin; ¥16,500–¥19,800 ($118–$141) triple. Western-style breakfast ¥900 ($6.40) extra. AE, JCB, V.

Remodeled in 1985, this hotel started out primarily as a business hotel but is trying to change its image to attract tourists. Most of the rooms are twins, and they are simple but bright, with large windows.

KOBE UNION HOTEL, 2-1-9 Nunobiki-cho, Chuo-ku, Kobe 651. Tel. 078/222-6500. Fax 078/242-0220. 167 rms. A/C MINIBAR TV TEL **Directions:** A 10-minute walk from Sannomiya or Shin-Kobe stations.

$ Rates: ¥6,900–¥7,400 ($49–$53) single; ¥12,000–¥12,500 ($86–$89) double/twin. AE, JCB, V.

Kobe Union Hotel, located about halfway between Sannomiya and Shin-Kobe stations, is next to Lawson Food Store, a 24-hour convenience store. They're used to foreigners here and have one Western restaurant. Rooms are small and simple but pleasant with large double-pane windows that open, TV with video, hairdryer, minibar, and hot-water pot. Check-in is at 2:30pm.

KOBE WASHINGTON HOTEL, 2-11-5 Shimoyamatedori, Chuo-ku, Kobe 650. Tel. 078/331-6111. Fax 078/331-6651. 218 rms. A/C MINIBAR TV TEL **Directions:** A 7-minute walk northwest of Sannomiya Station, on Ikuta Shinmichi St.

$ Rates: ¥8,400 ($60) single; ¥15,900 ($113) double/twin. AE, DC, JCB, MC, V.

As part of a nationwide business hotel chain, the Kobe Washington Hotel is a reliable and high-quality place to stay. The rooms are tiny but nicely decorated with modern furniture and come with minibar, TV with pay video (bilingual in twins and doubles), clock, and piped-in music. Panels on the windows slide shut for complete darkness. Three restaurants serve Japanese and Western food, including shabu-shabu; its ninth-floor restaurant/bar is a steakhouse with views of the city.

SANNOMIYA TERMINAL HOTEL, Kumoi-Dori 8-chome, Chuo-ku, Kobe 651. Tel. 078/291-0001. Fax 078/291-0020. 190 rms. A/C TV TEL **Directions:** Located above JR Sannomiya Station.

$ Rates: ¥8,800–¥12,000 ($57–$86) single; ¥16,700 ($119) double; ¥17,000–¥19,000 ($121–$136) twin. AE, DC, JCB, MC, V.

You can't get any closer to Sannomiya Station than this hotel, located practically on top of the JR Sannomiya Station. This very convenient and upper-scale business hotel has check-in at 1pm instead of 3pm, as with most business hotels. Rooms are fairly large and spotlessly clean, and feature TV with CNN cable and pay video, a radio, a pot for heating water, and double-pane windows to shut out noise from train traffic.

Long-staying guests in deluxe twins and doubles are provided with scales—perhaps so they can monitor their weight gain as they gorge themselves on Kobe's scrumptious food in the Japanese and French restaurants. Only the twins, doubles, and deluxe singles have a minibar, but there are vending machines in case you're searching for liquid other than water.

BUDGET

KOBE YMCA HOTEL, 2-7-15 Kano-cho, Chuo-ku, Kobe 650. Tel. 078/ 241-7205. 14 rms (all with bath). A/C TV **Directions:** Between Sannomiya and Shin-Kobe stations, about a 10-minute walk from each.

$ Rates (including breakfast, tax, and service charge): ¥6,200–¥8,800 ($44–$63) single; ¥11,000–¥16,500 ($78–$118) twin. YMCA member ¥300 ($2.15) discount. No credit cards.

Sandwiched in between the two Green Hill Hotels about equidistant from Sannomiya and Shin-Kobe stations, this hotel is used primarily for banquets, weddings (yes, you can get married here at the YMCA), and teaching classes. It has only 4 single rooms and 10 twins with a bare, dormitory look to them, but they all have a minuscule bathroom, coin-operated TV, and a pot for heating water. Men, women, and families are welcome.

Youth Hostel

YOUTH HOSTEL KOBE MUDOJI 174, 100 Shinchi, Fukuchi, Yamada-cho, Kita-ku, Kobe 651-12. Tel. 078/581-0250. 40 beds. **Bus:** From Minotani Station, then a 15-minute walk.

$ Rates (per person): ¥2,000 ($14.30) member; ¥2,500 ($17.85) nonmember. Breakfast ¥450 ($3.20); dinner ¥750 ($5.35). No credit cards.

Since there is no youth hostel located in Kobe, this one may be your best bet. Located north of Kobe past Mt. Rokkozan, it occupies part of a temple, with sleeping on futon. Meals are also Japanese style, and there's a coin-operated laundry machine.

WHERE TO DINE

Kobe is famous for its beef, so tender that the best cuts virtually melt in your mouth. Unlike countries like Australia and the United States, where cattle graze in open fields, in villages around Kobe the cattle are hand-fed barley, corn, rice, bran, molasses, rapeseed oil, and soybean meal. The rumor that cattle are fed beer is untrue—they may, however, get one bottle each as a farewell present just before being sent off to the slaughterhouse. There are only a few head of cattle per household, so each gets a lot of individual attention. For exercise the cattle are used for labor, and after the workout are washed and massaged with water and straw brushes.

With a sizable foreign population, Kobe is also a good place to dine on international cuisine, including Indian and Chinese food. The greatest concentration of Chinese restaurants is in Chinatown, called Nankinmachi by the locals, south of Motomachi Station. Occupying the former hot spot of sailor bars and pubs, this pedestrian-laned area boasts about 30 restaurants, most with plastic-food displays outside their doors. Simply walk around and pick one. Kobe also has its share of inexpensive fast-food joints.

In addition to the many Japanese and Western restaurants listed below, be sure to read the nightlife section. Many bars serve meals and snacks that are sometimes cheaper than those served at restaurants.

EXPENSIVE

ALAIN CHAPEL, 31st floor of Portopia Hotel, 6-10-2 Minatojima, Port Island. Tel. 303-5201.
   Cuisine: FRENCH. **Reservations:** Recommended. **Transportation:** Portliner monorail to Shiminhiroba Station.
$ Prices: Set-dinner courses ¥11,000–¥18,000 ($78.55–$128.55); set lunch ¥7,000 ($50). AE, DC, JCB, MC, V.

Open: Lunch daily 11:30am–2pm; dinner daily 5–9:30pm.

For elegant French dining, Alain Chapel is an excellent choice. In a stately drawing-room setting of square pillars, chandeliers, flowers, and white tapered candles on each table, this restaurant serves the creations of French chef Alain Chapel. The set meals are popular with the Japanese clientele. If you decide to dine à la carte, you might start with lobster salad and then try either Kobe beef or duck in foie gras. Average dinner checks, including wine, tax, and service, are generally around ¥17,000 ($121.40) per person.

Top off your meal with a drink or a coffee at Plein d'Etoiles, which is a floor below Alain Chapel. This lounge features piano music and a band every night, for which it charges a ¥650 ($4.65) cover charge. Cocktails, served until 11:50pm, start at ¥900 ($6.45).

KITANO, 1-5-7 Kitano-cho. Tel. 222-5121.
   Cuisine: FRENCH/CONTINENTAL. **Reservations:** Recommended. **Directions:** A 10-minute walk from Shin-Kobe Station.
$ **Prices:** Appetizers ¥1,300–¥1,800 ($9.30–$12.85); set-dinner courses ¥10,000–¥13,000 ($71.40–$92.85); set lunches ¥3,300–¥5,500 ($23.55–$39.30).
   Open: Lunch daily 11am–2:30pm (last order); dinner daily 5–10:30pm (last order).

Located on a hill overlooking the city, this well-known restaurant offers dining with a view. It's especially popular with middle-aged Japanese women, who come to take advantage of the daily lunch special, called Queen's Lunch, for ¥3,300 ($23.55)—and yes, you guys can order it, too. There are also set steak lunches and dinners. The dinner menu also includes sole, turbot, lobster, chicken, filet mignon, and scallops.

MISONO, 1-7-6 Kitanagasa Dori. Tel. 331-2890.
   Cuisine: STEAKHOUSE. **Reservations:** Recommended. **Directions:** A 2-minute walk northwest of Sannomiya Station, on Ikuta Shinmichi St., across from Higashimon St.
$ **Prices:** Set-dinner courses ¥12,000–¥18,000 ($85.70–$128.55); set lunch ¥2,200 ($15.70). AE, DC, JCB, MC, V.
   Open: Lunch Mon–Sat 11:30am–2pm; dinner 5–10pm. Sun 11:30am–10pm.

One of Kobe's most famous steakhouses, Misono claims to have originated teppanyaki steak back in 1945, a style of cooking that uses flat hot plates and today is a favorite not only in Japan but in other countries as well. A modern restaurant, Misono uses Kobe beef from cattle raised in mountain villages about 40 miles north of the city. Seated at tables with hot plates, diners are treated to meals prepared by master chefs right at their table—without, however, the hoopla that usually accompanies such a performance in Japanese restaurants elsewhere in the world.

OKAGAWA, 1-115-2 Kitano-cho. Tel. 222-3511.
   Cuisine: TEMPURA. **Reservations:** Recommended. **Station:** Shin-Kobe, a few minutes' walk away.
$ **Prices:** Tempura set course ¥8,800 ($63); shabu-shabu or sukiyaki ¥7,700 ($55); kaiseki ¥11,000 ($78.55). AE, DC, JCB, V.
   Open: Daily 11am–9pm.

Okagawa occupies a rather new and dignified building up on the bluffs of Kitano, not far from Shin-Kobe Station and about a 5-minute taxi ride from Sannomiya Station. It specializes in tempura, but also serves shabu-shabu or sukiyaki and a kaiseki menu. Although the restaurant is modern, it has latticed wood, shoji screens, and flower arrangements—coolly elegant and emphasizing the Japanese tradition of simplicity. In addition to various tatami rooms, its two tempura counters command good views of the city. A tempura set lunch is available for ¥4,400 ($31.40).

MODERATE

GANDHARA, 4th floor of Nikaku Building, 1-2-3 Kitanagsa Dori. Tel. 391-4975.

Cuisine: INDIAN. **Directions:** A 1-minute walk north of JR Sannomiya Station.

$ Prices: Curries ¥1,100–¥1,400 ($7.85–$10); set-dinner courses ¥2,800–¥5,500 ($29–$39.30); set lunch ¥1,700 ($12.15). AE, DC, JCB, MC, V.

Open: Daily 11am–10pm.

This Indian restaurant is conveniently located just north of Sannomiya Station, next to Shakey's. Its portions are not as generous as those at the other Indian restaurants that follow, but it is easy to find and the curries are slightly cheaper. The best deal is the lunch special, which comes with chicken curry, vegetable curry, rice, Indian bread, shish kebab, salad, and dessert. This place is decorated with Indian knickknacks you never see in restaurants in India. Another Gandhara restaurant in Kobe is located in Kitano.

GAYLORD, basement of Meiji Seimei Building, 8-3-7 Isogami Dori. Tel. 251-4359.

Cuisine: INDIAN. **Directions:** A 5-minute walk south of JR Sannomiya Station.

$ Prices: Curries ¥1,500–¥2,000 ($10.70–$14.30); set-dinner courses ¥3,300–¥5,000 ($23.55–$35.70); set lunches ¥1,300–¥2,300 ($9.30–$16.40). AE, DC, JCB, MC, V.

Open: Lunch Mon–Fri 11:30am–2:30pm; dinner Mon–Fri 5–9:30pm. Sat–Sun and hols 11:30am–9:30pm.

One of the best-known Indian restaurants in Kobe, Gaylord is on Flower Road between the Sanwa and Kyowa banks and across from the Flower Clock. With its low lighting, candles, wood-paneled ceiling, Indian artwork, and piped-in sitar music, this place is classier than your usual Indian restaurant. Other franchise Gaylord restaurants are in Bombay, New Delhi, Hong Kong, London, San Francisco, and Los Angeles.

The extensive menu includes such delights as shrimp cooked in mild gravy with coconut, marinated lamb pieces cooked in cream and spices, and tandoori fish, chicken, or mutton. Vegetarian selections vary and include saffron-flavored rice with nuts and fruit, Bengal beans cooked in sharp spices, spiced lentils cooked with cream, and spinach and cheese cooked in spices. It's customary to order one dish per person and then share. If you're by yourself, you can order one of the set menus starting at ¥3,300 ($23.55). Since that was my case, I ordered the mini-tandoori set course, which came with fish and chicken tandoori, shish kebab, Indian bread, salad, chicken curry, a dry vegetable dish (in this case potato and cabbage), rice, and tea or coffee. Lunch specials, starting at ¥1,400 ($10), are served every day except Sunday and holidays.

IRORIYA, 3-chome Kitano-cho. Tel. 231-6777.

Cuisine: SHABU-SHABU/SUKIYAKI. **Directions:** A 12-minute walk north of Sannomiya Station on Kitano-zaka Road.

$ Prices: Sukiyaki or shabu-shabu ¥4,900 ($35); udon suki ¥3,000 ($21.40). AE, JCB, V.

Open: Daily noon–10pm (last order 9:30pm).

A rather formal establishment, this is another well-known restaurant serving Kobe beef but specializing in shabu-shabu and sukiyaki. Take off your shoes at the front entryway, where they'll be whisked out of sight. Then a kimono-clad woman will lead you through this rather large restaurant to your dining table and your own private hearth. All interior artwork is done by the owner of the restaurant. If you don't care for beef, you may wish to order the *udon suki*, which consists of noodles, seafood, and vegetables cooked together and eaten straight out of the pot.

KINRYUKAKU, 7th floor of Kobe Shinbun Kaikan Building. Tel. 221-1616.

Cuisine: CHINESE. **Directions:** A 1-minute walk southwest of Sannomiya Station.

$ Prices: Dishes ¥700–¥3,000 ($5–$21.40); set-dinner courses ¥8,800 ($62.85); set lunch ¥1,100 ($7.85). AE, JCB, MC, V.

Open: Daily 11:30am–8:30pm.

This restaurant, across from Sannomiya Station, serves Cantonese food in a more luxurious setting than that of the usual Chinese restaurant. The English translation of its name is "Golden Dragon," the chef is Chinese, and the dishes include many different varieties of pork, chicken, seafood, vegetables, and noodles. The best bargain is the set-lunch menu, available every day except Sunday and holidays, which allows you to select two main dishes from a list of 10, plus pickles, soup, and rice. Since most à la carte dishes are meant for two to three persons, ask for the Japanese menu if you're dining alone—it offers smaller portions, with dishes averaging ¥800 ($5.70).

RAJA, 2-7-4 Sakaemachi Dori. Tel. 332-5253.
   Cuisine: INDIAN. **Directions:** A 3-minute walk south of Motomachi Station.
$ Prices: Curries ¥1,200–¥2,200 ($8.55–$15.70); set-dinner courses ¥2,900–¥4,900 ($20.70–$35); set lunches ¥1,100–¥2,200 ($7.85–$15.70). AE, DC, JCB, V.
   Open: Lunch Thurs–Tues 11:30am–2:30pm; dinner Thurs–Tues 5–9pm.
A few minutes' walk south of Motomachi and just west of Chinatown, this small establishment is rather trendy in its simplicity; my only complaint is that the tables are squeezed too closely together, but that's probably to accommodate everyone who wants to eat here. At any rate, the menu offers the usual tandoori chicken, seafood, mutton, and vegetable curries.

SKY RESTAURANT, 11th floor of Oriental Hotel, on Kyomachi St. Tel. 331-8111.
   Cuisine: FRENCH/CONTINENTAL. **Transportation:** A 5-minute taxi ride south of Sannomiya Station.
$ Prices: Set-dinner courses ¥6,000–¥12,000 ($42.85–$85.70); set lunches ¥2,400–¥4,500 ($17.15–$32.15). AE, DC, JCB, MC, V.
   Open: Lunch daily noon–2pm; dinner daily 5–10pm.
With three walls of glass, this restaurant lets the port and city serve as its decorative background, while nightly piano music adds to the mood. Set-dinner menus start at ¥6,000 ($42.85), but for steak with truffle sauce and lobster, expect to spend more than ¥12,000 ($85.70). A specialty of the house is the roast rib of Kobe beef; other dishes include seafood, chicken, veal, and lamb.

WANG THAI, 2nd floor of President Arcade, 2-14-22 Yamamoto Dori Ave. Tel. 222-2507.
   Cuisine: THAI. **Directions:** A 15-minute walk northwest of Sannomiya Station, on Yamamoto Dori Ave.
$ Prices: Dishes ¥1,000–¥2,000 ($7.15–$14.30). AE, DC, MCB, V.
   Open: Lunch Thurs–Tues 11am–2:30pm; dinner Thurs–Tues 5:30–9:30pm.
   Closed: Wed except on national hols.
Claiming to be the first Thai restaurant in the Kansai area (which encompasses Kobe, Osaka, and Kyoto), Wang Thai offers an extensive menu in English, its almost 100 items including pork, beef, seafood, rice, noodle, and vegetarian selections. Most popular is the chicken wrapped in bamboo leaf, but I found the chicken curry with peanuts, potatoes, and herbs equally delicious. It would be tempting to order a variety of dishes and really splurge, but if you're on a budget you can eat here for less than ¥2,000 ($14.30). It's located across the street from the Casablanca Club.

BUDGET

MASAYA HONTEN, 1-8-21 Nakayamate Dori. Tel. 331-4178.
   Cuisine: NOODLES. **Directions:** A few minutes' walk north of Sannomiya Station on Kitano-zaka.
$ Prices: ¥800–¥4,000 ($5.70–$28.55). No credit cards.
   Open: Daily 11am–1am.
This well-known noodle restaurant in Kobe has been dishing out noodles for more than 30 years and is easy to spot by the waterwheel and plastic-food display case outside its front door (there's another display case inside). Since the menu is in Japanese only, make your choice from one of these cases before sitting down. Dishes available include tempura with noodles (tempura soba), pork cutlet with noodles

(tonkatsu soba), and curry noodles, all costing less than ¥200 ($8.55). Sukiyaki served with noodles is available for less than ¥4,000 ($28.55). A good place for night owls, since it stays open late.

STEAKLAND KOBE ⑭, 1-8-2 Kitanagasa Dori. Tel. 332-1787.
Cuisine: STEAKS. **Directions:** Across from Hankyu Sannomiya Station, to the north.
$ Prices: Steaks ¥2,000–¥4,000 ($14.30–$28.55); steak set dinner ¥4,400 ($31.40); set lunch ¥1,400 ($10). No credit cards.
Open: Daily 11am–10pm.

If you want to eat teppanyaki steak but can't afford the high prices of Kobe beef, one of the cheapest places you can go is Steakland Kobe, on the street facing the north side of Hankyu Sannomiya Station. Lunch specials, served from 11am to 3pm, begin at only ¥1,400 ($10) for steak cooked on the hot plate in front of you, miso soup, rice, Japanese pickles, and a vegetable. At dinner, steaks begin at ¥2,999 ($14.30), but Kobe beef is more expensive, with Kobe-beef steak dinners starting at ¥4,400 ($31.40).

THREE LITTLE PIGS, 4-7-14 Kano-cho. Tel. 321-5858.
Cuisine: INTERNATIONAL. **Directions:** A 5-minute walk north of Sannomiya Station.
$ Prices: Dishes ¥600–¥1,500 ($4.30–$10.70); set dinners ¥3,000–¥5,000 ($21.40–$35.70). No credit cards.
Open: Dinner daily 5–10pm (last order).

Popular with Kobe's younger generation is this cozy and intimate restaurant just southeast of the Yamate Kansen and Kitano-zaka intersection. Cavernlike, with three tiny floors of dining, it offers an eclectic selection of cuisine, from salads and rice onigiri rolls to omelets and various seafood dishes. Both Japanese and Western food is available, but since the menu is in Japanese only, it's best to look around at what others are eating.

YAMADA NO KAKASI, 3-9-6 Sannomiya-cho. Tel. 391-0769 or 391-0360.
Cuisine: KUSHIKATSU. **Directions:** A 5-minute walk southeast of Motomachi Station.
$ Prices: Skewers ¥200–¥400 ($1.40–$2.85); "kakasi course" set menu ¥1,600 ($11.40). JCB, V.
Open: Lunch Mon and Wed–Fri 11am–3pm; dinner Mon and Wed–Fri 5–9pm. Sat, Sun, and hols 11am–9pm.

This cozy kushikatsu restaurant is on the western edge of the Sannomiya Center Gai covered shopping arcade. A very narrow and small establishment, it consists of a long counter and some tables in the back. All the wood gleams, and added touches of pottery make you feel you're in the country instead of in the middle of Kobe. The man who has been operating this eatery for the past quarter of a century makes 25 different kinds of kushikatsu, depending on the season. You can order different skewers, but the easiest thing to do is simply to order the "kakasi course" set menu, which consists of 10 sticks. Your man behind the counter will select the ingredients himself, and since the food is supposed to be eaten hot, he'll serve one stick at a time. If you're still hungry at the end of the meal, you can always order a few skewers more. The specialty here is the delicately breaded shrimp and garlic skewer. Other morsels include asparagus wrapped in bacon, mushrooms, potatoes with cheese, chicken wrapped in mint leaf, and lotus root. Highly recommended.

SPECIALTY DINING

Fast Food

Shakey's, just north of Sannomiya Station, serves an all-you-can-eat lunch Monday through Saturday from 11am to 3pm (closed holidays) for only ¥650 ($4.65). In the same vicinity is a **McDonald's.**

A Dining Complex

Underneath the Shinkobe Oriental Hotel next to Shin-Kobe Station is a huge shopping complex with more than 30 food and beverage outlets. Called **OPA** (short for Oriental Park Avenue), this modern-day maze offers everything from Tex-Mex, sushi, and Japanese nouvelle cuisine to Italian, Chinese, and seafood cuisine. I can't claim to have tried them all (I never would have made it to the rest of this book), but I can vouch for the salad bar at Central Station, second floor (tel. 262-2731), decorated in a train motif. A trip through the salad bar (one of the best I've seen in Japan) costs ¥1,000 ($7.15) as your main meal. The specialty here is steak, but other items on the menu include turkey, chicken, prawns, fish, and lobster. Daily hours are 11am to 2am (last order at 1:30am).

A Special Coffee Shop

Nishimura, 1-26-3 Nakayamate Dori (tel. 221-1872), is a good place to go for a cup of coffee. Located on the corner of Hunter-Zaka and Yamate Kansen roads, it's open daily from 8:30am to 11pm, with coffee starting at ¥400 ($2.85) for such blends as Colombian, mocha, and Jamaican. In addition to this branch, there are six other Nishimura coffee shops in Kobe.

EVENING ENTERTAINMENT

Kobe has a wide selection of English-style pubs, bars, expatriate hangouts, and nightclubs. All the establishments below are easily accessible to foreigners and are within walking distance of Sannomiya Station.

THE CLUB & MUSIC SCENE

THE CASABLANCA CLUB, 3-1-6 Kitano-cho, on Yamamoto Dori Ave. (also called Ijinki Dori Ave.). Tel. 241-0200.
This is actually a membership club with a great dinner special available also to nonmembers (¥3,300 or $23.55), which includes your choice of chicken, fish, veal, or beef, plus soup, salad, rice or pita bread, dessert, and coffee. If you don't eat dinner, there's a ¥1,500 ($10.70) drink minimum per person. The interior is an elegant cool white, with a grand piano, palm trees, and pictures of Bogart and Bacall. There's nightly entertainment and dancing. Open: Daily 5pm–midnight.
Admission: ¥1,000 ($7.15) nonmember. **Prices:** Beer ¥750 ($5.35), cocktails ¥1,100 ($7.85).

SONE, 1-24-10 Nakayamate Dori on Kitano-zaka Street. Tel. 221-2055.
Much older and more established is Sone, which has been a jazz hangout for more than 25 years. It has its own in-house jazz band, which plays mainly classics and well-known tunes to an appreciative Japanese audience. Snacks and sandwiches are available. Open: Daily 5:30pm–1am (until midnight Sun).
Admission: Music charge ¥900 ($6.40). **Prices:** Beer ¥750 ($5.35), cocktails ¥1,000 ($7.15).

KENTO'S, 3-10-18 Shimoyamate Dori. Tel. 392-2181.
With more than 20 locations in Japan, Kento's has been a great hit among the Japanese, with live bands playing oldies but goldies from the 1950s and '60s. It's located on Tor Road just north of where it intersects with Ikuta Shinmichi Street (near the Washington Hotel). Open: Daily 5pm–2:30am.
Admission: ¥1,400 ($10) music charge; ¥1,400 ($10) table charge. Guests must buy at least one drink and one food item. **Prices:** Beer ¥750 ($5.35). Spaghetti, salads, seafood, desserts, and snacks ¥1,000 ($7.15).

COPACABANA, 2-1-13 Nakayamate Dori. Tel. 332-6694.

In the basement of the Akai Fusha-no-Aru Building, on Yamate Kansen Road north of Sannomiya Station (next to Second Chance), this is one of Kobe's most famous entertainment hot spots. It features Brazilian and other Latin American music, but the real draw is probably the almost-nude female dancer who entertains the many sailors who come here. The place is small, with a brightly colored interior. Open: Mon–Sat 6pm–3am.

Admission: ¥1,100 ($7.85) entrance fee; ¥800 ($5.70) obligatory table snack.
Prices: Beer ¥770 ($5.50), cocktails ¥1,000 ($7.15).

THE BAR SCENE

KING'S ARMS, 4-2-15 Isobedori. Tel. 221-3774.

This English-style pub is popular with Kobe's foreigners. Located south of Sannomiya Station on Flower Road, not far from the New Port Hotel, it started out in 1950 as an exclusive club for American and British military personnel. After it went public, it became a favorite hangout for sailors and travelers passing through town, and has since mellowed into a cozy and well-established eating and drinking spot catering to all kinds of people, including the businessmen who stop here after work for a drink and a study of the daily newspaper. Its walls are decorated with beer coasters, bills of various currencies from around the world, and business cards of former patrons. Churchill's portrait gazes sternly down upon the bar.

While the first floor is for serious drinking, the second floor is for dining—on steak, stewed beef, grilled chicken, roast beef sandwiches, and such. A la carte main dishes are in the ¥1,700 to ¥2,500 ($12.15 to $17.85) range. Lunch specials begin at ¥1,000 ($7.15). Beer costs ¥450 ($3.20), and cocktails are ¥900 ($6.40). Open: Daily 11:30am–11pm (10pm Sun and hols) (last food order 9pm).

DANNY BOY, 2-10-1 Nakayamate Dori. Tel. 231-6566.

This English-style pub popular with the Japanese is a quiet place to escape the noisy crowds of Kobe's nightlife—a respectable and somewhat plush establishment. It's located north of Sannomiya Station at the corner of Hunter-Zaka and Yamate Kansen roads. There's an English menu here, with such choices as pizza, teriyaki steak, and beef Stroganoff starting at ¥1,100 ($7.85). Beer costs ¥650 ($4.65), and cocktails are ¥750 ($5.35). Open: Daily 11:30am–1am.

THE ATTIC, 4-1-12 Kitano-cho. Tel. 222-1586.

The Attic is in the Ijinkan Club Building on the—where else?—top floor. It's crammed with all kinds of things often relegated to the attic and then promptly forgotten—tennis shoes, racquets, football helmets, license plates, a cello, guitars, and assorted junk. It's owned by local celebrity Marty Kuehnert, a broadcaster of English-language sports shows. Munchies include hamburgers, barbecued chicken, and steak sandwiches. Happy hour is from 6 to 7:30pm Tuesday and Thursday, with two drinks for the price of one. Most main dishes cost ¥1,000 ($7.15), beer is ¥650 ($4.65), and cocktails are ¥850 ($6.05). Open: Wed–Mon 6pm–2am.

Admission: 20% service charge for nonmembers. Weekend ¥500 ($3.55) cover charge.

ATTIC JUNIOR, Fix 213 Building, 2-13-14 Yamamoto Dori. Tel. 261-8459.

Across the street (Ijinkan Dori) from, and catercorner to, The Attic is Attic Junior, a sports bar where the latest U.S. basketball, baseball, and football games and play-offs are zoomed in by satellite. The whole place is plastered with old *Sports Illustrated* covers and American sports memorabilia. Beer is ¥650 ($4.65). Open: Daily 6pm–2am.

Admission: 10% service charge for nonmembers.

ASAHI BIERHAUS, north of Hankyu Sannomiya Station in basement of Eki Mae Building. Tel. 332-0593.

A good place for a hearty beer or two is in this Japanese interpretation of a German beer hall, designed to resemble such an establishment with all kinds of corny statements in German—one translation reads "In heaven there's no beer, that's why I drink it here." German beer-garden music plays in the background, and the waitresses even wear dirndls. If you're hungry, the menu includes roulade, sausage and sauerkraut, German fried potatoes, and pizza, with most items under ¥1,400 ($10). A small mug of beer is ¥450 ($3.20). Open: Daily noon–10pm. Closed: Third Mon of month Nov–Apr.

IROHANIHOHETO, 1-9-17 Kitanagasa Dori. Tel. 321-1688.

Located just north of Hankyu Sannomiya Station on a small side street is this inexpensive yakitori-ya. One of a chain of drinking establishments that cater primarily to young Japanese, it's identified outside its door with a sign that says ANTIQUE PUB RESTAURANT, but there's nothing antique about it. Its prices are cheap, with most dishes of fish, sashimi, soup, yakitori, and much, much more available for less than ¥500 ($3.55). Beer costs ¥450 to ¥600 ($3.20 to $4.30). Open: Daily 5:30pm–3:30am.

SECOND CHANCE, 2nd floor of Takashima Building, 2-1-12 Nakayamate Dori. Tel. 391-3544.

This all-nighter on Yamate Kansen Road is a small, one-room bar favored by young night owls who don't mind the rather sparse furnishings. I must admit my own recollections of this place are a bit fuzzy, but I do remember music ranging from the Doors to the Talking Heads. This is where people congregate when the other bars have had the good sense to close down for the night. Beer is ¥550 ($3.90), and cocktails are ¥750 ($5.35). Open: daily 6pm–5am.

---

6. MOUNT KOYA

465 miles W of Tokyo; 124 miles S of Osaka

GETTING THERE   By Train   The easiest way to get to Koyasan is from Osaka. Ordinary express (kyuko) trains of the Nankai Line depart from Osaka's Namba Station every half hour and cost ¥1,100 ($7.85) one way. The trip south takes about 1 hour and 40 minutes. If you want to ride in luxury, take one of the limited-express cars with reserved seats, costing ¥730 ($5.20) extra and taking about 1 hour and 20 minutes. After the train ride (the last stop is called Gokurakubashi), you continue your trip to the top of Mt. Koya by cable car. The price of the cable car is included in your train ticket.

ESSENTIAL INFORMATION   The **area code** for Mt. Koya, lying in Wakayama Prefecture, is 0736.

At the top of Koyasan is Koyasan Eki Station, where you'll find a booth of the local tourist office, the **Koyasan Tourist Association's,** whose main office (tel. 0736/56-2616) is located approximately in the center of Koyasan. At both tourist offices you can pick up a map of Koyasan and book a room in a temple. Both offices are open daily from 8:30am to 5pm, with slightly shorter hours in winter. Mt. Koya's complete address is 600 Koya-san, Koya-cho, Ito-gun, Wakayama Prefecture.

GETTING AROUND   Outside the station you can board a **bus** that follows the main street of Koyasan all the way to the Okunoin-mae or Ichinohashi-guchi (also called Ichinohasi) bus stop. It passes almost all the sites along the way, as well as most temples accommodating visitors and the Koyasan Tourist Association's main office.

If you've harbored visions of wooden temples nestled in among the trees whenever you've thought of Japan, the sacred mountain of Mt. Koya is the place to go. It's all there—head-shaven monks, religious chantings at the crack of dawn, the wafting of incense, temples, towering cypress trees, tombs, and early-morning mist rising above the treetops. Mt. Koya, called Koyasan by the Japanese, is one of Japan's most sacred places and is the mecca of the Shingon Esoteric sect of Buddhism. Standing 3,000 feet above the world, the top of Mt. Koya is home to about 120 Shingon Buddhist temples scattered through the mountain forests. Some 50 of these temples offer accommodations to visitors, making it one of the best places in Japan to observe temple life firsthand.

Koyasan became a place of meditation and religious learning more than 1,170 years ago, when Kukai, known posthumously as Kobo Daishi, was granted the mountaintop by the imperial court in 816 as a place to establish his Shingon sect of Buddhism. Kobo Daishi was a charismatic priest who spent 2 years in China studying Esoteric Buddhism and introduced the Shingon sect in Japan upon his return. Revered for his excellent calligraphy, his humanitarianism, and his teachings, Kobo Daishi remains today one of the most beloved figures in Japanese Buddhist history. When he died in the 9th century, he was laid to rest in a mausoleum on Mt. Koya. His followers believe that Kobo Daishi is not dead but simply in a deep state of meditation, awaiting the arrival of the last Bodhisatva (Buddha messiahs). According to popular belief, priests opening his mausoleum decades after his death found his body still warm. Through the centuries many of Kobo Daishi's followers, wishing to be close at hand when the great priest awakens, have had huge tombs or tablets constructed close to Kobo Daishi's mausoleum, and many have had their ashes interred here. Pilgrims over the last thousand years have included emperors, nobles, and common people, all climbing to the top of the mountain to pay their respects. Women, however, were barred from entering the sacred grounds of Koyasan until 1872.

WHAT TO SEE & DO

⭐ The most awe-inspiring and magnificent of Koyasan's many structures and temples, **Okunoin** contains the mausoleum of Kobo Daishi. The most dramatic way to approach Okunoin is from the Ichinohashi-guchi bus stop, where a pathway leads 1 mile to the mausoleum. Swathed in a respectful darkness of huge cypress trees that form a canopy overhead are monument after monument, tomb after tomb, all belonging to faithful followers from past centuries.

I don't know whether being here will affect you the same way, but I was awestruck by the hundreds of tombs, the iridescent green moss, the shafts of light streaking through the treetops, the stone lanterns, and the gnarled bark of the old cypress trees. Together, they present a dramatic picture representing a thousand years of Japanese Buddhist history. If you're lucky you won't meet many people along this pathway. (Tour buses fortunately park at a newer entrance to the mausoleum at the bus stop called Okunoin-mae. I absolutely forbid you to take this newer and shorter route, since its crowds lessen the impact of this place considerably. Rather, make sure you take the path to the farthest left, which begins near Ichinohashi bus stop. Much less traveled, it's also much more impressive). At any rate, be sure to return to the mausoleum at night—the stone lanterns are lit (now electrically), creating a mysterious and powerful effect.

At the end of the pathway is the **Lantern Hall,** which houses about 11,000 lanterns. Two sacred fires, which reportedly have been burning since the 11th century, are kept safely inside. The mausoleum itself is behind the Lantern Hall. Buy a white candle, light it, and wish for anything you want. Then sit back and watch respectfully as Buddhists come to chant and pay respects to one of Japan's greatest Buddhist leaders.

As for other things to see, **Kongobuji Temple** ⒁ is close to the tourist office and is the headquarters of the Shingon sect in Japan. The entrance fee of ¥350 ($2.50) allows you to wander around the old wooden structure. On the temple grounds is a large and magnificent rock garden. Imagine the effort spent in getting those huge boulders to their present site. If it's raining, consider yourself lucky—the wetness adds a sheen and color to the rocks.

Another important site is the **Danjogaran Complex,** an impressive sight with a huge main hall (*kondo*); a large vermilion-colored pagoda (*daito*), which many consider to be Koyasan's most magnificent structure; and the oldest building on Mt. Koya, the Fudodo, built in 1198. Next to the complex is the **Reihokan Museum** ⒁, with such treasures of Koyasan on display as wooden Buddha sculptures, scrolls, art, and implements. It's open daily April through October from 8am to 5pm, and November through March from 8:30am to 4:30pm. Admission is ¥500 ($3.55).

A little out of the way from the other sites are the Tokugawa Mausolea, where two Tokugawa shoguns were laid to rest. Visit these only if you have extra time.

WHERE TO STAY

Although this community of 7,000 residents has the usual stores, schools, and offices of any small town, there are no hotels here—the only place you can stay at is a temple, and I strongly suggest you do so. Japanese who come here have almost always made reservations beforehand, so you should do the same. You can make one by calling the temple directly or through travel agencies such as JTB. You can also make reservations upon arrival in Koyasan at the Tourist Association offices described above, but that may be a bit risky during peak travel seasons. At last check, the Koyasan Tourist Association indicated it would make reservations only for those who come in personally to its office.

Prices for an overnight stay, including two vegetarian meals, are the same for all temples on Koyasan and range from ¥7,500 to ¥11,000 ($53 to $78.55) per person, depending on the room. Tax is extra.

Your room will be tatami and may include a nice view of a garden. Living at the temple are high school students and college students attending Koyasan's Buddhist university; they will bring your meals to your room, make up your futon, and clean your room. The morning service is at 6am. (You don't have to attend but I recommend that you do.) Both baths and toilets are communal, and meals are at set times. Because the students must leave for school, breakfast is usually served by 7:30am. Incidentally, Buddhist monks are vegetarians, not teetotalers, and because beer and sake are made of rice and grain, they're readily available at the temples for an extra charge. Below are just a few of the dozens of temples open for overnight guests.

EKOIN ⑮⓪**. Tel. 0736/56-2514.** 36 rms (none with bath). **Bus:** Ichinohashi-guchi stop.
$ Rates (per person, including two meals): ¥7,500–¥11,000 ($53–$78.55). No credit cards.
This 100-year-old temple has beautiful grounds and is nestled in a wooded slope. The place is known for its excellent Buddhist cuisine, and the master priest will give zazen meditation lessons if his schedule permits. Twenty rooms here have TV; 25 have telephones.

FUMONIN TEMPLE ⑮①**. 0736/56-2224.** 35 rms (none with bath). **Bus:** Senjuinbashi bus stop.
$ Rates (per person, including two meals): ¥7,500–¥11,000 ($53–$78.55). No credit cards.
Centrally located near the Tourist Association, this temple has a small but beautiful garden created by the same person who designed the garden at Nijo Castle in Kyoto. (Other temples with famous gardens include Hosenin and Tentokuin.) Seven rooms have TV; 35 have telephones.

RENGEJOIN TEMPLE ⑮②**. Tel. 0736/56-2233.** 48 rms (none with bath). **Bus:** Isshinguchi bus stop.
$ Rates (per person, including two meals): ¥7,500–¥11,000 ($53–$78.55). No credit cards.
★ This temple is owned by a priest whose wife and son speak English, so a lot of foreigners are directed here—it's a good place to meet people. There's also a nice garden here, and this is one of the few temples that will probably take you in without a reservation. Ten rooms have TV.

SHOJOSHININ ⑮③**. Tel. 0736/56-2006.** 20 rms (none with bath). **Bus:** Ichinohashi-guchi stop.
$ Rates (per person, including two meals): ¥7,500–¥11,000 ($53–$78.55). No credit cards.

This temple has a great location at the beginning of the tomb-lined pathway to Okunoin, making it convenient for your late-night stroll to the mausoleum. The present temple buildings date from about 150 years ago, but the temple was first founded about 1,000 years ago. A large wooden structure with rooms overlooking a small garden and pond, it's usually full in August and peak seasons, so make reservations early. About half the rooms have TV; three-fourths have telephones.

7. HIMEJI

400 miles W of Tokyo; 81 miles W of Kyoto; 54 miles E of Okayama

GETTING THERE   By Train   About 4 hours from Tokyo, 1 hour from Kyoto, and ½ hour from Okayama by the Shinkansen bullet train.

By Bus   It takes 9 hours to travel from Shibuya Bus Terminal in Tokyo to Himeji Station.

ESSENTIAL INFORMATION   The **area code** for Himeji, lying in Hyogo Prefecture, is 0792.

The **Himeji City Tourist Information Center** (tel. 0792/85-3792) is at a central exit of the station's north side, to the left after you exit from the ticket gate. It's open daily from 9am to 5pm and offers maps in English. If you're stopping in Himeji only for a few hours to see the castle, deposit your luggage in the coin lockers just beside the tourist office or underneath the Shinkansen tracks.

The main reason tourists come to Himeji is to see its beautiful castle, which embodies better than any other the best in Japan's military architecture.

WHAT TO SEE & DO

THE TOP ATTRACTIONS

HIMEJI CASTLE, Honmachi. Tel. 85-1146.

Perhaps the most beautiful castle in all of Japan, Himeji Castle is nicknamed "White Heron Castle" in reference to its white walls, which stretch out on either side of the main donjon and resemble a white heron poised in flight over the plain. Whether it looks to you like a heron or just a castle, the view of the white five-story donjon under a blue sky is striking. This is also one of the few castles in Japan that has remained virtually undamaged since its completion centuries ago, surviving even the World War II bombings that laid Himeji city in ruins. Himeji Castle is about a 10-minute walk straight north of the station and is connected to the station by a wide boulevard, Otemae Dori. You can see the castle immediately upon leaving the station.

Originating as a fort in the 14th century, Himeji Castle took a more majestic form in 1581, when a three-story donjon was built by Hideyoshi Toyotomi during one of his military campaigns in the district. In the early 1600s the castle became the residence of Terumasa Ikeda, one of Hideyoshi's generals and a son-in-law of Tokugawa Ieyasu. He remodeled the castle into its present five-story structure. With its extensive gates, three moats, and turrets, it had one of the most sophisticated defense systems in Japan. The maze of passageways leading to the donjon was so complicated that intruders would find themselves trapped in dead ends. The castle walls were constructed with square or circular holes to allow muzzles of guns to poke through; the rectangular holes were for archers. There were also drop chutes where stones or boiling water could be dumped on enemies trying to scale the walls.

On weekends, there are sometimes volunteer guides hanging around the ticket office who are willing to give you a guided tour of the castle for free. It gives them an opportunity to practice their English. Often college students, they can tell you the history of the castle and relate old castle gossip. But even if you go on your own, you won't have any problems learning about the history of the castle, since the city of Himeji has done a fine job of placing English explanations throughout the castle grounds. Allow about 1½ hours here.

Admission: ¥500 ($3.55).

Open: Daily 9am–5pm in summer, daily 9am–4pm in winter.

HYOGO PREFECTURAL MUSEUM OF HISTORY, 68 Honmachi. Tel. 88-9011.

Just behind Himeji Castle to the northeast is the Hyogo Prefectural Museum of History. If you're coming here from the castle, take the Karamete exit from the castle, follow the circular drive to the right, and then turn left in front of the redbrick building (the city art museum). The history museum is straight ahead. It exhibits materials from prehistoric times to the present day, with many explanations in English. Some of the displays allow hands-on experience, such as traditional Japanese toys and Bunraku puppets with strings you can pull to move eyebrows and other facial features. If you're here on Sunday or a national holiday, you can even try on a samurai period costume (samurai outfits were amazingly heavy). Displays include those devoted to castles in Japan and around the world, with videos in English describing the structure and layout of Himeji Castle; children's games of yesteryear; and Shoshazan Enkyoji, a famous temple complex on nearby Enkyo Mountain.

Admission: ¥200 ($1.40).

Open: Tues–Sun 10am–5pm.

HIMEJI SHIMIN KAIKAN, 112 Sosha Honmachi. Tel. 84-2800.

If you're at all interested in Japanese flower arrangement, the tea ceremony, or the proper way to wear a kimono, you'll want to take advantage of the free cultural classes held here Monday through Friday. Classes are offered on an alternating basis, so the best thing to do is drop by the tourist office in the train station for an English-language leaflet complete with a schedule and a map of how to get there.

Admission: Free.

Open: Mon–Fri 1:30pm–3:30pm. **Directions:** A 7-minute walk from Himeji Station, east of the main road leading to Himeji Castle.

NEARBY ATTRACTIONS

If you have time for an excursion, board bus no. 6 or 8 from in front of Himeji Station (to the right after exiting from the station's central exit) and ride it for 25 minutes to **Shoshazan Enkyoji.** Founded in the Heian Period (12th century), this large complex of temples contains a thousand years of Buddhist history in its precincts, including the Kongo Satta Buddha, sculpted in 1395, and the Yakushido, the oldest surviving structure dating from the Kamakura Period (early 14th century). The easiest way to reach the temple complex from the bus stop (called Shosha) is by ropeway, which costs ¥300 ($2.15) one way. There are also horse-drawn carriages available for the same price.

WHERE TO STAY

Himeji lacks an adequate supply of good accommodations. In fact, some of the worst hotels I've seen in Japan are in Himeji. Your safest bet is to stick to the recommendations listed below.

EXPENSIVE

BANRYU ⑭, 135 Shimodera-machi, Himeji 670. Tel. 0792/85-2112. 20 rms (11 with bath). A/C TV TEL **Directions:** A 15-minute taxi ride from Himeji Station.

$ Rates (per person, including two meals): ¥16,500 ($118) without bath; ¥20,000 ($143) with bath and garden view. AE, JCB, V.

A traditional ryokan about a 15-minute walk from Himeji Castle, it is surrounded by a wood-and-stone wall, has a modest but peaceful garden, and caters to foreigners. A pleasant place with large rooms and some antiques, it's about 30 years old. Western breakfasts are served upon request.

MODERATE

HIMEJI CASTLE HOTEL, 210 Hojyo, Himeji 670. Tel. 0792/84-3311. Fax 0792/84-3729. 207 rms. A/C MINIBAR TV TEL **Directions:** A 10-minute walk from the south (Shinkansen) exit of Himeji Station.
$ Rates: ¥6,600–¥10,000 ($47–$71) single; ¥16,500 ($118) double; ¥15,500–¥25,000 ($110–$178) twin. AE, DC, JCB, MC, V.

Opened in 1975, this is considered one of Himeji's best tourist hotels. I especially like the cheapest twins—they were made by joining two single rooms together, so that beds are in one room and a couch is in the other, and so that there are two bathrooms and two television sets. This could be a lifesaver for couples or friends who have been traveling together a bit too long. Facilities include an outdoor swimming pool, which charges ¥1,500 ($10.70) for a dip, and a Western restaurant called Chateau, which serves set lunches starting at ¥1,500 ($10.70) and set dinners at ¥3,300 ($23.55).

HOTEL OKUUCHI, 3-56 Higashi Nobusue, Himeji 670. Tel. 0792/22-8000. Fax 0792/85-0306. 315 rms. A/C MINIBAR TV TEL **Directions:** A 10-minute walk south of Himeji Station.
$ Rates: ¥6,500–¥7,000 ($46–$50) single; ¥12,000–¥13,300 ($86–$95) twin. AE, V.

Down the street from the Castle Hotel, this place has an indoor swimming pool guests can use for free all year. A little more than half of this business-type hotel's rooms are singles, and most of the rest are twins. Rooms are small but are equipped with push-button phone, alarm clock, radio, minibar, hot-water pot, and TV with pay video. Because of the construction of the building, most rooms have absolutely no view—if that's important to you, be sure to specify your wishes. The hotel's two restaurants serve Japanese and Chinese cuisine.

HOTEL SUNROUTE NEW HIMEJI (155), 241 Ekimae-cho, Himeji 670. Tel. 0792/23-1111. Fax 0792/23-7100. 40 rms. A/C MINIBAR TV TEL **Directions:** A 1-minute walk north of Himeji Station, across street from station's central exit.
$ Rates: ¥5,500–¥7,000 ($39–$50) single; ¥13,500 ($96) double; ¥13,500–¥14,800 ($96–$106) twin. Japanese-style rooms: ¥14,800 ($106) double. AE, DC, JCB, MC, V.

Opened in 1983, when it took over an existing hotel, this Sunroute has recently renovated facilities, including a Chinese restaurant and a cheerful coffee shop. Rooms are equipped with the usual alarm clock, minibar, hot-water pot and tea, and TV with pay video, and windows are large, with sliding panels for complete darkness. The cheapest singles have tiny glazed windows that can't open, so if sunshine is important to you, pay the higher price. In summer there's a rooftop beer garden here open daily from 5 to 9pm.

BUDGET

HOTEL HIMEJI PLAZA, 158 Toyozawa-cho, Himeji 670. Tel. 0792/81-9000. 218 rms (168 with bath, 50 with toilet only). A/C MINIBAR TV TEL **Directions:** A 1-minute walk from south (Shinkansen) exit of Himeji Station.
$ Rates (including tax and service): ¥6,000 ($43) single with toilet only, ¥6,800–¥7,300 ($48–$52) single with bath; ¥10,800–¥12,800 ($77–$91) double/twin with bath. AE, DC, JCB, MC, V.

This business hotel is your best bet for a good place close to the station—look for the white building with a clock on top of the front façade. Rooms are bright and cheerful, with hot-water pot for tea, TV with pay video, clock, minibar, and semidouble-size beds. The windows are glazed but can be opened. There's a coin-operated laundry in the hotel, a public bath and sauna (for men only), soda and beer machines, and one Western-style restaurant. The staff is friendly and courteous.

HOTEL SUNROUTE HIMEJI ⑮, **195-9 Ekimae-cho, Himeji 670. Tel. 0792/85-0811.** Fax 0792/84-1025. 89 rms (all with bath). A/C MINIBAR TV TEL **Directions:** A 1-minute walk northeast of Himeji Station's central exit (turn right out of the exit).

$ Rates (including service): ¥7,000 ($50) single; ¥11,000–¥13,500 ($78–$96) twin; ¥12,900 ($92) double; ¥15,500 ($111) triple. AE, DC, JCB, MC, V.

The front desk and lobby are on the fourth floor of this white building, which opened as a hotel in the mid-1970s. It features rooms with heavy curtains that can be drawn to shut out any light, a hot-water pot for tea, a minibar, and TV with pay video. Rooms facing the railroad tracks are fitted with double-pane windows to screen out train noises. During summer months there's a rooftop beer garden here open daily from 5 to 9pm, with mugs of beer starting at ¥550 ($3.90). The hotel's one restaurant serves Japanese food, plus a Western-style buffet breakfast for ¥1,000 ($7.15).

Youth Hostel

YOUTH HOSTEL TEGARAYAMA SEINEN-NO-IE, 58 Nishi-nobuse, Himeji 670. Tel. 0792/93-2716. 32 beds. **Bus:** A 10-minute ride from Himeji Station, then a 10-minute walk.

$ Rates (per person): ¥1,700 ($12.15). No credit cards. No meals are served here, no one speaks English, and the woman I talked to was not very receptive. Youth-hostel cards aren't required, and there's a coin-operated laundry machine.

WHERE TO DINE

Parallel and to the right of Otemae-Dori, the main drag from Himeji Station to the castle, is a covered shopping arcade called Miyukidori, with lots of restaurants and coffee shops. There's even a McDonald's if you're interested.

FUKUTEI ⑮, **75 Kameimachi. Tel. 23-0981.**
Cuisine: VARIED JAPANESE. **Directions:** About a 4-minute walk from Himeji Station, about halfway down Miyukidori arcade on a side street.
$ Prices: Set meals ¥1,500–¥2,500 ($10.70–$17.85); set lunch ¥1,000 ($7.15). JCB, V.
Open: Fri–Wed 11am–9:30pm.

This popular restaurant offers a wide assortment of Japanese food, including sashimi, tempura, noodles, eel, and sushi. A great deal is the hearty teishoku obento lunch for around ¥1,000 ($7.15), served until 2pm. It usually includes sashimi, tempura, soup, rice, and pickled vegetables. There's also a mini-kaiseki available for lunch at the same price. If you come for dinner, you can eat for less than ¥2,000 ($14.30). A refuge for shoppers, Fukutei has soothing Japanese instrumental music playing in the background. If you have the map in English from the tourist office, this restaurant is indicated by number 77 and is wrongly spelled "Hukutei" (unless they've corrected the map by the time you get there).

MAMPUKU ⑮, **Hakurocho. Tel. 22-3901.**
Cuisine: EEL. **Directions:** An 8-minute walk north of Himeji Station.
$ Prices: ¥800–¥1,800 ($5.70–$12.85). No credit cards.
Open: Fri–Wed 10am–5pm.

Mampuku is a small and plain-looking restaurant located on the left-hand side of Otemae-Dori Avenue, as you go from the station to the castle. It's just before the last stoplight leading to the castle grounds and has blue curtains in front of its door and a plastic-food display case. An eel shop, but also serving noodles, sushi, tempura, and other Japanese food, it's convenient if you've stopped in Himeji only a few hours to visit the castle.

MINATO-AN ⑮, **Tatemachi. Tel. 22-1171.**

Cuisine: UDON NOODLES. **Directions:** A 5-minute walk from Himeji Station.
$ **Prices:** ¥600–¥800 ($4.30–$5.70). No credit cards.
Open: Thurs–Tues 11am–8:30pm.

This small neighborhood noodle shop, identified by number 69 on the map issued by the tourist office, is on a back street to the west of Otemae-Dori Avenue, the main street leading from the station to the castle. Across from a tiny neighborhood shrine and located on a corner, the restaurant has pictures of a black-and-red bucket, as well as a plastic-food display case, outside. The specialty here is udon noodles served in a wooden bucket. Other noodle dishes include somen, ramen, tempura udon, and curry udon. The menu is in Japanese only, so make your choice from the plastic goodies on display. In any case, no matter what you choose, you're sure to be satisfied—the food here is simple but delicious.

C.P. NEWS, Gofukumachi 16. Tel. 82-7510.
Cuisine: VARIED WESTERN. **Directions:** A 5-minute walk north of Himeji Station.
$ **Prices:** ¥600–¥800 ($4.30–$5.70); set lunch ¥800 ($5.70). No credit cards.
Open: Daily 11:30am–midnight. **Closed:** Second and fourth Tues of month.

Not far from the Miyukidori shopping arcade and across from Taiyo Kobe Bank is one of the trendiest restaurant/bars in town. It looks as if it had been imported from Tokyo, with its sparse, art deco style, triangular tables, young staff, and young clientele. It offers sandwiches, spaghetti, pizza, salads, curry rice, and more. It also serves coffee, tea, beer, and alcoholic concoctions.

SPECIALTY DINING

If you're here in summer, there are **beer gardens** on the roofs of the Hotel Sunroute Himeji, the Hotel Sunroute New Himeji, and the Festa department store, which is right above Himeji Station itself. Hours for all are 5 to 9pm, and snacks are available in addition to beer.

Beside Mampuku, an eel restaurant described above, is an **obento counter** selling box lunches of eel, curry rice, hamburgers, and more for about ¥500–¥600 ($3.55–$4.30) per lunch. Since it's on the way to Himeji Castle, you might want to stop here to pick up your lunch for a picnic on the castle's park grounds.

8. OKAYAMA

454 miles W of Tokyo; 136 miles W of Kyoto; 100 miles E of Hiroshima

GETTING THERE By Train Okayama is a major stop on the Shinkansen bullet line about 4 hours from Tokyo, 1½ hours from Kyoto, and less than 1 hour from Hiroshima.

By Bus There are three overnight buses leaving daily from Shinjuku and Shinagawa stations in Tokyo, arriving in Okayama the next day. There is also an express bus service from Osaka.

ESSENTIAL INFORMATION The **area code** for Okayama City, lying in Okayama Prefecture, is 0862.

Before leaving Tokyo, stop by the Tourist Information Center and pick up a leaflet called *Okayama and Kurashiki.*

The **Okayama Tourist Information Office** (tel. 0862/22-2912) is inside the Okayama Station building, near the central exit of the east side (look for the signs). The tourist office window is well marked in English and is open daily from 8:30am to 8pm. They're well prepared for foreign visitors with excellent brochures and a map in English.

GETTING AROUND   Okayama's sights are all clustered within walking distance of each other and are east of Okayama Station. The easiest way to sightsee is to take a **streetcar** from Okayama Station bound for Higashiyama, and to disembark after about 8 minutes at the Shiroshita tram stop. From there, **walk** to the Orient Museum, then Korakuen Garden, Okayama Castle, the Yumeji Art Museum, and the Hayashibara Museum of Art. Allow at least 5 hours to tour all of these sights.

With the opening of the Seto Ohashi Bridge in the spring of 1988, Okayama Prefecture has leaped into the tourism spotlight. Japanese from all over the country have come to marvel over this bridge, measuring almost 6 miles in length and connecting Okayama Prefecture on Honshu island with Sakaide on Shikoku island. Whereas it used to take an hour by ferry to reach Shikoku, the double-decker bridge for trains and cars cuts travel time down to just 15 minutes. For the Japanese, the Seto Ohashi Bridge is one of the most important attractions of Okayama Prefecture and the Seto Inland Sea.

For those of you less interested in bridges, Okayama is important for other reasons as well. In Okayama city, there's one of the most beautiful gardens in Japan. In nearby Kurashiki, covered later in this chapter, there's an old section of the town that's one of the most picturesque places in the country. And scattered through Okayama Prefecture are so-called International Villas, built by the prefecture especially for foreigners and located primarily in rural areas, with rates that are amazingly low.

WHAT TO SEE & DO

KORAKUEN GARDEN, 1-5 Korakuen. Tel. 72-1147.

Okayama's claim to fame is its Korakuen Garden, considered to be one of Japan's three most beautiful landscaped gardens (the other two are in Kanazawa and Mito). Completed in 1700 after 14 years of work, its 28 acres are graced with a pond, running streams, pine trees, plum and cherry trees, bamboo groves, and tea plantations. The surrounding hills, as well as Okayama's famous black castle, are incorporated into the design of the garden. Its name, Korakuen, means "the garden for taking pleasure later," which has its origins in an old saying: "Bear sorrow before the people; take pleasure after them." This garden differs from most Japanese gardens in that it has large expanses of grassy open areas, a rarity in crowded Japan.

Admission: ¥250 ($1.80).

Open: Apr–Sept 7:30am–6pm, Oct–Mar 8am–5pm.

OKAYAMA CASTLE [OKAYAMAJO], 2-1-1 Marunouchi. Tel. 25-2096.

Across the river from Korakuen Park and over a footbridge, Okayamajo was originally built in the 16th century. Destroyed in World War II and rebuilt in 1966, this unique castle has earned the nickname "Crow Castle" because of its black color, painted deliberately so as to contrast with neighboring Himeji's famous White Heron castle. Like most castles, this one houses swords, samurai gear, and palanquins. Unlike castles of yore, however, this one comes with an elevator that whisks you up to the top floor of the donjon, from which you have a view of the park and the city beyond. If you feel like indulging in whimsical fantasies deserving of children's fairy tales, you can rent paddleboats in the shape of swans or tea cups in the river below the castle.

Admission: ¥250 ($1.80).

Open: Daily 9am–5pm.

ORIENT MUSEUM [ORIENTO BIJUTSUKAN], 9-31 Tenzincho. Tel. 32-3636.

This museum, designed in the style of an Islamic mosque, exhibits about 2,000 items of artwork from the ancient Orient, including pottery, glassware, and metalwork from Asia, Iran, Syria, and ancient Mesopotamia.

Admission: ¥200 ($1.40).

Open: Tues–Sun 9am–5pm.

HAYASHIBARA MUSEUM OF ART [HAYASHIBARA BIJUTSUKAN], 2-7-15 Marunouchi. Tel. 23-1733.

About a 5-minute walk from Okayama Castle, this museum contains relics belonging to the former feudal owners of the castle, the Ikeda clan, including furniture, swords, pottery, lacquerware, Noh costumes, and armor.
Admission: ¥300 ($2.15).
Open: Daily 9am–5pm.

YUMEJI ART MUSEUM [YUMEJI-KYODO BIJUTSUKAN], 2-1-32 Hama. Tel. 71-1000.

North of Korakuen Park and across the river is the Yumeji Art Museum, dedicated to the works of Takehisa Yumeji. Born in Okayama Prefecture in 1884, Yumeji is sometimes referred to as Japan's Toulouse-Lautrec and is credited with developing the fin de siècle art nouveau movement in Japan. This collection includes some of his most famous works, including watercolors, oils, and woodblock prints.
Admission: ¥600 ($4.30).
Open: Apr–Nov daily 9am–6pm, Dec–Mar Tues–Sun 9am–5pm.

WHERE TO STAY

EXPENSIVE

HOTEL NEW OKAYAMA, 1-1-25 Ekimae-cho, Okayama City 700. Tel. 0862/23-8211. Fax 0862/23-1172. 82 rms. A/C MINIBAR TV TEL Directions: Across from Okayama Station's east exit.

$ Rates: ¥11,000–¥14,300 ($78–$102) single; ¥21,000–¥39,000 ($150–$278) double/twin. AE, DC, JCB, MC, V.

This spacious hotel, located right next to Okayama's train station, has a large lobby on the sixth floor. Rooms are luxuriously appointed, with large windows, covered with shoji-like screens; semidouble-size beds; and radio, minibar, and alarm clock, among other amenities. The cheapest singles face an inner courtyard and have absolutely no view, so it may be worth it to spring for the higher-priced rooms.

Dining/Entertainment: The hotel has both Japanese and Western restaurants, and from May to mid-August there's a beer garden on the hotel's roof from 5 to 9pm.
Services: Free newspaper, same-day laundry service.
Facilities: Shopping arcade, art gallery.

OKAYAMA KOKUSAI HOTEL, 4-1-16 Kadota Honmachi, Okayama City 703. Tel. 0862/73-7311. Fax 0862/71-0292. 334 rms. A/C MINIBAR TV TEL Directions: A 15-minute taxi ride from station.

$ Rates: ¥10,000–¥14,800 ($71–$106) single; ¥18,000–¥20,000 ($121–$143) double; ¥18,000–¥20,000 ($128–$143) twin. AE, DC, JCB, MC, V.

This Western-style hotel has a resortlike holiday atmosphere, and is located above the city on a wooded hill. It also has the most psychedelic elevators I've ever seen—their walls are lined with fabric of colorful silk threads in wavy patterns. Rooms face the city or the woods—city views are more dramatic and expensive. Rooms are comfortable and feature a radio, an alarm clock, and a refrigerator stocked with everything from beer to "titbits"—which turn out to be nuts. The TV has a pay video channel, including movies in English, sports, and adult movies. The staff here is friendly and courteous.

Dining/Entertainment: Restaurants serve Japanese, French, and Chinese cuisine, including L'Arc en Ciel on the 13th floor, with panoramic views of the city. There's also a rooftop beer garden with romantic views of the city lights, open from the end of June through August.
Facilities: Outdoor swimming pool, open from mid-July to the end of August.

MODERATE

CULTURE HOTEL, 1-3-2 Gankunan-cho, Okayama City 700. Tel. 0862/ 55-1122. 93 rms. A/C TV TEL Directions: A 5-minute taxi ride from Okayama Station, or a 15-minute walk.

$ Rates: ¥6,500–¥7,000 ($46–$50) single; ¥12,000 ($86) double/twin. Japanese-style rooms: ¥13,000–¥16,500 ($93–$118). AE, JCB, MC, V.

⭐ This is an excellent choice for a modestly priced hotel. It is a rather striking
white building, and its lobby uses white bricks in a number of imaginative
ways—chipped to form patterns, buckled, or pulled out from the wall in relief.
⑨ Water from an inside fountain empties into a stream that runs through the
lobby lounge to an outside waterfall and small garden. I wish more moderately
priced hotels would put as much excitement into their designs as this one.
Rooms are pleasantly decorated with cheerful flowered wallpaper and have a clock,
radio, and hot-water pot. There are also eight Japanese-style rooms. Used primarily by
wedding parties in preparation for elaborate receptions held at the hotel, some of
them look onto a small private garden. The hotel's one restaurant serves Western
food.

**OKAYAMA PLAZA HOTEL, 2-3-12 Hama, Okayama City 703. Tel. 0862/
72-1201.** Fax 0862/73-1557. 85 rms. A/C TV TEL **Bus:** Okaden bus from Gate
9 at Okayama Station to Yumeiji-kyodo Bijutsukan-mae stop.
$ Rates: ¥7,500 ($53) single; ¥14,000–¥16,500 ($100–$118) double; ¥14,000–
¥15,500 ($100–$111) twin. AE, JCB, MC, V.
Located just north of Korakuen Gargen, this hotel has a lobby featuring a gigantic
wind chime—glass chandeliers in front of the main door sway in the breeze and make
a music of their own. Rooms are large with semidouble-size beds, but the bathrooms
are fairly small.

**HOTEL SUNROUTE ⑯, 1-3-12 Shimoishi, Okayama City 700. Tel.
0862/32-2345.** Fax 0862/25-6556. 123 rms. A/C MINIBAR TV TEL **Directions:** A 10-minute walk southwest of Okayama Station.
$ Rates: ¥6,300–¥6,900 ($45–$49) single; ¥11,000–¥13,000 ($78–$93)
double/twin; ¥16,000 ($114) triple. AE, DC, JCB, MC, V.
This chain business hotel is in a redbrick building and has one Western-style
restaurant. Rooms are basic, with TV with pay video, clock, hot-water pot and tea
bags.

**OKAYAMA TERMINAL HOTEL, 1-5 Ekimoto-cho, Okayama City 700. Tel.
0862/33-3131.** Fax 0862/33-3144. 114 rms. A/C TV TEL **Directions:** Beside
Okayama Station, to right as you leave from east exit.
$ Rates: ¥7,000–¥9,300 ($50–$66) single; ¥12,900–¥15,500 ($92–$111) dou-
ble; ¥12,000–¥16,500 ($78–$118) twin. AE, DC, JCB, MC, V.
Your average business hotel, this white building right beside Okayama Station houses
rooms with hot water for tea, radio, and clock, among other amenities. The front desk
is on the third floor, and rooms feature double-pane windows to shut out traffic noise.

**WASHINGTON HOTEL, 3-6 Honmachi, Okayama City 700. Tel. 0862/31-
9111.** Fax 0862/21-0048. 210 rms. A/C MINIBAR TV TEL **Directions:** A
5-minute walk east of Okayama Station on Momotaro Odori.
$ Rates: ¥7,000–¥8,000 ($50–$57) single; ¥13,500–¥14,000 ($96–$100) dou-
ble; ¥13,500–¥17,300 ($96–$123) twin. AE, DC, JCB, MC, V.
Opened in 1988, the Washington Hotel has a second-floor lobby. Rooms—167 of
them singles, all featuring semidouble-size beds—are pleasant, with windows that
open, bilingual TV (operated by a bedside control panel), radio, and minibar, among
other amenities. Toilets are even equipped with bidetlike jets of water, the latest in
Japanese technology. Facilities here include a Chinese restaurant, a coffee shop, and a
live-music venue in the basement called Kento's, which features tunes from the '50s
and '60s.

BUDGET

**MATSUNOKI ⑯, 19-1 Ekimotomachi, Okayama City 700. Tel. 0862/53-
4111.** 59 rms (24 with bath). A/C MINIBAR TV TEL **Directions:** A 2-minute
walk west of Okayama Station.

$ Rates (per person): ¥6,200 ($44) single; ¥5,200 ($37) twin. With two meals ¥8,400 ($60) per person. No credit cards.

A gleaming white building built in 1987, Matsunoki is situated behind the New Station Hotel. Owned and managed by a friendly family, it has 25 Japanese-style tatami rooms and 4 Western-style singles and twins, all equipped with deep Japanese tub, Western toilet, hairdryer, and other amenities; those that face east toward the station even have their own little balcony. Meals are served in a cheerful communal dining hall. Incidentally, there are 19 more Japanese-style rooms in an older annex next door. All without private bathroom, these nevertheless go for about the same price.

Youth Hostel

YOUTH HOSTEL OKAYAMA-KEN SEINEN KAIKAN ⑯, **1-7-6 Tsukura-cho, Okayama City 700. Tel. 0862/52-0651.** 65 beds. A/C **Directions:** A 20-minute walk northwest of Okayama Station.

$ Rates: ¥2,300 ($16.40) member; ¥2,900 ($20.70) nonmember. Breakfasts ¥450 ($3.20). Dinner ¥850 ($6.05). No credit cards.

This youth hostel's 13 Japanese-style rooms sleep 3 to 10 persons per room. There are bicycles for rent, as well as laundry facilities.

ELSEWHERE IN OKAYAMA PREFECTURE

✪ ⑤ Although they're not located within the city limits of Okayama, you might consider treating yourself to a few days in the countryside by staying at one of the **International Villas.** Financed and maintained by the Okayama Prefectural Government, these small country inns are the brainstorm of Okayama's governor, who wished to repay the kindness he received from foreigners during his trips abroad as a youth. Thus, these villas are open only to foreigners, though accompanying Japanese guests are welcome. The cost of staying at one of the villas is only ¥3,000 ($21.40) per person for nonmembers and ¥2,500 ($17.85) for members. The cost of a membership card is ¥500 ($3.55) and is available at check-in at any villa—worth it if you're staying more than one night. Each villa is small, with only a half dozen or so guest rooms, and is outfitted with the latest in bathroom and kitchen facilities. These villas are so well constructed, in fact, that you would easily pay more than twice the rate if they were privately owned. You can cook your own food or visit one of the local restaurants.

There are six International Villas, most in small villages or in rural settings. One of the completed villas, modeled after a traditional soy-sauce warehouse, is located in a mountain village named **Fukiya,** an old copper-mining town that has changed little since the mid-19th century. In **Koshihata** and **Hattoji,** accommodations are in two 19th-century renovated thatched farmhouses, and in **Ushimado** guests stay in a modern open-beamed villa with sweeping views of the Seto Inland Sea—probably the most popular villa for visiting tourists. Also offering great views is the villa on **Shiraishi Island,** which offers beaches, shrines, and accommodations in an airy glass-and-wooden building. In **Takebe,** known for hot springs where visitors can enjoy nine different types of baths, guests stay in an innovative building constructed of wood and designed to resemble a traditional wooden barge. It also has an outdoor hot-spring bath. In short, these villas are remarkable—and maybe other prefectures will take their cue from Okayama and start building inexpensive lodgings. For more information on the International Villas, call the Okayama Prefectural Government's International Exchange Section at (0862)24-2111, ext. 2483.

WHERE TO DINE

As with all cities in Japan, you won't have any problems finding restaurants in Okayama. Many Japanese restaurants are clustered around Okayama Station, while the best Western restaurants are located in the hotels. Okayama's most famous dish is the Okayama Barazushi, made of Seto Inland Sea delicacies and fresh mountain vegetables. Traditionally served during festive occasions, it consists of a rice casserole laced with shredded ginger and cooked egg yolk and topped with a variety of goodies, including conger eel, shrimp, fish, lotus root, and bamboo.

EXPENSIVE

L'ARC EN CIEL, 13th floor of Okayama Kokusai Hotel, 4-1-16 Kadota Honmachi. Tel. 73-7311.

Cuisine: FRENCH. **Reservations:** Recommended. **Directions:** A 15-minute taxi ride from Okayama Station.

$ Prices: Appetizers ¥1,500–¥2,000 ($10.70–$14.30); main dishes ¥2,700–¥5,000 ($19.28–$35.70); set-dinner courses ¥6,500–¥16,500 ($46.40–$118); set lunches ¥1,600–¥2,700 ($11.40–$19.30). AE, DC, JCB, MC, V.

Open: Lunch daily 11:30am–2pm; dinner daily 5–10pm.

For relaxed and intimate dining, head for L'Arc en Ciel, located on top of a hill in the Kokusai Hotel, with sweeping views of the city (beautiful at sunset). A la carte dishes include filet of steak and lobster. Dishes here are imaginative and fun—I once had filet of sole in white cream sauce and was surprised to see it arrive with a small squid and a shrimp, and topped with shredded crab and carrots. A good place for a splurge.

MODERATE

GONTA-ZUSHI ⑯, 1-2-1 Nodaya-cho. Tel. 23-6442.

Cuisine: SUSHI. **Directions:** From Okayama Station, walk 5 minutes through Ekimae Shotengai covered shopping arcade until you reach a busy street. Gonta-Zushi is across this street on left corner.

$ Prices: Nigiri Matsu ¥2,200 ($15.70); sushi set meals ¥1,100–¥2,700 ($7.85–$19.30). AE, DC, JCB, V.

Open: Thurs–Tues 11am–11pm.

If you're hungry for sushi, you can't go wrong with Gonta-Zushi. The prices are reasonable, the food is excellent, and the atmosphere is typical sushi bar, with a long counter and sushi experts dressed in traditional garb. I had the Nigiri Matsu, which came with nigiri-zushi of conger eel, shrimp, squid, sea bream, tuna, and fish from the Seto Inland Sea, plus three *norimaki* (edible seaweed rolled around rice and pickled vegetables). If you order sushi à la carte, it will be served to you on large shiny leaves. Other choices include seafood kaiseki starting at ¥3,800 ($27.15) and the Matsurizushi (Okayama Barazushi) set for ¥1,400 ($10). They also sell sushi to go here starting at ¥500 ($3.55). Gonta-Zushi is recognizable by its white lanterns hanging in front of the door and green sign.

PETIT ("PUCHI") MARIE ⑯, 6-7 Nishikimachi. Tel. 22-9066.

Cuisine: FRENCH. **Directions:** A 5-minute walk east of Okayama Station.

$ Prices: Main dishes ¥1,500–¥2,700 ($10.70–$19.30); set meal ¥3,300 ($23.55); set lunch ¥730 ($5.20). No credit cards.

Open: Lunch Thurs–Tues 11:15am–2:45pm (last order); dinner Thurs–Tues 5–9pm (last order).

This tiny one-room establishment is so popular customers line up outside, and dining is on a first-come, first-served basis. The interior is corny but the food is fun. A beef stew cooked in red wine is popular, as is the very inexpensive set lunch.

BUDGET

SUISHIN ⑯, basement of Dai-ichi Central Building. Tel. 32-5101.

Cuisine: RICE CASSEROLES/FISH/VARIED JAPANESE. **Directions:** Across from Okayama Station's east exit, beside Takashimaya department store.

$ Prices: Rice casseroles ¥750 ($5.35); most dishes ¥1,500–¥2,500 ($10.70–$17.85). AE, JCB, MC, V.

Open: Thurs–Tues 11am–9pm.

There are lots of inexpensive restaurants in the basement of the Dai-ichi Central

Building, across from Okayama Station's east exit. Among the restaurants selling pizza, plus Chinese and Japanese cuisine, is Suishin, which specializes in kamameshi (rice casserole dishes) and fish from the Seto Inland Sea. This is a chain restaurant with headquarters in Hiroshima. Being a great fan of eel dishes, I chose the eel kamameshi, which came laced with bits of conger eel, ginger, and boiled egg yolk, with Japanese pickles on the side. The Japanese menu shows pictures of other dishes served, including cold shabu-shabu, tempura, sushi, and various eel dishes. A simply furnished and popular place, it gets quite busy at lunchtime.

AKATOGARASHI ⑯, **6-27 Togiya-cho. Tel. 25-7966.**
   Cuisine: ITALIAN. **Directions:** A 10-minute walk east of Okayama Station.
$ **Prices:** Main dishes ¥1,000–¥2,000 ($7.15–$14.30). No credit cards.
   Open: Lunch Tues–Sun 11am–3pm; dinner Tues–Sun 5–10pm. **Closed:** Every third Sun.
Akatogarashi means "hot pepper" in Japanese and is the name of this inexpensive Italian restaurant. A one-room place with white stucco walls, heavy ceiling beams, and Italian wine bottles as decoration, it's small and personable, and for some reason attracts mainly young Japanese females, who the manager here figures make up about 80% of his clientele. Available are different kinds of spaghetti and pizzas, as well as chicken, beef, lamb, and fish. There are also set dinners ranging from ¥2,700 to ¥5,500 ($19.30 to $39.30) and a lunch teishoku for ¥900 ($6.40). The restaurant is located east of Okayama Station—walk on Momotaro Dori (the street on which the streetcar runs), cross over the Nishigawa Greenway canal, and then take the third right (there's a stoplight at this corner).

OKABE, 1-10-1 Omotecho. Tel. 22-1404.
   Cuisine: TOFU. **Streetcar:** Shiroshita stop, then a 5-minute walk.
$ **Prices:** Set meals ¥850–¥1,200 ($6.05–$8.55); set lunch ¥750 ($5.35). No credit cards.
   Open: Lunch Mon–Sat 11:30am–3pm; dinner Mon–Sat 5–9pm. **Closed:** National hols.
In the heart of town just off the Omotecho covered shopping arcade is a very popular and informal eatery specializing in homemade tofu. It offers a great lunchtime Okabe Teishoku for ¥750 ($5.35), which consists mainly of tofu dishes, along with rice and pickled vegetables. Seating is along one long counter, behind which an army of women scurry to get out orders. This is one of Okayama's best-known restaurants.

SHOPPING

A sampling of products and crafts made in Okayama Prefecture can be seen at the **Okayama Prefectural Product Center (Okayama-ken Bussan Tenjijo)** ⑯, 1-3-1 Tamachi (tel. 25-4765), about a 10-minute walk from Okayama Station. It features Bizen pottery, rush-grass mats (*igusa*), wood carvings, colorful wooden masks, spirits and papier-mâché toys, and more. Closed holidays, it's open Monday through Saturday from 9am to 5pm.

For general shopping, at Okayama Station there's a large underground shopping arcade called **Ichibangai** with boutiques selling clothing, shoes, and accessories, and across from the station is **Takashimaya,** a department store. In addition, in the heart of the city is also the **Omotecho covered shopping arcade,** where you'll find **Tenmaya,** Okayama's largest department store.

9. KURASHIKI

16 miles W of Okayama

GETTING THERE By Train If you're arriving in Kurashiki by Shinkansen (which takes about 4½ hours from Tokyo and almost 2 hours from Kyoto), you'll arrive at Shin-Kurashiki Station, which is about 6 miles west of Kurashiki Station and the heart of the city. The local train between the stations runs about every 15 minutes.

If you're coming to Kurashiki from the east, it's easier to disembark from the Shinkansen in Okayama and transfer to a local train for the 17-minute ride directly to Kurashiki Station.

By Bus   Buses depart from Okayama Station to Kurashiki on a regular basis.

ESSENTIAL INFORMATION   The **area code** for Kurashiki, lying in Okayama Prefecture, is 0864.

Before leaving Tokyo, pick up the leaflet *Okayama and Kurashiki* at the Tourist Information Center.

In Kurashiki, the **tourist information office** (tel. 0864/26-8681) at Kurashiki Station has maps in English and will point you in the right direction to your hotel. It's located on the second floor of the station near the ticket wicket and is open daily from 9am to 5:30pm. There's another tourist information office, called the **Kurashiki-Kan** (tel. 0864/22-0542), located right on the canal, which also has maps and brochures. It's open from 9am to 5:30pm (5pm in winter) and is the only Western-looking wooden building in the area.

If I were forced to select the most picturesque town in Japan, Kurashiki would certainly be a top contender. In the heart of the city, clustered around a willow-fringed canal, is a delightful area of old buildings and ryokan perfect for camera buffs. As an administrative center of the shogunate in the 17th century, Kurashiki blossomed into a prosperous marketing town where rice, sake, and cotton were collected from the surrounding region and shipped off to Osaka and beyond. Back in those days, wealth was measured in rice, and large granaries were built in which to store the mountains of granules passing through the town. Canals were dug so that barges laden with grain could work their way to ships anchored in the Seto Inland Sea. *Kurashiki,* in fact, means "Warehouse Village." It's these warehouses still standing that give Kurashiki its distinctive charm. In addition, Kurashiki is known throughout Japan for its many art museums. The willow-lined canal with all the museums is only a 10-minute walk from Kurashiki Station, reached by walking south on Chuo Dori.

WHAT TO SEE & DO
BIKAN HISTORICAL AREA

Called the Bikan Historical Area, Kurashiki's old town is small, consisting of a canal lined with graceful willows and 200-year-old granaries made of black-tile walls topped with white mortar. Many of the granaries have been turned into museums, ryokan, restaurants, and boutiques selling hand-blown glass, papier-mâché toys, and mats and handbags made of igusa (rush grass).

Street vendors sell jewelry, their wares laid out beside the canal, and healthy young boys stand ready to give visitors rides in rickshaws. "I hear they're imported from Hong Kong," explains a resident who feels impelled to stop and point out Kurashiki's museums spread out along the canal. He's anxious that I don't miss a thing.

Another Kurashiki resident advises me that because of the crowds that descend upon Kurashiki during the day (about four million tourists come here a year), I should get up early in the morning before the shops and museums open and explore this tiny area while it's still under the magic of the early-morning glow. "Real lovers of Kurashiki come on Monday," he adds, "because that's when most everything is closed and there are less people." But no matter when you come, you're likely to fall under the city's spell. Even rain only enhances the contrasting black and white of the buildings. In other words, one of the most rewarding things to do in Kurashiki is simply to explore.

THE MUSEUMS

OHARA MUSEUM OF ART [OHARA BIJUTSUKAN], 1-1-15 Chuo. Tel. 22-0005.

⭐ A highlight of Kurashiki's Bikan Historical Area is its many fine museums, and foremost in this cultural oasis is the Ohara Museum of Art, which first opened in 1930 and is located right on the canal. The main building, a two-story stone structure resembling a Greek temple, is small but manages to contain the works of such European greats as Picasso, Matisse, Vlaminck, Chagall, Manet, Monet, Degas, Pissarro, Sisley, Toulouse-Lautrec, Gauguin, Cézanne, El Greco, Renoir, Corot, and Rodin. The founder of the museum, Ohara Magosaburo, believed that people even in remote Kurashiki should have the opportunity to view great works of art.

Other galleries on the museum grounds hold modern Japanese paintings, contemporary Japanese and Western art, ceramics, and woodblock prints, including prints by the famous Japanese artist Shiko Munakata, paintings by Ryusei Kishida, and ceramics by Shoji Hamada.

Admission: ¥600 ($4.30) allows entry to all galleries.
Open: Tues–Sun 9am–5pm.

KURASHIKI FOLKCRAFT MUSEUM [KURASHIKI MINGEI-KAN], 1-4-11 Chuo. Tel. 22-1637.

Continuing along the same side of the canal as the Ohara Museum of Art and rounding the curve to the right, you'll come to the Kurashiki Folkcraft Museum, easily identified by its sign in English. With the slogan USABILITY EQUALS BEAUTY, the museum contains folkcrafts not only from Japan but from various countries around the world, giving unique insight into the similarities and differences in cultures as reflected in the items they make and use in daily life. There are baskets made of straw, bamboo, willow, and other materials from Taiwan, Hawaii, Mexico, Sweden, Indonesia, England, Portugal, Germany, and Japan, and there are also ceramics, glass, textiles, and woodwork. The displays are housed in three old rice granaries.

Admission: ¥500 ($3.55).
Open: Mar–Nov Tues–Sun 9am–5pm; Dec–Feb Tues–Sun 9am–4:15pm.

JAPAN RURAL TOY MUSEUM [NIHON KYODOGANGU-KAN], 1-4-16 Chuo. Tel. 22-8058.

Almost next to the Folkcraft Museum is the Japanese Rural Toy Museum, a delightful and colorful display of traditional and antique toys from all over Japan and from various countries (the United States is represented by the cornhusk doll). Included are miniature floats, spinning tops, masks, and kites—2,000 items in all. A store at the entrance sells toys.

Admission: ¥310 ($2.20).
Open: Daily 8am–5pm.

KURASHIKI ARCHAEOLOGICAL MUSEUM [KURASHIKI KOKO-KAN], 1-3-13 Chuo. Tel. 22-1542.

This museum, also in an old granary, houses objects unearthed in the surrounding region, as well as relics of the Incas and Chinese.

Admission: ¥300 ($2.15).
Open: Mar–Nov Tues–Sun 9am–5pm; Dec–Feb Tues–Sun 9am–4:30pm.

OHASHI HOUSE [OHASHIKE JUTAKU], 3-21-31 Achi. Tel. 22-0007.

For a look at what life was like in Kurashiki during the Edo Period, visit this restored home, built in 1796 by a wealthy merchant family that made its fortune in rice and salt. It contains furniture and items used in business and home life during the period.

Admission: ¥300 ($2.15).
Open: Tues–Sun 9am–5pm.

OTHER ATTRACTIONS

A few minutes' walk from the canal and museums is a complex called **Kurashiki Ivy Square.** Built as a cotton mill by a local spinning company in 1888, this handsome redbrick complex shrouded in ivy has been renovated into a hotel, restaurants, museums, and a few boutiques and galleries selling crafts. It's especially romantic in the evening, when from the end of June to the end of August there's a beer garden in the inner courtyard, open daily from 6 to 9:30pm. Classical music wafts from loudspeakers built into the brick floors of the courtyard.

As for museums at Ivy Square, the **Kurabo Memorial Hall** shows the history of the old spinning company, which was Kurashiki's biggest employer for decades, providing jobs for many young women in the area. Perhaps the most interesting thing to see in this museum is a tape made more than 70 years ago showing life at the factory, including the women's dormitory, where many of the single women lived. The tape is located toward the end of the museum and is activated with the push of a button.

Nearby is **Ivy Gakkan,** a museum with a curious mixture of reproductions of the world's famous paintings (perhaps for art students who can't afford trips to see the real thing) and a section devoted to the history of Kurashiki. Interesting here are photographs of the city taken in the early 1900s.

Finally, the **Kojima Memorial Hall** contains more Western art of the Ohara collection, as well as paintings by Torajiro Kojima, who went to Europe to purchase most of the pieces in the Ohara museums. The Oriental Room of the Memorial Hall (with its own separate entrance) contains vases, pottery, glass, and some sculpture from ancient Egypt, Iran, Turkey, and other early cultures.

Entrance to Kurabo Memorial Hall, Ivy Gakkan, and Kojima Memorial Hall costs ¥400 ($2.85) for a combined ticket. Hours for all are 9am to 5pm, but the Kojima Memorial Hall is closed on Monday.

Near Ivy Square is the **Kurabo Orchid Center,** which displays 200 different varieties of orchids in every conceivable shape, color, and size. Daily hours here are 9am to 6pm, and admission is ¥300 ($2.15).

WHERE TO STAY

RYOKAN

TSURUGATA ⑯, **1-3-15 Chuo, Kurashiki 710. Tel. 0864/24-1635.** 13 rms (3 with bath, 10 with toilet only). A/C TV TEL **Directions:** A 15-minute walk from Kurashiki Station to Bikan Historical Area.

$ Rates (per person, including Japanese breakfast and dinner): ¥22,000–¥39,000 ($157–$278) per person. AE, DC, JCB, MC, V.

This ryokan, located in a 240-year-old building on the canal, was once a merchant's house and shop selling rice, cotton, and cooking oil. The rooms here have their own toilet, and there are public baths with instructions in English on how to use them, indicating that they're accustomed to foreign guests here. Rustic furniture, gleaming wood, and high ceilings are trademarks of this ryokan.

Tsurugata also maintains its own small restaurant, serving kaiseki, tempura, and sashimi. The kaiseki dinners here are lovely, beautifully arranged on various dishes and as delicious as they look. Open daily from 11:30am to 2:30pm and 5 to 7pm, it's a good place to stop off for lunch. Mini-kaiseki starts at ¥3,300 ($23.55) for lunch and ¥4,400 ($31.40) for dinner, while sashimi teishoku is ¥1,600 ($11.40).

RYOKAN KURASHIKI ⑯, **4-1 Honmachi, Kurashiki 710. Tel. 0864/22-0730.** 20 rms (9 with bath). A/C TV TEL **Directions:** A 15-minute walk from Kurashiki Station to Bikan Historical Area.

$ Rates (per person, including breakfast and dinner): ¥16,500–¥20,000 ($118–$143) without bath, ¥30,000 ($214) with bath. AE, JCB, MC, V.

The best place to stay to get a feeling of old Kurashiki is right in the heart of it—in one of the old warehouses, made up of an old mansion and three converted rice-and-sugar warehouses more than 250 years old. Located right on Kurashiki's picturesque willow-lined canal and filled with antiques, this ryokan has long, narrow corridors, nooks and crannies, and the peaceful sanctuary of an inner garden. There's no other ryokan in Japan quite like this one—it's fun simply walking through the corridors and looking at all the antiques. No two rooms are alike, and at the Terrace de Ryokan Kurashiki you can sip ceremonial green tea while looking out over a small garden. Even if you don't stay at this ryokan, you may wish to come treat yourself to green tea, which costs ¥620 ($4.40). It goes without saying that there are public communal baths. Western-style breakfasts are available.

MINSHUKU

TOKUSAN KAN ⑰, **6-21 Honmachi, Kurashiki 710. Tel. 0864/25-3056.**
19 rms (1 with bath). A/C TV **Directions:** A 15-minute walk from Kurashiki Station to Bikan Historical Area.

$ Rates (per person): ¥5,500 ($39) without meals; ¥6,500–¥14,000 ($46–$100) with breakfast and dinner. JCB.

A minshuku catering mainly to young Japanese, Tokusan Kan is located near the canal and Kurashiki Ivy Square. The Japanese-style rooms are divided into two separate buildings, one 90 years old and the other 200 years old, but both interiors have been totally renovated and are modern. Both buildings serve lunches to tour groups of Japanese, which can be quite noisy, assuming you want to hang around in your room.

KOKUMIN RYOKAN OHGUMA, 3-1-2 Achi, Kurashiki 710. Tel. 0864/22-0250. 13 rms (2 with bath). A/C TV TEL **Directions:** A 2-minute walk from Kurashiki Station.

$ Rates (per person): ¥4,400–¥6,000 ($31–$43) without meals; ¥6,500–¥11,000 ($46–$78) with breakfast and dinner. No credit cards.

If you wish to stay close to the station, this minshuku is located just across from Kurashiki Station. The entry to this small establishment with Japanese-style rooms is through a narrow shopping arcade, located to the right of the main road leading from the station (not the more obvious, large arcade, located to the left). The ryokan first opened more than 60 years ago, but most of the building dates from about 15 years ago. Its tatami rooms are simple but comfortable.

KAMOI ⑰, **1-24 Honmachi, Kurashiki 710. Tel. 0864/22-4898.** 16 rms (none with bath). A/C TV **Directions:** A 15-minute walk from Kurashiki Station.

$ Rates (per person): ¥4,000 ($28) without meals; ¥5,500–¥9,000 ($39–$64) with breakfast and dinner. No credit cards.

Kamoi is a minshuku located on a slope leading toward Tsurugatayama Park and Achi Shrine, right beside the stone torii gate that leads to the shrine. It's popular among young people, and its fourth-floor rooms have good views of the city. Since the owner of this minshuku is also owner and chef of a restaurant (described later), you can be assured that the food served here is especially good. Although the building was built about a decade ago, it follows an architectural style befitting old Kurashiki. Rooms are simple, with coin-operated TV. Western-style breakfast is served upon request.

MINSHUKU KAWAKAMI ⑰, **1-10-13 Chuo, Kurashiki 710. Tel. 0864/24-1221.** 11 rms (none with bath). A/C TV **Directions:** A 15-minute walk from Kurashiki Station to Bikan Historical Area.

$ Rates (per person): ¥3,900 ($28) without meals; ¥5,500 ($39) with breakfast and dinner. No credit cards.

A NOTE ON JAPANESE SYMBOLS

Many hotels, restaurants, and other establishments in Japan do not have signs giving their names in English letters. As an aid to the reader, Appendix C lists the Japanese symbols for all such places described in this guide. Each set of symbols has a number, which corresponds to the number that appears inside an oval next to the establishment's name in the text. Thus, to find the Japanese symbols for, say, Osaka's **Hotel Hokke Club** ⑬, refer to number 138 in the appendix.

Located on a tiny side street just off the Kurashiki canal and not far from the Japan Rural Toy Museum, this minshuku features simple Japanese-style rooms, with coin-operated TV and air conditioning. Western-style breakfasts are available.

HOTELS

KURASHIKI KOKUSAI HOTEL, 1-1-44 Chuo, Kurashiki 710. Tel. 0864/ 22-5141. Fax 0864/22-5192. 106 rms. A/C MINIBAR TV TEL **Directions:** A 10-minute walk from Kurashiki Station, on Chuo Dori.

$ Rates: ¥9,900 ($71) single; ¥15,500–¥19,000 ($111–$136) double; ¥15,500–¥22,000 ($111–$157) twin. AE, DC, JCB, MC, V.

If you prefer to sleep in a bed rather than on a futon, this is Kurashiki's most popular Western-style hotel—and it's easy to see why. This delightful hotel, built in 1963, blends into its surroundings, with black-tile walls set in white mortar. Inside the hotel's lobby are two huge woodblock prints by Japanese artist Shiko Munakata. Commissioned by the hotel, *Great Barriers of the Universe* is his largest piece.

The atmosphere of the hotel is decidedly old-fashioned, which only adds to the charm. If you prefer more modern surroundings, however, ask for a room in the much newer annex, which features mainly twins with slightly upgraded facilities. The hotel is located behind the Ohara Museum of Art, and its back rooms have a pleasant view of the museum, greenery, and the black-tile roofs of the old granaries. It's a convenient location for exploring the old town. All rooms come with radio, TV, minibar, hot-water pot and tea bags. The more expensive rooms face the back of the hotel, and have the most pleasant views.

Dining/Entertainment: There's a pleasant Western-style restaurant, a Japanese-style restaurant with a tempura corner, a bar, and a beer garden in the backyard open from mid-July to end of August.

Services: Free newspaper, same-day laundry service.

HOTEL KURASHIKI, 1-1-1 Achi, Kurashiki 710. Tel. 0864/26-6111. Fax 0864/26-6163. 139 rms. A/C MINIBAR TV TEL **Directions:** A minute's walk from Kurashiki Station.

$ Rates: ¥8,000–¥9,300 ($57–$66) single; ¥15,500–¥35,000 ($111–$250) twin; ¥21,500 ($153) triple. AE, DC, JCB, MC, V.

If you prefer a place near the station, you can't get any closer than this combination business/tourist hotel, part of the Japan Railways Group. The rooms in this modern, spotless, and attractive hotel are pleasantly decorated with flowered bedspreads and cheerful pastels of green or pink and have nicely tiled bathrooms instead of the usual one-unit cubbyholes of most business hotels. Windows are of double-pane glass to shut out noise, and there are both Japanese and Western restaurants.

KURASHIKI TERMINAL HOTEL ⑰, **1-7-2 Achi, Kurashiki 710. Tel. 0864/26-1111.** Fax 0864/26-9001. 212 rms. A/C TV TEL **Directions:** A minute's walk from Kurashiki Station.

$ Rates: ¥6,500–¥8,200 ($43–$58) single; ¥13,000–¥14,300 ($93–$102) twin; ¥15,900–¥17,500 ($113–$125) triple. AE, DC, JCB, MC, V.

Another business hotel near the station, the Kurashiki Terminal Hotel occupies the top floors of a redbrick building, with a lobby on the ninth floor. Its rooms, on the 10th through 12th floors, come with TV with pay video, minibar, alarm clock, and double-pane windows. On the ninth floor is a restaurant serving both Japanese and Western food, as well as a buffet-style breakfast costing ¥1,000 ($7.15). Vending machines dispense beer and soda, and hot water for tea is free.

KURASHIKI IVY SQUARE HOTEL, 7-2 Honmachi, Kurashiki 710. Tel. 0864/22-0011. Fax 0864/24-0515. 180 rms (52 with bath). A/C MINIBAR TV TEL **Directions:** A 15-minute walk from Kurashiki Station.

$ Rates: ¥6,500–¥7,500 ($46–$53) single without bath, ¥9,500–¥10,700 ($68–$76) single with bath; ¥11,000–¥12,500 ($78–$89) twin without bath, ¥14,800–¥17,000 ($106–$121) twin with bath; ¥18,000 ($128) double with bath; ¥13,200–¥16,500 ($94–$118) triple without bath. AE, DC, JCB, MC, V.

★ Another interesting place to stay and a good choice in this price category, this hotel is located in the converted cotton mill on Ivy Square. The rooms have a somewhat stark but country feel, and come with the usual minibar, clock, and hot water for tea, among other amenities, plus toilet. All doubles are with bath, while triples are without. Much of the architectural style of the old mill has been left intact. The best rooms face a tiny expanse of green grass and an ivy-covered wall. Pleasant restaurants serve Japanese and Western food.

EL PASO INN, 1-9-4 Chuo, Kurashiki 710. Tel. 0864/21-8282. 30 rms (all with bath). A/C MINIBAR (in most rooms) TV TEL **Directions:** A 15-minute walk from Kurashiki Station.

$ Rates (including service): ¥6,000 ($43) single; ¥10,900 ($78) for two in a semidouble-size bed; ¥12,000 ($86) twin; ¥17,500 ($125) triple; ¥24,000 ($171) quad. AE, JCB, MC, V.

Not far from the Ohara Museum of Art and the Bikan Historical Area is the El Paso Inn, which opened in 1987 and appeals mainly to the younger set with its simple, breezy architecture reminiscent of the American Southwest. It features a pleasant, contemporary restaurant with seating under a glass-domed inner courtyard. Rooms are simple, with tiny bathrooms, and those on the third floor facing north have the best view. There are bicycles available free of charge to hotel guests.

YOUNG INN KURASHIKI, 1-14-8 Achi, Kurashiki 710. Tel. 0864/25-3411. 39 rms (4 with bath). A/C TV **Directions:** A 1-minute walk from south exit of Kurashiki Station.

$ Rates: ¥3,800 ($27) single occupancy in twin without bath, ¥6,500 ($46) single occupancy in twin with bath; ¥6,500 ($46) twin without bath, ¥7,500 ($53) twin with bath. No credit cards.

If all the hostelries suggested above are full, you might try a rather different kind of place called Young Inn Kurashiki. A redbrick building behind the Terminal Hotel, it has a youth-hostel feel and seems more European than Japanese. Painted in bright primary colors, it looks as though it might have been rather chic at one time but has faded somewhat with neglect. Informal, it caters mainly to young people, with two to three beds per room; the beds are arranged on different levels in bunk-bed style. In fact, the three-bed rooms on the fifth floor have to be seen to be believed—the third bed is about 10 feet off the floor and you have to climb a ladder to reach it. Definitely for the nimble unafraid of heights.

YOUTH HOSTELS

KURASHIKI YOUTH HOSTEL, 1537-1 Mukoyama, Kurashiki 710. Tel. 0864/22-7355. 60 beds. A/C **Directions:** A 30-minute walk south of Kurashiki Station, past Bikan Historical Area.

$ Rates: ¥2,300 ($16.40) per person; ¥700 ($5) extra without membership card. Breakfast ¥450 ($3.20); dinner ¥850 ($6.05). No credit cards.

This youth hostel, located in Mukoyama Park, has a policy of accepting card-carrying members only, but has been known to let in unknowing foreign nonmembers who show up forlornly on their doorstep. What you do with that bit of information is up to you. There are eight persons to a room, and there are laundry facilities.

WHERE TO DINE

WISTERIA, Kurashiki Kokusai Hotel, 1-1-44 Chuo. Tel. 22-5141.
Cuisine: WESTERN. **Directions:** A 10-minute walk south of Kurashiki Station, on Chuo Dori.
$ Prices: Set dinners ¥4,500–¥7,500 ($32.15–$53.55); set lunches ¥1,600–¥3,300 ($11.40–$23.55). AE, DC, JCB, MC, V.
Open: Lunch daily 11am–2pm; dinner daily 6–9pm.

For Western dining close to the canal, this place offers a pleasant setting with large windows. Lunch includes such dishes as seafood, salads, spaghetti, sandwiches, and beef or shrimp curry, with most dishes between ¥1,000 and ¥1,800 ($7.15 and $12.85), as well as set lunches. The dinner menu includes seafood, roast duck with peach, stewed beef, grilled salmon, lobster, and steaks. If it's available, try the *sawara* (a locally caught fish) in champagne.

KIYUTEI, 1-2-20 Chuo. Tel. 22-5140.

Cuisine: STEAKS. **Directions:** A 15-minute from Kurashiki Station, in Bikan Historical Area.

$ Prices: Main dishes ¥1,000–¥2,000 ($7.15–$14.30); steak dinners ¥2,700–¥6,600 ($19.30–$47.15). AE, DC, JCB, MC, V.

Open: Tues–Sun 11am–9pm (last order 8:30pm).

Kiyutei is located across from the main entrance of the Ohara Museum of Art at the head of the canal. Enter through the front gate, pass through the small courtyard, and go into a small room dominated by a counter with cooks grilling steaks, the specialty of the house. Steak dinners, which come with soup, salad, and rice or roll, are available, as well as grilled lobster or salmon, stewed beef with soup, hamburger steak, spaghetti, fried shrimp, and grilled chicken. There's an English menu.

KAMOI ⑰, 1-3-17 Chuo. Tel. 22-0606.

Cuisine: SUSHI. **Directions:** A 15-minute walk from Kurashiki Station, in Bikan Historical District.

$ Prices: Set meals ¥1,300–¥2,200 ($9.30–$15.70). No credit cards.

Open: Tues–Sun 9am–6pm.

⑤ This sushi restaurant is run by the man who has a minshuku of the same name. It's located in a 200-year-old rice granary along Kurashiki's willow-fringed canal, across from the Ohara Museum of Art. Inside, the stark-white walls and dark wooden beams are decorated with such antiques as cast-iron teapots, old rifles, gourds, and samurai hats. Since the menu is in Japanese, you can select from the plastic-food display outside the front door. In addition to sushi set meals, there are also tempura, eel, and daikonzushi, a local rice dish covered with vegetables and seafood and commonly served during festivals. During winter the same dish is served warm and is called *nukuzushi*. The cost of both rice casseroles is ¥1,000 ($7.15).

TSUTA, Ivy Square. Tel. 22-0011.

Cuisine: VARIED JAPANESE. **Directions:** A few minutes' walk from Bikan Historical District.

$ Prices: Set meals ¥2,000–¥3,000 ($14.30–$21.40); kaiseki ¥5,500–¥8,800 ($39.30–$62.85). AE, DC, JCB, MC, V.

Open: Lunch daily 11:30am–2pm; dinner daily 5–9:30pm.

Tsuta means "ivy" in Japanese, a reference to the fact that the restaurant is in Ivy Square, and serves local Kurashiki specialties, including special rice dishes, fish, obento, sukiyaki, shabu-shabu, and farm products. Set in the converted spinning factory, it has high ceilings and is airy and bright. The most popular dish consists of rice with red beans, sashimi, fried tofu, and vegetables and is called *obento rikyu*.

RESTAURANT IVY, Ivy Square. Tel. 22-0011.

Cuisine: WESTERN. **Directions:** A few minutes' walk from Bikan Historical District.

$ Prices: Main dishes ¥1,000–¥2,500 ($7.15–$17.85); set meals ¥2,000–¥4,900 ($14.30–$35). AE, DC, JCB, MC, V.

Open: Daily 11:30am–9:30pm.

Next to Tsuta in Ivy Square is this restaurant, which serves Western fare. Decorated with an ivy theme—even the tablecloths and napkins are green with designs of vines—it also has the high ceiling of the original factory. Set menus range from a minute hamburger-steak course to sirloin or tenderloin steak dinners. A la carte main dishes include salmon or shrimp, scallops, chicken, pork ginger, beef teriyaki, and beef Stroganoff. Less expensive dishes include beef or shrimp curry, mixed pilaf, spaghetti, and sandwiches for ¥1,000 to ¥1,500 ($7.15 to $10.70).

SPECIALTY DINING

After visiting the Ohara Museum of Art you might wish to stop in at the **El Greco Coffeehouse** (tel. 22-0297) next door. An ivy-colored stone building, it's

Kurashiki's most famous coffee shop and is simply decorated with a wooden floor, wooden tables and benches, and vases of fresh flowers. It serves coffee, green tea, milkshakes, ice cream, and cake from 10am to 5pm. It's closed Monday.

10. MATSUE

570 miles W of Tokyo; 116 miles NW of Okayama;
251 miles NE of Hakata (Fukuoka)

GETTING THERE By Train The easiest way to reach Matsue is from Okayama via a 3-hour train ride. There's also one daily express to Matsue directly from Hiroshima (a beautiful ride, by the way), and one train a day from Hakata Station in Fukuoka.

ESSENTIAL INFORMATION The **area code** for Matsue, lying in Shimane Prefecture, is 0852.

At the Tokyo or Kyoto Tourist Information Center, be sure to pick up the leaflet *Matsue and Izumo-Taisha Shrine*.

Upon arrival at Matsue Station, stop off at one of the **tourist information offices.** One is located in the station itself and is open daily from 8:30am to 7pm. An additional information office is located to the left after you leave the station by the north exit, and it's open daily from 9am to 5:30pm. Both locations have an English-language brochure with a good map of the city. If you have any questions, call the tourist office (tel. 0852/27-2598).

GETTING AROUND Although Matsue's sights are concentrated in one area of town and are easy to find on your own, you may want a **"goodwill guide"** to show you around, especially if you're going to Izumo-Taisha Shrine. Established by the Japan National Tourist Organization, the goodwill guide network is composed of volunteers with foreign-language abilities who act as guides in their city. All you have to do is pay their entrance fees into museums and sights—and it's nice if you buy them lunch too. If you wish to have guides (they're always assigned in pairs), apply the day before at one of the tourist information offices before 4pm.

Matsue's attractions lie to the north of the station, and although **buses** run virtually everywhere, you can easily cover the distances **on foot.**

With a population of about 140,000, Matsue lies near the northern coast of western Honshu in Shimane Prefecture. It's off the beaten track of most foreign tourists, who keep to a southerly route in their travels toward Kyushu. The Japanese, however, are quite fond of Matsue, and a fair number of them choose to spend their summer vacation at this pleasant small town. I'll always remember Matsue as the place where the local schoolchildren greet foreigners with "*konnichiwa*" (good afternoon) instead of the usual "*haro*" (hello), testimony to the fact that foreigners are still few and far between.

At last check with the Japan National Tourist Organization, only 1 of the more than 130 group tours organized by foreign tour operators included Matsue in its itinerary of Japan. And yet Matsue, hugging the shores of Lake Shinji, has a number of cultural assets that make a trip here worthwhile.

WHAT TO SEE & DO

MATSUE CASTLE

First built in 1611 and partly reconstructed in 1642, Matsue Castle (tel. 21-4030) was the only castle along this northern stretch of coast built for warfare rather than merely as a residence. It's also one of Japan's few remaining original castles—that is, it's not a reconstruction. Rising up from a hill with a good view of the city about a mile northwest of Matsue Station, the five-story donjon (which actually conceals six floors to give its warriors a fighting advantage) houses the usual daimyo and samurai gear, including armor, swords, and helmets belonging to the ruling Matsudaira clan.

Lafcadio Hearn, a European who lived in Matsue in the 1890s, adopted Japanese citizenship, and wrote extensively about Japan and the Japanese, said of Matsue Castle: "Crested at its summit, like a feudal helmet, with two colossal fishes of bronze lifting their curved bodies skyward from either angle of the roof and bristling with horned gables and gargoyled eaves and tilted puzzles of tiles roofing at every story, the creation is a veritable architectural dragon, made up of magnificent monstrosities."

As you walk through the castle up to the top floor, notice the staircase. Although it looks sturdy, it's light enough to be pulled up to halt enemy intrusions. And to think that the castle almost met its demise during the Meiji Restoration, when the ministry of armed forces auctioned it off. Luckily, former vassals of the clan pooled their resources and bought the castle keep. In 1927 the grounds were donated to the city. It is open daily from 8:30am to 5pm; admission is ¥310 ($2.20).

ATTRACTIONS NEAR THE CASTLE

Just south of Matsue Castle is the **Matsue Cultural Museum (Matsue Kyodo-kan)** ⑭ (tel. 22-3958), a white Western-style building erected in honor of Emperor Meiji in 1903. Open daily from 8:30am to 5pm and charging ¥155 ($1.10) admission, it displays crafts, utensils, and implements of everyday life from the Meiji Period, beginning in 1868 and extending through the early 1900s. There are old photographs, manuscripts, old obento lunch boxes, combs and hairpins, and tea-ceremony objects.

If you walk from Matsue Castle north along its moat, in about 5 minutes you'll come to a number of attractions. Stop off at **Teahouse Meimei-an** ⑮ (tel. 21-9863), one of Japan's most renowned and well-preserved thatch-roofed teahouses, which was built in 1779. It's located at the top of a flight of stairs from which you have a good view of Matsue Castle. For the entrance fee of ¥200 ($1.40) and an additional ¥300 ($2.15), you can have the bitter Japanese green tea and sweets served to you before moving off to your next destination. It's open daily from 9am to 5pm.

Buke Yashiki ⑯ (tel. 22-2243), a few minutes' walk from the teahouse, is an ancient samurai house open daily to the public from 8:30am to 5pm. Facing the castle moat, it was built in 1730 and belonged to the Shiomi family, one of the chief retainers of the feudal lord residing in the castle. High-ranking samurai, the Shiomi family lived pretty much like kings themselves, having separate servants' quarters and even a shed for their palanquin. Compared with samurai residences in wealthier regions of Japan, however, this samurai house is considered rather austere. As you walk around it, peering into rooms with their wooden walls slid open to the outside breeze, you'll see furniture and objects used in daily life by samurai during the Edo Period. Admission is ¥200 ($1.40).

On the same street as this samurai house are two more attractions. The **Tanabe Art Museum (Tanabe Bijutsukan)** ⑰ is a modern building housing changing exhibits of ceramics and artwork, particularly items used in the tea ceremony; open Tuesday through Sunday from 9am to 5pm (except Monday and days of exhibit changes). Its admission ranges from ¥500 to ¥750 ($3.55 to $5.35), depending on the exhibit. The **Hearn Memorial Hall (Hearn Kinenkan)** contains memorabilia of writer Lafcadio Hearn (1850–1904), including his desk, manuscripts, and smoking pipes. The Japanese are fascinated with this man who married a Japanese, became a Japanese citizen, and adopted the name Koizumi Yakumo. Writing a number of books about Japan, he was one of the first writers to give the Japanese the chance to see themselves through the eyes of a foreigner. His books still provide insight into Japanese life at the turn of the century and are available at all bookstores in Japan with an English section.

Since most Japanese will assume it's out of respect for Hearn that you've come to Matsue, you may want to read one of his books before coming here. His volume *Glimpses of Unfamiliar Japan* contains an essay called "In a Japanese Garden," in which he gives his impressions of Matsue, where he lived for 15 months before moving to Kumamoto to teach English. This memorial is open daily from 8:30am to 5pm and admission is ¥205 ($1.45). Near the memorial is a Japanese-style house where Hearn lived. Charging ¥150 ($1.05), it's open Thursday through Tuesday from 9am to 4:30pm (5pm in summer).

About a 15-minute walk west of Matsue Castle is **Gesshoji Temple** ⑰, the family temple of the Matsudaira clan. It was established back in 1664 by Matsudaira Naomasa, whose grandfather was the powerful Tokugawa Ieyasu. Nine generations of the Matsudaira clan are buried here. The temple is open daily from 8am to 6pm (5pm in winter), and admission is ¥300 ($2.15).

The most important religious structure in the vicinity of Matsue, however, is **Izumo-Taisha Shrine.** It's a 55-minute ride from Matsue-onsen Station to Izumo-Taisha-mae Station, with a change of trains at Kawato Station. The shrine is important because its site is the oldest in Japan. It's probably the most popular attraction in the area, but as with most things in Japan, the present shrine buildings date only from 1744 and 1874. Dedicated to the Shinto deity responsible for medicine and farming, the shrine is constructed in an ancient style, simple and dignified.

WHERE TO STAY

Accommodations in Matsue include ryokan, tourist hotels, and business hotels, most of them within walking distance of Matsue Station.

RYOKAN

MINAMI-KAN ⑰**, 14 Suetsugu Honmachi, Matsue 690. Tel. 0852/21-5131.** 12 rms (9 with bath). A/C MINIBAR TV TEL **Directions:** An 8-minute taxi ride from Matsue Station, or a 15-minute walk north.

$ Rates (per person, including breakfast and dinner): ¥17,500–¥30,000 ($125–$214) per person. Room in lake house: ¥35,000–¥45,000 ($250–$321). DC, JCB, MC, V.

Minami-Kan, located off the Kyomise covered shopping arcade in the heart of Matsue, has Japanese-style rooms that face Lake Shinji. Completely remodeled in 1985, it has modern rooms that come with fridge and other amenities. Western breakfasts are available. If you want to feel special, there are two rooms in a separate little house right beside the lake. Minami-kan is also renowned for its restaurant, described in the "Where to Dine" section, below.

HORAISO ⑱**, Tonomachi, Matsue 690. Tel. 0852/21-4337.** 10 rms (3 with bath). A/C MINIBAR TV TEL **Directions:** A 10-minute taxi ride from Matsue Station.

$ Rates (per person): ¥14,000–¥22,000 ($100–$157) with breakfast and dinner; ¥10,000 ($71) without meals. No credit cards.

⭐ Tucked away on a side street not far from Matsue Castle, this 50-year-old ryokan is guarded by a wall, an imposing wooden gateway, and a pine tree. Each room is different and faces an inner courtyard garden. This is one of the few ryokan that doesn't mind if you want to take your meals elsewhere. The higher-priced rooms are those with a private bathroom.

HOTELS

TOKYU INN, 590 Asahimachi, Matsue 690. Tel. 0852/27-0109. Fax 0852/25-1327. 181 rms. A/C MINIBAR TV TEL. **Directions:** Across street from Matsue Station's north exit.

$ Rates (including service): ¥7,400–¥8,000 ($53–$57) single; ¥13,800–¥16,500 ($98–$118) double/twin. AE, DC, JCB, MC, V.

One of Matsue's newer business hotels and part of a national chain, the Tokyu Inn offers rooms of adequate size that come with everything you'd need. Vending machines dispense beer, cold coffee, soda, and whisky. The front desk is courteous, and facilities include the Shangri-La restaurant, which serves both Western and

Japanese dishes. It's open from 11am to 2pm and 5 to 9pm, offering seafood, steaks, spaghetti, tempura, and sandwiches. Japanese-style obento lunch boxes cost ¥1,000 ($7.15). If you're on a budget or like sitting outside, Tokyu Inn also has a rooftop beer garden open in summer from 5:30 to 9pm. Beer starts at ¥550 ($3.90), and there's also an all-you-can-eat menu available for ¥3,300 ($23.55).

HOTEL ICHIBATA, 30 Chidori-cho, Matsue 690. Tel. 0852/22-0188. Fax 0852/22-0230. 138 rms. A/C MINIBAR TV TEL **Bus:** A 15-minute ride from Matsue Station to Matsue Onsen stop. **Directions:** A 30-minute walk from station, north over bridge and then to left.

$ Rates: ¥7,500 ($53) single; ¥12,000 ($86) double; ¥12,000 ($86) twin facing inland, ¥17,500 ($125) twin facing the lake. Japanese-style rooms: ¥18,000– ¥35,000 ($128–$250) double occupancy. AE, JCB, V.

Matsue's best-known tourist hotel is the Hotel Ichibata, in a part of town called Matsue Onsen, a hot-spring spa. It's not very conveniently located, since it's a hike from the station and a 20-minute walk to Matsue Castle. In addition, it's seen better days (it was built in 1968). Still, it does have hot-spring public baths on the seventh floor, with views over the nearby Lake Shinji. It also has a summertime beer garden on its front lawn, as well as one restaurant serving Japanese and Western fare. Rooms are equipped with clock, minibar, radio, and hot-water pot for tea. None of the singles or doubles have views of the lake, but all of the Japanese-style rooms do, including some combination-style rooms with both beds and tatami area.

MATSUE URBAN HOTEL ⑱, **590-3 Asahimachi, Matsue 690. Tel. 0852/22-0002.** 281 rms. A/C MINIBAR TV TEL **Directions:** Across street from Matsue Station's north exit.

$ Rates (including tax and service): ¥5,000 ($36) single; ¥7,300 ($52) semidouble for two persons; ¥9,600 ($68) twin. Annex: ¥5,000 ($36) single; ¥7,900 ($56) double. AE, DC, JCB, MC, V.

This hotel is a red building to the right of the Tokyu Inn, about a minute's walk from the train station. Although the 60 single rooms are rather small, with tiny windows, all beds are semidoubles, and the 10 twins are all corner rooms with large windows. Rooms are pleasant, with fridge, clock, and TV with pay video, but large people may have trouble fitting into the tiny tubs. There's a Japanese restaurant, as well as a Western restaurant that serves spaghetti and pilaf. The front desk is on the second floor.

If there are two of you and you want to sleep in the same bed, you're welcome to one of the single's semidouble-size beds. You're probably better off, however, moving to the Urban's new annex building next door, which offers single and double rooms. The phone number is the same as the one for the main hotel.

MATSUE PLAZA HOTEL ⑱, **469-1 Asahimachi, Matsue 690. Tel. 0852/ 26-6650.** 178 rms (all with bath). A/C TV TEL **Directions:** Across from Matsue Station's south exit.

$ Rates: ¥3,800–¥4,700 ($27–$33) single; ¥8,200 ($58) double/twin. Weekend discount on single rooms. JCB, MC, V.

Although most of Matsue's attractions and hotels are located north of the station, there are a couple inexpensive business hotels across the street from the station's south exit. This redbrick-and-brown business hotel, with its front desk located on the second floor, is a bit old, with worn carpets and small rooms, but prices are cheap. On weekends, when business traffic is slow, the price for single rooms drops a couple of hundred yen. No rooms have a great view, but those on the top floor are best. All rooms have windows that open, coin-operated TV with pay video, clock, and hot-water pot. Both Japanese and Western restaurants are located in the hotel building.

MATSUE MINAMI GUCHI HOTEL ⑱, **470-1 Asahimachi, Matsue 690. Tel. 0852/27-2000.** 43 rms (all with bath). A/C MINIBAR TV TEL **Directions:** Across street from Matsue's south exit.

$ Rates: ¥3,800–¥4,400 ($27–$31) single; ¥8,200 ($58) double/twin. No credit cards.

To the right of the Plaza Hotel is a white building on a corner that contains the Matsue Minami Guchi Hotel. Its name means "South Exit Hotel." The people working the front desk (on the second floor) are accommodating, and the guest rooms are typical business-hotel rooms with minibar and clock. Otherwise, not much to differentiate this business hotel from the one above.

YOUTH HOSTEL

MATSUE YOUTH HOSTEL ⑱, **1546 Kososhicho, Matsue 690-01. Tel. 0852/36-8620.** 52 beds. A/C **Directions:** Bus from Matsue Station to Matsue Onsen, transferring there to train to Furue Station, then a 10-minute walk. **Bus:** From Matsue Station to Furue, the last stop.

$ Rates (per person): ¥2,300 ($16.40) members, ¥2,800 ($20) nonmembers. Breakfast ¥450 ($3.20); dinner ¥850 ($6.05). No credit cards.

Although this hostel is officially for members only, it occasionally takes in foreigners without membership cards. However, it's a bit inconvenient to reach, since buses that go to Furue directly from Matsue Station are infrequent. Stop at the Matsue tourist office in the train station for directions to the hostel, which offers laundry facilities and bicycles for rent.

WHERE TO DINE

MINAMI-KAN ⑲, **14 Suetsugu Honmachi. Tel. 0852/21-5131.**
Cuisine: KAISEKI/LOCAL DISHES. **Reservations:** Recommended. **Directions:** A 15-minute walk north of Matsue Station, off Kyomise covered shopping arcade.

$ Prices: Set meals ¥3,800–¥8,800 ($27.15–$62.85); lunch specials ¥1,800–¥3,000 ($12.85–$21.40). DC, JCB, MC, V.
Open: Lunch daily 11:30am–2:30pm; dinner daily 5–9pm.

This restaurant, in the same building as the Minami-Kan ryokan (described above), is modern and sophisticated, with views of a gravel garden and the lake. Of the various set lunches, I especially recommend the mini-kaiseki Hanagoromo set lunch, with its various dishes of bite-size morsels. For dinner, there are set meals of various local specialties, including fish of Lake Shinji, and kaiseki.

KANEYASU ⑱, **Otesemba-cho. Tel. 21-0550.**
Cuisine: FISH/JAPANESE. **Directions:** A 2-minute walk directly north of Matsue Station, behind Meiji Seimei Building.

$ Prices: Dinners average ¥3,000 ($21.40); lunch teishoku ¥600 ($4.30). No credit cards.
Open: Mon–Fri 11:30am–9pm, Sat 5–7pm. **Closed:** Hols.

This modest one-counter place has good food and is run by motherly bustling women. It's been around for more than 20 years, and most of its customers are local working people, so avoid the noontime rush. It has a great lunch teishoku for ¥600 ($4.30) that includes a piece of *yakizakana* (grilled fish), vegetable, soup, tofu, rice, and tea. It's served from 10:30am to "whenever"; I came at 3pm and still got the lunch special. If you come for dinner and indulge in sake, sashimi, and grilled fish, expect to spend about ¥3,000 ($21.40). Highly recommended.

GINSEN ⑱, **Asahimachi. Tel. 21-2381.**
Cuisine: RICE CASSEROLES. **Directions:** A few minutes' walk from Matsue Station; take north exit and then turn right.

$ Prices: Kamameshi ¥850–¥1,000 ($6.05–$7.15); Hakozen teishoku ¥3,000 ($21.40). AE, DC, JCB, MC, V.
Open: Mon–Sat 11am–10pm.

This well-known and popular restaurant is located on the street that runs right in front of the station's north side. Its specialty is kamameshi (rice casseroles), which change with the season and may include such toppings as red snapper, oysters, eel, and other delicacies. The Hakozen teishoku includes kamameshi, sashimi, soup, rice, and numerous side dishes.

YAGUMOAN ⑱, Matsue Castle. Tel. 22-2400.
   Cuisine: SOBA NOODLES. **Directions:** North of Matsue Castle, facing moat.
$ **Prices:** Noodles ¥600–¥1,600 ($4.30–$11.40). AE, DC, JCB, MC, V.
   Open: Daily 9am–5pm.

A wonderful place to stop off for lunch if you're sightseeing north of Matsue Castle, this restaurant is located between the Buke Yashiki samurai house and the Tanabe Art Museum on the road bordering the castle moat. This lovely soba shop with a teahouselike atmosphere is surrounded by bamboo, bonsai, a Japanese garden, and a pond. The noodles here are all handmade. Surrounded by a stone wall with a large wooden entryway, part of this restaurant is 200 years old and is a former samurai residence. A plastic-food display case is located to the left as you step through the entryway.

SHOPPING

For one-stop shopping for locally crafted goods, visit the **Shimane Souvenir and Handcraft Center (Shimane-ken Bussankanko-kan),** Tonomachi (tel. 22-5758), just southeast of Matsue Castle, near the Ichibata department store in the Kenmin Kaikan Building. It sells everything from ceramics to furniture to toys and foodstuffs, all products of Shimane Prefecture. It's open daily from 9:30am to 6pm.

More local products are on sale at the **Matsue Folk Art Center (Matsue Meisan Center),** 212 Chidori-cho (tel. 21-5252), located next to the Ichibata Hotel in an area of town called Matsue Onsen. Open daily from 9am to 9pm, it also features a stage on the third floor where music, dance, and other traditional performing arts shows are given four times every day except in December. The cost is ¥450 ($3.20). Inquire at the tourist office for current showtimes.

11. HIROSHIMA

554 miles W of Tokyo; 235 miles W of Kyoto;
174 miles E of Hakata/Fukuoka

GETTING THERE By Train Hiroshima is 4½ hours from Tokyo by Shinkansen bullet train, 2 hours from Kyoto, and 1 hour and 20 minutes from Hakata Station.

By Bus Buses from Tokyo Station reach Hiroshima in 12 hours.

ESSENTIAL INFORMATION The **area code** for Hiroshima, lying in Hiroshima Prefecture, is 082.

Before leaving Tokyo, pick up a copy of the leaflet *Hiroshima and Miyajima* at the Tourist Information Center.

The Hiroshima **city tourist offices** are located both at Hiroshima Station, open daily from 9am to 5:30pm; and in the Rest House at the north end of Peace Memorial Park, open daily from 9:30am to 6pm April through September and from 8:30am to 5pm October through March. Both locations have a brochure and map in English. If you have any questions, call the tourist office at 082/261-1811.

ORIENTATION & GETTING AROUND The Hondori covered shopping arcade and its neighboring streets are considered the heart of the city and are located to the east of Peace Park. Close by is Nagarikawa, Hiroshima's nightlife district.

There are **tram** and **bus** lines running through the city, but you can make the circuit between Shukkei-en Garden, Hiroshima Castle, and Peace Memorial Park on **foot.** Shukkei-en Garden is 15 minutes from Hiroshima Station; Hiroshima Castle is 5 minutes from the garden; and from the castle to the park it's another 15-minute walk, passing the A-Bomb Dome on the way.

SPECIAL EVENTS Hiroshima's most important event is the peace demonstration held here every year on August 6.

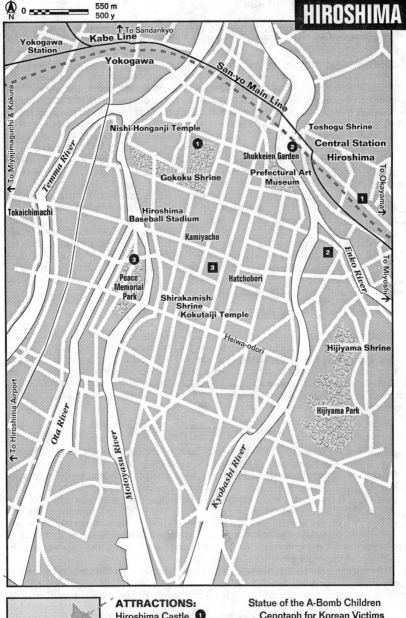

HIROSHIMA

To Sandankyo
Kabe Line
Yokogawa Station
Yokogawa
San-yo Main Line
Yokogawa Station
To Miyajimaguchi & Kokura
Temma River
Nishi-Honganji Temple
Toshogu Shrine
Central Station
Hiroshima
Shukkeien Garden
Prefectural Art Museum
Gokoku Shrine
To Okayama
Tokaichimachi
Hiroshima Baseball Stadium
Enko River
To Miyoshi
Kamiyacho
Peace Memorial Park
Hatchobori
Shirakamisha Shrine
Kokutaiji Temple
Hijiyama Shrine
Heiwa-odori
To Hiroshima Airport
Ota River
Motoyasu River
Kyobashi River
Hijiyama Park

JAPAN
Hiroshima
TOKYO

ATTRACTIONS:
Hiroshima Castle ❶
Peace Memorial Park: ❸
   Peace Memorial Museum
   Peace Memorial Hall
   Memorial Cenotaph
   Peace Flame
   A-Bomb Dome

Statue of the A-Bomb Children
   Cenotaph for Korean Victims
Shukkei-en Garden ❷

ACCOMMODATIONS:
Hiroshima City Hotel **2**
Hiroshima Kokusai Hotel **3**
Hiroshima Terminal Hotel **1**

With a population of approximately one million, Hiroshima looks just like any other up-and-coming city in Japan. Modern buildings, industry, the manufacture of cars and ships—the city is full of vitality and purpose, with a steady flow of both Japanese and foreign business executives in and out of the city.

But unlike other cities, Hiroshima's past is clouded: it has the unfortunate distinction of being the first city ever destroyed by an atomic bomb (the second city, and hopefully the last, was Nagasaki). It happened one clear summer morning, August 6, 1945, at 8:15, when three B-29s approached Hiroshima from the northeast. One of them passed over the central part of the city, dropped the bomb, and then took off at full speed. The bomb exploded 43 seconds later at an altitude of 1,900 feet in a huge fireball, followed by a mushroom cloud of smoke that rose 29,700 feet in the air.

There were approximately 400,000 people living in Hiroshima at the time of the bombing and about half of them lost their lives. The heat from the blast was so intense that it seared people's skin, while the pressure caused by the explosion tore clothes off bodies and caused the rupture and explosion of intestines and other internal organs. Flying glass tore through flesh like bullets, and fires broke out over the city. But that wasn't the end of it. Victims who survived the blast were subsequently exposed to huge doses of radioactivity. Their hair fell out, their gums bled, their white-blood cells decreased, and many died of leukemia or other forms of cancer. Even people who showed no outward signs of sickness suddenly died, creating a feeling of panic and helplessness in the survivors. And today, people still continue to suffer from the effects of the bomb, including a high incidence of cancer, disfigurement, scars, and keloid skin tissue.

WHAT TO SEE & DO

As you walk around Hiroshima today, you'll find it hard to imagine that the city was the scene of such widespread horror and destruction more than 45 years ago. On the other hand, Hiroshima does not have the old buildings, temples, and historical structures other cities have. But it draws a steady flow of travelers, who come to see Peace Memorial Park, the city's best-known landmark. Hiroshima is also the most popular gateway for cruises of the Seto Inland Sea and for trips to Miyajima, a jewel of an island covered later in this chapter.

PEACE MEMORIAL PARK

The main focus of Peace Memorial Park, in the center of the city, is **Peace Memorial Museum** (241-4004). The exhibit begins with a description of the atomic bomb that destroyed the city, the route that the American B-29s took to drop the bomb, and the intensity of the blast's epicenter. It then shows in graphic detail the effects of the blast on bodies, buildings, and materials. Most of the photographs in the exhibit are of burned and seared skin, charred remains of bodies, and people with open wounds. There's a bronze Buddha that was half melted in the blast, and melted glass and ceramics. There are also some granite steps that show a dark shadow where someone had been sitting at the time of the explosion—the shadow is all that remains of that person.

The museum opens at 9am and closes at 6pm May through November; it closes at 5pm December through April. Note that the ticket window closes a half hour before closing time. Admission fee is ¥50 (35¢). The exhibits all have excellent explanations in English.

Next to the museum is **Peace Memorial Hall,** where two documentaries in

---

IMPRESSIONS

We had found the awesome sight of a Hiroshima that was now even bigger than it had been before the bomb, far richer and more prosperous.
—JAMES CAMERON, POINT OF DEPARTURE, 1967

English are shown throughout the day on the second floor. One focuses on Hiroshima and the results of the bombing, while the second film takes a more scientific look at the atomic bombs in both Hiroshima and Nagasaki.

North of the museum is the **Memorial Cenotaph,** designed by Japan's famous architect Kenzo Tange (who also designed Tokyo's Akasaka Prince Hotel). Shaped like a figurine clay saddle found in ancient tombs, it shelters a stone chest, which in turn holds the names of those killed by the bomb. An epitaph, written in Japanese, carries the hopeful phrase, "Repose ye in Peace, for the error shall not be repeated." If you stand in front of the cenotaph, you have a view through the hollow arch of the Peace Flame and the Atomic-Bomb Dome. The **Peace Flame** will continue to burn until all atomic weapons vanish from the face of the earth and nuclear war is no longer a threat to humanity. The **A-Bomb Dome** is the skeletal ruins of the former Industrial Promotion Hall—it was left as a visual reminder of the death and destruction caused by the single bomb.

Also in the park is the **Statue of the A-Bomb Children,** dedicated to the war's most innocent victims, who died instantly in the blast or afterward from the effects of radiation. The statue is of a girl with outstretched arms, and rising above her is a crane, symbol of happiness and longevity in Japan. The statue is based on the true story of a young girl who suffered from the effects of radiation after the bombing in Hiroshima. She believed that if she could fold 1,000 paper cranes she would become well again. After folding her 964th crane, however, she died. Today, all Japanese children are familiar with her story, and around the memorial are streamers of paper cranes donated by schoolchildren from all over Japan.

Needless to say, visiting Peace Memorial Park is a rather sobering and depressing experience, but it's perhaps a necessary one. Every concerned individual should be informed of the effects of an atomic bomb and should be aware that what was dropped on Hiroshima is small compared to the hydrogen bombs of today.

Incidentally, just outside Peace Memorial Park, across the Honkawa River, is the **Cenotaph for Korean Victims.** It's a little-publicized fact that 20,000 Koreans (in other words, 10% of those who perished) were killed that fateful summer day, most of them brought to Japan as forced laborers. The monument reads: "The Korean victims were given no funerals or memorial services and their spirits hovered for years unable to pass on to heaven. . . ." It's significant that the cenotaph is outside the park—even today, Koreans and their descendants face discrimination in Japan. But I must also add that it was a concerned and conscientious Japanese woman who made sure I saw this monument.

HIROSHIMA CASTLE

Originally built in 1593 but destroyed in the atomic blast, Hiroshima Castle was reconstructed in 1958. Its five-story donjon, or keep, is a faithful reproduction of the original one. It's open from 9am to 5:30pm (4:30pm from October through March). Inside the castle is a history museum with a collection focusing on Japan's feudal days, with displays of samurai gear, models of old Hiroshima, and pictures of the past. Entrance to both the museum and castle is ¥300 ($2.15).

SHUKKEI-EN GARDEN

Near Hiroshima Station, Shukkei-en Garden was first laid out in 1620, with a pond constructed in imitation of a famous lake in China, Si Hu. The garden's name means

---

IMPRESSIONS

In the dying afternoon, I wander dying round the Park of Peace.
It is right, this squat, dead place, with its left-over air
Of an abandoned International Trade and Tourist Fair . . .
—JAMES KIRKUP, "NO MORE HIROSHIMAS," *THESE HORNED ISLANDS,* 1962

"landscape garden in miniature." The park is situated on the Ota River and includes streams, ponds, islets, and bridges—a pleasant respite from city traffic. Charging a ¥200 ($1.40) admission, Shukkei-en is open daily from 9am to 5:30pm (4:30pm from October through March).

THE SETO INLAND SEA

Hiroshima is also the usual departure point for day cruises on the Seto Inland Sea. Stretching between Honshu and the islands of Shikoku and Kyushu, the Inland Sea is dotted with more than 3,000 pine-covered islands and islets. Cruises are operated daily from March to the end of November by the **Setonaikai Kisen steamship company** (tel. 253-1212), and advance booking is required. One cruise departs from Miyajima daily at 8:30am, with a stop at Hiroshima before heading on to Kure, Yasura, Omishima Island, and Setoda. The trip from Miyajima or Hiroshima to Setoda is ¥6,380 ($45.55) one way. If it's winter or you're simply more interested in a shorter cruise, Setonaikai Kisen also offers a daily cruise throughout the year to the island of Miyajima, with departures at 11:45am. Cost of the round-trip cruise is ¥10,000 ($71.40), including lunch.

All the above cruises must be booked in advance, which you can do at several hotels, including the ANA Hotel Hiroshima. More information on these cruises is given in a leaflet called *Inland Sea and Shikoku,* available from the Tourist Information Center in either Tokyo or Kyoto.

WHERE TO STAY
EXPENSIVE

ANA HOTEL HIROSHIMA, 7-20 Nakamachi, Naka-ku, Hiroshima 730. **Tel. 082/241-1111,** or toll free 800/ANA HOTELS in U.S. and Canada. Fax 082/241-9123. 431 rms. A/C MINIBAR TV TEL **Directions:** 7-minute taxi ride from Hiroshima Station. **Streetcar:** 1 from Hiroshima Station to Chuden-mae stop.

$ Rates: ¥9,900–¥12,000 ($71–$86) single; ¥17,000–¥20,000 ($121–$143) double; ¥19,000–¥23,000 ($136–$164) twin. AE, DC, JCB, MC, V.

One of Hiroshima's premier hotels, the ANA Hotel Hiroshima is on the tree-lined Peace Boulevard (Heiwa Odori), just a 5-minute walk from Peace Memorial Park. It's lobby, overlooking a tiny garden with waterfalls, is carpeted and subdued, with a menagerie of glass birds hanging from the ceiling (modeled after the red-throated loon, the Hiroshima prefectural bird). Service at the hotel is excellent. Some 20% of the hotel's guests are foreigners, most of them Americans, and the large, comfortable rooms have facilities Westerners will appreciate, such as bilingual TV, with pay video and with one channel devoted to Kyodo news service in English, and the FEN English radio station. All the amenities you'd expect from a first-class hotel are included.

Dining/Entertainment: There are seven restaurants and bars, including those serving Japanese, Chinese, and French cuisine and teppanyaki steaks. A rooftop beer garden (open summer months from 5:30 to 9:30pm) and one of the two bars on the 22nd floor featuring live piano music nightly add to the hotel's entertainment.

Services: Free delivery of *Japan Times,* same-day laundry service.

Facilities: Health club with indoor swimming pool, exercise equipment, and sauna (fee: ¥5,000 or $35.70; ¥2,000 or $14.30 for use of pool alone).

MITAKISO ⑱, **1-7 Mitaki-cho, Nishi-ku, Hiroshima 733. Tel. 082/237-1402.** 12 rms (2 with bath, 10 with toilet only). A/C TV TEL **Directions:** A 15-minute taxi ride from Hiroshima Station.

$ Rates (per person, including breakfast and service): ¥20,000–¥38,000 ($143–$271). No credit cards.

This is a beautiful traditional Japanese inn, part of which is 70 years old. Its rooms are spread along an exquisite landscape garden with stunted pines, ponds, tiny maple trees, stone lanterns, and meandering streams. The best rooms are elegant and private, with sliding doors that open onto the garden. The least expensive rooms face away from the garden toward the street, but if you're traveling off-season you may be upgraded to a room with a garden view. Most rooms come with toilet only, but there are public baths. The ryokan is well known for its excellent cuisine. Its entrance is past a high stone wall and a massive stone lantern. A great place for a splurge.

MODERATE

HIROSHIMA CITY HOTEL, 1-4 Kyobashi-cho, Minami-ku, Hiroshima 732. Tel. 082/263-5111. Fax 082/262-2403. 169 rms. A/C TV TEL **Directions:** A 3-minute walk from Minami Guchi exit of Hiroshima Station, straight through underpass and over bridge; hotel will be on your right.
$ Rates: ¥6,900–¥7,700 ($49–$55) single; ¥11,500 ($82) double; ¥12,000–¥17,500 ($86–$125) twin. AE, JCB, MC, V.

If you wish to stick close to Hiroshima Train Station, this business hotel across from the Century City Hotel (you can see the Century City Hotel's sign from the train station if you look hard enough) is a good bet. Although it opened in the 1970s, it has since been renovated and looks much newer. Half of the rooms are singles, and the cheapest are the smallest I've seen (which, in Japan, says quite a lot), but all rooms come with bathroom, TV with the adult-oriented pay video, radio, and alarm clock. If you want a view, ask for a room above the ninth floor. Vending machines are on the fifth floor; you'll also find both a Western restaurant and a Japanese restaurant on the top floors.

HIROSHIMA KOKUSAI HOTEL, 3-13 Tatemachi, Naka-ku, Hiroshima 730. Tel. 082/248-2323. Fax 082/248-2622. 76 rms. A/C MINIBAR TV TEL **Streetcar:** 1, 2, or 6 from Hiroshima Station to Tatemachi stop, then a 5-minute walk.
$ Rates: ¥6,900 ($49) single; ¥11,500 ($82) twin; ¥12,500 ($89) double. AE, DC, JCB, MC, V.

Built in 1966, this well-known, established hotel is in the center of Hiroshima, within walking distance of Peace Memorial Park, Shukkei-en Garden, Hiroshima Castle, and the Hondori covered shopping arcade. Rooms are rather crowded in appearance, but they're comfortable and come with minibar, TV with pay video, clock, and radio. There are Japanese and Western restaurants, and smörgåsbord breakfasts are served for ¥1,000 ($7.15).

HIROSHIMA TERMINAL HOTEL, 1-5 Matsubara-cho, Minami-ku, Hiroshima 732. Tel. 082/262-1111. Fax 082/262-4050. 440 rms. A/C TV TEL **Directions:** Beside Hiroshima Station, Shinkansen exit.
$ Rates: ¥9,300–¥11,600 ($66–$83) single; ¥13,000–¥17,500 ($93–$125) double; ¥17,500–¥28,000 ($115–$200) twin. AE, V.

Despite its rather ordinary name, this is a great medium-range hotel, one of Hiroshima's newest, with a spacious marbled lobby. Each room offers push-button phone, alarm clock, TV with pay video, radio with FEN, hot-water pot, and hairdryer. The higher-priced rooms also come with minibar. There are 12 restaurants and bars, including a high-class okonomiyaki eatery, a good sushi bar, and a popular disco in the basement called Maharaja. The steakhouse on the 14th floor offers dining with a view.

HOTEL SILK PLAZA, 14-1 Hatchobori, Naka-ku, Hiroshima 730. Tel. 082/227-8111. Fax 082/227-8110. 231 rms. A/C MINIBAR TV TEL **Streetcar:** 1, 2, or 6 from Hiroshima Station to Hatchobori stop, then a few minutes' walk.
$ Rates: ¥6,200–¥6,500 ($44–$46) single; ¥12,000 ($86) double/twin. AE, DC, JCB, MC, V.

Hotel Silk Plaza is on Hakushima Dori Avenue, near three department stores. A locally owned hotel rather than part of a chain, it started out in 1974 as a business hotel, but after 5 years began catering to wedding receptions and now attracts foreign tourists as well. Single rooms all have semidouble-size bed, but the cheapest singles are not recommended, since they open toward a wall with windows of other guest rooms just 2 feet away. They also tend to be dark. The rooms facing the outside are much better. All rooms are very simple—TV with pay video, hot-water pot, clock, and refrigerator. There are both Western and Japanese restaurants, and a buffet-style breakfast is served for ¥1,000 ($7.15).

SERA BEKKAN ⑱, **4-20 Mikawa-cho, Naka-ku, Hiroshima 730. Tel. 082/248-2251.** 35 rms (all with bath). A/C TV TEL **Streetcar:** 1, 2, or 6 to Hatchobori stop, then a 5-minute walk.

$ Rates (per person, including breakfast and dinner): ¥13,000–¥27,000 ($93–$193). DC, JCB, MC.

This modern ryokan is located in the city center just off Namiki Dori Avenue. Although the building itself is far from traditional, the rooms themselves are Japanese style, with tatami mats, shoji screens, and a safe for valuables. There are large public baths. Dinner and breakfast are served in your room (Western-style breakfasts are available). Rates vary depending on the meal you order for dinner and the number of people staying in the rooms.

TOKYU INN, 3-17 Komachi, Naka-ku, Hiroshima 730. Tel. 082/244-0109. Fax 082/245-4467. 284 rms. A/C MINIBAR TV TEL **Streetcar:** 1 from Hiroshima Station to Chugoku-denryoku-mae stop, then a 1-minute walk.

$ Rates (including service charge): ¥7,300 ($52) single; ¥11,800 ($84) twin. AE, DC, JCB, MC, V.

Part of a nationwide chain of business hotels, this is a reliable medium-priced hotel, located near the Peace Boulevard and Rijo Dori intersection and just a 5-minute walk from Peace Memorial Park. About 80% of its clientele are Japanese businessmen. The hotel's restaurant serves a buffet-style Japanese and Western breakfast for ¥1,030 ($7.35), lunches for ¥550 to ¥2,800 ($3.90 to $20), and dinners from about ¥1,600 ($11.40).

BUDGET

MIKAWA RYOKAN, 9-6 Kyobashi-cho, Minami-ku, Hiroshima 732. Tel. 082/261-2719. 13 rms (none with bath). A/C TV TEL **Directions:** A 7-minute walk southwest of Hiroshima Station.

$ Rates: ¥3,600 ($26) single; ¥6,500 ($46) double; ¥10,000 ($71) triple. Japanese breakfast ¥700 ($5). AE, V.

This two-story ryokan, a member of the Japanese Inn Group, prefers advance reservations. Rooms are simple tatami and come with coin-operated bilingual TV, heater, and air conditioning. Check-in is at 5pm and the front doors close at 11pm. There's a coin-operated laundry facility.

RIJYO KAIKAN ⑲, **1-5-3 Otemachi, Naka-ku, Hiroshima 730. Tel. 082/245-2322.** 49 rms (all with bath). A/C TV TEL **Streetcar:** 1, 2, or 6 from Hiroshima Station to Kamiyacho stop, then a 3-minute walk.

$ Rates (per person): ¥4,900–¥5,700 ($35–$41) single; ¥4,600–¥4,900 ($33–$35) twin. Extra bed ¥1,000 ($7.15). Breakfast ¥700 ($5) extra. No credit cards.

Ⓢ An excellent place to stay if there's room. Located close to the Hondori covered shopping arcade and Peace Memorial Park, this ryokan is intended primarily as lodging for government office employees, but anyone can stay here if room permits. Opened in 1985, it's a modern structure of glass and brown tiles in an unusual triangular shape. Check-in isn't until 4pm here, and the front counter is located to the left as you enter the building. The rooms here are great for the price—bright, white, and cheerful, with hot-water pot, radio, TV, clock, and toilet and deep tub. There are both Japanese and Western restaurants and a self-service cafeteria named Maple, where you can get a cup of coffee for only ¥200 ($1.40). Breakfast consists of ham and eggs, bread, soup, salad, and coffee. If you want to stay here, it's safest to make a reservation 2 months in advance. Weekends are usually fully booked, but weekdays are generally not so full.

Youth Hostel

HIROSHIMA YOUTH HOSTEL ⑲, **1-13-6 Ushitashin-machi, Higashi-ku, Hiroshima 732. Tel. 082/221-5343.** 104 beds. A/C **Bus:** 22 from Hiroshima Station to Ushitashin-machi 1-chome stop (a 15-minute ride), then an 8-minute walk.

$ Rates (including sheets): ¥2,260 ($16.15). Breakfast ¥410 ($2.90); dinner ¥620 ($4.40). No credit cards.

This youth hostel is very easy to find: the bus even announces the youth-hostel stop in English, and from there you'll see signs directing you to the hostel. Located partway up a hill with good views, it accepts nonmembers. The staff all speak English, and they're enthusiastic about accepting foreigners (reservations in summer a must). Doors close at 9:30pm, but it's worth it to get back by 9pm, when a movie in English is shown every night.

WHERE TO DINE

In addition to the Japanese and Western restaurants listed below, the hotel section above also gives some information about buffets and meals. Incidentally, at the Hondori shopping arcade you'll also find a number of inexpensive and fast-food places, including McDonald's, Shakey's, and Mister Donut.

EXPENSIVE

AMAGI ⑲², 10-10 Kaminobori-cho. Tel. 221-2375.

Cuisine: KAISEKI/OBENTO. **Reservations:** At least 3 days in advance for kaiseki meals in private room. **Directions:** A 10-minute walk east of Hiroshima Station.

$ Prices: Dinner kaiseki courses ¥9,000–¥16,500 ($64–$118); lunch set meals ¥3,300–¥6,500 ($23.55–$46.40). No credit cards.

Open: Lunch Tues–Sun 11am–2pm; dinner Tues–Sun 5–9pm (last order 8pm). **Closed:** Last Sun of every month.

Amagi is a well-known modern restaurant specializing in kaiseki meals. It offers informal dining up on the second floor in a setting of cool and simple elegance. The lunch menu includes obento lunch boxes from ¥3,300 ($23.55), with full kaiseki courses starting at ¥6,500 ($46.40). Dinner offers elaborate kaiseki courses, and if you really feel like splurging, you can reserve your own private tatami room in the back of the restaurant in what used to be a ryokan years ago. Charges for a private room are ¥1,000 ($8) per person, and the minimum price of kaiseki meals here are ¥11,000 ($78.55) for lunch and ¥16,500 ($117.85) for dinner.

ATAGO, 7-20 Nakamachi. Tel. 241-1111.

Cuisine: TEPPANYAKI STEAKS. **Reservations:** Recommended. **Streetcar:** 1 to Chuden-mae, then a 2-minute walk.

$ Prices: Set dinner courses ¥5,500–¥14,000 ($39.30); set lunches ¥2,400–¥4,500 ($17.15–$32.15). AE, JCB, V.

Open: Lunch daily 11:30am–2pm; dinner daily 5–10pm.

This teppanyaki steak restaurant, next to the ANA Hotel on Peace Boulevard, is convenient if you're visiting the Peace Memorial Museum. It is strikingly modern with its marble tables and geometric lines, but kimono-clad waitresses bring drinks while chefs prepare steak and seafood before your eyes. Best are the lunch-time set courses starting at ¥2,400 ($17.15), which offer sirloin steak, salad, miso soup, rice, Japanese pickles, and sherbet.

CASTLE VIEW, 22nd floor of ANA Hotel, 7-20 Nakamachi. Tel. 241-1111.

Cuisine: FRENCH. **Reservations:** Recommended. **Streetcar:** 1 to Chuden-mae, then a 2-minute walk.

$ Prices: Set-dinner courses ¥7,500–¥14,000 ($53.55–$100); set lunches ¥3,300–¥6,500 ($23.55–$46.40). AE, DC, JCB, MC, V.

Open: Lunch daily 11:30am–2:30pm; dinner daily 5–10pm.

This restaurant is named for the view you'll have of the castle, but you have to look pretty hard to find it. Still, this is the second-tallest building in Hiroshima and you do have a fine view of the city. A small, elegant restaurant decorated in gold and light pink, with comfortable chairs and a single rose on each table, this establishment offers steaks and seafood and a variety of other main courses on its seasonal menu. Expect to spend about ¥6,000 to ¥10,000 ($42.85 to $71.40) and up per person if you order from the à la carte menu.

MODERATE

KANAWA ⑲⑶, **Motoyasu River. Tel. 241-7416.**
  Cuisine: OYSTERS. **Streetcar:** 1 to Chuden-mae stop.
$ Prices: Main dishes ¥1,000–¥2,500 ($7.15–$17.85); set meals ¥6,500–
  ¥15,000 ($46.40–$107.15). AE, JCB, V.
  Open: Lunch daily 11am–2pm; dinner daily 5–10pm. **Closed:** Every Sun
  Apr–Sep; first and third Sun Oct–Mar.

⭐ There are 10,000 rafts cultivating oysters in Hiroshima Bay, with a yearly output of 30,000 tons of shelled oysters. Needless to say, oysters are a Hiroshima specialty, and this houseboat moored on the Motoyasu River just off Peace (Heiwa) Boulevard not far from Peace Memorial Park is one of the best places to enjoy them. Although winter is the best time for fresh oysters, the owner of this restaurant has his own oyster rafts and freezes his best stock in January so that he's able to serve excellent oysters even in summer. This floating restaurant has been here more than 25 years, and dining is in tatami rooms with views of the river. The English menu lists oysters cooked about any way you like or can imagine. A la carte dishes include the popular baked oyster in its shell with lemon, tempura oyster, or oyster soup. If you feel like indulging, order one of the set courses that feature just oysters cooked in various ways, including in the shell, fried, in soup, and steamed.

**LE TRAIN BLUE, 14th floor of Kokusai Hotel, 3-13 Tatemachi. Tel.
248-2323.**
  Cuisine: WESTERN. **Streetcar:** 1, 2, or 6 from Hiroshima Station to Tatamachi
  stop, then a 5-minute walk.
$ Prices: Set-dinner courses ¥4,400–¥6,500 ($31.40–$46.40); set lunches
  ¥1,600–¥2,500 ($11.40–$17.85). AE, DC, JCB, V.
  Open: Daily 11:30am–midnight.

Ⓢ This is Hiroshima's only revolving restaurant, making a full turn every hour. It is fashioned after the dining car of a train (supposedly the Orient Express), and each table is placed beside the window, making for privacy with a view. Reasonably priced, Le Train Blue's à la carte menu lists steak, seafood, lamb, veal, and duck; but the best bargain is the weekly set-lunch course for ¥1,600 ($11.40). Another bargain is the ¥3,000 ($21.40) dinner special for women only, available every night except Saturday. You can also come here just for a drink; cocktails are ¥850 ($6.05) and beer starts at ¥650 ($4.65).

UNKAI, 5th floor of ANA Hotel, 7-20 Nakamachi. Tel. 241-1111.
  Cuisine: VARIED JAPANESE. **Streetcar:** 1 to Chuden-mae.
$ Prices: Main dishes ¥2,000–¥3,500 ($14.30–$25); set-dinner courses
  ¥5,000–¥15,000 ($35.70–$107.15); set lunches ¥2,200–¥5,500 ($15.70–
  $39.30). AE, DC, JCB, MC, V.
  Open: Daily 11:30am–10pm.

Another convenient restaurant if you're visiting Peace Memorial Park is this Japanese restaurant in the ANA Hotel. It overlooks a garden of stunted pine trees, azalea bushes, neatly arranged stones, and a pond full of golden carp—said to resemble Shukkei-en Garden in miniature. There's an English menu here, with such à la carte choices as tempura shrimp, abalone in butter served in its own shell, sashimi, rice porridge, and even the head of red snapper boiled in soy sauce. There are also set meals for such fare as shabu-shabu, tempura, kaiseki, and red-snapper sashimi. I had the Miyajima Course, which came with sashimi, sardines, clear soup, eggs of red snapper, a locally caught fish from the Seto Inland Sea, tempura, vegetables, bean-paste soup, Japanese pickles, rice, and fruit. Less expensive is lunchtime, when teishoku lunches are served until 2pm; offered at that time are soup, sashimi, pickles, rice, and dessert, along with main dishes that range from tempura to Japanese steak. You can also get noodles for ¥850 ($6.05), and for bigger appetites, there are obento lunch boxes for ¥3,300 ($23.55) and ¥5,500 ($39.30).

BUDGET

ANDERSON KITCHEN, 7-1 Hondori. Tel. 247-2403.
Cuisine: INTERNATIONAL. **Streetcar:** 1, 2, or 6 to Kamiyacho stop, then a 3-minute walk.
$ **Prices:** ¥600–¥1,200 ($4.30–$8.55); set meals ¥1,000–¥1,500 ($7.15–$10.70). No credit cards.
Open: Daily 11am–7:30pm (last order), one corner of the restaurant open until 10pm, serving French and Chinese food. **Closed:** Third Wed of every month.

This restaurant, located on a corner of the Hondori covered shopping arcade not far from Peace Memorial Park, is a popular cafeteria on the second floor above its own bakery with the same name. There are several counters specializing in different types of food—for example, salads and sandwiches, fried dishes such as grilled chicken, desserts—while one counter sells drinks. Just pick up a tray and select the items you want. You pay at the end of each counter.

CASPI, 2nd floor of Hotel Silk Plaza, 14-1 Hatchobori. Tel. 227-8111.
Cuisine: WESTERN. **Streetcar:** 1, 2, or 6 from Hiroshima Station to Hatchobori stop, then a few minutes' walk.
$ **Prices:** Set dinners ¥1,800–¥4,900 ($12.85–$35); set lunch ¥990 ($7.05). AE, JCB, MC, V.
Open: Lunch daily 11am–2:30pm; dinner daily 5–8:30pm (last order).
This simple restaurant serves a set lunch that's a great bargain. Its menu changes daily, but when I was there the special consisted of soup, salad, pork cutlet with vegetables, and coffee, with unlimited portions of salad.

MASUI, Hatchobori. Tel. 227-2983.
Cuisine: STEAKS/SHABU-SHABU-SUKIYAKI. **Streetcar:** 1, 2, or 6 to Hatchobori, then a 5-minute walk.
$ **Prices:** ¥900–¥4,000 ($6.45–$28.55); lunch teishoku ¥750 ($5.35). No credit cards.
Open: Thurs–Tues 11am–8:45pm. **Closed:** Second Tues of month.
A very inexpensive, popular restaurant serving beef dishes, Masui is near Chugoku Bank, which is close to the Silk Plaza Hotel in the middle of town. Individual small servings of shabu-shabu, for example, start at only ¥750 ($6) for pork and ¥1,300 ($10.40) for beef, while sukiyaki goes for ¥1,200 ($8.55). This two-story restaurant is especially crowded during lunchtime, when it churns out plate after plate of teishoku specials. The ¥750 ($5.35) teishoku gets you a hamburger patty, ham, omelet, pork cutlet, and rice, but if that's too expensive you can forgo the hamburger and get the other items for ¥650 ($4.65).

OKONOMI-MURA ⑲⑷, 5-21 Shin-tenchi. Tel. 241-8758.
Cuisine: OKONOMIYAKI. **Streetcar:** 1, 2, or 6 to Hatchobori stop, then a 5-minute walk.
$ **Prices:** ¥500–¥800 ($3.55–$5.70). No credit cards.
Open: Daily 11am–9pm, but some stalls stay open to midnight.

Although the people of Osaka claim to have made okonomiyaki popular among the masses, the people of Hiroshima claim to have made it an art. In any case, okonomiyaki is a kind of Japanese pancake, filled with cabbage, meat, and other fillings. Whereas in Osaka the ingredients are all mixed together, in Hiroshima each layer is prepared separately, which means the chefs have to be quite skilled at keeping the whole thing together. The best place in town to witness these short-order cooks at their trade is here. Its name means "okonomiyaki village" and that's what it is—a ramshackle building with two floors of about 14 individual stalls, each dishing out okonomiyaki (the food still remains a dish for the masses).

All stalls offer basically the same menu—just sit down at one of the counters and watch how the chef first spreads pancake mix on a hot griddle, then follows it with a layer of cabbage and bean sprouts, bacon, and then an egg on top. If you want, you can have yours with udon (thick white noodles) or soba (thin yellow noodles). Helpings are enormous. You'll find the place just off the Hondori shopping arcade near Shakey's. Highly recommended, it's one of Hiroshima's most beloved establishments.

RIJYO, in Rijyo Kaikan, 1-5-3 Otemachi. Tel. 245-2322.
   Cuisine: WESTERN. **Streetcar:** 1, 2, or 6 to Kamiyacho, then a 3-minute walk.
$ Prices: Set dinner course ¥1,700 ($12.15); set lunch ¥700 ($5). No credit cards.
   Open: Daily 7am–9pm.
Rijyo Kaikan, described under budget accommodations, has a bright and modern restaurant made cheerful by colorful wall hangings. It serves a variety of inexpensive dishes, including salmon steak, hamburger steak, roast beef, sirloin and tenderloin steaks, beef curry, pizza toast, sandwiches, and spaghetti, with most prices under ¥1,000 ($7.15). It's within a 5-minute walk of Peace Memorial Park, most easily reached via the Motoyasubashi bridge.

SUISHIN ⑯, 6-7 Tatemachi. Tel. 247-4411.
   Cuisine: RICE CASSEROLES. **Streetcar:** 1, 2, or 6 to Tatemachi, then a 3-minute walk.
$ Prices: Main dishes ¥1,000–¥2,500 ($7.15–$17.85); kamameshi (rice casseroles) ¥750. AE, DC, JCB, MC, V.
   Open: Thurs–Tues 11:20am–10pm (last order 9pm).
This is the main shop of a locally owned restaurant chain specializing in kamameshi (rice casseroles). First opened in 1950, this chain now has five locations in Hiroshima alone. The main shop, in the middle of town, has five floors of dining, and though the décor is rather simple, this place is very popular for its rice casseroles topped with such Hiroshima delicacies as oysters, mushrooms, sea bream, sea eels, shrimp, and chestnuts. It sells about 800 kamameshi per day, a number that swells to as many as 2,000 on Sunday. To deal with the demand, the restaurant owner invented his own conveyor-belt oven, which can cook 180 kamameshi in an hour. Other dishes include oysters, eel, globe fish, flatfish, and sardines. Lunch specials change daily and are available for ¥850 ($6.05) from 11:20am to 1:30pm. There are also take-out boxes of seafood and vegetables for ¥1,000 to ¥4,000 ($7.15 to $28.55), making this a good place to buy your picnic lunch.

12. MIYAJIMA

8 miles NW of Hiroshima

GETTING THERE   The easiest way to get to Miyajima is from Hiroshima. You can travel from Hiroshima by **train, streetcar,** or **bus,** all of which deposit you at Miyajimaguchi, from which it's just a 10-minute ferry ride to the island of Miyajima. If you have a Japan Rail Pass, you can ride free on the JR **ferry,** which leaves from the pier right in front of the train station.

ESSENTIAL INFORMATION   The area code for Miyajima, lying in Hiroshima Prefecture, is 0829.
   Before leaving Tokyo or Kyoto, drop by the Tourist Information Center for a copy of *Hiroshima and Miyajima.*
   In Miyajima stop off at the **Tourist Information Office** (tel. 0829/44-0008), located in the JR ferry terminal. Open every day from 8:30am to 5:15pm, it has a brochure in English with a map.

Easily reached in about 45 minutes from Hiroshima, Miyajima is a treasure of an island only 1.2 miles off the mainland in the Seto Island Sea. No doubt you've seen pictures of its most famous landmark—a huge red torii, or shrine gate, rising up out of the water. Erected in 1875 and made of camphor wood, it's the largest torii in Japan, measuring more than 53 feet tall, and guards Miyajima's main attraction, Itsukushima Shrine.

Miyajima is one of the most scenic spots in Japan, an exceptionally beautiful island that has been held sacred since ancient times. In the olden days no one was allowed to do anything so human as to give birth or die on the island, with the result that both the pregnant and the ill were quickly ferried across to the mainland. Even today there's no cemetery on Miyajima. Covered with cherry trees that illuminate the island with their snowy petals in spring, as well as with maple trees that emblazon it in reds in autumn, Miyajima is home to tame deer that roam freely through the village and to monkeys that swing through the woods. It's a delightful island on which to stroll around—but avoid coming on a weekend.

WHAT TO SEE & DO

Itsukushima Shrine is less than a 10-minute walk from the ferry pier along a narrow street lined with souvenir shops and restaurants. Founded back in 592 to honor three female deities, the wooden shrine is built out over the water so that when the tide is in it appears as though the shrine is floating. A brilliant vermilion, it contrasts starkly with the wooded hills in the background and the blue of the sky above, casting its reflection in the waters below. The majority of the buildings are thought to date from the 16th century, preserving the original style of 12th-century architecture, but they have been repaired repeatedly through the centuries. Most of the buildings of the shrine are closed, but from sunrise to sunset daily (usually 6:30am to 6pm in summer and to 5pm in winter) and for ¥300 ($2.15), you can walk along the 770-foot covered dock that threads its way past the outer part of the main shrine and the oldest Noh stage in Japan. From the shrine you have a good view of the red torii standing in the water. If you're lucky you might get to see bugako put on for one of the many tour groups that pass through. An ancient musical court dance, bugako was introduced to Japan centuries ago from India through China and Korea. The costume of the dancer is orange, matching the shrine around him.

Incidentally, I should also add that if you happen to see Itsukushima Shrine when the tide is in and it's seemingly floating on water, you should consider yourself very lucky indeed. Most of the time the lovely shrine is floating above nothing more glamorous than mud. That's when a little imagination comes in handy.

As you exit from the shrine, you'll find the **Miyajima Museum of Historic Treasures,** which contains replicas of national treasures (the real ones are safely locked away), old books, armor, and household items. Perhaps of more interest is the **Miyajima Municipal History and Folklore Museum,** a few minutes' walk from the shrine. This one has explanations in English to guide you through the 150-year-old house, which once belonged to a wealthy merchant. Open daily from 8:30am to 5pm, it features farm equipment, water jars, cooking objects, carved-wood boxes, furniture, and items used in daily life. Admission is ¥250 ($1.80).

Other attractions on Miyajima include an **aquarium;** 1,750-foot-high **Mount Misen,** the largest peak on the island and easily reached by cable car from Momijidani Park; and **beaches** for swimming.

WHERE TO STAY

Although you can visit Miyajima in a day from Hiroshima, it's a pleasant experience to stay overnight in a ryokan (there are no Western-style hotels).

IWASO RYOKAN ⑲⑤**, Miyajima, Saeki-gun 739-05. Tel. 0829/44-2233.**
45 rms (40 with bath). A/C TV TEL. **Directions:** A 15-minute walk from ferry pier.
$ Rates (per person, including two meals and service charge): ¥16,500–¥30,000 ($118–$214) per person. Cottage: ¥40,000 ($285) per person. AE, JCB, V.

This the most famous ryokan on the island, and with a history spanning more than 130 years, was also the first ryokan to open on Miyajima. It's highly recommended for a splurge, with the price dependent on the room, its view, and the meals you select. There are four price levels of dinners, and Western breakfasts are served on request. The newest part of the ryokan was built in 1981, and though some of its newer rooms have very peaceful and relaxing views of a stream and woods, I prefer the rooms dating from about 50 years ago (they have more individuality). But if you really want to go all out and live in style, there are also a couple of separate cottages more than 70 years old that are exquisitely decorated and come with old wooden tubs. You can open your shoji screens here to see maples, a gurgling brook, and woods, all in utter privacy. You'll be treated like royalty here, but of course you have to pay for it.

MIYAJIMA GRAND HOTEL, Miyajima, Saeki-gun 739-05. Tel. 0829/44-2411. 67 rms (all with bath). A/C TV TEL **Directions:** Free shuttle bus service from ferry pier.

$ Rates (per person, including two meals): ¥20,000 ($143) per person. Weekday and winter discounts. AE, JCB, V.

Completely renovated and reopened in 1985, this modern building looks like a hotel rather than a ryokan. Although most of its rooms are Japanese-style tatami rooms, it also has 10 combination rooms with both twin beds and separate tatami areas. This ryokan doesn't differ from other modern ryokan, except that in its lobby there's a rather unusual mix of green, light purple, and pink in the décor. Western breakfasts are served on request.

JYUKEISO (196)**, Miyajima, Saeki-gun 739-05. Tel. 0829/44-0300.** 13 rms (all with bath). A/C TV TEL **Directions:** A 20-minute walk from ferry pier.

$ Rates (per person, including breakfast, dinner, and service): ¥18,000 ($128). No credit cards.

If you're looking for a smaller ryokan that's a bit more moderately priced, this is a good choice. Although it's a hike from the ferry pier (it's in the same vicinity as Miyajima Lodge, listed below), it sits on a small hill and affords some pleasant views of Miyajima. In addition, the owner here speaks English. The ryokan was started some 50 years ago by his grandmother, though the present building is much more modern. All but one of the rooms are Japanese tatami rooms. Western breakfasts are available on request.

MIYAJIMA LODGE (197)**, Miyajima, Saeki-gun 739-05. Tel. 0829/44-0430.** 30 rms (18 with bath). A/C TV **Directions:** A 25-minute walk from ferry pier, beside Omoto Park.

$ Rates (per person, including breakfast and dinner): ¥5,900 ($42) without bath; ¥7,000 ($50) with bath. No credit cards.

For lower-priced accommodations, try this lodge, where the simply decorated rooms are the do-it-yourself kind, in which you lay out your futon yourself. Sheets and cotton kimono are provided in each room.

WHERE TO DINE

Since all ryokan serve both breakfast and dinner, the only meal you have to worry about is lunch.

MOMIJI (198)**, in Iwaso Ryokan. Tel. 0829/44-2233.**
   Cuisine: MINI-KAISEKI. **Directions:** A 15-minute walk from ferry pier.
$ Prices: Mini-kaiseki ¥2,000–¥3,300 ($14.30–$23.55). No credit cards.
   Open: Lunch Tues–Sun 11:30am–2pm.

Even if you don't stay at Iwaso Ryokan, Miyajima's most famous Japanese inn, you can stop off for lunch at its restaurant, a very pleasant modern place with clusters of paper-covered lanterns hanging from the ceiling and windows opening onto woods and a stream below. The specialty here is its mini-kaiseki lunches, as well as its *anagomeshi* (barbecued conger eel on rice) teishoku for ¥1,000 ($7.15).

FUJITAYA (199)**, Tel. 44-0151.**
   Cuisine: ANAGOMESHI. **Directions:** A 20-minute walk from ferry pier.
$ Prices: Anagomeshi teishoku ¥2,500 ($17.85). No credit cards.
   Open: Daily 11am–5pm.

This pleasant restaurant is located on the right side of the road leading toward Mt.

Misen and Daishoin as you exit from Itsukushima Shrine. It has a history of 80 years, but although the building itself is recent, a traditional atmosphere is created with a wooden ceiling, shoji lamps, and a back courtyard with a maple tree, moss-covered rocks, and water running from a bamboo pipe into a pool carved into a flat rock. Fujitaya serves only anagomeshi (barbecued conger eel on rice), available with side dishes (such as pickled vegetables), soup, and tea.

CHAPTER 14
SHIKOKU

The smallest of Japan's four main islands, Shikoku is also one of the least visited by foreigners. That's surprising considering the natural beauty of its rugged mountains, its mild climate, and its most famous monuments—88 sacred Buddhist temples. It's the wish of many Japanese to make a pilgrimage to all 88 temples at least once in their lifetime as a tribute to the great Buddhist priest Kobo Daishi, who was born in Shikoku in 774 and who founded the Shingon sect of Buddhism. Many Japanese make the trip upon retirement.

Such a pilgrimage has been popular since the Edo Period in the belief that a successful completion of the tour exonerates Buddhist followers from rebirth. It used to take several months to visit all 88 temples on foot, and even today you can see the pilgrims making their rounds dressed in white—only now they go by bus, which cuts traveling time down to 2 weeks.

SEEING SHIKOKU

I suggest you visit Shikoku on your travels through southern Japan. You could, for example, travel through Honshu to Kyushu and from Kyushu start back north via Shikoku, or vice versa. Ferries connect Shikoku to Beppu on Kyushu Island, as well as to Tokyo, Osaka, Kobe, and Hiroshima on Honshu Island. In fact, for centuries the only way to reach Shikoku was by boat, but the completion of one of the longest bridges in the world changed all that. Opened in 1988, the Seto Ohashi Bridge measures 5.83 miles from shore to shore and connects Kojima on Honshu with Sakaide on Shikoku. Those of you aboard the Shinkansen, therefore, need change trains only in Okayama for trains bound for either Takamatsu or Matsuyama on Shikoku. Whereas the journey from Tokyo Station to Shikoku used to take 6 to 7 hours, you can now cover the same distance in about 4½ hours. Incidentally, the Seto Ohashi Bridge took 10 years to construct and actually consists of six separate bridges that connect various islands of the Seto Inland Sea. The people of Shikoku consider the bridge one of their major tourist attractions.

1. TAKAMATSU

496 miles W of Tokyo; 44 miles S of Okayama

GETTING THERE   By Plane   1 hour and 10 minutes from Tokyo, 1 hour from Fukuoka, 2 hours and 10 minutes from Sapporo.

By Train   Trains depart from Okayama approximately twice an hour, reaching Takamatsu in 1 hour.

By Bus   Buses depart from Tokyo Station nightly, reaching Takamatsu in about 11 hours.

By Boat   Ferries connect Takamatsu with Osaka in 2 hours and 40 minutes.

ESSENTIAL INFORMATION   The **area code** for Takamatsu, lying in Kagawa Prefecture, is 0878.

WHAT'S SPECIAL ABOUT SHIKOKU

Buddhist Temples
- A total of 88 sacred temples ringing the island. A visit to all of them is Japan's most popular pilgrimage.

Parks
- Ritsurin Park, laid out in the 1600s and one of Japan's most outstanding landscaped gardens.

Architectural Highlights
- Matsuyama Castle, built almost 400 years ago.

- Dogo Onsen Honkan, a three-story wooden bathhouse built in 1894 and one of the most delightful public bathhouses in the country.
- Shikoku Mura Village, an open-air museum of 21 houses and buildings dating from the Edo Period.
- Kompira Grand Playhouse, Japan's oldest Kabuki theater.

If you want some detailed information on Shikoku, be sure to drop by the Tourist Information Center in Tokyo or Kyoto for a leaflet called *Inland Sea and Shikoku*.

The **Takamatsu City Information Office** (tel. 0878/51-2009) is located in the train station and is open every day except New Year's from 9am to 5pm. Stop here for an English-language map of the city and directions to your hotel.

ORIENTATION & GETTING AROUND The Takamatsu train station is located on the coast of the Seto Inland Sea, only a few minutes' walk from the pier where ferries depart for Honshu and Shodo islands. All of the hotels and restaurants listed below, as well as Ritsurin Park, are located south and southeast of the train station. Chuo-dori Street is the town's main avenue and runs south from the train station past Ritsurin Park, passing the Takamatsu Grand Hotel, the Tokyu Inn, and the Hotel Rich on the way. **Buses** and **trams** depart from in front of the station. The tram station, called Kotoden Chikko Station, is across the street from the train station, next to the Takamatsu Grand Hotel.

The second-largest town in Shikoku, Takamatsu is on the northeastern coast of the island overlooking the Seto Inland Sea. Takamatsu means "high pine," and the city served as the feudal capital of the powerful Matsudaira clan from 1642 until the Meiji Restoration in 1868. Takamatsu's most famous site is Ritsurin Park, one of the most outstanding gardens in Japan.

WHAT TO SEE & DO

The main attractions of Takamatsu are spread out in the city but are easily reached by bus, tram, or train from the train station.

RITSURIN PARK

Ritsurin Park (tel. 33-7411) was once the summer retreat of the Matsudaira family. Work on the park began in the 1600s, and it took about 100 years to complete. Using the backdrop of adjacent Mount Shiun in a principle known as "borrowed landscaping," the park incorporates the mountain into its overall design. Basically, the garden can be divided into two parts: a traditional, classical southern garden and a modern northern garden with wide grassy lawns.

The **southern garden** holds the most interest to visitors. Arranged around the prescribed six ponds and 13 scenic mounds, it represents what is called a strolling garden, in which each bend of the footpath—indeed, every new step—brings another perspective into view, another combination of rock, tree, and mountain. The garden is absolutely exquisite, and when I was there a mist was rolling off Mt. Shiun, lending a mysteriousness to the landscape. After all, what better fits the image of traditional Japan than mist and pine trees? Altogether, there are 1,500 pine trees and 500 cherry trees in Ritsurin Park, which you should tour in a counterclockwise fashion to appreciate fully the changing views.

Also in the park are a museum of local folk art and handcrafts, a zoo, and a shop where local products of Kagawa Prefecture are sold, including kites, masks, wood carvings, umbrellas, fans, and bamboo vases. Be sure to stop off at the park's teahouse for a cup of frothy green tea. Called Kikugetsu-tei, the teahouse dates from feudal days. There's a separate entrance charge to Kikugetsu-tei of ¥310 ($2.20); a cup of ceremonial tea costs another ¥300 ($2.15).

Ritsurin Park is open daily from sunrise to sunset, approximately 7am to 5pm in winter and 5:30am to 7pm June through August. The admission fee is ¥310 ($2.20), and the park is located about 10 minutes from Takamatsu train station by bus or tram—the tram stop is called Ritsurin-Koen. If you have a Japan Rail Pass, you might even consider going by JR train traveling in the direction of Tokushima; get off at Ritsurin-koen Kita Guchi, which is near the north entrance to the park.

SHIKOKU MURA VILLAGE

✪ Shikoku Mura Village (tel. 43-3111) is an open-air museum of 21 Shikoku houses dating from the Edo Period. The houses, which are picturesquely situated on the slope of Yashima Hill, include thatch-roofed homes of farmers and fishermen, a 150-year old rural Kabuki stage, a tea-ceremony house, and sheds for pressing sugar and for producing paper out of mulberry bark. There's also a suspended bridge made of vines, a familiar sight in Shikoku as a means for crossing the island's many gorges and ravines—if you look closely, however, you'll see that this one is reinforced by cables.

It takes at least an hour to stroll through the village, which is open daily from 8:30am to 4:30pm (5pm in summer). The admission fee is ¥500 ($3.55). I heartily recommend this village if you have not had the opportunity to see similar villages in Takayama or Kawasaki, since they convey better than anything else rural life in Japan in centuries past. Shikoku Mura Village is about a 20-minute tram ride from the Kotoden Chikko tram station. You can also get there by JR train traveling in the direction of Tokushima. The station for both is called Yashima.

OTHER SIGHTS

From Yashima Station close to Shikoku Mura Village you can take a cable car to the top of Yashima Plateau, where you'll find **Yashimaji Temple,** 84th of Shikoku's 88 sacred temples. Yashima is also famous as the site of a 12th-century battle between the rival clans of Taira and Minamoto as they fought for control over Japan. The Minamoto clan eventually won and established its shogunate court in Kamakura.

If you have some extra time and want to rest a few minutes, visit **Tamamo Park,** which is located behind the Takamatsu Grand Hotel close to the Takamatsu train station. The moats, gardens, and several three-story turrets are all that remain of what used to be an imposing castle belonging to the local warlords. There isn't a lot to see, but it's a pleasant place for a stroll or a picnic lunch if you're waiting for the next train.

One of Takamatsu's newest attractions is the **Takamatsu City Museum of Art (Takamatsu Bijutusukan),** Konyamachi 10-4 (tel. 23-1711). It's about a 10-minute walk south of Takamatsu Station: simply walk along Chuo-dori Street past the Hyogomachi covered shopping arcade, and turn left a couple of blocks later onto Bijutsukan Dori. The museum features a permanent exhibition of postwar Japanese art, as well as changing exhibitions of Japanese and Western artists. Cost of the permanent exhibit is ¥200 ($1.40), and the museum's hours are 9am to 5pm Tuesday through Sunday.

If you're spending several days in Takamatsu, there are several attractions in the surrounding countryside worthy of your attention. **Shodo Island (Shodoshima)** is the second-largest island in the Seto Inland Sea and is easily reached from the ferry pier close to the Takamatsu train station in about an hour. Most visitors come to Shodo Island to see its natural wonders, including Kankakei Gorge, which measures 3.7 miles long; a monkey park with more than 700 wild monkeys; and Shihozashi

Lookout, with its panoramic views of the Inland Sea. Shodo also contains a miniature replica of Shikoku's 88 sacred temples, located so close together on this small island that a pilgrimage on foot here takes only 5 days or so. An extensive network of public buses crisscrosses the island, but if you're on a tight schedule, you may wish to join one of the full or half-day sightseeing tours available. More information on Shodo Island can be obtained by calling the Shodoshima Tourist Office at 0879/62-1111.

One of the best historical side trips you can take is to **Kotohira,** home of Kotohiragu Shrine as well as the oldest Kabuki theater in Japan. It takes about an hour to reach Kotohira by train from Takamatsu Station, but that isn't the end of it—the shrine itself is at the top of 785 granite steps. If that's too much for you, you can hire porters who will take you only to the main gate (called Omon in Japanese), which is reached after climbing 365 steps. The cost of riding in one of these palanquins is ¥4,500 ($32) one way and ¥5,500 ($39) if you're carried back down.

At any rate, the long trek up to Kotohiragu Shrine begins by exiting from the Kotohira train station's only exit, taking a left after passing under the first torii gate, and then right on a narrow, shop-lined street. Presently you'll reach the first flight of stairs. If you're making a detour to the Kabuki theater described below, turn left after the 22nd step, from which the theater is only a 3-minute walk away; otherwise, continue climbing upwards—you should reach the main shrine after a 30-minute workout. You'll be rewarded with a sweeping view of the surrounding countryside, as well as the shrine itself. Popularly known as Kompira-San, Kotohiragu Shrine was originally founded in the 11th century but has been rebuilt many times, with the main shrine buildings re-erected about 100 years ago. Considered one of the biggest and oldest Shinto shrines in the country, it's popular with fishermen, who come here to pray for safe journeys at sea. Part of the shrine complex is filled with boat models and photographs of ships that have been placed under the deity's care. Notice also the paper cranes, symbolizing good luck, as well as the small slats of wood hanging from the beams. If you wish, you can buy one of these slats and write a wish upon it. On my last visit, I saw a plea for a better profit in a family's business, as well as a wish to become smarter.

Since you're in the vicinity, I highly recommend a visit to **Kompira Grand Playhouse,** known as **Kompira O-Shibai** ⑳ in Japanese. Open Wednesday through Monday from 9am to 5pm and charging an admission fee of ¥300 ($2.15), it is stunning in its simplicity and delightful in its construction. Since there was no electricity in 1835, when it was built, the sides of the hall are rows of shoji screens and wooden coverings, which could be opened and closed to control the amount of light reaching the stage. Notice the tatami seating, the paper lanterns, and the revolving stage, which was turned by eight men in the basement. You can also tour the various makeup and dressing rooms behind the stage. Most curious is the fact that although all actors in Kabuki are men, there's a separate dressing room for the actor who impersonated and played the part of a woman. Actual Kabuki plays are staged once a year in April, but as you may well imagine, tickets are hard to come by.

WHERE TO STAY

Because Takamatsu is not a big tourist destination, it doesn't have a wide selection of accommodations. Prices for rooms, however, are much lower here than in most cities in Japan.

HOTELS

These medium-range hotels all have rooms with private bath.

TAKAMATSU TOKYU INN, 9-9 Hyogo-machi, Takamatsu 760. Tel. 0878/21-0106. Fax 0878/21-0291. 191 rms. A/C MINIBAR TV TEL. **Directions:** A 7-minute walk south of Takamatsu Station.
$ Rates: ¥9,600 ($68) single; ¥15,000 ($107) double/twin. AE, DC, JCB, MC, V.
Located on Chuo-dori Street, next to the Hyogomachi covered shopping arcade, this is one of the newer hotels in town. The lobby is on the second floor, and its one restaurant serves Western fare. Rooms are clean, simple, and small but have all the

usual business-hotel amenities, including clock, TV, stocked fridge, and cotton kimono. Those facing Chuo-dori Street are fitted with double-pane windows to shut out traffic noise. None of the views are spectacular, but I'd choose a top-floor room facing west and the distant sea.

HOTEL RICH, 9-1 Furujinmachi, Takamatsu 760. Tel. 0878/22-3555. Fax 0878/22-7516. 126 rms. A/C MINIBAR TV TEL **Directions:** A 7-minute walk south of Takamatsu Station.

$ Rates: ¥7,000–¥8,000 ($50–$57) single; ¥13,500–¥23,600 ($96–$164) double/twin. AE, DC, JCB, MC, V.

Located almost directly across the street from the Tokyu Inn on Chuo-dori Street, this beige-brick hotel features three restaurants serving Japanese, Chinese, and French cuisine, as well as a bar. Rooms are similar to those in the Tokyu Inn.

TAKAMATSU GRAND HOTEL, 1-5-10 Kotobuki-cho, Takamatsu 760. Tel. 0878/51-5757. Fax 0878/21-9422. 136 rms. A/C MINIBAR TV TEL **Directions:** A 1-minute walk from Takamatsu Station.

$ Rates: ¥7,500–¥8,000 ($53–$57) single; ¥13,500 ($96) double; ¥13,500–¥23,000 ($96–$164) twin. AE, DC, JCB, MC, V.

In terms of location, price, and view, this is one of the best deals in town. A striped building on Chuo-dori Street, it's located near Takamatsu Station, the main artery for trains to the rest of Shikoku and for ferries from Honshu and Kyushu. Built in 1971, the hotel is on the edge of Tamamo Park, formerly the site of Takamatsu Castle and now an oasis of pine trees, three-story turrets, moats, and a classical garden. Both the lobby on the third floor and the Yashima Sky Restaurant on the seventh floor command sweeping views of the park. Rooms were recently renovated and come with the usual amenities. The higher-priced rooms facing the park have the nicest views. There are nine restaurants and a shopping arcade in the hotel complex.

TAKAMATSU PLAZA HOTEL ㉑, 7-Banchi, Tamamo-cho, Takamatsu 760. Tel. 0878/51-3655. 125 rms (all with bath). A/C TV TEL **Directions:** A 5-minute walk east of Takamatsu Station, near ferry docks.

$ Rates: ¥5,000–¥5,500 ($36–$39) single; ¥8,800 ($63) double/twin. AE, JCB, MC, V.

If all else fails, try this inexpensive, 10-story business hotel. Rooms are of adequate size, with the difference in price based on room size—so I recommend you ask for a room on a higher floor with a view of either the sea or Tamamo Park. The twin rooms don't have closets—just hooks on the wall for hanging clothes, as in olden days in Japan.

RYOKAN

HOTEL KAWAROKU, Hyakken-cho, Takamatsu 760. Tel. 0878/21-5666. Fax 0878/21-7301. 70 rms (all with bath). A/C MINIBAR TV TEL **Directions:** A 10-minute walk south of Takamatsu Station.

$ Rates: ¥14,300–¥22,000 ($102–$157) per person with two meals. Room only (without meals): ¥10,500 ($75) single; ¥13,000 ($93) twin. AE, JCB, MC, V.

First opened as a ryokan 110 years ago, this place was destroyed during an air raid in World War II, and is now a modern structure with 49 Japanese-style and 21 Western-style rooms, all with safe, TV, minibar, and the usual amenities. It's located close to the Mitsukoshi department store and several shopping arcades in the heart of the city. The Western-style rooms are white, bright, and clean, while the Japanese-style rooms are simply furnished and have that wonderful earthy smell of tatami. The hotel's one restaurant serves French cuisine (described in detail in the "Where to Dine" section, below); if you want Japanese food, it will be served in your room.

TOKIWA HONKAN ㉒, 1-8-1 Tokiwa-cho, Takamatsu 760. Tel. 0878/61-5577. 24 rms (12 with bath, 12 with toilet only). A/C MINIBAR TV TEL **Tram:** Kotodan Kawaramachi Station, then a 2-minute walk.

$ Rates (per person, including breakfast and dinner): ¥14,000–¥27,000 ($100–$193).

★ This traditional Japanese ryokan has a delightful inner courtyard reminiscent of those found around teahouses, with a pond, dwarf pine trees, golden carp, stone lanterns, wooden passageways, and vermilion railings. The ryokan is topped with a donjon, making it look like a shogun's castle. Built in 1954, the ryokan originally catered to foreigners, but it now receives only about 20 foreign guests a year. Rooms were completely renovated in 1987, so that they all now have a private toilet. Only half the rooms are equipped with a private bathtub, but public baths are located on each floor. There are also large communal baths separated for men and women.

WHERE TO DINE

Takamatsu is known throughout Japan for its *sanuki udon*—thick white noodles made from wheat flour. With Takamatsu as the center of this industry, there are as many as 400 sanuki manufacturers and more than 2,000 noodle shops in Kagawa Prefecture. It's been estimated that about 10% of the population eats sanuki noodles every day, a percentage that's about five times higher than in any other area of Japan. Takamatsu also has a fresh supply of fish from the Seto Inland Sea. If you want Western food in Takamatsu, your best bet is to dine at a hotel.

EXPENSIVE

LE BON 6, Hotel Kawaroku, Hyakken-cho. Tel. 21-5666.
   Cuisine: FRENCH. **Reservations:** Not necessary. **Directions:** A 10-minute walk south of Takamatsu Station.
$ **Prices:** Main dishes ¥2,500–¥6,000 ($17.85–$42.85); set courses ¥6,500–¥8,800 ($46.40–$62.85); set lunches ¥1,000–¥3,300 ($7.15–$23.55). AE, DC, JCB, MC, V.
   Open: Lunch daily 11:30am–1:30pm; dinner daily 5–8:30pm.
This is one of Takamatsu's best-known French restaurants. The Japanese chef here studied and worked for many years in both France and Belgium and, representing Japan, won a gold medal in 1982 at a world food contest held in Luxembourg. The emphasis at this restaurant is on food rather than on décor, and the menu includes seafood, beef, and lamb dishes. The chef takes special pride in his creations for the set meals, which change monthly and cost ¥6,500 ($46.40) and ¥8,800 ($62.85). These dishes are so beautifully arranged you almost hate to eat them. If you're on a budget, consider coming for one of the set lunches priced from ¥1,000 to ¥3,300 ($7.15–$23.55).

MODERATE

TENKATSU ⑳³, Hyogomachi. Tel. 21-5380.
   Cuisine: TEMPURA/SUSHI. **Reservations:** A necessity. **Directions:** A 10-minute walk south of Takamatsu Station on Chuo-dori, then a right at Hyogomachi covered shopping arcade. Walk through arcade; restaurant will be immediately on left.

A NOTE ON JAPANESE SYMBOLS

Many hotels, restaurants, and other establishments in Japan do not have signs giving their name in English letters. As an aid to the reader, Appendix C lists the Japanese symbols for all such places described in this guide. Each set of symbols has a number, which corresponds to the number that appears inside an oval next to the establishment's boldfaced name in the text. Thus, to find the Japanese symbols for, say, Osaka's **Hotel Hokke Club** ⑬⁸, refer to the number 138 in the appendix.

$ Prices: Dishes ¥1,000–¥2,500 ($7.15–$17.85); set meal ¥3,500 ($25). AE, DC, JCB, MC, V.
Open: Daily 11am–10pm.

This well-known tempura and sushi restaurant is in a modern-looking building with a plastic-food display case and a window where passersby can watch a chef prepare sushi. Inside the restaurant are tatami mats and tables, but I suggest sitting at the counter, which encircles a large pool filled with fish, mainly flatfish. As customers order their meals, fish are swooped out of the tanks with nets—they certainly couldn't be fresher. In fact, I saw some customers served a fish that was still quivering even though it had been sliced for sashimi. Although the menu here is in Japanese only, there are pictures accompanying some of the tempura and sushi courses. If you feel like splurging, there's a meal for ¥3,500 ($25) that features Japanese food in season, changing every month. Another specialty of the house is wine, served every month with something different in it. In March, for example, it's peach blossoms and in April cherry blossoms.

YASHIMA SKY RESTAURANT, 7th floor of Takamatsu Grand Hotel, 1-5-10 Kotobuki-cho. Tel. 51-5757.
Cuisine: WESTERN. **Directions:** A 1-minute walk from Takamatsu Station.
$ Prices: Main dishes ¥1,600–¥3,300 ($11.40–$23.55); set-dinner courses ¥3,500–¥6,000 ($25–$42.85); set lunches ¥900–¥3,800 ($6.40–$27.15). AE, DC, JCB, MC, V.
Open: Lunch daily 11:30am–2pm; dinner daily 5–8:30pm.

Enclosed on three sides by glass, this restaurant atop the Takamatsu Grand Hotel affords panoramic views of Tamamo Park and the harbor full of boats coming and going. Lunchtime offers three set meals available for ¥900 ($6.40), ¥2,700 ($19.30), and ¥3,800 ($27.15). The à la carte menu offers fondue, steak tartare, lobster thermidor, tenderloin and sirloin steaks, filet mignon, wienerschnitzel, shrimp pilaf, and sandwiches.

BUDGET

HANSUKE ㉔, Hyogomachi shopping arcade. Tel. 51-5653.
Cuisine: YAKITORI. **Directions:** A 10-minute walk south of Takamatsu Station on Chuo-dori St. to Hyogomachi.
$ Prices: ¥400–¥1,500 ($2.85–$10.70). No credit cards.
Open: Lunch Mon–Sat 11:30am–1pm; dinner Mon–Sat 4–10pm. **Closed:** National hols.

Unlike many of the other shops in the Hyogomachi covered shopping arcade, this yakitori-ya, just around the corner from the Tokyu Inn, has been in operation on this spot for more than 30 years, making it one of the oldest yakitori shops in town, if not the oldest. Simple and cheap, it's a greasy spoon in the true sense of the word; the grill looks as if it's been here from the beginning. The yakitori, however, is excellent and costs ¥400 ($2.85) for four skewers of chicken wedged between slices of onion. The establishment also serves eel, including kabayaki, a filet of eel, for ¥1,400 ($10). The real specialty of Hansuke, however, is its namesake, *hansuke*, which according to the shop owner means "heads of eel stuck on a skewer." Both I and the Japanese I was with thought it was one of the most unappetizing sights we had ever seen, but in a spontaneous burst of adventure we decided to try it. I don't want to spoil your own experience by telling you what it was like, but be prepared for lots of bones. A skewer of hansuke is a bargain at only ¥100 (70¢) a stick.

KANAIZUMI ㉕, Daikumachi. Tel. 21-6688.
Cuisine: SANUKI UDON. **Directions:** A 15-minute walk from Takamatsu Station.
$ Prices: Set meals ¥700–¥3,000 ($5–$21.40). AE, JCB, MC, V.
Open: Daily 10am–10pm. **Closed:** Second and fourth Mon of month.

This is the best place to watch sanuki udon being made. It's a bit classier than your usual noodle shop, and is easily recognizable from the outside by a huge paper lantern hanging in front of the restaurant and a front window where sanuki noodles are being made by hand. Although the menu is in Japanese, pictures accompany each set meal, which comes with noodles and a combination of various vegetables and meats. You can also order a bowl of noodles without side dishes for just ¥450 ($3.20). I had a set meal called Niku-nabe Udon, which cost ¥1,000 ($7.15) and consisted of a bowl of noodles, leeks, thin slices of beef, and rice cake in hot broth. I dipped each morsel first into a mixture of raw egg, just as one does with sukiyaki. It was good, but rice cakes take forever to chew. Be prepared also for slippery noodles and all that good-natured slurping that accompanies a meal in a noodle shop.

MARUICHI ⓜ, **1-4-13 Tokiwa-cho. Tel. 61-7623.**
    Cuisine: YAKITORI. **Tram:** Kotoden Kawaramachi Station, then a 1-minute walk; or a 15-minute walk from Takamatsu Station.
    $ Prices: ¥300–¥2,000 ($2.15–$14.30). No credit cards.
    Open: Mon–Sat 5–11pm.

★   Although technically a drinking establishment, this is also a great place for an inexpensive meal. Cozy and friendly, it is decorated with colorful kites, heavy wooden beams, and a stone floor. A Westerner living in Takamatsu introduced Maruichi to me and said it's a good place to meet the natives. An English menu lists octopus sashimi (if you've never tried it, this is a good place to do so), kimchi (Korean spiced cabbage) with pork, mushrooms with melted cheese, salads, and, of course, yakitori. An evening of eating, drinking, and merriment here should cost about ¥2,000 ($8) per person. Maruichi is easy to spot from the outside by its huge red lantern and blue curtains hanging in front of the door inscribed with YAKITORI IZAKA.

TAKAMATSU PLAZA HOTEL, 10th-floor restaurant, 7-Banchi, Tamamo-cho. Tel. 51-3655.
    Cuisine: WESTERN. **Directions:** A 5-minute walk east of Takamatsu Station, near ferry docks.
    $ Prices: Appetizers and salads ¥400–¥1,000 ($2.85–$7.15); main dishes ¥1,000–¥1,800 ($7.15–$12.85); set meals ¥2,000–¥3,300 ($15.70–$23.55). AE, JCB, MC, V.
    Open: Lunch daily 11am–2pm; dinner daily 5–9pm.

This restaurant, on the top floor of a business hotel, serves inexpensive Western fare typical of such establishments—but the difference here is that the dining room affords a view of the harbor. Dishes include spaghetti, pork, beef, and chicken main dishes, and changing set meals.

ZAIGOUDON-WARAYA, 91 Yashima-Nakamachi. Tel. 43-3115.
    Cuisine: SANUKI UDON NOODLES. **Tram:** Kotoden Yashima Station, then a 10-minute walk.
    $ Prices: Sanuki udon ¥400–¥2,300 ($2.85–$16.40). No credit cards.
    Open: Daily 10am–7pm.

Another noodle restaurant you might want to try—especially if you're going to Shikoku Mura Village—is located just below the village in a 100-year-old thatched house (look for the waterwheel and tables for outdoor seating). It features handmade noodles, with the combination udon and tempura dish especially popular.

---

2. MATSUYAMA

496 miles W of Tokyo; 120 miles E of Takamatsu; 132 miles SW of Okayama

GETTING THERE By Plane Flights connect Matsuyama with Tokyo, Osaka, Nagoya, and Fukuoka.

By Train The easiest way to reach Matsuyama is by train from Okayama on Honshu island, with eight departures daily; the trip takes 2 hours and 40 minutes. There are also eight trains a day from Takamatsu and the trip takes less than 3 hours.

By Bus Buses depart daily from Tokyo's Tokyo Station and Shinjuku Station, reaching Matsuyama 13 hours later.

By Boat Matsuyama is also linked to various ports on Honshu and Kyushu islands, including Kobe (trip time: 9 hr.), Osaka (10 hr., 35 min.), Beppu (4 hr.), and Hiroshima (1 hr., 15 min.). Buses departing from Matsuyama Port (Matsuyama Kanko Ko) reach Matsuyama Station in about 25 minutes.

ESSENTIAL INFORMATION The **area code** for Matsuyama, lying in Ehime Prefecture, is 0899. Its postal code is 790.

Information on how to reach Matsuyama and places of interest can be obtained in a leaflet called *Inland Sea and Shikoku,* available at the Tourist Information Center in either Tokyo or Kyoto.

The **Matsuyama City Tourist Information Office** (tel. 0899/31-3914) is located inside the Matsuyama JR Train Station and can be spotted easily with its sign in English. Open daily from 8:30am to 7:30pm, it has an excellent pamphlet and map in English.

ORIENTATION & GETTING AROUND Matsuyama Station is in the west end of town, and most points of interest spread to the east. **Streetcars** depart from the front of the station to such places as Dogo Spa and the Okaido Shopping Arcade, a covered pedestrian passageway lined with restaurants and shops, considered to be the heart of the city. Matsuyama Castle lies just northwest of Okaido, less than 1½ miles from the train station. Many **buses** and **commuter trains** bound for the suburbs depart from Matsuyama City Station, called Shi-eki in Japanese, which is linked to Matsuyama (JR Train) Station by streetcar.

Although Matsuyama is Shikoku's largest town, with a population of more than 420,000, it has the relaxed atmosphere of a small town. Located on the island's northwest coast, Matsuyama features one of Japan's best-preserved feudal castles and what I consider to be the most delightful public bathhouse in the country.

WHAT TO SEE & DO
THE TOP ATTRACTIONS

✪ **Matsuyama Castle** (tel. 21-4873) crowns the top of Katsuyama Hill right in the heart of the city. It was built by feudal lord Kato Yoshiakira about 385 years ago, later falling into the hands of the powerful Matsudaira family. Like most structures in Japan, Matsuyama Castle has suffered fire and destruction through the ages, but unlike many other castles (such as those in Osaka and Nagoya), this one is the real thing. There's only one entrance, a pathway leading through a series of gates that could be swung shut to trap attacking enemies. The three-story donjon houses a museum of armor and swords from the Matsudaira family. Surrounding the castle is a park, and if you're feeling energetic you can walk through the park to the castle in about 15 minutes. Otherwise, the easiest way to reach the castle is to take the streetcar to Ichibancho stop, walk 5 minutes north and then take a chair lift and a cable car on the east side of Katsuyama Hill. A ticket for ¥570 ($4.05) includes the round-trip ride to the top of the hill and entrance to the castle; otherwise admission is ¥260 ($1.85). The castle is open daily from 9am to 5pm (remember, as with all museums and attractions in Japan, you must enter a half hour before closing time).

Dogo Spa (Dogo Onsen), with a 3,000-year history, claims to be the oldest hot-spring spa in Japan. Located in the northeast part of the city, about a 20-minute tram ride from Matsuyama Station (take streetcar no. 5 to Dogo Onsen stop), Dogo Spa can accommodate about 9,000 people in 62 hotels and ryokan, which means that the narrow streets resound at night with the clatter of geta (wooden shoes) as vacationers go to the various bathhouses.

✪ Most of the hotels and ryokan in Dogo have their own *onsen* (hot-spring bath), but I suggest that no matter where you stay you make at least one trip to **Dogo Onsen Honkan** (tel. 21-5141), a wonderful, three-story public bathhouse built in 1894. A wooden structure with shoji screens, tatami rooms, creaking wooden stairways, and a white heron topping the crest of the roof, it is as much a social institution as it is a place to soak and scrub. On busy days as many as 4,000 people will pass through its front doors. The water here is transparent, colorless, tasteless, and alkaline. The hottest spring water coming into the spa is 120°F and coolest is 70°F—but don't worry, the waters are mixed to achieve a comfortable 108°F.

Bathing, however, is just a small part of the experience here. Most people come to relax, socialize, and while away an hour or more, and I suggest that you do the same. Although you can bathe for as little as ¥250 ($1.80), it's worth it to pay extra for the privilege of relaxing on tatami mats in a communal room on the second floor, dressed in a rented yukata (kimono), drinking tea from a lacquered tea set, and eating Japanese sweets. If the weather is fine, all the shoji screens are pushed open to let in a breeze, and as you sprawl out on the tatami, drinking your tea and listening to the clang of the streetcar and the clatter of wooden shoes, you can almost imagine you've somehow landed in ancient Japan. To my mind the whole scene resembles an old woodblock print that has suddenly sprung to life.

Cost of the bath, yukata, sweets, and tea is ¥620 ($4.40). Use of a smaller and therefore more private bath and lounging area where tea and sweets are also served costs ¥980 ($7). And if you really want to splurge, you can rent your own private tatami room on the third floor, which also comes with tea, sweets, and yukata, for ¥1,300 ($9.30).

Connected to the spa is another building, built in 1899 for the imperial family, and you can take a tour of its rooms for a couple of hundred yen. The spa is open from 6:30am (which is the arrival time of the first streetcar) until 11pm, but you must enter by 10pm. The ticket window for sweets, yukata, and tea closes at 9pm.

After your bath, you may want to visit **Ishiteji Temple,** about a 10-minute walk east of Dogo Onsen Station. Built in 1318, it's the 51st of Shikoku's 88 sacred temples and, with its blend of Chinese and Japanese styles, is a good example of architecture of the Kamakura Period. Notice the many straw sandals hanging on the temple gate. They are placed there by older Japanese in hopes of regaining new strength in their legs. There are, incidentally, seven other temples in Matsuyama that belong to the sacred 88, but Ishiteji is the most important and popular.

CRAFTS & CULTURE

Matsuyama is famous for several crafts, one of which is Iyo Kasuri, a cotton cloth dyed with Japanese indigo and worn traditionally as working attire by farm housewives. It was originated in the early 1800s by a woman named Kana Kagiya. If you're interested in seeing firsthand how this cloth is produced, then and now, you can visit **Mingei Iyo Kasuri Kaikan** (207), Kumanodai 1165 (tel. 22-0405), a small factory you can reach by bus from Matsuyama JR Station. It displays the processes of dyeing, machine weaving, and hand-weaving the blue cloth. Open daily from 8am to 5pm, it charges a small admission fee of ¥50 (35¢). You can even dye your own handkerchief for an extra ¥1,000 ($7.15). A shop sells Kasuri pillowcases, purses, clothing, hats, and bolts of cloth.

Another product of Ehime Prefecture is Tobe pottery, called Tobe-yaki in Japanese. Noted for its thick white porcelain painted with cobalt-blue designs, Tobe pottery is produced in the town of Tobe, which you can reach by bus in about 40 minutes from Matsuyama Shi-eki. There are several kilns open to the public, the best known of which is **Umeno-Seito-jo** (208), (tel. 62-2311), open Tuesday through Sunday, closed the second Sunday of the month and for a few days in mid-August. Hours are 8am to 5pm. Founded back in 1882 and now in its fourth generation of ownership by the Umeno family, it employs more than 100 people. You can watch all of the artisans except those who do the actual painting of the designs—the technique is a closely guarded secret. Inside the shop be sure to check out the bargain corner, where pieces with slight imperfections go for about half price. Another place you can shop for Tobe-yaki is at **Tobe-yaki Kanko Center** (209) (tel. 62-2070), open daily from 9am to 5pm. At both places you can try your hand in a workshop.

If you don't have time to visit the places where Kasuri cloth and Tobe-yaki are made, you can see both at the **Ehime Prefectural Products Hall (Ehime no Bussan)** (210), Ichibancho 4-chome (tel. 41 7584), not far from the ANA Zenniku Hotel at Kencho-mae tram stop. Open every day from 8:30am to 5pm except

Saturday afternoon, Sunday, and national holidays, it sells the products of Ehime Prefecture, including foodstuffs (such as sweets and honey), Tobe pottery, Kasuri cloth, masks, bamboo vases, lacquerware, cultivated pearls, and dolls. The dolls are shaped in an oval and are known as the princess doll, made in the image of Empress Jingu, who came to Dogo Spa in the second century when she was pregnant.

For less esoteric shopping, take a spin through Matsuyama's covered shopping arcade. I don't think there's a Japanese city left without one, but this arcade is especially long. It starts with the Okaido arcade next to Mitsukoshi department store (streetcar stop: Ichibancho), which eventually runs into the Gintengai covered arcade, which in turn dips underground into the Matsuchika Town underground shopping center near Shi-eki. You'll find a bewildering number of shops, boutiques, and inexpensive restaurants selling everything from hamburgers to tempura and sushi.

If you're interested in the performing arts, the newly opened **Ehime Prefectural Convention and Cultural Hall** (tel. 23-5111), designed by Kenzo Tange, has frequent concerts, dramas, and other performances. Check with your hotel or the tourist office for information on current productions.

And finally, if you're a devoted fan of Japanese swords and samurai armor, head straight for the hydrofoil that will whisk you to **Omishima** in about an hour. Here, on this unpretentious and rather neglected island, is Japan's most important sword and armor collection. As much as 80% of Japan's national treasure of swords and armor is kept at the shrine here, just as it has been for centuries. Many of the pieces were donated by the owners themselves, including armor once worn by Yoritomo Minamoto 800 years ago. You can also see the armor worn by female warrior Tsuruhime, a kind of Japanese Joan of Arc.

NEARBY ATTRACTIONS

If you have time for a side trip around Ehime Prefecture, I strongly recommend an excursion to the village of **Uchiko,** which has some fine old homes and buildings dating back to the Edo Period and the turn of the century. Whereas about 70% of Matsuyama was destroyed during World War II, Uchiko was left intact and a tiny part of the old city is a living memorial to the days of yore. Even the 50-minute train ride from Matsuyama JR Station is enjoyable as you weave through valleys of wooded hills. Be sure to pick up a map of the village at the Uchiko train station, even though it's in Japanese. A walk through the old part of town, known as Yokaichi, should take about an hour or two, depending on how often you stop along the way. Most of the older homes are clustered along one narrow street—there isn't a whole lot to see, but the walk is pleasant and some of the scenes make good photo essays. Note that most museums and buildings in Uchiko are closed on Wednesday.

The first important building on a walking tour of the city is **Uchikoza** ㉑, which is a Kabuki theater built in 1916. It was recently restored, and though it's not as grand as the one near Takamatsu described earlier in this chapter, it's a good example of how townspeople used to enjoy themselves years ago. It features a revolving stage and many windows that can be opened and closed to control the amount of light reaching the stage.

Other places of interest in Yokaichi include **Machi-ya Shiryokan** and **Kamihaga House,** old homes that have been restored and opened to the public. Built in 1894, Kamihaga House is especially grand, having once belonged to a merchant who made his fortune by exporting wax. During the Edo Period, Uchiko gained fame as a center of candlemaking and wax production, used both for lighting and for the styling of elaborate hairdos. Later the wax was applied to thread used in weaving and as an ingredient in vanishing cream, pomade, and shoe polish. At the worlds' fairs of 1894 in Chicago and 1900 in Paris, Uchiko wax won first prize for quality.

Today, only one man carries on this wax-making tradition, a man named Omori Yataro, who represents the fifth generation of candlemakers. Following the same techniques as those developed by his ancestors 200 years ago, he even collects his own haze berries (a kind of sumac) and makes his candles by hand. His workshop is open to the public, and in the mornings you can observe him at work.

WHERE TO STAY

There are choices for hotels in all price categories in Matsuyama. If you prefer to stay in a ryokan, head for Dogo Spa.

RYOKAN

FUNAYA ⑫, 1-33 Dogo Yunomachi, Matsuyama 790. Tel. 0899/47-0278. 43 rms (21 with bath). A/C TV TEL **Tram:** From Matsuyama Station to Dogo Onsen stop, then a 5-minute walk.

$ Rates (per person, including breakfast, dinner, and service charge): ¥24,000–¥40,000 ($171–$285). AE, DC, JCB, MC, V.

This is where the imperial family stays on visits to Dogo. Although it doesn't look like much from the outside, the inside is comfortable and pleasant. The present building dates from 1963, but the history of the ryokan itself goes back 140 years. The lobby and many of its rooms look out onto a garden. Thirty-eight of the ryokan's 43 rooms are tatami, two are furnished with twin beds, and three are combine beds and tatami areas. Facilities include an open-air bath.

KASUGAEN ⑬, 3-1 Saigidani-cho, Matsuyama 790. Tel. 0899/41-9156. 52 rms (all with bath). A/C MINIBAR TV TEL **Tram:** From Matsuyama Station to Dogo Onsen stop, from which it's a 5-minute walk.

$ Rates (per person, including breakfast, dinner, and service charge): ¥20,000 ($143). AE, DC, JCB, MC, V.

This ryokan in Dogo has mainly Japanese-style rooms, as well as combination rooms with both twin beds and tatami areas. Meals are elaborate kaiseki courses, with about 10 dishes served. There's an open-air bath.

HOTELS

Expensive

ANA ZENNIKU HOTEL, 3-2-1 Ichiban-cho, Matsuyama 790. Tel. 0899/33-5511. Fax 0899/21-6053. 333 rms. A/C MINIBAR TV TEL **Tram:** From Matsuyama Station to Kencho-mae stop, then a 2-minute walk.

$ Rates: ¥7,500–¥14,300 ($53–$102) single; ¥17,000–¥18,000 ($121–$128) double; ¥18,000–¥31,000 ($128–$221) twin. AE, DC, JCB, MC, V.

Matsuyama's premier hotel is in the heart of the city, just south of Matsuyama Castle and not far from the Okaido covered shopping arcade. It's only a 5-minute walk to the cable car going up to the castle, and streetcars heading for Dogo pass right in front of the hotel. Built in 1979, the hotel is spacious, cheerfully decorated, and offers 55 boutiques on four floors (including one selling Tobe-yaki). Rooms are large and well appointed, with TV, minibar, radio, clock, and desk.

Dining/Entertainment: There are six restaurants, bars, and lounges. The Unkai (Japanese), the Castle Grill (seafood and steaks), and Tohen (Chinese) restaurants are described in the "Where to Dine" section, below. There is a 14th-floor bar next to the Castle Grill for after-dinner drinks, and a rooftop beer garden.

Services: Free newspaper, same-day laundry service.

Facilities: Shopping arcade.

Moderate

THE KOKUSAI INTERNATIONAL HOTEL, 1-13 Ichiban-cho, Matsuyama 790. Tel. 0899/32-5111. Fax 0899/45-2055. 80 rms. A/C MINIBAR TV TEL **Tram:** From Matsuyama Station to Ichiban-cho stop, then a 3-minute walk.

$ Rates: ¥7,000 ($50) single; ¥11,000–¥20,000 ($78–$143) double/twin. AE, DC, JCB, MC, V.

Small, pleasant, and not far from the ANA Zenniku, this medium-priced hotel features rooms with radio, clock, TV, minibar, and large windows that let in lots of light. Even single rooms here have double beds, and some rooms have views of Matsuyama Castle. Yoshicho, the hotel's Japanese restaurant, serves kushikatsu, sashimi, sukiyaki, and tempura, while the hotel's Western restaurant offers sandwiches, fish, beef curry, spaghetti, and set meals, as well as teppanyaki steaks.

HOTEL SUNROUTE, 391-8 Miyatacho, Matsuyama 790. Tel. 0899/33-2811. Fax 33-2763. 110 rms. A/C TV TEL **Directions:** A 3-minute walk north of Matsuyama Station.

$ **Rates:** ¥6,500 ($46) single; ¥10,000–¥13,000 ($71–$93) double; ¥13,000–¥16,500 ($93–$118) twin; ¥18,500–¥20,000 ($132–$143) triple. AE, DC, JCB, MC, V.

This redbrick building, opened in 1986, is part of a nationwide chain of business hotels. Its rooms are reasonably priced and feature TV with coin-operated videos, radio, clock, hot-water pot for tea, and double-pane windows to shut out noises from the train station. The best views are from those rooms on the top floors facing east, which have a glimpse of the distant castle. On the hotel's roof is a covered beer garden, open rain or shine from 5pm to 9pm March through September. After paying an initial charge of ¥2,700 ($21.60), you can eat and drink as much as you like.

TAIHEI BUSINESS HOTEL ㉔, 3-1-15 Heiwa Dori, Matsuyama 790. Tel. 0899/43-3560. 140 rms (all with bath). A/C TV TEL **Directions:** A 10-minute taxi ride from Matsuyama Station.

$ **Rates:** ¥4,700–¥6,000 ($33–$43) single; ¥8,800 ($63) double; ¥9,000–¥13,000 ($64–$93) twin; ¥12,000–¥16,500 ($86–$118) triple. Japanese-style rooms: ¥4,500 ($32) per person. Buffet breakfasts ¥500 ($3.55) extra. No credit cards.

This rather interesting establishment is located at the northern base of Katsuyama Hill. Unlike the plastic, impersonal atmosphere of most business hotels, this one is rather eccentric—most rooms are decorated with old-fashioned wallpaper, worn flowered bedspreads, curtains, and shaggy rugs. The effect is cozy and pleasant, and rooms are great for the price. Buffet breakfasts, as well as set dinners starting at ¥900 ($6.40), are served in a cheerful dining area. There's a public bath and sauna, but it's for men only. If women happen to be in the majority, it becomes a women's-only facility, but I have the feeling that happens only rarely.

YOUTH HOSTEL

MATSUYAMA SHINSEN-EN YOUTH HOSTEL ㉕, 22-3 Dogohimezuka Otsu, Matsuyama 790. Tel. 0899/33-6366. 70 beds. A/C **Tram:** From Matsuyama Station to Dogo Onsen stop, then an 8-minute walk.

$ **Rates:** ¥2,500 ($17.85) member, ¥3,300 ($23.80) nonmember. Breakfast ¥450 ($3.20), dinner ¥750 ($5.35). No credit cards.

Its convenient location in Dogo Onsen Spa makes this a popular youth hostel among young Japanese. Facilities include bicycles for rent and a coin-operated laundry.

WHERE TO DINE

CASTLE GRILL, 14th floor of ANA Zenniku Hotel, 3-2-1 Ichiban-cho. Tel. 0899/33-5511.

Cuisine: SEAFOOD/STEAKS. **Reservations:** Recommended. **Tram:** Kenchomae, a few minutes' walk away.

$ **Prices:** Soups and appetizers ¥800–¥1,500 ($5.70–$10.70); main dishes ¥2,000–¥4,500 ($14.30–$32.15); set-dinner courses ¥5,500–¥11,000 ($30.30–$78.55); set lunches ¥1,000–¥3,800 ($7.15–$27.15). AE, DC, JCB, MC, V.

Open: Lunch Mon–Sat 11:45am–2:30pm; dinner Mon–Sat 5:30–9:30pm; Sun and hols 11:45am–9:30pm.

For fine hotel dining, the ANA Zenniku Hotel is a good choice for variety and convenience, since it's located right in the heart of the city, close to the castle and the shopping arcades. This is one of the most romantic Western restaurants in town, with candles and flowers on each table and a view in the valley below of a European-style castle built by a former lord, Bansuiso Mansion, which is lit up at night. If you order à la carte from the menu featuring primarily steaks and seafood, expect to spend about

¥7,000 ($50). After dinner, retire to the Blue Bell Lounge next door, with more views of the city and live piano music.

UNKAI, 6th floor of ANA Zenniku Hotel, 3-2-1 Ichiban-cho. Tel. 0899/ 33-5511.
  Cuisine: VARIED JAPANESE. **Reservations:** Recommended. **Tram:** Kencho-mae, a few minutes' walk away.
$ **Prices:** Set meals ¥5,000–¥12,000 ($35.70–$85.70). AE, DC, JCB, MC, V.
  Open: Lunch Mon–Sat 11:45am–2:30pm; dinner Mon–Sat 5–9:30pm; Sat and hols 11:45am–9:30pm.

This restaurant offers a variety of food, including sukiyaki, shabu-shabu, tempura, and sashimi. Although the menu is in Japanese only, there are pictures accompanying most of the set meals. A la carte dinners usually run about ¥5,000 ($45.70) per person; set lunches start at ¥1,500 ($10.70). The restaurant overlooks a small garden with a stream that is lit up at night.

TOHEN, 6th floor of ANA Zenniku Hotel, 3-2-1 Ichiban-cho. Tel. 0899/ 33-5511.
  Cuisine: CHINESE. **Reservations:** Recommended. **Tram:** Kencho-mae, a few minutes' walk away.
$ **Prices:** Main dishes ¥1,500–¥2,500 ($10.70–$17.85); set lunches ¥1,000–¥3,000 ($7.15–$21.40). AE, DC, JCB, MC, V.
  Open: Lunch Mon–Sat 11:45am–2:30pm; dinner Mon–Sat 5–9:30pm; Sun and hols 11:45am–9:30pm.

This restaurant is decorated in soothing peach tones and warm woods, and the most popular time to come is at lunch, when quick service will bring you set meals starting at ¥1,000 ($7.15). The dinner menu lists set courses for two people beginning at ¥7,000 ($50), with the à la carte menu offering shrimp, pork, beef, liver, kidney, duck, and chicken dishes that come in two sizes. If there are two of you, the practice is to order three small dishes and share.

BEER GARDEN, rooftop of ANA Zenniku Hotel, 3-2-1 Ichiban-cho. Tel. 0899/33-5511.
  Cuisine: JAPANESE/WESTERN. **Tram:** Kencho-mae, a few minutes' walk away.
$ **Prices:** ¥3,000 ($21.40) for all-you-can-eat buffet. No credit cards.
  Open: Dinner daily 5:30–9:30pm. **Closed:** Oct–May.

If you're on a budget or simply want to sit out under the sun or stars, try the ANA Zenniku's rooftop beer garden, which serves an all-you-can eat smörgåsbord of Western and Japanese food for ¥3,000 ($21.40) at the door and ¥2,900 ($20.70) if you purchase a ticket in advance at the hotel.

SHINHAMASAKU ㉖, Sanbancho 4-chome. Tel. 33-3030.
  Cuisine: VARIED JAPANESE. **Directions:** An 8-minute walk from Shi-eki-mae tram stop, or an 8-minute walk south of ANA Zenniku Hotel.
$ **Prices:** Set meals ¥1,000–¥11,000 ($7.15–$78.55). No credit cards.
  Open: Lunch daily 11am–3pm; dinner daily 4:30–8:30pm.

This modern restaurant located in the heart of town near the Matsuyama Central Post Office serves fresh seafood from the Seto Inland Sea and other local specialties, as well as shabu-shabu, kamameshi, and crab and eel dishes. The menu is in Japanese only but has pictures of the various set courses, most of which range from ¥1,000 ($7.15) to ¥3,000 ($21.40). Popular is the *Seiro bento* with tempura for ¥2,700 ($19.30), which includes about 20 different bite-size morsels, all served in a wooden box. Kaiseki set meals start at ¥3,800 ($27.15).

HYAKUMI ㉗, 2 Sanbancho. Tel. 45-1893.
  Cuisine: VARIED JAPANESE. **Tram:** Ichiban-cho, a 4-minute walk away.
$ **Prices:** Kamameshi ¥750 ($5.35); set meals ¥1,000–¥2,700 ($7.15–$19.30). JCB, MC, V.
  Open: Wed–Mon 11:30am–9pm; open Tues if national hol. **Closed:** Wed after national hol.

This restaurant is just off Okaido pedestrian shopping lane close to the ANA Zenniku

Hotel. Although it doesn't have an English menu, it has a plastic-food display case outside showing tempura, shabu-shabu, somen (noodles), kamameshi (rice casseroles), and other dishes. I've had the Bochan Teishoku, a rice casserole dish served with fish, soup, egg custard, and tea, for ¥1,800 ($12.85). The topping for your rice casserole is your choice—how about crab, shrimp, or fish? I've also tried the Higawari Teishoku, which means daily special and which changes every day. It's available until 2pm every day except Sunday and national holidays and costs ¥900 ($6.40). It usually consists of a variety of small dishes, and included soup, sashimi, tempura, pickled vegetables, beef, egg custard, and rice during my last visit. The ground floor provides counter seating, but I find the little cubicles with either tatami or table seating on the first floor much more festive.

CHAPTER 15

KYUSHU

The southernmost of Japan's four main islands, Kyushu offers a mild climate, such hot-spring spas as Beppu and Ibusuki, beautiful countryside, national parks, and warm, friendly people. Historians believe that Japan's earliest inhabitants lived in Kyushu before gradually pushing northward, and according to Japanese legend it was from Kyushu that the first emperor, Jimmu, began his campaign to unify Japan. Kyushu is therefore considered to be the cradle of Japanese civilization. And because Kyushu is the island closest to Korea and China, it has served through the centuries as a point of influx for both people and ideas from abroad, including those from the West.

Christian missionaries such as St. Francis Xavier succeeded in converting many Kyushu Japanese to Christianity. And in Nagasaki, small communities of Dutch and Chinese merchants were allowed to remain throughout Japan's 200-some years of isolation from the West. In short, Kyushu should be high on the list of any visitor to Japan. From its hot-sand baths to its volcanic peaks to its beaches and cosmopolitan cities, Kyushu offers some of the best attractions in Japan.

SEEING THE REGION

Most of Kyushu's towns are along the coast, which means that you can visit most cities and attractions by circling the island by train. You might, for example, wish to start out in Fukuoka, where its Hakata Station is the terminus for Shinkansen bullet trains from Tokyo. From there you can head south to Kagoshima, stopping at Beppu and Miyazaki along the way. From Kagoshima, consider taking the bus to Chiran to visit its famous samurai gardens and continuing by bus onward to Ubusuki, Kyushu's southernmost tip. From there, take the train northward along Kyushu's western coast to Kumamoto, where you can take a side trip to Mt. Aso in the middle of the island. Nagasaki is easily reached by train from Kumamoto, and you can complete your tour of Kyushu by taking a bus from Nagasaki to the mountain resort of Unzen. Complete your circuit of the island by returning to Fukuoka and boarding the Shinkansen bullet train bound for Honshu.

1. FUKUOKA

730 miles W of Tokyo; 281 miles W of Hiroshima

GETTING THERE By Plane International direct flights from Pusan, Seoul, Taipei, Hong Kong, Honolulu, Beijing, Shanghai, Colombo, Guam, Saipan, Singapore, Kuala Lumpur, Sydney, and Brisbane. Domestic flights connect Fukuoka with Tokyo in 1½ hours.

WHAT'S SPECIAL ABOUT KYUSHU

Hot-Spring Spas

- ☐ Beppu, with its 168 public bath-houses; open-air sand bathing; Takegawara bathhouse, built in the late 1800s; and Suginoi Palace, one of the largest bathhouses in Japan.
- ☐ Ibusuki, located on the southern tip of Kyushu and famous for its open-air sand bathing, the huge indoor Jungle Bath, and its tropical climate.
- ☐ Unzen, a resort town with hot sulphur springs 2,385 feet high in the mountains.

Castles

- ☐ Kumamoto Castle, originally constructed in the 1600s and now containing a museum.

Natural Spectacles

- ☐ The Hells of Beppu, boiling ponds created by volcanic activity.
- ☐ Mt. Aso, the largest crater basin in the world.
- ☐ Mt. Sakurajima, an active volcano in southern Kyushu.

Gardens

- ☐ Suizenji in Kumamoto, famous for its miniature reproductions of well-known landmarks along the old Tokaido Highway, including a miniature Mt. Fuji.
- ☐ Iso Garden in Kagoshima, laid out more than 300 years ago and used by former lords for poetry-composing parties.
- ☐ Six samurai gardens in Chiran, laid out in the 18th century.

Dining

- ☐ Kumamoto's local specialties, including grilled tofu, fish and taro with bean paste, lotus root, and basashi (raw horse meat).
- ☐ Internationally influenced cuisine of Nagasaki, including a spongecake with Portuguese origins and Shippoku, dishes native to Nagasaki that show Chinese, Japanese, and European influences.
- ☐ Satsuma cuisine of Kagoshima, which includes fish, pork, and chicken dishes unique to southern Kyushu.

Shopping

- ☐ Ningyo clay dolls of Hakata.
- ☐ Damascene and pearls, specialties of Kumamoto
- ☐ Oshima pongee, a type of Japanese silk produced in Kagoshima
- ☐ Satsuma pottery, first brought to Kyushu by Korean potters almost 400 years ago.

By Train Fukuoka's Hakata Station is the last stop on the Shinkansen bullet train from Tokyo, about 6 hours away; Hiroshima is 1½ hours away.

By Bus Night buses depart from Shinjuku Station, arriving in Tenjin 15 hours and 15 minutes later.

With a population of 1.2 million, Fukuoka is Kyushu's largest city and serves as a major international and domestic gateway to the island.

During Japan's feudal days, Fukuoka was actually divided into two distinct towns separated by the Nakagawa River. Fukuoka was where the samurai lived, since it was the castle town of the local feudal lord. Merchants lived across the river in Hakata, the commercial center of the area. Both cities were joined in 1889 under the common name of Fukuoka. Fukuoka's main train station, however, is in Hakata and is therefore called Hakata Station.

In the 13th century, Fukuoka was selected by Mongol forces under Kublai Khan as the best place to invade Japan. The first attack came in 1274, but the Japanese were able to repel the invasion. Convinced the Mongols would attack again, the Japanese built a 10-foot-high stone wall along the coast. The second invasion came in 1281.

Not only did the Mongols find the wall impossible to scale, but a typhoon blew in and destroyed the entire Mongol fleet. The Japanese called this gift from heaven "divine wind," or kamikaze, a word that took on a different meaning during World War II, when young Japanese pilots crashed their planes into American ships in a last-ditch attempt to win the war.

As an industrial and business center of Kyushu, Fukuoka is not considered much of a destination on the tourist circuit. However, you may find yourself making a one-night stopover here after an international flight or a day's train ride from Tokyo.

ORIENTATION

INFORMATION

The **area code** for Fukuoka, lying in Fukuoka Prefecture, is 092. An **international post office** is located next to Hakata Station.

Before leaving Tokyo or Kyoto, drop by the Tourist Information Center to pick up a leaflet called *Fukuoka*. It lists the major sights of the city. The **Fukuoka Tourist Information Office** (tel. 092/431-3003) is in Hakata Station. Open from 9am to 7pm, it has maps and a pamphlet in English.

CITY LAYOUT

Although Hakata Station is the terminus for the Shinkansen bullet train, with most of Fukuoka's hotels clustered nearby, the heart of Fukuoka is an area called **Tenjin,** which serves as the business center for the city. It's also home to several department stores, a large underground shopping arcade, coffee shops, and restaurants. Less than a 10-minute walk from Tenjin is **Nakasu,** Fukuoka's largest nightlife district, with lots of bars, restaurants, and small clubs.

GETTING AROUND

BY SUBWAY

The easiest method of transportation is by subway. One convenient subway line, for example, runs from Hakata Station to Tenjin (the third stop), passing Nakasukawabata on the way, the stop for the Nakasu nightlife district. This same line will also take you to Ohori-Koen Park.

BY BUS

The city's two bus terminals are located in Tenjin and at Hakata Station.

BY TRAIN

Whereas Hakata Station serves as the terminus for the Shinkansen and Japan Railways trains departing for the rest of Kyushu, Tenjin has its own station, called the Nishitetsu Fukuoka Station. This is where you board the train if you're going to Dazaifu.

IMPRESSIONS

Japan, a country combining a feverish proficiency in many of the habits of advanced civilization with uncompromising relics of feudal crystallization.
—GEORGE CURZON, *TALES OF TRAVEL*, 1923

WHAT TO SEE & DO

Shofukuji Temple is just a 10-minute walk northwest of Hakata Station. Thought to be the oldest Zen Buddhist temple in Japan, it was founded in 1195 by a priest named Eisai, who introduced Zen and tea seeds into Japan after studying 4 years in China.

Located about 15 minutes on foot from Hakata Station is **Sumiyoshi-jinja Shrine.** With 400-year-old buildings, it's one of Kyushu's oldest Shinto shrines and is dedicated to the guardians of seafarers. As it's favored by the Japanese as a good place for wedding ceremonies, you may be lucky and witness a traditional wedding in progress.

If you feel like being lazy, take the subway line from Hakata Station to the Ohori-Koen subway stop, just 10 minutes away. There you'll find **Ohori-Koen Park,** built on part of the outer defenses of the former Fukuoka Castle. Laid around a lake said to be a copy of Xi Hu in China, and dotted with small islands connected with bridges, it's a perfect place to relax with a picnic lunch. On the south side of the park is a traditional Japanese garden—constructed in 1984.

The nearby **Fukuoka City Art Museum** (Fukuoka Shiritsu Bijutsukan) (tel. 714-6051), in the southeastern part of the park facing the lake, contains modern and Buddhist art, tea-ceremony utensils, ancient weapons, and armor. It's open Tuesday through Sunday from 9:30am to 5:30pm. Admission is ¥200 ($1.40).

If you have time, the most popular thing to do in Fukuoka is to take a side trip to **Dazaifu Temmangu Shrine,** which you can reach in 35 minutes by taking the Nishi Nippon Tetsudo Line (called Nishitetsu for short) from Nishitetsu Fukuoka Station in Tenjin. Trains depart every 30 minutes and the station stop is called Dazaifu Station. Dazaifu Temmangu Shrine was established in 905, although the present main hall dates from 1590. It's dedicated to the god of scholarship, which is one reason why the shrine is so popular—high school students flock here to pray that they pass the tough entrance exams into universities. Planted with lots of plum trees, camphor trees, and irises, the extensive grounds surrounding the shrine can be explored on a rented bicycle.

WHERE TO STAY

Because most people make a stopover in Fukuoka for only one night, I've listed accommodations within walking distance of Hakata Station.

EXPENSIVE

ANA ZENNIKU HOTEL HAKATA, 3-3-3 Hakata-ekimae, Hakata-ku 812. Tel. 092/471-7111. Fax 092/472-7707. 354 rms. A/C MINIBAR TV TEL
Directions: A 4-minute walk from Hakata Guchi exit of Hakata Station.
$ Rates: ¥11,000–¥16,500 ($78–$118) single; ¥23,000 ($164) double; ¥21,000–¥32,000 ($150–$228) twin. Japanese-style suites: ¥27,000 ($193) two to three persons. AE, DC, JCB, MC, V.

One of the finest places to stay in town, this modern and sparkling-clean first-class hotel has everything you'd expect from a hotel of this stature. Its lobby is spacious and its rooms are bright and comfortable, with the usual pay video channels on TV, well-stocked minibar, radio, and large bathroom. Japanese-style suites have all the modern conveniences.

Dining/Entertainment: There are cocktail lounges, Chinese and Western restaurants, and a Japanese restaurant that is described in the "Where to Dine" section later in this chapter. An outside sidewalk café is open from 5pm to 9:30pm during summer months.

Services: Free newspaper, same-day laundry service.

Facilities: A health club with pool, sauna, and exercise equipment which you can use for ¥6,000 ($43), shopping arcade.

HAKATA MIYAKO HOTEL, 2-1 Hakata-eki Higashi, Hakata-ku 812. Tel.

092/441-3111. Fax 092/481-1306. 269 rms. A/C MINIBAR TV TEL **Directions:** A 1-minute walk from Hakata Station's south side.
$ Rates: ¥10,000–¥14,000 ($71–$100) single; ¥16,500–¥18,000 ($118–$128) double/twin. Japanese-style rooms: ¥18,500 ($132). AE, DC, JCB, MC, V.

This hotel is just in front of the Shinkansen bullet train exit of Hakata Station, on the south side. With the good name and legendary service of the Miyako hotel chain behind it, this hostelry has well-appointed rooms (some with bilingual TV). The hotel's six Japanese-style rooms, used most often as waiting rooms before wedding ceremonies and receptions held at the hotel, have cypress bathtubs.

Dining/Entertainment: Starlight, a French restaurant on the 12th floor, features live piano music, while Shikitei specializes in Kyoto-style dishes. There's also a cocktail lounge on the 12th floor, a bar on the 2nd floor, and a coffee shop.

Services: Free newspaper, same-day laundry service.

Facilities: Beauty parlor, souvenir shop, medical clinic.

MODERATE

HOTEL CENTRAZA HAKATA, 4-23 Hakataeki-Chuogai, Hakata-ku 812. Tel. 092/461-0111. Fax 092/461-0171. 198 rms. A/C MINIBAR TV TEL **Directions:** A 1-minute walk from Shinkansen (south) exit of Hakata Station.
$ Rates: ¥9,300–¥15,000 ($66–$107) single; ¥13,000–¥16,000 ($93–$114) double; ¥15,000–¥20,000 ($107–$143) twin. AE, DC, JCB, MC, V.

Located on the square in front of the Shinkansen exit of Hakata Station, this hotel has a spacious and marbled second-floor lobby, and all rooms have semidouble- or double-size beds, a TV control panel beside the bed, radio, clock, refrigerator, minibar, and hot-water pot. There's a small outdoor swimming pool, and in the basement is Gourmet City, with approximately a dozen restaurants.

CHISAN HOTEL HAKATA ⑱, **2-8-11 Hakata-ekimae, Hakata-ku 812. Tel. 092/411-3211.** Fax 092/473-8323. 289 rms. A/C MINIBAR TV TEL **Directions:** A 7-minute walk from Hakata Guchi exit of Hakata Station; walk straight out of station and hotel will be on right.
$ Rates (including tax and service): ¥7,900 ($56) single; ¥12,400 ($88) double; ¥13,500–¥15,800 ($96–$113) twin. AE, DC, JCB, MV, V.

This light-tiled triangular building is an efficient and dependable business hotel with good service and a friendly staff. Rooms come with TV with pay video, radio, clock, minibar, and hot-water pot and tea. The best rooms are the higher-priced twins. Located in the curve of the hotel's front façade, they offer large rounded windows and lots of space. The hotel's one restaurant serves a buffet breakfast of Japanese and Western food for ¥1,000 ($7.15).

CLIO COURT, 5-3 Hakataeki-Chuogai, Hakata-ku 812. Tel. 092/472-1111. Fax 092/474-3222. 203 rms. A/C MINIBAR TV TEL **Directions:** A 1-minute walk from Hakata Station, beside Shinkansen exit.
$ Rates: ¥11,000–¥16,000 ($78–$114) single; ¥13,000–¥20,000 ($93–$143) double; ¥15,400–¥23,000 ($110–$164) twin. AE, DC, JCB, MC, V.

One of Fukuoka's newest and best medium-priced hotels, this sleek and modern hotel features lots of chrome, mirrors, and white marble in its design. Its chic lobby is up on the third floor, and its rooms, all doubles and twins, are decorated in art deco styles. Few of the rooms have the same interior design—they're the creation of well-known female architect Rei Kurokawa. Rooms are large; even the bathrooms are roomy. The cheapest rooms, however, don't have any windows, and since there are no single rooms per se, single travelers are assigned to twin or double rooms at rates slightly less than for double occupancy.

Restaurants in the hotel serve French, Chinese, and Japanese cuisine. In the basement is an interesting setup called Clio Seven, which is essentially one large room divided into seven different bars and restaurants, including a sushi bar, a yakitori-ya, and an English-style pub. Clio Seven is open daily from 5pm to 1am.

MITSUI URBAN HOTEL ㉑, **2-8-15 Hakata-ekimae, Hakata-ku 812. Tel. 092/451-5111.** 310 rms. A/C MINIBAR TV TEL **Directions:** A 7-minute walk from Hakata Guchi exit of Hakata Station.
$ Rates: ¥7,400 ($52.85) single; ¥14,000 ($100) double/twin. AE, DC, JCB, MC, V.

Next to the Chisan Hotel, described above, is another business hotel, part of a nationwide hotel chain. This one was built more than a decade ago but still looks relatively new. The rooms are small but have large windows and contain everything you need.

BUDGET

TOYO HOTEL, 1-9-36 Hakata-eki Higashi, Hakata-ku 812. Tel. 092/474-1121. 274 rms (all with bath). A/C MINIBAR TV TEL **Directions:** A 2-minute walk north from Shinkansen exit of Hakata Station.
$ Rates (including tax and service charge): ¥7,200 ($51) single; ¥9,900 ($71) double; ¥11,000–¥14,000 ($78–$100) twin; ¥14,000–¥16,500 ($100–$118) triple. AE, DC, JCB, MC, V.

All beds in this comfortable business hotel are semidoubles, and the sofa in the twin rooms can be made into an extra bed. Some of the lower-floor twins face another building, making them rather dark. Ask for a room higher up; those facing north have the best view. Since this is a Japanese businessman's hotel, don't be too surprised to find vending machines selling magazines of questionable taste.

HAKATA GREEN HOTEL 2, 4-4 Hakataeki-Chuogai, Hakata-ku 812. Tel. 092/451-4111. Fax 092/451-4508. 569 rms (all with bath). A/C TV TEL **Directions:** A 2-minute walk from Shinkansen exit of Hakata Station.
$ Rates (including tax and service): ¥6,200 ($44) single; ¥9,000 ($64) twin; ¥8,200 ($58) double. AE, DC, JCB, MC, V.

Not far from the Toyo Hotel are the Hakata Green Hotels 1 and 2. Green Hotel 2 is newer and nicer, so when making your reservation make sure your reservation is for Green Hotel 2 (the hotels have the same phone number and fax number). It has mainly singles, but some twins and doubles are available. Rooms, tiny and without closets, are white, bright, and clean, and come with coin-operated TV, clock, a plug-in pressing board to keep businessmen's pants nicely pressed (you can also use it on skirts), and large windows that open. There's a tiny drying rack in the bathroom to hang up wet clothes. Machines in the hallway dispense free hot tea.

The ground-floor Japanese restaurant, Ginroku, is decorated with Japanese kites and traditional décor, and it has modern pop music. It's open daily from 7 to 10am and from 11am to 1:30pm. In the evenings it's a reasonably priced yakitori-ya, offering skewered chicken, sashimi, baked potatoes, flatfish, and corn on the cob. You can eat here for less than ¥1,500 ($10.70).

Youth Hostels

DAZAIFU YOUTH HOSTEL ㉒, **Sanjo 1-18-1, Dazaifu 818-01. Tel. 092/922-8740.** 24 beds. A/C **Directions:** A 12-minute walk from Dazaifu Station.
$ Rates: ¥2,400 ($17.15) member, ¥600 ($4.30) extra for nonmember. Breakfast ¥450 ($3.20); dinner ¥850 ($6.05). No credit cards.

This two-story youth hostel is located in Dazaifu, home of the famous Daizaifu Temmangu Shrine. Facilities include tennis courts and coin-operated laundry machines.

YAKIYAMA YOUTH HOSTEL, Yakiyama, Izuka City 820. Tel. 09482/22-6385. 90 beds. **Bus:** From Nishitetsu-Fukuoka Bus Center in Tenjin (50-minute ride), then a 10-minute walk; or from Hakata Station, bus from platform 12 to Yakiyama Pass.
$ Rates: Oct–Apr ¥2,050 ($14.65); May–Sept ¥1,800 ($12.85). Breakfast ¥500 ($3.55); dinner ¥800 ($5.70). No credit cards.

This hostel, which accepts members only, is located between Fukuoka and Izuka City on Yakiyama Pass. There are two hiking courses nearby, both 2 hours long.

WHERE TO DINE

TSUKUSHINO, 15th floor of ANA Zenniku Hotel Hakata, 3-3-3 Hakata-ekimae. Tel. 092/471-7111.
Cuisine: VARIED JAPANESE/LOCAL SPECIALTIES. **Reservations:** Recommended. **Directions:** A 5-minute walk from Hakata Guchi exit of Hakata Station.
$ Prices: Kaiseki ¥7,700–¥20,000 ($55–$143); lunch set meals ¥1,200–¥5,000 ($8.55–$39.30). AE, DC, JCB, MC, V.
Open: Daily 11:30am–10pm.

Although most first-class hotels feature Western restaurants on their top floors, the ANA Zenniku Hotel has given its Japanese restaurant, Tsukushino, with its views of the city, the premier spot on the 15th floor. A beautifully sculpted bonsai pine graces the entrance to the restaurant, designed to resembles a village lane. Overhanging eaves and traditional tiled roofs extend from the ceiling, and in the center of the restaurant is a glass-enclosed courtyard with raked gravel and bushes. The English menu describes each dish. Mizutaki, for example, is a Fukuoka specialty described as chicken boiled in light broth with various Japanese vegetables and tofu. Kaiseki offerings change every 2 months. There are also shabu-shabu, sashimi dishes, and a separate tempura counter. Lunch is much cheaper, with teishoku specials beginning at ¥1,200 ($8.55) and served until 2pm. Most popular is the Tsukushino obento lunch box for ¥2,700 ($19.30), which includes sashimi, boiled vegetables, and lots more.

STARLIGHT, Hakata Miyako Hotel, 2-1 Hakata-eki Higashi. Tel. 092/441-3111.
Cuisine: WESTERN. **Reservations:** Recommended. **Directions:** A 1-minute walk from Shinkansen exit of Hakata Station.
$ Prices: Set dinner courses ¥6,500–¥11,000 ($46.40–$78.55). AE, DC, JCB, MC, V.
Open: Dinner daily 5–10:30pm.

Western dining at the Miyako Hotel is done in style at the 12th-floor Starlight. There's live piano music nightly and at one end of the restaurant is a cocktail bar where you can retire for drinks after dinner. If you order seafood or steak main dishes from the large leather-bound menu, expect to spend about ¥10,000 ($71.40) per person.

SHIKITEI, Hakata Miyako Hotel, 2-1 Hakata-eki Higashi. Tel. 092/441-3111.
Cuisine: KYOTO CUISINE/LOCAL DISHES. **Directions:** A 1-minute walk from Shinkansen exit of Hakata Station.
$ Prices: Set meals ¥3,800–¥10,000 ($27.15–$71.40); set lunches ¥1,600–¥3,800 ($11.40–$27.15). AE, DC, JCB, MC, V.
Open: Lunch daily 11:30am–2pm; dinner daily 5–9:30pm.

With the Miyako chain's most famous hotel located in Kyoto, it's not surprising that this hotel's Japanese restaurant, Shikitei, specializes in Kyoto-style dishes. Set meals start at ¥3,800 ($27.15) for sashimi, tempura, and mizutaki and rise to ¥6,500 ($46.40) for shabu-shabu and sukiyaki. Kyoto kaiseki selections start at ¥5,500 ($39.30). During lunch there are also obento lunch box specials.

GYOSAI ㉒, 3-chome Hakata-ekimae. Tel. 441-9780.
Cuisine: SASHIMI/SEAFOOD. **Directions:** A 7-minute walk from Hakata Guchi exit; walk straight from station and restaurant will be on your left.
$ Prices: ¥1,000–¥2,500 ($7.15–$17.85); lunch teishoku ¥650 ($4.65). JCB.
Open: Lunch Mon–Sat 11:30am–1:30pm; dinner Mon–Sat 5–10:30pm.

Specializing in Japanese seafood, this restaurant is located across the street from the Chisan Hotel (its sign says OKI DOKI). Actually, it's one of four Gyosai restaurants in Fukuoka—two are in the Tenjin shopping area and another one is located not far from Hakata Station. (There's even a Gyosai in New York City.) You can get a plate of assorted sashimi here for ¥1,600 ($11.40). The menu is in Japanese only, so the easiest thing to do is order one of the set meals, which are shown in a brochure with pictures and range from ¥4,000 to ¥7,000 ($28.55 to $50). The lunch teishoku, served from 11:30am to 1:30pm, is very reasonable at ¥650 ($4.65) and consists of fried and raw fish, vegetables, pickles, soup, and rice.

GOURMET CITY, basement of Hotel Centraza, 4-23 Hakataeki-Chuogai. Tel. 461-0111.
　　Cuisine: WESTERN/JAPANESE. **Directions:** A 1-minute walk from shinkansen exit of Hakata Station.
　$ Prices: ¥700–¥2,500 ($5–$17.85). No credit cards.
　　Open: Daily 11am–11pm.
For inexpensive dining close to the station, try Gourmet City, with approximately a dozen establishments offering everything from sushi, Chinese food, and steaks to ice cream and beer. Restaurants are chic and well designed, with plastic-food displays and lunch specials priced mostly under ¥1,500 ($10.70).

SHOPPING

You don't have to venture far from Hakata Station to go shopping. In fact, the **Izutsuya department store** is located right above the station itself. Incidentally, on top of the department store is a rooftop beer garden open mid-April through August from 5 to 10pm. Radiating out from the station are underground shopping arcades. Deitos is located under the Shinkansen tracks and is comprised of various souvenir shops selling cakes, woven handbags, and Hakata's famous clay ningyo dolls.

Another large shopping area is in Tenjin, third stop on the subway line from Hakata Station. There's a huge underground shopping mall here, called **Tenjin Chikagai,** which stretches some 1,300 feet north to south. There are also many boutiques, department stores, specialty shops, coffee shops, and restaurants in the area.

---

2. BEPPU

762 miles SW of Tokyo, 116 miles SE of Fukuoka

GETTING THERE　By Plane　The nearest airport is Oita, an hour's bus ride away; ANA flights from Tokyo's Haneda airport takes about 1½ hours.

By Train　From Tokyo by Shinkansen to Kokura, then transfer to a limited express bound for Beppu, the trip taking 7 or 8 hours. There are also approximately 19 trains a day from Hakata Station in Fukuoka, the trip taking 2½ hours.

By Bus　From Osaka to Beppu, the bus trip takes 10 hours.

By Ferry　Ferries make regular runs to Beppu from Osaka, Hiroshima, Kobe, and Matsuyama.

ESSENTIAL INFORMATION　The **area code** for Beppu, lying in Oita Prefecture, is 0977; the **postal code** is 874.

The Tourist Information Center in either Tokyo or Kyoto has a free leaflet called *Beppu and Vicinity,* with information on this area of Kyushu as well as on transportation within it.

Once in Beppu be sure to stop by the **Beppu Tourist Information Office** (tel. 0977/24-2838), which is located at Beppu Station and is open daily from 9am to 6pm. You can pick up an excellent brochure called *The Smile of Japan—Beppu,* with such useful information as what to see in the area, which local buses to take, the opening and closing hours for the major sights, and a map of the city. Another information office, called the **Foreign Tourist Information Service,** is located about a 2-minute walk from Beppu Station on the second floor of the Frosen Building (tel.

0977/23-1119). It's operated by English-speaking volunteers and offers tourist information and advice.

GETTING AROUND The easiest ways to get around Beppu are **bus** and **taxi**. If you plan on doing a lot of sightseeing by bus, there's a 1-day bus pass with the strange name of "My Beppu Free," which nonetheless costs ¥800 ($5.70) and allows unlimited travel on Kamenoi Company buses within the city. If you're short of time, you may want to join one of the many organized tours.

Some 12 million people come to Beppu every year to relax and rejuvenate themselves, and they do so in a number of unique ways. They sit in mud baths up to their necks; they bury themselves in hot black sand; they soak in hot springs; and on New Year's they bathe in water filled with floating orange peels. With more than 3,000 hot springs spewing forth 140,000 tons of water daily, and a total of 168 public bathhouses, Beppu is one of Japan's best-known spa resorts.

Bathing reigns supreme here—and I suggest you join in the fun. After all, visiting Beppu without enjoying the baths would be like going to a famous restaurant with your own TV dinner. Beppu itself, not a very large town, is situated on Kyushu's east coast in a curve of Beppu Bay. It is bounded on one side by the sea and on the other by steep hills and mountains. Steam rises everywhere throughout the city, escaping from springs and pipes and giving the town an otherworldly appearance. Indeed, eight of the hot springs look so much like hell that that's what they're called—Jigoku, the Hells. But rather than a place most people try to avoid, the Hells are a major tourist attraction. In fact, everything in Beppu is geared toward tourism, and if you're interested in rubbing elbows with Japanese on vacation, this is one of the best places to do so.

WHAT TO SEE & DO

There are many kinds of springs and baths with various mineral contents that help in ailments from rheumatism to skin disease. If all you want is a quick dip in a hot-spring bath in between train rides, you have no farther to go than **Eki-mae Onsen,** which is just a minute's walk from Beppu Station's main exit and which also features a Jacuzzi. If you have a specific ailment, call the hot-springs section of the tourist office (tel. 21-1111) to ask which baths would help you most. The pamphlet *The Smile of Japan,* described above, also has information on the various baths and their specific benefits. Otherwise, if you're simply here for the experience of the baths, there are two I particularly recommend.

SUGINOI PALACE

Most of the Japanese inns, hotels, and even private homes are tapped into Beppu's hot springs, but no matter where you stay you should visit Suginoi Palace, which adjoins the Suginoi Hotel. This is one of the most fantastic and fantasy-provoking baths in all of Japan, and also one of the largest. Two separate bathing areas are housed in what look like airplane hangars, one for men and one for women. Filled with lush tropical plants and pools of various sizes and temperatures, one of the baths features a benevolent-looking Buddha sitting atop a giant fish bowl full of carp, while the other boasts a large red torii gate similar to ones you see at Shinto shrines. If you come 2 days in a row you can see both baths, as men and women alternate facilities daily. The baths also feature a steam room, a sauna, an outdoor pool, a Korean-style heated floor upon which you can lie down and relax, a pit with hot sand in which to bury yourself, and even a so-called "coffee bath" with real coffee in it, thought to aid the complexion.

The baths are open to the public daily from 9am to 9pm at a cost of ¥1,800 ($12.85). If you're staying at the Suginoi Hotel, you can use the baths daily for free from 9am to 10:30pm. In addition to its huge bathhouses, Suginoi Palace offers an outdoor waterfall and pond filled with greedy carp (buy some fish food and you'll see what I mean—they almost jump out of the water in their feeding frenzy). There's also a small landscaped garden, a beautiful display of bonsai plants, a play area with amusement-park rides for children, a miniature golf course, and bowling lanes. There's even a variety show, with two performances daily. (*Note:* The variety show is included in the admission price to the baths, but occasionally big-name entertainers appear and admission prices go up regardless of whether or not you attend the show. To avoid having to pay extra, it might be prudent to check the price). Especially good is the **Suginoi Museum,** which charges a separate admission fee of ¥500 ($3.55). Its collection is worth more than ¥10 billion and includes a varied selection of samurai armor, Japanese antique weapons, toilet sets, ceramics, lacquerware, religious artifacts, clocks, and other items dating from the Edo Period.

A HOT-SAND BATH

✪ One of the unique things you can do in Beppu is take a bath in hot sand, and one of the best places to do it is at **Takegawara Bathhouse.** Built in 1879, it's one of the oldest public baths in the city. The inside of the building resembles an ancient gymnasium. Bathing areas are separate for men and women, and are dominated by a pit filled with black sand. The attendants are used to foreigners here and will instruct you to strip, wash yourself down, and then lie down in a hollow they've dug in the sand. You should bring your own towel, which you should use to cover your vital parts. An attendant will then shovel sand on top of you and pack you in until only your head and feet are sticking out. I personally didn't find the sand all that hot, but it is relaxing as the heat soaks into your body. You stay buried for 10 minutes, contemplating the wooden ceiling high above and hoping you don't get an itch somewhere. When the time is up, the attendant will tell you to stand up, shake off the sand, and then jump into a bath of hot water. The cost of this bathing experience is ¥600 ($4.30), and daily hours are 6:30am to 9pm.

Open-air sand baths are also offered at **Beppu Beach (Shoningahama),** reportedly good for muscle pain, rheumatism, and neuralgia. You keep on your yukata for the burial here, and the experience also costs ¥600 ($4.30). Daily hours are 8:30am to 6pm, with slightly shorter hours in winter. You can reach Beppu Beach via bus no. 24 or 26, departing from the main exit on the east side of Beppu Station; you can also reach it on a local commuter train to Daigoku Station.

THE HELLS

As for sightseeing, you might as well join everyone else and go to the Hells. These Hells are boiling ponds created by volcanic activity. Six of them are clustered close together in the Kannawa area within walking distance of each other and can be toured in about an hour or so. One ¥1,500 ($10.70) ticket allows entrance to all eight Hells; otherwise, the separate entrance fee to each one is ¥300 ($2.15). You can also join a 2-hour tour of the Hells for ¥3,000 ($23.20), but it's conducted in Japanese only. Each Hell has its own attraction. Umi Jigoku, or Sea Hell, has the color of sea water. Chinoike Jigoku, the Blood-Pond Hell, is blood-red in color because of the red clay dissolved in the hot water. Yama Jigoku features animals living in its hot spring, and Oniyama Jigoku is where crocodiles are bred. Tatsumaki Jigoku, or Waterspout Hell, has one of the largest geysers in Japan, and with a temperature of 221°F it's hotter than any other hot spring in Beppu.

TAKASAKIYAMA MOUNTAIN

On Beppu's southern border, about a 15-minute bus ride from Beppu Station, rises Takasakiyama Mountain. Its peak is home to more than 1,800 monkeys, which come down every day to feed, returning to their home by late afternoon. They wander freely among the visitors, and humans are advised not to challenge them by looking directly into their eyes. Admission to this attraction is ¥500 ($3.55), and daily hours are 8:30am to 5pm in winter, 8am to 5:30pm in summer.

COOL FOR KIDS

If you have children traveling with you or simply are fond of zoos, you may be interested in visiting **African Safari**, a drive-through nature park with a road that winds through bare grassland. Bears, baboons, elephants, rhinos, zebras, camels, bison, giraffes, lions, tigers, and other exotic animals are allowed to roam in their own restricted areas, separated by fences so that they don't eat each other. Humans are confined to their cars or special buses. Entrance to the park is ¥2,200 ($15.70), while bus rides through the park cost ¥420 ($3) extra. Best, however, is to pay extra for the ¥1,000 ($7.15) caged bus that features slots of food for the various animals so that you can watch them eat at close range. The prices for children are ¥1,200 ($8.55) for admission and ¥720 ($5.15) for the caged bus. The zoo, which features 1,300 animals belonging to 69 different species, is open daily from 9am to 5pm (9:30am to 4pm from November 16 to March 15).

To reach African Safari, take bus no. 41 or 43 from Beppu Station. The trip takes about 50 minutes. Incidentally, the bus passes through an interesting part of Beppu called Myoban, where you'll notice a number of straw huts along the side of the road. These huts are built above hot springs and protect the formation of white powderlike sulphur deposits, called *yunohana* in Japanese. You can buy the powder and add it to your bath at home for an instant hot-spring experience.

WHERE TO STAY

EXPENSIVE

SUGINOI HOTEL, Kankaiji, Beppu 874. Tel. 0977/24-1141. Fax 0977/21-0010. 590 rms. A/C MINIBAR TV TEL **Bus:** From Beppu Station to Suginoi Palace stop. **Directions:** An 8-minute taxi ride from Beppu Station.

$ Rates (per person, including buffet breakfast and dinner in Western or Japanese restaurant): ¥22,000–¥33,000 ($157–$236) single occupancy; ¥18,500–¥23,000 ($132–$164) double occupancy; ¥20,000–¥21,000 ($143–$150) triple occupancy. Off-season discount ¥2,000 ($14.30) on above rates. AE, DC, JCB, MC, V.

This is probably the best-known hotel in Beppu, famous for its gigantic baths. A huge complex situated on a wooded hill with a sweeping view of the city and sea below, it's one of the most popular places to stay for both Japanese and foreign visitors. Popular also with group tours, it's a lively and noisy hotel filled with good-natured vacationers. In other words, if you like being in the middle of the action, this is the place for you. The hotel is divided into an older east wing and a new west wing known as Hana. Both Western- and Japanese-style rooms are available, but the drawback of the Western-style rooms is that they face inland and therefore miss out on the view of the city. On the other hand, they're also slightly cheaper. Some combination-style rooms featuring both beds and a separate tatami area are also available, with fantastic views of the sea. All rooms are modestly furnished and come with a safe for valuables, among other amenities.

Dining/Entertainment: Restaurants include the Shangrila, which serves Western food, and the Silver Hat, a Japanese restaurant located on the 15th floor of the east wing. There are also a coffee shop and a tea lounge.

Facilities: Suginoi Palace with huge baths, Suginoi Museum, landscaped garden, children's amusement park, miniature golf, and bowling alley; shopping arcade; games room; beauty salon; outdoor swimming pool.

KANNAWAEN ㉒, **Kannawa, Beppu 874. Tel. 0977/66-2111.** 17 rms (4 with bath). A/C TV TEL **Directions:** A 15-minute taxi ride from Beppu Station.

$ Rates (per person, including breakfast, dinner, and service charge): ¥20,000–¥35,000 ($143–$250). No credit cards.

If it's peace and quiet you're searching for, this is a wonderful ryokan hidden away on a lushly landscaped hill not far from the Hells. It actually consists of six separate houses spread around its grounds, and its tatami rooms with shoji screens look out onto carefully tended gardens, hot springs, bamboo, streams, bonsai, stone lanterns, and flowers. This is the perfect place to escape the crowds and to relax in an open-air bath set among rocks and trees. Most rooms do not have a private bathroom, but the beauty of the surrounding countryside more than makes up for it. I highly recommend this place.

Incidentally, if the ryokan itself is too expensive for you, you can come here just to use its open-air bath, open to the public daily from noon to 3pm and 9 to 10:30pm for ¥500 ($3.55). Since it's close to the Hells, you might want to come here after battling the crowds.

MODERATE

NIPPAKU HOTEL, 26-12-3 Kitahama, Beppu 874. Tel. 0977/23-2291. Fax 0977/23-2293. 72 rms (29 with bath). A/C TV TEL **Directions:** A 10-minute walk from Beppu Station.

$ Rates (including tax and service): ¥8,800 ($63) single without bath; ¥12,700 ($91) twin without bath, ¥13,900 ($66) twin with bath. AE, DC, JCB, MC, V.

They're used to foreigners at this reasonably priced tourist hotel, and the front-desk staff speaks English. Rooms are nicely but modestly furnished, and facilities include a restaurant and hot-spring public baths. Both Japanese- and Western-style rooms are available.

TENJUSO ㉓, Minami-soencho 6 Kumi, Beppu 874. Tel. 0977/23-0131. 20 rms (8 with bath). A/C TV TEL **Directions:** A 5-minute taxi ride from Beppu Station.

$ Rates (per person, including breakfast and dinner): ¥6,500–¥15,000 ($46–$107). No credit cards.

A very reasonably priced ryokan, this traditional inn is more than 50 years old and is hidden from the rest of the world by an old stone wall. Each tatami-style room is different and some have private baths, but in any case you'll want to try the hot-spring public bath. The more expensive rooms have a bathroom and a view of the sea, and three rooms have a minibar.

BUDGET

GREEN BUSINESS HOTEL ㉔, 1-3-11 Kitahama, Beppu 874. Tel. 0977/ 25-2244. 53 rms (all with bath). A/C TV TEL **Directions:** A 2-minute walk from Beppu Station.

$ Rates: ¥4,900 ($35) single; ¥6,500 ($46) double; ¥8,800 ($63) twin. No credit cards.

This relatively new business hotel has rooms that are much larger than those of the average business hotel. Rooms come with coin-operated TV and radio, and those facing the front of the hotel even come with tiny balcony.

KAGETSU, Tanoyucho 7-22, Beppu 874. Tel. 0977/24-2355. 10 rms (all with bath). A/C TV TEL **Directions:** A 1-minute walk from west exit of train station (turn left out of station).

$ Rates (per person): ¥3,000 ($21) per person. No credit cards.

Ⓢ Kagetsu offers probably the best deal in all of Beppu—the room rate is about the lowest I've come across in my travels through Japan. Even more astonishing is that each of the rooms, both Western and Japanese style, comes with its own private bathroom, TV, central heating, and air conditioning. And as if that weren't enough, Mrs. Takayama gives out free tickets to the local public bath, even though her own water is supplied from the natural hot springs. No meals are served, but there are plenty of restaurants in the area. I wish every city had a Kagetsu.

KOKAGE, 8-9 Ekimaecho, Beppu 874. Tel. 0977/23-1753. Fax 0977/23-3895. 16 rms (10 with bath). A/C TV TEL **Directions:** A 2-minute walk from main exit of Beppu Station.

$ Rates: ¥3,800 ($27) single with bath; ¥6,500 ($46) twin without bath, ¥7,500

($53) twin with bath; ¥10,000 ($71) triple without bath, ¥11,000 ($78) triple with bath. Breakfast ¥800 ($5.70); Japanese dinner ¥1,800 ($12.85). AE, V.

In operation for more than 20 years, this minshuku is run by a friendly older gentleman who speaks a few words of English and is a member of the Japanese Inn Group. There are 11 Japanese-style rooms, 1 combination room with bed and tatami area, 3 twin rooms, and 1 double room. Rooms are old and a bit worn, but they are furnished with kimono, towels, hot water for tea, and coin-operated heater and air conditioner. There's a public hot-spring bath, and meals are served in a homey dining room with a cluttered but interesting collection of hanging lamps and clocks.

SAKAEYA ㉕, **Ida, Kannawa, Beppu 874. Tel. 0977/66-6234.** 17 rms (none with bath). A/C MINIBAR TV TEL **Directions:** A 10-minute taxi ride from Beppu Station.

$ Rates (per person): ¥3,800 ($27) room only; ¥5,500 ($39) including breakfast; ¥8,500 ($61) including breakfast and dinner. No credit cards.

⭐ This is one of the best budget places to stay near the Hells and the oldest minshuku in the city. The oldest rooms date from the Meiji Period (1868–1912) and feature old radiators heated naturally from hot springs. Another relic is the stone oven in the open courtyard, which uses steam from hot springs for cooking (many older homes in Beppu still use such ovens). Use of the oven is free in case you want to cook your own meals; there's also a modern kitchen you can use. Most of the rooms, all Japanese style, have sinks, and all come with cotton yukata. This establishment is popular with young Japanese, especially during Golden Week at the beginning of May and during New Year's. If the minshuku is full, the owner here says he'll be happy to relocate you in another minshuku close by.

Youth Hostel

BEPPU YOUTH HOSTEL, Kankaiji 2, Beppu 874. Tel. 0977/23-4116. Fax 0977/22-0086. 150 beds. A/C **Bus:** 14 from Beppu Station to Suginoi Palace (a 20-minute ride), then a 4-minute walk.

$ Rates: ¥2,300 ($16.40) member with youth hostel card; ¥3,000 ($21.40) nonmember. Breakfast ¥400 ($2.85); dinner ¥850 ($6.05). No credit cards.

This youth hostel is close to the Suginoi Hotel, and since you have to fork out money for the bus ride, you're much better off staying at Kagetsu, described above, if you don't have a youth hostel card. In any case, there are both tatami rooms and bunk beds, and facilities include hot-spring baths and a coin laundry.

WHERE TO DINE

CHIKUDEN ㉖, **1-6-1 Kitahama. Tel. 25-2277.**
   Cuisine: SASHIMI/BLOWFISH. **Directions:** A 10-minute walk from Beppu Station's main exit.
$ Prices: Sashimi set meal ¥3,300 ($23.55). No credit cards.
   Open: Daily 5pm–midnight.

An economically priced restaurant, Chikuden serves a variety of sashimi, including fugu (blowfish, a Beppu specialty), sea bream, and abalone, at reasonable prices. The menu is in Japanese only, but if you want a plate with a variety of sashimi, ask for the moriawase for ¥3,300 ($23.55). A plate of fugu sashimi also costs ¥3,300 ($23.55). Sukiyaki is also served. The ground floor has tatami and counter seating, while the second floor has four private tatami rooms for groups.

JIN ㉗, **1-15-7 Kitahama. Tel. 21-1768.**
   Cuisine: GRILLED FOODS. **Directions:** A 5-minute walk from Beppu Station's main exit.
$ Prices: ¥500–¥1,500 ($3.55–$10.70). No credit cards.
   Open: Daily 5pm–midnight.

If you're looking for a quick, inexpensive dinner near the train station, you'll find plenty of them in and around the main exit. Jin is one of these, easily reached by walking from the station straight down the shop-lined street under the awnings all the way to the end. Jin is on the right, across the street from the Tokiwa department store, and is easily recognizable by its row of red lanterns hanging from its eaves. It's a lively robatayaki featuring grilled foods, including skewered meats and vegetables and fish. A platter of sashimi costs ¥1,000 ($7.15).

AMAMIJAYA ㉒, **1-4 Jissoji. Tel. 67-6024.**
   Cuisine: NOODLES. **Directions:** A 15-minute walk from the cluster of six Hells.
$ Prices: ¥450–¥650 ($3.20–$4.65). No credit cards.
   Open: Thurs–Tues 10am–10pm.
In addition to fugu, another specialty of Beppu is flat noodles. Amamijaya, which means "Sugar Tea House," serves noodles that are made by hand by the owner. Filled with local crafts and toys hanging on its walls, this inexpensive shop offers *dangojiro* (flat noodles and vegetable soup), *yaseiuma* (a sweet dish of flat noodles covered with powdered soy beans and sugar), *mochi* (Japanese rice cake), and *zosui* (rice porridge with plums), among other dishes.

---

3. MOUNT ASO

31 miles E of Kumamoto; 835 miles SW of Tokyo

GETTING THERE   By Train   Aso Station is 1 hour from Kumamoto and 2½ hours from Beppu.

By Bus   The most popular and pleasant route is by bus along the 186-mile-long Trans-Kyushu Highway, which links Beppu with Mt. Aso, Kumamoto, and Nagasaki. Sightseeing buses departing several times daily from both Kumamoto and Beppu are operated by the Kyushu Kokusai Kanko Bus Company. A timetable for buses departing from both Beppu and Kumamoto is provided in the leaflet *Kumamoto and Mt. Aso,* available at the Tourist Information Centers in Kyoto and Tokyo. The buses pass through rice paddies, tobacco and wheat fields, and bamboo groves, and skirt around waterfalls, streams, and hot springs. They all stop at Aso Station and allow a half hour for sightseeing at Mt. Aso's West Station. Since this is hardly enough time to visit both the museum there and take the cable car to the summit, if you're a volcano buff you may want to purchase a one-way ticket to Mt. Aso, spend an hour or two at the top, and then take one of the local buses back down to Aso Station.

ESSENTIAL INFORMATION   The **area code** for Mt. Aso, lying in Kumamoto Prefecture, is 0967.

GETTING AROUND   There are several resort towns at Mt. Aso circling Nakadake, the most famous and only active volcanic cone in the region, including Aso, Takamori, and Aso-Shimoda. If you're interested in going to the top of Nakadake, the approach is from Aso Station in Aso. From Aso Station you can board a **bus** for the 40-minute ride to Aso West Station (Asosan Nishi), from which you can take a **ropeway** to the top of the crater. There are nine buses daily running both ways between Aso Station and Aso West Station. The last bus departs Aso West Station at 5pm, but you'd be wise to check on this.

In the center of Kyushu between Beppu and Kumamoto is the Mt. Aso National Park, encompassing two groups of mountains, volcanic Mt. Aso and Mt. Kuju, as well as grasslands, forests, and hot springs. Although Mt. Kuju is the largest mountain on the island, the chief attraction of the park is Mt. Aso—it possesses the largest crater basin in the world. Measuring 11 miles from east to west, almost 15 miles from north to south, and 74½ miles in circumference, Mt. Aso must have been one mighty mountain before blowing its stack—larger even than Mt. Fuji. Today five volcanic cones sit in the Mt. Aso crater basin. One of them, Nakadake, is still active, constantly spewing forth high-temperature gas and sulfurous fumes. Every once in a while it even explodes (the latest eruption occurring in 1979). At the base of Nakadake at Aso West Station is the Mt. Aso Volcanic Museum. The entrance fee is ¥820 ($5.85), and the highlights are two cameras that have been placed on the walls of the active volcanic cone so that you can see the latest activity. There's also a 15-minute show depicting Mt. Aso National Park during the various seasons.

WHERE TO STAY

Because of its high altitude, Mt. Aso National Park is an ideal summer retreat, with a number of hot-spring resorts spread throughout the Aso crater basin.

IN ASO & VICINITY

RYOKAN MIMURA ㉙, Uchinomaki, Aso-machi, Aso-gun 869-22. Tel. 0967/32-0835. 17 rms (12 with bath). A/C MINIBAR TV TEL **Directions:** A 10-minute taxi ride from Aso Station.

$ Rates (per person, including breakfast and dinner): ¥22,000–¥50,000 ($132–$357). No credit cards.

⭐ This new and elegant ryokan, spread on the ridge of a hill, is the epitome of simplified beauty, with flower arrangements in each room, wooden beams, and views of the countryside or a manicured garden. Four rooms have twin beds, with separate tatami areas, for those who prefer to sleep in beds. Some of the rooms also have Japanese-style deep wooden tubs, which smell wonderful when filled with piping hot water. There are also separate hot-spring baths for men and women, with large windows overlooking the countryside below.

The rates charged depend largely on the meals you order for breakfast and dinner. But no matter the price range, the food served is as elegant as the ryokan itself and is the highlight of a stay here. The meals are beautifully displayed, using items from nature—a sprig from an azalea bush may serve as a chopstick holder, while cedar leaves or a delicate maple leaf may be used to enhance individual dishes. My sashimi came in a small ice igloo complete with pebbles in the bottom. My meal also included basashi (raw horse meat), considered a great delicacy in Kyushu. Diced crab was served in its shell, which acted as its bowl, and fish was fried on a hot flat stone.

ASO NO TSUKASA VILLA PARK HOTEL, Kurokawa, Aso-machi, Aso-gun 869-22. Tel. 0967/34-0811. 139 rms (102 with bath). A/C MINIBAR TV TEL **Directions:** A 3-minute taxi ride, or a 10-minute walk from Aso Station.

$ Rates (per person, including breakfast, dinner, and service): ¥13,000–¥36,000 ($92.85–$257). AE, DC, JCB, MC, V.

If you want to stay near Aso Station, you might want to try this modern brick hotel, which first opened more than 20 years ago but was completely rebuilt and renovated in 1984. The price differences are reflected in room size, furnishings, and meals. The cheapest rooms have no private bathroom, while the most expensive ones feature a wooden tub. Most of the rooms are Japanese style, but there are also combination rooms with a bedroom, a living room, and a separate tatami area, large enough for the whole family. Facilities include hot-spring baths, tennis courts, an outdoor pool, horses for rent, and a botanical garden. Its restaurant, Papiyon, features local beef from the Aso area, known as Higo beef.

ASO YOUTH HOSTEL ㉚, 9222-2 Bochu, Aso-machi. Aso-gun 869-22. Tel. 0967/34-0804. 60 beds. **Directions:** A 15-minute walk from Aso Station.

$ Rates (per person): ¥2,000 ($14.30) member and nonmember. Breakfast ¥400 ($2.85); dinner ¥600 ($4.30). No credit cards.

This two-story concrete youth hostel offers just the basics of beds and laundry facilities.

PENSION VILLAGE

Not far from Aso near a small town called Uchinomaki are a dozen or so Western-style pensions, collectively called "Pension Mura" by the locals (Pension

Village). Pensions differ from minshuku in that their rooms contain beds instead of futon, but they are also small, family-run affairs with only a handful of rooms. Rooms in all the pensions here average about ¥7,500 ($53) per person, including breakfast and dinner.

PENSION ASO NO TOKEI-DAI, Uchinomaki, Aso-machi, Aso-gun 869-22. Tel. 0967/32-2236. 9 rms (1 with bath). A/C **Directions:** 5-minute taxi ride from Uchinomaki Station.

$ **Rates** (per person, including breakfast and dinner): ¥7,500 ($53). AE, JCB, MC, V.

The owner of this modern pension speaks some English and will refer you to one of the other nearby pensions if his place is full. If you call from the station, someone from the pension will come pick you up.

IN TAKAMORI

On the other side of Mt. Aso is another resort town, called Takamori. Since there's no bus service from here to the summit, this place is better for those who appreciate the beauty of massive volcanoes from afar.

MINAMI ASO KOKUMIN KYUKA MURA ㉛, Takamori. Tel. 0967/62-2111. 80 rms (29 with bath). TV TEL **Bus:** From Takamori Station to front of Kokumin Kyuka Mura.

$ **Rates** (per person): ¥2,700 ($19.30) without bath; ¥4,900 ($35) with bath. Breakfast and dinner ¥3,000 ($21.40) extra. No credit cards.

This National Vacation Village is popular with school groups and families because of the great view it commands of Mt. Aso. It features tennis courts, bikes for rent, public baths, and a botanical garden. The rooms are typical of national vacation villages— simple tatami rooms with TV, futon and sheets, and yukata cotton kimono. The place is usually packed during July and August, but otherwise you should be able to get a room. It's wise to make reservations in advance.

IN ASO-SHIMODA

MINAMI ASO KOKUMIN SHUKUSHA ㉜, Aso-Shimoda. Tel. 0967/67-0078. 19 rms (none with bath). TV **Directions:** A 15-minute taxi ride from Aso-Shimoda Station.

$ **Rates** (per person, including breakfast, dinner and tax): ¥5,900 ($42). No credit cards.

Near Aso-Shimoda you'll find a People's Lodge, with rates cheaper than the National Vacation Village described above. There are only three buses daily from Aso-Shimoda Station, so it might be best to take a taxi. All the rooms have balconies, some with splendid views, and come with coin-operated TV, yukata cotton kimono, sheets, and futon. Not far from the lodge is a picturesque open-air bath beside a pounding waterfall, where men and women bathe together.

WHERE TO DINE

IN ASO

PAPIYON, Aso No Tsukasa Villa Park Hotel, Kurokawa, Aso-machi. Tel. 0967/34-0811.
Cuisine: STEAKS. **Reservations:** Recommended. **Directions:** A 3-minute taxi ride, or a 10-minute walk from Aso Station.

$ **Prices:** Steak courses ¥3,000–¥6,000 ($21.40–$42.85). AE, DC, JCB, MC, V.
Open: Daily 11am–9pm.

A good lunchtime choice, this restaurant features local beef from the Aso area, known as Higo beef. This restaurant buys whole cows so that it can slice the beef itself. The texture of the meat is unique, and is much different from that of the beef back home. The menu is in Japanese only, with steak courses including soup, rice, and salad. Also available is raw Higo beef and smoked salmon.

NEARBY PLACES TO EAT

DENGAKU NO SATO ㉝**, Takamori. Tel. 62-1899.**
   Cuisine: LOCAL SPECIALTIES. **Directions:** A 5-minute taxi ride from Takamori Station.
$ Prices: Dengaku teishoku ¥1,500 ($10.70). No credit cards.
   Open: Daily 10am–7pm.

Housed in a 120-year-old thatched farmhouse, this wonderful rustic restaurant in Takamori has tatami seating around individual hibachis built into the wooden floor. Its specialty is *dengaku* (food skewered on sticks). You cook your dengaku yourself by sticking the skewers into the ashes surrounding the blaze in your hibachi. Order the dengaku teishoku, and you'll have a variety of skewered items, including fish, taro, tofu, and mountain crabs that you pop whole into your mouth—delicious and crunchy. You can also order *kappozake,* which is sake heated in a hollow bamboo beside your fire.

4. KUMAMOTO

804 miles W of Tokyo; 118 miles S of Fukuoka

GETTING THERE   By Train   Trains depart from Hakata Station several times an hour, reaching Kumamoto in about 1½ hours.

By Bus   In addition to express buses that travel between Hakata Station and Kotsu Center in Kumamoto, there are overnight buses from Osaka, Kyoto, Kobe, and Nagoya.

Located roughly halfway down Kyushu's western side, Kumamoto boasts a fine castle and a landscaped garden, both from the first half of the 17th century. Once one of Japan's most important castle towns, Kumamoto today is a progressive city with a population of 624,000. In an effort to attract both domestic and foreign enterprises, the city is planning a technopolis—a technological research city—to be built close to its airport by 1995. With other technopolises being planned for such cities in Kyushu as Kagoshima, Oita, and Miyazaki, the island has given itself a nickname: Silicon Island.

ORIENTATION

INFORMATION

The **area code** for Kumamoto, lying in Kumamoto Prefecture, is 096.
   The leaflet *Kumamoto and Mt. Aso,* distributed by the **Tourist Information Center** in Kyoto and Tokyo, contains information on how to get to Kumamoto and places of interest in the city.

IMPRESSIONS

The Japanese should have no concern with business.
—RUDYARD KIPLING, *FROM SEA TO SEA*, 1889

The **tourist information center,** open daily from 9am to 5:30pm, is in front of Kumamoto Station (tel. 096/352-3743) and has a good English map and brochure of the city.

CITY LAYOUT

Kumamoto Station is not in the city's downtown section, but it's easy to get there by streetcar no. 2, which departs from in front of the station. Downtown is northeast of Kumamoto Station, centered around several covered shopping streets called **Shimotori** and **Sunroad Shinshigai,** which are located to the south and southeast of Kumamoto Castle. There are many shops, bars, and restaurants in the area. Nearby is **Kotsu Center,** from which all buses in the city depart, and the location of several business hotels listed below.

GETTING AROUND

Streetcar no. 2, which departs from Kumamoto Station and passes Kotsu Center, will also take you to both the castle (stop: Kumamoto-jo-mae) and the Suizenji Garden (stop: Suizenji-Koen-mae).

WHAT TO SEE & DO

✪ Completed in 1607, **Kumamoto Castle** is massive—it took 7 years to build. It was constructed under the direction of Kato Kiyomasa, a great warrior who fought alongside Tokugawa Ieyasu in a battle in 1600 and who was rewarded for his loyalty with land in what is today Kumamoto. To make the castle walls impossible for enemies to scale, they were built with curves and topped with an overhang. Furthermore, the castle was built atop a hill and had three main buildings, 49 towers, 29 gates, and 18 two-story gatehouses. Passing into the possession of the Hosokawa family in 1632, the castle remained an important stronghold for the Tokugawa shogunate throughout its 250 years of rule, particularly in campaigns against powerful and independent-minded lords in southern Kyushu.

Much of the castle was destroyed in 1877 during the Seinan Rebellion led by Saigo Takamori, a samurai who was unhappy with the new policies of the Meiji government in which ancient samurai rights were rescinded. Saigo led a troop of samurai in an attack on the castle and its imperial troops. The battle raged for 53 days before government reinforcements finally arrived and quelled the rebellion. When the smoke cleared, most of the castle lay in smoldering ruins, ravaged by fire.

The castle was reconstructed in 1960 of ferroconcrete, and although it's not nearly as massive as before, it's still quite impressive. The interior houses a museum with elaborately decorated palanquins, armor of feudal lords, swords, former possessions of both Kato Kiyomasa and the Hosokawa family, and artifacts from the Seinan Rebellion. There are also displays of such locally made products as pottery and toys. Open daily from 8:30am to 5:30pm (4:30pm in winter), it charges an admission of ¥200 ($1.40) for the castle grounds. If you want to go inside the castle, it costs ¥300 ($2.15) more.

Not far from the castle are two museums worth seeing. The **Kumamoto Prefectural Art Museum (Kumamoto Kenritsu Bijutsukan)** (tel. 352-2111), open Tuesday through Sunday from 9:30am to 4:30pm, displays fine art, as well as replicas of burial tombs that have been excavated in the prefecture. Nearby is the **Kumamoto Municipal Museum (Kumamoto Shiritsu Hakubutsukan)** (tel. 324-3500), open Tuesday through Sunday from 9am to 4:30pm. It houses collections devoted to the humanities and the natural and physical sciences, and also contains a planetarium.

✪ **Suizenji Garden,** laid out in 1632 by the Hosokawa family, wraps itself around a cold spring-fed lake. Incorporated into the garden's design are famous scenes in miniature from the 53 stages of the ancient Tokaido Highway, which connected Kyoto and Tokyo and which were immortalized in Hiroshige's famous woodblock prints. Most recognizable is cone-shaped Mt. Fuji. The park is small—almost disappointingly so. One wishes it stretched on and on. To assuage disappointment, stop off at the 400-year-old thatch-roofed teahouse beside the pond, transported from the imperial grounds in Kyoto. Inside, ceremonial green tea is served while you sit and contemplate the view. If you want to sit on tatami inside the teahouse, it costs ¥500 ($3.55). If you're content sitting outside at a table under the shelter of trees, it costs ¥400 ($2.85). Entrance to the park is ¥200 ($1.40) between 7:30am and 6pm (8:30am and 5pm in winter); after that, it's free, but only the main gate remains open. If you want to do some moon gazing, this is the place.

Although it's located on the outskirts of Kumamoto, about 30 minutes by bus from Kotsu Center, if you're at all interested in handcrafted items used in everyday life from various countries around the world, you'll enjoy the **Kumamoto International Folk Art Museum (Tatsuda machi-Kamitatsuda)** (tel. 338-7504). This museum displays furniture, pottery, weavings, toys, and other handcrafted items from such diverse countries as India, Peru, Greece, Korea, Mexico, Egypt, and Japan. As items used in everyday life both now and in former times, many of them are rustic but beautifully made. The museum is open Tuesday through Sunday from 9am to 4pm and charges an admission of ¥350 ($2.50). If you're going by bus, get off at Sannomiya bus stop.

WHERE TO STAY

Accommodations in Kumamoto are hotels rather than ryokan. Many of the hotels, however, have Japanese-style rooms in case you'd rather sleep on futon and tatami. There are also some inexpensive minshuku. There are several medium- and budget-priced business hotels located in the downtown section close to Kotsu Center bus depot.

EXPENSIVE

KUMAMOTO CASTLE HOTEL, 4-2 Joto-cho, Kumamoto 860. Tel. 096/326-3311. Fax 096/326-3324. 208 rms. A/C MINIBAR TV TEL **Streetcar:** 2 from Kumamoto Station to Shiyakusho-mae stop, then a 3-minute walk.
$ Rates: ¥9,300–¥11,500 ($66–$83) single; ¥14,800 ($106) double; ¥16,500–¥21,500 ($118–$153) twin. Japanese-style rooms: ¥27,000–¥40,000 ($193–$285) double occupancy. AE, DC, JCB, MC, V.

This tall brick hotel is located just east of Kumamoto Castle, with some rooms offering good views of the castle grounds. A subdued, quiet, and conservative hotel, it is popular with middle-aged Japanese and has rooms with the usual TV (Japanese only), minibar, and hot-water pot with tea.

Dining/Entertainment: Four restaurants in the hotel serve Western, French, and Chinese cuisine, including the Loire on the 11th floor, with views of the Castle.
Services: Same-day laundry service.

NEW SKY HOTEL, 2 Higashiamidaji-cho, Kumamoto 860. Tel. 096/354-2111. Fax 096/354-8973. 358 rms. A/C MINIBAR TV TEL **Directions:** A 10-minute walk northeast of Kumamoto Station, or streetcar 2 one stop to Gionbashi stop, then a few minutes' walk.
$ Rates: ¥8,500–¥12,000 ($61–$86) single; ¥16,500 ($119) double; ¥16,500–¥22,000 ($118–$157) twin. Japanese-style rooms: ¥12,000 ($86) double occupancy. AE, DC, JCB, MC, V.

This 25-story high-rise is one of Kumamoto's best hotels. Its rooms are divided between an older west wing and a more modern east wing, and they're stocked with a lot of thoughtful amenities, including a laundry rope in the bathroom (a welcome sight if you've been on the road awhile), a hot-water pot for tea, bilingual TV (in the new wing only), alarm clock, radio, bedside control panels, and an extra phone in the bathroom. With the no. 2 streetcar running right in front of the hotel, there is easy access to both Kumamoto Castle and Suizenji Garden.

Dining/Entertainment: Japanese, Chinese, and Western restaurants, including the Leodor, an elegant restaurant on the 25th floor serving steaks and seafood.

Services: *Japan Times* delivered to your room in the morning (it's always a day late in Kyushu); same-day laundry service.

Facilities: Beauty salon, barbershop, shopping arcade, sightseeing desk, health club with workout equipment and indoor 25-meter swimming pool (fee: ¥3,000 or $21.40; pool only ¥720 or $5.15), sauna and public bath (free of charge).

MODERATE

CHISAN HOTEL KUMAMOTO, 4-39 Karashimacho, Kumamoto 860. Tel. 096/322-3911. Fax 096/356-5229. 201 rms. A/C MINIBAR TV TEL **Directions:** A few minutes' walk from Kotsu Center, or streetcar 2 from Kumamoto Station to Karashimacho stop.

$ Rates: ¥7,000 ($50) single; ¥12,000 ($86) double; ¥13,000 ($93) twin. AE, JCB, MC, V.

First on my list of business hotels is Chisan Hotel Kumamato, which opened in 1984 as part of the Chisan hotel chain. Its lobby is pleasantly decorated with marble, brass railings, and stained glass, and the rooms are simply but tastefully decorated and come with minibar, TV, and hot-water pot for tea. The electricity in the room works only when you insert your key into a pocket beside the door (this not only saves energy but saves time searching for misplaced keys). The hotel's one restaurant, decorated with masks from Africa, serves Western food.

KOTSU CENTER HOTEL, 3-10 Sakuramachi, Kumamoto 860. Tel. 096/326-8828 or 354-1111. Fax 096/354-1120. 116 rms. A/C MINIBAR TV TEL **Directions:** Located above Kotsu Center.

$ Rates: ¥5,800–¥7,400 ($41–$53) single; ¥11,500 ($82) double; ¥12,000–¥15,000 ($86–$107) twin; ¥16,500 ($118) triple. AE, DC, JCB, MC, V.

This hotel is located right in the Kotsu Center itself, with a third-floor lobby that is usually buzzing with activity from Japanese group tours. There's a French as well as a Szechuan restaurant, and from May through August there's a rooftop beer garden open daily from 5 to 9:30pm. Rooms are basic but comfortable, with minibar, TV with pay videos, hairdryer, and hot-water pot for tea. The lowest-priced single rooms don't have windows and aren't recommended.

MARUKO HOTEL, 11-10 Kamitori-cho, Kumamoto 860. Tel. 096/353-1241. Fax 096/353-1217. 35 rms (all with bath). A/C TV TEL **Streetcar:** 2 from Kumamoto Station to Torichosuji stop, then an 8-minute walk through Kamitori shopping arcade.

$ Rates: ¥7,000 ($50) single; ¥13,000 ($93) twin; ¥18,000 ($128) triple. AE, DC, JCB, MC, V.

A member of the Japanese Inn Group, it's much larger than most in this group and is also more expensive. It's located in the heart of the city, just off the Kamitori covered shopping arcade, and is owned and managed by a petite, gracious woman who is happy to receive foreign guests. Forty-one of its rooms are Japanese tatami rooms, with a pleasant sitting alcove next to large windows. There are also a couple of Western-style rooms and a couple of combination rooms with both beds and tatami. All rooms come with TV with video, hot water for tea, safe for valuables, refrigerator, kimono, and air conditioning, among other amenities. Both Western and Japanese meals are available, with breakfast ranging from ¥800 to ¥1,500 ($5.70 to $10.70) and dinner from ¥3,000 to ¥6,000 ($21.40 to $42.85).

BUDGET

KUMAMOTO STATION HOTEL (234), 1-3-6 Nihongi, Kumamoto 860. Tel. 096/325-2001. 75 rms (all with bath). A/C TV TEL **Directions:** A few minutes' walk from Kumamoto Station; walk straight out of station, cross bridge in front, then turn immediately right. Hotel is first building on right, beside small river.

$ Rates: ¥5,900 ($42) single; ¥10,300 ($73) double/twin. Japanese-style rooms:

¥13,000 ($93) double occupancy; ¥16,500 ($118) triple. Breakfast ¥600 ($4.30) extra. No credit cards.

This is your best bet if you want to stay in a business hotel within walking distance of Kumamoto Station. It has 50 single rooms, 21 twins, and three Japanese-style rooms, and a small restaurant/coffee shop.

TOKYU INN, 7-25 Shinshigai, Kumamoto 860. Tel. 096/322-0109. Fax 096/322-3050. 138 rms (all with bath). A/C MINIBAR TV TEL **Directions:** Across street from Kotsu Center; or streetcar 2 from Kumamoto Station to Karashimacho stop.

$ Rates: ¥7,000 ($50) single; ¥10,300 ($73.55) double; ¥10,500–¥11,000 ($75–$78) twin. AE, JCB, MC, V.

This business hotel is across the street from the Kotsu Center right next to the Sunroad Shinshigai covered shopping arcade. Its rooms are small but contain everything you need, including TV, minibar, and cotton kimono. There's a Western as well as a Japanese/Korean restaurant, and vending machines that dispense pop and beer.

Youth Hostels

KUMAMOTO SHIRITSU YOUTH HOSTEL ㉟, 5-15-55 Shimazaki-machi, Kumamoto 860. Tel. 096/352-2441. 64 beds. A/C **Bus:** From platform 36 of Kotsu Center bus terminal to Kuriyama Youth Hostel Mae bus stop (50-minute ride).

$ Rates (per person): ¥1,600 ($11.40) member and nonmember. Air conditioning or heating ¥200 ($1.40) extra. Breakfast ¥400 ($2.85); dinner ¥600 ($4.30). No credit cards.

Located in a residential area, this youth hostel has 32 beds for women and 32 beds for men. The man in charge here speaks English. Incidentally, on the map issued by the tourist office, this establishment is identified as the Municipal Youth Hostel.

SUIZENJI YOUTH HOSTEL ㊱, 1-2-10 Hakusan, Kumamoto 860. Tel. 096/371-9193. 30 beds. A/C **Streetcar:** 2 from station to Misotenjinmae stop (25-minute ride), then a 2-minute walk.

$ Rates (per person): ¥2,200 ($15.70) member; ¥2,900 ($20.70) nonmember. Breakfast ¥450 ($3.20). No credit cards.

This two-story concrete youth hostel offers both beds and futon accommodations. No dinners are served; there are laundry facilities.

WHERE TO DINE

Kumamoto's specialties include dengaku (delicacies such as fish, taro, and tofu coated with bean paste and grilled at a fire), *karashi renkon* (lotus root that has been boiled, filled with a mixture of bean paste and mustard, and then deep-fried), and basashi (raw horse meat that is sliced thin and then dipped in soy sauce flavored with ginger or garlic).

EXPENSIVE

LEODOR, 25th floor of New Sky Hotel, 2 Higashiamidaji-cho. Tel. 354-2111.
  Cuisine: FRENCH. **Reservations:** Recommended. **Streetcar:** 2 to Gionbashi stop, then a 3-minute walk. **Directions:** A 10-minute walk north of Kumamoto Station.
  $ Prices: Set-dinner courses ¥6,500–¥11,000 ($46.40–$78.55); set lunches ¥3,800 ($27.15). AE, DC, JCB, MC, V.
  Open: Lunch daily 11:30am–2pm; dinner daily 5–10pm.

For elegant dining with a view, head for Leodor, high above Kumamoto on the 25th floor of the New Sky Hotel. A white piano (with nightly entertainment from 7 to 8:30pm) dominates the dining hall, which has purple tablecloths and carpet; elaborate tableware and flowers on every table enhance meals of steak, fish, and lamb. There are set meals available for both lunch and dinner, but if you order from the seasonal à la carte menu, expect to spend about ¥10,000 ($71.40) per person for dinner, including wine.

LOIRE, 11th floor of Kumamoto Castle Hotel, 4-2 Joto-cho. Tel. 326-3311.

Cuisine: FRENCH. **Reservations:** Recommended. **Streetcar:** 2 to Shiyakusho-mae stop, then a 3-minute walk.

$ Prices: Set-dinner courses ¥4,900–¥11,000 ($35–$78.55); set lunches ¥1,300–¥7,000 ($9.30–$50). AE, DC, JCB, MC, V.

Open: Lunch daily 11:30am–2pm; dinner daily 5–10pm.

This restaurant overlooks Kumamoto Castle and is a convenient place for lunch if you're visiting the castle or the Kumamoto Traditional Crafts Center. The menu is short, offering primarily set meals that change with the seasons but usually include choices in seafood and beef dishes.

MODERATE

GINNAN, in Kumamoto Castle Hotel, 4-2 Joto-cho. Tel. 326-3311.

Cuisine: TEMPURA/SEAFOOD. **Streetcar:** 2 to Shiyakusho-mae, then a 3-minute walk.

$ Prices: Set meals ¥2,700–¥11,000 ($19.30–$78.55); set lunch ¥1,000 ($7.15). AE, DC, JCB, MC, V.

Open: Lunch daily 11:30am–2pm; dinner daily 4:30–9:30pm.

Another good choice for dining in the vicinity of the castle and the Kumamoto Traditional Crafts Center is the Castle Hotel's Japanese restaurant. A fish tank at this restaurant's entrance displays shrimp, flatfish, and eels happily swimming around, unaware of their impending fate, and the Japanese menu has pictures of its offerings, of which the tempura set dinner is the most popular.

KOHRIN, in New Sky Hotel, 2 Higashiamidaji-cho. Tel. 354-2111.

Cuisine: VARIED JAPANESE. **Streetcar:** 2 to Gionbashi stop. **Directions:** A 10-minute walk north of Kumamoto Station.

$ Prices: Set meals ¥3,500–¥11,000 ($25–$78.55). AE, DC, JCB, MC, V.

Open: Lunch daily 11:30am–2pm; dinner daily 5–10pm.

This excellent restaurant has a menu in Japanese only, with set meals that include local specialties, sushi, tempura, and seasonal kaiseki dishes. I highly recommend the course of *seishoho-yaki*—Japanese steak wrapped in bamboo and served with side dishes of basashi, mustard lotus, sashimi, red snapper, pickled vegetables from the region of Mt. Aso, and rice. For an after-dinner drink, top off your meal with shochu, for which Kumamoto is famous. If you come here for lunch, you can have noodles—try the tempura soba for ¥1,000 ($7.15). Another good lunchtime choice is the Kohrin teishoku, for ¥2,000 ($14.30), which includes sashimi, tempura, sushi, soba noodles, and side dishes.

SENRI (237), Suizenji Garden. Tel. 384-1824.

Cuisine: LOCAL SPECIALTIES/VARIED JAPANESE. **Streetcar:** 2 to Suizenji-Koen-mae stop.

$ Prices: Set-dinner courses ¥4,900 and up ($35); set lunches ¥2,200 ($15.70). No credit cards.

Open: Daily 11am–10pm.

You can try Kumamoto's local dishes at this restaurant right in Suizenji Garden, which is a good place to stop off for lunch or dinner while visiting the famous garden. Although the menu is in Japanese only, there's a pamphlet available with pictures. Teishoku set lunches all cost ¥2,200 ($15.70) each, and choices include eel, river fish, tempura, and basashi. Along with your choice of main dish are side dishes of a vegetable, soup, rice, and tea. Dinners cost ¥4,900 ($35) and up and include the same items as in the lunch teishoku, plus extra dishes. Dining is in small tatami rooms, located to the right after you enter the front door. The choice rooms face the garden. It's best to make a reservation to dine here. Incidentally, connected to this restaurant is its cheaper dining room (to the left if you face the building, with a plastic-food display case outside in front), which offers the same eel, river fish, tempura, and basashi lunch teishoku for about ¥500 ($4) less than in the private tatami rooms described above.

BUDGET

AOYAGI ㉘, 1-2-10 Shimotori. Tel. 353-0311.
   Cuisine: VARIED JAPANESE/LOCAL SPECIALTIES. **Streetcar:** 2 to Torichosuji stop, then walk through Shimotori shopping arcade.
$ Prices: Set meals ¥1,400–¥2,500 ($10–$17.85); kaiseki ¥4,500 ($32.15). No credit cards.
   Open: Daily 11:30am–11pm.
Everyone in Kumamoto knows this restaurant, located in the downtown area just off the Shimotori shopping arcade. It has a plastic-food display case outside its front door showing dishes of sushi, tempura, basashi, and kamameshi (rice casseroles). You can also take out box lunches of sushi for ¥1,000 ($7.15) and up. There are three floors of dining.

BEER GARDEN, in Kotsu Center Hotel. Tel. 354-1111.
   Cuisine: VARIED. **Directions:** Above Kotsu Center Hotel.
$ Prices: ¥300–¥500 ($2.15–$3.55). No credit cards.
   Open: Dinner daily 5–9:30pm. **Closed:** Sept–Apr.
If the weather's warm and your main interest is drinking beer outdoors, head for the roof of this conveniently located beer garden at the Kotsu Center bus depot. It has its share of fake palm trees and Astro-turf, but it also offers panoramic views of the city. Beer starts at ¥450 ($3.20) and snacks include grilled chicken, sausage, french fries, *edamame* (soybeans), and other fare.

GOEMON ㉙, 1-7-3 Shimotori. Tel. 354-2266.
   Cuisine: VARIED JAPANESE/LOCAL SPECIALTIES. **Streetcar:** 2 to Torichosuji stop.
$ Prices: ¥200–¥600 ($1.40–$4.30); set meals ¥1,400–¥2,750 ($10–$19.65). No credit cards.
   Open: Sun–Fri 11:30am–11pm; Sat 11:30am–midnight.
Located downtown near the Shimotori shopping arcade, this is technically a drinking establishment, but it serves a variety of inexpensive dishes and is popular with a lively young crowd, especially on weekends. A la carte dishes of dengaku, flatfish, sashimi, green-tea noodles, and much more range from a mere ¥100 (70¢) for rice balls to ¥500 ($3.55) for raw tuna. There are also set meals. The menu is in Japanese only, but it has some pictures; the best thing to do is simply to look around at what others are eating. This establishment has a rustic feel to it, and although it's tatami seating, some of the tables have leg wells underneath for your feet. Take off your shoes at the front door and deposit them in a locker, just as you would at a bathhouse.

KIMURA-SO ㉚, Suizenji Garden. Tel. 384-1864.
   Cuisine: CARP. **Streetcar:** 2 to Suizenji-Koen-mae stop.
$ Prices: Fried carp or carp sushi ¥650 ($4.65); set meal ¥2,200 ($15.70). No credit cards.
   Open: Daily 11am–9pm. **Closed:** One day a month, but not on a certain day.
Just a few steps away from Senri (described above), and also located in Suizenji Garden, this restaurant features inexpensive dining outside in a pavilion built over a pond, with a partial view of the garden. Carp is its specialty, which you can have raw or fried. Also on the menu are grilled shrimp, eel, tonkatsu, and basashi.

SHOPPING

One of Kumamoto's most famous products is its damascene, in which gold and silver are inlaid on an iron plate to form patterns of flowers, bamboo, and other designs. Originally used to adorn armor, damascene today is used in such accessories as jewelry and tie clasps. Another Kumamoto product is the Yamaga lantern, made of gold paper and used during the Yamaga Lighted Lantern Festival, held in August. Other products include Amakusa pearls, pottery, toys, and bamboo items.

✪ A wonderful place to see Kumamoto Prefecture's products and learn how they are made is the **Kumamoto Traditional Crafts Center** ㉑, 3-35 Chiba-jo (tel. 324-4930), next to Kumamoto Castle, near the Kumamoto Castle Hotel. Confusingly enough, it's identified on the English map given out by the tourist office as the Industrial Art Museum—hopefully someone will get around to correcting this someday. A spacious and attractive brick building, the center devotes its second floor to handmade craftwork from all over the prefecture, along with displays on how the items are made. Although explanations are in Japanese only, the displays are so well laid out and the rooms are so bright and cheerful that much is self-explanatory. At the display on the bow and arrow, for example, you can see the intricate steps involved in its production. Other displays include those on pottery, bamboo products, fans (haven't you ever wondered how they're made?), toys, furniture, wooden rice barrels, damascene, and kitchen knives sharp enough to chop through bone. Most items aren't hidden away behind glass but are out in the open. Entrance here is ¥190 ($1.35) and worth every yen.

The first floor of the Traditional Crafts Center is free and serves as a gallery where locally made products are sold, including those wonderful kitchen knives, furniture, ceramics, toys, paper lanterns, and damascene. Unfortunately, the center can ship only purchases that have a total value less than ¥60,000 ($480), and even then only to about eight large cities in the United States. The center is open Tuesday through Sunday from 9am to 5pm.

Another place selling local products is the **Display Hall of Kumamoto Products (Kumamoto-ken Bussankan)** ㉒, on the third floor of the Sangyo Bunka Kaikan Building, downtown next to the Kotsu Center. This store, open daily from 10am to 6pm (except on the second and fourth Mondays of the month), sells pottery, toys, knives, paper lanterns, damascene, Amakusa pearls, spirits, and confectioneries.

For more shopping, in the heart of downtown there are covered shopping arcades, called **Shimotori** and **Sunroad Shinshigai,** where you'll find the usual clothing boutiques, gift shops, shoe stores, restaurants, and coffee shops.

---

5. NAGASAKI

825 miles W of Tokyo; 95 miles SW of Fukuoka

GETTING THERE   By Train   Trains depart Hakata Station in Fukuoka approximately every half hour, with travel time of approximately 2½ hours. From Tokyo, take the Shinkansen bullet train to Hakata Station, transferring there for a train to Nagasaki; travel time is 8 to 9½ hours, depending on the type of train and connections.

Nagasaki lies on the northwest coast of Kyushu. Unlike Kumamoto, Kagoshima, or many other well-known cities in Japan, Nagasaki does not have a castle or famous landscaped garden. Rather, Nagasaki's charm is much more subtle, lying in the city itself. Many people in Japan—including foreign residents—consider Nagasaki one of the country's most beautiful cities. It's a town of hills rising from the harbor, of houses perched on terraced slopes, of small streets, distinctive neighborhoods, and a people extremely proud of their city. Without a doubt, it's one of Japan's most livable cities.

Perhaps to the untrained foreign eye Nagasaki may look like any other modern Japanese town, but there's no other city in Japan quite like it. In a nation as homogeneous as Japan, Nagasaki from a historical perspective is its most cosmopolitan city, with a unique blend of outside cultures interwoven into its architecture, food, and festivals. Centuries ago, Nagasaki's bay, sheltered by islands, made it a natural as a safe place to anchor ships. It opened its harbor to European vessels in 1571 and became a port of call for Portuguese and Dutch ships. Chinese merchants moved here and set up their own community. Along with traders came Christian missionaries, primarily from Portugal and Spain, who found many converts among the Japanese in Nagasaki. And during Japan's more than 200 years of isolation, only Nagasaki was allowed to conduct trade with outsiders and thus served as the nation's window on the rest of the world. Even today Japanese come to Nagasaki for a dose of the city's intermingled cultures.

If you're looking for a typical Japanese city, Nagasaki isn't the place. If you're searching for something more than just typical—something special—then Nagasaki won't disappoint you.

ORIENTATION

INFORMATION

The **area code** for Nagasaki, lying in Nagasaki Prefecture, is 0958.

Information on Nagasaki and its attractions is given in *Nagasaki and Unzen*, a leaflet available at the Tourist Information Center in Tokyo and Kyoto.

At Nagasaki Station the **Nagasaki City Office of Tourist Information** (tel. 0958/22-1954 or 23-3631) maintains an information window, located just past the ticket-gate exit, which distributes maps in English. It's open daily from 8am to 5pm. An even better map, however, is available just across the street from the train station in the office of the **Nagasaki Prefecture Tourist Federation** (tel. 0958/26-9407), on the second floor of the Kotsu Sangyo Building. This office can provide information on all of Nagasaki Prefecture, including Unzen.

CITY LAYOUT

Along with Kobe and Sapporo, Nagasaki is one of Japan's most navigable cities, and there are lots of signs in English that point the way to attractions. Nagasaki Station is not considered the downtown part of the city. Rather, most nightspots, shops, and restaurants are located southeast of the station, clustered around an area that contains Shianbashi Dori, Kanko Dori Street, and the Hamanomachi shopping arcade. Peace Park and its museum on the atomic bomb are located north of Nagasaki Station.

GETTING AROUND

BY STREETCAR

The easiest way to get around the city is by streetcar. Four lines run through the heart of the city and most stops are written in English. The streetcars are ancient one-wagon affairs, retired to Nagasaki from other cities that considered them too slow and old fashioned. And yet in Nagasaki, streetcars have their own lanes of traffic, so that during rush hour they're usually the fastest things on the road. It costs a mere ¥100 (70¢) to ride one; pay at the front when you get off. You can also buy a ¥500 ($3.55) ticket at major hotels that allows unlimited rides for 1 day on the city's streetcars. If you're buying individual tickets, you're allowed to transfer to another line only at Tsukimachi Station. Otherwise, you must buy a separate ticket each time you board a tram.

ON FOOT

You can also get around Nagasaki easily on foot, certainly the most intimate way to experience the city and its atmosphere. You can walk from the Hamanomachi shopping district to Glover Garden, for example, in 15 to 20 minutes, passing Chinatown, Dejima, and the Dutch Slope on the way. Shianbashi Dori, located just off the streetcar stop of the same name, is just a few minutes' walk from Hamanomachi shopping arcade.

IMPRESSIONS

The Japanese have done with their past. They want to be somebody else and something else than what they have been and still partly are.
—BASIL HALL CHAMBERLAIN, *THINGS JAPANESE*, 1890

BY BUS

Nagasaki also has buses, but destinations are in Japanese only, and who knows where the heck they're going. Stick to the streetcars.

WHAT TO SEE & DO

All of Nagasaki's major attractions are connected with the city's diversified and sometimes tragic past. The city is perhaps best known as the second city—and, we hope, the last city—to be destroyed by an atomic bomb.

NISHIZAKA HILL

After Nagasaki opened its port to European vessels, Christian missionaries came to the city to convert the Japanese to Christianity. Gradually, however, the Japanese rulers began to fear that these Christian missionaries would try to exert political and financial influence through their converts. Who wasn't to say that conversion to Christianity was just the first step toward colonialization? So in 1587 the shogun Hideyoshi Toyotomi officially banned Christianity. In 1597, 26 Christians (20 Japanese and 6 foreigners) were arrested in Kyoto and Osaka, marched through the snow to Nagasaki, and crucified on Nishizaka Hill as examples of what would happen to offenders. Through the ensuing years, there were more than 600 documented cases of Christians being put to death in the Nishizaka area. In 1862 the 26 martyrs were named saints by the pope. Today on Nishizaka Hill, about a 3-minute walk from Nagasaki Station, there's a monument dedicated to the saints with statues of the 26 martyrs carved in stone relief. There's also a small museum housing artifacts relating to the history of Christianity in Japan, as well as ashes of three of the saints. Perhaps most amazing about the history of Christianity in Japan is that the religion was practiced secretly by the faithful throughout Japan's isolation policy, surviving more than 200 years underground without the benefits of a church or clergy.

DEJIMA

When the Tokugawa shogunate adopted a national policy of isolation in the 1630s, only Nagasaki was allowed to remain open as a port of trade with foreigners. Since the Portuguese and Spaniards were associated with the outlawed Christian religion, only the Dutch and the Chinese were allowed to continue trading. The Dutch were confined to a tiny man-made island called Dejima, and the only people allowed to cross the bridge into the Dutch community were Japanese prostitutes and traders.

Today, Dejima is little more than a streetcar stop, having long ago become part of the mainland in the city's land reclamation projects. If you're interested, however, the **Nagasaki Municipal Dejima Museum** (reached by taking streetcar no. 1 to Dejima stop) houses materials relating to the Dutch during their seclusion on the island. It's free and is open Tuesday through Sunday from 9am to 5pm. Behind the museum is a model of how the island used to look when the Dutch lived there.

Incidentally, the Dejima Museum also serves as the temporary quarters of the **Nagasaki Museum of History and Folklore** while the latter's permanent home (the former Hongkong Shanghai Bank, constructed in 1908) is being renovated. Since no one seems to know exactly how long the renovation will take, it would be wise to check with the tourist office before making a trip just to see this museum. It exhibits crafts and daily utensils common in Nagasaki between the mid-18th century and the mid-20th century, including hand mirrors, hair ornaments, Chinese objects, some lacquerware, old furniture, gramophones, and even a plastic-food replica of Nagasaki's most famous meal, the *shippoku,* a feast usually shared by four or more people. Hours are 9am to 5pm Tuesday through Sunday.

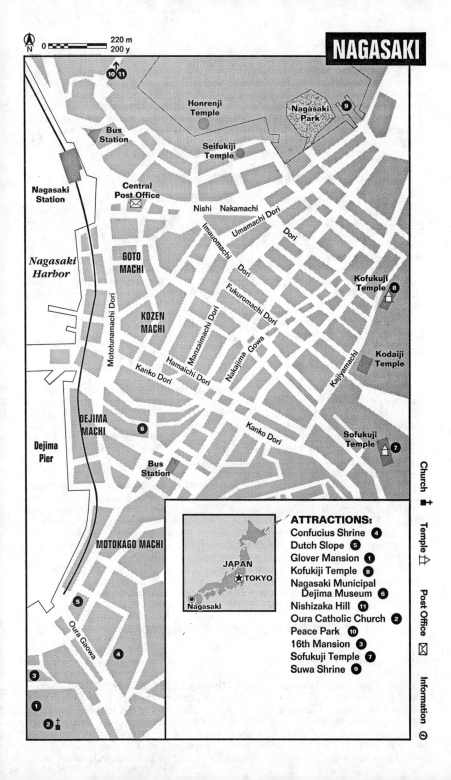

THE PORT

If you're interested in seeing the results of Nagasaki's history as a trading port, walk to nearby Ohato Port Terminal (tel. 26-6236) or take streetcar no. 1 to the Ohato stop. There you can board a boat for a 50-minute trip through the town's modern harbor. The never-ending commentary is in Japanese, but you can see for yourself the Mitsubishi shipyards, where massive boats are both built and repaired. Boats depart daily at 11:40am and 3:15pm, with more boats added in peak season, but you'd be wise to check the schedule beforehand. Cost of the cruise is ¥770 ($5.50).

GLOVER GARDEN & VICINITY

After Japan opened its doors to the rest of the world, Nagasaki emerged as one of the more progressive cities in the country, with many foreign residents. A number of Western-style houses built during the Meiji Period (1868–1912) still survive and have been moved to a large park called Glover Garden (tel. 22-8223) on a hill overlooking Nagasaki and the harbor. The stone and clapboard houses have sweeping verandas, Western parlors, the most modern conveniences of the time—and Japanese-style roofs. The most famous house is the **Glover Mansion,** built in 1863 and romanticized as the home of Madame Butterfly (a fictitious character). Thomas Glover, married to a Japanese, was a remarkable Englishman who, among other things, financially backed and managed ship-repair yards in Nagasaki, brought the first steam locomotive to Japan, opened the first mint in Japan, sold guns and ships, and exported tea.

Also located on the grounds is the **Nagasaki Traditional Performing Arts Museum,** which displays floats and dragons used in Nagasaki's most famous festival, the autumn Okunchi Festival, held in autumn. The highlight of the museum is an excellent film of the colorful parade.

Entrance to Glover Garden and the museum is ¥600 ($4.30), and daily hours are 8am to 6pm (8:30am to 5pm December through February). To reach it, take streetcar no. 5 to Oura Tenshudoshita stop. After entering the grounds you might be a little shocked to see moving escalators carved into the hillside. While an outdoor escalator in a garden might seem somewhat bizarre, the Japanese point out that it's there for the benefit of senior citizens who might find the climb up the hill too strenuous. At any rate, the views from here are among the best in the city, offering a good look at both the town, its harbor, and the shipyards.

Next to Glover Garden is the **16th Mansion (Jurokuban-kan Mansion)** (tel. 22-0016), built in 1860 by the American government as the first mansion in Japan for its consular staff. It houses glassware, chinaware, and religious objects from Nagasaki's early years. Some of the pieces of Imari chinaware on display have pictures of Europeans on them. Destined for Western markets, they prove that the Japanese were willing and able to adapt their products for an outside market even then. The entrance fee is ¥400 ($2.85), and daily hours are 8:30am to 5pm.

Within a few minutes' walk from Glover Garden are the **Oura Catholic Church** (tel. 23-2628), Japan's oldest Gothic wooden church, built in 1865 to commemorate the 26 Christian martyrs, and **Dutch Slope (Oranda-zaka),** a cobbled road lined with wooden houses built by former Dutch residents.

TEMPLES, SHRINES & BRIDGES

The legacy left by Nagasaki's many Chinese residents is best enjoyed at the city's many Chinese restaurants (refer to the "Where to Dine" section, below) and best seen at its Chinese-style temples. Not far from the Oura Church mentioned above are the colorful **Confucius Shrine** and the **Historical Museum of China,** which charges an admission of ¥500 ($4) to see its artifacts, on loan from the Chinese National Museum of History in Beijing. Nagasaki's most famous temple, however, is **Sofukuji Temple,** which dates back to 1629 and is known for its Ming Dynasty architecture. It's located about a 7-minute walk from the Hamanomachi downtown shopping district or is easily reached by taking streetcar no. 1 or 4 to Shokakujishita stop. From Sofukuji Temple, I recommend a pleasant 20-minute walk north along narrow streets to **Kofukuji Temple,** the first Obaku-Zen Buddhist temple in Japan, founded by a Chinese priest in 1629. From there the nearest streetcar stop is Kokaidomae.

Although the Okunchi Festival has Chinese roots, it's celebrated at **Suwa Shrine,** a Shinto shrine that was built to promote Shintoism when the feudal government was trying to stamp out Christianity. Today, the shrine symbolizes better than anything else the spiritual heart of the Japanese community. When Japanese women turn 33 and men turn 40, they come here to pray for good health and a long life. The shrine sells fortunes in English. If you're satisfied with your fortune, keep it. If you're not, tie it to the branch of a tree and the fortune is conveniently negated. Suwa Shrine is a few minutes' walk from the Suwa Jinja-mae streetcar stop, reached by streetcar no. 3 or 4.

In addition to the temples described above, the Chinese also left their mark on Nagasaki with the construction of several bridges. Most famous of these is the so-called **Megane-bashi,** or **Spectacles Bridge,** named after the reflection the two-arched bridge casts in the water. I wouldn't know, however, because I've never seen the Nakashima River larger than a trickle. It does occasionally flood, as in 1982, when it wiped out several old bridges. These have now been reconstructed, along with a promenade complete with benches and children's playgrounds. Since it's only a 5-minute walk from the Hamanomachi shopping arcade, you might wish to come here with some take-out sushi and enjoy a picnic. The Megane-bashi, by the way, was built in 1634 by a Chinese Zen priest named Mozi of Kofukuji Temple. It's the oldest stone-arched bridge in Japan and is one of Nagasaki's most photographed objects. The nearest streetcar stops are Nigiwai-bashi and Kokaidomae on lines 3, 4, and 5.

PEACE PARK

✪ On August 9, 1945, at 11:02am, American forces dropped an atomic bomb over Nagasaki, 3 days after they had dropped a bomb over Hiroshima. Exploding 1,600 feet above ground, it destroyed about a third of the city, killed an estimated 75,000 people, and injured 75,000 more. Today, Nagasaki's citizens are among the most vigorous peace activists in the world, and Peace Park, located north of Nagasaki Station, serves as a reminder of that fateful day and a warning about the destructiveness of the atomic bomb. Every year on the anniversary of the bombing, a peace demonstration is held in Peace Park.

At one end of Peace Park a black stone pillar marks the exact epicenter of the atomic blast. Ironically enough, the bomb exploded almost directly over a Catholic church. At the other end of the park is the 30-foot-high Peace Statue, representing male deity. Although the exact meaning of the statue is left to individual interpretation, one hand points to the sky from whence the bomb came (meant as a warning?) and the other hand points to the horizon (representing the future?).

Next to Peace Park is a museum, the **Nagasaki International Cultural Hall** (popularly called the **Atomic Bomb Museum**) (tel. 44-1231). It contains objects, photos, and artifacts showing the devastation caused by the atomic bomb. It's by no means pleasant, but something every concerned individual should see. The International Cultural Hall is open daily from 9am to 6pm April through October, closing an hour earlier November through March. Entrance fee is ¥50 (35¢). Located in the basement of the same building but containing an entirely different kind of collection is the **Nagasaki Municipal Museum,** which charges ¥100 (70¢) admission. It features artifacts relating to the Edo Period and Japanese Christianity. Peace Park can be reached by streetcar no. 1 or 3; disembark at Matsuyama tram stop.

NAGASAKI HOLLAND VILLAGE

If you're in Nagasaki for more than a day and you want to take a side trip, you might want to visit one of Nagasaki's newest attractions—Nagasaki Holland Village, a living proof of how adept the Japanese are at imitation. They have reconstructed a replica of a Dutch village, with each building a faithful copy of an original back in the Netherlands. Although I was a bit skeptical about visiting an imitation Dutch village in Japan, I must admit that the grounds and craftsmanship are beautifully done. Even Holland itself doesn't always look this pristine. Contained in the village are a porcelain museum, with an exact replica of a room in West Berlin's Charlottenburg Palace that has an elaborate display of china made in both China and Arita, Japan; a museum dedicated to the Dutch in Nagasaki's history; churches; and china shops, craft shops, souvenir boutiques, and more. There's even a cheese shop selling Dutch imports—it once managed to sell three tons of cheese in a day. That could well be a world record.

Nagasaki Holland Village is an hour away by bus from Nagasaki Station. Admission is a bit steep, at ¥2,570 ($18.35), and bus fare is ¥630 ($4.80). At Nagasaki Station there's a special information office for the Holland Village where you can buy your ticket, called a "passport." The best time to visit is of course in the spring, when—what else?—it's tulip season.

WHERE TO STAY

Nagasaki has very reasonably priced hotels. The busiest time of the year is in May, when Nagasaki is brimming with busloads of schoolchildren who come here on class excursions.

EXPENSIVE

HOTEL NEW NAGASAKI, 14-5 Daikoku-machi, Nagasaki 850. Tel. 0958/26-8000. Fax 0958/26-6162. 149 rms. A/C MINIBAR TV TEL **Directions:** A 1-minute walk from Nagasaki Station.
$ Rates: ¥20,000 ($143) single; ¥23,000 ($164) double/twin. AE, DC, JCB, MC, V.

One of Nagasaki's newest and most deluxe hotels, the Hotel New Nagasaki has a convenient location right next to the train station. Its marble lobby is light and airy, and rooms are outfitted with hot-water pot, hairdryer, TV, and cable radio with more than 400 stations, including the American armed forces network FEN. Many rooms also have connections for facsimile machines.

Dining/Entertainment: Seven restaurants range from Western to Chinese and Japanese, including a Kobe steakhouse.

Services: Free newspaper, same-day laundry service.

Facilities: Fitness club, indoor swimming pool, sauna.

NAGASAKI TOKYU HOTEL, 1-18 Minamiyamate-machi, Nagasaki 850. Tel. 0958/25-1501. Fax 0958/23-5167. 224 rms. A/C MINIBAR TV TEL **Streetcar:** 1 from Nagasaki Station to Tsukimachi, then 5 to Oura Kaigan stop, from which it's a few minutes' walk.
$ Rates: ¥10,500–¥12,500 ($75–$89) single; ¥20,000 ($143) double; ¥20,000–¥24,000 ($143–$171) twin. AE, DC, JCB, MC, V.

Although the lobby of this hotel, located near Glover Garden, is sparsely furnished (with its bare white walls and stained-glass windows, it reminds me of the inside of a church—which fits in with Nagasaki's history), the rooms are comfortable and come with a tiny balcony and bilingual TV. Since rates are based on room size rather than view, ask for a room facing Glover Garden.

Dining/Entertainment: French food is served in the Glover restaurant, along with views of the harbor. Ohura features both Japanese and Chinese cuisine, and there's one bar.

Services: Free newspaper.

Facilities: Souvenir shop.

SAKAMOTO-YA ㉔, 2-13 Kanaya-machi, Nagasaki 850. Tel. 0958/26-8211. Fax 0958/25-5944. 15 rms (all with bath). A/C MINIBAR TV TEL **Directions:** A 5-minute walk southeast of Nagasaki Station.
$ Rates (per person, including breakfast, dinner, and service charge): ¥15,500–¥33,000 ($111–$235). AE, DC, JCB, MC.

★ If you want to sleep in a ryokan, this beautiful 90-year-old ryokan (Nagasaki's oldest) is right in the heart of the city and is a wonderful place to stay. Most of the rooms have a Japanese-style bathtub made of wood, as well as artwork on the walls. The best room is the Pine Room (Matsu No Ma), which even has its own private little garden. Rates here vary according to the room and the meals served. If you want, you can order shippoku, a Nagasaki specialty consisting of a variety of dishes showing European and Chinese influences, for ¥5,000 ($35.70) more. Western breakfasts are also served on request.

MODERATE

HOLIDAY INN, 6-24 Doza-machi, Nagasaki 850. Tel. 0958/28-1234, or toll free 800/HOLIDAY in the U.S. Fax 0958/28-0178. 84 rms. A/C MINIBAR TV TEL **Streetcar:** 1 from Nagasaki Station to Kanko Dori stop, then a 1-minute walk.

$ Rates: ¥10,500–¥11,500 ($75–$82) single; ¥16,000–¥18,000 ($114–$128) double; ¥18,000–¥23,000 ($114–$164) twin. Children under 12 stay free in parents' room. AE, DC, JCB, MC, V.

This hotel is conveniently located just off Kanko Dori Street, close to the Hamanomachi shopping arcade in the heart of the city. You can walk from the hotel to most sites, including Glover Mansion and Sofukuji and Kofukuji temples. All rooms have double-, queen-, or king-size beds. Rooms are large and bright, and come with the usual TV, minibar, and alarm clock. The hotel's restaurant serves Japanese cuisine. There's also a cocktail bar.

NAGASAKI GRAND HOTEL, 5-3 Manzai-machi, Nagasaki 850. Tel. 0958/23-1234. Fax 0958/22-1793. 126 rms. A/C MINIBAR TV TEL **Streetcar:** 1 from Nagasaki Station to Hamanomachi stop, then a 4-minute walk.

$ Rates: ¥9,300 ($66) single; ¥14,300 ($102) double; ¥15,500–¥18,000 ($111–$128) twin. Japanese-style rooms: ¥25,000 ($178) double occupancy. AE, DC, JCB, MC, V.

This fine older hotel is conveniently located near the Hamanomachi shopping district. Its rooms are soothingly decorated in soft pastels of mauve or pea green and come with what you'd expect from a hotel of this category—hot-water pot, TV, minibar, and alarm clock. The single rooms, with unusual layouts utilizing space to its utmost, are especially pleasant. There are also three Japanese-style rooms. In addition to the hotel's three restaurants, there's a great beer garden right outside the lobby that is surrounded by palm trees and azaleas. It's open mid-April to the end of August daily from 5 to 10pm.

NAGASAKI WASHINGTON HOTEL, 9-1 Shinchi-machi, Nagasaki 850. Tel. 0958/28-1211. Fax 0958/25-8023. 176 rms. A/C MINIBAR TV TEL **Streetcar:** 1 from Nagasaki Station to Tsukimachi stop, then a 3-minute walk.

$ Rates: ¥8,000 ($57) single; ¥15,000 ($107) double; ¥16,500 ($118) twin. AE, DC, JCB, MC, V.

This chain hotel is located on the edge of the city's tiny Chinatown, about a 2-minute walk from the Hamanomachi shopping district. The rooms in this 10-story brick building are slightly more expensive than those in the average business hotel, but the rooms are large and come equipped with TV, alarm clock, minibar, radio, and Japanese-style deep tub. Panels in the windows can be closed for complete darkness. To save energy, electricity is generated only when the key card is inserted into the bedside panel. The hotel's 10th-floor restaurant, with views of the city, specializes in steaks. There's also a coffee shop and Japanese restaurant.

PARK SIDE HOTEL, 14-1 Heiwa-machi, Nagasaki 852. Tel. 0958/45-3191. Fax 0958/46-5550. 56 rms. A/C TV TEL **Streetcar:** 1 or 3 from Nagasaki Station to Matsuyama stop, then a 4-minute walk through Peace Park.

$ Rates: ¥6,900 ($49) single; ¥13,500 ($96) twin; ¥11,500 ($82) double. AE, DC, JCB, MC, V.

This pleasant and small hotel located next to Peace Park is a favorite with long-term guests, both because they enjoy its quiet location and because they can jog early in the morning in the park. The Western-style restaurant has big windows overlooking the greenery of the park, which is ablaze with cherry blossoms in spring. There's also a Japanese restaurant and a bar, and since this hotel is the tallest building in the area, its rooftop beer garden (open May to the end of August daily from 5 to 9pm) offers a good view of the vicinity and of the surrounding hills radiating into the distance. The rooms have semidouble-size beds and double-pane windows.

HOTEL NEW TANDA, 2-24 Tokiwa-machi, Nagasaki 850. Tel. 0958/27-6121. Fax 0958/26-1704. 161 rms. A/C MINIBAR TV TEL **Streetcar:** 1 from Nagasaki Station to Tsukimachi; then 5 to Shiminbyoin stop, from which it's a few minutes' walk.

$ Rates: ¥8,000–¥10,000 ($57–$71) single; ¥13,700–¥18,000 ($98–$128) double; ¥16,000–¥19,000 ($114–$136) twin; ¥20,000 ($143) triple. AE, DC, JCB, MC, V.

This brick hotel is located at the bottom of Dutch Slope, about a 7-minute walk to either Glover Garden or the Hamanomachi shopping district. Popular with foreign visitors, it has one Western-style restaurant, a bar, and a combination pub/restaurant. In summer there's a rooftop beer garden, where you can look out over the harbor. Room rates are based on location, view, and furnishings.

HOTEL STATION ROYAL AJISAI ⑳, 7-3 Daikoku-machi, Nagasaki 850. Tel. 0958/22-2222. Fax 0958/22-9608. 82 rms. A/C TV TEL **Directions:** A 1-minute walk from Nagasaki Station, across street.

$ Rates: ¥7,500 ($53) single; ¥11,000 ($78) double; ¥15,400 ($110) twin; ¥20,000 ($143) triple. Japanese–style rooms: ¥20,000 ($143) double occupancy; ¥30,000 ($214) quad. DC, JCB, MC, V.

This modern brick building across the street from Nagasaki Station is a cross between a business and a tourist hotel. It is locally owned by a Japanese who has eight hotel properties in Nagasaki, and its rooms come with just the basics, including double-pane windows to shut out train traffic. The most expensive twins are large corner rooms with big windows that open onto a balcony and offer sweeping views. The best deal, however, is a large Japanese-style room with two beds plus a separate tatami area—good for a family, large group, or the entertaining of friends. The hotel has one coffee shop and one Japanese-style restaurant.

BUDGET

CAPSULE INN NAGASAKI ⑳, 2-11 Daikoku-machi, Nagasaki 850. Tel. 0958/21-1099. 30 beds. A/C TV **Directions:** A 2-minute walk from Nagasaki Station, behind Nishikyushu Daiichi Hotel.

$ Rates (per person): ¥2,900 ($20.70). AE, DC, JCB, V.

If you're male and are content with just the basics, you might wish to try this functional capsule hotel. Each unit is no larger than a coffin—but nevertheless outfitted with a TV set. Obviously, noisy neighbors are the main setback, though at these prices you might not care.

HOTEL IBIS, 8-19 Kabasima-machi, Nagasaki 850. Tel. 0958/24-2171. Fax 0958/22-5582. 87 rms (all with bath). A/C MINIBAR TV TEL **Directions:** A 10-minute walk south of Nagasaki Station, or two stops on streetcar 1 to Ohato stop.

$ Rates: ¥5,700–¥6,200 ($41–$44) single; ¥9,600 ($68) double; ¥10,500–¥12,000 ($75–$86) twin; ¥16,500 ($118) triple. Western breakfast ¥800 ($5.70). AE, DC, V.

Rooms are simple at this reasonably priced business hotel, located within walking distance of Nagasaki Station, the Ohato Port Terminal with its harbor tours, and Hamanomachi shopping district. Rooms are small but have all the basics.

MINSHUKU SIEBOLD, 1-2-11 Sakurababa, Nagasaki 850. Tel. 0958/22-5623. 5 rms (none with bath). A/C TV TEL **Streetcar:** 3 from Nagasaki Station to Shindaiku Machi, then a 1-minute walk.

$ Rates (per person): ¥4,500 ($32) without meals; ¥4,900 ($35) including breakfast; ¥6,000 ($43) with two meals. No credit cards.

If you're on a tight budget or prefer the intimacy of a minshuku, the Siebold (sometimes pronounced "Shibolt" by the Japanese) is one of the best places to stay, offering simply furnished Japanese-style rooms. The woman who runs the place doesn't speak much English, but her husband, who works at a travel agency, does and is happy to recommend inexpensive yakitori-ya in the neighborhood.

MINSHUKU TANPOPO, 21-7 Hoeicho, Nagasaki 852. Tel. 0958/61-6230. 13 rms (none with bath). A/C TV **Station:** Urakami JR (one station north of Nagasaki Station), a 15-minute walk away.
$ Rates: ¥3,600 ($26) single; ¥6,500 ($46) twin; ¥10,000 ($71) triple. Breakfast ¥500 ($3.55); dinner ¥1,500 ($10.70). AE.

Although located in a four-story concrete building, this minshuku offers simple tatami rooms at very reasonable rates. Situated about halfway between Nagasaki Station and Peace Park on the east side of the Urakami River, it offers free parking and laundry facilities. If you let the owners know you're coming and call from the station, they'll pick you up. Minshuku Tanpopo is a member of the Japanese Inn Group.

NISHIKYUSHU DAIICHI HOTEL ㉔, 2-1 Daikoku-machi, Nagasaki 850. Tel. 0958/21-1711. Fax 0958/23-8745. 83 rms (all with bath). A/C TV TEL **Directions:** A 1-minute walk from Nagasaki Station, across street.
$ Rates: ¥6,500 ($46) single; ¥10,300 ($73) double; ¥10,500 ($75) twin; ¥13,200 ($94) triple. AE, DC, JCB, MC, V.

This business hotel across the street from Nagasaki Station has comfortable rooms with the usual TV (with pay video for adult entertainment) and alarm clock, but the bathrooms are minuscule. Some of the singles are dark because of an adjoining building, so it might be prudent to ask about the various options available. The hotel's restaurant serves a Western breakfast.

SANSUI-SO ㉔, 2-25 Ebisu-machi, Nagasaki 850. Tel. 0958/24-0070. Fax 0958/22-1952. 29 rms (all with bath). A/C TV TEL **Directions:** A few minutes' walk southeast of Nagasaki Station.
$ Rates (per person): ¥5,500 ($39) without meals; ¥8,500 ($60.70) with breakfast and dinner. DC, JCB, V.

Six of the rooms at this inexpensive Japanese-style accommodation are Western style, and all rooms are outfitted with coin-operated TV, heater, and air conditioner. Facilities include a public bath and a laundry machine.

Youth Hostels

NAGASAKI KENRITSU YOUTH HOSTEL ㉔, 2 Tateyama-cho, Nagasaki 850. Tel. 0952/23-5032. 132 beds. A/C **Directions:** A 12-minute walk southeast of Nagasaki Station.
$ Rates (per person): ¥2,100 ($15) member and nonmember. Breakfast ¥500 ($3.55); dinner ¥700 ($5). No credit cards.

This is the most conveniently located youth hostel in Nagasaki, and you don't have to be a youth hostel member to stay here. There are laundry facilities.

NAGASAKI NANPOEN YOUTH HOSTEL, 320 Hamahira-cho, Nagasaki 850. Tel. 0958/23-5526. 20 beds. A/C **Bus:** A 6-minute ride from Nagasaki Station, to Hamahira-cho stop.
$ Rates (per person): ¥2,100 ($15) members only. ¥400 ($2.85) breakfast; ¥650 ($4.65) dinner. No credit cards.

This small youth hostel, which sleeps guests on futons and is open to members only, is located up on a hill northeast of Nagasaki Station. The night view is beautiful.

NAGASAKI ORANDA-ZAKA YOUTH HOSTEL, 288, 6-14 Higashiyamate-cho, Nagasaki 850. Tel. 0958/22-2730. 55 beds. A/C **Streetcar:** 1 from Nagasaki Station to Tsukimachi; then 5 to Ishibashi (last stop), from which it's a 3-minute walk.
$ Rates (per person): ¥2,100 ($15) members only. Breakfast ¥450 ($3.20); dinner ¥650 ($4.65). No credit cards.

This youth hostel accepts members only and is located within a 10-minute walk of Glover Garden and Oura Catholic Church. It has laundry facilities.

URAGAMI-GA-OKA YOUTH HOSTEL, 6-14 Miyoshi-machi, Nagasaki

850. Tel. 0958/47-8473. 42 beds. A/C **Streetcar:** 1 or 3 from Nagasaki Station to Ohashi stop, then a 4-minute walk.
$ Rates (per person): ¥2,100 ($15) member; ¥2,800 ($20) nonmember. Breakfast ¥450 ($3.20); dinner ¥750 ($5.35). No credit cards.

This youth hostel, open to both members and nonmembers, is located one streetcar stop north of Peace Park. Its public bath offers a great view of the city, and facilities include laundry machines.

WHERE TO DINE

Nagasaki's most famous food is actually a whole meal of various courses with Chinese, European, and Japanese influences. Called shippoku, it's a feast generally shared by a group of four or more persons and includes such dishes as fish soup, sashimi, and fried, boiled, and vinegared seasonal delicacies from land and sea. Another Nagasaki specialty is *champon,* a thick Chinese noodle usually served in soup.

Nagasaki's nightlife district centers on a small street near Hamanomachi known as Shianbashi Dori, which begins just off the streetcar stop of the same name and is easily recognizable by its neon arch of a bridge and palm trees. Lined with pink plastic flowers, this street shimmers with the lights of various drinking establishments and yakitori-ya, which are often the cheapest places to go for a light dinner.

EXPENSIVE

FUKIRO ⓺, **146 Kami Nishiyama-machi. Tel. 22-0253.**
Cuisine: SHIPPOKU/KAISEKI. **Reservations:** Essential. **Streetcar:** 3 or 4 to Suwa Jinjamae, then a few minutes' walk.
$ Prices: Set meals from ¥8,500 ($60.70). DC.
Open: Lunch daily 11:30am–3pm; dinner daily 5pm–midnight.

This elegant old wooden restaurant is on a small cliff not far from Suwa Shrine. In a building 180 years old, it specializes in shippoku served in private tatami rooms, as well as kaiseki. Set courses start at ¥8,500 ($60.70), but there's virtually no limit to how high they can go. When making your reservation, it's best to state how much you wish to pay. The chef will go from there.

KAGETSU ⓺, **Maruyama-cho. Tel. 22-0191.**
Cuisine: SHIPPOKU/KAISEKI. **Reservations:** Required at least a week in advance. **Streetcar:** 1 or 4 to Shianbashi, then a few minutes' walk.
$ Prices: Shippoku or kaiseki set course ¥20,000 ($143), including tax and service charge. DC, V.
Open: Noon–7:30pm. **Closed:** On alternate Mon and Sun.

A wonderful but very expensive place to try shippoku, Kagetsu was first established in 1618 and is one of Japan's longest-running restaurants. The oldest part of the present building is about 300 years old. A wooden structure set back from the road, which is the center of Nagasaki's night scene of sailors' bars and strip cabarets, Kagetsu is an oasis of dignified old Japan, with kimono-clad waitresses shuffling down wooden corridors and serving guests in tatami rooms. Formerly a geisha house, it even has a stone-floored room designed for a table and chairs where foreign patrons could be entertained.

Behind the restaurant is a 300-year-old garden. I'll never forget my evening stroll here as a half moon rose above gnarled, stunted pines. The back of the restaurant, consisting mainly of glass, was all lit up, so that I could see into a multitude of private tatami rooms all on different levels. Guests were seated on the floor on cushions, and women in kimonos were playing the gracious hostess, pouring drinks and laughing behind their hands, and from the eaves outside the restaurant hung lighted lanterns. If it hadn't been for the fact that the men wore business suits, I would have sworn it looked exactly like a woodblock print of old Japan.

Needless to say, this restaurant is very popular and sometimes is booked up to a full month in advance. There must be at least two of you if you want to eat shippoku or kaiseki.

MODERATE

DEJIMA RESTAURANT, 7th floor of Grand Hotel, 5-3 Manzai machi. Tel. 23-1234.

Cuisine: WESTERN/SHIPPOKU. **Streetcar:** 1, 3, or 4 to Hamanomachi stop, then a 4-minute walk.
$ Prices: Set meals ¥4,900–¥9,000 ($35–$64.30). AE, DC, JCB, MC, V.
Open: Daily 11am–9pm.

If sitting on the floor puts your legs to sleep, you can enjoy a shippoku meal in Western surroundings at this hotel restaurant, which has set meals of steak, fish, daily specials, and shippoku. The latter consists of swordfish in diced soybean sauce, various seasonal hors d'oeuvres, minced veal soup, fresh seafood, brisket of pork, seafood and vegetable fritter, chicken hollandaise, cold beef, Chinese pilaf, dessert, and coffee.

HAMAKATSU ㉑, 6-50 Kajiya-machi. Tel. 26-8321.

Cuisine: SHIPPOKU. **Streetcar:** 1 or 4 to Shianbashi stop, then a 2-minute walk.
$ Prices: Main dishes ¥500–¥800 ($3.55–$5.70); shippoku set meals ¥4,100–¥15,000 ($29.30–$107.15). AE, DC, JCB, MC, V.
Open: Daily 11:30am–8:40pm (last order).

There must be at least two of you to order the reasonably priced shippoku meals at this modern restaurant. So if you're by yourself, you can order a smaller set menu that will give you a variety of local specialties, including tempura with green-tea noodles, fried and boiled dishes, sashimi, and more. Set meals are served on the second floor; the first floor is devoted to inexpensive à la carte dishes of both Japanese and Chinese origin, with most items under ¥700 ($5). Although the menu is in Japanese and changes seasonally, each dish is accompanied by a photo. Included are such items as steamed dumplings, tofu dishes, cold chicken, raw beef, and chili shrimp.

OBINATA, 3-19 Funadaiku-machi. Tel. 26-1437.

Cuisine: ITALIAN. **Streetcar:** 1 or 4 to Shianbashi stop, then a 1-minute walk.
$ Prices: Pastas and main dishes ¥1,000–¥3,300 ($7.15–$23.55). AE.
Open: Mon–Sat 5pm–1am.

One of my favorite restaurants, Obinata has a warm, earthy feel to it, due perhaps to its heavy wooden beams, large bouquets of flowers, candelabra, and classical music playing softly in the background—an oasis of old Europe in the heart of Kyushu. It's located behind the Fukusaya castella shop, just off the nightlife street called Shianbashi Dori. The atmosphere is cozy and the service is a delight. The menu lists such main dishes as steak, Southern fried chicken with bacon, filet of beef goulash, Japanese steak, spaghetti, lasagne, and pizza. Dishes are creative and fun, the restaurant's own interpretations. Expect to pay about ¥6,000 ($43) if you go all out and order an appetizer, main dish, and wine (there's a wide selection of Bordeaux, Moselle, and Rhine wines), but you can eat more cheaply if you stick to pastas.

OHURA, Tokyu Hotel, 1-18 Minamiyamate-machi. Tel. 25-1501.

Cuisine: JAPANESE/CHINESE. **Streetcar:** 5 to Oura Tensudoshita, then a few minutes' walk.
$ Prices: Shippoku ¥3,400–¥4,500 ($24.30–$32.15); set courses ¥6,500–¥10,000 ($46.40–$71.40). AE, DC, JCB, MC, V.
Open: Lunch daily 11:30am–2:30pm; dinner daily 5–9:30pm (last order).

This restaurant, located in the basement of the Tokyu Hotel, is a pleasant and quiet place to stop for a meal if you're visiting Glover Garden. It serves shippoku (colorful pictures depict the various courses available) and Japanese and Chinese selections, including tempura, fried sweet-and-sour pork, shredded pork with green pepper, and assorted fried noodles Nagasaki style. The lunch menu lists dishes that average ¥800 to ¥1,500 ($5.70 to $10.70). The dinner menu is more extensive and slightly pricier; expect to spend about ¥3,000 ($21.40) or ¥4,000 ($28.55) if you order à la carte.

SAKURA HOUSE, 6-15 Kajiya-machi. Tel. 26-0229.

   Cuisine: WESTERN/FRENCH. **Streetcar:** 1 or 4 to Shianbashi, then a 3-minute walk.

$ **Prices:** Main dishes ¥1,300–¥2,200 ($9.30–$15.70); set-dinner courses ¥2,700–¥8,000 ($19.30–$57.15); set lunch ¥1,500 ($10.70). AE, DC, JCB, MC, V.

   Open: Daily 11:30am–midnight (last order 11pm).

Although it's one of Nagasaki's newer and trendy restaurants, it resembles a much older establishment from the 1930s or '40s. Decorated with half-paneled walls, wooden floors, and a wooden bar counter, it's located close to Hamanomachi, and not far from Hamakatsu, described above. Its menu lists soups, salads, seafood, chicken, duck, beef, pork, and lamb selections. Since it calls itself a restaurant/bar, you can also come here for just a drink and listen to background music of jazz or swing.

TOKIWA, Nagasaki View Hotel, 2-33 Oura-machi. Tel. 24-2211.

   Cuisine: SUSHI. **Streetcar:** 5 to Oura Kaigan, then a 1-minute walk.

$ **Prices:** Set meal ¥2,700 ($19.30); lunch teishoku ¥1,400–¥1,600 ($10–$11.45). AE, DC, JCB, MC, V.

   Open: Lunch daily 11:30am–2pm; dinner daily 5–9pm.

If you're hungering for raw fish, it doesn't come any fresher than at this conveniently located restaurant between Hamanomachi and Glover Garden in the Nagasaki View Hotel. Tokiwa features a wooden counter surrounding a pool filled with live fish. When its number is up, a fish is scooped out of the water and then prepared right before your very eyes. Sometimes the fish is gutted and fileted, with only the head, heart, and skeleton left intact, so that the sashimi can be arranged around the alive and still-quivering animal and delivered to the customer's table. Barring that, you might opt for one of the lunch teishoku beginning at ¥1,400 ($10), which range from sashimi teishoku to tempura teishoku.

BUDGET

BHARATA, 2-10 Yasaka St., Aburaya-machi. Tel. 24-9194.

   Cuisine: INDIAN. **Streetcar:** 1 or 4 to Shianbashi, then a 1-minute walk.

$ **Prices:** Curries ¥1,000–¥1,200 ($7.15–$8.55); set courses ¥1,400–¥2,900 ($10–$20.70). AE, DC, JCB, MC, V.

   Open: Lunch Tues–Fri 11:30am–3pm, dinner Tues–Fri 5–10pm. Sat–Sun 11:30am–10pm.

A craving for hot and spicy food can be satisfied at Bharata, located close to the Hamanomachi shopping arcade just off Kajiya-machi Street on the second floor of a brick building. An inexpensive establishment with modest décor, it serves Indian food: curry dishes of beef, chicken, kofta (meatballs), shrimp, and fish include Indian bread or pilaf, chutney, and salad. There's a set vegetarian meal with various small dishes for ¥1,400 ($10) and a nonvegetarian set meal for ¥2,900 ($20.70).

KOUZANROU ㉕, 12-1 Shinchi-machi. Tel. 21-3735.

   Cuisine: CHINESE. **Streetcar:** 1 to Tsukimachi or Kanko Dori stops, from which it's about a 5-minute walk.

$ **Prices:** Champon ¥700–¥900 ($5–$6.45); main dishes ¥900–¥1,600 ($6.45–$11.45). No credit cards.

   Open: Daily 11am–9pm (last order 8:30pm).

A popular Chinese restaurant located in the heart of Nagasaki's small Chinatown, it serves a mostly Chinese clientele and its most popular dish is champon. If you order such à la carte dishes as spring rolls, champon, or sweet-and-sour pork, most of which are under ¥1,300 ($9.30), you'll dine in the restaurant's simply furnished ground-floor dining area of tables and chairs. If you feel like splurging, you can order a set meal of various dishes, which range in price from ¥3,300 to ¥10,000 ($23.55 to $71.40), and can opt for being escorted upstairs to your private tatami room. During lunch there's a set meal available for ¥2,200 ($15.70) as well.

Kouzanrou is so successful that it's opened a smaller shop right next to the Nagasaki train station (to the right after exiting from the station). Very modern and sleek in design, it also offers champon and is open daily from 11am to 9pm.

SHIKAIRO, 4-5 Matsugae-cho. Tel. 22-1296.
   Cuisine: CHINESE. **Streetcar:** 5 to Oura Kaigan stop, then a 2-minute walk.
$ Prices: Champon ¥800 ($5.70); set courses ¥3,000–¥20,000 ($21.40–$71.40). JCB.
   Open: Lunch daily 11:30am–3pm; dinner daily 5–9:30pm (last order 8pm).

⭐ If you're interested in eating champon Chinese noodles, this is the Chinese restaurant that created them. First opened back in 1899, it moved into its present building in 1973. Located close to the Tokyu Hotel and Glover Garden, it's a large white building topped with a rounded dome and offering four floors of dining. It can accommodate as many as 1,500 people, and caters to large groups and receptions. Knowing where to go for a meal would be confusing if it weren't for the ground-floor welcoming committee, who are eager to point the way. Come to think of it, however, you might still be confused, because the numbers for floors in the elevator are written in kanji only. Assuming that you do eventually end up in the right dining hall, you'll find yourself in a large and noisy room surrounded by lots of other hungry souls. There are more than 30 items on the English menu, including barbecued pork, braised shark fin with shredded meat, chicken with bamboo shoots and onion, fried noodles, and, of course, champon. If you order à la carte, expect to spend from ¥2,000 to ¥3,000 ($14.30 to $21.40) per person.

YAGURA-CHAYA ㉝, 6-38 Motoshikkui-machi. Tel. 22-0984.
   Cuisine: YAKITORI/VARIED JAPANESE. **Streetcar:** 1 or 4 to Shianbashi, then a 3-minute walk.
$ Prices: ¥300–¥650 ($2.15–$4.65). MC, V.
   Open: Dinner Sun–Thurs 5pm–midnight, Fri and Sat 5pm–2am.
Actually a drinking establishment offering inexpensive dishes, this place is located right next to a live-music house called Kento's. It sports dark-stained heavy wooden beams that give it a respectable farmhouse feeling, an atmosphere amplified by the dolls, straw sandals, kites, paper lanterns, umbrellas, and other things suspended from the walls and ceiling. The menu is extensive—unfortunately written in Japanese only—and includes baked fish, skewers of yakitori, chicken nuggets, sashimi, baked corn, pizza, sashimi, salads, tofu, and much more. Most items are priced under ¥500 ($3.55). Beer and shochu start at ¥400 ($2.85).

YAGURA-SUSHI ㉞, Hamanomachi covered shopping arcade on stretch closest to Megane-bashi. Tel. 22-1813.
   Cuisine: SUSHI. **Streetcar:** 4 or 5 to Hamanomachi stop, then a 4-minute walk.
$ Prices: Sushi teishoku ¥700 ($5). No credit cards.
   Open: Fri–Wed 9am–9pm.
To find this place in the Hamanomachi covered shopping arcade, look for its traditional-looking storefront, with a window showing the sushi experts at work and a sign in English saying TRY OUR DELICIOUS SUSHI FOR ONE. There's a small dining area; most people you'll see standing in line, however, are waiting for take-out orders, with lunch boxes starting at ¥600 ($4.30). This is a good place to buy a picnic lunch, and you can eat it near Megane-bashi bridge.

SPECIALTY DINING

If you're having a Big Mac attack, **McDonald's** is located in the Hamanomachi shopping district, on Kanko Dori Avenue next to the Holiday Inn.

SHOPPING

Locally made Nagasaki products include cultured pearls and coral objects. A convenient place to shop for Nagasaki products is the **Local Products Hall**

(Nagasaki-ken Bussankan), across the street from Nagasaki Station on the second floor of the Kotsu Sangyo Building. Look for the sign outside that says NAGASAKI PREFECTURE TOURIST FEDERATION.

Another good place for shopping is the **Hamanomachi shopping arcade,** near the Nishi-Hamanomachi and Kanko Dori streetcar stops. Located centrally downtown, this covered arcade has clothing boutiques, restaurants, accessory stores, and shops specializing in local handicrafts.

Another famous product of Nagasaki is its castella (*kasutera*), a spongecake with Portuguese origins. Japanese visitors to Nagasaki can't leave without buying castella for co-workers and friends back home. There are cake shops throughout the city, and the most famous is **Fukusaya,** 3-1 Fundaiku-machi (tel. 21-2938), not far from the Hamanomachi shopping arcade. Fukusaya is located in a 200-year-old building and has a history that stretches back even further. It's open daily from 8:30am to 8pm; closed the second Thursday of each month.

EVENING ENTERTAINMENT

Kento's, Motoshikkui-machi (tel. 21-3453) features "oldies but goldies," primarily American hits from the 1950s and '60s, sung by Japanese bands—the music is loud. Open daily from 6pm to midnight. Admission is ¥1,500 ($10.70), then each customer is required to buy at least one food dish and one drink. Dishes range from ice cream to spaghetti and salads, all under ¥1,000 ($7.15), while drinks start at ¥650 ($4.65).

6. UNZEN

41 miles SE of Nagasaki

GETTING THERE   By Bus   The easiest way to get to Unzen is by Kenci Bus from Nagasaki. Buses leave about every hour or so from the bus terminal across the street from Nagasaki Station. The ride takes about 2 hours and costs ¥1,700 ($12.15) one way.

ESSENTIAL INFORMATION   The **area code** for Unzen, lying in Nagasaki Prefecture, is 0957.

Before leaving Tokyo or Kyoto, be sure to stop by the Tourist Information Center to pick up the free leaflet *Nagasaki and Unzen,* which describes places of interest in Unzen and the Shimabara Peninsula.

In Unzen, the **tourist office** (tel. 0957/73-3434) is located in the heart of Unzen Spa not far from the Hells. Open daily from 9am to 5pm, it has a rudimentary but adequate map in English of Unzen and the surrounding area. Nearby is the **Unzen Visitor's Center** with natural history displays of the national park.

Unzen Spa is a small resort town 2,385 feet above sea level in the pine-covered hills of the Shimabara Peninsula. Because of its high altitude and cool mountain air, its great scenery and hot sulfur springs, Unzen became popular in the 1880s as a summer resort for American and European visitors, who came from Shanghai, Hong Kong, and Singapore to escape the oppressive humid summer heat. They arrived in Unzen by bamboo palanquin from Obama, 7 miles away. The fact that there were foreigners here explains why Unzen has one of Japan's oldest golf courses, dating from 1913.

WHAT TO SEE & DO

In 1934 the area around Unzen became **Unzen National Park,** named after what was thought to be an extinct volcano, Mt. Unzen. In 1991, however, Mt. Unzen erupted, killing several dozen people on its eastern slope. Unzen Spa, on the opposite side, was untouched and remains the area's most popular resort town.

Unzen Spa literally bubbles with activity as sulfurous hot springs erupt into surface cauldrons of scalding water in an area known as **the Hells (Jigoku).** Indeed, in the

1600s these cauldrons were used for hellish punishment as Christians were boiled alive here after Christianity was outlawed in Japan. Today, Unzen Spa has more than 30 solfataras and fumaroles. The Hells are a favorite hangout of huge black ravens, and the barren land has been baked a chalky white through the centuries. There are pathways leading through the hot springs where sulfur vapors rise thick to veil pine trees on surrounding hills. Old women in bonnets sell eggs that have been boiled in the hot springs for ¥50 (35¢) apiece. They also sell corn on the cob for ¥350 ($2.50) an ear.

I like Unzen Spa because it's small and navigable. It consists basically of just a few streets with hotels and ryokan spread along them, a welcome relief if you've been spending a few hectic weeks rushing through big cities and catching buses and trains. Only 1,700 people live here, and from the town a number of hiking paths wind into the tree-covered hills. If you feel like taking an excursion, buses leave about every hour for **Nitta Pass,** about a 20-minute ride away. The fare is ¥700 ($5) round trip. From Nitta Pass you can take a ropeway up higher to **Mt. Myoken** for a better view, but the best thing to do in my opinion is to take the footpath that runs from Nitta Pass and skirts the mountain along a tree-shaded path. The first 15 or 20 minutes of the path is fairly easy, and that's all you may care to exert yourself. If you're ready for some real climbing, however, continue along the path for another half hour or so where it leads starkly uphill to the summit of Mt. Fugen, Unzen's highest peak at 4,462 feet above sea level and the peak that erupted in 1991. There, on a clear day, you'll be rewarded with splendid views of other volcanic peaks as far away as Mt. Aso in the middle of Kyushu. Also on Mt. Fugen is Fugen Shrine, which is about a 20-minute hike from the peak. Allow at least 2 hours for the hike from Nitta Pass to Mt. Fugen and back.

For sports, you can play golf at Unzen's famous and Japan's oldest **public golf course** (tel. 73-3368), open daily from 8am to 5pm. Total charge for the nine-hole course, including greens fees, tax, and caddy, is ¥7,340 ($52.40) on weekdays and ¥9,500 ($67.85) on weekends and holidays. There's also a shorter nine-hole course (good for beginners) charging ¥2,900 ($20.70). Unzen Spa also has **public tennis courts,** which are free—your only obligation is to rake the dirt court when you finish playing.

Keep in mind that, as with many resort areas in Japan, Unzen tends to be crowded during Golden Week in early May, during New Year's, and in July and August. The best times of year are late April to June, when the azalea bushes are in glorious bloom, and in late October and early November, when the maple leaves turn brilliant reds.

WHERE TO STAY & DINE

With the exception of the budget accommodation listed at the end of this section, all the ryokan and hotels listed here are within easy walk of bus stops along the route followed by the bus from Nagasaki. Tell the bus driver where you're staying, and he'll drop you off at the nearest stop.

EXPENSIVE

MIYAZAKI RYOKAN ㉕, 320 Unzen, Obamacho, Minami-Takaki-gun 854-06. Tel. 0957/73-3331. 107 rms (all with bath). A/C MINIBAR TV TEL
$ Rates (per person, including breakfast, dinner, and service charge): ¥20,000–¥30,000 ($143–$214). AE, DC, JCB, MC, V.
One of the largest Japanese inns in Unzen, this modern structure overlooks a manicured traditional garden, with hills and sulfur vapors rising in the background. All rooms come with TV with pay video, safe for valuables, alarm clock, and minibar.

IMPRESSIONS

The Japanese assimilate rather than imitate.
—JAMES KIRKUP, *THESE HORNED ISLANDS,* 1962

In addition to Japanese-style tatami rooms, there are also combination rooms that feature twin beds and a separate tatami area. The meals served in this ryokan are excellent. Breakfasts (Western style, if desired) are served in a communal dining area, but dinners are served in the individual guest rooms in true ryokan fashion. Room prices are the same regardless of which direction the rooms face, so I'd advise securing one that faces the hot springs and wooded hills rather than the village. The views from these rooms are among the best in Unzen. As expected, this ryokan has large hot-spring public-bath facilities.

UNZEN KANKO HOTEL, 320 Unzen, Obamacho, Minami-Takaki-gun 854-06. Tel. 0957/73-3263. Fax 0957/73-3419. 60 rms. TV TEL
$ Rates: Western–style rooms: ¥7,500–¥9,000 ($53–$64) single; ¥15,000–¥22,000 ($107–$157) double/twin. Japanese-style rooms: ¥27,000–¥40,000 ($193–$286). Combination rooms: ¥22,000 ($157). AE, DC, JCB, MC, V.

If you're the least bit romantic, you won't be able to resist staying at this old-fashioned mountain lodge, built in 1935 of stone and wood and covered in ivy. The rooms are rustic and old-fashioned too, with heavy ceiling-to-floor curtains tied back to reveal a balcony, brass doorsills, a high ceiling, and wooden beams. There are 50 Western-style rooms, eight newer Japanese-style tatami rooms, and two combination rooms that come with both bed and tatami area.

Dining/Entertainment: Even if you don't stay at the hotel, you may want to come here for a meal. The dining hall is large, with wooden paneling and wooden floors, white tablecloths, and flowers on each table. Open for lunch from noon to 1:30pm and for dinner starting at 6pm, with last orders taken at 8pm, it serves set menus of both Japanese and Western selections starting at ¥4,400 ($31.40). The Western set meal for ¥5,500 ($39.30), for example, will bring you hors d'oeuvres, soup, lobster, the main dish and vegetables, a salad, a roll or rice, ice cream, and coffee or tea. There's also a small à la carte menu that includes such dishes as filet mignon, chicken, pork cutlets, lobster, sole, fried shrimp, and spaghetti. Spaghetti costs ¥900 ($6.40). Also on the hotel grounds is a tempura restaurant called Gyo En, located just to the right as you enter the hotel's cedar-lined driveway. A small house with one room for dining, it's open daily from 6 to 8:30pm, with set meals ranging from ¥4,400 to ¥5,500 ($31.40 to $39.30).

Facilities: Hot-spring sulfur baths, billiard tables, table tennis, and electronic games. The hotel also has a couple of racquets you can use in case you want to swing at balls down at the public tennis courts.

YUMEI HOTEL, 380 Obamacho, Minami-Takaki-gun 854-06. Tel. 0957/ 73-3206. 72 rms (all with bath). A/C MINIBAR TV TEL
$ Rates (per person, including breakfast, dinner, and service charge): Weekdays ¥14,000 ($104); weekends and peak season ¥17,500 ($125); combination rooms ¥20,000–¥50,000 ($143–$357). AE, DC, JCB, MC, V.

First opened about 100 years ago during the Meiji Period by the present owner's grandfather, the Yumei Hotel is a moderately priced ryokan in Unzen. The present building was constructed in 1983 and renovated in 1987. All rooms come with safe for valuables, minibar, and TV with adult video; those on the fifth floor come with a large balcony. Most of the rooms are Japanese style, but 20 are combination style, with both beds and a separate tatami area.

Dining/Entertainment: Dinners are served in each guest's room, while breakfasts are served in a communal dining room.

Facilities: Hot-spring baths open 24 hours a day, swimming pool open from July through August, bowling alley, and public tennis courts next door.

MODERATE

KASEYA RYOKAN ㉖, **Unzen, Obamacho, Minami-Takaki-gun 854-06. Tel. 0957/73-3321.** 13 rms (none with bath). A/C TV TEL
$ Rates (per person, including breakfast, dinner, and service charge): ¥8,500–¥11,000 ($61–$78). No credit cards.

This economically priced ryokan, dating back to 1909, has been totally remodeled. All rooms are Japanese style and are simply decorated, with a high ceiling and flower arrangements in each room. There are three communal public sulfur baths, one each for men and for women, and a smaller bath for families. Western-style breakfasts are available.

BUDGET

SEIUNSO KOKUMIN SHUKUSHA ㉕⑦, **500-1 Unzen, Obamacho, Minami Takaki-gun 854-06. Tel. 0957/73-3273.** 52 rms (15 with bath). TV TEL
Directions: A 30-minute walk from Unzen Spa.
$ Rates (per person, including breakfast, dinner, and service charge): ¥6,000 ($43) without bath; ¥7,000 ($50) with bath. No credit cards.
Formerly a youth hostel, this place still offers the least expensive accommodations in Unzen Spa. Because it is about a 30-minute walk from the spa, the staff will pick guests up if they telephone from the bus stop in Unzen. The higher-priced rooms have their own private bathroom and balcony, but the view from the cheaper rooms is no less grand. All rooms have coin-operated TV. There's a hot-spring public bath here, as well as a public outdoor bath not far from Seiunso. There are also laundry facilities. You should try to make reservations 3 months in advance for New Year's and August, the most crowded times of the year.

7. KAGOSHIMA

927 miles SW of Tokyo; 197 miles S of Fukuoka;
123 miles S of Kumamoto; 214 miles SW of Beppu

GETTING THERE   By Plane   Kagoshima's international airport connects Kyushu with Hong Kong and Korea, while domestic flights give easy access to Tokyo (flight time: 1 hr., 50 min.), Nagoya (flight time: 1 hr., 25 min.), Osaka (flight time: 1 hr., 10 min.), and Hiroshima (flight time: 1 hr., 10 min.).

BY TRAIN   12 hours from Tokyo, 8 hours from Osaka, and about 4 hours from Fukuoka. All trains passing through Kagoshima make two stops, at both Kagoshima Station and Nishi Kagoshima Station. Kagoshima Station is the closest station to Iso Garden, the Sakurajima Ferry Terminal, Shigetomiso, Hirayama Ryokan, Nakazono Ryokan, and the Shiroyama Kanko Hotel, listed below. If you're heading for any of the other hotels described below, you should get off the train at Nishi Kagoshima Station.

By Ferry   Ferry service daily from Osaka, arriving in Kagoshima the next day (travel time: 21 hr.), costing ¥10,000 ($71.40).

With a population of more than half a million, Kagoshima is a city of palm trees, flowering trees and bushes, wide avenues, and people who are like the weather—warm, mild-tempered, and easygoing. Because of its relative isolation at the southern tip of Japan, far away from the capitals of Kyoto and Tokyo, Kagoshima through the centuries has developed an independent spirit that has fostered a number of great men and accomplishments. Foremost is the Shimazu clan, a remarkable family that for 29 generations (695 years) ruled over Kagoshima and its vicinity before the Meiji Restoration in 1868. Much of Japan's early contact with the outside world was via Kagoshima, first with China and then with the Western world. Japan's first contact with Christianity occurred in Kagoshima when St. Francis Xavier landed here in 1549. Although he stayed only 10 months, he converted more than 600 Japanese to Christianity.

By the mid-19th century, as the Tokugawa shogunate began losing strength and the confidence of the people, the Shimazu family was already looking toward the future and the modernization of Japan. In the mid-1850s the Shimazus built the first

Western-style factory in the country, employing 200 men to make cannons, glass, ceramics, landmines, ships, and farming tools. In 1865, while Japan's doors were still officially closed to the outside world and all contact with foreigners was forbidden, the Shimazus smuggled 19 young men to Britain so that they could learn foreign languages and technology. After these men returned to Japan, they became a driving force in the Meiji Restoration and the modernization of Japan.

Another historical figure who played a major role during the Meiji Restoration was Takamori Saigo, who was born in Kagoshima Prefecture. A philosopher, scholar, educator, and poet, he helped restore Emperor Meiji to power, but because he was also a samurai he subsequently became disillusioned when the ancient rights of the samurai class were rescinded and the wearing of swords was forbidden. He led a force of samurai against the government in what is called the Seinan Rebellion, but was defeated. He then withdrew to Shiroyama in Kagoshima, where he committed suicide in 1877. Today, Saigo has many fans among the Japanese, and on Shiroyama Hill you can visit the cave where he committed suicide.

ORIENTATION
INFORMATION

The **area code** for Kagoshima, lying in Katoshima Prefecture, is 0992. An **international post office** is located at the Nishi Kagoshima Station.

Information on Kagoshima is given in *Southern Kyushu,* a leaflet distributed by the Tourist Information Centers in Tokyo and Kyoto.

In Kagoshima there are **tourist information centers** at both Nishi Kagoshima Station (tel. 0992/53-2500) and Kagoshima Station (tel. 0992/22-2500), as well as at the airport. The centers are open daily from 8:30am to 5pm. The staffs speak English and has good maps in English. The **Kagoshima Prefectural Tourist Office** is located in the Sangyo Kaikan Building, 9-1 Meizancho (tel. 0992/23-5771); here you can obtain information on the city as well as the prefecture, including Ibusuki and Chiran.

CITY LAYOUT

The downtown section of Kagoshima is the area between Nishi Kagoshima and Kagoshima stations, with **Tenmonkan-Dori Street** (a covered shopping arcade) serving as the heart of the city. You can walk from one station to the other in less than 30 minutes, but there is also a streetcar connecting the two.

GETTING AROUND

If you think you'll be doing a lot of traveling by streetcar, you might want to invest in a 1-day pass for ¥500 ($3.55), valid for travel on Kagoshima's two **tram lines** and on some city **buses.** Passes can be purchased at the tourist office in Nishi Kagoshima Station.

WHAT TO SEE & DO

With ties to Naples, Italy, as its sister city, Kagoshima bills itself as the "Naples of the Orient." That's perhaps stretching things a bit too far, but Kagoshima is balmy most of the year and it even has its own Mt. Vesuvius—**Mt. Sakurajima,** an active volcano across Kinko Bay, continuously puffs steam into the sky and occasionally covers the city with fine soot and ash. In 1914, Sakurajima had a whopper of an eruption and belched up 3 billion tons of lava. When the eruption was over, the townspeople were surprised to discover that the flow of lava had been so great that it blocked the 1,666-foot-wide channel separating the volcano from a neighboring peninsula. Sakurajima, which had once been an island, was now part of the mainland.

Magnificent from far away and impressive if you're near the top, Sakurajima can be visited by a ferry that leaves every 15 minutes from a pier close to Kagoshima Station.

It takes 15 minutes to reach Sakurajima. Oddities of Sakurajima include the fact that its rich soil produces the world's largest radishes, averaging about 37 pounds but sometimes weighing in at 80 pounds, and the world's smallest oranges, only 1.2 inches in diameter. There are walking paths through lava fields close to Sakurajima's ferry pier, but because Sakurajima is sparsely populated, with only limited public transportation, you might want to join a tour operated by Japan Railways that visits lava fields and lookouts around the volcano in 1 hour and 45 minutes. JR buses depart twice daily, at 9:30am and 1:30pm, from the ferry dock on Sakurajima. It would be prudent to check the departure times to make sure they haven't changed. Price of the tour is ¥1,700 ($12.15), but it's free if you have a Japan Rail Pass.

✪ Whereas Sakurajima, rising dramatically out of the bay, is Kagoshima's best-known landmark, **Iso Garden** (tel. 47-1551) is its most widely visited attraction. These gardens of the Shimazu clan, laid out more than 300 years ago, incorporated Sakurajima and Kinko Bay into the design scheme. Open daily from 8:30am to 5:30pm (5pm in winter), with an admission fee of ¥620 ($4.40), Iso Garden features a particularly idyllic spot where the 21st lord of the Shimazu family held famous poem-composing garden parties. Guests seated themselves on stones beside a gently meandering rivulet and were requested to have completed a poem by the time a cup filled with sake came drifting by on the tiny brook. Ah, those were the days!

Next to Iso Garden, and included in its entrance fee, is the **Shokoshuseikan Museum,** built in the mid-1850s as Japan's first modern factory. It houses about 300 items relating to the almost 700-year history of the Shimazu clan, including palanquins used to carry lords to Edo (present-day Tokyo), everyday items the family used, and photographs. I find the photographs showing the Shimazu family dressed in Western-style fashions particularly interesting. Iso Garden is located about 10 minutes by bus from Kagoshima Station and 30 minutes by bus from Nishi Kagoshima Station.

Another museum worth visiting is the **City Art Museum (Kagoshima Shiritsu Bijutsukan)** (tel. 24-3400), which has a collection of contemporary paintings by artists born in Kagoshima Prefecture, including Seiki Kuroda, Takeji Fujishima, and Wada Eisaku. A small selection of paintings by Western artists is also displayed, as well as pottery, glass, bronzes, and other works of art. The permanent exhibition is small, but special exhibitions are also held here. Open Tuesday through Sunday from 9am to 5pm; admission is ¥200 ($1.40). It's located in the heart of the city between the two train stations. The nearest streetcar stop is Asahi Dori. Only a few minutes' walk away from the City Art Museum, and with the same hours, is the **Kagoshima Prefectural Museum of Culture (Reimeikan)** (tel. 22-5100). One of the finest prefectural museums in the country, it was built on the former site of Tsurumaru Castle, of which only the moat remains. The museum traces the history of the people of Kagoshima over the last 40,000 years, with exhibits devoted to topography and natural history, archeological finds, and the society and culture of old Satsuma. Admission here is ¥250 ($1.80).

NEARBY ATTRACTIONS

If you have an extra morning or afternoon, I suggest taking an excursion to **Chiran,** a small village 19 miles south of Kagoshima. Surrounded by wooded hills and rows of neatly cultivated tea plantations, it's one of the 102 castle towns that once bordered the Shimazu kingdom during the Edo Period. Although the castle is no longer standing, six old gardens and samurai houses have been carefully preserved by descendants.

Apparently, the village headman of Chiran had the opportunity to travel with his lord Shimazu to Kyoto and Edo in the mid-1700s, taking along with him some of his

---

IMPRESSIONS

Ambiguity interests the Japanese a good deal more than does logic.
—D. J. ENRIGHT, *THE WORLD OF DEW,* 1955

local samurai as retainers. The headman and his retainers were so impressed with the sophisticated culture of Kyoto and Edo that they invited gardeners to Chiran to construct a series of gardens on the samurai estates surrounding the castle.

Some of these gardens remain intact, and are located on a delightful road called Samurai Lane, which is lined with moss-covered stone walls and hedges. Since descendants of the samurai are still living in the houses, only the gardens are open to the public. There are three types of gardens here: the miniature artificial hill style, in which a central pond symbolizes the sea and rocks the mountains; the "dry" garden, in which the sea is symbolized not by water but by white sand that is raked to give it rippling movements of water; and the "borrowed scenery" garden, in which surrounding mountains and scenery are incorporated into the general garden design. Although the gardens are small, they are exquisite and charming. Notice, for example, how the tops of hedges are cut to resemble rolling hills, blending with the shapes of mountains in the background.

The six gardens open to the public are indicated by a white marker in front of each entry gate. All six can be visited for ¥300 ($2.15), and it should take about an hour to see them all. Pay the entry fee for all six at the first garden you visit; you'll be given a pamphlet containing a map and a description of the gardens in English.

Chiran can be reached in about 75 minutes from Yamagataya Bus Station, next to the Yamagataya department store in downtown Kagoshima. Although Chiran is located midway between Ibusuki and Kagoshima, there are unfortunately no public buses going onward to Ibusuki. If you want to visit Chiran and continue on to Ibusuki, it's best to join one of the organized tours that depart from Kagoshima, stop briefly in Chiran, and end in Ibusuki. The cost of such a tour, conducted in Japanese only, is ¥3,590 ($25.65). Tour buses depart from Nishi Kagoshima Station at 10:10am and include stops at Lake Ikeda and Mt. Kaimon, at a thought-provoking museum dedicated to the kamikaze pilots of World War II, and at the Ibusuki Jungle Bath (part of the Ibusuki Kanko Hotel), in addition to the short walk through Chiran. The bus reaches the Ibusuki Jungle Bath at around 5pm, where you can soak at leisure—your tour ticket includes local bus transportation to Ibusuki Station, which you can use when you want.

WHERE TO STAY

Hotels in Kagoshima offer a good selection of dining for both Japanese and Western cuisine.

EXPENSIVE

SHIGETOMISO ㉕㊈, **31-7 Shimazu-cho, Kagoshima 890. Tel. 0992/47-3155.** 15 rms (all with bath). A/C MINIBAR TV TEL **Directions:** A 20-minute walk or 5-minute taxi ride from Kagoshima Station.

$ Rates (per person, including breakfast, dinner, and service): ¥22,000–¥40,000 ($157–$286). AE, DC, JCB, MC, V.

One of Kagoshima's most beautiful ryokan, this was once a villa for the ruling Shimazu clan. Spreading along a gentle slope of a hill in a profusion of flowering plants, with a garden and a waterfall, this enchanting ryokan overlooks the bay in a storybook setting. Its oldest rooms date from the 1820s, and through the decades a number of stories, myths, and legends have arisen to add to their mystique. One room, for example, is said to have belonged to the lord's mistress; here you can see a wooden pillar marred by tiny holes—apparently made by the mistress as she stabbed it with her hairpin out of frustration caused by the lord's too infrequent visits. Another room is colored a unique reddish tinge, derived from the blood of pigs brought from Okinawa. There's a closet where the clan could hide during attack, and the ceiling of one hallway was constructed deliberately low to thwart downward blows of enemy swords. In more recent history, the James Bond movie *You Only Live Twice* has a sequence filmed in one of the ryokan's rooms. In short, the whole ryokan is a museum in itself and contains antiques that once belonged to the Shimazu family. All rooms come with private bathroom, peace, and tranquillity. Highly recommended if you can afford it.

SHIROYAMA KANKO HOTEL, 41-1 Shinshoin-cho, Kagoshima 890. Tel. 0992/24-2211. Fax 0992/24-2222. 496 rms. A/C MINIBAR TV TEL **Directions:** A 15-minute taxi ride from either Nishi Kagoshima Station or Kagoshima Station.

$ Rates: ¥10,000 ($71) single; ¥15,000 ($107) double; ¥17,500 ($125) twin. AE, DC, JCB, MC, V.

Kagoshima's foremost hotel, the Shiroyama Kanko Hotel sits 353 feet high atop the wood-covered Shiroyama Hill and commands a fine view of the city below and Sakurajima across the bay. Rooms are pleasant and comfortable, although the singles are slightly small. The best rooms face the volcano.

Dining/Entertainment: The Sky Lounge on the seventh floor features seafood and steaks, along with a great view of the city and Sakurajima. In addition to Japanese and Chinese restaurants, there's also a pleasant outdoor beer garden that is open during the summer months.

Facilities: Indoor swimming pool and sauna (free for guests), fitness gym, souvenir shops (selling such locally made products as silk pongee, Satsuma pottery, yaku cedar, and confectioneries), art gallery, bakery, beauty salon, travel agency.

MODERATE

Unless otherwise stated, all hotels in this category have private bathroom.

KAGOSHIMA HAYASHIDA HOTEL, 12-22 Higashisengoku-cho, Kagoshima 892. Tel. 0992/24-4111. Fax 0992/24-4553. 198 rms. A/C MINIBAR TV TEL **Directions:** A 10-minute walk from either Nishi Kagoshima or Kagoshima Station. **Streetcar:** Tenmonkan-Dori stop, a 1-minute walk away.

$ Rates: ¥8,500 ($61) single; ¥12,000 ($86) double; ¥14,000 ($100) twin. AE, DC, JCB, MC, V.

Located right in the heart of downtown near the Tenmonkan-Dori arcade, this hotel follows what appears to be a Space Age theme. It's built around an inner garden atrium called Space Garden, and the inside guest rooms possess views of the atrium through one-way mirrors. Although these rooms facing the inside tend to be dark, they're much quieter than those facing the outside streets. Rooms are small but of modern design, and are equipped with TV, clock, and radio.

Inside the Space Garden, with its sunroof, plants, and trees, are four restaurants serving Japanese, Cantonese, French, and Western cuisine. Meals average about ¥3,000 ($21.40) and up, and daily hours are 11am to 2:30pm to 5 to 10pm. A Filipino band performs in the center of the atrium in the summer.

KAGOSHIMA SUN ROYAL HOTEL, 1-8-10 Yojiro, Kagoshima 890. Tel. 0992/53-2020. Fax 0992/55-0186. 304 rms (260 with bath). A/C MINIBAR TV TEL **Bus:** 16 from Nishi Kagoshima Station (ask driver to tell you where to get off).

$ Rates: ¥5,300 ($38) single without bath, ¥8,200 ($58) single with bath; ¥9,500 ($68) twin without bath, ¥16,500 ($118) twin with bath; ¥19,000 ($136) double. Japanese-style rooms: ¥18,000 ($128). AE, JCB, MC, V.

This hotel is located in a new section of town with modern buildings and wide avenues called Kamaoike. Its only drawback is that it's a bit far from the center, but city buses departing from Nishi Kagoshima reach the hotel in 20 minutes. Its rooms come with TV with pay video, clock, music, and minibar, and all the double, twin, and Japanese-style rooms face the sea and have a balcony. Singles face only inland and do not have a balcony; the cheapest singles come without bathtub or shower but with toilet and sink. I personally prefer the Japanese-style rooms with their tatami sitting alcoves beside the balcony. There's a great *onsen* (hot-spring bath) on the 13th floor, separated for men and women. You can look out over Mt. Sakurajima as you bathe. Restaurants include the Phoenix Sky Lounge on the 13th floor, serving Western food and boasting a view of the sea, and a Japanese restaurant where kaiseki and local dishes are served for about ¥2,500 to ¥6,000 ($17.85 to $42.85).

KAGOSHIMA TOKYU HOTEL, 22-1 Kamoike Shinmachi, Kagoshima 890. Tel. 0992/57-2411. Fax 0992/57-6083. 206 rms. A/C MINIBAR TV TEL **Bus:** 10 from Nishi Kagoshima Station to Noukyo Kaikan-mae stop.

$ Rates: ¥7,900–¥10,000 ($56–$71) single; ¥15,000–¥21,000 ($107–$150) twin; ¥17,500 ($125) double. AE, DC, JCB, MC, V.

This first-rate medium-priced hotel, also located in the new section of town, Kamoike, is built right on the waterfront, with a good view of the volcano. Its twins and doubles face the water, and each has a veranda, great for sitting out in the morning and watching the sun rise over Sakurajima. Singles (without balcony) all face inland. There's an outdoor swimming pool open during the warmer months (usually from about May to September) and an outdoor Jacuzzi, fed by natural hot springs and open year round.

The hotel's Japanese restaurant, Yamabuki, serves tempura, sashimi, and local dishes; its Western restaurant, Hibiscus, serves steak, lobster, sandwiches, curries, and pilaf. If you're in the mood for teppanyaki steak, try the hotel's Steak House Fresia, where the chef prepares your food before your very eyes.

BUDGET

BUSINESS HOTEL GASTHOF, 7-3 Chuo-cho, Kagoshima 890. Tel. 0992/ 52-1401. 56 rms (all with bath). A/C TV TEL **Directions:** A 3-minute walk from Nishi Kagoshima Station.

$ Rates (including tax and service): ¥6,300 ($45) single; ¥7,500 ($53) double; ¥9,300 ($66) twin; ¥13,000 ($93) triple. Breakfast ¥700–¥1,000 ($5–$7.15). No credit cards.

Although it looks rather uninteresting from the outside, the lobby of this inexpensive hotel is quite another story. It reminds me of some forgotten pawnshop, with its glass cases packed with antiques (some several centuries old), old knives, ceramics, and pottery, as well as its fish tanks. More likely than not, three small dogs will greet you from atop the check-in counter. None of the stuff is for sale—it's all there simply for your viewing pleasure. The rooms are very basic and a bit worn, but they're adequate; and the location is convenient.

HIRAYAMA RYOKAN ㉟, 6-7 Meizancho, Kagoshima 890. Tel. 0992/ 22-4489. 18 rms (none with bath). A/C TV TEL **Directions:** A 5-minute walk from Kagoshima Station.

$ Rates (per person): ¥3,800 ($27) without meals; ¥4,700 ($33) with breakfast; ¥6,500 ($46) with breakfast and dinner. No credit cards.

This is a Japanese-style business hotel, which means that its accommodations are all tatami rooms rather than bedrooms. The building is old and the hallways could use a good vacuuming, but the tatami rooms are fine and come with coin-operated TV and air conditioning. Meals are Japanese and are served in a dining hall. The people running the place are pleasant and understand some English.

NAKAZONO RYOKAN, 1-18 Yasui-cho, Kagoshima 892. Tel. 0992/26-5125. 15 rms (none with bath). A/C TV. **Directions:** A 7-minute walk from Kagoshima Station. **Streetcar:** Shiyakusho-mae stop, from which it's a 1-minute walk.

$ Rates (including tax and service): ¥4,400 ($31) single; ¥8,300 ($59) double; ¥11,500 ($82) twin. Breakfast ¥1,000–¥1,500 ($7.15–$10.70); dinner ¥2,500 ($17.85). AE.

A member of the Japanese Inn Group, this simple ryokan has a convenient location and offers laundry facilities and tatami rooms with coin-operated TV. Some rooms have a refrigerator. For guests who are interested, a tea ceremony is available in the ryokan's tearoom.

PARK HOTEL ㉠, 15-24 Chuo-cho, Kagoshima 890. Tel. 0992/51-1100. 70 rms (all with bath). A/C TV TEL **Directions:** A 2-minute walk from Nishi Kagoshima Station.

$ Rates (including tax and service): ¥6,500 ($46) single; ¥10,000 ($71) double; ¥11,000 ($78) twin. AE, DC, JCB, V.

A number of business hotels have opened in Kagoshima in the past few years, most of them located close to Nishi Kagoshima Station. The Park Hotel is one of these. All of its rooms are Western style and come with semidouble-size beds, TV with adult videos, windows that can be opened, hot water for tea, and, for a business hotel, an uncommonly large bathroom. All but 12 of its rooms are singles. There are six doubles and six twins. Its one restaurant serves both Western and Japanese food, with selections including shabu-shabu, obento lunch boxes, spaghetti, sirloin steak, and hamburger steak.

STATION HOTEL NEW KAGOSHIMA, 6-5 Chuo-cho, Kagoshima 890. Tel. 0992/53-5353. Fax 0992/52-3882. 210 rms (all with bath). A/C TV TEL
   Directions: A 2-minute walk from Nishi Kagoshima Station.
$ Rates (including tax and service charge): ¥5,700 ($41) single; ¥10,000 ($71) double/twin. Japanese-style rooms: ¥11,000 ($78) double occupancy. AE, DC, JCB, V.
The rooms here are basic but adequate. Eight Japanese-style rooms are available. A restaurant on the eighth floor called Star Dust serves both Japanese and Western food; there's also a Chinese restaurant. The ninth floor boasts a beer garden (open in summer).

Youth Hostel

SAKURAJIMA YOUTH HOSTEL ㉖①, Hakama-goshi, Kagoshima 891-14. Tel. 0992/93-2150. 100 beds. A/C **Directions:** A 5-minute walk from ferry pier on Sakurajima.
$ Rates (per person): ¥1,850 ($13.20) member and nonmember. Heating and air-conditioning charges ¥200 ($1.40) extra. Breakfast ¥410 ($2.90); dinner ¥620 ($4.40). No credit cards.
This youth hostel is on the slope of the Sakurajima volcano, making it a great place for a holiday. There's a sports facility and public hot springs near the hostel, and if you're really adventurous, you can even bathe in the sea. There are laundry facilities.

WHERE TO DINE

While in Kagoshima, be sure to try its local dishes, known as Satsuma cooking (Satsuma was the original name of the Kagoshima area). This style of cooking supposedly has its origins in food cooked on battlefields centuries ago, but if that's the case I'm sure it's improved greatly since then.

MODERATE

KUMASOTEI ㉖②, 6-10 Higashisengoku-cho. Tel. 22-6356.
   Cuisine: LOCAL SPECIALTIES. **Streetcar:** Tenmonkan-Dori stop, a 5-minute walk away.
$ Prices: Satsuma set courses ¥4,500–¥6,000 ($32.15–$42.85); kaiseki set dinner ¥4,000 ($28.55); kaiseki lunch ¥2,200 ($15.70). AE, DC, JCB, MC, V.
   Open: Lunch daily 11am–2:30pm; dinner daily 5–10pm.
A good place to try local Satsuma dishes is at this well-known restaurant, located in the center of town between Nishi Kagoshima and Kagoshima stations. It reminds me more of a private home or ryokan, since dining is in individual tatami rooms. If there isn't a crowd, you'll probably have your own private room; otherwise, you'll share. The main menu is in Japanese, but there's a smaller menu in English that features Satsuma specialties, including *Satsuma-age* (ground fish that has been deep-fried), *torisashi* (raw chicken, and not as bad as it sounds), *tonkotsu* (pork that has been boiled for several hours in shochu and brown sugar—absolutely delicious), *zakezushi* (rice that has been soaked in sake all day and then mixed with such things as vegetables and shrimp), bonito baked with salt, *awameshi* (rice mixed with wheat and undoubtedly very healthy), and *Satsume-jiru* (miso soup with chicken and locally grown vegetables). *Kibinago* is a small fish belonging to the herring family caught in

the waters around Kagoshima. A silver color with brown stripes, it is often eaten raw—arranged on a dish so that it looks like a chrysanthemum. This restaurant also serves kaiseki.

SKY LOUNGE, 7th floor of Shiroyama Kanko Hotel, 41-1 Shinshoin-cho. Tel. 0992/24-2211.
   Cuisine: WESTERN. **Directions:** A 15-minute taxi ride from Nishi Kagoshima Station or Kagoshima Station.
$ Prices: Main dishes ¥1,500–¥3,500 ($10.70–$25); set-dinner courses ¥5,500–¥8,000 ($39.30–$57.15); set lunch ¥2,000 ($14.30). AE, DC, JCB, MC, V.
   Open: Daily 11am–11:30pm.

For Western dining with a view, you can't beat this restaurant, located high above the city atop the Shiroyama Kanko Hotel. It's especially wonderful at dusk as the lights come on below and Sakurajima slowly fades into darkness. The restaurant's à la carte selections include fried or grilled shrimp, sole filet, lobster thermidor, green-pepper steak, veal cutlet, spaghetti, and sandwiches. There are also set meals available for both lunch and dinner.

BUDGET

NOBORUYA ㉓, 2-15 Horie-cho. Tel. 26-6690.
   Cuisine: RAMEN NOODLES. **Directions:** A 15-minute walk from Kagoshima Station or Nishi Kagoshima Station.
$ Prices: Noodles ¥900 ($6.45). No credit cards.
   Open: Mon–Sat 11am–7pm.

★ This popular and inexpensive restaurant in the center of town is Kagoshima's best-known ramen, or noodle, shop. Since only one dish is served, there's no problem ordering. A big bowl of ramen comes with noodles (made fresh every day) and slices of pork, and is seasoned with garlic. You also get pickled radish (supposedly good for the stomach) and tea. As you eat your ramen at the counter, you can watch women peeling garlic and cooking huge pots of noodles over gas flames. A great place to soak in local atmosphere.

SATSUMA ㉔, 10-4 Chuo-chu. Tel. 52-2661.
   Cuisine: LOCAL SPECIALTIES. **Directions:** Across street from Nishi Kagoshima Station.
$ Prices: ¥500–¥1,000 ($3.55–$7.15); set meals ¥600–¥2,750 ($4.30–$19.65). No credit cards.
   Open: Lunch Tues–Sun 10am–3pm; dinner Tues–Sun 5:30–10pm.

This tiny, modestly priced restaurant serving Satsuma food has a large red lantern and white curtains outside its door. A cozy and wonderfully cluttered establishment, it has room for only about 10 people on its ground floor and another 10 people on its second floor. Featured, as at Kumasotei (above), are torisashi, kibinago, Satsuma-jiru soup, Satsuma-age, and tonkotsu.

SHOPPING

If you're interested in shopping in Kagoshima, local products include *oshima pongee*, Japanese silk made into such items as clothing, handbags, and wallets; shochu, an alcoholic drink made from such ingredients as sweet potatoes and drunk either cold on the rocks or mixed with boiling water; furniture, statues, and chests made from *yaku* cedar; and Satsuma pottery—probably Kagoshima's most famous product. It's been produced in the Kagoshima area for more than 380 years, first by Korean potters brought here to practice their trade. Satsuma pottery comes in two styles, black and white. White Satsuma pottery is more elegant and was used by former lords; the black pottery, on the other hand, was used by the townspeople in everyday life.

   In Kagoshima's downtown area are several department stores—Yamagataya, Mitsukoshi, and Takashimaya—where you can shop for local products. There are also souvenir shops in the downtown area, including a covered shopping arcade called Tenmonkan-Dori.

Another good place to shop for local items is the **Display Hall of Kagoshima Products** in the Sangyo Kaikan Building, 9-1 Meizancho (tel. 25-6120). Open Monday through Friday from 8:30am to 5pm and on Saturday until 12:30pm, this one-room shop is located in Kagoshima's downtown and sells such goods as tinware, handmade knives, Satsuma pottery, glassware, oshima pongee, yaku cedar, shochu, and other items from Kagoshima Prefecture.

There are many Satsuma pottery factories in the Kagoshima area. Most easily accessible is **Kinko Togei 298,** 2-2-3 Taniyamako (tel. 61-1019), where you can observe production of Satsuma pottery and make purchases from its showroom. The factory will ship or airmail your purchases home. Open daily from 8:30am to 5:15pm, it can be reached by train or tram from Nishi Kagoshima Station. If you're going by train, get off at Sakanoue Station; from there it's either a 20-minute walk or a 5-minute taxi ride. If you want to go by streetcar, get off at Taniyama Station; from there it's a 10-minute taxi ride.

8. IBUSUKI

31 miles S of Kagoshima

GETTING THERE **By Train** It takes 1 hour from Kagoshima by train.

By Bus It takes 1½ hours by bus from Kagoshima's Yamagataya Bus Center in the heart of the city, near Asahi Dori tram stop. You can also join a sightseeing bus tour from Kagoshima, with stops in Chiran and other points along the way. See the Kagoshima section for more information.

ESSENTIAL INFORMATION The area code for Ibusuki, lying in Kagoshima Prefecture, is 0993.

Be sure to get the leaflet *Southern Kyushu* from the Tourist Information Center in Tokyo or Kyoto.

Upon arrival in Ibusuki, stop by the **tourist information counter** (tel. 0993/22-4114) at Ibusuki Station to pick up a map in Japanese with some English on it. There's also an English brochure available with a brief rundown of sightseeing attractions in the area around Ibusuki. The information counter is open daily from 9am to 7:30pm.

At the southern tip of the Satsuma Peninsula, Ibusuki (pronounced "*ee*-boo-ski") is southern Kyushu's most famous hot-spring resort. With a pleasant average temperature of 64.5°F, it's a region of lush vegetation, flowers, and palm trees—and of course, hot springs.

The town of Ibusuki is spread along the coast, and there are public buses that run through the main streets. The town isn't large, and taxis are readily available.

WHAT TO SEE & DO

The most popular thing to do is to have yourself buried up to your neck in hot black sand, and the best place to do this is at **Surigahama Public Beach,** located about 5 minutes from Ibusuki Station by bus. After paying ¥510 ($3.65), you'll be supplied with a yukata cotton kimono and towel. Change into the yukata in the changing room and then walk down to the beach. One of the women there will dig you a shallow grave. Lie down, arrange your yukata so that no vulnerable areas are left exposed, and then lie still while she piles sand on top of you. It's quite a funny sight, actually, to see nothing but heads sticking out of the ground. Bodies are heated by hot springs that surface close to the ground before running into the sea. It's best to go when the tide is low so you can get closer to the sea. The water is alkali saline, a hot 185°F, and helps in gastroenteric troubles, neuralgia, and female disorders. After your sand bath, go indoors for a hot-spring bath. The Surigahama sand baths are open every day from 8:30am to 9pm (8pm in winter).

Other hot-spring and sand baths are found in the spa hotels spread along Ibusuki's

6-mile-long beach. The biggest indoor baths are the **Ibusuki Kanko Hotel's Jungle Bath,** a huge affair with pools of various shapes and sizes surrounded by tropical plants. If you've been to Beppu's Suginoi Palace baths, however, this one may be somewhat of a letdown. The women's baths are much smaller than the men's, although no one objects if women want to use the men's baths instead. Use of the Jungle Bath is free to hotel guests; all others must pay a ¥620 ($4.40) entrance fee. There are also indoor hot-sand baths here, for which everyone (including hotel guests) must pay an extra ¥1,030 ($7.35). To visit the area surrounding Ibusuki, it's best to either join a tour group (conducted in Japanese only) or rent a car. Public bus lines are neither extensive nor frequent. Popular destinations include **Nagasakibana Point,** Kyushu's southernmost point and the location of a bird and animal park with variety shows; and **Lake Ikeda,** Kyushu's largest lake. It has a depth of 820 feet, not to mention gigantic eels. Some of these eels weigh 33 pounds and measure about 6 feet in length. If you're interested in seeing these creatures, souvenir shops and stops along the lake have some on display in big tanks.

Another destination is **Kaimon Natural Park,** located at the foot of Mt. Kaimon. There's a rest house here serving snacks and inexpensive food, and an 18-hole golf course. Greens fees are ¥13,000 ($92.85) on weekdays, ¥20,000 ($142.85) on Saturday, and ¥21,000 ($150) on Sunday and holidays. Now you know why golf in Japan is a luxury sport. For more information on golfing, call the golf course at 32-3141.

WHERE TO STAY

Most of Ibusuki's hotels and ryokan are located along its 6-mile beach. Because this is a resort area, accommodations are more expensive than in the cities.

EXPENSIVE

HOTEL HAKUSUIKAN ㉖, **Tarahama-kaigon, Ibusuki 891-04. Tel. 0993/ 22-3131.** 210 rms (182 with bath, 28 with toilet only). A/C MINIBAR TV TEL
Directions: A 5-minute taxi ride from Ibusuki Station.
$ Rates (per person, including breakfast, dinner, and service charge): ¥14,000–¥38,000 ($100–$271). AE, DC, JCB, MC, V.
A long driveway lined with pine trees sets the mood for this modern and elegant Japanese-style inn on the beach. Its resortlike setting is further enhanced by two swimming pools, an indoor hot-sand bath, an outdoor beer garden (open in summer), a bar, a practice golf course, and a beautifully constructed outdoor hot spring, with separate areas for men and women. Although the majority of rooms are Japanese-style tatami rooms, there are also 40 Western-style twins and 71 combination rooms with both beds and separate tatami areas. All rooms face the sea. The best rooms have their own balcony and a Japanese-style deep tub made of hinoki cypress, while the least expensive rooms are in an older building and come with toilet only. Breakfasts are Western-style buffets. This is a very pleasant place to stay and a perfect getaway.

IBUSUKI KANKO HOTEL, 3755 Juni-cho, Ibusuki 891-04. Tel. 0993/22-2131. Fax 0993/24-3215. 627 rms (554 with bath). A/C MINIBAR TV TEL
Directions: A 5-minute taxi ride from Ibusuki Station.
$ Rates: ¥13,000–¥22,000 ($93–$157) double or single in Western-style room with bath. Japanese-style rooms: ¥11,000 ($78) double occupancy without bath; ¥17,000 ($121) with bath. AE, DC, JCB, MC, V.
This is Ibusuki's best-known spa hotel, a self-contained resort on 125 acres of lush tropical grounds with pleasant walking trails throughout. The hotel is very popular with Japanese tour groups, both for its huge Jungle Bath with various baths and pools and its evening entertainment. The hotel tries to imitate a Hawaiian resort—the staff even wears Hawaiian shirts to help create the mood.
The hotel has 460 Western-style twin rooms (there are no singles), all with bathroom, and 167 Japanese tatami rooms with and without bath. All the rooms have either a full or partial view of the sea and come with their own balcony—the best rooms in my opinion are the ones that also have views of the wonderful garden. The

Japanese-style rooms are located in an older building with a less magnificent view. Nights at the Kanko Hotel are nice, with the sound of the waves and of the frogs croaking in the lotus pond.

Dining/Entertainment: The hotel has nine food-and-beverage outlets. For Western dining, try the Sky Lounge on the 10th floor, with a panoramic view of the water; it's open daily from 7am to 11:30pm. The average dinner costs about ¥6,000 ($42.85). The Japanese restaurant, Okonomi, serves tempura, sushi, and local dishes.

A particularly entertaining place to dine is the Jungle Park Restaurant Theater, a huge dinner theater featuring live variety shows usually from—you guessed it—Hawaii. The Japanese guests show up in outfits provided in the hotel rooms—blue-flowered pajamalike shirts and shorts for the men and pink-flowered shifts for the women. If you really want to join in the fun, wear the same. The food is Japanese barbecue style, and you cook your thin slices of beef and vegetables at your table on a hot griddle over a gas flame. Dinner begins at ¥4,500 ($32.15), and showtime is 6:30 to 8pm.

Another dinnertime show, the Mexican Acapulco Diving Show, features platform divers from Mexico who plunge more than 100 feet through the air into the sea. Diners watch the spectacle from a glass-enclosed restaurant/theater right on the beach, and the price here is also ¥4,500 ($32.15) for the show and dinner.

Facilities: Outdoor swimming pools, tennis courts, bowling arcade, shopping arcade, private beach, and huge hot-spring baths (described above). The hotel even has a delightful small art museum called the Iwasaki Museum of Art, and the collection contains French and Japanese paintings by such artists as Henri Matisse, Seiki Kuroda, and Takeji Fujishima. Next to the art museum is a newly opened museum featuring art and antiques from Japan and China, including cloisonné, ivory, and ceramics. The museums are open daily from 8am to 6pm and are in themselves worth a trip to the Kanko Hotel.

SHUSUIEN ㊥, **5-27-27 Yunohama, Ibusuki 891-04. Tel. 0993/23-4141.** 41 rms (all with bath). A/C MINIBAR TV TEL **Directions:** A 5-minute taxi ride from Ibusuki Station.

$ Rates (per person, including breakfast, dinner, and service): ¥20,000–¥63,000 ($143–$450). DC, JCB, MC, V.

✪ If you want to stay in a ryokan, Shusuien is renowned both for its excellent service and its cuisine. In annual competitions held by Japanese travel agencies in which 100 top accommodations are rated, Shusuien has consistently won first prize for its cooking and third for its service. Although small, it employs a staff of 120. This is a good place to stay if you want to be pampered and don't want to spend your holidays with group tours of jovial vacationers. The most expensive rooms face the sea, have their own balcony, and are higher up. The less expensive rooms face inland and have no balcony. Needless to say, this ryokan is elegant yet refined in its setting. Used to foreign businessmen, it serves Western-style breakfasts on request.

Dining/Entertainment: It has one bar and one restaurant, Shimazu-han, where you can try its award-winning cuisine even if you don't stay here.

Services: Free newspaper.

Facilities: Shopping arcade.

MODERATE

HOTEL KAIRAKUEN, 5-26-4 Yunohama, Ibusuki 891-04. Tel. 0993/22-3121. 61 rms (all with bath). A/C TV **Directions:** A 20-minute walk or a 5-minute taxi ride from Ibusuki Station.

$ Rates (per person, including breakfast, dinner, and service): ¥8,000–¥16,000 ($57–$114). JCB.

This inexpensive combination hotel-ryokan is located right next to the Surigahama sand baths on the beach. The majority of its rooms are Japanese-style tatami rooms, though there are also two Western-style rooms and four combination rooms with both beds and tatami areas. Although the hotel's building is old and a bit run-down, the price is right. The best rooms are those that face the sea, and the absolute best room is no. 408, which is located on a corner of the building; it has lots of windows and features both beds and a tatami area, making it perfect for families. All rooms have a private bath that features water directly from the hot springs, and rooms facing the sea have a window above the tub so you can look out on the water as you bathe. Dinner is served in your room, while Japanese breakfasts are served in a communal dining area.

BUDGET

IBUSUKI KOKUMIN KYUKA-SON ㉗, Higashikata, Shiomi-cho, Ibusuki 891-04. Tel. 0993/22-3211. 65 rms (7 with bath, 58 with toilet only). A/C TV TEL **Bus:** Shuttle buses depart from in front of Ibusuki Station after every train arrival. **Directions:** A 10-minute taxi ride from Ibusuki Station.

$ Rates (per person): ¥4,900 ($35) without meals or bath; ¥7,300 ($52) without bath but with breakfast and dinner; ¥8,800 ($63) with bath, breakfast and dinner. No credit cards.

This National People's Village is located right at the water's edge and offers reasonably priced accommodations. Tennis courts, rental bikes, and hot-spring baths make this a very popular place to stay, especially during the summer vacation months of July and August, on New Year's, in March during spring vacation, and in May during school trips. Otherwise, you can probably get a room here. Rooms are basic, and some that face the sea even have a balcony. Eight of the rooms are Western style. You can reach the village by the village's own bus, recognizable by three circles of green, red, and blue, which is the symbol of National People's Villages.

MARUTOMI ㉘, 5-24-15 Yunohama, Ibusuki 891-04. Tel. 0993/22-5579. 7 rms (none with bath). A/C TV **Directions:** A 5-minute taxi ride from Ibusuki Station.

$ Rates (per person, including breakfast and dinner): ¥5,500 ($39). No credit cards.

Located close to the Surigahama sand baths, on a tiny road that leads inland just across the street from the baths, this inexpensive establishment is a family-run minshuku, and since the owner here is a fisherman, you can count on fresh seafood. The rooms are all Japanese style and feature chips of camphor wood, which give the rooms a pleasant outdoor smell. There's a coin-operated laundry machine and a small tiled bathtub with water from a hot spring.

WHERE TO DINE

SHIMAZU-HAN, Hotel Shusuien, 5-27-27 Yunohama. Tel. 23-4141.
  Cuisine: JAPANESE. **Reservations:** Recommended. **Directions:** A 5-minute taxi ride from Ibusuki Station.
$ Prices: Set-dinner courses ¥2,700–¥6,000 ($19.30–$42.85); set lunches ¥1,600–¥4,000 ($11.45–$28.55). DC, JCB, MC, V.
  Open: Lunch daily noon–2pm; dinner daily 6–11pm.

This is probably the best place in town to have lunch. In fact, Japanese visitors staying in other ryokan in Ibusuki will request room-only rates so that they can enjoy dinner here at the award-winning Shimazu-han. Although the food served in its restaurant is not as extensive or expensive as that served to its ryokan guests, meals here are a pleasure, served in eight private tatami rooms on plates that have been chosen with care to match both the seasons and the food displayed. Dishes are served in courses rather than all at once, and start at ¥1,600 ($11.45) for lunch. Although the menu is in Japanese only, there are photos for each course. The most popular set meal is the Shimazu Gozen for ¥3,500 ($25), which includes sashimi, tempura, fish, soup, egg custard, vegetables, rice, and other dishes. Be sure to order a cup of plum shochu (*ume shu*)—it's the best shochu I've ever had.

AOBA ㉙, 1-2-11 Minato. Tel. 22-3356.
  Cuisine: VARIED JAPANESE. **Directions:** A 1-minute walk from Ibusuki Station.
$ Prices: ¥400–¥1,200 ($2.85–$8.55). No credit cards.
  Open: Daily 11am–9:30pm.
For an inexpensive meal near Ibusuki Station, take a left out of the station and look for

a small shop on the main street with white curtains over its door and a display of plastic food. This pleasant and informal eatery offers tempura, eel, local specialties, noodles, and more, with both table and tatami seating available. There's a lunch teishoku offered until 2pm for ¥1,100 ($7.85).

CHOZYUAN Ⓐ⃝ **, Kaimon-cho, Tosenkyo. Tel. 22-3155.**
   Cuisine: SOMEN NOODLES. **Bus:** Eight departures daily from Ibusuki Station (a 30-minute ride).
$ **Prices:** Noodles ¥500 ($3.55). No credit cards.
   Open: Daily May–June 10am–7pm, July–Aug 10am–9pm, Sept–Apr 10am–5pm.

★ If you're adventurous, this is a fun restaurant in the countryside. Serving as a lunch stop for some of the organized tours of the area (including the Kagoshima-to-Ibusuki bus tour described in the previous section), it specializes in somen, or cold noodles. Seating is under a pavilion beside a man-made waterfall, so you eat to the accompaniment of running water and Japanese traditional music playing in the background. In the middle of your table is a large round container with water swirling around in a circle. When you get your basket of noodles, dump them into the cold water; then fish them out with your chopsticks, dip them in soy sauce, and enjoy. There are also four set menus starting at ¥1,100 ($7.85), which come with such things as grilled trout, vegetables, and soup. You can also try carp sashimi. Be sure to keep the wrapper your chopsticks came in—it's a souvenir bookmark.

9. MIYAZAKI

897 miles SW of Tokyo; 252 miles SE of Fukuoka; 78 miles W of Kagoshima

GETTING THERE **By Plane** 1½ hours from Tokyo, then a 15-minute ride to the center of town.

By Train From Tokyo, take the Shinkansen bullet train to Kokura, transferring there to a limited express (trip time: approximately 11 hr.). There are direct trains from Hakata Station in Fukuoka (trip time: about 7 hr.), Beppu (trip time: 3 hr., 45 min.); and Kagoshima (trip time: 3 hr.).

By Bus Eight buses depart daily from Fukuoka for Miyazaki (trip time: almost 5 hr.).

ESSENTIAL INFORMATION The **area code** for Miyazaki, lying in Miyazaki Prefecture, is 0985.
   Before leaving Tokyo or Kyoto, be sure to pick up the leaflet *Miyazaki and Vicinity* at the Tourist Information Center.
   For a map of the city in English, stop off at the **tourist information center** at either the airport or JR Miyazaki Station. The airport office is open daily from 7:30am to 8:30pm, while the train station information center is open daily from 9am to 5:30pm.
   For detailed information on Miyazaki Prefecture, drop by the **prefectural tourist office** (called *kanko kyokai* in Japanese), located just off Tachibana-dori Street at 2-7-18 Tachibanadori (tel. 0985/25-4676). Open Monday through Friday from 8:30am to 5pm and on Saturday from 8:30am to 12:30pm, it has information on Aya, Aoshima, Udo Shrine, and other attractions.

With a population of 280,000, Miyazaki is one of the largest and most important cities in southern Kyushu and serves as the government seat of Miyazaki Prefecture. Yet Miyazaki feels isolated and somewhat neglected by the rest of Japan. Tokyo seems far away, and most foreigners who happen to land at Kagoshima's international airport tend to head north for Kumamoto, missing Miyazaki altogether. Japanese honeymooners, who used to favor Miyazaki over most other domestic destinations a decade ago, are now flocking to the shores of Hawaii and Australia.

And yet Miyazaki is a perfect place to relax, swim in the Pacific Ocean, get in some rounds of golf, and savor some of the local delicacies. Temperatures here are the second warmest in Japan, after Okinawa, and flowers bloom throughout the year. You won't see many foreigners here, and the natives will treat you warmly and kindly. If you want to unwind and pamper yourself for a few days, Miyazaki is a good place to do it. And if you have the energy for sightseeing, Miyazaki Prefecture offers some historical and natural attractions.

The main street in town is Tachibana-dori Street, lined with shops, department stores, and restaurants. Many buses serving other parts of town, as well as Miyazaki Prefecture, make stops along this main thoroughfare. There's also a large bus terminal south of the Oyodo River close to Minami Miyazaki Station.

WHAT TO SEE & DO

Although all of the sights listed below are accessible by public transportation, they are quite spread out. You may, therefore, want to join an organized tour, even though it will be conducted in Japanese only. At least it gets you to each destination and you won't have to worry about time schedules and bus stops. A tour operated by Miyazaki Kotsu Bus Company that departs at 8:50am daily from the bus terminal near Minami Miyazaki Station visits Miyazaki Shrine, Heiwadai Park, an amusement park for children, Aoshima Island, Horikiri Pass, Cactus Park, and Udo Shrine. The tour lasts 7 hours and costs ¥4,630 ($33.05).

The most important shrine in town is **Miyazaki Shrine,** dedicated to the first emperor of Japan, Emperor Jimmu, who was the first leader of the Yamoto courts. Peacefully surrounded by woods and cedar trees and about a 15-minute bus ride from Tachibana-dori Street, the shrine is austerely plain and is built from cedar. Be sure to visit the nearby **Miyazaki Prefectural Museum (Miyazaki-ken Sogo Hakubutsukan),** open Tuesday through Sunday from 8:30am to 5pm. It houses collections of ancient clay images, stone implements, ancient pottery, and folkloric items.

Archeological digs in Miyazaki Prefecture have unearthed a multitude of ancient burial mounds and clay figures known as *haniwa.* Replicas of these ancient mounds and haniwa clay figures can be seen in **Haniwa Garden,** most easily reached by taxi in about 15 minutes from Miyazaki Station. Approximately 400 of these clay figures have been placed between trees on mounds covered with moss. I especially like the haniwa with the simple face and body and the O-shaped mouth; it's said to represent a dancing woman. A one-room exhibition house displays some items found in ancient burial mounds, and if you want you can buy a small clay replica to take home with you.

Haniwa Garden is located in a large park called Heiwadai Park, in which you'll also find the **Tower of Peace.** Having a pedestal built with stones donated from countries around the world, it was constructed with the help of volunteers and was finished—ironically enough—in 1940.

If you want to see real burial mounds, head for Saitobaru, where there are more than 300 5th- and 6th-century tombs. Most of the mounds are now covered with grass and trees, so there isn't a lot to see. There is, however, the **Saitobaru Museum,** which displays excavated swords, mirrors, bead jewelry, clay pots, stone coffins, tools, and haniwa. The haniwa were buried along with deceased lords to symbolize court retainers who would serve him after death. There are also scale models of several of the burial mounds, including models of the two largest mounds, where the emperor's ancestors were buried. Saitobaru can be reached in about an hour by bus from the bus terminal near Minami Miyazaki Station or from downtown.

Also an hour's bus ride from Miyazaki is **Aya,** a village of about 7,300 people known for its production of traditional handcrafts. It boasts five kilns, a glass-blowing factory, at least a dozen wood-carving shops, two bamboo-craft makers, and three weaving shops. A recently constructed crafts center displays and sells the products of these establishments.

Next to the crafts center is **Aya Castle,** a reproduction of the original Aya Castle built 650 years ago. Made of fir trees, the castle is tiny compared to most in Japan and contains a few artifacts, such as samurai uniforms and swords. Because both the castle and the crafts center are small and located an hour away from Miyazaki, I suggest you visit Aya only if you have a special interest in crafts or have no other chance to see a Japanese castle. Both the center and castle are located about a 10-minute walk from the center of Aya town on top of a peaceful wooded hill. Hours are 9am to 5pm daily; the entrance fee is ¥310 ($2.20).

One of the most famous sights associated with Miyazaki is **Aoshima,** a tiny island less than a mile in circumference and connected to the mainland via a walkway. Although Aoshima is located about 25 minutes south by train from Miyazaki Station, it's considered part of Miyazaki city. There's a small shrine on the island, and the beaches nearby are the most popular among the people of Miyazaki for swimming in July and August.

If you follow the coast from Aoshima farther south, you'll come to **Nichinan Coast,** famous for its eroded, rippling waves of rock, said to resemble a washboard. There's a local bus from Miyazaki that travels along this beautiful coastline (and passes through Aoshima), going all the way to Udo in about 1½ hours (the name of the bus stop is Udo).

✪ Here you'll find **Udo Shrine,** located about a 15-minute walk from the bus stop. Dedicated to the father of Emperor Jimmu, this vermilion-colored shrine is actually located in a cave beside the ocean, with an exhilarating view. Udo Shrine is famous among young couples who come here to pray for success and harmony in marriage. Behind the shrine are cave formations thought to resemble breasts, and milk candy is a specialty of the shops near the shrine. If you'd like to make a wish, purchase a piece of clay pottery from the shrine and look for a rock shaped like a turtle and topped with a white circle of rope. If you can toss the pottery piece so that it stays inside the circle, your wish will come true. Women are supposed to throw right-handed; men are to throw left-handed.

WHERE TO STAY

EXPENSIVE

SUN HOTEL PHOENIX, 3083 Hamayama Shioji, Miyazaki 880-01. Tel. 0985/39-3131. Fax 0985/39-6496. 296 rms. A/C MINIBAR TV TEL **Directions:** A 15-minute taxi ride from Miyazaki Station.

$ Rates: ¥10,500–¥12,500 ($75–$89) single/double; ¥17,500–¥26,000 ($125–$186) twin. Japanese-style rooms: ¥18,500–¥30,000 ($132–$214) double occupancy. AE, DC, JCB, MC, V.

The most relaxing and luxurious places to stay in Miyazaki are the Sun Hotel Phoenix and the slightly cheaper Seaside Hotel Phoenix, located side by side and under the same ownership. Both of the hotels are isolated, are surrounded by many acres of land and by the sea, and offer a number of recreational diversions. Built about 15 years ago, the Sun Hotel Phoenix is the more deluxe of the two hotels, with higher prices charged for rooms facing the sea. Its 203 Western-style rooms are roomy, with bedside reading lamps, hairdryer, minibar, clock, radio, and kimono. There are also 93 Japanese-style rooms.

Dining/Entertainment: Restaurant Sky Blue, on the ninth floor, has unobstructed views of the Pacific, pine woods, and the golf course below. Open from 11am to 3pm and 5 to 10pm, it offers lunch courses from ¥2,200 ($15.70) and dinner courses from ¥5,500 ($39.30) for steaks or seafood. The à la carte menu includes gratin, sandwiches, seafood, stewed beef, pilaf, curry, and spaghetti. The hotel's Japanese restaurant on the second floor features seafood and sashimi, with teishoku beginning at ¥4,500 ($32.15). There are also a sushi bar, a cocktail bar, and a coffee shop.

Facilities: Shops, tennis courts, bowling lanes, zoo, children's playground, outdoor swimming pool (open in summer only), public bath, and golf-driving range. The 27-hole golf course is famous in Japan and is much cheaper than courses near Tokyo. Greens fees (including tax and caddy) are ¥25,000 ($178) on weekdays and ¥30,000 ($214) on Saturday and Sunday. Rental of clubs costs about ¥2,000

($14.30). The hotel has a much cheaper course in the mountains, where fees (including caddy) are ¥13,500 ($96) on weekdays and ¥19,000 ($136) on weekends. Next to the hotel complex is a wonderful area of woods and ponds, and bicycles are available for rent.

MODERATE

HOTEL PHOENIX, 2-1-1 Matsuyama, Miyazaki 880. Tel. 0985/23-6111.
Fax 0985/26-4535. 117 rms. A/C MINIBAR TV TEL **Directions:** A 5-minute taxi ride from Miyazaki Station.
$ Rates: ¥8,800 ($63) single; ¥10,500–¥12,500 ($75–$89) double; ¥13,000–¥18,500 ($93–$132) twin. AE, DC, JCB, V.
Also under the same ownership as the Sun Hotel Phoenix and the Seaside Hotel Phoenix, but in town, is the Hotel Phoenix, located right beside the Oyodo River. Rooms that face the river cost slightly more. There's a small outdoor pool open in July and August; unfortunately, this is located right outside the lobby's window, so there's no hiding those extra pounds. A beer garden on the roof, open May to mid-September daily from 5:30 to 10pm, has a great view of the river, city, and the hills beyond. Beer starts at ¥600 ($4.30). There's also a Western restaurant, a Japanese restaurant, and a cocktail bar.

MIYAZAKI ORIENTAL HOTEL, 2-10-22 Hiroshima, Miyazaki 880. Tel. 0985/27-3111. 102 rms. A/C MINIBAR TV TEL **Directions:** A 2-minute walk from Miyazaki Station.
$ Rates: ¥5,500 ($39) single; ¥8,800 ($63) double; ¥10,000 ($71) twin. JCB, V.
If you're looking for a business hotel close to the station, you might want to try this one, built in 1975. Its rooms seem a bit old and could use some cheerful renovations, but prices are reasonable. Ninety of its rooms are single, and rates with meals are also available. There's someone at the front desk who speaks English, and the hotel's one restaurant serves Chinese food. Rooms come with minibar, hairdryer, pants-presser, and clock.

SEASIDE HOTEL PHOENIX, 3083 Hamayama Shioji, Miyazaki 880-01. Tel. 0985/39-1111. Fax 0985/39-1639. 196 rms (all with bath). A/C MINIBAR TV TEL **Directions:** A 15-minute taxi ride from Miyazaki Station.
$ Rates: ¥8,800 ($63) single; ¥8,800–¥11,000 ($63–$78) double; ¥15,000–¥22,000 ($107–$157) twin. Japanese-style rooms: ¥14,000–¥24,000 ($100–$171) double occupancy. AE, DC, JCB, V.
This hotel, 2 years older than the Sun Hotel Phoenix, described above, has an almost equal number of Western and Japanese rooms. It has both Japanese and Western restaurants, and guests can use the facilities of the Sun Hotel Phoenix.

BUDGET

AOSHIMA KOKUMIN SHUKUSHA ㉗, 2-12-36 Aoshima, Miyazaki 889-22. Tel. 0985/65-1533. 57 rms (5 with bath). A/C TV TEL **Train:** From Miyazaki Station to Aoshima Station (a 25-minute ride), then a 3-minute walk.
$ Rates (per person): Japanese-style rooms: ¥3,500 ($25) without bath, ¥5,000 ($36) with bath. Western-style rooms: ¥5,000 ($36) without bath. Breakfasts ¥800 ($5.70). No credit cards.
If you're a sun worshiper, you may want to stay at this public lodge located right next to tiny Aoshima Island. All of its rooms face the ocean, and the beach for swimming is only a 5-minute walk away. All of its 49 Japanese-style rooms (5 with private bathroom) have a balcony, but its 8 Western-style rooms come without a balcony or bathroom. Popular with Japanese families, this kokumin shukusha is heavily booked during New Year's, Golden Week in May, and July and August, so make reservations if you plan to travel during these times. Supper costs ¥1,600 ($12.80) and up.

MINSHUKU TAKE, 4-1-15 Aoshima, Miyazaki 889-22. Tel. 0985/65-1420. 6 rms (none with bath). A/C TV **Train:** From Miyazaki Station to Aoshima Station, then a 5-minute walk.

$ Rates: ¥3,300 ($23) single; ¥6,500 ($46) twin; ¥10,000 ($71) triple. Breakfast ¥500 ($3.55); dinner ¥1,500 ($10.70). AE, MC, V.

Also located in Aoshima, not far from the kokumin shukusha described above, this two-story minshuku is a member of the Japanese Inn Group. Its owners will pick you up at the station if you let them know you're coming. There's a coin-operated laundry, and Aoshima's beaches and attractions are within easy walking distance. All rooms are Japanese style, simple and pleasant.

WHERE TO DINE

Miyazaki's subtropical climate is conducive to the growth of a number of vegetables and fruits, including sweet pumpkins, oranges, cucumbers, green peppers, shiitake mushrooms, and chestnuts.

Especially popular is shochu, made from sweet potatoes, buckwheat, or corn. The two restaurants listed below specialize in imaginative dishes made with locally grown vegetables, fruit, and other produce. They are located close together just off Tachibana-dori Street.

GYOSANTEI ㉒, **basement of Shokokaikan Building, Higashi 1-chome. Tel. 24-7070.**
   Cuisine: LOCAL SPECIALTIES. **Directions:** A 15-minute walk from Miyazaki Station.
$ Prices: Set meals ¥3,800–¥7,500 ($27.15–$53.55). JCB, V.
   Open: Lunch Mon–Sat 11:30am–2pm; dinner Mon–Sat 5–10pm.

Although the stairwell doesn't look like much, this is an attractive restaurant with wooden floors, tatami mats, leg wells under the tables, and waitresses dressed in kimonos. Notice the two little mounds of salt on either side of the restaurant's door—they symbolize purification. Just as in the olden days, there's a split length of bamboo inside the leg well on which to rest your stockinged feet, and the menu is written on a scroll. I suggest you order one of the courses featuring local food. The Himukazen course, for example, which means "facing the sun," changes according to what's in season and what the cook decides to create, but it always includes as its main dish a pumpkin filled with chicken and radish and topped with hard-boiled egg yolk, with a raw yolk plopped on top (which nevertheless slowly cooks from the heat)—meant to resemble the sun. Side dishes might include salmon rolled inside Japanese radish, raw flying fish served with freshly grated wasabi (horseradish), fried prawn with dried mushrooms used as a coating instead of flour, or Miyazaki melon. It's truly a restaurant of culinary surprises, making dining here a pleasure.

SUGI NO KO ㉓, **Tachibana-dori 2-1-4. Tel. 22-5798.**
   Cuisine: LOCAL SPECIALTIES. **Directions:** A 15-minute walk from Miyazaki Station.
$ Prices: Set meals ¥3,800–¥10,000 ($27.15–$71.40); set lunch ¥2,700 ($19.30). AE, DC, JCB, MC, V.
   Open: Lunch Mon–Sat 11:30am–2pm; dinner Mon–Sat 4–11pm.

The owner of this third-floor restaurant creates all his own dishes and has even produced a book of his recipes. The dining area displays haniwa dolls and other crafts of Miyazaki Prefecture, and there are also private tatami rooms. The menu is written in Japanese only, so the best thing to do is to order one of the set meals. At lunch, for example, the Miyazaki Gyuu Teishoku comes with Miyazaki beef seasoned with soy sauce and served with four different sauces, vegetables, soup, rice, and fruit. One of the side dishes featured during my visit was delicate tofu filled with pungent mustard.

SHOPPING

The **Miyazaki-ken Bussankan,** located just off Tachibana-dori Street at 1-6 Miyata-cho (tel. 0985/25-4676), is a good place to shop for wooden trays, bowls, ceramics, masks, haniwa clay reproductions, swords, lacquerware, and other crafts made in Miyazaki Prefecture. Open Monday through Friday from 8:30am to 6pm and on Saturday from 8:30am to 12:30pm.

CHAPTER 16

NORTHERN JAPAN — HOKKAIDO

Because so many of Japan's historical events took place in Kyoto, Tokyo, and other cities in southern Honshu, most tourists to Japan never venture farther north than Tokyo. True, northern Japan does not have the temples, shrines, gardens, and castles of southern Japan, but it does have spectacular scenery. Matsushima, about 3 hours north of Tokyo, is considered one of Japan's most scenic spots, with pine-covered islets dotting its bay. Farther north is Hokkaido, the northernmost of Japan's four main islands.

HOKKAIDO

Hokkaido's landscape is strikingly different from that of any other place in Japan. With more than 30,000 square miles, Hokkaido makes up about 21% of Japan's total land mass and yet has only 5% of its population. In other words, Hokkaido has what the rest of Japan doesn't—space. Considered the country's last frontier, Hokkaido didn't begin opening up to development until after the Meiji Restoration in 1868, when the government began encouraging Japanese to migrate to the island. Even today Hokkaido has a frontier feel to it, and many young Japanese come here to backpack, ski, camp, and tour across the countryside on motorcycles or bicycles. There are dairy farms and silos and broad, flat fields of wheat, corn, potatoes, and rice. Then the land puckers up to craggy and bare volcanoes, gorges, and hills densely covered with trees. There are clear spring lakes, mountain ranges, rugged wilderness, wild animals, and rare plants. About 7% of Hokkaido is preserved as national and prefectural parks.

With winters that are long and severe, Hokkaido has its main tourist season in August, when days are cool and pleasant, with an average temperature of 70°F. And while the rest of the nation is under the deluge of the rainy season, Hokkaido's summers are usually bright and clear. In winter, ski enthusiasts flock to slopes near Sapporo and to resorts such as Daisetsuzan National Park. And February marks the annual Sapporo Snow Festival, with its huge ice and snow sculptures.

The people of Hokkaido are considered to be as open and hearty as the wide expanse of land around them. Hokkaido is also home of the Ainu, the native inhabitants of the island. Not much is known about their origins, but the Ainu arrived in Hokkaido approximately 800 years ago. It's not even clear whether they're Asian or Caucasian, but they're of different racial stock than the Japanese. They are round-eyed and light-skinned, and Ainu males can grow thick beards and mustaches. Traditionally the Ainu lived as hunters and fishermen, but after Hokkaido opened up to development they were gradually assimilated into Japanese society, taking Japanese names and adopting the Japanese language and clothing. Like Native Americans, they were often discriminated against and their culture was largely destroyed. Today, there

WHAT'S SPECIAL ABOUT HOKKAIDO

Natural Spectacles
- ☐ Mt. Hakodate, reached by cable car and famous for its night view of Hakodate.
- ☐ Lake Toya, a typical caldera lake, boasting a depth of 590 feet.
- ☐ Active volcanoes, including Mt. Usu and Showa-Shinzen.
- ☐ Sounkyo Gorge, with rock walls rising almost 500 feet and a series of waterfalls.
- ☐ Akan National Park, with its breeding grounds of red-crested cranes.

Hot-Spring Spas
- ☐ Toyako Onsen, on the shores of Lake Toya and featuring the magnificent Sun Palace Hotel, complete with indoor and outdoor baths, swimming pool, and waterslides.

- ☐ Noboribetsu, one of Japan's most famous hot-spring resorts.
- ☐ Akanko Onsen in Akan National Park.

Regional Food & Drink
- ☐ Sapporo Beer, produced in Sapporo since 1876.
- ☐ Hokkaido local products, including hairy crab, corn on the cob, and potatoes.
- ☐ Genghis Khan, a dish of mutton and vegetables that you barbecue at your own table.

---

are an estimated 15,000 Ainu still living in Hokkaido. Some of them earn their living from tourism, selling Ainu wood carvings and other crafts, as well as performing traditional dances and songs.

SEEING HOKKAIDO

Public transportation around Hokkaido is by train and bus. In addition to regular bus lines, there are sightseeing buses linking national parks and major attractions. Although they are more expensive than trains and regular buses, they offer unparalleled views of the countryside. Keep in mind that bus schedules fluctuate with the seasons, as some lines don't run during the snowy winter months.

If you plan to do a lot of traveling in Hokkaido and you are not traveling by Japan Rail Pass, you can purchase a **special pass** issued by Japan Railways that allows unlimited travel on its trains and buses in Hokkaido. The pass can be purchased in Japan anywhere except Hokkaido, with several options available. A 20-day Hokkaido JR Pass, for example, costs ¥40,000 ($286) and includes a round-trip ticket from the place of departure (say, Tokyo) to Hokkaido. A 5-day pass costs ¥14,000 ($100) and a 10-day pass costs ¥22,000 ($157). These two tickets allow 20% discounts on round-trip tickets from the place of departure to Hokkaido.

Because distances are long and traffic is rather light, Hokkaido is one of the few places in Japan where driving your own car is actually recommended. Because it's expensive, however, it's economical only if there are several of you. Rates for 1 day of car rental begin at ¥8,000 ($57) for the first 220 kilometers (136 miles), with each additional day costing ¥5,500 ($39.30) for 100 kilometers (62 miles). Car-rental agencies are found throughout Hokkaido as well as at Chitose Airport outside Sapporo.

Incidentally, travel to Hokkaido by land is generally via Shinkansen bullet train from Ueno or Tokyo Station in Tokyo to Morioka, followed by limited express from Morioka to Aomori on the northern tip of Honshu Island. For centuries the only way to continue from Aomori to Hokkaido was by boat, but the opening of the Seikan Tunnel (April 1988) now allows the entire trip to be made by train. Whereas the ferry ride to Hakodate, on Hokkaido, used to take 4 hours, the train ride by tunnel takes less than 3 hours—45 minutes of which is in the tunnel. At any rate, the entire trip from Tokyo to Hakodate via train should take about 8 hours. The fastest way to reach Hokkaido, of course, is to fly.

As for the best route through Hokkaido, the first stop is usually Hakodate, a convenient one-night stopover. From there you can board a local train bound for Sapporo, stopping off at Shikotsu-Toya National Park along the way. After spending a few days in Sapporo, take the train to Kamikawa, transferring there to a bus that will take you directly to Sounkyo Onsen in Daisetsuzan National Park. From Sounkyo Onsen you can then continue your trip by taking a bus to Rubeshibe, transferring there to a train to Bihoro. From Bihoro, sightseeing buses depart for Akan National Park, where you can then spend the night at Lake Akan. From Akan you may wish to return to Tokyo by plane from Kushiro Airport.

---

1. MATSUSHIMA

234 miles NE of Tokyo

GETTING THERE   By Train   From Tokyo you can take the Tohoku Shinkansen from Ueno or Tokyo Station to Sendai, which will take from 2 to 2½ hours, depending on the number of stops. In Sendai, change to the JR Senseki Line—it's well marked in English, so you shouldn't have any difficulty changing trains in Sendai. It takes about 25 minutes by express train to reach Matsushima Kaigan Station.

By Boat   A popular way to get to Matsushima is to take the Senseki train line from Sendai only as far as Hon-Shiogama (about 18 minutes by express). From there you can catch a sightseeing boat to Matsushima Kaigan Pier. See "What to See & Do," below.

ESSENTIAL INFORMATION   The **area code** for Matsushima and Sendai, both lying in Miyagi Prefecture, is 022.

Before leaving Tokyo, be sure to stop by the Tourist Information Center for a free leaflet called *Sendai, Matsushima, and Hiraizumi*. It has a map of Matsushima Bay and tells of attractions in and around Matsushima.

Upon arrival in Matsushima, stop off at one of the **Matsushima Tourist Association Offices,** located at both Matsushima Kaigan train station and at Matsushima Kaigan Pier (tel. 022/354-2618). You can pick up a brochure with a map in English and get directions to your hotel. Daily hours for both are 8:30am to 5pm. The train station and pier are about a 10-minute walk apart.

SPECIAL EVENTS   The **Tanabata Festival** is held August 6 to 8 in Sendai, and the **Toronagashi Festival** takes place August 15 and 16 in Matsushima.

Because the trip to Hokkaido is such a long one, the most pleasant way to travel is to break up the journey with an overnight stay in Matsushima in northern Honshu. Matsushima means "Pine-clad Islands," and that's exactly what this region is. More than 200 pine-covered islets and islands dot Matsushima Bay, giving it the appearance of a giant pond in a Japanese landscape garden. Twisted and gnarled pines sweep upward from volcanic tuff and white sandstone, creating bizarre and beautiful shapes. Matsushima is so dear to Japanese hearts that it is considered one of the three most scenic spots in Japan (the other two are Miyajima in Hiroshima Bay and Amanohashidate on the north coast of Honshu)—and was so designated about 270 years ago in a book written by a Confucian philosopher of the Edo government. Basho (1644–94), the famous Japanese haiku poet, was so struck by Matsushima's beauty that it's almost as though he were at a loss for words when he wrote: "Matsushima, Ah! Matsushima! Matsushima!"

I have no doubt that Matsushima was indeed awesomely and strikingly beautiful during Basho's time, as well as during the time it was selected as one of Japan's three most scenic spots, but motorboats have been invented since then, and although they offer the closest view of the islands, all those boats plying the water somehow detract from the mood that evoked such ecstasy in Basho long ago. Still, Matsushima itself is a pleasant small town on the waters of Matsushima Bay and makes a worthwhile stop if you're on your way north to Hokkaido.

All of Matsushima's major attractions are within walking distance of both the train station and the pier, and you can cover the whole area on foot in half a day of leisurely sightseeing.

WHAT TO SEE & DO

Arriving in Matsushima by **sightseeing boat** is a good introduction to the bay, as you pass pine-covered islands and oyster rafts along the way. Board the boat in Hon-Shiogama for the 1-hour trip to Matsushima Kaigan Pier, which costs ¥1,500 ($10.70) one way. Unfortunately, the commentary is in Japanese only (a good time to break out the Walkman unless you've become oblivious to noise by now). And believe it or not, a couple of the boats are shaped like a huge peacock and a dragon. Boats leave from both Hon-Shiogama and Matsushima Kaigan piers about every half hour between 8am and 4pm in summer, but only once an hour in winter. If you're going in the off-season, be sure to check the schedule (tel. 022/362-2431).

Even if you don't arrive by boat, you might still want to take a boat trip in the bay. Regular sightseeing boats make 40-minute trips around the bay and back and charge ¥2,000 ($14.30) per person. You can also charter one of the smaller motorboats— which, judging by the number of them leaving the pier every few minutes, seems to be the most popular way to see Matsushima. Charter motorboats cost ¥4,500 ($32.15) for a tour lasting 20 minutes, ¥11,000 ($78.55) for 60 minutes, and ¥16,500 ($117.85) for 2 hours. You can see more of the islands on these smaller craft than you can on the regular sightseeing boats.

In addition to the boat trips, there are four spots spread around Matsushima that are historically considered the best for viewing Matsushima's islands. These spots are called Otakamori, Tomiyama, Tamonzan, and Ogidani. The closest is **Ogidani,** a 10-minute taxi ride away from the pier. I personally don't think it's worth the time or effort to make it to each of these four lookouts. You can get as much a feel for Matsushima's beauty simply by visiting the more easily accessible attractions listed below. If you feel like hiking to a lookout, **Sokanzan Lookout** is about a 30-minute hike from Matsushima Kaigan Pier and offers a panoramic view of the region.

✪ Matsushima's best-known structure is **Zuiganji Temple** ㉔, the most famous Zen temple in the northern part of Japan. Located just a few minutes' walk away, from Matsushima Kaigan Pier, its entrance is shaded by tall cedar trees. On the right side of the pathway leading to the temple are caves and grottoes dug out by priests long ago. Adorned with Buddhist statues and memorial tablets, they were used for practicing zazen (sitting meditation). Zuiganji Temple was founded in 1606 by the order of Date Masamune, the most powerful and important lord of northern Honshu. Unifying the region known as Tohoku, Date built his castle in nearby Sendai, and today almost all sites in and around Sendai and Matsushima are tied to the Date family. It took hundreds of workers 6 years to build the temple, which was

IMPRESSIONS

[A]n Ainu woman on Hokkaido went up to [my friend] and asked him indignantly: "What is it that is peculiar about us? Why do Japanese people look at us as if we were freaks?" She had tattooed round her lips and chin an enormous blue mustache, and a blue beard.
—ALEXANDER CAMPBELL, *THE HEART OF JAPAN,* 1962

constructed in the *shoin-zukuri* style typical of the Momoyama Period and served as the family temple of the Date clan.

An adjoining treasure hall, the **Seiryuden,** displays items belonging to the temple and the Date family, while the main hall contains elaborately carved wooden doors, transoms, and painted sliding doors—and at last check this was one of the few temples that still allowed flash photography (in its outer corridor). Admission is ¥500 ($3.55), and hours vary according to the season. The longest hours are from April to September, when it's open daily from 7:30am to 5pm. In winter, hours are 8am to 3:30 or 4pm.

Next to Zuiganji Temple (to the left if you're facing Zuiganji) is **Entsuin** ㉗, a lesser-known temple also built more than 300 years ago by the Date clan. Open from 8am to 5pm throughout the year and charging a ¥300 ($2.15) admission, it features a small rock garden, a beautiful rose garden, and a small temple housing an elaborate statue of Lord Date Mitsumune, grandson of Lord Date Masamune, who founded the Sendai fief. Depicted here on horseback, Mitsumune was reportedly poisoned and died at the tender age of 19. The statues surrounding him represent retainers who committed ritual suicide to follow their master into death. The statues and small temple are located at the back of the temple grounds, past the rose garden. Tour groups seem to bypass this temple, making it a peaceful retreat away from the crowds that sometimes descend on Matsushima.

Under the supervision of Zuiganji Temple is **Godaido,** a small wooden worship hall on a tiny island not far from the pier. Connected to the mainland by a short bridge, its grounds are open night and day and are free, but there's not much to see. The hall's interior is open to the public only every 33 years. (It won't be open again until August 20, 2006.) Godaido is often featured in brochures of Matsushima, making this delicate wooden temple one of the town's best-known landmarks.

Kanrantei, the "Water-Viewing Pavilion," is just a short walk from the pier. A simple wooden teahouse, it was used by generations of the Date family for such aesthetic pursuits as viewing the moon and watching the ripples on the tide. Originally it belonged to warlord Hideyoshi Toyotomi as part of his estate at Fushimi Castle near Kyoto, but he presented it to the Date family at the end of the 16th century. Kanrantei is open daily from 8am to 5pm. The entrance fee is ¥200 ($1.40). For an additional ¥300 ($2.15) you can drink ceremonial green tea while sitting upon the teahouse tatami and contemplating the bay, its islands, and the boats carving ribbons through the water. After drinking your tea, wander through the small museum, which contains artifacts belonging to the Date family. I found particularly interesting a screen painted long ago showing Matsushima—even then there were boats winding between the islands. Who knows, maybe the motorboats of today will someday look quaint and old-fashioned to generations hence.

Just a couple of minutes beyond Kanrantei on the southern edge of Matsushima is **Oshima,** a small island once used as a retreat by priests. At one time, there used to be many caves with carvings of scriptures, Buddhist images, and sutras, but today the island and its remaining stone images and structures are rather neglected and forgotten. There's no fee, no gate, and the island never closes. It's a nice quiet spot to sit and view the harbor. Because it was a Buddhist retreat, women were forbidden to enter Oshima until after the Meiji Restoration in 1868.

Next to Oshima is an aquarium called **Marine Pier** ㉘, open daily from 9am to 5pm and charging ¥1,100 ($7.85) for adults and ¥550 ($3.90) for children (tel. 354-2020). Although rather small, it has penguins, turtles, crocodiles, octopuses, sea otters, moray eels, and ocean sunfish. This place appeals mainly to kids, who also enjoy the aquarium's miniature train, carousel, and monorail.

At the other end of Matsushima is **Fukuurajima,** another island connected to the mainland, this time by a long red concrete bridge with orange-colored railings. It's a botanical garden of sorts, with several hundred labeled plants and trees, but mostly it's unkempt and overgrown—which comes as a surprise in cultivated Japan. It takes less than an hour to walk completely around the island. Between the hours of 8am and 6pm (4pm in winter) you must pay ¥100 (70¢) admittance; after hours you can enter for free.

As for destinations outside Matsushima, if you have time you may want to visit **Kinkazan Island,** accessible in about 2 hours by ferry from Ishinomaki. Kinkazan is a small island, with a pyramid-shaped mountain and woods inhabited by deer and monkeys. A shrine called Koganeyama is located halfway up the mountain.

WHERE TO STAY

Because this is a tourist town, accommodations in Matsushima are not cheap, especially during the peak months of May through November. For the Tanabata Festival, held August 6 to 8 in Sendai, and the Toronagashi Festival, held August 15 and 16 in Matsushima, rooms are usually fully booked a half year in advance. Rates are generally cheaper during the off-season months (from December through April). Almost all accommodations here are in ryokan, which means you're generally expected to take your dinner and breakfast there. Because Matsushima tends to be expensive, I've included some budget accommodations in nearby Sendai at the end of this section. If you stay there, you could make a day trip to Matsushima, only 25 minutes away.

IN MATSUSHIMA

Expensive

HOTEL SOHKAN, Isozaki, Aza Hama 1-1, Matsushima, Miyagi-gun 981-02. Tel. 022/354-2181. 134 rms. A/C MINIBAR TV TEL **Directions:** A 5-minute taxi ride from boat pier.

$ Rates (per person, including breakfast, dinner, and service charge): Japanese-style rooms: ¥16,000–¥50,000 ($114–$357). Western-style rooms: ¥16,000–¥27,000 ($114–$193). Off-season discount available. AE, DC, JCB, MC, V.

Despite the "hotel" in its name, this is a modern and comfortable ryokan located on the edge of Matsushima. Catering mainly to Japanese groups, it offers a koto concert in the early evening in its lobby, played by a woman in a traditional kimono. Although the majority of rooms are Japanese style, there are also a few Western-style rooms available that can sleep up to four people and even have bilingual TV. You have your choice of Japanese or Western breakfast and dinner.

Dining/Entertainment: In addition to Japanese and Western restaurants, there's also a karaoke bar, in which people from the audience stand up and sing a variety of songs while accompanied by taped instrumental music. It's a fun place to watch Japanese enjoying themselves.

Facilities: Public baths, a couple of golf holes for practice or beginners, and a 210-foot-high tower from which for ¥350 ($2.50) you can have a view over all of Matsushima.

MATSUSHIMA CENTURY HOTEL, 9 Aza Senzui, Matsushima, Miyagi-gun 981-02. Tel. 022/354-4111. 117 rms. A/C MINIBAR TV TEL **Directions:** A 10-minute walk from Matsushima Kaigan Station; a 3-minute walk from pier.

$ Rates (per person, including breakfast, dinner, and service charge): ¥38,000–¥50,000 ($271–$357) in peak season; ¥17,500–¥27,000 ($125–$193) in winter. Room only (no meals): ¥20,000–¥27,000 ($143–$193) double occupancy. AE, DC, JCB, MC, V.

A NOTE ON JAPANESE SYMBOLS

Many hotels, restaurants, and other establishments in Japan do not have signs giving their names in English letters. As an aid to the reader, Appendix C lists the Japanese symbols for all such places described in this guide. Each set of symbols has a number, which corresponds to the number that appears inside an oval next to the establishment's boldfaced name in the text. Thus, to find the Japanese symbols for, say, Osaka's **Hotel Hokke Club** ⑬⑧, refer to number 138 in the appendix.

This glittering white hotel opened on the shore of Matsushima in 1984 and is a cool oasis conveniently located in the middle of town between the pier and Fukuurajima Island. It's a sleek place appealing especially to the young. Approximately half the rooms are Japanese style, and all of these face the bay and have their own balcony. The Western-style rooms, sunny and cheerful and decorated in pastels and white, face only inland and have no balcony. If you opt to stay at the hotel without taking your meals here, you'll be placed in one of these.

Dining/Entertainment: Its karaoke bar charges a ¥2,700 ($19.30) cover, including one free drink. La Saison is a good place to come for lunch or dinner. Open from 11:30am to 2:30pm and from 6 to 9pm, this Western seafood restaurant is decorated with white latticed wood and ferns. You can order such dishes as sole, fried shrimp, scallops, steak, and beef Stroganoff à la carte, but especially good are the set-lunch courses starting at ¥1,500 ($10.70).

Facilities: Outdoor swimming pool, modern public baths, sauna—all overlooking the bay.

TAIKANSO ㉗, **10-76 Aza Inuta, Matsushima, Miyagi-gun 981-02. Tel. 022/354-2161.** 215 rms (198 with bath). A/C MINIBAR TV TEL **Directions:** A 15-minute walk or a 5-minute taxi ride from Matsushima Kaigan Station.

$ Rates (per person, including breakfast, dinner, and service charge): Western- and combination-style rooms: ¥16,500–¥35,000 ($118–$250). Japanese-style rooms: ¥20,000–¥35,000 ($143–$250). Peak season rates ¥2,000 ($14.30) extra. AE, DC, JCB, MC, V.

Accommodating 1,500 people, Taikanso sprawls atop a plateau surrounded by pine-covered hills and offers the best view in town. Both Western- and Japanese-style rooms are available, most with private bathroom. Pleasantly bright, they come with minibar, TV with pay video, and safe for valuables. Rates vary according to the season and whether your room faces the sea or the wooded mountains (which are also quite nice), and whether your room has tatami or beds. All of the Japanese-style rooms face the sea. Combination-style rooms have both beds and a tatami area.

Dining/Entertainment: The hotel has a nightclub with floor shows nightly. Restaurants include a noodle shop, with noodle dishes starting at ¥1,000 ($7.15); a Japanese seafood restaurant that serves sashimi and tempura, ranging in price from about ¥1,500 to ¥2,500 ($10.70 to $17.85); and a seventh-floor Western restaurant, called Shiosai, with probably the best view in town of both Matsushima Bay and the surrounding pine-covered hills. It's worth the 30-minute walk from Matsushima's pier just for the view. The food itself is nothing to write home about but is reasonably priced, with main dishes of curry, pilaf, spaghetti, and seafood, as well as Japanese dishes, priced at less than ¥2,000 ($14.30). Steak and lobster dinners start at ¥6,500 ($46.40), while a daily lunch special is available for ¥1,600 ($11.40). Hours are 11am to 9pm.

Facilities: Public baths overlooking island-studded bay; outdoor swimming pool.

Moderate

KONNOYA ㉘, **38-1 Fugendo, Matsushima, Miyagi-gun 981-02. Tel. 022/354-3006.** 26 rms (18 with bath). A/C MINIBAR TV TEL **Directions:** A 15-minute walk from Matsushima Kaigan train station; a 5-minute walk from pier.

$ Rates (per person, including breakfast, dinner, and service charge): ¥13,000 ($93) without bath; ¥14,000 ($100) with bath. ¥3,000 ($21.40) extra on weekends. Winter discount available. No credit cards.

This moderately priced, clean, modern ryokan is about a 5-minute walk inland from the pier. All rooms are Japanese style and come with safe for valuables, coin-operated TV, and refrigerator, among other amenities.

MATSUSHIMA KANKO HOTEL ㉘, **near Matsushima Kaigan Pier, Matsushima, Miyagi-gun 981-02. Tel. 022/354-2121.** 28 rms (7 with bath). MINIBAR TV TEL **Directions:** A 10-minute walk from Matsushima Kaigan Station; a 1-minute walk from pier.

$ Rates (per person, with breakfast, dinner, and service charge): ¥8,800–¥30,000 ($63–$214). JCB.

This is the best choice if you want to stay in an old-fashioned ryokan. It's popularly called Matsushima-jo, which means Matsushima Castle. Indeed, as Matsushima's oldest ryokan (built about 100 years ago), it does rather resemble a castle with its sloping tiled roof, white walls, and red railings. Inside, it's airy and delightful, with old wooden banisters polished from decades of human hands. Its walls are decorated with woodblock prints by the famous artist Hiroshige, as well as photographs of stern-faced Japanese who have stayed here in the past. Keep in mind that rooms come only with fans, not air conditioning, and tend to be drafty in winter, and that the communal toilets are Japanese style. However, rooms do come with sink, coin-operated TV, and minibar, and those on the third floor have views of the water. It has a convenient location directly behind Godaido worship hall, just a minute from Matsushima Kaigan Pier. The public bath mixes underground salt water with tap water. Western breakfasts are served on request.

RYOKAN KOZAKURA ㉘, near Matsushima Kaigan Pier on town's main street, Matsushima, Miyagi-gun 981-02. Tel. 022/354-2518. 12 rms (2 with bath). A/C MINIBAR TV TEL **Directions:** A 10-minute walk from Matsushima Kaigan Station, a 3-minute walk from pier.
$ Rates (per person, with breakfast, dinner, and service charge): ¥7,500 ($53.50) without bath; ¥12,000 ($86) with bath. Peak season ¥3,000 ($21.40) extra. JCB, V.
This simple concrete Japanese-style inn has a convenient location and offers inexpensive tatami rooms. Rooms are simple but come with TV, air conditioner, heater, and refrigerator, and meals are served in your own room.

Budget

MATSUSHIMA YOUTH HOSTEL ㉙, Miyato Island, Narusei-cho, Miyagi-gun 981-02. Tel. 0225/88-2220. 124 beds. **Train:** Senseki Line from Matsushima Kaigan Station (a 15-minute ride) to Nobiru Station, then a 15-minute walk.
$ Rates (per person): ¥2,300 ($16.40) member; ¥700 ($5) extra nonmember. Breakfast ¥450 ($3.30); dinner ¥850 ($6.05). No credit cards.
This hostel sleeps an average of eight persons per room in bunk beds. In addition to tennis courts and rental bicycles, there's a beach near the hostel.

IN SENDAI

JAPANESE INN AISAKI, 5-6 Kitame-machi, Aoba-ku, Sendai 980. Tel. 022/264-0700. Fax 022/227-6067. 16 rms (2 with bath). A/C TV TEL **Directions:** A 12-minute walk from Sendai Station, behind Central Post Office.
$ Rates: ¥4,400 ($31.40) single without bath, ¥5,500 ($39) single with bath; ¥7,700 ($55) twin without bath, ¥10,000 ($71) twin with bath; ¥13,000 ($93) triple with bath. Breakfast ¥700 ($5); dinner ¥1,500 ($10.70). AE, MC, V.
A member of the Japanese Inn Group, this simple inn offers both Western- and Japanese-style rooms with bilingual cable TV. Coin-operated laundry facilities are available.

SENDAI CHITOSE YOUTH HOSTEL, 6-3-8 Odawara, Sendai 983. Tel. 022/222-6329. 50 beds. **Bus:** From Sendai Station, platform 17 or 19 (a 10-minute ride), then a 3-minute walk. **Directions:** A 20-minute walk from Sendai Station's west exit.
$ Rates (per person): ¥2,300 ($16.40) member; ¥700 ($5) extra nonmember. Breakfast ¥450 ($3.20); dinner ¥750 ($5.35). No credit cards.
This is the closest youth hostel to Sendai Station, located in a quiet neighborhood. All rooms are tatami style, and meals are hearty. Facilities include rental bicycles and coin-operated laundry machines.

YOUTH HOSTEL SENDAI AKAMON, 61 Kawauchi-Kawamae-cho, Sendai

980. Tel. 022/264-1405. 70 beds. **Bus:** 9 or 16 from Sendai Station (a 15-minute ride), then a 5-minute walk.
$ Rates (per person): ¥2,300 ($16.40) member; ¥700 ($5) extra nonmember. Breakfast ¥400 ($2.85); dinner ¥750 ($5.35). No credit cards.
This youth hostel is located near Hirose River, offering hiking and boating opportunities. Its rooms are Japanese style.

SENDAI ONAI YOUTH HOSTEL, 1-9-35 Kashiwagi, Sendai 981. Tel. 022/234-3922. 15 beds. **Bus:** From Sendai Station, platform 24 (a 15-minute ride), then a 2-minute walk.
$ Rates (per person): ¥2,100 ($15) member; ¥700 ($5) extra nonmember. Breakfast ¥400 ($2.85); dinner ¥750 ($5.35). No credit cards.
Rental bicycles and vegetarian meals are available at this small youth hostel offering Japanese-style accommodations.

SENDAI-DOCHUAN YOUTH HOSTEL, 31 Kitayashiki, Onoda, Sendai 982. Tel. 022/247-0511. 24 beds. **Subway:** From Sendai Station a 12-minute ride, then an 8-minute walk.
$ Rates (per person): ¥2,500 ($17.85) member; ¥700 ($5) extra nonmember. Breakfast ¥450 ($3.20); dinner ¥850 ($6.05). No credit cards.
Recently renovated, this hostel seems more like a hotel, offering both beds and futon accommodations. Facilities include tennis courts, bicycles for rent, and coin-operated laundry machines.

WHERE TO DINE

Since all ryokan serve breakfast and dinner, the only meal you probably have to think about is lunch. There are several restaurants in Matsushima and you shouldn't have any trouble locating one. The one below is a good choice for lunch.

DONJIKI CHAYA (282), across street from Entsuin Temple. Tel. 354-5855.
Cuisine: NOODLES/ODANGO. **Directions:** A 5-minute walk from Matsushima Kaigan Station or pier.
$ Prices: Noodles ¥350–¥650 ($2.50–$4.65). No credit cards.
Open: Summer 9:30am–5pm daily; winter 9:30am–5pm only on weekends and hols.
This noodle shop is a convenient place for a light, inexpensive lunch. Located across the street from Entsuin Temple and easy to spot because of its thatched roof, it was built about 300 years ago and offers tatami seating and sliding doors pushed wide open in the summertime. In addition to noodles, it also serves *odango*—pounded rice balls covered with sesame, red-bean, or soy sauce.

---

2. HAKODATE

557 miles NE of Tokyo; 177 miles SW of Sapporo

GETTING THERE   By Train   From Tokyo, take the Shinkansen bullet train to Morioka (trip time: 3½ hr.); then transfer to direct train for Hakodate (trip time: about 4 hr.). There is also a night train that departs Tokyo around 7pm, arriving in Hakodate the next morning at 6:30am. Hakodate is about 4 hours by train from Sapporo, Hokkaido's largest town.

ESSENTIAL INFORMATION   The **area code** for Hakodate, lying in Hokkaido Prefecture, is 0138.
Before leaving Tokyo or Kyoto, be sure to pick up a flyer called *Southern Hokkaido* at the Tourist Information Center. Its strolling tours include Hakodate's

old Western-looking buildings, constructed back in the days when the town first opened as an international port.

The Hakodate **tourist office** (tel. 0138/23-5440) is just to the right after you exit from the Hakodate train station. Open from 9am to 7pm (5pm in winter), the office has information and an excellent map of Hakodate written in English.

The southern gateway to Hokkaido, Hakodate is about as far as you can get in a day if you're arriving in Hokkaido from Tokyo by train. Not a destination in and of itself, Hakodate makes a good one-night stopover because it has one nighttime attraction and one early-morning attraction, which means that you can easily see a little of the city before setting out to your next destination.

WHAT TO SEE & DO

Hakodate is probably most famous for its night view from atop **Mt. Hakodate,** which rises 1,100 feet just 1¾ miles southwest of Hakodate Station. Few vacationing Japanese spend the night in Hakodate without taking the cable car to the top of this lava cone, which was formed by the eruption of an undersea volcano. From the peak, the lights of Hakodate shimmer and glitter like jewels spilled on black velvet. You can reach the foot of Mt. Hakodate via a 5-minute streetcar ride from Hakodate Station to the stop named Jyujigai. From there you can take the cable car to the top for ¥1,200 ($8.55) round trip. From mid-April to mid-October, it runs every 10 minutes from 9am to 10pm, with shorter hours during the cold winter season. On the peak is an informal restaurant where you can indulge in a drink or snack while admiring the spectacular view, as well as the usual souvenir shops.

The next morning, visit the **morning market** before taking the train out of town. The market spreads out just south of the train station Monday through Saturday from about 5am to noon. Walk around and look at the variety of food for sale, especially the hairy crabs for which Hokkaido is famous.

If you have more time on your hands and are interested in renovated buildings dating from before the turn of the century, continue walking from the morning market in the direction of Mt. Hakodate until you come to a group of brick warehouses that have been converted into shops and restaurants (refer to the "Where to Dine" section, below, for more information). In succession, you'll find Union Square, Bay Hakodate, and History Plaza, all well done with exposed beams and original walls. In a country where old buildings are often bulldozed to make way for modern ones, Hakodate's waterfront redevelopment is a welcome change.

If you still have some extra time, you might consider a 1-hour boat trip around the harbor. Hakodate, along with Nagasaki, Kobe, and Yokohama, was one of the first ports open to foreigners in 1859. Boats leave several times a day from the end of April to the end of October and cost ¥1,100 ($7.85). Contact the tourist office at the train station for more information.

WHERE TO STAY

Because it's not a major tourist destination, Hakodate does not have a lot in the way of accommodations. Most of its hotels are near the train station.

EXPENSIVE

HAKODATE KOKUSAI HOTEL, 5-10 Otemachi, Hakodate 040. Tel. 0138/ 23-8751. Fax 0138/23-0239. 225 rms. A/C MINIBAR TV TEL **Directions:** A 5-minute walk from station (turn right out of station).

$ Rates: ¥9,300–¥13,000 ($66–$93) single; ¥18,000–¥25,000 ($128–$178) twin; ¥23,000–¥25,000 ($164–$178) double. Japanese-style rooms: ¥25,000 ($178). Combination rooms ¥27,000 ($193). AE, DC, JCB, MC, V.

Although located in a part of town full of junkyards and roads with potholes, this is the city's most expensive hotel. It has both Japanese- and Western-style rooms that are a good value for the money. All rooms come with TV, clock, radio, and minibar. The most expensive twins and doubles are deluxe rooms larger than standard rooms and facing the busy harbor. The twins have semidouble-size beds.

Dining/Entertainment: On the eighth floor are Matsumae, a Japanese restaurant, and Vue Mer, a Western restaurant—both with good views of the harbor. There are also a casual restaurant serving Western food, a Chinese restaurant, a coffee shop, and a bar.

Facilities: Shopping arcade, beauty salon.

HARBORVIEW HOTEL, 14-10 Wakamatsu-cho, Hakodate 040. Tel. 0138/22-0111. Fax 0138/23-0154. 190 rms. A/C MINIBAR TV TEL **Directions:** A 1-minute walk from Hakodate Station.
$ Rates: ¥8,800–¥9,000 ($63–$64) single; ¥14,000–¥15,000 ($100–$107) double; ¥17,500–¥25,000 ($125–$178) twin. AE, DC, JCB, MC, V.

This tall brick building located just to the right as you exit from Hakodate Station is one of the city's newest hotels. Despite its name, none of its 190 rooms squarely face the harbor, though those closest to the waterfront do afford views of the water. Rooms are small but pleasant, complete with minibar and thermos of water and tea, among other amenities. Since room rates are based on room size, ask for a room on one of the top floors, where you have a view of the whole city.

Dining/Entertainment: On the 13th floor are both a bar (open from 6pm to 2pm) and a Western restaurant. There are also Japanese and Chinese restaurants and a coffee shop.

MODERATE

HOTEL KIKUYA, 8-23 Wakamatsu-cho, Hakodate 040. Tel. 0138/26-1144. Fax 0138/22-0867. 27 rms (all with bath). A/C MINIBAR TV TEL **Directions:** A 3-minute walk south of Hakodate Station.
$ Rates: ¥6,000 ($43) single; ¥11,000 ($78) twin. Japanese-style rooms: ¥6,500 ($46) per person. Winter discount available. No credit cards.

The front desk at this reasonably priced hotel is on the second floor. Various kinds of rooms are available. They're small but adequate, and come with coin-operated TV and clock. The hotel's small restaurant serves both Japanese and Western food.

BUDGET

HAKODATE AKAI BOSHI, 3-22 Asahi-cho, Hakodate 040. Tel. 0138/26-4035. 5 rms (none with bath). TV **Directions:** A 13-minute walk or 5-minute taxi ride from Hakodate Station.
$ Rates (per person): ¥3,300 ($23). No credit cards.

This is a great place to stay. Spotlessly clean and cheerful, it's run by the Yamada family, who speak a little English and offer four Japanese-style rooms and one Western-style room, all outfitted with coin-operated TV. Facilities include a public shower and bathtub and a coin-operated laundry machine. No meals are served, but there's a small kitchen for guest use, and you're allowed to eat store-bought food in your room. Make reservations to stay here at least 3 days before your arrival, and keep in mind that the inn sometimes closes for part of the winter season, from November through March.

MINSHUKU FUKUISO 283, 30-16 Wakamatsu-cho, Hakodate 040. Tel. 0138/26-8239. 14 rms (none with bath). A/C MINIBAR TV TEL **Directions:** A 5-minute walk from Hakodate Station.
$ Rates (per person): ¥4,000 ($28) without meals; ¥6,500 ($46) with breakfast and dinner. No credit cards.

The rooms here are Japanese style and simply decorated, with the basics of air conditioning, heater, coin-operated TV, and cotton kimono. Although the proprietor here doesn't speak much English, things are pretty self-explanatory. The minshuku has its own public baths. To reach it, turn left on the road in front of the station (the one with the tram trails. Fukuiso is a couple of blocks down on the left side, past the crossroad with the planted median strip.

WHERE TO DINE

VUE MER, 8th floor of Hakodate Kokusai Hotel, 5-10 Otemachi. Tel. 0138/23-8751.
> **Cuisine:** FRENCH/WESTERN. **Directions:** A 5-minute walk south of Hakodate Station.
> **$ Prices:** Main dishes ¥1,000–¥3,500 ($7.15–$25); set-dinner course ¥6,000 ($42.85). AE, DC, JCB, MC, V.
> **Open:** Dinner daily 5pm–12:30am (last order).

If you feel like eating Western food, try the Kokusai Hotel's premier restaurant, the Vue Mer, which has a great view and an extensive wine and cocktail menu. It's the perfect place to come for a late dinner—you might want to come here after an evening stroll atop Mt. Hakodate. Its à la carte menu lists seafood, steaks, and pastas.

BAY RESTAURANT AND MARKET, 11-5 Toyokawa-cho. Tel. 22-1300.
> **Cuisine:** SEAFOOD. **Directions:** A 10-minute walk south of Hakodate Station.
> **$ Prices:** Set-dinner course ¥2,700 ($19.30); set lunch ¥1,600 ($11.40). No credit cards.
> **Open:** Lunch daily 11:30am–3pm; dinner daily 5:30–9:30pm.

★ This is my favorite restaurant among the several in the renovated brick warehouses along the waterfront. It's an airy locale, with exposed ceiling beams, brick walls, and simple but hip furniture. Serving mainly seafood, it offers set lunches and dinners with a trip through the salad bar, as well as a large selection of à la carte dishes from a menu that, unfortunately, is in Japanese only. For lunch you might want to try the teriyaki chicken or seafood-grill set meal, or the all-you-can eat salad bar. From the dinner menu, you might want to try fried shrimp with chili sauce, spicy tofu salad Chinese style, or tuna salad with coconut milk. There's also a raw-seafood bar where you can choose from the fresh seafood on display and then specify if you want it grilled, fried, or even simply raw. There are even tables outside by a canal for dining in fine weather.

MATSUMAE, 8th floor of Hakodate Kokusai Hotel, 5-10 Otemachi. Tel. 0138/23-8751.
> **Cuisine:** JAPANESE SEAFOOD. **Directions:** A 5-minute walk south of Hakodate Station.
> **$ Prices:** Set-dinner courses ¥1,700–¥6,500 ($12.15–$46.40); set lunches ¥750–¥1,600 ($5.35–$11.40). AE, DC, JCB, MC, V.
> **Open:** 11:30am–9:30pm (last order).

Also in the Kokusai Hotel, and with good views of the harbor, Matsumae is a Japanese seafood restaurant offering a variety of dishes from sashimi to tempura to broiled flatfish and squid, with à la carte prices starting at about ¥1,100 ($7.85). There are also lots of Hokkaido specialties, such as spring salmon, crab, and shrimp. In any case, there's an English menu, so you shouldn't have any difficulty ordering. Special lunch teishoku, served until 2pm, range from about ¥750 ($5.35) to ¥1,600 ($11.40) and may include tempura or sashimi in addition to side dishes.

HAKODATE BEER HALL, History Plaza, Motomachi. Tel. 27-1010.
> **Cuisine:** SNACKS/BEER. **Directions:** A 10-minute walk south of Hakodate Station.
> **$ Prices:** ¥900–¥3,000 ($6.40–$21.40). AE, JCB, V.
> **Open:** Daily 11:30am–10:30pm (last order 10pm).

This popular beer hall, located in a renovated brick warehouse along the waterfront, serves both dark and regular Sapporo beer along with seafood, sausages, fried noodles, and a range of other dishes displayed in its plastic-food case. Lunch teishoku, served until 2pm, include spaghetti, beef curry, fried noodles, obento lunch boxes, and other choices, ranging in price from about ¥700 to ¥1,500 ($5 to $10.70). A plate of assorted sausages costs ¥2,000 ($14.30), while teppanyaki is available for ¥3,000 ($21.40).

3. SAPPORO

731 miles NE of Tokyo; 177 miles NE of Hakodate

GETTING THERE   By Plane   If you're arriving at Sapporo's Chitose Airport, you can reach downtown Sapporo by either the airport limousine bus or by train from Japan Railways' Chitose Airport Station. Flights take 1½ hours from Tokyo, 2 hours from Hiroshima, and approximately 4 hours from Fukuoka (with a change of planes in Tokyo).

By Train   There are three overnight trains daily from Tokyo to Sapporo, taking about 16 hours.

ESSENTIAL INFORMATION   The **area code** for Sapporo, lying in Hokkaido Prefecture, is 011.

Sapporo is one of Japan's newest cities. A little more than a century ago, it was nothing more than a scattering of huts belonging to Ainu and Japanese families. All of Hokkaido, in fact, was a vast wilderness, largely unsettled, rich in timber and land. With the dawning of the Meiji Period, however, the government decided to colonize the island, and in 1869 it established the Colonization Commission. The area of Sapporo, which comes from the Ainu word meaning "big, dry river," was chosen as the site for the new capital from which to administer the land, and in 1871 construction of the city began.

During the Meiji Period, Japan looked eagerly toward the West for technology, ideas, and education, and Hokkaido was no exception. Between 1871 and 1884, 76 foreign technicians and experts, including 46 Americans, who had had experience in colonization were brought to this Japanese wilderness to aid in the island's development.

Sapporo was laid out in a grid pattern of uniform blocks similar to that of American cities. In 1875 the Sapporo Agricultural College was founded to train youths in skills useful to Hokkaido's colonization and development. Among the Americans invited to Hokkaido was William S. Clark, who taught for a year at the agricultural college. He is most remembered for what he said upon leaving: "Boys, be ambitious."

Ambitious they were. The Sapporo of today has grown to 1.6 million residents, making it the largest city north of Tokyo. In 1972, Sapporo was introduced to the world when the Winter Olympics were held here, and its many fine ski slopes continue to attract winter vacationers. In August, when the rest of Japan is sweltering under uncomfortably humid temperatures, Sapporo stays pleasantly cool.

With its nearby Chitose Airport, Sapporo serves as a springboard to Hokkaido's national parks and lakes. And yet despite all Sapporo has to offer and despite its size and importance, I've seen few foreigners in Sapporo even in August. For most visitors to Japan, Sapporo and the rest of Hokkaido remain virtually undiscovered.

ORIENTATION

INFORMATION

Pick up a flyer called *Sapporo and Vicinity* from the Tourist Information Center in either Tokyo or Kyoto.

Upon arrival in Sapporo, stop by the **tourist office** at Sapporo Station, in the underground passageway of the south exit, near the subway station. Daily hours are from 9am to 5pm, and you can pick up a map of the city and find directions to your hotel. If you have any questions during your stay, call the **Sapporo Tourism Department** at 211-2376.

In addition, the **Sapporo International Communication Plaza,** on the third floor of the MN Building, across from the Clock Tower (tel. 211-2105), provides information and maintains a staff of volunteer interpreters Monday through Saturday from 9am to 5pm. The Plaza also stocks a number of foreign publications, including *The New York Times, Time,* and *Newsweek.*

CITY LAYOUT

After the jumble of most Japanese cities, with their incomprehensible address systems, Sapporo will come as a welcome surprise. Its streets are laid out in a grid pattern, making the city easy to navigate. Addresses in Sapporo refer to blocks that follow one another in logical, numerical order.

The center of Sapporo is **Odori (Main Street),** a tree-lined avenue that bisects the city into north and south sections. North 1st, therefore, refers to the street one block north of Odori, as well as the entire block to the north of that street. Addresses in Sapporo are generally given by block. N1 W4, for example, is the address for the Sapporo Grand Hotel and means that it's located a block north of Odori and four blocks west of West 1st Street. (West 1st Street runs along the west bank of the Soseigawa River, while East 1st Street runs along the east bank.) If you want to be more technical about it, the entire, formal address of the hotel would read N1-jo W4-chome. "Jo" runs from north to south, while "chome" goes from east to west. Street signs are in English. Most of Sapporo's attractions and hotels lie south of Sapporo Station.

GETTING AROUND

Transportation in Sapporo is via **bus,** a few **subway** lines, and one **streetcar** line. Sapporo is also easy to cover **on foot.** You can, for example, walk south from Sapporo Station to Odori Park in less than 10 minutes and on to Susukino, Sapporo's nightlife district, in another 7 or 8 minutes.

For information on subways and buses in Sapporo, drop by the **Sapporo Transportation Information Office,** located underground at the Odori Station concourse. Open daily from 8am to 7pm, it also has maps of the city and can answer sightseeing inquiries.

SPECIAL EVENTS

Sapporo's annual **Snow Festival** is held from the first Wednesday to the following Sunday in February. Its mammoth snow and ice sculptures attract visitors from around the world.

WHAT TO SEE & DO

One of the first things you should do in Sapporo is simply walk around. Starting from Sapporo Station, take the street leading directly south called **Eki-mae Dori Street** (which is also West 4). This is one of Sapporo's main thoroughfares, and takes you through the heart of the city. Four blocks south of the station, turn left on N1 and after a block you'll find Sapporo's most famous landmark, **Clock Tower.** This Western-style wooden building was built in 1878 as a drill hall for the Sapporo Agricultural College (now Hokkaido University). The large clock at the top was made in Boston and was installed in 1881. In summer it attracts tourists even at night; they hang around the outside gates just to listen to it strike the hour. Inside the tower is a local-history museum with some old photographs of Sapporo and displays outlining the city's development. Although the explanations are in Japanese only, the museum is free and is open Tuesday through Sunday from 9am to 4pm (closed national holidays).

If you continue walking one block south of the Clock Tower, you'll reach **Odori,** a wide boulevard stretching almost a mile from east to west. In the middle of the boulevard is a wide median strip that has been turned into a park with trees, flower beds, and fountains. This is where much of the Sapporo Snow Festival is held in early February, when packed snow is carved to form statues, palaces, and fantasies. One snow structure may require as much as 300 six-ton truckloads of snow, brought in from the surrounding mountains. The Snow Festival also displays intricate ice carvings, done with so much attention to detail that it's almost a crime the carvings must melt. First begun in 1950 to add a bit of spice and life to the cold winter days, the Snow Festival now features about 150 large and small snow statues and draws about 2.2 million visitors a year.

Odori Park is also the scene of the **Summer Festival,** celebrated with beer gardens set up the length of the park from mid-July to mid-August and open every evening beginning at 5pm. Various Japanese beer companies set up their own booths and tables under the trees, while vendors put up stalls selling fried noodles, corn on the cob, and other goodies. Live bands serenade the beer drinkers under the stars. It all resembles the cheerful confusion of a German beer garden, which isn't surprising, considering that Munich is one of Sapporo's sister cities (Portland, Oregon, is another one).

From Odori Park you can continue your walk either above or below ground. Appreciated especially during inclement weather and during Hokkaido's long cold winters are two underground shopping arcades. Underneath Odori Park from Odori Subway Station all the way to the TV tower in the east is **Aurora Town,** with its boutiques and restaurants. Even longer is **Pole Town,** 1,300 feet of shops, almost 100 in all. Pole Town extends from Odori Subway Station south all the way to Susukino, Sapporo's nightlife amusement center, where you can find many restaurants and pubs (refer to the "Where to Dine" section, below). Before reaching Susukino, however, you may want to emerge at **Sanchome** (you'll see escalators going up), where you'll find more shopping at the Tanuki-koji covered shopping arcade.

Backtracking now toward the station, your last stop should be the **Botanical Garden (Shokubutsu-en),** the entrance to which is at N3 W8. Open Tuesday through Sunday from 9am to 4pm (April 29 to September 30) and from 9am to 3:30pm (October 1 to November 3), it has 5,000 varieties of plants arranged in marshland, herb, and alpine gardens, a greenhouse, and other sections. With lots of trees and grassy lawns, it's a good place for a summer afternoon picnic. Admission is ¥400 ($2.85). In winter, only the greenhouse is open.

OTHER THINGS TO SEE

✪ Although it's not within easy walking distance of Sapporo Station, you should make the **Sapporo Beer Factory** part of your sightseeing itinerary. The factory is directly east of Sapporo Station, about 10 minutes by bus. Sapporo Beer is famous throughout Japan, and the brew has been produced here ever since the first factory opened in 1876. Tours are held daily throughout the year, with the first tour starting at 8:40am and the last at 4:40pm during peak summer months. It's best to make reservations beforehand to avoid having to wait (tel. 731-4368). Although tours are conducted in Japanese only, a few of the guides speak English, so ask whether it's possible to have an English interpreter at the time you make your reservation. Free of charge, tours last approximately an hour.

The tour begins with a walk through the brewery, where you'll be struck by how few humans work in the factory. The process is fully automated in assembly lines—the main human function is merely to watch to make sure nothing goes haywire. Following the brewery tour is a short stop in the **Sapporo Museum,** where you'll see old beer posters, photographs, and other memorabilia. Then comes

SAPPORO

N

To Shin-Totsugawa ↑

SASSHO LINE

Race Course

← To Otaru & Hakodate

HAKODATE MAIN LINE

To Asahigawa & Hakodate →

Soen

Kita-Juhachijo

Kita-Junijo

Sapporo

1

3 **2**

2

1

Kita Gojo

Botanical Garden

3

Eki-mae Dori

4 **5**

Clock Tower Bldg.

4

Kita Ichijo

Odori   Odori Park

5

Odori

Hokkaiji

TOZAI SUBWAY LINE

Nishi-Juhachome

Maruyama-Koen

To Chitose Airport →

6 Tanuki Koji Shopping Arcade

Tanuki Koji

Susukino

☐ Ryukoji Temple

Nishi Nijutchome

Higashi-Hongaiji Temple

7 Maruyama Hill

Minami Kujo

Nishi Juitchome

Nakajima-Koen

Nakajima Park

Toyochira River

Minami Juyojo

Gokoku Shrine

Minami Jushichijo

Sapporo ○

JAPAN

★ TOKYO

ATTRACTIONS:
Botanical Garden
(Shokubtsu-en) **3**
Clock Tower **4**
Eki-mae Dori **2**
Maruyama Hill ski area **7**
Odori Park **5**
Sapporo Beer Factory &
Sapporo Museum **1**
Tanuki Koji Shopping Arcade **6**

ACCOMMODATIONS:
ANA Hotel Sapporo **2**
Keio Plaza Hotel **1**
New Otani **5**
Sapporo Grand Hotel **4**
Sapporo Tokyu Inn **3**

the fun part—you get to sample the brew. If after the tour you want to stick around and drink more of it (it often seems to work that way), you'll find the Sapporo Beer Hall on the grounds, and in summer months there's even an outdoor beer garden. Refer to the "Where to Dine" section, below, for details.

If you have time, you should also consider visiting **Nopporo Forest Park (Nopporo Shinrin Koen),** where you'll find a 330-foot tower (built in 1970 to commemorate Hokkaido's centennial) and two other attractions. The **Historical Museum of Hokkaido (Kaitaku Kinenkan)** houses collections detailing Hokkaido's development from prehistoric to modern times (including Ainu artifacts). The admission charge is ¥250 ($1.80) and hours are 9am to 4:30pm Tuesday through Sunday; closed national holidays. The **Historical Village of Hokkaido (Kaitaku-no-Mura)** is an open-air museum of historical houses, including homes, farmhouses, a school, a hostel, and a shrine. With the same hours as the Historical Museum, it charges ¥510 ($3.65) admission (¥410 or $2.90 in winter). You can reach Nopporo Park via the JR bus from Sapporo Station in 50 minutes.

SKIING

The slopes around Sapporo offer skiing from early December to late April. Since you can fly directly to Sapporo from many cities in Japan, it's a popular winter destination. The **Teine Olympia Ski Grounds** are located about an hour from Sapporo by bus. This was the site of the alpine, bobsled, and toboggan events in the Sapporo Winter Olympic Games of 1972. Other skiing areas within 30 minutes of Sapporo are **Mt. Moiwa, Mt. Arai,** and **Maruyama.** Most sites provide ski-rental equipment for approximately ¥3,500 ($25) per day, but keep in mind that sizes are generally smaller than in the West.

WHERE TO STAY

Because the 1972 Winter Olympics were held in Sapporo, the city has a large selection of fine hotels in various price categories. Sapporo's heaviest tourist season is during summer and during the annual Snow Festival held in early February. If you plan to attend the Snow Festival, book your hotel room at least 6 months in advance. At other times during the year, you should have no problem finding a room, but it's always wise to make a reservation in advance. During winter (excluding the time of the Snow Festival), some upper- and medium-priced hotels lower their room rates, sometimes by as much as 40%. That should come as welcome news to you ski enthusiasts. Be sure to ask for a discount.

EXPENSIVE

ANA HOTEL SAPPORO (also called Zenniku Hotel) ㉔, **N3 W1, Chuo-ku, Sapporo 060.** Tel. 011/221-4411. Fax 011/222-7624. 460 rms. A/C MINIBAR TV TEL **Directions:** A 5-minute walk southeast of Sapporo Station.

$ Rates: ¥14,000–¥20,000 ($100–$143) single; ¥23,000–¥27,000 ($164–$193) double; ¥23,000–¥33,000 ($164–$236) twin. AE, DC, JCB, MC, V.

This gleaming white hotel, rising high in Sapporo's skyline, has the kind of rooms travelers can appreciate: five lamps in its larger rooms so you don't have to read in the dark, bilingual TV sets that swivel and have pay video, an extra phone in the bathroom, two layers of curtains for complete darkness, and such amenities as a hot-water pot for tea, a minibar, a radio, and an alarm clock.

Dining/Entertainment: Top of Sapporo, on the 26th floor, is a French restaurant with views of the city. Chinese and Japanese restaurants are on the 25th floor, also with views of the city, while in the basement is Satohoro, a restaurant specializing in Hokkaido dishes. After dinner, retire to the sky lounge Sapporo View, where there's piano music every night except Sunday.

Services: Same-day laundry service.

Facilities: Sauna.

CENTURY ROYAL HOTEL, N5 W5, Chuo-ku, Sapporo 060. Tel. 011/221-

2121. Fax 011/231-2538. 336 rms. A/C MINIBAR TV TEL **Directions:** A 1-minute walk from Sapporo Station.

$ Rates: ¥14,800 ($106) single; ¥21,000-¥24,500 ($150-$175) double; ¥24,500-¥27,000 ($175-$193) twin. AE, DC, JCB, MC, V.

The Century Royal Hotel's excellent location next to the train station is its main selling point. Another is its revolving restaurant on the 23rd floor. Otherwise, rooms are fairly basic, with minibar, music, and alarm clock, among other amenities, and windows with double panes to shut out noise.

Dining/Entertainment: Rondo, a revolving restaurant on the 23rd floor, offers the best dining view in the city. There's also a Japanese restaurant serving Hokkaido specialties, a coffee shop, and bar.

Services: Same-day laundry service.

Facilities: Gift and souvenir shops.

KEIO PLAZA HOTEL, N5 W7, Chuo-ku, Sapporo 060. Tel. 011/271-0111. Fax 011/221-5450. 525 rms. A/C MINIBAR TV TEL **Directions:** A 3-minute walk west of Sapporo Station.

$ Rates: ¥14,000-¥17,000 ($100-$121) single; ¥19,000-¥30,000 ($136-$214) double; ¥25,000-¥30,000 ($178-$214) twin. AE, DC, JCB, MC, V.

This graceful hostelry has a white-and-light-green lobby that gives way to bold colors in the bedrooms, which are accented with striped bedspreads in primary colors. Rooms are what you'd expect in an upper-class hotel, including double-pane windows to block out noise, TV with pay video, hot-water pot, clock, and radio. The sink area has lots of room. Keep in mind that the cheapest doubles have only a semidouble-size bed; those with a full-size double bed begin at ¥27,000 ($193). This is an attractive hotel all around.

Dining/Entertainment: There are 13 bars and restaurants.

Services: Same-day laundry service.

Facilities: Indoor swimming pool, sauna and fitness gym (fee charged).

NEW OTANI, N2 W1, Chuo-ku, Sapporo 060. Tel. 011/222-1111. Fax 011/222-5521. 340 rms. A/C MINIBAR TV TEL **Directions:** A 6-minute walk southeast of Sapporo Station.

$ Rates: ¥15,000 ($107) single; ¥25,500-¥28,000 ($182-$200) twin; ¥27,000-¥29,000 ($193-$207) double; ¥27,000-¥30,000 ($193-$214) triple. AE, DC, JCB, MC, V.

Located just south of the ANA Hotel, the New Otani features rooms decorated in soothing pastels, with bilingual TV with pay video, radio, alarm clock, fridge, and double-pane windows that open. Bathrooms have larger-than-average tubs.

Dining/Entertainment: The Four Seasons restaurant offers French, Chinese, and Japanese cuisine, while Rendezvous, a convenient lobby coffee shop, is open from 7am to 10pm (the hot tuna sandwich, by the way, is delicious).

Services: Same-day laundry service.

Facilities: Medical center; Asahi Culture Center (with traditional art exhibitions); rental bicycles, golf clubs, and skis.

SAPPORO GRAND HOTEL, N1 W4, Chuo-ku, Sapporo 060. Tel. 011/261-3311. Fax 011/222-5164. 585 rms. A/C MINIBAR TV TEL **Directions:** A 6-minute walk south of Sapporo Station.

$ Rates: ¥13,000 ($93) single; ¥20,500 ($146) double; ¥22,500 ($161) twin. AE, DC, JCB, MC, V.

This dignified hotel, with more than 50 years of excellent service, is usually where VIPs stay when they come to Sapporo. Rooms in the newer annex (which opened in 1984) are very chic, with contemporary furniture and bilingual TV with pay video. There are large desks with lots of working space, semidouble-size beds in the single and twin rooms, and tiled bathrooms with marble-topped counters. Rooms in the older part of the hotel are also very nice and have been updated.

Dining/Entertainment: The hotel has an exceptional French restaurant, a beer hall, several bars, and Japanese restaurants.

Services: Same-day laundry service.

Facilities: Shopping arcade, sauna.

SAPPORO KORAKUEN HOTEL, Odori W8, Chuo-ku, Sapporo 060. Tel. 011/261-0111. Fax 011/261-5650. 305 rms. A/C MINIBAR TV TEL **Directions:** A 5-minute taxi ride or a 15-minute walk southwest of Sapporo Station.
$ Rates: ¥14,800 ($106) single; ¥22,000–¥23,000 ($157–$164) double; ¥22,000–¥35,000 ($157–$250) twin. AE, DC, JCB, MC, V.

This hotel is located right on Odori, the heart of the city. In fact, this would be the place to be during the Snow Festival (no single rooms, however, face the park). Its lobby flaunts space with an inner atrium that stretches 14 stories high (imagine what the heating bill must be). Rooms are small and slightly feminine in appearance, with a decor of soft pastels, and include all the amenities you'd expect, such as TV with remote control, hot-water thermos, hairdryer, clothesline in the bathroom, and radio.

Dining/Entertainment: Three restaurants serving Japanese, Chinese, and Western fare, the latter with a view of Odori Park.
Services: Same-day laundry service.
Facilities: Fitness club (fee charged).

MODERATE

All these hotels offer rooms with private bathroom.

CHISAN HOTEL SAPPOROSHINKAN, N2 W2, Chuo-ku, Sapporo 060. Tel. 011/222-6611. Fax 011/222-6617. 162 rms. A/C MINIBAR TV TEL **Directions:** A 5-minute walk south of Sapporo Station.
$ Rates: ¥9,400 ($67) single; ¥18,000 ($128) twin; ¥14,000 ($100) double. AE, DC, JCB, MC, V.

This pleasant business hotel opened in 1984—don't confuse it with the older Chisan, just a 30-second walk away (with rooms that are outdated and less cheerful, making the newer annex a much better deal). The rooms here come with the usual dark furniture and purple- and pink-striped bedcover that is the trademark of Chisan chain hotels. Panels close over the windows for darkness, and other facilities include TV with pay video, minibar, and semidouble-size beds. The hotel contains one Japanese restaurant.

NAKAMURAYA RYOKAN ⑳, N3 W7, Chuo-ku, Sapporo 060. Tel. 011/241-2111. Fax 011/241-2118. 32 rms (all with bath). A/C MINIBAR TV TEL **Directions:** A 7-minute walk southwest of Sapporo Station.
$ Rates: Japanese rates: ¥18,500 ($132) one person, including breakfast and dinner; ¥26,000 ($186) two persons, including breakfast and dinner. Special rates for foreigners: ¥7,700 ($55) one person without meals; ¥14,000 ($100) two persons without meals; ¥20,000 ($143) three persons without meals. AE, MC, V.

If you want to stay in a ryokan, this is a modern and comfortable Japanese inn located next to the entrance of the Botanical Garden. Most of the rooms are Japanese style, and all come with minibar, TV, and clock. I prefer the Japanese rooms to the Western ones—their simplicity is in sharp contrast to the old carpeting and odd color combination in the Western rooms. This ryokan is a member of the Japanese Inn Group, so if you make a booking in advance and mention Japanese Inn Group, you'll receive a much lower rate as a foreigner. Prices do not include meals, but they are available for ¥1,000 ($7.15) for breakfast and ¥5,000 ($35.70) extra for dinner. There's also a cafeteria. Although rooms have their own tub, you might want to take advantage of the hot-spring public baths here.

SAPPORO TOKYU INN, S4 W5, Chuo-ku, Sapporo 064. Tel. 011/531-0109. Fax 011/531-2387. 574 rms. A/C MINIBAR TV TEL **Subway:** From Sapporo Station to Susukino stop, then a 1-minute walk.
$ Rates (including service charge): ¥8,800–¥10,500 ($63–$75) single; ¥16,200–¥18,200 ($116–$130) double; ¥16,900–¥19,000 ($121–$136) twin. AE, DC, JCB, MC, V.

If you want to be close to the nightlife action in Susukino, this is the best choice in the area. A member of the Tokyu hotel chain, this redbrick business hotel has a total of 18 restaurants, including those in an adjoining basement shopping arcade. Rooms are spotlessly clean and tastefully decorated in muted browns, and come with TV and clock. Vending machines with beer and soda are located in the hallways. Notice the tiny dots beside each door, which are the room number in Braille. They're for the hotel's masseurs, who are often blind in Japan.

HOTEL SUNFLOWER SAPPORO, S5 W3, Chuo-ku, Sapporo 064. Tel. 011/512-5533. Fax 011/511-1060. 233 rms. A/C TV TEL **Subway:** From Sapporo Station to Susukino stop (two stops), then a 1-minute walk.

$ Rates (including tax and service): ¥9,300 ($66) single; ¥11,000 ($78) double; ¥16,500 ($118) twin. AE, DC, JCB, MC, V.

Located in the Susukino nightlife district, this is a good place to stay if you like carousing through the bars at night—it's not far to crawl back to your hotel. Based on its facilities and atmosphere, I would classify this establishment as a business hotel, but because of its location it caters to both businesspeople and tourists. The rooms are tiny and unexciting, with TV with pay video and a minuscule bathroom. The single rooms have glazed windows, so you can't see out; but even if you open the windows there isn't much to see, so I guess it doesn't matter. The hotel serves a popular and good buffet dinner, which offers a variety of Western, Japanese, Chinese, and local Hokkaido specialties for only ¥2,700 ($19.30) Monday through Saturday from 5 to 9pm and on Sunday from 4 to 9pm.

HOTEL SUNROUTE NEW SAPPORO, S2 W6, Chuo-ku, Sapporo 060. Tel. 011/251-2511. Fax 011/251-2513. 334 rms. A/C MINIBAR TV TEL **Subway:** From Sapporo Station to Susukino stop, then a 4-minute walk.

$ Rates: ¥10,000–¥11,000 ($71–$78) single; ¥17,500 ($125) double; ¥18,500–¥26,000 ($132–$186) twin; ¥24,000 ($171) triple. AE, DC, JCB, MC, V.

This pleasant modern business hotel is located on the Tanuki-koji covered shopping street in the center of town. Sporting a souvenir shop and Japanese and Western restaurants, it offers typical business-type rooms with TV and adult video, music, minibar, alarm clock, and hot-water pot.

WASHINGTON HOTEL 2, N5 W6, Chuo-ku, Sapporo 060. Tel. 011/222-3311. 202 rms. A/C MINIBAR TV TEL **Directions:** A 3-minute walk west of Sapporo Station.

$ Rates (including service charge): ¥9,300–¥9,800 ($66–$70) single; ¥17,400–¥20,500 ($124–$146) double; ¥17,700–¥20,500 ($126–$146) twin. AE, DC, JCB, MC, V.

Part of a reliable national hotel chain, the Washington Hotel has two locations in Sapporo, both close to the train station. This is the newer of the two—a bit more pleasant in its facilities. Rooms have rattan furniture, TV with video, minibar, hot-water pot, music, and alarm clock. Unlike most business hotels with check-in at 3 or 4pm, the Washington's check-in is 2pm. Restaurants include a coffee shop; a combination steak restaurant and bar called Gaslight, found in many Washington hotels; and a bar on the 10th floor.

WASHINGTON HOTEL 1, N4 W4, Chuo-ku, Sapporo 060. Tel. 011/251-3211. 434 rms. A/C TV TEL **Directions:** A 1-minute walk from Sapporo Station, across street.

$ Rates (including service charge): ¥6,500–¥9,600 ($46–$68) single; ¥17,000–¥20,500 ($121–$146) twin; ¥18,600 ($134). AE, DC, JCB, MC, V.

The cheaper and older of the two Washington hotels, this one has a lobby on the second floor, up the escalator. I don't advise the cheapest singles unless you hate sunshine, since they have no windows and are extremely dark. Slightly more expensive are those that face a rather drab inside courtyard, but at least you have a window. Why not splurge and go for one of the best singles in the house, which are larger and face toward the outside? Rooms have TV with pay video, hot-water pot and tea, and a tiny bathroom; those that face the station have double-pane windows to shut out noise.

Vending machines in the hallways dispense beer, snacks, and soft drinks; there are also Western and Japanese restaurants.

BUDGET

Youth Hostels

SAPPORO HOUSE YOUTH HOSTEL, N6 W6, Kita-ku, Sapporo 001. Tel. 011/726-4235. 124 beds. **Directions:** A 7-minute walk west of Sapporo Station; turn right out of south exit, walk three blocks, and then turn right again. Hostel is just beyond railroad tracks, on right.

$ Rates (per person): ¥2,300 ($16.40) member and nonmember. Breakfast ¥450 ($3.20); dinner ¥850 ($6.05). No credit cards.

The sign outside this white concrete building—the closest youth hostel to Sapporo Station—is in Japanese only, but look for the sign with "YH" on it. Sleeping accommodations are both beds and futon, and even in August they often have space. Rental bicycles are available.

SAPPORO MIYAGAOKA YOUTH HOSTEL, N1 14-chome Miyanomori, Chuo-ku, Sapporo 064. Tel. 011/611-9016. 52 beds. **Subway and Bus:** Subway from Sapporo to Odori stop, transferring there to Higashi-nishi Line heading west. Get off at Maruyama Koen stop, transferring there to bus.

$ Rates (per person): ¥2,400 ($17.15) member and nonmember. Breakfast ¥450 ($3.20); dinner ¥850 ($6.05). No credit cards.

This youth hostel is open only in summer, from July 1 through August. It's located near a park with tennis courts, west of the city.

SAPPORO SHIRITSU LIONS YOUTH HOSTEL, N1 18-chome Miyano-mori, Chuo-ku, Sapporo 064. Tel. 011/611-4709. 100 beds. **Subway and Bus:** Subway from Sapporo Station to Odori stop, transferring there to Higashi-nishi Line heading west. Get off at Maruyama Koen stop, transferring there to bus.

$ Rates: ¥2,400 ($17.15) member; ¥3,100 ($22.15) nonmember. Breakfast ¥450 ($3.20); dinner ¥850 ($6.05). No credit cards.

Not far from the Miyagaoka Youth Hostel, above, this hostel is also located near Maruyama Koen Park.

WHERE TO DINE

Hokkaido's specialties include crab, corn on the cob, potatoes, Genghis Khan (also spelled "Jingisukan"), Chinese noodles, salmon, and Ishikari Nabe. Genghis Khan is a dish of mutton and vegetables that you grill yourself, while Ishikari Nabe is a stew of salmon and other Hokkaido vegetables, also cooked at your table. As for Western food, your best bet is to dine in one of the many fine restaurants in Sapporo's top hotels.

EXPENSIVE

GRAND CHEF, Grand Hotel, N1 W4. Tel. 261-3311.
Cuisine: FRENCH. **Reservations:** Not necessary. **Directions:** A 6-minute walk south of Sapporo Station.

$ Prices: Set-dinner courses ¥11,000–¥20,000 ($78–$143); set lunches ¥3,300–¥5,500 ($23.55–$39.30). AE, DC, JCB, MC, V.

Open: Lunch daily 11:30am–2pm; dinner daily 5–10pm.

This excellent French restaurant is elegantly and cheerfully decorated in pink, white, and gray, and specializes in Hokkaido food cooked Western style. The à la carte dinner menu changes annually but always includes selections of seafood, such as scallops, sole, or salmon, as well as steak, lamb, chicken, and duck. Expect to spend about ¥6,500–¥11,000 ($46.40–$78.55) if you order à la carte. There are also special dinner courses and set lunches.

TOP OF SAPPORO, 26th floor of ANA Hotel (Zenniku Hotel), N3 W1. Tel. 221-4411.

> **Cuisine:** FRENCH. **Reservations:** Recommended. **Directions:** A 5-minute walk southeast of Sapporo Station.
>
> **$ Prices:** Set-dinner courses ¥5,500–¥9,000 ($39.30–$64.30); set lunches ¥2,000–¥4,500 ($14.30–$32.15). AE, DC, JCB, MC, V.
>
> **Open:** Lunch daily 11:30am–2:30pm; dinner daily 5–10pm.

This small, intimate, and tastefully decorated restaurant offers meals that change every 2 months and include Hokkaido delicacies cooked in a French style. A la carte dishes, for which you'll probably spend ¥8,000 ($57.15) for a complete meal, include broiled lobster, cream style king crab with sea urchin, roast lamb, and steak.

MODERATE

KURUMAYA, 25th floor of ANA Hotel (Zenniku Hotel), N3 W1. Tel. 221-0608.

> **Cuisine:** VARIED JAPANESE. **Directions:** A 5-minute walk southeast of Sapporo Station.
>
> **$ Prices:** Main dishes ¥900–¥6,000 ($6.40–$42.85). AE, DC, JCB, MC, V.
>
> **Open:** Daily 11:30am–9:30pm.

If you want to dine in elegant surroundings with a view of the city, the 25th floor of the ANA Hotel (Zenniku Hotel) has both a Japanese and a Chinese restaurant. Kurumaya, the Japanese restaurant, has an English menu and includes a shabu-shabu dinner course for ¥5,800 ($41.40), a sukiyaki meal for ¥6,000 ($42.85), and broiled Matsuzaka beef with Japanese peppers for ¥4,600 ($32.85). Other items include tempura, sashimi, salmon, noodles, rice porridge, and kaiseki.

RONDO, 23rd floor of Century Royal Hotel, next to Sapporo Station, N5 W5. Tel. 221-2121.

> **Cuisine:** WESTERN. **Directions:** A 1-minute walk from Sapporo Station.
>
> **$ Prices:** Main dishes ¥2,000–¥5,000 ($14.30–$35.70); set-dinner courses ¥6,500–¥16,500 ($46.40–$117.85); set lunches ¥2,200–¥5,000 ($15.70–$35.70). AE, DC, JCB, MC, V.
>
> **Open:** Daily 11:30am–11pm.

This revolving restaurant, conveniently located near Sapporo Station atop the Century Royal Hotel, makes a complete turn every hour and has an English menu complete with photos. Tables are all located at windows so that everyone gets the best view in the house. Even if you don't eat here, it's a good place to come on a fine clear day for a cup of coffee or an evening cocktail. The varied menu includes spaghetti, sandwiches, curry rice, grilled half chicken, pork chops, steak, crab gratin, and lobster gratin. Cocktails start at ¥880 ($6.30).

BUDGET

IROHANIHOHETO ⑧¹, S5 W4. Tel. 521-1682.

> **Cuisine:** VARIED JAPANESE. **Subway:** Susukino Station, a 3-minute walk away.
>
> **$ Prices:** ¥250–¥600 ($1.80–$4.30). No credit cards.
>
> **Open:** Sun–Fri 5pm–12:30am, Sat 5pm–3am.

This eating and drinking establishment in the Susukino area is part of a Sapporo chain that has since spread all over Japan. It's popular everywhere with young Japanese because of its low prices. As in most Irohanihoheto shops, this one is decorated in a rustic country style, with heavy wooden beams and folkcraft hanging from the rafters. The menu is in Japanese only, but there are some pictures; an alternative is to look at what others around you are eating. There are nearly 100 items on the menu, including yakitori, tofu dishes, oden, sashimi, vegetables, sausage, nikujaga (potato-and-beef stew), salads, buttered corn, fried fish, and more. Beer starts at ¥400 ($2.85).

Other Irohanihoheto branches in Sapporo can be found at S4 W2 and at S6 W3, both in the Susukino area; and at N3 W3, just a few minutes' south of Sapporo Station.

SAPPORO BIER GARTEN, N6 E9. Tel. 742-1531.

Cuisine: GENGHIS KHAN. **Directions:** A 5-minute taxi ride from Sapporo Station.

$ **Prices:** ¥300–¥1,000 ($2.15–$7.15); all-you-can-eat Genghis Khan ¥3,300 ($23.55). AE, DC, JCB, MC, V.

Open: Garden, June–Aug daily 5–9pm; beer hall, daily 11:30am–9pm.

I can't imagine going to Sapporo without dropping by the Sapporo Bier Garten, which is spread out under broad-leafed acacia trees. If it's winter or early in the day, you can dine in the Sapporo Beer Hall, an old ivy-covered brick building built in 1889 as the Sapporo brewery. The interior is also brick, with a wood floor and wood beams, making for a very congenial atmosphere. I personally prefer the second floor, where you dine underneath a huge old mash tub once used in brewing beer. By the way, though I haven't seen it myself, the management tells me that from January 20 to mid-February there's a snow igloo built outside in which you can sit and drink beer too.

The specialty of the house is Genghis Khan, which you cook yourself on a hot skillet at your table. The best deal in the house is the King Viking, which for ¥3,300 ($23.55) gives you as much Genghis Khan and as much draft beer as you can consume in a 2-hour period. A regular, single serving of Genghis Khan costs ¥1,000 ($7.15). Other dishes include buttered corn on the cob, potatoes, and crab. Draft beer starts at ¥450 ($3.20) for a small mug.

SATOHORO ⑳, basement of ANA Hotel (Zenniku Hotel), N3 W1. Tel. 221-4411.

Cuisine: HOKKAIDO SPECIALTIES. **Directions:** A 5-minute walk southeast of Sapporo Station.

$ **Prices:** Set-dinner courses ¥5,000–¥10,000 ($35.70–$71.40); set lunches ¥1,000–¥3,500 ($7.15–$25). AE, DC, JCB, MC, V.

Open: Daily 11:30am–10pm.

Near Sapporo Station in the basement of the ANA hotel, this restaurant serves Hokkaido specialties at reasonable prices. Simply decorated with wood and bamboo, it serves frozen salmon (*benishake ruibe*), potatoes in butter (*imo batta*), crab salad, local fish, and other dishes. A crab rice dish or crab salad costs ¥1,000 ($7.15), but if you feel like splurging you can order one of the set meals.

SUNTORY BEER BENIZAKURA GARDEN, Sumikawa 389-769, Minami-ku. Tel. 582-4411.

Cuisine: GENGHIS KHAN. **Subway:** Nanboku Line to Makomanai Station, then a 5-minute taxi ride or take one of Suntory shuttle buses that run between Makomanai Station and beer garden every 30 minutes.

$ **Prices:** ¥500–¥1,300 ($3.55–$9.30); all-you-can-eat Genghis Kahn ¥3,300 ($23.55). DC, JCB, MC.

Open: Daily 11:30am–9pm.

Not to be outdone by the Sapporo beer company, Suntory opened its own beer garden in 1985, on the south edge of town. Although the restaurant itself is bright and airy, you can dine outside by the lotus pond in fine weather. Be sure to wander through the gardens, which extend back behind the restaurant and consist of ponds and a waterfall. A single order of Genghis Khan costs ¥1,000 ($7.15), and Suntory beer starts at ¥450 ($3.20). For ¥3,300 ($23.55) you can eat all the Genghis Khan and drink as much beer as you want over a 2-hour period. Mild or spicy sauces for dipping morsels of mutton and vegetables are available.

TAJ MAHAL, S1 W2. Tel. 231-1168.

Cuisine: INDIAN. **Subway:** A 5-minute walk from Odori Station.

$ **Prices:** Curries ¥900–¥1,700 ($6.40–$12.15); set-dinner courses ¥2,000–¥6,000 ($14.30–$42.85); set lunch ¥800 ($5.70). AE, DC, JCB, V.

Open: Daily 11am–10pm (last order).

The main shop of this Indian restaurant is near Odori and the Mitsukoshi department store. In addition to its tandoori and kebabs are chicken, lamb, and vegetable curries (no pork or beef is served).

Taj Mahal also has a branch at N2 W3, near the Grand Hotel, about a 5-minute walk from Sapporo Station.

SPECIALTY DINING

Another well-known restaurant in Sapporo is **Hyosetsu-No-Mon** ㉘, S5 W2 (tel. 521-3046), which specializes in giant king crab caught in the Japan Sea north of Hokkaido. Actually, there are three restaurants here side by side in Sapporo's Susukino nightlife district. The main shop is the one farthest west (the first one you'll reach if you're walking from the Susukino subway station). The menu is easy enough—it's almost entirely of king crab, which comes in a variety of styles with prices to match. Set courses start at ¥7,000 ($50), and they include a cooked crab, sashimi, crab soup, crab tempura, and vegetables. Other meals range all the way up to ¥10,000 ($71.40), increasing the portion of crab and number of side dishes. You can also order à la carte for fried king crab claws, deep-fried king crab, tempura king crab, grilled king crab, and crabmeat chowder, with average meals ranging from ¥3,000 to ¥6,000 ($21.40 to $42.85). Other à la carte selections include various sashimi, raw sea urchin, salmon eggs, and raw crab organs. This main shop is open daily from 11am to 11pm.

Next to the main restaurant is its Western restaurant, where a small band provides entertainment nightly. The interior of this place is imitation European, although exactly which country it's imitating is hard to say. Menus from various countries hang on its walls, and the menus here all come with photographs so that foreigners have no problems ordering. It serves king crab à la carte dishes ranging from ¥1,000 to ¥3,300 ($7.15 to $23.55), including crab fondue and crab gratin. Other dishes include steak, sausage, pork, and potatoes, with prices mostly under ¥900–¥2,200 ($6.40–$15.70). Open daily from 5pm to midnight.

✪ The third Hyosetsu-no-Mon restaurant serves the same food as the main shop, above, but this one has two floor shows nightly as well, one at 6pm and the second at 8pm, and it's best to make a reservation. The show starts off with a classical dance, followed by contemporary and folk dances, and costs only ¥800 ($5.70) extra in addition to dinner, so it's worth coming here for a meal. This establishment is filled with Japanese tourists on holiday in Hokkaido and is great fun. You sit on the floor here to eat your meal in a dining hall reminiscent of old Kabuki theaters.

Sapporo is famous for its ramen (Chinese noodles), and the most popular place to eat them is on a tiny, narrow street in Susukino popularly known as **Ramen Yokocho.** Located just one block east of Susukino subway station before you get to the Hotel Sunflower, it's an alleyway of noodle shop after noodle shop—16 in all. It doesn't matter which one you choose—just look to see where there's an empty seat. The shops are all very small affairs consisting of a counter and some chairs. Most are open from 11am to midnight and their closed days are staggered, so you're sure to find some open. Noodles generally begin at ¥700 ($5) for a steaming bowlful.

4. THE NATIONAL PARKS OF HOKKAIDO

Much of Hokkaido's wilderness has been set aside in national parks. Of these, Shikotsu-Toya, Daisetsuzan, and Akan national parks are the best known, offering a wide range of activities from hiking to skiing to bathing at hot-spring resorts.

SHIKOTSU-TOYA NATIONAL PARK

If you have only a couple of days to spare to visit a national park in Hokkaido, Shikotsu-Toya National Park is the closest to Sapporo and therefore the easiest for the short-term visitor. It's also the first national park you'll reach if you've entered Hokkaido via train to Hakodate. This 381-square-mile national park encompasses lakes, volcanoes, and the famous hot-spring resorts of Toyako Spa and Noboribetsu Spa. In the village of Shiraoi, a museum and village commemorate the native Ainu and their culture.

Be sure to pick up a copy of *Southern Hokkaido*, put out by the Tourist Information Center in either Tokyo or Kyoto. It lists places of interest throughout the national park. As for traveling to and within the park, there's a bus from Sapporo that goes directly to Toyako Spa on Lake Toya. From Toyako Spa you can then proceed by bus to Noboribetsu and then back to Sapporo; from Noboribetsu you can also take a train to Shiraoi and back to Sapporo. There are also Japan Railways trains that run directly from Hakodate to Toya Station (from Toya Station it's a 15-minute bus ride to Lake Toya), and on to Noboribetsu, Shiraoi, and Sapporo.

TOYAKO SPA

Hugging the shores of Lake Toya, Toyako Spa (also called **Toyako Onsen;** *onsen* means "spa" is a small resort town with a sprinkling of ryokan, souvenir shops, and not much more. However, you don't come here for Toyako Spa itself, but for **Lake Toya,** the shining blue jewel of Shikotsu-Toya National Park. Surrounded on all sides by hills, Lake Toya is almost perfectly round. It is a typical caldera lake—that is, a lake that has formed within the collapsed crater of an extinct volcano. Approximately 590 feet deep, Lake Toya is invitingly clear and cool and never freezes over even in the dead of winter. In the middle of the lake are four thickly wooded islets, casting mirror images of themselves in the water below.

Most people stay in Toyako Onsen only one night. It's enough time to relax and do the few things the place has to offer. If you happen to stay two nights, you'll find your ryokan deserted after check-out time until the next crowd arrives at check-in time.

Getting There

If you're arriving by train from Sapporo (about 2 hours) or from Hakodate (a little over 2 hours), you'll arrive at Toya Station, about 4½ miles from Toyako Onsen. Since there is no train station in Toyako Onsen, you should transfer at Toya Station to a bus bound for the Toyako Onsen bus terminal, or you can take a taxi from Toya Station to Toyako Onsen for about ¥2,000 ($14.30).

You can also reach Toyako Onsen directly by either Donan or Jotetsu Bus Company from Sapporo. The trip takes 2 hours and 40 minutes and costs ¥2,550 ($18.20) one way.

Orientation

Essential Information The **area code** for Toyako Onsen is 01427.

The Toyako Onsen **tourist association** (tel. 01427/5-2446) is down the hill toward the lake, about a minute's walk away from the bus terminal. It's open daily from 9am to 5pm. Unfortunately, there's no map in English, but the spa is so small you shouldn't have any difficulty finding your way around. Walking is the best way to get around town, which stretches along one main road following the curve of the lake.

Getting Around

Buses for Showa-Shinzan and Takinous Camp depart from the bus terminal, so inquire there about the schedule. Buses aren't very frequent.

What to See & Do

The most popular thing to do is take a **boat ride** across the clear lake to a couple of the islands in the middle. Charging ¥1,200 ($8.55), the boat pulls into two small docks, the first at an island where there are some deer and winding footpaths, the second at another island where there's a natural history museum (which, unfortunately, has explanations in Japanese only and is therefore of little interest to foreign visitors). If you decide to disembark at either of these islands, you can catch the next boat in about a half hour. If you stay on the boat for the entire trip, it takes about an hour. Along the shore of Toyako Spa are also several docks where you can rent rowboats and paddleboats.

If it's August and hot, the temptation to simply jump into the lake and cool off will be almost too hard to resist. You may be astonished to learn, however, that there are no swimming facilities in Toyako Onsen itself. In fact, hardly any lakes in Hokkaido allow swimming, because they are considered too cold and dangerous for humans. Desperate for a swim, I once took a bus ride 20 minutes around the lake to **Takinoue Camp** (tel. 01426/6-2121), one of the few places where swimming is allowed. There's a small sandy beach here and a few parents playing with their children, making it a good place to jump in and play too. Incidentally, you can also camp here for ¥300 ($2.15) per person. There are even tents for rent at ¥850 ($6.05) that sleep five persons, but you must have your own sleeping bag and camping supplies.

The huge **public baths** of the Sun Palace Hotel, located on the edge of Toyako Spa and described in the "Where to Stay" section, below, are open to the general public every day from 10am to 4pm (and only to hotel guests after 4pm). They feature a huge indoor pool filled with hot-spring water and complete with artificial waves and even water slides. You wear your swimming suit here, but there are also hot-spring bathing facilities (separated for men and women) that include saunas. Incidentally, the swimming pool also has an outdoor area where you can sun yourself. If you've never been to one of Japan's huge public baths, it's worth the ¥2,000 ($14.30) entry fee, which becomes ¥2,500 ($17.85) on Sunday and public holidays. Hotel guests use the facilities for free.

There are two very active volcanoes on the shores of Lake Toya not far from Toyako Spa. **Mt. Usu,** which towers over the tiny spa, erupted in August 1977, blanketing 80% of Hokkaido in volcanic ash and dumping enough ash on Toyako Onsen itself that the people literally had to dig their way out of it. Chronicling Mt. Usu's eruption is the **Abuta Volcano Science Museum (Abuta Kazan Kagaku-kan)** (tel. 5-4400), conveniently located right above the Toyako Onsen bus terminal. Open daily from 9am to 5pm and charging ¥400 ($2.85) for admission, it depicts the 1977 eruption with photographs and lava-rock displays. Although explanations are in Japanese only, a pamphlet is available in English, setting forth the important facts. The most interesting aspect of the museum is the "experience room," which seats 350 persons around a large panoramic model of Lake Toya and Mt. Usu. During the experience, a rumbling begins directly below you and seats shake and shimmy, approximating what it must feel like to experience a volcano. Following is a film (again, in Japanese only) showing the Usu eruption, the evacuation of Toyako Onsen, and the ashes covering the town. The whole experience emphasizes Japan's volcanic origins and how its people have always lived in the shadows of volcanoes and earthquakes.

The other famous volcano in the vicinity is **Showa-Shinzan,** which first erupted in 1945. Before then it was nothing more than a flat farm field. Over 2 years, however, the ground began to rise, volcanic eruptions shook the area, and lava rose, resulting in the fledgling volcano. Showa-Shinzan still spouts billowing clouds of smoke. If you're interested in getting a close-up view, you can reach Showa-Shinzan by buses that depart from the Toyako Onsen bus terminal. A small museum at the foot of the volcano documents its birth. You can also catch a glimpse of the volcano from afar if you take the boat ride out onto Lake Toya.

One other thing worth mentioning is the nightly **fireworks** displays put on by the town of Toyako Onsen from June through August—that is, if they're still going on.

IMPRESSIONS

Japan is a great people. Her masons ply with stone,
her carpenters with wood, her smiths with iron,
and her artists with life, death, and all the eye
can take in.
—RUDYARD KIPLING, FROM SEA TO SEA, 1889

Although the town has managed to put on fantastic shows the past few years, such displays are extremely costly and as of now it's not certain whether they'll be carried on during the summers of 1992 and 1993. If so, however, they're worth seeing. The show begins at about 8:40pm and fireworks are set off from boats in the lake.

Where to Stay

The best rooms in town are those that face the lake, with its picturesque islands. Of course, these rooms are also the most expensive. This being a resort town for the Japanese, accommodations are largely in Japanese-style inns, where you're expected to take your dinner and breakfast. The busiest tourist season is from May to October; rates are generally higher during these months.

SUN PALACE HOTEL, Aza Toyako-Onsen-machi, Abutacho, Abuta-gun 049-57. Tel. 01427/5-4126. Fax 01427/5-2875. 459 rms. A/C MINIBAR TV TEL **Directions:** Take a right out of bus terminal and walk 30 minutes; or take a local bus to Sun Palace bus stop in front of hotel.

$ Rates (per person, including breakfast, dinner, and service charge): ¥17,000–¥26,000 ($121–$186) summer season; ¥13,000–¥20,000 ($93–$143) off-season. AE, DC, JCB, MC, V.

This is the most elaborate and conspicuous hotel in Toyako Onsen. Isolated on the edge of town on the shores of the lake, it's quite a hike from the bus terminal if you have baggage; and since local buses are infrequent, the easiest way to get there is by taxi. Its lobby features a spectacular light fixture made of gold-colored twisted metal sheets that rise out of a pond and spread up and out into the ceiling. With the largest public bath in town, including waterslides and other attractions for children, this is a good family hotel that appeals widely to both adults and kids. Rooms, all facing the lake, come in Japanese and Western style, with TV, a safe for valuables, and a minibar. The cheapest rooms are quite simple, while the more expensive ones are larger and better furnished. The main thing you're paying for at this hotel is its public facilities.

Dining/Entertainment: One restaurant, a coffee shop, and bar.

Facilities: Huge public baths (both inside and out), large indoor pool.

MANSEIKAKU ⟨288⟩, Aza Toyako-Onsen-machi, Abutacho, Abuta-gun 049-57. Tel. 01427/5-2171. Fax 01427/5-2271. 246 rms. A/C MINIBAR TV TEL **Directions:** A 15-minute walk from bus terminal; or take a local bus to Chuo Dori bus stop in front of hotel.

$ Rates (per person, including breakfast, dinner, and service charge): ¥17,000–¥40,000 ($121–$285) summer season; ¥15,000–¥36,000 ($107–$257) off-season. AE, DC, JCB, MC, V.

Another first-class hotel in town, this large, handsome brown-brick building is at the water's edge. Rooms are modern and comfortable, and some even come with their own balcony. Most of the rooms are Japanese-style tatami. There are also Western-style rooms with beds, but most of these rooms face inland. Combination rooms, on the other hand, with both beds and a tatami area, are lakeside. Breakfast is served buffet style, and for dinner you have a choice of a Japanese meal served in your room or a Western-style buffet in the hotel's European restaurant.

Dining/Entertainment: European restaurant, coffee shop, disco, karaoke bar (where guests sing along to their favorite tunes).

Facilities: Tennis court, indoor pool, large indoor and outdoor public baths. A woman's bath on the eighth floor features a small outdoor hot-spring bath (called *rotenburo* in Japanese), which, if you ask me, would be a perfect spot from which to watch the fireworks. Right beside the hotel is a boat dock where you can rent paddleboats and take charter motorboats around the lake.

PARK HOTEL, Aza Toyako-Onsen-machi, Abutacho, Abuta-gun 049-57. Tel. 01427/5-2445. 167 rms (131 with bath). MINIBAR TV TEL **Directions:** A 5-minute walk from bus terminal (walk one block toward lake and then turn right).

$ Rates (per person, including breakfast, dinner, and service charge): ¥15,000–¥20,000 ($107–$143) summer season; ¥11,000–¥16,000 ($78–$118) off-season. AE, DC, JCB, V.

This waterfront hotel boasts tennis courts, a pleasant public bath filled with tropical plants, a game room, bowling lanes, and a bar with laser shows. Half the rooms facing the water have a veranda of sorts—but you have to crawl over the windowsill to get outside. The other rooms have windows only. Since the hotel's Western-style rooms—all twins—face only inland, the Japanese rooms here are better by far, especially since they're the same price. There are also bathroom-less Japanese rooms facing inland.

TOYAKO ONSEN HOTEL, Aza Toyako-Onsen-machi, Abutacho, Abuta-gun 049-57. Tel. 01427/5-2222. 76 rms (20 with bath). MINIBAR TV TEL
   Directions: A 20-minute walk from bus terminal (from terminal, walk one block toward lake and then turn right).
$ Rates (per person, including breakfast, dinner, and service charge): ¥14,000–¥16,500 ($100–$118) summer season; ¥9,000–¥12,000 ($64–$86) off-season. AE, JCB, V.

At this somewhat older ryokan, the only facilities for guests are rather nice public baths, and rooms were recently renovated with new wallpaper and tatami mats. The big plus here is that all rooms facing the lake have a balcony, perfect for watching the fireworks. All rooms have a toilet, and a few have a tub as well. Although 15 Western-style rooms are available, none of them face the lake; a few combination rooms (with both beds and a tatami area), however, do have lake views.

TAKATSU RYOKAN ㉘, Aza Toyako-Onsen-machi, Abutacho, Abuta-gun 049-57. Tel. 01427/5-3088. 10 rms (2 with bath). TV TEL **Directions:** A 2-minute walk from bus terminal (turn left out of terminal and walk across bridge).
$ Rates (per person, including breakfast, dinner, and service charge): ¥6,500–¥10,000 ($46–$71). No credit cards.

If you want to stay in Toyako Onsen but can't afford a hotel on the lake's edge, you might try this ryokan, which is located a block inland. No English is spoken, but the proprietress says she gets by. All rooms are Japanese style except for one twin, and all rooms come with TV and fridge.

HOTEL NEW TOYAKO ㉙, Aza Toyako-Onsen-machi, Abutacho, Abuta-gun 049-57. Tel. 01427/5-2818. 15 rms (2 with bath). TV TEL **Directions:** A 1-minute walk from bus terminal, near tourist office (walk one block downhill toward lake).
$ Rates (per person, including breakfast, dinner, and service charge): ¥6,500–¥13,000 ($46–$93). No credit cards.

This combination business hotel/minshuku has clean and basic rooms, including a dozen Japanese-style rooms, two twins, and one double. Only the twin rooms have a private bath and toilet.

SHOWA-SHINZAN YOUTH HOSTEL ㉛, 103 Sobetsu-onsen, Sobetsu cho, 052-01. Tel. 01427/5-2283. 67 beds. **Bus:** From Toyako Onsen bus terminal to Showa-Shinzan Toza-an Guchi stop (an 8-minute ride).
$ Rates (per person): ¥2,300 ($16.40) member; ¥3,000 ($21.40) nonmember. Breakfast ¥450 ($3.20); dinner ¥750 ($5.35). No credit cards.

Located at the foot of the Showa-Shinzan volcano, this is the closest youth hostel to Toyako Onsen. In addition to rental bicycles and laundry facilities, it also has hot-spring baths, for which there's an obligatory ¥100 (70¢) charge.

Where to Dine

Since you'll be taking dinner and breakfast at your hotel, you have only lunch to worry about.

SENDOAN, 2nd floor of Wakasaimo. Tel. 5-2782.
   Cuisine: VARIED JAPANESE. **Directions:** A 3-minute walk from bus terminal (walk one block downhill toward lake, turn left and cross bridge; the restaurant is immediately to your right).
$ Prices: Set meals ¥1,200–¥1,600 ($8.55–$11.40). No credit cards.
   Open: Spring-autumn daily 11am–8pm; winter daily 11am–6pm.

This pleasant and attractive modern restaurant is on the water's edge just west of the main boat dock (to the left if you're facing the lake). You sit on tatami beside huge windows overlooking the lake. The menu is in Japanese only, but you can make your selection from the plastic-food display case. This is primarily a tempura and soba restaurant, with a variety of other selections as well. Set meals include shrimp tempura, salmon teishoku, obento lunch box, and tempura soba.

BOYOTEI, 36-12 Toyako Onsen-machi. Tel. 5-2311.
    Cuisine: WESTERN. **Directions:** A 3-minute walk from bus terminal (walk one block downhill toward lake and turn right).
$ Prices: ¥700–¥1,800 ($5–$12.85). No credit cards.
    Open: Spring–autumn daily 10am–10pm; winter daily 10am–7pm.

    Not far from the tourist office, this is a rather interesting-looking café set back from the town's main road behind an overgrown garden. A wooden sign hanging outside over the sidewalk says KAFE RESTAURANT. Opened more than 40 years ago before the large hotels across the street were built to block the view, it now seems rather hidden and forgotten. The interior looks as if it hasn't changed much over the decades, and is filled with knickknacks. A good, cozy place for a morning coffee, lunch, or an evening drink, it even has some tables and chairs outside. The menu has pork chops, hamburger steak, fried salmon, macaroni chicken gratin, macaroni crabmeat gratin, beef curry, spaghetti, and sandwiches. There are also set lunches and dinners. Various kinds of coffees start at ¥450 ($3.20), and beer starts at ¥650 ($4.65). The restaurant even has Guinness.

RESTAURANT PARK, 2nd floor of Park Hotel. Tel. 5-2445.
    Cuisine: JAPANESE/WESTERN. **Directions:** A 5-minute walk from bus terminal (walk one block downhill toward lake and turn right).
$ Prices: ¥700–¥1,700 ($5–$12.15). AE, DC, JCB, V.
    Open: Lunch daily 10am–3pm.
This informal and simply decorated place serves hamburger steak, curry dishes, noodles, sandwiches, and other choices.

NOBORIBETSU SPA

Famous for the variety of its hot-water springs, Noboribetsu Spa (called **Noboribetsu Onsen** in Japanese) is one of Japan's best-known spa resorts. It boasts 11 different types of hot water and gushes 10,000 tons a day. With temperatures ranging between 113°F and 197°F, the waters contain all kinds of minerals, including sulfur, salt, iron, and gypsum, and are thought to help relieve such disorders as high blood pressure, rheumatism, arthritis, eczema, and even constipation. Noboribetsu's name comes from the Ainu word meaning "white muddy river."

Getting There

Noboribetsu Onsen is about a 15-minute bus ride from the town of Noboribetsu and its Noboribetsu Station, which is where you'll arrive if you come by train. Noboribetsu Station lies on the main train line that runs between Hakodate and Sapporo, about 2½ hours from Hakodate, 45 minutes from Toya Station, and 1 hour and 10 minutes from Sapporo. There are also direct buses from Sapporo and Toyako Onsen to Noboribetsu Onsen.

Orientation

Essential Information The **area code** for Noboribetsu Onsen is 0143.
    The **tourist office** (tel. 0143/84-3311) is on Noboribetsu Onsen's main street just a minute north of the bus depot. It's open daily from 9am to 6pm. There's a pamphlet and map in English, but you may not encounter anyone here who speaks English. Luckily, the town is so small that you shouldn't have any problem getting around. The busiest tourist season is May to October and during New Year's, which is when hotel rates are at their highest.

What to See & Do

✪ Although all the spa hotels and ryokan have their own taps into the spring water, the most famous hotel bath in town is at the **Daiichi Takimotokan,** a monstrous bathing hall with more than a dozen pools containing different mineral contents at various temperatures. Recently remodeled, it's an elaborate affair with hot-spring baths both indoors and out, a Jacuzzi, saunas, steam rooms, and waterfall massage (this is one of my favorites—you simply sit under the shooting water and let it pummel your neck and shoulders).

The baths are separated for men and women, but there's an indoor pool with mixed bathing, so be sure to bring your swimsuit. My only complaint is that the workers cleaning the walls and floors of the bathhouses are men, a couple of whom were none too discreet in their stares. The Japanese women paid them no attention, so I guess we're supposed to do the same. At any rate, visiting the baths here is the best favor you can do yourself while in Noboribetsu. If you're staying at the Daiichi Takimotokan hotel, you can use the baths free of charge at any time. Otherwise, the baths are open to the public daily from 9am to 3pm (that is, you must enter by 3pm). The charge is ¥2,000 ($14.30).

To get an idea of what all this hot water looks like, visit **Hell Valley (Jigokudani),** at the north edge of town past the Daiichi Takimotokan hotel. A volcanic crater 1,485 feet in diameter, the huge depression is full of bubbling and boiling hot water and rock formations of orange and brown. If you walk along the concrete path that winds along the left side of the crater (called Hell Valley Promenade) and follow it as it swings farther to the left, you'll soon see a picnic area with a narrow footpath that leads off to the right through lush woods. If you follow it for about 10 minutes, you'll come to a lookout point over a large pond of hot bubbling water called Ohyunuma (the lookout is across the highway). If you want to take a different route back, follow the path that leads to the right just as you recross the highway. This pathway, called Funamiya Promenade, traces the backbone of several ridges all the way back into town, passing a number of small stone deities on the way.

Another attraction is **Lake Kuttara.** It's an unspoiled caldera lake a few miles from Noboribetsu Onsen and ranks as the second clearest in Japan (the clearest is considered to be Masshu in Akan National Park). Because the water is very cold, swimming is forbidden, but you can rent rowboats. The water is beautiful and wooded hills rise on all sides.

There's also a small restaurant at Lake Kuttara where you can eat ramen, tempura, soba, and trout. Unfortunately, there are only three buses a day that come here from Noboribetsu Onsen, leaving the spa at 9:30am, 11am, and 3:50pm. Each bus makes a 20-minute stop at the lake before returning to Noboribetsu Onsen. If this isn't enough time for you, you might want to take the early bus to the lake and return on a later one. Be sure to check on the latest schedule. Buses run from June 1 to October 22 only.

Incidentally, you'll also see advertisements for a bear park and Ainu village attraction. The best thing about this place is the trip via ropeway—the bear park occupies one of the tallest hills around. The hundred or so bears, however, are crowded together in a cement pen, and the Ainu "village" is mainly for souvenirs. I personally think you're better off spending your money elsewhere.

If you find yourself at Noboribetsu Station with some time on your hands, you might want to check out the Hokkaido Marine Park (tel. 83-3800), about 10 minutes from the station on foot. Opened in 1990, it is one of the largest aquariums in northern Japan. Admission is ¥1,900 ($13.55), and it's open daily from 8:30am to 9pm in summer and from 9am to 5pm in winter.

Where to Stay

As with many Japanese resorts, hotel and ryokan rates depend on the season and in some cases even the day of the week. Weekend rates are generally higher, especially May to October and during New Year's.

DAIICHI TAKIMOTOKAN, Noboribetsu Onsen 059-05. Tel. 0143/84-2111. Fax 0143/84-2202. 396 rms (350 with bath). MINIBAR TV TEL **Directions:** A 5-minute walk from bus terminal, beside Hell Valley.

$ Rates (per person, including breakfast, dinner, and service charge): ¥21,000–¥30,000 ($150–$214) summer season on weekdays; ¥27,000–¥37,000 ($193–$264) summer season on weekends; ¥16,000–¥20,000 ($114–$143) off-season. AE, DC, JCB, MC, V.

Because of its large bathing hall with the various pools, this is Noboribetsu Onsen's best-known ryokan. First opened 130 years ago, today it is a large, modern hotel. Guests are entitled to use the pools free anytime night or day. Only eight of the ryokan's rooms are Western style; the rest are all Japanese-style tatami. As with most first-class ryokan in Hokkaido's resort areas, rooms come with fan (only 72 rooms have air conditioning), TV with pay video, minibar, and safe for valuables.

GRAND HOTEL, Noboribetsu Onsen 059-05. Tel. 0143/84-2101. 259 rms (all with bath). A/C MINIBAR TV TEL **Directions:** A 1-minute walk from bus terminal.

$ Rates: Western-style rooms: ¥16,500 ($118) per person, including breakfast and dinner; ¥22,000 ($157) for two persons without meals. Japanese-style rooms: ¥19,000 ($136) per person, including breakfast and dinner. ¥2,000 ($14.30) extra Sat night. AE, JCB, V.

Rivaling Daiichi Takimotokan in terms of size, facilities, and comfort is the Grand Hotel, spread along the slope of a hill just above the bus terminal. Ninety-two of its rooms are twins, where you can stay without meals if you wish. This hotel sports a nice public bath. Though not as large as Takimotokan's, it is more elegant. The men's section has baths both indoors and outdoors, complete with waterfall and Roman goddess statues. As for the women's section, sorry—no outdoor pool, waterfall, or goddesses. However, it's large and bright, and there are saunas for both sexes.

TAKIMOTO INN, Noboribetsu Onsen 059-05. Tel. 0143/84-2205. 47 rms (all with bath). TV TEL **Directions:** A 5-minute walk from bus terminal.

$ Rates (per person, including breakfast, dinner, and service charge): ¥13,000–¥14,000 ($93–$100) late spring to early autumn, weekends, and New Year's; ¥11,000 ($78) off-season. AE, DC, JCB, MC, V.

Across the street from Daiichi Takimotokan is this small, comfortable, and moderately priced Western-style hotel. All of the rooms are twins, which are colorfully decorated—some with larger-than-life-size flowers splashed onto the wallpaper—but otherwise fairly basic, with a small bathroom and TV with pay video. The main advantage to staying here is that you can use Daiichi Takimotokan's famous baths for free.

KIYOMIZU, Noboribetsu Onsen 059-05. Tel. 0143/84-2145. Fax 0143/84-2146. 20 rms (none with bath). TV TEL **Directions:** A 2-minute walk from bus terminal.

$ Rates: ¥4,900–¥6,500 ($35–$46) single; ¥8,800–¥12,000 ($63–$86) twin; ¥11,500–¥16,000 ($82–$114) triple. Japanese or Western breakfast ¥1,000 ($7.15); dinner ¥2,000–¥3,000 ($14.30–$21.40). AE, DC, JCB, MC, V.

★ This is a small, reasonably priced, and very friendly ryokan on Noboribetsu Onsen's main street. A member of the Japanese Inn Group, it offers modestly furnished Japanese-style rooms. If you opt to have meals, they're served in your room. The owner, Mr. Iwai, speaks very good English and can answer your questions regarding Noboribetsu and the surrounding area. There are small hot-spring baths in the ryokan, and the public toilets are Japanese style. Incidentally, Mr. Iwai plans to add another 40 rooms in a nearby annex by the summer of 1992, featuring both a hot-spring bath on the seventh floor, with views of the surrounding countryside, and an open-air bath.

RYOKAN HANAYA, Noboribetsu Onsen 059-05. Tel. 0143/84-2521. 18 rms (none with bath). MINIBAR TV TEL **Bus:** From Noboribetsu Station to Hanaya-mae stop.

$ Rates: ¥3,800 ($27) single; ¥7,700 ($55) twin; ¥11,000 ($78) triple. Japanese or Western breakfast ¥1,000 ($7.15); dinner ¥2,000 ($14.30). AE.

This simple two-story ryokan is located at the edge of Noboribetsu Onsen, about a 5-minute walk from the bus terminal (if you're arriving by bus, get off before reaching the bus terminal—ask the bus driver to let you know where). A member of the Japanese Inn Group, it has hot-spring public baths, and meals are served in your room.

KIKUSUI ㉒, **Noboribetsu Onsen 059-05. Tel. 0143/84-2437.** 9 rms (none with bath). TV **Bus:** From Noboribetsu Station to Chugaku-mae stop, then a 5-minute walk.

$ Rates (per person, including breakfast and dinner): ¥6,500 ($46). No credit cards.

Although a bit far from Noboribetsu Onsen, you might consider staying here or at the minshuku described below if you're on a budget. Both are simple minshuku run by families who also manage adjoining temples, and the husband of this minshuku's owner is a Buddhist monk. Since neither of these minshuku have hot-spring baths (they do have regular public baths, however), you'll have to hike into town (about 30 minutes) to Takimotokan if you want the real thing. Note that these two minshuku are located on the route of the bus that travels between Noboribetsu Station and Noboribetsu Onsen, so if you're coming from the train station, there's no need to go all the way to the spa. Buses are infrequent, so check the schedule. Personally, I like this area's isolation.

NOBORIBETSU-SO ㉓, **Noboribetsu Onsen 059-05. Tel. 0143/84-3352.** 5 rms (none with bath). TV **Bus:** From Noboribetsu Station toward Noboribetsu Onsen to "Chugaku-mae" stop, then a 5-minute walk.

$ Rates (per person, including breakfast and dinner): ¥6,000 ($43). No credit cards.

Not far from the Kikusui and smaller, this minshuku also has public baths without the benefit of hot springs. For more information on how to get here, refer to the information on Kikusui above.

KANNONJI ㉔, **Noboribetsu Onsen 059-05. Tel. 0143/84-2359.** 25 beds. **Directions:** A 7-minute walk from the bus terminal.

$ Rates (per person): ¥2,300 ($16.40) member; ¥3,300 ($23.55) nonmember. Breakfast ¥400 ($2.85); dinner ¥850 ($6.05). No credit cards.

✪ Kannonji is run by a very friendly group of people who delight in receiving foreign guests. Rooms are all tatami, and diversions include a TV and karaoke. There are laundry facilities and a hot-spring bath, and coffee is available free in the small dining room. The dinners are especially good—notably a one-pot stew with chicken, egg, and vegetables called nabe.

AKASHIYA YOUTH HOSTEL ㉕, **Noboribetsu Onsen 059-05. Tel. 0143/84-2616.** 55 beds. **Directions:** A 2-minute walk from bus terminal.

$ Rates (per person): ¥2,300 ($16.40) member; ¥3,300 ($23.55) nonmember. Breakfast ¥400 ($2.85); dinner ¥850 ($6.05). No credit cards.

Just a couple of minutes' walk from the bus terminal, this youth hostel accommodates guests in both beds and tatami. It features a hot-spring bath and laundry facilities.

YOUTH HOSTEL RYOKAN KANEFUKU ㉖, **Noboribetsu Onsen 059-05. Tel. 0143/84-2565.** 40 beds. **Directions:** A 7-minute walk from bus terminal.

$ Rates (per person): ¥2,000 ($14.30) member; ¥3,000 ($21.40) nonmember. Breakfast ¥450 ($3.20); dinner ¥750 ($5.35). No credit cards.

Located a few minutes farther out of town than the other hostels listed here, this youth hostel is slightly cheaper. Unfortunately, there is no hot-spring bath here—only baths with water of the regular kind. There are laundry facilities.

Where to Dine

POPLAR RESTAURANT, Takimoto Inn. Tel. 84-2205.
   Cuisine: WESTERN. **Directions:** A 5-minute walk from bus terminal, near Hell Valley.
$ Prices: ¥700–¥1,700 ($5–$12.15). AE, DC, JCB, MC, V.
   Open: Lunch daily 11am–2pm.

If you find yourself looking for a place to stop for lunch, or a draft beer, or coffee, this restaurant serves inexpensive Western dishes. The Japanese menu with pictures lists such choices as beefsteak, pork chops, hamburger steak, fried shrimp, fried scallops, sandwiches, curry rice, shrimp gratin, and spaghetti.

SHIRAOI

On your way between Sapporo and Noboribetsu you might wish to visit Shiraoi, where a mock Ainu village of thatched houses has been set up and where demonstrations and dances are performed by Ainu. Particularly interesting is the museum, which contains crafts, utensils, and clothing, realistically depicting what life was like for the Ainu before the Japanese assimilated them into their society. Explanations are in English. Entrance fee is ¥515 ($3.65), and daily hours are 8am to 5pm (8:30am to 4:30pm November through March). If you want to know more about the Ainu, pick up a booklet called *The Ainu Museum,* which describes their life-style, religious beliefs, and customs.

DAISETSUZAN NATIONAL PARK

Although I find it difficult to rank nature in terms of beauty, there are some who maintain that Daisetsuzan National Park is the most spectacular of Hokkaido's parks. With its tall mountains covered with fir and birch trees and sprinkled with wildflowers, its river gorge laced with waterfalls and hiking trails throughout, Daisetsuzan National Park is the perfect place to come if you've been itching to get some exercise in relatively unspoiled countryside. Lying in the center of Hokkaido, this national park, Japan's largest, contains three volcanic mountain groups, including the highest mountain in Hokkaido, Mt. Asahi, at 7,513 feet. Hiking in summer and skiing in winter are the primary pursuits of the region.

SOUNKYO ONSEN

Nestled at the very edge of Sounkyo Gorge, Daisetsuzan's most famous natural attraction, Sounkyo Onsen is the perfect base for exploring the national park. Although the town itself is rather unattractive, with its cluster of souvenir shops and unimaginative buildings, its soothing hot springs and magnificent scenic backdrop make coming here worthwhile. In addition, Sounkyo Onsen serves as the starting point for bicycle trips along Sounkyo Gorge and for the cable car trip to the top of a neighboring peak. Sounkyo is one of my favorite places in all of Hokkaido.

Getting There

The only way to reach Sounkyo Onsen by public transportation is by bus. If you're coming from Sapporo, take the train as far as Kamikawa (2½ hours), then transfer to a bus for a 30-minute ride that will take you directly to Sounkyo. There are also buses connecting Sounkyo Onsen with Asahigawa and Rubeshibe, both about a 2-hour ride away.

Orientation

Essential Information   The **area code** for Sounkyo Onsen is 01658.

The **tourist information office,** called the **PR Center** (tel. 01658/5-3350), is located in a modern-looking wooden building downhill from the bus station. You can see it from the bus depot. No one speaks English here and maps of the village are in Japanese only, but the staff can point you in the direction of your ryokan or even make ryokan reservations for you. They also have a brochure in English describing the national park and its attractions. The office is open daily from 9am to 5pm (10:30am to 3:30pm November through April). In any case, the village is so tiny you won't have any difficulty getting around.

What to See & Do

✪ Souukyo Gorge is a river valley hemmed in on both sides by rock walls rising almost 500 feet high. Almost perpendicular in places, the gorge extends for about 12 miles, offering spectacular views with each bending curve. The best way to see the gorge is on a bicycle, which you can rent from stalls beside the bus terminal and a number of other places for ¥1,200 ($8.55) a day. There's a designated route you're supposed to follow (maps provided), and altogether the trip to the end of the route and back should take no longer than 2½ hours.

The first part of the trip by bicycle is unfortunately on a sidewalk next to a highway strung with cars. The highway winds along a rushing river past a couple of waterfalls until finally the highway disappears into a dark tunnel—which is where I'm convinced it belongs anyway. At this point the gorge belongs to cyclists and hikers and becomes quite narrow. You then pass through a tunnel yourself and emerge at the turning point of your trip where you'll find—what else?—souvenir shops, soda machines, and vendors selling corn on the cob. This is where tour buses pull in for a quick look.

If you're interested in hiking, or even if you're not, take the cable car from Sounkyo Onsen to the lofty peak of **Kuro-dake Mountain.** The trip takes 7 minutes and costs ¥1,390 ($9.90) round trip. From the cable-car station, walk a few minutes farther up the mountain, where you'll come to a chair lift. This costs ¥250 ($1.80) one way and takes 15 minutes, swinging you past lush forests of fir and birch. At the end of the lift, where the hiking paths begin, there's a hut where you sign your name and give your route so that tabs can be kept on people who are on the mountain. If you're not feeling overly ambitious, you can hike an hour and reach the peak of Kuro-dake, 6,500 feet high, where if the weather is clear you'll be rewarded with views of the surrounding mountain ranges.

If you feel like taking a day's hike, there's a circular path along the top of mountain ridges that you can hike in about 7 hours. And if you're really into hiking and wish to carry your backpack with you, a popular route is to walk from the Sounkyo chair lift over Mt. Asahi, Hokkaido's tallest mountain, and on to another chair lift that will take you down to Asahidake Onsen, a spa where you can spend the night. This trip takes 8 to 10 hours, so set out early. Be sure to pick up a map showing the hiking trails. It's in Japanese only, but since the trails are also marked in Japanese only, having an English map wouldn't do you much good. The hiking path isn't considered that strenuous, but you do need sturdy walking shoes. If you're going for just a short hike, tennis shoes are fine. The tops of the mountains are really beautiful here, covered with wildflowers and alpine plant life. It would be a shame to come to Sounkyo and not spend a few hours amid its lofty peaks.

From November to May the mountains become a skier's haven, especially for beginners (advanced skiiers will not find the slopes here challenging). Although you can rent skis up on the mountain at the cable-car station, keep in mind that your feet may be too big. Skis and boots rent for ¥3,300 ($23.55) and up. A day's cable-car and chair-lift ticket cost ¥3,000 ($21.40) at last check, but note that prices are expected to rise. The lift operations vary according to the month, but are open daily from about 8 or 9am to 4 or 4:30pm in winter and from 6am to 8pm in summer. The lifts shut down entirely for 2 weeks beginning in mid-February for maintenance work.

If you have time to kill, you might also consider dropping in on the **Sounkyo Museum Daisetsuzan National Park.** Its explanations are in Japanese only, but you'll see some aerial reliefs of the area, stuffed animals, butterflies, insects, and birds. Admission is ¥200 ($1.40).

Where to Stay

If you want to stay here in August, make reservations in advance. Incidentally, most families who live here run several operations that might include a ryokan, an adjoining restaurant, and a souvenir shop. The army of young Japanese college-age guys you see working in the area come from other parts of Japan to work in Sounkyo for the summer. They may not know a lot about the area, but most of them speak some English.

SOUNKYO PRINCE HOTEL CHOYOTEI, Sounkyo 078-17. Tel. 01658/5-

3241. 271 rms (all with bath). MINIBAR TV TEL **Directions:** An 8-minute walk from bus terminal.

$ Rates (per person, including breakfast, dinner, and service charge): ¥20,000–¥27,000 ($143–$193) summer season; ¥16,500–¥27,000 ($118–$193) off-season. AE, DC, JCB, MC, V.

This hotel offers the most expensive accommodations in town and boasts a good view of the gorge from its location atop a ridge. Both Japanese-style and combination rooms are available, pleasant and elegantly simple with minibar, safe for valuables, and TV with adult video. The higher rates are charged for rooms with views of the gorge. Facilities include a modern, comfortable lobby with views of a rock garden, an electronic-game room, a souvenir shop, noodle and sushi counters, and public baths on the top floor overlooking the gorge.

TAISETSU HOTEL, Sounkyo 078-17. Tel. 01658/5-3211. 250 rms (175 with bath). A/C TV TEL **Directions:** An 8-minute walk from bus terminal.

$ Rates (per person, including breakfast, dinner, and service charge): ¥16,500–¥22,000 ($118–$157) summer season; ¥11,000–¥22,000 ($78–$157) off-season. AE, DC, JCB, MC, V.

Just across the street from the Sounkyo Prince Hotel Choyotei, this large white hotel on a hill above the town is another great place to stay, especially if you can get a room on a top floor facing the gorge. Rates depend on the size of your room and its view. The most expensive rooms face the gorge, while the cheapest rooms have a toilet but no bath. Western breakfasts are available on request. Most rooms are tatami, but four Western-style rooms are also available. The hot-spring public baths here are large and consist of several different pools. As is often the case, however, the men's bath commands a better view than the women's.

GRAND HOTEL ㉗**, Sounkyo 078-17. Tel. 01658/5-3111.** 191 rms (all with bath). MINIBAR TV TEL **Directions:** A 2-minute walk from bus terminal.

$ Rates (per person, including breakfast, dinner, and service charge): ¥14,000–¥20,000 ($100–$143). 10% winter discount. AE, JCB, V.

Situated beside the highway that runs through Sounkyo Gorge, this older hotel was recently renovated. The lobby, with its marbled pillars and white walls, is cheerful though a bit overdone; the public spa baths are quite nice, with large windows, white tile, and stone. There are also outdoor baths, separated for men and women. Higher rates are for top-floor rooms with views of the surrounding mountain ranges.

PENSION YUKARA ㉘**, Sounkyo 078-17. Tel. 01658/5-3216.** 7 rms (none with bath). TV TEL **Directions:** A 6-minute walk from bus terminal.

$ Rates (per person, including breakfast, dinner, and service charge): ¥9,600 ($68) in Aug; ¥8,500 ($61) rest of year. AE, DC, JCB, MC, V.

The spotlessly clean, white, bright, and cute style of this pension is meant to appeal to young Japanese girls. Its rooms include both twins and tatami rooms, and they are decorated with pastel-colored wallpaper and lots of pink. There's a coin laundry here, but the drawback to this place is that it doesn't have a hot-spring bath—just regular bath water. Breakfast and dinner are Western style.

TSUCHIYA ㉙**, Sounkyo 078-17. Tel. 01658/5-3517.** 50 rms (none with bath). TV TEL **Directions:** A 3-minute walk from bus terminal.

$ Rates (per person, including breakfast, dinner, and service charge): ¥6,500–¥9,300 ($46–$66). No credit cards.

This hotel prides itself on being the largest minshuku in Hokkaido, for whatever that's worth. Rooms are located in a main building and an annex. Facilities include hot-spring baths, a coin laundry, and very clean Japanese-style rooms. Western breakfasts are available.

KITAGAWA ㉚**, Sounkyo 078-17. Tel. 01658/5-3515 and 5-3231.** 12 rms (none with bath). TV TEL **Directions:** Less than a 3-minute walk from bus terminal.

$ Rates (per person, including breakfast, dinner, and service charge): ¥6,500 ($46). No credit cards.

This clean and pleasant minshuku offering Japanese-style accommodations attracts mainly young Japanese. Located above a souvenir shop and restaurant of the same name, it has both a coin laundry and hot-spring baths.

ONOZUKA ③①, **Sounkyo 078-17. Tel. 01658/5-3308.** 8 rms (none with bath). TV **Directions:** A 3-minute walk from bus terminal.

$ Rates (per person, including breakfast, dinner, and service charge): ¥6,300–¥6,500 ($45–$46). No credit cards.

This simple minshuku has a small number of Japanese-style rooms, but it does have its own hot-spring baths, as well as a coffee shop on the ground floor. Western-style breakfasts are available if ordered the night before.

SOUNKYO YOUTH HOSTEL ③②, **Sounkyo 078-17. Tel. 01658/5-3418.** 90 beds. **Directions:** A 10-minute walk from bus terminal, past Taisetsu hotel.

$ Rates (per person): ¥2,250 ($16.05) member and nonmember. ¥150 ($1.05) extra heating charge in winter. Breakfast ¥450 ($3.20); dinner ¥850 ($6.05). No credit cards.

Located on top of a hill above the city, this hostel offers both beds and futon. Unfortunately, it doesn't have hot springs, but it does have a public bath and laundry facilities.

GINSENKAKU YOUTH HOSTEL ③③, **Sounkyo 078-17. Tel. 01658/5-3003.** 99 beds. **Directions:** About a 5-minute walk from bus terminal.

$ Rates (per person): ¥2,300 ($16.40) member; ¥3,300 ($23.55) nonmember. Breakfast ¥450 ($3.20); dinner ¥750 ($5.35). No credit cards.

This youth hostel is in the center of the village and has its own hot-spring bath, for which it charges an extra ¥150 ($1.05) if you're staying in the youth hostel and ¥500 ($3.55) if you're not. There are laundry facilities, and accommodations are futon.

AKAN NATIONAL PARK

Spreading through the eastern end of Hokkaido, Akan National Park features volcanic mountains, dense forests of subarctic primeval trees, and three caldera lakes, including Lake Akan. The best place to stay in the park is at Akanko Onsen, a small hot-spring resort on the edge of Lake Akan. It makes a good base from which to explore both the Akan National Park and the Red-Crested Crane National Park nearby.

Because Akan National Park lies at the eastern extremity of Hokkaido, you may wish to fly back to Tokyo. Kushiro Airport is 1 hour and 20 minutes away by bus from Akanko Onsen. The plane trip from Kushiro to Tokyo takes about 1½ hours.

As for Akanko Onsen itself, it's small, and walking is the best way to get around. It consists primarily of one main street that snakes along the lake, with ryokan and souvenir shops on both sides.

GETTING THERE

Since there's no train station at Akanko, transportation to the resort town is by bus from Kushiro or Bihoro. Bihoro is approximately 5 hours from Sapporo by train. If you're coming from Sounkyo, take the bus to Rubeshibe, from which it's less than an hour's train ride onward to Bihoro. In addition to regular buses that run from Bihoro to Akanko, there are also sightseeing buses that take in the most important sights along the way, offering the best way to see the national park. See below for more details.

ORIENTATION

Essential Information   The **area code** for Akanko Onsen is 0154.

If you have any questions concerning Akan National Park itself, drop by the **Visitor's Center,** with displays (unfortunately in Japanese only) of natural wonders pertaining to the park.

You can also stop at the **tourist association** (tel. 0154/67-2254), located just a minute's walk from the Akanko Onsen bus terminal in the direction of the lake. You can pick up a pamphlet in English about Akan National Park here and make reservations for hotels, ryokan, and minshuku. It's open daily from 9am to 6pm. There's also a small tourist window next to the boat pier where you buy tickets for boat rides on Lake Akan.

WHAT TO SEE & DO

Your sightseeing in Akan National Park should begin before reaching Akanko Onsen, which lies in the southern part of the park. The best way to see the national park, if you're not renting a car, is to board an **Akan sightseeing bus** in Bihoro, which is north of the park. That way you'll travel all the way through the park and see the most important natural wonders. The bus trip takes 5 hours, making stops at several scenic spots along the way, including Kusshoro and Mashu lakes. Kusshoro is one of Japan's largest mountain lakes, while Mashu is considered to be one of the most beautiful. A deep crater lake with the clearest water in Japan, Mashu was called "lake of the devil" by the Ainu because no water flows either into it or out of it. Surely Mashu is one of Japan's least-spoiled lakes—because of the steep, 660-foot-high rock walls ringing the lake, it has remained inaccessible to humanity (the bus stops at two observation platforms high above the lake). The bus trip costs ¥5,490 ($39.20) and is called the Panorama Course. At last check, buses departed from Bihoro three times daily, at 8:45am, 10:45am, and 12:25pm from the end of April to mid-October. In winter, only one bus departs daily. In any case, be sure to check departures ahead of time, since bus schedules change. In addition to sightseeing buses, there are also regular, direct buses that travel between Bihoro and Akan in about 70 minutes. For more information, call 0152/3-4182.

As for things to do in Akanko, the most popular activity is to take a boat cruise around **Lake Akan.** Lake Akan is famous for its very rare spherical green weed, called *marimo*. It's a spongelike ball of duckweed that grows 2 to 5 inches in diameter. Found in only a few places in the world, marimo is formed when many separate and stringy pieces of weed at the bottom of the lake roll around and eventually come together to form a ball. The ball grows larger and larger until sooner or later it breaks apart, whereby the whole process starts over again. On your boat cruise you'll make a stop at a small island on the lake where a marimo museum has been set up, consisting of duckweed in a few tanks, together with explanations of how they're formed. Supposedly, when the sun shines the marimo rises to the surface of the water, giving Lake Akan a wonderful green shimmer. However, the only marimo I ever saw was in the museum's tanks and in tanks of souvenir shops around town—even though the sun was shining. Perhaps you'll have better luck. The boat trip takes 1½ hours and costs ¥1,020 ($7.30).

While you're out on your boat trip, you'll notice two cone-shaped volcanoes, **O-Akandake** to the east and **Me-Akandake** to the south. Both are popular destinations for hikers. O-Akandake is dormant and it's about a 4½ hour hike to the summit from Akanko Onsen. Me-Akandake, the highest mountain in the Akan area, is active and is covered with primeval forests of spruce and fir. There's a trail leading to Me-Akandake from the west end of the town, and it takes about 4 hours to reach the top, from which you have panoramic views of the surrounding area.

A shorter hike follows a trail to **Mt. Hakutozan,** from which you also have a good view of the town and lake. It takes about 2 hours to reach Akan's skiing area and another 30 minutes to reach Mt. Hakutozan, a grassy and moss-covered knobby hill that remains warm throughout the year because of thermal activity just below the surface. The woods of birch and pine here are beautiful, and what's more, you'll probably find yourself all alone.

Incidentally, behind the park's Visitor's Center, described earlier, is a catwalk leading through marshy woods and connecting with a trail that terminates on the lake's shore. Here you'll find some bubbly hot-mud ponds, a grassy area good for picnics, and a rock-enclosed hot spring that empties right into the lake.

If you're in Akan in the winter, you may want to take advantage of its artificial snow atop the town's one skiing hill, with two runs that are good for beginners. The season runs from about the end of November until May.

If you haven't seen any Ainu dances yet, you might want to pay a visit to **Ainu Kotan Village** (tel. 67-2727), which is a souvenir-shop-lined street leading to a thatch-roofed lodge where you can see Ainu performing traditional dances. Costing ¥600 ($4.30), shows are performed about six times a day from May to the end of October and last half an hour.

By the way, since Akanko Onsen is a hot-spring spa, it would be a shame to come all this way and not partake of its waters. If you're staying somewhere that doesn't have hot springs, you can visit the public hot springs, called **Marimo Yu,** located across the street from the main boat dock. Open daily from 10am to 9pm, it charges a ¥250 ($1.80) admission.

Red-crested cranes are the prefectural birds of Hokkaido, and south of Akan is a breeding ground for these graceful and beautiful animals. **Tancho-zuru Shizen Koen (Red-crested Crane Natural Park)** (tel. 0154/56-2219) is a marshy area set aside for breeding and raising the crane. Open throughout the year daily from 9am to 5pm (4pm in winter), it charges ¥300 ($2.15) for visitors to observe the birds behind high mesh fences. You'll be surprised at how large these birds actually are. The crane park is 1 hour and 15 minutes by bus from the Akanko Onsen bus terminal; get off at the Tsuru-koen bus stop. By the way, this is the same bus that goes from Akanko to Kushiro Airport. The bus makes a 15-minute stop at this park, which is enough time to take a quick look at the birds before continuing on to the airport.

If you happen to be in Akan in the winter, you'll have the extra delight of visiting **Tancho-no-Sato,** private grounds where red-crested cranes court, mate, and live in the winter months from November to March. This is the best place to photograph the birds in action. It's a 42-minute bus ride from Akanko Onsen bus terminal.

WHERE TO STAY

Expensive

HOTEL AKANKOSO, Aza Akankohan, Akancho, Akan-gun 085-04. Tel. 0154/67-2231. 97 rms (all with bath). MINIBAR TV TEL **Directions:** A 5-minute walk from bus terminal.

$ Rates (per person, including breakfast, dinner, and service charge): ¥20,000–¥22,000 ($143–$157) summer season; ¥9,000–¥12,000 ($64–$86) winter season. AE, DC, JCB, V.

Located right next to the boat dock on the water's edge, this small hotel has a variety of Japanese-style rooms, as well as combination rooms, the best of which face the lake. The hotel's large communal hot-spring baths on the fifth floor are nicely laid out in brick and have views of the lake.

NEW AKAN HOTEL, Aza Akankohan, Akancho, Akan-gun 085-04. Tel. 0154/67-2121. 298 rms (292 with bath). MINIBAR TV TEL **Directions:** A 5-minute walk from bus terminal.

$ Rates (per person, including breakfast, dinner, and service charge): ¥14,000–¥29,000 ($100–$207) summer season; ¥11,000–¥20,000 ($78–$143) winter season. AE, DC, JCB, MC, V.

Situated on a shady spot beside Lake Akan, this hotel winds along the curve of the lake in a series of wings built at various stages in the past 20 years. The newest addition is the Annex Crystal, with very pleasant rooms featuring bay windows looking out on shade trees and the lake beyond. These rooms are the most expensive rates above, and come with nicely finished tile bathroom, hairdryer, minibar, radio, clock, hot-water pot, TV with coin video, and even pants presser (for pants and skirts). Both Japanese-style and Western-style rooms are available.

Dining/Entertainment: Among the several restaurants and bars, the Crystal Restaurant in the Annex Crystal is a good place to come for lunch. Its English menu offers sandwiches, spaghetti, beef curry, shrimp or crab pilaf, noodles, and more, at ¥700 to ¥1,600 ($5 to $11.40) for most items, as well as daily specials for ¥2,200 ($15.70). The restaurant has a very nice view of shade trees and lake and is open from 11am to 9pm.

Facilities: Souvenir shops and large public hot-spring baths.

Moderate

AKAN GRAND HOTEL ⑳, **Aza Akankohan, Akancho, Akan-gun 085-04.
Tel. 0154/67-2531.** 221 rms (all with bath). MINIBAR TV TEL **Directions:** A
9-minute walk from bus terminal.

$ Rates (per person, including breakfast, dinner, and service charge): ¥20,000–
¥27,000 ($143–$193) summer season for a room facing the lake,
¥13,000–¥22,000 ($93–$157) for a room facing inland; ¥11,000–¥22,000
($78–$157) winter season. AE, DC, JCB, MC, V.

This white hotel on the lake's edge offers rooms that face the water (obviously more
expensive) and those that face inland. Both Japanese-style tatami rooms and
combination rooms are available. Rooms are modern and clean, and come with the
usual TV with pay video, minibar, and clock. The public baths here are fairly unique
and have a large fish tank built into the wall.

**AKAN VIEW HOTEL, Aza Akankohan, Akancho, Akan-gun 085-04. Tel.
0154/67-3131.** 228 rms (all with bath). MINIBAR TV TEL **Directions:** A
6-minute walk from bus terminal.

$ Rates (per person, including breakfast, dinner, and service charge): ¥12,000–
¥17,000 ($86–$121) summer season; ¥7,000–¥13,000 ($50–$93) winter season. AE, DC, JCB, V.

This is the spa's newest place to stay and, despite its name, one of the few hotels
without a view of the lake. It's back from the waterfront, more inland than the other
hotels, and most of its rooms are Western-style twins, though 28 Japanese-style rooms
are also available. One of the best things about this hotel is that it has large indoor
pools, one for swimming laps and one for children, as well as the usual hot-spring
baths, open from 7am to 9pm. Even if you're not staying at the hotel, you can use the
facilities for ¥700 ($5) on weekdays and ¥1,030 ($7.35) on weekends and holidays.
Other facilities include tennis courts and bicycles for rent. Although none of the
rooms have a view of the water, the best rooms, in my opinion, are those that face
east, facing some woods and a creek.

HOTEL ICHIKAWA ⑳, **Aza Akankohan, Akancho, Akan-gun 085-04. Tel.
0154/67-2011.** 94 rms (54 with bath). MINIBAR TV TEL **Directions:** An
8-minute walk from bus terminal.

$ Rates (per person, including breakfast, dinner, and service charge): ¥16,500
($118) summer season; ¥14,000 ($100) winter season. MC, V.

Located right on the water's edge, this ryokan is a very reasonably priced place, and
the front-desk personnel are friendly. One advantage to staying here is Shigeru
Dameon Takada, a young Japanese man whose family owns the ryokan and who
speaks very good English. He told me that he'd be very happy to help foreigners with
any questions they might have regarding Akan—which could be quite useful, since
hardly anyone in Akan speaks English. All rooms are Japanese style, except two twins.
Rooms on the top (sixth) floor command the best views. The hot-spring public baths
on the first floor are very modern and face the lake. If you're here in summer, be sure
to take the hotel's pontoon boat for a 2-hour sunset cruise on the lake, complete with
barbecue dinner and a glass of wine for ¥5,000 ($35.70) per person. The hotel can
make arrangements for fishing, waterskiing, and snow skiing and will even tailor day
trips to other lakes and hiking destinations to your own desires.

Budget

MINSHUKU GINREI ⑳, **Aza Akankohan, Akancho, Akan-gun 085-04.
Tel. 0154/67-2597.** 9 rms (none with bath). TV **Directions:** A 10-minute walk
from bus terminal.

$ Rates (per person, including breakfast, dinner, and service charge): ¥5,500
($39). No credit cards.

Located on the west edge of town, this minshuku has simple rooms that come with
coin-operated TV. There's no view and no hot-spring bath, but the man who runs this
place welcomes foreigners.

MINSHUKU KIRI, Aza Akankohan, Akancho, Akan-gun 085-04. Tel. 0154/67-2755. 9 rms (none with bath). TV **Directions:** An 8-minute walk from bus terminal.

$ Rates (per person, including breakfast, dinner, and service charge): ¥5,500 ($39). No credit cards.

This minshuku is across the street from the Hotel Ichikawa. Look for the wooden sign hanging above the door with the English written very small. The nine Japanese-style rooms here are simple, with coin-operated TV. The bathtubs here are wooden and the water is from hot springs.

MINSHUKU YAMAGUCHI ⑳, **Aza Akankohan, Akancho, Akan-gun 085-04. Tel. 0154/67-2555.** 10 rms (none with bath). TV **Directions:** A 10-minute walk from bus terminal.

$ Rates (per person, including breakfast, dinner, and service charge): ¥5,300 ($38). No credit cards.

As with most minshuku, this family-run lodge on the west edge of town is small, with just 10 Japanese-style rooms. The advantage to staying here is that it has a hot-spring communal bath. Rooms come with coin-operated TV and are simple but cozy. From the dining room you have a peaceful view of some woods and, in winter when the leaves are gone, a view of the lake.

AKANKOHAN YOUTH HOSTEL, Aza Akankohan, Akancho, Akan-gun 085-04. Tel. 0154/67-2241. 58 beds. **Directions:** A 4-minute walk from bus terminal.

$ Rates (per person): ¥2,100 ($15) member; ¥3,100 ($22.15) nonmember. Breakfast ¥450 ($3.20); dinner ¥750 ($5.35). No credit cards.

Next to the boat sightseeing dock, this hostel is old and a bit run-down, offering both bed and tatami accommodations. It has hot-spring baths, laundry facilities, and bicycles for rent. Note, however, that it's open only in summer, from June through October.

ANGEL YOUTH HOSTEL ⑳, **Aza Akankohan, Akancho, Akan-gun 085-04. Tel. 0154/67-2309.** 90 beds. **Directions:** A 15-minute walk from bus terminal.

$ Rates (per person): ¥2,300 ($16.40) member; ¥3,300 ($23.55) nonmember. Hot-spring baths ¥150 ($1.05) extra. Breakfast ¥450 ($3.20); dinner ¥750 ($5.35). No credit cards.

This hostel is farther out of town, but the building is newer and in better shape than that of the Akankohan. If you call from the bus terminal, someone will come pick you up. There are also bicycles for rent here, making it easy to get back and forth to town. The place has its own hot-spring bath and laundry facilities.

A. BASIC PHRASES & VOCABULARY

Needless to say, it takes years to become fluent in Japanese, particularly in written Japanese, with its thousands of *kanji,* or Chinese characters, and many *hiragana* and *katakana* characters. Knowing just a few words of Japanese, however, not only is useful but will delight the Japanese you meet during your trip.

In pronouncing the following vocabulary, keep in mind that there's very little stress on individual syllables (pronunciation of Japanese is often compared to Italian). Here is an approximation of some of the sounds of Japanese:

a	as in f*a*ther
e	as in p*e*n
i	as in s*ee*
o	as in *o*h
oo	long *o* as in *ooo*h
u	as in b*oo*k
g	as in *g*ift at the beginning of words; like *ng* in si*ng* in the middle or at the end of a word

Vowel sounds are normally short; when they are long, as the final *o* in *domo arigatoo* (thank you), they are pronounced double, in which case you hold the vowel a bit longer. Vowel length can change the meaning of a word; for example, *okashi* (short *i*) means "a sweet," whereas *okashii* (long *i*) means "strange." As you can see, even a slight mispronunciation of a word can result in confusion or hilarity. (Incidentally, jokes in Japanese are almost always plays on words.)

The vowels *i* and *u* are sometimes just whispered or not pronounced at all, depending on their location in a word or sentence. For example: *Doo-itashi-mash'te* (you're welcome); *Ohayo gozaimas'* (good morning); *Wakarimas' ka* (do you understand)?; *Ikura des' ka* (how much)?; *S'ki des'* (I like it).

GENERAL WORDS & PHRASES

Good morning	**Ohayo gozaimasu**
Good afternoon	**Kon-nichi-wa**
Good evening	**Kon-ban-wa**
Good night	**Oyasumi-nasai**
Hello	**Haro (or Kon-nichi-wa)**
Good-bye	**Sayonara (or bye-bye!)**
Excuse me, I'm sorry	**Sumimasen**
Thank you	**Domo arigatoo**
You're welcome	**Doo-itashi-mashite**
Please (go ahead)	**Doozo**
Yes	**Hai**
No	**I-ie**
Foreigner	**Gaijin**
Japanese person	**Nihonjin**
Japanese language	**Nihongo**
American person	**Amerikajin**
English language	**Eigo**

Do you understand?	**Wakarimasu ka?**
I understand	**Wakarimasu**
I don't understand	**Wakarimasen**
Just a minute, please	**Chotto matte kudasai**
How much?	**Ikura desu ka?**
Where?	**Doko desu ka?**
When?	**Itsu desu ka?**
Expensive	**Takai**
Cheap	**Yasui**
I like it	**Suki desu**

TRAVELING

Train station	**Eki**
Airport	**Kuukoo**
Subway	**Chika-tetsu**
Bus	**Bus-u**
Taxi	**Takushi**
Airplane	**Hikooki**
Ferry	**Ferri**
Train	**Densha**
Bullet train	**Shinkansen**
Limited express train	**Tokkyu**
Ordinary express train	**Kyuko**
Local train	**Futsu**
Ticket	**Kippu**
Exit	**Deguchi**
Entrance	**Iriguchi**
North	**Kita**
South	**Minami**
East	**Higashi**
West	**Nishi**
Left	**Hidari**
Right	**Migi**
Straight ahead	**Massugu (or zutto)**
Far	**Toi**
Near	**Chikai**
Can I walk there?	**Aruite ikemasu ka?**
Street	**Dori (or michi)**
Tourist information office	**Kanko annaijo**
Map	**Chizu**
Police box	**Koban**
Post office	**Yubin-kyoku**
Stamp	**Kitte**
Bank	**Ginko**
Hospital	**Byooin**
Toilet	**Toire, Ben joh, Goh fu joh, O teh ahmai**
Hot-spring spa	**Onsen**
Bath	**Ofuro**
Public bath	**Sento**
Drugstore	**Kusuriya**

FOOD & LODGING

Restaurant	**Resutoran**
I'd like to make a reservation	**Yoyaku onegai shimasu**
For one person	**Hitori**

For two people	**Futari**
Menu	**Menyu**
Tea	**Ocha**
Coffee	**Koohi**
Water	**Mizu**
Lunch or daily special	**Teishoku**
Lunch box	**Obento**
Delicious	**Oishii**
Thank you for the meal	**Gochisoo-sama deshita**
Hotel	**Hoteru**
Japanese-style inn	**Ryokan**
Youth hostel	**Yusu hosuteru**
Cotton kimono	**Yukata**
Room	**Heya**
Does that include meals?	**Shokuji wa tsuite imasu ka?**
Key	**Kagi**
Balcony	**Baranda**

TIME

Now	**Ima**
Later	**Ato de**
Today	**Kyoo**
Tomorrow	**Ashita**
Day after tomorrow	**Asatte**
Yesterday	**Kinoo**
Which day?	**Nan-nichi desu ka?**
Daytime	**Hiruma**
Morning	**Asa**
Night	**Yoru**
Afternoon	**Gogo**
Sunday	**Nichiyoobi**
Monday	**Getsuyoobi**
Tuesday	**Kayoobi**
Wednesday	**Suiyoobi**
Thursday	**Mokuyoobi**
Friday	**Kinyoobi**
Saturday	**Doyoobi**
January	**Ichi-gatsu**
February	**Ni-gatsu**
March	**San-gatsu**
April	**Shi-gatsu**
May	**Go-gatsu**
June	**Roku-gatsu**
July	**Shichi-gatsu**
August	**Hachi-gatsu**
September	**Kyuu-gatsu**
October	**Juu-gatsu**
November	**Juuichi-gatsu**
December	**Juuni-gatsu**

NUMBERS

1	**Ichi**		6	**Roku**
2	**Ni**		7	**Shichi (or nana)**
3	**San**		8	**Hachi**
4	**Shi**		9	**Kyuu**
5	**Go**		10	**Juu**

11	**Juuichi**	60	**Rokujuu**
12	**Juuni**	70	**Nanajuu**
20	**Nijuu**	80	**Hachijuu**
30	**Sanjuu**	90	**Kyuuju**
40	**Shijuu (or yonjuu)**	100	**Hyaku**
50	**Gojuu**	1,000	**Sen**

B. GLOSSARY OF TERMS

ARCHITECTURE & INTERIOR DESIGN

Donjon Castle keep

Fusuma Sliding paper doors

Futon Japanese mattress

Gassho-zukuri Roofs built at steep angles, usually thatched and found in regions with heavy snowfalls

Jinja Shinto shrine

Kotatsu A heating element placed under a low table (which is covered with a blanket) for keeping one's legs warm; used in place of a heater in traditional Japanese homes

Minshuku Inexpensive lodging in a private home; the Japanese equivalent of a European pension

Ryokan Japanese-style inn

Shitamachi Old downtown area of Tokyo

Shoji White paper sliding windows

Tatami Rice mats

Tera (or dera) Temple

Tokonoma A small, recessed alcove in a Japanese room used to display a flower arrangement, scroll, or art object

Torii Entrance gate of a Shinto shrine, consisting usually of two poles topped with one or two crossbeams

Zabuton Floor cushions

COLLOQUIALISMS

Saavice Service, meaning "free of charge"

Salaryman A white-collar worker who receives a fixed salary

Nomi-ya A drinking establishment

O.L. Pronounced *O-eru*, initials for "office lady," or secretary

Yakitori-ya A drinking establishment that serves *yakitori*, skewered foods

Yakuza Japanese gangsters

CULTURE & PERFORMING ARTS

Bunraku Traditional Japanese puppet theater

Cha-no-yu Japanese tea ceremony

Ikebana Japanese flower arrangement

Kabuki Traditional Japanese drama, in which all the roles are performed by men

Kyogen Short comic reliefs, performed in between Noh plays

Noh Traditional Japanese drama, originally for the upper classes

MENU SAVVY

Ayu A small river fish; a delicacy of western Japan

Basashi Raw horse meat; a specialty of Kyushu

Champon Nagasaki-style Chinese noodles, served usually in soup
Chu-hi Shochu (*see below*) mixed with soda water and flavored with syrup and lemon
Dengaku Lightly grilled tofu (*see below*) coated with a bean paste
Dojo A small, eel-like river fish
Fugu Pufferfish (also known as blowfish or globefish)
"Genghis Khan" Mutton and vegetables grilled at your table
Gohan Rice
Gyoza Chinese fried pork dumplings
Jibuni A winter stew of chicken and vegetables; a specialty of Kanazawa
Kaiseki A formal Japanese meal consisting of many courses and served originally during the tea ceremony
Kamameshi A rice casserole topped with seafood, meat, or vegetables
Kushiage (also kushikatsu or kushiyaki) Deep-fried skewers of chicken, beef, seafood, and vegetables
Kyo-ryoori (also Kyo-ryori) Kyoto-style cuisine, including Kyo-kaiseki
Maguro Tuna
Makizushi Sushi (*see below*), vegetables, and rice rolled inside dried seaweed
Miso A soybean paste, used as a seasoning in soups and sauces
Miso-shiru Miso soup
Mochi Japanese rice cake
Nabemono A single-pot dish of chicken, beef, pork, or seafood, stewed with vegetables
Natto Fermented soybeans
Nikujaga A beef, potato, and carrot stew, flavored with sake (*see below*) and soy sauce; popular in winter
Oden Fish cakes, hard-boiled eggs, and vegetables, simmered in a light broth
Okonomiyaki A thick pancake filled with meat, fish, shredded cabbage, and vegetables or noodles, often cooked by diners at their table
Ramen Thick, yellow Chinese noodles, served in a hot soup
Sake Rice wine
Sansai Mountain vegetables, including bracken and flowering fern
Sashimi Raw seafood
Shabu-shabu Thinly sliced beef quickly dipped in boiling water and then dipped in a sauce
Shippoku A variety of dishes of Chinese, European, and Japanese origin; a specialty of Nagasaki
Shochu Japanese whiskey, made from rice, wheat, or potatoes
Shojin-ryoori Japanese vegetarian food, served at Buddhist temples
Shoyu Soy sauce
Shumai Steamed Chinese pork dumplings
Soba Buckwheat noodles
Somen Fine white wheat vermicelli, eaten cold in summer
Sukiyaki A Japanese fondue of thinly sliced beef cooked in a sweetened soy sauce with vegetables
Sushi (also nigiri-zushi) Raw seafood placed on top of vinegared rice
Tempura Deep-fried food coated in a batter of egg, water, and wheat flour
Teppanyaki Japanese-style steak, seafood, and vegetables cooked by a chef on a smooth, hot tableside grill
Tofu Soft bean curd
Tonkatsu Deep-fried pork cutlets
Udon Thick white wheat noodles
Unagi Grilled eel
Wasabi Japanese horseradish, served with sushi
Yakisoba Chinese fried noodles, served with sautéed vegetables
Yakitori Charcoal-grilled chicken, vegetables, and other specialties, served on bamboo skewers
Yudofu Tofu simmered in a pot at your table

C. A LIST OF JAPANESE SYMBOLS

TOKYO

1. Seifuso
   聖富荘

2. Shimizu Bekkan
   しみず別館

3. Kinsen
   金扇

4. Sushiko
   寿司幸

5. Kushi Colza
   串コルザ

6. Ohmatsuya
   大松屋

7. Suehiro
   スエヒロ

8. Sushi Sei
   寿司清

9. Atariya
   当りや

10. Donto
    どんと

11. Hayashi
    はやし

12. Inakaya
    田舎家

13. Zakuro
    ざくろ

14. Kushinobo
    串の坊

15. Tsunahachi
    つな八

16. Negishi
    ねぎし

17. Fukuzushi
    福鮨

18. Takamura
    篁

19. Gonin Byakusho
    五人百姓

20. Hassan
    八山

21. Shabu Zcn
    しゃぶ禅

22. Ganchan
    がんちゃん

23. Torigin
    鳥ぎん

24. Tamura
    田村

25. Tentake
    天竹

26. Edogin
    江戸銀

27. Sushi Dai
    寿司大

28. Mugitoro
    むぎとろ

29. Kuremutsu
    暮六つ

30. Komagata Dojo
    駒形どじょう

31. Chinya
    ちんや

32. Daikokuya
    大黒家

33. Keyaki
    欅

34. Namiki
    並木薮

35. Izu'ei
伊豆栄
36. Genrokusushi
元禄寿司
37. Seiyo Hiroba
せいよう広場
38. Kandagawa
神田川
39. Yabu-Soba
やぶそば
40. Tonki
とんき
41. Kappa Tengoku
かっぱ天国
42. Lupin
ルパン
43. Anyo
あんよ
44. Volga
ボルガ

KAMAKURA

45. Miyokawa
御代川
46. Monzen
門前
47. Kayagi-ya
茅木屋
48. Nakamura-an
なかむら庵
49. Raitei
檑亭

HAKONE

50. Ryuguden
龍宮殿
51. Ichinoyu
一の湯
52. Sugiyochi Ryokan
杉よし旅館

ATAMI

53. Hotel New Akao
ホテルニューアカオ
54. Kiunkaku
起雲閣

SHIMODA

55. Haji
はじ

DOGASHIMA

56. Ginsuiso
銀水荘
57. Kaikomaru
海晃丸

KYOTO

58. Kinmata
近又
59. Ryokan Rikiya
力弥
60. Rokuharaya Inn
六波羅屋
61. Myokenji Temple
妙顕寺
62. Myorenji Temple
妙蓮寺
63. Izusen
泉仙
64. Misogigawa
禊川
65. Izumoya
いづもや
66. Bio-Tei
びお亭
67. Ganko Sushi
がんこ寿司
68. Gontaro
権太呂
69. Musashi
むさし

70. Sancho
サンチョ

71. Zu Zu
厨厨

72. Hyotei
瓢亭

73. Mikaku
みかく

74. Minoko
美濃幸

75. Isobe
いそべ

76. Okutan
奥丹

77. Ladies' Hotel Chorakukan
長楽館

78. Goemonjaya
五衛ェ門茶屋

79. Koan
高庵

80. Nakamuraro
中村楼

81. Irohanihoheto
いろはにほへと

82. Kodaiji Rakusho Tea Room
洛匠

83. Zenrinji Temple
永観堂 禅林寺

84. Tanakaya
田中弥

85. Taku Taku
磔磔

86. Suishin Honten
酔心本店

NARA

87. Kikusuiro
菊水楼

88. Furuichi
古市

89. Harishin
はり新

TAKAYAMA

90. Kinkikan
金亀館

91. Asunaro
あすなろ

92. Ryokan Hishuya
飛州屋

93. Seiryu
清龍

94. Hida Gasshoen
飛驒合掌苑

95. Hachibei
八兵衛

96. Kakusho
角正

97. Bandai Kado Mise
萬代角店

98. Suzuya
寿々屋

99. Jizake-ya
地酒屋

100. Kofune
小舟

SHIRAKAWA-GO

101. Seikatsu Shiryokan
生活資料館

102. Myozenji
明善寺

103. Doburoku Matsuri no Yakata
どぶろく祭りの館

104. Kandaya
かんだ屋

105. Magoemon
孫右ェ門

106. Otaya
大田屋
107. Yosobe
よそべえ
108. Juemon
十右ェ門
109. Irori
いろり
110. Kitanosho
基太の庄

MATSUMOTO

111. Matsumoto Folkcraft Museum (Matsumoto Mingei-kan)
松本民芸館
112. Hotel Ikyu
一休
113. Nishiya Ryokan
西屋旅館

MAGOME & TSUMAGO

114. Magome
馬籠
115. Tsumago
妻籠

NAGOYA

116. Yamamoto-ya Honten
山本屋本店
117. Yaegaki Tempura House
八重垣
118. Kisoji
木曽路
119. Kishimentei
きしめん亭

ISE-SHIMA NATIONAL PARK

120. Yamadakan
山田館
121. Ise City Hotel
伊勢シティホテル

122. Hoshidekan
星出館
123. Kimpokan
錦浦館
124. Ishiyama-So
石山荘
125. Youth Hostel Taikoji
ユースホステル 太江寺

KANAZAWA

126. Miyabo
みやぼ
127. Kanazawa Castle Inn
キャッスルイン金沢
128. Yogetsu
陽月
129. Kanazawa Youth Hostel
金沢ユースホステル
130. Matsui Youth Hostel
松井ユースホステル
131. Miyoshian
三芳庵
132. Tozan
東山
133. Takeda
竹田
134. Zeniya
銭屋
135. Hamacho
浜長
136. Kitama
きたま
137. Kaga Tobi
加賀鳶

OSAKA

138. Hotel Hokke Club
ホテル法華クラブ
139. Shin-Osaka Sen-i City
センイ シティ ホテル

140. Hattori Ryokuchi Youth Hostel
服部緑地ユースホステル

141. Osaka-Shiritsu Nagai Youth Hostel
大阪市立長居ユースホステル

142. Kaen
花宴

143. Ebi Doraku
えび道楽

144. Kani Doraku
かに道楽

145. Kuidaore
くいだおれ

KOBE

146. Kitagami Hotel
北上ホテル

147. Steakland Kobe
ステーキランド KOBE

MT. KOYA

148. Kongobuji Temple
金剛峯寺

149. Reihokan Museum
霊宝館

150. Ekoin
恵光院

151. Fumonin Temple
普門院

152. Rengejoin Temple
蓮華定院

153. Shojoshinin
清浄心院

HIMEJI

154. Banryu
播龍

155. Hotel Sunroute New Himeji
ホテル サンルート ニュー姫路

156. Hotel Sunroute Himeji
ホテル サンルート 姫路

157. Fukutei
福亭

158. Mampuku
万福

159. Minato-an
三七十庵

OKAYAMA

160. Hotel Sunroute
ホテル サンルート 岡山

161. Matsunoki
まつのき旅館

162. Youth Hostel Okayama-ken Seinen Kaikan
ユースホステル 岡山県青年会館

163. Gonta-Zushi
権太寿し

164. Petit ("Puchi") Marie
プチマリエ

165. Suishin
酔心

166. Akatogarashi
赤とうがらし

167. Okayama Prefectural Product Center (Okayama-ken Bussan Tenjijo)
岡山県物産展示場

KURASHIKI

168. Tsurugata
鶴形

169. Ryokan Kurashiki
旅館くらしき

170. Tokusan Kan
特産館

171. Kamoi
カモ井

172. Minshuku Kawakami
民宿かわかみ

173. Kurashiki Terminal Hotel
倉敷ターミナルホテル

MATSUE

174. Matsue Cultural Museum (Matsue Kyodokan)
松江郷土館
175. Teahouse Meimei-an
明々庵
176. Buke Yashiki
武家屋敷
177. Tanabe Art Museum (Tanabe Bijutsukan)
田部美術館
178. Gesshoji Temple
月照寺
179. Minami-Kan
皆美館
180. Horaiso
蓬莱荘
181. Matsue Urban Hotel
松江アーバンホテル
182. Matsue Plaza Hotel
松江プラザホテル
183. Matsue Minami Guchi Hotel
松江南口ホテル
184. Matsue Youth Hostel
松江ユース・ホステル
185. Kaneyasu
かねやす
186. Ginsen
銀扇
187. Yagumoan
八雲庵

HIROSHIMA

188. Mitakiso
三瀧荘
189. Sera Bekkan
世羅別館
190. Rijyo Kaikan
鯉城会館
191. Hiroshima Youth Hostel
広島ユースホステル
192. Amagi
あまぎ
193. Kanawa
かなわ
194. Okonomi-Mura
お好み村

MIYAJIMA

195. Iwaso Ryokan
岩惣旅館
196. Jyukeiso
聚景荘
197. Miyajima Lodge
宮島ロッジ
198. Momiji
もみじ
199. Fujitaya
ふじたや

TAKAMATSU

200. Kompira O-Shibai
金毘羅大芝居
201. Takamatsu Plaza Hotel
高松プラザホテル
202. Tokiwa Honkan
常磐本館
203. Tenkatsu
天勝
204. Hansuke
半助
205. Kanaizumi
かな泉
206. Maruichi
まるいち

MATSUYAMA

207. Mingei Iyo Kasuri Kaikan
民芸伊予かすり会館

208. Umeno-Seito-jo
梅野精陶所

209. Tobe-yaki Kanko Center
砥部焼観光センター

210. Ehime Prefectural Products Hall
(Ehime no Bussan)
愛媛の物産

211. Uchikoza
内子座

212. Funaya
ふなや

213. Kasugaen
春日園

214. Taihei Business Hotel
ビジネスホテル泰平

215. Matsuyama Shinsen-en Youth
Hostel
松山神泉園ユースホステル

216. Shinhamasaku
新浜作

217. Hyakumi
佰味

FUKUOKA

218. Chisan Hotel Hakata
チサンホテル博多

219. Mitsui Urban Hotel
三井アーバンホテル

220. Dazaifu Youth Hostel
太宰府ユースホステル

221. Gyosai
魚菜

BEPPU

222. Kannawaen
神和苑

223. Tenjuso
天寿荘

224. Green Business Hotel
グリーン ビジネス ホテル

225. Sakaeya
サカエ屋

226. Chikuden
ちくでん

227. Jin
仁

228. Amamijaya
甘味茶屋

MT. ASO

229. Ryokan Mimura
旅館みむら

230. Aso Youth Hostel
阿蘇ユースホステル

231. Minami Aso Kokumin Kyuka
Mura
南阿蘇国民休暇村

232. Minami Aso Kokumin Shukusa
南阿蘇国民宿舎

233. Dengaku no Sato
田楽の里

KUMAMOTO

234. Kumamoto Station Hotel
熊本ステーションホテル

235. Kumamoto Shiritsu Youth Hostel
熊本市立ユースホステル

236. Suizenji Youth Hostel
水前寺ユースホステル

237. Senri
泉里

238. Aoyagi
青柳

239. Goemon
五右衛門

240. Kimura-so
きむら荘

241. Kumamoto Traditional Crafts
Center
熊本県伝統工芸館

276. Marine Pier
マリンピア

277. Taikanso
大観荘

278. Konnoya
今野屋

279. Matsushima Kanko Hotel
松島観光ホテル

280. Ryokan Kozakura
旅館小桜

281. Matsushima Youth Hostel
松島ユースホステル

282. Donjiki Chaya
どんじき茶屋

HAKODATE

283. Minshuku Fukuiso
民宿ふく井荘

SAPPORO

284. Zenniku Hotel (Ana
Hotel Sapporo)
全日空ホテル

285. Nakamuraya Ryokan
中村屋旅館

286. Satohoro
さとほろ

287. Hyosetsu-no-Mon
氷雪の門

SHIKOTSU-TOYA NATIONAL PARK

288. Manseikaku
万世閣

289. Takatsu Ryokan
多佳津旅館

290. Hotel New Toyako
ホテルニュー洞爺湖

291. Showa-Shinzan Youth Hostel
昭和新山ユースホステル

292. Kikusui
菊水

293. Noboribetsu-so
のぼりべつ荘

294. Kannonji
観音寺

295. Akashiya Youth Hostel
あかしやユースホステル

296. Youth Hostel Ryokan Kanefuku
ユースホステル旅館金福

DAISETSUZAN NATIONAL PARK

297. Grand Hotel
グランドホテル

298. Pension Yukara
ペンション ユーカラ

299. Tsuchiya
つちや

300. Kitagawa
北川

301. Onozuka
おのづか

302. Sounkyo Youth Hostel
層雲峡ユースホステル

303. Ginsenkaku Youth Hostel
銀泉閣ユースホステル

AKAN NATIONAL PARK

304. Akan Grand Hotel
阿寒グランドホテル

305. Hotel Ichikawa
ホテル市川

306. Minshuku Ginrei
民宿ぎんれい

307. Minshuku Yamaguchi
民宿山口

308. Angel Youth Hostel
エンジェル ユースホステル

D. THE METRIC SYSTEM

LENGTH

1 millimeter (mm)	=	.04 inches (*or* less than 1/16 in.)
1 centimeter (cm)	=	.39 inches (*or* just under 1/2 in.)
1 meter (m)	=	39 inches (*or* about 1.1 yards)
1 kilometer (km)	=	.62 miles (*or* about 2/3 of a mile)

To convert kilometers to miles, multiply the number of kilometers by 0.62. Also use to convert speeds from kilometers per hour (kmph) to miles per hour (m.p.h.).
To convert miles to kilometers, multiply the number of miles by 1.61. Also use to convert speeds from m.p.h. to kmph.

CAPACITY

1 liter (l)	=	33.92 fluid ounces = 2.1 pints = 1.06 quarts
	=	.026 U.S. gallons
1 Imperial gallon	=	1.2 U.S. gallons

To convert liters to U.S. gallons, multiply the number of liters by 0.26.
To convert U.S. gallons to liters, multiply the number of gallons by 3.79.
To convert Imperial gallons to U.S. gallons, multiply the number of Imperial gallons by 1.2.
To convert U.S. gallons to Imperial gallons, multiply the number of U.S. gallons by 0.83.

WEIGHT

1 gram (g)	=	0.035 ounces (*or* about a paperclip's weight)
1 kilogram (kg)	=	35.2 ounces
	=	2.2 pounds
1 metric ton	=	2,205 pounds = 1.1 short ton

To convert kilograms to pounds, multiply the number of kilograms by 2.2.
To convert pounds to kilograms, multiply the number of pounds by 0.45.

AREA

1 hectare (ha)	=	2.47 acres		
1 square kilometer (km²)	=	247 acres	=	.39 square miles

To convert hectares to acres, multiply the number of hectares by 2.47.
To convert acres to hectares, multiply the number of acres by 0.41.
To convert square kilometers to square miles, multiply the number of square kilometers by 0.39.
To convert square miles to square kilometers, multiply the number of square miles by 2.6.

TEMPERATURE

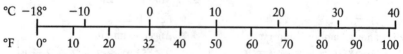

To convert degrees Celsius to degrees Fahrenheit, multiply °C by 9, divide by 5, and add 32 (example: 20°C × 9/5 + 32 = 68°F).
To convert degrees Fahrenheit to degrees Celsius, subtract 32 from °F, multiply by 5, then divide by 9 (example: 85°F − 32 × 5/9 = 29.4°C).

E. SIZE CONVERSIONS

The following charts should help you to choose the correct clothing sizes in Japan. Sizes, however, can vary, so the best guide is simply to try things on.

WOMEN'S DRESSES, COATS & SKIRTS

American	3	5	7	9	11	12	13	14	15	16	18
Japanese	36	38	38	40	40	42	42	44	44	46	48

WOMEN'S BLOUSES & SWEATERS

American	10	12	14	16	18	20
Japanese	38	40	42	44	46	48

WOMEN'S STOCKINGS

American	8	8½	9	9½	10	10½
Japanese	1	2	3	4	5	6

WOMEN'S SHOES

American	5	6	7	8	9	10
Japanese	36	37	38	39	40	41

MEN'S SUITS

American	34	36	38	40	42	44	46	48
Japanese	44	46	48	50	52	54	56	58

MEN'S SHIRTS

American	14½	15	15½	16	16½	17	17½	18
Japanese	37	38	39	41	42	43	44	45

MEN'S SHOES

American	7	8	9	10	11	12	13
Japanese	39½	41	42	43	44½	46	47

MEN'S HATS

American	6⅞	7⅛	7¼	7⅜	7½	7⅝
Japanese	55	56	58	59	60	61

CHILDREN'S CLOTHING

American	3	4	5	6	6X
Japanese	98	104	110	116	122

CHILDREN'S SHOES

American	8	9	10	11	12	13	1	2	3
Japanese	24	25	27	28	29	30	32	33	34

INDEX

GENERAL INFORMATION

DESTINATIONS

KEY TO ABBREVIATIONS: B = Budget; C = Capsule Hotel; E = Expensive; Hs = Hostel; J = Japanese-Style; M = Moderate; Mn = Minshuku; R = Ryokan; $ = Super-Value Choice; VE = Very Expensive; YH = Youth Hostel; * = an Author's Favorite

NOW, SAVE MONEY ON ALL YOUR TRAVELS!
Join Frommer's™ Dollarwise® Travel Club

Saving money while traveling is never easy, which is why the **Dollarwise Travel Club** was formed 32 years ago to provide cost-cutting travel strategies, up-to-date travel information, and a sense of community for value-conscious travelers from all over the world.

In keeping with the money-saving concept, the annual membership fee is low—$25 for U.S. residents and $35 for residents of Canada, Mexico, and other countries—and is immediately exceeded by the value of your benefits, which include:

1. Any TWO books listed on the following pages;
2. Plus any ONE Frommer's City Guide;
3. A subscription to our quarterly newspaper, *The Dollarwise Traveler;*
4. A membership card that entitles you to purchase through the Club all Frommer's publications for 33% to 40% off their retail price.

The eight-page **Dollarwise Traveler** tells you about the latest developments in good-value travel worldwide and includes the following columns: **Hospitality Exchange** (for those offering and seeking hospitality in cities all over the world); and **Share-a-Trip** (for those looking for travel companions to share costs).

Aside from the various Frommer's Guides, the Gault Millau Guides, and the Real Guides you can also choose from our Special Editions, which include such titles as *Caribbean Hideaways* (the 100 most romantic places to stay in the Islands); and *Marilyn Wood's Wonderful Weekends* (a selection of the best mini-vacations within a 200-mile radius of New York City).

To join this Club, send the appropriate membership fee with your name and address to: Frommer's Dollarwise Travel Club, 15 Columbus Circle, New York, NY 10023. Remember to specify which single city guide and which two other guides you wish to receive in your initial package of member's benefits. Or tear out the pages, check off your choices, and send them to us with your membership fee.

FROMMER BOOKS
PRENTICE HALL TRAVEL   Date_____
15 COLUMBUS CIRCLE
NEW YORK, NY 10023

Friends: Please send me the books checked below.

FROMMER'S™ COMPREHENSIVE GUIDES
(Guides listing facilities from budget to deluxe, with emphasis on the medium-priced)

☐ Alaska	$14.95	☐ Italy	$19.00
☐ Australia	$14.95	☐ Japan & Hong Kong	$17.00
☐ Austria & Hungary	$14.95	☐ Morocco	$18.00
☐ Belgium, Holland & Luxembourg	$14.95	☐ Nepal	$18.00
☐ Bermuda & The Bahamas	$17.00	☐ New England	$17.00
☐ Brazil	$14.95	☐ New Mexico	$13.95
☐ California	$18.00	☐ New York State	$19.00
☐ Canada	$16.00	☐ Northwest	$16.95
☐ Caribbean	$17.00	☐ Puerta Vallarta (avail. Feb. '92)	$14.00
☐ Carolinas & Georgia	$17.00	☐ Portugal, Madeira & the Azores	$14.95
☐ Colorado (avail. Jan '92)	$14.00	☐ Scandinavia	$18.95
☐ Cruises (incl. Alaska, Carib, Mex, Hawaii, Panama, Canada & US)	$16.00	☐ Scotland (avail. Feb. '92)	$17.00
		☐ South Pacific	$20.00
☐ Delaware, Maryland, Pennsylvania & the New Jersey Shore (avail. Jan. '92)	$19.00	☐ Southeast Asia	$14.95
		☐ Switzerland & Liechtenstein	$19.00
☐ Egypt	$14.95	☐ Thailand	$20.00
☐ England	$17.00	☐ Virginia (avail. Feb. '92)	$14.00
☐ Florida	$17.00	☐ Virgin Islands	$13.00
☐ France	$15.95	☐ USA	$16.95
☐ Germany	$18.00		

0891492

FROMMER'S CITY GUIDES

(Pocket-size guides to sightseeing and tourist accommodations and facilities in all price ranges)

☐ Amsterdam/Holland	$8.95	☐ Minneapolis/St. Paul	$8.95
☐ Athens	$8.95	☐ Montréal/Québec City	$8.95
☐ Atlanta	$8.95	☐ New Orleans	$8.95
☐ Atlantic City/Cape May	$8.95	☐ New York	$12.00
☐ Bangkok	$12.00	☐ Orlando	$12.00
☐ Barcelona	$12.00	☐ Paris	$8.95
☐ Belgium	$7.95	☐ Philadelphia	$11.00
☐ Berlin	$10.00	☐ Rio	$8.95
☐ Boston	$8.95	☐ Rome	$8.95
☐ Cancún/Cozumel/Yucatán	$8.95	☐ Salt Lake City	$8.95
☐ Chicago	$9.95	☐ San Diego	$8.95
☐ Denver/Boulder/Colorado Springs	$8.95	☐ San Francisco	$12.00
☐ Dublin/Ireland	$10.00	☐ Santa Fe/Taos/Albuquerque	$10.95
☐ Hawaii	$12.00	☐ Seattle/Portland	$12.00
☐ Hong Kong	$7.95	☐ St. Louis/Kansas City	$9.95
☐ Las Vegas	$8.95	☐ Sydney	$8.95
☐ Lisbon/Madrid/Costa del Sol	$8.95	☐ Tampa/St. Petersburg	$8.95
☐ London	$12.00	☐ Tokyo	$8.95
☐ Los Angeles	$8.95	☐ Toronto	$8.95
☐ Mexico City/Acapulco	$8.95	☐ Vancouver/Victoria	$7.95
☐ Miami	$8.95	☐ Washington, D.C.	$12.00

FROMMER'S $-A-DAY® GUIDES

(Guides to low-cost tourist accommodations and facilities)

☐ Australia on $40 a Day	$13.95	☐ Israel on $40 a Day	$13.95
☐ Costa Rica, Guatemala & Belize		☐ Mexico on $45 a Day	$18.00
on $35 a Day	$15.95	☐ New York on $65 a Day	$15.00
☐ Eastern Europe on $25 a Day	$16.95	☐ New Zealand on $45 a Day	$16.00
☐ England on $50 a Day	$17.00	☐ Scotland & Wales on $40 a Day	$18.00
☐ Europe on $45 a Day	$19.00	☐ South America on $40 a Day	$15.95
☐ Greece on $35 a Day	$14.95	☐ Spain on $50 a Day	$15.95
☐ Hawaii on $70 a Day	$18.00	☐ Turkey on $40 a Day	$22.00
☐ India on $40 a Day	$20.00	☐ Washington, D.C., on $45 a Day	$17.00
☐ Ireland on $40 a Day	$17.00		

FROMMER'S CITY $-A-DAY GUIDES

☐ Berlin on $40 a Day	$12.00	☐ Madrid on $50 a Day (avail. Jan '92)	$13.00
☐ Copenhagen on $50 a Day	$12.00	☐ Paris on $45 a Day	$12.00
☐ London on $45 a Day	$12.00	☐ Stockholm on $50 a Day (avail. Dec. '91)	$13.00

FROMMER'S FAMILY GUIDES

☐ California with Kids	$16.95	☐ San Francisco with Kids	$17.00
☐ Los Angeles with Kids	$17.00	☐ Washington, D.C., with Kids (avail. Jan	
☐ New York City with Kids (avail. Jan '92)	$18.00	'92)	$17.00

SPECIAL EDITIONS

☐ Beat the High Cost of Travel	$6.95	☐ Marilyn Wood's Wonderful Weekends	
☐ Bed & Breakfast—N. America	$14.95	(CT, DE, MA, NH, NJ, NY, PA, RI, VT)	$11.95
☐ Caribbean Hideaways	$16.00	☐ Motorist's Phrase Book (Fr/Ger/Sp)	$4.95
☐ Honeymoon Destinations (US, Mex &		☐ The New World of Travel (annual by	
Carib)	$14.95	Arthur Frommer for savvy travelers)	$16.95

(TURN PAGE FOR ADDITONAL BOOKS AND ORDER FORM)

0891492

☐ Paris Rendez-Vous . . . .$10.95   ☐ Travel Diary and Record Book $5.95
☐ Swap and Go (Home Exchanging) . . . . .$10.95   ☐ Where to Stay USA (from $3 to $30 a
                                                                    night) $13.95

FROMMER'S TOURING GUIDES

(Color illustrated guides that include walking tours, cultural and historic sites, and practical information)

☐ Amsterdam $10.95	☐ New York $10.95
☐ Australia $12.95	☐ Paris $8.95
☐ Brazil $10.95	☐ Rome $10.95
☐ Egypt $8.95	☐ Scotland $9.95
☐ Florence $8.95	☐ Thailand $12.95
☐ Hong Kong $10.95	☐ Turkey $10.95
☐ London $12.95	☐ Venice $8.95

GAULT MILLAU

(The only guides that distinguish the truly superlative from the merely overrated)

☐ The Best of Chicago $15.95	☐ The Best of Los Angeles $16.95
☐ The Best of Florida $17.00	☐ The Best of New England $15.95
☐ The Best of France $16.95	☐ The Best of New Orleans $16.95
☐ The Best of Germany $18.00	☐ The Best of New York $16.95
☐ The Best of Hawaii $16.95	☐ The Best of Paris $16.95
☐ The Best of Hong Kong $16.95	☐ The Best of San Francisco $16.95
☐ The Best of Italy $16.95	☐ The Best of Thailand $17.95
☐ The Best of London $16.95	☐ The Best of Toronto $17.00

☐ The Best of Washington, D.C. $16.95

THE REAL GUIDES

(Opinionated, politically aware guides for youthful budget-minded travelers)

☐ Amsterdam $9.95	☐ Mexico $11.95
☐ Berlin $11.95	☐ Morocco $12.95
☐ Brazil $13.95	☐ New York $9.95
☐ California & the West Coast $11.95	☐ Paris $9.95
☐ Czechoslovakia $13.95	☐ Peru $12.95
☐ France $12.95	☐ Poland $13.95
☐ Germany $13.95	☐ Portugal $10.95
☐ Greece $13.95	☐ San Francisco $11.95
☐ Guatemala $13.95	☐ Scandinavia $14.95
☐ Hong Kong $11.95	☐ Spain $12.95
☐ Hungary $12.95	☐ Turkey $12.95
☐ Ireland $12.95	☐ Venice $11.95
☐ Italy $13.95	☐ Women Travel $12.95
☐ Kenya $12.95	☐ Yugoslavia $12.95

ORDER NOW!

In U.S. include $2 shipping UPS for 1st book; $1 ea. add'l book. Outside U.S. $3 and $1, respectively.

Allow four to six weeks for delivery in U.S., longer outside U.S. We discourage rush order service, but orders arriving with shipping fees plus a $15 surcharge will be handled as rush orders.

Enclosed is my check or money order for $_____

NAME _____

ADDRESS _____

CITY _____ STATE _____ ZIP _____